Social Research Methods

Social Research Methods

Alan Bryman

third edition

OXFORD
UNIVERSITY PRESS

OXFORD

UNIVERSITY PRESS

Great Clarendon Street, Oxford ox2 6DP

Oxford University Press is a department of the University of Oxford.
It furthers the University's objective of excellence in research, scholarship,
and education by publishing worldwide in

Oxford New York

Auckland Cape Town Dar es Salaam Hong Kong Karachi
Kuala Lumpur Madrid Melbourne Mexico City Nairobi
New Delhi Shanghai Taipei Toronto

With offices in

Argentina Austria Brazil Chile Czech Republic France Greece
Guatemala Hungary Italy Japan Poland Portugal Singapore
South Korea Switzerland Thailand Turkey Ukraine Vietnam

Oxford is a registered trade mark of Oxford University Press
in the UK and in certain other countries

Published in the United States
by Oxford University Press Inc., New York

First edition 2001
Second edition 2004
This edition 2008

British Library Cataloguing in Publication Data

Data available

Library of Congress Cataloging in Publication Data

Data available

Library of Congress Cataloging-in-Publication Data

Bryman, Alan.
Social research methods / Alan Bryman.— 3rd ed.
p. cm.
Text accompanied by a companion web site.
ISBN-13: 978–0–19–920295–9
1. Social sciences—Research. 2. Social sciences—Methodology. I. Title.
H62.B787 2008
300.72—dc22
2008003361

Typeset by Graphicraft Limited, Hong Kong
Printed in Italy
on acid-free paper by
L.E.G.O. S.p.A.

ISBN 978–0–19–920295–9

3 5 7 9 10 8 6 4

Acknowledgements

Many people have helped me with this book, many of them unwittingly. Generations of research methods students at Loughborough University and the University of Leicester have plied me with ideas through their questioning of what I said to them. I wish to thank several people at or connected with OUP: Tim Barton for suggesting to me in the first place that I might like to think about writing a book like this; Angela Griffin for her editorial help during the passage of the first edition of this book; Patrick Brindle and Katie Allan for their help and suggestions during the preparation of the revised edition; Angela Adams for her constant support and encouragement with the revised and this third edition; Hilary Walford for her attention to detail when copy-editing the manuscript; and Helen Tyas, Sarah Brett and Lucy Hyde for help with various aspects of this edition. I also wish to thank Alan Beardsworth for his helpful and always constructive comments on drafts of the first edition of the book and Michael Billig for valuable comments on part of the first edition. I would like to say a big thank you to Emma Bell who worked with me on the first and revised editions of the business school adaptation of this book, *Business Research Methods*. Many of the changes that have been incorporated in the present edition were developed in conjunction with her. I also wish to thank Alan Radley, Darrin Hodgetts, and Andrea Cullen for their permission to include two photographs from their study of images of homelessness and to Sarah Pink for her permission to use an image from her research on women and bullfighting. I also wish to thank the *Nottingham Evening Post* for their kind permission to reproduce two newspaper articles in Chapter 12. The photograph in Plate 17.6 is Copyright DaimlerChrysler Corporation and is used with permission. I wish to thank the students who completed the questionnaires that were used for preparing the 'Student experience' features of this new edition. I also wish to thank the reviewers who prepared helpful comments on the previous edition for Oxford University Press.

As usual, Sue, Sarah, and Darren have supported me in many ways and put up with my anxieties and with my sudden disappearances to my study. When Sarah became a university student herself, she gave me many insights into a consumer's perspective on a book like this, for which I am grateful. Everyone except me is, of course, absolved of any responsibility for any of the book's substantive deficiencies.

Brief contents

Part Four   585

Detailed contents

Part Four 585

About the author

Alan Bryman was appointed Professor of Organizational and Social Research in the School of Management at the University of Leicester in August 2005. He is currently Head of the School. Prior to his move to Leicester, he was Professor of Social Research at Loughborough University for 31 years.

His main research interests are in leadership especially in higher education, research methods (particularly mixed methods research), and the 'Disneyization' and 'McDonaldization' of modern society. In 2003–2004 he completed a project on mixed methods research, as part of the Economic and Social Research Council's Research Methods Programme.

He has published widely in the field of Social Research, including: *Quantitative Data Analysis with SPSS 12 and 13: A Guide for Social Scientists* (Routledge, 2005) with Duncan Cramer; *Business Research Methods* (Oxford University Press, second edition 2007) with Emma Bell; *The SAGE Encyclopedia of Social Science Research Methods* (Sage, 2004) with Michael Lewis-Beck and Tim Futing Liao; *The Disneyization of Society* (Sage, 2004); *Handbook of Data Analysis* (Sage, 2004) with Melissa Hardy; and *Understanding Research for Social Policy and Practice* (Policy Press, 2004) with Saul Becker.

He has contributed articles to a range of academic journals including *Journal of Management Studies*; *Human Relations*; *International Journal of Social Research Methodology*; *Leadership Quarterly*, and *American Behavioural Scientist*. He is also on the editorial board of *Leadership*; *The Leadership Quarterly*; *Qualitative Research in Organizations and Management: An International Journal*, and the *Journal of Mixed Methods Research*. He has recently completed research into effective leadership in higher education, a project funded by the Leadership Foundation for Higher Education.

Introducing the students

For many readers of this book one of the main reasons for using it will be to enable you to undertake a research project of your own, perhaps for the first time. With this in mind, I have included boxed features entitled 'Student experience' which are based on the experiences of undergraduate and postgraduate social science students who have done a research project, usually as part of their final year dissertation. The aim of these features is to provide insight and advice based on the experiences of real students in their own words, or in other words, to 'tell it like it is', as Nichols and Beynon (1977) have put it. This feature is based on a set of questionnaires completed by eight undergraduate and four postgraduate students from a variety of different UK university social science departments in the UK. The main point of this feature is to provide you with insights into the experiences of student researchers. Profiles of each of the students are given below, and the original questionnaires can be downloaded in the form of podcasts from the Online Resource Centre at: **www.oxfordtextbooks.co.uk/orc/brymansrm3e/**.

I will now introduce the students who have provided input that has informed the writing of the 'Student experience' feature of this book. I am extremely grateful to them for being willing to share their experiences of doing a research project and hope that sharing what they have learned from this process with the readers of this book will enable others to benefit from their experience.

Rebecca Barnes

Rebecca Barnes was in the final stages of writing up her PhD in the School of Sociology and Social Policy, University of Nottingham. Rebecca's thesis examined the issue of violence and abuse in women's same-sex intimate relationships. Her research is one of only a few studies on this topic in the UK. Rebecca adopted a qualitative methodology, conducting semi-structured, in-depth interviews with 40 women who self-defined as having been abused in a previous same-sex relationship. She carried out her interviews across England and parts of Wales, using online avenues and various forms of advertising to recruit her sample. Rebecca's research experiences have fuelled her interest in methodological issues, and in particular, the ethical issues which are raised by 'sensitive' research. She has since been appointed Lecturer in Sociology at the University of Derby, where much of her teaching relates to research methods.

Jez Clark

Jez Clark graduated in 2007 with First Class Honours from the University of East Anglia, Norwich. Jez studied Politics with Media with a final year internship at an advertising agency at which he wrote on the evolution of political advertising. During his second year Jez undertook a 'Methods of Social Research' project exploring student perceptions of academic provision and support during university. His report focused on the academic issues and problems that individuals may face, and examined whether the UEA advisory system was providing adequate support. The information was collected by questionnaire, using a combination of systematic probability and stratified random sampling. The data taken from these were collated and analysed (if answers could be coded) using the SPSS programme; uncoded, 'open' responses were independently assessed.

Hannah Creane

Hannah Creane completed her undergraduate degree in Sociology with Law at Durham University. She finished her studies in 2007. The aim of Hannah's research project was to explore the generational changes within childhood. Hannah had always been interested in the development of the person from child to adult, and in particular the social construction of childhood. This interest was furthered after carrying out a pilot project in 2005 exploring the importance of sibling relationships in the development of the child. Hannah's project was based on the question of what makes a child a child as opposed to an adult, and to what extent this has changed across the generations. Her research was based on nine semi-structured interviews; she chose this research method in order to avoid limiting the response of the people she was interviewing. She created three distinct age brackets: 0–29, 30–59, and 60+, and then interviewed three people from each age bracket in order to ensure an equal representation for each generation.

Cornelius Grebe

Cornelius did a PhD in Social Policy and Administration at the University of Nottingham. His thesis used qualitative research to analyse German reconciliation of paid employment and care work policy. Cornelius combined a contextual social constructionist paradigm of enquiry with a feminist point of view analysing parental leave, childcare, anti-discrimination, and working time policies. He was interested in how policy 'solutions' shape our understanding of the social 'problem' of the incompatibility of paid employment and care work. Cornelius employed documentary analysis concentrating on enacted and proposed legislation.

Sarah Hanson

In 2006 Sarah completed a three-year BA honours degree in English and Sociology at the University of Derby. In her final year Sarah focused her dissertation on the sociological impact of women's magazines, through a combination of contextual and coded analysis. By using a system of content analysis that was fair and unbiased, Sarah was able to discover other meanings behind the structure of the magazines' front covers. Well-documented theories of feminism and the construction of gender and stereotypes allowed Sarah to decode the results and she was thus able to break down the magazine covers to disclose their true meaning.

Gareth Matthews

Gareth completed a BA in Sociology at the University of Nottingham in 2002, and then went on to complete an MA in Research Methods. Over this time he developed an interest in industrial sociology and, more specifically, Marxist approaches to labour process analysis, both of which stemmed from his personal experience in a variety of work settings. At present he is writing a thesis on the employment of migrant workers in the UK's hospitality industry, drawing on data from in-depth interviews held with employers and managers of hotels, bars, and restaurants in the Brighton and Hove area. The research seeks to challenge many of the connections that have recently been forged between the theoretical, analytical, and methodological approach to the study of the labour process, with a particular emphasis on the potential role of economic-geographical perspectives in reasserting the notion of 'place' into a revitalised empirical agenda.

Sophie Mason

Sophie Mason studied at the University of East Anglia undertaking a three-year course for a BA in Society, Culture and Media. In 2005–2006 she carried out a research project, which formed an integral part of her course. Her project was based on the views and experiences of students at the University of East Anglia. The project involved both qualitative and quantitative research on an individual and group scale, which required excellent organizational skills. Sophie felt it was important to consider the views of students from all demographics in order to gain a reliable understanding of individuals' university experiences. The project spanned three months from initial proposal to completion.

Lily Taylor

Lily Taylor completed her undergraduate degree in 2007 from the University of East Anglia, achieving a 2:1 in Society, Culture and Media. During her time studying Lily primarily directed her units towards those focused on social research. Lily's quantitative research project explored areas surrounding academic life at the UEA and focused in depth on student debt. The research methodology consisted of a questionnaire with a mixture of open- and closed-ended questions, conducted in university accommodation and around campus, using a random sampling technique. Exploring factors such as gender differences, living arrangements, degree courses, and part-time jobs enabled Lily to distinguish groups of people who were more likely to come out of university in debt than others, and the degree to which they were worried about this.

Erin Sanders

Erin recently completed her MSc in Gender and Politics at Birkbeck College, University of London. She became interested in how women were affected by development politics, and began investigating how sex workers were impacted by policies implemented in various developing countries. Her thesis research project focused on Thai NGOs that were working with female sex workers, investigating to what extent the organizations were representing women's interests. Her study was qualitative and incorporated feminist methodologies; semi-structured interviews were carried out with NGO representatives and sex workers in Bangkok and Chiang Mai. Erin is now working on her PhD at the University of Nottingham, exploring female tourism in Thailand.

Jack Sayers

Jack Sayers is a student at the University of East Anglia, Norwich, where he is studying for a Philosophy and Politics BA. In his second year of the program he studied the unit *Methods of Social Research*, in which he created his report. Jack's research was part of a group project that examined student satisfaction with university accommodation—interviewing those staying in halls of residences to attain their results. Jack's report emphasised the services provided by the university, both within the halls of residences, and the university itself. He compared the satisfaction levels of male and female participants to find out whether there was any deviation in their views.

Isabella Robbins

Isabella embarked on her first degree following the birth of her third child, and a twenty-five year career as a professional nurse. She studied Sociology in order to help her make sense of her world. Having obtained a BA Hons in Sociology at the University of Nottingham, she took up an ESRC 1+3 studentship at the University of Nottingham. Her research interest concerns contemporary motherhood and the particular issue of how mothers account for their vaccination decisions. Her interest in this stems from her own experience of motherhood and the inherent contradictions and challenges of mothering. In order to explore this issue, she undertook a qualitative research study. She has just submitted her PhD thesis.

Joe Thomson

 Joe Thomson studied at the University of East Anglia for a BA degree in Politics with Media. In his second year, Joe was encouraged to embark on a unit which would revolve around social research and individual project work based on the surrounding university environment. Like Jack Sayers, Joe's project had the objective of trying to gauge and understand the perspectives of UEA students regarding accommodation and campus facilities. His report focussed upon a comparison of experiences between international and UK/EU students, which highlighted issues such as security, inter-flat relationships, and services provided by the accommodation office. In order to carry out his research, Joe used a questionnaire design, as well as a combination of sampling methods: stratified random sampling and systematic probability sampling. Data gathered from interviews were coded and then analysed using SPSS.

Guide to the book

About the book

Focus of the book

This book has been written with two groups of readers in mind. First, undergraduates in subjects such as sociology, social policy, human geography, and education who at some point in their degree take a course, and often more than one course, in the area of research methods. The book covers a wide range of research methods, approaches to research, and ways of carrying out data analysis, so it is likely to meet the needs of the vast majority of students in this position. Research methods are not tied to a particular nation; many if not most of the principles transcend national boundaries. However, in writing the book, I have given it a decidedly British emphasis. This means that I have used British examples of research whenever possible or appropriate.

The second group, which in most cases overlaps with the first, comprises undergraduates and postgraduates who do a research project as part of the requirement for their degree programmes. This can take many forms, but one of the most common is that a small-scale research project is carried out and a dissertation based on the investigation is presented. In addition, students are often expected to carry out mini-projects in relation to certain modules. Chapter 3 has been written specifically for students doing research projects. This chapter thus builds on earlier discussion of research questions in Chapter 2, reinforcing a topic that is central to the whole process of doing research. The accent in the chapters in Parts Two and Three is on the practice of social research and as such these chapters will be extremely useful in helping students make informed decisions about doing their research. In addition, when each research method is examined, its uses and limitations are explored in order to help students to make these decisions. Chapter 27 provides advice on writing up research.

In addition to providing students with practical advice on doing research, the book also explores the nature of social research. This means that it attends to issues relating to fundamental concerns about what doing social research entails. For example:

- Is a natural science model of the research process applicable to the study of society?
- If not, why not?
- Why do some people feel it is inappropriate to employ such a model?
- If we do use a natural science model, does that mean that we are making certain assumptions about the nature of social reality?
- Equally, do those writers and researchers who reject such a model have an alternative set of assumptions about the nature of social reality?
- What kind or kinds of research findings are regarded as legitimate and acceptable?
- To what extent do values have an impact on the research process?
- Should we worry about the feelings of people outside the research community concerning what we do to people during our investigations?

These and many other issues impinge on research in a variety of ways and will be confronted at different stages throughout the book. While knowing how to do research —how best to design a questionnaire, how to observe, how to analyse documents, and so on—is crucial to an education in research methods, so too is a broad appreciation of the wider issues that impinge on the practice of social research. Thus, so far as I am concerned, the role of an education in research methods is not just to provide the skills that will allow you to do your own research, but also to provide you with the tools for a critical appreciation of how research is done and with what assumptions. One of the most important abilities that an understanding of research methods and methodology provides is an awareness of the need not to take evidence that you come across (in books, journals, and so on) for granted.

Why use this book?

There are likely to be two main circumstances in which this book is likely to be in your hands at the moment. One is that you have to study one or more modules in research methods for a degree in one of the social sciences or there are methodological components to one of your substantive modules (e.g. a module in the sociology of work). The other is that you have to conduct an investigation in a social scientific field, perhaps for a dissertation or project report, and you need some guidelines about how to approach your study. This book may find itself in your hands for either or both of these reasons during the course of doing your degree. It may be that you are wondering why you need to study research methods as a field and why people like the author of this book do social research at all. In the rest of this section, I will try briefly to address these issues and concerns but before that, what do we mean by social research?

What is meant by 'social research'?

The term 'social research' denotes in this book *academic* research on topics relating to questions relevant to the social scientific fields, like sociology, human geography, social policy, politics, and criminology. Thus, I mean research that draws on the social sciences for conceptual and theoretical inspiration. Such research may be motivated by developments and changes in society, such as the rise of concerns about security or of binge-drinking, but it will employ social scientific ideas to illuminate those changes.

Why do social research?

The rationale for doing social research has been outlined in the previous sub-section to a certain extent. Academics conduct such research because in the course of reading the literature on a topic or when reflecting on what is going on in modern social life, questions occur to them. They may notice a gap in the literature or an inconsistency between a number of studies or an unresolved issue in the literature. These provide common circumstances that act as springboards for social research in academic circles. Another is when there is a development in society that provides an interesting point of departure for the investigation of a research question. For example, noting the widespread use of text messaging, a researcher might be interested in studying how far it has affected the nature and quality of interaction in social life. In exploring this kind of issue, the researcher is likely to draw upon the literature on technology and on social interaction to provide insights into how to approach the issue. As I say in chapter 1, there is no single reason why people do social research of the kind emphasized in this book, but at its core, it is done because there is an aspect of our understanding of what goes on in society that is to some extent unresolved.

Why is it important to study methods?

To some students, there does not seem a great deal of point to studying research methods. They might take the view that if they have to conduct an investigation, why not adopt a 'need to know' approach? In other words, why not just look into how to do your research when you are on the verge of carrying out your investigation? Quite aside from the fact that this is an extremely risky approach to take, it neglects the opportunities that a training in research methods offers. In particular, you need to bear in mind the following:

- A training in research methods sensitizes you to the *choices* that are available to social researchers. In other words, it makes you aware of the range of research methods that can be employed to collect data and the variety of approaches to the analysis of data. Such an awareness will help you to make the most appropriate choices for your project since you need to be aware of when it is appropriate or inappropriate to employ particular techniques of data collection and analysis.

- A training in research methods provides you with an awareness of the 'dos' and 'don'ts' when employing a particular approach to collecting or analysing data. Thus, once you have made your choice of research method (for example, a questionnaire), you need to be aware of the practices you should follow in order to implement that method properly. You also need to be aware of the many pitfalls to be avoided.

- A training in research methods provides you with insights into the overall research process. It provides a general vantage point for understanding how research is done. As such, it illuminates the various stages of research, so that you can plan your research and think about such issues as how your research methods will connect with your research questions.

- A training in research methods provides you with an awareness of what constitutes good and poor research. It therefore provides a platform for developing a critical awareness of the limits and limitations of research that you read. This can be helpful in providing a critical appreciation of research that you read for substantive modules in fields like the sociology of work or of the family.

- The skills that a training in research methods imparts are transferable ones. Knowing about how to sample, how to design a questionnaire, how to conduct semi-structured interviewing or focus groups and so on are skills that are relevant to research in other spheres (such as firms, public sector organizations etc.).

- Studying research methods by using this book exposes you to a multitude of examples from real-life research. I have always learned a lot by reading research and finding out how others have carried out research and what lessons they seem to have learned. In view of this, the book is full of examples. I have tried to illustrate most of my major points with an example and often more than one. Most of our examples derive from published research and it is clearly the case that you will find it difficult to generate research of an equivalent level because of your limited resources, time, and experience. On the other hand, you can get close and it is important to learn about the benchmarks that good practice in published work provide. In your own research, it may be that, to use a well-known term devised by Herbert Simon (1960), you will need to *satisfice*. (Simon devised this term to forge a contrast with the model of rational decision making that was pervasive in economics. He argued that, when working in organizations, people satisfice when they make decisions rather than find the most appropriate means to achieve given ends. Satisficing means that the search for an appropriate course of action is governed by the principle of looking for what is satisfactory, rather than by what is optimal.) The important issue is to know in what ways you are needing to satisfice and what the implications are of doing so.

Thus, I feel that a training in research methods has much to offer and that readers of this book will recognize the opportunities and advantages that it provides.

Erin Sanders, one of the students who have contributed to this book, herself expresses the usefulness of a knowledge of research methods for a student embarking on a research project:

> I think students often read a good deal around their subject and have a working knowledge of the literature about their topic—but rarely read about methods and methodologies. Knowing about research methods is incredibly helpful when conducting research, and too often it is left out of the research process.

Structure of the book

Social research has many different traditions, one of the most fundamental of which is the distinction between quantitative and qualitative research. This distinction lies behind the structure of the book and the way in which issues and methods are approached.

The book is divided into four parts.

Part One comprises five scene-setting chapters. It deals with basic ideas about the nature of social research.

- Chapter 1 examines such issues as the nature of the relationship between theory and research and the degree to which a natural science approach is an appropriate framework for the study of society. It is here that the distinction between quantitative and qualitative research is first encountered. They are presented as different *research strategies* with different ways of conceptualizing how people and society should be studied. It is also shown that there is more to the distinction between them than whether an investigation includes the collection of quantitative data.

- In Chapter 2, the idea of a *research design* is introduced. This chapter allows an introduction to the basic frameworks within which social research is carried out, such as social survey research, case study research, and experimental research. These two chapters provide the basic building blocks for the rest of the book.

- Chapter 3 takes you through the mains steps that are involved in planning and designing a research project and offers advice on how to manage this process. It also includes a discussion of *research questions*— what they are, why they are important, and how they come to be formulated.

- Chapter 4 is designed to help you to get started on your research project by introducing the main steps in conducting a critical review of the literature.

- Chapter 5 considers the ways in which ethical issues impinge on researchers and the kinds of principles that are involved.

Part Two contains ten chapters concerned with quantitative research.

- The first chapter explores the nature of quantitative research and as such provides a context for the later chapters. The next four chapters are largely concerned with aspects of social survey research.

- Chapter 7 deals with sampling issues—how to select a sample and the considerations that are involved in assessing what can be inferred from different kinds of sample. It also contains at the beginning an introduction to survey research which acts as a backdrop to the discussion of sampling and to the subject matter of the following three chapters.

- Chapter 8 is concerned with the kind of interviewing that takes place in survey research, that is, structured interviewing.

- Chapter 9 covers the design of questionnaires. This involves a discussion of how to devise self-completion questionnaires, such as postal questionnaires.

- Chapter 10 examines the issue of how to ask questions for questionnaires and structured interviews.

- Chapter 11 covers structured observation, which is a method that has been developed for the systematic observation of behaviour.

- Chapter 12 presents content analysis, a method that provides a rigorous framework for the analysis of a wide range of documents.

- Chapter 13 deals with the analysis of data collected by other researchers and by official bodies. The emphasis then switches to the ways in which we can analyse quantitative data.

- Chapter 14 presents a range of basic tools for the analysis of quantitative data. The approach taken is non-technical. The emphasis is upon how to choose a method of analysis and how to interpret the findings. No formulae are presented.

- Chapter 15 shows you how to use computer software— in the form of SPSS, the most widely used software for analysing quantitative data—in order to implement the techniques you learned in Chapter 14.

Part Three contains eight chapters on aspects of qualitative research.

- Chapter 16 has the same role in relation to Part Three as Chapter 6 has in relation to Part Two. It provides an overview of the nature of qualitative research and as such provides the context for the other chapters in this Part.

- Chapter 17 is concerned with ethnography and participant observation, which is the source of some of the most well-known studies in social research. The two terms are often used interchangeably and refer to the immersion of the researcher in a social setting.

- Chapter 18 deals with the kinds of interview that qualitative researchers conduct, which is typically semi-structured interviewing or unstructured interviewing.

- Chapter 19 explores the focus group method, whereby groups of individuals are interviewed on a specific topic.

- Chapter 20 examines two ways in which qualitative researchers analyse language: conversation analysis and discourse analysis.

- Chapter 21 deals with the examination of documents in qualitative research. The emphasis then shifts to the analysis of qualitative data.

- Chapter 22 explores some approaches to the analysis of qualitative data.

- Chapter 23 shows you how to use computer software— a relatively new development in qualitative research— to assist with your analysis.

It is striking that certain issues recur across Parts Two and Three: interviewing, observation, documents, and data analysis. However, as you will see, quantitative and qualitative research constitute contrasting approaches to such activities.

Part Four contains chapters that go beyond the quantitative/qualitative research contrast.

- Chapter 24 deals with some of the ways in which the distinction between quantitative and qualitative research is less fixed than is sometimes supposed.

- Chapter 25 presents some ways in which quantitative and qualitative research can be combined to produce what is referred to as mixed methods research.

- Chapter 26 is concerned with the use of the Internet as a context or platform for conducting research.

- Chapter 27 has been included to help with writing up research, an often neglected area of the research process.

The third edition

This third edition contains both major and minor differences from the second edition. The major revisions are:

- A new chapter on *reviewing the literature* as the starting point for doing social research (Chapter 4). I know from talking with my own students and from supervising dissertation students that reviewing the literature can often be a cause for concern for them.

- Several chapters include *tips and skills* as mentioned in the previous section.

- *Student experience* features to illuminate students' own encounters with the social research process.

- Chapter 25 has been completely rewritten to take account of my own investigations into mixed methods research and the work of others who have been interested in this fast-growing area. I am grateful to some of the readers of the revised edition who suggested that I do this.

Minor revisions include:

- New sections on such topics as: the use of the telephone in qualitative interviewing; thematic analysis; recent discussions of quality criteria for qualitative research; and writing up mixed methods research.

- Many sections have been expanded and updated to include important developments such as the Economic and Social Research Council's *Research Ethics Framework* and the Department of Health's *Research Governance Framework for Health and Social Care*.

- All sections have been updated where appropriate. Chapter 26, which is concerned with the use of the Internet in social research, has undergone quite a lot of revisions, as this is an area of research methodology where a number of developments have taken place.

- New examples have been introduced and some from the previous editions have been replaced.

How to use the book

The book can be used in a number of different ways. However, I would encourage all readers at least to look at the chapter guide at the beginning of each chapter so that they can be sure whether they in fact need the material covered there and also to gain a sense of the range of issues the book does in fact address.

- **Wider philosophical and methodological issues**. If you do not need to gain an appreciation of the wider philosophical context of enquiry in social research, Chapter 1 can largely be ignored. If an emphasis on such issues *is* something you are interested in, Chapter 1 along with Chapter 24 should be a particular focus of attention.

- **Survey research**. Chapters 7 through 10 deal with the kinds of topics that need to be addressed in survey research. In addition, Chapter 14 examines ways of analysing the kinds of data that are generated by survey researchers. Also, sections in Chapter 26 explore issues to do with the conduct of surveys via e-mail or the World Wide Web.

- **Practical issues concerned with doing quantitative research**. This is the province of the whole of Part Two. In addition, you would be advised to read Chapter 2, which maps out the main research designs employed, such as experimental and cross-sectional designs that are frequently used by quantitative researchers.

- **Practical issues concerned with doing qualitative research**. This is the province of the whole of Part Three. In addition, you would be advised to read Chapter 2, which maps out the main research designs employed, such as the case study which is frequently employed in qualitative research.

- **Analysing data**. Chapters 14 and 22 explore the analysis of quantitative and qualitative research data respectively, while Chapters 15 and 23 introduce readers to the use of computer software in this connection. It may be that your module on research methods does not get into issues to do with analysis, in which case these chapters would be omitted.

- **Formulating research questions**. As I have already said in this Guide, I see the asking of research questions as fundamental to the research process. Advice on what research questions are, how they are formulated, where they come from, and so on is provided in chapter 3.

- **Doing your own research project**. I hope that the whole of this book will be relevant to students doing their own research projects or mini-projects, but Chapter 3 is the one where specific advice relating to this issue is located. In addition, I would alert you to the practical tips that have been devised and the checklists of points to remember.

- **Writing**. This issue is very much connected with the last point. It is easy to forget that your research has to be *written up*. This is as much a part of the research process as the collection of data. Chapter 27 discusses a variety of issues to do with writing up research.

- **Wider responsibilities of researchers**. It is important to bear in mind that as researchers we bear responsibilities to the people and organizations that are the recipients of our research activities. Ethical issues are raised at a number of points in this book and Chapter 5 is devoted to a discussion of them. The fact that an entire chapter has been given over to a discussion of ethics is a measure of their importance in terms of the need to ensure that all researchers should be ethically sensitive.

- **The quantitative/qualitative research contrast**. The distinction between quantitative and qualitative research is used in two ways: as a means of organizing the research methods and methods of analysis available to you; and as a way of introducing some wider philosophical issues about social research. Chapter 1 outlines the chief areas of difference between quantitative and qualitative research. These are followed up in Chapter 16. I also draw attention to some of the limitations of adhering to an excessively strict demarcation between the two research strategies in Chapter 24, while Chapter 25 explores ways of integrating them. If you do not find it a helpful distinction, these chapters can be avoided or skimmed.

- **The Internet**. The Internet plays an increasingly important role in the research process. At various junctures I provide important websites where key information can be gleaned. I also discuss in Chapter 4 the use of the Internet as a route for finding references for your *literature review*, itself another important phase of the research process. You will discover that many of the references that you find when you do an online search will then themselves be accessible to you in electronic form. Finally, Chapter 26 discusses the use of the Internet as a source of material that can be analysed and as a platform for doing research in the form of such research methods as web surveys, electronic focus groups, and email surveys.

Guided tour of textbook features

Research in focus features

It is often said that the three most important features to look for when buying a house are location, location, location. A parallel for the teaching of research methods is examples, examples, examples! Research in focus features are designed to provide a sense of place for the theories and concepts being discussed in the chapter text, by providing real examples of published research.

Chapter guide

Each chapter begins with a chapter guide that alerts readers to what they can expect to have learned by the end of each chapter. This provides a route map of what is to follow.

Key concept features

This feature explains key terms, for instance by asking 'What is . . . ?', or by listing a series of important points about a particular issue or topic. These features will help you build up a terminology about research methods which you can then apply in your own work and to provide further explanation of ideas that may be difficult to understand. Key concepts are indicated in blue type for quick reference and are defined in the Glossary.

Tips and skills features

These features provide guidance and advice on key aspects of the research process and are intended to help you to avoid making certain mistakes which I have found students commonly make, based on my experience of talking to and supervising them. Tips and skills features also give information that is intended to help you to acquire the skills that are needed to become a competent and social researcher.

◌ Student experience features

Student experience features draw on interviews with real research students from a variety of universities around the UK, and provide valuable windows into the research practices and problems of students who have gone before you. These features will help you to anticipate and resolve research problems as you move through your dissertation or project.

◌ Checklists

Most chapters include checklists of issues that should be borne in mind when engaging in certain activities (such as doing a literature review, devising a structured interview schedule, or conducting a focus group). They are meant to alert you to key points you will have encountered in the text so that you can be reminded of what to look out for or consider when doing your own research.

◌ Thinking deeply features

Social research methods can sometimes be complex: thinking deeply features contain further discussion of a topic or issue as a way of encouraging you to think about it in greater depth or helping to explain current debates or important discussions that have gone on between researchers. This feature is intended to take you beyond the introductory level and to raise your awareness of some of the complexities involved in using social research methods.

◌ Key points

At the end of each chapter there is a set of significant points that are particularly crucial for you to take note of. They are meant to alert you to issues that are especially important and to jog your memory about the areas that have been covered.

◌ Glossary

At the end of the book is a glossary of definitions of central terms. Many repeat definitions in the key concept features, but they also provide a convenient way of knowing what is meant by key terms. Glossary terms are also highlighted in blue text in the chapters.

◌ Questions for review

At the end of each chapter there is also a series of questions to help you to test your understanding of key concepts and ideas.

Guided tour of the ORC: lecturer resources

http://www.oxfordtextbooks.co.uk/orc/brymansrm3e/

This textbook is accompanied by a full suite of online resources which are freely available to adopting lecturers. Our comprehensive supplements will save you time in preparing lectures, planning seminars, and creating assessments for your students. To register for a password, simply follow the steps on the *Social Research Methods* homepage. ○

Deductive and inductive theory

- Deductivism:
  - theory --> data
  - explicit hypothesis to be confirmed or rejected
  - quantitative research
- Inductivism:
  - data --> theory
  - generalizable inferences from observations
  - qualitative research /grounded theory

© Oxford University Press, 2008. All rights reserved.   OXFORD *Higher Education*

○ PowerPoint slides

A suite of customizable PowerPoint slides has been included for use in lecture presentations. Arranged by chapter theme and tied specifically to the lecturer's guide, the slides may also be used as handouts in class.

○ Lecturer's guide

A comprehensive lecturer's guide has been included to assist both new and experienced instructors in their teaching. The guide includes reading guides, lecture outlines, further coverage of difficult concepts, and teaching activities, and is accompanied by instructions on how the guide may be most effectively implemented in the teaching programme.

◯ Case studies

Each chapter is accompanied by a case study, complete with 3–5 discussion questions. These can be used in seminars or as assignments, to stimulate group work, and independent critical thinking.

Figure 2.4

The longitudinal design

◯ Figures and tables from the text

All figures and tables from the text are provided in high resolution format for downloading into presentation software or for use in assignments and exam material.

◯ Test bank

This customizable resource contains 10 questions per chapter with answers and 100 words of feedback per question, allowing you to create your own personalized testing sessions. These can be used to monitor students' understanding and progress during the term, or in formal assessment at the end of the course.

Guided tour of the ORC: student resources

http://www.oxfordtextbooks.co.uk/orc/brymansrm3e/

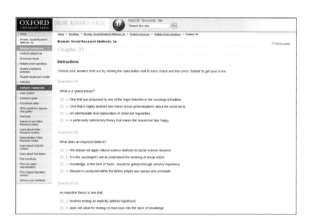

○ Multiple choice questions

The best way to reinforce your understanding of research methods is through frequent and cumulative revision. To aid you in this, a bank of self-marking multiple choice questions has been provided for each chapter of the text, and includes instant feedback on your answers to help strengthen your knowledge of key research concepts.

○ Annotated web links

A series of annotated web links to the best social research websites, organized by chapter, enables you to extend your understanding by reading the latest perspectives on social research issues.

○ Student researcher's toolkit

This toolkit is divided into two main parts:

1. A interactive research project guide which takes you step-by-step through each of the key research phases, ensuring that you do not overlook any research step, and providing guidance and advice on every aspect of social research from dealing with your supervisor to ways of organizing and writing your dissertation for maximum effect.

2. Dos and don'ts of social research: a quick practical checklist drawn from experience of common pitfalls.

○ Student experience podcasts

Learn from the real research experiences of students who have just completed their own research projects! Download podcasts explaining in detail about the research projects of 8 undergraduate and 4 postgraduate (MA and PhD) students from a range of degree courses throughout the UK. Learn about the research processes they went through and the problems they resolved as they moved through each research phase. The questionnaires are also available on the ORC as Word documents.

○ Guide to using Excel in data analysis

Using Excel to an advanced level can be one of the trickiest aspects of a research project. This interactive guide takes you through step-by-step from the very first stages of using Excel to more advanced topics such as charting, regression, and statistical significance.

Online Resource Centre authors

PowerPoint slides authored by Susie Scott, University of Sussex

Lecturer's guide authored by Susie Scott, University of Sussex

Case studies authored by Susie Scott, University of Sussex and updated by Tom Owens, International Business School, Budapest

Test bank authored by Susie Scott, University of Sussex

Multiple choice questions authored by Susie Scott, University of Sussex and updated by Tom Owens, International Business School, Budapest

Annotated web links authored by Susie Scott, University of Sussex and updated by Tom Owens, International Business School, Budapest

Student researcher's toolkit authored by Susie Scott, University of Sussex

Guide to using Excel in data analysis authored by David Whigham, Glasgow Caledonian University

Tom Owens, International Business School, Budapest, authored the PowerPoint slides and lecturer's guide for chapters 15 and 23, and all **ORC resources for chapter 4**, *Reviewing the literature* (apart from the test bank which is authored by Susie Scott).

Abbreviations

ASA	American Sociological Association
BCS	British Crime Survey
BFI	British Film Institute
BHPS	British Household Panel Survey
BPS	British Psychological Society
BSA	British Social Attitudes [survey]
BSA	British Sociological Association
BSE	Bovine Spongiform Encelphalopathy
CA	conversation analysis
CAPI	computer-assisted personal interviewing
CAQDAS	computer-assisted/aided qualitative data analysis software
CATI	computer-assisted telephone interviewing
CCTV	closed-circuit television
CDA	critical discourse analysis
CF	cystic fibrosis
CJD	Creuzfeld Jacob Disease
CV	curriculum vitae
DA	discourse analysis
ECA	ethnographic content analysis
EFS	Expenditure and Food Survey
ENT	ear, nose, throat
EPPI	Evidence for Policy and Practice Information and Coordinating Centre
ESRC	Economic and Social Research Council
FES	Family Expenditure Survey
FIAC	Flanders Interaction Analysis Categories
FMD	Foot and Mouth Disease
GHS	General Household Survey
HALS	Health and Lifestyle Survey
HETUS	Harmonized European Time Use Studies
HISS	hospital information support system
HRT	hormone replacement therapy
IBSS	International Bibliography of the Social Sciences
ICI	Imperial Chemical Industries
ISSP	International Social Survey Programme
ISP	Internet service provider
IT	information technology
LFS	Labour Force Survey
MUD	multi-user domain
NCDS	National Child Development Study
NFS	National Food Survey

NUD*IST	Non-Numerical Unstructured Data Indexing Searching and Theorizing
NVIVO	QSR NUD*IST Vivo
ONS	Omnibus Survey
ORACLE	Observational Research and Classroom Learning Evaluation
RCT	randomized controlled trial
REC	Research Ethics Committee
REF	*Research Ethics Framework*
RGF	*Research Governance Framework for Health and Social Care*
SCELI	Social Change and Economic Life Initiative
SCPR	Social and Community Planning Research
SE	standard error [of the mean]
SPSS	Statistical Package for the Social Sciences
SRA	Social Research Association
SSCI	Social Sciences Citation Index
TB	tuberculosis
TDM	Total Design Method
WERS	Workplace Employee Relations Survey
WoK	Web of Knowledge

Part One

Part One of this book is concerned with two ideas that will recur again and again during the course of this book—the idea of research strategy and the idea of research design. Chapter 1 outlines a variety of considerations that impinge on the practice of social research and relates these to the issue of research strategy. Two research strategies are identified: quantitative and qualitative research. Chapter 2 identifies the different kinds of research design that are employed in social research. Chapters 3 and 4 are concerned with providing advice to students on some of the issues that they need to consider if they have to prepare a dissertation based upon a relatively small-scale research project. Chapter 3 deals with planning and formulating research questions, including the principles and considerations that need to be taken into account in designing a small-scale research project, while Chapter 4 is about how to get started in reviewing the literature. Chapter 5 deals with ethics in social research.

These chapters provide some basic conceptual building blocks that you will return to at many points in the book. Some of the issues in Chapters 1 and 2 may seem remote from the issues of research practice dealt with in Chapters 3, 4, and 5, but they are in fact important and fundamental aspects of how we think about social research.

Social research strategies

Chapter outline

Chapter guide

The chief aim of this chapter is to show that a variety of considerations enter into the process of doing social research. The distinction that is commonly drawn among writers on and practitioners of social research between *quantitative research* and *qualitative research* is explored in relation to these considerations. This chapter explores:

- the nature of the **relationship** between theory and research, in particular whether theory guides research (known as a *deductive* approach) or whether theory is an outcome of research (known as an *inductive* approach);

- *epistemological* issues—that is, ones to do with what is regarded as appropriate knowledge about the social world; one of the most crucial aspects is the question of whether or not a natural science model of the research process is suitable for the study of the social world;

- *ontological* issues—that is, ones to do with whether the social world is regarded as something external to social actors or as something that people are in the process of fashioning;

- the ways in which these issues relate to the widely used distinction in the social sciences between two types of *research strategy*: **quantitative** and **qualitative research**; there is also a preliminary discussion, which will be followed up in Chapter 24, that suggests that, while quantitative and qualitative research represent different approaches to social research, we should be wary of driving a wedge between them;

- the ways in which *values* and *practical issues* also impinge on the social research process.

Introduction

This book is about social research. It attempts to equip people who have some knowledge of the social sciences with an appreciation of how social research should be conducted and what it entails. The latter project involves situating social research in the context of sociology, which in turn means attending to the question of its role in the overall enterprise of the discipline. It would be much easier to 'cut to the chase' and explore the nature of methods of social research and provide advice on how best to choose between and implement them. After all, many people might expect a book with the title of the present one to be concerned mainly with the ways in which the different methods in the social researcher's arsenal can be employed.

But the practice of social research does not exist in a bubble, hermetically sealed off from the social sciences and the various intellectual allegiances that their practitioners hold. Two points are of particular relevance here.

First, methods of social research are closely tied to different visions of how social reality should be studied. Methods are not simply neutral tools: they are linked with the ways in which social scientists envision the connection between different viewpoints about the nature of social reality and how it should be examined. However, it is possible to overstate this point. While methods are not neutral, they are not entirely suffused with intellectual inclinations either. Secondly, there is the question of how research methods and practice connect with the wider social scientific enterprise. Research data are invariably collected in relation to something. The 'something' may be a burning social problem or, more usually, a theory.

This is not to suggest that research is entirely dictated by theoretical concerns. One sometimes finds simple 'fact-finding' exercises published. Fenton *et al.* (1998) conducted a quantitative **content analysis** of social research reported in the British mass media. They examined national and regional newspapers, television and radio, and also magazines. They admit that one of the main reasons for conducting the research was to establish the amount and types of research that are represented. Sometimes, such exercises are motivated by a concern about a pressing social problem. McKeganey and Barnard (1996) conducted qualitative research involving observation and interviews with prostitutes and their clients in Glasgow. One factor that seems to have prompted this research was the concern about the role of prostitutes in spreading HIV infection (McKeganey and Barnard 1996: 3). Another scenario occurs when research is done on a topic when a specific opportunity arises. The interest of Westergaard *et al.* (1989) in the effects of redundancy seems to have been profoundly motivated by the opportunity that arose when a Sheffield steel company, which was close to their institutional base at the University of Sheffield, made a large number of people redundant. The firm's management approached the authors a year after the redundancies to conduct research on what had happened to the individuals who had been made redundant. The authors conducted social survey research using a structured interview approach on most of those made redundant. Of course, the authors were influenced by theories about and previous research on unemployment, but the specific impetus for the research on the effects of redundancy was not planned. Yet another stimulus for research can arise out of personal experiences. Lofland and Lofland (1995) note that many research publications emerge out of the researcher's personal biography, such as Zukin's (1982) interest in loft living arising out of her living in a loft in New York City. Another example is O'Reilly's (2002) investigation of British expatriates living on the Costa del Sol in Spain, which stemmed from her and her partner's dream of moving to the area themselves, which in fact they eventually did. Certainly, my own interest in Disney theme parks can be traced back to a visit to Disney World in Florida in 1991 (Bryman 1995, 1999), while my interest in the representation of social science research in the mass media (Fenton *et al.* 1998) can almost certainly be attributed to a wounding experience with the press reported in Haslam and Bryman (1994).

By and large, however, research data achieve significance in sociology when viewed in relation to theoretical concerns. This raises the issue of the nature of the relationship between theory and research.

Student experience
Personal experience as a basis for research interests

For her research, Isabella Robbins was interested in the ways in which mothers frame decisions regarding vaccinations for their children. This topic had a particular significance for her. She writes:

> As the mother of three children I have encountered some tough decisions regarding responsibility towards my children. Reading sociology, as a mature student, gave me the tools to help understand my world and to contextualize some of the dilemmas I had faced. In particular, I had experienced a difficult decision regarding the vaccination status of my children.

*To read more about Isabella's research experiences, go to the Online Resource Centre that accompanies this book at **http://www.oxfordtextbooks.co.uk/orc/brymansrm3e/**.*

Theory and research

Characterizing the nature of the link between theory and research is by no means a straightforward matter. There are several issues at stake here, but two stand out in particular. First, there is the question of what form of theory one is talking about. Secondly, there is the matter of whether data are collected to test or to build theories. Theory is important to the social researcher because it provides a backcloth and rationale for the research that is being conducted. It also provides a framework within which social phenomena can be understood and the research findings can be interpreted.

What type of theory?

The term 'theory' is used in a variety of different ways, but its most common meaning is as an explanation of observed regularities, for example, why sufferers of schizophrenia are more likely to come from working-class than middle-class backgrounds, or why work alienation varies by technology. But such theories tend not to be the stuff of courses in sociological theory, which typically focus much more on theories with a higher level of abstraction. Examples of such theories include structural-functionalism, **symbolic interactionism**, critical theory, poststructuralism, structuration theory, and so on. What we see here is a distinction between theories of the former type, which are often called *theories of the middle range* (Merton 1967),

and *grand theories*, which operate at a more abstract and general level. According to Merton, grand theories offer few indications to researchers as to how they might guide or influence the collection of empirical evidence. So, if someone wanted to test a theory or to draw an inference from it that could be tested, the level of abstractness is likely to be so great that the researcher would find it difficult to make the necessary links with the real world. There is a paradox here, of course. Even highly abstract ideas, such as Parsons's notions of 'pattern variables' and 'functional requisites', must have some connection with an external reality, in that they are likely to have been generated out of Parsons's reading of research or his reflections upon that reality or others' writings on it. However, the level of abstractness of the theorizing is so great as to make it difficult for them to be deployed in research. For research purposes, then, Merton argues that grand theories are of limited use in connection with social research, although, as the example in Research in focus 1.1 suggests, an abstract concept like social capital (Bourdieu 1984) can have some pay-off in research terms. Instead, middle-range theories are 'intermediate to general theories of social systems which are too remote from particular classes of social behavior, organization and change to account for what is observed and to those detailed orderly descriptions of particulars that are not generalized at all' (Merton 1967: 39).

Research in focus 1.1
Grand theory and social research

Butler and Robson (2001) used Bourdieu's **concept** of social capital as a means of understanding gentrification of areas of London. While the term 'social capital' has acquired an everyday usage, Butler and Robson follow Bourdieu's theoretical use of it, which draws attention to the social connectedness and the interpersonal resources that those with social capital can draw on to pursue their goals. While the term has attracted the interest of social policy researchers and others concerned with social exclusion, its use in relation to the middle class has been less prominent, according to Butler and Robson. Bourdieu's treatment implies that those with social capital cultivate significant social connections and then draw upon those connections as resources for their goals. Butler and Robson conducted **semi-structured interviews** with 'gentrifiers' in each of three inner London areas. Of the three areas, Telegraph Hill was the strongest in terms of social capital. According to the authors, this is revealed in 'its higher levels of voluntary co-operation and sense of geographically focused unity' (Butler and Robson 2001: 2159). It is the recourse to these networks of sociality that accounts for the successful gentrification of Telegraph Hill. Battersea, one of the other two areas, entails a contrasting impetus for gentrification in Bourdieu's terms. Here, economic capital was more significant for gentrification than the social capital that was important in Telegraph Hill. The role of economic capital in Battersea can be seen in the 'competitive access to an increasingly desirable and expensive stock of housing and an exclusive circuit of schooling centred on private provision' (Butler and Robson 2001: 2159). In the former, it is sociality that provides the motor for gentrification, whereas in Battersea it is through market forces and is only partially influenced by patterns of social connectedness. This study is an interesting example of the way in which a relatively high-level theoretical notion—social capital and its kindred concept of economic capital—associated with a social theorist can be employed to illuminate research questions concerning the dynamics of modern urban living.

By and large, then, it is not grand theory that typically guides social research. Middle-range theories are much more likely to be the focus of empirical enquiry. In fact, Merton formulated the idea as a means of bridging what he saw as a growing gulf between theory (in the sense of grand theory) and empirical findings. This is not to say that there were no middle-range theories before he wrote: there definitely were, but what Merton did was to seek to clarify what is meant by 'theory' when social scientists write about the relationship between theory and research.

Middle-range theories, unlike grand ones, operate in a limited domain, whether it is juvenile delinquency, racial prejudice, educational attainment, or the labour process (see Research in focus 1.2). They vary somewhat in their range of application. For example, labelling theory represents a middle-range theory in the sociology of deviance. Its exponents sought to understand deviance in terms of the causes and effects of the societal reaction to deviation. It was held to be applicable to a variety of different forms of deviance, including crime and mental illness. By contrast, Cloward and Ohlin's (1960) differential association theory was formulated specifically in connection with juvenile delinquency, and in subsequent years this tended to be its focus. Middle-range theories, then, fall somewhere between grand theories and empirical findings. They represent attempts to understand and explain a limited aspect of social life.

Research in focus 1.2
Labour process theory: a middle-range theory

In the sociology of work, labour process theory can be regarded as a middle-range theory. The publication of *Labor and Monopoly Capital* (Braverman 1974) inaugurated a stream of thinking and research around the idea of the labour process and in particular on the degree to which there has been an inexorable trend towards increasing control over the manual worker and the deskilling of manual labour. A conference volume of much of this work was published as *Labour Process Theory* (Knights and Willmott 1990). P. Thompson (1989) describes the theory as having four elements: the principle that the labour process entails the extraction of surplus value; the need for capitalist enterprises constantly to transform production processes; the quest for control over labour; and the essential conflict between capital and labour. Labour process theory has been the focus of considerable empirical research (e.g. Knights *et al.* 1985).

Even the grand/middle-range distinction does not entirely clarify the issues involved in asking the deceptively simple question of 'what is theory?'. This is because the term 'theory' is frequently used in a manner that means little more than the background literature in an area of social enquiry. To a certain extent, this point can be taken to apply to fact-finding exercises such as those referred to above. The analysis of the representation of social research in the media by Fenton *et al.* (1998) was undertaken against a background of similar analyses in the USA and of studies of the representation of natural science research in the media in several different countries. In many cases, the relevant background literature relating to a topic fuels the focus of an article or book and thereby acts as the equivalent of a theory, as with the research referred to in Research in focus 1.3. The literature in a certain domain acts as the spur to an enquiry. The literature acts as an impetus in a number of ways: the researcher may seek to resolve an inconsistency between different findings or between different interpretations of findings; the researcher may have spotted a neglected aspect of a topic; certain ideas may not previously have been tested a great deal (such as the notion that recycling may be gendered, which prompted the investigation in Research in focus 1.3); the researcher may feel that existing approaches being used for research on a topic are deficient, and so provides an alternative approach; and so on.

Research in focus 1.3
Background literature as theory: recycling and the domestic division of labour

Oates and McDonald (2006) conducted a **postal questionnaire** survey of households in Sheffield that had agreed to participate in a trial whereby they were given blue 'wheelie bins' in which paper waste could be deposited. The survey was conducted three years after the scheme had been launched. The questionnaire was primarily concerned with the matter of who within households is involved in recycling activities. A total of 1,532 questionnaires was mailed out to participants in the trial. The researchers received back 469 usable questionnaires, which comprised 31 per cent of all those sent out. They expected that recycling activity would be highly gendered, in a manner similar to other domestic tasks. The authors found 'a clear gender difference in [the] data, as the domestic division of labour literature might predict. However, there is also a significant amount of joint activity which was not anticipated. . . . [Men] are more likely to participate in recycling as part of a joint initiative and activity than they are to do it alone.' (Oates and McDonald (2006: 427)

People sometimes suggest that researchers find what they expect to find. This is an interesting example of a set of findings that are only partially in tune with the researchers' expectations! However, the main point to register is that it is the literature on the domestic division of labour that forms the starting point of this study, as the quotation above indicates. Interestingly, in the article in which this research is reported, much of this literature is referred to in a section with the subtitle 'Theories and trends in the domestic division of labour'.

Social scientists are sometimes prone to being somewhat dismissive of research that has no obvious connections with theory—in either the grand or middle-range senses of the term. Such research is often dismissed as naive *empiricism* (see Key concept 1.1). It would be harsh, not to say inaccurate, to brand as naive empiricism the numerous studies in which the publications-as-theory strategy is employed, simply because their authors have not been preoccupied with theory. Such research is conditioned by and directed towards research questions that arise out of an interrogation of the literature. The data collection and analysis are subsequently geared to the illumination or resolution of the research issue or problem that has been identified at the outset. The literature acts as a proxy for theory. In many instances, theory is latent or implicit in the literature.

Key concept 1.1
What is empiricism?

The term 'empiricism' is used in a number of different ways, but two stand out. First, it is used to denote a general approach to the study of reality that suggests that only knowledge gained through experience and the senses is acceptable. In other words, this position means that ideas must be subjected to the rigours of testing before they can be considered knowledge. The second meaning of the term is related to this and refers to a belief that the accumulation of 'facts' is a legitimate goal in its own right. It is this second meaning that is sometimes referred to as 'naive empiricism'.

Indeed, research that appears to have the characteristics of the fact-finding exercise should not be prematurely dismissed as naive empiricism either. McKeganey and Barnard's (1996) research on prostitutes and their clients is a case in point. On the face of it, even if one strips away the concern with HIV infection, the research could be construed as naive empiricism and perhaps of a rather prurient kind. However, this again would be a harsh and probably inaccurate judgement. For example, the authors relate their research findings to the literature reporting other investigations of prostitutes in a number of different countries. They also illuminate their findings by drawing on ideas that are very much part of the sociologist's conceptual tool kit. One example is Goffman's (1963) notion of 'stigma' and the way in which the stigmatized individual seeks to manage a spoiled identity; another is Hochschild's (1983) concept of 'emotional labour', a term she coined to denote the way in which airline flight attendants need to express positive emotions as part of the requirements for their jobs. In doing so, they contrive a demeanour of friendliness when dealing with passengers, some of whom may be extremely difficult.

It is not possible to tell from McKeganey and Barnard's (1996) report whether the concepts of stigma and emotional labour influenced their data collection. However, raising this question invites consideration of another question: in so far as any piece of research is linked to theory, what was the role of that theory? Up to this point, I have tended to write as though theory is something that guides and influences the collection and analysis of data. In other words, research is done in order to answer questions posed by theoretical considerations. But an alternative position is to view theory as something that occurs after the collection and analysis of some or all of the data associated with a project. We begin to see here the significance of a second factor in considering the relationship between theory and research—whether we are referring to deductive or inductive theory.

Deductive and inductive theory

Deductive theory represents the commonest view of the nature of the relationship between theory and social research. The researcher, on the basis of what is known about in a particular domain and of theoretical considerations in relation to that domain, deduces a hypothesis (or hypotheses) that must then be subjected to empirical scrutiny. Embedded within the hypothesis will be concepts that will need to be translated into researchable entities. The social scientist must both skilfully deduce a hypothesis and then translate it into operational terms. This means that the social scientist needs to specify how data can be collected in relation to the concepts that make up the hypothesis.

This view of the role of theory in relation to research is very much the kind of role that Merton had in mind in connection with middle-range theory, which, he argued, 'is principally used in sociology to guide empirical inquiry' (Merton 1967: 39). Theory and the hypothesis deduced from it come first and drive the process of gathering data (see Research in focus 1.4 for an example of a deductive approach to the relationship between theory and data). The sequence can be depicted as one in which the steps outlined in Figure 1.1 take place.

The last step involves a movement that is in the opposite direction from deduction—it involves *induction*, as the researcher infers the implications of his or her findings for the theory that prompted the whole exercise. The findings are fed back into the stock of theory and the research findings associated with a certain domain of enquiry. This can be seen in the case of the final reflections of Butler and Robson's (2001) study of gentrification in three areas of London when they write:

Each of the three groups has played on its strengths, where it has them. Gentrification, given this, cannot in any sense be considered to be a unitary phenomenon, but needs to be examined in each case according to its own logic and outcomes. The concept of social capital, when used as an integrated part of an extended conceptual framework for the apprehension of all forms of middle-class capital relations, can thus play an important part in discriminating between differing types of social phenomena. (Butler and Robson 2001: 2160)

In these final reflections they show how their findings and the interpretations of those findings can be fed back into both the stock of knowledge concerning gentrification in cities and, in the third of the three sentences, the concept of social capital and its uses.

However, while this element of inductiveness un-doubtedly exists in the approach outlined, it is typically deemed to be predominantly deductive in orientation. Moreover, it is important to bear in mind that, when this deductive approach, which is usually associated with quan-titative research, is put into operation, it often does not fol-low the sequence outlined in its pure form. As previously noted, 'theory' may be little more than the literature on a certain topic in the form of the accumulated knowledge gleaned from books and articles. Also, even when theory or theories can be discerned, explicit hypotheses are not always deduced from them in the way that Kelley and De Graaf (1997) did in Research in focus 1.4. A further point to bear in mind is that the deductive process appears very linear—one step follows the other in a clear, logical sequence. However, there are many instances where this is not the case: a researcher's view of the theory or litera-

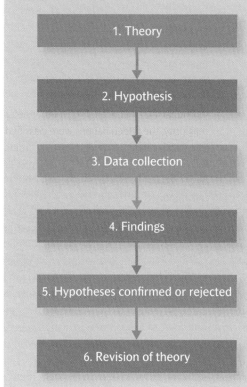

Figure 1.1

The process of deduction

1. Theory

2. Hypothesis

3. Data collection

4. Findings

5. Hypotheses confirmed or rejected

6. Revision of theory

ture may have changed as a result of the analysis of the collected data; new theoretical ideas or findings may be published by others before the researcher has generated his or her findings; or, as in the case of Layder *et al.* (1991), the relevance of a set of data for a theory may become apparent *after* the data have been collected.

Research in focus 1.4
A deductive study

Kelley and De Graaf (1997) show that a number of studies have examined the factors that have an impact upon individuals' religious beliefs, such as parents, schools, and friends, but they also argue that there are good grounds for thinking that the nation into which one is born will be an important cross-cultural factor. These reflections constitute what they refer to as the 'theory' that guided their research and from which the following hypothesis was derived: 'People born into religious nations will, in proportion to the orthodoxy of their fellow-citizens, acquire more orthodox beliefs than otherwise similar people born into secular nations' (Kelley and De Graaf 1997: 641). There are two central concepts in this hypothesis that would need to be measured: national religiosity (whether it is religious or secular) and individual religious orthodoxy. The authors hypothesized further that the religious orientation of the individual's family (whether devout or secular) would affect the nature of the relationship between national religiosity and religious orthodoxy.

To test the hypotheses, a **secondary analysis** of data deriving from survey research based on large **samples** from fifteen nations was conducted. UK readers will be interested to know that the British and Northern Irish (and Irish Republic) data were derived from the British Social Attitudes survey for 1991 (Jowell *et al.* 1992). Religious orthodoxy was measured by four survey questions concerned with religious belief. The questions asked about (1) whether the person believed in God, (2) his or her past beliefs about God, (3) how close the individual felt to God, and (4) whether he or she felt that God cares about everyone. To measure national religiosity, the fifteen nations were classified into one of five categories ascending from secular to religious. The classification was undertaken according to 'an unweighted average of parental church attendance . . . and religious belief in the nation as a whole' (Kelley and De Graaf 1997: 647). Family religious orientation was measured on a **scale** of five levels of parental church attendance. The hypotheses were broadly confirmed and the authors conclude that the 'religious environment of a nation has a major impact on the beliefs of its citizens' (Kelley and De Graaf 1997: 654). Some of the implications of the findings for theories about international differences in religiosity are then outlined.

This study demonstrates the process whereby hypotheses are deduced from existing theory and these then guide the process of data collection so that they can be tested.

This may all seem rather surprising and confusing. There is a certain logic to the idea of developing theories and then testing them. In everyday contexts, we commonly think of theories as things that are quite illuminating but that need to be tested before they can be considered valid or useful. In point of fact, however, while the process of deduction outlined in Figure 1.1 does undoubtedly occur, it is better considered as a general orientation to the link between theory and research. As a general orientation, its broad contours may frequently be discernible in social research, but it is also the case that we often find departures from it. However, in some research *no* attempt is made to follow the sequence outlined in Figure 1.1. Some researchers prefer an approach to the relationship between theory and research that is primarily *inductive*. With an inductive stance, theory is the *outcome* of research. In other words, the process of induction involves drawing generalizable inferences out of observations. Figure 1.2 attempts to capture the essence of the difference between inductivism and deductivism.

However, just as deduction entails an element of induction, the inductive process is likely to entail a modicum of deduction. Once the phase of theoretical reflection on a set of data has been carried out, the researcher may want

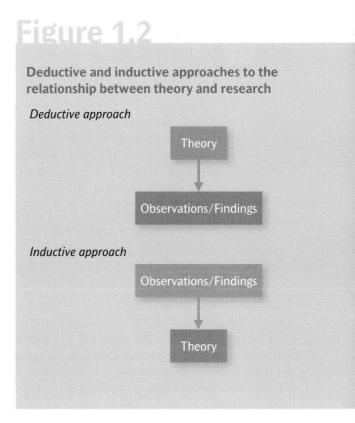

Figure 1.2

Deductive and inductive approaches to the relationship between theory and research

Deductive approach

Theory

Observations/Findings

Inductive approach

Observations/Findings

Theory

to collect further data in order to establish the conditions in which a theory will and will not hold. Such a general strategy is often called *iterative*: it involves a weaving back and forth between data and theory. It is particularly evident in *grounded theory*, which will be examined in Chapter 22, but in the meantime the basic point is to note that induction represents an alternative strategy for linking theory and research, although it contains a deductive element too.

However, as with 'theory' in connection with the deductive approach to the relationship between theory and research, we have to be cautious about the use of the term in the context of the inductive strategy too. While some researchers undoubtedly develop theories, equally it is necessary to be aware that very often what one ends up with can often be little more than empirical generalizations of the kind Merton (1967) wrote about. Research in focus 1.5 is an example of research that can be classified as inductive in the sense that it develops a theory out of interview data deriving from men suffering from chronic illness concerning what determines successful coping mechanisms for males afflicted with such a condition. In fact, the analytic strategy adopted by the author (Charmaz 1997) was grounded theory, and it is certainly the case that many of the most prominent examples of inductive research derive from this tradition (see the other chapters in Strauss and Corbin 1997b, from which Charmaz's example was taken).

Research in focus 1.5
An inductive study

Charmaz (1991, 1997) has been concerned to examine a number of aspects of the experiences of people with chronic illness. One phase of her research has entailed the examination specifically of men with such a condition. In one of her reports (Charmaz 1997), she discusses the results of her research into twenty men suffering from chronic illness. The bulk of her data derives from semi-structured interviews. In order to bring out the distinctiveness of men's responses, she compared the findings relating to men with a parallel study of women with chronic illness. She argues that a key component of men's responses is that of a strategy of *preserving self*. Although the experience of chronic illness invariably necessitates a change of lifestyle that itself occasions a change in personal identity, the men sought to preserve their sense of self by drawing on 'essential qualities, attributes, and identities of [the] past self' (Charmaz 1997: 49). By contrast, women were less reliant in their strategies of preserving self on the recapturing of past identities. She relates her theoretical reflections of her data to her male respondents' notions of masculine identity. Her emphasis on the idea of preserving self allows her to assess the factors that lie behind whether a man with chronic illness will 'reconstruct a positive identity or sink into depression' (Charmaz 1997: 57). If they were unable to have access to actions that would allow their sense of past self to be extended into the future (for example, through work), the probability of their sinking into depression was enhanced.

In this study, the inductive nature of the relationship between theory and research can be seen in the way that Charmaz's theoretical ideas (such as the notion of 'preserving self') derive from her data rather than being formed before she had collected her data.

Charmaz's (1997) research is an interesting illustration of an inductive approach. Two points are particularly worth noting about it. First, as previously noted, it uses a grounded theory approach to the analysis of data and to the generation of theory. This approach, which was first outlined by Glaser and Strauss (1967), is often regarded as especially strong in terms of generating theories out of data. This contrasts with the nature of many supposedly inductive studies, which generate interesting and illuminating findings but whose theoretical significance is not entirely clear. They provide insightful empirical generalizations, but little theory. Secondly, in much the same way that the deductive strategy is associated with a quantitative research approach, an inductive strategy of linking data and theory is typically associated with a qualitative research approach. It is not a coincidence that Charmaz's (1997) research referred to in Research in focus 1.5 is based on in-depth, semi-structured interviews that produced qualitative data in the form of respondents' detailed answers to her questions. However, as will be shown below, this characterization of the inductive strategy as associated with qualitative research is not entirely straightforward: not only does much qualitative research

not generate theory, but also theory is often used at the very least as a background to qualitative investigations.

It is useful to think of the relationship between theory and research in terms of deductive and inductive strategies. However, as the previous discussion has implied, the issues are not as clear-cut as they are sometimes presented. To a large extent, deductive and inductive strategies are possibly better thought of as tendencies rather than as a hard-and-fast distinction. But these are not the only issues that impinge on the conduct of social research.

Epistemological considerations

An epistemological issue concerns the question of what is (or should be) regarded as acceptable knowledge in a discipline. A particularly central issue in this context is the question of whether the social world can and should be studied according to the same principles, procedures, and

ethos as the natural sciences. The position that affirms the importance of imitating the natural sciences is invariably associated with an epistemological position known as *positivism* (see Key concept 1.2).

Key concept 1.2
What is positivism?

Positivism is an epistemological position that advocates the application of the methods of the natural sciences to the study of social reality and beyond. But the term stretches beyond this principle, though the constituent elements vary between authors. However, positivism is also taken to entail the following principles:

1. Only phenomena and hence knowledge confirmed by the senses can genuinely be warranted as knowledge (the principle of *phenomenalism*).

2. The purpose of theory is to generate hypotheses that can be tested and that will thereby allow explanations of laws to be assessed (the principle of *deductivism*).

3. Knowledge is arrived at through the gathering of facts that provide the basis for laws (the principle of *inductivism*).

4. Science must (and presumably can) be conducted in a way that is value free (that is, *objective*).

5. There is a clear distinction between scientific statements and normative statements and a belief that the former are the true domain of the scientist. This last principle is implied by the first because the truth or otherwise of normative statements cannot be confirmed by the senses.

A natural science epistemology: positivism

The doctrine of positivism is extremely difficult to pin down and therefore to outline in a precise manner, because it is used in a number of different ways by authors. For some writers, it is a descriptive category—one that describes a philosophical position that can be discerned in research—though there are still disagreements about what it comprises; for others, it is a pejorative term used to describe crude and often superficial data collection.

It is possible to see in the five principles in Key concept 1.2 a link with some of the points that have already been raised about the relationship between theory and research. For example, positivism entails elements of both a deductive approach (principle 2) and an inductive strategy (principle 3). Also, a fairly sharp distinction is drawn between theory and research. The role of research is to test theories and to provide material for the development of laws. But either of these connections between theory and research carries with it the implication that it is possible to collect observations in a manner that is not influenced by pre-existing theories. Moreover, theoretical terms that are not directly amenable to observation are not considered genuinely scientific; they must be susceptible to the rigours of observation. All this carries with it the implication of greater epistemological status being given to observation than to theory.

It should be noted that it is a mistake to treat positivism as synonymous with science and the scientific. In fact, philosophers of science and of the social sciences differ quite sharply over how best to characterize scientific practice, and since the early 1960s there has been a drift away from viewing it in positivist terms. Thus, when writers complain about the limitations of positivism, it is not entirely clear whether they mean the philosophical term or a scientific approach more generally. *Realism* (in particular, *critical realism*), for example, is another philosophical position that purports to provide an account of the nature of scientific practice (see Key concept 1.3).

Key concept 1.3
What is realism?

Realism shares two features with positivism: a belief that the natural and the social sciences can and should apply the same kinds of approach to the collection of data and to explanation, and a commitment to the view that there is an external reality to which scientists direct their attention (in other words, there is a reality that is separate from our descriptions of it). There are two major forms of realism:

- *Empirical realism* simply asserts that, through the use of appropriate methods, reality can be understood. This version of realism is sometimes referred to as *naive realism* to reflect the fact that it is often assumed by realists that there is a perfect (or at least very close) correspondence between reality and the term used to describe it. As such, it 'fails to recognise that there are enduring structures and generative mechanisms underlying and producing observable phenomena and events' and is therefore 'superficial' (Bhaskar 1989: 2). This is perhaps the most common meaning of the term. When writers employ the term 'realism' in a general way, it is invariably this meaning to which they are referring.

- *Critical realism* is a specific form of realism whose manifesto is to recognize the reality of the natural order and the events and discourses of the social world and holds that 'we will only be able to understand—and so change—the social world if we identify the structures at work that generate those events and discourses. . . . These structures are not spontaneously apparent in the observable pattern of events; they can only be identified through the practical and theoretical work of the social sciences'. (Bhaskar 1989: 2)

Critical realism implies two things. First, it implies that, whereas positivists take the view that the scientist's conceptualization of reality actually directly reflects that reality, realists argue that the scientist's conceptualization is simply a way of knowing that reality. As Bhaskar (1975: 250) has put it: 'Science, then, is the systematic attempt to express in thought the structures and ways of acting of things that exist and act independently of thought.' Critical realists acknowledge and accept that the categories they employ to understand reality are likely to be provisional. Thus, unlike naive realists, critical realists recognize that there is a distinction between the objects that are the focus of their enquiries and the terms they use to describe, account for, and understand them. Secondly, by implication, critical realists unlike positivists are perfectly content to admit into their explanations theoretical terms that are not directly amenable to observation. As a result, hypothetical entities that account for regularities in the natural or social orders (the 'generative mechanisms' to which Bhaskar refers) are perfectly admissible for realists, but not for positivists. For critical realists, it is acceptable that generative mechanisms are not directly observable, since they are admissable on the grounds that their effects are observable. What makes critical realism *critical* is that the identification of generative mechanisms offers the prospect of introducing changes that can transform the status quo. Research in focus 24.1 provides an example of research using a critical realist approach. This example can be read profitably at this stage even though it is in a much later chapter.

The crux of the epistemological considerations that form the central thrust of this section is the rejection by some writers and traditions of the application of the canons of the natural sciences to the study of social reality. A difficulty here is that it is not easy to disentangle the natural science model from positivism as the butt of their criticisms. In other words, it is not always clear whether they are inveighing against the application of a general natural scientific approach or of positivism in particular. There is a long-standing debate about the appropriateness of the natural science model for the study of society, but, since the account that is offered of that model tends to have largely positivist overtones, it would seem that it is positivism that is the focus of attention rather than other accounts of scientific practice (such as critical realism—see Key concept 1.3).

Interpretivism

Interpretivism is a term given to a contrasting epistemology to positivism (see Key concept 1.4). The term subsumes the views of writers who have been critical of the application of the scientific model to the study of the social world and who have been influenced by different intellectual traditions, which are outlined below. They share a view that the subject matter of the social sciences —people and their institutions—is fundamentally different from that of the natural sciences. The study of the social world therefore requires a different logic of research procedure, one that reflects the distinctiveness of humans as against the natural order. Von Wright (1971) has depicted the epistemological clash as being between positivism and *hermeneutics* (a term that is drawn from theology and that, when imported into the

social sciences, is concerned with the theory and method of the interpretation of human action). This clash reflects a division between an emphasis on the *explanation* of human behaviour that is the chief ingredient of the positivist approach to the social sciences and the *understanding* of human behaviour. The latter is concerned with the empathic understanding of human action rather than with the forces that are deemed to act on it. This contrast reflects long-standing debates that precede the emergence of the modern social sciences but find their expression in such notions as the advocacy by Max Weber (1864–1920) of an approach referred to in his native German as *Verstehen* (which means understanding). Weber (1947: 88) described sociology as a 'science which attempts the interpretive understanding of social action in order to arrive at a causal explanation of its course and effects'. Weber's definition seems to embrace both explanation *and* understanding here, but the crucial point is that the task of 'causal explanation' is undertaken with reference to the 'interpretive understanding of social action' rather than to external forces that have no meaning for those involved in that social action.

One of the main intellectual traditions that has been responsible for the anti-positivist position has been *phenomenology*, a philosophy that is concerned with the question of how individuals make sense of the world around them and how in particular the philosopher should bracket out preconceptions in his or her grasp of that world. The initial application of phenomenological ideas to the social sciences is attributed to the work of Alfred Schutz (1899–1959), whose work did not come to the notice of most English-speaking social scientists until the translation from German of his major writings in the 1960s, some twenty or more years after they had been

Key concept 1.4
What is interpretivism?

Interpretivism is a term that usually denotes an alternative to the positivist orthodoxy that has held sway for decades. It is predicated upon the view that a strategy is required that respects the differences between people and the objects of the natural sciences and therefore requires the social scientist to grasp the subjective meaning of social action. Its intellectual heritage includes: Weber's notion of *Verstehen*; the hermeneutic–phenomenological tradition; and symbolic interactionism.

written. His work was profoundly influenced by Weber's concept of *Verstehen*, as well as by phenomenological philosophers, like Husserl. Schutz's position is well captured in the following passage, which has been quoted on numerous occasions:

> The world of nature as explored by the natural scientist does not 'mean' anything to molecules, atoms and electrons. But the observational field of the social scientist—social reality—has a specific meaning and relevance structure for the beings living, acting, and thinking within it. By a series of common-sense constructs they have pre-selected and pre-interpreted this world which they experience as the reality of their daily lives. It is these thought objects of theirs which determine their behaviour by motivating it. The thought objects constructed by the social scientist, in order to grasp this social reality, have to be founded upon the thought objects constructed by the common-sense thinking of men [and women!], living their daily life within the social world. (Schutz 1962: 59)

Two points are particularly noteworthy in this quotation. First, it asserts that there is a fundamental difference between the subject matter of the natural sciences and the social sciences and that an epistemology is required that will reflect and capitalize upon that difference. The fundamental difference resides in the fact that social reality has a meaning for human beings and therefore human action is meaningful—that is, it has a meaning for them and they act on the basis of the meanings that they attribute to their acts and to the acts of others. This leads to the second point—namely, that it is the job of the social scientist to gain access to people's 'common-sense thinking' and hence to interpret their actions and their social

world from their point of view. It is this particular feature that social scientists claiming allegiance to phenomenology have typically emphasized. In the words of the authors of a research methods text whose approach is described as phenomenological: 'The phenomenologist views human behavior . . . as a product of how people interpret the world. . . . In order to grasp the meanings of a person's behavior, *the phenomenologist attempts to see things from that person's point of view*' (Bogdan and Taylor 1975: 13–14, emphasis in original).

In this exposition of *Verstehen* and phenomenology, it has been necessary to skate over some complex issues. In particular, Weber's examination of *Verstehen* is far more complex than the above commentary suggests, because the empathetic understanding that seems to be implied above was not the way in which he applied it (Bauman 1978), while the question of what is and is not a genuinely phenomenological approach to the social sciences is a matter of some dispute (Heap and Roth 1973). However, the similarity in the writings of the hermeneutic–phenomenological tradition and of the *Verstehen* approach, with their emphasis upon social action as being meaningful to actors and therefore needing to be interpreted from their point of view, coupled with the rejection of positivism, contributed to a stream of thought often referred to as interpretivism (e.g. J. A. Hughes 1990).

Verstehen and the hermeneutic–phenomenological tradition do not exhaust the intellectual influences on interpretivism. The theoretical tradition in sociology known as *symbolic interactionism* has also been regarded by many writers as a further influence. Again, the case is not clearcut. The implications for empirical research of the ideas of the founders of symbolic interactionism, in particular George Herbert Mead (1863–1931), whose discussion of the way in which our notion of self emerges through an appreciation of how others see us, have been hotly debated. There was a school of research, known as the Iowa school, that has drawn heavily on Mead's concepts and ideas, but has proceeded in a direction that most people would prefer to depict as largely positivist in tone (Meltzer *et al*. 1975). Moreover, some writers have argued that Mead's approach is far more consistent with a natural science approach than has typically been recognized (McPhail and Rexroat 1979). However, the general tendency has been to view symbolic interactionism as occupying similar intellectual space to the hermeneutic–phenomenological tradition and so broadly interpretative in approach. This tendency is largely the product of the writings of Herbert Blumer, a student of Mead's who acted as his mentor's spokesman and interpreter, and his followers (Hammersley 1989; R. Collins 1994). Not only did Blumer coin the term symbolic interaction; he also provided a gloss on Mead's writings that has decidedly interpretative overtones. Symbolic interactionists argue that interaction takes place in such a way that the individual is continually interpreting the symbolic meaning of his or her environment (which includes the actions of others) and acts on the basis of this imputed meaning. In research terms, according to Blumer (1962: 188), 'the position of symbolic interaction requires the student to catch the process of interpretation through which [actors] construct their actions', a statement that brings out clearly his views of the research implications of symbolic interactionism and of Mead's thought.

It should be appreciated that the parallelism between symbolic interactionism and the hermeneutic–phenomenological tradition should not be exaggerated. The two are united in their antipathy for positivism and have in common an interpretative stance. However, symbolic interactionism is, at least in the hands of Blumer and the many writers and researchers who have followed in his wake, a type of social theory that has distinctive epistemological implications; the hermeneutic–phenomenological tradition, by contrast, is best thought of as a general epistemological approach in its own right. Blumer may have been influenced by the hermeneutic–phenomenological tradition, but there is no concrete evidence of this. There are other intellectual currents that have affinities with the interpretative stance, such as the working-through of the ramifications of the works of the philosopher Ludwig Wittgenstein (Winch 1958), but the hermeneutic–phenomenological, *Verstehen*, and symbolic interactionist traditions can be considered major influences.

Taking an interpretative stance can mean that the researcher may come up with surprising findings, or at least findings that appear surprising if a largely external stance is taken—that is, a position from outside the particular social context being studied. Research in focus 1.6 provides an interesting example of this possibility.

Of course, as the example in Research in focus 1.6 suggests, when the social scientist adopts an interpretative stance, he or she is not simply laying bare how members of a social group interpret the world around them. The social scientist will almost certainly be aiming to place the interpretations that have been elicited into a social scientific frame. There is a double interpretation going on: the researcher is providing an interpretation of others' interpretations. Indeed, there is a third level of interpretation going on, because the researcher's interpretations have to be further interpreted in terms of the concepts, theories, and literature of a discipline. Thus, taking the example in Research in focus 1.6, Foster's (1995) suggestion that Riverside is not perceived as a high crime area by residents is her interpretation of her subjects' interpretations. She then had the additional job of placing her interesting findings into a social scientific frame, which she accomplished by relating them to existing concepts and discussions in criminology of such things as informal social control, neighbourhood watch schemes, and the role of housing as a possible cause of criminal activity.

The aim of this section has been to outline how epistemological considerations—especially those relating to the question of whether a natural science approach, and in particular a positivist one, can supply legitimate knowledge of the social world—are related to research practice. There is a link with the earlier section in that a deductive approach to the relationship between theory and research is typically associated with a positivist position. Key concept 1.2 does try to suggest that inductivism is also a feature of positivism (third principle), but, in the working-through of its implementation in the practice of social research, it is the deductive element (second principle) that tends to be emphasized. Similarly, the third level of interpretation that a researcher engaged in interpretative research must bring into operation is very much part of the kind of inductive strategy described in the previous section. However, while such interconnections between epistemological issues and research practice exist, it is important not to overstate them, since they represent tendencies rather than definitive points of correspondence. Thus, particular epistemological principles and research practices do not necessarily go hand in hand in a neat unambiguous manner. This point will be made again on several occasions and will be a special focus of Chapter 24.

Research in focus 1.6
Interpretivism in practice

Foster (1995) conducted ethnographic research using **participant observation** and semi-structured interviews in a housing estate in East London, referred to as Riverside. The estate had a high level of crime, as indicated by **official statistics** on crime. However, she found that residents did not perceive the estate to be a high crime area. This perception could be attributed to a number of factors, but a particularly important reason was the existence of 'informal social control'. People expected a certain level of crime, but felt fairly secure because informal social control allowed levels of crime to be contained. Informal social control comprised a number of different aspects. One aspect was that neighbours often looked out for each other. In the words of one of Foster's interviewees: 'If I hear a bang or shouting I go out. If there's aggravation I come in and ring the police. I don't stand for it.' Another aspect of informal social control was that people often felt secure because they knew each other. Another respondent said: 'I don't feel nervous . . . because people do generally know each other. We keep an eye on each others properties . . . I feel quite safe because you know your neighbours and you know they're there . . . they look out for you'. (Foster 1995: 575)

Ontological considerations

Questions of social ontology are concerned with the nature of social entities. The central point of orientation here is the question of whether social entities can and should be considered objective entities that have a reality external to social actors, or whether they can and should be considered social constructions built up from the perceptions and actions of social actors. These positions are frequently referred to respectively as *objectivism* and *constructionism*. Their differences can be illustrated by reference to two of the most common and central terms in social science—organization and culture.

Objectivism

Objectivism is an ontological position that implies that social phenomena confront us as external facts that are beyond our reach or influence (see Key concept 1.5).

We can discuss organization or *an* organization as a tangible object. It has rules and regulations. It adopts standardized procedures for getting things done. People are appointed to different jobs within a division of labour. There is a hierarchy. It has a mission statement. And so on. The degree to which these features exist from organization to organization is variable, but in thinking in these terms we are tending to the view that an organization has a reality that is external to the individuals who inhabit it. Moreover, the organization represents a social order in that it exerts pressure on individuals to conform to the requirements of the organization. People learn and apply the rules and regulations. They follow the standardized procedures. They do the jobs to which they are appointed. People tell them what to do and they tell others what to do. They learn and apply the values in the mission statement. If they do not do these things, they may be reprimanded or even fired. The organization is therefore a constraining force that acts on and inhibits its members.

The same can be said of culture. Cultures and subcultures can be viewed as repositories of widely shared values and customs into which people are socialized so that they can function as good citizens or as full participants. Cultures and subcultures constrain us because we internalize their beliefs and values. In the case of both organization and culture, the social entity in question comes across as something external to the actor and as having an almost tangible reality of its own. It has the characteristics of an object and hence of having an objective reality. To a very large extent, these are the 'classic' ways of conceptualizing organization and culture.

Key concept 1.5
What is objectivism?

Objectivism is an ontological position that asserts that social phenomena and their meanings have an existence that is independent of social actors. It implies that social phenomena and the categories that we use in everyday discourse have an existence that is independent or separate from actors.

Constructionism

However, we can consider an alternative ontological position—*constructionism* (Key concept 1.6). This position challenges the suggestion that categories such as organization and culture are pre-given and therefore confront social actors as external realities that they have no role in fashioning.

Let us take organization first. Strauss *et al.* (1973), drawing on insights from symbolic interactionism, carried out research in a psychiatric hospital and proposed that it was best conceptualized as a 'negotiated order'. Instead of taking the view that order in organizations is a pre-existing characteristic, they argue that it is worked at. Rules were far less extensive and less rigorously imposed than might be supposed from the classic account of organization. Indeed, Strauss *et al.* prefer to refer to them as 'much less like commands, and much more like general understandings' (1973: 308). Precisely because relatively little of the spheres of action of doctors, nurses, and other personnel was prescribed, the social order of the hospital was an outcome of agreed-upon patterns of action that were themselves the products of negotiations between the different parties involved. The social order is in a constant state of change because the hospital is 'a place where numerous agreements are continually being

Key concept 1.6
What is constructionism?

Constructionism is an ontological position (often also referred to as **constructivism**) that asserts that social phenomena and their meanings are continually being accomplished by social actors. It implies that social phenomena and categories are not only produced through social interaction but that they are in a constant state of revision. In recent years, the term has also come to include the notion that researchers' own accounts of the social world are constructions. In other words, the researcher always presents a specific version of social reality, rather than one that can be regarded as definitive. Knowledge is viewed as indeterminate. The discussion of **postmodernism** in Chapter 27 further examines this viewpoint. This sense of constructionism is usually allied to the ontological version of the term. In other words, these are linked meanings. Both meanings are antithetical to *objectivism* (see Key concept 1.5), but the second meaning is also antithetical to *realism* (see Key concept 1.3). The first meaning might be thought of usefully as constructionism in relation to the social world; the second as constructionism in relation to the nature of knowledge of the social world (and indeed the natural world).

Increasingly, the notion of constructionism in relation to the nature of knowledge of the social world is being incorporated into notions of constructionism, but in this book I will be using the term in relation to the first meaning, whereby constructionism is presented as an ontological position in relating to social objects and categories—that is, one that views them as socially constructed.

terminated or forgotten, but also as continually being established, renewed, reviewed, revoked, revised. . . . In any pragmatic sense, this is the hospital at the moment: this is its social order' (Strauss *et al.* 1973: 316–17). The authors argue that a preoccupation with the formal properties of organizations (rules, organizational charts, regulations, roles) tends to neglect the degree to which order in organizations has to be accomplished in everyday interaction, though this is not to say that the formal properties have *no* element of constraint on individual action.

Much the same kind of point can be made about the idea of culture. Instead of seeing culture as an external reality that acts on and constrains people, it can be taken to be an emergent reality in a continuous state of construction and reconstruction. Becker (1982: 521), for example, has suggested that 'people create culture continuously. . . . No set of cultural understandings . . . provides a perfectly applicable solution to any problem people have to solve in the course of their day, and they therefore must remake those solutions, adapt their understandings to the new situation in the light of what is different about it.' Like Strauss *et al.*, Becker recognizes that the constructionist position cannot be pushed to the extreme: it is necessary to appreciate that culture has a reality that 'persists and antedates the participation of particular people' and shapes their perspectives, but it is not an inert objective reality that possesses only a sense of constraint: it acts as a point of reference but is always in the process of being formed.

Neither the work of Strauss *et al.* nor that of Becker pushes the constructionist argument to the extreme. Each admits to the pre-existence of their objects of interest (organization and culture respectively). However, in each case we see an intellectual predilection for stressing the active role of individuals in the social construction of social reality. Not all writers adopting a constructionist

position are similarly prepared to acknowledge the existence or at least importance of an objective reality. Walsh (1972: 19), for example, has written that 'we cannot take for granted, as the natural scientist does, the availability of a preconstituted world of phenomena for investigation' and must instead 'examine the processes by which the social world is constructed.' Constructionism essentially invites the researcher to consider the ways in which social reality is an ongoing accomplishment of social actors rather than something external to them and that totally constrains them.

Constructionism also suggests that the categories that people employ in helping them to understand the natural and social world are in fact social products. The categories do not have built-in essences; instead, their meaning is constructed in and through interaction. Thus, a category like 'masculinity' might be treated as a social construction. This notion implies that, rather than being treated as a distinct inert entity, masculinity is construed as something whose meaning is built up during interaction. That meaning is likely to be a highly ephemeral one, in that it will vary by both time and place. This kind of stance frequently displays a concern with the language that is employed to present categories in particular ways. It suggests that the social world and its categories are not external to us, but are built up and constituted in and through interaction. This tendency can be seen particularly in **discourse analysis**, which is examined in Chapter 20. As Potter (1996: 98) observes: 'The world . . . is *constituted* in one way or another as people talk it, write it and argue it.' This sense of constructionism is highly antithetical to realism (see Key concept 1.3). Constructionism frequently results in an interest in the representation of social phenomena. Research in focus 1.7 provides an illustration of this idea in relation to the representation of the breast cancer epidemic in the USA.

Research in focus 1.7
Constructionism in action

Lantz and Booth (1998) have shown that breast cancer can be treated as a social construction. They note that US data show a rise in the incidence of the disease since the early 1980s, which has led to the depiction of the trend as an epidemic. The authors examined a variety of popular magazines using **qualitative content analysis** (see Key concept 12.1 for a brief description of this method). They note that many of the articles draw attention to the lifestyles of modern women, such as delaying first births, diet and alcohol consumption, and having careers. The authors argue that the articles:

ascribe blame to individual behaviors by listing a wide array of individual risk factors (many of which are not behaviors of 'traditional' women), and then offering prudent prescriptions for prevention. Women are portrayed as victims of an insidious disease, but also as victims of their own behaviors, many of which are related to the control of their own fertility. . . . These articles suggest that nontraditional women experience pathological repercussions within their bodies and, in turn, may be responsible for our current epidemic of breast cancer. (Lantz and Booth 1998: 915–16)

This article suggests that, as a social category, the breast cancer epidemic is being represented in popular magazines in a particular way—one that blames the victims and the lifestyles of modern women in particular. This is in spite of the fact that fewer than 20 per cent of cases of breast cancer are in women under the age of 50. Lantz and Booth's study is fairly representative of a constructionist ontology in suggesting that the epidemic is not simply being construed as a social fact but is being ascribed a particular meaning (one that blames the victims of the disease). In this way, the representation of the disease in popular magazines forms an important element in its social construction.

Constructionism is also frequently used as a term that reflects the indeterminacy of our knowledge of the social world (see Key concept 1.6 and the idea of constructionism in relation to the nature of knowledge of the social world). However, in this book, I will be using the term in connection with the notion that social phenomena and categories are social constructions.

Relationship to social research

Questions of social ontology cannot be divorced from issues concerning the conduct of social research. Ontological assumptions and commitments will feed into the ways in which research questions are formulated and research is carried out. If a research question is formulated in such a way as to suggest that organizations and cultures are objective social entities that act on individuals, the researcher is likely to emphasize the formal properties of organizations or the beliefs and values of members of the culture. Alternatively, if the researcher formulates a research problem so that the tenuousness of organization and culture as objective categories is stressed, it is likely that an emphasis will be placed on the active involvement of people in reality construction. In either case, it might be supposed that different approaches to the design of research and the collection of data will be required.

Research strategy: quantitative and qualitative research

Many writers on methodological issues find it helpful to distinguish between quantitative and qualitative research. The status of the distinction is ambiguous, because it is almost simultaneously regarded by some writers as a fundamental contrast and by others as no longer useful or even simply as 'false' (Layder 1993: 110). However, there is little evidence to suggest that the use of the distinction is abating and even considerable evidence of its continued, even growing, currency. The quantitative/qualitative distinction will be employed a great deal in this book, because it represents a useful means of classifying different methods of social research and because it is a helpful umbrella for a range of issues concerned with the practice of social research.

On the face of it, there would seem to be little to the quantitative/qualitative distinction other than the fact that quantitative researchers employ measurement and qualitative researchers do not. It is certainly the case that there is a predisposition among researchers along these lines, but many writers have suggested that the

Table 1.1

Fundamental differences between quantitative and qualitative research strategies		
	Quantitative	Qualitative
Principal orientation to the role of theory in relation to research	Deductive; testing of theory	Inductive; generation of theory
Epistemological orientation	Natural science model, in particular positivism	Interpretivism
Ontological orientation	Objectivism	Constructionism

differences are deeper than the superficial issue of the presence or absence of quantification. For many writers, quantitative and qualitative research differ with respect to their epistemological foundations and in other respects too. Indeed, if we take the areas that have been the focus of the last three sections—the connection between theory and research, epistemological considerations, and ontological considerations—quantitative and qualitative research can be taken to form two distinctive clusters of *research strategy*. By a research strategy, I simply mean a general orientation to the conduct of social research. Table 1.1 outlines the differences between quantitative and qualitative research in terms of the three areas.

Thus, quantitative research can be construed as a research strategy that emphasizes quantification in the collection and analysis of data and that:

- entails a deductive approach to the relationship between theory and research, in which the accent is placed on the testing of theories;

- has incorporated the practices and norms of the natural scientific model and of positivism in particular; and

- embodies a view of social reality as an external, objective reality.

By contrast, qualitative research can be construed as a research strategy that usually emphasizes words rather than quantification in the collection and analysis of data and that:

- predominantly emphasizes an inductive approach to the relationship between theory and research, in which the emphasis is placed on the generation of theories;

- has rejected the practices and norms of the natural scientific model and of positivism in particular in preference for an emphasis on the ways in which individuals interpret their social world; and

- embodies a view of social reality as a constantly shifting emergent property of individuals' creation.

There is, in fact, considerably more to the quantitative/qualitative distinction than this contrast. In Chapters 6 and 16 the nature of quantitative and then qualitative research respectively will be outlined in much greater detail, while in Chapters 24 and 25 the contrasting features will be further explored. In particular, a number of distinguishing features flow from the commitment of the quantitative research strategy to a positivist epistemology and from the rejection of that epistemology by practitioners of the qualitative research strategy. In other words, the three contrasts in Table 1.1 are basic, though fundamental, ones.

However, the interconnections between the different features of quantitative and qualitative research are not as straightforward as Table 1.1 and the previous paragraph imply. While it is useful to contrast the two research strategies, it is necessary to be careful about hammering a wedge between them too deeply. It may seem perverse to introduce a basic set of distinctions and then suggest that they are problematic. A recurring theme of this book is that discussing the nature of social research is just as complex as conducting research in the real world. You may discover general tendencies, but they are precisely that—tendencies. In reality, the picture becomes more complicated the more you delve.

For example, it is common to describe qualitative research as concerned with the generation rather than the testing of theories. However, there are examples of studies in which qualitative research has been employed to test rather than to generate theories. For example, Adler and Adler (1985) were concerned to explore the issue of whether participation in athletics in higher education in the USA is associated with higher or lower levels of academic achievement, an issue on which the existing literature was inconsistent. This is an illustration of the use of the existing literature on a topic being employed as a kind of proxy for theory. The first author was a participant observer for four years of a basketball programme in a university, and both authors carried out 'intensive, taped interviews' with players. The authors' findings do lead them to conclude that athletic participation is likely to result in lower academic achievement. This occurs because the programme participants gradually drift from idealistic goals about their academic careers, and a variety of factors lead them to become increasingly detached from academic work. For example, one student is quoted as saying: 'If I was a student like most other students I could do well, but when you play the calibre of ball we do, you just can't be an above-average student. What I strive for now is just to be an average student. . . . You just can't find the time to do all the reading' (Adler and Adler 1985: 247). This study shows how, although qualitative research is typically associated with generating theories, it can also be employed for testing them.

Moreover, it is striking that, although the Adler and Adler study is broadly interpretivist in epistemological orientation, with its emphasis on how college athletes view their social situation, the findings have objectivist, rather than constructionist, overtones. For example, when the authors describe the students' academic performance as 'determined less by demographic characteristics and high school experiences than by the structure of their college experiences' (Adler and Adler 1985: 249), they are positing a social world that is 'out there' and that has a formal, objective quality. It is an example of qualitative research in the sense that there is no quantification or very little of it, but it does not have *all* the other features outlined in Table 1.1. Similarly, the previously mentioned study by Westergaard *et al.* (1989) of the effects of redundancy was a quantitative study in the sense of being

concerned to measure a wide variety of concepts, but exhibited little evidence of a concern to test theories of unemployment or of a stressful life event like redundancy. Instead, its conclusions revolve around seeking to understand how those made redundant responded to the experience in terms of such things as their job-search methods, their inclination to find jobs, and their political attitudes. As such, it has interpretivist overtones in spite of being an exercise in quantitative research.

The point that is being made in this section is that quantitative and qualitative research represent different research strategies and that each carries with it striking differences in terms of the role of theory, epistemological issues, and ontological concerns. However, the distinction is not a hard-and-fast one: studies that have the broad characteristics of one research strategy may have a characteristic of the other. Not only this, but many writers argue that the two can be combined within an overall research project, and Chapter 25 examines precisely this possibility. In Chapter 25, I will examine what is increasingly referred to as *mixed methods research*. This term is widely used nowadays to refer to research that combines methods associated with both quantitative and qualitative research. Chapter 25 will explore the different ways in which social researchers combine these two research strategies.

In Research in focus 1.8, there is an example of a mixed methods study. I am presenting it here partly to provide an early insight into the possibility of doing mixed methods research, but also to show how a wedge need not and should not be driven between quantitative and qualitative research. By contrasting the two approaches, it is easy to see them as incompatible. As the example in Research in focus 1.8 shows, they can be fruitfully combined within a single project. This point will be amplified further throughout Chapter 25.

Research in focus 1.8
Mixed methods research—an example

In 2001 Britain was profoundly affected by the Foot and Mouth Disease (FMD), which had a big impact on people's movements. Poortinga *et al.* (2004) were interested in how far the public trusted the information the government was supplying and how it perceived the risks associated with the disease. Such issues were of interest in part because the researchers felt that the ways in which the public responds to a crisis was an important topic, but also because the issues connect with the influence in recent years of the notion of the 'risk society' (Beck 1992), which has attracted a good deal of sociological attention. At the height of the disease during 2–5 April 2001, the researchers conducted a survey by administering a **self-completion questionnaire** (see Chapter 9) to samples in two contrasting areas: Bude in Cornwall and Norwich in Norfolk. These two areas were chosen because they were very differently affected by FMD. The questionnaire covered the following areas: level of agreement with statements about the outbreak of the disease (e.g. 'My main concerns about FMD are to do with the possible impacts on human health'); perceptions of who was to blame; level of agreement with statements about the government's handling of FMD; degrees of trust in various sources of information about the disease; and personal information, such as any connection with the farming or tourist industries. In addition, a qualitative research method—**focus groups** (see Chapter 19)—was employed. In May and June 2001, these groups were convened and members of the groups were asked about the same kinds of issues covered in the questionnaire. Focus group participants were chosen from among those who had indicated in their questionnaire replies that they were willing to be involved in a focus group discussion. Three focus group discussions took place. While the questionnaire data were able to demonstrate the variation in such things as trust in various information sources, the focus groups revealed 'valuable additional information, especially on the reasons, rationalizations and arguments behind people's understanding of the FMD issue' (Poortinga *et al.* 2004: 86). As a result, the researchers were able to arrive at a more complete account of the FMD crisis than could have been obtained by either a quantitative or a qualitative research approach alone. This and other possible advantages of mixed methods research will be explored further in Chapter 25.

Influences on the conduct of social research

We are beginning to get a picture now that social research is influenced by a variety of factors. Figure 1.3 summarizes the influences that have been examined so far, but has added two more—the impact of *values* and of *practical considerations*.

Values

Values reflect either the personal beliefs or the feelings of a researcher. On the face of it, we would expect that social scientists should be value free and objective in their research. After all, one might want to argue that research that simply reflected the personal biases of its practitioners could not be considered valid and scientific because it was bound up with the subjectivities of its practitioners. Such a view is held with less and less frequency among social scientists nowadays. Émile Durkheim (1858–1917) wrote that one of the corollaries of his injunction to treat social facts as things was that all 'preconceptions must be eradicated' (Durkheim 1938: 31). Since values are a form of preconception, his exhortation was at least implicitly to do with suppressing them when conducting research. His position is unlikely to be regarded as credible nowadays, because there is a growing recognition that it is not feasible to keep the values that a researcher holds totally in check. These can intrude at any or all of a number of points in the process of social research:

- choice of research area;
- formulation of research question;
- choice of method;
- formulation of research design and data collection techniques;
- implementation of data collection;

Figure 1.3

Influences on social research

Theory   Practical considerations   Epistemology

Social research

Values   Ontology

- analysis of data;
- interpretation of data;
- conclusions.

There are, therefore, numerous points at which bias and the intrusion of values can occur. Values can materialize at any point during the course of research. The researcher may develop an affection or sympathy, which was not necessarily present at the outset of an investigation, for the people being studied. It is quite common, for example, for researchers working within a qualitative research strategy, and in particular when they use participant observation or very intensive interviewing, to develop a close affinity with the people whom they study to the extent that they find it difficult to disentangle their stance as social scientists from their subjects' perspective. This possibility may be exacerbated by the tendency that Becker (1967) identified for sociologists in particular to be very sympathetic to underdog groups. Equally, social scientists may be repelled by the people they study. The social anthropologist Colin Turnbull (1973) reports the results of his research into an African tribe known as the Ik. Turnbull was appalled by what he witnessed: a loveless (and for him unlovable) tribe that left its young and very old to die. While Turnbull was able to point to the conditions that had led to this state of affairs, he was very honest in his disgust for what he witnessed, particularly during the period of his initial sojourn among the tribe. However, that very disgust is a product of Western values about the family, and it is likely, as he acknowledged, that these will have influenced his perception of what he witnessed.

Another position in relation to the whole question of values and bias is to recognize and acknowledge that research cannot be value free but to ensure that there is no untrammelled incursion of values in the research process and to be self-reflective and so exhibit *reflexivity* about the part played by such factors. As Turnbull (1973: 13) put it at the beginning of his book on the Ik: 'the reader is entitled to know something of the aims, expectations, hopes and attitudes that the writer brought to the field with him, for these will surely influence not only how he sees things but even what he sees.' Researchers are increasingly prepared to forewarn readers of their biases and assumptions and how these may have influenced the subsequent findings. There has been a growth since the mid-1970s of collections of inside reports of what doing a piece of research was really like, as against the generalities presented in social research methods textbooks (like this one!). These collections frequently function as 'confessions', an element of which is often the writer's preparedness to be open about his or her personal biases. This point will be taken up further in Chapter 27.

Still another approach is to argue for consciously value-laden research. This is a position taken by some feminist writers who have argued that only research on women that is intendedly *for* women will be consistent with the wider political needs of women. Mies (1993: 68) has argued that in feminist research the 'postulate of *value free research*, of neutrality and indifference towards the research objects, has to be replaced by *conscious partiality*, which is achieved through partial identification with the research objects' (emphases in original).

Student experience
The influence of feminism on research questions

Sarah Hanson is very clear about the influence of feminism on her research and on her research questions in particular.

> My research project focused on the representation of women through the front covers of five women's magazines, combining the application of feminist theory with the decoding practices of content analysis. Throughout the project I wanted to understand the nature of women's magazines, the influences they have on women's sense of self and identity and the role the magazines play. I asked: do women's magazines support or destroy women's identity and do they encourage self-respect or self-scrutiny? I wanted to combine theory with fact, focusing on the meanings behind the presentation of images and text.

Similarly, for her research on NGOs (non-governmental organizations) and sex workers in Thailand, Erin Sanders wrote that she 'employed a feminist methodology—and as such attempted to engage with my research participants, particularly the sex workers, as a "friend" rather than as a "researcher" '. She also writes:

I chose to use a feminist methodology because I wanted to eliminate the power imbalance in the research relationship. As there are a number of power issues with a 'White', 'Western' woman interviewing 'Non-White', 'Non-Western' sex workers, I had hoped a feminist methodology . . . would help redress some of the power issues.

 To read more about Sarah's and Erin's research experiences, go to the Online Resource Centre that accompanies this book at http://www.oxfordtextbooks.co.uk/orc/brymansrm3e/.

The significance of feminism in relation to values goes further than this, however. In particular, several feminist social researchers around the early 1980s proposed that the principles and practices associated with quantitative research were incompatible with feminist research on women. For writers like Oakley (1981), quantitative research was bound up with male values of control that can be seen in the general orientation of the research strategy—control of the research subject/respondent and control of the research context and situation. Moreover, the research process was seen as one-way traffic, in which researchers extract information from the people being studied and give little, or more usually nothing, in return. For many feminists, such a strategy bordered on exploitation and was incompatible with feminism's values of sisterhood and non-hierarchical relationships between women. The antipathy towards quantitative research resulted in a preference for qualitative research among feminists. Not only was qualitative research seen as more consistent with the values of feminism; it was seen as more adaptable to those values. Thus, feminist qualitative research came to be associated with an approach in which the investigator eschewed a value-neutral approach and engaged with the people being studied as people and not simply as respondents to research instruments. The stance of feminism in relation to both quantitative and qualitative approaches demonstrates the ways in which values have implications for the process of social investigation. In more recent years, there has been a softening of the attitudes of feminists towards quantitative research. Several writers have acknowledged a viable and acceptable role for quantitative research, particularly when it is employed in conjunction with qualitative research (Jayaratne and Stewart 1991; Oakley 1998). This issue will be picked up in Chapters 16, 24, and 25.

There are, then, different positions that can be taken up in relation to values and value freedom. Far fewer writers overtly subscribe to the position that the principle of objectivity can be put into practice than in the past. Quantitative researchers sometimes seem to be writing in a way that suggests an aura of objectivity (Mies 1993),

but we simply do not know how far they subscribe to such a position. There is a greater awareness today of the limits to objectivity, so that some of the highly confident, not to say naive, pronouncements on the subject, like Durkheim's, have fallen into disfavour. A further way in which values are relevant to the conduct of social research is through the following ethical principles or standards. This issue will be followed up in Chapter 5.

Practical considerations

Nor should we neglect the importance and significance of *practical issues* in decisions about how social research should be carried out. There are a number of different dimensions to this issue. For one thing, choices of research strategy, design, or method have to be dovetailed with the specific research question being investigated. If we are interested in teasing out the relative importance of a number of different causes of a social phenomenon, it is quite likely that a quantitative strategy will fit our needs, because, as will be shown in Chapter 6, the assessment of cause is one of its keynotes. Alternatively, if we are interested in the world views of members of a certain social group, a qualitative research strategy that is sensitive to how participants interpret their social world may be the direction to choose. If a researcher is interested in a topic on which no or virtually no research has been done in the past, the quantitative strategy may be difficult to employ because there is little prior literature from which to draw leads. A more exploratory stance may be preferable, and, in this connection, qualitative research may serve the researcher's needs better, since it is typically associated with the generation rather than the testing of theory (see Table 1.1) and with a relatively unstructured approach to the research process (see Chapter 16). Another dimension may have to do with the nature of the topic and of the people being investigated. For example, if the researcher needs to engage with individuals or groups involved in illicit activities, such as violence (Patrick 1973), pilferage (Ditton 1977), or drug dealing (P. A. Adler 1985), it is unlikely that a social survey would gain the confidence of the subjects involved or achieve the necessary rapport. It is not surprising, therefore, that researchers in these areas have tended to use a qualitative strategy. By contrast, it does not seem likely that the hypothesis in the research described in Research in focus 1.4 could have been tested with a qualitative method like participant observation.

While practical considerations may seem rather mundane and uninteresting compared with the lofty realm inhabited by the philosophical debates surrounding such discussions about epistemology and ontology, they are important ones. All social research is a coming-together of the ideal and the feasible. Because of this, there will be many circumstances in which the nature of the topic or of the subjects of an investigation and the constraints on a researcher loom large in decisions about how best to proceed.

Student experience
A practical consideration in the choice of research method

One of the factors that influenced Rebecca Barnes's choice of the semi-structured interview for her study of violence in women's same-sex intimate relationships was that she felt that the topic is a highly sensitive area and that she therefore needed to be able to observe her interviewees' emotional responses.

> I felt that, given the sensitivity of the research topic, semi-structured, in-depth interviews would be most appropriate. This gave me the opportunity to elicit women's accounts of abuse in a setting where I was able to observe their emotional responses to the interview and endeavour to minimize any distress or other negative feelings that might result from participating in the research.

To read more about Rebecca's research experiences, go to the Online Resource Centre that accompanies this book at **http://www.oxfordtextbooks.co.uk/orc/brymansrm3e/**.

Key points

- Quantitative and qualitative research constitute different approaches to social investigation and carry with them important epistemological and ontological considerations.

- Theory can be depicted as something that precedes research (as in quantitative research) or as something that emerges out of it (as in qualitative research).

- Epistemological considerations loom large in considerations of research strategy. To a large extent, these revolve around the desirability of employing a natural science model (and in particular positivism) versus interpretivism.

- Ontological considerations, concerning objectivism versus constructionism, also constitute important dimensions of the quantitative/qualitative contrast.

- Values may impinge on the research process at different times.

- Practical considerations in decisions about research methods are also important factors.

- Feminist researchers have tended to prefer a qualitative approach, though there is some evidence of a change of viewpoint in this regard.

Questions for review

Theory and research

- If you had to conduct some social research now, what would the topic be and what factors would have influenced your choice? How important was addressing theory in your consideration?
- Outline, using examples of your own, the difference between grand and middle-range theory.
- What are the differences between inductive and deductive theory and why is the distinction important?

Epistemological considerations

- What is meant by each of the following terms: positivism; realism; and interpretivism? Why is it important to understand each of them?
- What are the implications of epistemological considerations for research practice?

Ontological considerations

- What are the main differences between epistemological and ontological considerations?
- What is meant by objectivism and constructionism?
- Which theoretical ideas have been particularly instrumental in the growth of interest in qualitative research?

Research strategy: quantitative and qualitative research

- Outline the main differences between quantitative and qualitative research in terms of: the relationship between theory and data; epistemological considerations; and ontological considerations.
- To what extent is quantitative research solely concerned with testing theories and qualitative research with generating theories?

Influences on the conduct of social research

- What are some of the main influences on social research?

Online Resource Centre

http://www.oxfordtextbooks.co.uk/orc/brymansrm3e/

Visit the Online Resource Centre that accompanies this book to enrich your understanding of social research strategies. Consult web links, test yourself using multiple choice questions, and gain further guidance and inspiration from the Student Researcher's Toolkit.

2

Research designs

Chapter outline

Chapter guide

In focusing on the different kinds of **research design**, we are paying attention to the different frameworks for the collection and analysis of data. A research design relates to the criteria that are employed when evaluating social research. It is, therefore, a framework for the generation of evidence that is suited both to a certain set of criteria and to the research question in which the investigator is interested. This chapter is structured as follows.

- **Reliability**, **replication**, and **validity** are presented as criteria for assessing the quality of social research. The latter entails an assessment in terms of several criteria covered in the chapter: **measurement validity**; **internal validity**; **external validity**; and **ecological validity**.

- The suggestion that such criteria are mainly relevant to **quantitative** research is examined, along with the proposition that an alternative set of criteria should be employed in relation to **qualitative research**. This alternative set of criteria, which is concerned with the issue of **trustworthiness**, is outlined briefly.

- Five prominent research designs are then outlined:
  - experimental and related designs (such as the **quasi-experiment**);
  - **cross-sectional design**, the most common form of which is **survey research**;
  - **longitudinal design** and its various forms, such as the panel study and the cohort study;
  - **case study** design;
  - **comparative design**.

- Each research design is considered in terms of the criteria for evaluating research findings.

Introduction

In the previous chapter, the idea of *research strategy* was introduced as a broad orientation to social research. The specific context for its introduction was the distinction between quantitative and qualitative research as different research strategies. However, the decision to adopt one or the other strategy will not get you far along the road of doing a piece of research. Two other key decisions will have to be made (along with a host of tactical decisions about the way in which the research will be carried out and the data analysed). These decisions concern choices about *research design* and *research method*. On the face of it, these two terms would seem to mean the same thing, but it is crucial to draw a distinction between them (see Key concepts 2.1 and 2.2).

Research methods can be and are associated with different kinds of research design. The latter represents a structure that guides the execution of a research method and the analysis of the subsequent data. The two terms are often confused. For example, one of the research designs to be covered in this chapter—the case study—is very often referred to as a *method*. As we will see, a case study entails the detailed exploration of a specific case, which could be a community, organization, or person. But, once a case has been selected, a research method or research methods are needed to collect data. Simply selecting an organization and deciding to study it intensively are not going to provide data. Do you observe? Do you conduct interviews? Do you examine documents? Do you administer questionnaires? You may in fact use any or all of these research methods, but the crucial point is that choosing a case study approach will not in its own right provide you with data.

Key concept 2.1
What is a research design?

A *research design* provides a framework for the collection and analysis of data. A choice of research design reflects decisions about the priority being given to a range of **dimensions** of the research process. These include the importance attached to:

- expressing causal connections between **variables**;
- generalizing to larger groups of individuals than those actually forming part of the investigation;
- understanding behaviour and the meaning of that behaviour in its specific social context;
- having a temporal (i.e. over time) appreciation of social phenomena and their interconnections.

Key concept 2.2
What is a research method?

A research method is simply a technique for collecting data. It can involve a specific instrument, such as a **self-completion questionnaire** or a **structured interview schedule**, or **participant observation** whereby the researcher listens to and watches others.

In this chapter, five different research designs will be examined: experimental design and its variants, including quasi-experiments; cross-sectional or survey design; longitudinal design; case study design; and comparative design. However, before embarking on the nature of and differences between these designs, it is useful to consider some recurring issues in social research that cut across some or all of these designs.

Criteria in social research

Three of the most prominent criteria for the evaluation of social research are *reliability*, *replication*, and *validity*. Each of these terms will be treated in much greater detail in later chapters, but in the meantime a fairly basic treatment of them can be helpful.

Reliability

Reliability is concerned with the question of whether the results of a study are repeatable. The term is commonly used in relation to the question of whether the measures that are devised for **concepts** in the social sciences (such as poverty, racial prejudice, deskilling, religious ortho-

doxy) are consistent. In Chapter 6 we will be looking at the idea of reliability in greater detail, in particular the different ways in which it can be conceptualized. Reliability is particularly at issue in connection with quantitative research. The quantitative researcher is likely to be concerned with the question of whether a measure is stable or not. After all, if we found that IQ tests, which were designed as measures of intelligence, were found to fluctuate, so that people's IQ scores were often wildly different when administered on two or more occasions, we would be concerned about it as a measure. We would consider it an unreliable measure—we could not have faith in its consistency.

Replication

The idea of reliability is very close to another criterion of research—*replication* and more especially *replicability*. It sometimes happens that researchers choose to replicate the findings of others. There may be a host of different reasons for doing so, such as a feeling that the original results do not match other evidence that is relevant to the domain in question. In order for replication to take place, a study must be capable of replication—it must be replic-*able*. This is a very obvious point: if a researcher does not spell out his or her procedures in great detail, replication is impossible. Similarly, in order for us to assess the reliability of a measure of a concept, the procedures that constitute that measure must be replicable by someone else. Ironically, replication in social research is not common. In fact, it is probably truer to say that it is quite rare. When Burawoy (1979) found that by accident he was conducting case study research in a US factory that had been studied three decades earlier by another researcher (Donald Roy), he thought about treating his own investigation as a replication. However, the low status of replication in academic life persuaded him to resist this option. He writes: 'I knew that to replicate Roy's study would not earn me a dissertation let alone a job. . . . [In] academia the real reward comes not from replication but from originality!' (Burawoy 2003: 650). Nonetheless, an investigation's capacity to be replicated—replicability—is highly valued by many social researchers working within a quantitative research tradition. See Research in focus 6.7 for an example of a replication study.

Validity

A further and in many ways the most important criterion of research is *validity*. Validity is concerned with the integrity of the conclusions that are generated from a piece of research. As we shall do for reliability, we will be examining the idea of validity in greater detail in later chapters, but in the meantime it is important to be aware of the main types of validity that are typically distinguished:

- *Measurement validity*. This criterion applies primarily to quantitative research and to the search for measures of social scientific concepts. Measurement validity is also often referred to as *construct validity*. Essentially, it is to do with the question of whether a measure that is devised of a concept really does reflect the concept

that it is supposed to be denoting. Does the IQ test really measure variations in intelligence? If we take the study reported in Research in focus 1.4, there are three concepts that needed to be measured in order to test the hypotheses: national religiosity, religious orthodoxy, and family religious orientation. The question then is: do the measures really represent the concepts they are supposed to be tapping? If they do not, the study's findings will be questionable. It should be appreciated that measurement validity is related to reliability: if a measure of a concept is unstable in that it fluctuates and hence is unreliable, it simply cannot be providing a valid measure of the concept in question. In other words, the assessment of measurement validity presupposes that a measure is reliable. If a measure is unreliable because it does not give a stable reading of the underlying concept, it cannot be valid, because a valid measure reflects the concept it is supposed to be measuring.

- *Internal validity*. This form of validity relates mainly to the issue of **causality**, which will be dealt with in greater detail in Chapter 6. Internal validity is concerned with the question of whether a conclusion that incorporates a causal **relationship** between two or more variables holds water. If we suggest that *x* causes *y*, can we be sure that it is *x* that is responsible for variation in *y* and not something else that is producing an apparent causal relationship? In the study examined in Research in focus 1.4, the authors were quoted as concluding that 'the religious environment of a nation has a major impact on the beliefs of its citizens' (Kelley and De Graaf 1997: 654). Internal validity raises the question: can we be sure that national religiosity really does cause variation in religious orientation and that this apparent causal relationship is genuine and not produced by something else? In discussing issues of causality, it is common to refer to the factor that has a causal impact as the *independent variable* and the effect as the *dependent variable* (see Key concept 2.3). In the case of Kelley and De Graaf's research, the 'religious environment of a nation' was an independent variable and 'religious belief' was the dependent variable. Thus, internal validity raises the question: how confident can we be that the independent variable really is at least in part responsible for the variation that has been identified in the dependent variable?

Key concept 2.3
What is a variable?

A variable is simply an attribute on which cases vary. 'Cases' can obviously be people, but they can also include things such as households, cities, organizations, schools, and nations. If an attribute does not vary, it is a *constant*. If all manufacturing organizations had the same ratio of male to female managers, this attribute of such organizations would be a constant and not a variable. Constants are rarely of interest to social researchers. It is common to distinguish between different types of variable. The most basic distinction is between *independent variables* and *dependent variables*. The former are deemed to have a causal influence on the latter. In addition, it is important to distinguish between variables—whether independent or dependent— in terms of their measurement properties. This is an important issue in the context of quantitative data analysis. In Chapter 14, a distinction is drawn between the following types of variable: **interval/ratio variables**; **ordinal variables**; **nominal variables**; and **dichotomous variables**. See page 321 for an explanation of these main types and Table 14.1 for brief descriptions of them.

- *External validity*. This issue is concerned with the question of whether the results of a study can be generalized beyond the specific research context. In Oates and McDonald's (2006) research on gender in relation to recycling responsibilities in Sheffield households that was referred to in Research in focus 1.3, data were collected from 469 couples. Can their findings about the gendered nature of recycling responsibilities be generalized beyond these 469 couples? In other words, if the research was not externally valid, it would apply to the 469 couples and to no other couples. If it was externally valid, we would expect it to apply more generally to heterosexual couples. It is in this context that the issue of how people are selected to participate in research becomes crucial. This is one of the main reasons why quantitative researchers are so keen to generate representative samples (see Chapter 7).

- *Ecological validity*. This criterion is concerned with the question of whether social scientific findings are applicable to people's everyday, natural social settings. As Cicourel (1982: 15) has put it: 'Do our instruments capture the daily life conditions, opinions, values, attitudes, and knowledge base of those we study as expressed in their natural habitat?' This criterion is concerned with the question of whether social research sometimes produces findings that may be technically valid but have little to do with what happens in people's everyday lives. If research findings are ecologically *in*valid, they are in a sense *artefacts* of the social scientist's arsenal of data collection and analytic

tools. The more the social scientist intervenes in natural settings or creates unnatural ones, such as a laboratory or even a special room to carry out interviews, the more likely it is that findings will be ecologically invalid. The findings deriving from a study using questionnaires may have measurement validity and a reasonable level of internal validity, and they may be externally valid, in the sense that they can be generalized to other samples confronted by the same questionnaire, but the unnaturalness of the fact of having to answer a questionnaire may mean that the findings have limited ecological validity.

Relationship with research strategy

One feature that is striking about most of the discussion so far is that it seems to be geared mainly to quantitative rather than to qualitative research. Both reliability and measurement validity are essentially concerned with the adequacy of measures, which are most obviously a concern in quantitative research. Internal validity is concerned with the soundness of findings that specify a causal connection, an issue that is most commonly of concern to quantitative researchers. External validity *may* be relevant to qualitative research, but the whole question of representativeness of research subjects with which the issue is concerned has a more obvious application to the realm of quantitative research, with its preoccupation with sampling procedures that maximize the opportunity for generating a representative sample. The issue of ecological validity relates to the naturalness of the research approach and seems to have considerable relevance to both qualitative and quantitative research.

Some writers have sought to apply the concepts of reliability and validity to the practice of qualitative research (e.g. LeCompte and Goetz 1982; Kirk and Miller 1986; Peräkylä 1997), but others argue that the grounding of these ideas in quantitative research renders them inapplicable to or inappropriate for qualitative research. Writers like Kirk and Miller (1986) have applied concepts of validity and reliability to qualitative research but have changed the sense in which the terms are used very slightly. Some qualitative researchers sometimes propose that the studies they produce should be judged or evaluated according to different criteria from those used in relation to quantitative research. Lincoln and Guba (1985) propose that alternative terms and ways of assessing qualitative research are required. For example, they propose *trustworthiness* as a criterion of how good a qualitative study is. Each aspect of trustworthiness has a parallel with the previous quantitative research criteria.

- *Credibility*, which parallels internal validity—i.e. how believable are the findings?
- *Transferability*, which parallels external validity—i.e. do the findings apply to other contexts?
- *Dependability*, which parallels reliability—i.e. are the findings likely to apply at other times?
- *Confirmability*, which parallels objectivity—i.e. has the investigator allowed his or her values to intrude to a high degree?

These criteria will be returned to in Chapter 16.

Hammersley (1992*a*) occupies a kind of middle position here, in that, while he proposes validity as an important criterion (in the sense that an empirical account must be plausible and credible and should take into account the amount and kind of evidence used in relation to an account), he also proposes *relevance* as a criterion. Relevance is taken to be assessed from the vantage point of the importance of a topic within its substantive field or the contribution it makes to the literature on that field. The issues in these different views have to do with the different objectives that many qualitative researchers argue are distinctive about their craft. The distinctive features of qualitative research will be examined in later chapters.

However, it should also be borne in mind that one of the criteria previously cited—ecological validity—may have been formulated largely in the context of quantitative research, but is in fact a feature in relation to which qualitative research fares rather well. Qualitative research often involves a *naturalistic* stance (see Key concept 2.4). This means that the researcher seeks to collect data in naturally occurring situations and environments, as opposed to fabricated, artificial ones. This characteristic probably applies particularly well to ethnographic research, in which participant observation is a prominent element of data collection, but it is sometimes suggested that it applies also to the sort of interview approach typically used by qualitative researchers, which is less directive than the kind used in quantitative research (see e.g. Research in focus 1.4). We might expect that much qualitative research is stronger than quantitative investigations in terms of ecological validity.

Key concept 2.4
What is naturalism?

Naturalism is an interesting example of a mercifully rare instance of a term that not only has different meanings, but also has meanings that can actually be contradictory! It is possible to identify three different meanings.

- *Naturalism means viewing all objects of study—whether natural or social ones—as belonging to the same realm and a consequent commitment to the principles of natural scientific method.* This meaning, which has clear affinities with **positivism**, implies that all entities belong to the same order of things, so that there is no essential difference between the objects of the natural sciences and those of the social sciences (Williams 2000). For many naturalists, this principle implies that there should be no difference between the natural and the social sciences in the ways in which they study phenomena. This version of naturalism essentially proposes a unity between the objects of the natural and the social sciences and that because of this, there is no reason for social scientists not to employ the approaches of the natural scientist.

- *Naturalism means being true to the nature of the phenomenon being investigated.* According to Matza, naturalism is 'the philosophical view that strives to remain true to the nature of the phenomenon under study' (1969: 5) and 'claims fidelity to the natural world' (1969: 8). This meaning of the term represents a fusion of elements of an interpretivist **epistemology** and a **constructionist ontology**, which were examined in Chapter 1. Naturalism is taken to recognize that people attribute meaning to behaviour and are authors of their social world rather than passive objects.

- *Naturalism is a style of research that seeks to minimize the intrusion of artificial methods of data collection.* This meaning implies that the social world should be as undisturbed as possible when it is being studied (Hammersley and Atkinson 1995: 6).

The second and third meanings overlap considerably, in that it could easily be imagined that, in order to conduct a naturalistic enquiry in the second sense, a research approach that adopted naturalistic principles in the third sense would be required. Both the second and third meanings are incompatible with, and indeed opposed to, the first meaning. Naturalism in the first sense is invariably viewed by writers drawing on an interpretivist epistemology as not 'true' to the social world, precisely because: it posits that there are no differences between humans and the objects of the natural sciences; it therefore ignores the capacity of humans to interpret the social world and to be active agents; and, in its preference for the application of natural science methods, it employs artificial methods of data collection. When writers are described as *anti-naturalists*, it is invariably the first of the three meanings that they are deemed to be railing against.

By and large, these issues in social research have been presented because some of them will emerge in the context of the discussion of research designs in the next section, but in a number of ways they also represent background considerations for some of the issues to be examined. They will be returned to later in the book.

Research designs

In this discussion of research designs, five different types will be examined: experimental design; cross-sectional or survey design; longitudinal design; case study design; and comparative design. Variations on these designs will be examined in their relevant subsections.

Experimental design

True **experiments** are quite unusual in sociology, but are employed in related areas of enquiry, such as social psychology and organization studies, while researchers in social policy sometimes use them in order to assess the impact of new reforms or policies. Why, then, bother to introduce experimental designs at all in the context of a book about social research? The chief reason, quite aside from the fact that they are sometimes employed, is that a true experiment is often used as a yardstick against which non-experimental research is assessed. Experimental research is frequently held up as a touchstone because it engenders considerable confidence in the robustness and trustworthiness of causal findings. In other words, true experiments tend to be very strong in terms of internal validity.

Manipulation

If experiments are so strong in this respect, why then do social researchers not make far greater use of them? The reason is simple: in order to conduct a true experiment, it is necessary to *manipulate* the independent variable in order to determine whether it does in fact have an influence on the dependent variable. Experimental subjects are likely to be allocated to one of two or more **experimental groups**, each of which represents different types or levels of the independent variable. It is then possible to establish how far differences between the groups are responsible for variations in the level of the dependent variable. Manipulation, then, entails intervening in a situation to determine which of two or more things happens to subjects. However, the vast majority of independent variables with which social researchers are concerned cannot be manipulated. If we are interested in the effects of gender on work experiences, we cannot *manipulate* gender so that some people are made male and others female. If we are interested in the effects of variations in social class on social and political attitudes or on health, we cannot allocate people to different social class groupings. As with the huge majority of such variables, the levels of social engineering that would be required are beyond serious contemplation.

Before moving on to a more complete discussion of experimental design, it is important to introduce a basic distinction between the *laboratory experiment* and the *field experiment*. As its name implies, the laboratory experiment takes place in a laboratory or in a contrived setting, whereas field experiments occur in real-life settings, such as in classrooms and organizations, or as a result of the implementation of reforms or new policies. It is experiments of the latter type that are most likely to touch on areas of interest to social researchers. In order to illustrate the nature of manipulation and the idea of a field experiment, Research in focus 2.1 describes a well-known piece of research.

Research in focus 2.1
A field experiment

As part of a programme of research into the impact of self-fulfilling prophecies (e.g. where someone's beliefs or expectations about someone else influence how the latter behaves), Rosenthal and Jacobson (1968) conducted research into the question of whether teachers' expectations of their students' abilities in fact influence the school performance of the latter. The research was conducted in a lower-class locality in the USA with a high level of children from minority group backgrounds. In the spring of 1964, all the students completed a test that was portrayed as a means of identifying 'spurters'—that is, students who were likely to excel academically. At the beginning of the following academic year, all the teachers were notified of the names of the students who had been identified as spurters. In fact, 20 per cent of the schoolchildren had been identified as spurters. However, the students had actually been administered a conventional IQ test and the so-called spurters had been selected randomly. The test was readministered eight months after the original one. The authors were then able to compare the differences between the spurters and the other students in terms of changes in various measures of academic performance, such as IQ scores, reading ability, and intellectual curiosity. Since there was no evidence for there being any difference in ability between the spurters and the rest, any indications that the spurters did in fact differ from their peers could be attributed to the fact that the teachers had been led to expect the former would perform better. The findings show that such differences did in fact exist, but that the differences between the spurters and their peers tended to be concentrated in the first two or three years of schooling.

Classical experimental design

The research in Research in focus 2.1 includes most of the essential features of what is known as the classical experimental design, which is also often referred to as the *randomized experiment* or *randomized controlled trial* (RCT). Two groups are established, and it is this that forms the experimental manipulation and therefore the independent variable—in this case, teacher expectations.

The spurters form what is known as the *experimental group* or *treatment group* and the other students form a *control group*. The experimental group receives the *experimental treatment*—teacher expectancies—but the control group does not receive an experimental treatment. The dependent variable—student performance —is measured before and after the experimental manipulation, so that a before-and-after analysis can be

Figure 2.1

Classical experimental design (*with illustration of the effect of teacher expectancies on IQ*)

conducted (see Figure 2.1). Moreover, the spurters and the non-spurters were assigned randomly to their respective groups. Because of this use of **random assignment** to the experimental and control groups, the researchers were able to feel confident that the only difference between the two groups was the fact that teachers expected the spurters to fare better at school than the others. They would have been confident that, if they did establish a difference in performance between the two groups, it was due to the experimental manipulation alone.

In order to capture the essence of this design, the following simple notation will be employed:

Obs An **obs**ervation made in relation to the dependent variable; there may well be two or more observations, such as IQ test scores and reading grades before (the *pre-test*) and after (the *post-test*) the experimental manipulation.

Exp The **exp**erimental treatment (the independent variable), such as the creation of teacher expectancies. **No Exp** refers to the absence of an experimental treatment and represents the experience of the control group.

T The **t**iming of the observations made in relation to the dependent variable, such as the timing of the administration of an IQ test.

Classical experimental design and validity

What is the purpose of the control group? Surely it is what happens to the spurters (the experimental group) that really concerns us? In order for a study to be a true experiment, it must control (in other words, eliminate) the pos-

sible effects of rival explanations of a causal finding, such as that teacher expectancies have an impact on student performance. We might then be in a position to take the view that such a study is internally valid. The presence of a control group *and* the random assignment of subjects to the experimental and control groups enable us to eliminate such rival explanations. To see this, consider some of the rival explanations that might occur if there was *no* control group. There would then have been a number of potential threats to internal validity (see Research in focus 2.2). These threats are taken from Campbell (1957) and Cook and Campbell (1979), but not all the threats to internal validity they refer to are included.

In the case of each of these threats to internal validity, each of which raises the prospect of a rival interpretation of a causal finding, the presence of a control group coupled with random assignment allows us to eliminate these threats. As a result, our confidence in the causal finding, that teacher expectancies influence student performance, is greatly enhanced.

However, simply because research is deemed to be internally valid does not mean that it is beyond reproach or that at least questions cannot be raised about it. When a quantitative research strategy has been employed, the other criteria can be applied to evaluate a study. First, there is the question of measurement validity. In the case of the Rosenthal and Jacobson study, there are potentially two aspects to this. One is the question of whether academic performance has been adequately measured. Measures like reading scores seem to possess *face validity*, in the sense that they appear to exhibit a

Research in focus 2.2
Threats to internal validity (and their application to the Rosenthal and Jacobson (1968) study)

The following is a list of possible threats to the internal validity of an investigation and how each is mitigated in the Rosenthal and Jacobson (1968) study by virtue of its being a true experiment.

- *History*. This refers to events other than the manipulation of teacher expectancies that may occur in the environment and which could have caused the spurters' scores to rise. The actions of the school head to raise standards in the school may be one such type of event. If there were no control group, we could not be sure whether it was the teachers' expectancies or the head's actions that were producing the increase in spurters' grades. If there is a control group, we are able to say that history would have an effect on the control group subjects too, and therefore differences between the experimental and control groups could be attributed to the effect of teacher expectancies alone.

- *Testing*. This threat refers to the possibility that subjects may become more experienced at taking a test or may become sensitized to the aims of the experiment as a result of the pre-test. The presence of a control group, which presumably would also experience the same effect, allows us to discount this possibility if there is a difference between the experimental and control groups.

- *Instrumentation*. This threat refers to the possibility that changes in the way a test is administered could account for an increase (or decrease) in scores between the pre-test and post-test—e.g. if slight changes to the test had been introduced. Again, if there is a control group, we can assume that testing would have affected the control group as well.

- *Mortality*. This relates to the problem of attrition in many studies that span a long period of time, in that subjects may leave. School students may leave the area or move to a different school. Since this problem is likely to afflict the control group too, it is possible to establish its significance as a threat relative to the impact and importance of teacher expectancies.

- *Maturation*. Quite simply, people change and the ways in which they change may have implications for the dependent variable. The students identified as spurters may have improved anyway, regardless of the effect of teacher expectancies. Maturation should affect the control group subjects as well. If we did not have a control group, it could be argued that any change in the students' school performance was attributable to the possibility that they would have improved anyway. The control group allows us to discount this possibility.

- *Selection*. If there are differences between the two groups, which would arise if they had been selected by a non-random process, variations between the experimental and control groups could be attributed to pre-existing differences in their membership. However, since a random process of assignment to the experimental and control groups was employed, this possibility can be discounted.

- *Ambiguity about the direction of causal influence*. The very notion of an independent variable and dependent variable presupposes a direction of causality. However, there may be occasions when the temporal sequence in a study is unclear, so that it is not possible to establish which variable affects the other. Since the creation of teacher expectancies preceded the improvements in academic achievement in the earlier years of school, in the Rosenthal and Jacobson study the direction of causal influence is clear.

correspondence with what they are measuring. However, given the controversy surrounding IQ tests and what they measure (Kamin 1974), we might feel somewhat uneasy about how far gains in IQ test scores can be regarded as indicative of academic performance.

Similarly, to take another of the authors' measures—intellectual curiosity—how confident can we be that this too is a valid measure of academic performance? Does it really measure what it is supposed to measure? The second question relating to measurement validity is whether the experimental manipulation really worked. In other words, did the random identification of some schoolchildren as spurters adequately create the conditions for the self-fulfilling prophecy to be examined? The procedure very much relies on the teachers being

taken in by the procedure, but it is possible that they were not all equally duped. If so, this would contaminate the manipulation.

Secondly, is the research externally valid? This issue is considered in Research in focus 2.3.

Research in focus 2.3
Threats to external validity (and their application to the Rosenthal and Jacobson (1968) study)

Campbell (1957) and Cook and Campbell (1979) identify five major threats to the external validity and hence **generalizability** of an investigation.

- *Interaction of selection and treatment.* This threat raises the question: to what social and psychological groups can a finding be generalized? Can it be generalized to a wide variety of individuals who might be differentiated by ethnicity, social class, region, gender, and type of personality? In the case of the Rosenthal and Jacobson study, the students were largely from lower social class groups and a large proportion were from ethnic minorities. This might be considered a limitation to the generalizability of the findings.

- *Interaction of setting and treatment.* This threat relates to the issue of how confident we can be that the results of a study can be applied to other settings. In particular, how confident can we be that Rosenthal and Jacobson's findings are generalizable to other schools? There is also the wider issue of how confident we can be that the operation of self-fulfilling prophecies can be discerned in non-educational settings. In fact, Rosenthal and others have been able to demonstrate the role and significance of the self-fulfilling prophecy in a wide variety of different contexts (Rosnow and Rosenthal 1997), though this still does not answer the question of whether the specific findings that were produced can be generalized. One set of grounds for being uneasy about Rosenthal and Jacobson's findings is that they were allowed an inordinate amount of freedom for conducting their investigation. The high level of cooperation from the school authorities was very unusual and may be indicative of the school being somewhat atypical, though whether there is any such thing as a 'typical school' is highly questionable.

- *Interaction of history and treatment.* This threat raises the question of whether the findings can be generalized to the past and to the future. The Rosenthal and Jacobson research was conducted forty years ago. How confident can we be that the findings would apply today? Also, their investigation was conducted at a particular juncture in the school academic year. Would the same results have obtained if the research had been conducted at different points in the year?

- *Interaction effects of pre-testing.* As a result of being pre-tested, subjects in an experiment may become sensitized to the experimental treatment. Consequently, the findings may not be generalizable to groups that have *not* been pre-tested, and, of course, in the real world people are rarely pre-tested in this way. The findings may therefore be partly determined by the experimental treatment as such and partly by how pre-test sensitization has influenced the way in which subjects respond to the treatment. This may have occurred in the Rosenthal and Jacobson research, since all students were pre-tested at the end of the previous academic year.

- ***Reactive effects*** *of experimental arrangements.* People are frequently, if not invariably, aware of the fact that they are participating in an experiment. Their awareness may influence how they respond to the experimental treatment and therefore affect the generalizability of the findings. Since Rosenthal and Jacobson's subjects do not appear to have been aware of the fact that they were participating in an experiment, this problem is unlikely to have been significant. The issue of *reactivity* and its potentially damaging effects is a recurring theme in relation to many methods of social research.

Thirdly, are the findings ecologically valid? The fact that the research is a field experiment rather than a laboratory experiment seems to enhance this aspect of the Rosenthal and Jacobson research. Also, the fact that the students and the teachers seem to have had little if any appreciation of the fact that they were in fact participating in an experiment may also have enhanced ecological validity, though this aspect of the research raises enormous *ethical* concerns, since deception seems to have been a significant and probably necessary feature of the investigation. The question of ethical issues is in many ways another dimension of the validity of a study and will be the focus of Chapter 5. The fact that Rosenthal and Jacobson made intensive use of various instruments to measure academic performance might be considered a source of concerns about ecological validity, though this is an area in which most if not all quantitative research is likely to be implicated.

A fourth issue that we might want to raise relates to the question of replicability. The authors lay out very clearly the procedures and measures that they employed. If anyone sought to carry out a replication, he or she could obtain further information from them should they need it. Consequently, the research is replicable, although there has not been an exact replication. Clairborn (1969) conducted one of the earliest replications and followed a procedure that was very similar to Rosenthal and Jacobson's. The study was carried out in three middle-class, suburban schools, and the timing of the creation of teacher expectancies was different from that in the original Rosenthal and Jacobson study. Clairborn failed to replicate Rosenthal and Jacobson's findings. This failure to replicate casts doubt on the external validity of the original research and suggests that the first three threats referred to in Research in focus 2.3 may have played an important part in the differences between the two sets of results.

The classical experimental design is the foundation of the randomized controlled trial, which has increasingly become the gold standard research design in health-related fields. With an RCT, the aim is to test 'alternative ways of handling a situation' (Oakley 2000: 18). This may entail comparing the impact of an intervention with what would have happened if there had been no intervention or comparing the impacts of different kinds of intervention (such as different forms of treatment of an illness). It is randomization of experimental participants that is crucial, as it means that the members of the different groups in the experiment are to all intents and purposes alike.

The laboratory experiment

Many experiments in fields like social psychology are laboratory experiments rather than field experiments. One of the main advantages of the former over the latter is that the researcher has far greater influence over the experimental arrangements. For example, it is easier to assign subjects randomly to different experimental conditions in the laboratory than to do the same in an ongoing, real-life organization. The researcher therefore has a higher level of control, and this is likely to enhance the internal validity of the study. It is also likely that laboratory experiments will be more straightforward to replicate, because they are less bound up with a certain milieu that is difficult to reproduce.

However, laboratory experiments like the one described in Research in focus 2.4 suffer from a number of limitations. First, the external validity is likely to be difficult to establish. There is the interaction of setting and treatment, since the setting of the laboratory is likely to be unrelated to real-world experiences and contexts. Also, there is likely to be an interaction of selection and treatment. In the case of Howell and Frost's (1989) study described in Research in focus 2.4, there are a number of difficulties: the subjects were students, who are unlikely to be representative of the general population, so that their responses to the experimental treatment may be distinctive; they were volunteers, and it is known that volunteers differ from non-volunteers (Rosnow and Rosenthal 1997: ch. 5); and they were given incentives to participate, which may further demarcate them from others, since not everyone is equally amenable to the blandishments of inducements. There will have been no problem of interaction effects of pre-testing, because, like many experiments, there was no pre-testing. However, it is quite feasible that reactive effects may have been set in motion by the experimental arrangements. Secondly, the ecological validity of the study may be poor, because we do not know how well the findings are applicable to the real world and everyday life. However, while the study may lack what is often called *mundane realism*, it may nonetheless enjoy *experimental realism* (Aronson and Carlsmith 1968). The latter means that the subjects are very involved in the experiment and take it very seriously.

Quasi-experiments

A number of writers have drawn attention to the possibilities offered by *quasi-experiments*—that is, studies that have certain characteristics of experimental designs but

Research in focus 2.4
A laboratory experiment

Howell and Frost (1989) were interested in the possibility that charismatic leadership, a term associated with Max Weber's (1947) types of legitimate authority, is a more effective approach to leadership in organizations than other types of leadership. They conducted a laboratory experiment that compared the effectiveness of charismatic leadership as against two other approaches—consideration and structuring. A number of hypotheses were generated, including: 'Individuals working under a charismatic leader will have higher task performance than will individuals working under a considerate leader' (Howell and Frost 1989: 245).

One hundred and forty-four students volunteered for the experiment. Their course grades were enhanced by 3 per cent for agreeing to participate. They were randomly assigned to work under one of the three types of leadership. The work was a simulated business task. All three leadership approaches were performed by two female actresses. In broad conformity with the hypotheses, subjects working under charismatic leaders scored generally higher in terms of measures of task performance than those working under the other leaders, particularly the considerate leader.

that do not fulfil all of the internal validity requirements. A large number of different types of quasi-experiments have been identified (Cook and Campbell 1979), and it is not proposed to cover them here. A particularly interesting form of quasi-experiment occurs in the case of 'natural experiments'. These are 'experiments' in the sense of entailing manipulation of a social setting, but as part of a naturally occurring attempt to alter social arrangements.

In such circumstances, it is invariably not possible to assign subjects randomly to experimental and control groups. An example is provided in Research in focus 2.5. The absence of random assignment in the research casts a certain amount of doubt on the study's internal validity, since the groups may not have been equivalent. However, the results of such studies are still compelling, because they are not artificial interventions in social life and

Research in focus 2.5
A quasi-experiment

Since the mid-1980s, a group of researchers has been collecting medical and psychiatric data on a cohort of over 10,000 British civil servants. The first wave of data collection took place between late 1985 and early 1988 and comprised clinical measurement (e.g. blood pressure, ECG, cholesterol) and a self-completion questionnaire that generated data on health, stress, and minor psychiatric symptoms. Further measurements of the same group took place in 1989/90 and 1992/3. The decision in the mid-1980s by the then UK government to transfer many of the executive functions of government to executive agencies operating on a more commercial basis than previously afforded the opportunity to examine the health effects of a major organizational change. Ferrie *et al.* (1998) report the results of their Phase 1 and Phase 3 data. They distinguished between three groups: those experiencing a change; those anticipating they would be affected by the change; and a 'control group' of those unaffected by the change. The authors found significant adverse health effects among those experiencing and anticipating change compared to the control group, although the extent of the effects of the major organizational change (or its anticipation) varied markedly between men and women. This study uses a quasi-experimental design, in which a control group is compared to two treatment groups. It bears the hallmarks of a classical experimental design, but there is no random assignment. Subjects were not randomly assigned to the three groups. Whether they were affected (or anticipated being affected by the changes) depended on decisions deriving from government and civil service policy.

Research in focus 2.6
A natural experiment

The effects of television violence on children is one of the most contested areas of social research and one that frequently causes the media to become especially shrill. St Helena in the South Atlantic provided a fascinating laboratory for the examination of the various claims when television was introduced to the island for the first time in the mid-1990s. The television viewing habits of a large sample of schoolchildren and their behaviour are being monitored and will continue to be monitored for many years to come. The project leader, Tony Charlton, was quoted in *The Times* as saying: 'The argument that watching violent television turns youngsters to violence is not borne out . . . The children have been watching the same amounts of violence, and in many cases the same programmes, as British children. But they have not gone out and copied what they have seen on TV' (Midgley 1998: 5). A report of the findings in *The Times* in April 1998 found that 'the shared experience of watching television made them less likely to tease each other and to fight, and more likely to enjoy books' (Frean 1998: 7). The findings derive from 900 minutes of video footage of children at play during school breaks, diaries kept by around 300 of the children, and ratings by teachers. The reports of the research in academic journals confirm that there was no evidence to suggest that the introduction of television had led to an increase in anti-social behaviour (e.g. Charlton *et al.* 1998, 1999).

because their ecological validity is therefore very strong. Most writers on quasi-experimentation discount natural experiments in which there is no control group or basis for comparison (Cook and Campbell 1979), but occasionally one comes across a single group natural experiment that is particularly striking (see Research in focus 2.6). Experimental designs and more especially quasi-experimental designs have been particularly prominent in *evaluation research* studies (see Key concept 2.5 and Research in focus 2.7).

Key concept 2.5
What is evaluation research?

Evaluation research, as its name implies, is concerned with the evaluation of such occurrences as social and organizational programmes or interventions. The essential question that is typically asked by such studies is: has the intervention (e.g. a new policy initiative or an organizational change) achieved its anticipated goals? A typical design may have one group that is exposed to the treatment, that is the new initiative, and a control group that is not. Since it is often neither feasible nor ethical to assign research participants randomly to the two groups, such studies are usually quasi-experimental. The use of the principles of experimental design are fairly entrenched in evaluation research, but other approaches have emerged in recent years. Approaches to evaluation based on qualitative research have emerged. While there are differences of opinion about how qualitative evaluation should be carried out, the different views typically coalesce around a recognition of the importance of an in-depth understanding of the context in which an intervention occurs and the diverse viewpoints of the stakeholders (Greene 1994, 2000).

Pawson and Tilley (1997) advocate an approach that draws on the principles of *critical realism* (see Key concept 1.3) and that sees the outcome of an intervention as the result of generative mechanisms and the contexts of those mechanisms. A focus of the former element entails examining the causal factors that inhibit or promote change when an intervention occurs. Pawson and Tilley's approach is supportive of the use of both quantitative and qualitative research methods. Tilley (2000) outlines an early example of the approach in the context of an evaluation of closed-circuit television (CCTV) in car parks. He observes that there are several mechanisms by which CCTV might deter car crime, such as deterrence of offenders, greater usage of car parks, which in itself produces surveillance, more effective use of security staff, and drivers become more sensitive to car security. Examples of contexts are: patterns of usage (such as if the car park is one that fills up and empties during rush-hour periods or one that is in more constant use); blind spots in car parks; and the availability of other sources of car crime for potential offenders. In other words, whether the mechanisms have certain effects is affected by the contexts within which CCTV is installed. The kind of evaluation research advocated by Pawson and Tilley maps these different combinations of mechanism and context in relation to different outcomes.

Research in focus 2.7
A quasi-experimental evaluation

Koeber (2005) reports the findings of a quasi-experiment in which he evaluated the use of multimedia presentations (PowerPoint) and a course website (Blackboard) for teaching introductory sociology at a US university. One group of students acted as the experimental group in that it was taught using these two forms of presenting learning materials simultaneously; the other group acted as a control group and did not experience the multimedia and website methods. There was no random assignment, but in several respects the two groups were comparable. Therefore, this is not a true experiment, but it has the features of a typical quasi-experiment in that the researcher tried to make the two treatments as comparable as possible. It is an evaluation study, because the researcher is seeking to evaluate the utility of the two teaching methods. The findings are interesting, in that it was found that there was no significant evidence of a difference in the performance of students (measured by their final grades for the course) between those who experienced the newer methods and those who experienced the more traditional ones. However, those students who were taught with the newer methods tended to perceive the course in more favourable terms, in that they were more likely to perceive various aspects of the course (e.g. course design, rapport with students, and the value of the course) in a positive way. Also, the experimental groups were less likely to perceive the course demands as difficult and to view the course workload as high.

Significance of experimental design

As was stated at the outset, the chief reason for introducing the experiment as a research design is because it is frequently considered to be a yardstick against which quantitative research is judged. This occurs largely because of the fact that a true experiment will allow doubts about internal validity to be allayed and reflects the considerable emphasis placed on the determination of causality in quantitative research. As we will see in the next section, cross-sectional designs of the kind associated with survey research are frequently regarded as limited, because of the problems of unambiguously imputing causality when using such designs.

Logic of comparison

However, before exploring such issues, it is important to draw attention to an important general lesson that an examination of experiments teaches us. A central feature of any experiment is the fact that it entails a *comparison*: at the very least it entails a comparison of results obtained by an experimental group with those engendered by a control group. In the case of the Howell and Frost (1989) experiment in Research in focus 2.4 there is no control group: the research entails a comparison of the effects of three different forms of leadership. The advantage of carrying out any kind of comparison like this is that we understand the phenomenon that we are interested in better when we compare it with something else that is similar to it. The case for arguing that charismatic leadership is an effective, performance-enhancing form of leadership is much more persuasive when we view it in relation to other forms of leadership. Thus, while the specific considerations concerning experimental design are typically associated with quantitative research, the potential of comparison in social research represents a more general lesson that transcends matters of both research strategy and research design. In other words, while the experimental design is typically associated with a quantitative research strategy, the specific logic of comparison provides lessons of broad applicability and relevance. This issue is given more specific attention below in relation to the comparative design.

Cross-sectional design

The cross-sectional design is often called a survey design, but the idea of the survey is so closely connected in most people's minds with questionnaires and structured interviewing that the more generic-sounding term *cross-sectional design* is preferable. While the research methods associated with surveys are certainly frequently employed within the context of cross-sectional research, so too are many other research methods, including **structured observation, content analysis, official statistics**, and **diaries**. All these research methods will be covered in later chapters, but in the meantime the basic structure of the cross-sectional design will be outlined.

The cross-sectional design is defined in Key concept 2.6. A number of elements of this definition have been emphasized.

- *More than one case.* Researchers employing a cross-sectional design are interested in variation. That variation can be in respect of people, families, organizations, nation states, or whatever. Variation can be established only when more than one case is being examined. Usually, researchers employing this design will select a lot more than two cases for a variety of reasons: they are more likely to encounter variation in all the variables in which they are interested; they can make finer distinctions between cases; and the requirements of sampling procedure are likely to necessitate larger numbers (see Chapter 7).
- *At a single point in time.* In cross-sectional design research, data on the variables of interest are collected more or less simultaneously. When an individual completes a questionnaire, which may contain fifty or more variables, the answers are supplied at essentially the same time. This contrasts with an experimental design. Thus, in the classical experimental design, someone in the experimental group is pre-tested, then exposed to

the experimental treatment, and then post-tested. Days, weeks, months, or even years may separate the different phases. In the case of the Rosenthal and Jacobson (1968) study, eight months separated the pre- and post-testing of the schoolchildren in the study.

- *Quantitative or quantifiable data.* In order to establish variation between cases (and then to examine associations between variables—see the next point), it is necessary to have a systematic and standardized method for gauging variation. One of the most important advantages of quantification is that it provides the researcher with a consistent benchmark. The advantages of quantification and of measurement will be addressed in greater detail in Chapter 6.
- *Patterns of association.* With a cross-sectional design it is possible to examine relationships only between variables. There is no time ordering to the variables, because the data on them are collected more or less simultaneously, and the researcher does not (invariably because he or she cannot) manipulate any of the variables. This creates the problem referred to in Research in focus 2.2 as 'ambiguity about the direction of causal influence'. If the researcher discovers a relationship between two variables, he or she cannot be certain whether this denotes a causal relationship, because the features of an experimental design are not present. All that can be said is the variables are related. This is not to say that it is not possible to draw causal inferences from research based on a cross-sectional design. As will be shown in Chapter 14, there are a number of ways in which the researcher is able to draw certain inferences about causality, but these inferences rarely have the credibility of causal findings deriving from an experimental design. As a result, cross-sectional research invariably lacks the internal validity that one finds in most experimental research (see the examples in Research in focus 2.8 and Thinking deeply 2.1).

Key concept 2.6
What is a cross-sectional research design?

A cross-sectional design entails the collection of data on *more than one case* (usually quite a lot more than one) and at *a single point in time* in order to collect a body of *quantitative* or *quantifiable data* in connection with two or more variables (usually many more than two), which are then examined to detect *patterns of association*.

Research in focus 2.8
Cross-sectional design and internal validity: an example based on the Health and Lifestyle Survey

Blaxter (1990) reports some of the findings of a large-scale cross-sectional study in which data were collected by three methods: a structured interview; physiological data on each respondent carried out by a nurse; and a self-completion questionnaire. Data were collected from a *random sample* of around 9,000 individuals. At one point Blaxter shows that there is a relationship between whether a person smokes and his or her diet. But how are we to interpret this relationship? Blaxter is quite properly cautious and does not infer any kind of causal relationship between the two. On the basis of the data, we cannot conclude whether smoking causes diet or whether diet causes smoking or whether the association between the two is actually an artefact of a third variable, such as a commitment or indifference to a 'healthy' lifestyle. There is, therefore, an ambiguity about the direction of causal influence.

Thinking deeply 2.1
Direction of causality: is sex good for you?

An article in the *Guardian*'s Health section reviewed evidence about whether sex is good for you. At one point, the author refers to a study of men that seems to suggest that sex does bring health benefits, but she also has to acknowledge the problem of the direction of cause and effect.

> A study of 1,000 men in Caerphilly found that those who had two or more orgasms a week halved their mortality risk compared with those who had orgasms less than once a month. But while the authors concluded that sex seems to have a protective effect on men's health, it is always possible that the association is the other way around—people who are ill are less likely to have sex in the first place.
> (Houghton 1998: 14)

In this book, the term 'survey' will be reserved for research that employs a cross-sectional research design and in which data are collected by questionnaire or by structured interview (see Key concept 2.7 overleaf). This will allow me to retain the conventional understanding of what a survey is while recognizing that the cross-sectional research design has a wider relevance—that is, one that is not necessarily associated with the collection of data by questionnaire or by structured interview.

Reliability, replicability, and validity

How does cross-sectional research measure up in terms of the previously outlined criteria for evaluating quantitative research: reliability, replicability, and validity?

- The issues of reliability and measurement validity are primarily matters relating to the quality of the measures that are employed to tap the concepts in which the researcher is interested, rather than matters to do with a research design. In order to address questions of the quality of measures, some of the issues outlined in Chapter 6 would have to be considered.

- Replicability is likely to be present in most cross-sectional research to the degree that the researcher spells out procedures for: selecting respondents; designing measures of concepts; administering research instruments (such as structured interview or self-completion questionnaire); and analysing data. Most quantitative research based on cross-sectional

Key concept 2.7
What is survey research?

Survey research comprises a cross-sectional design in relation to which data are collected predominantly by questionnaire or by structured interview on *more than one case* (usually quite a lot more than one) and at *a single point in time* in order to collect a body of *quantitative* or *quantifiable data* in connection with two or more variables (usually many more than two), which are then examined to detect *patterns of association*.

research designs specifies such procedures to a large degree.

- Internal validity is typically weak. As has just been suggested above, it is difficult to establish causal direction from the resulting data. Cross-sectional research designs produce associations rather than findings from which causal inferences can be unambiguously made. However, procedures for making causal inferences from cross-sectional data will be referred to in Chapter 14, though most researchers feel that the resulting causal findings rarely have the internal validity of those deriving from experimental designs.

- External validity is strong when, as in the case of research like Blaxter's (1990) study of Health and Lifestyles, the sample from which data are collected has been randomly selected. When non-random methods of sampling are employed, external validity becomes questionable. Sampling issues will be specifically addressed in Chapter 7.

- Since much cross-sectional research makes a great deal of use of research instruments, such as self-completion questionnaires and structured **observation schedules**, ecological validity may be jeopardized because the very instruments disrupt the 'natural habitat', as Cicourel (1982) puts it (see quotation on page 33).

Non-manipulable variables

As was noted at the beginning of the section on experimental design, in much if not most social research it is not possible to manipulate the variables in which we are interested. This is why most quantitative social research employs a cross-sectional research design rather than an experimental one. If we wanted internally valid findings in connection with the smoking—diet relationship investigated by Blaxter (1990) (see Research in focus 2.8), we would need to manipulate one of the variables. For example, if we believed that smoking influences diet (perhaps because smoking is an expensive habit, which may

affect people's ability to afford certain kinds of food), we might envisage an experiment in which we took the following steps:

- select a random sample of members of the public who do not smoke;

- establish their current dietary habits;

- randomly assign them to one of three experimental treatments: heavy smokers, moderate smokers, and non-smokers (who act as a control group); and

- after a certain amount of time establish their dietary habits.

Such a research design is almost laughable, because practical and ethical considerations are bound to render it unworkable. We would have to turn some people into smokers, and, in view of the evidence of the harmful effects of smoking, this would be profoundly unethical. Also, in view of the evidence about the effects of smoking, it is extremely unlikely that we would find people who would be prepared to allow themselves to be turned into smokers. We might offer incentives for them to become smokers, but that might invalidate any findings about the effects on diet if we believe that economic considerations play an important role in relation to the effects of smoking on diet. This research is essentially unworkable.

Moreover, some of the variables in which social scientists are interested, and which are often viewed as potentially significant independent variables, simply cannot be manipulated, other than by extreme measures. To more or less all intents and purposes, our ethnicity, age, gender, and social backgrounds are 'givens' that are not really amenable to the kind of manipulation that is necessary for a true experimental design. A man might be able to present himself through dress and make-up as a woman to investigate the impact of gender on job opportunities, as Dustin Hoffman's character did in the film *Tootsie*, but it is unlikely that we would find a sufficient number of men to participate in a meaningful experiment to allow such an issue to be investigated (although Thinking deeply 2.2 and 2.3 provide interesting cases of the manipulation of seemingly non-manipulable variables). Moreover, it could be reasonably argued that, even if we could bring this research design to fruition, the researcher would be examining the effects of only the external signs of gender and would be neglecting its more subjective and experiential aspects. Similarly, while the case of a white man presenting himself as a black man in Thinking deeply 2.3 is interesting, it is doubtful whether a brief sojourn as a person of colour could

adequately capture the experience of being black in the American South. Such an experience is formed by many years of personal experience and the knowledge that it will be an ongoing experience. Thus, although the cases described in Thinking deeply 2.2 and 2.3 provide interesting cases of manipulating apparently non-manipulable variables—gender and ethnicity—it is doubtful whether they could meaningfully be applied to an experimental context, not least because it is doubtful whether sufficient numbers of people could be found to endure the discomforts and inconvenience.

Thinking deeply 2.2
Manipulating a non-manipulable variable: gender

Norah Vincent, a New York journalist, spent a year disguised as a man whom she named 'Ned'. She reported her experiences in a book (Vincent 2006). She received help from friends with experience of make-up in the theatre, who assisted her with her facial appearance, and she received training in exhibiting a male voice. To exhibit a gender-appropriate body, she found a way to 'bind' her breasts and developed a masculine walk. She also 'ate and drank as much protein as [she] could shove down [her] neck' and acquired a 'prosthetic penis' (Vincent 2006: 13), as well as acquiring a new wardrobe. Vincent then entered the male world, working as a man, visiting strip clubs, socializing with other men, and dating women.

Thinking deeply 2.3
Manipulating a non-manipulable variable: ethnicity

In the 1950s John Howard Griffin (1961) blackened his face and visible parts of his body and travelled around the American South as a person of colour. He behaved appropriately by keeping his eyes averted to show due deference to whites. He was treated as a black man in a number of ways, such as by having to use water fountains designated for 'coloreds'. Griffin's aim was to experience what it was like being a black person in a period and region of racial segregation.

On the other hand, the very fact that we can regard certain variables as givens provides us with a clue as to how we can make causal inferences in cross-sectional research. Many of the variables in which we are interested can be *assumed* to be temporally prior to other variables. For example, we can assume that, if we find a relationship between ethnic status and alcohol consumption, that the former is more likely to be the independent variable because it is temporally prior to alcohol consumption. In

other words, while we cannot manipulate ethnic status, we can draw causal inferences from cross-sectional data.

Structure of the cross-sectional design

The cross-sectional research design is not easy to depict in terms of the notation previously introduced, but Figure 2.2 captures its main features, except that in this case Obs simply represents an observation made in relation to a variable.

Figure 2.2

A cross-sectional design

$$T_1$$
$$Obs_1$$
$$Obs_2$$
$$Obs_3$$
$$Obs_4$$
$$Obs_5$$
$$\ldots$$
$$Obs_n$$

Figure 2.3

The data rectangle in cross-sectional research

	Obs_1	Obs_2	Obs_3	Obs_4	$\ldots$	Obs_n
$Case_1$						
$Case_2$						
$Case_3$						
$Case_4$						
$Case_5$						
$\ldots$						
$Case_n$						

Figure 2.2 implies that a cross-sectional design comprises the collection of data on a series of variables (Obs_1 Obs_2 Obs_3 Obs_4 Obs_5 . . . Obs_n) at a single point in time, T_1. The effect is to create what Marsh (1982) referred to as a 'rectangle' of data that comprises variables Obs_1 to Obs_n and cases $Case_1$ to $Case_n$, as in Figure 2.3. For each case (which may be a person, household, city, nation, etc.) data are available for each of the variables, Obs_1 to Obs_n, all of which will have been collected at T_1. Each **cell** in the matrix will have data in it.

Cross-sectional design and research strategy

This discussion of the cross-sectional design has placed it firmly in the context of quantitative research. Also, the evaluation of the design has drawn on criteria associated with the quantitative research strategy. It should also be noted, however, that qualitative research often entails a form of cross-sectional design. A fairly typical form of such research is when the researcher employs **unstruc**-tured interviewing or **semi-structured interviewing** with a number of people. Research in focus 2.9 provides an illustration of such a study.

While emphatically within the qualitative research tradition, the study described in Research in focus 2.9 bears many research design similarities with cross-sectional studies within a quantitative research tradition, like Blaxter (1990). Moreover, it is a very popular mode of qualitative research. The research was not preoccupied with such criteria of quantitative research as internal and external validity, **replicability**, measurement validity, and so on. In fact, it could be argued that the conversational interview style made the study more ecologically valid than research using more formal instruments of data collection. It is also striking that the study was concerned with the factors that influence food selection, like

Research in focus 2.9
Qualitative research within a cross-sectional design

Beardsworth and Keil (1992) carried out a study of the dietary beliefs and practices of vegetarians. They write that their intention was to contribute 'to the analysis of the cultural and sociological factors which influence patterns of food selection and avoidance. The specific focus is on contemporary vegetarianism, a complex of interrelated beliefs, attitudes and practices . . .' (1992: 253). The authors carried out 'relatively unstructured interviews', which were 'guided by an inventory of issues' with seventy-six vegetarians and vegans in the East Midlands (1992: 261). Respondents were identified through a *snowball sampling* approach. The interviews were taped and transcribed, yielding a large corpus of qualitative data.

vegetarianism. The very notion of an 'influence' carries a strong connotation of causality, suggesting that qualitative researchers are interested in the investigation of causes and effects, albeit not in the context of the language of variables that so pervades quantitative research. Also, the emphasis was much more on elucidating the *experience* of something like vegetarianism than is often the case with quantitative research. However, the chief point in providing the illustration is that it bears many similarities to the cross-sectional design in quantitative research. It entailed the interviewing of quite a large number of people and at a single point in time. Just as with many quantitative studies using a cross-sectional design, the examination of early influences on people's past and current behaviour is based on their retrospective accounts of factors that influenced them in the past.

Longitudinal design(s)

The longitudinal design represents a distinct form of research design. Because of the time and cost involved, it is a relatively little-used design in social research, so it is not proposed to allocate a great deal of space to it. In the form in which it is typically found in social science subjects such as sociology, social policy, and human geography, it is usually an extension of survey research based on a self-completion questionnaire or structured interview research within a cross-sectional design. Consequently, in terms of reliability, replication, and validity, the longitudinal design is little different from cross-sectional research. However, a longitudinal design can allow some insight into the time order of variables and therefore may be more able to allow causal inferences to be made.

With a longitudinal design a sample is surveyed and is surveyed again on at least one further occasion. It is common to distinguish two types of longitudinal design: the *panel study* and the *cohort study*. With the former type, a sample, often a randomly selected national one, is the focus of data collection on at least two (and often more) occasions. Data may be collected from different types of case within a panel study framework: people, households, organizations, schools, and so on. An illustration of this kind of study is the British Household Panel Survey (BHPS) (see Research in focus 2.10).

Research in focus 2.10
The British Household Panel Survey

The British Household Panel Survey (BHPS) began in 1991 when a national representative sample of 10,264 individuals in 5,538 households were interviewed for the first time in connection with six main areas of interest:

- household organization;
- labour market behaviour;
- income and wealth;
- housing;
- health; and
- socio-economic values.

Panel members are interviewed annually. As a result of the continuous interviewing, it is possible to highlight areas of social change. For example, Laurie and Gershuny (2000) show that there have been changes in the ways in which couples manage their money. Over a relatively short five-year period (1991–5), there was a small decline in the proportion of men having a final say in financial decisions and a corresponding small increase in those reporting equal say, although interestingly these trends refer to aggregated replies of partners—around a quarter of partners give different answers about who has the final say!

For further information see **http://www.iser.essex.ac.uk/ulsc/bhps/** (accessed on 2 July 2007).

The BHPS is to be replaced by the UK Household Longitudinal Survey, which will be based on a much larger panel of households. See **http://www.iser.essex.ac.uk/ukhls/** (accessed on 2 July 2007). It will include a much larger sample of households—in the region of 40,000.

In a cohort study, either an entire cohort of people or a random sample of them is selected as the focus of data collection. The cohort is made up of people who share a certain characteristic, such as all being born in the same week or all having a certain experience, such as being unemployed or getting married on a certain day or in the same week. The National Child Development Study is an example of a cohort study (see Research in focus 2.11). More recently, a new cohort study—the ESRC Millennium Cohort Study (see Research in focus 2.12)—began at the turn of the present millennium.

Research in focus 2.11
The National Child Development Study

The National Child Development Study (NCDS) is based on all 17,000 children born in Great Britain in the week of 3–9 March 1958. The study was initially motivated by a concern over levels of perinatal mortality, but the data collected reflect a much wider range of issues than this focus implies. Data were collected on the children and their families at age 7. In fact, the study was not originally planned as a longitudinal study. The children and their families have been followed up at ages 11, 16, 23, 33, 41–2, and 46. Data are collected in relation to a number of areas, including: physical and mental health; family; parenting; occupation and income; and housing and environment.

For further information, see Fox and Fogelman (1990); Hodges (1998); and
http://www.esds.ac.uk/longitudinal/access/ncds/ (accessed on 2 July 2007).

Research in focus 2.12
The Millennium Cohort Study

This cohort study, known as the Child of the New Century, collects data relating to a sample of all children born in England and Wales over a twelve-month period from 1 September 2000 and all children born in Scotland and Northern Ireland from 1 December 2000. The sample is based on electoral wards, which have been disproportionately stratified (see Chapter 7 for more on this term) to ensure a good representation of the four countries, the relative wealth of the different areas, and ethnic minority groups. Interviews are conducted by computer-assisted personal interviewing (CAPI), and there is a self-completion questionnaire that is also computer-assisted. Data are collected from mothers and, where possible, fathers or father figures. Data are collected by interview from the mother on such issues as: parenthood; childcare; parental and baby's health; housing; and interests; by questionnaire, data are collected on areas such as domestic tasks; relationship with partner; and mental health. Questions for fathers deal with similar issues. The first wave of data collection took place during 2001–3. Since then, there have been two further waves of data collection (2004–5 and a further one beginning 2006). Information on the study can be found in
http://www.cls.ioe.ac.uk/studies.asp?section=000100020001 (accessed on 2 July 2007).

Panel and cohort studies share similar features. They have a similar design structure: Figure 2.4 portrays this structure and implies that data are collected in at least two waves on the same variables on the same people.

Both panel and cohort studies are concerned with illuminating social change and with improving the understanding of causal influences over time. The latter means that longitudinal designs are somewhat better able to deal

Figure 2.4

The longitudinal design

T_1	$\ldots$	T_n
Obs_1		Obs_1
Obs_2		Obs_2
Obs_3		Obs_3
Obs_4		Obs_4
Obs_5		Obs_5
$\ldots$		$\ldots$
Obs_n		Obs_n

with the problem of 'ambiguity about the direction of causal influence' that plagues cross-sectional designs. Because certain potentially independent variables can be identified at T_1, the researcher is in a better position to infer that purported effects that are identified at T_2 or later have occurred *after* the independent variables. This does not deal with the entire problem about the ambiguity of causal influence, but it at least addresses the problem of knowing which variable came first. In all other respects, the points made above about cross-sectional designs are the same as those for longitudinal designs.

Panel and cohort designs differ in important respects too. A panel study, like the BHPS, that takes place over many years can distinguish between age effects (the impact of the ageing process on individuals) and cohort effects (effects due to being born at a similar time), because its members will have been born at different times. A cohort study, however, can distinguish only ageing effects, since all members of the sample will have been born at more or less the same time. Also, a panel study, especially one that operates at the household level, needs rules to inform how to handle new entrants to households (for example, as a result of marriage or elderly relatives moving in) and exits from households (for example, as a result of marriage break-up or children leaving home).

Panel and cohort studies share similar problems. First, there is the problem of sample attrition through death, moving, and so on, and through subjects choosing to withdraw at later stages of the research. Menard (1991) cites the case of a study of adolescent drug use in the USA in which 55 per cent of subjects were lost over an eight-year period. However, attrition rates are by no means always as high as this. In 1981 the National Child

Development Study managed to secure data from 12,537 members of the original 17,414 cohort, which is quite an achievement bearing in mind that twenty-three years would have elapsed since the birth of the children. In 1991 data were elicited from 11,407. The problem with attrition is largely that those who leave the study may differ in some important respects from those who remain, so that the latter do not form a representative group. There is some evidence from panel studies that the problem of attrition declines with time (Berthoud 2000*a*); in other words, those who do not drop out after the first wave or two of data collection tend to stay on the panel. Secondly, there are few guidelines as to when is the best juncture to conduct further waves of data collection. Thirdly, it is often suggested that many longitudinal studies are poorly thought out and that they result in the collection of large amounts of data with little apparent planning. Fourthly, there is evidence that a *panel conditioning* effect can occur whereby continued participation in a longitudinal study affects how respondents behave. Menard (1991) refers to a study of family caregiving in which 52 per cent of respondents indicated that they responded differently to providing care for relatives as a result of their participation in the research.

Surveys, like the General Household Survey, the British Social Attitudes survey, and the British Crime Survey (see Table 13.1), that are carried out on a regular basis on samples of the **population** are not truly longitudinal designs because they do not involve the same people being interviewed on each occasion. They are perhaps better thought of as involving a repeated cross-sectional design or trend design in which samples are selected on each of several occasions. They are able to chart change but they cannot address the issue of the direction of cause and effect because the samples are always different.

It is easy to associate longitudinal designs more or less exclusively with quantitative research. However, qualitative research sometimes incorporates elements of a longitudinal design. This is especially noticeable in ethnographic research when the **ethnographer** is in a location for a lengthy period of time or when interviews are carried out on more than one occasion to address change. As an example of the latter, Smith *et al.* (2004) describe a study of young people's experiences of citizenship in which 110 young people were interviewed in depth in 1999 and then re-interviewed in each of the following two years to examine changes in their lifestyles, feelings, and opinions, as well as their future ambitions, in relation to citizenship issues. Only 64 young people participated in all three waves of data collection, suggesting quite a high level of sample attrition in this style of research.

Most longitudinal studies will be planned from the outset in such a way that sample members can be followed up at a later date. However, it can happen that the idea of conducting a longitudinal study occurs to the researchers at a later date. Provided there are good records, it may be possible to follow up sample members for a second wave of data collection or even for further waves. Research in focus 2.13 provides an extremely unusual but fascinating example of a longitudinal design from the USA with both planned and unplanned elements. This is also an interesting illustration of a mixed methods study, in that it combines quantitative and qualitative research.

Research in focus 2.13
A planned and unplanned longitudinal design

In the 1940s Sheldon and Eleanor Glueck of the Harvard Law School conducted a study concerned with how criminal careers begin and are maintained. The study entailed a comparison of 500 delinquents and 500 non-delinquents in Massachusetts. The two samples were matched in terms of several characteristics, such as age, ethnicity, and the socio-economic status of the neighbourhoods from which they were drawn. The sample was aged around 14 at the time and was followed up at ages 25 and 32. The data were collected by various means: interviews with the 1,000 participants, their families, and various key figures in their lives (e.g. social workers and school teachers); observations of the home; and records of various agencies that had any connection with the participants and their families. Obviously, data concerning criminal activity were collected for each individual by examining records relating to court appearances and parole. While all these sources of data produced quantitative information, qualitative data were also collected through answers to **open questions** in the interviews. Around the mid-1990s Laub and Sampson (2003, 2004) began to follow up the 500 men who had been in the delinquent sample. By this time, they would have been aged 70. Records of death and criminal activity were searched for all 500 men, so that patterns of ongoing criminal activity could be gleaned. Further, they managed to find and then interview 52 of the original delinquent sample. These cases were selected on the basis of their patterns of offending over the years, as indicated by the criminal records. The interviews were **life history interviews** to uncover key turning points in their lives and to find out about their experiences. This is an extremely unusual example of a longitudinal study that contains planned elements (the original wave of data collection followed by the ones eleven and eighteen years later) and an unplanned element conducted by Laub and Sampson many years later.

Case study design

The basic case study entails the detailed and intensive analysis of a single case. As Stake (1995) observes, case study research is concerned with the complexity and particular nature of the case in question. Some of the best-known studies in sociology are based on this kind of design. They include research on:

- a single community, such as Whyte's (1955) study of Cornerville in Boston, Gans's (1962) study of the East End of Boston, M. Stacey's (1960) research on Banbury, and O'Reilly's (2000) research on a community of Britons living on the Costa del Sol in Spain;

- a single school, such as studies by Ball (1981) and by Burgess (1983) on Beachside Comprehensive and Bishop McGregor respectively;

- a single family, like Lewis's (1961) study of the Sánchez family or Brannen and Nilsen's (2006) investigation of a family of low-skilled British men, which contained four generations in order to uncover changes in 'fathering' over time;

- a single organization, such as studies of a factory by writers such as Burawoy (1979), Pollert (1981), and Cavendish (1982), or of management in organizations like Pettigrew's (1985) work on Imperial Chemical Industries (ICI), or of pilferage in a single location like a bakery (Ditton 1977), or of a single police service (Holdaway 1983; see Research in focus 2.14);

- a person, like the famous study of Stanley, the 'jack-roller' (Shaw 1930); such studies are often characterized as using the life history or biographical approach (see Key concept 18.1); and

- a single event, such as the Cuban Missile Crisis (Allison 1971), a vicious rape attack (Winkler 1995), the events surrounding the media reporting of a specific issue area (Deacon, Fenton, and Bryman 1999), and the Balinese cockfight (Geertz 1973b).

Research in focus 2.14
A case study

Holdaway (1982, 1983) was a police officer who was also conducting doctoral research on his own police service, which was located in a city. His main research method was **ethnography**, whereby he was a participant observer who observed interaction, listened to conversations, examined documents, and wrote up his impressions and experiences in **field notes**. Holdaway's superiors did not know that he was conducting research on his own force, so that he was a **covert researcher**. This is a controversial method on ethical grounds (see Chapters 5 and 17). Holdaway's research provides insights into the nature of police work and the occupational culture with which officers surround themselves.

What is a case?

The most common use of the term 'case' associates the case study with a location, such as a community or organization. The emphasis tends to be upon an intensive examination of the setting. There is a tendency to associate case studies with qualitative research, but such an identification is not appropriate. It is certainly true that exponents of the case study design often favour qualitative methods, such as participant observation and unstructured interviewing, because these methods are viewed as particularly helpful in the generation of an intensive, detailed examination of a case. However, case studies are frequently sites for the employment of *both* quantitative and qualitative research, an approach that will receive attention in Chapter 25. Indeed, in some instances, when an investigation is based exclusively upon quantitative research, it can be difficult to determine whether it is better described as a case study or as a cross-sectional research design. The same point can often be made about case studies based upon qualitative research.

As an illustration of the difficulties of writing about case studies, consider the study described in Thinking deeply 2.4. Ostensibly, it is similar to Beardsworth and Keil's (1992) study of vegetarians in that it is a piece of

qualitative research within a cross-sectional design framework (see Research in focus 2.9). However, it has been described as providing 'case-study evidence' by Davies *et al.* (1994: 157), presumably on the grounds that the fieldwork was undertaken in a single location. I would prefer to reserve the term 'case study' for those instances where the 'case' is the focus of interest in its own right. The study in Thinking deeply 2.4 is no more a case study of Kidderminster than Beardsworth and Keil's (1992) research is based on a case study of the East Midlands. McKee and Bell's (1985) research is concerned with the experience of unemployment among the forty-five couples whom they interviewed. It is not concerned with Kidderminster as such. The town provides a kind of backdrop to the findings rather than a focus of interest in its own right. The crucial point is that Kidderminster is not the unit of analysis; rather it is the sample that is the unit of analysis.

Similarly, Powell and Butterfield (1997) present a quantitative analysis of promotion decisions in a US government department. They were concerned to investigate how far race had an impact on promotions within the department. The researchers found that race did not have a direct effect on promotion, but it did have an indirect effect. This occurred because race had an impact on two

Thinking deeply 2.4
What is the unit of analysis?

McKee and Bell (1985: 387) examined forty-five couples in a single location (Kidderminster in the West Midlands) in order to examine 'the impact of male unemployment on family and marital relations'. They describe their research instrument as an 'unstructured, conversational interview style'. In most cases, husbands and wives were interviewed jointly. The interviews were very non-directive, allowing the couples considerable freedom to answer in their own terms and time. Their research focused on the range of problems faced by unemployed families, the processes by which they cope, and the variations in their experiences. Thus the focus was very much on the experience of unemployment from the perspective of the couples. The authors show, for example, that the impact of husbands' unemployment on their wives is often far greater than is usually appreciated, since research frequently takes the unemployed person as the main hub of the enquiry. Couples often reported changes to the domestic division of labour, which in turn raised questions for them about images of masculinity and identity.

Is this study a case study of unemployment in Kidderminster or is it better thought of as a cross-sectional design study of unemployed men and their wives? As I suggest in the text, it is not terribly helpful to think of it as a case study, because Kidderminster is not the unit of analysis. It is about the responses to unemployment among a sample of individuals; the fact that the interviewees were located in Kidderminster is not significant to the research findings. However, it is not always easy to distinguish whether an investigation is of one kind rather than another. As these reflections imply, it is important to be clear in your own mind what your unit of analysis is.

variables—whether the applicant was employed in the hiring department and the number of years of work experience—which in turn affected promotion. The impact of race on these two variables was such that people of colour were disadvantaged with respect to promotion. Once again, we see here a study that has the hallmarks of both a cross-sectional design and a case study, but this time the research strategy was a quantitative one. As with the McKee and Bell (1985) research, it seems better to describe it as employing a cross-sectional design rather than a case study, because the case itself is not the apparent object of interest: it is little more than a location that forms a backdrop to the findings.

Similarly, I would tend to argue that the study of redundant steelworkers by Westergaard *et al.* (1989) is a case study of the effects of redundancy in which a quantitative research strategy was employed with clear indications of a cross-sectional design. With a case study, the case is an object of interest in its own right, and the researcher aims to provide an in-depth elucidation of it. Unless a distinction of this or some other kind is drawn, it becomes impossible to distinguish the case study as a special research design, because almost any kind of research

can be construed as a case study: research based on a national, random sample of the population of Great Britain would have to be considered a case study of Great Britain! However, it also needs to be appreciated that, when specific research illustrations are examined, they can exhibit features of more than one research design. What distinguishes a case study is that the researcher is usually concerned to elucidate the unique features of the case. This is known as an *idiographic* approach. Research designs like the cross-sectional design are known as *nomothetic* in that they are concerned with generating statements that apply regardless of time and place. However, an investigation may have elements of both (see Research in focus 2.15).

With experimental and cross-sectional designs, the typical orientation to the relationship between theory and research is a **deductive** one. The research design and the collection of data are guided by specific research questions that derive from theoretical concerns. However, when a qualitative research strategy is employed within a cross-sectional design, as in Beardsworth and Keil's (1992) research, the approach tends to be **inductive**. In other words, whether a cross-sectional design is inductive

Research in focus 2.15
A cross-sectional design with case study elements

Sometimes, an investigation may have both cross-sectional and case study elements. For example, Leonard (2004) was interested in the utility of the notion of social capital for research into neighbourhood formation. As such, she was interested in similar issues to the study in Research in focus 1.1. She conducted her study in a Catholic housing estate in West Belfast, where she conducted semi-structured interviews with 246 individuals living in 150 households. Her findings relate to the relevance of the concept of social capital, so that the research design looks like a cross-sectional one. However, on certain occasions she draws attention to the uniqueness of Belfast with its history in recent times of conflict and the search for political solutions to the problems there. At one point she writes: 'In West Belfast, as the peace process develops, political leaders are charged with connecting informal community networks to more formal institutional networks' (Leonard 2004: 939). As this comment implies, it is more or less impossible in a case like this to generate findings concerning community formation without reference to the special characteristics of Belfast and its troubled history.

or deductive tends to be affected by whether a quantitative or a qualitative research strategy is employed. The same point can be made of case study research. When the predominant research strategy is qualitative, a case study tends to take an inductive approach to the relationship between theory and research; if a predominantly quantitative strategy is taken, it tends to be deductive.

Reliability, replicability, and validity

The question of how well the case study fares in the context of the research design criteria cited early on in this chapter—measurement validity, internal validity, external validity, ecological validity, reliability, and replicability—depends in large part on how far the researcher feels that these are appropriate for the evaluation of case study research. Some writers on case study research, like Yin (2003), consider that they are appropriate criteria and suggest ways in which case study research can be developed to enhance its ability to meet the criteria; for others, like Stake (1995), they are barely mentioned, if at all. Writers on case study research whose point of orientation lies primarily with a qualitative research strategy tend to play down or ignore the salience of these factors, whereas those writers who have been strongly influenced by the quantitative research strategy tend to depict them as more significant.

However, one question on which a great deal of discussion has centred concerns the *external validity* or *generalizability* of case study research. How can a single case possibly be representative so that it might yield findings that can be applied more generally to other cases? For

example, how could the findings from Holdaway's (1982, 1983) research, referred to in Research in focus 2.14, be generalizable to all police services in Great Britain? The answer, of course, is that they cannot. It is important to appreciate that case study researchers do not delude themselves that it is possible to identify typical cases that can be used to represent a certain class of objects, whether it is factories, mass media reporting, police services, or communities. In other words, they do *not* think that a case study is a sample of one.

Types of case

Following on from the issue of external validity, it is useful to consider a distinction between different types of case that is sometimes made by writers. Yin (2003) distinguishes five types.

- The *critical case*. Here the researcher has a well-developed theory, and a case is chosen on the grounds that it will allow a better understanding of the circumstances in which the **hypothesis** will and will not hold. The study by Festinger *et al.* (1956) of a religious cult whose members believed that the end of the world was about to happen is an example. The fact that the event did not happen by the appointed day allowed the researchers to test the authors' propositions about how people respond to thwarted expectations.

- The *extreme* or *unique case*. The unique or extreme case is, as Yin observes, a common focus in clinical studies. Margaret Mead's (1928) well-known study of growing up in Samoa seems to have been motivated by her belief that the country represented a unique case. She argued that, unlike most other societies, Samoan youth do not suffer a period of anxiety and stress in adolescence. The factors associated with this relatively trouble-free period in their lives were of interest to her, since they might contain lessons for Western youth. Fielding (1982) conducted research on the extreme right-wing organization the National Front. While the National Front was not unique on the British political scene, it was extremely prominent at the time of his research and was beginning to become an electoral force. As such, it held an intrinsic interest that made it essentially unique.

- The *representative* or *typical case*. I prefer to call this an *exemplifying* case, because notions of representativeness and typicality can sometimes lead to confusion. With this kind of case, 'the objective is to capture the circumstances and conditions of an everyday or commonplace situation' (Yin 2003: 41). Thus a case may be chosen because it exemplifies a broader category of which it is a member. The notion of exemplification implies that cases are often chosen not because they are extreme or unusual in some way but because either they epitomize a broader category of cases or they will provide a suitable context for certain research questions to be answered. An illustration of the first kind of situation is Lynd and Lynd's (1929, 1937) classic community study of Muncie, Indiana, in the USA, which they dubbed 'Middletown' precisely because it seemed to typify American life at the time. A more recent instance occurred when the philosopher Julian Baggini (2007) spent several months living in Rotherham because its social characteristics seemed to typify Englishness. The second rationale for selecting exemplifying cases is that they allow the researcher to examine key social processes. For example, a researcher may seek access to an organization because it is known to have implemented a new technology and he or she wants to know what the impact of that new technology has been. The researcher may have been influenced by various theories about the relationship between technology and work and by the considerable research literature on the topic, and as a result seeks to examine the implications of some of these theoretical and empirical deliberations in a particular research site. The case merely provides an apt context for the working-through of these research questions. To take a concrete example, Russell and Tyler's (2002) study of one store in the 'Girl Heaven' UK chain of retail stores for 3–13-year-old girls does not appear to have been motivated by the store being critical, unique, or by it providing a context that had never before been studied, but was to do with the capacity of the research site to illuminate the links between gender and consumption and the commodification of childhood in modern society.

- The *revelatory case*. The basis for the revelatory case exists 'when an investigator has an opportunity to observe and analyse a phenomenon previously inaccessible to scientific investigation' (Yin 2003: 42). As examples, Yin cites Whyte's (1955) study of Cornerville, and Liebow's (1967) research on unemployed blacks.

- The *longitudinal case*. Yin suggests that a case may be chosen because it affords the opportunity to be investigated at two or more junctures. However, many case studies comprise a longitudinal element, so that it is more likely that a case will be chosen both because it is appropriate to the research questions on one of the other four grounds and also because it can be studied over time.

Any case study can involve a combination of these elements, which can best be viewed as rationales for choosing particular cases. For example, Margaret Mead's (1928) classic study of growing up in Samoa has been depicted above as an extreme case, but it also has elements of a critical case because she felt that it had the potential to demonstrate that young people's responses to entering their teenage years are not determined by nature alone. Instead, she used growing up in Samoa as a critical case to demonstrate that culture has an important role in the development of humans, thus enabling her to cast doubt on notions of biological determinism.

It may be that it is only at a very late stage that the singularity and significance of the case becomes apparent (Radley and Chamberlain 2001). Flyvbjerg (2003) provides an example of this. He shows how he undertook a study of urban politics and planning in Aalborg in Denmark, thinking it was a critical case. After conducting his fieldwork for a while, he found it was in fact an extreme case. He writes as follows:

> Initially, I conceived of Aalborg as a 'most likely' critical case in the following manner: if rationality and urban planning were weak in the face of power in Aalborg, then, most likely, they would be weak anywhere, at least in Denmark, because in Aalborg

the rational paradigm of planning stood stronger than anywhere else. Eventually, I realized that this logic was flawed, because my research [on] local relations of power showed that one of the most influential 'faces of power' in Aalborg, the Chamber of Industry and Commerce, was substantially stronger than their equivalents elsewhere. Therefore, instead of a critical case, unwittingly I ended up with an extreme case in the sense that both rationality and power were unusually strong in Aalborg, and my case study became a study of what happens when strong rationality meets strong power in the area of urban politics and planning. But this selection of Aalborg as an extreme case happened to me, I did not deliberately choose it. (Flyvbjerg 2003: 426)

Thus, we may not always appreciate the nature and significance of a 'case' until we have subjected it to detailed scrutiny.

One of the standard criticisms of the case study is that findings deriving from it cannot be generalized. Exponents of case study research counter suggestions that the evidence they present is limited because it has restricted external validity by arguing that it is not the purpose of this research design to generalize to other cases or to populations beyond the case. This position is very different from that taken by practitioners of survey research. Survey researchers are invariably concerned to be able to generalize their findings to larger populations and frequently use random sampling to enhance the representativeness of the samples on which they conduct their investigations and therefore the external validity of their findings. Case study researchers argue strenuously that this is not the purpose of their craft.

Case study as intensive analysis

Instead, case study researchers tend to argue that they aim to generate an intensive examination of a single case, in relation to which they then engage in a theoretical analysis. The central issue of concern is the quality of the theoretical reasoning in which the case study researcher engages. How well do the data support the theoretical arguments that are generated? Is the theoretical analysis incisive? For example, does it demonstrate connections between different conceptual ideas that are developed out of the data? The crucial question is not whether the findings can be generalized to a wider universe but how well the researcher generates theory out of the findings (Mitchell 1983; Yin 2003). Such a view places case study research firmly in the inductive tradition of the relationship between theory and research. However, a case study design is not necessarily associated with an inductive approach, as can be seen in the research by Adler and Adler (1985), which was referred to in Chapter 1. Thus, case studies can be associated with both theory generation and theory testing. Further, as Williams (2000) has argued, case study researchers are often in a position to generalize by drawing on findings from comparable cases investigated by others. This issue will be returned to in Chapter 16.

Longitudinal research and the case study

Case study research frequently includes a longitudinal element. The researcher is often a participant of an organization or member of a community for many months or years. Alternatively, he or she may conduct interviews with individuals over a lengthy period. Moreover, the researcher may be able to inject an additional longitudinal element by analysing archival information and by retrospective interviewing. Research in focus 2.16 provides an illustration of such research.

Research in focus 2.16
A case study of ICI

Pettigrew (1985) conducted research into the use of organizational development expertise at Imperial Chemical Industries (ICI). The fieldwork was conducted between 1975 and 1983. He carried out 'long semistructured interviews' in 1975–7 and again in 1980–2. During the period of the fieldwork he also had fairly regular contact with members of the organization. He writes: 'The continuous real-time data collection was enriched by retrospective interviewing and archival analysis . . .' (1985: 40).

Another way in which a longitudinal element occurs is when a case that has been studied is returned to at a later stage. A particularly interesting instance of this is the Middletown study that was mentioned previously. The town was originally studied by Lynd and Lynd in 1924–5 (I ynd and Lynd 1929) and was restudied to discern trends and changes in 1935 (Lynd and Lynd 1937). In 1977 the community was restudied yet again (Bahr *et al.* 1983), using the same research instruments but with minor changes. Burgess (1987) was similarly concerned with continuity and change at the comprehensive school he had studied in the early 1970s (Burgess 1983) when he returned to study it ten years later. However, as he observes, it is difficult for the researcher to establish how far change is the result of real differences over the two time periods or of other factors, such as different people at the school, different educational issues between the two time periods, and the possible influence of the initial study itself.

Comparative design

It is worth distinguishing one further kind of design: comparative design. Put simply, this design entails studying two contrasting cases using more or less identical methods. It embodies the logic of comparison in that it implies that we can understand social phenomena better when they are compared in relation to two or more meaningfully contrasting cases or situations. The comparative design may be realized in the context of either quantitative or qualitative research. Within the former, the data collection strategy will take the form outlined in Figure 2.5. This figure implies that there are at least two cases (which may be organizations, nations, communities, police forces, etc.) and that data are collected from each usually within a cross-sectional design format.

One of the more obvious forms of such research is in cross-cultural or cross-national research. In a useful definition, Hantrais (1996) has suggested that such research occurs:

when individuals or teams set out to examine particular issues or phenomena in two or more countries with the express intention of comparing their manifestations in different socio-cultural settings (institutions, customs, traditions, value systems, life styles, language, thought patterns), using the same research instruments either to carry out secondary analysis of national data or to conduct new empirical

Figure 2.5

A comparative design

$$T_1$$

Case 1:
Obs_1
Obs_2
Obs_3
Obs_4
Obs_5
...
Obs_n

Case n:
Obs_1
Obs_2
Obs_3
Obs_4
Obs_5
...
Obs_n

work. The aim may be to seek explanations for similarities and differences or to gain a greater awareness and a deeper understanding of social reality in different national contexts.

The research by Kelley and De Graaf (1997), referred to in Research in focus 1.4, is an illustration of cross-cultural research that entails a secondary analysis of survey evidence collected in fifteen nations. A further example is Gallie's (1978) survey research on the impact of advanced automation on comparable samples of industrial workers in both England and France. Gallie was able to show that national traditions of industrial relations were more important than technology in explaining worker attitudes and management–worker relations, a finding that was important in terms of the technological determinism thesis that was still current at the time.

Cross-cultural research is not without problems such as: managing and gaining the funding for such research (see Thinking deeply 2.5); ensuring, when existing data, such as **official statistics** or survey evidence, are submitted to a secondary analysis, that the data are comparable in terms of categories and data-collection methods; ensuring, when new data are being collected, that the need to translate data-collection instruments (for example, interview schedules) does not undermine genuine comparability; and ensuring that samples of respondents or organizations are equivalent. This last problem raises the further difficulty that, even when translation is carried out competently, there is still the potential problem of an insensitivity to specific national and cultural contexts. On the other hand, cross-cultural research helps to reduce the risk of failing to appreciate that social science findings are often, if not invariably, culturally specific. For example, Crompton and Birkelund (2000) conducted research using semi-structured interviewing with comparable samples of male and female bank managers in Norway and Britain. They found that, in spite of more family-friendly policies in Norway, bank managers in both countries struggle to manage career and domestic life. It might have been assumed that countries with greater attachment to such policies would ease these pressures, but comparative, cross-cultural research of this kind shows how easy it is to make such an erroneous inference.

Thinking deeply 2.5
Forms of cross-cultural research

As its name implies, cross-cultural research entails the collection and/or analysis of data from two or more nations. Possible models for the conduct of cross-cultural research are as follows.

1. A researcher, perhaps in conjunction with a research team, collects data in a number of countries. Gallie's (1978) research on the impact of advanced automation on industrial workers is an illustration of this model in that he took comparable samples of industrial workers from two oil refineries in both England and France.

2. A central organization coordinates a portion of the work of national organizations. The article by Kelley and De Graaf (1997) that is cited in this chapter provides an example of this model.

3. A secondary analysis is carried out of data that are comparable, but where the coordination of their collection is limited or non-existent. This kind of cross-cultural analysis might occur if researchers seek to ask survey questions in their own country that have been asked in another country. The ensuing data may then be analysed cross-culturally. A further form of this model is through the secondary analysis of officially collected data, such as unemployment statistics. Wall's (1989) analysis of the living arrangements of the elderly in eighteen European countries is an example of such research. The research uncovered considerable diversity in terms of such factors as whether the elderly lived alone and whether they were in institutional care. However, this approach is beset with problems associated with the deficiencies of many forms of official statistics (see Chapter 13) and problems of cross-national variations in official definitions and collection procedures.

4. Teams of researchers in participating nations are recruited by a person or body that coordinates the programme, or alternatively researchers in different countries with common interests make contact and coordinate their investigations. Each researcher or group of researchers has the responsibility of conducting the investigation in his/her/their own country. The work is coordinated in order to ensure comparability of research questions, of survey questions, and of procedures for administering the research instruments (e.g. Crompton and Birkelund 2000). This model differs from (2) above in that it usually entails a specific focus on certain research questions. An example can be found in Research in focus 25.6.

5. Although not genuinely cross-cultural research in the sense of a coordinated project across nations, another form can occur when a researcher compares what is known in one country with new research in another country. For example, Richard Wright, a US criminologist who has carried out a considerable amount of research into street robberies in his own country, was interested in how far findings relating to this crime would be similar in the UK. In particular, US research highlighted the role of street culture in the motivation to engage in such robbery. He was involved in a project that entailed semi-structured interviews with imprisoned street robbers in south-west England (Wright *et al.* 2006). In fact, the researchers found that street culture played an important role in the UK context in a similar way to that in the USA.

Comparative research should not be treated as solely concerned with comparisons between nations. The logic of comparison can be applied to a variety of situations. The Social Change and Economic Life Initiative, referred to in Research in focus 6.1, entailed identical studies (mainly involving survey research) in six contrasting labour markets, which were chosen to reflect different patterns of economic change in the early to mid-1980s and in the then recent past. By choosing meaningful contrasts, the significance of the different patterns for a variety of experiences of both employers and employees could be portrayed. Such designs are not without problems: the differences that are observed between the contrasting cases may not be due exclusively to the distinguishing features of the cases. Thus, some caution is necessary when explaining contrasts between cases in terms of differences between them.

In terms of issues of reliability, validity, replicability, and generalizability, the comparative study is no different from the cross-sectional design. The comparative design is essentially two or more cross-sectional studies carried out at more or less the same point in time.

The comparative design can also be applied in relation to a qualitative research strategy. When this occurs, it takes the form of a multiple-case study (see Research in focus 2.16). In recent years, a number of writers have argued for a greater use of case study research that entails the investigation of more than one case. Indeed, in certain social science fields, like organization studies, this has become a common research design in its own right. Essentially, a multiple-case (or multi-case) study occurs whenever the number of cases examined exceeds one. The main argument in favour of the multiple-case study is that it improves theory building. By comparing two or more cases, the researcher is in a better position to establish the circumstances in which a theory will or will not hold (Eisenhardt 1989; Yin 2003). Moreover, the comparison may itself suggest concepts that are relevant to an emerging theory.

Research in focus 2.17
A multiple-case study of British companies

In their study of the factors that contribute to competitive success among large British companies, Pettigrew and Whipp (1991) adopted a multiple-case study approach. They examined eight companies, which were made up of a successful and an unsuccessful company in each of three commercial sectors (automobile manufacturing; merchant banking; and book publishing). An additional company drawn from life insurance was also included in the sample. By strategically choosing companies in this way, they could establish the common and differentiating factors that lay behind the successful management of change.

Research in focus 2.17 describes one approach to selecting cases for a multiple-case study. In this illustration, cases were selected on the basis that they represented extreme types—namely, successful and unsuccessful firms, and their operation in certain commercial sectors. Research in focus 2.18 provides another example. In this second example, cases were selected on the basis of quantitative indicators of economic deprivation. For example, both the economically deprived areas in Edinburgh and

Glasgow were in the top 5 per cent of deprived areas in Scotland. With case selection approaches such as these, the findings that are common to the cases can be just as interesting and important as those that differentiate them. It is also worth pointing out that, although Research in focus 2.16 and 2.17 both used a comparative design using a multiple-case study approach, the former employed a predominantly qualitative research strategy, whereas the latter used a predominantly quantitative one.

Research in focus 2.18
A multiple-case study of Scottish neighbourhoods

Atkinson and Kintrea (2001) were interested in the implications of what are known as *area effects*. Area effects, as their name implies, are to do with the implications of living or working in an area for life chances and attitudes. The issue with which these authors were concerned was to do with the implications of area effects for the experience of poverty among those who are economically deprived. More specifically, is the experience of poverty worse if one lives in a poor area than if one lives in an economically mixed area? Are those who are economically disadvantaged more likely to experience social exclusion in one type of area rather than another (i.e. economically deprived or mixed)? The researchers selected an economically disadvantaged area and an economically and socially mixed area in Glasgow for comparison. They selected a similar pair of areas in Edinburgh, thus allowing a further element of comparison because of the greater buoyancy of this city compared to Glasgow. Thus, four areas were selected altogether and samples in each were questioned using a survey instrument. The quantitative comparisons of the data led the researchers to conclude that, by and large, it is 'worse to be poor in a poor area than one which is socially mixed' (Atkinson and Kintrea 2001: 2295).

However, not all writers are convinced about the merits of multiple-case study research. Dyer and Wilkins (1991), for example, argue that a multiple-case study approach tends to mean that the researcher pays less attention to the specific context and more to the ways in which the cases can be contrasted. Moreover, the need to forge comparisons tends to mean that the researcher needs to develop an explicit focus at the outset, whereas critics of the multiple-case study argue that it may be advantageous to adopt a more open-ended approach in many instances. These concerns about retaining contextual insight and a rather more unstructured research approach are very much associated with the goals of the qualitative research strategy (see Chapter 16).

The key to the comparative design is its ability to allow the distinguishing characteristics of two or more cases to act as a springboard for theoretical reflections about contrasting findings. It is something of a hybrid, in that in quantitative research it is frequently an extension of a cross-sectional design and in qualitative research it is frequently an extension of a case study design. It even exhibits certain features that are similar to experiments and quasi-experiments, which also rely on the capacity to forge a comparison.

Bringing research strategy and research design together

Finally, we can bring together the two research strategies covered in Chapter 1 with the research designs outlined in this chapter. Table 2.1 shows the typical form associated with each combination of research strategy and research design and a number of examples that either have been encountered so far or will be covered in later chapters. Table 2.1 refers also to research methods that will be encountered in later chapters, but that have not been referred to so far. The Glossary will give you a quick reference to terms used that are not yet familiar to you.

The distinctions are not always perfect. In particular, in some qualitative research it is not obvious whether a study is an example of a longitudinal design or a case study design. Life history studies, research that concentrates on a specific issue over time (e.g. Deacon, Fenton,

Table 2.1

Research strategy and research design		
Research design	**Research strategy**	
	Quantitative	Qualitative
Experimental	*Typical form*. Most researchers using an experimental design employ quantitative comparisons between experimental and control groups with regard to the dependent variable. *Examples*. Research in focus 2.2, 2.4.	No typical form. However, Bryman (1988*a*: 151–2) notes a study in which qualitative data on schoolchildren were collected within a quasi-experimental research design.
Cross-sectional	*Typical form*. Survey research or structured observation on a sample at a single point in time. Content analysis on a sample of documents. *Examples*. Research in focus 2.8, 7.1, 7.4, 11.2, 12.1, 12.2.	*Typical form*. Qualitative interviews or focus groups at a single point in time. Qualitative content analysis of a set of documents relating to a single period. *Examples*. Research in focus 2.9, 18.2; Thinking deeply 2.4.
Longitudinal	*Typical form*. Survey research on a sample on more than one occasion, as in panel and cohort studies. Content analysis of documents relating to different time periods. *Examples*. Research in focus 2.10, 2.11, 2.12.	*Typical form*. Ethnographic research over a long period, qualitative interviewing on more than one occasion, or qualitative content analysis of documents relating to different time periods. Such research warrants being dubbed longitudinal when there is a concern to map change. *Examples*. Research in focus 2.16, 16.4.
Case study	*Typical form*. Survey research on a single case with a view to revealing important features about its nature. *Examples*. The choice by Goldthorpe *et al.* (1968) of Luton as a site for testing the thesis of *embourgeoisement*; the study of Westergaard *et al.* (1989) of the effects of redundancy at a Sheffield steel plant (Research in focus 6.2).	*Typical form*. The intensive study by ethnography or qualitative interviewing of a single case, which may be an organization, life, family, or community. *Examples*. Research in focus 1.6, 2.13, 17.1, 20.3.
Comparative	*Typical form*. Survey research in which there is a direct comparison between two or more cases, as in cross-cultural research. *Examples*. Research in focus 1.4, 7.5; Gallie (1978).	*Typical form*. Ethnographic or qualitative interview research on two or more cases. *Examples*. Research in focus 2.17, 2.18, 16.6, 17.2.

and Bryman 1999), and ethnography in which the researcher charts change in a single case are examples of studies that cross the two types. Such studies are perhaps better conceptualized as longitudinal case studies rather than as belonging to one category of research design or another. A further point to note is that there is no typical form in the qualitative research strategy/experimental research design cell. Qualitative research in the context of true experiments is very unusual. However, as noted in the table, Bryman (1988*a*) refers to a qualitative study by Hall and Guthrie (1981), which employed a quasi-experimental design.

Key points

- There is an important distinction between a research method and a research design.
- It is necessary to become thoroughly familiar with the meaning of the technical terms used as criteria for evaluating research: reliability; validity; replicability; and the types of validity (measurement, internal, external, ecological).
- It is also necessary to be familiar with the differences between the five major research designs covered: experimental; cross-sectional; longitudinal; case study; and comparative. In this context, it is important to realize that the term 'experiment', which is often used somewhat loosely in everyday speech, has a specific technical meaning.
- There are various potential threats to internal validity in non-experimental research.
- Although the case study is often thought to be a single type of research design, it in fact has several forms. It is also important to be aware of the key issues concerned with the nature of case study evidence in relation to issues like external validity (generalizability).

Questions for review

- In terms of the definitions used in this book, what are the chief differences between each of the following: a research method; a research strategy; and a research design?

Criteria in social research

- What are the differences between reliability and validity and why are these important criteria for the evaluation of social research?
- Outline the meaning of each of the following: measurement validity; internal validity; external validity; and ecological validity.
- Why have some qualitative researchers sought to devise alternative criteria from reliability and validity when assessing the quality of investigations?
- Why have some qualitative researchers *not* sought to devise alternative criteria from reliability and validity when assessing the quality of investigations?

Research designs

- What are the main research designs that have been outlined in this chapter?
- A researcher reasons that people who read broadsheet newspapers are likely to be more knowledgeable about personal finance than readers of tabloid newspapers. He interviews 100 people about the newspapers they read and their level of financial knowledge. Sixty-five people read tabloids and thirty-five read broadsheets. He finds that the broadsheet readers are on average considerably more knowledgeable about personal finance than tabloid readers. He concludes that reading broadsheets enhances levels of knowledge of personal finance. Assess his reasoning.

Experimental design

● 'The main importance of the experimental design for the social researcher is that it represents a model of how to infer causal connections between variables.' Discuss.

● Following on from the last question, if experimental design is so useful and important, why is it not used more?

● What is a quasi-experiment?

Cross-sectional design

● In what ways does the survey exemplify the cross-sectional research design?

● Assess the degree to which the survey researcher can achieve internally valid findings.

● To what extent is the survey design exclusive to quantitative research?

Longitudinal design(s)

● Why might a longitudinal research design be superior to a cross-sectional one?

● What are the main differences between panel and cohort designs in longitudinal research?

Case study design

● What is a case study?

● Is case study research exclusive to qualitative research?

● What are some of the principles by which cases might be selected?

Comparative design

● What are the chief strengths of a comparative research design?

● Why might comparative research yield important insights?

Online Resource Centre

http://www.oxfordtextbooks.co.uk/orc/brymansrm3e/

Visit the Online Resource Centre that accompanies this book to enrich your understanding of research designs. Consult web links, test yourself using multiple choice questions, and gain further guidance and inspiration from the Student Researcher's Toolkit.

3

Planning a research project and formulating research questions

---

Chapter outline

---

i Chapter guide

The goal of this chapter is to provide advice to students on some of the issues that they need to consider if they have to prepare a dissertation based upon a relatively small-scale project. Increasingly, social science students are required to produce such a dissertation as part of the requirements for their degrees. In addition to help with the conduct of research, which will be the aim of the chapters that come later in this book, more specific advice on tactics in carrying out and writing up social research for a dissertation can be useful. It is against this background that this chapter has been written. The chapter explores a wide variety of issues, such as:

- advice on timing;
- advice on generating research questions;
- advice on conducting a project;
- advice on writing a research proposal.

Introduction

This chapter has been written to provide some advice for readers who might be carrying out a research project of your own. The chapters that follow in Parts Two, Three, and Four of this book will then provide more detailed information about the choices available to you and how to implement them. But beyond this, how might you go about conducting a small project of your own? I have in mind here the kind of situation that is increasingly common among degree programmes in the social sciences —the requirement to write a dissertation often of around 8,000 to 15,000 words. In particular, I have in mind the needs of undergraduate students, but it may be that students on postgraduate degree programmes will also find some of the observations I make helpful. Also, the advice is really concerned with students conducting projects with a component of empirical research in which they collect new data or perhaps conduct a secondary analysis of existing data.

Getting to know what is expected of you by your institution

Your institution or department will have specific requirements concerning a wide variety of different features that your dissertation should comprise and a range of other matters relating to it. These include such things as: the form of binding; how it is to be presented; whether an abstract is required; how big the page margins should be; the format for referencing; number of words; perhaps the structure of the dissertation; how much advice you can get from your supervisor; whether or not a proposal is required; plagiarism; deadlines; how much (if any) financial assistance you can expect; and so on.

The advice here is simple: *follow the requirements, instructions, and information you are given*. If anything in this book conflicts with your institution's guidelines and requirements, ignore this book! I very much hope this is not something that will occur very much, but if it does, keep to the guidelines your institution gives you.

Thinking about your research area

The chances are that you will be asked to start thinking about what you want to do research on well before you are due to start work on your dissertation. It is worth giving yourself a good deal of time. As you are doing your various modules, begin to think about whether there are any topics that might interest you and that might provide you with a researchable area.

Using your supervisor

Most institutions that require a dissertation or similar component allocate students to supervisors. Institutions vary quite a lot in what can be expected of supervisors; in other words, they vary in terms of what kinds of and how much assistance supervisors will give to students allocated to them. Equally, students vary a great deal in how frequently they see their supervisors and in their use of them. My advice here is simple: use your supervisor to the fullest extent that you are allowed and follow the pointers you are given by him or her. Your supervisor will almost certainly be someone who is well versed in the research process and who will be able to provide you with help and feedback at all stages of your research, subject to your institution's strictures in this regard. If your supervisor is critical of your research questions, your interview schedule, drafts of your dissertation, or whatever, try to respond positively. Follow the suggestions that he

or she provides, since the criticisms will invariably be accompanied by reasons for the criticisms and suggestions for revision. It is not a personal attack. Supervisors regularly have to go through the same process themselves when they submit an article to a peer-refereed journal or apply for a research grant or give a conference paper. So respond to criticisms and suggestions positively and be glad that you are being given the opportunity to address deficiencies in your work before it is formally examined.

A further point is that students who get stuck at the start of their dissertations or who get behind with their work sometimes respond to the situation by avoiding their supervisors. They then get caught up in a vicious circle that results in their work being neglected and perhaps rushed at the end. Try to avoid this situation by confronting the fact that you are experiencing difficulties in getting going or are getting behind and seek out your supervisor for advice.

Student experience
Using supervisors

Several students wrote about the role that their supervisors played in their research projects. Isabella Robbins mentions that her supervisor played an important role in relation to her analysis of her qualitative data.

> The emerging themes were strong and in that sense the analysis was not problematic, but I guess the problems came in mapping the analysis onto the theory. My way of dealing with this was to talk about the analysis at supervisions and to incorporate the ideas that came of these discussions.

Cornelius Grebe provided the following advice about relationships with supervisors:

> I have learned to be very clear about my expectations of my supervisors: what kind of professional and personal relationship I thrive in and what form of support exactly I need from them.

*To read more about Isabella's and Cornelius's research experiences, go to the Online Resource Centre that accompanies this book at **http://www.oxfordtextbooks.co.uk/orc/brymansrm3e/**.*

Managing time and resources

All research is constrained by time and resources. There is no point in working on research questions and plans that cannot be seen through because of time pressure or because of the costs involved. Two points are relevant here.

1. Work out a timetable—preferably in conjunction with your supervisor—detailing the different stages of your research (including the review of the literature and writing up). The timetable should specify the different stages and the calendar points at which you should start and finish them. Some stages are likely to be ongoing—for example, searching the literature for new references (see below)—but that should not prove an obstacle to developing a timetable.

2. Find out what, if any, resources can be put at your disposal for carrying out your research. For example, will you receive help from your institution with such things as travel costs, photocopying, secretarial assistance, postage, stationery, and so on? Will the institution be able to loan you hardware such as recording equipment and transcription machines if you need to record and transcribe your interviews? Has it got the software you need, such as SPSS or a qualitative data analysis package like NVivo? This kind of information will help you to establish how far your research design and methods are financially feasible and practical. The imaginary 'gym study' used in Chapter 15 is an example of an investigation that

Student experience
Managing time

One of the most difficult aspects of doing a research project for many students is managing their time. Sarah Hanson was explicit on this point:

> Never underestimate how long it will take you to complete a large project like a dissertation. Choose a topic you have passion about. The more you enjoy your research the more interesting it will be to read. Be organized: post-it notes, folders, wall planners, anything that keeps you on track from day to day will help you not to be distracted from the purpose of your study.

Both Hannah Creane and Lily Taylor felt that, unless your time is managed well, the analysis phase tends to be squeezed—often with undesirable consequences. Indeed, it is my experience too from supervising students' dissertations that they allow far too little time for data analysis and writing up. Here is what Hannah and Lily respectively wrote in response to a question asking what one single bit of advice they would give to others.

> Get your research done as soon as possible. The process of analysis is pretty much an ongoing one and can take a very long time, so the sooner you have all your data compiled the better. It also means that you have more time to make more extensive analysis rather than just noticing the surface emergent trends.

> Make sure you give yourself enough time to carry out the project, don't underestimate the amount of time data analysis can take!

Similarly, Rebeccca Barnes wrote that, if she was doing her research again:

> I would also allocate more time for data analysis and writing, as largely because of the long period of time which it took to recruit participants, these phases of my research were subject to considerable time pressures.

To read more about Sarah's, Hannah's, Lily's, and Rebecca's research experiences, go to the Online Resource Centre that accompanies this book at http://www.oxfordtextbooks.co.uk/orc/brymansrm3e/.

would be feasible within the kind of time frame usually allocated to undergraduate and postgraduate dissertations. However, it would require such facilities as: typing up the questionnaire, which nowadays students can usually do for themselves with the help of word-processing programs; photocopying covering letters and questionnaires; postage for sending the questionnaires out and for any follow-up letters to non-respondents; return postage for the questionnaires; and the availability of a quantitative data analysis package like SPSS.

Student experience
Devising a timetable for writing up

Lily Taylor found it helpful to have a timetable of deadlines for the different sections of the report she had to write.

> I produced a first draft of my report and made sure that I got it done in plenty of time before the deadline. I was then able to go over my work and make the necessary changes. I made sure that I had a check list with mini deadlines for each section, this made sure that I kept on top of my work and progressed at a steady rate.

Isabella Robbins writes that she 'devised a writing up timetable with a plan of the thesis'. Cornelius Grebe adopted a similar approach to his writing up. He writes: 'I agreed submission dates for individual draft chapters with my supervisors.'

To read more about Lily's, Isabella's, and Cornelius's research experiences, go to the Online Resource Centre that accompanies this book at **http://www.oxfordtextbooks.co.uk/orc/brymansrm3e/**.

Formulating suitable research questions

Many students want to conduct research into areas that are of personal interest to them. This is not a bad thing at all and, as I noted in Chapter 1, many social researchers start from this point as well (see also Lofland and Lofland 1995: 11–14). However, you must move on to develop research questions. This recommendation applies to qualitative research as well as quantitative research. As is explained in Chapter 16, qualitative research is more open-ended than quantitative research, and in Chapter 17 I refer to some notable studies that appear not to have been driven by specific research questions. However, very open-ended research is risky and can lead to the collection of too much data and, when it comes to writing up, to confusion about your focus. So, unless your supervisor advises you to the contrary, I would definitely formulate some research questions, even if they turn out to be somewhat less specific than the kinds we often find in quantitative research. In other words, what is it about your area of interest that you want to know?

Research questions are, therefore, important. No research questions or poorly formulated research questions will lead to poor research. If you do not specify clear research questions, there is a great risk that your research will be unfocused and that you will be unsure about what your research is about and what you are collecting data for. It does not matter how well you design a questionnaire or how skilled an interviewer you are; you must be clear about your research questions. Equally, it does not matter whether your research is for a research grant of £250,000, a doctoral thesis, or a small mini-project. Research questions are crucial because they will:

- guide your literature search;
- guide you in deciding what data you need to collect;
- guide your analysis of your data;
- guide your writing-up of your data;
- stop you from going off in unnecessary directions and tangents.

Therefore, research questions have many uses and you should resist the temptation of not formulating them or delaying their formulation. But do remember that your research questions must have a clear social scientific (for example, sociological) angle.

Thinking deeply 3.1
Marx's sources of research questions

Marx (1997) suggests the following as possible sources of research questions.

- Intellectual puzzles and contradictions.
- The existing literature.
- **Replication**.
- Structures and functions. For example, if you point to a structure such as a type of organization, you can ask questions about the reasons why there are different types and the implications of the differences.
- Opposition. Marx identifies the sensation of feeling that a certain theoretical perspective or notable piece of work is misguided and of exploring the reasons for your opposition.
- A social problem. But remember that this is just the source of a research question; you still have to identify social scientific (e.g. sociological) issues in relation to a social problem.
- 'Gaps between official versions of reality and the facts on the ground' (Marx 1997: 113). An example here is something like Delbridge's (1998) fascinating ethnographic account of company rhetoric about Japanized work practices and how they operate in practice.
- The counter-intuitive. For example, when common sense seems to fly in the face of social scientific truths.
- 'Empirical examples that trigger amazement' (Marx 1997: 114). Marx gives, as examples, deviant cases and atypical events.
- New methods and theories. How might they be applied in new settings?
- 'New social and technical developments and social trends' (Marx 1997: 114).
- Personal experience.
- Sponsors and teachers. But do not expect your teachers to provide you with detailed research questions.

Marx (1997) has suggested a wide range of possible sources of research questions (see Thinking deeply 3.1). As this list makes clear, research questions can derive from a wide variety of contexts. Figure 3.1 brings out the main steps in developing research questions. Research questions in quantitative research are sometimes more specific than in qualitative research. Indeed, some qualitative researchers advocate a very open approach with no research questions. This is a very risky approach and can result in collecting lots of data without a clear sense of what to observe or what to ask your interviewees. There is a growing tendency for qualitative researchers to advocate a somewhat more focused approach to their craft (e.g. Hammersley and Atkinson 1995: 24–9).

As Figure 3.1 implies, we usually start out with a general research area that interests us. It may derive from any of several sources:

- *Personal interest/experience*. As I pointed out in Chapter 1, my interest in theme parks can be traced back to a visit to Disney World in Orlando in 1991 and my interest in the representation of social science research in the mass media to a wounding encounter with the press.
- *Theory*. Someone might be interested in testing or exploring aspects of labour process theory or in the theory of the risk society.
- *The research literature*. Studies relating to a research area like modern consumerism might stimulate an

Figure 3.1

Steps in selecting research questions

Research area
Concerns about risk

↓

Select aspect of research area
Variations in concerns about risk

↓

Research questions
What areas of risk are of greatest concern among people? Does concern about risk vary by age, gender, social class, and education? Do parents tend to worry about risk more than non-parents? What is the main source of people's knowledge about issues relating to risk (newspapers, television, family)? Do concerns about risk have an impact on how people conduct their daily lives and if so in what ways? Do worries about risk result in fatalism?

↓

Select research questions
What areas of risk are of greatest concern among people? Does concern about risk vary by age, gender, social class, and education? Do parents tend to worry about risk more than non-parents?

Student experience
Theory as an influence on research questions

Rebecca Barnes's interest in feminist theories relating to patriarchy influenced her selection of woman-to-woman partner abuse as a focus for her enquiries.

> I became interested in the topic of woman-to-woman partner abuse as an undergraduate. My first encounter with this subject area took the form of a theoretical engagement with feminist explanations for domestic violence—primarily emphasizing patriarchy—and the ways in which emerging knowledge about violence and abuse in female same-sex relationships challenges this understanding. It was as a result of this first encounter that I became aware of the scarcity of research in this area, particularly in the UK, where this subject was virtually uncharted territory. I was at this point interested in pursuing postgraduate study, and thus decided to conduct my own UK-based study of woman-to-woman partner abuse for my Ph.D.

Theoretical ideas stimulated Gareth Matthews's interest in migrant labour. In his case, it was labour process theory that was the focus of his theoretical enquiry.

> Primarily, my interest stems from a more general interest in Marxist labour process theory, which I believe to be highly relevant to an understanding of the content of modern work-forms as well as the claims that are

made by academics about these. Since Braverman published *Labour and Monopoly Capital* in 1974, the labour process debate has taken many twists and turns, and the 'core' elements of the theory are now somewhat different from those expounded by Braverman. I do not seek simply to reiterate the importance of Braverman's formulation, but instead have attempted to explore the space between this and more modern theoretical propositions—in the light of real and perceived changes in the world of work and workers. . . . Essentially, my approach stems from the belief that the employment relation cannot simply be 'read off' from analyses of the content of jobs, and that it must instead be examined through an analysis of forces that operate at various levels (i.e. the workplace, the labour market, the state, etc.), and from the interaction between these forces and employers' necessarily contradictory aims and pressures.

 To read more about Rebecca's and Gareth's research experiences, go to the Online Resource Centre that accompanies this book at http://www.oxfordtextbooks.co.uk/orc/brymansrm3e/.

interest in the nature of the shopping experience in contemporary society.

- *Puzzles*. An interesting example of this can be found in a research article by Hodson (2004) in which he employs data from the Workplace Ethnography Project (see Research in focus 12.4). In this article he notes that writings on modern work imply two rather inconsistent views concerning the extent to which workplaces today are a source of social fulfilment. Some writers construe modern workplaces as intrinsically attractive environments to which people are drawn; others writers view people's commitment to social life at the workplace as stemming from job and career insecurities. Hodson set up these two different points of view explicitly as essentially rival hypotheses. Similarly, Wright *et al.* (2006) collected semi-

structured interview data on street robbers in the UK to shed light on two different views of the motivation for engaging in this crime. One view, which draws on rational choice theory, depicts street robbery as motivated by a trade-off between the desire for financial gain against the necessity to reduce the likelihood of detection. The other view of street robbery portrays it as a cultural activity from which perpetrators derived an emotional thrill and which helped to sustain a particular lifestyle.

- *New developments in society*. Examples might include the rise of the Internet and the diffusion of new models of organization, e.g. call centres.
- *Social problem*. An example might be the impact of asylum-seekers being viewed as a social problem by some sectors of society. This seems to have been one

 ## Student experience
New developments in society as a spur to research questions

Lily Taylor was interested in the role of debt on the student experience. What, in other words, is the impact of top-up fees on students' experiences of higher education?

Increasingly today more students are put off university because of the amount of debt most students will leave with. Particularly with the topical debate at the time over the tuition fee system and top-up fees, I believed it was an interesting area to look at. Students are supposed to be concerned and worried about essay deadlines and attending lectures and seminars, yet finance today seems to be the main anxiety for most university students.

 To read more about Lily's research experiences, go to the Online Resource Centre that accompanies this book at http://www.oxfordtextbooks.co.uk/orc/brymansrm3e/.

of the main factors behind the work of Lynn and Lea (2003), who examined the discourses surrounding the notion of the asylum-seeker in the UK.

These sources of interest are not mutually exclusive. For example, the investigation reported in Research in focus 1.1 was motivated by at least two of the above sources: an interest in exploring the concept of social capital (theory) and understanding the process of gentrification (a new development in society).

As these types of source suggest, in research we often start out with a general research area that interests us. This research area has to be narrowed down so that we can develop a tighter focus out of which research questions can be developed. We can depict the process of generating research questions as a series of steps that are suggested in Figure 3.1. The series of stages is meant to indicate that, when developing research questions, the researcher is involved in a process of progressive focusing down so that we move from a general research area down to specific research questions. In making this movement, we have to recognize that:

- We cannot answer all the research questions that occur to us. This is not just to do with issues of time and the cost of doing research. It is very much to do with the fact that we must keep a clear focus so that our research questions must relate to each other and form a coherent set of issues.

- We therefore have to select from the possible research questions that we arrive at.

- In making our selection, we should be guided by the principle that the research questions we choose should be related to one another. If they are not, our research will probably lack focus and we may not make as clear a contribution to understanding as would be the case if research questions were connected. Thus, in the example in Figure 3.1, the research questions relating to risk are closely connected.

In Tips and skills 'Criteria for evaluating research questions' some suggestions are presented about the kinds of considerations that should be taken into account when developing your own research questions.

Student experience
The nature of research questions

Some of the students worked with quite explicit and narrowly formulated research questions. For example, Rebecca Barnes writes:

> My research questions were: What forms and dynamics of abuse do women experience in same-sex relationships? What opportunities and challenges do women experience with respect to seeking support for woman-to-woman partner abuse? What impacts does being abused by a female partner have upon women's identities and biographies? How are women's accounts of woman-to-woman partner abuse similar to and different from heterosexual women's accounts of partner abuse?

Isabella Robbins was similarly explicit about her research questions:

1. How do mothers frame their decisions regarding childhood vaccination? In particular, do they present this as a matter of moral obligation (to their child/to the community)?

2. Do mothers consider they have a choice regarding childhood vaccination? If so, in what sense do they see this as a choice and what, if any, constraints do they identify as they seek to exercise that choice?

3. How do women place themselves and their decisions about childhood vaccination, in terms of the discourse of risk, responsibility, autonomy, and expertise?

4. What role do women accord to partners, mothers, siblings, and professionals in their decision-making about childhood vaccination?

Others opted for research questions that were somewhat more general and wider in focus. Erin Sanders writes of her research questions for her study:

What are the policy goals of women's NGOs in Thailand? How do these goals relate to the needs of women in the sex industry?

In a similar vein, Gareth Matthews writes:

My research questions were quite general. (i) what is the role of migrant workers in the UK's hospitality sector? (ii) What can this tell us about the relevance and usefulness of Marxist labour process theory?

Gareth went on to write:

These questions stem from my theoretical concerns, and a desire for the thesis to be guided by the findings and theoretical developments in relation to these findings during the course of the research. I did not want to begin with a specific hypothesis, and then to proceed by attempting to 'prove' or 'disprove' this, but sought instead to start with a general theoretical belief about work, and then to remain open-minded so as to allow the direction of research to be guided by the qualitative findings as they unfolded.

To read more about Rebecca's, Isabella's, Erin's, and Gareth's research experiences, go to the Online Resource Centre that accompanies this book at **http://www.oxfordtextbooks.co.uk/orc/brymansrm3e/**.

Tips and skills
Criteria for evaluating research questions

Research questions for a dissertation or project exhibit the following characteristics.

- They should be *clear*, in the sense of being intelligible.

- They should be *researchable*—that is, they should allow you to do research in relation to them. This means that they should not be formulated in terms that are so abstract that they cannot be converted into researchable terms.

- They should have some *connection(s) with established theory and research*. This means that there should be a literature on which you can draw to help illuminate how your research questions should be approached. Even if you find a topic that has been scarcely addressed by social scientists, it is unlikely that there will be no relevant literature (e.g. on related or parallel topics).

- Your research questions should be *linked* to each other. Unrelated research questions are unlikely to be acceptable, since you should be developing an argument in your dissertation. You could not very readily construct a single argument in relation to unrelated research questions.

- They should at the very least hold out the prospect of being able to make an *original contribution*—however small—to the topic.

- The research questions should be *neither too broad* (so that you would need a massive grant to study them) *nor too narrow* (so that you cannot make a reasonably significant contribution to your area of study).

If you are stuck about how to formulate research questions (or indeed other phases of your research), it is always a good idea to look at journal articles or research monographs to see how other researchers have formulated them. Also, look at past dissertations for ideas as well. Marx (1997) has suggested a wide range of sources of research questions (see Thinking deeply 3.1).

Writing your research proposal

In preparation for your dissertation you may be required to write a short proposal or plan outlining what your research project will be about and how you intend to go about it. This is a useful way of preparing for your research and it will encourage you to think about many of the issues that are covered in the next section. In addition to outlining your proposed research design and methods, the topic area in which your study is going to be located, and the research questions that you intend to address, the proposal will ask you to demonstrate some knowledge of the literature in your chosen field, for example by identifying several key authors or important research studies. This information may be used as the basis for allocating a supervisor who is knowledgeable in your area of research interest or who has experience with your proposed research approach. The proposal is also a useful basis for discussion of your research project with your supervisor, and, if it includes a timetable for the project, this can provide a basis for planning regular meetings with your supervisor to review your progress. Developing a timetable can be very important in making you think about aspects of the overall research process like the different stages of your research and their timing and in giving you a series of ongoing goals to aim for. Even if you are not required to produce a research proposal, it is worthwhile constructing a timetable for your research and asking your supervisor to look at it, so that you can assess how (un)realistic your goals are and whether you are allowing enough time for each of the components of the research process.

When writing a research proposal, there are a number of issues that you will probably need to cover.

- What is your research topic or, alternatively, what are your research objectives?

- Why is your research topic (or why are those research objectives) important?

- What is your research question or what are your research questions?

- What does the literature have to say about your research topic/objectives and research question(s)?

- How are you going to go about collecting data relevant to your research question(s)? In other words, what research methods are you intending to use?

- Why are the research methods/sources you have selected the appropriate ones for your research question?

- What resources will you need to conduct your research (e.g. postage, travel costs, software) and how will those resources be funded?

- What is your timetable for the different stages of the project?

- What problems do you anticipate in doing the research (e.g. access to organizations)?

- What are the possible ethical problems associated with your research?

- How will you analyse your data?

Writing a proposal is therefore useful in getting you started on your research project and encouraging you to set realistic objectives for your research project. In some higher education institutions, the research proposal may form part (albeit a small one) of the overall assessment of the dissertation or report that is produced out of the project. While the research proposal is a working document and the ideas that you set out in it can be refined and developed as your research progresses, it is important to bear in mind that if you keep changing your mind about your area of research interest and research design you will be using up valuable time needed to complete the dissertation within the deadline.

Preparing for your research

Do not begin your data collection until you have identified your research questions reasonably clearly. Develop your data-collection instruments with these research questions at the forefront of your thinking. If you do not do this, there is the risk that your results will not allow you to illuminate the research questions. If at all possible, conduct a small pilot study to determine how well your research instruments work.

You will also need to think about access and sampling issues. If your research requires you to gain access to or the cooperation of one or more closed settings like an organization, you need to confirm at the earliest opportunity that you have the necessary permission to conduct your work. You also need to consider how you will go about gaining access to people. These issues lead you into sampling considerations, such as the following.

- Who do you need to study in order to investigate your research questions?
- How easily can you gain access to a sampling frame?
- What kind of sampling strategy will you employ (e.g. probability sampling, quota sampling, theoretical sampling, convenience sampling)?
- Can you justify your choice of sampling method?

Also, while preparing for your data collection, you should consider whether there are any possible ethical problems associated with your research methods or your approach to contacting people (see Chapter 5).

Doing your research and analysing your results

Since doing your research and analysing your results are what the bulk of this book will be about, it is not necessary at this stage to go into detail, but here are some useful hints about practicalities.

- Keep good records of what you do. A research diary can be helpful here, but there are several other things to bear in mind. For example, if you are doing a survey by postal questionnaire, keep good records of who has replied, so that you know who should be sent reminders. If participant observation is a component of your research, remember to keep good field notes and not to rely on your memory.

- Make sure that you are thoroughly familiar with any hardware you are using in collecting your data, such as tape recorders for interviewing, and make sure it is in good working order (e.g. batteries that are not flat or close to being flat).

- Do not wait until all your data have been collected to begin coding. This recommendation applies to both quantitative and qualitative research. If you are

conducting a questionnaire survey, begin coding your data and entering them into SPSS or whatever package you are using after you have put together a reasonably sized batch of completed questionnaires. In the case of qualitative data, such as interview transcripts, the same point applies, and, indeed, it is a specific recommendation of the proponents of grounded theory that data collection and analysis should be intertwined.

- Remember that the transcription of recorded interviews takes a long time. Allow at least six hours' transcription for every one hour of recorded interview talk, at least in the early stages of transcription.

- Become familiar with any data analysis packages as soon as possible. This familiarity will help you to establish whether you definitely need them and will ensure that you do not need to learn everything about them at the very time you need to use them for your analysis.

- Do not at any time take risks with your personal safety (see Tips and skills 'Safety in research').

Tips and skills
Safety in research

In the middle of December 2002 a 19-year-old female student who had just started a degree course in sociology and community studies at Manchester Metropolitan University went missing. It was believed that, in order to complete a coursework assignment, she had gone to conduct a **life history interview** with a person aged over 50. Since she was interested in the homeless, it was thought that she had gone to interview a homeless person. Because of concerns about her safety, her tutor had advised her to take a friend and to conduct the interview in a public place. In fact, she had not gone to conduct the interview and to everyone's relief turned up in Dublin. There is an important lesson in this incident: you must bear in mind that social research may on occasions place you in potentially dangerous situations. You should avoid taking personal risks at all costs and you should resist any attempts to place yourself in situations where personal harm is a real possibility. Just as you should ensure that no harm comes to research participants (as prescribed in the discussion of ethical principles in Chapter 5), individuals involved in directing others' research should not place students and researchers in situations in which they might come to harm. Equally, lone researchers should avoid such situations. Sometimes, as with the interviews with the homeless, there is some possibility of being in a hazardous situation, in which case, if the researcher feels confident about going ahead with the interview, he or she needs to take precautions before going ahead with the interview. The advice given by the student's tutor—to take someone with her and to conduct the interview in a public place—was very sensible for a potentially dangerous interview. If you have a mobile telephone, keep it with you and keep it switched on. Personal attack alarms may also be useful. You should also make sure that, if your interviews or your periods of observation are part of a programme of work, you establish a routine whereby you keep in regular contact with others. However, there are situations in which there is no obvious reason to think that a situation may be dangerous, but where the researcher is faced with a sudden outburst of abuse or threatening behaviour. This can arise when people react relatively unpredictably to an interview question or to being observed. If there are signs that such behaviour is imminent (e.g. through body language), begin a withdrawal from the research situation. Further guidelines on these issues can be found in Craig *et al.* (2000).

Lee (2004) draws an important distinction between two kinds of danger in fieldwork: ambient and situational. The former refers to situations that are avoidable and in which danger is an ingredient of the context. Fieldwork in conflict situations of the kind encountered by the researcher who took on the role of a bouncer (Hobbs *et al.* 2003) would be an example of this kind of danger. Situational danger occurs 'when the researcher's presence or activities evoke aggression, hostility or violence from those within the setting' (Lee 2004: 1285). While problems surrounding safety may be easier to anticipate in the case of ambient danger, they are less easy to foresee in connection with situational danger. However, that is not to say that ambient danger is entirely predictable. It was only some time after she began her research in a hospital laboratory that Lankshear (2000) realized that there was a possibility of her being exposed to dangerous pathogens.

Sources: P. Barkham and R. Jenkins, 'Fears for Fresher who Vanished on Mission to talk to the Homeless', *The Times*, 13 Dec. 2002; S. McIntyre, 'How did Vicky Vanish?', *Daily Mail*, 13 Dec. 2002; R. Jenkins, 'Wasteland Search for Missing Student', *The Times*, 14 Dec. 2002.

Checklist

Planning a research project

○ Do you know what the requirements for your dissertation are, as set out by your university or department?

○ Have you made contact with your supervisor?

○ Have you allowed enough time for planning, doing, and writing up your research project?

○ Do you have a clear timetable for your research project with clearly identifiable milestones for the achievement of specific tasks?

○ Have you got sufficient financial and practical resources (e.g. money to enable travel to research site, recording device) to enable you to carry out your research project?

○ Have you formulated some research questions and discussed these with your supervisor?

○ Are the research questions you have identified capable of being answered through your research project?

○ Do you have the access that you require in order to carry out your research?

○ Are you familiar with the data analysis software that you will be using to analyse your data?

○ Have you allowed others to comment on your work so far and responded to their feedback?

○ Have you checked out whether there are likely to be any ethical issues that might be raised in connection with your research?

○ Have you allowed enough time for getting clearance through an ethics committee, if that is required for your research?

Key points

● Follow the dissertation guidelines provided by your institution.

● Thinking about your research subject can be time consuming, so allow plenty of time for this aspect of the dissertation process.

● Use your supervisor to the fullest extent allowed and follow the advice offered by him or her.

● Plan your time carefully and be realistic about what you can achieve in the time available.

● Formulate some research questions to express what it is about your area of interest that you want to know.

● Writing a research proposal is a good way of getting started on your research project and encouraging you to set realistic objectives.

● Consider access and sampling issues at an early stage and consider testing your research methods by conducting a pilot study.

● Keep good records of what you do in your research as you go along and don't wait until all your data have been collected before you start coding.

Questions for review

Managing time and resources

- Why is it important to devise a timetable for your research project?

Formulating suitable research questions

- What are the main sources of research questions?
- What are the main steps involved in developing research questions?
- What criteria can be used to evaluate research questions?

Writing your research proposal

- What is the purpose of the research proposal and how can it be useful?

Online Resource Centre

http://www.oxfordtextbooks.co.uk/orc/brymansrm3e/

Visit the Online Resource Centre that accompanies this book to enrich your understanding of planning a research project and formulating research questions. Consult web links, test yourself using multiple choice questions, and gain further guidance and inspiration from the Student Researcher's Toolkit.

4

Getting started: reviewing the literature

Chapter outline

Chapter guide

The goal of this chapter is to provide guidance for students on how to get started on their research project. Once you have identified your research questions (see Chapter 3), the next step in any research project is to search the existing literature and write a literature review. The principal task at this early stage involves reviewing the main ideas and research relating to your chosen area of interest. This provides the basis for the writing of a literature review, which forms an important part of the dissertation. This chapter will advise students on how to go about searching the literature and engaging critically with the ideas of other writers. It will also help you to understand some of the expectations of the literature review and give you some ideas about how to assess the quality of existing research.

Reviewing the existing literature

Why do you need to review the existing literature? The most obvious reason is that you want to know what is already known about your area of interest so that you do not simply 'reinvent the wheel'. Your literature review is where you demonstrate that you are able to engage in scholarly review based on your reading and understanding of the work of others in the same field. Beyond this, using the existing literature on a topic is a means of developing an argument about the significance of your research and where it leads. The simile of a *story* is also sometimes used in this context (see Thinking deeply 4.1). Whatever different understandings of the literature review process you adopt, it is important to be clear about the goal that the process is directed towards achieving. A competent review of the literature is at least in part a means of affirming your credibility as someone who is knowledgeable in your chosen area. This is not simply a matter of reproducing the theories and opinions of other scholars, but also being able to interpret what they have

written, possibly by using their ideas to support a particular viewpoint or argument. The purpose of exploring the existing literature should be to identify the following issues.

- What is already known about this area?
- What concepts and theories are relevant to this area?
- What research methods and research strategies have been employed in studying this area?
- Are there any significant controversies?
- Are there any inconsistencies in findings relating to this area?
- Are there any unanswered research questions in this area?

This last issue points to the possibility that you will be able to revise and refine your research questions in the process of reviewing the literature.

Tips and skills
Ways of conceptualizing a literature review

Bruce's (1994) study of research students' early experiences of the dissertation literature review identified six qualitatively different ways in which the review process was experienced or understood by postgraduates. The six conceptions included:

1. *List.* The literature review is understood as a list comprising pertinent items representing the literature of the subject.

2. *Search.* The review is a process of identifying relevant information and the focus is on finding or looking, which may involve going through sources (e.g. article, database) to identify information.

3. *Survey.* Students also see the literature review as an investigation of past and present writing or research on a subject; this investigation may be active (critical/analytical) or passive (descriptive).

4. *Vehicle.* The review is also seen as having an impact on the researcher, because it is seen as a vehicle for learning that leads to an increase in his or her knowledge and understanding. Within this conception the review acts as a sounding board through which the student can check ideas or test personal perceptions.

5. *Facilitator.* The literature review can be understood as directly related to the research that is about to be or is being undertaken, the process helping the researcher to identify a topic, support a methodology, provide a context or change research direction. The review thus helps to shape the course of the student's research.

6. *Report.* The review is understood as a written discussion of the literature, drawing on previously conducted investigations. The focus is on 'framing a written discourse about the literature which may be established as a component part of a thesis or other research report' (1994: 223).

These six conceptions reflect the varying relationship between the student and the literature, the earlier ones being more indirect—the student works with items that represent the primary literature, such as bibliographic citations—and the latter conceptions being more direct—the student works with source material, rather than, for example, a representative abstract. The conceptions can also be seen as cumulative, since a student who adopts the facilitator conception may also continue to hold the conception of the literature review as a survey. Bruce therefore recommends that students be encouraged to adopt the higher-level conceptions (3–6), because through these other ways of experiencing the literature review (1–3) become more meaningful.

Getting the most from your reading

Since a great deal of time during the early stages of your research project will be taken up with reading the existing literature in order to write your review, it is important to make sure that the process of reading is also preparing you for this. Getting the most out of your reading involves developing your skills in being able to read actively and critically. When you are reading the existing literature try to do the following.

- Take good notes, including the details of the material you read. It is infuriating to find that you forgot to record the volume number of an article you read and that needs to be included in your Bibliography. This may necessitate a trip to the library on occasions when you are already hard pressed for time.

- Develop critical reading skills. In reviewing the literature you should do more than simply summarize what you have read. You should, whenever appropriate, be critical in your approach. It is worth developing these skills and recording relevant critical points in the course of taking notes. Developing a critical approach is not necessarily one of simply criticizing the work of others. It entails moving beyond mere description and asking questions about the significance of the work. It entails attending to such issues as: How does the item relate to others you have read? Are there any apparent strengths and deficiencies—perhaps in terms of methodology or in terms of the credibility of the conclusions drawn? What theoretical ideas have influenced the item?

- Use your review of the literature as a means of showing why your research questions are important. For example, if one of your arguments in arriving at your research questions is that, although a lot of research has been done on X (a general topic or area, such as the secularization process, female entrepreneurship, or employee absenteeism), little or no research has been done on X_1 (an aspect of X), the literature review is the point where you can justify this assertion. Alternatively, it might be that there are two competing positions with regard to X_1 and you are going to investigate which one provides a better understanding. In the literature review, you should outline the nature of the differences between the competing positions. The literature review, then, allows you to locate your own research within a tradition of research in an area. Indeed, reading the literature is itself often an important source of research questions.

- Bear in mind that you will want to return to much of the literature that you examine in the discussion of your findings and conclusion.

- Do not try to get everything you read into a literature review. Trying to force everything you have read into your review (because of all the hard work involved in uncovering and reading the material) is not going to help you. The literature review must assist you in developing an argument, and bringing in material of dubious relevance may undermine your ability to get your argument across.

- Bear in mind that reading the literature is not something that you should stop doing once you begin designing your research. You should continue your search for and reading of relevant literature more or less throughout your research. This means that, if you have written a literature review before beginning your

data collection, you will need to regard it as provisional. Indeed, you may want to make quite substantial revisions of your review towards the end of writing up your work.

- Further useful thoughts about how to develop the literature can be found in Thinking deeply 4.1. The different ways of construing the literature that are presented in this box are derived from a review of qualitative studies of organizations, but the approaches identified have a much broader applicability, including quantitative research.

- The study referred to in Thinking deeply 4.2 contains some useful implications from a study of Ph.D. examiners' reports for conducting a literature review. One of the most central implications of it is to emphasize the importance of having a comprehensive coverage of the literature. While comprehensive coverage might be an expectation for Ph.D. candidates, this may be more difficult to achieve for undergraduate and postgraduate dissertations. At the very least, it implies that making sure that key references are included in the review is essential.

Thinking deeply 4.1
Presenting literature in articles based on qualitative research on organizations

Further useful advice on relating your own work to the literature can be gleaned from an examination of the ways in which articles based on qualitative research on organizations are composed. In their examination of such articles, Golden-Biddle and Locke (1993, 1997) argue that good articles in this area develop a story—that is, a clear and compelling framework around which the writing is structured. This idea is very much in tune with Wolcott's (1990*a*: 18) recommendation to 'determine the basic story you are going to tell'. Golden-Biddle and Locke's research suggests that the way the author's position in relation to the literature is presented is an important component of storytelling. They distinguish two processes in the ways that the literature is conveyed.

1. **Constructing intertextual coherence**. This refers to the way in which existing knowledge is represented and organized; the author shows how contributions to the literature relate to each other and the research reported. The techniques used are:
   - *Synthesized coherence* puts together work that is generally considered unrelated; theory and research previously regarded as unconnected are pieced together. There are two prominent forms:
     i. the organization of very incompatible references (bits and pieces);
     ii. connections are forged between established theories or research programmes.
   - *Progressive coherence* portrays the building up of an area of knowledge around which there is considerable consensus.

- *Non-coherence* recognizes that there have been many contributions to a certain research programme, but that there is considerable disagreement among practitioners.

Each of these strategies is designed to leave room for a contribution to be made.

2. **Problematizing the situation**. The literature is then subverted by locating a problem. The following techniques were identified:

   - *Incomplete*. The existing literature is not fully complete; there is a gap.
   - *Inadequate*. The existing literature on the phenomenon of interest has overlooked ways of looking at it that can greatly improve our understanding of it; alternative perspectives or frameworks can then be introduced.
   - *Incommensurate*. This argues for an alternative perspective that is superior to the literature as it stands. It differs from 'inadequate problematization' because it portrays the existing literature as 'wrong, misguided, or incorrect' (Golden-Biddle and Locke 1997: 43).

The key point about Golden-Biddle and Locke's account of the way the literature is construed in this field is that it is used by writers to achieve a number of things.

- They can demonstrate their competence by referring to prominent writings in the field (Gilbert 1977).
- They develop their version of the literature in such a way as to show and to lead up to the contribution they will be making in the article.
- The gap or problem in the literature that is identified corresponds to the research questions.

The idea of writing up one's research as storytelling acts as a useful reminder that reviewing the literature, which is part of the story, should link seamlessly with the rest of the article and not be considered as a separate element.

Thinking deeply 4.2
What do examiners look for in a literature review?

Holbrook *et al.* (2007) conducted an analysis of examiners' reports on Ph.D. theses. They analysed 1,310 reports relating to 501 theses in Australia (a Ph.D. thesis is examined by at least two examiners). These reports are naturally occurring documents, in that examiners have to provide these reports as part of the process of examining a Ph.D. candidate. In the course of writing a report, examiners frequently if not invariably comment on the literature review. While these findings are obviously specific to a Ph.D., the features that examiners look for are also applicable in general terms to other kinds of writing, such as an undergraduate or a postgraduate dissertation.

The reports were analysed using computer-assisted qualitative data analysis software, which will be covered in Chapter 23. The analysis of these reports suggests that comments concerning the literature review were of three basic kinds:

1. *Comments about coverage of the literature*. This was by far the most common type of comment and signals whether the candidate has covered and made sense of a broad swathe of the literature.
2. *Identification of errors*. This type of comment relates to such things as references being omitted from the bibliography, misreporting of references, and inconsistent presentation of referencing and quotations.

3. *Comments about 'use and application' of the literature.* Although this was the least common of the types of comment made by examiners, it attracts the bulk of the attention of Holbrook *et al.* It is made up of a number of subcategories of comment:

- the literature is used (or not used) to develop and sustain an argument;
- clear familiarity with the literature;
- the development of a critical assessment of the literature (the ability to 'weigh up the literature and subject it to critical appraisal, ideally to lead to a new or interesting perspective' (Holbrook *et al.* 2007: 348));
- connecting the literature to findings;
- demonstrating an appreciation of the disciplinary context of the literature.

One of the main themes running through these latter remarks is that the student does not just summarize the literature in a routine way, simply because he or she knows that a literature review has to be undertaken. Instead, examiners look for evidence that the candidate *uses* the literature—to develop an argument, to connect with his or her findings, or to develop a distinctive stance on the subject. However, undoubtedly, the thing that disconcerts examiners most is evidence of poor coverage of the literature, as it signals a lack of engagement with and full appreciation of the subject.

Systematic review

In recent years, considerable thought has been lavished on the notion of *systematic review* (see Key concept 4.1). This is an approach to reviewing the literature that adopts explicit procedures. It has emerged as a focus of interest for two main reasons. One is that it is sometimes suggested that many reviews of the literature tend to 'lack thoroughness' and reflect the biases of the researcher (e.g. Tranfield *et al.* 2003). Proponents of systematic review suggest that adopting explicit procedures make

such biases less likely to surface. Second, in fields like medicine, there has been a growing movement towards evidence-based solutions to illnesses and treatments. Systematic reviews of the literature are often seen as an accompaniment to evidence-based approaches, as their goal is to provide advice for clinicians and practitioners based on all available evidence. Such reviews are deemed to be valuable for decision-makers, particularly in areas where there is conflicting evidence concerning treatments (as in the case of medicine).

Key concept 4.1
What is a systematic review?

Systematic review has been defined as 'a replicable, scientific and transparent process . . . that aims to minimize bias through exhaustive literature searches of published and unpublished studies and by providing an audit trail of the reviewer's decisions, procedures and conclusions' (Tranfield *et al.* 2003: 209). Such a review is often contrasted with the traditional **narrative review**, which is the focus of the next section. The proponents of systematic review are more likely to generate unbiased and comprehensive accounts of the literature, especially in fields in which the aim is to understand whether a particular intervention has particular benefits, than those using the traditional review, which is often depicted by them as haphazard. A systematic review that includes only quantitative studies is a **meta-analysis** (see Key concept 4.2). In very recent times, the development of systematic review procedures for qualitative studies has attracted a great deal of attention, especially in the social sciences. **Meta-ethnography** (see Key concept 4.3) is one such approach to the synthesis of qualitative findings, but currently there are several different methods, none of which is in widespread use (Mays *et al.* 2005).

The systematic review approach is beginning to diffuse into other areas, like social policy, so that policy-makers and others can draw on reviews that summarize the balance of the evidence in certain areas of practice. Tranfield and colleagues contrast systematic review with what they describe as 'traditional narrative reviews' (the subject of the following section). An example of systematic review is given in Research in focus 4.1. However, advocates of systematic review acknowledge that, unlike medical science, social scientific fields are often characterized by low consensus concerning key research questions, because of the different theoretical approaches. Moreover, medical science is often concerned with research questions to do with answers to the question 'What works?'. Such questions are fairly well suited to systematic review in fields like social policy, but are less often encountered in other social science fields like sociology.

Nonetheless, systematic review has attracted a great deal of attention in recent years, so it is worth exploring some of its main steps. Millar (2004) provides a useful generic summary of these steps.

1. The purpose of the review must be defined. The review needs an explicit statement of purpose so that decisions about the inclusion and exclusion of studies can be made in a consistent way. It is often argued that, for a systematic review, the researcher and his or her team should assemble a panel to advise them on the precise formulation of the research issue(s) to be examined and also to assist with suggestions for keywords for Step 3 (below).

2. Establish criteria to guide the selection of studies. The reviewer might want to restrict the review to studies published only in a particular time period or to studies that derive from one region or nation rather than another. Another criterion might be the kind of research design or research method used. In some fields, like medicine, there is an unequivocal hierarchy of research approaches that are relevant to the 'What works?' question. This means that only articles that entail a true experimental design—often called randomized controlled trials or RCTs—will be included, as only research based on such designs generates unambiguous findings about cause and effect. However, in most of the social sciences there is far less consensus about what is the appropriate approach to research.

3. The reviewer should seek out and incorporate within the review all studies that meet the criteria spelled out in Step 2. The search will be based on keywords and terms relevant to the purpose defined in Step 1. The search

strategy must be described in terms that allow it to be replicated. Based on the strict application of the inclusion criteria formulated at Stage 2, the information search will lead to the production of a list of all the published outputs on which the review will be based. An issue that relates to inclusion and exclusion is that the reviewer has to consider which kinds of publication outlets should be incorporated. It is tempting to search for research published only in articles in peer-reviewed journals, because they are relatively easy to find using databases like the Social Sciences Citation Index using keywords. However, to rely solely on peer-reviewed journal articles would imply omitting other sources of evidence, most notably, studies reported in books, in articles in non-peer-reviewed journals, and in what is often referred to as 'grey literature' (for example, conference papers and reports by various bodies).

4. Key features of each study should be identified. A formal protocol should be used to record features like: date when the research was conducted; location; sample size; data collection methods; and the main findings. Exponents of systematic review invariably advocate that only high-quality research should be included in systematic reviews, and it is often recommended that explicit quality criteria are established for deciding which studies should be included and which should be excluded. Only studies that conform to the quality criteria would be included.

5. A synthesis of the results then has to be produced. With a meta-analysis, this phase will involve producing summary statistics from the quantitative data supplied with each study. In the case of other kinds of systematic review, such as those based on qualitative research, Millar (2004: 143) writes that the synthesis 'is often done in the form of summary tables, which provide an overview of the key characteristics of the studies reviewed'. Tranfield *et al.* (2003) argue that the review document should be accessible and readable, so that it will be easier for the practitioner to understand the research and therefore more likely that it will be translated into practice.

Tranfield *et al.* (2003) suggest that the systematic review process provides a more reliable foundation on which to design research, because it is based on a more comprehensive understanding of what we know about a subject. It is therefore likely to be relevant to researchers as a way of summarizing findings, so that it is not just practitioners who benefit from systematic reviews. Proponents of systematic review also recommend the

Research in focus 4.1
Healthy eating among young people

Shepherd *et al.* (2006) have published an account of the procedures they used to examine the barriers to healthy eating among young people aged 11–16 years and the factors that facilitate healthy eating. In Table 4.1 I have outlined the steps identified by Millar (2004) and the corresponding procedures and practices in the review by Shepherd *et al.* These authors used methods for systematic review that have been developed by the Evidence for Policy and Practice Information and Coordinating Centre (EPPI) at the Institute of Education, University of London. The EPPI has a very comprehensive website that details its approach and its main methods and provides full reports of many of the systematic reviews its members have conducted (**http://eppi.ioe.ac.uk/cms/** (accessed on 18 June 2007)).

One of the features that is especially noteworthy concerning the summary in Table 4.1 is that intervention studies (e.g. training parents in nutrition and evaluating the outcomes of such an intervention) and non-intervention studies (e.g. a cohort or an interview study) were separated out. Assessing the quality of studies is an important component of a systematic review, so that only reliable evidence forms the basis for such things as policy changes. Different quality criteria were employed for the two types of study. In the case of the non-intervention studies, the following seven criteria were used:

(i) an explicit account of theoretical framework and/or the inclusion of a literature review which outlined a rationale for the intervention;

(ii) clearly stated aims and objectives;

(iii) a clear description of the context which includes detail on factors important for interpreting the results;

(iv) a clear description of the sample;

(v) a clear description of the methodology, including systematic data collection methods;

(vi) analysis of the data by more than one researcher and

(vii) the inclusion of sufficient original data to mediate between data and interpretation (Shepherd *et al.* 2006: 242).

As a result of the application of these seven quality criteria and the ones for the intervention studies, just 22 outcome evaluations and 8 non-intervention studies were included in the systematic review. It is quite common for systematic reviews to end up being based on quite small numbers of studies, because the explicit criteria for inclusion coupled with the quality criteria represent standards that very few investigations can meet. Regarding the findings of the non-intervention studies, the authors report that several barriers to and facilitators of healthy eating were identified. For example, they write: 'Facilitating factors included information about nutritional content of foods/better labeling, parents and family members being supportive; healthy eating to improve or maintain one's personal appearance, will-power and better availability/lower pricing of healthy snacks' (Shepherd *et al.* 2006: 255).

approach for its transparency; in other words, the grounds on which studies were selected and how they were analysed are clearly articulated and are potentially replicable. However, it also has to be appreciated that not all areas of literature lend themselves to a systematic review approach, because they are not always concerned with research questions to do with exploring whether a certain independent variable has certain kinds of effects. Meta-analysis of quantitative studies requires this kind of research question, but qualitative studies and indeed some sorts of quantitative investigation are not necessarily in this format.

Table 4.1

Steps in systematic review in connection with a systematic review of barriers to, and facilitators of, healthy eating among young people (Shepherd *et al.* 2006)	
Steps in systematic review	Corresponding practices in Shepherd *et al.* (2006)
1. The purpose of the review must be defined	A. Review question: 'What is known about the barriers to, and facilitators of, healthy eating among young people?' (Shepherd *et al.* 2006: 243).
2. Establish criteria to guide the selection of studies	B. In addition to being about 'the barriers to, and facilitators of, healthy eating among young people', the review had to be: either an outcome evaluation (usually to evaluate the outcome of an intervention) or a non-intervention study (e.g. an interview study) in the UK, in English. Further, guidelines were formulated separately for these two types of study. In the case of non-intervention studies, it had to: be about attitudes, views, experiences, etc. of healthy eating; provide insights into respondents' own definitions of healthy eating and factors affecting it; and 'privilege young people's views' (Shepherd *et al.* 2006: 241).
3. The reviewer should seek out and incorporate within the review all studies that meet the criteria spelled out in Step 2.	C. A total of 7,048 reports were identified, of which 135 reports (relating to 116 studies) got through the first round of screening. Of the 116 studies, 75 were intervention studies, 32 were non-intervention studies, and 9 were prior systematic reviews.
4. Key features of each study should be identified.	D. 'Data for each study were entered independently by two researchers into a specialized database' (Shepherd *et al.* 2006: 241). Separate quality criteria were employed for intervention and non-intervention studies. Application of the full set of criteria outlined in B and of the quality criteria, resulted in just 22 outcome evaluations and 8 non-intervention studies being included in the systematic review.
5. A synthesis of the results then has to be produced.	E. Separate syntheses were conducted for the two types of study and a third synthesis for the intervention and non-intervention studies jointly. The authors write of this third synthesis: 'a matrix was constructed which laid out the barriers and facilitators identified by young people [in the non-intervention studies] alongside descriptions of the interventions included in the in-depth systematic review of outcome evaluations. The matrix was stratified by four analytical themes to characterize the levels at which the barriers and facilitators appeared to be operating: the school, family and friends, the self and practical and material resources' (Shepherd *et al.* 2006: 241).

Key concept 4.2
What is meta-analysis?

Meta-analysis involves summarizing the results of a large number of quantitative studies and conducting various analytical tests to show whether or not a particular **variable** has an effect. This provides a means whereby the results of large numbers of quantitative studies of a particular topic can be summarized and compared. The aim of this approach is to establish whether or not a particular variable has a certain effect by comparing the results of different studies. Meta-analysis thus involves pooling the results from various studies in order to estimate an overall effect by correcting the various **sampling** and **non-sampling errors** that may arise in relation to a particular study. In a sense, a meta-analysis lies between two kinds of activity covered in this book: doing a literature review of existing studies in an area in which you are interested (the focus of this chapter), and conducting a **secondary analysis** of other researchers' data (see the section on 'Other researchers' data' in Chapter 13). However, the technique relies on all the relevant information being available for each of the studies examined. Since not all the same information relating to methods of study and sample size is included in published papers, meta-analysis is not always feasible. Meta-analysis is vulnerable to what is known as the 'file drawer problem'. This occurs when a researcher conducts a study, finds that the independent variable does not have the intended effect, but has difficulty publishing his or her findings. As a result, it is often suggested that the findings are simply filed away in a drawer. If the file drawer problem has occurred in a field of research, the findings of a meta-analysis will be biased in favour of the independent variable being found to have a certain effect, as some of the findings that contradict that effect will not be in the public domain.

Research in focus 4.2
A meta-analysis of the effectiveness of teamwork

A meta-analysis conducted by Gully *et al.* (2002) sought to test the proposition that team *efficacy*, a team's belief that it can successfully perform a particular task, and team *potency*, a team's general belief in its capabilities across tasks and contexts, are positively related to team performance. They also wanted to examine the impact of *interdependence* (defined as the task, goal, and outcome interconnections between team members) on this relationship. They hypothesized that team efficacy would be more strongly related to performance when interdependence within a team was high.

Studies were identified using computer and manual searches of management-related journals and abstracting and indexing databases. Gully and his colleagues also contacted researchers working in the field to find out about projects that they were currently involved with and they searched conference proceedings for relevant papers. Sixty-seven studies were identified as suitable for meta-analysis. Each was read and coded according to the size of the effect relating team efficacy or potency to performance and was rated for aspects of interdependence. The researchers explored the **reliability** of the measurement instruments that had been used and took the sample size into account in their analysis of the studies.

Results of the analysis indicated that team efficacy and potency are related positively to performance. In addition, although interdependence was found to moderate the relationship between team efficacy and performance, interdependence was not found to affect the relationship between team potency and performance. These findings led the authors to conclude that the characteristics of the task environment are an important influence on the relationship between team efficacy and performance. In particular, when there is a high degree of interdependence—i.e. coordination, communication, and cooperation among team members—team efficacy is more strongly related to performance.

Key concept 4.3
What is meta-ethnography?

Meta-ethnography is a method that is used to achieve interpretative synthesis of qualitative research and other secondary sources, thus providing a counterpart to meta-analysis in quantitative research (Noblit and Hare 1988). It can be used to synthesize and analyse information about a phenomenon that has been extensively studied, such as lay experiences of diabetes (see Research in focus 4.3). However, this is where the similarity ends, because meta-ethnography 'refers not to developing overarching generalizations but, rather, translations of qualitative studies into one another' (1988: 25). Noblit and Hare base their approach on the idea that all social science explanation is comparative, involving the researcher in a process of translating existing studies into their own world view, and through this they create a reading of other people's readings about a subject. Meta-ethnography involves a series of seven phases that overlap and repeat as the synthesis progresses.

1. Getting started. This involves the researcher in identifying an intellectual interest that the qualitative research might inform by reading interpretative accounts.

2. Deciding what is relevant to the initial interest. Unlike positivists, interpretative researchers are not concerned with developing an exhaustive list of studies that might be included in the review. Instead the primary intent is to determine what accounts are likely to be credible and interesting to the intended audience for the synthesis.

3. Reading the studies. This involves the detailed, repeated reading of the studies, rather than moving to analysis of their characteristics.

4. Determining how the studies are related. This stage entails 'putting together' the various studies by determining the relationships between them and the metaphors used within them.

5. Translating the studies into one another. This phase is concerned with interpreting the meaning of studies in relation to each other: are they directly comparable or 'reciprocal' translations (so that the concepts used by each study are translated one-by-one into concepts used by the others); do they stand in opposition to each other as 'refutational' translations; or do they taken together represent a line of argument that is neither 'reciprocal' nor 'refutational'?

6. Synthesizing translations. The researcher compares the different translations and shows how they relate to each other. This may involve grouping them into different types.

7. Expressing the synthesis. This involves translating the synthesis into a form that can be comprehended by the audience for which it is intended.

Crucial to understanding this approach is that the synthesis is focused primarily on the interpretations and explanations offered by studies that are included, rather than on the data that these studies are based on. Meta-ethnography thus translates the interpretations of one study into the interpretations of another one.

Research in focus 4.3
A meta-ethnography of lay experiences of diabetes

Campbell *et al.* (2003) report their approach to conducting a meta-ethnography of studies within the medical sociology field of lay experiences of diabetes and diabetes care. A search came up with ten articles based on qualitative research that addressed this area. Three were excluded for quite different reasons: one turned out not to be based on qualitative research; the evidence in another was appraised as being too weak to warrant inclusion; and the findings of the third paper turned out to be in one of the seven papers that would be included. The seven papers could be grouped into three 'clusters': response to diabetes and treatment; how patients and practitioners differ in perceptions of the disease; and the connections between beliefs about the causes of diabetes and how they managed the disease. One of the themes to emerge among the four articles in the first of these three clusters was the link between control and 'strategic cheating'. Campbell *et al.* note that one study noted the significance of people's sense of control of the disease, which they accomplished through managing it strategically. Such people are referred to as 'copers'. Another study made a similar point between those who felt they were in control of their diet and those described as 'buffeted' by it. Their stance on this issue affected their perception of diabetes, with the former group having a less negative image of it. Some people were able to manage their diet strategically in a flexible way, which was sometimes perceived as 'cheating without guilt'. These reflections were then linked to findings across the two other studies in this group. The authors write:

> Looking across these four studies it would seem that strategic cheating, departing from medical advice in a thoughtful and intelligent way, in order to achieve a balance between the demands of diabetes and the way the person wants to live their life, was associated with a feeling of confidence, less guilt, acceptance of the diabetes and improved glucose levels. (Campbell *et al.* 2003: 678)

In addition, six concepts were found from the seven studies to be significant for the diabetes sufferers in terms of helping them to achieve a balance between controlling the disease and also having some control over their lives—for example, the need to adopt a less subservient approach to medical practitioners. Interestingly, the authors were able to derive insights from their meta-ethnography that were not present in any of the articles.

Tips and skills
Using systematic review in a student research project

The systematic review approach does contain some elements that cannot easily be applied in a student research project because of limitations of time and resources. For example, you are unlikely to be able to assemble a panel of experts in methodology and theory to meet you regularly and discuss the boundaries of the review. However, there are some aspects of the approach that can be applied to students' research. For example, meeting your supervisor regularly during the planning stage of your literature review to define the boundaries of the subject and to come up with likely search terms is extremely useful. Your supervisor's knowledge of the subject can be invaluable at this stage. Also, a systematic review approach to the literature requires a transparent way of searching for and examining the literature as well as keeping records of what you have done. These are also feasible for a student research project.

However, one of the limitations of systematic review stems from situations where research questions are not capable of being defined in terms of the effect of a particular variable, or when the subject boundaries are more fluid and open or subject to change. This is often the case in many areas of social research. Another criticism of the approach is that it can lead to a bureaucratization of the process of reviewing the literature, because it is more concerned with the technical aspects of how it is done than with the analytical interpretations generated by it. A third potential limitation of the approach relates to its application to qualitative research studies and in particular to the methodological judgments that inform decisions about quality and so determine the inclusion or exclusion of an article from a literature review. These stem from differences between qualitative and quantitative research in relation to the criteria used to assess their methodological quality (see Chapters 6 and 16). The systematic approach assumes that an objective judgement about the quality of an article can be made. Particularly in relation to qualitative research, there is little consensus on how the quality of studies should be carried out, an issue that will be returned to in Chapter 16. Moreover, some researchers would say that they measure the quality of published research in terms of what they find interesting—this may or may not include empirical study, but such a view is not compatible with the systematic approach, which requires articles to be evaluated in terms of methodological criteria. In addition, researchers in the medical sciences have found that the process of identifying relevant qualitative studies is more time consuming and cannot be done on the basis of the abstract or summary in the way that quantitative research studies can (Jones 2004). Finally, whether or not the systematic review approach makes sense to you depends somewhat on your epistemological position (see Chapter 1). As Noblit and Hare (1988: 15) state: 'Positivists have had more interest in knowledge synthesis than interpretivists. For them, knowledge accumulates. The problem has been how best to accomplish that accumulation.' For these reasons, researchers who adopt an interpretative approach to understanding the social sciences and use qualitative methods may find the systematic review approach more problematic. Similar concerns have been expressed by educational researchers about the suitability of systematic review in an area of study that is quite different from the medical field where it was developed (see Thinking deeply 4.3).

Thinking deeply 4.3
Debates about the role of systematic review in education research

Debates about the role of systematic review in education research are of potential relevance to social policy researchers because of the similarities shared between these two applied fields of study. Both education and social policy research draw on a range of social science disciplines, involve the study of practitioners, and are sometimes criticized for not focusing sufficiently on the concerns of practitioners and policy-makers. Evans and Benefield (2001) have argued that the medical model of systematic review can be adapted for application in education research. This would enable researchers to 'say something more precise and targeted' about the effectiveness of specific interventions, or in other words to provide evidence about 'what works' (2001: 538). Systematic reviews would thus help to make research evidence more usable.

However, Hammersley (2001) criticizes the assumption in systematic review about the superiority of the positivist model of research, which is expressed through the methodological criteria applied in evaluating the **validity** of studies (**experiments** being more highly valued), and through the explicit procedures used to produce reviews that are intended to be 'objective'. This 'takes little or no account of the considerable amount of criticism that has been made of that model since at least the middle of the twentieth century' (2001: 545). Moreover, Hammersley suggests that the dichotomy portrayed between rational rule-following, systematic review and irrational judgement, narrative review is overstated because even the simplest rule following involves an element of interpretation. He concludes:

> What all this means, I suggest, is that producing a review of the literature is a distinctive task in its own right. It is not a matter of 'synthesising data'; or, at least, there is no reason why we should assume that reviewing *must* take this form. Rather, it can involve judging the validity of the findings and conclusions of particular studies, and thinking about how these relate to one another, and how their interrelations can be used to illuminate the field under investigation. This will require the reviewer to draw on his or her tacit knowledge, derived from experience, and to *think* about the substantive and methodological issues, not just to apply replicable procedures. (Hammersley 2001: 549)

MacLure (2005: 409) suggests that the recent prioritization of systematic review in education research is worrying because 'it is hostile to anything that cannot be seen, and therefore controlled, counted and quality assured'; it thus degrades the status of reading, writing, thinking, and interpreting as activities that are crucial to the development of analysis and argument. Although systematic review has so far not been as widely adopted in social research, the concerns expressed by education researchers are of potential relevance, particularly to qualitative researchers. However, one of the most interesting aspects of Hammersley's (2001) critique is that he implies that systematic review is inconsistent with its own principles in that there appears to be no or very little evidence that systematic reviews lead to better evidence (and therefore presumably to better evidence-based practice)!

Narrative review

Rather than reviewing the literature to find out what their research project can add to existing knowledge about a subject, interpretative researchers (see Chapter 1 for an explanation of interpretivism) can have quite different reasons for reviewing the literature on a particular subject, since their purpose is to enrich human discourse (Geertz 1973a) by generating understanding rather than by accumulating knowledge. The literature review is for them a means of gaining an initial impression of the topic area that they intend to understand through their research. The process of reviewing the literature is thus a more uncertain process of discovery, in that you might not always know in advance where it will take you! Narrative reviews therefore tend to be less focused and more wide-ranging in scope than systematic reviews. They are also invariably less explicit about the criteria for exclusion or inclusion of studies. An example of a narrative review is given in Research in focus 4.4.

Research in focus 4.4
A narrative review of qualitative research on leadership

A few years ago, I conducted a literature review of qualitative research that had been undertaken on leadership (Bryman 2004*b*). Leadership research is a field that has been dominated over the years by quantitative investigations, so it struck me as potentially interesting to examine the growing number of qualitative studies that were appearing. I decided to examine only articles that had appeared in journals that publish only articles that have been reviewed by peers. There were two main reasons for this: peer-reviewed articles can be searched relatively easily through online databases like the Social Sciences Citation Index (SSCI, about which more will be said below), and peer review offers an element of quality control, since only articles that have gone through the process of peer review are accepted for publication. Peer review weeds out articles that are not of sufficient quality for a journal either by rejecting them outright or by insisting that authors implement substantial revisions in response to referees' concerns. In addition, I included in my review articles that I already knew and I hand searched the *Leadership Quarterly*, one of the main outlets for research articles. I also examined the bibliographies of some articles for further candidates for inclusion. This general area was of interest to me as I have long been interested in both qualitative research and the field of leadership. I did not have a specific focus to my review, although I was interested in general terms in the question of how similar qualitative research was to the quantitative research that dominated the field of leadership.

I presented my main findings in a table that outlined: the year of publication; the sector in which the research was conducted; the research design; the research methods used; the nature of the key findings; and the kinds of leadership style and leader behaviour that were emphasized in each study. On the basis of my findings, I suggested that qualitative research differed from the quantitative studies in the following ways: qualitative studies were more likely to emphasize leaders as people who promote change or who change their behaviour as leaders in response to change; qualitative studies were more likely to emphasize the ways that leaders have to take context into account; they were also more inclined to emphasize senior leaders rather than lower-level leaders; qualitative studies were more likely to emphasize different kinds of leadership from the quantitative studies; qualitative studies were less cumulative, in the sense that they tended not to build on each other's findings; some qualitative studies made relatively scant use of the existing literature; qualitative studies were more likely to stress the significance of the language of leadership; and they were more likely than quantitative studies to question the very idea of leadership. I also pointed to two ways in which qualitative and quantitative studies did not differ: they both tend to ignore informal leadership, and when qualitative studies relate the behaviour of leaders to outcomes (like morale) within a **cross-sectional design**, the findings could look strikingly similar in form to quantitative ones. In the subtitle of my article, I called it a 'critical but appreciative review'. It was critical in that it pointed to some overall deficiencies in qualitative research on leadership, such as a tendency not to be cumulative, because qualitative researchers' findings are not built upon by subsequent qualitative research. However, it was also appreciative, because I pointed to some of the distinctive contributions that qualitative research has made to the field.

If your approach to the relationship between theory and research is inductive rather than deductive (see Chapter 1), setting out all the main theoretical and conceptual terms that define your area of study prior to data collection is extremely problematic, because theory is the outcome of the study, rather than the basis for it. Hence, in the process of researching a topic, researchers may discover issues that they did not previously anticipate as likely to be important to their area of study. As a result, they become aware of the limitations of the topic area that they originally intended to inform, and this can lead them towards an unanticipated understanding of it (Noblit and Hare 1988). Interpretative researchers are thus more likely than deductive researchers to change their view of the theory or literature as a result of the analysis of collected data and so they require greater flexibility to modify the boundaries of their subject of study as they go along. This means that narrative review may be more suitable for qualitative researchers whose research strategy is based on an interpretative epistemology, and

for them systematic review should not be automatically accepted as a better way of dealing with the literature.

Most reviews are of the narrative kind, regardless of whether they are meant to be springboards for the reviewer's own investigation (for example, when the literature is reviewed as a means of specifying what is already known in connection with a research topic, so that research questions can be identified that the reviewer will then examine) or are ends in their own right (as a means of summarizing what is known in an area). When we examine some examples of writing up research in Chapter 27, we will see that the literature relevant to the researcher's area of interest is always reviewed as a means of establishing why the researcher conducted the research and what its contribution is likely to be. Such reviews are still mainly narrative reviews. However, the gap between systematic and narrative reviews is beginning to narrow, as sometimes some of the procedures associated with systematic reviews are incorporated into a narrative review.

Thinking deeply 4.4
Incorporating systematic review practices into narrative reviews

It is always risky to speculate, but I have a hunch that some narrative reviews will incorporate some of the practices associated with systematic review. Even though some writers like those mentioned in Thinking deeply 4.3 object to systematic review for its tendency towards a mechanical approach to reviewing the literature, it could be that some reviewers will be attracted to its emphasis on such features as transparency about how searches were conducted and/or comprehensiveness in the literature search. This is especially likely to be the case when reviewers work on their own, as systematic review requires more than one person to assist in such steps as: the formulation of research questions, the selection of keywords, and the assessment of quality.

An example is Glasby and Lester's (2005) narrative review of mental health inpatient services in the UK. The authors searched seven online databases (including the SSCI) using keywords that included 'mental health' in conjunction with 'hospital, inpatient, bed, ward, forensic, gender and ethnicity' (Glasby and Lester 2005: 865). Other sources of articles were explored as well. Abstracts of articles were examined to determine whether they were relevant to the review. These procedures seem very much in tune with those of systematic review, but Glasby and Lester rejected the use of tight quality assessment criteria because too few studies end up being included in a review. The authors write that: 'Thirty-seven documents relating directly to hospital inpatient services, fifty-one relating to forensic mental health services and sixty-one relating to the experiences of women and minority ethnic groups were included in the review' (Glasby and Lester 2005: 866). This is almost certainly a much larger number of studies than would have been included in a systematic review. Although this means that Glasby and Lester included studies that would probably have failed the quality tests employed in a systematic review, our confidence in the inferences they make from the literature is not necessarily damaged because of this, because they were able to generate those inferences from a larger number of studies.

Tips and skills
Reasons for writing a literature review

The following is a list of reasons for writing a literature review.

- You need to know what is already known in connection with your research area because you do not want to be accused of reinventing the wheel.
- You can learn from other researchers' mistakes and avoid making the same ones.
- You can learn about different theoretical and methodological approaches to your research area.
- It may help you to develop an analytic framework.
- It may lead you to consider the inclusion of variables in your research that you might not otherwise have thought about.
- It may suggest further research questions for you.
- It will help with the interpretation of your findings.
- It gives you some pegs on which to hang your findings.
- It is expected!

Student experience
Importance of doing a literature review

Lily Taylor does not appear to need convincing about the necessity of doing a literature review. As she notes:

> Looking at significant work that related to mine was good in the sense that it enabled me to look at the use of methodology and access key concepts and characteristics of the work.

To read more about Lily's research experiences, go to the Online Resource Centre that accompanies this book at **http://www.oxfordtextbooks.co.uk/orc/brymansrm3e/**.

Searching the existing literature

Usually, students will have in mind a few initial references when they begin on a project. These will probably come from recommended reading in course modules, or from textbooks. The bibliographies provided at the end of textbook chapters or articles will usually provide you with a raft of further relevant references that can also be followed up. A literature search relies on careful reading of books, journals, and reports in the first instance. After identifying a few keywords that help to define the bound-

aries of your chosen area of research (see below), electronic databases of published literature can be searched for previously published work in the field.

Electronic databases

Online bibliographical databases accessible on the Internet are an invaluable source of journal references. An increasing number of these will also provide access to the full text of an article in electronic format—these are usually referred to as e-journals. You will need to find out whether your institution can give you a user name and password to gain access to these databases, so look on your library's homepage, or ask a member of library staff.

Probably the single most useful source for the social sciences is the Social Sciences Citation Index (SSCI), which fully indexes over 1,700 major social science journals covering all social science disciplines dating back to 1970. To gain access to this website, most UK users will need an Athens username and password. It can be accessed from the ISI Web of Knowledge (WoK) home page at the following address: http://wok.mimas.ac.uk/ (accessed on 2 July 2007). The Citation indexes collectively are also known as Web of Science.

The SSCI database provides references and abstracts, and some libraries add full-text links for articles from some of the most important social science journals published worldwide. It is therefore very useful as an initial source in your literature search, because, if you search the database effectively, you can be relatively confident that you have covered the majority of recent academic journals that may have published articles on your topic of interest. Here are some introductory guidelines for searching SSCI.

- Click on GO beside Web of Science.

- Choose Social Science Citation Index by unticking the Science and Arts sections.

- Click ON GENERAL SEARCH. Note that the default is to search 1970 to date; you can change this by using the pull down menus.

- You can then search by TOPIC or by AUTHOR.

A feature of SSCI is its complete coverage of journal contents, so in addition to research and scholarly articles it also contains book reviews and editorial material, which invariably can be identified through keyword searches. You will need to experiment with the use of keywords, because this is usually the way in which databases like these are searched, though author searches are also possible. Finally a feature that is often useful is the 'Times cited' link. If you find an article that is relevant to your dissertation, then you can click to see which other articles have cited it. This does two things. First it allows you to see how an article has been used in more recent research, and in particular whether it has been challenged. Second, it gives an impression of whether the article and the ideas in it have been developed with new data. For example, at the time of writing this chapter (21 June 2007), my paper published in 1999 in the journal *Sociological Review* on the Disneyization of society has been cited in twenty-two other papers about related subjects, such as emotional labour and retailing. However, it is important to realize that articles in other journals may have cited the article. The reason that these would not turn up in an SSCI search is that those responsible for it operate a screening process, which means that by no means all

Student experience
Strategies for finding references

The students who supplied information concerning their strategies for doing their literature reviews used a variety of approaches. As well as searching the journals, Erin Saunders got help from her supervisor and others.

> I was recommended a number of relevant texts by my supervisor—and from there I located other sources by using the bibliographies of these texts. As well, I did an extensive journal search for articles that were related to my topic. I also contacted a number of academics in the field to ask for specific suggestions. Then I read as much of the literature as I could, identifying key themes and ideas.

Hannah Creane's approach was to focus on key names in the sociological literature on childhood.

> Initially I read a few core textbooks that cover the general aspects of sociology, and picked out from them the main names of sociologists who have written about childhood and, in particular, childhood as a social construction. From there I read the books of some of the key names within the field of childhood study, and

just simply kept looking up the names of sociologists whom they had referenced. I kept going like this until I felt I had enough literature to back up my findings and theories that I made in the light of my own research.

Rebecca Barnes proceeded by identifying key texts and then using bibliographies.

Once I started to locate the core texts, this process gathered more momentum, since I was able to draw on bibliographies in those sources to identify other relevant references.

 To read more about Erin's, Hannah's, and Rebecca's research experiences, go to the Online Resource Centre that accompanies this book at **http://www.oxfordtextbooks.co.uk/orc/brymansrm3e/**.

journals achieve entry into the database. The screening process takes into account the reputation and impact of the journal concerned.

You can also use the CITED REF SEARCH to search for articles that cite an article that you know about already. This can help you find other related research and also see what other authors thought of your original article. This is particularly useful if your article is a few years old.

Also very useful is Scopus, which is available at http://www.scopus.com/scopus/home.url (accessed on 2 July 2007).

Scopus describes itself as 'the largest abstract and citation database of research literature and quality web sources'. You will need an Athens or other username and password to get into the database. The 'General Search' may meet your initial needs. This allows you to search in terms of keywords and/or authors. You need to specify the date range of articles you wish to search for (it goes back to 1960) and to untick the subject areas not relevant to your search. Scopus tends to include a wider range of journals than SSCI. Like SSCI, it will bring up the abstract, as well as the full reference when a particular item is selected for further examination.

Also useful for searching for references is Google Scholar—see Tips and skills 'Using information on the Web' for details of how to use this search tool.

Nowadays, many academic publishers have begun to offer full-text versions of articles in their journals through their own websites; Cambridge University Press (Cambridge Journals Online) and Sage (HighWire) are the two most prominent examples. Again you will need to check with your librarian to find out which of these resources you can use and how to access them. The INGENTA website offers full-text versions from various publishers, and you will be able to access full-text versions of articles in journals to which your library subscribes. In addition to scholarly books and journals, newspaper archives can provide a valuable supplemen-

tary resource through which to review the emergence of new topics in areas of social concern. Most newspapers require subscription to be able to search their online databases (e.g. *Financial Times*, *Daily* and *Sunday Telegraph*, *The Times*). However, most academic libraries will have a subscription to some individual newspapers or to a service such as Proquest or Lexis Nexis, which allows you to search several newspapers at once; you may need a password to access them. Newspapers and periodicals can be a rich source of information about certain topics that make good stories for journalists, such as social problems, policy initiatives, or trade union disputes. The level of analysis can also be high. For an academic dissertation they should always be seen as secondary to published literature in books and journals, but it takes some time for academic articles to be published, so for recent events newspapers may be the only source of information.

A word of warning about using Google and other search engines for research. Internet search engines are very useful for researching all sorts of things. However, they merely find sites, they do not evaluate them, so be prepared to look critically at what you have found. Remember that anyone can put information on the Web, so when looking at websites, you need to evaluate whether the information you have found is useful. The following points are worth considering.

- Who is the author of the site and what is their motive for publishing?

- Where is the site located? The URL can help you here. Is it an academic site (.ac) or a government site (.gov), a non-commercial organization (.org) or a commercial one (.com or .co)?

- How recently was the site updated? Many sites will give you a last updated date, but you can get clues as to whether a page is being well maintained by whether the links are up to date and by its general appearance.

Try to confine your literature search to reliable websites, such as those mentioned in this chapter. For more on this issue, see Tips and skills 'Using information on the Web'.

The catalogue of your own institution is an obvious route to finding books, but so too are the catalogues of other universities. COPAC contains the holdings of twenty-seven of the largest university research libraries plus the British Library. It can be found at http://www.copac.ac.uk/copac (accessed on 2 July 2007). A well-known website like amazon can also be extremely helpful for searching for books.

Tips and skills
Using email alerts

One way of expanding your literature search is through email alerts. These supply you with an email when an issue of a journal that you are interested in is published. You can also be sent email alerts when articles with certain keywords or written by particular authors are published. One of the main ways of setting up email alerts is through Zetoc, through the British Library. You will need to sign in with a username and password. An Athens username and password will usually achieve this. To find Zetoc, go to **http://zetoc.mimas.ac.uk/** (accessed on 25 June 2007).

Tips and skills
Using information on the Web

The Internet provides an enormous and richly varied source of freely available information about social research that can be quickly and easily accessed without the need for university agreements to gain access to them. However, there is a difficulty in relying on this, because the strength of the Internet in providing access to huge amounts of information is also its weakness, in that it can be very difficult to differentiate what is useful and reliable from that which is too simplistic, too commercially oriented, too highly opinionated, or just not sufficiently academic. The worst thing that can happen is that you end up quoting from sources from the Web that are quite simply misleading and incorrect. Therefore, it is important to be selective in your use of information on the Internet and to build up a list of favourite websites that you can check regularly for information.

However, such sources have to be evaluated critically. For example, while writing this chapter, I encountered the following definition of qualitative research in Wikipedia, which is very popular among students.

> Qualitative research is one of the two major approaches to *research methodology* in *social sciences*. Qualitative research involves an indepth understanding of *human behaviour* and the *reasons* that govern human behaviour. Unlike *quantitative research*, qualitative research relies on reasons behind various aspects of *behaviour*. Simply put, it investigates the why and how of *decision-making*, as compared to what, where, and when of quantitative research. Hence, the need is for smaller but focused *samples* rather than large *random samples*, which qualitative research categorizes into patterns as the primary basis for organizing and reporting results (**http://en.wikipedia.org/wiki/Qualitative_research** (accessed on 12 February 2007)).

This is a very misleading characterization of both quantitative and qualitative research. It implies that quantitative researchers are not concerned with examining the 'reasons behind various aspects of behaviour'.

This is a quite extraordinary notion. The whole point of the preoccupation with **causality** and the very notions of independent and **dependent variables** that are part of the basic vocabulary of quantitative research (see Chapter 6) would suggest the opposite: quantitative researchers are deeply concerned about exploring the reasons behind behaviour. Also, qualitative researchers are concerned to explore 'what, where, and when', in that they frequently engage in descriptions of what is happening at certain events or on particular occasions, where they take place, and often draw inferences about their timing. Further, quantitative researchers 'categorize . . . data into patterns', but the nature and character of those patterns assume a different form. This is a very poor definition and characterization of qualitative research and demonstrates the risk of using Web sources in an unquestioning way. Wikipedia contains some very good entries but it has to be treated with caution, as do Web sources generally.

Searching tool

Google has a really useful product called 'Google Scholar', which can be accessed from the Google home page. This product provides a simple way to search broadly for academic literature. Searches are focused on peer-reviewed papers, theses, books, abstracts, and articles, from academic publishers, professional societies, preprint repositories, universities, and other scholarly organizations. Google Scholar also enables you to see how often an item has been cited by other people. This can be very useful in assessing the importance of an idea or a particular scholarly writer. See **http://scholar.google.com**.

Current affairs

For case study analyses and keeping up to date on current social issues the BBC News website is reasonably well balanced and quite analytical: **http://www.bbc.co.uk**.

Statistics on social trends

The National Statistics office makes a huge amount of data about social trends available on its website: **http://www.statistics.gov.uk/**. The statistics on Internet use at the beginning of Chapter 26 are gleaned by examining this website.

European statistics relating to specific countries, industries, and sectors can be found on Europa, the portal to the European Union website: **http://europa.eu.int**.

Other useful websites that are relevant to research methods

Teaching Resources and Materials for Social Scientists: **http://tramss.data-archive.ac.uk/**
Intute: **http://www.intute.ac.uk/services.html**
Exploring online research methods: **http://www.geog.le.ac.uk/ORM/**
(All websites mentioned in this box were accessed on 2 July 2007.)

Student experience
Literature review as ongoing

The literature review is often viewed as a distinct phase in the research process, but in fact it is often an ongoing component of a research project. While email alerts like Zetoc alerts (see Tips and skills 'Using email alerts') may be a useful way of keeping on top of the literature, they also mean that the literature review may not draw to a close at an early stage. Rebecca Barnes found that searching the literature was an ongoing process.

Although at the beginning of my Ph.D., I dedicated a more prolonged period of time to searching for and reviewing literature, this process has been an ongoing part of the research process. I used electronic databases such as Cambridge Sociological Abstracts to identify sources which could be useful, and I was also fortunate in stumbling across a bibliography of sources for same-sex domestic violence on the Internet. . . . I also subscribe to Zetoc alerts, which means that rather than having to spend time regularly updating the literature which I have, I am informed of many new articles as soon as they are published.

Rebecca's experience is not unusual. Isabella Robbins, who is doing a Ph.D., describes the literature review as feeling like 'a process that has been ongoing for about six years', while Sarah Hanson suggests that it can be difficult to bring the review to a close.

The only difficulty I encountered was that I couldn't stop reading; I had finished my literature review and had started writing my dissertation, but I kept stumbling upon book after book, which then had to be encompassed into the literature review. I ended up writing and rewriting my literature review.

To read more about Rebecca's, Isabella's and Sarah's research experiences, go to the Online Resource Centre that accompanies this book at http://www.oxfordtextbooks.co.uk/orc/brymansrm3e/.

Keywords and defining search parameters

For all these online databases, you will need to work out some suitable keywords that can be entered into the search engines and that will allow you to identify suitable references. Journal articles often include lists of keywords. When you find two or three articles that are relevant to your research and that have lists of keywords, it may be useful to use some of these keywords that are relevant to your research for searching for other articles. You will also need to think of synonyms or alternative terms and try to match your language to that of the source you are searching. For example, in the example in Research in focus 4.4, I used 'manage*' and 'administrat*' as well as 'leader*'. This is not because I think that management and administration are the same as leadership but because I realized quite early on that some authors use these terms either as synonyms for leadership or in very similar ways. Be prepared to experiment and to amend your keywords as your research progresses; you may find as you search the literature that there are other ways of describing your subject.

Tips and skills
Keywords

For all kinds of review—narrative or systematic—using keywords for searching online databases of articles is crucial. However, it is not as easy as it seems. For example, though the authors of the article in Research in focus 4.1 searched the literature thoroughly using keywords, they note that, after they had completed the meta-ethnography on lay experiences of diabetes, they 'were made aware of a meta-ethnography based on 43 qualitative reports concerned with the "lived experience of diabetes" ' (Campbell *et al.* 2003: 683). Not only were they unable to uncover this article, which had been published in 1998, through their search, but also the authors of the other meta-ethnography had included only three of the seven articles Campbell *et al.* had used. Searching for keywords requires some experimentation and should not be regarded as a one-off exercise. For example, if you are interested in 'the role of women in the management of banks' your keywords would be: WOMEN and MANAG* and BANK*.

Thus, 'manag*' would capture manag*er*, manag*ers*, manag*ing*, and manag*ement*, because the asterisk acts as a wild card that searches for all words beginning 'manag . . .'.

In most databases, typing in the title of your project, or a sentence or long phrase, as your search term is not advisable, as, unless someone has written something with the same title, you are unlikely to find very much. You need to think in terms of keywords (see Tips and skills 'Keywords').

Use the HELP provided in the databases themselves to find out how to use your keywords to best effect. The advice on using 'operators' such as AND, OR, and NOT can be especially helpful.

In some areas of research, there are very many references. Try to identify the major ones and work outwards from there. Move on to the next stage of your research at the point that you identified in your timetable, so that you can dig yourself out of the library. This is not to say that your search for the literature will cease, but that you need to force yourself to move on. Seek out your supervisor's advice on whether you need to search the literature much more. Figure 4.1 outlines one way of searching the literature. The most important thing to remember, as the note at the end of the figure suggests, is to keep a good record of the process so that you can keep track of what you have done.

 # Referencing your work

Referencing the work of others is an important academic convention because it emphasizes that you are aware of the historical development of your subject, particularly if you use the Harvard (or author–date) method, and shows that you recognize that your own research builds on the work of others. Referencing in your literature review is thus a way of emphasizing your understanding and knowledge of the subject. In other parts of your dissertation referencing will serve somewhat different purposes—for example, it will show your understanding of methodological considerations or help to reinforce your argument. A reference is also sometimes described as a citation and the act of referencing as citing.

As I mentioned earlier on in this chapter, a key skill in writing your literature review will therefore be to keep a record of what you have read, including all the bibliographic details about the article or book that will go into your bibliography or references. For larger research projects it can be useful to use note cards or software packages that are designed specifically for this purpose such as Procite or Endnote, but for a student research project it will probably be sufficient to keep an electronic record of all the items that you have read in a Word document, although you should bear in mind that you may not include all of these in your final bibliography. However, the main thing to make sure of is that you keep your bibliographic records up to date and do not leave this until the very end of the writing-up process, when you will probably be under significant time pressure.

Your institution will probably have its own guidelines as to which style of referencing you should use in your dissertation and if it does you should definitely follow them. However, the two main methods used are:

- *Harvard* or author–date. The essence of this system is that, whenever you paraphrase the argument or ideas of an author or authors in your writing, you add in parentheses immediately afterwards the surname of the author(s) and the year of publication. If you are quoting the author(s), you put quotation marks around the quotation and after the year of publication you include the page number where the quotation is from. All books, articles, and other sources that you have cited in the text are then given in a list of references at the end of the dissertation in alphabetical order. This is by far the most common referencing system in social research and the one that we follow in this book. It is, therefore, the style that we would encourage you to use if your university does not require you to follow its own guidelines.

- *Footnote or numeric*. This approach involves the use of superscript numbers in the text that refer to a note at the foot of the page or the end of the text, where the reference is given in full together with the page number if it is a direct quotation. If a source is cited more than once, an abbreviated version of the reference is given in any subsequent citation. As well as being used to refer to sources, footnotes and endnotes are often used to provide additional detail, including comments from the writer about the source being cited. This is a particular feature of historical writing. One of the advantages of the footnote or numeric method is that

Figure 4.1

One way of searching the literature

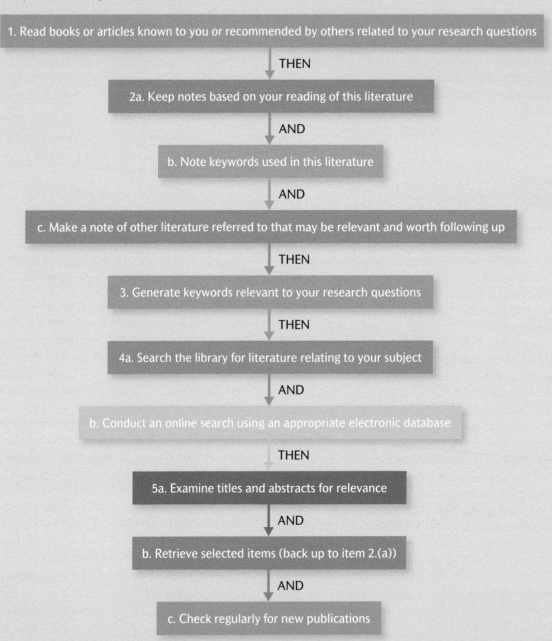

1. Read books or articles known to you or recommended by others related to your research questions

THEN

2a. Keep notes based on your reading of this literature

AND

b. Note keywords used in this literature

AND

c. Make a note of other literature referred to that may be relevant and worth following up

THEN

3. Generate keywords relevant to your research questions

THEN

4a. Search the library for literature relating to your subject

AND

b. Conduct an online search using an appropriate electronic database

THEN

5a. Examine titles and abstracts for relevance

AND

b. Retrieve selected items (back up to item 2.(a))

AND

c. Check regularly for new publications

Note: At each stage, keep a record of what you have done and your reasons for certain decisions. This will be useful to you for remembering how you proceeded and for writing up a description and justification of your literature search strategy, which can form part of your methods section. When making notes on literature that you read, make notes on content and method, as well as relevance, and keep thinking about how each item will contribute to your critical review of the literature.

it can be less distracting to the reader in terms of the flow of the text than the Harvard method, where sometimes particularly long strings of references can make a sentence or a paragraph difficult for the reader to follow. Furthermore, software packages like Word make the insertion of notes relatively simple, and many students find that this is a convenient way of referencing their work. However, when students use this method, they often use it incorrectly, as it is quite difficult to use

it well, and they are sometimes unsure whether or not also to include a separate bibliography. The footnote approach to referencing does not necessarily include a bibliography, but this can be important in the assessment of students' work (see Thinking deeply 4.2). As not having a bibliography is a potential disadvantage to this style of referencing, your institution may recommend that you do not use it.

Tips and skills
The Harvard and footnote approaches to referencing

The examples below show some fictitious examples of referencing in published work. Note that in published articles there is usually a list of references at the end, whereas in books this may be called a bibliography. The punctuation of references—such as where to place a comma, or whether to capitalize a title in full or just the first word—varies considerably from source to source. For example, with Harvard referencing, in some books and journals the surname of the author is separated from the date in the text with a comma—for example (Name, 1999)—but in others, like this book, there is no comma. However, the main thing is to be consistent. Select a format for punctuating your references, such as the one adopted by a leading journal in your subject area, and then stick to it.

An example of a Harvard reference to a book

In the text:
As Name and Other (1999) argue, motivation is a broad concept that comprises a variety of intrinsic and extrinsic factors . . .

. . . and in the bibliography or list of references:
Name, A. and Other, S. (1999), *Title of Book in Italics*. Place of Publication: Publisher.

An example of a Harvard reference with a direct quotation from a book

In the text:
However, the importance of intrinsic factors often tends to be overlooked since 'studies of motivation have tended predominantly to focus on the influence of extrinsic factors' (Name and Other 1999: 123).

. . . and in the bibliography or list of references:
Name, A. and Other, S. (1999), *Title of Book in Italics*. Place of Publication: Publisher.

An example of a Harvard reference to a journal article

In the text:
Research by Name (2003) has drawn attention to the importance of intrinsic factors in determining employee motivation.

... and in the bibliography or list of references:

> Refers to volume (issue) numbers

Name, A. (2003), 'Title of Journal Article', *Journal Title,* 28(4): 109–38.

Issue numbers are often not included, as in the case of the References in this book.

An example of a Harvard reference to a chapter in an edited book

In the text:

As Name (2001) suggests, individual motivation to work is affected by a range of intrinsic and extrinsic factors . . .

. . . and in the bibliography or list of references:

Name, A. (2001), 'Title of Book Chapter', in S. Other (ed.), *Title of Book in Italics.* Place of Publication: Publisher, pp. 124–56.

> Abbreviation for 'Editor'

An example of a secondary reference using the Harvard Method

In the text:

Individual motivation to work is affected by a range of intrinsic and extrinsic factors (Name 1993 cited in Other 2004).

. . . and in the bibliography or list of references:

Name, A. (1993), *Title of Book in Italics.* Place of Publication: Publisher, cited in S. Other (2004), *Title of Textbook in Italics.* Place of Publication: Publisher.

An example of a Harvard reference to an Internet site

In the text:

Scopus describes itself as 'the largest abstract and citation database of research literature and quality web sources' (Scopus 2007).

. . . and in the bibliography or list of references:

Scopus (online). Available from **http://info.scopus.com/** (accessed on 21 June 2007).

Note: it is very important to give the date of access, as some websites change frequently (or even disappear!).

An example of a footnote reference to a book

In the text:

On the other hand, research by Name and Other[3] has drawn attention to the influence of intrinsic factors on employee motivation . . .

. . . and in the footnotes:

[3] A. Name, *Title of Book in Italics*. Place of Publication, Publisher, 2000, pp. 170–7.

An example of a footnote reference to an Internet site

In the text:

Scopus describes itself as 'the largest abstract and citation database of research literature and quality web sources'.[39]

. . . and in the footnotes:

[39] Scopus (online). Available from **http://info.scopus.com/** (accessed 21 June 2007).

Bear in mind that it is essential when preparing your own referencing in the text and the bibliography or list of references, that *you follow the conventions and style that are recommended by your institution for preparing an essay, dissertation, or thesis.*

Tips and skills
Using bibliographic software

ProCite, EndNote, and Reference Manager are three of the leading windows-based software tools used for publishing and managing bibliographies. Your university may have a site licence for one of these packages. They are used by academic researchers, information specialists, and students to create bibliographic records equivalent to the manual form of index cards. This allows you to compile your own personal reference database. These records can then be automatically formatted to suit different requirements—for example, to comply with the referencing requirements of a particular scholarly journal. A further advantage to the software is that it can enable you to export references directly from databases such as the Social Sciences Citation Index (SSCI). The software also has search options that help you to locate a particular reference, although the extent of these features varies from one package to another.

In the long run, this can save you time and effort and reduce the possibility of errors. However, for a student research project it may not be worthwhile for you to take the time to learn how to use this software if it is only to be used for the dissertation. On the other hand, if knowledge of the software may be useful to you in the longer term, for example, if you are thinking of going on to pursue an academic career by doing a Ph.D., or if you are intending to work in a field where research skills are valued, then it may be worth learning how to use the software. More details about these products can be found on the following websites:

www.procite.com
www.endnote.com
www.refman.com

However, if you do not have access to one of these packages, similar software is offered free to students and can be downloaded from the Internet. One of these is BiblioExpress, a simplified version of the package Biblioscape. This package offers the main features associated with bibliographic referencing software and provides extensive user support from its website, which includes a free downloadable user manual. BiblioExpress enables you to do most of the main things needed for a student research project but does not require very much computing memory, so it can even be run from a floppy disk. For more details go to *www.biblioscape.com/biblioexpress.htm*

All web pages mentioned in this box were accessed on 15 July 2007.

Thinking deeply 4.5
The problem of using secondary literature sources

Be careful when using second-hand accounts of theories or findings. It is well known that these are sometimes misleadingly represented in publications—though hopefully not in this book! An interesting case is the *Affluent Worker* research that is described later in this book in Research in focus 22.8. This research entailed a survey in the 1960s of predominantly affluent workers in three firms in Luton. It is regarded as a classic of British sociology. One of the authors of the books that were published from this research conducted a search for books and articles that discussed the findings of this research. Platt (1984) shows that several authors misinterpreted the findings. Examples of such misinterpretation follow.

- *The study was based on just car workers*. It was not—only one of the three companies was a car firm.
- *The study was based on just semi-skilled or mass production workers*. It was not—there were a variety of skill levels and technological forms among the manual sample.
- *The research 'found' instrumentalism*, i.e. an instrumental orientation to work. This is misleading—instrumentalism was an inference about the data, not a finding as such.

The point of this discussion is the need to be vigilant about possibly recycling incorrect interpretations of theoretical ideas or research findings.

The role of the bibliography

What makes a good bibliography or list of references? You might initially think that length is a good measure, since a longer bibliography containing more references might imply that the author has been comprehensive in his or her search of the existing literature. This is undoubtedly true, but only up to a point, since it is also important for the bibliography to be selectively focused—it should not include everything that has ever been written about a subject but instead should reflect the author's informed judgement of the importance and suitability of sources. This incorporates some of the judgements about quality that were discussed earlier on in this chapter. One common proxy for quality is the reputation of the journal in which an article is published. However, although this is a useful indicator, we recommend that it is not one that you rely on exclusively, since there might be articles in lesser-status journals—for instance, those targeted at practitioners—that have relevance to your subject. But it is important to be aware of these judgements of quality and to seek the advice of your supervisor in making them. Another important feature of a good bibliography relates to secondary referencing. This is when you refer to an article or book that has been cited in another source such as a textbook and you do not, or cannot, access the original article or book from which it was taken. However, relying heavily on secondary references can be problematic, because you are dependent upon the interpretation of the original text that is offered by the authors of the secondary text. This may be adequate for some parts of your literature review, but it is a bit like the game Chinese Whispers, in that there is always the potential for different interpretations of the original text, and this increases the further removed you are from the original source. So it is a good idea to be cautious in the use of secondary references and to go back to the original source if you can, particularly if the reference is an important one for your subject. Thinking deeply 4.5 gives an example of how an author's work can be referenced in ways that involve reinterpretation and misquotation long after the date of publication. A further feature of a good bibliography stems from the relationship between the list of references at the end and the way in which they are used in the main body of the text. It should go without saying that it is not very helpful to include references in a list of references that are not even mentioned in the text. If references are integrated into the text in a way that shows you have read them in detail and understood the theoretical perspective from which they are written, this is much more impressive than if a reference is inserted into the text in a way that does not closely relate to what is being said in the text. Finally, Barnett (1994) argues that a good bibliography gives no indication of the quality of a piece of work, pointing out that some of the most influential academic books ever written do not even include one. Drawing on the ideas of Bourdieu (1984), he suggests that the main purpose of the bibliography is to enable you to understand the habitus that the author is claiming to reside in, this being about understanding the beliefs and dispositions of the author combined with the constraints associated with his or her situation.

Tips and skills
Helping your supervisor to understand your literature review

If you are planning to give a first draft of your literature review to your supervisor for him or her to comment on, make sure that you include your list of references in this version. Otherwise your supervisor will not know what literature you have used to compile the review, and this will make it harder for him or her to comment meaningfully on the quality of your work.

Avoiding plagiarism

An issue to bear in mind when writing up your literature review is the need to avoid plagiarizing the work that you are reading. Plagiarism is a notoriously slippery concept. To plagiarize is defined in *The Concise Oxford Dictionary* as to 'take and use another person's (thoughts, writings, inventions . . .) as one's own'. The Wikipedia definition refers to plagiarism as 'the passing off of another's work as if it were one's own, by claiming credit for something that was actually done by someone else' (consulted on 27 July 2006). The same source refers to it as a 'serious and punishable academic offense'. Plagiarism does not just relate to the literature you read in the course of preparing an essay or report. Taking material in a wholesale and unattributed way from sources like essays written by others or from websites is also a context within which plagiarism can occur. Further, it is possible to self-plagiarize, as when a person lifts material that he or she has previously written and passes it off as original work. Plagiarism is commonly regarded as a form of academic cheating and as such differs little if at all in the minds of many academics from other academic misdemeanours such as fabricating research findings.

There is a widespread view that plagiarism among students is increasing in incidence, though whether this is in fact the case is difficult to establish unambiguously. Indeed, it is difficult to establish how widespread plagiarism is, and there are quite substantial variations in estimates of its prevalence. It is widely viewed that the Internet is one of the main—if not *the* main—motor behind the perceived increase in the prevalence of plagiarism. The ease with which text can be copied from web-sites, e-journal articles, e-books, online essays sold commercially, and numerous other sources and then pasted into essays is often viewed as one of the main factors behind the alleged rise in plagiarism cases among students in UK universities and elsewhere.

There are several difficulties with plagiarism as an issue in higher education. One is that universities vary in their definitions of what plagiarism is (Stefani and Carroll 2001). Further, they vary in their response to it when it is uncovered. They also vary in both the type and severity of punishment. Further, within any university, academic and other staff differ in their views of the sinfulness of plagiarism and how it should be handled (Flint *et al.* 2006). There is also evidence that students are less convinced than academic staff that plagiarism is wrong and that it should be punished.

In view of all these uncertainties of both definition of and the response to plagiarism, students may wonder whether they should take issues of plagiarism seriously. My answer is that they most definitely should take it seriously. Academic work places a high value on the originality of the work that is presented in any kind of output. To pass someone else's ideas and/or writings off as your own is widely regarded as morally dubious at best. Thus, while there are several grey areas with regard to plagiarism, as outlined in the previous paragraph, it is important not to overstate its significance. There *is* widespread condemnation of plagiarism in academic circles and it *is* nearly always punished when found in the work of students (and indeed that of others). You should therefore avoid plagiarizing the work of others at all costs. So concerned are universities about the growth in the number of plagiarism cases that come before examination boards and the likely role of the Internet in facilitating it that they are making more and more use of plagiarism detection software, which trawls the Internet for such things as strings of words (for example, Turnitin UK; see http://www.jiscpas.ac.uk/turnitinuk.php (accessed on 21 June 2007) for more information). Thus, as several writers (e.g. McKeever 2006) have observed, the very technological development that is widely perceived as promoting the incidence of plagiarism—the Internet—is increasingly the springboard for its detection. Even well-known and ubiquitous search engines like Google are sometimes employed to detect student plagiarism through the search for unique strings of words.

The most important issue from the student's point of view is that he or she should avoid plagiarism at all costs, as the penalties may be severe, regardless of the student's own views on the matter. First, do not 'lift' large sections of text without making it clear that they are in fact quotations. This makes it clear that the text in question is not your own work but that you are making a point by quoting someone. It is easy to get this wrong. In June 2006 it was reported that a plagiarism expert at the London School of Economics had been accused of plagiarism in a paper he published on plagiarism! A paragraph was found that copied verbatim a published source by someone else and that had not been acknowledged properly as from another source. The accused person defended himself by saying that this was due to a formatting error. It is common practice in academic publications to indent a large section of material that is being quoted, thus:

> The most important issue from the student's point of view is that they should avoid plagiarism at all costs, as the penalties may be severe, regardless of the student's own views on the matter. First, do not 'lift' large sections of text without making it clear that they are in fact quotations. This makes it clear that the text in question is not your own work but that you are making a point by quoting someone. It is easy to get this wrong. In June 2006 it was reported that a plagiarism expert at the London School of Economics had been accused of plagiarism in a paper he published on plagiarism! A paragraph was found that copied verbatim a published source by someone else and that had not been acknowledged properly as from another source. The accused person defended himself by saying that this was due to a formatting error. It is common practice in

> academic publications to indent a large section of material that is being quoted. (Bryman 2008: 108)

The lack of indentation meant that the paragraph in question looked like it was his own work. While it may be that this is a case of 'unintentional plagiarism' (Park 2003), distinguishing the intentional from the unintentional is by no means easy. Either way, the credibility and possibly the integrity of the author may be undermined. It is also important to realize that, for many if not most institutions, simply copying large portions of text and changing a few words will also be regarded as plagiarism.

Second, do not pass other people's ideas off as your own. This means that you should acknowledge the source of any ideas that you present that are not your own. It was this aspect of plagiarism that led to the case reported in Thinking deeply 4.6. Here, the accusers did not suggest that Dan Brown had taken large chunks of text from their work and presented it as his own. Instead, they accused him of lifting their ideas. However, Dan Brown *did* acknowledge his use of their historical work on the grail myth, though only in a general way in a list of acknowledgments, as novelists mercifully do not continuously reference ideas they use in their work. Brown's accusers lost their case, but there have been other high-profile cases of plagiarism that *have* been proved. For example, in 2003, the UK Prime Minister's Director of Communications and Strategy issued a briefing to journalists on the concealment of weapons in Iraq. This was found to have been copied from several sources and became known as the 'dodgy dossier'. The fact that so much of it had been taken from the work of others undermined its credibility in the eyes of others.

One of the most important messages of this section will hopefully be that you should guard against plagiarism at all costs. But it should also be clear that you should find out what your university and possibly departmental guidelines on the matter are. Quite aside from the rights and wrongs of plagiarism, it is not likely to impress your tutor if it is clear from reading the text that large chunks of your essay or report have been lifted from another source with just your own words interspersing the plagiarized text. In fact, that is often in my experience a giveaway—the contrast in styles is frequently very apparent and prompts the tutor to explore the possibility that some or much of the assignment you submit has in fact been plagiarized. Nor is it likely to impress most tutors if much of the text has been lifted but a few words changed here and there, along with a sprinkled few written by you.

Thinking deeply 4.6
Plagiarism and copyright in *The Da Vinci Code*

The bestselling novel by Dan Brown *The Da Vinci Code* was the focus of a recent ground-breaking High Court trial in 2006 that had significant implications for the understanding of plagiarism and copyright within the publishing industry. Brown was accused by two historians, Baigent and Leigh, who are the authors of an earlier non-fiction book entitled *The Holy Blood and the Holy Grail*, of infringement of copyright by having plagiarized the central theme that forms the basis of his plot. However, Brown's defence argued that authors have for centuries recycled ideas from other books and that the ideas in dispute are too general to be protected by copyright law. The case was further complicated by the fact that the publisher, Random House, was responsible for the publication of both books. Commenting on the case, Professor Lisa Jardine, from Queen Mary, University of London, was quoted as saying 'They are not going to win. I don't think plagiarism any longer holds up. We live in a world of cut and paste' (Smith 2006). In a witness statement to the court, Brown claimed he had read the claimants' book but not until he had already formulated the ideas and storyline for his novel. The judge rejected claims that Dan Brown's book was in breach of copyright, although he did concede that a comparison of the two books did show some limited copying of the text. Sales of both books rose during the trial, which took place shortly before the release of a feature film based on Brown's book.

However, there have also been other recent cases where charges of plagiarism in novels have been made with an outcome less favourable to the author accused. For example, teenage American novelist Viswanathan, author of *How Opal Mehta Got Kissed, Got Wild, and Got a Life*, was accused of plagiarizing sections of passages from another novel by Kinsella called *Can you Keep a Secret*, including entire sentences that were found to be virtually identical. Viswanathan claimed that the similarity was unintentional and attributed it to her photographic memory. The book was subsequently withdrawn from sale and the author's $500,000 contract with the publisher Little Brown & Company cancelled after it was found that there were also passages by other writers, including work by Salman Rushdie and Megan McCafferty. The key question, according to Lawson (2006), is whether the young novelist knew what she was doing and whether she accepts it was plagiarism. He also contends that the case highlights some of the pressures that novelists are placed under by publishers to make their mark in a market where they are competing against other forms of entertainment.

Although both these cases highlight the contested nature of charges of plagiarism, including the importance of ascertaining the author's intent, which is very difficult to do, they also draw attention to the moral judgement and significant penalties that may be levelled at an author if plagiarism is shown to have occurred. Although university students are not in a situation of risking multi-million-dollar deals in the same way as these novelists, the impact of plagiarism if it is shown to be significant can be highly detrimental in terms of their education and career prospects.

Sources: D. Smith, 'Da Vinci Trial Pits History against Art', *Observer,* 26 Feb. 2006; Anon., 'Brown Wins Da Vinci Code Case', *Guardian*, 7 April 2006; S. Goldenberg, 'Star Young Author Admits Unconscious Plagiarism', *Guardian*, 26 April 2006; M. Lawson, 'Fingers in the Word Till', *Guardian*, 6 May 2006.

However, equally it has to be said that frequent quoting with linking sentences by you is not likely to impress either. When I have been presented with essays of that kind, I have frequently said to the student concerned that it is difficult to establish just what his or her own thoughts on the issue are.

Try therefore to express your ideas in your own words and acknowledge properly those ideas that are not your own. Plagiarism is something you may get away with once or twice, but it is so imprinted on the consciousness of many of us working in universities nowadays that you are unlikely to get away with it regularly.

It is also extremely irritating to find that your own work has been plagiarized. I was asked to act as an external examiner of a doctoral thesis and found that large sections of one of my books had been taken and presented as the student's own work. I found this extremely annoying. A colleague to whom I mentioned the incident remarked that the only thing worse than plagiarism is incompetent plagiarism—incompetent because the student had plagiarized the work of someone he or she knew would be the external examiner. However, on reflection, the colleague was mistaken. Plagiarism is wrong—regardless of whether it is competently implemented or not. It is precisely for this reason that, in May 2007, Google banned advertisements from companies that write customized essays for students (http://news.bbc.co.uk/1/hi/education/6680457.stm (accessed on 21 June 2007)). Advice on plagiarism can usually be found in handbooks provided by students' institutions, as well as from http://www.jiscpas.ac.uk/ and http://www.plagiarism.org/ (both accessed on 21 June 2001).

One final point to note is that plagiarism is like a moving target. What it is, how it should be defined, how it can be detected, how it should be penalized: all these issues and others are in a state of flux as I write this chapter. It is very much a shifting situation precisely because of the perception that it is increasing in frequency. The penalties can be severe, and, as I have witnessed when students have been presented with evidence of their plagiarism, it can be profoundly embarrassing and distressing for them. The message is simple: do not do it and make sure that you know exactly what it is and how it is defined at your institution so that you do not inadvertently commit the sin of plagiarism.

Checklist

Questions to ask yourself when reviewing the literature

○ Is your list of references up to date in your current areas of interest? Are there new areas of interest that you need to search on?

○ What literature searching have you done recently?

○ What have you read recently? Have you found time to read?

○ What have you learned from the literature? Has this changed in any way your understanding of the subject in which you are working?

○ Is what you have read going to influence your research design in any way? Has it given you ideas about what you need to consider and incorporate?

○ Have you been writing notes on what you have read? Do you need to reconsider how what you have read fits into your research?

Source: adapted from Bruce (1994).

Key points

● Writing a literature review is a means of reviewing the main ideas and research relating to your chosen area of interest.

● A competent literature review confirms you as someone who is competent in the subject area.

- A great deal of the work of writing a literature review is based upon reading the work of other researchers in your subject area; key skills can be acquired to help you get the most from your reading.

- Systematic review is a method that is gaining in popularity in social research as a way of enhancing the reliability of literature searching and review.

- Narrative review is a more traditional approach that has advantages of flexibility, which can make it more appropriate for inductive research and qualitative research designs.

Questions for review

Reviewing the existing literature

- What are the main reasons for writing a literature review?
- How can you ensure that you get the most from your reading?
- What are the main advantages and disadvantages associated with systematic review?
- What type of research questions is systematic review most suited to addressing?
- What are the main reasons for conducting a narrative literature review?
- In what type of research is narrative review most appropriate?

Searching the existing literature

- What are the main ways of finding existing literature on your subject?
- What is a keyword and how is it useful in searching the literature?

Referencing your work

- Why is it important to reference your work?
- What are the main referencing styles used in academic work and which of these is preferred by your institution?
- What is the role of the bibliography and what makes a good one?

Avoiding plagiarism

- What is plagiarism?
- Why is it taken so seriously by researchers?

Online Resource Centre

http://www.oxfordtextbooks.co.uk/orc/brymansrm3e/

Visit the Online Resource Centre that accompanies this book to enrich your understanding of reviewing the literature. Consult web links, test yourself using multiple choice questions, and gain further guidance and inspiration from the Student Researcher's Toolkit.

5

Ethics and politics in social research

Chapter outline

Chapter guide

Ethical issues arise at a variety of stages in social research. This chapter deals with the concerns about ethics that might arise in the course of conducting research. The professional bodies concerned with the social sciences have been keen to spell out the ethical issues that can arise, and some of their statements will be reviewed in this chapter. Ethical issues cannot be ignored as they relate directly to the integrity of a piece of research and of the disciplines that are involved. While ethical issues constitute the main emphasis of this chapter, related issues to do with the politics of research are also discussed. This chapter explores:

- some famous, even infamous, cases in which transgressions of ethical principles have occurred, though it is important not to take the view that ethical concerns arise only in relation to these extreme cases;
- different stances that can be and have been taken on ethics in social research;
- the significance and operation of four areas in which ethical concerns particularly arise: whether harm comes to participants; informed consent; invasion of privacy; and deception;
- some of the difficulties associated with ethical decision-making;
- some of the main political dimensions of research, from gaining access to research situations to the publication of findings.

Introduction

Discussions about the ethics of social research bring us into a realm in which the role of values in the research process becomes a topic of concern. They revolve around such issues as:

- How should we treat the people on whom we conduct research?
- Are there activities in which we should or should not engage in our relations with them?

Questions about ethics in social research also bring in the role of professional associations, such as the British Sociological Association (BSA) and the Social Research Association (SRA), which have formulated codes of ethics. The BSA's and SRA's codes will be referred to on several occasions.

Statements of professional principles are frequently accessible from the Internet. Some of the most useful codes of ethics can be found at the following Internet addresses.

- British Sociological Association (BSA), *Statement of Ethical Practice*: http://www.britsoc.co.uk/user_doc/ Statement%20of%20Ethical%20Practice.pdf
- Social Research Association (SRA), *Ethical Guidelines*: http://www.the-sra.org.uk/documents/pdfs/ ethics03.pdf
- British Psychological Society (BPS), *Code of Conduct, Ethical Principles, and Guidelines*: http:// www.bps.org.uk/about/rules5.cfm
- American Sociological Association (ASA), *Code of Ethics*: http://www.asanet.org/galleries/default-file/ Code%20of%20Ethics.pdf

All these statements were accessed on 2 July 2007.

Writings about ethics in social research are frequently frustrating for four reasons.

1. Writers often differ quite widely from each other over ethical issues and questions. In other words, they differ over what is and is not ethically acceptable.

2. The main elements in the debates do not seem to move forward a great deal. The same kinds of points that were made in the 1960s were being rehashed in the late 1990s and at the start of the present century. One thing that *has* changed is that ethical issues are nowadays more central to discussions about research than ever before. This may be due to a greater sensitivity to ethical issues, but it is also to do with a greater concern among representatives of universities, research funding bodies, and professional associations to exhibit good ethical credentials. One social scientist has turned sociological thinking onto the current research environment by suggesting that concerns about ethical issues today have the characteristics of a 'moral panic' (Van den Hoonaard 2001).

3. Debates about ethics have often accompanied well-known, not to say notorious, cases of alleged ethical transgression. They include: the study of a religious cult by a group of disguised researchers (Festinger *et al.* 1956); the use of pseudo-patients in the study of mental hospitals (Rosenhan 1973; Research in focus 11.5); Rosenthal and Jacobson's (1968) field **experiment** to study teacher expectations in the classroom (Research in focus 2.1); and Holdaway's (1982, 1983; Research in focus 2.14) covert **ethnography** of a police force. The problem with this emphasis on notoriety is that it can be taken to imply that ethical concerns reside only in such extreme cases, when in fact the potential for ethical transgression is much more general than this. See Research in focus 5.1 and 5.2 for two cases that have acquired a celebrated status for their notoriety. It is striking that the research referred to in Research in focus 5.1 and 5.2 relates to investigations that occurred some decades ago. One of the reasons that authors (like me!) keep returning to these two cases is partly to do with the starkness of their ethical transgressions, but it is also to do with the fact that it would be difficult and most probably impossible to find such clear-cut cases of bad ethical practices in more recent years. That is a product of the greater ethical awareness among social researchers as well as the greater significance of ethical guidelines and research ethics committees nowadays. That it is not to say that research like Humphreys's in Research in focus 5.1 or Milgram's in Research in focus 5.2 is inconceivable today, but that it is a lot less likely to occur.

4. Related to this last point is the fact that these extreme and notorious cases of ethical violation tend to be associated with particular research methods—notably disguised observation and the use of deception in experiments. Again, the problem with this association of ethics with certain studies (and methods) is that it implies that ethical concerns only or even primarily reside in some methods but not others. As a result, the impression can be gleaned that other methods, such as **questionnaires** or overt observation, are immune from ethical problems. That is not the case. For example, conducting questionnaire or overt observation research with children will raise a lot of ethical issues that may not be the case when the research is on adults.

Research in focus 5.1
The infamous case of the sociologist as voyeur

An investigation that has almost achieved particular notoriety because of its ethics (or lack of them, some might argue) is Humphreys's (1970) infamous study of homosexual encounters in public toilets ('tearoom trade'). Humphreys's research interest was in impersonal sex, and, in order to shed light on this area, he took on the role of 'watchqueen'—that is, someone who watches out for possible intruders while men meet and engage in homosexual sex in public toilets. As a result of his involvement in these social scenes, Humphreys was able to collect the details of active participants' car licence numbers. He was then able to track down their names and addresses and ended up with a **sample** of 100 active tearoom-trade participants. He then conducted an interview survey of a sample of those who had been identified and of a further sample that acted as a point of comparison. The **interview schedule** was concerned with health issues and included some questions about marital sex. In order to reduce the risk of being remembered, Humphreys waited a year before contacting his respondents and also changed his hair style.

Research in focus 5.2
The infamous case of the psychologist as Nazi concentration camp commandant

Milgram (1963) was concerned with the circumstances associated with the use of brutality in the Nazi concentration camps of the Second World War. In particular, he was interested in the processes whereby a person can be induced to cause extreme harm to another by virtue of being ordered to do so. To investigate this issue further, Milgram devised a laboratory experiment. Volunteers were recruited to act out the role of teachers who punished learners (who were accomplices of the experimenter) by submitting them to electric shocks when they gave incorrect answers to questions. The shocks were not, of course, real, but the teachers/volunteers were not aware of this. The level of electric shock was gradually increased with successive incorrect answers, until the teacher/volunteer refused to administer more shocks. Learners had been trained to respond to the rising level of electric shock with simulated but appropriate howls of pain. In the room was a further accomplice of Milgram's who cajoled the teacher/volunteer to continue to administer shocks, suggesting that it was part of the study's requirements to continue and that they were not causing permanent harm, in spite of the increasingly shrill cries of pain. Milgram's study shows that people can be induced to cause very considerable pain to others, and as such he saw it as shedding light on the circumstances leading to the horrors of the concentration camp.

This is not the only experiment in which Milgram engaged in ethically dubious practices. Milgram used the 'lost letter technique', which entails deception and a lack of informed consent. As a means of measuring community orientations to political groups and other social institutions, Milgram and his co-researchers deposited unmailed letters in a variety of locations in a city (Milgram *et al.* 1965). The researchers wanted to create a situation in which a person must decide whether to post an apparently lost letter. Do finders ignore it or do they find a postbox so that it can reach its destination? Each envelope bore the name of the addressee, a box number address, and a stamp. Four addresses were used: Friends of the Nazi Party; Friends of the Communist Party; Medical Research Associates; and a personal letter. The researchers then kept a record of the proportion of each type of letter that was posted on to each of the four addresses. Letters to the last two addresses were far more likely to be posted on than those to the first two. This technique represents an **unobtrusive method** that would be categorized as an example of 'contrived observation' (see Key concept 11.2).

In this chapter, I will introduce the main ethical issues and debates about ethics. I am not going to try to resolve them, because they are not readily capable of resolution. This is why the ethical debate has scarcely moved on since the 1960s. What *is* crucial is to be aware of the ethical principles involved and of the nature of the concerns about ethics in social research. It is only if researchers are aware of the issues involved that they can make informed decisions about the implications of certain choices. If nothing else, you should be aware of the possible opprobrium that will be coming your way if you make certain kinds of choice. My chief concern lies with the ethical issues that arise in relations between researchers and research participants in the course of an investigation. This focus by no means exhausts the range of ethical issues and dilemmas that arise, such as those that might arise in relation to the funding of social research or how findings are used by non-researchers. However, the ethical issues that arise in the course of doing research are the ones that are most likely to impinge on students. Writers on research ethics adopt different stances concerning the ethical issues that arise in connection with relationships between researchers and research participants. Key concept 5.1 outlines some of these stances.

Key concept 5.1
Stances on ethics

Authors on social research ethics can be characterized in terms of the stances they take on the issue. The following stances can be distinguished.

- *Universalism.* A universalist stance takes the view that ethical precepts should never be broken. Infractions of ethical principles are wrong in a moral sense and are damaging to social research. This kind of stance can be seen in the writings of Erikson (1967), Dingwall (1980), and Bulmer (1982). Bulmer does, however, point to some forms of what appears to be disguised observation that may be acceptable. One is retrospective covert observation, which occurs when a researcher writes up his or her experiences in social settings in which he or she participated but not as a researcher. An example would be Van Maanen (1991*b*), who wrote up his experiences as a ride operator in Disneyland many years after he had been employed there in vacation jobs. Even a universalist like Erikson (1967: 372) recognizes that it 'would be absurd . . . to insist as a point of ethics that sociologists should always introduce themselves as investigators everywhere they go and should inform every person who figures in their thinking exactly what their research is all about'.

- *Situation ethics.* E. Goode (1996) has argued for deception to be considered on a case-by-case basis. In other words, he argues for what Fletcher (1966: 31) has called a 'situation ethics', or more specifically 'principled relativism', which can be contrasted with the universalist ethics of some writers. This argument has two ways of being represented.

  1. *The end justifies the means.* Some writers argue that, unless there is some breaking of ethical rules, we would never know about certain social phenomena. Fielding (1982) essentially argues for this position in relation to his research on the National Front, an extreme right-wing organization that was becoming politically influential in the 1970s. Without some kind of disguised observation, this important movement and its appeal would not have been studied. This is usually linked to the second form of a situationist argument in relation to social research ethics.

  2. *No choice.* It is often suggested that we have no choice but to engage in dissimulation on occasions if we want to investigate the issues in which we are interested. This view can be discerned in the writings of Holdaway (1982) and Homan (Homan and Bulmer 1982).

- *Ethical transgression is pervasive.* It is often observed that virtually all research involves elements that are at least ethically questionable. This occurs whenever participants are not given absolutely all the details on a piece of research, or when there is variation in the amount of knowledge about research. Punch (1994: 91), for example, observes that 'some dissimulation is intrinsic to social life and, therefore, to fieldwork'. He quotes Gans (1962: 44) in support of this point: 'If the researcher is completely honest with people about his activities, they will try to hide actions and attitudes they consider undesirable, and so will be dishonest. Consequently, the researcher must be dishonest to get honest data.'

- *Anything goes (more or less).* The writers associated with arguments relating to situation ethics and a recognition of the pervasiveness of ethical transgressions are arguing not for an 'anything-goes' mentality, but for a certain amount of flexibility in ethical decision-making. However, Douglas (1976) has argued that the kinds of deception in which social researchers engage are trivial compared to those perpetrated by powerful institutions in modern society (such as the mass media, the police, and industry). His book is an inventory of tactics for deceiving people so that their trust is gained and they reveal themselves to the researcher. Very few researchers subscribe to this stance. Denzin (1968) comes close to an anything-goes stance when he suggests that social researchers are entitled to study anyone in any setting provided the work has a 'scientific' purpose, does not harm participants, and does not deliberately damage the discipline. The harm-to-participants criterion can also be seen in the case reported in Research in focus 5.3.

- *Deontological versus consequentialist ethics.* Another distinction that has attracted interest in recent years is between deontological and consequentialist ethics. Deontological ethics considers certain acts as wrong (or good) in and of themselves. Consequentialist ethics looks at the consequences of an act for guidance of whether it is right or wrong. In relation to the consideration of ethical issues in social research, deontological arguments tend to prevail—in terms of the issues covered below, deceiving research participants or *not* providing them with the opportunity for informed consent are regarded as ethically wrong. Consequentialist arguments do sometimes surface, however. For example, you sometimes see the argument that an activity like covert observation is wrong because it can harm the reputation of the profession of social research or of an organization. As such, other social researchers would be adversely affected by the ethically dubious decision to engage in covert observation.

Tips and skills
Ethics committees

In addition to needing to be familiar with the codes of practice produced by several professional associations such as the British Sociological Association, the American Sociological Association, and the Social Research Association, you should be acquainted with the ethical guidelines of your university or college. Most higher education organizations have ethics committees that issue guidelines about ethical practice. These guidelines are often based on or influenced by the codes developed by professional associations. Universities' and colleges' guidelines will provide indications of what are considered ethically unacceptable practices. Sometimes you will need to submit your proposed research to an ethics committee of your university or college. This is likely to occur if there is some uncertainty about whether your proposed research is likely to be in breach of the guidelines or if you want to go ahead with research that you know is ethically dubious but you wish to obtain permission to do it anyway. The ethical guidelines and the ethics committee are there to protect research participants, but they are also involved in protecting institutions, so that researchers will be deterred from behaving in ethically unacceptable ways that might rebound on institutions. Such behaviour could cause problems for institutions if ethically inappropriate behaviour gave rise to legal action against them or to adverse publicity. However, ethics committees and their guidelines are there to help and protect researchers too, so that they are less likely to conduct research that could damage their reputations.

One of the main approaches used by ethics committees is to ask researchers to indicate whether their research entails certain procedures or activities (which are often derived from professional guidelines like the BSA's *Statement of Ethical Practice* or the Economic and Social Research Council (ESRC)'s *Research Ethics Framework* (*REF*) (see Tips and skills 'The ESRC's *Research Ethics Framework*'), such as disguised observation, so that effectively they self-declare whether they are likely to engage in ethically dubious practices. If they indicate that they are in fact likely to engage in such a practice, the proposed research is then 'flagged' for full scrutiny by the ethics committee. In such an instance, the researcher is required to provide a full account of the research and the rationale for using the ethically dubious practice(s). This can slow down research a great deal and can of course result in the committee refusing to allow it to proceed.

In recent years, research ethics committees (often called Institutional Review Boards in the USA) have become quite controversial. Some writers see them as too influenced by a natural science model of the research process and as therefore inimical to social research and to **qualitative research** in particular (Lincoln and Tierney 2004). Further, they are sometimes seen as having gone too far in terms of their role of protecting institutions from litigious disgruntled research participants (Van Den Hoonard 2001). Further, it has been suggested that they divert attention from the need to be constantly vigilant for ethical problems that might arise in the course of doing research (Guillemin and Gillam 2004). In other words, there is a concern that, once the researcher has jumped over the bureaucratic hurdle of the ethics committee, he or she may feel that the ethical issues have been covered. This is clearly not the case, as ethical issues can and invariably do arise at all stages of the research process.

Ethical principles

Discussions about ethical principles in social research, and perhaps more specifically transgressions of them, tend to revolve around certain issues that recur in different guises, but they have been usefully broken down by Diener and Crandall (1978) into four main areas:

1. whether there is *harm to participants*;
2. whether there is a *lack of informed consent*;
3. whether there is an *invasion of privacy*;
4. whether *deception* is involved.

I will look at each of these in turn, but it should be appreciated that these four principles overlap somewhat. For example, it is difficult to imagine how the principle of informed consent could be built into an investigation in which research participants were deceived. However, there is no doubt that these four areas form a useful classification of ethical principles in and for social research.

Harm to participants

Research that is likely to harm participants is regarded by most people as unacceptable. But what is harm? Harm can entail a number of facets: physical harm; harm to participants' development; loss of self-esteem; stress; and 'inducing subjects to perform reprehensible acts', as Diener and Crandall (1978: 19) put it. In several studies that we have encountered in this book, there has been real or potential harm to participants.

- In the Rosenthal and Jacobson (1968) study (Research in focus 2.2), it is at least possible that the pupils who had not been identified as 'spurters' who would excel in their studies were adversely affected in their intellectual development by the greater attention received by the spurters.

- In the Festinger *et al.* (1956) study of a religious cult, it is quite likely that the fact that the researchers joined the group at a crucial time—close to the projected end of the world—fuelled the delusions of group members.

- Many of the participants in the Milgram (1963) experiment on obedience to authority (Research in focus 5.2) experienced high levels of stress and anxiety as a consequence of being incited to administer electric shocks. It could also be argued that Milgram's

observers were 'inducing subjects to perform reprehensible acts'. Indeed, yet another series of studies in which Milgram was involved placed participants in positions where they were being influenced to steal (Milgram and Shotland 1973).

- Many of the participants in Humphreys's (1970) research (see Research in focus 5.1) were married men who are likely to have been fearful of detection as practising homosexuals. It is not inconceivable that his methods could have resulted in some of them becoming identified against their will.

The BSA *Statement of Ethical Practice* enjoins researchers to 'anticipate, and to guard against, consequences for research participants which can be predicted to be harmful' and 'to consider carefully the possibility that the research experience may be a disturbing one'. Similar sentiments are expressed by the SRA's *Ethical Guidelines*, for example, when it is advocated that the 'social researcher should try to minimize disturbance both to subjects themselves and to the subjects' relationships with their environment'.

The issue of harm to participants is further addressed in ethical codes by advocating care over maintaining the confidentiality of records. This means that the identities and records of individuals should be maintained as confidential. This injunction also means that care needs to be taken when findings are being published to ensure that individuals are not identified or identifiable. The case of a study of an American town, Springdale (a pseudonym), by Vidich and Bensman (1968) is instructive in this regard. The research was based on Vidich's participant observation within the town for over two years. The published book on the research was uncomplimentary about the town and many of its leaders and was written in what many people felt was a rather patronizing tone. To make matters worse, it was possible to identify individuals through the published account. The town's inhabitants responded with a Fourth of July Parade in which many of the inhabitants wore badges with their pseudonyms, and an effigy of Vidich was set up so that it was peering into manure. The townspeople also responded by announcing their refusal to cooperate in any more social research. The inhabitants were clearly upset by the publication and to that extent were harmed by it. This example also touches on the issue of privacy, which will be addressed below.

As this last case suggests, the issue of confidentiality raises particular difficulties for many forms of qualitative research. In quantitative research, it is relatively easy to make records anonymous and to report findings in a way that does not allow individuals to be identified. However, this is often less easy with qualitative research, where particular care has to be taken with regard to the possible identification of persons and places. The use of pseudonyms is a common recourse, but may not elimi-

nate entirely the possibility of identification. This issue raises particular problems with regard to the secondary analysis of qualitative data (see Chapter 22), since it is very difficult, though by no means impossible, to present field notes and interview transcripts in a way that will prevent people and places from being identified. As Alderson (1998) has suggested, the difficulty is one of being able to ensure that the same safeguards concerning confidentiality can be guaranteed when secondary analysts examine such records as those provided by the original primary researcher.

Tips and skills
Data protection

One aspect of confidentiality and the management of it is that, in the UK, the Data Protection Act (1998) confers obligations on people and organizations who hold personal data on others and it confers rights on those about whom such information is held. The Information Commissioner's website points out the following about the Act:

> Firstly, it [the Data Protection Act] states that anyone who processes personal information must comply with eight principles, which make sure that personal information is:
>
> - Fairly and lawfully processed
> - Processed for limited purposes
> - Adequate, relevant and not excessive
> - Accurate and up to date
> - Not kept for longer than is necessary
> - Processed in line with your rights
> - Secure
> - Not transferred to other countries without adequate protection
>
> The second area covered by the Act provides individuals with important rights, including the right to find out what personal information is held on computer and most paper records. (**http://www.ico.gov.uk/ what_we_cover/data_protection/the_basics.aspx** (accessed on 12 February 2007)).

These principles are important to bear in mind, as it is clear that it is easy to fall foul of them when conducting social research. However, Section 33 of the Act effectively exempts personal information collected for research purposes from some of these principles. According to this section, the researcher must ensure that 'the data are not processed to support measures or decisions with respect to particular individuals' and that 'the data are not processed in such a way that substantial damage or substantial distress is, or is likely to be, caused to any data subject' (**http://www.opsi.gov.uk/ACTS/acts1998/80029--e.htm#33** (accessed on 12 February 2007)). Also important is that it is stipulated that research is exempt only if 'the results of the research or any resulting statistics are not made available in a form that identifies data subjects or any of them' (**http://www.opsi.gov.uk/ACTS/acts1998/80029--e.htm#33** (accessed on 12 February 2007)). This stipulation again points to the importance of ensuring that confidentiality is ensured and that individuals are not identifiable.

Responsibilities of researchers with respect to confidentiality are also laid down in the *Research Governance Framework for Health and Social Care* (*RGF*) of 2005. The *RGF* is concerned to provide a framework for research in the fields of health and social care that reduces risks and ensures the well-being of research participants. The *RGF* is meant to cover all research that takes place in organizations like hospitals or social care agencies and as such includes any social research that takes place in such locations. For example, it is stipulated in Section 3.5.1 that researchers are responsible for 'protecting the integrity and confidentiality of clinical and other records and data generated by the research' (**http://www.dh.gov.uk/assetRoot/04/12/24/27/04122427.pdf** (accessed on 12 February 2007)).

Holmes (2004) provides some important and useful suggestions about how to protect confidentiality and participants' data. Her tips include:

- not storing participants' names and addresses or letter correspondence on hard drives;
- using identifier codes on data files and storing the list of participants and their identifier codes separately in a locked cabinet;
- ensuring that transcribers sign a letter saying they will conform to the Data Protection Act;
- ensuring transcripts do not include participants' names;
- keeping copies of transcripts in a locked cabinet.

The central point of this Tips and skills feature is to reinforce the point that there is an environment that takes confidentiality and data protection issues very seriously and that it is important for students and researchers generally to be attuned to their obligations and what is required of them.

The need for confidentiality can present dilemmas for researchers. Westmarland (2001) has discussed the dilemmas she faced when observing violence by the police towards people being held in custody. She argues that, while a certain level of violence might be deemed acceptable, in part to protect the officers themselves and the public, there is an issue of at what point it is no longer acceptable and the researcher needs to inform on those involved. Moreover, such a reasonable level of violence may be consistent with the police occupational culture. The problem for the ethnographer is compounded by the fact that blowing the whistle on violence may result in a loss of the researcher's credibility among officers, premature termination of the investigation, or inability to gain access in the future. In the process, career issues are brought to the fore for the researcher, which connects with the discussion of political issues towards the end of this chapter. Similarly, in a feminist study of girls' experiences of violence, Burman *et al.* (2001: 455) encountered some distressing revelations that prompted them to ask 'exactly what, and how much, should be disclosed, to whom, and how should this be done'. Thus, the important injunction to protect confidentiality may create dilemmas for the researcher that are by no means easy to resolve.

The issue of confidentiality is clearly a very important one in its own right. Israel and Hay (2004) treat it as a separate principle of ethics in its own right. As they observe, if researchers do not observe the confidentiality of what is said to them, 'who would talk to them in the future?' (Israel and Hay 2004: 94). Thus, quite aside from the intrinsic wrongness of not keeping confidences, there is the consequentialist argument that it could harm generations of future researchers.

One of the problems with the harm-to-participants principle is that it is not possible to identify in all circumstances whether harm is likely, though that fact should not be taken to mean that there is no point in seeking to protect them from harm. Kimmel (1988) notes in this connection the example of the Cambridge-Summerville Youth Study. In 1939 an experiment was conducted on boys aged 5–13 who were either identified as likely to become delinquent or were average in this regard. The 506 boys were equally divided in terms of this characteristic. They were randomly assigned either to an experimental group in which they received preventative counselling or to a no-treatment control group. In the mid-1970s the records were re-examined and were quite shocking: 'Treated subjects were more likely than controls to evidence signs of alcoholism and serious mental illness, died at a younger age, suffered from more stress-related diseases, tended to be employed in lower-prestige occupations, and were more likely to commit second crimes' (Kimmel 1988: 19).

In other words, the treatment brought about a train of negative consequences for the group. This is an extreme example and relates to experimental research, which is not a research design that is commonly employed in social research (see Chapter 2), but it does illustrate the difficulty of anticipating harm to respondents. The ASA *Code of Ethics* suggests that, if there is any prospect of harm to participants, informed consent, the focus of the next section, is essential: 'Informed consent must be obtained when the risks of research are greater than the risks of everyday life. Where modest risk or harm is anticipated, informed consent must be obtained.'

Lack of informed consent

The issue of informed consent is in many respects the area within social research ethics that is most hotly debated. The bulk of the discussion tends to focus on what is variously called disguised or covert observation. Such observation can involve covert participant observation (Key concept 17.2), or simple or contrived observation (Key concept 11.2), in which the researcher's true identity is unknown. The principle means that prospective research participants should be given as much information as might be needed to make an informed decision about whether or not they wish to participate in a study. Covert observation transgresses that principle, because participants are not given the opportunity to refuse to cooperate. They are involved, whether they like it or not.

Lack of informed consent is a feature of the research in Research in focus 5.1 and 5.2. In Humphreys's research informed consent is absent, because the men for whom he acted as a watchqueen were not given the opportunity to refuse participation in his investigation. Similar points can be made about several other studies previously encountered in this book, such as Festinger *et al.* (1956), Rosenthal and Jacobson (1968), Patrick (1973), Rosenhan (1973), Fielding (1981, 1982), and Holdaway (1982, 1983). The principle of informed consent also entails the implication that, even when people know they are being asked to participate in research, they should be fully informed about the research process. As the SRA *Ethical Guidelines* suggests:

Inquiries involving human subjects should be based as far as practicable on the freely given informed consent of subjects. Even if participation is required by law, it should still be as informed as possible. In voluntary inquiries, subjects should not be under the impression that they are required to participate. They should be aware of their entitlement to refuse at any stage for whatever reason and to withdraw data just supplied. Information that would be likely to affect a subject's willingness to participate should not be deliberately withheld, since this would remove from subjects an important means of protecting their own interests.

Similarly, the BSA *Statement* says:

As far as possible participation in sociological research should be based on the freely given informed consent of those studied. This implies a responsibility on the sociologist to explain as fully as possible, and in terms meaningful to participants, what the research is about, who is undertaking and financing it, why it is being undertaken, and how it is to be promoted.

Thus, while Milgram's experimental subjects were volunteers and therefore knew they were going to participate in research, there is a lack of informed consent, because they were not given full information about the nature of the research and its possible implications for them.

However, as Homan (1991: 73) has observed, implementing the principle of informed consent 'is easier said than done'. At least two major points stand out here.

- It is extremely difficult to present prospective participants with absolutely all the information that might be required for them to make an informed decision about their involvement. In fact, relatively minor transgressions probably pervade most social research, such as deliberately underestimating the amount of time that an interview is likely to take so that people are not put off being interviewed and not giving absolutely all the details about one's research for fear of contaminating people's answers to questions.

- In ethnographic research, the researcher is likely to come into contact with a wide spectrum of people, and ensuring that absolutely everyone has the opportunity for informed consent is not practicable, because it would be extremely disruptive in everyday contexts. For example, in the passage from Punch's field notes in

Research in focus 17.7, the meandering cyclist could not be given the opportunity for informed consent. Punch was not a disguised participant observer so far as the police were concerned, but *was* disguised in connection with many of those with whom the police had encounters in the course of his fieldwork. Also, even when all research participants in a certain setting are aware that the ethnographer is a researcher, it is doubtful whether they are all similarly (let alone identically) informed about the nature of the research.

In spite of the widespread condemnation of violations of informed consent and the view that covert observation is especially vulnerable to accusations of unethical practice in this regard, studies using the method still appear periodically (e.g. Fielding 1982; Taylor 1999). The defence is usually of the 'end-justifies-the-means' kind, which is further discussed below. What is interesting in this present context is that the BSA *Statement* essentially leaves the door ajar for covert observation. The phrase 'as far as possible' regarding informed consent in the last quotation from the *Statement* does this, but the BSA then goes even further in relation to covert research:

> There are serious ethical and legal issues in the use of covert research but the use of covert methods may be justified in certain circumstances. For example, difficulties arise when research participants change their behaviour because they know they are being studied. Researchers may also face problems when access to spheres of social life is closed to social scientists by powerful or secretive interests. . . . However, covert methods violate the principles of informed consent and may invade the privacy of those being studied. Participant or non-participant observation in non-public spaces or experimental manipulation of research participants without their knowledge should be resorted to only where it is impossible to use other methods to obtain essential data. . . . In such studies it is important to safeguard the anonymity of research participants. Ideally, where informed consent has not been obtained prior to the research it should be obtained post-hoc.

While this statement hardly condones the absence of informed consent associated with covert research, it is not unequivocally censorious either. It recognizes that covert research 'may avoid certain problems' and refers, without using the term, to the possibility of reactivity associated with overt observational methods. It also

recognizes that covert methods can help to get over the difficulty of gaining access to certain kinds of setting. The passage entails an acknowledgement that informed consent is jeopardized, along with the privacy principle (see below), but implies that covert research can be used 'where it is impossible to use other methods to obtain essential data'. The difficulty here clearly is how a researcher is to decide whether it is in fact impossible to obtain data other than by covert work. I suspect that, by and large, covert observers typically make their judgements in this connection on the basis of the *anticipated* difficulty of gaining access to a setting or of encountering reactivity problems, rather than as a response to difficulties they have actually experienced. For example, Holdaway (1982: 63) has written that, as a police officer, his only alternatives to covert participant observation were either equally unethical (but less desirable) or 'unrealistic'. Similarly, Homan justified his use of covert participant observation of a religious sect on the grounds that sociologists were viewed very negatively by group members and therefore 'it seemed probable that the prevalence of such a perception would prejudice the effectiveness of a fieldworker declaring an identity as sociologist' (Homan and Bulmer 1982: 107). The issue of the circumstances in which violations of ethical principles, like informed consent, are deemed acceptable will reappear in the discussion below.

The principle of informed consent is also bound up to some extent with the issue of harm to participants. Erikson has suggested that, if the principle is not followed and if participants are harmed as a result of the research, the investigator is more culpable than if they did not know. For example, he writes: 'If we happen to harm people who have agreed to act as subjects, we can at least argue that they knew something of the risks involved . . .' (Erikson 1967: 369). While this might seem like a recipe for seeking a salve for the sociologist's conscience, it does point to an important issue—namely, that the social researcher is more likely to be vilified if participants are adversely affected when they were not willing accomplices than when they were. However, it is debatable whether that means that the researcher is any less culpable for that harm. Erikson implies they are less culpable, but this is a potential area for disagreement.

Informed consent forms

Increasingly, researchers prefer to obtain the informed consent of research participants by getting them to sign informed consent forms. For her postgraduate research on lesbian and gay awareness training, Peel (2004) used a consent form that outlined the purposes of the research and its background. The form then notified prospective interviewees that:

- their participation was voluntary;
- they were free to refuse to answer any of the questions;
- they could withdraw from the interview at any time; and
- they could withdraw their data within two weeks of the interview.

She also notified them that the interview would be recorded, that nobody but she and her supervisors would listen to the interview, that small sections might be heard by a few others, that it would be transcribed but all identifying information would be removed, and that parts of the interview might be used in her thesis and/or publications. Prospective interviewees were then asked to sign the form to confirm their consent.

The advantage of such forms is that they give respondents the opportunity to be fully informed of the nature of the research and the implications of their participation at the outset. Further, the researcher has a signed record of consent if any concerns are subsequently raised by participants or others. The chief possible problem is that the requirement to sign the form may prompt rather than alleviate concerns on the part of prospective participants, so that they end up declining to be involved.

Student experience
Informed consent forms

For Rebecca Barnes, 'ethical issues were a paramount concern, especially given the extremely sensitive and emotive nature of the topic'. She designed a participant information sheet and a consent form 'in order to make participants aware of their rights, and to advise them of the possible negative consequences of participating in the research'. Erin Sanders writes that she did not develop a consent form:

> because the women I interviewed didn't read English and I can't write in Thai, I didn't have a signed consent form. I was able to get verbal consent—but now I feel it might have been better to have a document translated into Thai—so that they understood the research—but also understood their rights and the steps that would be taken to safeguard their identities.

To read more about Rebecca's and Erin's research experiences, go to the Online Resource Centre that accompanies this book at **http://www.oxfordtextbooks.co.uk/orc/brymansrm3e/**.

Invasion of privacy

This third area of ethical concern relates to the issue of the degree to which invasions of privacy can be condoned. The right to privacy is a tenet that many of us hold dear, and transgressions of that right in the name of research are not regarded as acceptable. It is very much linked to the notion of informed consent, because, to the degree that informed consent is given on the basis of a detailed understanding of what the research participant's involvement is likely to entail, he or she in a sense acknowledges that the right to privacy has been surrendered for that limited domain. The BSA *Statement* makes a direct link in the

passage quoted on page 122 when it suggests: 'covert methods violate the principles of informed consent and may invade the privacy of those being studied.' Of course, the research participant does not abrogate the right to privacy entirely by providing informed consent. For example, when people agree to be interviewed, they will frequently refuse to answer certain questions on whatever grounds they feel are justified. Often, these refusals will be based on a feeling that certain questions delve into private realms, which respondents do not wish to make public, regardless of the fact that the interview is in private. Examples might be questions about income, religious beliefs, or sexual activities.

Covert methods are usually deemed to be violations of the privacy principle on the grounds that participants are not being given the opportunity to refuse invasions of their privacy. Such methods also mean that they might reveal confidences or information that they would not have revealed if they had known about the status of the confidant as researcher. The issue of privacy is invariably linked to issues of anonymity and confidentiality in the research process, an area that has already been touched on in the context of the question of whether harm comes to participants. The BSA *Statement* forges this kind of connection: 'The anonymity and privacy of those who participate in the research process should be respected. Personal information concerning research participants should be kept confidential. In some cases it may be necessary to decide whether it is proper or appropriate to record certain kinds of sensitive information.'

Raising issues about ensuring anonymity and confidentiality in relation to the recording of information and the maintenance of records relates to all methods of social research. In other words, while covert research may pose certain kinds of problem regarding the invasion of privacy, other methods of social research are implicated in possible difficulties in connection with anonymity and confidentiality. This was clearly the case with the Springfield research (Vidich and Bensman 1968), which was based on open participant observation. The issue here was that the absence of safeguards concerning the protection of the identity of some members of the community meant that certain matters about them came into the public domain that should have remained private.

Student experience
Anonymity and confidentiality

Rebecca Barnes writes that, in the participant information sheet she prepared, she stopped short of *guaranteeing* anonymity and confidentiality.

> I assured participants that I would do my utmost to uphold confidentiality and anonymity, but I was cautious about guaranteeing confidentiality and anonymity. Factors outside a researcher's control such as theft of confidential documents make such guarantees misleading. Nonetheless, I did do everything that I could to ensure confidentiality and anonymity, such as using pseudonyms in transcripts and beyond; storing interview tapes, transcripts, and participants' contact details separately. Also, when I transcribed the interviews, I altered specific details that could make a participant identifiable, such as the area in which they live, their occupation, and other details such as pubs or nightclubs that participants referred to. I ensured that the details that I changed did not change the meaning of participants' words in any way.

To read more about Rebecca's research experiences, go to the Online Resource Centre that accompanies this book at http://www.oxfordtextbooks.co.uk/orc/brymansrm3e/.

Deception

Deception occurs when researchers represent their work as something other than what it is. The two studies by Milgram referred to in Research in focus 5.2 involve deception. In the obedience-to-authority experiment, participants are led to believe they are administering real electric shocks. In the lost-letter study, deception occurs because people who place the lost letters in a postbox, so that they will be sent to their destinations, believe they are sending letters that have been accidentally lost rather than ones that have been deposited for a social psychological experiment. Deception in various degrees is probably quite widespread in such research, because researchers often want to limit participants' understanding of what the research is about so that they respond more naturally to the experimental treatment.

However, deception is by no means the exclusive pre-serve of social psychology experiments. E. Goode (1996), for example, placed four fake and slightly different dating advertisements in periodicals. He received nearly 1,000 replies and was able to conduct a content analysis of them. Several of the studies referred to in this book entail deception: Rosenthal and Jacobson (1968) deceived teachers into believing that particular children in their charge were likely to excel at school, when they had in fact been randomly selected; Festinger *et al.* (1956) deceived cult members that they were in fact real con-verts; Rosenhan's (1973) associates deceived admissions staff at mental hospitals that they were mentally ill; and Holdaway (1982) deceived his superiors and peers that he was functioning solely as a police officer.

The ethical objection to deception seems to turn on two points. First, it is not a nice thing to do. While the SRA *Guidelines* recognizes that deception is widespread in social interaction, it is hardly desirable. Second, there is the question of professional self-interest. If social researchers became known as snoopers who deceived people as a matter of professional course, the image of our work would be adversely affected and we might experience difficulty in gaining financial support and the cooperation of future prospective research participants. As the SRA *Guidelines* puts it: 'It remains the duty of social

researchers and their collaborators, however, not to pur-sue methods of inquiry that are likely to infringe human values and sensibilities. To do so, whatever the method-ological advantages, would be to endanger the reputation of social research and the mutual trust between social researchers and society which is a prerequisite for much research.' Similarly, Erikson (1967: 369) has argued that disguised observation 'is liable to damage the reputation of sociology in the larger society and close off promising areas of research for future investigators'.

One of the chief problems with the discussion of this aspect of ethics is that deception is, as some writers observe, widespread in social research (see the stance 'Ethical transgression is pervasive' in Key concept 5.1). It is rarely feasible or desirable to provide participants with a totally complete account of what your research is about. As Punch (1979) found in the incident referred to in Research in focus 17.7, he could hardly announce to the youth or the meandering cyclist that he was not in fact a police officer and then launch into a lengthy account of his research. Bulmer (1982), whose stance is predomin-antly that of a universalist in ethics terms (see Key con-cept 5.1), nonetheless recognizes that there are bound to be instances such as this and deems them justifiable. However, it is very difficult to know where the line should be drawn here.

 # Ethics and the issue of quality

Possibly one of the most interesting developments in con-nection with ethical issues is that a criterion of the ethical integrity of an investigation is its *quality*. For example, the ESRC's *REF* states that 'Research should be designed, reviewed and undertaken in a way that ensures its integrity and quality' (para. 3.2.1) and immediately goes on to say that 'This principle is at the heart of the *REF*'. See Tips and skills 'The ESRC's *Research Ethics Framework*' for more on this set of guidelines. Similarly a list of criteria for assessing the quality of qualitative research studies includes the criterion 'Evidence of consideration of eth-ical issues' (Spencer *et al.* 2003). This list of criteria was devised in connection with a report produced for the UK Government's Cabinet Office. Also, the *RGF* referred to in Tips and skills 'Data protection' states that 'research which is not of sufficient quality to contribute something use-ful to existing knowledge is unethical' (Department of

Health 2005: para. 2.3.1). Whether this link that is increasingly being forged between ethical integrity and research quality is a distinctively UK orientation, as hinted at by Israel and Hay (2004: 52), is an interesting question.

Anyone intending to conduct social research at a site associated with the National Health Service (NHS) or that involves NHS personnel or patients will face the additional hurdle of having to secure ethical clearance from a Research Ethics Committee (REC). There is a national framework of RECs in the UK, and it is a re-quirement under the *RGF* to secure clearance. Before 1 April 2007 the system was run by the Central Office of Research Ethics Committees, but it is now under the National Research Ethics Service, which is part of the National Patient Safety Agency. The latter's website con-tains a great deal of information concerning the process of applying for ethical clearance for research involving the NHS and a variety of documents about its procedures (http://www.nres.npsa.nhs.uk/index.htm (accessed 25 June 2007)). Three points should be noted about the system by anyone thinking of conducting social research that will require clearance by a REC. First, it is a slow process, so plenty of time needs to be allowed. Second, only around 15 per cent of applications are given clearance without further consideration. Most applications (around 64 per cent) result in issues being raised to which the applicant has to respond. Around 6 per cent are declined first time around. The rest are either considered by the REC not to be part of their remit or are withdrawn (Dixon-Woods *et al.* 2007). Third, RECs frequently raise issues about the quality of the research (see Thinking deeply 5.1).

Thinking deeply 5.1
Ethics and quality in a study of REC letters

Angell *et al.* (2008) conducted a content analysis (see Key concept 12.1 for a brief description of this technique) of 141 letters written on behalf of RECs. These were letters written to applicants seeking ethical clearance to proceed with research involving the NHS. The letters analysed were either of two types: letters that signalled either an unfavourable decision (i.e. the research could not go ahead because of concerns about ethical issues) or a provisional decision (i.e. clarification of certain issues was required or the applicant needed to indicate that he or she would change certain procedures in line with the REC's recommendations). Angell *et al.* found that issues relating to the quality of the proposed research, which the authors refer to as 'scientific issues', were raised in the context of 74 per cent of the letters analysed. The three most common concerns were: concerns about the sample; issues relating to the choice of methods; and concerns about the research question. For example, in the case of issues relating to the choice of methods, the most common complaint from RECs was that the rationale for the choice of method was unclear. However, they frequently also made judgements about the appropriateness of a method or how it was to be implemented. The point of this research is that it demonstrates that, at least as far as RECs are concerned, the distinction between ethics and scientific quality is not a stable one and that they frequently shade into each other. Thus, what is and is not an ethical issue is by no means a clear-cut matter.

Student experience
Not doing research involving the NHS

The ethical approval process can be very offputting for students. This was certainly the case for Isabella Robbins, who decided not to go through the NHS to conduct her investigation of childhood vaccinations because of the problems of getting ethical clearance.

I avoided using state organizations—e.g. the NHS—because of the lengthy and problematic system of gaining ethical approval. I was advised to approach self-help and informal groups. I sent a letter of introduction to leaders and chairpersons of organizing committees running these groups, outlining the aims and objectives of my project. I prepared a leaflet outlining my research and I asked group leaders to post leaflets and posters in the halls where these groups are held.

To read more about Isabella's research experiences, go to the Online Resource Centre that accompanies this book at http://www.oxfordtextbooks.co.uk/orc/brymansrm3e/.

The point of this brief section is only partly to draw attention to the way in which ethical issues are becoming entangled with matters of research quality, because there is a significant implication of this development. This implication is that it is increasingly likely that committees charged with the task of considering applications for ethical clearance will be commenting on the quality of researchers' proposed procedures. If quality is deemed to be a component of the ethical domain, it is at the very least distinctly possible that applicants for ethical clearance will find themselves having to defend decisions to do with their sampling, their interview guide, or their questionnaire on technical grounds, in addition to the areas, like those previously covered, that are part of the traditional domain of ethical considerations (for example, informed consent or harm to participants).

Tips and skills
The ESRC's *Research Ethics Framework*

In the UK context, the publication by the Economic and Social Research Council (ESRC) in 2005 of a document outlining its position on ethical issues and proving guidance on ethical matters was very significant. The ESRC is the major agency in the UK for funding social scientific research. It provides funding both for research projects, usually carried out by academics applying for support for significant investigations, and for postgraduate research in the form of studentships. The *Research Ethics Framework* (*REF*) outlines the Council's requirements in terms of ethical practice(s) for the research it supports. There is a broader perspective too, in that the ESRC intends through the *REF* to influence the ethical practices of social science research generally; in other words, it intends the influence of the *REF* to extend beyond research it supports. The *REF* lays down six principles of ethical research.

1. As noted above, ethical research is of a high quality. Thus, if a study is poorly designed, quite aside from the fact that it almost certainly would not receive financial support from the ESRC, it is unethical.

2. 'Research staff and subjects must be informed fully about the purpose, methods and intended possible uses of the research, what their participation entails and what risks, if any, are involved.'

3. Confidentiality of information must be maintained and anonymity of participants respected.

4. The involvement of research participants must be entirely voluntary.

5. 'Harm to participants must be avoided.'

6. 'The independence of research must be made clear, and any conflicts of interest or partiality must be explicit.' This draws attention to the possible role of affiliation bias to which some writers on ethics in research draw attention (Bell and Bryman 2007).

It is striking that the inclusion of the issue of quality in principle 1, of research staff in principle 2, and of possible conflicts of interest in principle 6 extend the reach of ethical issues when compared to those explored by Diener and Crandall (1978), which were reviewed above.

Also of considerable significance are the ESRC's proposals for the ways in which ethical issues should be given due consideration. The following are the main points concerning the Council's expectations regarding the process of handling ethical issues.

- ESRC does not expect ethical approval to have been obtained before submitting a proposal for funding. However, applicants need to specify what ethical approval is needed and how it will be achieved.

- When a proposal is peer-reviewed, reviewers and assessors are asked to comment on the self-assessment. This may lead to rejection if reviewers or assessors feel the self-assessment is wholly inadequate.

- If the application is successful, the ESRC will not release funds until there is a written confirmation from the institution where the research is to be conducted that the ethical approval outlined in the self-assessment has been completed.

- In some cases, only an 'expedited review' will be required. This will be when the risk of harm to participants or others is small. It will normally involve a member (or possibly more) of a research ethics committee conducting the review.

- When full ethical review is deemed to be needed, a research ethics committee will conduct such a review. The ESRC has laid down guidelines concerning who should be members of such committees.

- Institutions must ensure that there are mechanisms in place to monitor ongoing research projects so that any changes to the ethical issues involved in an investigation can be addressed. This provision is meant to ensure that ethical approval is an ongoing activity.

It is interesting to note the ESRC's views on what kinds of research would *not* be viewed as appropriate for expedited review—that is, projects that involve more than what is referred to as 'minimal risk' of harm to participants or others connected to the research. Examples they provide are research involving:

- vulnerable groups;

- groups that necessitate permission from a gatekeeper;

- deception or lack of full informed consent;

- access to records or personal/confidential information;

- possible 'psychological stress, anxiety or humiliation' (para. 1.2.2);

- intrusive interventions.

There are many other observations that could be made about the *REF*, but these are particularly salient ones. I have spent some time on it because it is likely to influence many universities' and colleges' practices with regard to ethical review. As such, it is likely to implicate many students conducting research projects of various kinds and levels.

 # The difficulties of ethical decision-making

The difficulty of drawing the line between ethical and unethical practices can be revealed in several ways. The issue of some members of social settings being aware of the researcher's status and the nature of his or her investigation has been mentioned on several occasions (though see Research in focus 5.3 for an interesting illustration of this issue). Manuals about interviewing are full of advice about how to entice interviewees to open up about themselves. Interviewers frequently err on the low side when asked how long an interview will take. Women may use their identity as women to influence female interviewees in in-depth interviews to probe into their lives and reveal inner thoughts and feelings, albeit with a commitment to feminist research (Oakley 1981; Finch 1984). Qualitative research is frequently very open-ended, and, as a result, research questions are either loose or not specified, so that it is doubtful whether ethnographers in particular are able to inform others accurately about the nature of their research. Perhaps, too, some interviewees find the questions we ask unsettling or find the cut and thrust of a **focus group** discussion stressful, especially if they inadvertently reveal more than they might have intended.

There are, in other words, many ways in which there is the potential for deception and, relatedly, lack of informed consent in social research. These instances are, of course, a very far cry from the deceptions perpetrated in the research summarized in Research in focus 5.1 and 5.2, but they point to the difficulty of arriving at ethically informed decisions. Ethical codes give advice on patently inappropriate practices, though sometimes leaving some room for manœuvre, as we have seen, but less guidance on marginal areas of ethical decision-making. Indeed, guidelines may even be used by research participants *against* the researcher when they seek to limit the boundaries of a fieldworker's investigation (Punch 1994).

It also has to be recognized that there is sometimes a clash between the ethically desirable and the practical. For example, it was previously noted that some researchers like to secure the informed consent of research participants by asking them to sign a consent form. However, it has been shown that the requirement to sign such a form reduces prospective participants' willingness to be involved in survey research. For example, one of the most recent studies from the USA shows that 13 per cent of respondents were willing to participate in a study but not if they were required to sign a consent form (Singer 2003). The problem then is that, if signed consent is insisted upon, it seems likely that the resulting sample will be biased (see Chapter 7 for a discussion of sampling bias). This has led Groves *et al.* (2004) to recommend that, for survey research, it is the interviewer who should sign the form, indicating that the respondent has given his or her verbal informed consent.

Research in focus 5.3
Ethics and research on prostitution

O'Connell Davidson and Layder (1994) discuss the research into prostitution in which the former author was engaged (and which forms part of the research reported in O'Connell Davidson 1998). She was conducting small-scale ethnographic research on a prostitute (Desirée, a pseudonym), who worked from home, along with her receptionists and clients. While Desirée and her receptionists were fully aware of O'Connell Davidson's status, the clients were not. The authors acknowledge the invasion of the clients' privacy and the lack of informed consent but say they are 'untroubled' by the intrusion O'Connell Davidson's presence represented. This is because the clients were anonymous to her and she was not 'in a position to secure, store or disclose information that could harm them' (O'Connell Davidson and Layder 1994: 214). Thus, the fact that there was no harm to participants is regarded as the litmus test of the ethical status of the research. In addition, we are given a version of the 'Ethical transgression is pervasive' stance (see Key concept 5.1): 'Virtually all social research is intrusive and exploitative to some degree' (O'Connell Davidson and Layder 1994: 215). However, there is an additional and interesting twist to this discussion of ethics. O'Connell Davidson acknowledges her commitment to and sympathy for Desirée and her receptionists. But these sentiments do not extend to the clients:

> I have no wish to advance their interests through the research, no personal liking and no real sympathy for them. I have a professional obligation to preserve their anonymity and to ensure that they are not harmed by my research, but I feel no qualms about being less than frank with them, and no obligation to allow them to choose whether or not their actions are recorded. (O'Connell Davidson and Layder 1994: 215)

In other words, rights of informed consent and of not being deceived are differentially distributed in society according to these authors. In such circumstances, the researcher sets him- or herself up as the judge of which individuals or groups 'deserve' ethical treatment, a view that has far-reaching implications.

New media and difficult decisions

The Internet has also thrown up new dimensions of ethical decision-making for social researchers. For example, it is very tempting to use newsgroups, chatrooms, listservs, email discussion groups, and so on as interesting fodder for examining interaction or a focus of interest. In Internet circles such 'lurking' is extremely frowned upon. However, quite aside from such condemnation, it is ethically debatable how far it is acceptable to treat such ongoing interactions as 'documents' that are ripe for analysis. When participants have not given their assent to having their postings used in this way, it could be argued that the principle of informed consent has been violated. However, it could also be claimed that, in some cases, such postings are in the public domain, much like letters to newspapers, so that seeking consent is unnecessary.

Whether electronic communications are public or private is currently a matter of some debate. Pace and Livingston (2005: 39) argue that such electronic communications should be used for research only if:

- the information is publically archived and readily available;
- no password is required to access the information;
- the material is not sensitive in nature;
- no stated site policy prohibits the use of the material.

These authors suggest that, if these conditions do not pertain, informed consent needs to be obtained and should be obtained without disrupting ongoing online activity. They also argue that identities and confidentiality must be protected. These guidelines are not without problems. For example, who decides whether material is 'sensitive in nature'? What is or is not sensitive is likely to be highly debatable, so treating it as a principle is not in the least straightforward. Issues like this bring out the difficulties associated with ethical decision-making. Internet research methods will be explored further in Chapter 26.

Research methods using visual media like photographs have become increasingly popular as embellishments of traditional techniques. An example is the rise of visual ethnography, which is discussed in Chapter 17. The growth of interest in visual research methods has almost certainly been stimulated by the popularity of digital cameras and the greater availability of camcorders. However, visual methods can also result in some difficult decisions too. It is clearly desirable to obtain the informed consent of those who appear in photographs, but it may not be possible to do this for absolutely everyone who appears. Some people may be in the background and may have moved off before they can be asked to provide their informed consent. Further, the significance of a photograph may become apparent only when the visual and non-visual data are being analysed and by then it may not be possible to establish informed consent with those affected. In my book on Disneyization (Bryman 2004), I would very much have liked to use a photograph I took while in the Asia region of Disney's Animal Kingdom in Orlando, Florida. I had taken a photograph of one of the 'cast members' who was dressed in thematically appropriate attire because he had been holding an insect that had intrigued both of us. It occurred to me later that it would have been an excellent illustration of the use of the body in theming, but I felt it was inappropriate to use it because of the lack of informed consent.

Politics in social research

However, ethics are by no means the only context within which issues to do with wider principles are relevant to and intrude into social research. In a sense, ethical issues are part of a wider consideration of the role that values play in the research process. But the ways in which values are relevant is not just to do with the ethical dimensions of research. In Chapter 1, in the section on 'Influences on the conduct of social research', it was noted that values intrude in all phases of the research process—from the choice of a research area to the formulation of conclusions. This means that the social researcher is never conducting an investigation in a moral vacuum—who he or she is will influence a whole variety of presuppositions that in turn have implications for the conduct of social research. This view is widely accepted among social researchers, and one hears increasingly less frequently claims that social research can be conducted in a wholly objective, value-neutral way. While quantitative research is sometimes depicted as committed to objectivity (e.g. Lincoln and Guba 1985), it is not at all clear that nowadays this principle is as widely endorsed among quantitative researchers as a desirable and feasible feature as qualitative researchers would have us believe.

For some writers on social research, a 'conscious partiality', as Mies (1993: 68) calls it, is celebrated. Particularly among feminist researchers, to do research on women in an objective, value-neutral way would be undesirable (as well as being difficult to achieve) because it would be incompatible with the values of feminism. Instead, many feminist researchers advocate a stance that extols the virtues of a commitment to women and exposing the conditions of their disadvantage in a male-dominated society. Much of such research has been concerned to change the situation of women, as well as to heighten our understanding of the disadvantages from which they suffer.

Considerations of this kind begin to draw attention to the way in which *politics* (in the non-party-political sense of the working-through of power and contests over its exercise) plays an important role in social research. Politics becomes important in different contexts and ways.

- Social researchers are sometimes put in the position where they *take sides*. This is precisely what many feminist researchers do when they focus on women's disadvantages in the family, the workplace, and elsewhere, and on the possibilities for improving their position. However, some writers have argued that this process of taking sides is pervasive in much sociology (see Thinking deeply 5.2).

- Related to this point is the issue of *funding* research. Much social research is funded by organizations such as firms and government departments. Such organizations frequently have a vested interest in the outcomes of the research. The very fact that some research is funded, while other research is not, suggests that political issues may be involved, in that we might anticipate that such organizations will seek to invest in studies that will be useful to them and that will be supportive of their operations and world views. Frequently, they are proactive, in that they may contact researchers to carry out an investigation or they will launch a call for researchers to tender bids for an investigation in a certain area. When social researchers participate in such exercises, they are participating in a political arena because they are having to tailor their research concerns and even research questions to a body that defines or at least influences those research concerns and research questions. Bodies like government departments (such as the Home Office) are going to be influenced by notions of relevance to their work and by their understanding of ministers' concerns. As a result, as Hughes (2000) observes in relation to research in the field of crime, an investigation of gun crimes among Britain's 'underclass' is more likely to be looked upon favourably for funding than one concerned with state-related misdemeanours. Morgan (2000) points out that research funded by the Home Office typically: is empirical; adopts quantitative research; is concerned with the costs and benefits of a policy or innovation; is short-termist (in the sense that the cost–benefit analysis is usually concerned with immediate impacts rather than longer-term ones); and is uncritical (in the sense that government policy is not probed but is concerned with the effectiveness of ways of implementing policy). In addition, many agencies restrict what researchers are able to write about their findings by insisting on seeing drafts of all proposed publications. Even bodies like the UK's major funder of social research, the Economic and Social Research Council (ESRC), increasingly mould their research programmes to what are perceived to be areas of concern in society and seek to involve non-academics as evaluators and audiences for research. Such features are related to the fact that the ESRC is itself involved in a political process of seeking to secure a continuous stream of funding from government, and being able to demonstrate relevance is one way of indicating standing in this regard.

- Gaining *access* is also a political process. Access is usually mediated by gatekeepers, who are concerned about the researcher's motives: what the organization can gain from the investigation, what it will lose by participating in the research in terms of staff time and other costs, and potential risks to its image. Often, gatekeepers will seek to influence how the investigation takes place, what kinds of questions can be asked, who can and who cannot be the focus of study, the amount of time to be spent with each research participant, the interpretation of findings, and the form of any report to the organization itself. Reiner (2000*b*) suggests that the police, for example, are usually concerned about how they are going to be represented in publications in case they are portrayed unfavourably to agencies to which they are accountable. Firms are also invariably concerned about issues of how they are going to be represented. Consequently, gaining access is almost always a matter of negotiation, and as such inevitably turns into a political process. The results of this negotiation are often referred to as 'the research bargain'.

- Once in the organization, researchers often find that *getting on* in organizations entails a constant process of negotiation and renegotiation of what is and is not permissible. In other words, there may be several layers of gatekeepers in any research project, so that issues of access become an ongoing feature of research. For example, for their research on cargo vessels, Sampson and Thomas (2003: 171) sought initial access through shipowning or managing companies, but found that 'the *key* gatekeeper is invariably the captain'. Captains varied in the degree of willingness to accommodate the researchers' investigative and other needs, and their chief officers, who represented a further layer of access, were frequently delegated responsibility for dealing with the fieldworkers. These officers also varied a great deal, with the researchers quoting one case in which the chief officer wanted to call a meeting about how the interviews should be conducted and another giving a much freer rein. Moreover, researchers are often treated with suspicion and reticence because of uncertainty about their motives, such as whether they are really working for management. It is unwise to assume that, simply because gatekeepers have given the researcher access, they will have a smooth passage in their subsequent dealings with the people they study. Some research participants, perhaps because they are suspicious or because they doubt the utility of social research, will obstruct the research process. Researchers may also find themselves becoming embroiled in the internal politics of organizations as factional disputes rear their heads and sometimes they may become pawns in such clashes if groups attempt to enlist them in getting over a particular viewpoint.

• When research is conducted in *teams*, politics may loom large, since the different career and other objectives of team members and their different (and sometimes divergent) perceptions of their contributions may form a quite separate political arena. However, this is unlikely to be a set of circumstances that will affect most undergraduate or postgraduate students. On the other hand, supervisors of postgraduate research and undergraduate dissertations may them-

selves be evaluated in terms of the number of postgraduate students seen through to completion or in terms of the quality of undergraduate dissertations for which they were responsible. Therefore, wider political processes of this kind may be relevant to many of this book's readers.

• There may be pressure to restrict the *publication* of findings. Hughes (2000) cites the case of a study of plea-bargaining in the British criminal justice system as a case in point. The researchers had uncovered what were deemed at the time to be disconcerting levels of informal bargaining, which were taken to imply that the formal judicial process was being weakened. The English legal establishment sought to thwart the dissemination of the findings and was persuaded to allow publication to go ahead only when a panel of academics confirmed the validity of the findings.

• The *use* made of findings by others can be the focus of further political machinations. In the 1960s a study that showed the persistence of streaming and social-class differentials in a comprehensive school (at a time when comprehensive schooling was a political issue, having just been introduced by the then Labour government) was used by right-wing writers on education at the time as a critique of the case for comprehensive schooling.

These are just a small number of ways in which we can talk about a politics of the research process.

Thinking deeply 5.2
Taking sides in social research: the Becker–Gouldner dispute

In the late 1960s there was an interesting dispute between two sociologists who were leaders in the field in the USA and beyond: Howard S. Becker (1928–) and Alvin Gouldner (1920–80). Their debate raised many issues concerning the role of values and politics in research, but the issue of taking sides in research is a particularly interesting aspect of their dispute. Becker (1967) argued that it is not possible to do research that is unaffected by our personal sympathies. When we conduct research, we are often doing so in the context of hierarchical relationships (police–criminal, managers–workers, warders–prisoners, doctors–patients, teachers–students). Becker felt that it is difficult in the context of such relationships not to take sides; instead, the bigger dilemma is deciding which side we are on. Becker recognized that within the field in which he conducted his research at the time—the sociology of deviance—the sympathies of many practitioners lay with the underdogs in these hierarchical relationships. At the very least, the sociologist of deviance may seek to express or represent the point of view of criminals, prisoners, mental patients, and others, even if they do not go as far as to identify with them. However, when sociologists of deviance take the perspective of such groups, Becker argued they are more likely to be accused of bias, because they are ascribing credibility to those whom society shuns and in many cases abhors. Why is a study stressing the underdog's perspective more likely to be regarded as biased? Becker proffered two reasons: because members of the higher group are widely seen as having an exclusive right to define the way things are in their sphere and because they are regarded as having a more complete picture. In other words, credibility is differentially distributed in society.

Gouldner (1968) argued that Becker exaggerated the issues he described in that by no means all research entails the need to take sides. He also argued that it was a mistake to think that, simply because the researcher takes the point of view of a section of society seriously, he or she necessarily sympathizes with that group. Much more recently, Liebling (2001) has argued that it is possible to see the merits of more than one side. Taking the case of prison research in the UK, she shows that not only is it possible to recognize the virtues of different perspectives, but it is also possible to do so without incurring too much wrath on either side—in her case, prison officials and prisoners.

Checklist

Issues to consider in connection with ethical issues

○ Have you read and incorporated into your research the principles associated with at least one of the major professional associations mentioned in this book?

○ Have you read and incorporated the requirements for doing ethical research in your institution?

○ Have you found out whether all proposed research needs to be submitted to the body in your institution that is responsible for the oversight of ethical issues?

○ If only certain types of research need to be submitted, have you checked to see whether your proposed research is likely to require clearance?

○ Have you checked to ensure that there is no prospect of any harm coming to participants?

○ Does your research conform to the principle of informed consent, so that research participants understand:

  ○ what the research is about?

  ○ the purposes of the research?

  ○ who is sponsoring it?

  ○ the nature of their involvement in the research?

  ○ how long their participation is going to take?

  ○ that their participation is voluntary?

  ○ that they can withdraw from participation in the research at any time?

  ○ what is going to happen to the data (e.g. how it is going to be kept)?

○ Are you confident that the privacy of the people involved in your research will not be violated?

○ Do you appreciate that you should not divulge information or views to your research participants that other research participants have given you?

○ Have you taken steps to ensure that your research participants will not be deceived about the research and its purposes?

○ Have you taken steps to ensure that the confidentiality of data relating to your research participants will be maintained?

○ Once the data have been collected, have you taken steps to ensure that the names of your research participants and the location of your research (such as the name of the organization(s) in which it took place) are not identifiable?

○ Does your strategy for keeping your data in electronic form comply with data protection legislation?

○ Once your research has been completed, have you met obligations that were a requirement of doing the research (e.g. submitting a report to an organization that allowed you access)?

Key points

- This chapter has been concerned with a limited range of issues concerning ethics in social research, in that it has concentrated on ethical concerns that might arise in the context of collecting and analysing data. My concern has mainly been with relations between researchers and research participants. Other ethical issues can arise in the course of social research.

- While the codes and guidelines of professional associations provide some guidance, their potency is ambiguous and they often leave the door open for some autonomy with regard to ethical issues.

- The main areas of ethical concern relate to: harm to participants; lack of informed consent; invasion of privacy; and deception.

- Covert observation and certain notorious studies have been particular focuses of concern.

- The boundaries between ethical and unethical practices are not clear-cut.

- Writers on social research ethics have adopted several different stances in relation to the issue.

- While the rights of research participants are the chief focus of ethical principles, concerns about professional self-interest are also of concern.

- Ethical issues sometimes become difficult to distinguish from ones to do with the quality of research.

- The Internet and other new media have opened up new arenas for ethical decision-making.

- There are political dimensions to the research process that link with the place of values.

- The political dimensions of research are concerned with issues to do with the role and exercise of power at the different stages of an investigation.

Questions for review

- Why are ethical issues important in relation to the conduct of social research?
- Outline the different stances on ethics in social research.

Ethical principles

- Does 'harm to participants' refer to physical harm alone?
- What are some of the difficulties that arise in following this ethical principle?
- Why is the issue of informed consent so hotly debated?
- What are the main difficulties of following this ethical principle?
- Why is the privacy principle important?
- Why does deception matter?
- How helpful are notorious studies like Milgram's electric shock experiments and Humphreys's study in terms of understanding the operation of ethical principles in social research?

Ethics and the issue of quality

- Why do issues to do with ethics sometimes become difficult to distinguish from issues to do with the quality of research?
- Is it possible to maintain a distinction between ethics and research quality?

The difficulties of ethical decision-making

- To what extent do new media throw up new areas of ethical concern?
- How easy is it to conduct ethical research?
- Read one of the ethical guidelines referred to in this chapter. How effective is it in guarding against ethical transgressions?

Politics in social research

- What is meant by suggesting that politics plays a role in social research?
- In what ways does politics manifest itself in social research?

Online Resource Centre

http://www.oxfordtextbooks.co.uk/orc/brymansrm3e/

Visit the Online Resource Centre that accompanies this book to enrich your understanding of ethics and politics in social research. Consult web links, test yourself using multiple choice questions, and gain further guidance and inspiration from the Student Researcher's Toolkit.

Part Two

Part Two of this book is concerned with quantitative research. Chapter 6 sets the scene by exploring the main features of this research strategy. Chapter 7 discusses the ways in which we sample people on whom we carry out research. Chapter 8 focuses on the structured interview, which is one of the main methods of data collection in quantitative research and in survey research in particular. Chapter 9 is concerned with another prominent method of gathering data through survey research—questionnaires that people complete themselves. Chapter 10 provides guidelines on how to ask questions for structured interviews and questionnaires. Chapter 11 discusses structured observation, a method that provides a systematic approach to the observation of people. Chapter 12 addresses content analysis, which is a distinctive and systematic approach to the analysis of a wide variety of documents. Chapter 13 discusses the possibility of using, in your own research, data collected by other researchers or official statistics. Chapter 14 presents some of the main tools you will need to conduct quantitative data analysis. Chapter 15 shows you how to use computer software in the form of SPSS—a very widely used package of programs—to implement the techniques learned in Chapter 14.

These chapters will provide you with the essential tools for doing quantitative research. They will take you from the very general issues to do with the generic features of quantitative research to the very practical issues of conducting surveys and analysing your own data.

The nature of quantitative research

Chapter outline

Chapter guide

This chapter is concerned with the characteristics of **quantitative research**, an approach that has been the dominant strategy for conducting social research. Its influence has waned slightly since the mid-1970s, when **qualitative research** became increasingly influential. However, it continues to exert a powerful influence in many quarters. The emphasis in this chapter is very much on what quantitative research typically entails, though at a later point in the chapter the ways in which there are frequently departures from this ideal type are outlined. This chapter explores:

- the main steps of quantitative research, which are presented as a linear succession of stages;
- the importance of **concepts** in quantitative research and the ways in which measures may be devised for concepts; this discussion includes a discussion of the important idea of an *indicator*, which is devised as a way of measuring a concept for which there is no direct measure;
- the procedures for checking the **reliability** and **validity** of the measurement process;
- the main preoccupations of quantitative research, which are described in terms of four features: measurement; **causality**; **generalization**; and **replication**;
- some criticisms that are frequently levelled at quantitative research.

Introduction

In Chapter 1, quantitative research was outlined as a distinctive **research strategy**. In very broad terms, it was described as entailing the collection of numerical data, as exhibiting a view of the **relationship** between theory and research as **deductive** and a predilection for a natural science approach (and of **positivism** in particular), and as having an objectivist conception of social reality. A number of other features of quantitative research were outlined, but in this chapter we will be examining the strategy in much more detail.

It should be abundantly clear by now that the description of the research strategy as 'quantitative research' should not be taken to mean that quantification of aspects of social life is all that distinguishes it from a qualitative research strategy. The very fact that it has a distinctive **epistemological** and **ontological** position suggests that there is a good deal more to it than the mere presence of numbers. In this chapter, the main steps in quantitative research will be outlined. We will also examine some of the principal preoccupations of the strategy and how certain issues of concern among practitioners are addressed, like the concerns about **measurement validity**.

The main steps in quantitative research

Figure 6.1 outlines the main steps in quantitative research. This is very much an ideal-typical account of the process: it is probably never or rarely found in this pure form, but it represents a useful starting point for getting to grips with the main ingredients of the approach and the links between them. Research is rarely as linear and as straightforward as the figure implies, but its aim is to do no more than capture the main steps and to provide a rough indication of their interconnections.

Figure 6.1

The process of quantitative research

1. Theory
2. Hypothesis
3. Research design
4. Devise measures of concepts
5. Select research site(s)
6. Select research subjects/respondents
7. Administer research instruments/collect data
8. Process data
9. Analyse data
10. Findings/conclusions
11. Write up findings/conclusions

Some of the chief steps have been covered in Chapters 1 and 2. The fact that we start off with theory signifies that a broadly deductive approach to the relationship between theory and research is taken. It is common for outlines of the main steps of quantitative research to suggest that a **hypothesis** is deduced from the theory and is tested. This notion has been incorporated into Figure 6.1. However, a great deal of quantitative research does not entail the specification of a hypothesis, and instead theory acts loosely as a set of concerns in relation to which the social researcher collects data. The specification of hypotheses to be tested is particularly likely to be found in experimental research. Other **research designs** sometimes entail the testing of hypotheses. In Chapter 1 a **cross-sectional design** using **social survey research** instruments that were used as an example (see Research in focus 1.4) involved hypothesis testing. However, as a rule, we tend to find that step 2 is more likely to be found in experimental research.

The next step entails the selection of a research design, a topic that was explored in Chapter 2. As we have seen, the selection of research design has implications for a variety of issues, such as the **external validity** of findings and researchers' ability to impute causality to their findings. Step 4 entails devising measures of the concepts in which the researcher is interested. This process is often referred to as *operationalization*, a term that originally derives from physics to refer to the operations by which a concept (such as temperature or velocity) is measured (Bridgman 1927). Aspects of this issue will be explored below in this chapter.

The next two steps entail the selection of a research site or sites and then the selection of subjects/respondents. (Experimental researchers tend to call the people on whom they conduct research 'subjects', whereas social survey researchers typically call them 'respondents'.) Thus, in social survey research an investigator must first be concerned to establish an appropriate setting for his or her research. A number of decisions may be involved. The well-known *Affluent Worker* research undertaken by Goldthorpe *et al.* (1968: 2–5) involved two decisions about a research site or setting. First, the researchers needed a community that would be appropriate for the testing of the 'embourgeoisement' thesis (the idea that affluent workers were becoming more middle class in their attitudes and lifestyles). As a result of this consideration, Luton was selected. Second, in order to come up with a **sample** of 'affluent workers' (Step 6), it was decided that people working for three of Luton's leading employers should be interviewed. Moreover, the researchers wanted the firms selected to cover a range of production technologies, because of evidence at that time that technologies had implications for workers' attitudes and behaviour. As a result of these considerations, the three firms were selected. Industrial workers were then sampled, also in terms of selected criteria that were to do with the researchers' interests in embourgeoisement and in the implications of technology for work attitudes and behaviour. Research in focus 6.1 provides a more recent example of research that involved similar deliberations about selecting research sites and sampling respondents. In experimental research, these two steps are likely to include the assignment of subjects into control and treatment groups.

Research in focus 6.1
Selecting research sites and sampling respondents: the Social Change and Economic Life Initiative

The Social Change and Economic Life Initiative (SCELI) involved research in six labour markets: Aberdeen, Coventry, Kirkaldy, Northampton, Rochdale, and Swindon. These labour markets were chosen to reflect contrasting patterns of economic change in the early to mid-1980s and in the then recent past. Within each locality, three main surveys were carried out.

- *The Work Attitudes/Histories Survey*. Across the six localities a **random sample** of 6,111 individuals was interviewed using a **structured interview schedule**. Each interview comprised questions about the individual's work history and about a range of attitudes.

- *The Household and Community Survey*. A further survey was conducted on roughly one-third of those interviewed for the Work Attitudes/Histories Survey. Respondents and their partners were interviewed by structured interview schedule, and each person also completed a **self-completion questionnaire**. This survey was concerned with such areas as the domestic division of labour, leisure activities, and attitudes to the welfare state.

- *The Baseline Employers' Survey*. Each individual in each locality interviewed for the Work Attitudes/Histories Survey was asked to provide details of his or her employer (if appropriate). A sample of these employers was then interviewed by structured interview schedule. The interview schedules covered such areas as the gender distribution of jobs, the introduction of new technologies, and relationships with trade unions.

The bulk of the results was published in a series of volumes, including Penn *et al.* (1994) and A. M. Scott (1994). This example shows clearly the ways in which researchers are involved in decisions about selecting both research site(s) and respondents.

Step 7 involves the administration of the research instruments. In experimental research, this is likely to entail pre-testing subjects, manipulating the **independent variable** for the **experimental group**, and post-testing respondents. In cross-sectional research using social survey research instruments, it will involve interviewing the sample members by structured interview schedule or distributing a self-completion questionnaire. In research using **structured observation**, this step will mean an observer (or possibly more than one) watching the setting and the behaviour of people and then assigning categories to each element of behaviour.

Step 8 simply refers to the fact that, once information has been collected, it must be transformed into 'data'. In the context of quantitative research, this is likely to mean that it must be prepared so that it can be quantified. With some information this can be done in a relatively straightforward way—for example, for information relating to such things as people's ages, incomes, number of years spent at school, and so on. For other variables, quantification will entail *coding* the information—that is, transforming it into numbers to facilitate the quantitative analysis of the data, particularly if the analysis is going to be carried out by computer. Codes act as tags that are placed on data about people to allow the information to be processed by the computer. This consideration leads into Step 9—the analysis of the data. In this step, the researcher is concerned to use a number of techniques of quantitative data analysis to reduce the amount of data collected, to test for relationships between variables, to develop ways of presenting the results of the analysis to others, and so on.

On the basis of the analysis of the data, the researcher must interpret the results of the analysis. It is at this stage that the 'findings' will emerge. The researcher will consider the connections between the findings that emerge out of Step 8 and the various preoccupations that acted as the impetus of the research. If there is a hypothesis, is it supported? What are the implications of the findings for the theoretical ideas that formed the background to the research?

Then the research must be written up. It cannot take on significance beyond satisfying the researcher's personal curiosity until it enters the public domain in some way by being written up as a paper to be read at a conference or as a report to the agency that funded the research or as a book or journal article for academic social researchers. In writing up the findings and conclusions, the researcher is doing more than simply relaying what has been found to others: readers must be convinced that the research conclusions are important and that the findings are robust. Thus, a significant part of the research process entails convincing others of the significance and validity of one's findings.

Once the findings have been published, they become part of the stock of knowledge (or 'theory' in the loose sense of the word) in their domain. Thus, there is a feedback loop from Step 11 back up to Step 1. The presence of an element of both deductivism (Step 2) and inductivism (the feedback loop) is indicative of the positivist foundations of quantitative research. Similarly, the emphasis on the translation of concepts into measures (Step 4) is symptomatic of the principle of phenomenalism (see Key concept 1.2) that is also a feature of positivism. It is to this important phase of translating concepts into measures that we now turn. As we will see, certain considerations follow on from the stress placed on measurement in quantitative research. By and large, these considerations are to do with the validity and reliability of the measures devised by social scientists. These considerations will figure prominently in the following discussion.

As noted at the outset of presenting the model in Figure 6.1, this sequence of stages is a kind of ideal-typical account that is probably rarely found in this pure form. At the end of this chapter, the section 'Is it always like this?' deals with three ways in which the model may not be found in practice.

Concepts and their measurement

What is a concept?

Concepts are the building blocks of theory and represent the points around which social research is conducted. Just think of the numerous concepts that have already been mentioned in relation to research examples cited so far in this book:

> structure, agency, social class, job search method, deskilling, emotional satisfaction, religious orthodoxy, religious orientation, preservation of self, informal social control, negotiated order, culture, academic achievement, teacher expectations, charismatic leadership, healthy lifestyle, conversion.

Each represents a label that we give to elements of the social world that seem to have common features and that strike us as significant. As Bulmer (1984: 43) succinctly puts it, concepts 'are categories for the organisation of ideas and observations'. One item mentioned in Chapter 2 but omitted from the list of concepts above is IQ. It has been omitted because it is not a concept! It is a *measure* of a concept—namely, intelligence. This is a rare case of a social scientific measure that has become so well known that the measure and the concept are almost as synonymous as temperature and the centigrade or Fahrenheit scales, or as length and the metric scale. The concept of intelligence has arisen as a result of noticing that some people are very clever, some are quite clever, and still others are not at all bright. These variations in what we have come to call the concept of 'intelligence' seem important, because we might try to construct theories to explain these variations. We may try to incorporate the concept of intelligence into theories to explain variations in things like occupational or educational performance. Similarly, with something like social mobility, we notice that some people improve their socio-economic position relative to their parents, others stay roughly the same, and others are downwardly mobile. Out of such considerations, the concept of social mobility is reached.

If a concept is to be employed in quantitative research, it will have to be measured. Once they are measured, concepts can be in the form of independent or **dependent variables**. In other words, concepts may provide an explanation of a certain aspect of the social world, or they may stand for things we want to explain. A concept like social mobility may be used in either capacity: as a possible explanation of certain attitudes (are there differences between the downwardly mobile and others in terms of their political dispositions or social attitudes?) or as something to be explained (what are the causes of variation in social mobility?). Equally, we might be interested in evidence of changes in amounts of social mobility over time or in variations between comparable nations in levels of social mobility. As we start to investigate such issues, we are likely to formulate theories to help us understand why, for example, rates of social mobility vary between countries or over time. This will in turn generate new concepts, as we try to tackle the explanation of variation in rates.

Why measure?

There are three main reasons for the preoccupation with measurement in quantitative research.

1. Measurement allows us to delineate *fine differences* between people in terms of the characteristic in question. This is very useful, since, although we can often distinguish between people in terms of extreme categories, finer distinctions are much more difficult to recognize. We can detect clear variations in levels of job satisfaction—people who love their jobs and people who hate their jobs—but small differences are much more difficult to detect.

2. Measurement gives us a *consistent device* or yardstick for making such distinctions. A measurement device provides a consistent instrument for gauging differences.

This consistency relates to two things: our ability to be consistent over time and our ability to be consistent with other researchers. In other words, a measure should be something that is influenced neither by the timing of its administration nor by the person who administers it. Obviously, saying that the measure is not influenced by timing is not meant to indicate that measurement readings do not change: they are bound to be influenced by the process of social change. What it means is that the measure should generate consistent results, other than those that occur as a result of natural changes. Whether a measure actually possesses this quality has to do with the issue of *reliability*, which was introduced in Chapter 2 and which will be examined again below.

3. Measurement provides the basis for *more precise estimates of the degree of relationship between concepts* (for example, through **correlation** analysis, which will be examined in Chapter 14). Thus, if we measure both job satisfaction and the things with which it might be related, such as stress-related illness, we will be able to produce more precise estimates of how closely they are related than if we had not proceeded in this way.

Indicators

In order to provide a measure of a concept (often referred to as an *operational definition*, a term deriving from the idea of operationalization), it is necessary to have an indicator or indicators that will stand for the concept (see Key concept 6.1). There are a number of ways in which indicators can be devised:

- through a question (or series of questions) that is part of a structured interview schedule or self-completion questionnaire; the question(s) could be concerned with the respondents' report of an attitude (e.g. job satisfaction) or their social situation (e.g. poverty) or a report of their behaviour (e.g. leisure pursuits);

- through the recording of individuals' behaviour using a structured **observation schedule** (e.g. pupil behaviour in a classroom);

- through **official statistics**, such as the use of Home Office crime statistics to measure criminal behaviour;

- through an examination of mass media content through **content analysis**—for example, to determine changes in the salience of an issue, such as AIDS, in the mass media (Beharrell 1993).

Indicators, then, can be derived from a wide variety of different sources and methods. Very often the researcher has to consider whether one indicator of a concept will be sufficient. This consideration is frequently a focus for social survey researchers. Rather than have just a single indicator of a concept, the researcher may feel that it may be preferable to ask a number of questions in the course of a structured interview or a self-completion questionnaire that tap a certain concept (see Research in focus 6.2 and 6.3 for examples).

Key concept 6.1
What is an indicator?

It is worth making two distinctions here. First, there is a distinction between an *indicator* and a *measure*. The latter can be taken to refer to things that can be relatively unambiguously counted, such as personal income, household income, age, number of children, or number of years spent at school. Measures, in other words, are quantities. If we are interested in some of the causes of variation in personal income, the latter can be quantified in a reasonably direct way. We use indicators to tap concepts that are less directly quantifiable. If we are interested in the causes of variation in job satisfaction, we will need indicators that will stand for the concept. These indicators will allow job satisfaction to be measured, and we can treat the resulting quantitative information as if it were a measure. An indicator, then, is something that is devised or already exists and that is employed *as though it were a measure of a concept*. It is viewed as an indirect measure of a concept, like job satisfaction. An IQ test is a further example, in that it is a battery of indicators of the concept intelligence. We see here a second distinction between *direct* and *indirect* indicators of concepts. Indicators may be direct or indirect in their relationship to the concepts for which they stand. Thus, an indicator of marital status has a much more direct relationship to its concept than an indicator (or set of indicators) relating to job satisfaction. Sets of attitudes always need to be measured by batteries of indirect indicators. So too do many forms of behaviour. When indicators are used that are not true quantities, they will need to be coded to be turned into quantities. Directness and indirectness are not qualities inherent to an indicator: data from a survey question on amount earned per month may be a direct measure of personal income, but, if we treat it as an indicator of social class, it becomes an indirect measure. The issue of indirectness raises the question of where an indirect measure comes from—that is, how does a researcher devise an indicator of something like job satisfaction? Usually, it is based on common-sense understandings of the forms the concept takes or on anecdotal or qualitative evidence relating to that concept.

Research in focus 6.2
A multiple-indicator measure of a concept

The research on the effects of redundancy by Westergaard *et al.* (1989), which was referred to in Chapters 1 and 2, was conducted by structured interview with 378 steel workers who had been made redundant. One of the authors' interests was whether their respondents' commitment to work varied according to whether they were still unemployed at the time of the interview or had found work or had retired. In order to measure commitment to employment, the authors gave their respondents ten statements and asked them to indicate their level of agreement or disagreement on a seven-point **scale** running from 'Yes, I strongly agree' to 'No, I strongly disagree'. There was a middle point on the scale that allowed for a neutral response. This approach to investigating a cluster of attitudes is known as a *Likert scale*, though in many cases researchers use a five-point rather than a seven-point scale for responses. See Key concept 6.2 for a description of what a Likert scale entails. The ten statements were as follows.

1. Work is necessary, but rarely enjoyable.

2. Having a job is not very important to me.

3. I regard time spent at work as time taken away from the things I want to do.

4. Having a job is/was important to me only because it brings in money.

5. Even if I won a great deal of money on the pools I'd carry on working.

6. If unemployment benefit were really high I would still prefer to work.

7. I would hate being on the dole.

8. I would soon get bored if I did not go out to work.

9. The most important things that have happened to me involved work.

10. Any feelings I've had in the past of achieving something worthwhile have usually come through things I've done at work.

In fact, the authors found that their respondents' replies did not differ a great deal in terms of whether they had found work since being made redundant or were still unemployed or had taken retirement.

Key concept 6.2
What is a Likert scale?

The investigation of attitudes is a prominent area in much survey research. One of the most common techniques for conducting such an investigation is the *Likert scale*, named after Rensis Likert, who developed the method. The Likert scale is essentially a multiple-indicator or multiple-item measure of a set of attitudes relating to a particular area. The goal of the Likert scale is to measure intensity of feelings about the area in question. In its most common format, it comprises a series of statements (known as 'items') that focus on a certain issue or theme. Each respondent is then asked to indicate his or her level of agreement with the statement. Usually, the format for indicating level of agreement is a 5-point scale going from 'strongly agree' to 'strongly disagree', but 7-point scale and other formats are used too. There is usually a middle position of 'neither agree nor disagree' or 'undecided' indicating neutrality on the issue. Each respondent's reply on each item is scored, and then the scores for each item are aggregated to form an overall score. Normally, since the scale measures intensity, the scoring is carried out so that a high level of intensity of feelings in connection with each indicator receives a high score (for example, on a 5-point scale, a score of 5 for very strong positive feelings about an issue and a score of 1 for very negative feelings). The measure of commitment to work referred to in Research in focus 6.2 is an example of a Likert scale. Variations on the typical format of indicating degrees of agreement are scales referring to frequency (for example, 'never' through to 'always') and evaluation (for example, 'very poor' through to 'very good').

There are several points to bear in mind about the construction of a Likert scale. The following are particularly important.

- The items must be statements and not questions.
- The items must all relate to the same object (job, organization, ethnic groups, unemployment, sentencing of offenders, etc.).
- The items that make up the scale should be interrelated (see the discussion of 'Internal reliability' in this chapter and Key concept 6.3).

It is useful to vary the phrasing so that some items imply a positive view of the phenomenon of interest and others a negative one. Thus, in the example in Research in focus 6.2, some items imply a negative view of work (e.g. 'Having a job is not very important to me') and others a positive view of work (e.g. 'I would soon get bored if I did not go out to work'). This variation is advised in order to identify respondents who exhibit *response sets* (see the sections on 'Response sets' in Chapters 8 and 9).

Using multiple-indicator measures

What are the advantages of using a multiple-indicator measure of a concept? The main reason for their use is a recognition that there are potential problems with a reliance on just a single indicator:

- It is possible that a single indicator will incorrectly classify many individuals. This may be due to the wording of the question or it may be a product of misunderstanding. But if there are a number of indicators, if people are misclassified through a particular question, it will be possible to offset its effects.

- One indicator may capture only a portion of the underlying concept or be too general. A single question may need to be of an excessively high level of generality and so may not reflect the true state of affairs for the people replying to it. Alternatively, a question may cover only one aspect of the concept in question. For example, if you were interested in job satisfaction, would it be sufficient to ask people how satisfied they were with their pay? Almost certainly not, because

most people would argue that there is more to job satisfaction than just satisfaction with pay. A single indicator such as this would be missing out on such things as satisfaction with conditions, with the work itself, and with other aspects of the work environment. By asking a number of questions the researcher can get access to a wider range of aspects of the concept.

- You can make much finer distinctions. Taking the Westergaard *et al.* (1989) measure of commitment to work as an example (see Research in focus 6.2), if we just took one of the indicators as a measure, we would be able to array people only on a scale of 1 to 7, assuming that answers indicating no commitment were assigned 1 and answers indicating a very high level of commitment were assigned 7, the five other points being scored 2, 3, 4, 5, and 6. However, with a multiple-indicator measure of ten indicators the range is 10 (10×1) – 70 (10×7). Key concept 6.2 provides some information about the kind of scale (a Likert scale) that was used in the study by Westergaard *et al.*

Research in focus 6.3
A multiple-indicator measure of another concept

In Kelley and De Graaf's (1997) research on religious beliefs, two of the main concepts in which they were interested—national religiosity and family religious orientation—were each measured by a single indicator (see Research in focus 1.4). However, religious orthodoxy was measured by four survey questions, answers to which were aggregated for each respondent to form a 'score' for that person. Answers to each of the four questions were given a score and then aggregated to form a religious belief score. The four questions were as follows.

1. Please indicate which statement below comes closest to expressing what you believe about God:
   - I don't believe in God.
   - I don't know whether there is a God and I don't believe there is any way to find out.
   - I don't believe in a personal God, but I do believe in a higher power of some kind.
   - I find myself believing in God some of the time, but not at others.
   - While I have doubts, I feel that I do believe in God.
   - I know God really exists and I have no doubts about it.

2. Which best describes your beliefs about God?
   - I don't believe in God and I never have.
   - I don't believe in God, but I used to.
   - I believe in God now, but I didn't used to.
   - I believe in God now and I always have.

3. How close do you feel to God most of the time?
   - Don't believe in God.
   - Not close at all.
   - Not very close.
   - Somewhat close.
   - Extremely close.

4. There is a God who concerns Himself with every human being, personally.
   - Strongly agree.
   - Agree.
   - Neither agree nor disagree.
   - Disagree.
   - Strongly disagree.

Dimensions of concepts

One elaboration of the general approach to measurement is to consider the possibility that the concept in which you are interested comprises different dimensions. This view is particularly associated with Lazarsfeld (1958). The idea behind this approach is that, when the researcher is seeking to develop a measure of a concept, the different aspects or components of that concept should be considered. This specification of the dimensions of a concept would be undertaken with reference to theory and research associated with that concept. Examples of this kind of approach can be discerned in Seeman's (1959) delineation of five dimensions of alienation (powerlessness, meaninglessness, normlessness, isolation, and self-estrangement). Bryman and Cramer (2008) demonstrate the operation of this approach with reference to the con-

cept of 'professionalism'. The idea is that people scoring high on one dimension may not necessarily score high on other dimensions, so that for each respondent you end up with a multidimensional 'profile'. Research in focus 6.4 demonstrates the use of dimensions in connection with the concept of 'deskilling' in the sociology of work.

However, in much if not most quantitative research, there is a tendency to rely on a single indicator of concepts. For many purposes this is quite adequate. It would be a mistake to believe that investigations that use a single indicator of core concepts are somehow deficient. In any case, some studies, like Kelley and De Graaf (1997, see Research in focus 6.3), employ both single- and multiple-indicator measures of concepts. What *is* crucial is whether measures are reliable and whether they are valid representations of the concepts they are supposed to be tapping. It is to this issue that we now turn.

Research in focus 6.4
Specifying dimensions of a concept: the case of deskilling

This example is taken from social survey research primarily concerned with social class in Britain by Marshall *et al.* (1988). The research was based on structured interviews with a national, random sample of individuals. One of the researchers' areas of interest was Braverman's (1974) deskilling thesis (see Research in focus 1.2). Based on a reading of the literature on this topic at the time, the authors argued that two important components or *dimensions* of deskilling on which they were able to shed light were 'skill as complexity and skill as freedom', which 'are central to the thesis that work is being proletarianized through the deskilling of tasks' (Marshall *et al.* 1988: 116). 'Skill as complexity' was measured by a single interview question asking respondents whether their current jobs required more, less, or about the same amount of skill as when they first started. 'Skill as freedom' was measured by seven indicators that were treated separately and not aggregated. The questions entailed asking respondents about such things as whether they were able to reduce the pace of their work or to initiate new tasks in their work. Neither dimension comprised measures that offered significant support for the deskilling thesis.

Reliability and validity

Although the terms 'reliability' and 'validity' seem to be almost synonymous, they have quite different meanings in relation to the evaluation of measures of concepts, as was seen in Chapter 2.

Reliability

As Key concept 6.3 suggests, reliability is fundamentally concerned with issues of consistency of measures. There are at least three different meanings of the term. These are outlined in Key concept 6.3 and elaborated upon below.

Stability

The most obvious way of testing for the stability of a measure is the *test–retest* method. This involves administering a test or measure on one occasion and then readministering it to the same sample on another occasion, i.e.

$$T_1 \qquad T_2$$
$$Obs_1 \qquad Obs_2$$

We should expect to find a high correlation between Obs_1 and Obs_2. Correlation is a measure of the strength of the relationship between two variables. This topic will be covered in Chapter 14 in the context of a discussion about quantitative data analysis. Let us imagine that we develop a multiple-indicator measure that is supposed to tap a concept that we might call 'designerism' (a preference for buying goods and especially clothing with 'designer' labels). We would administer the measure to a sample of respondents and readminister it some time later. If the correlation is low, the measure would appear to be unstable, implying that respondents' answers cannot be relied upon.

Key concept 6.3
What is reliability?

Reliability refers to the consistency of a measure of a concept. The following are three prominent factors involved when considering whether a measure is reliable:

- *Stability*. This consideration entails asking whether a measure is stable over time, so that we can be confident that the results relating to that measure for a sample of respondents do not fluctuate. This means that, if we administer a measure to a group and then readminister it, there will be little variation over time in the results obtained.

- *Internal reliability*. The key issue is whether the indicators that make up the **scale** or **index** are consistent—in other words, whether respondents' scores on any one indicator tend to be related to their scores on the other indicators.

- *Inter-observer consistency*. When a great deal of subjective judgement is involved in such activities as the recording of observations or the translation of data into categories and where more than one 'observer' is involved in such activities, there is the possibility that there is a lack of consistency in their decisions. This can arise in a number of contexts, for example: in content analysis where decisions have to be made about how to categorize media items; when answers to open-ended questions have to be categorized; or in structured observation when observers have to decide how to classify subjects' behaviour.

However, there are a number of problems with this approach to evaluating reliability. Respondents' answers at T_1 may influence how they reply at T_2. This may result in greater consistency between Obs_1 and Obs_2 than is in fact the case. Second, events may intervene between T_1 and T_2 that influence the degree of consistency. For example, if a long span of time is involved, changes in the economy or in respondents' personal financial circumstances could influence their views about and predilection for designer goods. For example, Berthoud (2000*b*) notes that an index of ill-health devised from the British Household Panel Survey (BHPS) achieved a high test–retest reliability. He notes that this is very encouraging, because 'some of the variation between tests (a year apart) will have been caused by genuine changes in people's health' (Berthoud 2000*b*: 170). There is no easy way of disentangling the effects of a lack of stability in the measure from 'real' changes in people's health over the year in question.

There are no clear solutions to these problems, other than by introducing a complex research design and so turning the investigation of reliability into a major project in its own right. Perhaps for these reasons, many if not most reports of research findings do not appear to carry out tests of stability. Indeed, longitudinal research is often undertaken precisely in order to identify social change and its correlates.

Internal reliability

This meaning of reliability applies to multiple-indicator measures like those examined in Research in focus 6.2 and 6.3. When you have a multiple-item measure in which each respondent's answers to each question are aggregated to form an overall score, the possibility is raised that the indicators do not relate to the same thing; in other words, they lack coherence. We need to be sure

that all our designerism indicators are related to each other. If they are not, some of the items may actually be unrelated to designerism and therefore indicative of something else.

One way of testing internal reliability is the *split-half* method. We can take the commitment to work measure developed by Westergaard *et al.* (1989) as an example (see Research in focus 6.2). The ten indicators would be divided into two halves with five in each group. The indicators would be allocated on a random or an odd–even basis. The degree of correlation between scores on two halves would then be calculated. In other words, the aim would be to establish whether respondents scoring high on one of the two groups also scored high on the other group of indicators. The calculation of the correlation will yield a figure, known as a coefficient, that varies between 0 (no correlation and therefore no internal consistency) to 1 (perfect correlation and therefore complete internal consistency). It is usually expected that a result of 0.80 and above implies an acceptable level of internal reliability. Do not worry if the figures appear somewhat opaque. The meaning of correlation will be explored in much greater detail later on. The chief point to carry away with you at this stage is that the correlation establishes how closely respondents' scores on the two groups of indicators are related.

Nowadays, most researchers use a test of internal reliability known as *Cronbach's alpha* (see Key concept 6.4). Its use has grown as a result of its incorporation into computer software for quantitative data analysis.

Inter-observer consistency

The idea of inter-observer consistency is briefly outlined in Key concept 6.3. The issues involved are rather too advanced to be dealt with at this stage and will be touched on briefly in later chapters. Cramer (1998:

Key concept 6.4
What is Cronbach's alpha?

To a very large extent we are leaping ahead too much here, but it is important to appreciate the basic features of what this widely used test means. Cronbach's alpha is a commonly used test of internal reliability. It essentially calculates the average of all possible split-half reliability coefficients. A computed alpha coefficient will vary between 1 (denoting perfect internal reliability) and 0 (denoting no internal reliability). The figure 0.80 is typically employed as a rule of thumb to denote an acceptable level of internal reliability, though many writers work with a slightly lower figure. In the case of the commitment to work scale devised by Westergaard *et al.* (1989: 93), alpha was 0.70, which they refer to as 'a satisfactory level'. In the case of Kelley and De Graaf's (1997) measure of religious orthodoxy, which comprised four indicators, alpha was 0.93. The alpha levels varied between 0.79 and 0.95 for each of the fifteen national samples that make up the data. Berthoud (2000*b*: 169) writes that a minimum level of 0.60 is 'good' and cites the case of an index of ill-health used in the BHPS that achieved a level of 0.77.

ch. 14) provides a very detailed treatment of the issues and appropriate techniques.

Validity

As noted in Chapter 2, the issue of measurement validity has to do with whether a measure of a concept really measures that concept (see Key concept 6.5). When people argue about whether a person's IQ score really measures or reflects that person's level of intelligence, they are raising questions about the measurement validity of the IQ test in relation to the concept of intelligence. Similarly, one often hears people say that they do not believe that the Retail Price Index really reflects inflation and the rise in the cost of living. Again, a query is being raised in such comments about measurement validity. And whenever students or lecturers debate whether formal examinations provide an accurate measure of academic ability, they too are raising questions about measurement validity.

Writers on measurement validity distinguish between a number of different types of validity. These types really reflect different ways of gauging the validity of a measure of a concept. These different types of validity will now be outlined.

Key concept 6.5
What is validity?

Validity refers to the issue of whether an indicator (or set of indicators) that is devised to gauge a concept really measures that concept. Several ways of establishing validity are explored in the text: **face validity**; **concurrent validity**; predictive validity; construct validity; and convergent validity. Here the term is being used as a shorthand for what was referred to as *measurement validity* in Chapter 2. Validity should therefore be distinguished from the other terms introduced in Chapter 2: **internal validity**; external validity; and **ecological validity**.

Face validity

At the very minimum, a researcher who develops a new measure should establish that it has *face validity*—that is, that the measure apparently reflects the content of the concept in question. Face validity might be established by asking other people whether the measure seems to be getting at the concept that is the focus of attention. In other words, people, possibly those with experience or expertise in a field, might be asked to act as judges to determine whether on the face of it the measure seems to reflect the concept concerned. Face validity is, therefore, an essentially intuitive process.

Concurrent validity

The researcher might seek also to gauge the *concurrent validity* of the measure. Here the researcher employs a *criterion* on which cases (for example, people) are known to differ and that is relevant to the concept in question. A new measure of job satisfaction can serve as an example. A criterion might be absenteeism, because some people are more often absent from work (other than through illness) than others. In order to establish the concurrent validity of a measure of job satisfaction, we might see how far people who are satisfied with their jobs are less likely than those who are not satisfied to be *absent* from work. If a lack of correspondence was found, such as there being no difference in levels of job satisfaction among frequent absentees, doubt might be cast on whether our measure is really addressing job satisfaction.

Predictive validity

Another possible test for the validity of a new measure is *predictive validity*, whereby the researcher uses a *future* criterion measure, rather than a contemporary one, as in the case of concurrent validity. With predictive validity, the researcher would take future levels of absenteeism as the criterion against which the validity of a new measure of job satisfaction would be examined. The difference from concurrent validity is that a future rather than a simultaneous criterion measure is employed.

Construct validity

Some writers advocate that the researcher should also estimate the *construct validity* of a measure. Here, the researcher is encouraged to deduce hypotheses from a theory that is relevant to the concept. For example, drawing upon ideas about the impact of technology on the experience of work, the researcher might anticipate that people who are satisfied with their jobs are less likely to work on routine jobs; those who are not satisfied are more likely to work on routine jobs. Accordingly, we could investigate this theoretical deduction by examining the relationship between job satisfaction and job routine. However, some caution is required in interpreting the absence of a relationship between job satisfaction and job routine in this example. First, either the theory or the deduction that is made from it might be misguided. Second, the measure of job routine could be an invalid measure of that concept.

Convergent validity

In the view of some methodologists, the validity of a measure ought to be gauged by comparing it to measures of the same concept developed through other methods. For example, if we develop a questionnaire measure of how much time managers spend on various activities (such as attending meetings, touring their organization, informal discussions, and so on), we might examine its validity by tracking a number of managers and using a structured observation schedule to record how much time is spent in various activities and their frequency.

An interesting instance of convergent *in*validity is described in Thinking deeply 6.1. In this example, the British Crime Survey (BCS) was consciously devised to provide an alternative measure of levels of crime so that it would act as a check on the official statistics. The two sets of data are collected in quite different ways: the official crime statistics are collected as part of the bureaucratic processing of offenders in the course of the activities of members of the British criminal justice system, whereas the BCS entails the collection of data by interview from a national sample of possible victims of crime. In the case reported in Thinking deeply 6.1 a lack of convergent validity was found. However, the problem with the convergent approach to testing validity is that it is not possible to establish very easily which of the two measures represents the more accurate picture. The BCS is not entirely flawless in its approach to the measurement of crime levels, and, in any case, the 'true' picture with regard to the volume of crime at any one time is an almost entirely metaphysical notion (Reiner 2000). While the authors of the news item were able to draw on bits of anecdotal evidence to support their thesis that the figures were being massaged and this together with the BCS evidence casts doubt on the official statistics, it would be a mistake to hold that the survey evidence necessarily represents a definitive and therefore unambiguously valid measure.

Thinking deeply 6.1
A case of convergent *in*validity: Home Office crime statistics

An article in the *Sunday Times* (Burrell and Leppard 1994) proclaimed the government's claims about the fall in crime a sham. The opening paragraph put the point as follows.

> The government's much heralded fall in crime is a myth. Hundreds of thousands of serious crimes have been quietly dropped from police records as senior officers massage their statistics to meet new Home Office targets. . . . Crime experts say at least 220,000 crimes, including burglary, assault, theft and car crimes, vanished from official statistics last year as a result of police manipulation of the figures.

What gave the 'crime experts' and the reporters the confidence to assert that the much-trumpeted fall in crime was a myth because the figures on which the claim was made had been massaged? The answer is that data from the British Crime Survey (BCS) had 'recently reported that actual crime rose faster over the past two years than during the 1980s' (see Research in focus 7.2 for details of the BCS). In each case, a large, randomly selected sample of individuals is questioned by structured interview. The survey is not based on a panel research design, because the same people are not interviewed with each wave of data collection. The BCS is an example of what is known as a 'victimization survey'. With this kind of survey, a sample of a **population** is questioned about its experiences as victims of crime. The idea is that unreported crime and other crime that does not show up in the official statistics will be revealed. The categories of crime used in the survey are meant to reflect those reported in the official statistics (Coleman and Moynihan 1996: 83–6). The 1994 survey found that there had been a marked increase in most categories of crime. Since the *Sunday Times* article, there have been several other newspaper exposés of the fiddling of crime figures by the police (Reiner 2000*a*).

Research in focus 6.5 provides a brief account of a new scale using the Likert procedure and some of the ways in which reliability and validity were assessed.

Reflections on reliability and validity

There are, then, a number of different ways of investigating the merit of measures that are devised to represent social scientific concepts. However, the discussion of reliability and validity is potentially misleading, because it would be wrong to think that all new measures of concepts are submitted to the rigours described above. In fact, most typically, measurement is undertaken within a stance that Cicourel (1964) described as 'measurement by fiat'. By the term 'fiat', Cicourel was referring not to a well-known Italian car manufacturer but to the notion of 'decree'. He meant that most measures are simply asserted. Fairly straightforward but minimal steps may be taken to ensure that a measure is reliable and/or valid, such as testing for internal reliability when a multiple-indicator measure has been devised and examining face

validity. But in many if not the majority of cases in which a concept is measured, no further testing takes place. This point will be further elaborated below.

It should also be borne in mind that, although reliability and validity are analytically distinguishable, they are related because validity presumes reliability. This means that, if your measure is not reliable, it cannot be valid (see page 32). This point can be made with respect to each of the three criteria of reliability that have been discussed. If the measure is not stable over time, it simply cannot be providing a valid measure. The measure could not be tapping the concept it is supposed to be related to if the measure fluctuated. If the measure fluctuates, it may be measuring different things on different occasions. If a measure lacks internal reliability, it means that a multiple-indicator measure is actually measuring two or more different things. Therefore, the measure cannot be valid. Finally, if there is a lack of inter-observer consistency, it means that observers cannot agree on the meaning of what they are observing, which in turn means that a valid measure cannot be in operation.

Research in focus 6.5
Developing a Likert scale: the case of attitudes to vegetarians

Chin *et al.* (2002) describe how they went about developing a scale designed to measure pro- or anti-vegetarian attitudes. They note that non-vegetarians sometimes see vegetarianism as deviant and that, as a result, vegetarians are sometimes regarded with suspicion if not hostility. The authors developed a scale comprising 33 items. Each item is a statement to which the respondent is asked to indicate strength of agreement or disagreement on a 7-point scale. The items were arrived at following: interviews with both vegetarians and non-vegetarians; reviewing the literature on vegetarianism; field observations (though it is not clear of what or whom); brainstorming within the team; and examining attitude scales on other forms of prejudice for possible wording and presentation. The items were meant to tap four areas:

- forms of behaviour in which vegetarians engage that are viewed as irritating; e.g. 'Vegetarians preach too much about their beliefs and eating habits' (possibly a double-barrelled item—see Chapter 10);
- disagreement with vegetarians' beliefs; e.g. 'Vegetarians are overly concerned with animal rights';
- health-related aspects of being a vegetarian; e.g. 'Vegetarians are overly concerned about gaining weight';
- appropriate treatment of vegetarians; e.g. 'It's O.K. to tease someone for being a vegetarian'.

The scale was tested out on a sample of university undergraduates in the USA. Some items from the scale were dropped because they exhibited poor internal consistency with the other items. Cronbach's alpha was conducted for the remaining 21 items and found to be high at 0.87 (see Key concept 6.4). The construct validity (see above on the meaning of this term) of the scale was also tested by asking the students to complete other scales that the researchers predicted would be associated with pro- or anti-vegetarian attitudes. One method was that the authors hypothesized that people with authoritarian attitudes would be more likely to be anti-vegetarians. This was confirmed, although the relationship between these two variables was very small. However, contrary to their hypothesis, the scale for attitudes towards vegetarianism was *not* found to be related to political conservatism. The scale emerges as internally reliable (see Key concept 6.3 on the meaning of this term) but as being of slightly questionable construct validity.

Research in focus 6.6
Assessing the internal reliability and the concurrent and predictive validity of a measure of organizational climate

Patterson *et al.* (2005) describe the way they went about validating a measure they developed of organizational climate. This is a rather loose concept that was first developed in the 1960s and 1970s to refer to the perceptions of an organization by its members. Four main dimensions of climate were developed based around the following notions.

1. *Human relations model.* Feelings of belonging and trust in the organization and the degree to which there is training, good communication, and supervisory support.

2. *Internal process model*. The degree of emphasis on formal rules and on traditional ways of doing things.

3. *Open systems model*. The extent to which flexibility and innovativeness are valued.

4. *Rational goal model*. The degree to which clearly defined objectives and the norms and values associated with efficiency, quality, and high performance are emphasized.

An Organizational Climate Measure, comprising 95 items in a 4-point Likert format (definitely false, mostly false, mostly true, definitely true) was developed and administered to employees in 55 UK organizations, with 6,869 completing a questionnaire—a response rate of 57 per cent. A **factor analysis** (see Key concept 6.6) was conducted to explore the extent to which there were distinct groupings of items that tended to go together. This procedure yielded seventeen scales, such as autonomy, involvement, innovation and flexibility, and clarity of organizational goals.

The *internal reliability* of the scales was assessed using Cronbach's alpha, showing that all scales were at a level of 0.73 or above. This suggests that the measure's constituent scales were internally reliable.

Concurrent validity was assessed following **semi-structured interviews** with each company's managers in connection with their organization's practices. The interview data were coded to provide criteria against which the validity of the scales could be gauged. In most cases, the scales were found to be concurrently valid. For example, the researcher examined the correlation between a scale designed to measure the emphasis on tradition and the degree to which practices associated with the 'new manufacturing paradigm' (Patterson *et al.* 2005: 397) were adopted, as revealed by the interview data. The correlation was −0.42, implying that those firms that were perceived as rooted in tradition tended to be less likely to adopt new manufacturing practices. Here the adoption of new manufacturing practices was treated as a criterion to assess the extent to which the scale measuring perceptions of tradition really was addressing tradition. If the correlation had been small or had been positive, the concurrent validity of the scale would have been in doubt.

To assess *predictive validity*, the researchers asked a senior **key informant** at each company to complete a questionnaire one year after the main survey had been conducted. The questionnaire was meant to address two of the measure's constituent scales, one of which was the innovation and flexibility scale. It asked the informants to assess their companies in terms of its innovativeness in a number of areas. For example, the correlation between the innovation and flexibility scale and informants' assessments of their companies in terms of innovativeness with respect to products achieved a correlation of 0.53. This implies that there was indeed a correlation between perceptions of innovativeness and flexibility and a subsequent indicator of innovativeness.

The main preoccupations of quantitative researchers

Both quantitative and qualitative research can be viewed as exhibiting a set of distinctive but contrasting preoccupations. These preoccupations reflect **epistemologically** grounded beliefs about what constitutes acceptable knowledge. In this section, four distinctive preoccupations that can be discerned in quantitative research will be outlined and examined: measurement, causality, generalization, and replication.

Measurement

The most obvious preoccupation is with measurement, a feature that is scarcely surprising in the light of much of the discussion in the present chapter so far. From the position of quantitative research, measurement carries a number of advantages that were previously outlined. It is not surprising, therefore, that issues of reliability and validity are a concern for quantitative researchers, though this is not always manifested in research practice.

Causality

There is a very strong concern in most quantitative research with explanation. Quantitative researchers are rarely concerned merely to describe how things are, but are keen to say why things are the way they are. This emphasis is also often taken to be a feature of the ways in which the natural sciences proceed. Thus, researchers are often not only interested in a phenomenon like racial prejudice as something to be described, for example, in terms of how much prejudice exists in a certain group of individuals, or what proportion of people in a sample are highly prejudiced and what proportion are largely lacking in prejudice. Rather, they are likely to want to explain it, which means examining its causes. The researcher may seek to explain racial prejudice in terms of personal characteristics (such as levels of authoritarianism) or in terms of social characteristics (such as education, or social mobility experiences). In reports of research you will often come across the idea of 'independent' and 'dependent' variables, which reflect the tendency to think in terms of causes and effects. Racial prejudice might be regarded as the dependent variable, which is to be explained, and authoritarianism as an independent variable, and which therefore has a causal influence upon prejudice.

When an experimental design is being employed, the independent variable is the variable that is manipulated. There is little ambiguity about the direction of causal influence. However, with cross-sectional designs of the kind used in most social survey research, there is ambiguity about the direction of causal influence in that data concerning variables are simultaneously collected. Therefore, we cannot say that an independent variable precedes the dependent one. To refer to independent and dependent variables in the context of cross-sectional designs, we must *infer* that one causes the other, as in the example concerning authoritarianism and racial prejudice in the previous paragraph. We must draw on common sense or theoretical ideas to infer the likely temporal precedence of variables. However, there is always the risk that the inference will be wrong (see Research in focus 25.5, for an example of this possibility).

The concern about causality is reflected in the preoccupation with internal validity that was referred to in Chapter 2. There it was noted that a criterion of good quantitative research is frequently the extent to which

there is confidence in the researcher's causal inferences. Research that exhibits the characteristics of an experimental design is often more highly valued than cross-sectional research, because of the greater confidence that can be enjoyed in the causal findings associated with the former. For their part, quantitative researchers who employ cross-sectional designs are invariably concerned to develop techniques that will allow causal inferences to be made. Moreover, the rise of longitudinal research like the British Household Panel Survey almost certainly reflects a desire on the part of quantitative researchers to improve their ability to generate findings that permit a causal interpretation.

Generalization

In quantitative research the researcher is usually concerned to be able to say that his or her findings can be generalized beyond the confines of the particular context in which the research was conducted. Thus, if a study of racial prejudice is carried out by a questionnaire with a number of people who answer the questions, we often want to say that the results can apply to individuals other than those who responded in the study. This concern reveals itself in social survey research in the attention that is often given to the question of how one can create a representative sample. Given that it is rarely feasible to send questionnaires to or interview whole populations (such as all members of a town, or the whole population of a country, or all members of an organization), we have to sample. However, we will want the sample to be as representative as possible in order to be able to say that the results are not unique to the particular group upon whom the research was conducted; in other words, we want to be able to generalize the findings beyond the cases (for example, the people) that make up the sample. The preoccupation with generalization can be viewed as an attempt to develop the lawlike findings of the natural sciences.

Probability sampling, which will be explored in Chapter 7, is the main way in which researchers seek to generate a representative sample. This procedure largely eliminates bias from the selection of a sample by using a process of random selection. The use of a random selection process does not guarantee a representative sample, because, as will be seen in Chapter 7, there are factors that operate over and above the selection system used that can jeopardize the representativeness of a sample. A related consideration here is this: even if we did have a representative sample, what would it be representative *of*. The simple answer is that it will be representative of the population from which it was selected. This is certainly the answer that sampling theory gives us. Strictly speaking, we cannot generalize beyond that population. This means that, if the members of the population from which a sample is taken are all inhabitants of a town, city, or region, or are all members of an organization, we can generalize only to the inhabitants or members of the town, city, region, or organization. But it is very tempting to see the findings as having a more pervasive applicability, so that, even if the sample were selected from a large city like Birmingham, the findings would be relevant to all similar cities. We should not make inferences beyond the population from which the sample was selected, but researchers frequently do so. The concern to be able to generalize is often so deeply ingrained that the limits to the generalizability of findings are frequently forgotten or sidestepped.

Student project
Generalizability in a student project

For his team-based survey research on students at his university, Joe Thompson felt that issues to do with reliability and validity were important. In particular, it appears from the following comment that the generalizability of the findings was especially significant.

> Again, the main considerations were reliability and validity of the research. Thus the methods used reflected this; the questionnaire went through a modification period where we as a group not only tested it on our sample but also received information from staff who worked within the area our research project was aimed at. We knew that the sample had to be representative of the whole university, so the number of members from the group interviewing students from different halls was in ratio to the number of students who lived within those residences.

To read more about Joe's research experiences, go to the Online Resource Centre that accompanies this book at http://www.oxfordtextbooks.co.uk/orc/brymansrm3e/.

The concern with generalizability or external validity is particularly strong among quantitative researchers using cross-sectional and longitudinal designs. There is a concern about generalizability among experimental research, as the discussion of external validity in Chapter 2 suggested, but users of this research design usually give greater attention to internal validity issues.

Replication

The natural sciences are often depicted as wishing to reduce to a bare minimum the contaminating influence of the scientist's biases and values. The results of a piece of research should be unaffected by the researcher's special characteristics or expectations or whatever. If biases and lack of objectivity were pervasive, the claims of the natural sciences to provide a definitive picture of the world would be seriously undermined. As a check upon the influence of these potentially damaging problems, scientists may seek to replicate—that is, to reproduce—each other's experiments. If there was a failure to replicate, so that a scientist's findings repeatedly could not be reproduced, serious questions would be raised about the validity of his or her findings. Consequently, scientists often attempt to be highly explicit about their procedures so that an experiment is capable of replication. Likewise, quantitative researchers in the social sciences often regard replication, or more precisely the ability to replicate, as an important ingredient of their activity. It is easy to see why: the possibility of a lack of objectivity and of the intrusion of the researcher's values would appear to be much greater when examining the social world than when the natural scientist investigates the natural order. Consequently, it is often regarded as important that the researcher spells out clearly his or her procedures so that they can be replicated by others, even if the research does not end up being replicated.

Whether research is in practice replicated is another matter. Replication is not a high-status activity in the natural and social sciences, because it is often regarded as a pedestrian and uninspiring pursuit. It is striking that in the example referred to in Research in focus 6.7, the exercise is referred to as a 'replication *and extension* of several previous studies' (emphasis added), conveying the impression that it is not *just* a replication.

Moreover, standard replications do not form the basis for attractive articles, so far as many academic journal editors are concerned. Consequently, replications of research appear in print far less frequently than might be supposed. A further reason for the low incidence of published replications is that it is difficult to ensure in social science research that the conditions in a replication are precisely the same as those that pertained in an original study. So long as there is some ambiguity about the degree to which the conditions relating to a replication are the same as those in the initial study, any differences in findings may be attibutable to the design of the replication rather than to some deficiency in the original study. To some extent, this is the case with the research referred to in Research in focus 6.7. Nonetheless, it is often regarded as crucial that the methods taken in generating a set of findings are made explicit, so that it is *possible* to replicate a piece of research. Thus, it is replicability that is often regarded as an important quality of quantitative research.

Research in focus 6.7
Replicating a study of cartoons

Davis (2003: 412) conducted what she refers to as a 'replication and extension of several previous studies'. The replication was of previous research—particularly that of Smith (1994)—that conducted content analyses of the characters in commercial cartoons that are broadcast in between children's television programmes in the USA. Content analysis is a technique that aims to provide quantitative analyses of different kinds of content in a systematic fashion. It is covered in detail in Chapter 12. Davis (2003) was especially interested in the extent to which the cartoon characters exhibited sex-role stereotyping. Based on previous research, Davis deduced several hypotheses concerning the sex role stereotyping of the cartoon characters in the 1990s. Examples of such hypotheses are:

- 'characters in major roles will be more likely to be male than characters in minor roles' (2003: 411)

- 'the character will be more likely to be male if the activity is an individual activity than a group activity' (2003: 411)

- 'characters in activities with high amounts of movement will be more likely to be male than those characters who are portrayed with low amounts of movement' (2003: 411)

Davis depicts her research as partly a replication and partly an extension, because Smith's research was concerned with children's television progammes in general, whereas hers is just concerned with animated cartoon programmes. She analysed the content of cartoons shown in one month of 1995. A cartoon entered the sample just once, no matter how many times it was shown. Through this process, there were 167 cartoons and 478 characters that were analysed. Her findings confirmed that advertising through cartoons aimed at children do indeed entail sex-role stereotyping. However, she also writes:

As this project largely replicated Smith's research, it shows the need for continued replication of this kind of analysis, as some of the findings in Smith's research were not reproduced in the analysis. The differences could be a function of the more narrowly defined sample of television programming from which the advertisements were drawn, or they could show a change in advertisers' methods of advertising their products to children. (Davis 2003: 421)

This research shows that a replication can be very valuable in establishing that the findings from a study should not be too readily accepted at face value. On the other hand, the second sentence in this quotation demonstrates how difficult it is to interpret the findings of a replication study. It is difficult to know how to interpret any divergences in the findings. Instead, as Davis implies, it is not that the original findings are 'wrong' but that it could be that, when applied to a different kind of sample, the same kind of analysis yields different findings or that there has been a change in advertisers' practices. It is common for there to be ambiguities of this kind with replications in social research.

The critique of quantitative research

Over the years, quantitative research along with its epistemological and ontological foundations has been the focus of a great deal of criticism, particularly from exponents and spokespersons of qualitative research. To a very large extent, it is difficult to distinguish between different kinds of criticism when reflecting on the different critical points that have been proffered. These include: criticisms of quantitative research in general as a research strategy; criticisms of the epistemological and ontological foundations of quantitative research; and criticisms of specific methods and research designs with which quantitative research is associated.

Criticisms of quantitative research

To give a flavour of the critique of quantitative research, four criticisms will be covered briefly.

1. *Quantitative researchers fail to distinguish people and social institutions from 'the world of nature'.* The phrase 'the world of nature' is from the writings of Schutz (1962) and the specific quotation from which it has been taken can be found on page 16 above. Schutz and other phenomenologists charge social scientists who employ a natural science model with treating the social world as if it were no different from the natural order. In so doing, they draw attention to one of positivism's central tenets—namely, that the principles of the scientific method can and should be applied to all phenomena that are the focus of investigation. As Schutz argues, this tactic is essentially to imply that this means turning a blind eye to the differences between the social and natural world. More particularly, as was observed in Chapter 1, it therefore means ignoring and riding roughshod over the fact that people interpret the world around them, whereas this capacity for self-reflection cannot be found among the objects of the natural sciences ('molecules, atoms, and electrons', as Schutz put it).

2. *The measurement process possesses an artificial and spurious sense of precision and accuracy.* There are a number of aspects to this criticism. For one thing, it has been argued that the connection between the measures developed by social scientists and the concepts they are supposed to be revealing is assumed rather than real; hence, Cicourel's (1964) notion of 'measurement by fiat'. Testing for validity in the manner described in the previous section cannot really address this problem, because the very tests themselves entail measurement by fiat. A further way in which the measurement process is regarded by writers like Cicourel as flawed is that it presumes that when, for example, members of a sample respond to a question on a questionnaire (which is itself taken to be an indicator of a concept), they interpret the key terms in the question similarly. For many writers, respondents simply do not interpret such terms similarly. An often used reaction to this problem is to use questions with fixed-choice answers, but this approach merely provides 'a solution to the problem of meaning by simply ignoring it' (Cicourel 1964: 108).

3. *The reliance on instruments and procedures hinders the connection between research and everyday life.* This issue relates to the question of ecological validity that was raised in Chapter 2. Many methods of quantitative research rely heavily on administering research instruments to subjects (such as structured interviews and self-completion questionnaires) or on controlling situations to determine their effects (such as in experiments). However, as Cicourel (1982) asks, how do we know if survey respondents have the requisite knowledge to answer a question or whether they are similar in their sense of the topic being important to them in their everyday lives? Thus, if respondents answer a set of questions designed to measure racial prejudice, can we be sure that they are equally aware of what it is and what its manifestations are and can we be sure that it is of equal concern to them in the ways in which it connects with everyday life? One can go even further and ask how well their answers relate to their everyday lives. People may answer a question designed to measure racial prejudice, but respondents' actual behaviour may be at variance with their answers (Thinking deeply 11.2).

4. *The analysis of relationships between variables creates a static view of social life that is independent of people's lives.* Blumer (1956: 685) argued that studies that aim to bring out the relationships between variables omit 'the process of interpretation or definition that goes on in human groups'. This means that, for example, we do not know how an apparent relationship between two or more variables has been produced by the people on whom the

research was conducted. This criticism incorporates the first and third criticisms that have been referred to—that the meaning of events to individuals is ignored and that we do not know how such findings connect to everyday contexts—but adds a further element—namely, that it creates a sense of a static social world that is separate from the individuals who make it up. In other words, quantitative research is seen as carrying an objectivist ontology that reifies the social world.

We can see in these criticisms the application of a set of concerns associated with a qualitative research strategy that reveals the combination of an interpretivist epistemological orientation (an emphasis on meaning from the individual's point of view) and a **constructionist** ontology (an emphasis on viewing the social world as the product of individuals rather than as something beyond them). The criticisms may appear very damning, but, as we will see in Chapter 16, quantitative researchers have a powerful battery of criticisms of qualitative research in their arsenal as well!

Is it always like this?

One of the problems with characterizing any research strategy, research design, or research method is that to a certain extent one is always outlining an ideal-typical approach. In other words, one tends to create something that represents that strategy, design, or method, but that may not be reflected in its entirety in research practice. This gap between the ideal type and actual practice can arise as a result of at least two major considerations. First, it arises because those of us who write about and teach research methods cannot cover every eventuality that can arise in the process of social research, so that we tend to provide accounts of the research process that draw upon common features. Thus, a model of the process of quantitative research, such as that provided in Figure 6.1, should be thought of as a general *tendency* rather than as a definitive description of all quantitative research. A second reason why the gap can arise is that, to a very large extent when writing about and teaching research methods, we are essentially providing an account of *good practice*. The fact of the matter is that these practices are often not followed in the published research that students are likely to encounter in the substantive courses that they will be taking. This failure to follow the procedures

associated with good practice is not necessarily due to incompetence on the part of social researchers (though in some cases it can be!), but is much more likely to be associated with matters of time, cost, and feasibility—in other words, the pragmatic concerns that cannot be avoided when one does social research.

Reverse operationism

As an example of the first source of the gap between the ideal type and actual research practice we can take the case of something that I have referred to as 'reverse operationism' (Bryman 1988a: 28). The model of the process of quantitative research in Figure 6.1 implies that concepts are specified and measures are then provided for them. As we have noted, this means that indicators must be devised. This is the basis of the idea of 'operationism' or **operationalism**, a term that derives from physics (Bridgman 1927), and that implies a deductive view of how research should proceed. However, this view of research neglects the fact that measurement can entail much more of an **inductive** element than Figure 6.1 implies. Sometimes, measures are developed that in turn lead to conceptualization. One way in which this can occur is when a statistical technique known as *factor analysis* is employed (see Key concept 6.6). In order to measure the concept of 'charismatic leadership', a term that owes a great deal to Weber's (1947) notion of charismatic authority, Conger and Kanungo (1998) generated twenty-five items to provide a multiple-item measure of the concept. These items derived from their reading of existing theory and research on the subject, particularly in connection with charismatic leadership in organizations. When the items were administered to a sample of respondents and the results were factor analysed, it was found that the items bunched around six factors, each of which, to all intents and purposes, represents a dimension of the concept of charismatic leadership:

1. strategic vision and articulation behaviour;

2. sensitivity to the environment;

3. unconventional behaviour;

4. personal risk;

5. sensitivity to organizational members' needs;

6. action orientation away from the maintenance of the status quo.

The point to note is that these six dimensions were not specified at the outset: the link between conceptualization and measurement was an inductive one. Nor is this an unusual situation so far as research is concerned (Bryman 1988*a*: 26–8).

Key concept 6.6
What is factor analysis?

Factor analysis is employed in relation to multiple-indicator measures to determine whether groups of indicators tend to bunch together to form distinct clusters, referred to as factors. Its main goal is to reduce the number of variables with which the researcher needs to deal. It is used in relation to multiple-item measures, like Likert scales, to see how far there is an inherent structure to the large number of items that often make up such measures. Researchers sometimes use factor analysis to establish whether the dimensions of a measure that they expect to exist can be confirmed. The clusters of items that are revealed by a factor analysis need to be given names (e.g. innovation and flexibility or autonomy in the example in Research in focus 6.6). It is a complex technique that is beyond the level at which this book is pitched (see Bryman and Cramer 2008: ch. 13), but it has considerable significance for the development of measures in many social scientific fields.

Reliability and validity testing

The second reason why the gap between the ideal type and actual research practice can arise is because researchers do not follow some of the recommended practices. A classic case of this tendency is that, while, as in the present chapter, much time and effort are expended on the articulation of the ways in which the reliability and validity of measures should be determined, often these procedures are not followed. There is evidence from analyses of published quantitative research in organization studies (Podsakoff and Dalton 1987), a field that draws extensively on ideas and methods used in the social sciences, that writers rarely report tests of the

stability of their measures and even more rarely report evidence of validity (only 3 per cent of articles provided information about measurement validity). A large proportion of articles used Cronbach's alpha, but, since this device is relevant only to multiple-item measures, because it gauges internal consistency, the stability and validity of many measures that are employed in the field of organization studies are unknown. This is not to say that the measures are necessarily *un*stable and *in*valid, but that we simply do not know. The reasons why the procedures for determining stability and validity are rarely used are almost certainly the cost and time that are likely to be involved. Researchers tend to be concerned with substantive issues and are less than enthusiastic about engaging in the kind of development work that would be required for a thoroughgoing determination of measurement quality. However, what this means is that Cicourel's (1964) previously cited remark about much measurement in sociology being 'measurement by fiat' has considerable weight.

The remarks on the lack of assessment of the quality of measurement should not be taken as a justification for readers to neglect this phase in their work. My aim is merely to draw attention to some of the ways in which practices described in this book are not always followed and to suggest some reasons why they are not followed.

Sampling

A similar point can be made in relation to sampling, which will be covered in the next chapter. As we will see, good practice is strongly associated with *random* or *probability sampling*. However, quite a lot of research is based on **non-probability samples**—that is, samples that have not been selected in terms of the principles of probability sampling, to be discussed in Chapter 7. Sometimes the use of non-probability samples will be due to the impossibility or extreme difficulty of obtaining **probability samples**. Yet another reason is that the time and cost involved in securing a probability sample are too great relative to the level of resources available. And yet a third reason is that sometimes the opportunity to study a certain group presents itself and represents too good an opportunity to miss. Again, such considerations should not be viewed as a justification and hence a set of reasons for ignoring the principles of sampling to be examined in the next chapter, not least because not following the principles of probability sampling carries implications for the kind of statistical analysis that can be employed (see Chapter 14). Instead, my purpose as before is to draw attention to the ways in which gaps between recommendations about good practice and actual research practice can arise.

Key points

- Quantitative research can be characterized as a linear series of steps moving from theory to conclusions, but the process described in Figure 6.1 is an ideal type from which there are many departures.

- The measurement process in quantitative research entails the search for indicators.

- Establishing the reliability and validity of measures is important for assessing their quality.

- Quantitative research can be characterized as exhibiting certain preoccupations, the most central of which are: measurement; causality; generalization; and replication.

- Quantitative research has been subjected to many criticisms by qualitative researchers. These criticisms tend to revolve around the view that a natural science model is inappropriate for studying the social world.

Questions for review

The main steps in quantitative research

- What are the main steps in quantitative research?

- To what extent do the main steps follow a strict sequence?

- Do the steps suggest a deductive or inductive approach to the relationship between theory and research?

Concepts and their measurement

● Why is measurement important for the quantitative researcher?

● What is the difference between a measure and an indicator?

● Why might multiple-indicator approaches to the measurement of concepts be preferable to those that rely on a single indicator?

Reliability and validity

● What are the main ways of thinking about the reliability of the measurement process? Is one form of reliability the most important?

● 'Whereas validity presupposes reliability, reliability does not presuppose validity.' Discuss.

● What are the main criteria for evaluating measurement validity?

The main preoccupations of quantitative researchers

● Outline the main preoccupations of quantitative researchers. What reasons can you give for their prominence?

● Why might replication be an important preoccupation among quantitative researchers, in spite of the tendency for replications in social research to be fairly rare?

The critique of quantitative research

● 'The crucial problem with quantitative research is the failure of its practitioners to address adequately the issue of meaning.' Discuss.

● How central is the adoption by quantitative researchers of a natural science model of conducting research to the critique by qualitative researchers of quantitative research?

Is it always like this?

● Why do social researchers sometimes not test the validity and/or reliability of measures that they employ?

 Online Resource Centre

http://www.oxfordtextbooks.co.uk/orc/brymansrm3e/

Visit the Online Resource Centre that accompanies this book to enrich your understanding of the nature of quantitative research. Consult web links, test yourself using multiple choice questions, and gain further guidance and inspiration from the Student Researcher's Toolkit.

Sampling

Chapter outline

Chapter guide

This chapter and the three that follow it are very much concerned with principles and practices associated with **social survey** research. Sampling principles are not exclusively concerned with survey research; for example, they are relevant to the selection of documents for **content analysis** (see Chapter 12). However, in this chapter the emphasis will be on sampling in connection with the selection of people who would be asked questions by interview or **questionnaire**. The chapter explores:

- the role of sampling in relation to the overall process of doing survey research;
- the related ideas of **generalization** (also known as **external validity**) and of a representative **sample**; the latter allows the researcher to generalize findings from a sample to a **population**;
- the idea of a *probability sample*—that is, one in which a random selection process has been employed;
- the main types of probability sample: the **simple random sample**; the **systematic sample**; the **stratified random sample**; and the multi-stage **cluster sample**;
- the main issues involved in deciding on sample size;
- different types of **non-probability sample**, including quota sampling, which is widely used in market research and opinion polls;
- potential sources of error in survey research.

Introduction to survey research

This chapter is concerned with some important aspects of conducting a survey, but it presents only a partial picture, because there are many other steps. In this chapter we are concerned with the issues involved in selecting individuals for survey research, although the principles involved apply equally to other approaches to **quantitative research**, such as content analysis. The next three chapters deal with the data collection aspects of conducting a survey, while Chapters 11 and 12 deal with issues to do with the analysis of data.

Figure 7.1 aims to outline the main steps involved in doing survey research. Initially, the survey will begin with general research issues that need to be investigated. These are gradually narrowed down so that they become research questions, which may take the form of hypotheses, but this need not necessarily be the case. The movement from research issues to research questions is likely to be the result of reading the literature relating to the issues, such as relevant theories and evidence.

Once the research questions have been formulated, the planning of the fieldwork can begin. In practice, decisions relating to sampling and the research instrument will overlap but are presented in Figure 7.1 as part of a sequence. The figure is meant to illustrate the main phases of a survey, and these different steps (other than those to do with sampling, which will be covered in this chapter) will be followed through in the next three chapters and in Chapters 14 and 15.

The survey researcher needs to decide what kind of population is suited to the investigation of the topic and also needs to formulate a research instrument and how it should be administered. By 'research instrument' is meant simply something like a **structured interview schedule** or a **self-completion questionnaire**. Moreover, there are several different ways of administering such instruments. Figure 7.2 outlines the main types that are likely to be encountered. Types 1 through 4 are covered in Chapter 8. Types 5 and 6 are covered in Chapter 9. Types 7 through 9 are covered in Chapter 26 in the context of the use of the Internet generally.

Figure 7.1

Steps in conducting a social survey

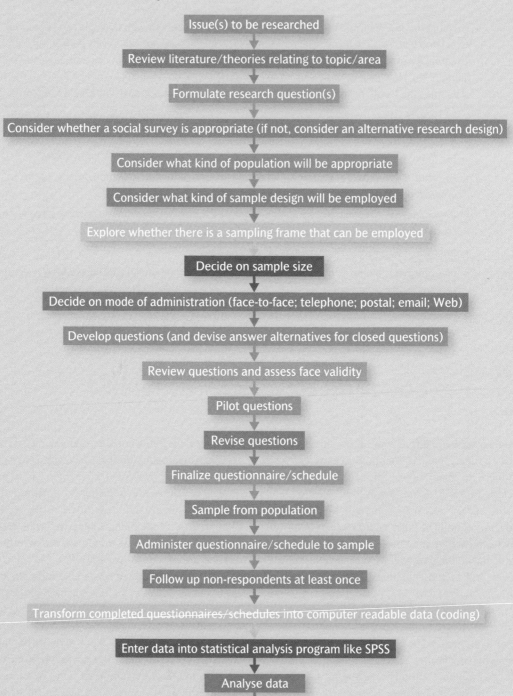

Figure 7.2

Figure 7.2

Main modes of administration of a survey

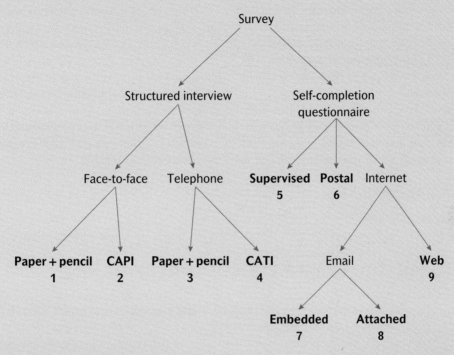

CAPI is computer-assisted personal interviewing
CATI is computer-assisted telephone interviewing

Introduction to sampling

Many of the readers of this book will be university or college students. At some point in your stay at your university (I will use this term from now on to include colleges) you may have wondered about the attitudes of your fellow students to various matters, or about their behaviour in certain areas, or something about their backgrounds. If you were to decide to examine any or all of these three areas, you might consider conducting structured interviews or sending out questionnaires in order to find out about their behaviour, attitudes, and backgrounds. You will, of course, have to consider how best to design your interviews or questionnaires, and the issues that are involved in the decisions that need to be made about designing these research instruments and administering them will be the focus of Chapters 8–10. However, before

getting to that point you are likely to be confronted with a problem. Let us say that your university is quite large and has around 9,000 students. It is extremely unlikely that you will have the time and resources to conduct a survey of all these students. It is unlikely that you would be able to send questionnaires to all 9,000 and even more unlikely that you would be able to interview all of them, since conducting survey research by interview is considerably more expensive and time consuming, all things being equal, than by postal questionnaire (see Chapter 9). It is almost certain that you will need to *sample* students from the total population of students in your university.

The need to sample is one that is almost invariably encountered in quantitative research. In this chapter

I will be almost entirely concerned with matters relating to sampling in relation to social survey research involving data collection by structured interview or questionnaire. Other methods of quantitative research involve sampling considerations, as will be seen in Chapters 11 and 12, when we will examine **structured observation** and content analysis respectively. The principles of sampling involved are more or less identical in connection with these other methods, but frequently other considerations come to the fore as well.

But will any old sample suffice? Would it be sufficient to locate yourself in a central position on your campus (if it has one) and then interview the students who come past you and whom you are in a position to interview? Alternatively, would it be sufficient to go around your student union asking people to be interviewed? Or again to send questionnaires to everyone on your course?

The answer, of course, depends on whether you want to be able to *generalize* your findings to the entire student body in your university. If you do, it is unlikely that any of the three sampling strategies proposed in the previous paragraph would provide you with a *representative sample* of all students in your university. In order to be able to generalize your findings from your sample to the population from which it was selected, the sample must be representative. See Key concept 7.1 for an explanation of key terms concerning sampling.

Key concept 7.1
Basic terms and concepts in sampling

- *Population*: basically, the universe of units from which the sample is to be selected. The term 'units' is employed because it is not necessarily people who are being sampled—the researcher may want to sample from a universe of nations, cities, regions, firms, etc. (Finch and Hayes (1994), for example, based part of their research upon a random sample of wills. Their population, therefore, was a population of wills.) Thus, 'population' has a much broader meaning than the everyday use of the term, whereby it tends to be associated with a nation's entire population.

- *Sample*: the segment of the population that is selected for investigation. It is a subset of the population. The method of selection may be based on a probability or a non-probability approach (see below).

- **Sampling frame**: the listing of all units in the population from which the sample will be selected.

- *Representative sample*: a sample that reflects the population accurately so that it is a microcosm of the population.

- *Sampling bias*: a distortion in the representativeness of the sample that arises when some members of the population (or more precisely the sampling frame) stand little or no chance of being selected for inclusion in the sample.

- *Probability sample*: a sample that has been selected using random selection so that each unit in the population has a known chance of being selected. It is generally assumed that a *representative sample* is more likely to be the outcome when this method of selection from the population is employed. The aim of probability sampling is to keep **sampling error** (see below) to a minimum.

- *Non-probability sample*: a sample that has not been selected using a random selection method. Essentially, this implies that some units in the population are more likely to be selected than others.

- *Sampling error*: error in the findings deriving from research due to the difference between a sample and the population from which it is selected. This may occur even though a probability sample has been employed.

- **Non-sampling error**: error in the findings deriving from research due to the differences between the population and the sample that arise either from deficiencies in the sampling approach, such as an inadequate sampling frame or **non-response** (see below), or from such problems as poor question wording, poor interviewing, or flawed processing of data.

- *Non-response*: a source of non-sampling error that is particularly likely to happen when individuals are being sampled. It occurs whenever some members of the sample refuse to cooperate, cannot be contacted, or for some reason cannot supply the required data (for example, because of mental incapacity).

- *Census*: the enumeration of an entire population. Thus, if data are collected in relation to all units in a population, rather than in relation to a sample of units of that population, the data are treated as census data. The phrase '*the* census' typically refers to the complete enumeration of all members of the population of a nation state—that is, a national census. This form of enumeration occurs once every ten years in the UK. However, in a statistical context, like the term *population*, the idea of a census has a broader meaning than this.

Why might the strategies for sampling students previously outlined be unlikely to produce a representative sample? There are various reasons, of which the following stand out.

- The first two approaches depend heavily upon the availability of students during the time or times that you search them out. Not all students are likely to be equally available at that time, so the sample will not reflect these students.

- They also depend on the students going to the locations. Not all students will necessarily pass the point where you locate yourself or go to the student union, or they may vary hugely in the frequency with which they do so. Their movements are likely to reflect such things as where their halls of residence or accommodation are situated, or where their departments are located, or their social habits. Again, to rely on these locations would mean missing out on students who do not frequent them.

- It is possible, not to say likely, that your decisions about which people to approach will be influenced by your judgements about how friendly or cooperative the people concerned are likely to be or by how comfortable you feel about interviewing students of the same (or opposite) gender to yourself, as well as by many other factors.

- The problem with the third strategy is that students on your course by definition take the same subject as each other and therefore will not be representative of all students in the university.

In other words, in the case of all of the three sampling approaches, your decisions about whom to sample are influenced too much by personal judgements, by prospective respondents' availability, or by your implicit criteria for inclusion. Such limitations mean that, in the language of survey sampling, your sample will be *biased*. A biased sample is one that does not represent the population from which the sample was selected. Sampling bias will occur if some members of the population have little or no chance of being selected for inclusion in the sample. As far as possible, bias should be removed from the selection of your sample. In fact, it is incredibly difficult to remove bias altogether and to derive a truly representative sample. What needs to be done is to ensure that steps are taken to keep bias to an absolute minimum.

Three sources of bias can be identified (see Key concept 7.1 for an explanation of key terms).

1. *If a non-probability or non-random sampling method is used.* If the method used to select the sample is not random, there is a possibility that human judgement will affect the selection process, making some members of the population more likely to be selected than others. This source of bias can be eliminated through the use of probability/random sampling, the procedure for which is described below.

2. *If the sampling frame is inadequate.* If the sampling frame is not comprehensive or is inaccurate or suffers from some other kind of similar deficiency, the sample that is derived cannot represent the population, even if a random/probability sampling method is employed.

3. *If some sample members refuse to participate or cannot be contacted—in other words, if there is non-response.* The problem with non-response is that those who agree to participate may differ in various ways from those who do not agree to participate. Some of the differences may be significant to the research question or questions. If the data are available, it may be possible to check how far, when there is non-response, the resulting sample differs from the population. It is often possible to do this in terms of characteristics such as gender or age, or, in the case of something like a sample of university students, whether the sample's characteristics reflect the entire sample in terms of faculty membership. However, it is usually impossible to determine whether differences exist between the population and the sample after non-response in terms of 'deeper' factors, such as attitudes or patterns of behaviour.

Sampling error

In order to appreciate the significance of sampling error for achieving a representative sample, consider Figures 7.3–7.7. Imagine we have a population of 200 people and we want a sample of 50. Imagine as well that one of the variables of concern to us is whether people watch soap operas and that the population is equally divided between those who do and those who do not. This split is represented by the vertical line that divides the population into two halves (Figure 7.3). If the sample is representative we would expect our sample of 50 to be equally split in terms of this variable (Figure 7.4). If there is a small amount of sampling error, so that we have one person too many who does not watch soap operas and one too few who does, it will look like Figure 7.5. In Figure 7.6 we see a rather more serious degree of over-representation of people who do not watch soaps. This time there are three too many who do not watch them and three too few who do. In Figure 7.7 we have a very

Figure 7.4

A sample with no sampling error

Watch soaps	Do not watch soaps

Figure 7.3

Watching soap operas in a population of 200

Watch soaps	Do not watch soaps

Figure 7.5

A sample with very little sampling error

Watch soaps	Do not watch soaps

Figure 7.6

A sample with some sampling error

Watch soaps   Do not watch soaps

Figure 7.7

A sample with a lot of sampling error

Watch soaps   Do not watch soaps

serious over-representation of people who do not watch soaps, because there are 35 people in the sample who do not watch them, which is much larger than the 25 who should be in the sample.

It is important to appreciate that, as suggested above, probability sampling does not and cannot eliminate sampling error. Even with a well-crafted probability sample, a degree of sampling error is likely to creep in. However, probability sampling stands a better chance than non-probability sampling of keeping sampling error in check so that it does not end up looking like the outcome featured in Figure 7.7. Moreover, probability sampling allows the researcher to employ **tests of statistical significance** that permit inferences to be made about the sample from which the sample was selected. These will be addressed in Chapter 14.

Types of probability sample

Imagine that we are interested in levels of alcohol consumption among university students and the variables that relate to variation in levels of drinking. We might decide to conduct our research in a single nearby university. This means that our population will be all students in that university, which will in turn mean that we will be able to generalize our findings only to students of that university. We simply cannot assume that levels of alcohol consumption and their correlates will be the same in other universities. We might decide that we want our research to be conducted only on full-time students, so that part-time students are omitted. Imagine too that there are 9,000 full-time students in the university.

Simple random sample

The simple random sample is the most basic form of probability sample. With random sampling, each unit of the population has an equal probability of inclusion in the sample. Imagine that we decide that we have enough money to interview 450 students at the university. This means that the probability of inclusion in the sample is

$$\frac{450}{9{,}000}, \text{ i.e. 1 in 20}$$

This is known as the *sampling fraction* and is expressed as

$$\frac{n}{N}$$

where n is the sample size and N is the population size.

The key steps in devising our simple random sample can be represented as follows.

1. Define the population. We have decided that this will be all full-time students at the university. This is our N and in this case is 9,000.

2. Select or devise a comprehensive sampling frame. It is likely that the university will have an office that keeps records of all students and that this will enable us to exclude those who do not meet our criteria for inclusion—i.e. part-time students.

3. Decide your sample size (n). We have decided that this will be 450.

4. List all the students in the population and assign them consecutive numbers from 1 to N. In our case, this will be 1 to 9,000.

5. Using a table of random numbers, or a computer program that can generate random numbers, select n (450) different random numbers that lie between 1 and N (9,000).

6. The students to which the n (450) random numbers refer constitute the sample.

Two points are striking about this process. First, there is almost no opportunity for human bias to manifest itself. Students would not be selected on such subjective criteria as whether they looked friendly and approachable. The selection of whom to interview is entirely mechanical. Second, the process is not dependent on the students' availability. They do not have to be walking in the interviewer's proximity to be included in the sample. The process of selection is done without their knowledge. It is not until they are contacted by an interviewer that they know that they are part of a social survey.

Step 5 mentions the possible use of a table of random numbers. These can be found in the appendices of many statistics books. The tables are made up of columns of five-digit numbers, such as:

09188
90045
73189
75768

54016
08358
28306
53840
91757
89415

The first thing to notice is that, since these are five-digit numbers and the maximum number that we can sample from is 9,000, which is a four-digit number, none of the random numbers seems appropriate, except for 09188 and 08358, although the former is larger than the largest possible number. The answer is that we should take just four digits in each number. Let us take the last four digits. This would yield the following:

9188
0045
3189
5768
4016
8358
8306
3840
1757
9415

However, two of the resulting numbers—9188 and 9415 —exceed 9,000. We cannot have a student with either of these numbers assigned to him or her. The solution is simple: we ignore these numbers. This means that the student who has been assigned the number 45 will be the first to be included in the sample; the student who has been assigned the number 3189 will be next; the student who has been assigned the number 5768 will be next; and so on.

However, this somewhat tortuous procedure may be replaced in some circumstances by using a *systematic sampling* procedure (see next section) and more generally can be replaced by enlisting the computer for assistance (see Tips and skills 'Generating random numbers').

Systematic sample

A variation on the simple random sample is the systematic sample. With this kind of sample, you select units directly from the sampling frame—that is, without resorting to a table of random numbers.

We know that we are to select 1 student in 20. With a systematic sample, we would make a random start between 1 and 20 inclusive, possibly by using the last two

Tips and skills
Generating random numbers

The method for generating random numbers described in the text is what might be thought of as the classic approach. However, a far neater and quicker way is to generate random numbers on the computer. For example, the following website provides an online random generator which is very easy to use: http://www.mdani.demon.co.uk/para/random.htm (accessed on 25 July 2007).

If we want to select 450 cases from a population of 9,000, specify 450 after **Generate**, the digit 1 after **pseudo-random numbers between** and 9000 after **and**. You will also need to specify from a drop-down menu 'with no repeats'. This means that no random number will be selected more than once. Then simply click on **GO** and the 450 random numbers will appear in a box below **OUTPUT**. You can then copy and paste the random numbers into a document.

digits in a table of random numbers. If we did this with the ten random numbers above, the first relevant one would be 54016, since it is the first one where the last two digits yield a number of 20 or below, in this case 16. This means that the sixteenth student on our sampling frame is the first to be in our sample. Thereafter, we take every twentieth student on the list. So the sequence will go:

16, 36, 56, 76, 96, 116, etc.

This approach obviates the need to assign numbers to students' names and then to look up names of the students whose numbers have been drawn by the random selection process. It is important to ensure, however, that there is no inherent ordering of the sampling frame, since this may bias the resulting sample. If there is some ordering to the list, the best solution is to rearrange it.

Stratified random sampling

In our imaginary study of university students, one of the features that we might want our sample to exhibit is a proportional representation of the different faculties to which students are attached. It might be that the kind of discipline a student is studying is viewed as relevant to a wide range of attitudinal features that are relevant to the study of drinking. Generating a simple random sample or a systematic sample *might* yield such a representation, so that the proportion of humanities students in the sample is the same as that in the student population and so on. Thus, if there are 1,800 students in the humanities faculty, using our sampling fraction of 1 in 20, we would expect to have *90* students in our sample from this fac-

ulty. However, because of sampling error, it is unlikely that this will occur and that there will be a difference, so that there may be, say, 85 or 93 from this faculty.

Because it is almost certain that the university will include in its records the faculty in which students are based, or indeed may have separate sampling frames for each faculty, it will be possible to ensure that students are accurately represented in terms of their faculty membership. In the language of sampling, this means stratifying the population by a criterion (in this case, faculty membership) and selecting either a simple random sample or a systematic sample from each of the resulting strata. In the present example, if there are five faculties we would have five strata, with the numbers in each stratum being one-twentieth of the total for each faculty, as in Table 7.1, which also shows a hypothetical outcome of using a simple random sample, which results in a distribution of students across faculties that does not mirror the population all that well.

The advantage of stratified sampling in a case like this is clear: it ensures that the resulting sample will be distributed in the same way as the population in terms of the stratifying criterion. If you use a simple random or systematic sampling approach, you *may* end up with a distribution like that of the stratified sample, but it is unlikely. Two points are relevant here. First, you can conduct stratified sampling sensibly only when it is relatively easy to identify and allocate units to strata. If it is not possible or it would be very difficult to do so, stratified sampling will not be feasible. Second, you can use more than one stratifying criterion. Thus, it may be that you would want to stratify by both faculty and gender or faculty and

Table 7.1

The advantages of stratified sampling			
Faculty	Population	Stratified sample	Hypothetical simple random or systematic sample
Humanities	1,800	90	85
Social sciences	1,200	60	70
Pure sciences	2,000	100	120
Applied sciences	1,800	90	84
Engineering	2,200	110	91
TOTAL	9,000	450	450

whether students are undergraduates or postgraduates. If it is feasible to identify students in terms of these stratifying criteria, it is possible to use pairs of criteria or several criteria (such as faculty membership plus gender plus undergraduate/postgraduate).

Stratified sampling is really feasible only when the relevant information is available. In other words, when data are available that allow the ready identification of members of the population in terms of the stratifying criterion (or criteria), it is sensible to employ this sampling method. But it is unlikely to be economical if the identification of population members for stratification purposes entails a great deal of work because there is no available listing in terms of strata.

Student experience
Probability sampling for a student project

Joe Thompson describes the sampling procedure that he and the other members of his team used for their study of students living in halls of residence at the University of East Anglia as a stratified random sample. The following description suggests that they employed a systematic sampling approach for finding students within halls.

Stratified random sampling was used to decide which halls of residence each member of the research team would go to and obtain questionnaire responses. This sampling method was the obvious choice as it meant there could be no fixing/bias to which halls the interviewee would go to and also maintained the representative nature of the research.

The stratified random sampling method known as the 'random walk process' was used when conducting the interviews. Each member of the research group was assigned a number between 4 and 8 as a sampling fraction gap: I was assigned the number 7 and 'Coleman house block 1' as my accommodation block. This meant that, when conducting my interviews, I would go to Coleman house and knock on the 7th door, and then the 14th door, adding 7 each time, until I had completed five interviews. If I encountered a lack of response from the 6th door, I would return to the first flat but add one each time to avoid periodicity. This sampling method was determined by the principles of standardization, reliability, and validity.

To read more about Joe's research experiences, go to the Online Resource Centre that accompanies this book at http://www.oxfordtextbooks.co.uk/orc/brymansrm3e/.

Multi-stage cluster sampling

In the example we have been dealing with, students to be interviewed are located in a single university. Interviewers will have to arrange their interviews with the sampled students, but, because they are all close together (even in a split-site university), they will not be involved in a lot of travel. However, imagine that we wanted a *national* sample of students. It is likely that interviewers would have to travel the length and breadth of the UK to interview the sampled students. This would add a great deal to the time and cost of doing the research. This kind of problem occurs whenever the aim is to interview a sample that is to be drawn from a widely dispersed population, such as a national population, or a large region, or even a large city.

One way in which it is possible to deal with this potential problem is to employ *cluster sampling*. With cluster sampling, the primary sampling unit (the first stage of the sampling procedure) is not the units of the population to be sampled but groupings of those units. It is the latter groupings or aggregations of population units that are known as *clusters*. Imagine that we want a nationally representative sample of 5,000 students. Using simple random or systematic sampling would yield a widely dispersed sample, which would result in a great deal of travel for interviewers. One solution might be to sample universities and then students from each of the sampled universities. A probability sampling method would need to be employed at each stage. Thus, we might randomly sample ten universities from the entire population of universities, thus yielding ten clusters, and we would then interview 500 randomly selected students at each of the ten universities.

Now imagine that the result of sampling ten universities gives the following list:

- Glasgow Caledonian
- Edinburgh
- Teesside
- Sheffield
- University College Swansea
- Leeds Metropolitan
- University of Ulster
- University College London
- Southampton
- Loughborough

This list is fine, but interviewers could still be involved in a great deal of travel, since the ten universities are quite a long way from each other. North American and Australian readers who examine this last comment by looking at a map of the United Kingdom may view the universities as in fact very close to each other!

One solution is likely to be to group all UK universities by standard region (see Research in focus 7.1 for an example of this kind of approach) and to randomly sample two standard regions. Five universities might then be sampled from each of the two lists of universities and then 500 students from each of the ten universities. Thus, there are separate stages:

- group UK universities by standard region and sample two regions;
- sample five universities from each of the two regions;
- sample 500 students from each of the ten universities.

Research in focus 7.1
An example of a multi-stage cluster sample

For their study of social class in modern Britain, Marshall *et al.* (1988: 288) designed a sample 'to achieve 2,000 interviews with a random selection of men aged 16–64 and women aged 16–59 who were not in full-time education'.

- Sampling parliamentary constituencies
  — Parliamentary constituencies were ordered by standard region (there are eleven).
  — Constituencies were allocated to one of three population density bands within standard regions.
  — These subgroups were then reordered by political party voted to represent the constituency at the previous general election.

- These subgroups were then listed in ascending order of percentage in owner–occupation.
- 100 parliamentary constituencies were then sampled.
- Thus, parliamentary constituencies were stratified in terms of four variables: standard region; population density; political party voted for in last election; and percentage of owner–occupation.
- Sampling polling districts
  - Two polling districts were chosen from each sampled constituency.
- Sampling individuals
  - Nineteen addresses from each sampled polling district were systematically sampled.
  - One person at each address was chosen according to a number of pre-defined rules.

In a sense, cluster sampling is always a multi-stage approach, because one always samples clusters first, and then something else—either further clusters or population units—is sampled.

Many examples of multi-stage cluster sampling entail stratification. We might, for example, want to stratify universities in terms of whether they are 'old' or 'new' universities—that is, those that received their charters after the 1991 White Paper for Higher Education, *Higher Education: A New Framework*. In each of the two regions, we would group universities along the old/new university criterion and then select two or three universities from each of the two strata per region.

Research in focus 7.1 provides an example of a multi-stage cluster sample. It entailed three stages: the sampling of parliamentary constituencies, the sampling of polling districts, and the sampling of individuals. In a way, there are four stages, because addresses are sampled from polling districts and then individuals are sampled from each address. However, Marshall *et al.* (1988) present their sampling strategy as involving just three stages. Parliamentary constituencies were stratified by four criteria: standard region, population density, voting behaviour, and owner–occupation.

The advantage of multi-stage cluster sampling should be clear by now: it allows interviewers to be far more geographically concentrated than would be the case if a simple random or stratified sample were selected. The advantages of stratification can be capitalized upon because the clusters can be stratified in terms of strata. However, even when a very rigorous sampling strategy is employed, sampling error cannot be avoided, as the example in Research in focus 7.2 shows.

Research in focus 7.2
The 1992 British Crime Survey

The British Crime Survey (BCS) is a regular survey, funded by the Home Office, of a national sample drawn from the populations of England and Wales. The survey was conducted on eight occasions between 1982 and 2000 and annually since 2001. In each instance, over 10,000 people were interviewed. The main object of the survey is to glean information on respondents' experiences of being victims of crime. There is also a self-report component in which a selection of the sample are interviewed on their attitudes to crime and to report on crimes they have committed. Before 1992, the BCS used the electoral register as a sampling frame. Relying on a register of the electorate as a sampling frame is not without problems in spite of appearing robust: it omits any persons who are not registered, a problem that was exacerbated by the Community Charge (poll tax), which resulted in a significant amount of non-registration, as some people sought to avoid detection in order not to have to pay the tax. In 1992 the Postcode Address File was employed as a sampling frame and has been used since then. Its main advantage over the electoral register as a sampling frame is that it is updated more frequently. It is not perfect, because the homeless will not be accessible through it. The sample itself is a stratified multi-stage cluster sample. The sampling procedure produced 13,117 residential addresses. Like most surveys, there was some non-response, with 23.3 per cent of the 13,117 addresses not resulting in a 'valid' interview. Just under half of these cases were the result of an outright refusal. In spite of the fact that the BCS is a rigorously selected and very large sample, an examination of the 1992 survey by Elliott and Ellingworth (1997) shows that there is some sampling error. By comparing the distribution of survey respondents with the 1991 census, they show that certain social groups are somewhat under-represented, most notably: owner–occupiers, households in which no car is owned, and male unemployed. However, Elliott and Ellingworth show that, as the level of property crime in postcode address sectors increases, the response rate (see Key concept 7.2) decreases. In other words, people who live in high crime areas tend to be less likely to agree to be interviewed. How far this tendency affects the BCS data is difficult to determine, but the significance of this brief example is that, even when a sample of this quality is selected, the existence of sampling and non-sampling error cannot be discounted. The potential for a larger spread of errors when levels of sampling rigour fall short of a sample like that selected for the BCS is, therefore, considerable.

The qualities of a probability sample

The reason why probability sampling is such an important procedure in social survey research is that it is possible to make inferences from information about a random sample to the population from which it was selected. In other words, we can generalize findings derived from a sample to the population. This is not to say that we treat the population data and the sample data as the same. If we take the example of the level of alcohol consumption in our sample of 450 students, which we will treat as the number of units of alcohol consumed in the previous

seven days, we will know that the mean number of units consumed by the sample ($\bar{x}$) can be used to estimate the population mean (μ) but with known margins of error. The mean, or more properly the **arithmetic mean**, is the simple average.

In order to address this point it is necessary to use some basic statistical ideas. These are presented in Tips and skills 'Generalizing from a random sample to the population' and can be skipped if just a broad idea of sampling procedures is required.

Tips and skills
Generalizing from a random sample to the population

Let us say that the sample mean is 9.7 units of alcohol consumed (the average amount of alcohol consumed in the previous seven days in the sample). A crucial consideration here is: how confident can we be that the mean level of alcohol consumption of 9.7 units is likely to be found in the population, even when probability sampling has been employed? If we take an infinite number of samples from a population, the sample estimates of the mean of the variable under consideration will vary in relation to the population mean. This variation will take the form of a bell-shaped curve known as a *normal distribution* (see Figure 7.8). The shape of the distribution implies that there is a clustering of sample means at or around the population mean. Half the sample means will be at or below the population mean; the other half will be at or above the population mean. As we move to the left (at or lower than the population mean) or the right (at or higher than the population mean), the curve

Figure 7.8

The distribution of sample means

Notes: 95 per cent of sample means will lie within the shaded area. SE = standard error of the mean.

tails off, implying fewer and fewer samples generating means that depart considerably from the population mean. The variation of sample means around the population mean is the *sampling error* and is measured using a statistic known as the **standard error of the mean**. This is an estimate of the amount that a sample mean is likely to differ from the population mean.

This consideration is important because sampling theory tells us that 68 per cent of all sample means will lie between + or − one standard error from the population mean and that 95 per cent of all sample means will lie between + or − 1.96 standard errors from the population mean. It is this second calculation that is crucial, because it is at least implicitly employed by survey researchers when they report their statistical findings. They typically employ 1.96 standard errors as the crucial criterion in how confident they can be in their findings. Essentially, the criterion implies that you can be 95 per cent certain that the population mean lies within + or − 1.96 sampling errors from the sample mean.

If a sample has been selected according to probability sampling principles, we know that we can be 95 per cent certain that the population mean will lie between the sample mean + or − 1.96 multiplied by the standard error of the mean. This is known as the *confidence interval*. If the mean level of alcohol consumption in the previous seven days in our sample of 450 students is 9.7 units and the standard error of the mean is 1.3, we can be 95 per cent certain that the population mean will lie between

$$9.7 + (1.96 \times 1.3)$$

and

$$9.7 - (1.96 \times 1.3)$$

i.e. between 12.248 and 7.152.

If the standard error was smaller, the range of possible values of the population mean would be narrower; if the standard error was larger, the range of possible values of the population mean would be wider.

If a stratified sample is selected, the standard error of the mean will be smaller because the variation between strata is essentially eliminated because the population will be accurately represented in the sample in terms of the stratification criterion or criteria employed. This consideration demonstrates the way in which stratification injects an extra increment of precision into the probability sampling process, since a possible source of sampling error is eliminated.

By contrast, a cluster sample without stratification exhibits a larger standard error of the mean than a comparable simple random sample. This occurs because a possible source of variability between students (i.e. membership of one university rather than another, which may affect levels of alcohol consumption) is disregarded. If, for example, some universities had a culture of heavy drinking in which a large number of students participated, and if these universities were not selected because of the procedure for selecting clusters, an important source of variability would have been omitted. It also implies that the sample mean would be on the low side, but that is another matter.

Sample size

As someone who is known as a teacher of research methods and a writer of books in this area, I often get asked questions about methodological issues. One question that is asked almost more than any other relates to the size of the sample—'how large should my sample be?' or 'is my sample large enough?' The decision about sample size is not a straightforward one: it depends on a number of considerations and there is no one definitive answer. This is frequently a source of great disappointment to those who pose such questions. Moreover, most of the time decisions about sample size are affected by considerations of time and cost. Therefore, invariably decisions about sample size represent a compromise between the constraints of time and cost, the need for precision, and a variety of further considerations that will now be addressed.

Absolute and relative sample size

One of the most basic considerations, and one that is possibly the most surprising, is that, contrary to what you might have expected, it is the *absolute* size of a sample that is important not its *relative* size. This means that a national probability sample of 1,000 individuals in the UK has as much validity as a national probability sample of 1,000 individuals in the USA, even though the latter has a much larger population. It also means that increasing the

size of a sample increases the precision of a sample. This means that the 95 per cent confidence interval referred to in Tips and skills 'Generalizing from a random sample to the population' narrows. However, a large sample cannot *guarantee* precision, so that it is probably better to say that increasing the size of a sample increases the *likely* precision of a sample. This means that, as sample size increases, sampling error decreases. Therefore, an important component of any decision about sample size should be how much sampling error one is prepared to tolerate. The less sampling error one is prepared to tolerate, the larger a sample will need to be. Fowler (1993) warns against a simple acceptance of this criterion. He argues that in practice researchers do not base their decisions about sample size on a single estimate of a variable. Most survey research is concerned to generate a host of estimates—that is, of the variables that make up the research instrument that is administered. He also observes that it is not normal for survey researchers to be in a position to specify in advance 'a desired level of precision' (Fowler 1993: 34). Moreover, since sampling error will be only one component of any error entailed in an estimate, the notion of using a desired level of precision as a factor in a decision about sample size is not realistic. Instead, to the extent that this notion does enter into decisions about sample size, it usually does so in a general rather than a calculated way.

Tips and skills
Sample size and probability sampling

As I have said in the text, the issue of sample size is the matter that most often concerns students and others. Basically, this is an area where size really does matter—the bigger the sample, the more representative it is likely to be (provided the sample is randomly selected), regardless of the size of the population from which it is drawn. However, when doing projects, students clearly need to do their research with very limited resources. You should try to find out from your department whether there are any guidelines about whether samples of a minimum size are expected. If there are no such guidelines, you will need to conduct your mini-survey in such a way as to maximize the number of interviews you can manage or the number of postal questionnaires you can send out, given the amount of time and resources available to you. Also, in many if not most cases, a truly random approach to sample selection may not be open to you. The crucial point is to be clear about and to justify what you have done. Explain the difficulties that you would have encountered in generating a random sample. Explain why you really could not include any more in your sample of respondents. But, above all, do not make claims about your sample that are not sustainable. Do not claim that it is representative or that you have a random sample when it is clearly not the case that either of these is true. In other words, be frank about what you have done. People will be much more inclined to accept an awareness of the limits of your sample design than claims about a sample that are patently false. Also, it may be that there are lots of good features about your sample—the range of people included, the good response rate, the high level of cooperation you received from the firm. Make sure you play up these positive features at the same time as being honest about its limitations.

Time and cost

Time and cost considerations become very relevant in this context. In the previous paragraph it is clearly being suggested that the larger the sample size the greater the precision (because the amount of sampling error will be less). However, by and large, up to a sample size of around 1,000, the gains in precision are noticeable as the sample size climbs from low figures of 50, 100, 150, and so on upwards. After a certain point, often in the region of 1,000, the sharp increases in precision become less pronounced, and, although it does not plateau, there is a slowing-down in the extent to which precision increases (and hence the extent to which the sample error of the mean declines). Considerations of sampling size are likely to be profoundly affected by matters of time and cost at such a juncture, since striving for smaller and smaller increments of precision becomes an increasingly uneconomic proposition. As Hazelrigg (2004: 85) succinctly puts it: 'The larger the size of the sample drawn from a population the more likely ($\bar{x}$) converges to μ; but the convergence occurs at a decelerating rate (which means that very large samples are decreasingly cost efficient).'

Non-response

However, considerations about sampling error do not end here. The problem of *non-response* should be borne in mind. Most sample surveys attract a certain amount of non-response. Thus, it is likely that only some members of our sample will agree to participate in the research. If it is our aim to ensure as far as possible that 450 students are interviewed and if we think that there may be a 20 per cent rate of non-response, it may be advisable to sample 540–50 individuals, on the grounds that approximately 90 will be non-respondents.

The issue of non-response, and in particular of refusal to participate, is of particular significance, because it has been suggested by some researchers that response rates to social surveys (see Key concept 7.2) are declining in many countries. This implies that there is a growing tendency towards people refusing to participate in social survey research. In 1973 an article in the American magazine *Business Week* carried an article ominously entitled 'The Public Clams up on Survey Takers'. The magazine asked survey companies about their experiences and found considerable concern about declining response rates. Similarly, in Britain, a report from a working party on the

Market Research Society's Research and Development Committee in 1975 pointed to similar concerns among market research companies. However, an analysis of this issue by T. W. Smith (1995) suggests that, contrary to popular belief, there is no consistent evidence of such a decline. Moreover, Smith shows that it is difficult to disentangle general trends in response rates from such variables as the subject matter of the research, the type of respondent, and the level of effort expended on improving the number of respondents to individual surveys. However, an overview of non-response trends in the USA based on non-response rates for various continuous surveys suggests that there is a decline in the preparedness of households to participate in surveys (Groves *et al.* 2004).

Key concept 7.2
What is a response rate?

The notion of a response rate is a common one in social survey research. When a social survey is conducted, whether by structured interview or by self-completion questionnaire, it is invariably the case that some people who are in the sample refuse to participate. The response rate is, therefore, the percentage of a sample that does, in fact, agree to participate. However, the calculation of a response rate is a little more complicated than this. First, not everyone who replies will be included: if a large number of questions are not answered by a respondent or if there are clear indications that he or she has not taken the interview or questionnaire seriously, it is better to employ only the number of *usable* interviews or questionnaires as the numerator. Similarly, it also tends to occur that not everyone in a sample turns out to be a suitable or appropriate respondent or can be contacted. Thus the response rate is calculated as follows:

$$\frac{\text{number of usable questionaires}}{\text{total sample} - \text{unsuitable or}} \times 100$$
$$\text{uncontactable members of the sample}$$

A further interesting issue in connection with non-response is that of how far researchers should go in order to boost their response rates. In Chapter 9, a number of steps that can be taken to improve response rates to postal questionnaires, which are particularly prone to poor response rates, are discussed. However, boosting response rates to interview-based surveys can prove expensive. Teitler *et al.* (2003) present a discussion of the steps taken to boost the response rate of a US sample that was hard to reach—namely, both parents of newly born children, where most of the parents were not married. They found that, although there was evidence that increasing the response rate from an initial 68 per cent to 80 per cent meant that the final sample resembled more closely the population from which the sample had been taken, diminishing returns undoubtedly set in. In other words, the improvements in the characteristics of the sample necessitated a disproportionate outlay of resources. However, this is not to say that steps should not be taken to improve response rates. For example, following up respondents who do not initially respond to a postal questionnaire invariably results in an improved response rate at little additional cost.

Research in focus 7.3
The problem of non-response

In December 2006 an article in *The Times* reported that a study of the weight of British children had been hindered because many families declined to participate. The study was commissioned by the Department of Health and found that, for example, among those aged 10 or 11, 14 per cent were overweight and 17 per cent were obese. However, *The Times* writer notes that a report compiled by the Department of Health on the research suggests that such figures are 'likely systematically to underestimate the prevalence of overweight and obesity' (quoted in Hawkes 2006: 24). The reason for this bias in the statistics is that parents were able to refuse to let their children participate, and those whose children were heavier were more likely to do so. As a result, the sample was biased towards those who were less heavy. The authors of the report drew the inference about sampling bias because they noted that, in areas where there was a better response rate, more children were recorded as obese than in areas where there was a poorer response rate.

Heterogeneity of the population

Yet another consideration is the homogeneity and heterogeneity of the population from which the sample is to be taken. When a sample is very heterogeneous, like a sample of a whole country or city, the population is likely to be highly varied. When it is relatively homogeneous, such as a population of students or of members of an occupation, the amount of variation is less. The implication of this is that, the greater the heterogeneity of a population, the larger a sample will need to be.

Kind of analysis

Finally, researchers should bear in mind the *kind of analysis* they intend to undertake. A case in point here is the contingency table. A contingency table shows the relationship between two variables in tabular form. It shows how variation in one variable relates to variation in another variable. To understand this point, consider the basic structure of a table in the study by Marshall *et al.* (1988) of social class in Britain. This research was referred to in Research in focus 7.1. The table is based on the 589 cohabiting couples (1,178 people) in which both partners are employed in paid work. The authors aim to show in the table how far couples are of the same or a different social class in terms of Goldthorpe's seven-category scheme for classifying social class. The result is a table in which, because each variable comprises 7 categories, there are 49 cells in the table (i.e. 7×7). In order for there to be an adequate number of cases in each cell, a fairly large sample was required. Imagine that Marshall *et al.* had conducted a survey on a much smaller sample in which they ended up with just 150 couples. If the same kind of analysis as Marshall *et al.* carried out was conducted, it would be found that these 150 couples would be very dispersed across the 49 cells of the table. It is likely that many of the cells would be empty or would have very small numbers in them, which would make it difficult to make inferences about what the table showed. In fact, quite a lot of the cells in the actual table in Marshall *et al.* have very small numbers in them (8 cells contain 1 or 0). This problem would have been even more pronounced if they had ended up with a much smaller sample of couples. Consequently, considerations of sample size should be sensitive to the kinds of analysis that will be subsequently required, such as the issue of the number of cells in a table. In a case such as this, a larger sample will be necessitated by the nature of the analysis to be conducted as well as the nature of the variables in question.

Types of non-probability sampling

The term 'non-probability sampling' is essentially an umbrella term to capture all forms of sampling that are not conducted according to the canons of probability sampling outlined above. It is not surprising, therefore, that the term covers a wide range of different types of sampling strategy, at least one of which—the quota sample—is claimed by some practitioners to be almost as good as a probability sample. In this section we will cover three main types of non-probability sample: the convenience sample; the snowball sample; and the quota sample.

Convenience sampling

A convenience sample is one that is simply available to the researcher by virtue of its accessibility. Imagine that a researcher who teaches education at a university is interested in the kinds of features that teachers look for in their headmasters. The researcher might administer a questionnaire to several classes of students, all of whom are teachers taking a part-time master's degree in education. The chances are that the researcher will receive all or almost all of the questionnaires back, so that there will be a good response rate. The findings may prove quite interesting, but the problem with such a sampling strategy is that it is impossible to generalize the findings, because we do not know of what population this sample is representative. They are simply a group of teachers who are available to the researcher. They are almost certainly not representative of teachers as a whole—the very fact they are taking this degree programme marks them off as different from teachers in general.

This is not to suggest that convenience samples should never be used. Let us say that our lecturer/researcher is developing a battery of questions that are designed to measure the leadership preferences of teachers. It is highly desirable to pilot such a research instrument before using it in an investigation, and administering it to a group who are not a part of the main study may be a legitimate way of carrying out some preliminary analysis of such issues as whether respondents tend to answer in identical ways to a question, or whether one question is often omitted when teachers respond to it. In other words, for this kind of purpose, a convenience sample may be acceptable though not ideal. A second kind of context in which it may be at least fairly acceptable to use a convenience sample is when the chance presents itself to gather data from a convenience sample and it represents too good an opportunity to miss. The data will not allow definitive findings to be generated, because of the problem of generalization, but it could provide a springboard for further research or allow links to be forged with existing findings in an area.

It also perhaps ought to be recognized that convenience sampling probably plays a more prominent role than is sometimes supposed. Certainly, in the field of organization studies it has been noted that convenience samples are very common and indeed are more prominent than are samples based on probability sampling (Bryman 1989a: 113–14). Social research is also frequently based on convenience sampling. Research in focus 7.4 and 7.5 contain examples of the use of convenience samples in social research. Probability sampling involves a lot of preparation, so that it is frequently avoided because of the difficulty and costs involved.

Research in focus 7.4
A convenience sample

Lucas (1997) describes a study of university students that was undertaken to find out about the extent and kinds of part-time employment among the students. Data were collected in spring 1995 from students in five of the seven faculties at Manchester Metropolitan University, where the author of the report was a lecturer. The specific degree programmes chosen were first degrees in: chemistry; combined studies; electrical engineering; history; hotel and catering management; illustration; law; psychology; and social science. Self-completion questionnaires were given out to students in the first, final, and either second or third years of their degrees (depending on whether the course lasted three or four years). The choice of subjects was designed to maximize the amount of variety in the type of degree programme and to provide similar numbers of males and females (since one gender frequently predominates in particular degree programmes). The questionnaire 'was issued, completed and collected at the end of class contact time by one of the researchers, or by a member of teaching staff' (Lucas 1997: 600–1). These procedures represent a very good attempt to generate a varied sample. It is a convenience sample, because the choice of degree programmes was selected purposively rather than randomly and because absentees from classes were unavailable to answer the questionnaires. On the other hand, because of the way questionnaires were administered, there was a very high rate of response among those students to whom the questionnaires were administered. An interesting question is whether absence from classes might be connected in some way to part-time working; in other words, might absence be due to students working at the time of the class or to students perhaps being too tired to go to the class because of their part-time work?

Research in focus 7.5
Another convenience sample

Miller *et al.* (1998) were interested in theories concerning the role of shopping in relation to the construction of identity in modern society. Since many discussions of this issue have been concerned with shopping centres (malls), they undertook a study that combined quantitative and **qualitative research** methods in order to explore the views of shoppers at two London shopping centres: Brent Cross and Wood Green. One phase of the research entailed structured interviews with shoppers leaving the centres. The interviews were conducted mainly during weekdays in June and July 1994. Shoppers were chiefly questioned as they left the main exits, though some questioning at minor exits also took place. The authors tell us: 'We did not attempt to secure a quota [see below] or random sample but asked every person who passed by, and who did not obviously look in the other direction or change their path, to complete a questionnaire' (Miller *et al.* 1998: 55). Such a sampling strategy produces a convenience sample because only people who are visiting the centre and who are therefore self-selected by virtue of their happening to choose to shop at these times could be interviewed.

Snowball sampling

In certain respects, snowball sampling is a form of convenience sample, but it is worth distinguishing because it has attracted quite a lot of attention over the years. With this approach to sampling, the researcher makes initial contact with a small group of people who are relevant to the research topic and then uses these to establish contacts with others. I used an approach like this to create a sample of British visitors to Disney theme parks (Bryman 1999).

Research in focus 7.6 describes the generation of a snowball sample of marijuana-users for what is often regarded as a classic study of drug use. Becker's comment on this method of creating a snowball sample is interesting: 'The sample is, of course, in no sense "random"'; it would not be possible to draw a random sample, since no one knows the nature of the universe from which it would have to be drawn' (Becker 1963: 46). What Becker is essentially saying here (and the same point applies to my study of Disney theme park visitors) is that there is no accessible sampling frame for the population from which

Research in focus 7.6
A snowball sample: Becker's study of marijuana users

In an article first published in 1953, Becker (1963) reports on how he generated a sample of marijuana-users. He writes:

> I conducted fifty interviews with marijuana users. I had been a professional dance musician for some years when I conducted this study and my first interviews were with people I had met in the music business. I asked them to put me in contact with other users who would be willing to discuss their experiences with me . . . Although in the end half of the fifty interviews were conducted with musicians, the other half covered a wide range of people, including laborers, machinists, and people in the professions. (Becker 1963: 45–6)

the sample is to be taken and that the difficulty of creating such a sampling frame means that such an approach is the only feasible one. Moreover, even if one could create a sampling frame of marijuana-users or of British visitors to Disney theme parks, it would almost certainly be inaccurate straight away, because this is a shifting population. People will constantly be becoming and ceasing to be marijuana-users, while new theme park visitors are arriving all the time.

The problem with snowball sampling is that it is very unlikely that the sample will be representative of the population, though, as I have just suggested, the very notion of a population may be problematic in some circumstances. However, by and large, snowball sampling is used not within a quantitative **research strategy**, but within a qualitative one: both Becker's and my study were carried out within a qualitative research framework. Concerns about external validity and the ability to generalize do not loom as large within a qualitative research strategy as they do in a quantitative research one (see Chapters 6 and 16). In qualitative research, the orientation to sampling is more likely to be guided by a preference for *theoretical sampling* than with the kind of statistical sampling that has been the focus of this chapter (see Key concept 17.5). There is a much better 'fit' between snowball sampling and the theoretical sampling strategy of qualitative research than with the statistical sampling approach of quantitative research. This is not to suggest that snowball sampling is entirely irrelevant to quantitative research: when the researcher needs to focus upon or to reflect relationships between people, tracing connections through snowball sampling may be a

better approach than conventional probability sampling (Coleman 1958).

Quota sampling

Quota sampling is comparatively rarely employed in academic social research, but is used intensively in commercial research, such as market research and political opinion polling. The aim of quota sampling is to produce a sample that reflects a population in terms of the relative proportions of people in different categories, such as gender, ethnicity, age groups, socio-economic groups, and region of residence, and in combinations of these categories. However, unlike a stratified sample, the sampling of individuals is not carried out randomly, since the final selection of people is left to the interviewer. Information about the stratification of the UK population or about certain regions can be obtained from sources like the Census and from surveys based on probability samples such as the General Household Survey, British Social Attitudes, and the British Household Panel Survey.

Once the categories and the number of people to be interviewed within each category (known as *quotas*) have been decided upon, it is then the job of interviewers to select people who fit these categories. The quotas will typically be interrelated. In a manner similar to stratified sampling, the population may be divided into strata in terms of, for example, gender, social class, age, and ethnicity. Census data might be used to identify the number of people who should be in each subgroup. The numbers to be interviewed in each subgroup will reflect the population. Each interviewer will probably seek out individuals who fit several subgroup quotas. Accordingly, an interviewer may know that among the various subgroups of people he or she must find, and interview, five Asian, 25–34-year-old, lower-middle-class females in the area in which the interviewer has been asked to work (say, the Wirral). The interviewer usually asks people who are available to him or her about their characteristics (though gender will presumably be self-evident) in order to determine their suitability for a particular subgroup. Once a subgroup quota (or a combination of subgroup quotas) has been achieved, the interviewer will no longer be concerned to locate individuals for that subgroup.

The choice of respondents is left to the interviewer, subject to the requirement of all quotas being filled, usually within a certain time period. Those of you who have ever been approached on the street by a person toting a clipboard and interview schedule and have been asked about your age, occupation, and so on, before being asked a series of questions about a product or whatever, have almost certainly encountered an interviewer with a quota sample to fill. Sometimes, he or she will decide not to interview you because you do not meet the criteria required to fill a quota. This may be due to a quota already having been filled or to the criteria for exclusion meaning that a person with a certain characteristic you possess is not required.

A number of criticisms are frequently levelled at quota samples.

- Because the choice of respondent is left to the interviewer, the proponents of probability sampling argue that a quota sample cannot be representative. It may accurately reflect the population in terms of superficial characteristics, as defined by the quotas. However, in their choice of people to approach, interviewers may be unduly influenced by their perceptions of how friendly people are or by whether the people make eye contact with the interviewer (unlike most of us who look at the ground and shuffle past as quickly as possible because we do not want to be bothered in our leisure time).

- People who are in an interviewer's vicinity at the times he or she conducts interviews, and are therefore available to be approached, may not be typical. There is a risk, for example, that people in full-time paid work may be under-represented and that those who are included in the sample are not typical.

- The interviewer is likely to make judgements about certain characteristics in deciding whether to approach a person, in particular, judgements about age. Those judgements will sometimes be incorrect—for example, when someone who is eligible to be interviewed, because a quota that he or she fits is unfilled, is not approached because the interviewer makes an incorrect judgement (for example, that the person is older than he or she looks). In such a case, a possible element of bias is being introduced.

- It has also been argued that the widespread use of social class as a quota control can introduce difficulties, because of the problem of ensuring that interviewees are properly assigned to class groupings (Moser and Kalton 1971).

- It is not permissible to calculate a standard error of the mean from a quota sample, because the non-random method of selection makes it impossible to calculate the range of possible values of a population.

All this makes the quota sample look a poor bet, and there is no doubt that it is not favoured by academic social researchers. It does have some arguments in its favour, however.

- It is undoubtedly cheaper and quicker than an interview survey on a comparable probability sample. For example, interviewers do not have to spend a lot of time travelling between interviews.

- Interviewers do not have to keep calling back on people who were not available at the time they were first approached.

- Because calling back is not required, a quota sample is easier to manage. It is not necessary to keep track of people who need to be recontacted or to keep track of refusals. Refusals occur, of course, but it is not necessary (and indeed it is not possible) to keep a record of which respondents declined to participate.

- When speed is of the essence, a quota sample is invaluable when compared to the more cumbersome probability sample. Newspapers frequently need to know how a national sample of voters feel about a certain topic or how they intend to vote at that time. Alternatively, if there is a sudden major news event, such as a terrorist incident like the London bombs of July 2005, the news media may seek a more or less instant picture of the nation's views about personal security or people's responses more generally. Again, a quota sample will be much faster.

- As with convenience sampling, it is useful for conducting development work on new measures or on research instruments. It can also be usefully employed in relation to exploratory work from which new theoretical ideas might be generated.

- Although the standard error of the mean should not be computed for a quota sample, it frequently is. As Moser and Kalton (1971) observe, some writers argue that the use of a non-random method in quota sampling should not act as a barrier to such a computation because its significance as a source of error is small when compared to other errors that may arise in surveys (see Figure 7.9). However, they go on to argue that at least with random sampling the researcher can calculate the amount of sampling error and does not have to be concerned about its potential impact.

There is some evidence to suggest that, when compared to random samples, quota samples often result in biases. They under-represent people in lower social strata, people who work in the private sector and manufacturing, and people at the extremes of income, and they over-represent women in households with children and people from larger households. On the other hand, it has to be acknowledged that probability samples are often biased too—for example, it is often suggested that they under-represent men and those in employment (Marsh and Scarbrough 1990; Butcher 1994).

Limits to generalization

One point that is often not fully appreciated is that, even when a sample has been selected using probability sampling, any findings can be generalized only to the population from which that sample was taken. This is an obvious point, but it is easy to think that findings from a study have some kind of broader applicability. If we take our imaginary study of alcohol consumption among students at a university, any findings could be generalized only to that university. In other words, you should be very cautious about generalizing to students at other universities. There are many factors that may imply that the level of alcohol consumption is higher (or lower) than among university students as a whole. There may be a higher (or lower) concentration of pubs in the university's vicinity, there may be more (or fewer) bars on the campus, there may be more (or less) of a culture of drinking at this university, or the university may recruit a higher (or lower) proportion of students with disposable income. There may be many other factors too. Similarly, we should be cautious of overgeneralizing in terms of locality. Lunt and Livingstone's (1992: 173) study of consumption habits was based on a postal questionnaire sent to '241 people living in or around Oxford during September 1989'. While the authors' findings represent a fascinating insight into modern consumption patterns, we should be cautious about assuming that they can be generalized beyond the confines of Oxford and its environs.

There could even be a further limit to generalization that is implied by the Lunt and Livingstone (1992) sample. They write that the research was conducted in September 1989. One issue that is rarely discussed in this context and that is almost impossible to assess is whether there is a time limit on the findings that are generated. Quite aside from the fact that we need to appreciate that the findings cannot (or at least should not) be generalized beyond the Oxford area, is there a point at which we have to say, 'well, those findings applied to the Oxford area then but things have changed and we can no longer assume that they apply to that or any other locality'? We are, after all, used to thinking that things have changed when there has been some kind of prominent change. To take a simple example: no one would be prepared to assume that the findings of a study in 1980 of university students' budgeting and personal finance habits would apply to students in the early twenty-first century. Quite aside from changes that might have occurred naturally, the erosion and virtual dismantling of the student grant system has changed the ways students finance their education, including perhaps a greater reliance on part-time work (Lucas 1997), a greater reliance on parents, and the use of loans. But, even when there is no definable or recognizable source of relevant change of this kind, there is none the less the possibility (or even likelihood) that findings are temporally specific. Such an issue is impossible to resolve without further research (Bryman 1989b).

Error in survey research

We can think of 'error', a term that has been employed on a number of occasions, as being made up of four main factors (Figure 7.9).

1. *Sampling error*. See Key concept 7.1 for a definition. This kind of error arises because it is extremely unlikely that one will end up with a truly representative sample, even when probability sampling is employed.

2. We can distinguish what might be thought of as *sampling-related error*. This is error that is subsumed under the category *non-sampling error* (see Key concept 7.1) but that arises from activities or events that are related to the sampling process and that are connected with the issue of **generalizability** or external validity of findings. Examples are an inaccurate sampling frame and non-response.

3. There is also error that is connected with the implementation of the research process. We might call this *data collection error*. This source of error includes such factors as: poor question wording in self-completion questionnaires or structured interviews; poor interviewing techniques; and flaws in the administration of research instruments.

4. Finally, there is *data processing error*. This arises from faulty management of data, in particular, errors in the *coding* of answers.

The third and fourth sources of error relate to factors that are not associated with sampling and instead relate much more closely to concerns about the validity of measurement, which was addressed in Chapter 6. However, the kinds of steps that need to be taken to keep these sources of error to a minimum in the context of social survey research will be addressed in the next three chapters.

Figure 7.9

Four sources of error in social survey research

Key points

- Probability sampling is a mechanism for reducing bias in the selection of samples.

- Ensure you become familiar with key technical terms in the literature on sampling such as: representative sample; random sample; non-response; population; sampling error; etc.

- Randomly selected samples are important because they permit generalizations to the population and because they have certain known qualities.

- Sampling error decreases as sample size increases.

- Quota samples can provide reasonable alternatives to random samples, but they suffer from some deficiencies.

- Convenience samples may provide interesting data, but it is crucial to be aware of their limitations in terms of generalizability.

- Sampling and sampling-related error are just two sources of error in social survey research.

Questions for review

- What do each of the following terms mean: population; probability sampling; non-probability sampling; sampling frame; representative sample; and sampling and non-sampling error?

- What are the goals of sampling?

- What are the main areas of potential bias in sampling?

Sampling error

- What is the significance of sampling error for achieving a representative sample?

Types of probability sample

- What is probability sampling and why is it important?

- What are the main types of probability sample?

- How far does a stratified random sample offer greater precision than a simple random or systematic sample?

- If you were conducting an interview survey of around 500 people in Manchester, what type of probability sample would you choose and why?

- A researcher positions herself on a street corner and asks 1 person in 5 who walks by to be interviewed. She continues doing this until she has a sample of 250. How likely is she to achieve a representative sample?

The qualities of a probability sample

- A researcher is interested in levels of job satisfaction among manual workers in a firm that is undergoing change. The firm has 1,200 manual workers. The researcher selects a simple random sample of 10 per cent of the population. He measures job satisfaction on a Likert scale comprising ten items. A high level of satisfaction is scored 5 and a low level is scored 1. The mean job satisfaction score is 34.3. The standard error of the mean is 8.57. What is the 95 per cent confidence interval?

Sample size

- What factors would you take into account in deciding how large your sample should be when devising a probability sample?
- What is non-response and why is it important to the question of whether you will end up with a representative sample?

Types of non-probability sample

- Are non-probability samples useless?
- In what circumstances might you employ snowball sampling?
- 'Quota samples are not true random samples, but in terms of generating a representative sample there is little difference between them, and this accounts for their widespread use in market research and opinion polling.' Discuss.

Limits to generalization

- 'The problem of generalization to a population is not just to do with the matter of getting a representative sample.' Discuss.

Error in survey research

- 'Non-sampling error, as its name implies, is concerned with sources of error that are not part of the sampling process.' Discuss.

Online Resource Centre

http://www.oxfordtextbooks.co.uk/orc/brymansrm3e/

Visit the Online Resource Centre that accompanies this book to enrich your understanding of sampling. Consult web links, test yourself using multiple choice questions, and gain further guidance and inspiration from the Student Researcher's Toolkit.

Structured
interviewing

Chapter outline

Chapter guide

The **structured interview** is one of a variety of forms of research interview, but it is the one that is most commonly employed in **survey research**. The goal of the structured interview is for the interviewing of respondents to be standardized so that differences between interviews in any research project are minimized. As a result, there are many guidelines about how structured interviewing should be carried out so that variation in the conduct of interviews is small. The chapter explores:

- the reasons why the structured interview is a prominent research method in survey research; this issue entails a consideration of the importance of standardization to the process of measurement;

- the different contexts of interviewing, such as the use of more than one interviewer and whether the administration of the interview is in person or by telephone;

- various prerequisites of structured interviewing, including: establishing rapport with the interviewee; asking questions as they appear on the **interview schedule**; recording exactly what is said by interviewees; ensuring there are clear instructions on the interview schedule concerning question sequencing and the recording of answers; and keeping to the question order as it appears on the schedule;

- problems with structured interviewing, including: the influence of the interviewer on respondents and the possibility of systematic bias in answers (known as *response sets*); the feminist critique of structured interview, which raises a distinctive cluster of problems with the method, is also examined.

Introduction

The interview is a common occurrence in social life, because there are many different forms of interview. There are job interviews, media interviews, social work interviews, police interviews, appraisal interviews. And then there are research interviews, which represent the kind of interview that will be covered in this and other chapters (such as Chapters 18 and 19). These different kinds of interview share some common features, such as the eliciting of information by the interviewer from the interviewee and the operation of rules of varying degrees of formality or explicitness concerning the conduct of the interview.

In the social research interview, the aim is for the interviewer to elicit from the interviewee or *respondent*, as he or she is frequently called in survey research, all manner of information: interviewees' own behaviour or that of others; attitudes; norms; beliefs; and values. There are many different types or styles of research interview, but the kind that is primarily employed in survey research is the structured interview, which is the focus of this chapter. Other kinds of interview will be briefly mentioned in this chapter but will be discussed in greater detail in later chapters.

The structured interview

The research interview is a prominent data-collection strategy in both quantitative and qualitative research. The survey is probably the chief context within which social researchers employ the structured interview (see Key concept 8.1) in connection with quantitative research, and it is this form of the interview that will be emphasized in this chapter. The structured interview is one of the two main ways of administering a survey research instrument and its main forms are briefly outlined in Figure 7.2. This figure should be consulted as a background to this chapter and Chapter 9.

Key concept 8.1
What is a structured interview?

A structured interview, sometimes called a *standardized interview*, entails the administration of an interview schedule by an interviewer. The aim is for all interviewees to be given exactly the same context of questioning. This means that each respondent receives exactly the same interview stimulus as any other. The goal of this style of interviewing is to ensure that interviewees' replies can be aggregated and this can be achieved reliably only if those replies are in response to identical cues. Interviewers are supposed to read out questions exactly and in the same order as they are printed on the schedule. Questions are usually very specific and very often offer the interviewee a fixed range of answers (this type of question is often called *closed*, *closed ended*, *pre-coded*, or *fixed choice*). The structured interview is the typical form of interview in survey research.

Thinking deeply 8.1
Common sources of error in survey research

There are many sources of error in survey research in addition to those associated with sampling. This is a list of the principal sources of error:

- a poorly worded question;
- the way the question is asked by the interviewer;
- misunderstanding on the part of the interviewee;
- memory problems on the part of the interviewee;
- the way the information is recorded by the interviewer;
- the way the information is processed, either when answers are **coded** or when data are entered into the computer.

The reason why survey researchers typically prefer the structured interview is that it promotes standardization of *both* the asking of questions *and* the recording of answers. This feature has two closely related virtues from the perspective of quantitative research: reducing error due to variation in the asking of questions, and greater accuracy in and ease of processing respondents' answers.

Reducing error due to interviewer variability

The standardization of both the asking of questions and the recording of answers means that, if it is properly executed, variation in people's replies will be due to 'true' or 'real' variation and not due to the interview context. To take a simple illustration, when we ask a question that is supposed to be an indicator of a concept, we want to keep error to a minimum, an issue that was touched on at the end of Chapter 7. We can think of the answers to a question as constituting the values that a variable takes. These values, of course, exhibit variation. This could be the question on alcohol consumption among students that was a focus of Chapter 7 at certain points. Students will vary in the number of alcohol units they consume (as in Figure 8.1). However, some respondents may be inaccurately classified in terms of the variable. There are a number of possible reasons for this (see Thinking deeply 8.1).

Most variables will contain an element of error, so that it is helpful to think of variation as made up of two components: true variation and error. In other words:

variation = true variation + variation due to error.

The aim is to keep the error component to a minimum (see Figure 8.2), since error has an adverse effect on the validity of a measure. If the error component is quite high (see Figure 8.3), validity will be jeopardized. The significance for error of standardization in the structured interview is that two sources of variation due to error—

Figure 8.2

A variable with little error

True variation

Variation due to error

Figure 8.3

A variable with considerable error

True variation

Variation due to error

the second and fifth in Thinking deeply 8.1—are likely to be less pronounced, since the opportunity for variation in interviewer behaviour in these two areas (asking questions and recording answers) is reduced.

The significance of standardization and of thereby reducing interviewer variability is this: assuming that there is no problem with an interview question due to such things as confusing terms or ambiguity (an issue that will be examined in Chapter 10), we want to be able to say as far as possible that the variation that we find is connected with true variation between interviewees and not to variation in the way a question was asked or the answers recorded in the course of the administration of a survey by structured interview. Variability can occur in either of two ways. First, *intra-interviewer variability*, whereby an interviewer is not consistent in the way he or she asks questions and/or records answers. Second, when there is more than one interviewer, there may be *inter-interviewer variability*, whereby interviewers are not consistent with each other in the ways they ask questions and/or record answers. Needless to say, these two sources of variability are not mutually exclusive; they can coexist, compounding the problem even further. In view of the significance of standardization, it is hardly surprising that some writers prefer to call the structured interview a *standardized interview* (e.g. Oppenheim 1992) or *standardized survey interview* (e.g. Fowler and Mangione 1990).

Figure 8.1

A variable

Variation

Accuracy and ease of data processing

Like self-completion questionnaires, most structured interviews contain mainly questions that are variously referred to as *closed, closed ended, pre-coded,* or *fixed choice*. This issue will be covered in detail in Chapter 10. However, this type of question has considerable relevance to the current discussion. With the closed question, the respondent is given a limited choice of possible answers. In other words, the interviewer provides respondents with two or more possible answers and asks them to select which one or ones apply. Ideally, this procedure will simply entail the interviewer placing a tick in a box by the answer(s) selected by a respondent or circling the selected answer or using a similar procedure. The advantage of this practice is that the potential for interviewer variability is reduced: there is no problem of whether the interviewer writes down everything that the respondent says or of misinterpretation of the reply given. If an *open* or *open-ended* question is asked, the interviewer may not write down everything said, may embellish what is said, or may misinterpret what is said.

However, the advantages of the closed question in the context of survey research go further than this, as we will see in Chapter 10. One advantage that is particularly significant in the context of the present discussion is that closed questions greatly facilitate the processing of data. When an open question is asked, the answers need to be sifted and *coded* in order for the data to be analysed quantitatively. Not only is this a laborious procedure, particularly if there is a large number of open questions and/or of respondents; it also introduces the potential for another source of error, which is the sixth in Thinking deeply 8.1: it is quite likely that error will be introduced as a result of variability in the coding of answers. When open questions are asked, the interviewer is supposed to write down as much of what is said as possible. Answers can, therefore, be in the form of several sentences. These answers have to be examined and then categorized, so that each person's answer can be aggregated with other respondents' answers to a certain question. A number will then be allocated to each category of answer, so that the answers can then be entered into a computer database and analysed quantitatively. This general process is known as coding and will be examined in greater detail in Chapter 10.

Coding introduces yet another source of error. First, if the rules for assigning answers to categories, collectively known as the *coding frame*, are flawed, the variation that is observed will not reflect the true variation in interviewees' replies. Second, there may be variability in the ways in which answers are categorized. As with interviewing, there can be two sources: *intra-coder variability*, whereby the coder varies over time in the way in which the rules for assigning answers to categories are implemented, and *inter-coder variability*, whereby coders differ from each other in the way in which the rules for assigning answers to categories are implemented. If either (or both) source(s) of variability occur, at least part of the variation in interviewees' replies will not reflect true variation and instead will be caused by error.

The closed question sidesteps this problem neatly, because respondents allocate *themselves* to categories. The coding process is then a simple matter of attaching a different number to each category of answer and of entering the numbers into a computer database. It is not surprising, therefore, that this type of question is often referred to as pre-coded, because decisions about the coding of answers are typically undertaken as part of the design of the schedule—that is, before any respondents have actually been asked questions. There is very little opportunity for interviewers or coders to vary in the recording or the coding of answers. Of course, if some respondents misunderstand any terms in the alternative answers with which they are presented, or if the answers do not adequately cover the appropriate range of possibilities, the question will not provide a valid measure. However, that is a separate issue and one that will be returned to in Chapter 10. The chief point to register about closed questions for the moment is that, when compared to open questions, they reduce one potential source of error *and* are much easier to process for quantitative data analysis.

Other types of interview

The structured interview is by no means the only type of interview, but it is certainly the main type that is likely to be encountered in survey research and in quantitative research generally. Unfortunately, a host of different terms have been employed by writers on research methodology to distinguish the diverse forms of research interview. Key concept 8.3 represents an attempt to capture some of the major terms and types.

All the forms of interview outlined in Key concept 8.2, with the exception of the *structured interview* and the *standardized interview*, are primarily used in connection with qualitative research, and it is in that context that they will be encountered again later in this book. They are rarely used in connection with quantitative research, and survey research in particular, because the absence of standardization in the asking of questions and recording of answers makes respondents' replies difficult to aggregate and to process. This is not to say that they have no role at all. For example, as we will see in Chapter 10, the unstructured interview can have a useful role in relation to developing the fixed-choice alternatives with which respondents are provided in the kind of closed question that is typical of the structured interview.

Key concept 8.2
Major types of interview

- *Structured interview*. See Key concept 8.1.

- *Standardized interview*. See Key concept 8.1.

- **Semi-structured interview**. This is a term that covers a wide range of instances. It typically refers to a context in which the interviewer has a series of questions that are in the general form of an interview schedule but is able to vary the sequence of questions. The questions are frequently somewhat more general in their frame of reference from that typically found in a structured interview schedule. Also, the interviewer usually has some latitude to ask further questions in response to what are seen as significant replies.

- *Unstructured interview*. The interviewer typically has only a list of topics or issues, often called an **interview guide** or *aide-mémoire*, that are to be covered. The style of questioning is usually informal. The phrasing and sequencing of questions will vary from interview to interview.

- *Intensive interview*. This term is employed by Lofland and Lofland (1995) as an alternative term to the unstructured interview. Spradley (1979) uses the term ethnographic interview to describe a form of interview that is also more or less synonymous with the unstructured interview.

- *Qualitative interview*. For some writers, this term seems to denote an unstructured interview (e.g. Mason 1996), but more frequently it is a general term that embraces interviews of both the semi-structured and unstructured kind (e.g. Rubin and Rubin 1995).

- *In-depth interview*. Like the term 'qualitative interview', this one sometimes refers to an unstructured interview but more often refers to both semi-structured and unstructured interviewing. The use of this term seems to be increasing.

- *Focused interview*. This is a term devised by Merton *et al.* (1956) to refer to an interview using predominantly open questions to ask interviewees questions about a specific situation or event that is relevant to them and of interest to the researcher.

- **Focus group**. This is the same as the focused interview, but interviewees discuss the specific issue in groups. See Key concept 19.1 for a more detailed definition.

- *Group interview*. Some writers see this term as synonymous with the focus group, but a distinction may be made between the latter and a situation in which members of a group discuss a variety of matters that may be only partially related.

- **Oral history interview**. This is an unstructured or semi-structured interview in which the respondent is asked to recall events from his or her past and to reflect on them (see also Key concept 18.1). There is usually a cluster of fairly specific research concerns to do with a particular epoch or event, so there is some resemblance to a focused interview.

- **Life history interview**. This is similar to the oral history interview, but the aim of this type of unstructured interview is to glean information on the entire biography of each respondent (see also Key concept 18.1).

Interview contexts

In an archetypal interview, an interviewer stands or sits in front of the respondent asking the latter a series of questions and writing down the answers. However, there are several possible departures from it, although this archetype is the most usual context for an interview.

More than one interviewee

In the case of group interviews or focus groups, there is more than one, and usually quite a few more than one, respondent or interviewee. Nor is this the only context in which more than one person is interviewed. McKee and Bell (1985), for example, interviewed couples in their study of the impact of male unemployment, while, in my research on visitors to Disney theme parks, not just couples but often their children took part in the interview as well (Bryman 1999). However, it is very unusual for structured interviews to be used in connection with this kind of questioning. In survey research, it is almost always a specific individual who is the object of questioning. Indeed, in survey interviews it is very advisable to discourage as far as possible the presence and intrusion of others during the course of the interview. Investigations in which more than one person is being interviewed tend to be exercises in qualitative research, though this is not always the case: Pahl's (1990) study of patterns of control of money among couples employed structured interviewing of couples and of husbands and wives separately.

More than one interviewer

This is a very unusual situation in social research, because of the considerable cost that is involved in dispatching two (or indeed more than two) people to interview someone. Bechhofer *et al.* (1984) describe research in which two people interviewed individuals in a wide range of occupations. However, while their approach achieved a number of benefits for them, their interviewing style was of the unstructured kind that is typically employed in qualitative research, and they argue that the presence of a second interviewer is unlikely to achieve any added value in the context of structured interviewing.

In person or by telephone?

A third way in which the archetype may not be realized is that interviews may be conducted by telephone rather than face-to-face. While telephone interviewing is quite common in commercial fields like market research, where it usually takes the form of computer-assisted telephone interviewing (CATI; see below), it is still far more customary to read reports of studies based on face-to-face interviews in academic social research, but see Research in focus 8.1 for an interesting example.

Research in focus 8.1
A telephone survey of the unemployed in Sweden

Nordenmark and Strandh (1999) report the findings of an interesting study of mental well-being among the unemployed in Sweden. Early in 1996 a national **random sample** of 3,500 was drawn from a register of all unemployed persons that is maintained by the Swedish Labour Market Board. A telephone survey was conducted with members of the **sample**. The response rate was 74 per cent. The interview schedule included questions on such issues as: 'mental well-being, the economy, work involvement, belief in the future, wage demands and job search behaviour' (Nordenmark and Strandh 1999: 585). Nearly two years later, those who had participated were re-interviewed by telephone with very similar questions. This is, therefore, an example of a *panel study*. The authors inform us that only part (around 6 per cent) of the 26 per cent who did not respond was due to a refusal to participate; the remainder was due to problems of contacting respondents.

There are several advantages of telephone over personal interviews.

- On a like-for-like basis, they are far cheaper and also quicker to administer. This arises because, for personal interviews, interviewers have to spend a great deal of time and money travelling between respondents. This factor will be even more pronounced when a sample is geographically dispersed, a problem that is only partially mitigated for personal interview surveys by strategies like cluster sampling. Of course, telephone interviews take time and hired interviewers have to be paid, but the cost of conducting a telephone interview will still be lower than a comparable personal one. Moreover, the general efficiency of telephone interviewing has been enhanced with the advent and widespread use in commercial circles of computer-assisted telephone interviewing (CATI).

- The telephone interview is easier to supervise than the personal interview. This is a particular advantage when there are several interviewers, since it becomes easier to check on interviewers' transgressions in the asking of questions, such as rephrasing questions or the inappropriate use of probes by the interviewer. Interviews can be tape-recorded so that data quality can be assessed, but this raises issues that relate to data protection and confidentiality, so that this procedure has to be treated cautiously.

- Telephone interviewing has a further advantage, which is to do with evidence (which is not as clear-cut as one might want) that suggests that, in personal interviews, respondents' replies are sometimes affected by characteristics of the interviewer (for example, class, ethnicity) and indeed by his or her mere presence (implying that the interviewees may reply in ways they feel will be deemed desirable by interviewers). The remoteness of the interviewer in telephone interviewing removes this potential source of bias to a significant extent. The interviewer's personal characteristics cannot be seen, and the fact that he or she is not physically present may offset the likelihood of respondents' answers being affected by the interviewer.

Telephone interviewing suffers from certain limitations when compared to the personal interview.

- People who do not own or who are not contactable by telephone obviously cannot be interviewed by telephone. Since this characteristic is most likely to be a feature of poorer households, the potential for sampling bias exists. Also, many people choose to be ex-directory—that is, they have taken action for their telephone numbers not to appear in a telephone directory. Again, these people cannot be interviewed by telephone. One likely solution to this last difficulty is *random digit dialling*. With this technique, the computer randomly selects telephone numbers within a predefined geographical area. Not only is this a random process that conforms to the rules about probability sampling examined in Chapter 7; it also stands a chance of getting at ex-directory households. But it cannot, of course, gain access to those without a telephone at all.

- Respondents with hearing impairments are much more likely to find telephone interviewing difficult for them than personal interviewing.

- The length of a telephone interview is unlikely to be sustainable beyond 20–25 minutes, whereas personal interviews can be much longer than this (Frey 2004).

- The question of whether response rates (see Key concept 7.2), are lower with surveys by telephone interview than with surveys by personal interview is unclear, in that there is little consistent evidence on this question. However, there is a general belief that telephone interviews achieve slightly lower rates than personal interviews (Frey and Oishi 1995; Shuy 2002; Frey 2004).

- There is some evidence to suggest that telephone interviews fare less well for the asking of questions about sensitive issues, such as drug and alcohol use, income, tax returns, and health. However, the evidence is not entirely consistent on this point, though it is probably sufficient to suggest that, when many questions of this kind are to be used, a personal interview may be superior (Shuy 2002).

- Developments in telephone communications such as the growing use of answerphones and other forms of call screening and of mobile phones have almost certainly had an adverse effect on telephone surveys in terms of response rates and the general difficulty of getting access to respondents through conventional landlines. Households that rely exclusively on mobile phones represent a particular difficulty.

- Telephone interviewers cannot engage in observation. This means that they are not in a position to respond to signs of puzzlement or unease on the faces of respondents when they are asked a question. In a personal interview, the interviewer may respond to such signs by restating the question or attempting to clarify the meaning of the question, though this has to be handled in a standardized way as far as possible. A further issue relating to the inability of the interviewer to observe is that, sometimes, interviewers may be asked to collect subsidiary information in connection with their visits (for example, whether a house is dilapidated). Such information cannot be collected when telephone interviews are employed.

- It is frequently the case that specific individuals in households or firms are the targets of an interview. In other words, simply anybody will not do. This requirement is likely to arise from the specifications of the population to be sampled, which means that people in a certain role or position or with particular characteristics are to be interviewed. It is probably more difficult to ascertain by telephone interview whether the correct person is replying.

- The telephone interviewer cannot readily employ visual aids such as show cards (see below) from which respondents might be asked to select their replies or to use diagrams or photographs.

- There is some evidence to suggest that the quality of data derived from telephone interviews is inferior to that of comparable face-to-face interviews. A series of experiments reported by Holbrook *et al.* (2003) on the mode of survey administration in the USA using long questionnaires found that respondents interviewed by telephone were more likely to: express no opinion or 'don't know' (see Chapter 10 for more on this issue); to answer in the same way to a series of linked questions; to express socially desirable answers; to be apprehensive about the interview; and to be more likely to be dissatisfied with the time taken by the interviews (even though they were invariably shorter than in the face-to-face mode). Also, telephone interviewees tended to be less engaged with the interview process. While these results should be viewed with caution, since studies like these are bound to be affected by such factors as the use of a large questionnaire on a national sample, they do provide interesting food for thought.

Computer-assisted interviewing

In recent years, increasing use has been made of computers in the interviewing process, especially in commercial survey research of the kind conducted by market research and opinion polling organizations. There are two main formats for computer-assisted interviewing: computer-assisted personal interviewing (CAPI) and computer-assisted telephone interviewing (CATI). A very large percentage of telephone interviews is conducted with the aid of personal computers. Among commercial survey organizations, almost all telephone interviewing is of the CATI kind nowadays, and this kind of interview has become one of the most popular formats for such firms. The main reasons for the growing use of CAPI has been that the increased portability and affordability of 'laptop' computers, and the growth in the number and quality of software packages that provide a platform for devising interview schedules, provide greater opportunity for them to be used in connection with face-to-face interviews.

With computer-assisted interviewing, the questions that comprise an interview schedule appear on the screen. As interviewers ask each question, they 'key in' the appropriate reply using the keyboard (for open questions) or using a mouse (for closed questions) and proceed to the next question. Moreover, this process has the great advantage that, when *filter questions* (see Tips and skills 'Instructions for interviewers in the use of a filter question') are asked, so that certain answers may be skipped as a result of a person's reply, the computer can be programmed to 'jump' to the next relevant question. This removes the possibility of interviewers inadvertently asking inappropriate questions or failing to ask ones that should be asked. As such, computer-assisted interviewing enhances the degree of control over the interview process and can therefore improve standardization of the asking and recording of questions. However, there is very little evidence to suggest that the quality of data deriving from computer-assisted interviews is demonstrably superior to comparable paper and pencil interviews (Couper and Hansen 2002). If the interviewer is out in the field all day, he or she can either take a disk with the saved data to the research office or send the data down a telephone line with the aid of a modem. It is possible that technophobic respondents may be a bit alarmed by their use, but, by and large, the use of computer-assisted interviewing seems destined to grow. My only personal experience with this technique was as a respondent in a market research survey: the laptop started to beep part of the way through the interview because the battery was about to expire and needed to be replaced with a back-up. An incident such as this could be disruptive to the flow of an interview and be alarming for technophobic respondents.

For their part, there is evidence that professional interviewers generally like computer-assisted interviewing, often feeling that it improves the image of their occupation, though there are many who are concerned about the problems that might arise from technical difficulties and the inconvenience of correcting errors with a computer as opposed to with a pen. One issue that sometimes disconcerts interviewers is the fact that they can see only part of the schedule at any one time (Couper and Hansen 2002).

CAPI and CATI have not infiltrated academic survey research to anything like the same degree that they have commercial survey research, although that picture is likely to change considerably because of the many advantages they possess. In any case, many of the large datasets that are used for secondary analysis (see Chapter 13 for examples) derive from computer-assisted interviewing studies undertaken by commercial or large social research organizations. One further point to register in connection with computer-assisted interviewing is that the section has not included Internet surveys. The reason for this is that such surveys are more properly considered as using self-completion questionnaires rather than structured interviewing (see Figure 7.2). With such surveys, there is no interviewer in the sense of a person who verbally asks questions. Internet surveys are covered in Chapter 26.

Conducting interviews

Issues concerning the conduct of interviews are examined here in a very general way. In addition to the matters considered here, there is clearly the important issue of how to word the interview questions themselves. This area will be explored in Chapter 10, since many of the rules of question-asking relate to self-completion questionnaire techniques like postal questionnaires as well as to structured interviews. One further general point to make here is that the advice concerning the conduct of interviews provided in this chapter relates to structured interviews. The framework for conducting the kinds of interviewing conducted in qualitative research (such as, unstructured and semi-structured interviewing and focus groups) will be handled in later chapters.

Know the schedule

Before interviewing anybody, an interviewer should be fully conversant with the schedule. Even if you are the only person conducting interviews, make sure you know it inside out. Interviewing can be stressful for interviewers, and it is possible that under duress standard interview procedures like filter questions (see Tips and skills 'Instructions for interviewers in the use of a filter question') can cause interviewers to get flustered and miss questions out or ask the wrong questions. If two or more interviewers are involved, they need to be fully trained to know what is required of them and to know their way around the schedule. Training is especially important in order to reduce the likelihood of interviewer variability in the asking of questions, which is a source of error.

Introducing the research

Prospective respondents have to be provided with a credible rationale for the research in which they are being asked to participate and for giving up their valuable time. This aspect of conducting interview research is of particular significance at a time when response rates to survey research appear to be declining, though, as noted in Chapter 7, the evidence on this issue is the focus of some disagreement. The introductory rationale may be either spoken by the interviewer or written down. In many cases, respondents may be presented with both modes. It comes in spoken form in such situations as when interviewers make contact with respondents on the street or when they 'cold call' respondents in their homes in person or by telephone. A written rationale will be required to alert respondents that someone will be contacting them in person or on the telephone to request an interview. Respondents will frequently encounter both forms—for example, when they are sent a letter and then when they ask the interviewer who turns up to interview them what the research is all about. It is important for the two accounts to be consistent, as this could be a test!

Introductions to research should typically contain the bits of information outlined in Tips and skills 'Topics and issues to include in an introductory statement'. Since interviewers represent the interface between the research and the respondent, they have an important role in maximizing the response rate for the survey. In addition the following points should be borne in mind.

- Interviewers should be prepared to keep calling back if interviewees are out or unavailable. This will require taking into account people's likely work and leisure habits—for example, there is no point in calling at home on people who work during the day. In addition, people living alone may be reluctant to answer the door when it is dark because of fear of crime.

- Be self-assured. You may get a better response if you presume that people will agree to be interviewed rather than that they will refuse.

- Reassure people that you are not a salesperson. Because of the tactics of certain organizations whose representatives say they are doing market or social research, many people have become very suspicious of people saying they would just like to ask you a few questions.

- Dress in a way that will be acceptable to a wide spectrum of people.

- Make it clear that you will be happy to find a time to suit the respondent.

Rapport

It is frequently suggested that it is important for the interviewer to achieve *rapport* with the respondent. This means that very quickly a relationship must be established that encourages the respondent to want (or at least be prepared) to participate in and persist with the interview. Unless an element of rapport can be established, some respondents may initially agree to be interviewed but then decide to terminate their participation because of the length of time the interview is taking or perhaps because of the nature of the questions being asked. While this injunction essentially invites the interviewer to be friendly with respondents and to put them at ease, it is important that this quality is not stretched too far. Too much rapport may result in the interview going on too long and the respondent suddenly deciding that too much time is being spent on the activity. Also, the mood of friendliness may result in the respondent answering questions in a way that is

Tips and skills
Topics and issues to include in an introductory statement

There are several issues to include in an introductory statement to a prospective interviewee. The following list comprises the principal considerations.

- Make clear the identity of the person who is contacting the respondent.

- Identify the auspices under which the research is being conducted—for example, a university, a market research agency.

- Mention any research funder, or, if you are a student doing an undergraduate or postgraduate dissertation or doing research for a thesis, make this clear.

- Indicate what the research is about in broad terms and why it is important, and give an indication of the kind of information to be collected.

- Indicate why the respondent has been selected—e.g. selected by a random process.

- Make it clear that participation is voluntary.

- Reassure the respondent that he or she will not be identified or be identifiable in any way. This can usually be achieved by pointing out that data are anonymized when they are entered into the computer and that analysis will be conducted at an aggregate level.

- Provide reassurance about the confidentiality of any information provided.

- Provide the respondent with the opportunity to ask any questions—e.g. provide a contact telephone number if the introduction is in the form of a written statement, or if in person simply ask if the respondent has any questions.

These suggestions are also relevant to the covering letter that accompanies postal questionnaires, except that researchers using this method need to remember to include a stamped-addressed envelope!

designed to please the interviewer. The achievement of rapport between interviewer and respondent is therefore a delicate balancing act. Moreover, it is probably somewhat easier to achieve in the context of the face-to-face interview than in the telephone interview, since in the latter the interviewer is unable to offer obvious visual cues of friendliness like smiling or maintaining good eye contact, which are also frequently regarded as conducive to gaining and maintaining rapport.

Asking questions

It was earlier suggested that one of the aims of the structured interview is to ensure that each respondent is asked exactly the same questions. Recall that in Thinking deeply 8.1 it was pointed out that variation in the ways a question is asked is a potential source of error in survey research. The structured interview is meant to reduce the likelihood of this occurring, but it cannot guarantee that this will not occur, because there is always the possibility that interviewers will embellish or otherwise change a question when it is asked. There is considerable evidence that this occurs, even among centres of social research that have a solid reputation for being rigorous in following correct methodological protocol (Bradburn and Sudman 1979). The problem with such variation in the asking of questions was outlined above: it is likely to engender variation in replies that does not reflect 'true' variation—in other words, error. Consequently, it is important for interviewers to appreciate the importance of keeping exactly to the wording of the questions they are charged with asking.

You might say: 'does it really matter?' In other words, surely small variations to wording cannot make a significant difference to people's replies? While the impact of variation in wording obviously differs from context to context and is in any case difficult to quantify exactly, experiments in question-wording suggest that even small variations in wording can exert an impact on replies (Schuman and Presser 1981). Three experiments in England conducted by Social and Community Planning Research concluded that a considerable number of interview questions is affected by interviewer variability. The researchers estimated that, for about two-thirds of the questions that were considered, interviewers contributed to less than 2 per cent of the total variation in each question (Collins 1997). On the face of it, this is a small amount of error, but the researchers regarded it as a cause for concern.

The key point to emerge, then, is the importance of getting across to interviewers the importance of asking questions as they are written. There are many reasons why interviewers may vary question-wording, such as reluctance to ask certain questions, perhaps because of embarrassment (Collins 1997), but the general admonition to keep to the wording of the question needs to be constantly reinforced when interviewers are being trained. It also needs to be borne in mind for your own research.

Recording answers

An identical warning for identical reasons can be registered in connection with the recording of answers by interviewers, who should write down respondents' replies as exactly as possible. Not to do so can result in interviewers distorting respondents' answers and hence introducing error. Such errors are less likely to occur when the interviewer has merely to allocate respondents' replies to a category, as in a closed question. This process can require a certain amount of interpretation on the part of the interviewer, but the error that is introduced is far less than when answers to open questions are being written down (Fowler and Mangione 1990).

Clear instructions

In addition to instructions about the asking of questions and the recording of answers, interviewers need instructions about their progress through an interview schedule. An example of the kind of context in which this is likely to occur is in relation to *filter questions*. Filter questions require the interviewer to ask questions of some respondents but not others. For example, the question:

> For which political party did you vote at the last general election?

presumes that the respondent did in fact vote. This option can be reflected in the fixed-choice answers that are provided, so that one of these is a 'did not vote' alternative. However, a better solution is not to presume anything about voting behaviour but to ask respondents whether they voted in the last general election and then to filter out those who did not vote. The foregoing question about the political party voted for can then be asked of those who did in fact vote. Similarly, in a study of meals, there is no point in asking vegetarians lots of questions about eating meat. It will probably work out best to filter vegetarians out and then possibly ask them a separate series of questions. Tips and skills 'Instructions for interviewers in the use of a filter question' provides a simple example in connection with an imaginary study of alcohol consumption. The chief point to register about this example is that it requires clear instructions for the interviewer. If such instructions are not provided, there is the risk that either respondents will be asked inappropriate questions (which can be irritating for them) or the interviewer will inadvertently fail to ask a question (which results in missing information).

Question order

In addition to warning interviewers about the importance of not varying the asking of questions and the recording of answers, they should be alerted to the importance of keeping to the order of asking questions. For one thing, varying the question order can result in certain questions being accidentally omitted, because the interviewer may forget to ask those that have been leapfrogged during the interview. Also, variation in question order may have an impact on replies: if some respondents have been previously asked a question that they should have been asked whereas others have not, a source of variability in the asking of questions will have been introduced and therefore a potential source of error.

Tips and skills
Instructions for interviewers in the use of a filter question

Each of the following questions includes an instruction to the interviewer about how to proceed.

1. Have you consumed any alcoholic drinks in the last twelve months?

     Yes _____

     No _____

     (if **No** proceed to question 4)

2. (*To be asked if interviewee replied* **Yes** *to question 1*)

     Which of the following alcoholic drinks do you consume most frequently?

     (Ask respondent to choose the category that he or she drinks most frequently and tick one category only.)

     Beer _____

     Spirits _____

     Wine _____

     Liquors _____

     Other _____   specify _____

3. How frequently do you consume alcoholic drinks?

     (Ask interviewee to choose the category that comes closest to his or her current practice.)

     Daily   _____

     Most days   _____

     Once or twice a week   _____

     Once or twice a month   _____

     A few times a year   _____

     Once or twice a year   _____

4. (*To be asked if interviewee replied* **No** *to question 1*)

     Have you ever consumed alcoholic drinks?

     Yes _____

     No _____

Quite a lot of research has been carried out on the general subject of question order, but few if any consistent effects on people's responses that derive from asking questions at different points in a questionnaire or interview schedule have been unveiled. Different effects have been demonstrated on various occasions. A study in the USA found that people were less likely to say that their taxes were too high when they had been previously asked whether government spending ought to be increased in a number of areas (Schuman and Presser 1981: 32). Apparently, some people perceived an inconsistency between wanting more spending and lower taxes, and adjusted their answers accordingly. Research on crime victimization in the USA suggests that earlier questions may affect the salience of later issues (Schuman and Presser 1981: 45). Respondents were asked whether they had been victims of crime in the preceding twelve months. Some respondents had been previously asked a series of questions about their attitudes to crime, whereas others had not. Those who had been asked about their attitudes reported considerably more crime than those who had not been asked.

Mayhew (2000) provides an interesting anecdote on question order in relation to the British Crime Survey. Each wave of the BCS has included the question:

Taking everything into account, would you say the police in this area do a good job or a poor job?

In 1988 this question appeared twice by mistake for some respondents! For all respondents it appeared early on, but for around half it also appeared later on in the context of questions on contact with the police. Of those given the question twice, 66 per cent gave the same rating, but 22 per cent gave a more positive rating to the police and just 13 per cent gave a less favourable one. Mayhew suggests that, as the interview wore on, respondents became more sensitized to crime-related issues and more sympathetic to the pressures on the police.

However, it is difficult to draw general lessons from such research, at least in part because experiments in question order do not always reveal clear-cut effects of varying the order in which questions are asked, even in cases where effects might legitimately have been expected. There are two general lessons.

1. Within a survey, question order should not be varied (unless, of course, question order is the subject of the study!).

2. Researchers should be sensitive to the possible implications of the effect of early questions on answers to subsequent questions.

The following rules about question order are sometimes proposed.

- Early questions should be directly related to the topic of the research, about which the respondent has been informed. This removes the possibility that the respondent will be wondering at an early stage in the interview why he or she is being asked apparently irrelevant questions. This injunction means that personal questions about age, social background, and so on should *not* be asked at the beginning of an interview.

- As far as possible, questions that are more likely to be salient to respondents should be asked early in the interview schedule, so that their interest and attention are more likely to be secured. This suggestion may conflict with the previous one, in that questions specifically on the research topic may not be obviously salient to respondents, but it implies that as far as possible questions relating to the research topic that are more likely to grab their attention should be asked at or close to the start of the interview.

- Potentially embarrassing questions or ones that may be a source of anxiety should be left till later. In fact, research should be designed to ensure that, as far as possible, respondents are not discomfited, but it has to be acknowledged that with certain topics this effect may be unavoidable.

- With a long schedule or questionnaire, questions should be grouped into sections, since this allows a better flow than skipping from one topic to another.

- Within each group of questions, general questions should precede specific ones. Tips and skills 'A sequence of questions on the topic of identity cards' provides an illustration of such a sequence, which follows the recommendations of Gallup (1947, cited in Foddy 1993: 61–2). The example is concerned to demonstrate how the approach might operate in connection with identity cards, which have been an area of discussion and some controversy in the UK in recent years. The question order sequence is designed with a number of features in mind. It is designed to establish people's levels of knowledge of identity cards before asking questions about it and to distinguish those who feel strongly about it from those who do not. According to Foddy (1993), the second question is always open ended, so that respondents' frames of references can be established with respect to the topic at hand. However, it seems likely that, if sufficient pilot research has been carried out, a closed question could be envisaged, a point that applies equally to question 4.

Tips and skills
A sequence of questions on the topic of identity cards

1. Have you heard of identity cards?

    Yes _____   No _____

2. What are your views about identity cards?

3. Do you favour or not favour identity cards?

    Favour _____   Not favour _____

4. Why do you favour (not favour) identity cards?

5. How strongly do you feel about this?

    Very strongly   _____

    Fairly strongly   _____

    Not at all strongly _____

- A further aspect of the rule that general questions should precede specific ones is that it has been argued that, when a specific question comes before a general one, the aspect of the general question that is covered by the specific one is discounted in the minds of respondents because they feel they have already covered it. Thus, if a question about how people feel about the amount they are paid precedes a general question about job satisfaction, there are grounds for thinking that respondents will discount the issue of pay when responding about job satisfaction.

- It is sometimes recommended that questions dealing with opinions and attitudes should precede questions to do with behaviour and knowledge. This is because it is felt that behaviour and knowledge questions are less affected by question order than questions that tap opinions and attitudes.

- During the course of an interview, it sometimes happens that a respondent provides an answer to a question that is to be asked later in the interview. Because of the possibility of a question order effect, when the interviewer arrives at the question that appears already to have been answered, it should be repeated.

However, question order effects remain one of the more frustrating areas of structured interview and questionnaire design, because of the inconsistent evidence that is found and because it is difficult to formulate **generalizations** or rules from the evidence that does point to their operation. An interesting discussion about question order took place some years ago in connection with the study of social class and is discussed in Thinking deeply 8.2.

Thinking deeply 8.2
A debate about question order

An interesting case of the issue of question order becoming a focus of controversy is provided by the research on social class by Marshall *et al.* (1988), which is referred to in more detail in Research in focus 7.1 and 8.2. In a critique of the research, Saunders (1989) argues that it reveals what he calls 'socialist preconceptions', implying that values overtly intruded into the research (see Figure 1.3). Saunders argues that one way in which this was revealed was the sheer weight of questions about social class prior to respondents being asked about the groups to which they saw themselves as belonging. Saunders (1989: 4) writes:

A glance at their questionnaire reveals that respondents were bombarded with questions about class right from the start of the interview. Following no fewer than 28 detailed questions about the class system, respondents were then asked if they thought they belonged to any social class and whether there was, by any chance, any other grouping they identified with apart from their class. Not surprisingly, most agreed that they did belong to one class or another . . . and that they could not think of any other identity . . . Armed with their 'findings', the authors then conclude that we are all class-oriented after all and that other identities are far less important.

Two of the book's authors replied with a spirited rebuttal. They reply that:

> the question about class was preceded by 30 substantive items. Six of these have no obvious relationship to the issue of social identities; for example, they elicit perceptions of Britain's economic performance . . . No less than 17 . . . were specifically designed to make interviewees see the world in terms other than those of social class. They invited people to think of themselves as consumers . . . as voters . . . as members of ethnic or gender groupings; as employees . . . in short, as everything but members of an identifiable social class. Interviewees were also asked whether there were 'any important conflicts in Britain today' before the word social class was ever mentioned. Then, and only then, were they quizzed about their perception of Britain as a specifically class society. (Marshall and Rose 1989: 5)

This is an interesting debate because it raises the issue of the role of values and bias in social research and also because it relates to the issue of question order while demonstrating the difficulty of being definitive about the issue. For example, while Marshall and Rose's reply is convincing, it might be that it is the *relative number* of questions about social class preceding questions of identity that may have been influential and to which Saunders alludes. Nonetheless, the debate usefully demonstrates the difficulty of producing conclusive evidence about question order effects.

Probing

Probing is a highly problematic area for researchers employing a structured interview method. It frequently happens in interviews that respondents need help with their answers. One obvious case is where it is evident that they do not understand the question—they may either ask for further information or it is clear from what they say that they are struggling to understand the question or to provide an adequate answer. The second kind of situation the interviewer faces is when the respondent does not provide a sufficiently complete answer and has to be probed for more information. The problem in either situation is obvious: the interviewer's intervention may influence the respondent, and the nature of interviewers' interventions may differ. A potential source of variability in respondents' replies that does not reflect 'true' variation is introduced—that is, error.

Some general tactics with regard to probes are as follows.

- If further information is required, usually in the context of an open-ended question, standardized probes can be employed, such as 'Could you say a little more about that?' or 'Are there any other reasons why you think that?' or simply 'mmmm . . . ?'.

- If the problem is that when presented with a closed question the respondent replies in a way that does not allow the interviewee to select one of the pre-designed answers, the interviewer should repeat the fixed-choice alternatives and make it apparent that the answer needs to be chosen from the ones that have been provided.

- If the interviewer needs to know about something that requires quantification, such as the number of visits to building societies in the last four weeks or the number of building societies in which the respondent has accounts, but the respondent resists this by answering in general terms ('quite often' or 'I usually go to the building society every week'), the interviewer needs to persist with securing a number from the respondent. This will usually entail repeating the question. The interviewer should not try to second guess a figure on the basis of the respondent's reply and then suggest that figure to him or her, since the latter may be unwilling to demur from the interviewer's suggested figure.

However, from the point of view of standardizing the asking of questions in surveys using structured interviewing, probing should be kept to a minimum (assuming it cannot be eliminated) because it introduces error. This occurs because it is impossible for interviewers to probe in a consistent manner and because interviewer effects are more likely to occur, whereby characteristics of the interviewer have an impact on the respondent's replies (Groves *et al.* 2004: 281–2).

Prompting

Prompting occurs when the interviewer suggests a possible answer to a question to the respondent. The key prerequisite here is that all respondents receive the same prompts. All closed questions entail standardized prompting, because the respondent is provided with a list of possible answers from which to choose. An unacceptable approach to prompting would be to ask an open question and to suggest possible answers only to some respondents, such as those who appear to be struggling to think of an appropriate reply.

During the course of a face-to-face interview, there are several circumstances in which it will be better for the interviewer to use 'show cards' rather than rely on reading out a series of fixed-choice alternatives. Show cards (sometimes called 'flash cards') display all the answers from which the respondent is to choose and are handed to the respondent at different points of the interview. Three kinds of context in which it might be preferable to employ

show cards rather than to read out the entire set of possible answers are as follows.

- There may be a very long list of possible answers. For example, respondents may be asked which daily newspaper they each read most frequently. To read out a list of newspapers would be tedious and it is probably better to hand the respondent a list of newspapers from which to choose.

- Sometimes, during the course of interviews, respondents are presented with a group of questions to which the same possible answers are attached. An example of this strategy is Likert scaling, an approach to attitude measurement that was discussed in Key concept 6.2. The components of a Likert scale are often referred to as *items* rather than as *questions*, since strictly speaking respondents are not being asked questions but are presented with statements to which they are asked to indicate their levels of agreement. See Research in focus 6.2 and 6.5 for examples. It would be excruciatingly dull to read out all 7 possible answers ten times. Also, it may be expecting too much of respondents to read out the answers once and then require them to keep the possible answers in their heads for the entire batch of questions to which they apply. A show card that can be used for the entire batch and to which respondents can constantly refer is an obvious solution. As was mentioned in Key concept 6.2, most Likert scales of this kind comprise 5 levels of agreement/disagreement and it is this more conventional approach that is illustrated in the show card in Tips and skills 'A show card'.

Tips and skills
A show card

Card 6

Strongly agree

Agree

Undecided

Disagree

Strongly disagree

- Some people are not keen to divulge personal details such as their age or their income. One way of neutralizing the impact of such questioning is to present respondents with age or income bands with a letter or number attached to each band. They can then be asked to say which letter/number applies to them (see Tips and skills 'Another show card'). This procedure will obviously not be appropriate if the research requires *exact* ages or incomes. It may be extendable to sensitive areas such as number of sexual partners or sexual practices for the same kinds of reason.

Tips and skills
Another show card

Card 11

1. Below 20
2. 20–29
3. 30–39
4. 40–49
5. 50–59
6. 60–69
7. 70 and over

Student experience
The need for structure in a survey interview

Joe Thompson's survey research on students and their views of accommodation and facilities at his university was part of a team project. After he and other members of his team had piloted the interview schedule, they decided that it was not sufficiently structured. They felt that they needed to impose more structure and decided to use show cards (he refers to them by their other common name 'cue cards').

The group therefore used opportunistic sampling to test if the questionnaire would be successful when applied in a social setting, having to give the questionnaire to one person over the week. The following week the group discussed the issues they had encountered when carrying out the pilot questionnaire, raising amongst others the concern of not having a standard interview procedure, which would mean that certain biases could affect the results. Therefore the group decided they would use cue cards when giving the options in answer to the question, so as to avoid leading questions, etc. After these changes were implemented, the final version of the questionnaire was produced.

To read more about Joe's research experiences, go to the Online Resource Centre that accompanies this book at http://www.oxfordtextbooks.co.uk/orc/brymansrm3e/.

Leaving the interview

Do not forget common courtesies like thanking respondents for giving up their time. But the period immediately after the interview is one in which some care is necessary in that sometimes respondents try to engage the interviewer in a discussion about the purpose of the interview. Interviewers should resist elaboration beyond their standard statement, because respondents may communicate what they are told to others, which may bias the findings.

Training and supervision

On several occasions, reference has been made to the need for interviewers to be trained. The standard texts on survey research and on interviewing practice tend to be replete with advice on how best to train interviewers. Such advice is typically directed at contexts in which a researcher hires an interviewer to conduct a large amount or even all the interviews. It also has considerable importance in research in which several interviewers (who may be either collaborators or hired interviewers) are involved in a study, since the risk of interviewer variability in the asking of questions needs to be avoided.

For many readers of this book who are planning to do research, such situations are unlikely to be relevant because they will be 'lone' researchers. You may be doing an undergraduate dissertation, or an exercise for a research methods course, or you may be a postgraduate conducting research for a Master's dissertation or for a thesis. Most people in such a situation will not have the luxury of being able to hire a researcher to do any interviewing (though you may be able to find someone to help you a little). When interviewing on your own, you must in a sense train yourself to follow the procedures and advice provided above. This is a very different situation from a large research institute or market research agency, which relies on an army of hired interviewers who carry out the interviews. Whenever people other than the lead researcher are involved in interviewing, they will need training and supervision in the following areas:

- contacting prospective respondents and providing an introduction to the study;
- reading out questions as written and following instructions in the interview schedule (e.g. in connection with filter questions);
- using appropriate styles of probing;
- recording exactly what is said;
- maintaining an interview style that does not bias respondents' answers.

Fowler (1993) cites evidence that suggests that training of less than one full day rarely creates good interviewers.

Supervision of interviewers in relation to these issues can be achieved by:

- checking individual interviewers' response rates;
- tape-recording at least a sample of interviews;
- examining completed schedules to determine whether any questions are being left out or if they are being completed properly;
- call-backs on a sample of respondents (usually around 10 per cent) to determine whether they were interviewed and to ask about interviewers' conduct.

Research in focus 8.2 provides an example of some of the ingredients of research involving multiple interviewers.

Research in focus 8.2
An example of research involving multiple interviewers

This example is taken from the study by Marshall *et al.* (1988), a team of sociologists from the University of Essex, of social class in modern Britain. The interviewing was carried out by a leading independent social research institute, Social and Community Planning Research (SCPR). The research aimed to achieve a sample of 2,000 respondents (1,770 was the number actually achieved; see Research in focus 7.1 for details of the sampling procedure).

One hundred and twenty-three interviewers were employed on the survey. Six full-time briefing sessions were held, all of which were attended by a member of the Essex team, and interviewers were also given a full set of written instructions. The first three interviews conducted by each interviewer were subjected to an immediate thorough checking in order that critical comments, where appropriate, could be conveyed. During the course of fieldwork the work of interviewers was subject to personal recall. Ten per cent of issued addresses were re-issued for recall . . . In addition, 36 interviewers were accompanied in the field by supervisors . . . (Marshall *et al.* 1988: 291)

Problems with structured interviewing

While the structured interview is a commonly used method of social research, certain problems associated with it have been identified over the years. These problems are not necessarily unique to the structured interview, in that they can sometimes be attributed to kindred methods, such as the self-completion questionnaire in survey research or even semi-structured interviewing in qualitative research. However, it is common for the structured interview to be seen as a focus for the identification of certain limitations, which are briefly examined below.

Characteristics of interviewers

There is evidence that interviewers' attributes can have an impact on respondents' replies, but, unfortunately, the literature on this issue does not lend itself to definitive generalizations. In large part, this ambiguity in the broader implications of experiments relating to the effects of interviewer characteristics is due to several problems, such as: the problem of disentangling the effects of interviewers' different attributes from each other (race, gender, socio-economic status); the interaction between the characteristics of interviewers and the characteristics of respondents; and the interaction between any effects observed and the topic of the interview. Nonetheless, there is undoubtedly some evidence that effects due to characteristics of interviewers can be discerned.

The ethnicity of interviewers is one area that has attracted some attention. Schuman and Presser (1981) cite a study that asked respondents to nominate two or three of their favourite actors or entertainers. Respondents were much more likely to mention black actors or entertainers when interviewed by black interviewers than when interviewed by white ones. Schuman

and Converse (1971) interviewed 619 black Detroiters shortly after Martin Luther King's assassination in 1968. The researchers found significant differences in the answers given between black and white interviewers in around one-quarter of the questions asked.

Although this proportion is quite disturbing, the fact that the majority of questions appear to have been largely unaffected does not give rise to a great deal of confidence that a consistent biasing factor is being uncovered. Similarly inconclusive findings tend to occur in relation to experiments with other sets of characteristics of interviewers. These remarks are not meant to play down the potential significance of interviewers' characteristics for measurement error, but to draw attention to the limitations of drawing conclusive inferences about the evidence. All that needs to be registered at this juncture is that almost certainly the characteristics of interviewers do have an impact on respondents' replies but that the extent and nature of the impact are not clear and are likely to vary from context to context.

Response sets

Some writers have suggested that the structured interview is particularly prone to the operation among respondents of what Webb *et al.* (1966: 19) call 'response sets', which they define as 'irrelevant but lawful sources of variance'. This form of response bias is especially relevant to multiple-indicator measures (see Chapter 6), where respondents reply to a battery of related questions or items, of the kind found in a Likert scale (see Key concept 6.2). The idea of a response set implies that people respond to the series of questions in a consistent way but one that is irrelevant to the concept being measured. Two of the most prominent types of response set are known as the 'acquiescence' (also known as the 'yeasaying' and 'naysaying' effect) and the 'social desirability' effect.

Acquiescence

Acquiescence refers to a tendency for some people consistently to agree or disagree with a set of questions or items. Imagine a respondent who replied with agreement to all the items in Research in focus 6.2. The problem is that agreement with some of the items implies a low level of commitment to work (items 1–4), whereas agreement with others implies a high level of commitment to work (items 5–10). One of the reasons why researchers who employ this kind of multiple-item measure use wordings that imply opposite stances (that is, some items implying a high level of commitment and others implying a low level of commitment to work) is to weed out those respondents who appear to be replying within the framework of an acquiescence response set.

Social desirability bias

The social desirability effect refers to evidence that some respondents' answers to questions are related to their perception of the social desirability of those answers. An answer that is perceived to be socially desirable is more likely to be endorsed than one that is not. This phenomenon has been demonstrated in studies on mental health using psychiatric inventories. These inventories are meant to be concerned not with chronic mental illness but with minor neuroses and anxieties. Research in New York by Dohrenwend (1966) noted that Puerto Ricans tended to score much higher on the inventory that he administered than other ethnic groups. He found that this tendency was not due to a higher level of mental illness in this ethnic group, but to the effect of social desirability in respondents' answers. Puerto Ricans were much less likely than the other ethnic groups to perceive the items in the inventory as undesirable. This meant that what the researcher had found was a link not between ethnicity and mental health, but between ethnicity and perceptions of the social desirability of mental health inventory items. Later research suggested that variation in the social desirability of mental illness symptoms was related to the perceived prevalence of those symptoms among the respondent's friends and acquaintances (Phillips 1973). The presence of social desirability effects has been demonstrated in other settings (e.g. Arnold and Feldman 1981).

In so far as these forms of response error go undetected, they represent sources of error in the measurement of concepts. However, while some writers have proposed outright condemnation of social research on the basis of evidence of response sets (e.g. Phillips 1973), it is important not to get carried away with such findings. We cannot be sure how prevalent these effects are, and to some extent awareness of them has led to measures to limit their impact on data (for example, by weeding out cases obviously affected by them or by instructing interviewers to limit the possible impact of the social desirability effect by not becoming overly friendly with respondents and by not being judgemental about their replies).

The problem of meaning

A critique of survey interview data and findings gleaned from similar techniques was developed by social scientists influenced by phenomenological and other interpretivist ideas of the kinds touched on in Chapter 1 (Cicourel 1964, 1982; Filmer *et al.* 1972; Briggs 1986; Mishler 1986). This critique revolves around what is often referred to in a shorthand way as the 'problem of meaning'. The kernel of the argument is that when humans communicate they do so in a way that not only draws on commonly held meanings but also simultaneously creates meanings. 'Meaning' in this sense is something that is worked at and achieved —it is not simply pre-given. Allusions to the problem of meaning in structured interviewing draw attention to the notion that survey researchers presume that interviewer and respondent share the same meanings of terms employed in the interview questions and answers. In fact, the problem of meaning implies that the possibility that interviewer and respondent may not be sharing the same meaning systems and hence imply different things in their use of words is simply sidestepped in structured interview research. The problem of meaning is resolved by ignoring it.

The feminist critique

The feminist critique of structured interviewing is difficult to disentangle from the critique launched against quantitative research in general, which was briefly outlined in Chapter 1. However, for many feminist social researchers the structured interview symbolizes more readily than other methods the limitations of quantitative research, partly because of its prevalence but also partly because of its nature. By 'its nature' is meant the fact that the structured interview epitomizes the asymmetrical relationship between researcher and subject that is seen as an ingredient of quantitative research: the researcher extracts information from the research subject and gives nothing in return. For example, standard textbook advice of the kind provided in this chapter implies that rapport is useful to the interviewer but he or she should guard against becoming too familiar. This means that questions asked by respondents (for example, about the research or about the topic of the research) should be politely but firmly rebuffed on the grounds that too much familiarity should be avoided and because the respondents' subsequent answers may be biased.

This is perfectly valid and appropriate advice from the vantage point of the canons of structured interviewing with its quest for standardization and for valid and reliable data. However, from the perspective of feminism, when women interview women a wedge is hammered between them that, in conjunction with the implication of a hierarchical relationship between the interviewer and respondent, is incompatible with its values. An impression of exploitation is created, but exploitation of women is precisely what feminist social science seeks to fight against. Oakley (1981) found in her research on childbirth that she was frequently asked questions by her respondents. It was these questions that typified the problems of being a feminist interviewing women.

> The dilemma of a feminist interviewer interviewing women could be summarised by considering the practical application of some of the strategies recommended in the textbooks for meeting interviewees' questions. For example, these advise that such questions as 'Which hole does the baby come out of?' 'Does an epidural ever paralyse women?' and 'Why is it dangerous to leave a small baby alone in the house?' should be met with such responses from the interviewer as 'I guess I haven't thought enough about it to give a good answer right now,' or 'a head-shaking gesture which suggests "that's a hard one"' (Goode and Hatt [1952: 198]).
> (Oakley, 1981: 48)

Such advice still appears in textbooks concerned with survey research. For example, Groves *et al.* (2004: 283) supply the following advice:

> 1. Interviewers should refrain from expressing views or opinions on the topics covered by the survey instrument.
>
> 2. Interviewers should refrain from presenting any personal information that might provide a bias for inferring what their preferences or values might be that are relevant to the content of the interview.
>
> 3. Although a little informal chatting about neutral topics, such as the weather or pets, may help to free up communication, for the most part, interviewers should focus on the task.

This is in fact good advice from the point of view of reducing error that might arise from the interviewer influencing or biasing the interviewee's replies. As such, it is likely to reduce error arising from the influence of the interviewer.

Oakley's point is that to act according to such canons of textbook practice would be irresponsible for a feminist in such a situation. It was this kind of critique of structured interviewing and indeed of quantitative research in general that ushered in a period in which a great many feminist social researchers found qualitative research more compatible with their goals and norms. In terms of interviewing, this trend resulted in a preference for forms of interviewing such as unstructured and semi-structured interviewing and focus groups. These will be the focus of later chapters. However, as noted in Chapter 1, there has been some softening of attitudes towards the role of quantitative research among feminist researchers. For example, Walby and Myhill (2001) have shown how surveys of violence against women that are dedicated to uncovering such violence (rather than general crime surveys like the BCS) reveal higher levels than are often thought to occur. By paying greater attention to issues like greater privacy in the interview and special training in sensitive interviewing, dedicated surveys in some countries have proved highly instructive about the causes and incidence of violence against women. Such research, which is based on structured interview, would not seem to be inconsistent with the goals of most feminist researchers and indeed may be of considerable significance for many women. Nonetheless, there is still a tendency for qualitative research to remain the preferred research strategy for many feminist researchers.

Key points

- The structured interview is a research instrument that is used to standardize the asking and often the recording of answers in order to keep interviewer-related error to a minimum.
- The structured interview can be administered in person or over the telephone.
- It is important to keep to the wording and order of questions when conducting survey research by structured interview.
- While there is some evidence that interviewers' characteristics can influence respondents' replies, the findings of experiments on this issue are somewhat equivocal.
- Response sets can be damaging to data derived from structured interviews and steps need to be taken to identify respondents exhibiting them.
- The structured interview symbolizes the characteristics of quantitative research that feminist researchers find distasteful: in particular, the lack of reciprocity and the taint of exploitation.

Questions for review

The structured interview

- Why is it important in interviewing for survey research to keep interviewer variability to a minimum?
- How successful is the structured interview in reducing interviewer variability?
- Why might a survey researcher prefer to use a structured rather than an unstructured interview approach for gathering data?
- Why do structured interview schedules typically include mainly closed questions?

Interview contexts

- Are there any circumstances in which it might be preferable to conduct structured interviews with more than one interviewer?
- 'Given the lower cost of telephone interviewing compared to face-to-face interviews, the former is generally preferable.' Discuss.

Conducting interviews

- Prepare an opening statement for a study of manual workers in a firm, to which access has already been achieved.
- To what extent is rapport an important ingredient of structured interviewing?
- How strong is the evidence that question order can significantly affect answers?
- How strong is the evidence that interviewers' characteristics can significantly affect answers?
- What is the difference between probing and prompting? How important are they and what dangers are lurking with their use?

Problems with structured interviewing

- What are response sets and why are they potentially important?
- What are the main issues that lie behind the critique of structured interviewing by feminist researchers?

Online Resource Centre

http://www.oxfordtextbooks.co.uk/orc/brymansrm3e/

Visit the Online Resource Centre that accompanies this book to enrich your understanding of structured interviewing. Consult web links, test yourself using multiple choice questions, and gain further guidance and inspiration from the Student Researcher's Toolkit.

Self-completion questionnaires

Chapter outline

Chapter guide

Questionnaires that are completed by respondents themselves are one of the main instruments for gathering data using a **social survey** design, along with the **structured interview** that was covered in the previous chapter. Probably the most common form is the mail or **postal questionnaire**. The term 'self-completion questionnaire' is often used because it is somewhat more inclusive than 'postal questionnaire'. This chapter explores:

- the advantages and disadvantages of the questionnaire in comparison to the structured interview;
- how to address the potential problem of poor response rates, which is often a feature of the postal questionnaire;
- how questionnaires should be designed in order to make answering easier for respondents and less prone to error;
- the use of diaries as a form of self-completion questionnaire.

Introduction

In a very real sense, the bulk of the previous chapter was about questionnaires. The structured interview is in many, if not most, respects a questionnaire that is administered by an interviewer. However, there is a tendency, which borders on a convention, to reserve the term 'questionnaire' for contexts in which a battery of usually **closed questions** is completed by respondents themselves.

Self-completion questionnaire or postal questionnaire?

The *self-completion questionnaire* is sometimes referred to as a *self-administered questionnaire*. The former term will be followed in this book. With a self-completion questionnaire, respondents answer questions by completing the questionnaire themselves. As a method, the self-completion questionnaire can come in several different forms. Probably the most prominent of these forms is the *postal* or *mail questionnaire*, whereby, as its name implies, a questionnaire is sent through the post to the respondent. The latter, following completion of the instrument, is usually asked to return it by post; an alternative form of return is when respondents are requested to deposit their completed questionnaires in a certain location, such as a box in a school common room or in a supervisor's office in a firm. 'Postal' is used rather than mail to distinguish questionnaires that are sent out through the postal system from email questionnaires, which are discussed in Chapter 26. The term 'self-completion questionnaire' also covers forms of administration, such as when a researcher hands out questionnaires to all students in a class and collects them back after they have been completed. For example, Smith and McVie (2003) describe their use of such an instrument for their longitudinal cohort study of crime in relation to transformations during youth and adolescent development among a large sample of young people in Edinburgh. They write:

> In general, questionnaires were completed by a whole class under the supervision of one or two researchers. . . . Desks were spaced out as much as possible, and in most cases questionnaires were completed in exam-like conditions, with talking strongly discouraged, and little or no overlooking of others' questionnaires. (Smith and McVie 2003: 183)

In this case, we can see that the questionnaire is self-administered but is neither sent out nor returned through the postal system. 'Self-completion questionnaire' is, therefore, a more inclusive term than 'postal questionnaire', though it is probably true to say that the latter is the most prominent form of the self-completion questionnaire.

In the discussion that follows, when points apply to more or less all forms of self-completion questionnaire, this term will be employed. When points apply specifically or exclusively to questionnaires sent through the post, the term 'postal questionnaire' will be used.

Evaluating the self-completion questionnaire in relation to the structured interview

In many ways, the self-completion questionnaire and the structured interview are very similar methods of social research. The obvious difference between them is that, with the self-completion questionnaire, there is no interviewer to ask the questions; instead, respondents must read each question themselves and answer the questions themselves. Beyond this obvious, but central, difference, they are remarkably similar. However, because there is no interviewer in the administration of the self-completion questionnaire, the research instrument has to be especially easy to follow and its questions have to be particularly easy to answer. After all, respondents cannot be trained in the way interviewers can be; nor do they know their way around a research instrument in the way a 'lone researcher' might.

As a result, self-completion questionnaires, as compared to structured interviews, tend to:

- have fewer open questions, since closed ones tend to be easier to answer;
- have easy-to-follow designs to minimize the risk that the respondent will fail to follow filter questions or will inadvertently omit a question;
- be shorter to reduce the risk of 'respondent fatigue', since it is manifestly easier for a respondent who becomes tired of answering questions in a long questionnaire to consign it to a waste paper bin rather than to terminate an interview.

Advantages of the self-completion questionnaire over the structured interview

Cheaper to administer

Interviewing can be expensive. The cheapness of the self-completion questionnaire is especially advantageous if you have a sample that is geographically widely dispersed. When this is the case, a postal questionnaire will be much cheaper, because of the time and cost of travel for interviewers. This advantage is obviously less pronounced in connection with telephone interviews, because of the lower costs of telephone charges relative to travel and time spent travelling. But, even in comparison to telephone interviewing, the postal questionnaire enjoys cost advantages.

Quicker to administer

Self-completion questionnaires can be sent out through the post or otherwise distributed in very large quantities at the same time. A thousand questionnaires can be sent out through the post in one batch, but, even with a team of interviewers, it would take a long time to conduct personal interviews with a sample of that size. However, it is important to bear in mind that the questionnaires do not all come back immediately and that they may take several weeks to be returned. Also, there is invariably a need to send out follow-up letters and/or questionnaires to those who fail to return them initially, an issue that will be returned to below.

Absence of interviewer effects

It was noted in Chapter 8 that various studies have demonstrated that characteristics of interviewers (and respondents) may affect the answers that people give. While the findings from this research are somewhat equivocal in their implications, it has been suggested that characteristics such as ethnicity, gender, and the social background of interviewers may combine to bias the answers that respondents provide. Obviously, since there is no interviewer present when a self-completion questionnaire is being completed, interviewer effects are eliminated. However, this advantage probably has to be regarded fairly cautiously, since few consistent patterns have emerged over the years from research to suggest what kinds of interviewer characteristics bias answers. Probably of greater importance to the presence of an interviewer is the tendency for people to be more likely to exhibit social desirability bias when an interviewer is present. Research by Sudman and Bradburn (1982) suggests that postal questionnaires work better than personal interviews when a question carries the possibility of such bias. There is also a tendency for respondents to under-report activities that induce anxiety or about which they are sensitive. Research summarized by Tourangeau and Smith (1996) strongly suggests that respondents tend to report more drug use and alcohol consumption and a higher number of sexual partners and of abortions in self-completion questionnaires than in structured interviews.

No interviewer variability

Self-completion questionnaires do not suffer from the problem of interviewers asking questions in a different order or in different ways.

Convenience for respondents

Self-completion questionnaires are more convenient for respondents, because they can complete a questionnaire when they want and at the speed that they want to go.

Disadvantages of the self-completion questionnaire in comparison with the structured interview

Cannot prompt

There is no one present to help respondents if they are having difficulty answering a question. It is always important to ensure that the questions that are asked are clear and unambiguous, but this is especially so with the self-completion questionnaire, since there is no interviewer to help respondents with questions they find difficult to understand and hence to answer. Also, great attention must be paid to ensure that the questionnaire is easy to complete; otherwise questions will be inadvertently omitted if instructions are unclear.

Cannot probe

There is no opportunity to probe respondents to elaborate an answer. Probing can be very important when open-ended questions are being asked. Interviewers are often trained to get more from respondents. However, this problem largely applies to open questions, which are not used a great deal in self-completion questionnaire research.

Cannot ask many questions that are not salient to respondents

Respondents are more likely than in interviews to become tired of answering questions that are not very salient to them, and that they are likely to perceive as boring. Because of the risk of a questionnaire being consigned to a waste paper bin, it is important to avoid including many non-salient questions in a self-completion questionnaire. However, this point suggests that, when a research issue *is* salient to the respondent, a high response rate is feasible (Altschuld and Lower 1984). This means that, when questions are salient, the self-completion questionnaire may be a good choice for researchers, especially when the much lower cost is borne in mind.

Difficulty of asking other kinds of question

In addition to the problem of asking too many questions that are not salient to respondents, as previously suggested, it is also important to avoid asking more than a very small number of open questions (because respondents frequently do not want to write a lot). Questions with complex structures, such as filters, should be avoided as far as possible (because respondents often find them difficult to follow).

Questionnaire can be read as a whole

Respondents are able to read the whole questionnaire before answering the first question. When this occurs, none of the questions asked is truly independent of the others. It also means that you cannot be sure that questions have been answered in the correct order. It also means that the problem of question order effects (see Chapter 8) may arise.

Do not know who answers

With postal questionnaires, you can never be sure whether the right person has answered the questionnaire. If a questionnaire is sent to a certain person in a household, it may be that someone else in that household completes the questionnaire. It is also impossible to have any control over the intrusion of non-respondents (such as other members of a household) in the answering of questions. Similarly, if a questionnaire is sent to a manager in a firm, the task may simply be delegated to someone else. This advantage of the structured interview over the postal questionnaire does not apply when the former is administered by telephone, since the same problem applies. There is a feeling among some commentators that when a self-completion questionnaire is administered over the Internet (a form of administration of questionnaires that is covered in Chapter 26), the problem of not knowing who is replying is exacerbated because of the propensity of some Web users to assume online identities (Couper 2004).

Cannot collect additional data

With an interview, interviewers might be asked to collect snippets of information about the home, school, firm, or whatever. This is not going to be possible in connection with a postal questionnaire, but if self-completion questionnaires are handed out in a school or firm, it is more feasible to collect such additional data.

Difficult to ask a lot of questions

As signalled above, because of the possibility of 'respondent fatigue', long questionnaires are rarely feasible. They may even result in a greater tendency for questionnaires not to be answered in the first place, since they can be offputting.

Not appropriate for some kinds of respondent

Respondents whose literacy is limited or whose facility with English is restricted will not be able to answer the questionnaire. The second of these difficulties cannot be entirely overcome when interviews are being employed, but the difficulties are likely to be greater with postal questionnaires.

Greater risk of missing data

Partially answered questionnaires are more likely, because of a lack of prompting or supervision, than in interviews. It is also easier for respondents actively to decide not to answer a question when on their own than when being asked by an interviewer. For example, questions that appear boring or irrelevant to the respondent may be especially likely to be skipped. If questions are not answered, this creates a problem of *missing data* for the variables that are created.

Lower response rates

One of the most damaging limitations is that surveys by postal questionnaire typically result in lower response rates (see Key concept 7.2) than comparable interview-based studies. The significance of a response rate is that, unless it can be proven that those who do not participate do not differ from those who do, there is likely to be the risk of bias. In other words, if, as is likely, there are differences between participants and refusals, it is probable that the findings relating to the sample will be affected. If a response rate is low, it seems likely that the risk of bias in the findings will be greater.

The problem of low response rates seems to apply particularly to postal questionnaires. Research in focus 7.4 describes a survey by self-completion questionnaire that was answered by all students to whom it was administered; the only non-respondents were those who were absent from the lecture. When a self-completion questionnaire is employed in this kind of context, it seems less vulnerable to the problem of a low response rate.

Mangione (1995: 60–1) has provided the following classification of bands of response rate to postal questionnaires:

over 85%	excellent
70–85%	very good
60–69%	acceptable
50–59%	barely acceptable
below 50%	not acceptable

Research in focus 9.1 reports a study that achieved an 'excellent' response rate.

Tips and skills
Response rates

Response rates are important because, the lower a response rate, the more questions are likely to be raised about the representativeness of the achieved sample. In a sense, this is likely to be an issue only with randomly selected samples. With samples that are not selected on the basis of a probability sampling method, it could be argued that the response rate is less of an issue because the sample would not be representative of a **population** even if everyone participated! Postal questionnaire surveys in particular are often associated with low response rates, and, as Mangione's classification illustrates, according to some authorities a response rate of below 50 per cent is not acceptable. On the other hand, many published articles report the results of studies that are well below this level. In an examination of published studies in the field of organizational research in the years 1979–83, Mitchell (1985) found a range of response rates of 30 to 94 per cent. Therefore, if you achieve a low response rate, do not despair. Although writers like Mangione (1995) may regard response rates of 30 per cent as unacceptable (and he may be right about this judgement), a great deal of published research also achieves low response rates. The key point is to recognize and acknowledge the implications of the possible limitations of a low response rate. On the other hand, if your research is based on a **convenience sample**, ironically it could be argued that a low response rate is less significant. Many students find postal and other forms of self-completion questionnaire attractive because of their low cost and quick administration. The point of this discussion is that you should not be put off using such techniques because of the prospect of a low response rate.

Research in focus 9.1
A monetary incentive

Lunt and Livingstone (1992) conducted a postal questionnaire survey into a variety of issues relating to the notion of consumerism. They were particularly interested in people's attitudes to money. In September 1989 they sent out 241 questionnaires to people living in or around Oxford. Each person was paid 'a nominal £2 for their time' (1992: 173). The questionnaire was long (twenty pages) and took between one and one-and-a-half hours to complete. In spite of its length, 219 returned the questionnaire, making a response rate of 91 per cent.

Steps to improve response rates to postal questionnaires

Because of the tendency for postal questionnaire surveys to generate lower response rates than comparable structured interview surveys (and the implications this has for the validity of findings), a great deal of thought and research has gone into ways of improving survey response. The following steps are frequently suggested.

- Write a good covering letter explaining the reasons for the research, why it is important, and why the recipient has been selected; mention sponsorship if any, and provide guarantees of confidentiality. The advice provided in Tips and skills 'Topics and issues to include in an introductory statement' (in Chapter 8) in connection with the kind of letter that might go out in advance of a respondent being asked to be interviewed can be followed to good effect.

- Postal questionnaires should always be accompanied by a stamped addressed envelope or, at the very least, return postage.

- Follow up individuals who do not reply at first, possibly with two or three further mailings. The importance of reminders cannot be overstated—they do work. My preferred approach has been to send out a reminder letter to non-respondents two weeks after the initial mailing, reasserting the nature and aims of the survey and suggesting that the person should contact a member of the research team or me to obtain a replacement copy of the questionnaire if the original one has been lost. Then, two weeks after that, all further non-respondents should be sent another letter along with a further copy of the questionnaire. These reminders have a demonstrable effect on the response rate. Some writers argue for further mailings of reminder letters to non-respondents. If a response rate is worryingly low, such further mailings would certainly be desirable.

- Unsurprisingly, shorter questionnaires tend to achieve better response rates than longer ones. However, this is not a clear-cut principle, because it is difficult to specify when a questionnaire becomes 'too long'. Also, the evidence suggests that the effect of the length of questionnaires on response rates cannot be separated very easily from the salience of the topic(s) of the research for respondents and from the nature of the sample. Respondents may be highly tolerant of questionnaires that contain many questions on topics that interest them.

- Clear instructions and an attractive layout improve postal questionnaire response rates. Dillman (1983), as part of what he calls the Total Design Method (TDM) for postal questionnaire research, recommends lower case for questions and upper case for closed answers.

- Do not allow the questionnaire to appear unnecessarily bulky. Dillman (1983) recommends a booklet format for the questionnaire and using the photocopier to reduce the size of the questionnaire to fit the booklet format. This approach also gives the impression of a more professional approach.

- As with structured interviewing (see Chapter 8), begin with questions that are more likely to be of interest to the respondent. This advice is linked to the issue of salience (see above) but has particular significance in the context of research that may have limited salience for the respondent.

- There is some controversy about how significant for response rates it is to personalize covering letters, by including the respondent's name and address (Baumgartner and Heberlein 1984). However, one of the features of the TDM approach advocated by Dillman (1983) is that these details are supplied on covering letters and each is individually signed.

- I am inclined to the view that in general postal questionnaires should comprise as few open questions as possible, since people are often deterred by the prospect of having to write a lot. In fact, many writers on the subject recommend that open questions are used as little as possible in self-completion questionnaires.

- Providing monetary incentives increases the response rate. These are more effective if the money comes with the questionnaire rather than if it is promised once the questionnaire has been returned. Apparently, respondents typically do not cynically take the money and discard the questionnaire! The evidence also suggests that quite small amounts of money have a positive impact on the response rate, but that larger amounts do not necessarily improve the response rate any further.

Designing the self-completion questionnaire

Do not cramp the presentation

Because of the well-known problem of low response rates to the postal questionnaire in particular, it is sometimes considered preferable to make the instrument appear as short as possible in order for it to be less likely to deter prospective respondents from answering. However, this is almost always a mistake. As Dillman (1983) observes, an attractive layout is likely to enhance response rates, whereas the kinds of tactics that are sometimes employed to make a questionnaire appear shorter than it really is—such as reducing margins and the space between questions—make it look cramped and thereby unattractive. Also, if questions are too close together, there is a risk of a tendency for them to be inadvertently omitted.

This is not to say that you should be ridiculously liberal in your use of space, as this does not necessarily provide for an attractive format either and may run the risk of making the questionnaire look bulky. As with so many other issues in social research, a steady course needs to be steered between possible extremes.

Clear presentation

Far more important than making a self-completion questionnaire appear shorter than is the case is to make sure that it has a layout that is easy on the eye, as Dillman emphasizes, and that it facilitates the answering of all questions that are relevant to the respondent. Dillman's recommendation of lower case for questions and upper case for closed answers is an example of one consideration, but at the very least a variety of print styles (e.g. different fonts, print sizes, bold, italics, and capitals) can enhance the appearance *but must be used in a consistent manner*. This last point means that you should ensure that you use one style for general instructions, one for headings, perhaps one for specific instructions (like 'Go to question 7'), one for questions, and one for closed answers. Mixing print styles, so that one style is sometimes used for both general instructions and questions, can be very confusing for respondents.

Vertical or horizontal closed answers?

Bearing in mind that most questions in a self-completion questionnaire are likely to be of the closed kind, one consideration is whether to arrange the fixed answers vertically or horizontally. Very often, the nature of the answers will dictate a vertical arrangement because of their sheer length. Many writers prefer a vertical format

whenever possible, because, in some cases where either arrangement is feasible, confusion can arise when a horizontal one is employed (Sudman and Bradburn 1982). Consider the following:

What do you think of the Prime Minister's performance in his job since he took office?

(*Please tick the appropriate response*)

Very ____ Good ____ Fair ____ Poor _____ Very ____
good   poor

There is a risk that, if the questionnaire is being answered in haste, the required tick will be placed in the wrong space—for example, indicating Good when Fair was the intended response. Also, a vertical format more clearly distinguishes questions from answers. To some extent, these potential problems can be obviated through the judicious use of spacing and print variation, but they represent significant considerations. A further reason why vertical alignments can be superior is that they are probably easier to code, especially when pre-codes appear on the questionnaire. Very often, self-completion questionnaires are arranged so that to the right of each question are two columns: one for the column in which data relating to the question will appear in a data matrix; the other for all the pre-codes. The latter allows the appropriate code to be assigned to a respondent's answer by circling it for later entry into the computer. Thus, the choice would be between the formats presented in Tips and skills 'Closed question with a horizontal format' and Tips and skills 'Closed question with a vertical format'. In the second case, not only is there less ambiguity about where a tick is to be placed; the task of coding is easier. However, when there is to be a battery of questions with identical answer formats, as in a Likert scale, a vertical format will take up too much space. One way of dealing with this kind of questioning is to use abbreviations with an accompanying explanation. An example can be found in Tips and skills 'Formating a Likert scale'. The four items are taken from an eighteen-item Likert scale designed to measure job satisfaction (Brayfield and Rothe 1951).

Tips and skills
Closed question with a horizontal format

What do you think of the Prime Minister's performance in his job since he took office?
(*Please tick the appropriate response*)

Very good ____ Good ____ Fair ____ Poor ____ Very poor ____ 5 4 3 2 1

Tips and skills
Closed question with a vertical format

What do you think of the Prime Minister's performance in his job since he took office?
(Please tick the appropriate response)

Very good	___	5
Good	___	4
Fair	___	3
Poor	___	2
Very poor	___	1

Tips and skills
Formatting a Likert scale

In the next set of questions, you are presented with a statement. You are being asked to indicate your level of agreement or disagreement with each statement by indicating whether you: Strongly Agree (SA), Agree (A), are Undecided (U), Disagree (D), or Strongly Disagree (SD).
(Please indicate your level of agreement by circling the appropriate response)

23. My job is like a hobby to me.
    SA   A   U   D   SD

24. My job is usually interesting enough to keep me from getting bored.
    SA   A   U   D   SD

25. It seems that my friends are more interested in their jobs.
    SA   A   U   D   SD

26. I enjoy my work more than my leisure time.
    SA   A   U   D   SD

Identifying response sets in a Likert scale

One of the advantages of using closed questions is that they can be pre-coded, thus turning the processing of data for computer analysis into a fairly simple task (see Chapter 10 for more on this). However, some thought has to go into the scoring of the items of the kind presented in Tips and skills 'Formatting a Likert scale'. We might, for example, score question 23 as follows:

Strongly agree = 5
Agree = 4
Undecided = 3
Disagree = 2
Strongly disagree = 1

Accordingly, a high score for the item (5 or 4) indicates satisfaction with the job and a low score (1 or 2) indicates low job satisfaction. The same applies to question 24. However, when we come to question 25, the picture is different. Here, agreement indicates a *lack* of job satisfaction. It is disagreement that is indicative of job satisfaction. We would have to reverse the coding of this item, so that:

Strongly agree = 1
Agree = 2
Undecided = 3
Disagree = 4
Strongly disagree = 5

The point of including such items is to identify people who exhibit response sets, like acquiescence (see Chapter 8). If someone were to agree with all eighteen items, when some of them indicated *lack* of job satisfaction, it is likely that the respondent is affected by a response set, and the answers are unlikely to provide a valid assessment of job satisfaction for that person.

Clear instructions about how to respond

Always be clear about how you want respondents to indicate their replies when answering closed questions. Are they supposed to place a tick by or circle or underline the appropriate answer, or are they supposed to delete inappropriate answers? Also, in many cases it is feasible for the respondent to choose more than one answer—is this acceptable to you? If it is not, you should indicate this in your instructions, for example:

> (*Please choose the one answer that best represents your views by placing a tick in the appropriate box.*)

If you do not make this clear and if some respondents choose more than one answer, you will have to treat their replies as if they had not answered. This possibility increases the risk of missing data from some respondents. If it is acceptable to you for more than one category to be chosen, you need to make this clear, for example:

> (*Please choose all answers that represent your views by placing a tick in the appropriate boxes.*)

It is a common error for such instructions to be omitted and for respondents either to be unsure about how to reply or to make inappropriate selections.

Keep question and answers together

This is a simple and obvious, though often transgressed, requirement—namely, that you should never split a question so that it appears on two separate pages. A common error is to have some space left at the bottom of a page into which the question can be slotted but for the closed answers to appear on the next page. Doing so carries the risk of the respondent forgetting to answer the question or providing an answer in the wrong group of closed answers (a problem that is especially likely when a series of questions with a common answer format is being used, as with a Likert scale).

Diaries as a form of self-completion questionnaire

When the researcher is specifically interested in precise estimates of different kinds of behaviour, the diary warrants serious consideration, though it is still a relatively underused method. The term 'diary' has somewhat different meanings in social research (see Key concept 9.1). It is the first of the three meanings—what H. Elliott (1997) calls the 'researcher-driven diary'—that is the focus of attention here, especially in the context of its use in relation to quantitative research. When employed in this way, the researcher-driven diary functions in a similar way to the self-completion questionnaire. Equally, it could be said that the researcher-driven diary is an alternative method of data collection to observation. It can be thought of as the equivalent of structured observation (see Chapter 11) in the context of research questions that are framed in terms of quantitative research. With diary methods, observation takes place because the person who completes the diary observes his or her own behaviour.

Corti (1993) distinguishes between 'structured diaries' and 'free-text diaries'. Either may be employed by quantitative researchers. The research on gender and time use in Research in focus 9.2 is an illustration of the structured diary. The specific kind of diary employed in this research is often referred to as a 'time-use diary', in that it is designed so that diarists can record more or less contemporaneously the amount of time engaged in certain activities, such as food preparation, childcare, selfcare, eating, and so on. Estimates of the amount of time spent in different activities are often regarded as more accurate than questionnaire estimates, because the events are less subject to memory problems or to the tendency to round up or down (Fisher and Layte 2004). However, a time use diary is more intrusive than answering a questionnaire, and it could be argued that it causes changes in behaviour. Sullivan also asked couples to record in the diary the amount of enjoyment they derived from the different activities. This information was also recorded simultaneously and was answered on a five-point scale, like a Likert scale.

Key concept 9.1
The diary in social research

There are three major ways in which the term 'diary' has been employed in the context of social research.

1. *The diary as a method of data collection*. Here the researcher devises a structure for the diary and then asks a sample of diarists to complete the instruments so that they record what they do more or less contemporaneously with their activities. H. Elliott (1997) refers to this kind of use of the diary as 'researcher-driven diary'. Such diaries can be employed for the collection of data within the context of both quantitative and qualitative research. Sometimes, the collection of data in this manner is supplemented by a personal interview in which the diarist is asked questions about such things as what he or she meant by certain remarks. This 'diary-interview', as it is often referred to (Zimmerman and Wieder 1977), is usually employed when diarists record their behaviour in prose form rather than simply indicating the amount of time spent on different kinds of activity.

2. *The diary as a document*. The diary in this context is written spontaneously by the diarist and not at the behest of a researcher. Diaries in this sense are often used by historians but have some potential for social researchers working on issues that are of social scientific significance. As Scott (1990) observes, the diary in this sense often shades into autobiography. Diaries as documents will be further addressed in Chapter 21.

3. *The diary as a log of the researcher's activities*. Researchers sometimes keep a record of what they do at different stages as an *aide-mémoire*. For example, the famous social anthropologist Malinowski (1967) kept an infamous log of his activities ('infamous' because it revealed his distaste for the people he studied and his inappropriate involvement with females). This kind of diary often shades into the writing of **field notes** by **ethnographers**, about which more is written in Chapter 17.

Research in focus 9.2
A diary study to examine gender and time use

Sullivan (1997) reports the findings of a study of the ways in which the experience of domestic time is gendered. She uses data derived from time-use diaries that were collected in the course of conducting research at the household level for the Social Change and Economic Life Initiative (SCELI) studies referred to in Research in focus 6.1. Data were collected from household members over a one-week period, producing diary information for approximately 1,300 individuals. Diarists indicated what they were doing for every fifteen minutes of the day. Because diaries were completed for several members of a household, it was possible to compare the diaries of others in the household to see if they engaged in certain activities simultaneously. The analysis in this article is based on only those couples for whom there were diary data on at least 6.7 days of valid information. This yields data on 408 couples.

Sullivan (1997: 225) writes:

> The diary booklet requested diarists to record both what they were doing at each point in time, and whether they were doing anything else at the same time, and the subsequent activity coding allows for up to four simultaneous activities in any one quarter hour. . . . Forty-one major groups of activities are recorded in the SCELI diaries, but for the purposes of this analysis the domestic tasks have been grouped into seven categories . . .

The seven categories were (in rank order of the frequency of overall time spent by women performing the task): cooking; cleaning/clothes care; childcare; shopping; gardening; odd jobs/DIY; and domestic travel. Through an analysis of such data, Sullivan is able to show such things as the differences between men and women and the proportion of time doing tasks together.

An example of a free-text diary is provided by Coxon's (1994) sexual diary, which was developed because of worries about the vagueness of answers to questions about sexual activity used in questionnaires and also because of the lack of context to replies. Coxon employed the diary method to study the ways in which gay men are responding to the risks of HIV/AIDS. One of several advantages of the diary method for this research was that it provided information on the time sequencing of events (for example, which practice followed which). This kind of information is much more difficult to glean from questionnaires. The diary method allowed Coxon to collect a variety of information from the written prose relating to sexual activity over a week. The method allowed the following kinds of information to be recorded and coded:

- nature of each item of sexual activity (e.g. anal intercourse, oral sex);
- details of the participants;
- whether the diarist was active or passive in the activity;
- whether the diarist or his partner achieved orgasm;
- whether drugs accompanied the practice;
- whether lubricants were used;
- what activities—sexual or otherwise—preceded each item of sexual activity;
- whether any other aids were employed;
- the location of the activity.

Crook and Light (2002) employed time-use diaries within a free-text format. University students were asked to keep a diary for a week of the different kinds of study and learning activity in which they engaged at different times of the day. The diaries were divided into fifteen-minute intervals, so that each student had to indicate for each interval 'details of their activity, location, and any study resources that might be in use' (Crook and Light

2002: 162). The various activities were grouped into three types: classes, private study, and social study (i.e. study with a peer). They were able to show the very different patterns and amounts of study typically undertaken during a day.

Using free-text recording of behaviour carries the same kinds of problem as those associated with coding answers to structured-interview open questions—namely, the time-consuming nature of the exercise and the risk of introducing error associated with the coding of answers (see Chapter 10 for a discussion of these issues). However, the free-text approach is less likely to be problematic when, as in the case of Coxon's (1994) research, diarists can be instructed about what is required and when the kinds of behaviour of interest are specific. It would be much more difficult to code free-text entries relating to a more general arena of types of behaviour of the kind studied by Sullivan (1997; see Research in focus 9.2). Structured diaries particularly lend themselves to examining cross-cultural differences in time use—see Research in focus 9.3 for an example.

Corti (1993) recommends that the person preparing the diary should

- provide explicit instructions for diarists;
- be clear about the time periods within which behaviour is to be recorded—i.e. day, twenty-four hours, week;
- provide a model of a completed section of a diary;
- provide checklists of 'items, events or behaviour' that can jog people's memory—but the list should not become too daunting in length or complexity;
- include fixed blocks of time or columns showing when the designated activities start and finish (for diaries of the kind used by Sullivan (1996), which show how people budget their time).

Research in focus 9.3
Harmonized European Time Use Studies project

Time-use diaries offer great opportunities for cross-cultural studies. The Harmonized European Time Use Studies (HETUS) project coordinates time-use diary studies among a wide range of European nations (see Fisher and Layte 2004). According to the HETUS website, the main criteria for the design of diaries is as follows:

The study recommends the collection of two diaries, one on a week day and one on a weekend day. The fieldwork is recommended to last 12 months to capture activities from all times of year. Diaries are recommended to include fixed 10 minute time slots, and that columns collect secondary information, who else is present, and location. (**http://www.timeuse.org/information/studies/data/eu-2000+.php** (accessed on 15 February 2007))

The diary is mainly completed on paper, but increasingly diaries of this kind can be completed on computer by clicking with a mouse. It presents people with a grid of time slots or time periods where they can complete the starting time of each activity, and then a series of columns. People write in descriptions of their activities, the location of activities, and the mode of transport in their own words, then the own-words records later are coded into activities. See Plate 9.1 for a sample one-day diary from the UK National Survey of Time Use, which is harmonized with HETUS.

Plate 9.1

Sample diary entry for the National Survey of Time Use

Time diary page as used in the UK 2000 Time Use Survey conducted by the Office for National Statistics (ONS). Reprinted with permission.

Advantages and disadvantages of the diary as a method of data collection

The studies that have been used to illustrate the use of diaries also suggest its potential advantages.

- When fairly precise estimates of the frequency and/or amount of time spent in different forms of behaviour are required, the diary almost certainly provides more valid and reliable data than questionnaires.

- When information about the sequencing of different types of behaviour is required, the diary is likely to perform better than questionnaires or interviews.

- The first two advantages could be used to suggest that structured observation would be just as feasible, but structured observation is probably less appropriate for producing data on behaviour that is personally sensitive, such as sexual behaviour. Moreover, although data on such behaviour can be collected by structured interview, it is likely that respondents will be less willing to divulge details of the kind revealed in Coxon's (1994) research. If such information were collected by questionnaire, there is greater risk of recall and rounding problems (see the first point in this list).

On the other hand, diaries may suffer from the following problems.

- They tend to be more expensive than personal interviews (because of the costs associated with recruiting diarists and of checking that diaries are being properly completed).

- Diaries can suffer from a process of attrition, as people decide they have had enough of the task of completing a diary.

- This last point raises the possibility that diarists become less diligent over time about their record keeping.

- There is sometimes failure to record details sufficiently quickly, so that memory recall problems set in.

However, diary researchers such as Coxon and Sullivan argue that the resulting data are more accurate than the equivalent data based on interviews or questionnaires.

Key points

- Many of the recommendations relating to the self-completion questionnaire apply equally or almost equally to the structured interview, as has been mentioned on several occasions.

- Closed questions tend to be used in survey research rather than open ones. Coding is a particular problem when dealing with answers to open questions.

- Structured interviews and self-completion questionnaires both have their respective advantages and disadvantages, but a particular problem with questionnaires sent by post is that they frequently produce a low response rate. However, steps can be taken to boost response rates for postal questionnaires.

- Presentation of closed questions and the general layout constitute important considerations for the self-completion questionnaire.

- The researcher-driven diary is a possible alternative to using questionnaires and interviews when the research questions are very specifically concerned with aspects of people's behaviour.

Questions for review

Self-completion questionnaire or postal questionnaire?

● Are the self-completion questionnaire and the postal questionnaire the same thing?

Evaluating the self-completion questionnaire in relation to the structured interview

● 'The low response rates frequently achieved in research with postal questionnaires mean that the structured interview is invariably a more suitable choice.' Discuss.

● What steps can be taken to boost postal questionnaire response rates?

Designing the self-completion questionnaire

● Why are self-completion questionnaires usually made up mainly of closed questions?

● Why might a vertical format for presenting closed questions be preferable to a horizontal format?

Diaries as a form of self-completion questionnaire

● What are the main kinds of diary used in the collection of social science data?

● Are there any circumstances when the diary approach might be preferable to the use of a self-completion questionnaire?

Online Resource Centre

http://www.oxfordtextbooks.co.uk/orc/brymansrm3e/

Visit the Online Resource Centre that accompanies this book to enrich your understanding of self-completion questionnaires. Consult web links, test yourself using multiple choice questions, and gain further guidance and inspiration from the Student Researcher's Toolkit.

Asking questions

Chapter outline

Chapter guide

This chapter is concerned with the considerations that are involved in asking questions that are used in structured interviews and questionnaires of the kinds discussed in the two previous chapters. As such, it continues the focus upon social survey research that began with Chapter 7. The chapter explores:

- the issues involved in deciding whether or when to use open or closed questions;
- the different kinds of question that can be asked in structured interviews and questionnaires;
- rules to bear in mind when designing questions;
- vignette questions in which respondents are presented with a scenario and are asked to reflect on the scenario;
- the importance of piloting questions;
- the possibility of using questions that have been used in previous survey research.

Introduction

To many people, how to ask questions represents the crux of considerations surrounding the use of social survey instruments such as the structured interview or the self-completion questionnaire. As the previous two chapters have sought to suggest, there is much more to the design and administration of such research instruments than how best to phrase questions. However, there is no doubt that the issue of how questions should be asked is a crucial concern for the survey researcher, and it is not surprising that this aspect of designing survey instruments has been a major focus of attention over the years and preoccupies many practising researchers.

Open or closed questions?

One of the most significant considerations for many researchers is whether to ask a question in an open or closed format. This distinction was first introduced in Chapter 8. The issue of whether to ask a question in an open or closed format is relevant to the design of both structured interview and self-completion questionnaire research.

With an open question respondents are asked a question and can reply however they wish. With a closed question they are presented with a set of fixed alternatives from which they have to choose an appropriate answer. All the questions in Tips and skills 'Instructions for interviewers in the use of a filter question' (in Chapter 8) are of

the closed kind. So too are the Likert-scale items in Research in focus 6.2 and Tips and skills 'Formatting a Likert scale' in Chapter 9; these form a particular kind of closed question. What, then, are some of the advantages and limitations of these two types of question format?

Open questions

Open questions present both advantages and disadvantages to the survey researcher, though, as the following discussion suggests, the problems associated with the processing of answers to open questions tend to mean that closed questions are more likely to be used.

Advantages

Although survey researchers typically prefer to use closed questions, open questions do have certain advantages over closed ones, as outlined in the list below.

- Respondents can answer in their own terms. They are not forced to answer in the same terms as those foisted on them by the response choices.
- They allow unusual responses to be derived. Replies that the survey researcher may not have contemplated (and that would therefore not form the basis for fixed-choice alternatives) are possible.
- The questions do not suggest certain kinds of answer to respondents. Therefore, respondents' levels of knowledge and understanding of issues can be tapped. The salience of issues for respondents can also be explored.
- They are useful for exploring new areas or ones in which the researcher has limited knowledge.
- They are useful for generating fixed-choice format answers. This is a point that will be returned to below.

Disadvantages

However, open questions present problems for the survey researcher, as the following list reveals.

- They are time-consuming for interviewers to administer. Interviewees are likely to talk for longer than is usually the case with a comparable closed question.
- Answers have to be 'coded', which is very time-consuming. Key concept 10.1 outlines the nature of coding and provides some considerations involved in its use. For each open question it entails reading through answers, deriving themes that can be employed to form the basis for codes, and then going through the answers again so that the answers can be coded for entry into a computer spreadsheet. The process is essentially identical to that involved in *content analysis*

and is sometimes called *post-coding* to distinguish it from *pre-coding*, whereby the researcher designs a coding frame in advance of administering a survey instrument and often includes the pre-codes in the questionnaire (as in Tips and skills 'Processing a closed question'). However, in addition to being time-consuming, post-coding can be an unreliable process, because it can introduce the possibility of variability in the coding of answers and therefore of measurement error (and hence lack of validity). This is a form of data-processing error (see Figure 7.9). Research in focus 10.1 and 10.2 deal with aspects of the coding of open questions.

- They require greater effort from respondents. Respondents are likely to talk for longer than would be the case for a comparable closed question, or, in the case of a self-completion questionnaire, would need to write for much longer. Therefore, it is often suggested that open questions have limited utility in the context of self-completion questionnaires. Because of the greater effort involved, many prospective respondents are likely to be put off by the prospect of having to write extensively, which may exacerbate the problem of low response rates with postal questionnaires in particular (see Chapter 9).
- There is the possibility in research based on structured interviews of variability between interviewers in the recording of answers. This possibility is likely to arise as a result of the difficulty of writing down verbatim what respondents say to interviewers. The obvious solution is to employ a tape recorder. However, it is not always practicable to employ one—for example, in a noisy environment. Also, the transcription of answers to tape-recorded open questions is immensely time-consuming and adds additional costs to a survey. The problem of transcription is one continually faced by qualitative researchers using semi-structured and unstructured interviews (see Chapter 18).

Key concept 10.1
What is coding?

Coding is a key stage in **quantitative research**. Many forms of data that are of interest to social scientists are essentially in an unstructured form. Examples are: answers to open questions in interviews and questionnaires; newspaper articles; television programmes; and behaviour in a school classroom. In order to quantify and analyse such materials, the social researcher has to code them. Coding entails two main stages. First, the unstructured material must be categorized. For example, with answers to an open question, this means that the researcher must examine people's answers and group them into different categories. Research in focus 10.1 provides some examples of this process. Second, the researcher must assign numbers to the categories that have been created. This is a largely arbitrary process, in the sense that the numbers themselves are simply tags that will allow the material to be processed quantitatively. Thus, when Schuman and Presser (1981; see Research in focus 10.3) asked a question about the features of a job that people most prefer, answers were grouped into eleven categories: pay; feeling of accomplishment; control of work; pleasant work; security; opportunity for promotion; short hours; working conditions; benefits; satisfaction; other responses. Each of these eleven categories would then need to be assigned a number, such as: 1 for pay; 2 for feeling of accomplishment; 3 for control of work; 4 for pleasant work; etc.

There is an important distinction between *pre-coding* and *post-coding*. Many closed questions in survey research instruments are pre-coded (see Tips and skills 'Processing a closed question' for an example). This means that respondents are being asked to assign themselves to a category that has already had a number assigned to it. Post-coding occurs when answers to an open question are being coded or when themes in newspaper articles concerned with a certain topic are being counted, as in **content analysis** (see Chapter 12).

When coding, three basic principles need to be observed (Bryman and Cramer 2008).

1. The categories that are generated must not overlap. If they do, the numbers that are assigned to them cannot be applied to distinct categories.

2. The list of categories must be complete and therefore cover all possibilities. If it is not, some material will not be capable of being coded. This is why coding a certain item of information, such as answers to an open question, sometimes includes a category of 'other'.

3. There should be clear rules about how codes should be applied, so that the person conducting the coding has instructions about the kinds of answers that should be subsumed under a particular code. Such rules are meant to ensure that those who are conducting the coding are consistent over time in how they assign the material to categories and, if more than one person is coding, are consistent with each other. The term 'coding frame' is often employed to describe the lists of codes that should be applied to unstructured data and the rules for their application. In content analysis and **structured observation**, the term 'coding manual' is often preferred to describe the lists of codes for each item of information and the rules to be employed.

Quantitative data are also sometimes *recoded*. For example, if we have data on the exact age of each person in a **sample**, we may want to group people into age bands. The rationale for doing this is described in Chapter 14 and the procedure of recoding with a computer program is described in Chapter 15.

Coding also occurs in **qualitative research**, but the role it plays and its significance are somewhat different there from quantitative research. Coding in qualitative research is described in Chapter 22 and the procedure for coding with a qualitative data analysis computer program is described in Chapter 23.

Research in focus 10.1
Coding an open question

Coding an open question usually entails reading and rereading **transcripts** of respondents' replies and formulating distinct themes in their replies. A *coding frame* then needs to be designed that identifies the types of answer associated with each question and their respective codes (i.e. numbers). A **coding schedule** may also be necessary to keep a record of rules to be followed in the identification of certain kinds of answer in terms of a theme. The numbers allocated to each answer can then be used in the computer processing of the data.

Charles and Kerr (1988) conducted interviews concerning the consumption of food in the home with 200 British women. Their interviews were of the semi-structured kind (see Key concept 8.2), so that the questions were open ended. Charles and Kerr were working within a qualitative **research strategy**, but, for several of the questions that they asked, they found it helpful to quantify respondents' answers. Thus, while the bulk of the presentation of their findings is in the form of passages from interview transcripts, which is the conventional way of presenting such findings in qualitative research (see Chapter 18), some of their findings were far more redolent of the kind typically encountered in quantitative research. As the authors say: 'The material that we have is . . . qualitative, as we included many open-ended questions which gave the women the chance to talk freely, and quantitative, as the sample was large enough to produce useful statistical data' (Charles and Kerr 1988: 7).

One of their analyses is a **contingency table** (see Chapter 14), which shows the relationship between social class of male partner and responsibility for meal preparation. The latter **variable** was coded so that five categories of responsibility were generated: self prepares all meals; self mainly, partner sometimes; either or both (50/50); self mainly with help from partner and/or children sometimes; and other. Men in classes I and II were more likely to participate than those in the other social classes. Another table shows the **relationship** between class and the occasions that alcohol is drunk at home. The latter variable comprised the following categories: Christmas and special occasions; Christmas, special occasions and when having company; at other times but not frequently; once a week or more; never drink at home; and other. These categories were generated after the data had been collected and essentially entailed a process of discerning likely categories and then systematically coding each respondent's answer to determine how it should be coded in terms of such considerations as responsibility for preparing meals or the occasions when alcohol is consumed in the home.

Research in focus 10.2
Coding a very open question

Foddy (1993) reports the results of an exercise in which he asked a small sample of his students 'Your father's occupation is (was) . . .' and requested three details: nature of business; size of business; and whether owner or employee. In answer to the size of business issue, the replies were particularly variable in kind, including: 'big', 'small', 'very large', '3,000 acres', 'family', 'multinational', '200 people', and 'Philips'. The problem here is obvious: you simply cannot compare and therefore aggregate people's replies. In a sense, the problem is only partly to do with the difficulty of coding an open question. It is also due to a lack of specificity in the question. If, instead, Foddy had asked 'How many employees are (were) there in your father's organization?', a more comparable set of answers should have been forthcoming. Whether his students would have known this information is, of course, yet another issue. However, the exercise does illustrate the potential problems of asking an open question, particularly one like this that lacks a clear reference point for gauging size.

Closed questions

The advantages and disadvantages of closed questions are in many respects implied in some of the considerations relating to open questions.

Advantages

Closed questions offer the following advantages to researchers.

- It is easy to process answers. For example, the respondent in a self-completion questionnaire or the interviewer using a structured **interview schedule** will place a tick or circle an answer for the appropriate response. The appropriate code can then be almost mechanically derived from the selected answer, since the pre-codes are placed to the side of the fixed-choice answers. See Tips and skills 'Processing a closed question' for an example based on Tips and skills 'Closed question with a vertical format' (in Chapter 9).

- Closed questions enhance the comparability of answers. With post-coding there is always a problem of knowing how far respondents' answers that receive a certain code are genuinely comparable. As previously noted, the assignment of codes to people's answers may be unreliable (see the sixth point in Thinking deeply 8.1). Checks are necessary to ensure that there is a good deal of agreement between coders and that coders do not change their coding conventions over time. Closed questions essentially circumvent this problem.

- Closed questions may clarify the meaning of a question for respondents. Sometimes, respondents may not be clear about what a question is getting at, and the availability of answers may help to clarify the situation for them.

- Closed questions are easy for interviewers and/or respondents to complete. Precisely because interviewers and respondents are not expected to write extensively and instead have to place ticks or circle answers, closed questions are easier and quicker to complete.

- In interviews, closed questions reduce the possibility of variability in the recording of answers in structured interviewing. As noted in Chapter 8, if interviewers do not write down exactly what respondents say to them when answering questions, a source of bias and hence of invalidity is in prospect. Closed questions reduce this possibility, though there is still the potential problem that interviewers may have to *interpret* what is said to them in order to assign answers to a category.

Disadvantages

However, closed questions exhibit certain disadvantages.

- There is a loss of spontaneity in respondents' answers. There is always the possibility that they might come up with interesting replies that are not covered by the fixed answers that are provided. One solution to this possible problem is to ensure that an open question is used to generate the categories (see Research in focus 10.3). Also, there may be a good case for including a possible response category of 'Other' and to allow respondents to indicate what they mean by this category.

Tips and skills
Processing a closed question

What do you think of the Prime Minister's performance in his job since he took office?
(Please tick the appropriate response)

Very good	____	5
Good	✓	④
Fair	____	3
Poor	____	2
Very poor	____	1

Research in focus 10.3
A comparison of results for a closed and an open question

Schuman and Presser (1981) conducted an **experiment** to determine how far responses to closed questions can be improved by asking the questions first as open questions and then developing categories of reply from respondents' answers. They asked a question about what people look for in work in both open and closed format. Different samples were used. They found considerable disparities between the two sets of answers (60 per cent of the open-format categories were not capable of being subsumed by the closed-format answers). They then revised the closed categories to reflect the answers they had received from people's open-ended answers. They readministered the open question and the revised closed question to two large samples of Americans. The question and the answers they received are as follows.

This next question is on the subject of work. People look for different things in a job. Which one of the following five things do you most prefer in a job? [closed question]. What would you most prefer in a job? [open question].

Closed format		Open format	
Answer	%	Answer	%
Work that pays well	13.2	Pay	16.7
Work that gives a feeling of accomplishment	31.0	Feeling of accomplishment	14.5
Work where there is not too much supervision and you make most decisions yourself	11.7	Control of work	4.6
Work that is pleasant and people are nice to work with	19.8	Pleasant work	14.5
Work that is steady + little chance of being laid off	20.3	Security	7.6
	96% of sample		57.9% of sample
		Opportunity for promotion	1.0
		Short hours/lots of free time	1.6
		Working conditions	3.1
		Benefits	2.3
		Satisfaction/liking a job	15.6
Other/DK/NA	4.0	Other responses	18.3

With the revised form for the closed question, Schuman and Presser were able to find a much higher proportion of the sample whose answers to the open question corresponded to the closed one. They argue that the new closed question was superior to its predecessor and is also superior to the open question. However, it is still disconcerting that only 58 per cent of respondents answering the open question could be subsumed under the same categories as those answering the closed one. Also, the distributions are somewhat different: for example, twice as many respondents answer in terms of a feeling of accomplishment with the closed format than with the open one. Nonetheless, the experiment demonstrates the desirability of generating forced-choice answers from open questions.

Student experience
Closed questions and quantitative data analysis

Joe Thompson and his fellow students who formed a team conducting research on students at their university favoured closed questions because of the ease with which they could be analysed using **SPSS**, the software that is covered in Chapter 15. When they reviewed the interview schedule they had devised after it had been piloted, they focused on such issues as:

> were there too many open or closed questions so not providing enough qualitative or quantitative data, or should the questions be on a dichotomous or ranking **scale**. As the results of the questionnaire were to be analysed using a data analysis computer program (SPSS), the group tended to favour closed questions to give definite answers that could be correlated to show trends.

However, Sophie Mason, who was also a member of a team doing survey research at Joe's university, felt that the combination of closed and open questions did offer certain advantages: 'By using both open and closed questions it was possible to gain the necessary statistics as well as opinions and experiences unique to each student.'

To read more about Joe's and Sophie's research experiences, go to the Online Resource Centre that accompanies this book at http://www.oxfordtextbooks.co.uk/orc/brymansrm3e/.

- It can be difficult to make forced-choice answers mutually exclusive. The fixed answers that respondents are provided should not overlap. If they do overlap, the respondents will not know which one to choose and so will arbitrarily select one or the other or alternatively may tick both answers. If a respondent were to tick two or more answers when one is required, it would mean that you would have to treat the respondent's answer as **missing data**, since you would not know which of the ticked answers represented the true one. One of the most frequently encountered forms of this problem can be seen in the following age bands:

    18–30
    30–40
    40–50
    50–60
    60 and over

    In which band would a 40-year-old position him- or herself?

- It is difficult to make forced-choice answers exhaustive. All possible answers should really be catered for, although in practice this may be difficult to achieve,

since this rule may result in excessively long lists of possible answers. Again, a category of 'Other' may be desirable to provide a wide range of answers.

- There may be variation among respondents in the interpretation of forced-choice answers. There is always a problem when asking a question that certain terms may be interpreted differently by respondents. If this is the case, then validity will be jeopardized. The presence of forced-choice answers can exacerbate this possible problem, because there may be variation in the understanding of key terms in the answers.

- Closed questions may be irritating to respondents when they are not able to find a category that they feel applies to them.

- In interviews, a large number of closed questions may make it difficult to establish rapport, because the respondent and interviewer are less likely to engage with each other in a conversation. The interview is more likely to have an impersonal feel to it. However, given the fact that the extent to which rapport is a desirable attribute of structured interviewing is somewhat difficult to determine (see Chapter 8), this is not necessarily too much of a problem.

Student experience
The dilemmas of open and closed questions

Joe Thompson encountered the classic dilemmas with the use of open and closed questions in the course of his research on students at the University of East Anglia. He writes:

As the results were analysed using SPSS, more closed questions were asked, which I feel restrains scope and didn't give the interviewee a chance for personal expression through providing a specific range of answers. This was an issue that was decided would be overlooked, as the most important thing was that the results could be analysed and patterns drawn. Although open questions provide more qualitative data, they are difficult to apply to any kind of scale and therefore are not easy to compare.

As he notes, closed questions do not readily give respondents 'a chance for personal expression', but the data deriving from them are easier to analyse. On the other hand, open questions may give richer qualitative data but are not easy to analyse for quantitative analysis.

To read more about Joe's research experiences, go to the Online Resource Centre that accompanies this book at http://www.oxfordtextbooks.co.uk/orc/brymansrm3e/.

Types of questions

It is worth bearing in mind that, when you are employing a structured interview or self-completion questionnaire, you will probably be asking several different types of question. There are various ways of classifying these, but here are some prominent types of question:

- *Personal factual questions*. These are questions that ask the respondent to provide *personal information*, such as age, education, occupation, marital status, income, and so on. This kind of question also includes questions about *behaviour*. Such factual questions may have to rely on the respondents' memories, as when they are asked about such things as frequency of church attendance, how often they visit the cinema, or when they last ate out in a restaurant.

- *Factual questions about others*. Like the previous type, this one asks for personal information about others, sometimes in combination with the respondent. An example of such a question would be one about household income, which would require respondents to consider their own incomes in conjunction with those of their partners. Charles and Kerr's (1988) question about who is involved in meal preparation (see Research in

focus 10.1) is one that asked wives what they and their husbands do when preparing meals. Indeed, a criticism of such research is precisely that it relies on the possibly distorted views of respondents concerning their own and others' behaviour (Beardsworth and Keil 1997). Like personal factual questions, an element of reliance on memory recall is likely to be present.

- *Informant factual questions*. Sometimes, we place people who are interviewed or who complete a questionnaire in the position of informants rather than of respondents answering questions about themselves. This kind of question can also be found in certain contexts, as when people are asked about such things as the size of the firm for which they work, who owns it, whether it employs certain technologies, and whether it has certain specialist functions. Such questions are essentially about characteristics of an entity of which they have knowledge, in this case, a firm. However, informant factual questions may also be concerned with behaviour: the Charles and Kerr (1988) questions are examples of this kind, in that the person being asked the question is being asked to reply about behaviour in terms of the household or family.

- *Questions about attitudes*. Questions about attitudes are very common in both structured interview and self-completion questionnaire research. The Likert scale is one of the most frequently encountered formats for measuring attitudes.

- *Questions about beliefs*. Respondents are frequently asked about their beliefs, possibly religious and political beliefs. Another form of asking questions about beliefs is when respondents are asked whether they believe that certain matters are true or false—for example, a question asking whether the respondent believes the UK is better off as a result of being a member of the European Community. Alternatively, in a survey about crime respondents might be asked to indicate whether they believe that the incidence of certain crimes is increasing.

- *Questions about normative standards and values*. Respondents may be asked to indicate what principles of behaviour influence them or they hold dear. The elicitation of such norms of behaviour is likely to have considerable overlap with questions about attitudes and beliefs, since norms and values can be construed as having elements of both.

- *Questions about knowledge*. Questions can sometimes be employed to 'test' respondents' knowledge in an area. For example, as part of their study of the role of the mass media in the public understanding of science, Hargreaves *et al.* (n.d.) asked survey respondents to answer a large number of knowledge questions relating to scientific issues. The questions were asked in 2002 of 1,000 respondents on two separate occasions to establish whether there had been any change in knowledge levels. One question asked: 'Some recent research has suggested that there might be a link between the MMR [mumps, measles, and rubella] vaccine and which medical disorder?' Respondents were given five response alternatives: blindness; dyslexia; Down's syndrome; autism; and don't know. More or less equal proportions of the sample (two-thirds) gave the correct answer of autism on each occasion.

Most structured interview schedules and self-completion questionnaires will comprise more than one, and often several, of these types of question. It is important to bear in mind the distinction between different types of question. There are a number of reasons for this.

- It is useful to keep the distinctions in mind because they force you to clarify in your own mind what you are asking about, albeit in rather general terms.
- It will help to guard against asking questions in an inappropriate format. For example, a Likert scale is entirely unsuitable for asking factual questions about behaviour.
- When building scales like a Likert scale, it is best not to mix different types of question. For example, attitudes and beliefs sound similar and you may be tempted to use the same format for mixing questions about them. However, it is best not to do this and instead to have separate scales for attitudes and beliefs. If you mix them, the questions cannot really be measuring the same thing, so that measurement validity is threatened.

Rules for designing questions

Over the years, numerous rules (and rules of thumb) have been devised in connection with the dos and don'ts of asking questions. In spite of this, it is one of the easiest areas for making mistakes. There are three simple rules of thumb as a starting point; beyond that the rules specified below act as a means of avoiding further pitfalls.

General rules of thumb

Always bear in mind your research questions

The questions that you will ask in your self-completion questionnaire or structured interview should always be geared to answering your research questions. This first rule of thumb has at least two implications. First, it means that you should make sure that you ask questions that relate to your research questions. Ensure, in other words, that the questionnaire questions you ask will allow your research questions to be addressed. You will definitely not want to find out at a late stage that you forgot to include some crucial questions. Second, it means that there is little point in asking questions that do not relate to your research questions. It is also not fair to waste your respondents' time answering questions that are of little value.

What do you want to know?

Rule of thumb number two is to decide exactly what it is you want to know. Consider the seemingly harmless question.

Do you have a car?

What is it that the question is seeking to tap? Is it car ownership? If it is car ownership, the question is inadequate, largely because of the ambiguity of the word 'have'. The question can be interpreted as: personally owning a car; having access to a car in a household; and 'having' a company car or a car for business use. Thus, an answer of 'yes' may or may not be indicative of car ownership. If you want to know whether your respondent owns a car, ask him or her directly about this matter. Similarly, there is nothing wrong with the question

How many children do you have?

However, if what you are trying to address is the standard of living of a person or household, the crucial issue is how many are living at home.

How would *you* answer it?

Rule of thumb number three is to put yourself in the position of the respondent. Ask yourself the question and try to work out how you would reply. If you do this, there is at least the possibility that the ambiguity that is inherent in the 'Do you have a car?' question will manifest itself, and its inability to tap car ownership would become apparent. Let us say as well that there is a follow-up question to the previous one:

Have you driven the car this week?

Again, this looks harmless, but if you put yourself in the role of a respondent, it will be apparent that the phrase 'this week' is vague. Does it mean the last seven days or does it mean the week in which the questioning takes place, which will, of course, be affected by such things as whether the question is being asked on a Monday or a Friday? In part, this issue arises because the question designer has not decided what the question is about. Equally, however, a moment's reflection in which you put yourself in the position of the respondent might reveal the difficulty of answering this question.

Taking account of these rules of thumb and the following rules about asking questions may help you to avoid the more obvious pitfalls.

Specific rules when designing questions

Avoid ambiguous terms in questions

Avoid terms such as 'often' and 'regularly' as measures of frequency. They are very ambiguous, because respondents

will operate with different frames of reference when employing them. Sometimes, their use is unavoidable, but when there is an alternative that allows actual frequency to be measured, this will nearly always be preferable. So, a question like:

How often do you usually visit the cinema?

Very often	____
Quite often	____
Not very often	____
Not at all	____

suffers from the problem that, with the exception of 'not at all', the terms in the response categories are ambiguous. Instead, try to ask about actual frequency, such as:

How frequently do you usually visit the cinema?
(*Please tick whichever category comes closest to the number of times you visit the cinema*)

More than once a week	____
Once a week	____
2 or 3 times a month	____
Once a month	____
A few times a year	____
Once a year	____
Less than once a year	____

Alternatively, you might simply ask respondents about the number of times they have visited the cinema in the previous four weeks.

Words like 'family' are also ambiguous, because people will have different notions of who makes up their family. As previously noted, words like 'have' can also be sources of ambiguity.

It is also important to bear in mind that certain common words, such as 'dinner' and 'book', mean different things to different people. For some, dinner is a midday snack, whereas for others it is a substantial evening meal. Similarly, some people refer to magazines or to catalogues and brochures as books, whereas others work with a more restricted definition. In such cases, it will be necessary to define what you mean by such terms.

Avoid long questions

It is commonly believed that long questions are undesirable. In a structured interview the interviewee can lose the thread of the question and in a self-completion questionnaire the respondent may be tempted to omit such questions or to skim them and therefore not give them sufficient attention. However, Sudman and Bradburn (1982) have suggested that this advice applies better to attitude questions than to ones that ask about behaviour. They argue that, when the focus is on behaviour, longer questions have certain positive features in interviews—for example, they are more likely to provide memory cues and they facilitate recall because of the time taken to complete the question. However, by and large, the general advice is to keep questions short.

Avoid double-barrelled questions

Double-barrelled questions are ones that in fact ask about two things. The problem with this kind of question is that it leaves respondents unsure about how best to respond. Take the question:

How satisfied are you with pay and conditions in your job?

The problem here is obvious: the respondent may be satisfied with one but not the other. Not only will the respondent be unclear about how to reply, but any answer that is given is unlikely to be a good reflection of the level of satisfaction with pay *and* conditions. Similarly,

How frequently does your husband help with cooking and cleaning?

suffers from the same problem. A husband may provide extensive help with cooking but be totally uninvolved in cleaning, so that any stipulation of frequency of help is going to be ambiguous and to create uncertainty for respondents.

The same rule applies to fixed-choice answers. In Research in focus 10.3, one of Schuman and Presser's (1981) answers is:

Work that is pleasant and people are nice to work with.

While there is likely to be a symmetry between the two ideas in this answer—pleasant work and nice people—there is no *necessary* correspondence between them. Pleasant work may be important for someone, but he or she may be relatively indifferent to the issue of how pleasant their co-workers are. A further instance of a double-barrelled question is provided in Thinking deeply 10.1.

Thinking deeply 10.1
Matching question and answers in closed questions (and some double-barrelled questions too)

While the first edition of this book was being prepared, I was reading a novel whose publisher had inserted a feedback questionnaire within its pages. At one point in the questionnaire there is a series of Likert-style items regarding the book's quality. In each case, the respondent is asked to indicate whether the attribute being asked about is: poor; acceptable; average; good; or excellent. However, in each case, the items are presented as questions, for example:

Was the writing elegant, seamless, imaginative?

The problem here is that an answer to this question is 'yes' or 'no'. At most, we might have gradations of yes and no, such as: definitely; to a large extent; to some extent; not at all. However, 'poor' or 'excellent' cannot be answers to this question. The problem is that the questions should have been presented as statements, such as:

Please indicate the quality of the book in terms of each of the following criteria:

The elegance of the writing:

Poor   _____

Acceptable   _____

Average   _____

Good   _____

Excellent   _____

Of course, I have changed the sense slightly here, because, as it is stated, a further problem with the question is that it is a double-barrelled question. In fact, it is 'treble-barrelled', because it actually asks about three attributes of the writing in one. The reader's views about the three qualities may vary. A similar question asks:

Did the plot offer conflict, twists, and a resolution?

Again, not only does the question imply a 'yes' or 'no', it actually asks about three attributes. How would you answer if you had different views about each of the three criteria?

It might be argued that the issue is a nit-picking one: someone reading the question obviously knows that he or she is being asked to rate the quality of the book in terms of each attribute. The problem is that we simply do not know what the impact might be of a disjunction between question and answer, so you may as well get the connection between question and answers right (and do not ask double- or treble-barrelled questions either!).

Avoid very general questions

It is easy to ask a very general question when in fact what is wanted is a response to a specific issue. The problem with questions that are very general is that they lack a frame of reference. Thus,

How satisfied are you with your job?

seems harmless but it lacks specificity. Does it refer to pay, conditions, the nature of the work, or all of these? If there is the possibility of such diverse interpretations, respondents are likely to vary in their interpretations too, and this will be a source of error. My favourite general question comes from Karl Marx's *Enquête ouvrière*, a questionnaire that was sent to 25,000 French socialists and others (though there is apparently no record of any being returned). The final (one-hundredth) question reads:

What is the general, physical, intellectual, and moral condition of men and women employed in your trade? (Bottomore and Rubel 1963: 218)

Avoid leading questions

Leading or loaded questions are ones that appear to lead the respondent in a particular direction. Questions of the kind 'Do you agree with the view that . . . ?' fall into this class of question. The obvious problem with such a question is that it is suggesting a particular reply to respondents, although invariably they do have the ability to rebut any implied answer. However, it is the fact that they might feel pushed in a certain direction that is undesirable. Such a question as:

Would you agree to cutting taxes further even though welfare provision for the most needy sections of the population might be reduced?

is likely to make it difficult for some people to answer in terms of fiscal probity. But, once again, Marx is the source of a favourite leading question:

If you are paid piece rates, is the quality of the article made a pretext for fraudulent deductions from wages? (Bottomore and Rubel 1963: 215)

Avoid questions that are actually asking two questions

The double-barrelled question is a clear instance of the transgression of this rule, but in addition there is the case of a question like:

Which political party did you vote for at the last general election?

What if the respondent did not vote? It is better to ask two separate questions:

Did you vote at the last general election?

Yes _____

No _____

If YES, which political party did you vote for?

Another way in which more than one question can be asked is with a question like:

How effective have your different job search strategies been?

Very effective _____

Fairly effective _____

Not very effective _____

Not at all effective _____

The obvious difficulty is that, if the respondent has used more than one job search strategy, his or her estimation of effectiveness will vary for each strategy. A mechanism is needed for assessing the success of each strategy rather than forcing respondents to average out their sense of how successful the various strategies were.

Avoid questions that include negatives

The problem with questions with 'not' or similar formulations in them is that it is easy for the respondent to miss the word out when completing a self-completion questionnaire or to miss it when being interviewed. If this occurs, a respondent is likely to answer in the opposite way from the one intended. There are occasions when it is impossible to avoid negatives, but a question like the following should be avoided as far as possible:

> Do you agree with the view that students should not have to take out loans to finance higher education?

Instead, the question should be asked in a positive format. Questions with double negatives should be totally avoided, because it is difficult to know how to respond to them. Oppenheim (1966) gives the following as an example of this kind of question:

> Would you rather not use a non-medicated shampoo?

It is quite difficult to establish what an answer of 'yes' or 'no' would actually mean in response to this question.

One context in which it is difficult to avoid using questions with negatives is when designing Likert-scale items. Since you are likely to want to identify respondents who exhibit response sets and will therefore want to reverse the direction of your question asking (see Chapter 9), the use of negatives will be difficult to avoid.

Avoid technical terms

Use simple, plain language and avoid jargon. Do not ask a question like:

> Do you sometimes feel alienated from work?

The problem here is that many respondents will not know what is meant by 'alienated', and furthermore are likely to have different views of what it means, even if it is a remotely meaningful term to them.

Consider the following question:

> The influence of the TUC on national politics has declined in recent years.
>
> Strongly agree   ____
>
> Agree   ____
>
> Undecided   ____
>
> Disagree   ____
>
> Strongly disagree   ____

The use of acronyms like TUC can be a problem, because some people may be unfamiliar with what they stand for.

Does the respondent have the requisite knowledge?

There is little point in asking respondents lots of questions about matters of which they have no knowledge. It is very doubtful whether meaningful data about computer use could be extracted from respondents who have never used or come into direct contact with one.

Make sure that there is a symmetry between a closed question and its answers

A common mistake is for a question and its answers to be out of phase with each other. Thinking deeply 10.1 describes such an instance.

Make sure that the answers provided for a closed question are balanced

A fairly common error when asking closed questions is for the answers that are provided to be unbalanced. For example, imagine that a respondent is given a series of options such as:

> Excellent   ____
>
> Good   ____
>
> Acceptable   ____
>
> Poor   ____

In this case, the response choices are balanced towards a favourable response. Excellent and Good are both positive; Acceptable is a neutral or middle position; and Poor is a negative response. In other words, the answers are loaded in favour of a positive rather than a negative reply, so that a further negative response choice (perhaps Very poor) is required.

Memory problems

Do not rely too much on stretching people's memories to the extent that the answers for many of them are likely to be inaccurate. It would be nice to have accurate replies to a question about the number of times respondents have visited the cinema in the previous twelve months, but it is highly unlikely that most will in fact recall events accurately over such a long space of time (other perhaps than those who have not gone at all or only once or twice in the preceding twelve months). It was for this reason that, in the similar question referred to above, the time frame was predominantly just one month.

Don't know

One area of controversy when asking closed questions is whether to offer a 'don't know' or 'no opinion' option. The issue chiefly relates to questions concerning attitudes. The chief argument for including the 'don't know' option is that *not* to include one risks forcing people to express views that they do not really hold. Converse and Presser (1986: 35–6) strongly advocate that survey respondents should be offered a 'don't know' option but argue that it should be implemented by using a filter question to filter out those who do not hold an opinion on a topic. This means that the interviewer needs to ask two questions, with the second question just relating to those respondents who do hold an opinion.

The alternative argument in connection with 'don't know' is that presenting it as an option allows respondents to select it when they cannot be bothered to think about the issue. In other words, presenting the option may prevent some respondents from doing the required thinking on an issue. A series of experiments conducted in the USA suggest that many respondents who express a lack of opinion on a topic do in fact hold an opinion (Krosnick *et al.* 2002). It was found that respondents with lower levels of education were especially prone to selecting the 'don't know' option and that questions that are later on in a questionnaire are more likely to suffer from a tendency for 'don't know' to be selected. The latter finding implies a kind of question order effect, a topic that was addressed in Chapter 8. It implies that respondents become increasingly tired or bored as the questioning proceeds and therefore become prone to laziness in their answers. The researchers conclude that data quality is not enhanced by the inclusion of a 'don't know' option and that it may even be the case that some respondents become inhibited from expressing an opinion that they probably hold. Consequently, these researchers err on the side of *not* offering a 'don't know' option unless it is felt to be absolutely necessary.

Tips and skills
Common mistakes when asking questions

Over the years, I have read many projects and dissertations based on structured interviews and self-completion questionnaires. I have noticed that a small number of mistakes recur. Here is a list of some of them.

- An excessive use of open questions. Students sometimes include too many open questions. While a resistance to closed questions may be understandable, although not something I would agree with, open questions are likely to reduce your response rate and will cause you analysis problems. Keep the number to an absolute minimum.

- An excessive use of yes/no questions. Sometimes students include lots of questions that provide just a yes/no form of response. This is usually the result of lazy thinking and preparation. The world rarely fits into this kind of response. Take a question like:

  Are you satisfied with opportunities for promotion in the firm?

  Yes   ____

  No   ____

  This does not provide for the possibility that respondents' feelings will not be a simple case of being satisfied or not. People invariably vary in the intensity of their feelings about such things. So why not rephrase it as:

  How satisfied are you with opportunities for promotion in the firm?

  Very satisfied   ____

  Satisfied   ____

  Neither satisfied nor dissatisfied   ____

  Dissatisfied   ____

  Very dissatisfied   ____

- Students often fail to give clear instructions on self-completion questionnaires about how the questions should be answered. Specify whether you want a tick, something to be circled or deleted, or whatever. If only one response is required, make sure you say so—for example, 'tick the answer that comes closest to your view'.

- Be careful about letting respondents choose more than one answer. Sometimes it is unavoidable, but questions that allow more than one reply are often a pain to analyse.

- In spite of the fact that I always warn about the problems of overlapping categories, students still formulate closed answers that are not mutually exclusive. In addition, some categories may be omitted. For example:

  How many times per week do you use public transport?

  1–3 times   _____

  3–6 times   _____

  6–9 times   _____

  More than 10 times   _____

  Not only does the respondent not know where to answer if his or her answer might be 3 or 6 times; there is no answer for someone who would want to answer 10.

- Students sometimes do not ensure the answers correspond to the question. For example:

  Do you regularly go to your gym?

  More than once a week   _____

  Once a week   _____

  2 or 3 times a month   _____

  Once a month   _____

  The problem here is that the answer to the question is logically either 'yes' or 'no'. However, the student quite sensibly wants to gain some idea of frequency (something that I would agree with in the light of my second point in this list!). The problem is that the question and the response categories are out of kilter. The question should be:

  How frequently do you go to your gym in any month?

  More than once a week   _____

  Once a week   _____

  2 or 3 times a month   _____

  Once a month   _____

If you never committed any of these 'sins', you would be well on the way to producing a questionnaire that would stand out from the rest, provided you took into account the other advice I give in this chapter as well!

Vignette questions

A form of asking mainly closed questions that has been used in connection with the examination of people's normative standards is the vignette technique. The technique essentially comprises presenting respondents with one or more scenarios and then asking them how they would respond when confronted with the circumstances of that scenario. Research in focus 10.4 describes a vignette that was employed in the context of a study of family obligations in Britain. The aim was to elicit respondents' normative judgements about how family members should respond to relatives who are in need and indeed *who* should do the responding.

Research in focus 10.4
A vignette to establish family obligations

Jim and Margaret Robinson are a married couple in their early forties. Jim's parents, who live several hundred miles away, have had a serious car accident and they need long-term daily care and help. Jim is their only son. He and his wife both work for the Electricity Board and they could both get transfers so they could work near his parents.

Card E

(a) From the card, what should Jim and Margaret do?
   Move to live near Jim's parents
   Have Jim's parents move to live with them
   Give Jim's parents money to help them pay for daily care
   Let Jim's parents make their own arrangements
   Do something else (SPECIFY)
   Don't know

(b) In fact, Jim and Margaret are prepared to move and live near Jim's parents, but teachers at their children's school say that moving might have a bad effect on their children's education. Both children will soon be taking O-levels [predecessors to the current GCSE examinations].

   What should Jim and Margaret do? Should they move or should they stay?
   Move
   Stay

(c) Why do you think they should move/stay?

Probe fully verbatim

(d) Jim and Margaret *do* decide to go and live near Jim's parents. A year later Jim's mother dies and his father's condition gets worse so that he needs full-time care.

   Should Jim or Margaret give up their jobs to take care of Jim's father? *IF YES*: Who should give up their job, Jim or Margaret?

   Yes, Jim should give up his job
   Yes, Margaret should give up her job
   No, neither should give up their jobs
   Don't know/Depends

Source: Finch (1987: 108).

The vignette is designed to tease out respondents' norms concerning family obligations in respect of several factors: the nature of the care (whether long or short term and whether it should entail direct involvement or just the provision of resources); the significance of geographical propinquity; the dilemma of paid work and care; and the gender component of who should give up a job if that was deemed the appropriate course of action. There is a gradual increase in the specificity of the situation facing Jim and Margaret and therefore the respondent. Initially, we are not aware of whether Jim and Margaret are prepared to move; then we know they are; and then we learn they do in fact decide to move, which leads to the question of whether one of them should become a full-time carer.

Many aspects of the issues being tapped by the series of questions could be accessed through attitude items, such as:

> When a working couple decide that one of them should care for parents, the wife should be the one to give up her job.
>
> Strongly agree _____
>
> Agree _____
>
> Undecided _____
>
> Disagree _____
>
> Strongly disagree _____

The advantage of the vignette over such an attitude question is that it anchors the choice in a situation and as such reduces the possibility of an unreflective reply. Finch (1987) also argues that, when the subject matter is a sensitive area (in this case, dealing with family relationships), there is the possibility that the questions may be seen as threatening by respondents. Respondents may feel that they are being judged by their replies. Finch argues that the fact that the questions are about other people (and imaginary ones at that) permits a certain amount of distance between the questioning and the respondent and results in a less threatening context. However, it is hard to believe that respondents will not feel that their replies will at least in part be seen as reflecting on them, even if the questions are not about them as such.

One obvious requirement of the vignette technique is that the scenarios must be believable, so that considerable effort needs to go into the construction of credible situations. Finch points to some further considerations in relation to this style of questioning. It is more or less impossible to establish how far assumptions are being made about the characters in the scenario (such as their ethnicity) and what the significance of those assumptions might be for the validity and comparability of people's replies. It is also difficult to establish how far people's answers reflect their own normative views or indeed how they themselves would act when confronted with the kinds of choices revealed in the scenarios. However, in spite of these reservations, the vignette technique warrants serious consideration when the research focus is concerned with an area that lends itself to this style of questioning.

 # Piloting and pre-testing questions

It is always desirable, if at all possible, to conduct a pilot study before administering a self-completion questionnaire or structured interview schedule to your sample. In fact, the desirability of piloting such instruments is not solely to do with trying to ensure that survey questions operate well; piloting also has a role in ensuring that the research instrument as a whole functions well. Pilot studies may be particularly crucial in relation to research based on the self-completion questionnaire, since there will not be an interviewer present to clear up any confusion. Also, with interviews, persistent problems may emerge after a few interviews have been carried out and these can then be addressed. However, with self-completion questionnaires, since they are sent or handed out in large numbers, considerable wastage may occur before any problems become apparent.

Here are some uses of pilot studies in survey research.

- If the main study is going to employ mainly closed questions, open questions can be asked in the pilot to generate the fixed-choice answers. Glock (1988), for example, extols the virtues of conducting qualitative interviews in preparation for a survey for precisely this kind of reason.

- Piloting an interview schedule can provide interviewers with some experience of using it and can infuse them with a greater sense of confidence.

- If everyone (or virtually everyone) who answers a question replies in the same way, the resulting data are unlikely to be of interest because they do not form a variable. A pilot study allows such a question to be identified.

- In interview surveys, it may be possible to identify questions that make respondents feel uncomfortable and to detect any tendency for respondents' interest to be lost at certain junctures.

- Questions that seem not to be understood (more likely to be realized in an interview than in a self-completion questionnaire context) or questions that are often not answered should become apparent. The latter problem of questions being skipped may be due to confusing or threatening phrasing, poorly worded instructions, or confusing positioning in the interview schedule or questionnaire. Whatever the cause might be, such missing data are undesirable and a pilot study may be instrumental in identifying the problem.

- Pilot studies allow the researcher to determine the adequacy of instructions to interviewers, or to respondents completing a self-completion questionnaire.

- It may be possible to consider how well the questions flow and whether it is necessary to move some of them around to improve this feature.

The pilot should not be carried out on people who might have been members of the sample that would be employed in the full study. One reason for this is that, if you are seeking to employ probability sampling, the selecting-out of a number of members of the population or sample may affect the representativeness of any subsequent sample. If possible, it is best to find a small set of respondents who are comparable to members of the population from which the sample for the full study will be taken.

 # Using existing questions

One final observation regarding the asking of questions is that you should also consider using questions that have been employed by other researchers for at least part of your questionnaire or interview schedule. This may seem like stealing and you would be advised to contact the researchers concerned regarding the use of questions they have devised. However, employing existing questions allows you to use questions that have in a sense been piloted for you. If any reliability and validity testing has taken place, you will know about the measurement qualities of the existing questions you use. A further advantage of using existing questions is that they allow you to draw comparisons with other research. This might allow you to indicate whether change has occurred or whether the findings apply to your sample. For example, if you are researching job satisfaction, using one of the standard job satisfaction scales would allow you to compare your findings with another researcher's. Alternatively, using the same questions as another researcher may allow you to explore whether the location of your sample appears to make a difference to the findings. While you need to be cautious about inferring too much from such comparisons between your own and other researchers' data, the findings can nonetheless be illuminating.

At the very least, examining questions used by others might give you some ideas about how best to approach your own questions, even if you decide not to make use of them as they stand. The use of existing questions is a common practice among researchers. For example, the researchers who developed the scale designed to measure attitudes to vegetarians (Research in focus 6.5) used several existing questions devised for measuring other concepts in which they were interested, such as measures of authoritarianism and political conservatism. These other measures had known properties in terms of their reliability and validity. Similarly, Walklate (2000: 194) describes how in developing a survey instrument to be administered to possible victims of crime, she and her colleagues used 'tried and tested questions taken from pre-existing criminal victimization surveys amended to take account of our own more localized concerns'.

The process of finding questions has been made a great deal easier by the creation of 'question banks', which act as repositories of questions employed in surveys and elsewhere. A very useful question bank can be found at the following address: http://qb.soc.surrey.ac.uk/ (accessed on 3 July 2007). The question bank includes questions from major surveys. They are presented in the context of the questionnaire in which they appeared and are accompanied by technical details. The search mechanism allows you to search for a particular questionnaire or it allows you to input keywords to find cases of the use of topics in questions. For the latter, select the **Search** button and then enter your keyword(s) or phrase as requested.

Tips and skills
Getting help in designing questions

When designing questions, as I suggested above, try to put yourself in the position of someone who has been asked to answer the questions. This can be difficult, because some (if not all!) of the questions may not apply to you—for example, if you are a young student doing a survey of retired people. However, try to think about how *you* would reply. This means concentrating not just on the questions themselves but also on the links between the questions. For example, do filter questions work in the way you expect them to? Then try the question out on some people you know, as in a pilot study. Ask them to be critical and to consider how well the questions connect to each other. Also, do look at the questionnaires and structured interview schedules that other experienced researchers have devised. They may not have asked questions on your topic, but the way they have asked the questions should give you an idea of what to do and what to avoid when designing such instruments.

Checklist

Issues to consider for your structured interview schedule or self-completion questionnaire

○ Have you devised a clear and comprehensive way of introducing the research to interviewees or questionnaire respondents?

○ Have you considered whether there are any existing questions used by other researchers to investigate this topic that could meet your needs?

○ Do the questions allow you to answer all your research questions?

○ Could any questions that are not strictly relevant to your research questions be dropped?

○ Have you tried to put yourself in the position of answering as many of the questions as possible?

○ Have you piloted the questionnaire with some appropriate respondents?

○ If it is a structured interview schedule, have you made sure that the instructions to yourself and to anyone else involved in interviewing are clear (e.g. with filter questions, is it clear which questions should be missed out)?

○ If it is a self-completion questionnaire, have you made sure that the instructions to respondents are clear (e.g. with filter questions, is it clear which questions should be missed out)?

○ Are instructions about how to record responses clear (e.g. whether to tick or circle or delete; whether more than one response is allowable)?

○ Have you included as few open questions as possible?

○ Have you allowed respondents to indicate levels of intensity in their replies, so that they are not forced into 'yes' or 'no' answers where intensity of feeling may be more appropriate?

○ Have you ensured that questions and their answers do not span more than one page?

○ Have socio-demographic questions been left until the end of the questionnaire?

○ Are questions relating to the research topic at or very close to the beginning?

○ Have you taken steps to ensure that the questions you are asking really do supply you with the information you need?

○ Have you taken steps to ensure that there are no:

    ○ Ambiguous terms in questions or response choices?

    ○ Long questions?

    ○ Double-barrelled questions?

    ○ Very general questions?

    ○ Leading questions?

    ○ Questions that are asking about two or more things?

    ○ Questions that include negatives?

    ○ Questions using technical terms?

○ Have you made sure that your respondents will have the requisite knowledge to answer your questions?

○ Is there an appropriate match between your questions and your response choices?

○ Have you made sure that your response choices are properly balanced?

○ Do any of your questions rely too much on your respondents' memory?

○ Have you ensured that there is a category of 'other' (or similar category such as 'unsure' or 'neither agree nor disagree') so that respondents are not forced to answer in a way that is not indicative of what they think or do?

If you are using a Likert-scale approach:

○ Have you included some items that can be reverse scored in order to minimize response sets?

○ Have you made sure that the items really do relate to the same underlying cluster of attitudes so that they can be aggregated?

○ Have you ensured that your response choices are exhaustive?

○ Have you ensured that your response choices do not overlap?

Key points

- While open questions undoubtedly have certain advantages, closed questions are typically preferable for a survey, because of the ease of asking questions and recording and processing answers.
- This point applies particularly to the self-completion questionnaire.
- Open questions of the kind used in qualitative interviewing have a useful role in relation to the formulation of fixed-choice answers and piloting.
- It is crucial to learn the rules of question-asking to avoid some of the more obvious pitfalls.
- Remember always to put yourself in the position of the respondent when asking questions and to make sure you will generate data appropriate to your research questions.
- Piloting or pre-testing may clear up problems in question formulation.

Questions for review

Open or closed questions?

- What difficulties do open questions present in survey research?
- Why are closed questions frequently preferred to open questions in survey research?
- What are the limitations of closed questions?
- How can closed questions be improved?

Types of question

- What are the main types of question that are likely to be used in a structured interview or self-administered questionnaire?

Rules for designing questions

- What is wrong with each of the following questions?

  What is your annual salary?

Below £10,000	_____
£10,000–15,000	_____
£15,000–20,000	_____
£20,000–25,000	_____
£25,000–30,000	_____
£30,000–35,000	_____
£35,000 and over	_____

Do you ever feel alienated from your work?

All the time   ____

Often   ____

Occasionally   ____

Never   ____

How satisfied are you with the provision of educational services and social services in your area?

Very satisfied   ____

Fairly satisfied   ____

Neither satisfied nor dissatisfied   ____

Fairly dissatisfied   ____

Very dissatisfied   ____

What is your marital status?

Single   ____

Married   ____

Divorced   ____

Vignette questions

- In what circumstances are vignette questions appropriate?

Piloting and pre-testing questions

- Why is it important to pilot questions?

Using existing questions

- Why might it be useful to use questions devised by others?

Online Resource Centre

http://www.oxfordtextbooks.co.uk/orc/brymansrm3e/

Visit the Online Resource Centre that accompanies this book to enrich your understanding of asking questions. Consult web links, test yourself using multiple choice questions, and gain further guidance and inspiration from the Student Researcher's Toolkit.

Structured observation

Chapter outline

Chapter guide

Structured observation is a method that is relatively underused in social research. It entails the direct observation of behaviour and the recording of that behaviour in terms of categories that have been devised prior to the start of data collection. This chapter explores:

- the limitations of survey research for the study of behaviour;
- the different forms of observation in social research;
- the potential of structured observation for the study of behaviour;
- how to devise an observation schedule;
- different strategies for observing behaviour in structured observation;
- sampling issues in structured observation research; with this method, the issue of sampling is to do not just with people but also with the sampling of time and contexts;
- issues of reliability and validity in structured observation;
- field stimulations, whereby the researcher actively intervenes in social life and records what happens as a consequence of the intervention, as a form of structured observation;
- some criticisms of structured observation.

Introduction

Structured observation is a method for systematically observing the behaviour of individuals in terms of a schedule of categories. It is a technique in which the researcher employs explicitly formulated rules for the observation and recording of behaviour. One of its main advantages is that it allows behaviour to be observed directly, unlike in survey research, which allows behaviour only to be inferred. In survey research, respondents frequently report their behaviour, but there are good reasons for thinking that such reports may not be entirely accurate. Structured observation constitutes a possible solution in that it entails the direct observation of behaviour.

Problems with survey research on social behaviour

Chapters 8 through 10 have dealt with several different aspects of survey research. In the course of outlining procedures associated with the survey, certain problems with the techniques with which it is typically associated have been identified. To some extent the deficiencies associated with the survey are recognized by practitioners, who have developed ways of dealing with them or at least of offsetting their impact to some degree. When survey techniques such as the structured interview or the self-completion questionnaire are employed in connection with the study of respondents' *behaviour*, certain characteristic difficulties are encountered, some of which have been touched on in earlier chapters. Tips and skills 'Problems with using survey research to investigate behaviour' identifies some of the difficulties entailed in using survey methods to research behaviour. The list is by no means exhaustive but it does capture some of the main elements.

Tips and skills
Problems with using survey research to investigate behaviour

- *Problem of meaning*. People may vary in their interpretations of key terms in a question (see Thinking deeply 11.1).
- *Problem of omission*. When answering the question, respondents may inadvertently omit key terms in the question (see Thinking deeply 11.1).
- *Problem of memory*. They may misremember aspects of the occurrence of certain forms of behaviour.
- *Social desirability effect*. They may exhibit a tendency towards replying in ways that are meant to be consistent with their perceptions of the desirability of certain kinds of answer.
- *Question threat*. Some questions may appear threatening and result in a failure to provide an honest reply.
- *Interviewer characteristics*. Aspects of the interviewer may influence the answers provided.
- *Gap between stated and actual behaviour*. How people say they are likely to behave and how they actually behave may be inconsistent (see Thinking deeply 11.2).

Thinking deeply 11.1
Accurate reporting of behaviour and the problems of meaning and omission

Belson (1981) has conducted detailed studies of how people interpret questions designed to gauge attitudes and behaviour. One question concerned with the latter was embedded in a structured **interview schedule** administered to fifty-nine British adults and went as follows:

> When you turn on your television in the evening, do you generally go on viewing till the end of the evening or do you just watch one or two programmes? (Belson 1981: 59)

Intensive interviews undertaken after the structured interviews had been carried out revealed that no respondents interpreted the question totally correctly. Twenty-five respondents arrived at incorrect interpretations; the rest were broadly correct but in varying degrees. A common problem was that the question was designed to refer to when the respondents themselves turned the television on. This was correctly interpreted by thirty-eight respondents, but fifteen interpreted the question to mean when the set was switched on—that is, not necessarily by the respondent (problem of meaning). Nine respondents appeared not to have taken any notice of the phrase 'when you turn on your television' (problem of omission). Similarly, ten failed to consider 'till the end of the evening' in their answers, while 'generally' spawned several interpretations. We see here problems of omission and meaning respectively.

Thinking deeply 11.2
Gap between stated and actual behaviour

This is one of the most infamous cases of problems of the gap between what people say they do (or are likely to do) and their actual behaviour. Questionnaires tap people's attitudes and reports of their behaviour, but one might legitimately question how well these relate to actual behaviour. A study of racial prejudice conducted many years ago by LaPiere (1934) illustrates this issue. He spent two years travelling with a young Chinese student and his wife to determine whether they were refused entry at hotels and restaurants. They twice crossed the USA. Of 66 hotels, they were refused entry once; of 184 restaurants and diners, none refused entry. LaPiere sought to eliminate himself as a possible contaminating influence by ensuring that he was not involved in gaining access to the various establishments and indeed seems to have sought to load the dice slightly in favour of being turned away:

> Whenever possible I let my Chinese friend negotiate for accommodation . . . or sent them into a restaurant ahead of me. In this way I attempted to 'factor' myself out. We sometimes patronized high-class establishments after a hard and dusty day on the road and stopped at inferior auto camps when in our most presentable condition. (LaPiere 1934: 232)

LaPiere then allowed six months to elapse and sent questionnaires to the hotels and restaurants they had visited. One of the questions asked: 'Will you accept members of the Chinese race as guests in your establishment?' Of the establishments that replied, 92 per cent of restaurants said no; and 91 per cent of hotels said no. LaPiere's simple though striking study clearly illustrates the gap that may exist between reports of behaviour and actual behaviour. It should also be noted that the question asked is somewhat unclear, a feature that is not usually remarked upon in connection with this widely cited study. 'Will you . . . ?' can be interpreted as asking the respondent to project into the future or to state the establishment's policy. Quite why the more obvious formulation of 'Do you . . . ?' was not used is not clear, though it is unlikely that this point has a significant bearing on the findings and their implications for survey research.

So why not observe behaviour?

An obvious solution to the problems identified is to observe people's behaviour directly rather than to rely on research instruments like questionnaires to elicit such information. In this chapter, I am going to outline a method called *structured observation* (see Key concept 11.1), also often called *systematic observation*.

Much like the interview (see Key concept 8.2), there are many different forms of observation approach in social research. Key concept 11.2 outlines some major ways of conducting observation studies in social research.

It has been implied that structured observation can be viewed as an alternative to survey methods of research. After all, in view of the various problems identified in Tips and skills 'Problems with using survey research to investigate behaviour', it would seem an obvious solution to observe people instead. However, structured observation has not attracted a large following and instead tends to be used in certain specific research areas, such as the behaviour of school teachers and pupils and interaction between them.

Key concept 11.1
What is structured observation?

Structured observation, often also called *systematic observation*, is a technique in which the researcher employs explicitly formulated rules for the observation and recording of behaviour. The rules inform observers about what they should look for and how they should record behaviour. Each person who is part of the research (we will call these people 'participants') is observed for a predetermined period of time using the same rules. These rules are articulated in what is usually referred to as an *observation schedule*, which bears many similarities to a structured interview schedule with **closed questions**. The aim of the observation schedule is to ensure that each participant's behaviour is systematically recorded so that it is possible to aggregate the behaviour of all those in the **sample** in respect of each type of behaviour being recorded. The rules that constitute the observation schedule are as specific as possible in order to direct observers to exactly what aspects of behaviour they are supposed to be looking for. The resulting data resemble questionnaire data considerably, in that the procedure generates information on different aspects of behaviour that can be treated as **variables**. Moreover, structured observation research is typically underpinned by a cross-sectional **research design** (see Key concept 2.6 and Figures 2.2 and 2.3).

Key concept 11.2
Major types of observation research

The following are the major forms of observational research in social research.

- *Structured observation*. See Key concept 11.1.
- *Systematic observation*. See Key concept 11.1.
- *Participant observation*. This is one of the best-known methods of research in the social sciences. It is primarily associated with **qualitative research** and entails the relatively prolonged immersion of the observer in a social setting in which he or she seeks to observe the behaviour of members of that setting (group, organization, community, etc.) and to elicit the meanings they attribute to their environment and behaviour. Participant observers vary considerably in how much they participate in the social settings in which they locate themselves. See Key concept 17.1 and Chapter 17 generally for a more detailed treatment.
- *Non-participant observation*. This is a term that is used to describe a situation in which the observer observes but does not participate in what is going on in the social setting. Structured observers are usually non-participants in that they are in the social setting being observed but rarely participate in what is happening. The term can also be used in connection with unstructured observation.
- *Unstructured observation*. As its name implies, unstructured observation does not entail the use of an observation schedule for the recording of behaviour. Instead, the aim is to record in as much detail as possible the behaviour of participants with the aim of developing a narrative account of that behaviour. In a sense, most participant observation is unstructured, but the term unstructured observation is usually employed in conjunction with non-participant observation.
- *Simple observation and contrived observation*. Webb *et al.* (1966) write about forms of observation in which the observer is unobtrusive and is not observed by those being observed. With simple observation, the observer has no influence over the situation being observed; in the case of contrived observation, the observer actively alters the situation to observe the effects of an intervention. These two types of observation are invariably forms of non-participant observation and can entail either structured or unstructured observation.

Central to any structured observation study will be the *observation schedule* or *coding scheme*. This specifies the categories of behaviour that are to be observed and how behaviour should be allocated to those categories. It is best to illustrate what this involves by looking at examples. One of the best-known schedules for the observation of classrooms is Flanders Interaction Analysis Categories (FIAC), devised by Flanders (1970). This scheme was developed in the USA, but has been employed fairly extensively in other countries. An observer watches a classroom during a lesson and every three seconds allocates a category number to the type of activity that takes place in that three-second period. (See Figure 11.1 for the different types of activity in the FIAC scheme.) In other words, in each and every minute, the observer will write down twenty numbers, each of which will relate directly to the coding scheme.

From such data a number of features can be derived. For example, it becomes possible to compare teachers' styles in terms of such things as the relative emphasis upon teachers doing the talking and pupils talking. One can also compare teachers in terms of the amounts of silence or confusion that take place in their lessons. It also becomes possible to compare classes in terms of these categories. In fact, we tend to find, using the FIAC scheme, that two-thirds of time in the classroom is made up of talk. Of that talk, two-thirds derives from the teacher. It is helpful in bringing about an understanding of what happens in lessons and can be useful in developing information about which styles seem most effective. For example, are better exam results achieved by teachers who exhibit a high level of talking relative to that of pupils, or are teachers who allow more pupil talk more effective? The scheme can also be used in teacher training in order to help trainees to become aware of features of their teaching style, and possibly to begin to question its appropriateness.

It is interesting to think about how a scheme like this might be employed in connection with higher education teaching and in particular in tutorials and seminars. In the following imaginary scheme, the focus is on the teacher. The categories might be:

Tutor

1. asking question addressed to group;
2. asking question addressed to individual;
3. responding to question asked by member of group;
4. responding to comment by member of group;

Figure 11.1

FIAC categories

Teacher talk	Response	1 Accepts feeling (e.g. accepts and clarifies an attitude or the feeling tone of a pupil) 2 Praises or encourages 3 Accepts or uses ideas of pupils
	Initiation	4 Asks questions 5 Lecturing 6 Giving direction 7 Criticizing or justifying authority
Pupil talk		8 Pupil talk—response 9 Pupil talk—initiation
Silence		10 Silence or confusion

5. discussing topic;
6. making arrangements;
7. silence.

Student(s)

8. asking question;
9. responding to question from tutor;
10. responding to comment from tutor;
11. responding to question from another student;
12. responding to comment from another student;
13. talking about arrangements.

We might want to code what is happening every five seconds. The coding sheet for a five-minute period in the tutorial might then look like Figure 11.2. We might try to relate the amount of time that the tutor is engaged in particular activities to such things as: number of students in the group; layout of the room; subject discipline; gender of tutor; age of tutor; and so on.

Figure 11.2

Coding sheet for imaginary study of university tutors

3	3	3	3	10	10	10	10	10	10	10	10
10	10	10	10	10	10	7	7	7	8	8	8
8	8	8	8	8	8	8	8	11	11	11	11
11	11	11	11	11	11	11	11	11	11	11	11
7	7	7	7	7	4	4	4	4	4	4	1

Note: Each cell represents a five-second interval and each row is one minute.

Research in focus 11.1
Observing behaviour in English schools

Blatchford *et al.* (2003) conducted research into the impact of class size on pupil behaviour. They were interested in the possibility that, as class sizes increase, pupil inattentiveness also increases, resulting in difficult relationships between the children. The observational component of this research was based on children in large and small reception classes (age 4–5 years). The authors describe their approach as involving:

direct, i.e. on-the-spot, observations of selected children in terms of previously developed categories and in terms of 5-minute observation sheets divided into continuous 10-second time samples. The schedule was child-based in the sense that one child at a time was observed . . . The schedule involved categories that provided a description of time spent in three 'social modes'—when with their teachers, other children and when not interacting. Within each of these three modes sub-categories covered work, procedural, social and off-task activity. . . . The aim was to observe [6 randomly chosen] children in each class five times per day, for 3 days. In the event the average number of completed observation sheets per child was 14 . . . In terms of time there were 69 minutes of observation per child.

The Blatchford *et al.* (2003) article emphasizes the data relating to interaction between children and 'off-task' behaviour. The interaction between children was observed and coded in terms of the following categories: task; procedure (class organization and management); social; mucking about; aggressive; help; and unclear.

The observation schedule

Devising a schedule for the recording of observations is clearly a crucial step in the structured observation project. The considerations that go into this phase are very similar to those involved in producing a structured interview schedule. The following considerations are worth taking into account.

- A clear focus is necessary. There are two aspects to this point. First, it should be clear to the observer exactly who or what (and possibly both) is to be observed. For example, if people are the focus of attention, the observer needs to know precisely who is to be observed. Also, the observer needs to know which if any aspects of the setting are to be observed and hence recorded. The second sense in which a clear focus is necessary is that the research problem needs to be clearly stated so that the observer knows which of the many things going on in any setting are to be recorded.

- As with the production of a closed question for a structured interview schedule or self-completion questionnaire, the forms taken by any category of behaviour must be both mutually exclusive (i.e. not overlap) and inclusive. Taking the earlier example of coding behaviour in a university tutorial, we might conceivably run into a problem of the thirteen categories not being exhaustive if a student knocks on the tutor's door and quickly asks him or her a question (perhaps about the tutorial topic if the student is from another of the tutor's groups). An observer unfamiliar with the ways of university life might well be unsure about whether this behaviour needs to be coded in terms of the thirteen categories or whether the coding should be temporarily suspended. Perhaps the best approach would be to have another category of behaviour to be coded that we might term 'interruption'. It is often desirable for a certain amount of unstructured observation to take place before the construction of the observation schedule and for there to be some piloting of it so that possible problems associated with a lack of inclusiveness can be anticipated.

- The recording system must be easy to operate. Complex systems with large numbers of types of behaviour will be undesirable. Much like interviewers using a structured interview schedule, observers need to be trained, but even so it is easy for an observer to become flustered or confused if faced with too many options.

- One possible problem with some observation schedules is that they sometimes require a certain amount of interpretation on the part of the observer. For example, it might be difficult to distinguish between a student responding to a question raised by another student and discussing the tutorial topic. To the extent that it may be difficult to distinguish between the two, a certain amount of interpretation on the part of the observer may be required. If such interpretation is required, there would need to be clear guidelines for the observer and considerable experience would be required (see Research in focus 11.2 for an illustration of a study in which a good deal of interpretation seems to have been necessary).

Research in focus 11.2
Observing jobs

Jenkins *et al.* (1975) report the results of an exploratory study employed to measure the nature of jobs. The research focused on several different types of job in a number of different types of organization. An observation schedule was devised to assess the nature of twenty aspects (**dimensions**) of the jobs in question. Most of the dimensions were measured through more than one **indicator**, each of which took the form of a question that observers had to answer on a six- or seven-point **scale**. These were then aggregated for each dimension. While the research has a predominantly psychological slant, many of the twenty dimensions relate to issues that have been raised in the sociology of work by labour process theorists and others (e.g. Braverman 1974). One dimension relates to 'Worker pace control' and comprises three observational indicators such as:

How much control does the employee have in setting the pace of his or her work?

Another dimension was 'Autonomy', which comprised four items, such as:

The job allows the individual to make a lot of decisions on his or her own.

Most of the observers were university students. The procedure for conducting the observations was as follows: 'Each respondent was observed twice for an hour. The observations were scheduled so that the two different observations were separated by at least 2 days, were usually made at different times of the day, and were always made by two different observers' (Jenkins *et al.* 1975: 173).

Strategies for observing behaviour

There are different ways of conceptualizing how behaviour should be recorded.

- We can record in terms of *incidents*. This means waiting for something to happen and then recording what follows from it. Essentially, this is what LaPiere (1934) did (see Thinking deeply 11.2), in that he waited for the Chinese couple to negotiate entry to each hotel or restaurant and then recorded whether they were allowed entry or not. I remember reading many years ago in a newspaper that someone placed a ladder over a pavement and then observed whether people preferred to go under the ladder or to risk life and limb in the face of oncoming traffic. A considerable number preferred the latter option, confirming the persistence of superstitious beliefs in an apparently secular society. Once again, an incident (someone approaching the ladder) triggered the observation. Research in focus 11.3 contains a more recent example of such 'research'. Observation of this kind is what Webb *et al.* (1966) would regard as an example of *contrived observation*, because the researchers fabricated the situation. The discussion later in this chapter of *field stimulations* provides further illustrations of this kind of research.

- We can observe and record in terms of *short periods* of time. This was the case with the research reported in Research in focus 11.1, where '5-minute observation sheets' were used. A slight variation on this theme can be found in the research reported in Research in focus 2.6. Children in St Helena were videotaped over a two-week period during their morning, lunchtime, and afternoon breaks. The tapes were then coded using

the Playgound Behaviour Observation Schedule which is an instrument for recording the occurrence of 23 behaviours (e.g. games; fantasy play; character imitation; anti-social and pro-social behaviour) and their behaviour groupings (i.e. whether the behaviour was undertaken by an individual, a pair, or with 3–5 or 6 or more children). . . . A separate Playgound Behaviour Observation Schedule was completed for each 30-second segment. (Charlton *et al.* 1998: 7)

- We can observe and record observations for quite *long periods* of time. The observer watches and records more or less continuously. The FIAC scheme adopts this strategy. Another example is the study of job characteristics by Jenkins *et al.* (1975), which entailed the observation of each worker on two occasions but for an hour on each occasion (see Research in focus 11.2): 'The observation hour was structured so that the observer spent 10 min becoming oriented to the job, 30 min observing specific job actions, and 20 min rating the job in situ. The observers then typically spent an additional 15 min away from the job completing observation instrument' (Jenkins *et al.* 1975: 174). This last study is an example of what Martin and Bateson (1986) refer to as '**continuous recording**', whereby the observer observes for extended periods, thus allowing the frequency and duration of forms of behaviour to be measured. They contrast this approach with **time sampling**.

- *Time sampling* is a further approach to the observation of behaviour. An example here would be a study of schools known as the ORACLE (Observational Research and Classroom Learning Evaluation) project (Galton *et al.* 1980). In this research, eight children (four of each gender) in each class in which observation took place were observed for around four minutes but on ten separate occasions. A mechanical device made a noise every twenty-five seconds, and, on each occasion this occurred, the observer made a note of what the teacher or pupils were doing in terms of the observation schedule. The sampling of time periods was random.

Research in focus 11.3
Is chivalry disappearing?

This is hardly research, but 'roadside tests' set up by the tyre firm Continental found that British male drivers were unwilling to help a 'woman described as blonde, in her mid-twenties and attractive' who was struggling to change a tyre (McVeigh 2006). These tests, which were a form of contrived observation, were set up in five British cities. Across the cities, 97 per cent of men zoomed past her, while she 'stood at the roadside clutching a spare wheel'. Chivalry was somewhat greater in Newcastle and among drivers of red cars! *The Times* columnist who reported this 'research' writes that a survey, for which no details are given, found that over half of British men claimed they would stop to help a woman struggling to change a tyre in such circumstances. This apparent gulf between actual and stated behaviour recalls the LaPiere study referred to in Thinking deeply 11.2.

Sampling

Just like survey research, structured observation necessitates decisions about sampling. However, with structured observation, issues surrounding sampling do not revolve solely around how to sample people. Several other sampling issues are involved.

Sampling people

When people are being sampled, considerations very similar to those encountered in Chapter 7 in respect of probability sampling come to the fore. This means that the observer will ideally want to sample on a random basis. In Croll and Moses' (1985) research on children with special educational needs, thirty-four classrooms from a number of different schools were selected for observation. All children were within the same age range. Initially, each teacher was interviewed to determine which children in his or her class were regarded as having special needs. In addition, tests of both reading ability and non-verbal reasoning were administered to children to identify those who appeared to have special needs, but who had not been identified by the teacher. Up to six children with special needs in each class were then randomly sampled as being the focus of structured observation; so too were four children who had not been identified as having special needs—these children acted as a kind of **control group**. In this way, 280 children were sampled, of whom 151 were identified as having special needs; the other 129 served as control subjects. The teachers did not know exactly which children were being observed. Each child was observed for a few minutes, after which the observer proceeded to the next child to be observed in a predetermined random order. In the end, each child was observed for a total of two hours. This was made up of a large number of short observation periods. In the research reported in Research in focus 11.1, the six students in each class were selected randomly but with the stipulation that three boys and three girls would be sampled. In the study of job characteristics (Research in focus 11.2), the individuals who were observed at work were randomly selected (Jenkins *et al.* 1975).

Sampling in terms of time

As implied by the idea of time sampling (see above), it is often necessary to ensure that, if certain individuals are sampled on more than one occasion, they are not always observed at the same time of the day. This means that, if particular individuals are selected randomly for observation on several different occasions for short periods, it is desirable for the observation periods to be randomly selected. For example, it would not be desirable for a certain pupil in a school classroom always to be observed at the end of the day. He or she may be tired and this will give a false impression of that pupil's behaviour. In the research reported in Research in focus 11.1, each child was observed at separate times on three different days. As a result, the researchers' ratings of any child are unlikely to be distorted by unusual behaviour that he or she might exhibit on just one or two occasions.

Further sampling considerations

The sampling procedures mentioned so far conform to probability sampling principles, because it is feasible to construct a sampling frame for individuals. However, this is not always possible for different kinds of reason. Studies in public areas, like the research on superstition mentioned above, do not permit random sampling, because we cannot very easily construct a sampling frame of people walking along a street. Similarly, it is not feasible to construct a sampling frame of interactions. Reiss (1976), for example, has written about the difficulty of developing a random sample of encounters between police officers and the public. The problem with doing structured observation research on such a topic is that it does not lend itself to the specification of a sampling frame, and therefore the researcher's ability to generate a probability sample is curtailed.

As suggested in Chapter 7, considerations relating to probability sampling derive largely from concerns surrounding the external validity (or generalizability) of findings. Such concerns are not necessarily totally addressed by resorting to probability sampling, however. For example, if a structured observation study is conducted over a relatively short span of time, issues of the representativeness of findings are likely to arise. If the research was conducted in schools, observations

conducted towards the end of the school year, when examinations are likely to loom large in the thinking of both teachers and students, may affect the results obtained compared to observations at a different point in the academic year. Consequently, consideration has to be given to the question of the timing of observation. This potential problem was dealt with in the ORACLE research by ensuring that teachers and each target pupil were observed on six occasions during each of the three school terms. Furthermore, how are the sites in which structured observation is to take place selected? Can we presume that they are themselves representative? Clearly, a random sampling procedure for the selection of schools may assuage any worries in this connection. However, in view of the difficulty of securing access to settings such as schools and business organizations, it is likely that the organizations to which access is secured may not be representative of the population of appropriate ones.

A further set of distinctions between types of sampling in structured observation have been drawn by Martin and Bateson (1986) between:

- '*ad libitum* sampling', whereby the observer records whatever is happening at the time;

- 'focal sampling', in which a specific individual is observed for a set period of time; the observer records all examples of whatever forms of behaviour are of interest in terms of a schedule;

- 'scan sampling', whereby an entire group of individuals is scanned at regular intervals and the behaviour of all of them is recorded at that time. This sampling strategy allows only one or two types of behaviour to be observed and recorded; and

- 'behaviour sampling', whereby an entire group is watched and the observer records who was involved in a particular kind of behaviour.

Most structured observation research seems to employ the first two types: Flanders's FIAC scheme is an example of *ad libitum* sampling; the research by Galton *et al.* (1980), Croll and Moses (1985), Blatchford *et al.* (2003; see Research in focus 11.1), Jenkins *et al.* (1975; see Research in focus 11.2), and the research by Buckle and Farrington (1994) cited in Research in focus 11.4 are illustrations of focal sampling.

Research in focus 11.4
A study of shoplifting

Buckle and Farrington (1994) report the results of a **replication** of an earlier study of shoplifting in a department store in Peterborough (Buckle and Farrington 1984). The replication was conducted in a similar store in Bedford. Customers were selected at random as they entered the store and followed by two observers until they left. The observers recorded such details as: cost of items bought; gender, race, and estimated age; and behaviour. In Peterborough 486 people formed the basis of the sample and in Bedford it was 502. Nine people shoplifted in Peterborough and six in Bedford. Somewhat surprisingly, shoplifters were more likely to be male and either under 25 (in Peterborough) or over 55 (in Bedford). Most shoplifters also purchased goods. Most shoplifting was of small items of relatively little monetary value. The sampling and observation strategies entailed random sampling of people followed by **continuous recording** for a short or long period depending on how long the person remained in the store.

Issues of reliability and validity

One writer has concluded that, when compared to interviews and questionnaires, structured observation 'Provides (*a*) more reliable information about events; (*b*) greater precision regarding their timing, duration, and frequency; (*c*) greater accuracy in the time ordering of variables; and (*d*) more accurate and economical reconstructions of large-scale social episodes' (McCall 1984: 277). This is a very strong endorsement for structured observation, but, as McCall notes, there are several issues of reliability and validity that confront practitioners of the method. Some of these issues are similar to those faced by researchers when seeking to develop measures in social research in general (see Chapter 6) and by survey research in particular. However, certain concerns are specific to structured observation.

Reliability

Practitioners of structured observation have been concerned with the degree of *inter-observer consistency*. Essentially, this issue entails considering the degree to which two or more observers of the same behaviour agree in terms of their coding of that behaviour on the observation schedule. The chief mechanism for assessing this component of reliability is a statistic called *kappa* (see Key concept 11.3; *this box can be ignored if you feel unsure about addressing more complex statistical issues at this stage*).

A second consideration in relation to reliability is the degree of consistency of the application of the observation schedule over time—that is, *intra-observer consistency*. This is clearly a difficult notion, because of the capacity and often necessity for people to behave in different ways on different occasions and in different contexts. Assessing the consistency of observation ratings across all possibilities is clearly a difficult undertaking. The procedures for assessing this aspect of reliability are broadly similar to those applied to the issue of inter-observer consistency. The Jenkins *et al.* (1975) research addressed the issue of inter-observer consistency over time and found that the measures fared even worse in this respect (Research in focus 11.2).

It is clearly not an easy matter to achieve reliability in structured observation. This is a point of some significance in view of the fact that validity presupposes reliability (see Chapter 6). Reliability may be difficult to achieve on occasions, because of the effects of such factors as observer fatigue and lapses in attention. However, this point should not be exaggerated, because the ORACLE researchers were able to achieve high levels of reliability for many of their measures, and indeed two critics of structured observation have written that 'there is no doubt that observers can be trained to use complex **coding schedules** with considerable reliability' (Delamont and Hamilton 1984: 32). (Using the Scott coefficient

Key concept 11.3
Cohen's kappa

This box can be ignored if you feel unsure about addressing more complex statistical issues at this stage.

Cohen's kappa is a measure of the degree of agreement over the coding of items by two people. As such, it could be applied to the coding of any textual information, as in the content analysis of newspaper articles or of answers to open interview questions, as well as to the coding of observation. Much like Cronbach's alpha (see Key concept 6.4) you will end up with a coefficient that will vary between 0 and 1. The closer the coefficient is to 1, the higher the agreement and the better the inter-observer consistency. A coefficient of 0.75 or above is considered very good; between 0.6 and 0.75, it is considered good; and between 0.4 and 0.6, it is regarded as fair. The meaning of kappa is that it measures the degree of agreement between observers beyond that which would occur by chance. Croll (1986) refers to a very similar statistic, the Scott coefficient of agreement, which can be interpreted in an identical way.

The values of kappa in the study of job characteristics referred to in Research in focus 11.2 were mainly in the 'fair' category. The two items referred to in Research in focus 11.2 achieved kappa values of 0.43 and 0.54 respectively (Jenkins *et al.* 1975). These are not very encouraging and suggest that the coding of job characteristics was not very reliable.

referred to in Key concept 11.3, it was found that the average inter-observer reliability level across the different components of pupil behaviour was 0.90.) The high levels of reliability may be due to the factors that are intrinsic to the school classroom and to the fact that there is a long tradition of structured observation research in schools, so that a fund of experience has been accumulated in this domain.

Validity

Measurement validity relates to the question of whether a measure is measuring what it is supposed to measure. The validity of any measure will be affected by:

- whether the measure reflects the concept it has been designed to measure (see Chapter 6), and
- error that arises from the implementation of the measure in the research process (see Chapter 8).

The first of these issues simply means that in structured observation it is necessary to attend to the same kinds of issues concerning the checking of validity (assessing face validity, concurrent validity, and so on) that are encountered in research based on interviews and questionnaires. The second aspect of validity—

error in implementation—relates to two matters in particular.

- Is the observation schedule administered as it is supposed to be? This is the equivalent of ensuring that interviewers using a structured interview schedule follow the research instrument and its instructions exactly as they are supposed to. If there is variability between observers or over time, the measure will be unreliable and therefore cannot be valid. Ensuring that observers have as complete an understanding as possible of how the observation schedule should be implemented is therefore crucial.

- Do people change their behaviour because they know they are being observed? This is an instance of what is known as the 'reactive effect' (Key concept 11.4). After all, if people adjust the way they behave because they know they are being observed (perhaps because they want to be viewed in a favourable way by the observer), their behaviour would have to be considered atypical. As a result, we could hardly regard the results of structured observation research as indicative of what happens in reality. As McCall (1984) notes, there is evidence that a reactive effect occurs in structured observation, but that by and large research participants become accustomed to being observed, so that the researcher essentially becomes less intrusive the longer he or she is present. Moreover, it should be borne in mind that frequently people's awareness of the observer's presence is offset by other factors. For example, teachers and students have many tasks to accomplish that reflect the demands of the classroom, so that the observer's ability to make a big impact on behaviour may be curtailed by the requirements of the situation.

Key concept 11.4
Reactive effect

Webb *et al.* (1966: 13) wrote about the 'reactive measurement effect', by which they meant that 'the research subject's knowledge that he is participating in a scholarly search may confound the investigator's data'. They distinguished four components of this effect.

1. *The guinea pig effect—awareness of being tested.* Examples of the kind of concern that Webb *et al.* were writing about are such effects as the research participant wanting to create a good impression or feeling prompted to behave in ways (or express attitudes) that would not normally be exhibited.

2. *Role selection.* Webb *et al.* argue that participants are often tempted to adopt a particular kind of role in research. An example is that there is a well-known effect in experimental research (but which may have a broader applicability) whereby some individuals seek out cues about the aims of the research and adjust what they say and do in line with their perceptions (which may of course be false) of those aims.

3. *Measurement as a change agent.* The very fact of a researcher being in a context in which no researcher is normally present may itself cause things to be different. For example, the fact that there is an observer sitting in the corner of a school classroom means that there is space and a chair being used that otherwise would be unoccupied. This very fact may influence behaviour.

4. *Response sets.* This is an issue that primarily relates to questionnaire and interview research and occurs when the respondent replies to a set of questions in a consistent but clearly inappropriate manner. Examples of this kind of effect are measurement problems like the social desirability effect and yeasaying and naysaying (consistently answering yes or no to questions or consistently agreeing or disagreeing with items regardless of the meaning of the question or item).

Reactive effects are likely to occur in any research in which participants know they are the focus of investigation. Webb *et al.* called for greater use of what they call *unobtrusive measures* or *non-reactive methods* that do not entail participants' knowledge of their involvement in research (see Key concept 13.3 for more information).

Field stimulations as a form of structured observation

Salancik (1979) has used the term 'field stimulation' to describe a form of observation research that shares many of the characteristics of structured observation. Although he classifies field stimulations as a qualitative method, they are in fact better thought of as operating with a **quantitative research strategy**, since the researcher typically seeks to quantify the outcomes of his or her interventions. In terms of the classification offered in Key concept 11.2, it is in fact 'contrived observation'. Part of LaPiere's study (see Thinking deeply 11.2) was a field stimulation: when he arranged for the Chinese couple to seek entry to the hotels and restaurants in order to observe the effects of their attempts, he was employing a field stimulation. A field stimulation, therefore, is a study in which the researcher directly intervenes in and/or manipulates a natural setting in order to observe what happens as a consequence of that intervention. However, unlike most structured observation, in a field stimulation participants do not know they are being studied. A famous field stimulation is described in Research in focus 11.5.

Research in focus 11.5
A field stimulation

David Rosenhan (1973) was one of eight people who sought to gain entry as patients to mental hospitals in the USA. Some of them—they are referred to as 'pseudo-patients'—sought entry to more than one hospital, so that twelve hospitals were approached. Each pseudo-patient was instructed to say that he or she was hearing voices. All successfully gained entry, in eleven of the twelve cases with a diagnosis of schizophrenia. As soon as they had succeeded in gaining entry, the pseudo-patients were instructed to cease exhibiting any symptoms. In spite of the fact that the pseudo-patients were all 'sane', it took many of them quite a long time to be released. The length of hospitalization varied between 7 and 52 days with a mean of 19 days. In four of the hospitals, pseudo-patients approached psychiatrists and nurses with a request for release, with no member of staff being approached more than once on any day. The pseudo-patients recorded the nature of the response to their requests: 71 per cent of psychiatrists responded by moving on with their heads averted and 88 per cent of nurses did likewise. Rosenhan regards this evidence as indicating that the mental patient becomes powerless and depersonalized. The study has been highly controversial, as many psychiatrists have sought to question its implications, while others have raised ethical issues of the kind addressed in Chapter 5 (such as the use of deception).

Some field stimulations can take the form of an experimental design (see Chapter 2). An example is a study by Daniel (1968) of racial discrimination in Britain in the 1960s. Daniel undertook conventional attitude studies among immigrant groups to establish levels of discrimination. In addition, he developed 'situation tests' to back up his findings. For example, in one set of situation tests he examined discrimination in the area of accommodation. Sixty advertisements for accommodation to let were selected from a number of regions. Advertisements stipulating 'no coloureds' or 'Europeans only' were deliberately excluded. At the time, it was not illegal for landlords to place such instructions in their advertisements. Each landlord was approached by each of the following: a West Indian; a white Hungarian; and a white Englishman. The applicants were presented with identical sets of characteristics, but they differed in terms of ethnicity. The applicant was requesting accommodation for a married couple with no children. In half of the applications (i.e. 30), the testers adopted 'professional roles'. In these roles they sought more expensive accommodation. In the other half, they adopted manual roles. In 15 of the 60 cases, all 3 applicants got the same information (e.g. let, still vacant). This means that discrimination occurred in the remaining 45 cases (see Table 11.1).

Daniel's research strongly suggests that, because the Hungarian was rarely discriminated against, it is colour rather than being a member of an ethnic minority as such that causes discrimination. Similar studies were conducted in relation to house purchase, employment, and car insurance. Interestingly, the researchers often found that these tests implied that discrimination was *greater* than had been indicated by the attitude surveys, presumably because it is difficult to know if you really have been discriminated against.

Table 11.1

Daniel's (1968) situation test: the case of accommodation	
Reaction to request for accommodation	No.
West Indian was told accommodation taken; both other applicants told it was vacant	38
West Indian was asked for higher rent than the others	4
West Indian and Hungarian were told accommodation let	2
West Indian and Hungarian were asked for higher rent	1
All applicants received the same information	15
TOTAL	60

While such research provides some quite striking findings and gets around the problem of **reactivity** by not alerting research participants to the fact that they are being observed, like the pseudo-patient study in Research in focus 11.5, ethical concerns are sometimes raised, such as the use of deception. Moreover, the extent to which an observation schedule can be employed is inevitably limited, because excessive use will blow the observer's cover. All that can usually be done is to engage in limited coding, in particular the nature of the effect of the intervention, as in the LaPiere (1934) and Daniel (1968) studies, or to include a limited amount of further observation, as in the Rosenhan (1973) research. In the case of the civility tests in Research in focus 11.6, the coding needed is minimal, as in the Daniel study, to the outcome—is the person smiled at, helped, let into the traffic jam, etc.

Research in focus 11.6
Studies of urban civility

In 2006 *The Times* reported the findings of a test of civility that was carried out by *Reader's Digest* reporters in thirty-five world cities (Hamilton 2006). The test involved three tests of politeness: does someone help when papers are dropped on a busy street?; how often do shop assistants say 'thank you' at the checkout?; and how often is a door held open for someone? New York came top with a score of 80 per cent and Bombay bottom (32 per cent). London came joint fifteenth with Lisbon and Paris with a score of 57 per cent, which is just above the average world politeness level of 55 per cent.

A similar test was reported the previous year for eight British cities (Britten 2005). There were four criteria: smiling at you at a checkout; holding the door open for you; helping you out when you drop a shopping bag; and letting another motorist into a traffic jam during the rush hour. Each of these tests was carried out ten times per city. Newcastle came top with a score of 77 per cent and Birmingham bottom with 43 per cent. London, which was also in the *Reader's Digest* study, came fifth with 54 per cent.

Each of these news reports can be viewed as based on field stimulations. Because participants in the research are not aware of the fact that they are in fact research participants, these represent *unobtrusive measures* of civility. See Key concept 13.3 for more on unobtrusive measures and methods.

Criticisms of structured observation

Although it is not extensively used in social research, structured observation has been quite controversial. Certain criticisms have been implied in some of the previous discussion of reliability and validity issues, as well as in connection with the issue of generalizability. However, certain other areas of criticism warrant further discussion.

- There is a risk of imposing a potentially inappropriate or irrelevant framework on the setting being observed. This point is similar to the problem of the closed question in questionnaires. This risk is especially great if the setting is one about which little is known. One solution is for the structured observation to be preceded by a period of unstructured observation, so that appropriate variables and categories can be specified.

- Because it concentrates upon directly observable behaviour, structured observation is rarely able to get at intentions behind behaviour. Sometimes, when intentions are of concern, they are imputed by observers. Thus, in the FIAC scheme (see Figure 11.1), the category 'teacher praises or encourages' means imputing a motive to something that the teacher says. In the ORACLE research, the observers had to interpret whether a child gazing out of the window was working or not (Galton *et al.* 1980; Delamont and Hamilton 1984). Essentially, the problem is that structured observation does not readily allow the observer to get a grasp of the meaning of behaviour.

- There is a tendency for structured observation to generate lots of fragments of data. The problem here can be one of trying to piece them together to produce an overall picture, or one of trying to find general themes that link the fragments of data together. It becomes difficult, in other words, to see a bigger picture that lies behind the segments of behaviour that structured observation typically uncovers. It has been suggested, for example, that the tendency for structured observation studies of managers at work to find little evidence of planning in their everyday work (e.g. Mintzberg 1973) is due to the tendency for the method to fragment a manager's activities into discrete parts. As a result, something like planning, which may be an element in many managerial activities, becomes obscured from view (Snyder and Glueck 1980).

- It is often suggested that structured observation neglects the context within which behaviour takes place. Delamont and Hamilton (1984), for example, note in connection with the ORACLE research that it was found that teachers' styles were related to their ages. However, they argue that such a finding can really be understood only 'if data are gathered on teacher careers and life histories of a kind eschewed by ORACLE' (1984: 9). Of course, were such data collected, this criticism would have little weight, but the tendency of structured observation researchers to concentrate on overt behaviour tends to engender this kind of criticism.

On the other hand . . .

It is clear from the previous section that there are undeniable limitations to structured observation. However, it also has to be remembered that, when overt behaviour is the focus of analysis and perhaps issues of meaning are less salient, structured observation is almost certainly more accurate and effective than getting people to report on their behaviour through questionnaires.

It may also be that structured observation is a method that works best when accompanied by other methods. Since it can rarely provide reasons for observed patterns of behaviour, if it is accompanied by another method that can probe reasons, it is of greater utility. Delamont (1976) in her research in a school found FIAC to be useful as a means of exploring differences in teaching style between teachers. However, she was able to get at some of the reasons for the quantitative differences that she discerned only because she had carried out some participant observation and semi-structured interviewing (two of the main methods of qualitative research) in various school classes. For example, she compared two Latin teachers who were similar in certain respects but differed in terms of 'the proportion of questioning to lecturing in their speech' (Delamont 1976: 108). These differences in teaching style reflected contrasting views about teaching and differences in personal demeanour. Blatchford (2005) reports that the structured observation data that were collected in the research reported in Research in focus 11.1 were part of a wider study of the impact of variations in class size. The other methods employed were: termly questionnaires administered to teachers to gauge their estimates of how they allocated time in classrooms between different activities; end-of-year questionnaires administered to teachers asking them about their experiences of the impact of class size; and case studies of small and large classes comprising some semi-structured observation of events and semi-structured interviews with teachers and the head teacher.

In laboratory experiments in fields like social psychology, observation with varying degrees of structure is quite commonplace, but in social research structured observation has not been frequently used. Perhaps one major reason is that, although interviews and questionnaires are limited in terms of their capacity to tap behaviour accurately, as noted above, they do offer the opportunity to reveal information about both behaviour *and* attitudes and social backgrounds. In other words, they are more flexible and offer the prospect of being able to uncover a variety of correlates of behaviour (albeit reported behaviour), such as social background factors. They can also ask questions about attitudes and investigate explanations that people proffer for their behaviour. As a result, researchers using questionnaires are able to gain information about some factors that may lie behind the patterns of behaviour they uncover. Also, not all forms of behaviour are liable to be accessible to structured observation and it is likely that survey research or researcher-driven diaries (see Key concept 9.1) are the only likely means of gaining access to them. However, greater use of structured observation may result in greater facility with the method, so that reliable measures of the kind developed in areas like education might emerge.

Checklist

Structured observation research

- ◯ Have you clearly defined your research questions?
- ◯ Is the sample to be observed relevant to your research questions?
- ◯ Can you justify your sampling approach?
- ◯ Does your observation schedule indicate precisely which kinds of behaviour are to be observed?
- ◯ Have your observation categories been designed so that there is no need for the observer to interpret what is going on?
- ◯ Have you made sure that the categories of behaviour do not overlap?
- ◯ Do all the different categories of behaviour allow you to answer your research questions?
- ◯ Have you piloted your observation schedule?
- ◯ Are the coding instructions clear?
- ◯ Are the categories of behaviour inclusive?
- ◯ Is it easy to log the behaviour as it is happening?

Key points

- Structured observation is an approach to the study of behaviour that is an alternative to survey-based measures.
- It comprises explicit rules for the recording of behaviour.
- Structured observation has tended to be used in relation to a rather narrow range of forms of behaviour, such as that occurring in schools.
- It shares with survey research many common problems concerning reliability, validity, and generalizability.

- Reactive effects have to be taken into account but should not be exaggerated.
- Field stimulations represent a form of structured observation but suffer from difficulties concerning ethics.
- Problems with structured observation revolve around the difficulty of imputing meaning and ensuring that a relevant framework for recording behaviour is being employed.

Questions for review

Problems with survey research on social behaviour

- What are the chief limitations of survey research with regard to the study of behaviour?

So why not observe behaviour?

- What are the chief characteristics of structured observation?
- To what extent does it provide a superior approach to the study of behaviour than questionnaires or structured interviews?

The observation schedule

- What is an observation schedule?
- 'An observation schedule is much like a self-completion questionnaire or structured interview except that it does not entail asking questions.' Discuss.
- Devise an observation schedule of your own for observing an area of social interaction in which you are regularly involved. Ask people with whom you normally interact in those situations how well they think it fits what goes on. Have you missed anything out?

Strategies for observing behaviour

- What are the main ways in which behaviour can be recorded in structured observation?

Sampling

- Identify some of the main sampling strategies in structured observation.

Issues of reliability and validity

- How far do considerations of reliability and validity in structured observation mirror those encountered in relation to the asking of questions in structured interviews and self-completion questionnaires?
- What is the reactive effect and why might it be important in relation to structured observation research?

Field stimulations as a form of structured observation

- What are field stimulations and what ethical concerns are posed by them?

Criticisms of structured observation

- 'The chief problem with structured observation is that it does not allow us access to the intentions that lie behind behaviour.' Discuss.
- How far do you agree with the view that structured observation works best when used in conjunction with other research methods?

Online Resource Centre

http://www.oxfordtextbooks.co.uk/orc/brymansrm3e/

Visit the Online Resource Centre that accompanies this book to enrich your understanding of structured observation. Consult web links, test yourself using multiple choice questions, and gain further guidance and inspiration from the Student Researcher's Toolkit.

Content analysis

Chapter outline

Chapter guide

Content analysis is an approach to the analysis of documents and texts (which may be printed or visual) that seeks to quantify content in terms of predetermined categories and in a systematic and replicable manner. It is a very flexible method that can be applied to a variety of different media. In a sense, it is not a research method in that it is an approach to the analysis of documents and texts rather than a means of generating data. However, it is usually treated as a research method because of its distinctive approach to analysis. This chapter explores:

* the kinds of research question to which content analysis is suited;
* how to approach the sampling of documents to be analysed;
* what kinds of features of documents or texts are counted;
* how to go about *coding*, which is probably the central and most distinctive stage of doing a content analysis;
* the advantages and disadvantages of content analysis.

Introduction

Imagine that you are interested in the amount and nature of the interest shown by the mass media, such as newspapers, in a major news item such as AIDS/HIV or mad cow disease (BSE). You might ask such questions as:

* When did news items on this topic first begin to appear?
* Which newspapers were fastest in generating an interest in the topic?
* Which newspapers have shown the greatest interest in the topic?
* At what point did media interest begin to wane?
* Have journalists' stances on the topic changed—for example, in terms of pro- versus anti-science or pro- versus anti-government.

If you want to know the answers to research questions such as these, you are likely to need to use content analysis to answer them.

Probably the best-known definition of content analysis is as follows:

> Content analysis is a research technique for the objective, systematic and quantitative description of the manifest content of communication. (Berelson 1952: 18)

Another well-known and apparently similar definition is:

> Content analysis is any technique for making inferences by objectively and systematically identifying specified characteristics of messages. (Holsti 1969: 14)

It is striking that both these definitions contain a reference to two qualities: objectivity and being systematic. The former quality means that, as with something like an observation schedule (Chapter 11), rules are clearly specified in advance for the assignment of the raw material (such as newspaper stories) to categories. Objectivity in this sense resides in the fact that there is transparency in the procedures for assigning the raw material to categories, so that the analyst's personal biases intrude as little as possible in the process. The content analyst is simply applying the rules in question. The quality of being systematic means that the application of the rules is done in a consistent manner so that bias is again suppressed. As a result of these two qualities, anyone could employ the rules and (hopefully) come up with the same results. The process of analysis is one that means that the results are not an extension of the analyst and his or her personal biases. The rules in question may, of course, reflect the researcher's interests and concerns and therefore these might be a product of subjective bias, but the key point is that, once formulated, the rules can be (or should be capable of being) applied without the intrusion of bias.

Berelson's definition also makes reference to 'quantitative description'. Content analysis is firmly rooted in the quantitative research strategy in that the aim is to produce quantitative accounts of the raw material in terms of the categories specified by the rules. The feature of quantification adds to the general sense of the systematic and objective application of neutral rules, so that it becomes possible to say with some certainty and in a systematic way that, for example, during a certain period in which it was potentially at the forefront of media attention, *The Times* and other broadsheet newspapers carried far more coverage of AIDS/HIV than tabloid newspapers, with the interesting exception of the *Sun* (Beharrell 1993).

Two other elements in Berelson's definition are striking especially when juxtaposed against Holsti's. First, Berelson refers to 'manifest content'. This means that content analysis is concerned with uncovering the apparent content of the item in question: what it is clearly about. Holsti makes no such reference, alluding only to 'specified characteristics'. The latter essentially opens the door to conducting an analysis in terms of what we might term 'latent content'—that is, with meanings that lie beneath the superficial indicators of content. Uncovering such latent content means interpreting meanings that lie beneath the surface, such as whether the impression is given that the author construes the AIDS/HIV issue as one solely of concern in relation to the gay community and its sexual practices or as having a broader set of implications that would include heterosexuals. A related distinction is sometimes made between an emphasis on the text (in particular, counting certain words) and an emphasis on

themes within the text, which entails searching for certain ideas within the text (Beardsworth 1980).

A second element in Berelson's definition not found in Holsti's is the reference to 'communication'. Berelson's (1952) book was concerned with communication research, a field that has been especially concerned with newspapers, television, and other mass media. Holsti refers somewhat more generally to 'messages', which raises the prospect of a quite wide applicability of content analysis beyond the specific boundaries of the mass media and mass communications. Content analysis becomes applicable to many different forms of unstructured information, such as transcripts of semi- and unstructured interviews (e.g. Bryman, Stephens, and A Campo 1996) and even qualitative case studies of organizations (e.g. Research in focus 12.4). Nor is it necessary for the medium being analysed to be in a printed form. Research has been conducted on:

- the visual images (as well as the text) of women's and men's magazines to examine the degree to which messages about bodily appearance are gendered (Malkin *et al.* 1999);

- gender roles in animated cartoons (Davis 2003; see Research in focus 6.7);

- radio and television news programmes (see Research in focus 12.1 for an example);

- the lyrics of popular songs to reveal changes in the representation of women (Maric 2002).

However, there is little doubt that the main use of content analysis has been in the examination of printed texts and documents and of mass media items in particular. In this regard, content analysis is one of a number of approaches to the examination of texts that have been developed over the years (see Key concept 12.1).

Key concept 12.1
What is content analysis?

Content analysis is an approach to the analysis of documents and texts that seeks to quantify content in terms of predetermined categories and in a systematic and replicable manner.

Content analysis can be usefully contrasted with two other approaches to the analysis of the content of communication:

- *Semiotics*. The study/science of signs. An approach to the analysis of documents and other phenomena that emphasizes the importance of seeking out the deeper meaning of those phenomena. A semiotic approach is concerned to uncover the processes of meaning production and how signs are designed to have an effect upon actual and prospective consumers of those signs. This approach will be explored in Chapter 21.

- *Ethnographic content analysis*. A term employed by Altheide (1996) to refer to an approach to documents that emphasizes the role of the investigator in the construction of the meaning of and in texts. It is also sometimes referred to as ***qualitative content analysis***. As with most approaches that are described as ethnographic, there is an emphasis on allowing categories to emerge out of data and on recognizing the significance for understanding meaning in the context in which an item being analysed (and the categories derived from it) appeared. This approach will be explored in Chapter 21.

When the term 'content analysis' is employed in this chapter, it will be referring to quantitative content analysis—that is, the first of the three forms of analysis referred to in this list, which is the kind of analysis to which Berelson (1952) and Holsti (1969) refer.

What are the research questions?

As with most quantitative research, it is necessary to specify the research questions precisely, as these will guide both the selection of the media to be content analysed and the coding schedule. If the research questions are not clearly articulated, there is a risk that inappropriate media will be analysed or that the coding schedule will miss out key dimensions. Most content analysis is likely to entail several research questions. The research referred to in Research in focus 12.1 was concerned with 'the reporting of social science research in the British mass media'. In itself this is not very specific and hardly directs you to a clear specification of the media to be examined or the development of a coding schedule. However, like most researchers, Fenton *et al.* (1998) had certain specific research questions in mind, such as:

- How much social science research is reported?

- Do certain mass media report a disproportionate amount of social science research?

- In what locations does social science research tend to get reported (for example, special features rather than general news items)?

- Do some topics receive greater attention than others?

- Are certain social science disciplines favoured by the mass media?

- Do the mass media tend to report research conducted by particular methods?

- What tends to prompt the reporting of social science research?

- Are researchers of a particular status (for example, professors) or from certain institutions (for example, prestigious universities) more likely to receive coverage than others?

Such questions seem to revolve around the questions of: *who* (gets reported); *what* (gets reported); *where* (does the issue get reported); *location* (of coverage within the items analysed); *how much* (gets reported); and *why* (does the issue get reported).

As with much content analysis, the researchers were just as interested in omissions in coverage as in what *does* get reported. For example, details about the status of the researcher(s) and about research methods were frequently omitted. Such omissions are in themselves potentially interesting, as they may reveal what is and is not important to reporters and their editors.

Another kind of issue that is frequently encountered in content analysis is one that was not a concern for the researchers looking at the reporting of social science research:

How far does the amount of coverage of the issue change over time?

This kind of research question is particularly asked by researchers who are keen to note trends in coverage to

Research in focus 12.1
An illustration of content analysis: social science research in the British mass media

Fenton *et al.* (1998) conducted a study using content analysis of the amount and nature of the reporting of social science research in the British mass media. A **sample** of eighty-one days of media coverage between 26 May 1994 and 31 March 1995 was taken. The authors state: 'Any media item that mentioned original research conducted by a social scientist or social scientific institution, whether domestic or foreign, was coded, along with any times in which a social scientist (as identified by the item) commented on social issues' (Fenton *et al.* 1998: 24). The media monitored comprised:

- 12 national newspapers—6 broadsheet and 6 tabloid newspapers; 5 of the 12 newspapers were Sunday papers;
- 4 local newspapers—1 costed and 1 free newspaper from each of Nottingham and Manchester;
- 5 magazines—2 weekly women's publications, 2 monthly women's publications, and 1 monthly men's publication;
- 13 national and local television news programmes covering all four terrestrial television channels broadcasting at the time;
- 6 weekly investigative journalism/social reportage television programmes;
- 5 weekly/daily television talk shows/magazine programmes;
- any prime time *ad hoc* television programmes deemed relevant;
- national radio news on both Radio 4 and Radio 5 Live;
- 9 national Radio 4 investigative journalism/social reportage/studio talk shows and magazine programmes;
- local radio news in two regions: BBC Radio Nottingham and BBC GMR;
- local radio current affairs on BBC GMR Talkback.

The researchers uncovered 466 cases of research being reported. A further 126 news items were coded in which social scientists acted as pundits. The researchers included the cases of 'punditry' in many of their analyses, because the number of items in which social science research featured in news items was considerably smaller than they had envisaged.

Each news item was coded in terms of a number of features, such as:

- the source of the item (e.g. which newspaper or television programme);
- the topic of the research;
- the social science discipline referred to in the news item;
- when no social science discipline was referred to, the 'inferred discipline';
- the professional status of the researcher;
- the main research method employed.

demonstrate ebbs and flows in media interest. An example of this kind of research is a study by Miller and Reilly (1995) of British newspaper coverage of 'food scares'. They show how newspaper coverage of the salmonella in eggs scare was the focus of a massive amount of coverage of salmonella over a period of around twenty days in December 1988 following the statements of a British government minister and the ensuing controversy. However, in the eleven months prior to that, salmonella had rarely been in the news, and in the subsequent twelve months the amount of coverage was sharply lower than it had been in December 1988. It petered out further over the next four years. However, this decline in coverage occurred in spite of public health evidence that the incidence of salmonella poisoning was increasing. Similarly, Beharrell (1993) has charted for the period 1988–91 the changes in the amount of UK newspaper coverage of AIDS/HIV issues.

Selecting a sample

There are several phases in the selection of a sample for content analysis. Because it is a method that can be applied to many different kinds of document, the case of applying it to the mass media will be explored here. However, the basic principles have a broader relevance to a wide range of applications of content analysis.

Sampling media

Many studies of the mass media entail the specification of a research problem in the form of 'the representation of X in the mass media'. The X may be trade unions, food scares, crime, drink driving, or social science research. But which mass media might one choose to focus upon? Will it be newspapers or television or radio or magazines, or whatever? And, if newspapers, will it be all newspapers or tabloids or broadsheets? And, if both tabloids and broadsheets, will it be all of them and will it include Sunday papers? If it will be a sample of newspapers, including Sunday ones, will these be national or local or both? And will it include free newspapers? And if newspapers, will all news items be candidates for analysis—for example, would feature articles and letters to the editor be included?

The research reported in Research in focus 12.1 chose to cover a very wide variety of mass media, which is just as well, since the authors were not able to locate a very large number of appropriate items (news items covering social science research). More typically, researchers will opt for one or possibly two of the mass media and may sample within that type or types. Beharrell's (1993) study of the reporting and representation of AIDS/HIV in the British mass media concentrated on all national and Sunday national newspapers from November 1988 to August 1991, as a result of which a sample of over 4,000 news items was created.

Sampling dates

Sometimes, the decision about dates is more or less dictated by the occurrence of a phenomenon. For example, the representation of NATO bombing raids in Serbia in 1999 will have been dictated by the inception of the raids. One could hardly examine the issue prior to the raids, though there may be an important consideration in deciding at what point the content analysis should cease, since discussions about the raids could continue for some time after the cessation of formal hostilities and may entail a reappraisal as a result of subsequent events.

With a research question that entails an ongoing general phenomenon, such as the representation of social science research or crime, the matter of dates is more open. The principles of probability sampling outlined in Chapter 7 can readily be adapted for sampling dates. For example, it is possible to generate a systematic sample of dates by randomly selecting one day of the week and then selecting every nth day thereafter. Alternatively, Monday newspapers could provide the first set of newspapers for inclusion, followed by Tuesday the following week, Wednesday the week after, and so on.

One important factor is whether the focus will be on an issue that entails keeping track of representation as it happens, in which case the researcher may begin at any time and the key decision becomes when to stop, or whether it is necessary to go backwards in time to select media from one or more time periods in the past. For example, if Jagger (1998) had wanted to examine whether there had been a marked change in the ways in which men and women represent themselves in dating advertisements (see Research in focus 12.2), she would obviously have needed to examine the columns of earlier years. She might have taken comparable samples from ten and twenty years earlier and perhaps even beyond. Warde

Research in focus 12.2
Finding love

Jagger (1998) reports a content analysis of 1,094 dating advertisements in two Scottish newspapers and two newspapers with a general readership throughout Britain. The sample of advertisements was chosen over two four-week periods: March 1996 and May 1996. Three research questions drove the study.

- What is 'the relative significance of resources and lifestyle choices as identity markers and desirable attributes for men and women' (1998: 799)?

- How far do men and women vary in the degree to which they market themselves and describe their preferred (or ideal) partners in terms of the body?

- How far are 'traditional stereotypes of masculinity and femininity . . . still in operation' (1998: 799)?

Jagger particularly noted the tendency for a considerable percentage of the advertisers to market themselves in terms of their lifestyle choices, a tendency that was not substantially affected by gender. She also found that women were far more likely than men to stress the importance of economic and other resources for their preferred partners. There was also a somewhat greater propensity for women to market themselves in terms of physical appearance. However, men were just as likely to market themselves as 'slim', suggesting that certain norms of bodily shape may no longer be exclusive to one gender. Jagger also found that men frequently market themselves in 'feminine' terms and women in 'masculine' terms—a rather surprising finding. More generally, her results point to the significance of the body in identity construction in modern society for both men and women. In a later publication, Jagger (2005) explores the ways in which consumer culture has had an impact on the representation of the self in this same sample of dating advertisements. She shows that the significance of a person's age and how that is represented varies for men and women.

(1997) was interested in changes in the representation of food (what should be eaten and how it should be eaten) in the food columns of women's magazines. He writes:

> My primary sources were the five most widely read women's weekly magazines and the five most widely read monthly magazines in each of two twelve-month periods in 1967–8 and 1991–2. The magazines were sampled at the mid-point of the months of November, February, May and August in each year, in order to control for seasonal variation in the contents of food columns. . . . From the selected magazines I drew a systematic sample of recipes. This produced 114 recipes in the earlier year, 124 in the later period[,] which, given their random selection, should be sufficient to make some generalizations about recipes and any changes over time. (Warde 1997: 44–5)

Three points stand out in this passage. First, there is the concern, which has just been alluded to, with being able to establish change by tracking back in time to earlier issues of the mass medium being analysed. Second, Warde wanted to ensure that the magazines were selected from four different points in each of the two twelve-month periods in order to ensure that seasonal factors did not overly influence the findings. If he had selected magazines just from November, there might have been a preoccupation with Christmas fare, while findings from magazines from a summer month might have been affected by the greater availability of certain foods, such as particular fruit. A decision was made to cover the four seasons in order to reduce the impact of such factors. Third, there is a clear concern to enhance the representativeness of the recipes and therefore the **generalizability** of the findings by using a probability sampling method in that a systematic sample was arrived at (see Chapter 7).

What is to be counted?

Obviously, decisions about what should be counted in the course of a content analysis are bound to be profoundly affected by the nature of the research questions under consideration. Content analysis offers the prospect of different kinds of 'units of analysis' being considered. The following kinds of units of analysis are frequently encountered and can be used as guides to the kinds of objects that might be the focus of attention. However, what you would actually *want* or *need* to count will be significantly dictated by your research questions.

Significant actors

Particularly in the context of mass media news reporting, the main figures in any news item and their characteristics are often important items to code. These considerations are likely to result in such persons as the following being recorded in the course of a content analysis.

- What kind of person has produced the item (e.g. general or specialist news reporter)?

- Who is or are the main focus of the item (e.g. politician, expert, government spokesperson, or representative of an organization)?

- Who provides alternative voices (e.g. politician, expert, government spokesperson, representative of an organization, or person in the street)?

- What was the context for the item (e.g. interview, release of a report, or an event such as an outbreak of hostilities or a minister's visit to a hospital)?

In the case of the content analysis of the reporting of social science research in the mass media (see Research in focus 12.1), the significant actors included:

- the author of the item (e.g. type of correspondent);

- the type of item (e.g. in the case of the press, whether the research was reported in a general article, feature article, or some other context);

- the details of the researcher who was most prominent in the item (e.g. personal details, status, and whether he or she was acting as a researcher or pundit in the context of the item);

- what prompted the item (e.g. launch of a report, new research initiative, or a conference);

- the details of the main (if any) commentators on the research;

- any other actors.

The chief objective in recording such details is to map the main protagonists in news reporting in an area and to begin to reveal some of the mechanics involved in the production of information for public consumption.

Words

While it may seem a dull activity, the counting of the frequency with which certain words occur is sometimes undertaken in content analysis. However, the use of some words rather than others can often be of some significance, because it can reveal the predilection for sensationalizing certain events. For example, Dunning *et al.* (1988) have noted a tendency for the British press in the late 1960s to sensationalize the reporting of disturbances at football matches. The use of such emotive words as 'hooligan' and 'lout', along with inferences about 'war', are clearly significant. Alternative, less dramatic terms could have been used. Instead, the florid accounts of violence at football matches may have created the kind of 'moral panic' that Cohen (1973) has written about. While Dunning *et al.* did not conduct a content analysis of such news reporting, their analysis points to the potential significance of the choice of certain words and the neglect of others. Jagger's (1998) study of dating advertisements (see Research in focus 12.2) counted such words as 'slim' and 'non-smoker' to uncover some of the characteristics deemed desirable.

A variation on the search for the occurrence of certain words is the examination of keywords in the context of other words. Hansen (1995) provides an interesting example in a study of the reporting of BSE (mad cow disease) in the *Today* newspaper. He found that news items in which BSE appeared often included other prominent words, such as 'beef', 'food', 'meat', 'pounds [£]', 'Government', and 'ban'. The frequency with which such words accompanied 'mad', 'cow', and 'disease' led Hansen (1995: 159) to infer that 'there is a clear indication . . . that the coverage focuses on: (1) the danger which the disease poses for a key component of the British diet, (2) on costs, and (3) on what the government is doing or should be doing about it'. The examination of such key accompanying words can then be a springboard for a more thematic analysis (see next section). Hansen notes that the frequent occurrence of certain words suggests certain types of 'discourse'. For example, he identifies a discourse concerned with the *transmission* of BSE (such words as: infected, catch, spread, etc.) and a discourse

emphasizing risk and threat (such words as: safe, risk, fears, danger, etc.). Tips and skills 'Counting words in electronic news reports' discusses the use of this kind of analysis in the context of electronic newspapers. An interesting example of a content analysis that emphasizes words can be found in Research in focus 12.3.

Tips and skills
Counting words in electronic news reports

The growing availability of the printed news media in electronic form, such as CD-ROM and in electronic databases, greatly facilitates the search for and counting of keywords in this kind of context. Most of the main UK newspapers and many overseas ones are available in electronic format either through their own websites or through a website like British Media Online (**http://www.wrx.zen.co.uk/britnews.htm** (accessed on 3 July 2007)), which acts as a launch pad for a host of different electronic newspapers. The newspapers can then usually be searched for keywords and phrases. You will probably need a password (for example, Athens authentication to access them), especially if you are seeking to access them away from your university or college.

Further, some simple analyses can be conducted using Lexis Nexis. This database comprises newspaper articles from a wide variety of newspapers. For example, Beardsworth and Bryman (2004) used Lexis Nexis Professional to search this database for the years 1985 to 2002 for the incidence of keywords relating to BSE, such as: Bovine Spongiform Encelphalopathy; BSE; CJD; and Creuzfeld Jacob Disease. They chart the number of reports using at least one of these terms in each newspaper per annum. Their analysis shows how there was a small surge of media reporting around 1990 and then a huge 'spike' in the mid-1990s, when it attracted a great deal of media interest, and then a trailing-off in the incidence of reporting. They also show how the statistics for beef and veal consumption in the UK display a corresponding pattern. This article demonstrates the use of a simple counting procedure that can be quite revealing and that is greatly facilitated by the availability of electronic (and in this case online) mass media.

Research in focus 12.3
A keyword analysis of postings to cancer websites

Seale *et al.* (2006) report the results of a study in which he retrieved all postings on a single day (20 April 2005) to online forums of the two most prevalent websites in the UK concerned with breast and prostate cancer. Keywords in this research were words that occur with unusual frequency compared with other words in the corpus that is analysed. In this case, Seale and his colleagues were interested in keyword frequency in the breast cancer postings as compared to the prostate cancer postings. The search for keywords was undertaken with specialist software called *Wordsmith* (**http://www.lexically.net/wordsmith/** (accessed on 3 July 2007)). Seale *et al.* (2006: 2582) then 'used this quantitative information to facilitate an interpretive, qualitative analysis focusing on the meanings of word clusters associated with keywords'. Thus, Seale and his colleagues use this quantitative analysis of words as a springboard for a more probing qualitative examination of the links between the words. They found that men with prostate cancer were more likely to use words associated with research (e.g. 'study'), treatment (e.g. 'radical prostatectomy'), and tests and diagnosis (e.g. 'biopsy') compared to women discussing breast cancer. By contrast, women discussing breast cancer were more likely to use keywords associated with feelings (e.g. 'scared') and people (e.g. 'family') and also to use superlatives (e.g. 'amazing'). Other differences were found but these are among the more striking ones. A further level of comparison was that Seale and his colleagues conducted the same kind of keyword analysis of transcripts of qualitative interviews with people suffering from both kinds of cancer. This allowed them to infer differences in keywords relating to the interview context and the more public one of Internet postings.

Subjects and themes

Frequently in a content analysis the researcher will want to code text in terms of certain subjects and themes. Essentially, what is being sought is a categorization of the phenomenon or phenomena of interest. For example, in the case of the content analysis of the reporting of social science research in the British mass media, Fenton *et al.* (1998) were concerned to classify the main social science discipline that formed the backcloth to the research being reported (Research in focus 12.1). This entailed a classification into one of seven types: sociology; social policy; economics; psychology; business and management; political science; and interdisciplinary. Research drawing on other social science disciplines was not included in the study. Another topic was the methodology of the research being reported, which resulted in research being classified in terms of such categories as: survey/mail questionnaire; interview; ethnography; and, of course, content analysis.

However, while such categorizations are often relatively straightforward, when the process of coding is thematic, a more interpretative approach needs to be taken. At this point, the analyst is searching not just for manifest content but latent content as well. It becomes necessary to probe beneath the surface in order to ask deeper questions about what is happening. In the research on social science research in the mass media (see Research in focus 12.1), each reported study was classified in terms of the subject area of the research (Fenton *et al.* 1998). Sixty-two categories were employed and were grouped into seven main areas: UK and overseas economy; UK and overseas government politics and policy; social integration and control; health; demographics; social analysis—general; and lifestyles. Another example of having to interpret derives from the researchers' examination of what they refer to as the 'inferred discipline' involved in a

reported piece of research. This issue arose because, in many cases (nearly 60 per cent of all news items in which social science research was reported), no social science discipline was mentioned in the news report, so that it was necessary to infer which discipline was involved.

Dispositions

A further level of interpretation is likely to be entailed when the researcher seeks to demonstrate a disposition in the texts being analysed. For example, it may be that the researcher wants to establish whether journalists, in the reporting of an issue in the news media, are favourably inclined or hostile towards an aspect of it, such as their stances on the government's handling of a food scare crisis. In the case of the study by Fenton *et al.* (1998; see Research in focus 12.1) of the reporting of social science research, each item was coded in terms of whether the editorial commentary on the research was positive, negative, or merely descriptive. In many cases, it was necessary to infer whether the editorial commentary was implicitly positive or negative if there were no manifest indications of such value positions. Such an analysis entails establishing whether a judgemental stance can be discerned in the items being coded and the nature of the judgement.

Another way in which dispositions may be revealed in content analysis is through the coding of ideologies, beliefs, or principles. Jagger (1998) coded dating advertisements in terms of whether gendered stereotypical categories of masculinity and femininity were employed when advertisers were describing themselves (see Research in focus 12.2). She came up with the surprising finding that women were more likely than men to advertise themselves in terms of a masculine stereotype, while men were more likely to advertise themselves in terms of a feminine stereotype.

Coding

As much of the foregoing discussion has implied, coding is a crucial stage in the process of doing a content analysis. There are two main elements to a content analysis coding scheme: designing a coding schedule and designing a coding manual. To illustrate its use, imagine a student interested in crime reporting in a local newspaper. The student chooses to focus on the reporting of crimes subject to court proceedings and where the victim is a person rather than an organization. To simplify the issue we will just have the following variables:

1. nature of the offence;
2. gender of perpetrator;
3. social class of perpetrator;
4. age of perpetrator;
5. gender of victim;
6. social class of victim;
7. age of victim;
8. depiction of victim;
9. position of news item.

Content analysts would normally be interested in a much larger number of variables than this, but a simple illustration like this can be helpful for getting across the operation of a coding schedule and a coding manual. Also, it is quite likely that the student would want to record the item so that the details of more than one offender and more than one victim are included. In other words, very often a crime will entail multiple perpetrators and/or victims, so that the details of each of the key figures (age, gender, occupation, depiction of victim) would need to be recorded. However, to keep the illustration simple, just one perpetrator and victim is assumed.

Coding schedule

The coding schedule is a form onto which all the data relating to an item being coded will be entered. Figure 12.1 provides an example of a coding schedule. The schedule is very much a simplification in order to facilitate the discussion of the principles of coding in content analysis and of the construction of a coding schedule in particular.

Each of the columns in Figure 12.1 is a dimension that is being coded. The column headings indicate the dimension to be coded. The blank cells on the coding form are the places in which codes are written in. One form would be used for each media item that was coded. The codes can then be transferred to a computer data file for analysis with a software package like SPSS (see Chapter 15).

Coding manual

On the face of it, the coding schedule in Figure 12.1 seems very bare and does not appear to provide much information about what is to be done or where. This is where the coding manual comes in. The coding manual is a statement of instructions to coders that also includes all the possible categories for each dimension being coded. It provides: a list of all the dimensions; the different categories subsumed under each dimension; the numbers (i.e. *codes*) that correspond to each category; and guidance on what each dimension is concerned with and any factors that should be taken into account in deciding how to allocate any particular code to each dimension. Figure 12.2 provides the coding manual that might correspond to the coding schedule in Figure 12.1. A coding manual includes all the dimensions that would be employed in

Figure 12.1

Coding schedule

Case number	Day	Month	Year	Nature of offence I	Gender of perpetrator	Occupation of perpetrator	Age of perpetrator	Gender of victim	Occupation of victim	Age of victim	Depiction of victim	Nature of offence II

Figure 12.2

Coding manual

Nature of offence I

1. Violence against the person
2. Sexual offences
3. Robbery
4. Burglary in a dwelling
5. Burglary other than in a dwelling
6. Theft from a person
7. Theft of pedal cycle
8. Theft from shops
9. Theft from vehicle
10. Theft of motor vehicle
11. Vehicle interference and tampering
12. Other theft and handling stolen goods
13. Fraud and forgery
14. Criminal damage
15. Drug offences
16. Other notifiable offences

Gender of perpetrator

1. Male
2. Female
3. Unknown

Occupation of perpetrator

1. I Higher grade professionals, administrators, and officials; managers in large establishments; large proprietors
2. II Lower-grade professionals, administrators, and officials; higher-grade technicians; managers in small business and industrial establishments; supervisors of nonmanual employees
3. IIIa Routine nonmanual employees in administration and commerce
4. IIIb Personal service workers
5. IVa Small proprietors, artisans, etc., with employees
6. IVb Small proprietors, artisans, etc., without employees
7. IVc Farmers and smallholders; self-employed fishermen
8. V Lower-grade technicians, supervisors of manual workers
9. VI Skilled manual workers
10. VIIa Semi-skilled and unskilled manual workers (not in agriculture)

11. VIIb Agricultural workers
12. Unemployed
13. Retired
14. Housewife
15. Student
16. Other
17. Unknown

Age of perpetrator

Record age (−1 if unknown)

Gender of victim

1. Male
2. Female
3. Unknown
4. Organization (if victim is an organization as in fraud cases)

Occupation of victim

Same as for occupation of perpetrator
If not applicable, code as 99

Age of victim

Record age (−1 if unknown; −2 if not applicable)

Depiction of victim

1. Victim responsible for crime
2. Victim partly responsible for crime
3. Victim not at all responsible for crime
4. Not applicable

Nature of offence II (code if second offence mentioned in relation to the same incident; code 0 if no second offence)
Same as for Nature of offence I

Position of news item

1. Front page
2. Inside
3. Back page

the coding process, indications of the guidance for coders, and the kinds of lists of categories that were created for each dimension.

The coding manual includes the occupation of both the perpetrator and the victim. It uses Goldthorpe's social class categorization and is based on the summary by Marshall *et al.* (1988: 22). To this scheme have been added three further categories that might be used in newspapers: unemployed; retired; and housewife. There is also a category of 'other'. The offences are categorized in terms of those used by the police in recording crimes notified to them according to Home Office rules. Much finer distinctions could be used, but, since the student may not be planning to examine a large sample of news items, broader categories might be preferable. They have the further advantage of being comparable to the Home Office data. Recorded crime statistics have been criticized for their lack of reliability and validity (see Chapter 13), but the comparison between such data and the reporting of crime in local newspapers would be potentially illuminating.

The coding schedule and manual permit two offences to be recorded when an incident entails more than one offence. If there are more than two, the student has to make a judgement concerning the most significant offence. The student should also treat as the first offence the main one mentioned in the article.

The coding manual is crucial because it provides coders with complete listings of all categories for each dimension they are coding and guidance about how to interpret the dimensions. It is on the basis of these lists and guidance that a coding schedule of the kind presented in Figure 12.1 will be completed. Even if you are a lone researcher, such as a student conducting a content analysis for a dissertation or thesis, it is important to spend a lot of time providing yourself with instructions about how to code. While you may not face the problem of inter-coder reliability, the issue of intra-coder reliability is still significant for you (see below).

Plates 12.1 and 12.2 provide examples of the kind of article that might appear. Both are from the *Nottingham Evening Post*.

The coding of the incident in Plate 12.1 would then appear as in Figure 12.1 and the data would be entered into a computer program like SPSS as follows:

123 27 12 02 1 1 17 46 1 17 –1 3 16 2

A form like that in Figure 12.3 would be completed for the news item and the data from each form would then be entered as a row of data in a computer program like SPSS. Note that the news item in Plate 12.2 contains a second offence, which has been coded as 16 under 'Nature of offence II'. Figure 12.4 contains the form that would be completed for the item in Plate 12.2. The following row of data would be created:

301 04 07 03 1 1 17 24 1 5 –1 3 0 2

Figure 12.3

Completed coding schedule for news item in Plate 12.1

Case number	Day	Month	Year	Nature of offence I	Gender of perpetrator	Occupation of perpetrator	Age of perpetrator	Gender of victim	Occupation of victim	Age of victim	Depiction of victim	Nature of offence II	Position of news item
123	27	12	02	1	1	17	46	1	17	–1	3	16	2

Figure 12.4

Completed coding schedule for news item in Plate 12.2

Case number	Day	Month	Year	Nature of offence I	Gender of perpetrator	Occupation of perpetrator	Age of perpetrator	Gender of victim	Occupation of victim	Age of victim	Depiction of victim	Nature of offence II	Position of news item
301	04	07	03	1	1	17	24	1	5	–1	3	0	2

Plate 12.1

Reporting a crime in local newspapers I

Dogs fighting led to assault

Owner guilty of chain attack and cruelty

By SEAN KENNY

IT began with a fight between two dogs — but ended when one owner faced assault and animal cruelty charges.

Conrad Aaron Martin, 46, of Leybourne Drive, Bestwood, attacked a dog and its owner with a chain when they met while out for a morning walk, Nottingham magistrates heard.

He was out with his English and Staffordshire bull terrier cross, on May 27 on the Hucknall Embankment in Bestwood when his pet met Rocco Lamagna's German shepherd dog, Lupo, out for his morning walk.

The terrier locked his teeth around Lupo's front leg and Mr Lamagna, of Bestwood, asked Martin to control his dog.

But, the court was told, Martin replied: "I'm going to kill you... and your dog."

Mr Lamagna told the court: "He got a massive chain and hit me and the dog with it.

"I tried to bend over my dog, I couldn't do anything. My dog was bleeding from his eye."

Mr Lamagna told the court he had not taken his dog along that route since the incident.

Talking to the *Post* after the trial, Mr Lamagna said: "The attack was totally unexpected.

"I'd just come out of hospital and was taking Lupo for a walk when his dog went for mine."

Mr Lamagna controlled his dog and tried to protect him: "Lupo's eye was bleeding and I tried to cover him to stop him getting bitten again.

"The vet's bill cost me £65.

"I used to walk Lupo down there all the time, but I never go there now."

Denied

The court heard that after Mr Lamagna reported the attack to the police, investigations led to an identity parade being organised.

Mr Lamagna immediately picked out Martin, the court was told.

Martin had denied the charges of assault and cruelty to animals, but was found guilty.

He told the court: "There's nothing I wouldn't do to defend my dog."

Magistrate Mrs Ann Allison said: "We accept Mr Lamagna was certain when he picked you out at the identity parade."

Martin has two previous convictions for affray whilst walking his dog, in November and December last year.

His sentence will be decided by the crown court.

FIGHT VICTIMS: Rocco Lamagna and his dog Lupo.   *C241202SO7-1*

From *Nottingham Evening Post*, 27 Dec. 2002, p. 12. Reprinted with kind permission of the publisher.

Plate 12.2

Reporting a crime in local newspapers II

Landlords hit out as pub attacker avoids jail

PUB ASSAULT: Injured landlord Paul Buxton and, left, his assailant Tom Turton

ANGRY licensees have blasted the "deplorable" sentence given to a violent customer.

Tom Turton, 24, poked his thumbs into landlord Paul Buxton's eyes after being asked to leave the Lady Bay pub in Trent Boulevard.

Turton, of Fourth Avenue, Sherwood Rise, was ordered to do 200 hours community service by Nottingham magistrates after admitting common assault. He was also told to pay £170 compensation and £55 costs.

The sentence has outraged members of the West Bridgford Pubwatch scheme, of which Mr Buxton is a member.

Letter

Today they were sending a letter to the Chairman of the Magistrates Bench which reads: "We are writing to express our disgust at the leniency of the sentence given to the accused Tom Turton. What kind of message are we giving out here?"

The landlords described the handling of the case, including numerous adjournments, as "deplorable".

The Pubwatch group is also taking legal advice about whether to appeal against the decision.

Alan Merryweather, the Pubwatch vice-chairman who runs the Test Match Inn in West Bridgford, said: "I don't know what guidelines the magistrates have, but Turton should have got a six month custodial sentence.

"We feel that reflects the severity of the injuries."

Assaulted landlord Paul Buxton said: "I don't think his sentence was stiff enough.

"He needs a short, sharp shock — but the message that's gone out is smack a landlord and you'll get away with it.

"No-one should go to work and get punched or poked in the eyes."

Magistrates heard that on Sunday, March 9, Turton had spent all afternoon and evening drinking in the Lady Bay pub, downing six or seven pints of lager.

At closing time, he became enraged when Mr Buxton jokingly told him to leave.

Dennis Quinn, prosecuting, told the court: "He deliberately stuck both thumbs in each of Mr Buxton's eyes.

"Mr Buxton said he could feel the thumbs in his eye sockets."

The landlord suffered cuts to the rear of his eyes. It has left him with occasional blurred vision and needing eye drops, but there will be no lasting damage.

Mr Turton was the first person to be banned from all 22 pubs within the West Bridgford Pubwatch.

Sundeep Soor, in mitigation, said it was Turton's first violent offence and he was very remorseful".

Disgust at 'lenient' sentence

ANGRY: Mr Buxton with the letter sent to magistrates and, above, the Lady Bay pub

Graham Hooper, Justices Clerk at Nottingham Magistrates' Court, said the maximum penalty for common assault is a £5,000 fine or six months in prison.

He added: "When a licensee or someone going about their business serving the public is assaulted that's seen as a fact which makes the offence more serious.

"But magistrates are required to look at the circumstances of the offender and consider each case on its merits."

From *Nottingham Evening Post*, 4 July 2003, p. 5. Reprinted with kind permission of the publisher.

Forms like these would be completed for each news item within the chosen period or periods of study.

Potential pitfalls in devising coding schemes

There are several potential dangers in devising a content analysis coding scheme, and they are very similar to the kinds of consideration that are involved in the design of structured interview and structured observation schedules.

- *Discrete dimensions*. Make sure that your dimensions are entirely separate; in other words, there should be no conceptual or empirical overlap between them. For example, in the research presented in Research in focus 12.1, it is necessary to be clear about the difference between discipline and topic of the research even though they have a similar ring.

- *Mutually exclusive categories*. Make sure that there is no overlap in the categories supplied for each dimension. If the categories are not mutually exclusive, coders will be unsure about how to code each item.

- *Exhaustive categories*. For each dimension, all possible categories should be available to coders.

- *Clear instructions*. Coders should be clear about how to interpret what each dimension is about and what factors to take into account when assigning codes to each category. Sometimes, these will have to be very elaborate. Coders should have little or no discretion in how to allocate codes to units of analysis.

- *Clarity about the unit of analysis*. For example, in the study of social science research in the mass media (see Research in focus 12.1), the authors found it necessary to operate with a clear distinction between the media item (e.g. a newspaper article) and the social science research being reported. Thus some of the data recorded were to do with the media item; other data

recorded were to do with the research being referred to. The researchers' content analysed up to three social science research profiles per media item, because often the media reporting of research referred to more than one investigation. In the study reported in Research in focus 6.7, 167 cartoons were sampled, but it was the *characters* in those cartoons that provided the units of analysis. As a result, characteristics of the 478 characters were coded and analysed. Similarly, in the imaginary study of the media reporting of crime in the local press, more than one offence per media item could be recorded. You need to be clear about the distinction between the media item (e.g. a newspaper article) and the topic being coded (an offence). In practice, a researcher is interested in both but needs to keep the distinction in mind.

In order to be able to enhance the quality of a coding scheme, it is highly advisable to pilot early versions of the scheme. Piloting will help to identify difficulties in applying the coding scheme, such as uncertainty about which category to employ when considering a certain dimension or discovering that no code is available to cover a particular case. Piloting will also help to identify any evidence that one category of a dimension tends to subsume an extremely large percentage of items. If this occurs, it may be necessary to consider breaking that category down so that it allows greater discrimination between the items being analysed.

The reliability of coding is a further potential area of concern. Coding must be done in a consistent manner. As with structured observation, coding must be consistent between coders (*inter-coder reliability*), and each coder must be consistent over time (*intra-coder reliability*). An important part of piloting the coding scheme will be testing for consistency between coders and, if time permits, intra-coder reliability. The process of gauging reliability is more or less identical to that briefly covered in the context of structured observation in Key concept 11.3.

Advantages of content analysis

Content analysis has several advantages, which are outlined below.

- Content analysis is a very transparent research method. The coding scheme and the sampling proce-

dures can be clearly set out so that replications and follow-up studies are feasible. It is this transparency that often causes content analysis to be referred to as an objective method of analysis.

- It can allow a certain amount of longitudinal analysis with relative ease. Several of the studies referred to above allow the researcher to track changes in frequency over time (Beharrell 1993; Miller and Reilly 1995; Warde 1997). For example, Warde's (1997) research entailed an analysis of women's magazines over two different time periods. Similarly, changes in emphasis in crime reporting in newspapers over two very different periods can be examined.

- Content analysis is often referred to favourably as an *unobtrusive method*, a term devised by Webb *et al.* (1966) to refer to a method that does not entail participants in a study having to take the researcher into account (see Key concept 13.3). It is therefore a *non-reactive method* (see Key concept 11.4 and 13.3). However, this point has to be treated with a little caution. It is certainly the case that, when the focus of a content analysis is upon things such as newspaper articles or television programmes, there is no **reactive effect**. Newspaper articles are obviously not written in the knowledge that a content analysis may one day be carried out on them. On the other hand, if the content

analysis is being conducted on documents such as interview transcripts or ethnographies (e.g. Hodson 1996; see Research in focus 12.4), while the process of content analysis does not itself introduce a reactive effect, the documents may have at least partly been influenced by such an effect.

- It is a highly flexible method. It can be applied to a wide variety of different kinds of unstructured information. While content analysis is often associated with the analysis of mass media outputs, it has a much broader applicability than this. Research in focus 12.4 presents an illustration of a rather unusual but none the less interesting application of content analysis.

- Content analysis can allow information to be generated about social groups to which it is difficult to gain access. For example, most of our knowledge of the social backgrounds of elite groups, such as senior clergy, company directors, and top military personnel, derives from content analyses of such publications as *Who's Who* and *Burke's Peerage* (Bryman 1974).

Student experience
The significance of the transparency of content analysis

For her research on the front covers of women's magazines, Sarah Hanson felt that the transparency of the research method she had chosen was significant. She writes:

My supervisor, Kristin, influenced my research methods a lot, as, having never done a study quite so large before, I needed a good way to organize my research and writing. By introducing Bryman's *Social Research Methods* (Second Edition) and the chapter on Content Analysis into my dissertation, I was able to do a lot of research within a controlled environment; my total word count for the research in my appendix tables was over 2,000 words. Content analysis allows for many different types of research and data collection to be easily carried out and studied, allowing you to work methodically throughout the decoding and analysis. By including content analysis in my dissertation, it allowed for easy reference throughout the text and allowed the marker to see the 'mathematical' workings, providing proof of how I came to my final conclusions.

It is nice to know one's work has an impact!

To read more about Sarah's research experiences, go to the Online Resource Centre that accompanies this book at **http://www.oxfordtextbooks.co.uk/orc/brymansrm3e/**.

Research in focus 12.4
A content analysis of qualitative research on the workplace

Hodson (1996: 724) reports the results of a content analysis of 'book-length ethnographic studies based on sustained periods of direct observation'. There is an excellent website in connection with the Workplace Ethnography Project, which can be found at **http://www.sociology.ohio-state.edu/rdh/Workplace-Ethnography-Project.html** (accessed on 19 February 2007). As a method, ethnography, which will be explored in detail in Chapter 17, entails a long period of **participant observation** in order to understand the culture of a social group. Hodson's content analysis concentrated on ethnographic studies of workplaces that had been published in book form (that is, published articles were excluded because they rarely included sufficient detail). Thousands of case studies were assessed for possible inclusion in the sample. The sample was made up of studies from different countries and included some well-known British ones (Beynon 1975; Nichols and Beynon 1977; Pollert 1981; Cavendish 1982). Early publications based on the content analysis derived from 86 ethnographies were selected, which meant that 106 cases were analysed (several published ethnographies were of more than one case). According to the Workplace Ethnography Project website **http://www.sociology.ohio-state.edu/rdh/Workplace-Ethnography-Project.html** (accessed on 19 February 2007), the current and probably final tally is described as follows: 'The study generated 204 ethnographic cases. These cases were derived from 156 separate books since the observations reported in some books allowed the coding of multiple cases.' The difference arises because newer ethnographies have been gradually incorporated into the database since this early article.

In Hodson (1996) each case was coded in terms of one of five types of workplace organization (craft, direct supervision, assembly line, bureaucratic, and worker participation). This was the **independent variable**. Various **dependent variables** and 'control' variables (variables deemed to have an impact on the **relationships** between independent and dependent variables) were also coded.

Here are two of the variables and their codes.

WORKERS:

Job satisfaction
1 = very low; 2 = moderately low; 3 = average;
4 = high; 5 = very high

Autonomy
1 = none (the workers' tasks are completely determined by others, by machinery or by organizational rules); 2 = little (workers occasionally have the chance to select among procedures or priorities); 3 = average (regular opportunities to select procedures or set priorities within definite limits); 4 = high (significant latitude in determining procedures and setting priorities); 5 = very high (significant interpretation is needed to reach broadly specified goals) (Hodson 1996: 728).

Hodson's findings suggest that some pessimistic accounts of worker participation schemes (for example, that they do not genuinely permit participation and do not necessarily have a beneficial impact on the worker) are incomplete. A more detailed treatment of this research can be found in Hodson (1999). Since this early 1996 publication, many others have been published in major journals, including the article on social fulfillment at the workplace (Hodson 2004), which was referred to on page 72 in Chapter 3. Through his test of the competing hypotheses, Hodson was able to show that there are gender and occupational status differences in the richness of social affiliation at work.

Not only does the website provide a list of publications deriving from the project (including downloadable pdf files of most of the articles) and all the coding information, you can download the data into SPSS, which is the software that will be covered in Chapter 15.

Disadvantages of content analysis

Like all research techniques, content analysis suffers from certain limitations, which are described below.

- A content analysis can only be as good as the documents on which the practitioner works. Scott (1990) recommends assessing documents in terms of such criteria as: authenticity (that the document is what it purports to be); credibility (whether there are grounds for thinking that the contents of the document have been or are distorted in some way); and representativeness (whether the documents examined are representative of all possible relevant documents, as, if certain kinds of document are unavailable or no longer exist, generalizability will be jeopardized). These kinds of consideration will be especially important to bear in mind when a content analysis is being conducted on documents like letters. These issues will be explored in further detail in Chapter 21.

- It is almost impossible to devise coding manuals that do not entail some interpretation on the part of coders. Coders must draw upon their everyday knowledge as participants in a common culture in order to be able to code the material with which they are confronted (Cicourel 1964; Garfinkel 1967). To the extent that this occurs, it is questionable whether it is justifiable to assume a correspondence of interpretation between the persons responsible for producing the documents being analysed and the coders (Beardsworth 1980).

- Particular problems are likely to arise when the aim is to impute latent rather than manifest content. In searching for traditional markers of masculinity and femininity (Research in focus 12.2) or inferring a social science discipline (Research in focus 12.1), the potential for an invalid conjecture being made is magnified.

- It is difficult to ascertain the answers to 'why?' questions through content analysis. For example, Jagger (1998: 807) found that 'the body of their partner, its attractiveness, shape and size, was of less importance to advertisers when in the buying mode [advertising for a partner]' than when in the selling mode (market-

ing oneself) (see Research in focus 12.2). Why? And finding that this was true of both men and women is, as Jagger suggests, even more surprising. But again, why? We can speculate, but our suggested answers can usually only be speculations. Similarly, Fenton *et al.* (1998) found that sociology was only the fourth most common discipline to be referred to when social science research was being reported (see Research in focus 12.1). However, Fenton *et al.* also inferred subject disciplines when they were not referred to explicitly by journalists. Sociology was by far the most frequent *inferred* discipline. Again, while this is an interesting finding, the reasons for it can only be speculated about (Fenton *et al.* 1998). Sometimes, users of content analysis have been able to shed some light on 'why?' questions raised by their investigations by conducting additional data collection exercises. Such exercises might include qualitative content analysis (e.g. Glasgow University Media Group 1976) and/or interviews with journalists and others (e.g. Fenton *et al.* 1998).

- Content analytic studies are sometimes accused of being atheoretical. It is easy to see why an atheoretical approach might arise. The emphasis in content analysis on measurement can easily and unwittingly result in an accent being placed on what is measurable rather than what is theoretically significant or important. However, content analysis is not necessarily atheoretical. Jagger (1998, 2005) placed her findings on dating advertisements in the context of current ideas about consumerism and the body. Fenton *et al.* (1998) conducted their content analysis within an overall approach that stressed the importance of studying the mass communication process from inception to reception and the importance of power and contestation within that process. Hodson's (1996) content analysis of workplace ethnographies was underpinned by theoretical ideas deriving from the work of influential writers such as Blauner (1964) and Edwards (1979) concerning developments in modes of workplace organization and their impacts on workers' experiences.

Checklist

Content analysis

- ◯ Have you clearly defined your research questions?
- ◯ Is the population of documents to be content analysed relevant to your research questions?
- ◯ Can you justify your sampling approach?
- ◯ Have you made sure that your dimensions do not overlap?
- ◯ Have you made sure that the categories used for each of your dimensions do not overlap?
- ◯ Are the categories you use for each dimension exhaustive?
- ◯ Do all the dimensions allow you to answer your research questions?
- ◯ Have you piloted your coding schedule?
- ◯ Are the coding instructions clear?
- ◯ If your research is based on the mass media, can you justify the time span of your coverage?
- ◯ Are you clear about the unit of analysis?

Key points

- ● Content analysis is very much located within the quantitative research tradition of emphasizing measurement and the specification of clear rules that exhibit reliability.
- ● While traditionally associated with the analysis of mass media content, it is in fact a very flexible method that can be applied to a wide range of phenomena.
- ● It is crucial to be clear about your research questions in order to be certain about your units of analysis and what exactly is to be analysed.
- ● You also need to be clear about what is to be counted.
- ● The coding schedule and coding manual are crucial stages in the preparation for a content analysis.
- ● Content analysis becomes particularly controversial when it is used to seek out latent meaning and themes.

Questions for review

- To what kinds of documents and media can content analysis be applied?
- What is the difference between manifest and latent content? What are the implications of the distinction for content analysis?

What are the research questions?

- Why are precise research questions especially crucial in content analysis?
- With what general kinds of research questions is content analysis concerned?

Selecting a sample

- What special sampling issues does content analysis pose?

What is to be counted?

- What kinds of things might be counted in the course of doing a content analysis?
- To what extent do you need to infer latent content when you go beyond counting words?

Coding

- Why is coding so crucial in content analysis?
- What is the difference between a coding schedule and a coding manual?
- What potential pitfalls need to be guarded against when devising coding schedules and manuals?

Advantages of content analysis

- 'One of the most significant virtues of content analysis is its immense flexibility in that it can be applied to a wide variety of documents.' Discuss.

Disadvantages of content analysis

- To what extent does the need for coders to interpret meaning undermine content analysis?
- How far are content analysis studies atheoretical?

Online Resource Centre

http://www.oxfordtextbooks.co.uk/orc/brymansrm3e/

Visit the Online Resource Centre that accompanies this book to enrich your understanding of Content analysis. Consult web links, test yourself using multiple choice questions, and gain further guidance and inspiration from the Student Researcher's Toolkit.

Secondary analysis and official statistics

Chapter guide

This chapter explores the possibilities associated with the analysis of data that have been collected by others. There are two main types discussed in this chapter:

- the **secondary analysis** of data collected by other researchers;
- the secondary analysis of **official statistics**—that is, statistics collected by government departments in the course of their work or specifically for statistical purposes.

This chapter explores:

- the advantages and disadvantages of carrying out secondary analysis of data collected by other researchers, particularly in view of many data sets being based on large, high-quality investigations that are invariably beyond the means of students;
- how to obtain such data sets;
- the potential of official statistics in terms of their **reliability** and **validity**;
- the growing recognition in recent years of the potential of official statistics after a period of neglect as a result of criticisms levelled at them;
- the notion that official statistics are a form of *unobtrusive method*—that is, a method that is not prone to a reaction on the part of those being studied to the fact that they are research participants.

Introduction

Many of the techniques we have covered so far—**survey research** by **questionnaire** or **structured interview**, **structured observation**, and **content analysis**—can be extremely time-consuming and expensive to conduct. Students in particular may have neither the time nor the financial resources to conduct very extensive research. Yet we know that large amounts of quantitative data are collected by social scientists and others. Moreover, many organizations, most notably government departments and their various representatives, collect data that are presented in statistical form and that may be usable by social scientists. Would it not be a good idea to analyse such data rather than collect new data? It would have the additional advantage for the long-suffering public that they would not be bothered by interviewers and by questionnaires popping through their letter boxes.

This is where *secondary analysis* comes in. Secondary analysis offers this kind of opportunity. Key concept 13.1 contains a brief definition of secondary analysis and raises one or two basic points about what it involves. As the opening paragraph suggests, we will in this chapter be concerned with two kinds of issue:

1. the secondary analysis of data that have been collected by other researchers;

2. the secondary analysis of data that have been collected by various institutions in the course of their business.

One prominent form of such data is official statistics concerned with areas of social life such as crime, unemployment, and strikes. The use of such official statistics for social research has been controversial, and aspects of the ensuing debate will be addressed below.

Key concept 13.1
What is secondary analysis?

Secondary analysis is the analysis of data by researchers who will probably not have been involved in the collection of those data, for purposes that in all likelihood were not envisaged by those responsible for the data collection. Secondary analysis may entail the analysis of either quantitative data (Dale *et al.* 1988) or qualitative data (Corti *et al.* 1995), but it is with the former that we will be concerned in this chapter. To some extent, it is difficult to know where primary and secondary analysis start and finish. If a researcher is involved in the collection of survey interview data and analyses some of the data, resulting in some publications, but then some time later decides to rework the data, it is not entirely clear how far the latter is primary or secondary analysis. Typically, secondary analysis entails the analysis of data that others have collected, but, as this simple scenario suggests, this need not necessarily be the case.

For example, I was involved in a secondary analysis of data on dietary choices, attitudes and practices among a **sample** of Leicestershire residents (Beardsworth *et al.* 2002). This analysis reflected my and the lead author's research interests. The analysis dealt with the significance of gender in nutritional attitudes and choices, which had not been the focus of previous analyses of these data. I had not been involved in the collection of the data or in design of the research, but the co-authors of the article that reported the analysis had been involved in these phases of the research. It is questionable whether for them it was a secondary analysis, but for me it certainly was. The analysis shows that women are more likely than men to adopt what we call a 'virtuous' pattern of eating, which acknowledges a sensitivity to, and preparedness to act in terms of, ethical and nutritional principles that are respected in many Western societies. The article also shows that these principles have a sinister component in that they frequently come to be associated among women with feelings of guilt, disordered eating patterns, and concerns about body shape.

Other researchers' data

There are several reasons why secondary analysis should be considered a serious alternative to collecting new data. These advantages of secondary analysis have been covered by Dale *et al.* (1988), from which I have borrowed most of the following observations. In considering the various advantages of secondary analysis, I have in mind the particular needs of the lone student conducting a small research project as an undergraduate or a more substantial piece of work as a postgraduate. However, this emphasis should definitely not be taken to imply that secondary analysis is really appropriate or relevant only to students. Quite the contrary: secondary analysis should be considered by all social researchers, and, indeed, the Economic and Social Research Council (ESRC) requires applicants for research grants who are proposing to col-

lect new data to demonstrate that relevant data are not already available in the UK Data Archive (see below).

My reason for emphasizing the prospects of secondary analysis for students is simply based on my personal experience that they tend to assume that any research they carry out has to entail the collection of primary data. Unless you are advised otherwise by your supervisor or by any documentation supplied by your department or university, it is worth giving serious consideration to doing a secondary analysis, because it will allow you to spend more time on the analysis and interpretation of data. Moreover, you simply will not be in a position to produce a data set of comparable quality, because of the lack of time and resources likely to be available to you. Further, as the outline in the next section of the advantages of secondary analysis suggests, you may be able to conduct analyses that would be inconceivable if you relied on data you collected yourself.

Advantages of secondary analysis

Secondary analysis offers numerous benefits to students carrying out a research project. These are outlined below.

- *Cost and time*. As noted at the outset, secondary analysis offers the prospect of having access to good quality data for a tiny fraction of the resources involved in carrying out a data collection exercise yourself. Numerous data sets are available from the Data Archive, which is housed at the University of Essex in Colchester. You do not even have to go to Colchester yourself to search for data. The Archive has a very good website, which can be searched in a variety of ways, such as keywords (see below).

- *High-quality data*. Many of the data sets that are employed most frequently for secondary analysis are of extremely high quality. By this I mean several things. First, the sampling procedures have been rigorous, in most cases resulting in samples that are as close to being representative as one is likely to achieve. While the organizations responsible for these studies suffer the same problems of survey non-response as anybody else, well-established procedures are usually in place for following up non-respondents and thereby keeping this problem to a minimum. Second, the samples are often national samples or at least cover a wide variety of regions of Great Britain or the UK. The

degree of geographical spread and the sample size of such data sets are invariably attained only in research that attracts quite substantial resources. It is certainly inconceivable that student projects could even get close to the coverage that such data sets attain. Third, many data sets have been generated by highly experienced researchers, and, in the case of some of the large data sets, like the General Household Survey (GHS), the British Social Attitudes (BSA) survey (see Research in focus 13.1), and the British Household Panel Survey (BHPS; see Research in focus 13.1 and 13.2), the data have been gathered by social research organizations that have developed structures and control procedures to check on the quality of the emerging data.

- *Opportunity for longitudinal analysis*. Partly linked to the last point is the fact that secondary analysis can offer the opportunity for longitudinal research, which, as noted in Chapter 2, is rather rare in the social sciences because of the time and cost involved. Sometimes, as with the BHPS, a panel design has been employed, and it is possible to chart trends and connections over time. Such data are sometimes analysed cross-sectionally, but there are obviously opportunities for longitudinal analysis as well. Also, with data sets such as the GHS and the BSA survey, where similar data are collected over time, usually because certain interview questions are recycled each year, trends (such as shifting opinions or changes in behaviour) can be identified over time. With such data sets, respondents differ from year to year, so that causal inferences over time cannot be readily established, but nonetheless it is still possible to gauge trends.

Research in focus 13.1
Religion in Britain and the 'believing without belonging' thesis

'Believing without belonging', as the phrase implies, is meant to suggest that religion has not declined in modern British society in terms of the extent to which religious beliefs are held; rather, the phrase suggests that it is allegiance to institutional religion that has declined, in that religious beliefs are still fairly robust. This thesis was explored by Voas and Crockett (2005), who conducted secondary analyses of both the BHPS and the BSA survey. For the BHPS analysis, the authors took waves 1 (1991) and 9 (1999–2000) focusing on three questions that are asked:

1. A question asking whether the respondent views him- or herself as belonging to any religion and, if so, which one. This is used to indicate a person's religious affiliation.

2. A question asking how often the respondent attends religious services or meetings. This is commonly used as an **indicator** of participation.

3. A question asking each respondent how much difference religious beliefs make to his or her life. Respondents answer on a **scale**: no difference; little difference; some difference; great difference. This question is taken to indicate strength of belief and its significance in the respondent's life.

The findings lead Voas and Crockett (2005: 15) to suggest that 'religious decline is principally the result of differences between generations: each age cohort is less religious than the last'. Also, the same data do not support the 'believing without belonging' thesis: if anything, religious belief is declining faster than belonging. They explored the BSA data, which could be examined over a much longer period (1983–2002). The data were examined as a continuous time series for each year for which there were data on religious affiliation and belief. They show that the dominant effect was a cohort effect; that is, each cohort (five cohorts were distinguished) was less religious (in terms of affiliation, attendance, and belief) than the previous one. Overall, then, these longitudinal data suggest that the 'believing without belonging' thesis cannot be supported empirically.

- *Subgroup analysis*. When large samples are the source of data (as in the GHS and BHPS), there is the opportunity to study what can often be quite sizeable subgroups. Very often, in order to study specialized categories of individuals, small localized studies are the only feasible way forward because of costs. Large data sets can frequently yield quite large nationally **representative samples**. For example, Arber and Gilbert (1989) used the 1980 GHS to isolate a sample of over 4,500 elderly people living in private households. In 1980, respondents aged 65 and over were asked various questions about their ability to perform certain tasks. This information was used to compile a disability **index**. Levels of disability could then be related to patterns of caring for the elderly. As Arber and Gilbert (1989: 75) observe: 'The large sample size, high response rate (82 per cent) and representative nature of the sample size make the GHS a valuable data source to complement, extend and systematically test findings and theoretical ideas derived from small, qualitative and localised studies.' While the data did not address the elderly in institutional care, it nonetheless provides a valuable source of high-quality data on the elderly. It is easy to see how a wide range of different subgroups could be identified for similar kinds of analysis.

Research in focus 13.2
Household work: an example of secondary analysis

Bond and Sales (2001) conducted a secondary analysis of wave 4 (1994) of the BHPS. They were interested in the organization of household work among couples where both members were of working age and were in paid work. Of the 9,481 adults interviewed during this wave of data collection, 981 couples met the researchers' criteria. Bond and Sales were interested in the **variables** associated with the amount of time men and women spent in household work and the level of sharing of household jobs. As regards the former of these **dependent variables**, the authors show, for example, that the amount of time spent in household tasks was negatively associated with the relative economic power of one's partner and that men tended to spend more time on domestic tasks the longer the hours of their partners in paid work. Sharing of tasks was greater among women working longer hours, but men take up only a small amount of the household work that does not get done as a result of women working. Moreover, men with greater economic power than their partners tended to share less than those without such power. A study like this allows an important topic to be illuminated through a relatively representative sample that would require a great deal of effort to compile.

- *Opportunity for cross-cultural analysis*. Cross-cultural research has considerable appeal at a time when social scientists are more attuned to the processes associated with globalization and to cultural differences. It is easy to forget that many findings should not be taken to apply to countries other than that in which the research was conducted. However, cross-cultural research presents barriers to the social scientist. There are obvious barriers to do with the cost and practical difficulties of doing research in a different country, especially when language and cultural differences are likely to be significant. The secondary analysis of comparable data from two or more countries provides one possible model for conducting cross-cultural research. In order for a cross-cultural analysis to be conducted, some coordination is necessary so that the questions asked are comparable. The research on religiosity described in Research in focus 1.4 and 6.3 by Kelley and De Graaf (1997) provides an example of such coordination. The authors describe the process as follows:

> Data are from the 1991 'Religion' module of the International Social Survey Programme (ISSP), an international consortium composed primarily of academic survey organizations . . . Each year, the ISSP creates a module containing exactly the same questions, answer categories, and sequencing for all countries surveyed. . . . The samples are all large, representative national samples of adults. The most common procedure is to hold face-to-face interviews with a stratified random sample . . . followed by a leave-behind self-completion questionnaire containing the ISSP module . . .
> (Kelley and De Graaf 1997: 642)

Kelley and De Graaf's results were based upon a secondary analysis of the data from the fifteen nations involved in the research. Opportunities for such cross-cultural analysis appear to be increasing. For example, core questions used in the Labour Force Survey are also used in equivalent surveys conducted by EU member states.

- *More time for data analysis*. Precisely because data collection is time-consuming, the analysis of data is often squeezed. It is easy to perceive the data collection as the difficult phase and to take the view that the analysis of data is relatively straightforward. This is not the case. Working out what to make of your data is no easy matter

and requires considerable thought and often a preparedness to consider learning about unfamiliar techniques of data analysis. While secondary analysis invariably entails a lot of data management—partly so that you can get to know the data and partly so that you can get it into a form that you need (see below)—and this phase should not be underestimated—the fact that you are freed from having to collect fresh data means that your approach to the analysis of data can be more considered than perhaps it might otherwise have been.

- *Reanalysis may offer new interpretations*. It is easy to take the view that, once a set of data has been analysed, the data have in some sense been drained of further insight. What, in other words, could possibly be gained by going over the same data that someone else has analysed? In fact, data can be analysed in so many different ways that it is very unusual for the range of possible analyses to be exhausted. Several possibilities can be envisaged. A secondary analyst may decide to consider the impact of a certain variable on the relationships between variables of interest. Such a possibility may not have been envisaged by the initial researchers. Second, the arrival of new theoretical ideas may suggest analyses that could not have been conceived of by the original researchers. In other words, the arrival of such new theoretical directions may prompt a reconsideration of the relevance of the data. Third, an alternative method of quantitative data analysis may be employed and offer the prospect of a rather different interpretation of the data. Fourth (and related to the last point), new methods of quantitative data analysis are continuously emerging. Disciplines such as statistics and econometrics are continually developing new techniques of analysis, while some techniques are developed within the social sciences themselves. As awareness of such techniques spreads, and their potential relevance is recognized, researchers become interested in applying them to new data sets.

- *The wider obligations of the social researcher*. For all types of social research, research participants give up some of their time, usually for no reward. It is not unreasonable that the public should expect that the data that they participate in generating should be mined to its fullest extent. However, much social research is chronically under-analysed. Primary researchers may feel they want to analyse only data relating to central research questions or lose interest as a new set of research questions interpose themselves into their imagination. Making data available for secondary analysis enhances the possibility that fuller use will be made of data.

Limitations of secondary analysis

The foregoing list of benefits of secondary analysis sounds almost too good to be true. In fact, there are not very many limitations, but the following warrant some attention.

- *Lack of familiarity with data.* When you collect your own data, when the data set is generated, it is hardly surprising that you are very familiar with the structure and contours of your data. However, with data collected by others, a period of familiarization is necessary. You have to get to grips with the range of variables, the ways in which the variables have been coded, and various aspects of the organization of the data. The period of familiarization can be quite substantial with large complex data sets and should not be underestimated.

- *Complexity of the data.* Some of the best-known data sets that are employed for secondary analysis, such as the BHPS, are very large in the sense of having large numbers of both respondents and variables. Sometimes, the sheer volume of data can present problems with the management of the information at hand, and, again, a period of acclimatization may be required. Also, some of the most prominent data sets that have been employed for secondary analysis are known as *hierarchical* data sets, such as the GHS and the BHPS. The difficulty here is that the data are collected and presented at the level of both the household and the individual, as well as other levels. The secondary analyst must decide which level of analysis is going to be employed. If the decision is to analyse individual-level data, the individual-level data must then be extracted from the data set. Different data will apply to each level. Thus, at the household level, the GHS provides data on such variables as number of cars and consumer durables, while, at the individual level, data on income and employment can be found. Dale (1987) was interested in life-cycle stages and employed household level data from the 1979 GHS to develop a typology of life-cycle stages, which included fourteen categories, and various correlates of the various categories, such as net disposable household income.

- *No control over data quality.* The point has been made on several occasions that secondary analysis offers the opportunity for students and others to examine data of far higher quality than they could collect themselves.

However, this point applies mainly to data sets such as the GHS, the BHPS (see Research in focus 2.10), the BCS (see Thinking deeply 6.1), the NCDS (see Research in focus 2.11), the Social Change in Economic Life Initiative (see Research in focus 6.1), and the BSA survey (see Research in focus 1.4). While the quality of data should never be taken for granted, in the case of such data sets it is reasonably assured, though that is not to say that they will necessarily meet all of a prospective secondary analyst's needs, since data may not have been collected on an aspect of a topic that would have been of considerable interest. With other data sets, somewhat more caution may be necessary in connection with data quality, although certain fundamental checks on quality are usually made by archives in which data are deposited.

- *Absence of key variables.* Because secondary analysis entails the analysis of data collected by others for their own purposes, it may be that one or more key variables may not be present. You may, for example, want to examine whether a relationship between two variables holds even when one or more *other* variables are taken into account. Such an analysis is known as *multivariate analysis*, an area that will be touched on in the next chapter. The inability to examine the significance or otherwise of a theoretically important variable can be frustrating and can arise when, for example, a theoretical approach that has emerged since the collection of the data suggests its importance. Obviously, when researchers collect primary data themselves, the prospect of this happening should be less pronounced.

Accessing the Data Archive

The UK Data Archive at the University of Essex is likely to be your main source of quantitative data for secondary analysis, although it may be that some of your lecturers will have data sets that they are prepared to put at your disposal. The best route for finding out about data held at the Archive is to examine its online catalogue. Access to this catalogue can be obtained by going to the Data Archive home page at http://www.data-archive.ac.uk/ (accessed on 3 July 2007), or by going directly to the catalogue search page at http://www.data-archive.ac.uk/search/searchStart.asp (accessed on 3 July 2007). This will bring up the search catalogue (see Plate 13.1). I asked for any studies with the keyword 'recycling', a topic that was attracting a lot of attention at the time I was revising this chapter. I clicked on the **GO** button. This

Plate 13.1

The UK Data Archive Search Catalogue

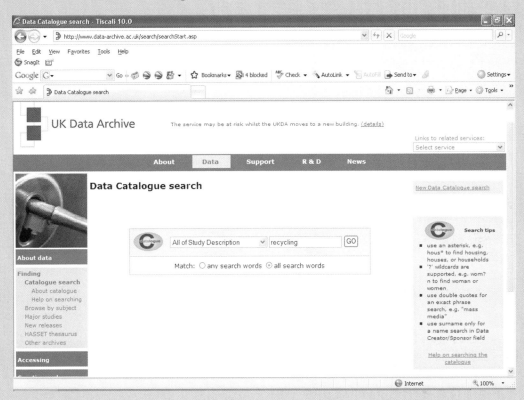

resulted in 13 studies being found (see Plate 13.2). This allows one to look at the documentation relating to any promising candidates for analysis and even order the data set concerned. The information provided typically gives a description of the study, along with a variety of particulars: sponsors; sampling details; method of data collection; main topics of the survey; and information about publications deriving from the study. It also informs you whether there are special conditions relating to access. With the one I specified, which was SN 5261—Scottish Household Survey, 2003–2004: Lite Version, I was told: 'The depositor has specified that registration is required and standard conditions of use apply.' Where there are special conditions, they normally involve signing an undertaking form. To order the data, you need to have set up an account, which will have resulted in your being given a user name and password that will allow you to download data. You will need to find out if there is an administrative charge for receiving the data, but it is likely that, if you are a student at or a member of staff in a

UK institution of higher education, there will be no charge or perhaps a nominal one. Online documentation is available towards the foot of the web page for the chosen study (see Plate 13.3, which also shows some of the information about the project that can be found on the Data Archive Website).

Information about searching for qualitative data for the purpose of conducting a secondary analysis can be found in Chapter 22. Qualitative data can be searched for through Qualidata, which, like the UK Data Archive, is located at the University of Essex, but, unlike the Archive, is not itself a repository of data.

A website that has been designed to increase the use of secondary analysis and that provides a variety of hyperlinks to useful sites is http://tramss.data-archive.ac.uk (accessed on 3 July 2007). Table 13.1 lists several large data sets that are accessible to students and would repay further investigation in terms of their potential use in the context of research questions in which you might be interested. Further information about these data sets can be

Plate 13.2

Results of a search

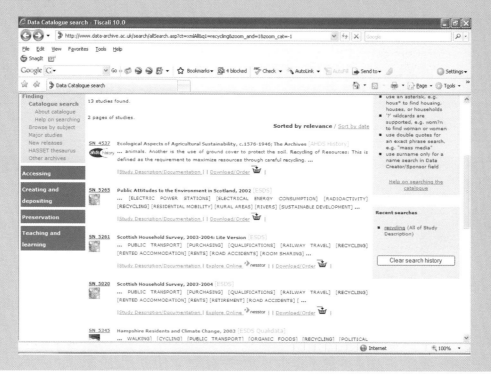

Plate 13.3

Description and documentation for the chosen data

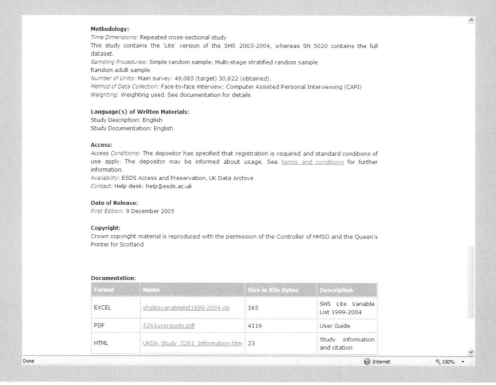

Table 13.1

Large data sets suitable for secondary analysis

Title	Data set details	Topics covered
British Crime Survey (BCS)	Irregular survey of randomly selected sample of people questioned by structured interview. The 2001–2 BCS had a target sample of 36,000 individuals. Began in 1982 and since then carried out in 1984, 1988, and 1992. Biennially between 1992 and 2000 and annually from 2001.	Experience of and attitudes to crime; fear of crime; risk of crime.
British Household Panel Survey (BHPS)	A panel study that began in 1991 and is conducted annually by interview and questionnaire with a national representative sample of around 10,000 individuals in just over 5,000 households. The same individuals are interviewed each year. The BHPS is to be replaced by the UK Household Longitudinal Survey, which will be based on a much larger panel of households. See http://www.iser.essex.ac.uk/ukhls/ (accessed on 2 July 2007).	Household organization; labour market behaviour; income and wealth; housing; health; socio-economic values.
British Social Attitudes (BSA) Survey	More or less annual survey since 1983 of a representative sample aged 18 and over by interview and questionnaire. Each survey comprises an hour-long interview and a self-completion questionnaire.	Wide range of areas of social attitudes and behaviour. Some areas are core ones asked annually; others are asked irregularly.
Expenditure and Food Survey (EFS)	A new survey, which began in April 2001, that combines and replaces the FES and NFS. Data are based on households, which are asked to complete diaries of expenditure and income over a two-week period. In addition, face-to-face interviews are conducted by CAPI.	Areas formerly covered by FES and NFS.
Family Expenditure Survey (FES)	Annual interviews from 1957 with members of around 10,000 households who kept diary records of expenditure and income over two-week period. It was replaced by the Expenditure and Food Survey in 2001.	Family expenditure and income.
General Household Survey (GHS)	Annual interviews since 1971 with members aged over 16 in over 8,000 randomly sampled households. No surveys were carried out in 1997–8, when the GHS was reviewed, and in 1999–2000, when it was revamped. Following this hiatus, the GHS has been resumed on an annual basis.	Standard issues such as education and health asked each year, plus additional items that vary annually. Huge variety of questions relating to social behaviour and attitudes.
Labour Force Survey (LFS)	Biennial interviews, 1973–83, and annual interviews, 1984–91, comprising a quarterly survey of around 15,000 addresses per quarter and an additional survey in March–May; since 1991 quarterly survey of around 60,000 addresses. Since 1998 core questions are also administered in member states of the European Union.	Hours worked, job search methods, training, and personal details such as nationality and gender.
Millennium Cohort Study	Study of 19,000 babies and their families born between 1 September 2000 and 31 August 2001 in England and Wales, and between 22 November 2000 and 11 January 2002 in Scotland and Northern Ireland. Data were collected by interview with parents when babies were 9 months and around 3 years old.	Continuity and change in each child's family and its parenting environment; assesses important aspects of the child's development.
National Child Development Study (NCDS)	Irregular but ongoing study of all 17,000 children born in Great Britain in the week of 3–9 March 1958. Since 1981 comprises interview and questionnaire. There have been six waves of data collection: 1965 (when members were aged 7 years), in 1969 (age 11), in 1974 (age 16), in 1981 (age 23), in 1985 (age 33), and in 1999–2000 (age 41–42).	Physical and mental health; family; parenting; occupation and income; housing and environment; etc.
National Food Survey (NFS)	First set up in 1940, this survey entailed interviews with a representative sample of households, and diary records for one week. In 1998 data were collected from both sources from 6,000 households. It was replaced by the Expenditure and Food Survey in 2001.	Nature of household; food shopping; meals.
ONS Omnibus Survey	A regular commercial survey by structured interview since 1990 of just under 2,000 people. Since 1990 it has been conducted eight times per year.	Core questions each year about respondents, plus modules (asked on behalf of participating organizations) on topics that change annually concerning, e.g. food safety, eating behaviour, personal finance, sports participation.
Workplace Employee Relations Survey (WERS)	This survey has been carried out in 1980, 1984, 1990, 1998, and 2004. Workplaces of ten or more employees are sampled, and interviews carried out with managers, worker representatives, and employees.	Pay determination; recruitment and training; equal opportunities; workplace change; work attitudes; management organization; employee representation; etc.

found via the Data Archive catalogue or by using Google or any other search engine to look for them.

In discussing secondary analysis in this chapter, I have tended to emphasize large data sets like the BHPS. However, it is worth bearing in mind that the Data Archive holds data deriving from a wide range of studies. If you enter 'Research methods' as your search term when searching the catalogue, one of the studies that comes up is a content analysis of journal articles that combine quantitative and qualitative research. This is a study I conducted in 2003–4 and which forms the basis for much of Chapter 25. However, this is in no sense a large data set like the ones that have been the focus of attention for much of the previous discussion. It is also worth keeping a look-out for interesting good quality studies that may not be archived. As mentioned in Chapter 12, the data from the Workplace Ethnography Project (Research in focus 12.4) can be easily downloaded and could form the basis of a very interesting secondary analysis project for someone with interests in areas like the sociology of work.

Official statistics

The use and analysis of official statistics for purposes of social research has been a very controversial area for many years. Agencies of the state, in the course of their business, are required to keep a running record of their areas of activity. When these records are aggregated, they form the official statistics in an area of activity. Thus, in Great Britain, the police compile data that form the crime rate (also known as 'notifiable crimes recorded by the police') and the Employment Service collects data that form the basis for the level of unemployment (also known as the 'claimant count'). These are just two, as it happens high-profile, sets of statistics that can be subsumed under the general category of 'official statistics'. Such statistics are frequently the cause of headlines in the mass media—for example, if there has been a sharp increase in the level of recorded crime or unemployment. But they would also seem to offer considerable potential for social researchers.

We could imagine such official statistics offering the social researcher certain advantages over some other forms of quantitative data, such as data based on surveys.

- The data have already been collected. Therefore, as with other kinds of secondary analysis of data (see above), considerable time and expense may be saved. Also, the data may not be based on samples, so that a complete picture can be obtained.

- Since the people who are the source of the data are not being asked questions that are part of a research project, the problem of *reactivity* will be much less pronounced than when data are collected by interview or questionnaire.

- There is the prospect of analysing the data both cross-sectionally and longitudinally. When analysing the data cross-sectionally, we could examine crime rates (and indeed the incidence of specific crimes) in terms of such standard variables as social class, income, ethnicity, age, gender, and region. Such analyses allow us to search for the factors that are associated with crime or unemployment. Also, we can analyse the data over time. Precisely because the data are compiled over many years, it is possible to chart trends over time and perhaps to relate these to wider social changes.

- There is the prospect as well of cross-cultural analysis, since the official statistics from different nation states can be compared for a specific area of activity. After all, a sociological classic of the stature of Durkheim's *Suicide* (Durkheim 1952) was the result of a comparative analysis of official statistics on suicide in several countries.

However, readers who recall Thinking deeply 6.1 will already be on their guard. The official statistics concerned with an area of social life like crime can be very misleading, because they record only those individuals who are processed by the agencies that have the responsibility for compiling the statistics. Crime and other forms of deviance have been a particular focus of attention and concern among critics of the use of official statistics. Figure 13.1 illustrates, in connection with crime and the crime rate, the kinds of factor that can lead to concern.

If we take a criminal offence as the starting point (step 1), we can consider the factors that might or might not result in its becoming part of the crime rate. An offence might become a candidate for inclusion in the crime rate as a result of either of two events (it might be that others can be envisaged but these two represent major

Figure 13.1

The social construction of crime statistics: eight steps

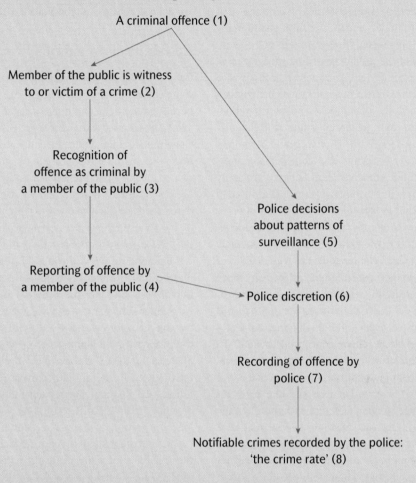

Source: adapted from a figure in Beardsworth *et al.* (n.d.)

possibilities). First, the crime may be seen by a member of the public or a member of the public may be a victim of a crime (step 2). However, a crime has to be recognized as such before it will be reported to the police (step 3). Even if it is recognized as a criminal offence, the member of the public (even if he or she is a victim) may choose not to bring the crime to the notice of the police. This means that, if a criminal act goes unnoticed, or is noticed but not recognized as criminal, or is noticed and recognized as criminal but not reported to the police, it will not enter the official statistics. Step 4 is the reporting of the crime to the police. Even then the crime may not be entered into the crime statistics, because the police have

considerable discretion about whether to proceed with a conviction and may choose to let the person off with a warning (step 6). They may be influenced by such factors as the severity of the crime, the perpetrator's previous record, the perpetrator's demeanour or suggestions of contrition, or their volume of work at the time.

Alternatively, a crime may be observed by the police as a result of their patterns of surveillance, which is a product of decisions about how best to deploy police officers (step 5). Once again, the crime may not become part of the crime rate because of the operation of police discretion. Thereafter, once the police exercise discretion in such a way as to lead them to seek a prosecution (step 6), the offence is recorded (step 7) and it becomes a 'notifiable crime recorded by the police' and as such part of the crime rate (step 8).

What are the implications of this process for the crime rate and for criminal statistics generally? For one thing, it means that a substantial amount of crime undoubtedly goes unrecorded as a result of: not coming to the attention of members of the public; not being recognized as criminal; not being reported; decisions regarding police surveillance that may result in some crimes being given lower priority; and the operation of police discretion. This undercurrent of unrecorded crime is frequently referred to as 'the dark figure' (Coleman and Moynihan 1996). Nor can crime be regarded as alone in this connection. Suicide statistics almost certainly fail to record many potential cases for inclusion and may even include a small number that are not in fact suicides (as a result of problems of deciding whether the 'victim' was involved in an accident or intended to commit suicide). It is extremely difficult to determine whether someone is the victim of suicide when there is no suicide note. Moreover, those responsible for concluding whether a death is a suicide or not may come under considerable pressure not to record it as such, possibly because of feelings of potential stigma or because of religious taboos concerning suicide. To push the point even further, the deficiencies of official statistics do not relate just to areas of deviant behaviour such as crime and suicide. For example, the 'claimant count', which is used to gain a picture each month of the level of unemployment, may misrepresent the 'real' level of unemployment: people who are unemployed but who do not claim benefits or whose claim is disallowed will not be counted in the statistics, while those who form part of the claimant count but who work in part of what is known as the 'black' or 'informal' economy (and who therefore are not really unemployed) *will* be included in the unemployment statistics.

Increasingly, official statistics and summaries of them are available via the Internet. National Statistics Online is a good springboard for access to a wide variety of official statistics and can be accessed at http://www.statistics.gov.uk (accessed on 3 July 2007).

Reliability and validity

Issues of reliability and validity seem to loom large in these considerations. Reliability seems to be jeopardized because definitions and policies regarding the phenomena to be counted vary over time. For example, the UK Government Home Office or police service policies may mean that more resources are to be put into surveillance of a certain area of crime, such as drugs or drink-driving. Moreover, as part of a crackdown, it may be that police officers are less likely to operate their discretion in such a way as to result in perpetrators being let off with a warning. The problem for the reliability of the crime statistics is that variations over time in levels of a particular crime may be due not to variations in the level of transgression but to variations in the propensity to expend resources on surveillance and to proceed with prosecution. Also, there may be changes over time in the definitions of crime or in the propensity of victims to proceed with a complaint. Such changes will clearly affect the degree to which fluctuations in the rate of occurrence of certain crimes reflect 'real' fluctuations in the incidence of those crimes or other factors (that is, variations over time in surveillance, operation of discretion, definition, propensity to report, and other factors). A further factor that can impair the reliability of crime statistics is 'fiddling' by police officers (see Thinking deeply 6.1 and 13.1). To the extent that such factors operate, the reliability of the crime data will be adversely affected and, as a result, validity will be similarly impaired.

Thinking deeply 13.1
Fiddling the crime figures

An article in *The Times* (Leake 1998) reported that there was growing evidence that senior police officers frequently massage the crime statistics for their forces. The author argued that many officers deliberately 'lose' crimes in order to make their detection rates look better. As a result, crime rates are often lower than they should be. The article cites the following methods of suppressing crimes:

- classifying multiple burglaries—for example, in a block of flats in one day—as a single incident;
- cataloguing multiple credit card or cheque card frauds as a single offence;
- excluding common assaults, when people are not seriously injured, from the figures for violent crime;
- excluding drug offences where people admit to offending but are only cautioned.

These methods of reducing the crime rate will adversely affect reliability, because it is not possible to compare the figures over different time periods because of variations over time in the propensity to massage the data. Validity will be similarly affected, in part because **measurement validity** presupposes reliability (see Chapter 6) and also because the figures cannot be regarded as providing a picture of the true level of crime.

Also, the problems with official statistics extend to the examination of the variables with which the crime rate is associated. For example, it might be assumed that, if an examination of regional differences demonstrates that the crime rate varies by the chief ethnic or social class composition of an area, this implies that ethnic status and social class are themselves related to crime. There are two problems with drawing such an inference. First, there is an analytic difficulty known as the *ecological fallacy* (see Key concept 13.2). Second, even if we could ignore the problem of the ecological fallacy (which we cannot, of course), we would still be faced with an issue that is related to the matter of validity. Variations between ethnic groups or social classes may be a product of factors other than variations between ethnic groups and social classes in their propensity to commit crimes. Instead, the variations may be due to such factors as: variations in the

likelihood of members of the public reporting a crime when the perpetrator is of one ethnic group or class rather than others; variations in the surveillance activities of the police so that areas with a high concentration of members of one ethnic group or class rather than others are more likely to be the focus of activity; variations between ethnic groups or social classes in the propensity of police officers to exercise discretion; and problems for the police of learning about and investigating certain crimes that are themselves related to ethnicity or class (for example, white-collar crime). Similarly, as Douglas (1967) observes in connection with suicide statistics, it is quite likely that variations between ethnic and religious groups in suicide rates may be a product at least in part of variations in the predilection of the families of suicide victims to put pressure on official figures like coroners not to treat a death as a suicide.

Key concept 13.2
What is the ecological fallacy?

The ecological fallacy is the error of assuming that inferences about individuals can be made from findings relating to aggregate data. Coleman and Moynihan (1996) provide the example of the relationship between ethnicity and crime. They observe that findings showing a higher incidence of crime in regions with high concentrations of ethnic minorities have been used to imply that members of such minority groups are more likely to commit crimes. However, research on this issue in the 1960s suggested that in fact members of ethnic minority groups were less likely to offend. The fallacy can arise for several reasons—for example, it may not be the members of the minority groups who are responsible for the high levels of offending.

Condemning and resurrecting official statistics

In the 1960s, in particular, there was a torrent of criticism of various kinds of official statistics, especially those con-

nected with crime and deviance. The various criticisms previously outlined were very much to the fore. In fact, so entrenched was the belief in many quarters that official statistics were of dubious value to social researchers that the view took root that they were virtually worthless.

Instead, it was recommended that social researchers should turn their attention to the investigation of the organizational processes that produce the various deficiencies identified by the various writers. In the words of the writers of one influential article, rates of crime and other forms of deviance 'can be viewed as indices of organizational processes rather than as indices of certain forms of behavior' (Kitsuse and Cicourel 1963: 137). The effect of this view was to consign official statistics to the sidelines of social research so that they became an object of research interest rather than a potential source of data, although research based on official statistics continued in certain quarters. It would also be wrong to think that the critique formulated by writers such as Kitsuse and Cicourel (1963) and Douglas (1967) was the sole reason for the neglect of official statistics during this period. The fact that official statistics, because they are a sideline for many state agencies, are invariably not tailored to the needs of social researchers can be considered a further limitation. In other words, it may be that the definitions of apparently similar or identical terms (such as unemployment or socio-economic class) employed by those responsible for compiling official statistics may not be commensurate with the definitions employed by social researchers.

An important article by Bulmer (1980) questioned the relative neglect of official statistics by British sociologists in particular and represented a turning point in the views of many researchers towards this source of data (Levitas and Guy 1996). For one thing, Bulmer argued that the critique of official statistics had largely revolved around the elaboration of criticisms surrounding statistics relating to crime and deviance. He observes that these are subject to special well-known problems and it would be wrong to generalize these problems to the full range of official statistics. Many official statistics may be flawed in certain respects, but the flaws are not necessarily as pronounced as those to do with crime and deviance. Moreover, the flaws in many of the official statistics not concerned with crime and deviance are probably no worse than the errors that occur in much measurement deriving from methods like surveys based on questionnaires and structured interviews. Indeed, some forms of official statistics are probably very accurate by almost any set of criteria, such as statistics relating to births, marriages, and deaths.

Bulmer also argues that, so far as some of the key variables in social research are concerned, the distance between the definitions employed by the compilers of official statistics and those employed by social researchers is not as great as is sometimes supposed. However, he notes that the case of social class is somewhat different. The development of the Registrar General's classification of social class groupings seems to have taken little notice of the schemes devised by sociologists, such as the influential Hall–Jones and Hope–Goldthorpe approaches. However, Bulmer notes that the Registrar General's classification nonetheless helpfully brings out clear divergences of socio-economic position between the groupings it comprises and is frequently employed by social researchers to make precisely this point. Bulmer points to the fact that data deriving from official statistics that show pronounced social class differences in mortality are extremely important and of considerable significance to medical and other sociologists. The data are not without problems and detractors, but there is a considerable willingness to use the statistics. The same applies to Inland Revenue data based on estate duties that have been employed to examine wealth distribution.

A further criticism of the rejection of various forms of official statistics is that it seems to imply that quantitative data compiled by social researchers are somehow error free or at least superior. However, as we have seen in previous chapters, while social researchers do their best to reduce the amount of error in their measurement of key concepts (such as through the standardization of the asking of questions and the recording of answers in survey research), it is not the case that the various measures that are derived are free of error. All social measurement is prone to error; what is crucial is taking steps to keep that error to a minimum. Therefore, to reject official statistics because they contain errors is misleading if in fact all measurement in social research contains errors. The problem here is that some official statistics are particularly prone to error, such as those relating to crime and deviance.

However, even here some caution is necessary. While data deriving from the British Crime Survey (BCS) may be employed to show that only a proportion of all crimes are notified to the police (see Thinking deeply 6.1), it would be wrong to conclude that the survey is an error-free yardstick. Coleman and Moynihan (1996) point to several measurement errors that are likely to afflict the BCS. For example, there is evidence to suggest that the BCS results in an overestimation of serious incidents through a process known as 'forward telescoping'. This means that serious incidents that are outside the recall period of twelve months (the period about which respondents are questioned) are erroneously considered to have occurred during that period. In other words, people have a tendency to believe that serious crimes of which they have been victims, but that occurred more than twelve months previously, actually occurred during the recall period. Coleman and Moynihan (1996) also point to errors arising from factors such as concealment in the course of interviewing. For example, there is some evidence to suggest that women are more likely to report sexual offences and domestic violence to the police (step 4 in Figure 13.1) than to a survey interviewer. In other words, dismissing official statistics on crime on the basis of survey evidence of the kind generated by the BCS is not without problems because it is not free of error itself.

It is clear that, following Bulmer's (1980) statement of the issue, the wholesale rejection of official statistics by many social researchers has been tempered. While there is widespread recognition and acknowledgement that problems remain with certain forms of official statistics (in particular those relating to crime and deviance), each set of statistics has to be evaluated for the purposes of social research on its own merits.

Official statistics as a form of unobtrusive method

One of the most compelling and frequently cited cases for the continued use of official statistics is that they can be considered a form of unobtrusive measure, although nowadays many writers prefer to use the term 'unobtrusive method' (Lee 2000). This term is derived from the notion of 'unobtrusive measure' coined by Webb *et al.*

(1966). In a highly influential book, Webb *et al.* argued that social researchers are excessively reliant on measures of social phenomena deriving from methods of data collection that are prone to *reactivity* (see Research in focus 2.3 and Key concept 11.4, where this idea is introduced). This means that, whenever people know that they are participating in a study (which is invariably the case with methods of data collection such as structured interviewing, self-administered questionnaire, and structured observation), a component of their replies or behaviour is likely to be influenced by their knowledge that they are being investigated. In other words, their answers to questions or the behaviour they exhibit may be untypical.

Official statistics fit fairly squarely in the second of the four types of unobtrusive measures outlined in Key concept 13.3. As noted in the box, this second grouping covers a very wide range of sources of data, which includes statistics generated by organizations that are not agencies of the state. This is a useful reminder that potentially interesting statistical data are frequently compiled by a wide range of organizations. An interesting use of such data is described in Research in focus 13.3. However, social researchers do not make a great deal of use of such data, and it is not irrelevant that the author referred to in the research presented in Research in focus 13.3 is an economist. There may be greater potential for searching out and mining statistical data produced by organizations that are relatively independent of the state.

Key concept 13.3
What are unobtrusive measures?

An unobtrusive measure is 'any method of observation that directly removes the observer from the set of interactions or events being studied' (Denzin 1970). Webb *et al.* (1966) distinguished four main types.

1. *Physical traces.* These are the 'signs left behind by a group' and include such things as graffiti and trash.

2. *Archive materials.* This category includes statistics collected by governmental and non-governmental organizations, diaries, the mass media, and historical records.

3. *Simple observation.* This refers to 'situations in which the observer has no control over the behavior or sign in question, and plays an unobserved, passive, and nonintrusive role in the research situation' (Webb *et al.* 1966: 112).

4. *Contrived observation.* This is the same as simple observation, but the observer either actively varies the setting in some way (but without jeopardizing the unobtrusive quality of the observation) or employs hidden hardware to record observations, such as video cameras.

Official statistics would be subsumed under Category 2, as would content analysis of media content of the kind described in Chapter 12. However, a content analysis like that described in Research in focus 12.3 would not be considered an example of an unobtrusive measure, because the material being content analysed (workplace **ethnographies**) derives from studies in which the data were generated in an obtrusive fashion. Structured observation of the kind covered in Chapter 11 will typically not fall into Categories 3 and 4, because the observer is usually known to those being observed. The study by Rosenhan (1973) described in Research in focus 11.5 is an illustration of contrived observation, because the pseudo-patients were not known to be researchers and they actively varied the situation by their own behaviour. The Daniel (1968) study described in Table 11.1 is also an example of contrived observation, because the 'actors' were not known to be researchers and by applying for rented accommodation they were actively varying the situation.

It is important to realize that Webb *et al.* (1966) were not intending that unobtrusive methods should supplant conventional methods. Instead, they argued that the problem they were identifying was the almost exclusive reliance upon methods that were likely to be affected by reactivity. Webb *et al.* argued for greater '**triangulation**' (see Key concept 16.4) in social research, whereby conventional (reactive) and unobtrusive (non-reactive) methods would be employed in conjunction. For example, they wrote that they were providing an inventory of unobtrusive methods, 'because they demonstrate ways in which the investigator may shore up reactive infirmities of the interview and questionnaire' (Webb *et al.* 1966: 174).

It is worth noting that unobtrusive methods or measures encapsulate at least two kinds of ways of thinking about the process of capturing data. First, many so-called unobtrusive measures are in fact *sources* of data, such as graffiti, diaries, media articles, and official statistics. Such sources require analysis in order to be rendered interesting to a social scientific audience. Second, it includes *methods* of data collection, such as simple and contrived observation. While the data generated by such methods of data collection also require analysis, the data have to be produced by the methods. The data are not simply out there awaiting analysis in the way in which diaries or newspaper articles are (although, of course, a great deal of detective work is often necessary to unearth such sources). This means that neither of the terms 'unobtrusive methods' or 'unobtrusive measures' captures the variety of forms terribly well. A further disadvantage of the term 'unobtrusive measure' is that it seems to imply a connection to quantitative research alone, whereas certain approaches employed by qualitative researchers may qualify as unobtrusive methods.

Lee (2000) has developed a classification of unobtrusive methods that differs slightly from that of Webb *et al.* (1966). He distinguishes the following kinds of data.

1. *Found data*. This category corresponds more or less exactly to *physical traces*.

2. *Captured data*. This category comprises both *simple observation* and *contrived observation*.

3. *Retrieved data: running records*. Records concerned with births, marriages and deaths are prominent cases of this kind of record, whereby records can be examined over quite long periods so that changes can be explored. He also includes in this category personal advertisements like marriage announcements and dating advertisements (see Research in focus 12.2 for an example of research using the latter), as are job advertisements.

4. *Retrieved data: personal and episodic records*. With this category, Lee has in mind three kinds of data: **personal documents** (letters, diaries, memoirs), visual images in the mass media (e.g. newspaper photographs and picture postcards), and 'documents produced through "institutional discovery" procedures' (Lee 2000: 87) (e.g. reports of inquiries into the factors that led to a disaster).

5. Lee also distinguishes *records produced through the Internet*, especially the various forms of computer-mediated communication, such as email and various kinds of message boards and chat rooms. In the years since Lee wrote, blogs (web logs) might be another kind.

Many of these different kinds of data are encountered elsewhere in this book, e.g. personal documents in Chapter 21 and computer-mediated communications in Chapters 21 and 26. Each of the different types that Webb *et al.* and Lee distinguish pose distinctive questions in terms of issues like the reliability of the evidence and the ethical issues involved.

Research in focus 13.3
Using unofficial statistics? The case of New York taxi cab drivers

Following his informal observation on the behaviour of New York taxi drivers (cabbies), Camerer (1997) was interested in testing two different theories about the relationship between the number of hours a cabby works and average hourly earnings. One theory—the law of supply—predicted that cabbies would want to work more when their average hourly earnings would be high (for example, during bad weather or on working days when more business people are around) rather than when they are low. The second theory—daily income targeting—suggests that cabbies set themselves an income target for the day and once that target is attained they stop work for the day. On good days (when hourly wages are higher) this theory simply means they will stop earlier. Camerer obtained taximeter readings from the New York Taxi and Limousine Commission. The data allowed 3,000 observations of cabbies' behaviour for 1988, 1990, and 1994. Tips are not recorded, so a guess had to be made about likely levels in this area. The data provided unequivocal support for the daily income targeting theory. However, further analysis revealed a difference between newer and more experienced drivers: the former behaved very much in line with income targeting theory; the more experienced drivers were much more varied and their overall levels of behaviour were closer to the law of supply theory, though not entirely in conformity with it. Overall, if cabbies obeyed the law of supply, their mean incomes would rise by around 15 per cent.

Key points

- Secondary analysis of existing data offers the prospect of being able to explore research questions of interest to you without having to go through the process of collecting the data yourself.

- Very often, secondary analysis offers the opportunity of being able to employ high-quality data sets that are based on large reasonably representative samples.

- Secondary analysis presents few disadvantages.

- The analysis of official statistics may be thought of as a special form of secondary analysis but one that is more controversial because of the unease about the reliability and validity of certain types of official data, especially those relating to crime and deviance.

- The problems associated with official data relating to crime and deviance should not be generalized to all official statistics. Many forms of official statistics are much less prone to the kinds of errors that are detectable in relation to crime and deviance data, but there remains the possible problem of divergences of definition between compilers of such data and social researchers.

- Official statistics represent a form of unobtrusive method and enjoy certain advantages (especially lack of reactivity) because of that.

Questions for review

- What is secondary analysis?

Other researchers' data

- Outline the main advantages and limitations of secondary analysis of other researchers' data.
- Examine recent issues of one of the British sociology journals, like *Sociology*. Locate an article that uses secondary analysis. How well do the advantages and limitations you outlined fit this article?
- Does the possibility of conducting a secondary analysis apply only to quantitative data produced by other researchers?

Official statistics

- Why have many social researchers been sceptical about the use of official statistics for research purposes?
- How justified is their scepticism?
- What reliability and validity issues do official statistics pose?
- What are unobtrusive methods or measures? What is the chief advantage of such methods?

Online Resource Centre

http://www.oxfordtextbooks.co.uk/orc/brymansrm3e/

Visit the Online Resource Centre that accompanies this book to enrich your understanding of secondary analysis and official statistics. Consult web links, test yourself using multiple choice questions, and gain further guidance and inspiration from the Student Researcher's Toolkit.

Quantitative data analysis

Chapter outline

Chapter guide

In this chapter, some of the basic, but nonetheless most frequently used methods for analysing quantitative data analysis will be presented. In order to illustrate the use of the methods of data analysis, a small imaginary set of data based on attendance at a gym is used. It is the kind of small research project that would be feasible for most students doing undergraduate research projects for a dissertation or similar exercise.

The chapter explores:

- the importance of *not* leaving considerations of how you will analyse your quantitative data until after you have collected all your data; you should be aware of the ways in which you would like to analyse your data from the earliest stage of your research;

- the distinctions between the different kinds of variable that can be generated in quantitative research; knowing how to distinguish types of variables is crucial so that you appreciate which methods of analysis can be applied when you examine variables and relationships between them;

- methods for analysing a single variable at a time (*univariate analysis*);

- methods for analysing relationships between variables (*bivariate analysis*);

- the analysis of relationships between three variables (*multivariate analysis*).

Introduction

In this chapter, some very basic techniques for analysing quantitative data will be examined. In the next chapter, the ways in which these techniques can be implemented using sophisticated computer software (SPSS for Windows) will be introduced. The formulae that underpin the techniques to be discussed will not be presented, since the necessary calculations can easily be carried out by using SPSS for Windows. Two chapters cannot do justice to these topics, and readers are advised to move as soon as possible on to books that provide more detailed and advanced treatments (e.g. Bryman and Cramer 2004).

Before beginning this exposition of techniques, I would like to give you advance warning of one of the biggest mistakes that people make about quantitative data analysis:

I don't have to concern myself with how I'm going to ana-lyse my survey data until after I've collected my data. I'll leave thinking about it till then, because it doesn't impinge on how I collect my data.

This is a common error that arises because quantitative data analysis looks like a distinct phase that occurs after the data have been collected (see, for example, Figure 6.1, in which the analysis of quantitative data is depicted as a late step—number 9—in quantitative research). Quantitative data analysis is indeed something that occurs typically at a late stage in the overall process and is also a distinct stage.

However, that does not mean that you should not be considering how you will analyse your data until then. In fact, you should be fully aware of what techniques you will apply at a fairly early stage—for example, when you are designing your questionnaire, observation schedule, coding frame, or whatever. The two main reasons for this are as follows.

- You cannot apply just any technique to any variable. Techniques have to be appropriately matched to the types of variables that you have created through your research. This means that you must be fully conversant with the ways in which different types of variable are classified.

- The size and nature of your **sample** are likely to impose limitations on the kinds of techniques you can use (see the discussion in Chapter 7 of the issue of 'Kind of analysis').

In other words, you need to be aware that decisions that you make at quite an early stage in the research process, such as the kinds of data you collect and the size of your sample, will have implications for the sorts of analysis that you will be able to conduct.

A small research project

The discussion of quantitative data analysis will be based upon an imaginary piece of research carried out by an undergraduate marketing student for a dissertation. The student in question is interested in the role of the sport and leisure industry and in particular, because of her own enthusiasm for leisure clubs and gyms, with the ways in which such venues are used and people's reasons for joining them. She has read an article that suggests that participant involvement in adult fitness programmes is associated with their attitudinal loyalty, comprising investment of time and money, social pressure from significant others, and internalization of or commitment to the fitness regime. She intends to use this theory as a framework for her findings. The student is also interested in issues relating to gender and body image, and she suspects that men and women will differ in their reasons for going to a gym and the kinds of activities in which they engage in the gym. Her final issue of interest relates to the importance of age in determining gym involvement. In particular, she has discovered that previous research has shown that older people tend to show higher levels of attitudinal loyalty to recreational activities more generally and she wants to find out if this finding also applies to involvement in leisure clubs and gyms.

She secures the agreement of a gym close to her home to contact a sample of its members by post. The gym has 1,200 members and she decides to take a **simple random sample** of 10 per cent of the membership (i.e. 120 members). She sends out **postal questionnaires** to members of the sample with a covering letter testifying to the gym's support of her research. One thing she wants to know is how much time people spend on each of the three main classes of activity in the gym: cardiovascular equipment, weights equipment, and exercises. She defines each of these carefully in the covering letter and asks members of the sample to keep a note of how long they spend on each of the three activities on their next visit. They are then requested to return the questionnaires to her in a pre-paid reply envelope. She ends up with a sample of 90 questionnaires—a response rate of 75 per cent.

Part of the questionnaire is presented in Tips and skills 'Part of a questionnaire used in study of gym users'. The entire questionnaire runs to four pages, but only twelve of the questions are provided here. Many of the questions (1, 3, 4, 5, 6, 7, 8, and 9) are pre-coded and the student simply has to circle the **code** to the far right of the question under the column 'code'. With the remainder of the questions, specific figures are requested, and she simply transfers the relevant figure to the code column. An example of a questionnaire that has been completed by a respondent and coded by the student is presented in Tips and skills 'A completed and processed questionnaire'.

Tips and skills
Part of a questionnaire used in study of gym users

Questionnaire   Code

  1. Are you male or female (please tick)?

      Male ____   Female ____   1   2

  2. How old are you?

     ____ years

3. Which of the following best describes your *main* reason for going to the gym? (please tick *one* only)

Relaxation	_____	1
Maintain or improve fitness	_____	2
Lose weight	_____	3
Meet others	_____	4
Build strength	_____	5
Other (please specify)	_____	6

4. When you go to the gym, how often do you use the cardiovascular equipment (jogger, step machine, bike, rower)? (please tick)

Always	_____	1
Usually	_____	2
Rarely	_____	3
Never	_____	4

5. When you go to the gym, how often do you use the weights machines (including free weights)? (please tick)

Always	_____	1
Usually	_____	2
Rarely	_____	3
Never	_____	4

6. How frequently do you usually go to the gym? (please tick)

Every day	_____	1
4–6 days a week	_____	2
2 or 3 days a week	_____	3
Once a week	_____	4
2 or 3 times a month	_____	5
Once a month	_____	6
Less than once a month	_____	7

7. Are you usually accompanied when you go to the gym or do you usually go on your own? (please tick *one* only)

On my own	_____	1
With a friend	_____	2
With a partner/spouse	_____	3

8. Do you have sources of regular exercise other than the gym?

Yes _____   No _____   1 2

*If you have answered **No** to this question, please proceed to question 10*

9. If you have replied **Yes** to question 8, please indicate the *main* source of regular exercise in the last six months from this list (please tick *one* only).

Sport	_____	1
Cycling on the road	_____	2
Jogging	_____	3
Long walks	_____	4
Other (please specify)	_____	5

10. During your last visit to the gym, how many minutes did you spend on the cardiovascular equipment (jogger, step machine, bike, rower)?

    _____ minutes

11. During your last visit to the gym, how many minutes did you spend on the weights machines (including free weights)?

    _____ minutes

12. During your last visit to the gym, how many minutes did you spend on other activities (e.g. stretching exercises)?

    _____ minutes

Tips and skills
A completed and processed questionnaire

Questionnaire   Code

1. Are you male or female (please tick)?

   Male __✓__   Female _____   ①2

2. How old are you?

   __21__ years   21

3. Which of the following best describes your *main* reason for going to the gym? (please tick *one* only)

Relaxation	_____	1
Maintain or improve fitness	__✓__	②
Lose weight	_____	3
Meet others	_____	4
Build strength	_____	5
Other (please specify)	_____	6

4. When you go to the gym, how often do you use the cardiovascular equipment (jogger, step machine, bike, rower)? (please tick)

Always	__✓__	①
Usually	_____	2
Rarely	_____	3
Never	_____	4

5. When you go to the gym, how often do you use the weights machines (including free weights)? (please tick)

Always	__✓__	①
Usually	_____	2
Rarely	_____	3
Never	_____	4

6. How frequently do you usually go to the gym? (please tick)

Every day	_____	1
4–6 days a week	_____	2
2 or 3 days a week	✓	③
Once a week	_____	4
2 or 3 times a month	_____	5
Once a month	_____	6
Less than once a month	_____	7

7. Are you usually accompanied when you go to the gym or do you usually go on your own? (please tick *one* only)

On my own	✓	①
With a friend	_____	2
With a partner/spouse	_____	3

8. Do you have sources of regular exercise other than the gym?

Yes _____   No ✓   1 ②

*If you have answered **No** to this question, please proceed to question 10*

9. If you have replied **Yes** to question 8, please indicate the *main* source of regular exercise in the last six months from this list (please tick *one* only).   O

Sport	_____	1
Cycling on the road	_____	2
Jogging	_____	3
Long walks	_____	4
Other (please specify)	_____	5

10. During your last visit to the gym, how many minutes did you spend on the cardiovascular equipment (jogger, step machine, bike, rower)?

33 minutes   33

11. During your last visit to the gym, how many minutes did you spend on the weights machines (including free weights)?

17 minutes   17

12. During your last visit to the gym, how many minutes did you spend on other activities (e.g. stretching exercises)?

5 minutes   5

Missing data

The data for all 90 respondents are presented in Tips and skills 'Gym survey data'. Each of the twelve questions is known for the time being as a variable number (var00001, etc.) Each variable number corresponds to the question number in Tips and skills 'Part of a question-naire used in study of gym users' (i.e. var00001 is question 1, var00002 is question 2, etc.) An important issue arises in the management of data as to how to handle 'missing data'. Missing data arise when respondents fail to reply to a question—either by accident or because they do not want to answer the question. Thus, respondent 24 has failed to answer question 2, which is concerned with age. This has been coded as a zero (0) and it will be important to ensure that the computer software is notified of this fact, since it needs to be taken into account during the analysis. Also, question 9 has a large number of zeros, because many people did not answer it, because they have been filtered out by the previous question (i.e. they do not have other sources of regular exercise). These have also been coded as zero to denote missing data, though strictly speaking their failure to reply is more indicative of the question not being applicable to them. Note also that there are zeros for var00010, var00011,

and var00012. However, these do *not* denote missing data but that the respondent spends zero minutes on the activity in question. Everyone has answered questions 10, 11, and 12, so there are in fact no missing data for these variables. If there had been missing data, it would be necessary to code missing data with a number that could not also be a true figure. For example, nobody has spent 99 minutes on these activities, so this might be an appropriate number as it is easy to remember and could not be read by the computer as anything other than missing data.

Tips and skills
Gym survey data

var00001	var00002	var00003	var00004	var00005	var00006	var00007	var00008	var00009	var00010	var00011	var00012
1	21	2	1	1	3	1	2	0	33	17	5
2	44	1	3	1	4	3	1	2	10	23	10
2	19	3	1	2	2	1	1	1	27	18	12
2	27	3	2	1	2	1	2	0	30	17	3
1	57	2	1	3	2	3	1	4	22	0	15
2	27	3	1	1	3	1	1	3	34	17	0
1	39	5	2	1	5	1	1	5	17	48	10
2	36	3	1	2	2	2	1	1	25	18	7
1	37	2	1	1	3	1	2	0	34	15	0
2	51	2	2	2	4	3	2	0	16	18	11
1	24	5	2	1	3	1	1	1	0	42	16
2	29	2	1	2	3	1	2	0	34	22	12
1	20	5	1	1	2	1	2	0	22	31	7
2	22	2	1	3	4	2	1	3	37	14	12
2	46	3	1	1	5	2	2	0	26	9	4
2	41	3	1	2	2	3	1	4	22	7	10
1	25	5	1	1	3	1	1	1	21	29	4
2	46	3	1	2	4	2	1	4	18	8	11
1	30	3	1	1	5	1	2	0	23	9	6
1	25	5	2	1	3	1	1	1	23	19	0
2	24	2	1	1	3	2	1	2	20	7	6
2	39	1	2	3	5	1	2	0	17	0	9
1	44	3	1	1	3	2	1	2	22	8	5
1	0	1	2	2	4	2	1	4	15	10	4
2	18	3	1	2	3	1	2	1	18	7	10
1	41	3	1	1	3	1	2	0	34	10	4
2	38	2	1	2	5	3	1	2	24	14	10
1	25	2	1	1	2	1	2	0	48	22	7
1	41	5	2	1	3	1	1	2	17	27	0
2	30	3	1	1	2	2	2	0	32	13	10
2	29	3	1	3	2	1	2	0	31	0	7

var00001	var00002	var00003	var00004	var00005	var00006	var00007	var00008	var00009	var00010	var00011	var00012
2	42	1	2	2	4	2	1	4	17	14	6
1	31	2	1	1	2	1	2	0	49	21	2
2	25	3	1	1	2	3	2	0	30	17	15
1	46	3	1	1	3	1	1	3	32	10	5
1	24	5	2	1	4	1	1	2	0	36	11
2	34	3	1	1	3	2	1	4	27	14	12
2	50	2	1	2	2	3	2	0	28	8	6
1	28	5	1	1	3	2	1	1	26	22	8
2	30	3	1	1	2	1	1	4	21	9	12
1	27	2	1	1	2	1	1	3	64	15	8
2	27	2	1	2	4	2	1	4	22	10	7
1	36	5	1	1	3	2	2	0	21	24	0
2	43	3	1	1	4	1	2	0	25	13	8
1	34	2	1	1	3	2	1	1	45	15	6
2	27	3	1	1	2	1	1	4	33	10	9
2	38	2	1	3	4	2	2	0	23	0	16
1	28	2	1	1	3	3	1	2	38	13	5
1	44	5	1	1	2	1	2	0	27	19	7
2	31	3	1	2	3	2	2	0	32	11	5
2	23	2	1	1	4	2	1	1	33	18	8
1	45	3	1	1	3	1	1	2	26	10	7
2	34	3	1	2	2	3	2	0	36	8	12
1	27	3	1	1	2	3	1	3	42	13	6
2	40	3	1	1	2	2	1	4	26	9	10
2	24	2	1	1	2	1	1	2	22	10	9
1	37	2	1	1	5	2	2	0	21	11	0
1	22	5	1	1	4	1	1	1	23	17	6
2	31	3	1	2	3	1	1	4	40	16	12
1	37	2	1	1	2	3	2	0	54	12	3
2	33	1	2	2	4	2	2	0	17	10	5
1	23	5	1	1	3	1	1	1	41	27	8
1	28	3	1	1	3	3	2	0	27	11	8
2	29	2	1	2	5	2	1	2	24	9	9
2	43	3	1	1	2	1	2	0	36	17	12
1	28	5	1	1	3	1	1	1	22	15	4
1	48	2	1	1	5	1	1	4	25	11	7
2	32	2	2	2	4	2	2	0	27	13	11
1	28	5	1	1	2	2	2	0	15	23	7
2	23	2	1	1	5	1	1	4	14	11	5
2	43	2	1	2	5	1	2	0	18	7	3
1	28	2	1	1	4	3	1	2	34	18	8
2	23	3	1	1	2	1	2	0	37	17	17
2	36	1	2	2	4	2	1	4	18	12	4
1	50	2	1	1	3	1	1	2	28	14	3
1	37	3	1	1	2	2	2	0	26	14	9
2	41	3	1	1	2	1	1	4	24	11	4
1	26	5	2	1	5	1	1	1	23	19	8
2	28	3	1	1	4	1	2	0	27	12	4
2	35	2	1	1	3	1	1	1	28	14	0
1	28	5	1	1	2	1	1	2	20	24	12

var00001	var00002	var00003	var00004	var00005	var00006	var00007	var00008	var00009	var00010	var00011	var00012
2	36	2	1	1	3	2	2	0	26	9	14
2	29	3	1	1	4	1	1	4	23	13	4
1	34	1	2	2	4	2	1	0	24	12	3
1	53	2	1	1	3	3	1	1	32	17	6
2	30	3	1	1	4	1	2	0	24	10	9
1	43	2	1	1	2	1	1	2	24	14	10
2	26	5	2	1	4	1	1	1	16	23	7
2	44	1	1	1	4	2	2	0	27	18	6
1	45	1	2	2	3	3	2	0	20	14	5

Types of variable

One of the things that might strike you when you look at the questions is that the kinds of information that you receive varies by question. Some of the questions call for answers in terms of real numbers: questions 2, 10, 11, and 12. Questions 1 and 8 yield either/or answers and are therefore in the form of dichotomies. The rest of the questions take the form of lists of categories, but there are differences between these too. Some of the questions are in terms of answers that are rank ordered: questions 4, 5, and 6. Thus we can say in the case of question 6 that the category 'every day' implies greater frequency than '4–6 days a week', which in turn implies greater frequency than '2 or 3 days a week', and so on. However, in the case of questions 3, 7, and 9, the categories are *not* capable of being rank ordered. We cannot say in the case of question 3 that 'relaxation' is more of something than 'maintain or improve fitness' or 'lose weight'.

These considerations lead to a classification of the different types of variable that are generated in the course of research. The four main types are:

- *Interval/ratio variables*. These are variables where the distances between the categories are identical across the range of categories. In the case of variables var00010 to var00011, the distance between the categories is one minute. Thus, a person may spend 32 minutes on cardiovascular equipment, which is 1 minute more than someone who spends 31 minutes on this equipment. That difference is the same as the difference between someone who spends 8 minutes and another who spends 9 minutes on the equipment. This is the highest level of measurement, and a very wide range

of techniques of analysis can be applied to interval/ratio variables. There is, in fact, a distinction between interval and ratio variables, in that the latter are **interval variables** with a fixed zero point. However, since most ratio variables exhibit this quality in social research (e.g. income, age, number of employees, revenue), they are not being distinguished here.

- *Ordinal variables*. These are variables whose categories can be rank ordered (as in the case of interval/ratio variables), but the distances between the categories are not equal across the range. Thus, in the case of question 6, the difference between the category 'every day' and '4–6 days a week' is not the same as the difference between '4–6 days a week' and '2 or 3 days a week', and so on. Nonetheless, we can say that 'every day' is more frequent than '4–6 days a week', which is more frequent than '2 or 3 days a week', etc. You should also bear in mind that, if you subsequently group an interval/ratio variable like var00002, which refers to people's ages, into categories (e.g. 20 and under; 21–30; 31–40; 41–50; 51 and over), you are transforming it into an ordinal variable.

- *Nominal variables*. These variables, also known as *categorical variables*, comprise categories that cannot be rank ordered. As noted previously, we cannot say in the case of question 3 that 'relaxation' is more of something than 'maintain or improve fitness' or 'lose weight'.

- *Dichotomous variables*. These variables contain data that have only two categories (e.g. gender). Their position in relation to the other types is slightly ambiguous, as they have only one interval. They therefore can

Table 14.1

Types of variable			
Type	Description	Examples in gym study	Variable Name in SPSS (see Chapter 15)
Interval/ratio	Variables where the distances between the categories are identical across the range	var00002 var00010 var00011 var00012	age cardmins weimins othmins
Ordinal	Variables whose categories can be rank ordered but the distances between the categories are not equal across the range	var00004 var00005 var00006	carduse weiuse frequent
Nominal	Variables whose categories cannot be rank ordered; also known as *categorical*	var00003 var00007 var00009	reasons accomp exercise
Dichotomous	Variables containing data that have only two categories	var00001 var00008	gender othsourc

be considered as having attributes of the other three types of variable. They look as though they are nominal variables, but because they have only one interval they are sometimes treated as ordinal variables. However, it is probably safest to treat them for most purposes as if they were ordinary nominal variables.

The four main types of variable and illustrations of them from the gym survey are provided in Table 14.1.

Multiple-indicator (or multiple-item) measures of concepts, like Likert scales (see Research in focus 6.2), strictly speaking produce ordinal variables. However, many writers argue that they can be treated as though they produce interval/ratio variables, because of the relatively large number of categories they generate. For a brief discussion of this issue, see Bryman and Cramer (2004: 71–3), who distinguish between 'true' interval/ratio variables and those produced by multiple-indicator measures.

Figure 14.1 provides guidance about how to identify variables of each type.

Univariate analysis

Univariate analysis refers to the analysis of one variable at a time. In this section, the commonest approaches will be outlined.

Frequency tables

A frequency table provides the number of people and the percentage belonging to each of the categories for the variable in question. It can be used in relation to all the different types of variable. An example of a frequency table is provided for var00003 in Table 14.2. Notice that nobody chose two of the possible choices of answer— 'meet others' and 'other'—so these are not included in the table. The table shows, for example, that 33 members of the sample go to the gym to lose weight and that they represent 37 per cent (percentages are often rounded up and

Figure 14.1

Deciding how to categorize a variable

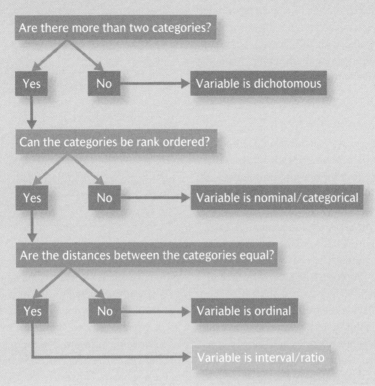

Table 14.2

Frequency table showing reasons for visiting the gym		
Reason	*n*	per cent
Relaxation	9	10
Maintain or improve fitness	31	34
Lose weight	33	37
Build strength	17	19
TOTAL	90	100

Table 14.3

Frequency table showing ages of gym members		
Age	*n*	per cent
20 and under	3	3
21–30	39	44
31–40	23	26
41–50	21	24
51 and over	3	3
TOTAL	89	100

down in frequency tables) of the entire sample. The procedure for generating a frequency table with SPSS is described on pages 348–51.

If an interval/ratio variable (like people's ages) is to be presented in a frequency table format, it is invariably the case that the categories will need to be grouped. When grouping in this way, take care to ensure that the cate-

gories you create do not overlap (for example, like this: 20–30, 30–40, 40–50, etc.). An example of a frequency table for an interval/ratio variable is shown in Table 14.3, which provides a frequency table for var00002, which is concerned with the ages of those visiting the gym. If we do not group people in terms of age ranges, there would be thirty-four different categories, which is too many to take in. By creating five categories, the distribution of ages is easier to comprehend. Notice that the sample totals 89 and that the percentages are based on a total of 89 rather than 90. This is because this variable contains one missing value (respondent 24). This means that this respondent has not replied to the question or has not replied in a manner that can be aggregated with the answers from the other respondents. The procedure for grouping respondents with SPSS is described on pages 345–7.

Diagrams

Diagrams are among the most frequently used methods of displaying quantitative data. Their chief advantage is that they are relatively easy to interpret and understand. If you are working with nominal or ordinal variables, the *bar chart* and the *pie chart* are two of the easiest methods to use. A bar chart of the same data presented in Table 14.2 is presented in Figure 14.2. Each bar represents the number of people falling in each category. This figure was produced with SPSS for Windows. The procedure for generating a bar chart with SPSS is described on page 351.

Another way of displaying the same data is through a pie chart, like the one in Figure 14.3. This also shows the relative size of the different categories but brings out as well the size of each slice relative to the total sample. The percentage that each slice represents of the whole sample is also given in this diagram, which was also produced

with SPSS for Windows. The procedure for generating a pie chart with SPSS is described on pages 351–2.

If you are displaying an interval/ratio variable, like var00002, a *histogram* is likely to be employed. Figure 14.4, which was also generated by SPSS for Windows, uses the same data and categories as Table 14.3. As with the bar chart, the bars represent the relative size of each of the age bands. However, note that, with the histogram, there is no space between the bars, whereas there is a

Figure 14.3

Pie chart showing main reasons for visiting the gym (SPSS output)

Figure 14.2

Bar chart showing main reasons for visiting the gym (SPSS output)

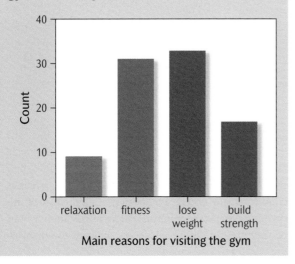

Figure 14.4

Histogram showing the ages of gym visitors (SPSS output)

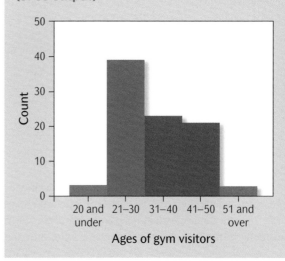

space between the bars of a bar chart. Histograms are produced for interval/ratio variables, whereas bar charts are produced for nominal and ordinal variables. The procedure for generating a histogram with SPSS is described on page 352.

Measures of central tendency

Measures of central tendency encapsulate in one figure a value that is typical for a distribution of values. In effect, we are seeking out an average for a distribution, but, in quantitative data analysis, three different forms of average are recognized.

- *Arithmetic mean*. This is the average as we understand it in everyday use—that is, we sum all the values in a distribution and then divide by the number of values. Thus, the arithmetic mean (or more simply the *mean*) for var00002 is 33.6, meaning that the average age of gym visitors is nearly 34 years of age. The mean should be employed only in relation to interval/ratio variables, though it is not uncommon to see it being used for ordinal variables as well.

- *Median*. This is the mid-point in a distribution of values. Whereas the mean is vulnerable to *outliers* (extreme values at either end of the distribution), which will exert considerable upwards or downwards pressure on the mean, by taking the mid-point of a distribution the median is not affected in this way. The median is derived by arraying all the values in a distribution from the smallest to the largest and then finding the middle point. If there is an even number of values, the median is calculated by taking the mean of the two middle numbers of the distribution. In the case of var00002, the median is 31. This is slightly lower than the mean, in part because some considerably older members (especially respondents 5 and 10) inflate the mean slightly. The median can be employed in relation to both interval/ratio and ordinal variables.

- *Mode*. This is the value that occurs most frequently in a distribution. The mode for var00002 is 28. The mode can be employed in relation to all types of variable.

The procedure for generating the mean, median, and mode with SPSS is described on page 352.

Measures of dispersion

The amount of variation in a sample can be just as interesting as the typical value of a distribution. For one thing, it becomes possible to draw contrasts between comparable distributions of values. For example, is there more or less variability in the amount of time spent on cardiovascular equipment as compared to weights machines?

The most obvious way of measuring dispersion is by the *range*. This is simply the difference between the maximum and the minimum value in a distribution of values associated with an interval/ratio variable. We find that the range for the two types of equipment is 64 minutes for the cardiovascular equipment and 48 minutes for the weights machines. This suggests that there is more variability in the amount of time spent on the former. However, like the mean, the range is influenced by outliers, such as respondent 60 in the case of var00010.

Another measure of dispersion is the *standard deviation*, which is essentially the average amount of variation around the mean. Although the calculation is somewhat more complicated than this, the standard deviation is calculated by taking the difference between each value in a distribution and the mean and then dividing the total of the differences by the number of values. The standard deviation for var00010 is 9.9 minutes and for var00011 it is 8 minutes. Thus, not only is the average amount of time spent on the cardiovascular equipment higher than for the weights equipment; the standard deviation is greater too. The standard deviation is also affected by outliers, but, unlike the range, their impact is offset by dividing by the number of values in the distribution. The procedure for generating the standard deviation with SPSS is described on page 352.

Bivariate analysis

Bivariate analysis is concerned with the analysis of two variables at a time in order to uncover whether the two variables are related. Exploring relationships between variables means searching for evidence that the variation in one variable coincides with variation in another variable. A variety of techniques is available for examining relationships, but their use depends on the nature of the two variables being analysed. Figure 14.5 attempts to portray the main types of bivariate analysis according to the types of variable involved.

Figure 14.5

Methods of bivariate analysis

	Nominal	Ordinal	Interval/ratio	Dichotomous
Nominal	Contingency table + chi-square (χ^2) + Cramér's V	Contingency table + chi-square (χ^2) + Cramér's V	Contingency table + chi-square (χ^2) + Cramér's V. If the interval/ratio variable can be identified as the dependent variable, compare means + eta	Contingency table + chi-square (χ^2) + Cramér's V
Ordinal	Contingency table + chi-square (χ^2) + Cramér's V	Spearman's rho (ρ)	Spearman's rho (ρ)	Spearman's rho (ρ)
Interval/ratio	Contingency table + chi-square (χ^2) + Cramér's V. If the interval/ratio variable can be identified as the dependent variable, compare means + eta	Spearman's rho (ρ)	Pearson's r	Spearman's rho (ρ)
Dichotomous	Contingency table + chi-square (χ^2) + Cramér's V	Spearman's rho (ρ)	Spearman's rho (ρ)	phi (ϕ)

Relationships not causality

An important point to bear in mind about all the methods for analysing relationships between variables is that it is precisely *relationships* that they uncover. As was noted in Chapter 2 in relation to cross-sectional designs, this means that you cannot infer that one variable causes another. Indeed, there are cases when what appears to be a causal influence working in one direction actually works in the other way. An interesting example of this problem of causal direction will be presented in Research in focus 25.5.

The example shows that Sutton and Rafaeli (1988) expected to find a relationship between the display of positive emotions (for example, smiling or friendliness on the part of checkout staff) in retail outlets and sales in those outlets. In other words, the display of positive emotions was deemed to have a causal influence on levels of retail sales. In fact, the relationship was found to be the other way round: levels of retail sales exerted a causal influence on the display of emotions (see Research in focus 25.5 for more detailed explanation of this study).

Sometimes, we may feel confident that we can infer a causal direction when a relationship between two variables is discerned—for example, if we find that age and voting behaviour are related. It is impossible for the way people vote to influence their age, so, if we do find the two variables to be related, we can infer with complete confidence that age is the independent variable. It is not uncommon for researchers, when analysing their data, to draw inferences about causal direction based on their assumptions about the likely causal direction among related variables, as Sutton and Rafaeli (1988) did in their study. Although such inferences may be based on sound reasoning, they can only be inferences, and there is the possibility that the real pattern of causal direction is the opposite of that which is anticipated.

Contingency tables

Contingency tables are probably the most flexible of all methods of analysing relationships in that they can be employed in relation to any pair of variables, though they

Table 14.4

Contingency table showing the relationship between gender and reasons for visiting the gym

Reasons	Gender			
	Male		Female	
	No.	%	No.	%
Relaxation	3	7	6	13
Fitness	15	36	16	33
Lose weight	8	19	25	52
Build strength	16	38	1	2
TOTAL	42		48	

Note: $\chi^2 = 22.726\ p < 0.0001$.

are not the most efficient method for some pairs, which is the reason why the method is not recommended in all of the cells in Figure 14.5. A contingency table is like a frequency table, but it allows two variables to be simultaneously analysed so that relationships between the two variables can be examined. It is normal for contingency tables to include percentages, since these make the tables easier to interpret. Table 14.4 examines the relationship between two variables from the gym survey: gender and reasons for visiting the gym. The percentages are *column percentages*—that is, they calculate the number in each cell as a percentage of the total number in that column. Thus, to take the top left-hand cell, the 3 men who go to the gym for relaxation are 7 per cent of all 42 men in the sample. Users of contingency tables often present the presumed independent variable (if one can in fact be presumed) as the column variable and the presumed dependent variable as the row variable. In this case, we are presuming that gender influences reasons for going to the gym. In fact, we know that going to the gym cannot influence gender. In such circumstances, it is column rather than row percentages that will be required. The procedure for generating a contingency table with SPSS is described on page 352.

Contingency tables are generated so that patterns of association can be searched for. In this case, we can see clear gender differences in reasons for visiting the gym. As our student anticipated, females are much more likely than men to go to the gym to lose weight. They are also somewhat more likely to go the gym for relaxation. By contrast, men are much more likely to go to the gym to build strength. There is little difference between the two genders in terms of fitness as a reason.

Pearson's *r*

Pearson's *r* is a method for examining relationships between interval/ratio variables. The chief features of this method are as follows:

- the coefficient will almost certainly lie between 0 (zero or no relationship between the two variables) and 1 (a perfect relationship)—this indicates the *strength* of a relationship;
- the closer the coefficient is to 1, the stronger the relationship; the closer it is to zero, the weaker the relationship;
- the coefficient will be either positive or negative—this indicates the *direction* of a relationship.

To illustrate these features consider Tips and skills 'Imaginary data from five variables to show different types of relationship', which gives imaginary data for five variables, and the scatter diagrams in Figures 14.6–14.9, which look at the relationship between pairs of interval/ratio variables. The scatter diagram for variables 1 and 2 is presented in Figure 14.6 and shows a perfect **positive relationship**, which would have a Pearson's *r* correlation of 1. This means that, as one variable increases, the other variable increases by the same amount and that no

Figure 14.6

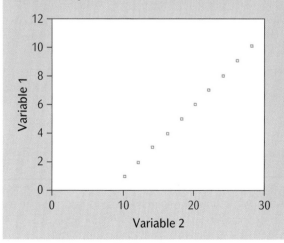

Scatter diagram showing a perfect positive relationship

Figure 14.7

Scatter diagram showing a perfect negative relationship

Figure 14.8

Scatter diagram showing two variables that are not related

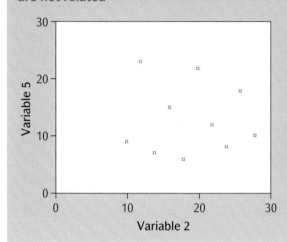

other variable is related to either of them. If the correlation was below 1, it would mean that variable 1 is related to at least one other variable as well as variable 2.

The scatter diagram for variables 2 and 3 (Figure 14.7) shows a perfect negative relationship, which would have a Pearson's *r* correlation of –1. This means that, as one variable increases, the other variable decreases and that no other variable is related to either of them.

If there was no or virtually no correlation between the variables, there would be no apparent pattern to the markers in the scatter diagram. This is the case with the relationship between variables 2 and 5. The correlation is virtually zero at –0.041. This means that the variation in each variable is associated with other variables than the ones present in this analysis. Figure 14.8 shows the appropriate scatter diagram.

Tips and skills
Imaginary data from five variables to show different types of relationship

| Variables | | | | |
1	2	3	4	5
1	10	50	7	9
2	12	45	13	23
3	14	40	18	7
4	16	35	14	15
5	18	30	16	6
6	20	25	23	22
7	22	20	19	12
8	24	15	24	8
9	26	10	22	18
10	28	5	24	10

Figure 14.9

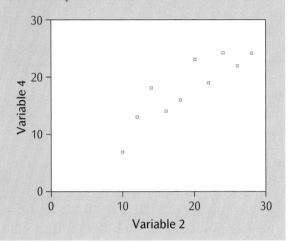

Scatter diagram showing a strong positive relationship

If a relationship is strong, a clear patterning to the variables will be evident. This is the case with variables 2 and 4, whose scatter diagram appears in Figure 14.9. There is clearly a positive relationship and in fact the Pearson's *r* value is 10.88 (usually, positive correlations are presented without the 1 sign). This means that the variation in the two variables is very closely connected, but that there is some influence of other variables in the extent to which they vary.

Going back to the gym survey, we find that the correlation between age (var00002) and the amount of time spent on weights equipment (var00011) is –0.27, implying a weak negative relationship. This suggests that there is a tendency such that, the older a person is, the less likely he or she is to spend much time on such equipment, but that other variables clearly influence the amount of time spent on this activity.

In order to be able to use Pearson's *r*, the relationship between the two variables must be broadly *linear*—that is, when plotted on a scatter diagram, the values of the two variables approximate to a straight line (even though they may be scattered, as in Figure 14.9) and do not curve. Therefore, plotting a scatter diagram before using Pearson's *r* is important, in order to determine that the nature of the relationship between a pair of variables does not violate the assumptions being made when this method of correlation is employed.

If you square a value of Pearson's *r*, you can derive a further useful statistic—namely the *coefficient of determi-*

nation, which expresses how much of the variation in one variable is due to the other variable. Thus, if *r* is –0.27, r^2 is 0.0729. We can then express this as a percentage by multiplying r^2 by 100. The product of this exercise is 7 per cent. This means that just 7 per cent of the variation in the use of cardiovascular equipment is accounted for by age. The coefficient of determination is a useful adjunct to the interpretation of correlation information.

The procedure for generating Pearson's *r* with SPSS is described on page 352 and the procedure for generating scatter diagrams with SPSS is described on pages 353–4.

Spearman's rho

Spearman's rho, which is often represented with the Greek letter ρ, is designed for the use of pairs of ordinal variables, but is also used, as suggested by Figure 14.5, when one variable is ordinal and the other is interval/ratio. It is exactly the same as Pearson's *r* in terms of the outcome of calculating it, in that the computed value of rho will be either positive or negative and will vary between 0 and 1. If we look at the gym study, there are three ordinal variables: var00004, var00005, and var00006 (see Table 14.1). If we use Spearman's rho to calculate the correlation between the first two variables, we find that the correlation between var00004 and var00005—frequency of use of the cardiovascular and weights equipment—is low at 0.2. A slightly stronger relationship is found between var00006 (frequency of going to the gym) and var00010 (amount of time spent on the cardiovascular equipment), which is 0.4. Note that the latter variable is an interval/ratio variable. When confronted with a situation in which we want to calculate the correlation between an ordinal and an interval/ratio variable, we cannot use Pearson's *r*, because both variables must be at the interval/ratio level of measurement. Instead, we must use Spearman's rho (see Figure 14.5). The procedure for generating Spearman's rho with SPSS is described on page 352.

Phi and Cramér's *V*

Phi (ϕ) and Cramér's *V* are two closely related statistics. The phi coefficient is used for the analysis of the relationship between two dichotomous variables. Like Pearson's *r*, it results in a computed statistic that varies between 0 and 1 or –1. The correlation between var00001 (gender) and var00008 (other sources of regular exercise) is 0.24, implying that males are somewhat more likely than females to have other sources of regular exercise, though the relationship is weak.

Cramér's *V* uses a similar formula to phi and can be employed with nominal variables (see Figure 14.5). However, this statistic can take on only a positive value, so that it can give an indication only of the strength of the relationship between two variables, not of the direction. The value of Cramér's *V* associated with the analysis presented in Table 14.4 is 0.50. This suggests a moderate relationship between the two variables. Cramér's *V* is usually reported along with a contingency table and a chi-square test (see below). It is not normally presented on its own. The procedure for generating phi and Cramér's *V* with SPSS is described on page 352.

Comparing means and eta

If you need to examine the relationship between an interval/ratio variable and a nominal variable, and if the latter can be relatively unambiguously identified as the independent variable, a potentially fruitful approach is to compare the means of the interval/ratio variable for each subgroup of the nominal variable. As an example, consider Table 14.5, which presents the mean number of minutes spent on cardiovascular equipment (var00010) for each of the four categories of reasons for going to the gym (var00003). The means suggest that people who go to the gym for fitness or to lose weight spend considerably more time on this equipment than people who go to the gym to relax or to build strength.

This procedure is often accompanied by a test of association between variables called *eta*. This statistic expresses the level of association between the two variables and, like Cramér's *V*, will always be positive. The level of eta for the data in Table 14.5 is 0.48. This suggests a moderate relationship between the two variables. Eta-squared expresses the amount of variation in the interval/ratio variable that is due to the nominal variable. In the case of this example, eta-squared is 22 per cent. Eta is a very flexible method for exploring the relationship between two variables, because it can be employed when one variable is nominal and the other interval/ratio. Also, it does not make the assumption that the relationship between variables is linear. The procedure for comparing means and for generating eta with SPSS is described on pages 354–8.

Table 14.5

Comparing subgroup means: time spent on cardiovascular equipment by reasons for going to the gym					
Time	Reasons				
	Relaxation	Fitness	Lose weight	Build strength	Total
Mean number of minutes spent on cardiovascular equipment	18.33	30.55	28.36	19.65	26.47
n	9	31	33	17	90

Multivariate analysis

Mutivariate analysis entails the simultaneous analysis of three or more variables. This is quite an advanced topic and it is recommended that readers examine a textbook on quantitative data analysis for an exposition of techniques (e.g. Bryman and Cramer 2004). There are three main contexts within which multivariate analysis might be employed.

Could the relationship be spurious?

In order for a relationship between two variables to be established, not only must there be evidence that there is a relationship but the relationship must be shown to be *non-spurious*. A spurious relationship exists when there appears to be a relationship between two variables, but

Figure 14.10

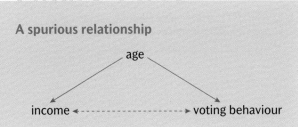

A spurious relationship

the relationship is not real: it is being produced because each variable is itself related to a third variable. For example, if we find a relationship between income and voting behaviour, we might ask: could the relationship be an artefact of age (see Figure 14.10)? The older one is, the more likely one is to earn more, while age is known to influence voting behaviour. If age were found to be producing the apparent relationship between income and voting behaviour, we would conclude that the relationship is spurious. An interesting possible case of a spurious relationship was highlighted in a very short report in *The Times* (1 October 1999, p. 2) of some medical findings. The article noted that there is evidence to suggest that women on hormone replacement therapy (HRT) have lower levels of heart disease than those not on this form of therapy. The article cites Swedish findings that suggest that the relationship may be due to the fact that women who choose to start the therapy are 'thinner, richer and healthier' than those who do not. These background factors would seem to affect both the likelihood of taking HRT *and* the likelihood of getting heart disease. A further illustration in connection with a health-related issue comes from another *Times* article (Hawkes 2003), which reports a relationship among men between frequency of shaving and likelihood of a heart attack or stroke. The reason appears to be that each of the variables (frequency of shaving and vulnerability to a heart attack or stroke) is affected by lifestyle and hormonal factors.

Could there be an intervening variable?

Let us say that we do not find that the relationship is spurious; we might ask *why* there is a relationship between two variables. For example, there have been several studies that have explored the relationship between an organization's market orientation and its business performance. However, the mixed nature of the findings to have emerged from these studies led Piercy *et al.* (2002) to suggest that there is a more complex relationship between these two variables than previous studies have assumed. In particular, they speculated that higher levels of market orientation are associated with higher levels of employee motivation, satisfaction, and commitment, which in turn leads to enhanced organizational performance. Employee attitudes are thus an *intervening variable*:

market → employee → organizational
orientation attitudes performance

An intervening variable allows us to answer questions about the bivariate relationship between variables. It suggests that the relationship between the two variables is not a direct one, since the impact of market orientation on organizational performance is viewed as occurring via employee attitudes.

Could a third variable moderate the relationship?

We might ask a question like: does the relationship between two variables hold for men but not for women? If it does, the relationship is said to be moderated by gender. We might ask in the gym study, for example, whether the relationship between age and whether visitors have other sources of regular exercise (var00008) is moderated by gender. This would imply that, if we find a pattern relating age to other sources of exercise, that pattern will vary by gender. Table 14.6 shows the relationship between age and other sources of exercise. In this table, age has been broken down into just three age bands to make the table easier to read. The table suggests that the 31–40 age group are less likely to have other sources of

Table 14.6

Contingency table showing the relationship between age and whether gym visitors have other sources of regular exercise (percentages)			
Other source of exercise	Age		
	30 and under	31–40	41 and over
Other source	64	43	58
No other source	36	57	42
n	42	23	24

Table 14.7

Contingency table showing the relationship between age and whether gym visitors have other sources of regular exercise for males and females (percentages)						
Other source of exercise	Gender					
	Male			Female		
	30 and under	31–40	41 and over	30 and under	31–40	41 and over
Other source	70	33	75	59	50	42
No other source	30	67	25	41	50	58
n	20	9	12	22	14	12

regular exercise than the 30 and under and 41 and over age groups. However, Table 14.7, which breaks the relationship down by gender, suggests that the pattern for males and females is somewhat different. Among males, the pattern shown in Table 14.7 is very pronounced, but for females the likelihood of having other sources of exercise declines with gender. It would seem that the relationship between age and other sources of exercise is moderated by gender. This example illustrates the way in which contingency tables can be employed for multivariate analysis. However, there is a wide variety of other techniques (Bryman and Cramer 2008: ch. 10). The procedure for conducting such an analysis with SPSS is described on page 358.

Statistical significance

One difficulty with working on data deriving from a sample is that there is often the lingering worry that, even though you have employed a probability sampling procedure (as in the gym survey), your findings will not be generalizable to the population from which the sample was drawn. As we saw in Chapter 7, there is always the possibility that *sampling error* (difference between the population and the sample that you have selected) has occurred, even when probability sampling procedures have been followed. If this happens, the sample will be unrepresentative of the wider population and therefore any findings will be invalid. To make matters worse, there is no feasible way of finding out whether they do in fact apply to the population! What you can do is to provide an indication of how confident you can be in your findings. This is where statistical significance and the various tests of statistical significance come in.

We need to know how confident we can be that our findings can be generalized to the population from which that sample was selected. Since we cannot be absolutely certain that a finding based on a sample will also be found in the population, we need a technique that allows us to establish how confident we can be that the finding exists in the population and what risk we are taking in inferring that the finding exists in the population. These two elements—confidence and risk—lie at the heart of tests of statistical significance (see Key concept 14.1). However, it is important to appreciate that tests of statistical significance can be employed only in relation to samples that have been drawn using probability sampling.

In Chapter 7 (see Tips and skills 'Generalizing from a random sample to the population'), in the context of the discussion of the standard error of the mean, we began to get an appreciation of the ideas behind statistical significance. For example, we know that the mean age of the gym sample is 33.6. Using the concept of the standard error of the mean, we can calculate that we can be 95 per cent confident that the population mean lies between 31.72 and 35.47. This suggests that we can determine in broad outline the degree of confidence that we can have in a sample mean.

Key concept 14.1
What is a test of statistical significance?

A test of statistical significance allows the analyst to estimate how confident he or she can be that the results deriving from a study based on a randomly selected sample are generalizable to the population from which the sample was drawn. When examining statistical significance in relation to the relationship between two variables, it also tells us about the risk of concluding that there is in fact a relationship in the population when there is no such relationship in the population. If an analysis reveals a statistically significant finding, this does not mean that that finding is intrinsically significant or important. The word 'significant' seems to imply importance. However, statistical significance is solely concerned with the confidence researchers can have in their findings. It does not mean that a statistically significant finding is substantively significant.

In the rest of this section, we will look at the tests that are available for determining the degree of confidence we can have in our findings when we explore relationships between variables. All the tests have a common structure.

- *Set up a null hypothesis*. This stipulates that two variables are not related in the population—for example, that there is *no* relationship between gender and visiting the gym in the population from which the sample was selected.

- *Establish the level of statistical significance that you find acceptable*. This is essentially a measure of the degree of risk that you might reject the null hypothesis (implying that there *is* a relationship in the population) when you should support it (implying that there is no relationship in the population). Levels of statistical significance are expressed as probability levels—that is, the probability of rejecting the null hypothesis when you should be confirming it. See Key concept 14.2 on

Key concept 14.2
What is the level of statistical significance?

The level of statistical significance is the level of risk that you are prepared to take that you are inferring that there is a relationship between two variables in the population from which the sample was taken when in fact no such relationship exists. The maximum level of risk that is conventionally taken in social research is to say that there are up to 5 chances in 100 that we might be falsely concluding that there is a relationship when there is not one in the population from which the sample was taken. This means that, if we drew 100 samples, we are recognizing that as many as 5 of them might exhibit a relationship when there is not one in the population. Our sample might be one of those five, but the risk is fairly small. This significance level is denoted by $p < 0.05$ (p means *probability*). If we accepted a significance level of $p < 0.1$, we would be accepting the possibility that as many as 10 in 100 samples might show a relationship where none exists in the population. In this case, there is a greater risk than with $p < 0.05$ that we might have a sample that implies a relationship when there is not one in the population, since the probability of our having such a sample is greater when the risk is 1 in 10 (10 out of 100 when $p < 0.1$) than when the risk is 1 in 20 (5 out of 100 when $p < 0.05$). Therefore, we would have greater confidence when the risk of falsely inferring that there is a relationship between 2 variables is 1 in 20, as against 1 in 10. But, if you want a more stringent test, perhaps because you are worried about the use that might be made of your results, you might choose the $p < 0.01$ level. This means that you are prepared to accept as your level of risk a probability of only 1 in 100 that the results could have arisen by chance (that is, due to sampling error). Therefore, if the results, following administration of a test, show that the results are statistically significant at the $p < 0.05$ level, but *not* the $p < 0.01$ level, you would have to confirm the null hypothesis.

Figure 14.11

Type I and Type II errors

this issue. The convention among most social researchers is that the maximum level of statistical significance that is acceptable is $p < 0.05$, which implies that there are fewer than five chances in 100 that you could have a sample that shows a relationship when there is not one in the population.

- *Determine the statistical significance of your findings* (i.e. use a statistical test like chi-square—see below).

- If your findings are statistically significant at the 0.05 level—so that the risk of getting a relationship as strong as the one you have found, when there is *no* relationship in the population, is no higher than 5 in 100—you would *reject* the null hypothesis. Therefore, you are implying that the results are unlikely to have occurred by *chance*.

There are in fact two types of error that can be made when inferring statistical significance. These errors are known as Type I and Type II errors (see Figure 14.11). A Type I error occurs when you reject the null hypothesis when it should in fact be confirmed. This means that your results have arisen by chance and you are falsely concluding that there is a relationship in the population when there is not one. Using a $p < 0.05$ level of significance means that we are more likely to make a Type I error than when using a $p < 0.01$ level of significance. This is because with 0.01 there is less chance of falsely rejecting the null hypothesis. However, in doing so, you increase

the chance of making a Type II error (accepting the null hypothesis when you should reject it). This is because you are more likely to confirm the null hypothesis when the significance level is 0.01 (1 in 100) than when it is 0.05 (1 in 20).

The chi-square test

The chi-square (χ^2) test is applied to contingency tables like Table 14.4. It allows us to establish how confident we can be that there is a relationship between the two variables in the population. The test works by calculating for each cell in the table an expected frequency or value—that is, one that would occur on the basis of chance alone. The chi-square value, which in Table 14.4 is 22.726, is calculated by calculating the differences between the actual and expected values for each cell in the table and then summing those differences (it is slightly more complicated than this, but the details need not concern us here). The chi-square value means nothing on its own and can be meaningfully interpreted only in relation to its associated level of statistical significance, which in this case is $p < 0.0001$. This means that there is only one chance in 10,000 of rejecting the null hypothesis (that is, inferring that there *is* a relationship in the population when there is no such relationship in the population). You could be extremely confident that there is a relationship between gender and reasons for visiting the gym among all gym members, since the chance that you have obtained a sample that shows a relationship when there is no relationship among all gym members is 1 in 10,000.

Whether a chi-square value achieves statistical significance depends not just on its magnitude but also on the number of categories of the two variables being analysed. This latter issue is governed by what is known as the 'degrees of freedom' associated with the table. The number of degrees of freedom is governed by the simple formula:

Number of degrees of freedom = (number of columns – 1)(number of rows – 1).

In the case of Table 14.5, this will be $(2 – 1)(4 – 1)$—that is, 3. In other words, the chi-square value that is arrived at is affected by the size of the table, and this is taken into account when deciding whether the chi-square value is statistically significant or not. The procedure for chi-square in conjunction with a contingency table with SPSS is described on page 352.

Correlation and statistical significance

Examining the statistical significance of a computed correlation coefficient, which is based on a randomly selected sample, provides information about the likelihood that the coefficient will be found in the population from which the sample was taken. Thus, if we find a correlation of –0.62, what is the likelihood that a relationship of at least that size exists in the population? This tells us whether the relationship could have arisen by chance.

If the correlation coefficient r is –0.62 and the significance level is $p < 0.05$, we can reject the null hypothesis that there is no relationship in the population. We can infer that there are only five chances in 100 that a correlation of at least –0.62 could have arisen by chance alone. You *could* have one of the five samples in 100 that shows a relationship when there is not one in the population, but the degree of risk is reasonably small. If, say, it was found that $r = –0.62$ and $p < 0.1$, there could be as many as ten chances in 100 that there is no correlation in the population. This would *not* be an acceptable level of risk for most purposes. It would mean that in as many as one sample in 10 we might find a correlation of –0.62 or above when there is not a correlation in the population. If $r = –0.62$ and $p < 0.001$, there is only one chance in 1,000 that no correlation exists in the population. There would be a very low level of risk if you inferred that the correlation had not arisen by chance.

Whether a correlation coefficient is statistically significant or not will be affected by two factors:

1. the size of the computed coefficient, and

2. the size of the sample.

This second factor may appear surprising. Basically, the larger a sample, the more likely it is that a computed correlation coefficient will be found to be statistically significant. Thus, even though the correlation between age and the amount of time spent on weights machines in the gym survey was found to be just –0.27, which is a fairly weak relationship, it is statistically significant at the $p < 0.01$ level. This means that there is only one chance in 100 that there is no relationship in the population. Because the question of whether a correlation coefficient is statistically significant depends so much on the sample size, it is important to realize that you should always examine *both* the correlation coefficient *and* the significance level. You should not examine one at the expense of the other.

This treatment of correlation and statistical significance applies to both Pearson's r and Spearman's rho. A similar interpretation can also be applied to phi and Cramér's V. SPSS automatically produces information regarding statistical significance when Pearson's r, Spearman's rho, phi, and Cramér's V are generated.

Comparing means and statistical significance

A test of statistical significance can also be applied to the comparison of means that was carried out in Table 14.5. This procedure entails treating the total amount of variation in the dependent variable—amount of time spent on cardiovascular equipment—as made up of two types: variation *within* the four subgroups that make up the independent variable and variation *between* them. The latter is often called the *explained variance* and the former the *error variance*. A test of statistical significance for the comparison of means entails relating the two types of variance to form what is known as the F statistic. This statistic expresses the amount of explained variance in relation to the amount of error variance. In the case of the data in Table 14.5, the resulting F statistic is statistically significant at the $p < 0.001$ level. This finding suggests that there is only one chance in 1,000 that there is no relationship between the two variables among all gym members. SPSS produces information regarding the F statistic and its statistical significance if the procedures described on page 354 are followed.

Checklist

Doing and writing up quantitative data analysis

○ Have you answered your research questions?

○ Have you made sure that you have presented only analyses that are relevant to your research questions?

○ Have you made sure that you have taken into account the nature of the variable(s) being analysed when using a particular technique (i.e. whether nominal, ordinal, interval/ratio, or dichotomous)?

○ Have you used the most appropriate and powerful techniques for answering your research questions?

○ If your sample has *not* been randomly selected, have you made sure that you have not made inferences about a population (or at least, if you have done so, have you outlined the limitations of making such an inference?)?

○ If your data are based on a cross-sectional design, have you resisted making unsustainable inferences about causality?

○ Have you remembered to code any missing data?

○ Have you commented on all the analyses you present?

○ Have you gone beyond univariate analysis and conducted at least some bivariate analyses?

○ If you have used a Likert scale with reversed items, have you remembered to reverse the coding of them?

Key points

● You need to think about your data analysis before you begin designing your research instruments.

● Techniques of data analysis are applicable to some types of variable and not others. You need to know the difference between interval/ratio, ordinal, nominal, and dichotomous variables.

● You need to think about the kinds of data you are collecting and the implications your decisions will have for the sorts of techniques you will be able to employ.

● Become familiar with computer software like SPSS before you begin designing your research instruments, because it is advisable to be aware at an early stage of difficulties you might have in presenting your data in SPSS.

● Make sure you are thoroughly familiar with the techniques introduced in this chapter and when you can and cannot use them.

● The basic message, then, is not to leave these considerations until your data have been collected, tempting though it may be.

● Do not confuse statistical significance with substantive significance.

Questions for review

- At what stage should you begin to think about the kinds of data analysis you need to conduct?
- What are missing data and why do they arise?

Types of variable

- What are the differences between the four types of variable outlined in this chapter: interval/ratio; ordinal; nominal; and dichotomous?
- Why is it important to be able to distinguish between the four types of variable?
- Imagine the kinds of answers you would receive if you administered the following four questions in an interview survey. What kind of variable would each question generate: dichotomous; nominal; ordinal; or interval/ratio?

    1. Do you enjoy going shopping?

        Yes ——

        No ——

    2. How many times have you shopped in the last month? Please write in the number of occasions below.

        ——

    3. For which kinds of items do you most enjoy shopping? Please tick one only.

        Clothes (including shoes) ——

        Food ——

        Things for the house ——

        Presents ——

        Entertainment (CDs, videos, etc.) ——

    4. How important is it to you to buy clothes with designer labels?

        Very important ——

        Fairly important ——

        Not very important ——

        Not at all important ——

Univariate analysis

- What is an outlier and why might one have an adverse effect on the mean and the range?
- In conjunction with which measure of central tendency would you expect to report the standard deviation: the mean; the median; or the mode?

Bivariate analysis

- Can you infer causality from bivariate analysis?
- Why are percentages crucial when presenting contingency tables?
- In what circumstances would you use each of the following: Pearson's r; Spearman's rho; phi; Cramér's V; eta?

Multivariate analysis

- What is a spurious relationship?
- What is an intervening variable?
- What does it mean to say that a relationship is moderated?

Statistical significance

- What does statistical significance mean and how does it differ from substantive significance?
- What is a significance level?
- What does the chi-square test achieve?
- What does it mean to say that a correlation of 0.42 is statistically significant at $p < 0.05$?

Online Resource Centre

http://www.oxfordtextbooks.co.uk/orc/brymansrm3e/

Visit the Online Resource Centre that accompanies this book to enrich your understanding of quantitative data analysis. Consult web links, test yourself using multiple choice questions, and gain further guidance and inspiration from the Student Researcher's Toolkit.

Using SPSS for Windows

Chapter outline

Chapter guide

In order to implement the techniques that you learned in Chapter 14, you would need to do either of two things: learn the underlying formula for each technique and apply your data to it, or use computer software to analyse your data. The latter is the approach chosen in this book for two main reasons.

1. It is closer to the way in which quantitative data analysis is carried out in real research nowadays.

2. It helps to equip you with a useful transferable skill.

You will be learning **SPSS** for Windows, which is the most widely used package of computer software for doing this kind of analysis. It is relatively straightforward to use. We will be continuing to refer to the techniques introduced in Chapter 14 and will continue to use the gym survey as an example.

This chapter largely operates in parallel to Chapter 14, so that you can see the links between the techniques learned there and the use of SPSS to implement them.

Introduction

This chapter aims to provide a familiarity with some basic aspects of SPSS for Windows, which is possibly the most widely used computer software for the analysis of quantitative data for social scientists. SPSS, which originally was short for Statistical Package for the Social Sciences, has been in existence since the mid-1960s and over the years has undergone many revisions, particularly since the arrival of personal computers. The version that was used in preparing this section was Release 15. From this point on, when referring to SPSS for Windows in the text, it will be called simply SPSS. The gym survey used in Chapter 14 will be employed to illustrate SPSS operations and methods of analysis. The aim of this chapter is to introduce ways of using SPSS to implement the methods of analysis discussed in Chapter 14.

SPSS operations will be presented in **bold**, for example, **Variable Name:** and **Analyze**. Names given to variables in the course of using SPSS will be presented in ***bold italics***, e.g. ***gender*** and ***reasons***. Labels given to values or to variables are also in bold but in a different font, e.g. **reasons for visiting** and **male**. Tips and Skills Basic operations in SPSS presents a list summarizing these. One further element in the presentation is that a right-pointing arrow ($\rightarrow$) will be used to denote 'click once with the left-hand button of your mouse'. This action is employed to make selections and similar activities.

Tips and skills
Basic operations in SPSS

- The **SPSS Data Editor**. This is the sphere of SPSS into which data are entered and subsequently edited and defined. It is made up of two screens: the **Data Viewer** and the **Variable Viewer**. You move between these two viewers by selecting the appropriate tab at the bottom of the screen.

- The **Data Viewer**. This is the spreadsheet into which your data are entered. When you start up SPSS, the **Data Viewer** will be facing you.

- The **Variable Viewer**. This is another spreadsheet, but this one displays information about each of the variables and allows you to change that information. It is the platform from which you provide for each variable such information as: the variable name; a variable label; and value labels (see below).

- The **Output**. When you perform an analysis or produce a diagram (called a 'chart' in SPSS), your output will be deposited here. The **Output Viewer** superimposes itself over the **Data Editor** after an analysis has been performed or a chart generated.

- A **Variable Name**. This is the name that you give to a variable, e.g. *gender*. The name must be no more than eight characters. Until you give a variable a name, it will be referred to as *var00001*, etc. When the variable has been given a name, it will appear in the column for that variable in the **Data View** window. It is generated from the **Variable Viewer**.

- A **Variable Label**. This is a label that you can give to a variable but which is not restricted to eight characters. Spaces can be used, e.g. **reasons for visiting**. The Label will appear in any output you generate. It is generated from the **Variable Viewer**.

- A **Value Label**. This is a label that you can attach to a **code** that has been used when entering data for all types of variables other than interval/**ratio variables**. Thus, for var00001, we would attach the label **male** to 1 and **female** to 2. When you generate output, such as a **frequency table** or chart, the labels for each value will be presented. This makes the interpretation of output easier. It is generated from the **Variable Viewer**.

- **Missing Values** . . . When you do not have data for a particular case when entering data for a variable (e.g. because a respondent has failed to answer that question), you must specify how you are denoting missing values for that variable. Missing values are generated from the **Variable Viewer**.

- **Recode**. A procedure that allows codes or numbers to be changed. It is especially helpful when you need to combine groups of people—for example, when producing age bands.

- **Compute** . . . A procedure that allows you to combine two or more variables to form a new variable.

- **Analyze**. This is the point on the menu bar above the **Data Editor** from which you choose (via a drop-down menu) which method of analysis you want to select. Note that, whenever an item on a menu appears with a right-pointing arrowhead after it, this means that, if you select that option, a further menu will follow on.

- **Graphs**. This is the point on the menu bar above the **Data Editor** from which you choose (via a drop-down menu) which chart you want to select.

- **Chart Editor**. When you produce a graph, you can edit it with the **Chart Editor**. To activate this editor, double-click anywhere in the graph. A small chart editor window will appear and your main graph will appear opaque until you exit the Editor. From the Editor, you can make various changes and enhancements to your graph.

Getting started in SPSS

Beginning SPSS

To start SPSS, double click on the **spsswin** icon on your computer screen. If there is no icon, → the Start button in the bottom left-hand corner of your screen. From the menu of programs, → **SPSS for Windows**. A follow-on menu will appear, from which you should select **SPSS 15.0 for Windows**. When SPSS loads, you *may* be faced with an opening dialog box with the title 'What do you want to do?' and a list of options. Many users prefer to disable this opening box. It is not important in relation to the following exposition, so → **Cancel**. You will then be faced with the **SPSS Data Editor**. This is made up of two components: **Data View** and **Variable View**. In the following discussion, these two screens are referred to as the **Data Viewer** and the **Variable Viewer**. You move between these two viewers by selecting the appropriate tab at the bottom of the screen. The **Data Viewer** is in the form of a spreadsheet grid into which you enter your data. The columns represent *variables*—in other words, information about characteristics of each person in the gym study sample. Until data are entered, each column simply has

var as its heading. The rows represent *cases*, which can be people (as in the example you will be working through) or any unit of analysis. Each block in the grid is referred to as a cell. Note also that when the data are in the SPSS spreadsheet, they will look different, for example, 1 will be 1.00.

Entering data in the **Data Viewer**

To input the data into the **Data Viewer**, make sure that the top left-hand cell in the grid is highlighted (Plate 15.1). If it is not highlighted, simply click once in that cell. Then, type the appropriate figure for that cell—that is, 1. This number goes directly into that cell and into the box beneath the toolbar. As an alternative to using the mouse, many people find it easier to use the arrow keys on their keyboard to move from cell to cell. If you make a mistake at any point, simply click once in the cell in question, type in the correct value, and click once more in that cell. When you have finished, you should end up in the bottom right-hand cell of what will be a perfect rectangle of data. Plate 15.2 shows the **Data Viewer** with the data from

Plate 15.1

The SPSS Data Viewer

Each column represents a variable

Each row represents a case

Plate 15.2

The Data Viewer with 'gym study' data entered

> The first row shows the data for the person who answered the questionnaire in Tips and skills A completed and processed questionnaire on pages 317–18.

	var00001	var00002	var00003	var00004	var00005	var00006	var00007	var00008	var00009	var00010	var00011	var00012
1	1.00	21.00	2.00	1.00	1.00	3.00	1.00	2.00	.00	33.00	17.00	5.00
2	2.00	44.00	1.00	3.00	1.00	4.00	3.00	1.00	2.00	10.00	23.00	10.00
3	2.00	19.00	3.00	1.00	2.00	2.00	1.00	1.00	1.00	27.00	18.00	12.00
4	2.00	27.00	3.00	2.00	1.00	2.00	1.00	2.00	.00	30.00	17.00	3.00
5	1.00	57.00	2.00	1.00	3.00	2.00	3.00	1.00	4.00	22.00	.00	15.00
6	2.00	27.00	3.00	1.00	1.00	3.00	1.00	1.00	3.00	34.00	17.00	.00
7	1.00	39.00	5.00	2.00	1.00	5.00	1.00	1.00	5.00	17.00	48.00	10.00
8	2.00	36.00	3.00	1.00	2.00	2.00	2.00	1.00	1.00	25.00	18.00	7.00
9	1.00	37.00	2.00	1.00	1.00	3.00	1.00	2.00	.00	34.00	15.00	.00
10	2.00	51.00	2.00	2.00	2.00	4.00	3.00	2.00	.00	16.00	18.00	11.00
11	1.00	24.00	5.00	2.00	1.00	3.00	1.00	1.00	1.00	.00	42.00	16.00
12	2.00	29.00	2.00	1.00	2.00	3.00	1.00	2.00	.00	34.00	22.00	12.00
13	1.00	20.00	5.00	1.00	1.00	2.00	1.00	2.00	.00	22.00	31.00	7.00
14	2.00	22.00	2.00	1.00	3.00	4.00	2.00	1.00	3.00	37.00	14.00	12.00
15	2.00	46.00	3.00	1.00	1.00	5.00	2.00	2.00	.00	26.00	9.00	4.00
16	2.00	41.00	3.00	1.00	2.00	2.00	3.00	1.00	4.00	22.00	7.00	10.00
17	1.00	25.00	5.00	1.00	1.00	3.00	1.00	1.00	1.00	21.00	29.00	4.00
18	2.00	46.00	3.00	1.00	2.00	4.00	2.00	1.00	4.00	18.00	8.00	11.00
19	1.00	30.00	3.00	1.00	1.00	5.00	1.00	2.00	.00	23.00	9.00	6.00
20	1.00	25.00	5.00	2.00	1.00	3.00	1.00	1.00	1.00	23.00	19.00	.00
21	2.00	24.00	2.00	1.00	1.00	3.00	2.00	1.00	2.00	20.00	7.00	6.00
22	2.00	39.00	1.00	2.00	3.00	5.00	1.00	2.00	.00	17.00	.00	9.00
23	1.00	44.00	3.00	1.00	1.00	3.00	2.00	1.00	2.00	22.00	8.00	5.00
24	1.00	.00	1.00	2.00	2.00	4.00	2.00	1.00	4.00	15.00	10.00	4.00
25	2.00	18.00	3.00	1.00	2.00	3.00	1.00	2.00	1.00	18.00	7.00	10.00
26	1.00	41.00	3.00	1.00	1.00	3.00	1.00	2.00	.00	34.00	10.00	4.00
27	2.00	38.00	2.00	1.00	2.00	5.00	3.00	1.00	2.00	24.00	14.00	10.00
28	1.00	25.00	2.00	1.00	1.00	2.00	1.00	2.00	.00	48.00	22.00	7.00
29	1.00	41.00	5.00	2.00	1.00	3.00	1.00	1.00	2.00	17.00	27.00	.00
30	2.00	30.00	3.00	1.00	1.00	2.00	2.00	2.00	.00	32.00	13.00	10.00
31	2.00	29.00	3.00	1.00	3.00	2.00	1.00	2.00	.00	31.00	.00	7.00

the gym survey entered (though only part of the set of data is visible, in that data relating to only some of the respondents are visible). The first row of data contains the coded answers from the completed questionnaire in Chapter 14 (see Tips and skills A completed and processed questionnaire).

In order to proceed further, you will find that SPSS works in the following typical sequence for defining variables and analysing your data.

1. You make a selection from the menu bar at the top of the screen, e.g. → **Analyze**.

2. From the menu that will appear, make a selection, e.g. → **Descriptive Statistics**.

3. This will bring up a ***dialog box*** in which you will usually inform SPSS of what you are trying to do—e.g. which variables are to be analysed.

4. Very often, you then need to convey further information and to do this you have to → a button that will bring up what is called, following Bryman and Cramer (2008), a ***sub-dialog box***.

5. You then provide the information in the sub-dialog box and then go back to the dialog box. Sometimes, you will need to bring up a further sub-dialog box and then go back to the dialog box.

When you have finished going through the entire procedure, → **OK**. The toolbar beneath the menu bar allows shortcut access to certain SPSS operations.

Defining variables: variable names, missing values, variable labels, and value labels

Once you have finished entering your data, you need to define your variables. The following steps will allow you to do this:

Plate 15.3

The **Variable Viewer**

To insert **Missing Labels** for **var00003**, click here

1. → the **Variable View** tab at the bottom of the **Data Viewer** (opens the **Variable Viewer** shown in Plate 15.3).

2. To provide a variable name, click on the current variable name (e.g. **var00003**) and type the name of the name you want to give it (e.g. **reasons**). Remember that this name must be no more than eight characters and you can**not** use spaces.

3. You can then give your variable a more detailed name, known in SPSS as a variable label. To do this, →

cell in the **Label** column relating to the variable for which you want to supply a variable label. Then, simply type in the variable label (i.e. **reasons for visiting**).

4. Then you will need to provide 'value labels' for variables that have been given codes. The procedure generally applies to variables that are not interval/ratio variables. The latter, which are numeric variables, do not need to be coded (unless you are grouping them in some way). To assign value labels, → in the **Values** column relating to the variable you are working on. A small

Plate 15.4

The Value Labels dialog box

Remember to click on **Add** after entering each **Value** and **Label**

button with three dots on it (▣) will appear. → ▣. The **Value Labels** dialog box will appear (Plate 15.4). → the box to the right of **Value** and begin to define the value labels. To do this, enter the value (e.g. **1**) in the area to the right of **Value** and then the value label (e.g. **relaxation**) in the area to the right of **Label**. Then → **Add**. Do this for each value. When you have finished → **OK**.

5. You will then need to inform SPSS of the value that you have nominated for each variable to indicate a missing value. In the case of *reasons*, the value is 0 (zero). To assign the missing value, → the cell for this variable in the **Missing** column. Again, → ▣. This will generate the **Missing Values** dialog box (Plate 15.5). In the **Missing Values** dialog box, enter the missing value (0) below **Discrete Missing Values** and then → **OK.**

In order to simplify the following presentation, *reasons* will be the only variable for which a variable label will be defined.

Recoding variables

Sometimes you need to recode variables—for example, when you want to group people. You would need to do this in order to produce a table like Table 14.3 for an interval/ratio variable like **var00002**, which we will give the variable name *age*. SPSS offers two choices: you can recode *age* so that it will be changed in the **Data View**, or you can keep *age* as it is and create a new variable. This latter option is desirable whenever you want to preserve the variable in question as well as create a new one. Since we may want to carry out analyses involving *age* as an interval/ratio variable, we will recode it so that a new variable, which we will call *agegp*, for *age* groups, will be created. The aim of the following operations is to create a new variable—*agegp*—which will comprise five age bands, as in Table 14.3.

1. → **Transform** → **Recode into Different Variables** **. . .** [opens **Recode into Different Variables** dialog box shown in Plate 15.6]

Plate 15.5

The Missing Values dialog box

Designates 0 as the missing value for the variable in question

Plate 15.6

The Recode into Different Variables dialog box

Original name of variable

Recoded name of variable

Click here to specify how values are to be recoded

Plate 15.7

The Recode into Different Variables: Old and New Values sub-dialog box

Recode into Different Variables: Old and New Values

Old Value
- Value:
- System-missing
- System- or user-missing
- Range:
  through
- Range, LOWEST through value:
- ⦿ Range, value through HIGHEST:
  51
- All other values

New Value
- ⦿ Value: 5
- System-missing
- Copy old value(s)

Old --> New:

Add	MISSING --> SYSMIS
	Lowest thru 20 --> 1
Change	21 thru 30 --> 2
	31 thru 40 --> 3
Remove	41 thru 50 --> 4
	51 thru Highest --> 5

☐ Output variables are strings   Width: 8
☐ Convert numeric strings to numbers ('5'->5)

[Continue] [Cancel] [Help]

---

2. → **age** → ▣ [puts *age* in **Input Variable->Output Variable:** box] → box below **Output Variable Name:** and type *agegp* → **Change** [puts *agegp* in the **Numeric Variable->Output Variable:** box] → **Old and New Values . . .** [opens **Recode into Different Variables: Old and New Values** sub-dialog box shown in Plate 15.7]

3. → the circle by **System- or user-missing** and by **System-missing** under **New Value**, if you have missing values for a variable, which is the case for this variable

4. → circle by **Range, LOWEST through value:** and type **20** in the box → box by **Value:** under **New Value** and type **1** → **Add** [the new value will appear in the box below **Old->New:**]

5. → first box by **Range** and type **21** and in box after **through** type **30** → box by **Value** under **New Value** and type **2** → **Add**

6. → first box by **Range** and type **31** and in box after **through** type **40** → box by **Value** under **New Value** and type **3** → **Add**

7. → first box by **Range** and type **41** and in box after **through** type **50** → box by **Value** under **New Value** and type **4** → **Add**

8. → circle by **Range, value through HIGHEST** and type **51** in the box → box by **Value** under **New Value** and type **5** → **Add** → **Continue** [closes the **Recode into Different Variables: Old and New Values** sub-dialog box shown in Plate 15.7 and returns you to the **Recode into Different Variables** dialog box shown in Plate 15.6]

9. → **OK**

The new variable *agegp* will be created and will appear in the **Data Viewer**. You would then need to generate **value labels** for the five age bands and possibly a **variable label** using the approach described above.

Computing a new variable

A person's total amount of time spent in the gym is made up of three variables: *cardmins*, *weimins*, and *othmins*. If we add these up, we should arrive at the total number of minutes spent on activities in the gym. In so doing, we will create a new variable *totalmin*. To do this, this procedure should be followed:

1. → **Transform** → **Compute Variable . . .** [opens the **Compute Variable** dialog box shown in Plate 15.8]

Plate 15.8

The Compute Variable dialog box

2. under **Target Variable:** type *totalmin*

3. from the list of variables at the left, → *cardmins* [puts *cardmins* in box beneath **Numeric Expression:**] → +; → *weimins* [puts *weimins* after + sign] → +; → *othmins* [puts *othmins* after + sign]

4. → **OK**

The new variable *totalmin* will be created and will appear in the **Data Editor**.

Now at last, we can begin to analyse the data!

Data analysis with SPSS

Generating a frequency table

To produce a frequency table like the one in Table 14.2:

1. → **Analyze** → **Descriptive Statistics** → **Frequencies** . . . [opens the **Frequencies** dialog box shown in Plate 15.9]

2. → **reasons for visiting** → ▣ [puts **reasons for visiting** in **Variables** box]

3. → **OK**

The table will appear in the **Output Viewer** (see Plate 15.10)

Plate 15.9

The Frequencies dialog box

Select variable(s) to be analysed from here

Click here to send selected variable(s) into **Variable[s]:** list

Plate 15.10

The Output Viewer with Frequency table

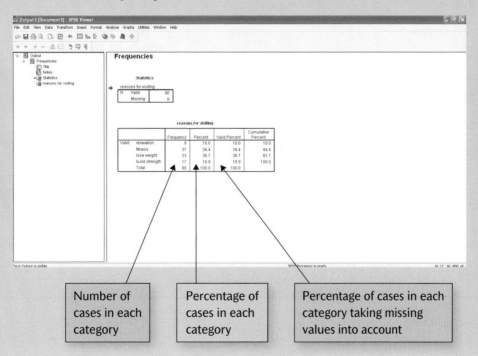

Number of cases in each category

Percentage of cases in each category

Percentage of cases in each category taking missing values into account

Plate 15.11

Using the **Chart Builder** to Generate a Bar Chart

Note that in the **Frequencies** dialog box, variables that have been assigned labels will appear in terms of their variable labels, but those that have not been assigned labels will appear in terms of their variable names. This is a feature of all dialog boxes produced via **Analyze** and **Graphs** (see below).

Generating a bar chart

To produce a bar chart like the one in Figure 14.2:

1. → **Graphs** → **Chart Builder** . . . [opens **Chart Builder** dialog box shown in Plate 15.11]

2. Make sure **Gallery** on the left hand side has been selected → **Bar** from the list below **Choose from:** → the format you want to select (the simplest is in the top left-hand corner 📊) and drag and drop it into the large area above it

3. → **reasons for visiting** from the list below **Variables:** and drop into the area (X-Axis?) below the chosen format → **OK** [the chart will appear in the **Output Viewer**]

4. If you want the numbers of respondents in each category to be indicated on the chart, double-click anywhere on the chart [opens the **Chart Editor**]

5. → **Elements** → **Show Data Labels** [opens the **Properties** sub-dialog box]

6. → **Count**

7. → **Apply**

Generating a pie chart

To produce a pie chart like the one in Figure 14.3:

1. → **Graphs** → **Chart Builder** . . .

2. Make sure **Gallery** on the left-hand side has been selected → **Pie/Polar** from the list below **Choose from:** → select the format you want (the simplest is in the top left-hand corner) and drag and drop it into the large area above it

3. → **reasons for visiting** from the list below **Variables:** and drop into the area (X-Axis?) below the chosen format → **OK** [the chart will appear in the **Output Viewer**]

4. In order to include percentages, as in Figure 14.3, *double-click* anywhere in the chart in order to bring up the **Chart Editor** (see Plate 15.12). The chart will appear in the **Chart Editor** and the main figure will become opaque

Plate 15.12

The **Chart Editor**

5. → **Elements** → **Show Data Labels** [opens the **Properties** sub-dialog box]

6. → **Per cent** from below **Displayed:**

7. → **Apply**

Your chart will be in colour, but, if you only have access to a monochrome printer, you can change your pie chart into patterns, which allows the slices to be clearer. This can be done through the **Chart Editor**.

Generating a histogram

In order to generate a histogram for an interval/ratio variable like *age*:

1. → **Graphs** → **Chart Builder** . . . [opens **Chart Builder** dialog box]

2. Make sure **Gallery** on the left-hand side has been selected → **Histogram** from the list below **Choose from:** → select the format you want (the simplest is in the top left-hand corner) and drag and drop it into the large area above it

3. → *age* from the list below **Variables:** and drop into the area (X-Axis?) below the chosen format → **OK** [the chart will appear in the **Output Viewer**]

This procedure will generate a histogram whose age bands are defined by the software. By double clicking on the diagram, the histogram can be edited using the **Chart Editor**. For example, colours can be changed or patterns inserted.

Generating the arithmetic mean, median, standard deviation, and range

To produce the mean, median, standard deviation, and the range for an interval/ratio variable like *age*, the following steps should be followed:

1. → **Analyze** → **Descriptive Statistics** → **Explore:** [opens the **Explore** dialog box]

2. → *age* → ☐ to the left of **Dependent List** [puts *age* in the **Dependent List** box] → **Statistics** under **Display** → **OK**

The output will also include the 95 per cent confidence interval for the mean, which is based on the standard error of the mean. The output can be found in Table 15.1. If you select **Plots** . . . the **Explore: Plots** sub-dialog box will appear and you can elect to generate a histogram. To do this, you will need to select either **Both** or **Plots** under **Display** on the **Explore** dialog box.

Generating a contingency table, chi-square, and Cramér's *V*

In order to generate a contingency table, like that in Table 14.4, along with a chi-square test and Cramér's *V*, the following procedure should be followed:

1. → **Analyze** → **Descriptive Statistics** → **Crosstabs** . . . [opens the **Crosstabs** dialog box shown in Plate 15.13]

2. → **reasons for visiting** → ☐ by Row(s): [**reasons for visiting** will appear in the Row(s): box] → *gender* → ☐ by Columns: [*gender* will appear in the **Columns:** box] → **Cells** . . . [opens **Crosstabs: Cell Display** sub-dialog box shown in Plate 15.14]

3. Make sure **Observed** in the **Counts** box has been selected. Make sure **Column** under **Percentages** has been selected. If either of these has not been selected, simply click at the relevant point. → **Continue** [closes **Crosstabs: Cell Display** sub-dialog box and returns you to the **Crosstabs** dialog box shown in Plate 15.13]

4. → **Statistics** [opens the **Crosstabs: Statistics** sub-dialog box shown in Plate 15.15]

5. → **Chi-square** → **Phi and Cramér's V** → **Continue** [closes **Crosstabs: Statistics** sub-dialog box and returns you to the **Crosstabs** dialog box shown in Plate 15.13]

6. → **OK**

The resulting output can be found in Table 15.2.

If you have a table with two dichotomous variables, you would use the same sequence of steps to produce phi.

Generating Pearson's *r* and Spearman's rho

To produce Pearson's *r* in order to find the correlations between *age*, *cardmins*, and *weimins*, follow these steps:

1. → **Analyze** → **Correlate** → **Bivariate** . . . [opens **Bivariate Correlations** dialog box shown in Plate 15.16]

2. → *age* → ☐ → *cardmins* → ☐ → *weimins* → ☐ [*age*, *cardmins*, and *weimins* should now be in the **Variable:** box] → **Pearson** [*if* not already selected] → **OK**

The resulting output is in Table 15.3.

To produce correlations with Spearman's rho, follow the same procedure but instead of selecting **Pearson**, you should → **Spearman** instead.

Table 15.1

Explore output for *age* (SPSS output)

Explore

Case Processing Summary

	Cases					
	Valid		Missing		Total	
	N	Percent	N	Percent	N	Percent
age	89	98.9%	1	1.1%	90	100.0%

Descriptives

			Statistic	Std. Error
age	Mean		33.5955	.94197
	95% Confidence	Lower Bound	31.7235	
	Interval for Mean	Upper Bound	35.4675	
	5% Trimmed Mean		33.3159	
	Median		31.0000	
	Variance		78.971	
	Std. Deviation		8.88656	
	Minimum		18.00	
	Maximum		57.00	
	Range		39.00	
	Interquartile Range		14.00	
	Skewness		.446	.255
	Kurtosis		−.645	.506

Generating scatter diagrams

Scatter diagrams, known as *scatterplots* in SPSS, are produced in the following way. Let us say that we want to plot the relationship between *age* and *cardmins*. There is a convention that, if one variable can be identified as likely to be the independent variable, it should be placed on the *x* axis—that is, the horizontal axis. Since *age* is bound to be the independent variable, we would follow these steps.

To produce a pie chart like the one in Figure 14.3:

1. → **Graphs** → **Chart Builder** . . .

2. Make sure **Gallery** on the left-hand side has been selected → **Scatter/Dot** from the list below **Choose from:** → the format you want (the simplest is in the top left-hand corner ☐) and drag and drop it into the large area above it

3. → *age* from the list below **Variables:** and drop into the area **X-Axis?** below the chosen format

4. → *cardmins* the list below **Variables:** and drop into the area **Y-Axis?** below the chosen format

5. → **OK** [the chart will appear in the **Output Viewer**]

A default scatter diagram is shown in Figure 15.1. The scatter diagram can then be edited by bringing up the **Chart Editor**. For example, the type and size of the markers can be changed by clicking anywhere in the chart in the **Chart Editor**. This brings up a **Properties** sub-dialog box that allows a variety of changes to the appearance of

Plate 15.13

The **Crosstabs** dialog box

Select and place here the variable that will make up the rows. This will be the dependent variable if it is possible and legitimate to make a claim about likely causality

Select and place here the variable that will make up the columns. This will be the independent variable if it is possible and legitimate to make a claim about likely causality

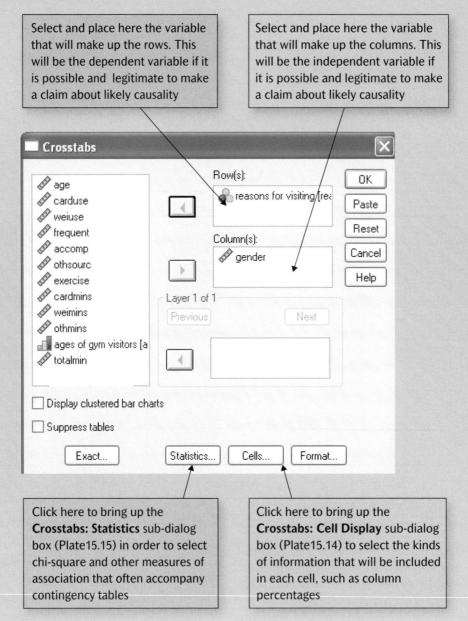

Click here to bring up the **Crosstabs: Statistics** sub-dialog box (Plate15.15) in order to select chi-square and other measures of association that often accompany contingency tables

Click here to bring up the **Crosstabs: Cell Display** sub-dialog box (Plate15.14) to select the kinds of information that will be included in each cell, such as column percentages

the diagram, such as colour and the nature of the points on the plot.

Comparing means and eta

To produce a table like Table 14.5, these steps should be followed:

1. → **Analyze** → **Compare Means** → **Means** . . . [opens the **Means** dialog box shown in Plate 15.18]

2. → *cardmins* → ⊡ to the left of Dependent List: → **reasons for visiting** → ⊡ to the left of Independent List: → **Options** . . . [opens the **Means: Options** sub-dialog box]

Plate 15.14

The Crosstabs: Cell Display sub-dialog box

Select this to show the number of cases in each cell in the table

Select to give the percentage of cases of each category of the column variable

Crosstabs: Cell Display

Counts
- ☑ Observed
- ☐ Expected

Continue
Cancel
Help

Percentages
- ☐ Row
- ☑ Column
- ☐ Total

Residuals
- ☐ Unstandardized
- ☐ Standardized
- ☐ Adjusted standardized

Noninteger Weights
- ◉ Round cell counts
- ○ Truncate cell counts
- ○ No adjustments
- ○ Round case weights
- ○ Truncate case weights

Plate 15.15

The Crosstabs: Statistics sub-dialog box

Select to provide the chi-square statistic for the contingency table

Select to generate phi and/or Cramér's V

Crosstabs: Statistics

- ☑ Chi-square
- ☐ Correlations

Continue
Cancel
Help

Nominal
- ☐ Contingency coefficient
- ☑ Phi and Cramér's V
- ☐ Lambda
- ☐ Uncertainty coefficient

Ordinal
- ☐ Gamma
- ☐ Somers' d
- ☐ Kendall's tau-b
- ☐ Kendall's tau-c

Nominal by Interval
- ☐ Eta

- ☐ Kappa
- ☐ Risk
- ☐ McNemar

- ☐ Cochran's and Mantel-Haenszel statistics
  Test common odds ratio equals: 1

Table 15.2

Contingency table for reasons for visiting by *gender*

Crosstabs

Case Processing Summary

| | Cases | | | | | |
| | Valid | | Missing | | Total | |
	N	Percent	N	Percent	N	Percent
reasons for visiting * gender	90	100.0%	0	.0%	90	100.0%

reasons for visiting * gender Crosstabulation

| | | | gender | | Total |
			1.00	2.00	
reasons for visiting	relaxation	Count	3	6	9
		% within gender	7.1%	12.5%	10.0%
	fitness	Count	15	16	31
		% within gender	35.7%	33.3%	34.4%
	lose weight	Count	8	25	33
		% within gender	19.0%	52.1%	36.7%
	build strength	Count	16	1	17
		% within gender	38.1%	2.1%	18.9%
Total		Count	42	48	90
		% within gender	100.0%	100.0%	100.0%

Chi-Square Tests

	Value	df	Asymp. Sig. (2-sided)
Pearson Chi-Square	22.726[a]	3	.000
Likelihood Ratio	25.805	3	.000
Linear-by-Linear Association	9.716	1	.002
N of Valid Cases	90		

a. 2 cells (25.0%) have expected count less than 5. The minimum expected count is 4.20.

Interpret the Pearson Chi-Square, which is the one whose value is referred to in the text

Table 15.2

Continued

Symmetric Measures

		Value	Approx. Sig.
Nominal by Nominal	Phi	.503	.000
	Cramer's V	.503	.000
N of Valid Cases		90	

a. Not assuming the null hypothesis.

b. Using the asymptotic standard error assuming the null hypothesis.

Shows strength of the relationship between the variables

Shows the level of statistical significance of the computed value of Cramér's *V*

Plate 15.16

The **Bivariate Correlations** dialog box

All variables to be correlated go here

Select **Pearson** or **Spearman** depending on the kinds of variables being analysed

Table 15.3

Correlations output for *age*, *weimins*, and *cardmins* (SPSS output)

Correlations

Correlations

		age	cardmins	weimins
age	Pearson Correlation	1	−.109	−.273**
	Sig. (2-tailed)		.311	.010
	N	89	89	89
cardmins	Pearson Correlation	−.109	1	−.161
	Sig. (2-tailed)	.311		.130
	N	89	90	90
weimins	Pearson Correlation	−.273**	−.161	1
	Sig. (2-tailed)	.010	.130	
	N	89	90	90

Correlations of $p < 0.05$ are 'flagged' with asterisks

**. Correlation is significant at the 0.01 level (2-tailed)

Shows strength of relationship between variables as indicated by Pearson's *r*

Shows level of statistical significance of computed value of Pearson's *r*

Shows number of cases involved in the calculation of a correlation, less any cases for which there are missing values for either or both variables

3. → **Anova table and eta** underneath Stastistics to First Layer → **Continue** [closes the **Means: Options** sub-dialog box and returns you to the **Means** dialog box shown in Plate 15.18] → **OK**

Generating a contingency table with three variables

To create a table like that in Table 14.7, you would need to follow these steps:

1. → **Analyze** → **Descriptive Statistics** → **Crosstabs** [opens the **Crosstabs** dialog box shown in Plate 15.13]

2. → *othsourc* → ▣ by **Row(s)**: [*othsourc* will appear in the **Row(s)**: box]

3. → *age3* [this is the name given to the newly created variable with *age* recoded into three categories] → ▣

by **Column(s)**: [*age3* will appear in the **Columns** box] → *gender* → ▣ beneath **Previous** [*gender* will appear in the box underneath **Layer 1 of 1**] → **Cells** [opens **Crosstabs: Cell Display** sub-dialog box shown in Plate 15.14]

4. Make sure **Observed** in the **Counts** box has been selected. Make sure Column under Percentages has been selected. If either of these has not been selected, simply click at the relevant point.

5. → **Continue** [closes **Crosstabs: Cell Display** sub-dialog box and returns you to the **Crosstabs** dialog box shown in Plate 15.13]

6. → **OK**

The resulting table will look somewhat different from Table 14.7 in that *gender* will appear as a row rather than as a column variable.

Plate 15.17

The **Simple Scatterplot** sub-dialog box

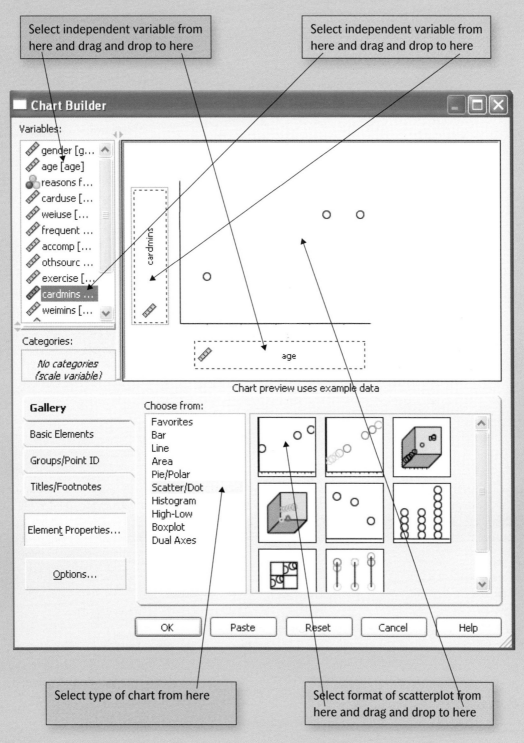

Select independent variable from here and drag and drop to here

Select independent variable from here and drag and drop to here

Select type of chart from here

Select format of scatterplot from here and drag and drop to here

Figure 15.1

Scatter diagram showing relationship between *age* and *cardmins* (SPSS output)

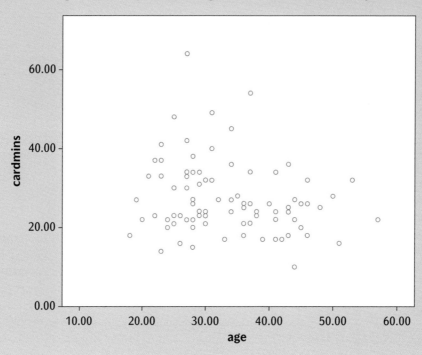

Plate 15.18

The **Means** dialog box

Further operations in SPSS

Saving your data

You will need to save your data for future use. To do this, make sure that the **Data Editor** is the active window. Then,

→ **File** → **Save As . . .**

The **Save Data As** dialog box will then appear. You will need to provide a name for your data, which will be placed after File Name: I called the file 'gym study'. You also need to decide where you are going to save the data—for example, onto a memory stick. To select the destination drive, → the **My Computer** button in the column to the left and then select the drive and folder into which you want to place your data. Then → **Save**.

Remember that this procedure saves your data *and* any other work you have done on your data—for example, value labels and recoded variables. If you subsequently use the data again and do more work on your data, such as creating a new variable, you will need to save the data again or the new work will be lost. SPSS will give you a choice of renaming your data, in which case you will have two files of data (one with the original data and one with any changes), or keeping the same name, in which case the file will be changed and the existing name retained.

Retrieving your data

When you want to retrieve the data file you have created, → **File** → **Open** → **Data. . . .** The **Open File** dialog box will appear. You then need to go to the location in which you have deposited your data to retrieve the file containing your data and then → **Open**. A shortcut alternative to this procedure is to → the first button on the toolbar (it looks like an open file), which brings up the **Open File** dialog box.

Printing output

To print all the output in the **SPSS Output Viewer**, make sure that the **Output 1 – SPSS Viewer** is the active window and then → **File** → **Print . . .** The **Print** dialog box will appear and then → **OK**. To print just some of your output, hold down the Ctrl button on your keyboard and click once on the parts you want to print. The easiest way to do this is to select all the elements you want in the output summary in the left-hand segment of the **Output Viewer** shown in Plate 15.10. Then bring up the Print dialog box. When the **Print** dialog box appears, make sure Selection under **Print range** has been selected. The third button on the toolbar (which appears as a printer) provides a shortcut to the **Print** dialog box.

Key points

- SPSS can be used to implement the techniques learned in Chapter 14 but learning new software requires perseverance and at times the results obtained may not seem to be worth the learning process.

- But it is worth it, it would take you far longer to perform calculations on a sample of around 100 than to learn the software.

- If you find yourself moving into much more advanced techniques, the time saved is even more substantial, particularly with large samples.

- It is better to become familiar with SPSS before you begin designing your research instruments, so you are aware of difficulties you might have in presenting your data in SPSS at an early stage.

Questions for review

Getting started in SPSS

- Outline the differences between: variable names, variable labels, and value labels.
- In what circumstances might you want to recode a variable?
- In what circumstances might you want to create a new variable?

Data analysis with SPSS

Using the gym survey data, create:

- a frequency table for *exercise*;
- a bar chart and pie chart for *exercise* and compare their usefulness;
- a histogram for *cardmins*;
- measures of central tendency and dispersion for *cardmins*;
- a contingency table and chi-square test for *exercise* and *gender*;
- Pearson's *r* for *age* and *cardmins*;
- Spearman's rho for *carduse* and *weiuse*;
- a scatter diagram for *age* and *cardmins*;
- a comparing means analysis for **totalmin** and **reasons for visiting**.

Online Resource Centre

http://www.oxfordtextbooks.co.uk/orc/brymansrm3e/

Visit the Online Resource Centre that accompanies this book to enrich your understanding of using SPSS for Windows. Consult web links, test yourself using multiple choice questions, and gain further guidance and inspiration from the Student Researcher's Toolkit.

Part Three

Part Three of this book is concerned with qualitative research. Chapter 16 sets the scene by exploring the main features of this research strategy. Chapter 17 deals with ethnography and participant observation, which are among the main ways of collecting qualitative data. Chapter 18 is concerned with the kind of interviewing that is carried out in qualitative research. Chapter 19 addresses the focus group method, which is an increasingly popular technique that allows groups of people to be interviewed. Chapter 20 explores two approaches to the study of language in social research: conversation analysis and discourse analysis. Chapter 21 explores the types of documents with which qualitative researchers tend to be concerned and approaches to examining them. Chapter 22 examines different approaches to qualitative data analysis and offers advice on how it can be carried out. Chapter 23 shows you how to use computer software in the form of NVivo to conduct the kind of analysis discussed in Chapter 22.

These chapters will provide you with the essential tools for doing qualitative research. They will take you from the very general issues to do with the generic features of qualitative research to the very practical issues of conducting your own observational studies or interviews and analysing your own data.

The nature of
qualitative research

Chapter outline

Chapter guide

Qualitative research is a research strategy that usually emphasizes words rather than quantification in the collection and analysis of data. As a research strategy it is inductivist, constructionist, and interpretivist, but qualitative researchers do not always subscribe to all three of these features. This chapter is concerned with outlining the main features of qualitative research, which has become an increasingly popular approach to social research. The chapter explores:

- the main steps in qualitative research; delineating the sequence of stages in qualitative research is more controversial than with quantitative research, because it exhibits somewhat less codification of the research process;

- the relationship between theory and research;

- the nature of concepts in qualitative research and their differences from concepts in quantitative research;

- how far reliability and validity are appropriate criteria for qualitative researchers and whether alternative criteria that are more tailored to the research strategy are necessary;

- the main preoccupations of qualitative researchers; five areas are identified in terms of an emphasis on: seeing through the eyes of research participants; description and context; process; flexibility and lack of structure; and concepts and theory as outcomes of the research process;

- some common criticisms of qualitative research;

- the main contrasts between qualitative and quantitative research;

- the stance of feminist researchers on qualitative research.

Introduction

We began Chapter 6 by noting that *quantitative* research had been outlined in Chapter 1 as a distinctive research strategy. Much the same kind of general point can be registered in relation to *qualitative* research. In Chapter 1 it was suggested that qualitative research differs from quantitative research in several ways. Most obviously, qualitative research tends to be concerned with words rather than numbers, but three further features were particularly noteworthy:

1. an inductive view of the relationship between theory and research, whereby the former is generated out of the latter;

2. an epistemological position described as interpretivist, meaning that, in contrast to the adoption of a natural scientific model in quantitative research, the stress is on the understanding of the social world through

an examination of the interpretation of that world by its participants; and

3. an ontological position described as constructionist, which implies that social properties are outcomes of the interactions between individuals, rather than phenomena 'out there' and separate from those involved in its construction.

As Bryman and Burgess (1999) observe, although there has been a proliferation of writings on qualitative research since the 1970s, stipulating what it is and is not as a distinct research strategy is by no means straightforward. They propose three reasons for this state of affairs.

1. As a term 'qualitative research' is sometimes taken to imply an approach to social research in which quantitative data are not collected or generated. Many writers on

Key concept 16.1
Four traditions of qualitative research

Gubrium and Holstein (1997) suggest four traditions of qualitative research.

1. *Naturalism*: seeks to understand social reality in its own terms; 'as it really is'; provides rich descriptions of people and interaction in natural settings.

2. *Ethnomethodology*: seeks to understand how social order is created through talk and interaction; has a naturalistic orientation.

3. *Emotionalism*: exhibits a concern with subjectivity and gaining access to 'inside' experience; is concerned with the inner reality of humans.

4. *Postmodernism*: emphasizes 'method talk'; is sensitive to the different ways social reality can be constructed. For more on postmodernism see Key concept 27.2.

We encountered the term 'naturalism' in Key concept 2.4. The use of the term here is more or less the same as the second meaning referred to in Key concept 2.4. The naturalist tradition has probably been the most common one over the years. The second tradition will be encountered in Chapter 20, when we will be looking at an approach to the collection of qualitative data known as *conversation analysis*. The more recent postmodern standpoint will be addressed in Chapter 27. The third tradition—emotionalism—has not become the focus of a significant stream of research and will not be emphasized in this book. However, the mere presence of these four contrasting traditions points to the difficulty of creating a definitive account of what qualitative research is and is not.

qualitative research are critical of such a rendition of qualitative research, because (as we will see) the distinctiveness of qualitative research does not reside solely in the absence of numbers.

2. Writers like Gubrium and Holstein (1997) have suggested that several different traditions in qualitative research can be identified (see Key concept 16.1). In addition, Key concept 16.2 suggests that there are distinctive stances within the qualitative research tradition.

3. Sometimes, qualitative research is discussed in terms of the ways in which it differs from quantitative research. A potential problem with this tactic is that it means that qualitative research ends up being addressed in terms of what quantitative research is *not*.

Silverman (1993) has been particularly critical of accounts of qualitative research that do not acknowledge the variety of forms that the research strategy can assume. In other words, writers like Silverman are critical of attempts to specify the nature of qualitative research as a general approach (see also Key concept 16.2).

However, unless we can talk to a certain degree about the nature of qualitative research, it is difficult to see how it is possible to refer to qualitative research as a distinctive research strategy. In much the same way that in Chapter 6 it was recognized that quantitative researchers employ different research designs, in writing about the characteristics of qualitative research we will need to be sensitive to the different orientations of qualitative researchers. Without at least a sense of what is common to a set of many if not most studies that might be described as qualitative, the very notion of qualitative research would be rendered problematic. Yet it is clear that, for many social scientists, it is a helpful and meaningful category that can be seen in a variety of ways. Examples are: the arrival of specialist journals, such as *Qualitative Sociology, Qualitative Research, Ethnography*, and *Qualitative Inquiry*; texts on qualitative research (e.g. Silverman 1993, 2000; Seale 1999); a *Handbook of Qualitative Research* (Denzin and Lincoln 1994, 2000, 2005*a*); and a series of books on different facets of qualitative research (the Sage Qualitative Research Methods Series).

Key concept 16.2
The Nine Moments of Qualitative Research

Denzin and Lincoln (2005*b*) have suggested that qualitative research has progressed through a number of stages. They portray this as a history of qualitative research in North America. It is not clear why the stages are presented as relating only to North America, but the distinctions are worth drawing attention to because they relate closely to the suggestion that there are different traditions of qualitative research.

1. *The traditional period*. The early twentieth century up to the Second World War. This phase refers to the work of social anthropologists and the Chicago School. It refers to in-depth studies of 'slices of life' that portrayed those who were studied as strange or alien. It was heavily imbued with **positivism**.

2. *Modernist phase*. Post-Second World War to early 1970s. During this period, qualitative researchers built on the work of the traditional period but at the same time sought to enhance the rigour of qualitative enquiries and began to reflect on the nature of their craft. These investigations also showed a tendency towards positivism.

3. *Blurred genres*. 1970–86. This was a period when a variety of epistemological and ontological approaches, as well as theoretical ideas, were being explored as plausible bases for qualitative enquiries. According to Denzin and Lincoln, we see in this period a continued proclivity towards positivism, but with the beginnings of an interpretivist self-consciousness, influenced by Geertz's (1973*a*) insistence that qualitative researchers are involved in interpretations of the interpretations of those on whom they conduct their investigations.

4. *Crisis of representation*. Mid-1980s onwards. Most of the key writings associated with this moment occurred in the 1980s. It refers to a period in which qualitative social researchers in general (though much of the writing stemmed initially from social anthropology) developed greater self-awareness concerning in particular the fact that their accounts of their fieldwork are just one way of representing reality and that, moreover, their representations are heavily influenced by their social locations. The 'crisis of representation' then is the recognition that the researcher's written work has limited scientific authority. These ideas will be encountered again in Chapter 27 in the section 'Writing ethnography'.

The next three phases refer to 'a triple crisis' stemming from the fourth moment above.

5. *Postmodern period of experimental ethnographic writing*. Mid-1990s. Heavily influenced by postmodernism (see Key concept 27.2), work under this heading is characterized by an awareness of the different ways of representing research participants (often referred to as 'the other') when writing up findings. Qualitative researchers have tried different ways of representing the people on whom they conduct their investigations.

6. *Post-experimental enquiry*. 1995–2000. This period is associated mainly with the emergence of AltaMira Press, a publisher of qualitative research that encourages experimental and interdisciplinary writing. It describes itself as having a 'focus on interdisciplinary work, breaking long-standing boundaries' (**http://www.altamirapress.com/RLA/About/** (accessed on 18 March 2007)).

7. *The methodologically contested present*. 2000–4. This refers to a period in which there is considerable disagreement about how qualitative research should be conducted and the directions it should be heading. It is very much associated with the arrival of journals like *Qualitative Inquiry* and *Qualitative Research* that provide forums for these debates. While Denzin and Lincoln date this period as 2000–4, there is a great deal of evidence to suggest that the contested methodological differences have not abated. One of the areas that has been a focus of the ongoing debates has been the issue of research quality criteria in relation to qualitative studies.

8. *Now*. 2005–. This period is characterized by a backlash against qualitative research with a reassertion in government circles of the value of traditional science. Some of these pressures are reviewed in Bryman (2007*a*).

9. *The fractured future.* Lincoln and Denzin (2005: 1123) also speculate about what the immediate future holds: 'Randomized field trials . . . will occupy the time of one group of researchers while the pursuit of a socially and culturally responsive, communitarian, justice-oriented set of studies will consume the meaningful working moments of the other.'

This time line of phases is useful because it highlights the difficulty of characterizing 'qualitative research'. As Silverman (1993) observes, the term covers a number of different research methods and approaches to qualitative data that differ considerably. On the other hand, Denzin and Lincoln's 'moments' have to be treated with some caution. First, it has to be borne in mind that work that could be depicted in terms very similar to the first two phases continues to be conducted. Indeed, many of the qualitative investigations that serve as illustrations in Part Three are of this type. Although qualitative researchers may be more self-conscious nowadays about their influence on the research process and the significance of how they write, many qualitative studies are still characterized by **realism**, at least to some degree. Second, Denzin and Lincoln's later phases are associated too much with particular events—the arrival of a new publisher or new journals —which looks strange when viewed in relation to the several decades with which the earlier moments are associated. Third, their ninth and final moment seems to be concerned with a rift in social research in general rather than within qualitative research as such.

Several reasons might be proposed for the unease among some writers concerning the specification of the nature of qualitative research. Two reasons might be regarded as having particular importance. First, qualitative research subsumes several diverse research methods that differ from each other considerably. The following are the main research methods associated with qualitative research.

- *Ethnography/participant observation.* While some caution is advisable in treating ethnography and participant observation as synonyms, in many respects they refer to similar if not identical approaches to data collection in which the researcher is immersed in a social setting for some time in order to observe and listen with a view to gaining an appreciation of the culture of a social group. It has been employed in such social research classics as Whyte's (1955) study of street corner life in a slum community and Gans's (1962) research on a similar group in the throes of urban redevelopment.

- *Qualitative interviewing.* This is a very broad term to describe a wide range of interviewing styles (see Key concept 8.2 for an introduction). Moreover, qualitative researchers employing ethnography or participant observation typically engage in a substantial amount of qualitative interviewing.

- Focus groups (see Key concept 8.2).

- Language-based approaches to the collection of qualitative data, such as discourse and conversation analysis.

- The collection and qualitative analysis of texts and documents.

Each of these approaches to data collection will be examined in Part Three. The picture with regard to the very different methods and sources that comprise qualitative research is made somewhat more complex by the fact that a multi-method approach is frequently employed. As noted above, researchers employing ethnography or participant observation frequently conduct qualitative interviews. However, they also often collect and analyse texts and documents as well. Thus, there is considerable variability in the collection of data among studies that are typically deemed to be qualitative. Of course, quantitative research also subsumes several different methods of data collection (these were covered in Part Two), but the inclusion of methods concerned with the analysis of language as a form of qualitative research implies somewhat greater variability.

A second reason why there is some resistance to a delineation of the nature of qualitative research is that the connection between theory and research is somewhat more ambiguous than in quantitative research. With the latter research strategy, theoretical issues drive the formulation of a research question, which in turn drives the collection and analysis of data. Findings then feed back into the relevant theory. This is rather a caricature, because what counts as 'theory' is sometimes little more than the research literature relating to a certain issue or area. In qualitative research, theory is supposed to be an outcome of an investigation rather than something that precedes it. However, some writers, like Silverman (1993: 24), have argued that such a depiction of qualitative research is 'out of tune with the greater sophistication of contemporary field research design, born out of accumulated knowledge of interaction and greater concern with issues of reliability and validity'. This is particularly the case with conversation analysis, an approach to the study of language that will be examined in Chapter 20. However, qualitative research is more usually regarded as denoting an approach in which theory and categorization emerge out of the collection and analysis of data. The more general point being made is that such a difference within qualitative research may account for the unease about depicting the research strategy in terms of a set of stages.

The main steps in qualitative research

The sequence outlined in Figure 16.1 provides a representation of how the qualitative research process can be visualized. In order to illustrate the steps, a published study by Foster (1995) of crime in communities will be used. This study was previously encountered in Research in focus 1.6.

- *Step 1. General research question(s).* The starting point for Foster's (1995) study of crime in communities, particularly ones that contain predominantly public housing, is the high levels of crime in poorer areas. To the extent that it is a focus of attention, it is frequently assumed that communities with high levels of crime

Figure 16.1

An outline of the main steps of qualitative research

1. General research questions
2. Selection of relevant site(s) and subjects
3. Collection of relevant data
4. Interpretation of data
5. Conceptual and theoretical work
5a. Tighter specification of the research question(s)
5b. Collection of further data
6. Writing up findings/conclusions

tend to have low levels of social control. But Foster argues that we know very little about how informal social control operates in such communities and what its significance for crime is. She also notes that council estates are frequently presumed to be crime prone but that there is little evidence on 'the diversity in experience and attitudes of residents within individual estates' (Foster 1995: 563). It would be easy to presume that, to the extent that council estates are prone to high crime levels, they exhibit low levels of social control. Thus Foster formulates a general set of concerns revolving around council estates and their crime-proneness and the possible role and dynamics of social control in the process. She also notes that some writers have suggested that the propensity to crime in council estates may be in part attributed to flaws in the design of the estates.

Thinking deeply 16.1
Research questions in qualitative research

Research questions in qualitative research are stated with varying degrees of explicitness. Sometimes, the research question is embedded within a general statement of the orientation of an article. Thus, the author of the research covered below in Research in focus 16.3 writes at the beginning of a long paragraph:

> The main proposition in this article is that different masculinities are produced through performances that draw on the different cultural resources that are available in each setting. (Swain 2004: 167)

Others opt for a more explicit treatment of research questions. Ashforth *et al.* (2007) were interested in the phenomenon of 'dirty work', a term first introduced nearly fifty years previously to refer to work that is tainted 'physically, socially or morally' (Hughes 1958: 122; quoted in Ashforth *et al.* 2007: 149). The researchers conducted **semi-structured interviews** with managers in eighteen such occupations in order to explore how the work is 'normalized', that is, how they develop ways of dealing with or reducing the significance of the taint of dirty work. After a discussion of the literature and their view of its implications for their own work, they write:

In summary, our research questions were:

> *Research Question 1. What normalization challenges do managers in dirty work occupations face?*
> *Research Question 2. What tactics do managers report using to normalize dirty work?* (Ashforth *et al.* 2007: 151; italicized in original)

One factor that may affect the degree of explicitness with which research questions are stated is the outlet in which the research is published. Ashforth *et al.* (2007) published this article in the *Academy of Management Journal*, which in the past has tended to publish mainly empirical articles deriving from quantitative research. It may be that Ashforth *et al.* chose this format for presenting their research questions so that it would exhibit some of the characteristics of research questions or hypotheses in quantitative research that tend to be stated explicitly. Another article in the same issue also stated the research questions very explicitly though they were not formatted to stand out in the same way.

> Thus, two research questions guided this article: (1) What conditions trigger organizational stakeholders and leaders to engage in sensegiving activities? and (2) What conditions enable sensegiving on the part of stakeholders and leaders motivated to engage in sensegiving activities? (Maitlis and Lawrence 2007: 59)

The researchers went on to investigate these two research questions by collecting qualitative data from semi-structured interviews, observation and examination of documents in connection with three British symphony orchestras.

- *Step 2. Selection of relevant site(s) and subjects.* The research was conducted on a London council estate (with the fictitious name 'Riverside'), which had a high level of crime and which exhibited the kinds of housing features that are frequently associated with a propensity to crime. Relevant research participants, such as residents, were identified.

- *Step 3. Collection of relevant data.* Foster describes her research as 'ethnographic'. She spent eighteen months 'getting involved in as many aspects of life there as possible from attending tenant meetings, the mothers and toddlers group, and activities for young people, to socializing with some of the residents in the local pub' (Foster 1995: 566). Foster also tells us that 'extended interviews' were conducted with forty-five residents of Riverside (and another London estate, but the majority were from Riverside) and twenty-five 'officials', such as police and housing officers. Foster's account of her research methods suggests that she is likely to have generated two types of data: fieldwork notes based on her ethnographic observation of life in the community and detailed notes (and most probably transcripts) of interviews undertaken.

- *Step 4. Interpretation of data.* One of the key findings to emerge from the data is the fact that, in spite of the fact that Riverside has a high crime rate, it is not perceived as a problem in this regard by Riverside residents. For example, she quotes from an interview with an elderly tenant: 'They used to say that they couldn't let the flats [apartments] here . . . but I mean as far as muggings or anything like that you don't hear of nothing like that even now' (Foster 1995: 568). Instead, housing problems loomed larger in the minds of residents than crime. She also found that 'hidden economy' crimes were prevalent on the estate and that much crime was tolerated by residents. She also observes that, contrary to expectations about estates like Riverside, there was clear evidence of informal social control mechanisms at work, such as shaming practices.

- *Step 5. Conceptual and theoretical work.* No new concepts seem to emerge from Foster's research, but her findings enable her to tie together some of the elements outlined above under Step 1. For example, she writes:

> Crime then need not be damaging *per se* providing other factors cushion its impact. On Riverside these included support networks in which tenants felt that someone was watching out for their properties and provided links with people to whom they could turn

> if they were in trouble. Consequently while generalized fears about crime remained prevalent, familiarity and support went some way to reducing the potential for hostile encounters. (Foster 1995: 580)

It is this step, coupled with the interpretation of data, that forms the study's findings.

- *Steps 5a. Tighter specification of the research question(s), and 5b. Collection of further data.* There is no specific evidence from Foster's account that she followed a process in which she collected further data after she had built up early interpretations of her data. When this occurs, as it sometimes does in research within a grounded theory framework, there can be an interplay between interpretation and theorizing, on the one hand, and data collection, on the other. Such a strategy is frequently referred to as an *iterative* one. She does write at one point that some residents and officials were interviewed twice and in some cases even three times in the course of her research. This raises the possibility that she was re-interviewing certain individuals in the light of her emerging ideas about her data, but this can only be a speculation.

- *Step 6. Writing up findings/conclusions.* There is no real difference between the significance of writing up in quantitative research and qualitative research, so that exactly the same points made in relation to step 11 in Figure 6.1 apply here. An audience has to be convinced about the credibility and significance of the interpretations offered. Researchers are not and cannot be simply conduits for the things they see and the words they hear. The salience of what researchers have seen and heard has to be impressed on the audience. Foster does this by making clear to her audience that her findings have implications for policies regarding estates and crime and for our understanding of the links between housing, community, and crime. A key point to emerge from her work, which she emphasizes at several points in the article and hammers home in her concluding section, is that being an insider to Riverside allowed her to see that a community that may be regarded by outsiders as having a high propensity towards crime should not be presumed to be seen in this way by members of that community.

Two particularly distinctive aspects of the sequence of steps in qualitative research are the highly related issues of the links between theory and concepts with research data. It is to these issues that we now turn.

Theory and research

Most qualitative researchers when writing about their craft emphasize a preference for treating theory as something that emerges out of the collection and analysis of data. As will be seen in Chapter 22, practitioners of grounded theory—a frequently cited approach to the analysis of qualitative data—especially stress the importance of allowing theoretical ideas to emerge out of one's data. But some qualitative researchers argue that qualitative data can and should have an important role in relation to the *testing* of theories as well. Silverman (1993), in particular, has argued that in more recent times qualitative researchers have become increasingly interested in the testing of theories and that this is a reflection of the growing maturity of the strategy. Certainly, there is no reason why qualitative research cannot be employed in order to test theories that are specified in advance of data collection. In any case, much qualitative research entails the testing of theories in the course of the research process. So, in Figure 16.1, the loop back from Step 5a, 'Tighter specification of the research question(s)', to Step 5b, 'Collection of further data', implies that a theoretical position may emerge in the course of research and may spur the collection of further data to test that theory. This kind of oscillation between testing emerging theories and collecting data is a particularly distinctive feature of grounded theory. It is presented as a dashed line in Figure 16.1, because it is not as necessary a feature of the process of qualitative research as the other steps.

One key point that is implied by Figure 16.1 is that the typical sequence of steps in qualitative research entails the generation of theories rather than the testing of theories that are specified at the outset. Silverman (1993) is undoubtedly correct that pre-specified theories *can be* and sometimes *are* tested with qualitative data, but the generation of theory tends to be the preferred approach.

Concepts in qualitative research

A central feature of Chapter 6 was the discussion of concepts and their measurement. For most qualitative researchers, developing measures of concepts will not be a significant consideration, but concepts are very much part of the landscape in qualitative research. However, the way in which concepts are developed and employed is often rather different from that implied in the quantitative research strategy. Blumer's (1954) distinction between 'definitive' and 'sensitizing' concepts captures aspects of the different ways in which concepts are thought about.

Blumer (1954) argued stridently against the use of definitive concepts in social research. The idea of definitive concepts is typified by the way in which, in quantitative research, a concept, once developed, becomes fixed through the elaboration of indicators. For Blumer, such an approach entailed the application of a straitjacket on the social world, because the concept in question comes to be seen exclusively in terms of the indicators that have been developed for it. Fine nuances in the form that the concept can assume or alternative ways of viewing the concept and its manifestations are sidelined. In other words, definitive concepts are excessively concerned with what is common to the phenomena that the concept is supposed to subsume rather than with variety. Instead, Blumer (1954: 7) recommended that social researchers should recognize that the concepts they use are sensitizing concepts in that they provide 'a general sense of reference and guidance in approaching empirical instances'. For Blumer, then, concepts should be employed in such a way that they give a very general sense of what to look for and act as a means for uncovering the variety of forms that the phenomena to which they refer can assume. In providing a critique of definitive concepts, it is clear that Blumer had in mind the concept-indicator model described in Chapter 6. In other words, his views entailed in large part a critique of quantitative research and a programmatic statement that would form a springboard for an alternative approach that nowadays we would recognize as qualitative research.

Blumer's distinction is not without its problems. It is not at all clear how far a very general formulation of a concept can be regarded as a useful guide to empirical enquiry. If it is too general, it will simply fail to provide a useful starting point because its guidelines are too broad; if too narrow, it is likely to repeat some of the difficulties Blumer identified in relation to definitive concepts. However, his general view of concepts has attracted some support, because his preference for not imposing pre-ordained schemes on the social world chimes with that of many qualitative researchers. As the example in Research in focus 16.1 suggests, the researcher frequently starts out with a broad outline of a concept, which is revised and narrowed during the course of data collection. For subsequent researchers, the concept may be taken up and revised as it is employed in connection with different social contexts or in relation to somewhat different research questions.

Research in focus 16.1
The emergence of a concept in qualitative research: the case of emotional labour

Hochschild's (1983) idea of emotional labour—labour that 'requires one to induce or suppress feelings in order to sustain the outward countenance that produces the proper state of mind in others' (1983: 7)—has become a very influential concept in the sociology of work and in the developing area of the sociology of emotions. Somewhat ironically for a predominantly qualitative study, Hochschild's initial conceptualization appears to have emerged from a **questionnaire** she distributed to 261 university students. Within the questionnaire were two requests: 'Describe a real situation that was important to you in which you experienced a deep emotion' and 'Describe as fully and concretely as possible a real situation that was important to you in which you either changed the situation to fit your feelings or changed your feelings to fit the situation' (1983: 13). Thus, although a **self-completion questionnaire** was employed, the resulting data were qualitative. The data were analyzed in terms of the idea of emotion *work*, which is the same as emotional labour but occurs in a private context. Emotional labour is essentially emotion work that is performed as part of one's paid employment. In order to develop the idea of emotional labour, Hochschild looked to the world of work. The main occupation she studied was the flight attendant. Several sources of data on emotional labour among flight attendants were employed. She gained access to Delta Airlines, a large American airline, and in the course of her investigations she:

- watched sessions for training attendants and had many conversations with both trainees and experienced attendants during the sessions;

- interviewed various personnel, such as managers in various sections, and advertising agents;

- examined Delta advertisements spanning thirty years;

- observed the flight attendant recruitment process at Pan American Airways, since she had not been allowed to do this at Delta;

- conducted 'open-ended interviews lasting three to five hours each with thirty flight attendants in the San Francisco Bay Area' (1983: 15).

In order to forge a comparison with a contrasting occupational group that is nonetheless also involved in emotional labour, Hochschild also interviewed five debt-collectors. In her book, she explores such topics as the human costs of emotional labour and the issue of gender in relation to it. It is clear that Hochschild's concept of emotional labour began as a somewhat imprecise idea that emerged out of a concern with emotion work and that was gradually developed in order to address its wider significance. The concept has been picked up by other qualitative researchers in the sociology of work. For example, Leidner (1993) has explored through ethnographic studies of a McDonald's restaurant and an insurance company the ways in which organizations seek to 'routinize' the display of emotional labour.

Sampling in qualitative research

In this book, sampling issues in qualitative research are discussed mainly in Chapters 17 and 18. As will become apparent from the sections on sampling in these two chapters, qualitative researchers typically engage in *purposive sampling* (see Key concept 17.4). This type of sampling is essentially to do with the selection of units (which may be people, organizations, documents, departments, etc.), with direct reference to the research questions being asked.

Probability sampling may be used in qualitative research (e.g. Rafaeli *et al.* 1997), though this is more likely to occur in interview-based rather than in ethnographic qualitative studies. There is no obvious rule of thumb that might be used to help the qualitative researcher in deciding when it might be appropriate to employ probability sampling, but two criteria might be envisaged. First, if it is highly significant or important for the qualitative researcher to be able to generalize to a wider population, probability sampling is likely to be a more compelling sampling approach. This might occur with audiences for one's work for whom generalizability in the traditional sense of the word is important. Second, if the research questions do not suggest that particular categories of people (or whatever the unit of analysis is) should be sampled, there may be a case for sampling randomly. This is not a likely or common occurrence, but, if it occurs, probability sampling warrants consideration.

When purposive sampling takes place in qualitative research, it often occurs at more than one level. For example, in the study of British symphony orchestras (Maitlis and Lawrence 2007) referred to briefly in Thinking deeply 16.1, there were two levels of sampling.

1. *Sampling of orchestras.* Three orchestras were selected, with the choice being based 'on the study's aims, seeking a balanced sample of organizations in which issues and processes could be compared but in which heterogeneity was also significant' (Maitlis and Lawrence 2007: 60). Maitlis and Lawrence argue that the three orchestras are based on three of the main categories of orchestra in Britain. These three types are based on the governance structure of the orchestra and its sources of revenue. The authors also point out that they selected only orchestras that were neither the weakest nor the strongest (aesthetically or financially) 'to increase the study's generalizabil-

ity' (Maitlis and Lawrence 2007: 60). What we see here in the selection of units of analysis is a combination of selection for heterogeneity (governance structure and revenue) and homogeneity (mid-level performance). In this way, the researcher is able to exert some control over the kinds of comparison that can be forged.

2. *Sampling of interviewees.* Interviews were conducted with: each orchestra's executive director and all members of its management team; its main conductor; and those musicians who were representatives on the orchestra's board and its orchestra committee, which represents musicians' interests. In addition, interviews were conducted with long-term members of the orchestra or who had previously been members of the board or orchestra committee. Musicians who expressed an interest were also interviewed (these latter interviews would be more characteristic of convenience rather than purposive sampling). A total of 120 interviews were conducted. In addition, the researchers attended meetings and rehearsals and examined numerous documents.

Sometimes, when conducting a mixed methods investigation involving both quantitative and qualitative research, the findings from a survey might be used as the basis for the selection of a purposive sample. For example, in a study of social policy researchers in the UK, an e-survey was conducted that sought respondents' views on a wide variety of issues concerning criteria for evaluating the quality of social policy research (Bryman *et al.* in press; Sempik *et al.* 2007). Respondents were asked whether they would be prepared to be interviewed by telephone so that issues could be probed more deeply and other issues that had not been explored in the e-survey could be addressed. Of the 251 researchers who replied to the online questionnaire 90 agreed to be interviewed. On the basis of their replies, 28 of the 90 researchers were interviewed by telephone using a semi-structured interview approach. The 28 interviewees were selected to reflect a variety of orientations to social policy research and to the evaluation of research quality. For example, one criterion was derived from where the respondent stood on the issue of whether he or she felt that social policy research should contribute to policy and practice or to knowledge or to a combination of both. This sampling strategy allowed interviewees to be selected purposively in terms of criteria that were central to the main topic of the research—the appraisal of research quality.

The term 'purposive sampling' covers a wide variety of approaches, as this brief discussion should make clear. Further examples and ways of thinking about it can be found in the next two chapters. What links them is that the sampling is conducted with reference to the goals of the research, so that units of analysis are selected in terms of criteria that will allow the research questions to be answered.

 # Reliability and validity in qualitative research

In Chapters 2 and 6 it was noted that reliability and validity are important criteria in establishing and assessing the quality of research for the quantitative researcher. However, there has been some discussion among qualitative researchers concerning their relevance for qualitative research. Moreover, even writers who do take the view that the criteria are relevant have considered the possibility that the meanings of the terms need to be altered. For example, the issue of measurement validity almost by definition seems to carry connotations of measurement. Since measurement is not a major preoccupation among qualitative researchers, the issue of validity would seem to have little bearing on such studies. As foreshadowed briefly in Chapter 2, a number of different stances have been taken by qualitative researchers in relation to these issues.

Adapting reliability and validity for qualitative research

One stance is to assimilate reliability and validity into qualitative research with little change of meaning other than playing down the salience of measurement issues. Mason (1996: 21), for example, in her book on qualitative research, argues that reliability, validity and generalizability (which is the main component of external validity —see Chapter 2) 'are different kinds of measures of the quality, rigour and wider potential of research, which are achieved according to certain methodological and disciplinary conventions and principles'. She sticks very close to the meaning that these criteria have in quantitative research, where they have been largely developed. Thus, validity refers to whether 'you are observing, identifying, or "measuring" what you say you are' (Mason 1996: 24). LeCompte and Goetz (1982) and Kirk and Miller (1986) also write about reliability and validity in relation to qualitative research but invest the terms with a somewhat

different meaning from Mason. LeCompte and Goetz write about the following.

- *External reliability*, by which they mean the degree to which a study can be replicated. This is a difficult criterion to meet in qualitative research, since, as LeCompte and Goetz recognize, it is impossible to 'freeze' a social setting and the circumstances of an initial study to make it replicable in the sense in which the term is usually employed (see Chapter 6). However, they suggest several strategies that can be introduced in order to approach the requirements of external reliability. For example, they suggest that a qualitative researcher replicating ethnographic research needs to adopt a similar social role to that adopted by the original researcher. Otherwise what a researcher conducting a replication sees and hears will not be comparable to the original research.

- *Internal reliability*, by which they mean whether, when there is more than one observer, members of the research team agree about what they see and hear. This is a similar notion to *inter-observer consistency* (see Key concept 6.3).

- *Internal validity*, by which they mean whether there is a good match between researchers' observations and the theoretical ideas they develop. LeCompte and Goetz argue that internal validity tends to be a strength of qualitative research, particularly ethnographic research, because the prolonged participation in the social life of a group over a long period of time allows the researcher to ensure a high level of congruence between concepts and observations.

- *External validity*, which refers to the degree to which findings can be generalized across social settings. LeCompte and Goetz argue that, unlike internal validity, external validity represents a problem for qualitative researchers because of their tendency to employ case studies and small samples.

As this brief treatment suggests, qualitative researchers have tended to employ the terms reliability and validity in very similar ways to quantitative researchers when seeking to develop criteria for assessing research.

Alternative criteria for evaluating qualitative research

However, a second position in relation to reliability and validity in qualitative research can be discerned. Some writers have suggested that qualitative studies should be judged or evaluated according to quite different criteria from those used by quantitative researchers. Lincoln and Guba (1985) and Guba and Lincoln (1994) propose that it is necessary to specify terms and ways of establishing and assessing the quality of qualitative research that provide an alternative to reliability and validity. They propose two primary criteria for assessing a qualitative study: *trustworthiness* and *authenticity*.

Trustworthiness

Trustworthiness is made up of four criteria, each of which has an equivalent criterion in quantitative research:

1. *credibility*, which parallels internal validity;
2. *transferability*, which parallels external validity;
3. *dependability*, which parallels reliability;
4. *confirmability*, which parallels objectivity.

A major reason for Guba and Lincoln's unease about the simple application of reliability and validity standards to qualitative research is that the criteria presuppose that a single absolute account of social reality is feasible. In other words, they are critical of the view (described in Chapter 1 as *realist*) that there are absolute truths about the social world that it is the job of the social scientist to reveal. Instead, they argue that there can be more than one and possibly several accounts.

Credibility

The significance of this stress on multiple accounts of social reality is especially evident in the trustworthiness criterion of *credibility*. After all, if there can be several possible accounts of an aspect of social reality, it is the feasibility or credibility of the account that a researcher arrives at that is going to determine its acceptability to others. The establishment of the credibility of findings entails both ensuring that research is carried out according to the canons of good practice *and* submitting research findings to the members of the social world who were studied for confirmation that the investigator has correctly understood that social world. This latter technique is often referred to as *respondent validation* or *member validation* (see Key concept 16.3). Another technique they recommend is *triangulation* (see Key concept 16.4).

Key concept 16.3
What is respondent validation?

Respondent validation, which is also sometimes called member validation, is a process whereby a researcher provides the people on whom he or she has conducted research with an account of his or her findings. The aim of the exercise is to seek corroboration or otherwise of the account that the researcher has arrived at. Respondent validation has been particularly popular among qualitative researchers, because they frequently want to ensure that there is a good correspondence between their findings and the perspectives and experiences of their research participants. The form that respondent validation can assume varies. There are several different forms of respondent validation.

- The researcher provides each research participant with an account of what he or she has said to the researcher in an interview and conversations, or of what the researcher observed by watching that person in the course of an observational study. For example, Bloor (1978, 1997) reports that he carried out observations of ear, nose, and throat (ENT) consultants concerning their approaches to making decisions about the assessment of patients. He submitted a report to each consultant on his or her practices.

- The researcher feeds back to a group of people or an organization his or her impressions and findings in relation to that group or organization. Bloor (1997) says that, for his research on therapeutic communities, he conducted group discussions (which were taped) with community members to gauge reactions to draft research reports.

- The researcher feeds back to a group of people or an organization some of his or her writings that are based on a study of that group or organization (e.g. articles, book chapters). Ball (1984) asked teachers in a school in which he had conducted ethnographic research to comment on draft articles and chapters, and similarly Willis (1977) asked the young working-class males who were the focus of his ethnography to comment on draft chapters, as did Skeggs (1994) for her parallel study of young working-class women (see Research in focus 17.8 for further details).

In each case, the goal is to seek confirmation that the researcher's findings and impressions are congruent with the views of those on whom the research was conducted and to seek out areas in which there is a lack of correspondence and the reasons for it. However, the idea is not without practical difficulties.

- Respondent validation may occasion defensive reactions on the part of research participants and even censorship.

- Bloor (1997: 45) observes that, because some approaches to enquiry may result in research participants developing relationships with the researcher of 'fondness and mutual regard', there may be a reluctance to be critical.

- It is highly questionable whether research participants can validate a researcher's analysis, since this entails inferences being made for an audience of social science peers. This means that, even though the first two methods of respondent validation may receive a corroborative response, the researcher still has to make a further leap, through the development of concepts and theories, in providing a social science frame for the resulting publications. If the third method of respondent validation is employed, it is unlikely that the social scientific analyses will be meaningful to research participants. Hobbs (1993) fed back some of his writings on entrepreneurship in London's East End to his informants, and it is clear that they made little sense of what he had written. Similarly, Skeggs (1994: 86) reports: ' "Can't understand a bloody word it says" was the most common response' (see Research in focus 17.8 for further details of this study).

Transferability

Because qualitative research typically entails the intensive study of a small group, or of individuals sharing certain characteristics (that is, depth rather than the breadth that is a preoccupation in quantitative research), qualitative findings tend to be oriented to the contextual uniqueness and significance of the aspect of the social world being studied. As Lincoln and Guba put it, whether findings 'hold in some other context, or even in the same context at some other time, is an empirical issue' (Lincoln and Guba 1985: 316). Instead, qualitative researchers are encouraged to produce what Geertz (1973a) calls *thick description*—that is, rich accounts of the details of a culture. Lincoln and Guba argue that a thick description provides others with what they refer to as a database for making judgements about the possible transferability of findings to other milieux.

Dependability

As a parallel to reliability in quantitative research, Lincoln and Guba propose the idea of dependability and argue that, to establish the merit of research in terms of this criterion of trustworthiness, researchers should adopt an 'auditing' approach. This entails ensuring that complete records are kept of all phases of the research process— problem formulation, selection of research participants, fieldwork notes, interview transcripts, data analysis decisions, and so on—in an accessible manner. Peers would then act as auditors, possibly during the course of the research and certainly at the end to establish how far proper procedures are being and have been followed. This would include assessing the degree to which theoretical inferences can be justified. Auditing has not become a popular approach to enhancing the dependability of qualitative research. A rare example is a study of behaviour at an American 'swap meet', where second-hand goods are bought and sold (Belk *et al*. 1988). A team of three researchers collected data over four days through observation, interviews, photography, and video-recording. The researchers conducted several trustworthiness tests, such as respondent validation and triangulation. But, in addition, they submitted their draft manuscript and entire data set to three peers, whose task 'was to criticize

the project for lack of sufficient data for drawing its conclusions if they saw such a void' (Belk *et al*. 1988: 456). The study highlights some problems associated with the auditing idea. One is that it is very demanding for the auditors, bearing in mind that qualitative research frequently generates extremely large data sets, and it may be that this is a major reason why it has not become a pervasive approach to validation.

Key concept 16.4
What is triangulation?

Triangulation entails using more than one method or source of data in the study of social phenomena. The term has been employed somewhat more broadly by Denzin (1970: 310) to refer to an approach that uses 'multiple observers, theoretical perspectives, sources of data, and methodologies', but the emphasis has tended to be on methods of investigation and sources of data. One of the reasons for the advocacy by Webb *et al*. (1966) of a greater use of **unobtrusive methods** was their potential in relation to a strategy of triangulation (see Key concept 13.3). Triangulation can operate within and across research strategies. It was originally conceptualized by Webb *et al*. (1966) as an approach to the development of measures of concepts, whereby more than one method would be employed in the development of measures, resulting in greater confidence in findings. As such, triangulation was very much associated with a quantitative research strategy. However, triangulation can also take place within a qualitative research strategy. In fact, **ethnographers** often check out their observations with interview questions to determine whether they might have misunderstood what they had seen. Bloor (1997) reports that he tackled the process of death certification in a Scottish city in two ways: interviewing clinicians with a responsibility for certifying causes of deaths, and asking the same people to complete dummy death certificates based on case summaries he had prepared. Increasingly, triangulation is also being used to refer to a process of cross-checking findings deriving from both quantitative and qualitative research (Deacon *et al*. 1998). Triangulation represents just one way in which it may be useful to think about the integration of these two research strategies and is covered in Chapter 25 in the context of **mixed methods research**.

Confirmability

Confirmability is concerned with ensuring that, while recognizing that complete objectivity is impossible in social research, the researcher can be shown to have acted in good faith; in other words, it should be apparent that he or she has not overtly allowed personal values or theoretical inclinations manifestly to sway the conduct of the research and findings deriving from it. Lincoln and Guba propose that establishing confirmability should be one of the objectives of auditors.

Authenticity

In addition to these four trustworthiness criteria, Lincoln and Guba suggest criteria of *authenticity*. These criteria

raise a wider set of issues concerning the wider political impact of research. These are the criteria:

- *Fairness*. Does the research fairly represent different viewpoints among members of the social setting?

- *Ontological authenticity*. Does the research help members to arrive at a better understanding of their social milieu?

- *Educative authenticity*. Does the research help members to appreciate better the perspectives of other members of their social setting?

- *Catalytic authenticity*. Has the research acted as an impetus to members to engage in action to change their circumstances?

- *Tactical authenticity*. Has the research empowered members to take the steps necessary for engaging in action?

The authenticity criteria are thought-provoking but have not been influential, and their emphasis on the wider impact of research is controversial. They have certain points of affinity with *action research* (see Key concept 16.5), which by and large has not been a popular form of social research, though it has had some impact in fields like organization studies and education. The emphasis on practical outcomes differentiates it from most social research.

Recent discussions about quality criteria for qualitative research

The main point of discussing Lincoln and Guba's ideas is that they differ from writers like LeCompte and Goetz in seeking criteria for evaluating qualitative research that represent a departure from those employed by quantitative researchers. The issue of research quality in relation to qualitative investigations has become a rather contested area in recent years, with several schemes of criteria being proposed as possible alternatives to reliability and validity as criteria and to schemes like Lincoln and Guba's list. For example, Yardley (2000) has proposed the following four criteria:

- *Sensitivity to context*: sensitivity not just to the context of the social setting in which the research is conducted but also to potentially relevant theoretical positions and ethical issues.

- *Commitment and rigour*: substantial engagement with the subject matter, having the necessary skills, and thorough data collection and analysis.

- *Transparency and coherence*: research methods clearly specified, clearly articulated argument, and a reflexive stance (see Key concept 27.4 on **reflexivity**).

- *Impact and importance*: importance of having an impact on and significance for theory, the community on which the research is conducted and for practitioners.

When compiling these criteria, Yardley had in mind health researchers who are likely to emphasize the impact of a study, which probably accounts for the presence of the last of these four criteria—impact and importance—which has some affinities with Lincoln and Guba's authenticity criteria.

Perhaps in response to the proliferation of different lists of qualitative research criteria and also because of the lack of agreed criteria, Spencer *et al.* (2003) have produced an extremely comprehensive list (see Thinking deeply 16.2). This list of quality criteria draws on the schemes that already existed at the time of their research and also on consultations with researchers in various fields. These consultations were in the form of semi-structured interviews and focus groups with practising researchers and writers on social research methods. In fact, I was one of the interviewees and also a focus group participant.

Thinking deeply 16.2
Using checklists for appraising quality in qualitative research?

Spencer *et al.* (2003) were commissioned to produce a report for the UK Government's Cabinet Office that aimed to provide a framework for assessing the quality of **evaluation research** studies that derived from qualitative investigations. Although their report focused upon evaluation research (see Key concept 2.5), they drew on considerations relating more generally to qualitative research, so that their scheme has a relevance beyond evaluation research.

The authors produced what is probably the most comprehensive list of criteria around. Here are the criteria that they suggest should be used when appraising the quality of a qualitative research study. In the case of each criterion, the original wording has been used.

1. How credible are the findings?
2. Has knowledge/understanding been extended by the research?

3. How well does the evaluation address its original aims and purposes?

4. Scope for drawing wider influences—how well is this explained?

5. How clear is the basis of the evaluative appraisal?

6. How defensible is the research design?

7. How well defended is the sample design/target selection of cases/documents?

8. Sample composition/case inclusion—how well is the eventual coverage described?

9. How well was the data collection carried out?

10. How well has the approach to, and formulation of, the analysis been conveyed?

11. Contexts of data sources—how well are they retained and portrayed?

12. How well has diversity of perspective and content been explored?

13. How well has detail, depth and complexity (richness?) of the data been conveyed?

14. How clear are the links between data, interpretation and conclusions—i.e. how well can the route to any conclusions be seen?

15. How clear and coherent is the reporting?

16. How clear are the assumptions/theoretical perspectives/values that have shaped the form and output of the evaluation?

17. What evidence is there of attention to ethical issues?

18. How adequately has the research process been documented?

Each of these eighteen criteria comes with 'quality indicators' that are designed to help in the appraisal of a study. What is not clear is how such a framework should be used. It has the appearance of a checklist, but as Spencer *et al.* (2003: 90) note, there is resistance within the qualitative research community to the possibly rigid application of any list of criteria that a checklist would entail. The researchers found that the idea of checklists of quality criteria were generally regarded rather negatively by interviewees. In fact, Spencer *et al.* do not promote their framework as a checklist, noting various concerns about their use in qualitative research, such at the risk of checklists becoming too prescriptive or of being applied too rigidly. However, the fact that the authors do not treat their work as leading to a checklist does not mean that the framework cannot or should not be used in that way. Indeed, around the same time that Spencer and his colleagues published their report, Michael Quinn Patton, a leading qualitative evaluation researcher, published online a list of criteria that *was* designed to be used as a checklist—see **http://www.wmich.edu/evalctr/checklists/qec.pdf** (accessed on 29 March 2007).

What do *you* think? Can checklists be valuable for appraising the quality of qualitative studies? If your answer is no, why is that? Is it something to do with the nature of qualitative research that makes checklists of quality inappropriate? Might checklists be more valuable in appraising the quality of quantitative research?

The full report by Spencer *et al.* can be found at **http://www.policyhub.gov.uk/docs/qqe_rep.pdf** (accessed on 29 March 2007).

Between quantitative and qualitative research criteria

Hammersley (1992*a*) lies midway between the preference for adapting quantitative research criteria and the preference for alternative quality criteria when assessing the quality of qualitative investigations. He proposes that validity is an important criterion but reformulates it somewhat. For Hammersley, validity means that an empirical account must be plausible and credible and should take into account the amount and kind of evidence used in relation to an account. In proposing this criterion, Hammersley's position shares with realism (see Key concept 1.3) the notion that there is an external social reality that can be accessed by the researcher. However, he simultaneously shares with the critics of the empirical realist position the rejection of the notion that such access is direct and in particular that the researcher can act as a mirror on the social world, reflecting its image back to an audience. Instead, the researcher is always engaged in representations or constructions of that world. The plausibility and credibility of a researcher's 'truth claims' then become the main considerations in evaluating qualitative research. Hammersley's *subtle realist* account, as he calls

it, entails recognizing that we can never be absolutely certain about the truth of any account, since we have no completely incontrovertible way of gaining direct access to the reality on which it is based. Therefore, he argues, 'we must judge the validity of claims [about truth] on the basis of the adequacy of the evidence offered in support of them' (1992*a*: 69). This means that an account can be held to be 'valid or true if it represents accurately those features of the phenomena that it is intended to describe, explain or theorise' (1992*a*: 69).

Key concept 16.5
What is action research?

There is no single type of action research, but broadly it can be defined as an approach in which the action researcher and members of a social setting collaborate in the diagnosis of a problem and in the development of a solution based on the diagnosis. It can take a variety of forms, from the action researcher being hired by a client to work on the diagnosis to and solution of a problem, to working with a group of individuals who are identified as needing to develop a capacity for independent action. The collection of data is likely to be involved in the formulation of the diagnosis of a problem and in the emergence of a solution. In action research, the investigator becomes part of the field of study. Action research can involve the collection of both quantitative and qualitative data. Gibson (2004: 5) describes a Canadian project that was interested in the social and cultural factors that have an impact on the prevention and treatment of tuberculosis (TB) among 'foreign-born and aboriginal populations'. The idea for the project came from a nurse in a TB clinic who garnered support from the groups most affected by the disease. An advisory committee, which drew its membership from the local community in a province of Alberta, as well as from community, government, and academic constituencies, was formed. Two representatives from each of the ten distinct socio-cultural communities were recruited and acted as research associates. Following training, they collected data through interviews and analysed some of the resulting data. Interviews were conducted in relation to four groups: TB sufferers; people on prophylaxis; people who refused prophylaxis; and 'those with a more distant history of TB in their country of origin or on aboriginal reserves' (Gibson 2004: 5). The research associates, members of the advisory committee, and academic staff analysed the interview data. The findings revealed that, while the health care system deals well will active TB cases, it is less effective in relation to prevention in relation to communities at risk. It also revealed that health professionals often fail to identify TB because it is not prevalent in Western nations. The advisory group then produced a plan to disseminate its findings and developed other initiatives including 'an information video, a community education nurse position, and TB fact sheet in their various languages' (Gibson 2004: 5).

Action research is more common in some social science areas than others. It is more common in fields such as business and management research and social policy than others. It is sometimes dismissed by academics for lacking rigour and for being too partisan in approach. However, it is advocated by some researchers because of its commitment to involving people in the diagnosis of and solutions to problems rather than imposing on them solutions to pre-defined problems.

Action research should not be confused with *evaluation research* (Key concept 2.5), which usually denotes the study of the impact of an intervention, such as a new social policy or a new innovation in organizations. The research referred to in Research in focus 16.6 was conducted broadly with an evaluation research frame of reference in that it was concerned to evaluate the impact of the introduction of performance appraisal in British universities.

Hammersley also suggests *relevance* as an important criterion of qualitative research. Relevance is taken to be assessed from the vantage point of the importance of a topic within its substantive field or the contribution it makes to the literature on that field. Hammersley also discusses the question of whether the concerns of practitioners (that is, people who are part of the social setting being investigated and who are likely to have a vested interest in the research question and the implications of findings deriving from it) might be an aspect of considerations of relevance. In this way, his approach touches on the kinds of consideration that are addressed by Guba and Lincoln's authenticity criteria (Lincoln and Guba 1985; Guba and Lincoln 1994). However, he recognizes that the kinds of research questions and findings that might be of interest to practitioners and researchers are likely to be somewhat different. As Hammersley notes, practitioners are likely to be interested in research that helps them to understand or address problems with which they are confronted. These may not be (and perhaps are unlikely to be) at the forefront of a researcher's set of preoccupations. However, there may be occasions when researchers can combine the two and may even be able to use this capability as a means of securing access to organizations in which they wish to conduct research (see Chapter 17 for a further discussion of access issues).

Overview of the issue of criteria

There is a recognition—albeit to varying degrees—that a simple application of the quantitative researcher's criteria of reliability and validity to qualitative research is not desirable, but writers vary in the degree to which they propose a complete overhaul of those criteria. Nor do the three positions outlined above—adapting quantitative research criteria, alternative criteria, and Hammersley's subtle realism—represent the full range of possible stances on this issue (Hammersley 1992a; Seale 1999). To a large extent, the differences between the three positions reflect divergences in the degree to which a realist position is broadly accepted or rejected. Writers on qualitative research who apply the ideas of reliability and validity with little if any adaptation broadly position themselves as realists—that is, as saying that social reality can be captured by qualitative researchers through their concepts and theories. Lincoln and Guba reject this view, arguing instead that qualitative researchers' concepts and theories are representations and that there may, therefore, be other equally credible representations

of the same phenomena. Hammersley's position occupies a middle ground in terms of the axis, with realism at one end and anti-realism at the other, in that, while acknowledging the existence of social phenomena that are part of an external reality, he disavows any suggestion that it is possible to reproduce that reality for the audiences of social scientific endeavour. Most qualitative researchers nowadays probably operate around the midpoint on this realism axis, though without necessarily endorsing Hammersley's views. Typically, they treat their accounts as one of a number of possible representations rather than as definitive versions of social reality. They also bolster those accounts through some of the strategies advocated by Lincoln and Guba, such as thick descriptions, respondent validation exercises, and triangulation.

To a certain extent, traditional quantitative research criteria have made something of a comeback since the late 1990s. One issue is to do with the perception of qualitative research. For one thing, to reject notions like reliability and validity could be taken by some constituencies (such as funding bodies) as indicative of a lack of concern with rigor, which is not a desirable impression to create. Consequently, there has been some evidence of increased concern with such issues. Armstrong *et al.* (1997) report the result of an exercise in what they call 'inter-rater reliability', which involved the analysis by six experienced researchers of a focus group transcript. The transcript related to research concerned with links between perceptions of disability and genetic screening. The focus group was made up of sufferers of cystic fibrosis (CF) and the participants were asked to discuss genetic screening. The raters were asked to extract prominent themes from transcripts, which is one of the main ways of analysing qualitative data (see Chapter 22). They tended to identify similar themes but differed in how themes were 'packaged'. One theme that was identified was 'visibility'. This theme was identified as a theme in transcripts by all researchers and refers to the invisibility of genetic disorders. The CF sufferers felt disadvantaged relative to other disabled groups because of the invisibility of their disorder and felt that the public were more sympathetic to and more inclined to recognize visible disabilities. However, some analysts linked it to other issues: two linked it with stigma; one to problems of managing invisibility. In a sense the results are somewhat inconclusive but are interesting for this discussion because they reveal an interest among qualitative researchers in reliability. A more recent and similar exercise is described in Research in focus 16.2.

Research in focus 16.2
Reliability for qualitative researchers

Gladney *et al.* (2003) report the findings of an exercise in which two multidisciplinary teams of researchers were asked to analyse qualitative interviews with eighty Texas school students. The interviews were concerned with reflections on violence on television; reasons for violence among some young people; and reasons for some young people *not* being violent. One group of raters read interview transcripts of the interviews; the other group listened to the audio-taped recordings. Thus, the dice were slightly loaded in favour of different themes being identified by the two groups. In spite of this there was remarkable consistency between the two groups in the themes identified. For example, in response to the question 'Why are some young people violent?', Group One identified the following themes: family/parental influence; peer influence; social influence; media influence; and coping. Group Two's themes were: the way they were raised; media influence; appearance; anger, revenge, protection; and environmental or peer influence. Such findings are quite reassuring and are interesting because of their clear interest in reliability in a qualitative research context. Interestingly, exercises such as this can be viewed as a form of what Lincoln and Guba (1985) call *auditing*.

Student experience
Thinking about reliability

Hannah Creane was concerned about the reliability of her categorization of her qualitative data and enlisted others to check out her thinking.

> There was a slight concern when I was grouping data together that my categorization was of an arbitrary nature, and so I could be making assumptions and theorizing on the basis of highly subjective categories. However, I tried to make sure that all the categories I used were relevant, and I checked them over with other people to make sure they made sense in relation to the research and the questions I was dealing with.

To read more about Hannah's research experiences, go to the Online Resource Centre that accompanies this book at **http://www.oxfordtextbooks.co.uk/orc/brymansrm3e/**.

The main preoccupations of qualitative researchers

As was noted in Chapter 6, quantitative and qualitative research can be viewed as exhibiting a set of distinctive but contrasting preoccupations. These preoccupations reflect epistemologically grounded beliefs about what constitutes acceptable knowledge. In Chapter 1, it was suggested that at the level of epistemology, whereas quantitative research is profoundly influenced by a natural science approach to what should count as acceptable knowledge, qualitative researchers are more influenced by *interpretivism* (see Key concept 1.4). This position can itself be viewed as the product of the confluence of three related stances: Weber's notion of *Verstehen*; symbolic interactionism; and phenomenology. In this section, five distinctive preoccupations among qualitative researchers will be outlined and examined.

Seeing through the eyes of the people being studied

An underlying premise of many qualitative researchers is that the subject matter of the social sciences (that is, people and their social world) does differ from the subject matter of the natural sciences. A key difference is that the objects of analysis of the natural sciences (atoms, molecules, gases, chemicals, metals, and so on) cannot attribute meaning to events and to their environment. However, people *do*. This argument is especially evident in the work of Schutz and can particularly be seen in the passage quoted on page 16, where Schutz draws attention to the fact that, unlike the objects of the natural sciences, the objects of the social sciences—people—are capable of attributing meaning to their environment. Consequently, many qualitative researchers have suggested that a methodology is required for studying people that reflects these differences between people and the objects of the natural sciences. As a result, many qualitative researchers express a commitment to viewing events and the social world through the eyes of the people that they study. The social world must be interpreted from the perspective of the people being studied, rather than as though those subjects were incapable of their own reflections on the social world. The epistemology underlying qualitative research has been expressed by the authors of one widely read text as involving two central tenets: '(1) . . . face-to-face interaction is the fullest condition of participating in the mind of another human being, and (2) . . . you must participate in the mind of another human being (in sociological terms, "take the role of the other") to acquire social knowledge' (Lofland and Lofland 1995: 16).

It is not surprising, therefore, that many researchers make claims in their reports of their investigations about having sought to take the views of the people they studied as the point of departure. This tendency reveals itself in frequent references to empathy and seeing through others' eyes. Here are some examples.

- Fielding (1982) carried out research on members of the National Front, a British extreme right-wing political party. In spite of his feelings of revulsion for the

racist doctrine, he sought to examine the party's position 'as a moral posture and its members' interpretations were to be illuminated by an empathetic immersion in their world. In the process of "telling it like it was for them", I could reproduce an account from which outsiders could understand the ideology's persuasiveness to people so placed' (Fielding 1982: 83).

- Armstrong (1993) carried out ethnographic research on football hooliganism through participant observation with Sheffield United supporters. He describes his work as located in '*Verstehende* sociology—trying to think oneself into the situations of the people one is interested in . . . in this case the "Hooligan". This approach involves recognizing social and historical phenomena as beyond any single or simple identifying cause and attempting to make sense from the social actors' viewpoint' (Armstrong 1993: 5–6).

- Like Armstrong, Taylor (1993), in relation to her ethnographic study of female injecting drug users, draws attention to the influence of Weber's idea of *Verstehen* on her research. The significance of the idea for her was that it meant that 'in order to understand social actions we must grasp the meaning that actors attach to their actions' (Taylor 1993: 7). She also acknowledges the influence of symbolic interactionism on her position.

- For their research on teenaged girls' views on and experiences of violence, Burman *et al.* (2001: 447) 'sought to ground the study in young women's experiences of violence, hearing their accounts and privileging their subjective views'.

This predilection for seeing through the eyes of the people studied in the course of qualitative research is often accompanied by the closely related goal of seeking to probe beneath surface appearances. After all, by taking the position of the people you are studying, the prospect is raised that they might view things differently from what an outsider with little direct contact might have expected. This stance reveals itself in:

- Foster's (1995) research on a high crime community, which was not perceived as such by its inhabitants;

- Skeggs's (1994: 74) study of young working-class women, showing that they were not 'ideological dupes of both social class and femininity';

- Taylor's (1993: 8) study of intravenous female drug users, showing the people she studied are not 'pathetic, inadequate individuals' but 'rational, active people making decisions based on the contingencies of

Student experience
Importance of seeing through research participants' eyes

Rebecca Barnes was attracted to qualitative research for her research on violence in same-sex relationships because there had only been a quantitative research in this area and because she wanted to understand the phenomenon in her research participants' own words.

I chose a qualitative research design for a number of reasons. First, I was aware that very little qualitative research exists in my field of research, and at the time that I started my research, I could not find any comprehensive qualitative studies of woman-to-woman partner abuse in the UK. Thus, I wanted my research to contribute towards filling this gap, on a national and international level. I also chose a qualitative research design because I wanted to achieve an in-depth understanding of the experiences of woman-to-woman partner abuse that women reported in their own words and using their own frames of reference. I also set out to achieve a more textured analysis of the dynamics of abuse and the different impacts that being abused has upon women, and how these may change over time.

To read more about Rebecca's research experiences, go to the Online Resource Centre that accompanies this book at http://www.oxfordtextbooks.co.uk/orc/brymansrm3e/.

both their drug using careers and their roles and status in society';

- Armstrong's (1993: 11) quest in his research on football hooliganism to 'see beyond mere appearances' and his finding that, contrary to the popular view, hooligans are not a highly organized group led by a clearly identifiable group of ringleaders;

- O'Reilly's (2000) ethnography of British expatriates on the Costa del Sol in Spain, in which she shows how the widely held view that this group is deeply dissatisfied with their lives in the sun and long to return is by no means an accurate portrayal in terms of how they view themselves and their situation.

The empathetic stance of seeking to see through the eyes of one's research participants is very much in tune with interpretivism and demonstrates well the epistemological links with phenomenology, symbolic interactionism, and *Verstehen*. However, it is not without practical problems. For example: the risk of 'going native' and losing sight of what you are studying (see Key concept 17.3); the problem of how far the researcher should go, such as the potential problem of participating in illegal or dangerous activities, which could be a risk in research like that engaged in by Taylor and Armstrong; and the

possibility that the researcher will be able to see through the eyes of only some of the people who form part of a social scene but not others, such as only people of the same gender. These and other practical difficulties will be addressed in the chapters that follow.

Description and the emphasis on context

Qualitative researchers are much more inclined than quantitative researchers to provide a great deal of descriptive detail when reporting the fruits of their research. This is not to say that they are exclusively concerned with description. They *are* concerned with explanation, and indeed the extent to which qualitative researchers ask 'why?' questions is frequently understated. For example, Skeggs (1997: 22) has written that her first question for her research on young working-class women was 'why do women, who are clearly not just victims of some ideological conspiracy, consent to a system of class and gender oppression which appears to offer few rewards and little benefit?' (see Research in focus 17.8 for further details of this study).

Many qualitative studies provide a detailed account of what goes on in the setting being investigated. Very often qualitative studies seem to be full of apparently trivial details. However, these details are frequently important for the qualitative researcher, because of their significance for their subjects and also because the details provide an account of the context within which people's behaviour takes place. It was with this point in mind that Geertz (1973a) recommended the provision of thick descriptions of social settings, events, and often individuals. As a result of this emphasis on description, qualitative studies are often full of detailed information about the social worlds being examined. On the surface, some of this detail may appear irrelevant, and, indeed, there is a risk of the researcher becoming too embroiled in descriptive detail. Lofland and Lofland (1995: 164–5), for example, warn against the sin of what they call 'descriptive excess' in qualitative research, whereby the amount of detail overwhelms or inhibits the analysis of data.

One of the main reasons why qualitative researchers are keen to provide considerable descriptive detail is that they typically emphasize the importance of the contextual understanding of social behaviour. This means that behaviour, values, or whatever must be understood in context. This recommendation means that we cannot understand the behaviour of members of a social group other than in terms of the specific environment in which they operate. In this way, behaviour that may appear odd or irrational can make perfect sense when we understand the particular context within which that behaviour takes place. The emphasis on context in qualitative research goes back to many of the classic studies in social anthropology, which often demonstrated how a particular practice, such as the magical ritual that may accompany the sowing of seeds, made little sense unless we understand the belief systems of that society. One of the chief reasons for the emphasis on descriptive detail is that it is often precisely this detail that provides the mapping of context in terms of which behaviour is understood. The propensity for description can also be interpreted as a manifestation of the naturalism that pervades much qualitative research (see Key concept 2.4 and 16.1), because it places a premium on detailed, rich descriptions of social settings.

Conducting qualitative research in more than one setting can be helpful in identifying the significance of context and the ways in which it influences behaviour and ways of thinking. Research in focus 16.3 provides an illustration of a multiple-case study that demonstrates this potential.

Research in focus 16.3
Contextual understanding in an ethnographic study of three schools

Swain (2004) conducted an ethnographic study of three junior schools in the UK in the late 1990s. Ethnography is discussed in the next chapter. Because it compared findings from three schools, this was a multiple-case study, which drew on the strengths of using a **comparative design** in that it was possible to explore the significance of context across the three schools. The schools were different in terms of the social characteristics of the pupils they recruited: Highwoods Independent's (the school names are pseudonyms) pupils were mainly upper middle class; pupils at Petersfield Junior were predominantly middle class; and Westmoor Abbey Junior's pupils were mainly working class. Swain (2004: 169) describes his data collection methods as involving non-participant observation of pupils in lessons and around the school and 'loosely structured interviews' with pupils based on 'nominated friendship groups'. In this article, Swain was interested in the ways in which boys construct what it means to be masculine in the school and draws primarily on data collected on boys rather than on girls. Swain shows that masculinity was inseparable from the achievement of status among school peer groups and that the body was the means of expressing masculinity. The significance of context emerges in connection with Swain's account of how the body was used to convey masculinity in the three schools: at Highwoods sport was the medium through which the body expressed masculinity; at Westmoor Abbey the emphasis was macho and frequently took on a violent tone; and at Petersfield it was speed and strength (predominantly in the playground rather than on the sports field). Context reveals itself in the different resources in the three schools that students must draw upon to perform masculinity

Emphasis on process

Qualitative research tends to view social life in terms of processes. This tendency reveals itself in a number of different ways. One of the main ways is that there is often a concern to show how events and patterns unfold over time. As a result, qualitative evidence often conveys a strong sense of change and flux. As Pettigrew (1997: 338) usefully puts it, process is 'a sequence of individual and collective events, actions, and activities unfolding over time in context'. Qualitative research that is based in ethnographic methods is particularly associated with this emphasis on process (although, ironically, British social anthropology, which is often associated with the early development of ethnographic research, is sometimes thought of as presenting a static picture of social reality by virtue of its association with functionalism). It is the element of participant observation that is a key feature of ethnography that is especially instrumental in generating this feature.

Ethnographers are typically immersed in a social setting for a long time—frequently years. Consequently, they are able to observe the ways in which events develop over time or the ways in which the different elements of a social system (values, beliefs, behaviour, and so on) interconnect. Such findings can inject a sense of process by seeing social life in terms of streams of interdependent events and elements (see Research in focus 16.4 for an example).

This is not to say, however, that ethnographers are the only qualitative researchers who inject a sense of process into our understanding of social life. It can also be achieved through semi-structured and **unstructured interviewing,** by asking participants to reflect on the processes leading up to or following on from an event. McKee and Bell (1985: 388; see also Thinking deeply 2.4), for example, show, through the use of a 'largely unstructured, conversational interview style' with forty-five couples in which the man was unemployed, the accommodations that are made over time by both husbands and wives to the fact of male unemployment. The various accommodations are not an immediate effect of unemployment but are gradual and incremental responses over time. The life history approach is an example of a form of qualitative research. One of the best-known studies of this kind is Lewis's (1961) study of a poor Mexican family. Lewis carried out extended taped interviews with the family members to reconstruct their life histories. For his study of disasters in the UK, and in particular of the fire at a holiday leisure complex on the Isle of Man, Turner (1994) employed published documents to arrive at a reconstruction of the events leading up to the fire and a theoretical understanding of those events. Thus, the emphasis on process in qualitative research can be seen in the use of quite different approaches to data collection.

Research in focus 16.4
Process in (strike) action

Waddington (1994) describes his experiences associated with his participant observation of a strike at the Ansells brewery in Birmingham in the 1980s. As a participant observer, he was involved in 'attending picket lines, mass meetings and planning discussions, and accompanying the strikers on flying picketing and intelligence gathering manœuvres' (1994: 113). In addition to observation, he carried out informal interviews and linked these data to other sources, such as 'material deriving from newspaper archives, company and trade union documents, letters and richly detailed minutes of trade union–management meetings' (1994: 115). As a result, he was able to show 'how the contemporary beliefs, values and attitudes of the workforce, and the mutual feelings of animosity and distrust between employees and management, were shaped by a sequence of historical events stretching back over 20 years' (1994: 115). We can see in this example the development of a sense of process in three ways: through observation of the strike over its entirety, so that developments and interconnections between events could be brought out; through connecting these events with historical and other data, so that the links between the strike and previous and other events and actions could be outlined; and through the sketching of the context (in the form of the past, as well as current beliefs and values) and its links with behaviour during the strike.

Flexibility and limited structure

Many qualitative researchers are disdainful of approaches to research that entail the imposition of predetermined formats on the social world. This position is largely to do with the preference for seeing through the eyes of the people being studied. After all, if a structured method of data collection is employed, since this is bound to be the product of an investigator's ruminations about the object of enquiry, certain decisions must have been made about what he or she expects to find and about the nature of the social reality that would be encountered. Therefore, the researcher is limited in the degree to which he or she can genuinely adopt the world view of the people being studied. Consequently, most qualitative researchers prefer a research orientation that entails as little prior contamination of the social world as possible. To do otherwise risks imposing an inappropriate frame of reference on people. Keeping structure to a minimum is supposed to enhance the opportunity of genuinely revealing the perspectives of the people you are studying. Also, in the process, aspects of people's social world that are particularly important to them, but that might not even have crossed the mind of a researcher unacquainted with it, are more likely to be forthcoming. As a result, qualitative research tends to be a strategy that tries not to delimit areas of enquiry too much and to ask fairly general rather than specific research questions (see Figure 16.1 and Thinking deeply 16.1).

Because of the preference for an unstructured approach to the collection of data, qualitative researchers adopt methods of research that do not require the investigator to develop highly specific research questions in advance and therefore to devise instruments specifically for those questions to be answered. Ethnography, with its emphasis on participant observation, is particularly well suited to this orientation. It allows researchers to submerge themselves in a social setting with a fairly general research focus in mind and gradually to formulate a narrower emphasis by making as many observations of that setting as possible. They can then formulate more specific research questions out of their collected data. Similarly, interviewing is an extremely prominent method in the qualitative researcher's armoury, but it is not of the kind we encountered in the course of most of Chapter 8—

namely, the structured interview. Instead, qualitative researchers prefer less structured approaches to interviewing, as we will see in Chapter 18. Blumer's (1954) argument for sensitizing rather than definitive concepts (that is, the kind employed by quantitative researchers) is symptomatic of the preference for a more open-ended, and hence less structured, approach.

An advantage of the unstructured nature of most qualitative enquiry (that is, in addition to the prospect of gaining access to people's world views) is that it offers the prospect of flexibility. The researcher can change direction in the course of his or her investigation much more easily than in quantitative research, which tends to have a built-in momentum once the data collection is under way: if you send out hundreds of postal questionnaires and realize after you have started to get some back that there is an issue that you would have liked to investigate, you are not going to find it easy to retrieve the situation. Structured interviewing and structured observation can involve some flexibility, but the requirement to make interviews as comparable as possible for survey investigations limits the extent to which this can happen. O'Reilly (2000) has written that her research on the British on the Costa del Sol shifted in two ways over the duration of her participant observation: from an emphasis on the elderly to expatriates of all ages; and from an emphasis on permanent residents to less permanent forms of migration, such as tourism. These changes in emphasis occurred because of the limitations of just focusing on the elderly and on permanent migrants, since these groups were not necessarily as distinctive as might have been supposed. Similarly, Kathleen Gerson has explained that, in her research on changing forms of the family, she conducted an early interview with a young man who had been brought up in his early years in a traditional household that underwent a considerable change during his childhood. This led her to change her focus from an emphasis on family structures to processes of change in the family (Gerson and Horowitz 2002). See Research in focus 16.5 for a further illustration of the ways in which the unstructured data collection style of qualitative research can be used to suggest alternative avenues of enquiry or ways of thinking about the phenomenon being investigated.

Research in focus 16.5
Flexibility in action

In the course of a study of young people with learning difficulties using qualitative interviews, Davies (1999) reports that she found that on many occasions her interviewees mentioned food in the course of conversations. Initially, she followed these conversations up largely in order to establish rapport with these young people. However, she gradually came to realize that in fact food was of considerable significance for her research, because it represented a lens through which her participants viewed their anxieties about the ways people attempted to control them. Food was also a focus for their strategies of resistance to control.

Research in focus 16.6
Emerging concepts

In the late 1980s and early 1990s, most UK universities were in the throes of introducing staff appraisal schemes for both academic and academic-related staff. Staff appraisal is employed to review the appraisee's performance and activities over a period of usually one or two years. Along with some colleagues, I undertook an evaluation of staff appraisal schemes in four universities (Bryman *et al.* 1994). The research entailed the collection of both quantitative and qualitative data within the framework of a comparative research design. The qualitative data were derived from large numbers of interviews with appraisers, appraisees, senior managers, and many others. In the course of conducting the interviews and analysing the subsequent data we became increasingly aware of a cynicism among many of the people we interviewed. This attitude revealed itself in several ways, such as: a view that appraisal had been introduced just to pacify the government; a belief that nothing happened of any significance in the aftermath of an appraisal meeting; the view that it was not benefiting universities; and a suggestion that many participants to the appraisal process were just going through the motions. As one of the interviewees said in relation to this last feature: 'It's like going through the motions of it [appraisal]. It's just get it over with and signed and dated and filed and that's the end of it' (quoted in Bryman *et al.* 1994: 180).

On the basis of these findings it was suggested that the attitudes towards appraisal and the behaviour of those involved in appraisal were characterized by *procedural compliance*, which was defined as 'a response to an organizational innovation in which the technical requirements of the innovation . . . are broadly adhered to, but where there are substantial reservations about its efficacy and only partial commitment to it, so that there is a tendency for the procedures associated with the innovation to be adhered to with less than a total commitment to its aims' (Bryman *et al.* 1994: 178).

Concepts and theory grounded in data

This issue has already been addressed in much of the exposition of qualitative research above. For qualitative researchers, concepts and theories are usually inductively arrived at from the data that are collected (see Research in focus 16.1 and 16.6).

The critique of qualitative research

In a similar way to the criticisms that have been levelled at quantitative research mainly by qualitative researchers, a parallel critique has been built up of qualitative research. Some of the more common ones follow.

Qualitative research is too subjective

Quantitative researchers sometimes criticize qualitative research as being too impressionistic and subjective. By these criticisms they usually mean that qualitative findings rely too much on the researcher's often unsystematic views about what is significant and important, and also upon the close personal relationships that the researcher frequently strikes up with the people studied. Precisely because qualitative research often begins in a relatively open-ended way and entails a gradual narrowing-down of research questions or problems, the consumer of the writings deriving from the research is given few clues as to why one area was the chosen area upon which attention was focused rather than another. By contrast, quantitative researchers point to the tendency for the problem formulation stage in their work to be more explicitly stated in terms of such matters as the existing literature on that topic and key theoretical ideas.

Difficult to replicate

Quantitative researchers also often argue that these tendencies are even more of a problem because of the difficulty of replicating a qualitative study, although replication in the social sciences is by no means a straightforward matter regardless of this particular issue (see Chapter 6). Precisely because it is unstructured and often reliant upon the qualitative researcher's ingenuity, it is almost impossible to conduct a true replication, since there are hardly any standard procedures to be followed. In qualitative research, the investigator him- or herself is the main instrument of data collection, so that what is observed and heard and also what the researcher decides to concentrate upon is very much a product of his or her predilections. There are several possible components of this criticism: what qualitative researchers (especially perhaps in ethnography) choose to focus upon while in the field is a product of what strikes them as significant, whereas other researchers are likely to empathize with

other issues; the responses of participants (people being observed or interviewed) to qualitative researchers is likely to be affected by the characteristics of the researcher (personality, age, gender, and so on); and, because of the unstructured nature of qualitative data, interpretation will be profoundly influenced by the subjective leanings of a researcher. Because of such factors, it is difficult—not to say impossible—to replicate qualitative findings. The difficulties ethnographers experience when they revisit grounds previously trodden by another researcher (often referred to as a 'restudy') do not inspire confidence in the replicability of qualitative research (Bryman 1994).

Problems of generalization

It is often suggested that the scope of the findings of qualitative investigations is restricted. When participant observation is used or when unstructured interviews are conducted with a small number of individuals in a certain organization or locality, they argue that it is impossible to know how the findings can be generalized to other settings. How can just one or two cases be representative of all cases? In other words, can we really treat Holdaway's (1982) research on the police in Sheffield as representative of all police forces, or Armstrong's (1998) research on Sheffield United supporters as representative of all football supporters, or Waddington's (1994) study of a strike as generalizable to all lengthy strikes? In the case of research based on interviews rather than participation, can we treat interviewees who have not been selected through a probability procedure or even quota sampling as representative? Are Taylor's (1993) female intravenous drug users typical of all members of that category or are Skeggs's (1994; see Research in focus 17.8) young working-class women typical?

The answer in all these cases is, of course, emphatically 'no'. A case study is not a sample of one drawn from a known population. Similarly, the people who are interviewed in qualitative research are not meant to be representative of a population, and indeed, in some cases, like female intravenous drug users, we may find it more or less impossible to enumerate the population in any precise manner. Instead, the findings of qualitative research are to generalize to theory rather than to populations. It is 'the cogency of the theoretical reasoning' (Mitchell 1983: 207), rather than statistical criteria, that is decisive in considering the generalizability of the findings of qualitative research. In other words, it is the quality of the theoretical inferences that are made out of qualitative data that is crucial to the assessment of generalization.

However, not all writers on the issue of generalization in relation to qualitative research (and case study research in particular) accept this view. Williams (2000: 215) has argued that, in many cases, qualitative researchers are in a position to produce what he calls *moderatum* generalizations—that is, ones in which aspects of the focus of enquiry (a group of drug users, a group of football hooligans, a strike) 'can be seen to be instances of a broader set of recognizable features'. In addition, Williams argues that not only is it the case that qualitative researchers *can* make such generalizations but that in fact they often *do* make them. Thus, when generating findings relating to the hooligans who follow a certain football club, a researcher will often draw comparisons with findings by other researchers relating to comparable groups. Indeed, the researcher may also draw comparisons and linkages with still other groups: followers of other professional sports teams or violent groups that are not linked to sport. When forging such comparisons and linkages, the researcher is engaging in *moderatum* generalization. *Moderatum* generalizations will always be limited and somewhat more tentative than those associated with statistical generalizations of the kind associated with probability sampling (see Chapter 7). On the other hand, they do permit a modicum of generalization and help to counter the view that generalization beyond the immedi-

ate evidence and the case is impossible in qualitative research.

These three criticisms reflect many of the preoccupations of quantitative research that were discussed in Chapter 6. A further criticism that is often made of qualitative research, but that is perhaps less influenced by quantitative research criteria, is the suggestion that qualitative research frequently lacks transparency in how the research was conducted.

Lack of transparency

It is sometimes difficult to establish from qualitative research what the researcher actually *did* and how he or she arrived at the study's conclusions. For example, qualitative research reports are sometimes unclear about such matters as how people were chosen for observation or interview. This deficiency contrasts sharply with the sometimes laborious accounts of sampling procedures in reports of quantitative research. However, it does not seem plausible to suggest that outlining in some detail the ways in which research participants are selected constitutes the application of quantitative research criteria. Readers have a right to know how far research participants were selected to correspond to a wide range of people. Also, the process of qualitative data analysis is frequently unclear (Bryman and Burgess 1994a). It is often not obvious how the analysis was conducted—in other words, what the researcher was actually doing when the data were analysed and therefore how the study's conclusions were arrived at. To a large extent, these areas of a lack of transparency are increasingly being addressed by qualitative researchers.

Is it always like this?

This was a heading that was employed in Chapter 6 in relation to quantitative research, but it is perhaps less easy to answer in relation to qualitative research. To a large extent, this is because qualitative research is less codified than quantitative research—that is, it is less influenced by strict guidelines and directions about how to go about data collection and analysis. As a result, and this may be noticed by readers of the chapters that follow this one, accounts of qualitative research are frequently less prescriptive in tone than those encountered in relation to quantitative research. Instead, they often exhibit

more of a descriptive tenor, outlining the different ways qualitative researchers have gone about research or suggesting alternative ways of conducting research or analysis based on the writer's own experiences or those of others. To a large extent, this picture is changing, in that there is a growing number of books that seek to make clear-cut recommendations about how qualitative research should be carried out.

However, if we look at some of the preoccupations of qualitative research that were described above, we can see certain ways in which there are departures from the practices that are implied by these preoccupations. One of the main departures is that qualitative research is sometimes a lot more focused than is implied by the suggestion that the researcher begins with general research questions and narrows it down so that theory and concepts are arrived at during and after the data collection. There is no *necessary* reason why qualitative research cannot be employed to investigate a specific research problem. For example, Hammersley *et al.* (1985) describe a study that was designed to explore the impact of external assessments on schools. More specifically, they wanted to examine the contention, which was based on other studies of schools, that 'external examinations lead to lecturing and note-taking on the part of secondary-school teachers and instrumental attitudes among their pupils' (Hammersley *et al.* 1985: 58). This contention was examined through a comparison of two schools that varied considerably in the emphasis they placed on examinations. This study exhibits a comparative research design (see Chapter 2), with its accent on a comparison of two cases. A related way in which qualitative research differs from the standard model is in connection with the notion of a lack of structure in approaches to collecting and analysing data. As will be seen in Chapter 20, techniques like conversation analysis entail the application of a highly codified method for analysing talk. Moreover, the growing use of computer-assisted qualitative data analysis software (CAQDAS), which will be the subject of Chapter 23, is leading to greater transparency in the procedures used for analysing qualitative data. This greater transparency may lead to more codification in qualitative data analysis than has previously been the case.

Some contrasts between quantitative and qualitative research

Several writers have explored the contrasts between quantitative and qualitative research by devising tables that allow the differences to be brought out (e.g. Halfpenny 1979; Bryman 1988*a*; Hammersley 1992*b*). Table 16.1 attempts to draw out the chief contrasting features:

- *Numbers vs. Words*. Quantitative researchers are often portrayed as preoccupied with applying measurement procedures to social life, while qualitative researchers are seen as using words in the presentation of analyses of society.

- *Point of view of researcher vs. Point of view of participants*. In quantitative research, the investigator is in the driving seat. The set of concerns that he or she brings to an investigation structures the investigation. In qualitative research, the perspective of those being studied—what they see as important and significant—provides the point of orientation.

- *Researcher is distant vs. Researcher is close*. This dimension is to do with the relationship between researchers and their research participants. In quantitative research, researchers are uninvolved with their subjects and in some cases, as in research based on postal questionnaires or on hired interviewers, may have no contact with them at all. Sometimes, this lack of a relationship with the subjects of an investigation is regarded as desirable by quantitative researchers, because they feel that their objectivity might be compromised if they become too involved with the people they study. The qualitative researcher seeks close involvement with the people being investigated, so

Table 16.1

Some common contrasts between quantitative and qualitative research	
Quantitative	Qualitative
Numbers	Words
Point of view of researcher	Points of view of participants
Researcher distant	Researcher close
Theory testing	Theory emergent
Static	Process
Structured	Unstructured
Generalization	Contextual understanding
Hard, reliable data	Rich, deep data
Macro	Micro
Behaviour	Meaning
Artificial settings	Natural settings

that he or she can genuinely understand the world through their eyes.

- *Theory and concepts tested in research vs. Theory and concepts emergent from data.* Quantitative researchers typically bring a set of concepts to bear on the research instruments being employed, so that theoretical work precedes the collection of data, whereas in qualitative research concepts and theoretical elaboration emerge out of data collection.

- *Static vs. Process.* Quantitative research is frequently depicted as presenting a static image of social reality with its emphasis on relationships between variables. Change and connections between events over time tend not to surface, other than in a mechanistic fashion. Qualitative research is often depicted as attuned to the unfolding of events over time and to the interconnections between the actions of participants of social settings.

- *Structured vs. Unstructured.* Quantitative research is typically highly structured, so that the investigator is able to examine the precise concepts and issues that are the focus of the study; in qualitative research the approach is invariably unstructured, so that the possibility of getting at actors' meanings and of concepts emerging out of data collection is enhanced.

- *Generalization vs. Contextual understanding.* Whereas quantitative researchers want their findings to be generalizable to the relevant population, the qualitative researcher seeks an understanding of behaviour, values, beliefs, and so on in terms of the context in which the research is conducted.

- *Hard, reliable data vs. Rich, deep data.* Quantitative data are often depicted as 'hard' in the sense of being robust and unambiguous, owing to the precision offered by measurement. Qualitative researchers claim, by contrast, that their contextual approach and their often prolonged involvement in a setting engender rich data.

- *Macro vs. Micro.* Quantitative researchers are often depicted as involved in uncovering large-scale social trends and connections between variables, whereas qualitative researchers are seen as being concerned with small-scale aspects of social reality, such as interaction.

- *Behaviour vs. Meaning.* It is sometimes suggested that the quantitative researcher is concerned with people's behaviour and the qualitative researcher with the meaning of action.

- *Artificial settings vs. Natural settings.* Whereas quantitative researchers conduct research in a contrived context, qualitative researchers investigate people in natural environments.

However, as we will see in Chapter 24, while these contrasts depict reasonably well the differences between quantitative and qualitative research, they should not be viewed as constituting hard-and-fast distinctions. As I show there, qualitative research can be employed to test theories, while quantitative research is often a good deal more exploratory than is typically assumed. Indeed, the section in Chapter 6 on 'reverse operationism' implies that in quantitative research concepts often emerge out of the data that are collected (see pages 160–1). Also, it is by no means always appropriate to characterize qualitative researchers as collecting their data in natural (rather than artificial) settings. This may be an appropriate depiction of research that entails participant observation, but a lot of qualitative research involves interviewing and interviews do not constitute natural settings, even though the interviews tend to be less structured than in survey research. Further, quantitative and qualitative research are not so poles apart that they cannot be combined, as the discussion in Chapter 25 of mixed methods research implies.

 # Some similarities between quantitative and qualitative research

It is also worth bearing in mind the ways in which quantitative and qualitative research are *similar* rather than different. Hardy and Bryman (2004) have pointed out that, although there clearly are differences between quantitative and qualitative research, it should also be recognized that there are similarities too. They draw attention to the following points:

- *Both are concerned with data reduction.* Both quantitative and qualitative researchers collect large amounts of data. These large amounts of data represent a problem for researchers, because they then have to distill the data. By reducing the amount of data, they can then begin to make sense of the data. In quantitative research, the process of data reduction takes the form of statistical analysis—something like a mean or a **frequency table** is a way of reducing the amount of data on large numbers of people. In qualitative data analysis, as will be seen in Chapter 22, qualitative researchers develop concepts out of their often rich data.

- *Both are concerned with answering research questions.* Although the nature of the kinds of research questions asked in quantitative and qualitative research are typically different (more specific in quantitative research, more open-ended in qualitative research), they are both fundamentally concerned with answering questions about the nature of social reality.

- *Both are concerned with relating data analysis to the research literature.* Both quantitative and qualitative researchers are typically concerned to relate their findings to points thrown up by the literature relating to the topics on which they work. In other words, the researcher's findings take on significance in large part when they are related to the literature.

- *Both are concerned with variation.* In different ways, both quantitative and qualitative researchers seek to uncover and then to represent the variation that they uncover. This means that both groups of researchers are keen to explore how people (or whatever the unit of analysis is) differ and to explore some of the factors connected to that variation, although, once again, the *form* that the variation takes differs.

- *Both treat frequency as a springboard for analysis.* In quantitative research, frequency is a core outcome of collecting data, as the investigator typically wants to reveal the relative frequency with which certain types of behaviour occur or how many newspaper articles emphasize a certain issue in their articles. In qualitative research, issues of frequency arise in the fact that, in reports of findings in publications, terms like 'often' or 'most' are commonly employed. Also, when analysing qualitative data, the frequency with which certain themes occur commonly acts as a catalyst for which ones tend to be emphasized when writing up findings.

- *Both seek to ensure that deliberate distortion does not occur.* Very few social researchers nowadays subscribe to the view that it is possible to be an entirely objective dispassionate student of social life. Further, sometimes researchers can be partisan (see Chapter 5). However, that does not imply that 'anything goes'. In particular, researchers seek to ensure that 'wilful bias' (Hammersley and Gomm 2000) or what Hardy and Bryman (2004: 7) call 'consciously motivated misrepresentation' does not occur.

- *Both argue for the importance of transparency.* Both quantitative and qualitative researchers seek to be clear about their research procedures and how their findings were arrived at. This allows others to judge the quality and importance of their work. In the past, it has sometimes been suggested that qualitative researchers could be opaque about how they went about their investigations, but increasingly transparency surfaces as an expectation.

- *Both must address the question of error.* In Chapter 8, readers were introduced to the significance of error for quantitative research (or, more specifically, survey research) and what steps are taken to reduce its likelihood. For the quantitative researcher, error must be reduced as far as possible so that variation that is uncovered is real variation and not the product of problems with how questions are asked or how research instruments are administered. In qualitative research, the investigator seeks to reduce error by ensuring that, for example, there is a good fit between his or her concepts and the evidence that has been amassed.

- *Research methods should be appropriate to the research questions.* This point is not addressed by Hardy and Bryman (2004), but a further issue is that both groups of researchers seek to ensure that, when they specify research questions, they select research methods and approaches to the analysis of data that are appropriate to those questions.

These tend to be rather general points of similarity, but they are an important corrective to any view that portrays them as completely different. There *are* differences between quantitative and qualitative research but that is not to say that there are no points of similarity.

Feminism and qualitative research

A further dimension that could have been included in the section on 'Some contrasts between quantitative and qualitative research' is that, in the view of some writers, qualitative research is associated with a feminist sensitivity, and that, by implication, quantitative research is viewed by many feminists as incompatible with feminism. This issue was briefly signposted in Chapter 1. The link between feminism and qualitative research is by no means a cut-and-dried issue, in that, although it became something of an orthodoxy among some writers, it has not found favour with all feminists. Indeed, there are signs at the time of writing that views on the issue are changing.

The notion that there is an affinity between feminism and qualitative research has at least two main components to it: a view that quantitative research is inherently incompatible with feminism, and a view that qualitative research provides greater opportunity for a feminist sensitivity to come to the fore. Quantitative research is frequently viewed as incompatible with feminism for the following reasons.

- According to Mies (1993), quantitative research suppresses the voices of women either by ignoring them or by submerging them in a torrent of facts and statistics.

- The criteria of valid knowledge associated with quantitative research are ones that turn women, when they are the focus of research, into objects. This means that women are again subjected to exploitation, in that knowledge and experience are extracted from them with nothing in return, even when the research is conducted by women (Mies 1993).

- The emphasis on controlling variables further exacerbates this last problem, and indeed the very idea of control is viewed as a masculine approach.

- The use of predetermined categories in quantitative research results in an emphasis on what is already known and consequently in 'the silencing of women's own voices' (Maynard 1998: 18).

- The criteria of valid knowledge associated with quantitative research also mean that women are to be researched in a value-neutral way, when in fact the goals of feminist research should be to conduct research specifically *for* women.

- It is sometimes suggested that the quest for universal laws is inconsistent with feminism's emphasis on the situated nature of social reality, which is seen as embedded in the various social identities (based on gender, ethnicity, sexual orientation, class, etc.) that are unique to individuals (Miner-Rubino *et al.* 2007).

By contrast, qualitative research has been viewed by many feminists as either more compatible with feminism's central tenets or as more capable of being adapted to those tenets. Thus, in contrast to quantitative research, qualitative research allows:

- women's voices to be heard;

- exploitation to be reduced by giving as well as receiving in the course of fieldwork;

- women *not* to be treated as objects to be controlled by the researcher's technical procedures; and

- the emancipatory goals of feminism to be realized. For example, Skeggs (2001: 429) has observed that one of the earliest principles on which feminist research was based was that it should 'alleviate the conditions of oppression'.

How qualitative research achieves these goals will be addressed particularly in relation to the next three chapters, since the issues and arguments vary somewhat from one method to the other. Skeggs (2001: 429–30) argues that the political goals of feminist research led to a preference for qualitative research 'to focus on women's experience and to listen and explore the shared meanings between women with an aim to reformulate traditional research agendas'. However, there are risks with this prioritization of women's experience. In feminist standpoint epistemology, a perspective that places a particular emphasis on experience from the standpoint of women, this prioritization is especially pronounced. However, as Letherby (2003: 46) has suggested, this position 'can and has been used to replace male supremacy with female supremacy and [to] support binary oppositions'. She suggests that, for many analysts, this is likely to be viewed as an unhelpful position to take.

In fact, the issue of qualitative research as providing the opportunity for a feminist approach has somewhat different aspects when looking at ethnography, qualitative

Student experience
Feminism and the research relationship

For Erin Sanders, the prospect of using a feminist approach drawing on qualitative research was attractive in terms of her personal value commitments. However, as this passage shows, she recognized that there are dilemmas and that the issue of feminist research being less exploitative than other approaches should not be exaggerated.

> A number of ethical questions emerged reinterviewing sex workers. Because I was employing feminist methodologies . . . I wanted to truly engage with the women that I spoke to, rather than employing a more positivist methodology that would mandate a sense of distance. I felt that feminist methodologies would allow a more balanced research experience—and would enable me to share information about myself to help offset the inherent power imbalance in the research relationship. However, it became evident to me that, employing a variety of 'traditional' feminist methodologies, there was still a power differential. I had hoped to avoid exploiting the women I interviewed for my own personal gain, but I am not sure that this actually happened. I'm not sure that it is ever possible to overcome the power imbalance in the research relationship, especially when I, as a 'White', 'Western' woman, research an 'Other'. From an ethical perspective, it seems to me that the research relationship fosters an exploitative relationship in a number of ways, and I will have to seriously consider how (or if) I can avoid these in future.

*To read more about Erin's research experiences, go to the Online Resource Centre that accompanies this book at **http://www.oxfordtextbooks.co.uk/brymansrm3e/**.*

---

interviewing, and focus groups—the topics of the next three chapters. However, it ought also to be recognized that there has been a softening of attitude among some feminist writers towards quantitative research in recent years. Examples of this softening are as follows.

- There is a recognition that many of the worst excesses of discrimination against women might not have come to light so clearly were it not for the collection and analysis of statistics revealing discrimination (Maynard 1994; Oakley 1998). The very presence of factual evidence of this kind has allowed the case for equal opportunities legislation to be made much more sharply, although, needless to say, there is much more that still needs to be done in this field.

- Quantitative research can be enlisted as an aid to implementing social change for feminists. Miner-Rubino *et al.* (2007) suggest that knowing about the distribution of attitudes and behaviour in a sample can be used to establish the most appropriate course of action for social change.

- As Jayaratne and Stewart (1991) and Maynard (1994, 1998) have pointed out, at the very least it is difficult to see why feminist research that combines quantitative and qualitative research would be incompatible with the feminist cause.

- There has also been a recognition of the fact that qualitative research is not *ipso facto* feminist in orientation. If, for example, ethnography, which is covered in the next chapter, provided for a feminist sensitivity, we would expect fields like social anthropology, which have been virtually founded on the approach, to be almost inherently feminist, which is patently not the case (Reinharz 1992: 47–8). If this is so, the question of appropriate approaches to feminist research would seem to reside in the *application* of methods rather than something that is inherent in them. Consequently, some writers have preferred to write about *feminist research practice* rather than about *feminist methods* (Maynard 1998: 128).

These issues will be returned to in the next three chapters.

Key points

- There is disagreement over what precisely qualitative research is.
- Qualitative research does not lend itself to the delineation of a clear set of linear steps.
- It tends to be a more open-ended research strategy than is typically the case with quantitative research.
- Theories and concepts are viewed as outcomes of the research process.
- There is considerable unease about the simple application of the reliability and validity criteria associated with quantitative research to qualitative research. Indeed, some writers prefer to use alternative criteria that have parallels with reliability and validity.
- Most qualitative researchers reveal a preference for seeing through the eyes of research participants.
- Several writers have depicted qualitative research as having a far greater affinity with a feminist standpoint than quantitative research can exhibit.

Questions for review

- What are some of the difficulties with providing a general account of the nature of qualitative research?
- Outline some of the traditions of qualitative research.
- How compelling is Denzin and Lincoln's (2005) marking out of distinct 'moments' in the history of qualitative research?
- What are some of the main research methods associated with qualitative research?

The main steps in qualitative research

- Does a research question in qualitative research have the same significance and characteristics as in quantitative research?

Theory and research

- Is the approach to theory in qualitative research inductive or deductive?

Concepts in qualitative research

- What is the difference between definitive and sensitizing concepts?

Sampling in qualitative research

- How does purposive sampling differ from random sampling?

Reliability and validity in qualitative research

- How have some writers adapted the notions of reliability and validity to qualitative research?
- Why have some writers sought alternative criteria for the evaluation of qualitative research?
- Evaluate Lincoln and Guba's criteria.
- Would it be useful to develop quality criteria into checklists?
- What is respondent validation?
- What is triangulation?

The main preoccupations of qualitative researchers

- Outline the main preoccupations of qualitative researchers.
- How do these preoccupations differ from those of quantitative researchers, which were considered in Chapter 6?

The critique of qualitative research

- What are some of the main criticisms that are frequently levelled at qualitative research?
- To what extent do these criticisms reflect the preoccupations of quantitative research?

Is it always like this?

- Can qualitative research be employed in relation to hypothesis testing?

Some contrasts between quantitative and qualitative research

- 'The difference between quantitative and qualitative research revolves entirely around the concern with numbers in the former and with words in the latter.' How far do you agree with this statement?

Some similarities between quantitative and qualitative research

- Does it make sense to describe quantitative and qualitative research as being characterized by both differences *and* similarities?

Feminism and qualitative research

- Why have many feminist researchers preferred qualitative research?
- Is there no role for quantitative research in relation to feminist research?

Online Resource Centre

http://www.oxfordtextbooks.co.uk/orc/brymansrm3e/

Visit the Online Resource Centre that accompanies this book to enrich your understanding of the nature of qualitative research. Consult web links, test yourself using multiple choice questions, and gain further guidance and inspiration from the Student Researcher's Toolkit.

Ethnography and participant observation

Chapter guide

Ethnography and participant observation entail the extended involvement of the researcher in the social life of those he or she studies. However, the former term is also frequently taken to refer to the written output of that research. The chapter explores:

- the problems of gaining access to different settings and some suggestions about how they might be overcome;
- the issue of whether a covert role is practicable and acceptable;
- the role of **key informants** for the **ethnographer**;
- the different kinds of roles that ethnographers can assume in the course of their fieldwork;
- sampling strategies in ethnography, in particular *theoretical sampling*, which is associated with the **grounded theory** approach to qualitative data analysis, which will be examined in Chapter 22;
- the role of **field notes** in ethnography and the varieties of forms they can assume;
- bringing ethnography to an end;
- the role of visual materials, which have attracted increased attention in recent years, in ethnography;
- the controversy about the nature of feminist ethnography.

Introduction

Discussions about the merits and limitations of participant observation have been a fairly standard ingredient in textbooks on social research for many years. However, for some time writers on research methods have preferred to write about ethnography rather than participant observation. It is difficult to date the point at which this change of terminology (though it is more than just this) occurred, but sometime in the 1970s ethnography began to become the preferred term. Before that, ethnography was primarily associated with social anthropological research, whereby the investigator visits a (usually) foreign land, gains access to a group (for example, a tribe or village), spends a considerable amount of time (often many years) with that group with the aim of uncovering its culture, watches and listens to what people say and do, engages people in conversations to probe specific issues of interest, takes copious field notes, and returns home to write up the fruits of his or her labours.

Key concept 17.1 represents an attempt to deal with some of these issues and to arrive at a working definition of ethnography. The seven bullet points at the end of Key concept 17.1 that make up the definition of ethnography featured there could be viewed as a simple process of join-

ing a group, watching what goes on, making some notes, and writing it all up. In fact, ethnography is nowhere nearly as straightforward as this implies. This chapter will outline some of the main decision areas that confront ethnographers, along with some of the many contingencies they face. However, it is not easy to generalize about the ethnographic research process in such a way as to provide definitive recommendations about research practice. As prefigured at the end of the previous chapter, the diversity of experiences that confront ethnographers and the variety of ways in which they deal with them does not readily permit clear-cut generalizations. The following comment in a book on ethnography makes this point well:

> Every field situation *is* different and initial luck in meeting good informants, being in the right place at the right time and striking the right note in relationships may be just as important as skill in technique. Indeed, many successful episodes in the field do come about through good luck as much as through sophisticated planning, and many unsuccessful episodes are due as much to bad luck as to bad judgement. (Sarsby 1984: 96)

Key concept 17.1
What are ethnography and participant observation?

Many definitions of ethnography and participant observation are very difficult to distinguish. Both draw attention to the fact that the participant observer/ethnographer immerses him- or herself in a group for an extended period of time, observing behaviour, listening to what is said in conversations both between others and with the fieldworker, and asking questions. It is possible that the term 'ethnography' is sometimes preferred because 'participant observation' seems to imply just observation, though in practice participant observers do more than simply observe. Typically, participant observers and ethnographers will gather further data through interviews and the collection of documents. It may be, therefore, that the apparent emphasis on observation in the term 'participant observation' has meant that an apparently more inclusive term would be preferable, even though in fact it is generally recognized that the method entails a wide range of methods of data collection and sources. Ethnography is also sometimes taken to refer to a study in which participant observation is the prevalent research method but that also has a specific focus on the culture of the group in which the ethnographer is immersed.

However, the term 'ethnography' has an additional meaning, in that it frequently simultaneously refers to both a method of research of the kind outlined above *and* the written product of that research. Indeed, 'ethnography' frequently denotes both a research process and the written outcome of the research. For example, consider the opening sentences of Taylor's (1993) book on female drug users, which was mentioned on several occasions in Chapter 16.

> This book provides an account of the lives and experiences of a group of female intravenous drug users in Glasgow. It is based on fifteen months' participant observation of the women in their own setting and on in-depth interviews carried out at the end of the observation period. It is the first full ethnographic account of the lifestyle of female drug users. (Taylor 1993: 1)

It is worth noting the following features.

- The book is subtitled *An Ethnography of a Female Injecting Community*. The term 'ethnography' therefore seems to apply both to the method of investigation and to the book itself. This is underlined by the phrase 'the first full ethnographic account'.

- The mention of the main data collection methods as participant observation *and* interviewing suggests that the ethnographic research comprises these two techniques of data collection but that interviewing is viewed as something separate from participant observation. In fact, participant observers frequently conduct interviews in the course of their research.

- The passage draws on several **qualitative research** motifs encountered in Chapter 16, such as the preference for seeing through the eyes of the people being studied (reference to 'lives and experiences') and a naturalistic stance ('in their own setting').

In this book, ethnography will be taken to mean a research method in which the researcher:

- is immersed in a social setting for an extended period of time;
- makes regular observations of the behaviour of members of that setting;
- listens to and engages in conversations;
- interviews informants on issues that are not directly amenable to observation or that the ethnographer is unclear about (or indeed for other possible reasons);

- collects documents about the group;
- develops an understanding of the culture of the group and people's behaviour within the context of that culture;
- and writes up a detailed account of that setting.

Thus, ethnography is being taken to include participant observation and is also taken to encapsulate the notion of ethnography as a written product of ethnographic research.

Tips and skills
Micro-ethnography

If you are doing research for an undergraduate project or masters dissertation, it is unlikely that you will be able to conduct a full-scale ethnography. Ethnographic research usually entails long periods of time in the field in an organization, as part of a community, or in the company of a group. Nevertheless, it may be possible to carry out a form of *micro-ethnography* (Wolcott 1990b). This would involve focusing on a particular aspect of a topic. For example, if you are interested in call centres, you might focus on the way staff manage to interact and discuss work problems in spite of continuously receiving calls and being monitored. A relatively short period of time (from a couple of weeks to a few months) could be spent in the organization—on either a full-time or a part-time basis—to achieve such a tightly defined topic.

However, this statement should not be taken to imply that forethought and an awareness of alternative ways of doing things are irrelevant. It is with this kind of issue that the rest of this chapter will be concerned. However, issues to do with the conduct of interviews by ethnographers will be reserved for Chapter 18.

Access

One of the key and yet most difficult steps in ethnography is gaining access to a social setting that is relevant to the research problem in which you are interested. The way in which access is approached differs along several **dimensions**, one of which is whether the setting is a relatively open one or a relatively closed one (Bell 1969). Hammersley and Atkinson (1995) make a similar distinction when they refer to 'public' settings as opposed to ones that are not public (see also Lofland and Lofland 1995). Closed, non-public settings are likely to be organizations of various kinds, such as firms, schools, cults, social movements, and so on. The open/public setting is likely to be everything else—that is, research involving communities, gangs, drug users, and so on.

Overt versus covert ethnography

One way to ease the access problem is to assume a *covert* role—in other words, not to disclose the fact that you are a researcher. This strategy obviates the need to negotiate access to organizations or to explain why you want to intrude into people's lives and make them objects of study. As we shall see, seeking access is a highly fraught business, and the adoption of a covert role removes some of the difficulties. These two distinctions—the open/public versus closed setting and the overt versus covert role—suggest, following Bell (1969), a fourfold distinction in forms of ethnography (see Figure 17.1, which contains for each of the four types examples that have been

Figure 17.1

Four forms of ethnography

	Open/public setting	Closed setting
Overt role	*Type 1* • Taylor's (1993) study of intravenous drug users • Foster's (1995) study of a high-crime community • Willis's (1977) study of working-class 'lads' • Giulianotti's (1995) research on football hooligans (Research in focus 17.2) • Hobbs's (1988, 1993) research on entrepreneurship in London's East End • Whyte's (1955) classic study of street corner life in a Boston slum area • O'Reilly's (2000) research on the British living on Spain's Costa del Sol	*Type 2* • Leidner's (1993) studies of a McDonald's restaurant and an insurance firm • Coffey's (1999) research in a UK accountancy firm • Burgess's (1983, 1987) research on a Roman Catholic comprehensive school • Barker's (1984) study of Moonies (a religious cult) • Waddington's (1994) study of a prolonged strike (Research in focus 16.4)
Covert role	*Type 3* • Patrick's (1973) study of a violent Glasgow gang	*Type 4* • Holdaway's (1982, 1983) study of a police force in which he was already a policeman • Research by Hobbs *et al.* (2003) on bouncers (see also Winlow *et al.* 2001) • Research by Mattley (2006) on working for a sex fantasy phone line

Note: This figure is a development of a table in Bell (1969).

encountered in earlier chapters or will be mentioned in this one).

Three points should be registered about Figure 17.1. First, the open/public setting versus closed setting distinction is not a hard-and-fast one. Sometimes, gaining access to groups can have a near formal quality, such as having to pacify a gang leader's anxieties about your goals. Also, organizations sometimes create contexts that have a public character, such as the meetings that are arranged for members or prospective recruits by social movements like religious cults or political movements like the National Front.

Secondly, the overt versus covert distinction is not without problems. For example, while an ethnographer may seek access through an overt route, there may be many people with whom he or she comes into contact who will not be aware of the ethnographer's status as a researcher. Atkinson (1981: 135) notes in connection with his research on the training of doctors in a medical

school that, although he was 'an "open" observer with regard to the doctors and students', he was 'a "disguised" observer with regard to the patients'. Also, some ethnographers move between the two roles (see Research in focus 17.1).

Another interesting case is provided by Glucksman (1994), who in the 1970s left her academic post to work on a factory assembly line in order to shed light on the reasons why feminism appeared not to be relevant to working-class women. In a sense, she was a covert observer, but her motives for the research were primarily political, and she says that, at the time she was undertaking the research, she had no intention of writing the book that subsequently appeared and that was published under a pseudonym (Cavendish 1982). After the book's publication, it was treated as an example of ethnographic research. Was she an overt or a covert observer (or neither or both)? Whichever description applies, this is an interesting case of what might be termed *retrospective ethnography*.

Research in focus 17.1
An example of the perils of covert observation: the case of field notes in the lavatory

Ditton's (1977) research on 'fiddling' in a bakery provides an interesting case of the practical difficulties of taking notes during covert observation as well as an illustration of an ethnographer who shifted his position from covert to overt observation at least in part because of those difficulties:

> Nevertheless, I *was* able to develop personal covert participant-observation skills. Right from the start, I found it impossible to keep everything that I wanted to remember in my head until the end of the working day . . . and so had to take rough notes as I was going along. But I was stuck 'on the line', and had nowhere to retire to privately to jot things down. Eventually, the wheeze of using innocently provided lavatory cubicles occurred to me. Looking back, all my notes for that third summer were on Bronco toilet paper! Apart from the awkward tendency for pencilled notes to be self-erasing from hard toilet paper . . . my frequent requests for 'time out' after interesting happenings or conversations in the bakehouse and the amount of time I was spending in the lavatory began to get noticed. I had to pacify some genuinely concerned workmates, give up totally undercover operations, and 'come out' as an observer—albeit in a limited way. I eventually began to scribble notes more openly, but still not in front of people when they were talking. When questioned about this, as I was occasionally, I coyly said that I was writing things down that occurred to me about 'my studies'. (Ditton 1977: 5)

In terms of the distinctions in Figure 17.1, Ditton moved from a Type 4 to a Type 2 form of ethnography.

A third point to note about Figure 17.1 is that entries are more numerous in the Types 1 and 2 **cells** than in the Types 3 and 4 cells. In large part, this reflects the fact that ethnographers are far more likely to be in an overt role than a covert one. There are several reasons for this situation. As Key concept 17.2 reveals, the reasons for the preference of most ethnographers for an overt role are to do with practical and ethical considerations, but the latter predominate in most researchers' thinking. Because of the ethical problems that beset **covert research** (and indeed some of the practical difficulties), the bulk of the discussion of access issues that follows will focus upon ethnographers seeking to employ an overt role.

Access to closed settings

As Van Maanen and Kolb (1985: 11) observe, 'gaining access to most organizations is not a matter to be taken lightly but one that involves some combination of strategic planning, hard work and dumb luck'. In selecting a particular social setting to act as a **case study** in which to conduct an ethnographic investigation, the researcher may employ several criteria. These criteria should be determined by the general research area in which he or she is interested. Very often a number of potential cases (and sometimes very many) will be relevant to your research problem. You may choose a certain case because of its 'fit' with your research questions, but there are no guarantees of success, as Van Maanen and Kolb's remark suggests. Sometimes, sheer perseverance pays off. Leidner (1993) was determined that one of the organizations in which she conducted ethnographic research on the routinization of service work should be McDonald's. She writes:

> I knew from the beginning that I wanted one of the case studies to be of McDonald's. The company was a pioneer and exemplar of routinized interaction, and since it was locally based, it seemed like the perfect place to start. McDonald's had other ideas, however, and only after tenacious pestering and persuasion did I overcome corporate employees' polite demurrals, couched in terms of protecting proprietary information and the company's image. (Leidner 1993: 234–5)

Key concept 17.2
What is the covert role in ethnography?

Advantages

- *There is no problem of access.* Adopting a covert role largely gets around the access problem, because the researcher does not have to seek permission to gain entry to a social setting or organization.

- *Reactivity is not a problem.* Using a covert role also reduces reactivity (see Research in focus 2.3 and Key concept 11.4), because participants do not know the person conducting the study is a researcher. Therefore, they are less likely to adjust their behaviour because of the researcher's presence.

Disadvantages

- *The problem of taking notes.* As Ditton (1977; see Research in focus 17.1) discovered, it is difficult and probably in some circumstances impossible to take notes when people do not realize you are conducting research. As we will see below, notes are very important to an ethnographer, and it is too risky to rely exclusively on your memory.

- *The problem of not being able to use other methods.* Ethnography entails the use of several methods, but, if the researcher is in a covert role, it is difficult to steer conversations in a certain direction for fear of detection and it is essentially impossible to engage in interviewing.

- *Anxiety.* The covert ethnographer is under constant threat of having his or her cover blown. Ethnography is frequently a stressful research method, and the worries about detection can add to those anxieties. Moreover, if the ethnographer *is* found out, the whole research project may be jeopardized.

- *Ethical problems.* Covert observation transgresses two important ethical tenets: it does not provide participants with the opportunity for **informed consent** (whereby they can agree or disagree to participate on the basis of information supplied to them) and it entails deception. It can also be taken to be a violation of the principle of privacy. Also, many writers take the view that, in addition to being potentially damaging to research participants, it can also harm the practice of research, because of fears about social researchers being identified by the public as snoopers or voyeurs if they are found out. Ethical issues are considered in greater detail in Chapter 5.

However

- As the main text points out, in some circumstances the overt/covert distinction may be a matter of degree.

- Also, a covert participant observer may reveal *some* aspects of his or her true identity. While Mattley (2006: 144) describes herself as a covert participant observer when she worked for and conducted ethnographic research on a sex fantasy phone line, she writes: 'I decided that I would be open about who I am, but not why I wanted to be hired.' Part of the way through the research, her supervisor suggested she should do a study of the callers. She asked the owner of the business about whether she could do this and he agreed, declining her offer to let him read anything she wanted to write about the work prior to publication. As he graphically put it: 'I hate to read that fucking stuff, I trust you, you won't fuck me over' (Mattley 2006: 146). However, with respect to her callers, Mattley was still a covert participant observer.

This kind of determination is necessary for any instance in which you want to study a specific organization, such as a particular religious sect or social movement. Rejection is likely to require a complete rethink.

However, with many research questions, several potential cases are likely to meet your criteria. Organizational researchers have developed a range of tactics, many of which may seem rather unsystematic in tone, but they are worth drawing attention to.

- Use friends, contacts, colleagues, academics to help you gain access; provided the organization is relevant to your research question, the route should not matter.

- Try to get the support of someone within the organization who will act as your champion. This person may be prepared to vouch for you and the value of your research. Such people are placed in the role of 'sponsors'.

- Usually you will need to get access through top management/senior executives. Even though you may secure a certain level of agreement lower down the hierarchy, you will usually need clearance from them. Such senior people act as 'gatekeepers'.

- Offer something in return (e.g. a report). This strategy carries risks in that it may turn you into a cheap consultant and may invite restrictions on your activities, such as insistence on seeing what you write. However, it helps to create a sense of being *trustworthy*. Some writers on research methodology do not recommend this approach, although, among researchers on formal organizations, it is commonplace.

- Provide a clear explanation of your aims and methods and be prepared to deal with concerns. Suggest a meeting at which you can deal with worries and provide an explanation of what you intend to do in terms that can readily be understood by others.

- Be prepared to negotiate—you will want complete access but it is unlikely you will be given a *carte blanche*.

- Be reasonably honest about the amount of people's time you are likely to take up. This is a question you will almost certainly be asked if you are seeking access to commercial organizations and probably to many not-for-profit ones too.

Access to open/public settings

Gaining access to public settings is beset with problems, many of which are similar in nature to access to closed settings. An example of the difficulties that await the researcher is one of Whyte's (1955) early encounters in the field in his classic case study *Street Corner Society*, when he was trying to make contacts during his early days in the field in Boston's North End. The following incident occurred in a hotel bar:

I looked around me again and now noticed a threesome: one man and two women. It occurred to me that here was a maldistribution of females which I might be able to rectify. I approached the group and opened with something like this: 'Pardon me. Would you mind if I join you?' There was a moment of silence while the man stared at me. He then offered to throw me downstairs. I assured him that this would not be necessary and demonstrated as much by walking right out of there without any assistance. (Whyte 1955: 289)

Sometimes, ethnographers will be able to have their paths smoothed by individuals who act as both sponsor and gatekeeper. In Whyte's case, the role played by 'Doc' has become the stuff of legend, and there is a temptation to seek out your Doc when attempting to gain access to a group. Indeed, when Gans (1962) decided to conduct ethnographic research in an area that was adjacent to the part of Boston on which Whyte had carried out his research, he visited Whyte 'to find out how [he] could meet a " Doc"' (Gans 1968: 311).

In seeking to gain access to one group of football hooligans, Giulianotti (1995; see Research in focus 17.2) actively sought out someone who could adopt this role for him, but, in gaining access to a second group, he was able to draw upon existing acquaintances who could ease his entrée into the group. We see here two common methods of gaining access to groups—via gatekeepers and via acquaintances who then act as sponsors. In seeking access to intravenous female drug users, Taylor (1993) consciously used a gatekeeper strategy. She contacted a local detached drug worker in the area, who introduced her to some local users and accompanied her on her first few research visits. A form of research bargain (see Research in focus 17.2) was set up in that Taylor agreed that the drug worker could refer clients to her if any of his clients said they would prefer to discuss issues with a female. Similarly, Hobbs (1988) says that he used his skills as a football coach to gain access to various entrepreneurial networks for his study of London's East End.

'Hanging around' is another common access strategy. As a strategy, it typically entails either loitering in an area until you are noticed or gradually becoming incorporated into or asking to join a group. The second of these was roughly the approach Whyte was taking, which nearly led to an encounter with a staircase. Wolf (1991) employed a hanging-around strategy in gaining access to outlaw bikers in Canada. On one occasion he met a group of them at a motorcycle shop and expressed an interest in 'hanging around' with them but tried to move too quickly in seeking

Research in focus 17.2
Access to football hooligans

Giulianotti (1995) sought access to two groups of football supporters engaged in hooligan activity: Aberdeen and Hibernian 'casuals', as the particular groups he was interested in termed themselves. Access to the Aberdeen casuals was reasonably smooth, in that he was a close friend of three of the forty-seven Aberdeen casuals who had been caught by the police at a notorious match in 1985. He had also gone to school and socialized with many of the first group of casuals to emerge in Aberdeen in the 1982–5 period. He also claims that in terms of 'age, attire, and argot' his personal characteristics were similar to those of the people he was studying. Gradually his contacts with Aberdeen casuals broadened out and eventually he 'began socializing freely with the gang at football matches, travelling to and from matches within the main grouping of the Aberdeen casuals' (Giulianotti 1995: 4). Access to the equivalent Hibernian (Hibs) supporters in Edinburgh was much more difficult for three reasons: absence of prior acquaintanceships; his Aberdonian background and accent; and a high level of negative newspaper publicity about the Hibs casuals at the time he was seeking access, which made the group sensitive to infiltration and people writing about them. Eventually, he was able to negotiate access to the group by striking what he, following Becker (1970), calls a 'research bargain': he provided the Hibs supporters with answers to questions about the Aberdeen 'casual scene', such as 'What do Aberdeen say about us?' (Giulianotti 1995: 6). This allowed him to establish among the Hibs supporters his reasons for studying the Aberdeen casuals as well. Giulianotti also actively sought out a gatekeeper who could ease his entry into the group. After some abortive attempts, he was finally introduced to someone at a game, and this contact allowed his access to further supporters to spread. Giulianotti (1995: 3) describes his overall research approach thus:

> The research . . . consists of regularly introducing myself to new research acquaintances; renegotiating association with familiar casuals; talking with them, drinking with them, and going to matches with them; generally participating with them in a variety of social situations; but disengaging myself from preparing for and participating in violence, within and outside of football match contexts.

information about and access to them and was forced to abandon his plans. Eventually, a hanging-around strategy resulted in him being approached by the leader of a biker group (Rebels MC), who acted as his sponsor. In order to bring this off, Wolf ensured that he was properly attired. Attention to dress and demeanour can be a very important consideration when seeking access to either public or closed settings.

As these anecdotes suggest, gaining access to social settings is a crucial first step in ethnographic research, in that, without access, your research plans will be halted in their tracks. It is also fraught with difficulties and in certain cases with danger—for example, when the research is likely to be on groups engaged in violent or criminal activities. Therefore, this discussion of access strategies can be only a starting point in knowing what kinds of approach can be considered.

Ongoing access

But access does not finish when you have made contact and gained an entrée to the group. You still need access to *people*. Simply because you have gained access to an organization does not mean that you will have an easy passage through the organization. Securing access is in many ways an ongoing activity. It is likely to prove a problem in closed contexts like organizations.

- People will have suspicions about you, perhaps seeing you as an instrument of top management (it is very common for members of organizations to believe that researchers are placed there to check up on them). When Sharpe (2000: 366) began research on prostitution in a red light area, she was quickly depicted as being 'anything from a social worker to a newspaper reporter with hidden cameras and microphones'.

When conducting her research on the British on the Costa del Sol, O'Reilly (2000) was suspected of being from the Department of Social Security and of being a tax inspector.

- People will worry that what they say or do may get back to bosses or to colleagues. Van Maanen (1991a) notes from his research on the police that, if you conduct ethnographic research among officers, you are likely to observe activities that may be deeply discrediting and even illegal. Your credibility among police officers will be determined by your reactions to situations and events that are known to be difficult for individuals.

- If people have these worries, they may go along with your research but in fact sabotage it, engaging in deceptions, misinformation, and not allowing access to 'back regions' (Goffman 1956).

There are three things you can do to smooth the path of ongoing access.

- Play up your credentials. Use your past work and experience; your knowledge of the organization and/or its sector; your understanding of their problems.

- Pass tests. Be non-judgemental when things are said to you about informal activities or about the organization; make sure information given to you does not get back to others, whether bosses or peers.

- You may need a role. If research involves quite a lot of participant observation, the role will be part of your position in the organization; otherwise, you will need to construct a 'front', by your dress, by your explanations about what you are doing there, by helping out occasionally with work or offering advice. Be consistent—do not behave ambiguously or inconsistently.

Similar considerations apply to research in public settings.

- Make sure you have thought about ways in which people's suspicions can be allayed. You will need a 'front', as Ditton (1977; Research in focus 17.1) had when referring to 'his studies'. Similarly, Giulianotti (see Research in focus 17.2) simply said that he was doing research on football supporters for a book.

- Be prepared for tests of either competence or credibility. Taylor (1993) reports that, at a drop-in centre at which she had been allowed to attend a meeting, 'proper cups' for tea were put out. Afterwards Taylor (1993: 15) was told that, if she had crooked her 'wee finger', as the leader of the centre had done, her informant 'would have put [Taylor] down in such a way that you'd never want to speak to us again'. When researching gang members in a poor community, Horowitz (Gerson and Horowitz 2002; see Research in focus 17.6) writes that she was frequently told 'confidential' stories (which turned out to be fictional) to determine whether she could keep a secret.

- Be prepared for changes in circumstances. Both Giulianotti (1995; Research in focus 17.2) and Armstrong (1993) found that sudden newspaper exposés of football hooliganism or evidence of police infiltration can engender worries that you are not what or who you say you are.

Key informants

One aspect of having sponsors or gatekeepers who smooth access for the ethnographer is that they may become *key informants* in the course of the subsequent fieldwork. The ethnographer relies a lot on informants, but certain informants may become particularly important to the research. They often develop an appreciation of the research and direct the ethnographer to situations, events, or people likely to be helpful to the progress of the investigation. Whyte's (1955) study is again an extreme example of this development. Whyte reports Doc as saying to him at one point: 'You tell me what you want to see, and we'll arrange it. When you want some information, I'll ask for it, and you listen. When you want to find out their philosophy of life, I'll start an argument and get it for you. If there's something else you want to get, I'll stage an act for you' (Whyte 1955: 292). Doc was also helpful in warning Whyte that he was asking too many questions, when he told him to 'go easy on that "who", "what", "why", "when", "where", stuff' (Whyte 1955: 303). Patrick (1973) was able to develop a similarly fruitful relationship with 'Tim' for his study of a violent gang in Glasgow. Taylor (1993) says that her period of participant observation was in relation to fifty female drug users and that intensive interviews were carried out with twenty-six women, but that eight of the women were key informants.

Key informants can clearly be of great help to the ethnographer and frequently provide a support that helps with the stress of fieldwork. However, it also needs to be borne in mind that they carry risks in that the ethnographer may develop an undue reliance on the key informant, and, rather than seeing social reality through the eyes of members of the social setting, the researcher is seeing social reality through the eyes of the key informant.

In addition, the ethnographer will encounter many people who will act as informants. Their accounts may be solicited or unsolicited (Hammersley and Atkinson 1995). Some researchers prefer the latter, because of its greater spontaneity and naturalism. Very often, research participants develop a sense of the kinds of events the ethnographer wants to see or encounters that it would be beneficial to be present at. Armstrong (1993) says that, while doing research on 'The Blades', a group of supporters of Sheffield United Football Club who were engaged in hooligan activity (see Chapter 16 for other references to this research), he would sometimes get tip-offs:

> 'We're all gonna' Leeds in a couple o' weeks . . . four coaches, Pond Street, town centre. If you're serious about this study you'll be down there on one of 'em.' I often travelled on the same coach as Ray [an informant]; he would then sit with me at matches and in pubs and point out Blades, giving me background information. Sometimes he would start conversations with Blades about incidents which he knew I wanted to know about and afterwards would ask 'Did you get

> all that down then?' . . . There was never one particular informant; rather, there were many Blades I could ring up and meet at any time, who were part of the core and would always welcome a beer and a chat about 'It', or tell me who I 'ought to 'ave a word wi'.
> (Armstrong 1993: 24–5)

Such unsolicited sources of information are highly attractive to the ethnographer because of their relative spontaneity, although, as Hammersley and Atkinson (1995: 130–1) observe, they may on occasions be staged for the ethnographer's benefit. Solicited accounts can occur in two ways: by interview (see Chapter 18) or by casual questioning during conversations (though in ethnographic research the boundary between an interview and a conversation is by no means clear-cut, as Burgess (1984) makes clear). When the ethnographer needs specific information concerning an issue that is not amenable to direct observation or that is not cropping up during 'natural' conversations, solicited accounts are likely to be the only way forward.

Roles for ethnographers

Related to the issue of ongoing access (or relationships in the field, as it is sometimes called) is the question of the kind of role the ethnographer adopts in relation to the social setting and its members. Several schemes have been devised by writers on research methods to describe the various roles that can be and have been adopted by ethnographers.

One of the most widely cited schemes is Gold's (1958) classification of participant observer roles, which can be arrayed on a continuum of degrees of involvement with and detachment from members of the social setting (see Figure 17.2). The four roles are:

1. *Complete participant.* According to Gold, the complete participant is a fully functioning member of the social setting and his or her true identity is not known to members. As such, the complete participant is a covert observer, like Holdaway (1982) and Mattley (2006).

2. *Participant-as-observer.* This role is the same as the complete participant one, but members of the social setting are aware of the researcher's status as a researcher. The

ethnographer is engaged in regular interaction with people and participates in their daily lives. All the studies referred to in Figure 17.1 as involving an overt role—whether in open/public or closed settings—are of this kind, as was Giulianotti's research (see Research in focus 17.2).

3. *Observer-as-participant.* In this role, the researcher is mainly an interviewer. There is some observation but very little of it involves any participation. Many of the studies covered in Chapter 18 are of this type. Ethnographic research on the police is often of this type, since the opportunities for genuine participation are few, because of considerations of legality and interrupting operational policing. Thus, as an observer-as-participant, Norris (1993: 126) has described how in this role he concentrated on gathering two types of data: 'naturally occurring inter-officer talk' and 'detailed descriptions of how officers handled "live" incidents'. See also Research in focus 17.3 for a further illustration.

4. *Complete observer.* In this role, the researcher does not interact with people. According to Gold, people do not

Figure 17.2

Gold's classification of participant observer roles

have to take the researcher into account. Examples can be found in studies using forms of observation that are unobtrusive in character.

Most writers would take the view that, since ethnography entails immersion in a social setting and fairly prolonged involvement, the complete observer role should not be considered as participant observation or ethnography at all, since participation is likely to be more or less entirely missing. Some writers might also question whether research based on the observer-as-participant role can genuinely be regarded as ethnography, but, since it is likely that certain situations are unlikely to be amenable to the immersion that is a key ingredient of the method, it could be argued that to dismiss it totally as an approach to ethnography is rather restrictive. It is significant in this context that Gold referred to the four roles in relation to conducting 'fieldwork', which has the potential for a broader meaning than either participant observation or ethnography.

Research in focus 17.3
An observer-as-participant in the Magic Kingdom

An interesting illustration of research that comes very close to the observer-as-participant role is Raz's (1999) study of Tokyo Disneyland. His main sources of data were: many visits to the theme park, including being part of several official and unofficial tours; interviews with current and former employees; a textual analysis of company guidebooks; and an examination of the reception of the park by visitors through a **focus group**. Raz's goal was to explore the meeting place of the forces of globalization, in the form of the familiar themes associated with the Disney company, and forces of the 'local', in the form of the distinctive character of Japanese culture. He draws on ideas like 'globalization' in order to develop an understanding of the ways in which the combination of global and local forces is played out and on Hochschild's (1983) **concept** of 'emotional labour' (see Research in focus 16.1) to develop an appreciation of the world of work for the Disney employee.

Each role carries its own advantages and risks. The issues concerning being a complete participant were covered in Key concept 17.2. According to Gold, the participant-as-observer role carries the risk of over-identification and hence of 'going native' (see Key concept 17.3), but offers the opportunity to get close to people. Gold argues that the observer-as-participant role carries the risk of not understanding the social setting and people in it sufficiently and therefore of making incorrect inferences. The complete observer role shares with complete participation the removal of the possible problem of reactivity, but it carries even further risks than the observer-as-participant role of failing to understand situations.

Gans (1968) has devised a classification of participant observer roles, but he views these as roles that will coexist in any project. In other words, the three roles he outlines will be employed at different times in the course of ethnographic research and for different purposes. The three roles are:

1. *total participant*, in which the ethnographer is completely involved in a certain situation and has to resume a researcher stance once the situation has unfolded and then write down notes;

2. *researcher-participant*, whereby the ethnographer participates in a situation but is only semi-involved, so that he or she can function fully as a researcher in the course of the situation;

3. *total researcher*, which entails observation without involvement in the situation, as in attendance at a public meeting or watching what is going on in a bar; when in this role, the researcher does not participate in the flow of events.

Key concept 17.3
What is 'going native'?

'Going native' refers to a plight that is supposed sometimes to afflict ethnographers when they lose their sense of being a researcher and become wrapped up in the world view of the people they are studying. The prolonged immersion of ethnographers in the lives of the people they study, coupled with the commitment to seeing the social world through their eyes, lie behind the risk and actuality of going native. Going native is a potential problem for several reasons but especially because the ethnographer can lose sight of his or her position as a researcher and therefore find it difficult to develop a social scientific angle on the collection and analysis of data. When Hobbs (1988: 6) writes in connection with his fieldwork on entrepreneurship in London's East End that he 'often had to remind himself that [he] was not in a pub to enjoy [himself] but to conduct an academic inquiry, and repeatedly woke up the following morning with an incredible hangover facing the dilemma of whether to bring it up or write it up', he may have been on the brink of going native.

However, it should not be assumed that going native is an inevitable risk associated with ethnography or indeed that it is the only risk to do with how participant observers relate to the social situations in which they find themselves. Lee-Treweek (2000) carried out research on auxiliary carers in two homes for the elderly. She describes how in one of these homes she had an almost completely opposite reaction to going native. She disliked the home and appears to have found the staff unappealing because of their lack of sympathy for and their uncaring approach to the elderly people for whom they were responsible. None the less, she felt that she 'was gathering good data, despite [her] feelings of being an outsider' (Lee-Treweek 2000: 120). The lesson of this story is that going native is not an inevitable accompaniment to ethnography.

The advantage of Gans's classification is that, like Gold's, it reflects degrees of involvement and detachment, but has the advantage that it deals only with overt observation and recognizes that ethnographers do not typically adopt a single role throughout their dealings. It is arguably the case that, even if it were possible to adopt a single ethnographic role over the entire course of a project, it is likely that it would be undesirable, because there would be a lack of flexibility in handling situations and people, and risks of excessive involvement (and hence of going native) or detachment would loom large. The issue of the kind of role(s) the ethnographer adopts is of considerable significance, because it has implications for field relationships in the various situations that are encountered.

Active or passive?

A further issue that is raised about any situation in which the ethnographer participates is the degree to which he or she should be or can be an active or a passive participant (Van Maanen 1978). Even when the ethnographer is in an observer-as-participant role, there may be contexts in which either participation is unavoidable or a compulsion to join in in a limited way may be felt. For example, Fine's (1996) research on the work of chefs in restaurants was carried out largely by semi-structured interview. In spite of his limited participation, he found himself involved in washing up in the kitchens to help out during busy periods. In many instances, the researcher has no choice. Researchers who do ethnographic research on the police, for example, unless they are covert observers like Holdaway (1982) or take steps to become police officers like Rubinstein (1973), are unlikely to be able to be active participants beyond offering fairly trivial assistance. An example of this can be found in an incident reported in Punch's field notes in connection with his research on the police in Amsterdam: 'Tom wanted to move the cars which were blocking the narrow and busy street in front of the station, and said sternly to the suspect, but with a smile at me behind his back, "You stay here with your hands up and don't try anything because this detective here [pointing at me] is keeping an eye on you." I frowned authoritatively' (Punch 1979: 8). Punch travelled with the officers in their cars but in civilian clothes and employed as a 'front' the role of a plain clothes policeman. On the other side of the coin, in taking the job of a bouncer, the participant observer is not going to have the luxury of deciding whether to become involved in fights, since these are likely to come with the territory (Winlow *et al*. 2001).

Sometimes, ethnographers may *feel* they have no choice in getting involved, because a failure to participate actively might indicate to members of the social setting a lack of commitment and lead to a loss of credibility. This can often lead to dilemmas on the part of ethnographers, especially when the activities in which they actively take part (or might do so) are illegal or dangerous (see Research in focus 17.4). On the other hand, many writers counsel against active participation in criminal or dangerous activities (Polsky 1967). Both Armstrong (1993) and Giulianotti (1995; see Research in focus 17.2) refused to participate in fights while doing research into football hooliganism. The latter writes: 'My own rules are that I will not get involved in fighting or become a go-between for the two gangs in organizing fights' (Giulianotti 1995: 10). Indeed, we see here a strong argument against covert research on criminals or those involved in dangerous activities, since it will be much more difficult for someone in such a role not to participate.

Research in focus 17.4
Active ethnography and illegal activity

In the context of his study of entrepreneurship (a euphemism for several kinds of legal and illegal activity) among East Enders in London, Hobbs (1988: 7, 15) admits he engaged in illegal activities:

> A refusal, or worse still an enquiry concerning the legal status of the 'parcel', would provoke an abrupt conclusion to the relationship. Consequently, I was willing to skirt the boundaries of criminality on several occasions, and I considered it crucial to be willingly involved in 'normal' business transactions, legal or otherwise. I was pursuing an interactive, inductive study of an entrepreneurial culture, and in order to do so I had to display entrepreneurial skills myself. . . . [My] status as an insider meant that I was afforded a great deal of trust by my informants, and I was allowed access to settings, detailed conversations, and information that might not otherwise have been available.

Sampling

The sampling of informants in ethnographic research is sometimes a combination of convenience sampling and snowball sampling (see Chapter 7 for an explanation of these terms). Much of the time ethnographers are forced to gather information from whatever sources are available to them. Very often they face opposition or at least indifference to their research and are relieved to glean information or views from whoever is prepared to divulge such details. This seems to have been the essence of Armstrong's (1993: 21) strategy in the context of football hooliganism when he tried to 'locate individuals within the group networks that constituted the Blades'. However, as the lengthy quotation from his work on page 410 suggests, he was regularly able to secure from his informants details of others whom it would be useful for him to consult. Similarly, Taylor (1993: 16) has written in connection with her study of female drug users that her research participants were:

> eventually obtained by a mix of 'snowballing techniques' . . . and my almost continuous presence in the area. . . . Rather than ask to be introduced or given names of others I could contact, when I met a woman I would spend as much time with her as she would allow, participating in her daily round, and through this come to meet others in her social circle. My continued presence in the area also led other women drug users to approach me when I was alone . . . In addition, the drug worker in the area would mention my presence and interest to women with whom he came in contact and facilitate introductions where possible.

Ethnographers who take on a role that is closer to that of observer-as-participant rely somewhat more on formally asking for names of others who might be relevant and who could be contacted.

Whichever of the two strategies is adopted, the question is raised as to the degree to which either can result in a **representative sample** of informants. Probability sampling is almost never used in ethnographic research and is rarely employed in qualitative research based on interviews.

In many cases, it is not feasible to conduct a probability sampling exercise because of the constraints of ongoing fieldwork and also because it can be difficult and often impossible to map 'the **population**' from which a **random sample** might be taken—that is, to create a **sampling frame**. Instead, ethnographers have to ensure that they gain access to as wide a range of individuals relevant to the research question as possible, so that many different perspectives and ranges of activity are the focus of attention.

Purposive sampling

Most sampling in qualitative research entails purposive sampling of some kind. This term is explained in Key concept 17.4, and one of its main forms—theoretical sampling—is examined in the next section and in Key concept 17.5.

In qualitative research, purposive sampling considerations often apply to the sampling of the cases in which the research will be conducted and then to people within those cases. Thus, in Swain's (2004) ethnographic study that was examined in Research in focus 16.2, it was important for him to study the construction of masculinity in schools of contrasting socio-economic background. Since his research question implied that the construction of masculinity draws on the cultural resources that are available in a setting, it was important to demonstrate the operation of this process of social construction by exploring different social settings, since the cultural resources would be different in each setting. Since friendship groups were likely to be important contexts within which masculinities were constructed and reinforced, the sampling of students for interview was implemented by drawing on nominated friendship groups. In this way, there were two levels of purposive sampling: of contexts/cases (i.e. the schools) and of students.

Theoretical sampling

One form of purposive sampling is *theoretical sampling* (see Key concept 17.5), advocated by Glaser and Strauss (1967) and Strauss and Corbin (1998) in the context of an approach to qualitative data analysis they developed known as grounded theory. In Glaser and Strauss's view, because of its reliance on statistical rather than theoretical criteria, probability sampling is not appropriate to

Key concept 17.4
What is purposive sampling?

Purposive sampling is a non-probability form of sampling. The researcher does not seek to sample research participants on a random basis. The goal of purposive sampling is to sample cases/participants in a strategic way, so that those sampled are relevant to the research questions that are being posed. Very often, the researcher will want to sample in order to ensure that there is a good deal of variety in the resulting **sample**, so that sample members differ from each other in terms of key characteristics. Because it is a non-probability sampling approach, purposive sampling does not allow the researcher to generalize to a population. Although a purposive sample is not a random sample, it is not a **convenience sample** either (see Chapter 7 on convenience sampling). A convenience sample is simply available by chance to the researcher, whereas in purposive sampling the researcher samples with certain research goals in mind. In purposive sampling, sites, like organizations, and people (or whatever the unit of analysis is) within sites are selected because of their relevance to understanding a social phenomenon. The researcher needs to be clear in his or her mind what the criteria are that will be relevant to the inclusion or exclusion of cases (whether 'cases' means sites, people, or something else). Examples of purposive sampling in qualitative research are snowball sampling (see Research in focus 7.6 for an example) and theoretical sampling (see Key concept 17.5). In **quantitative research**, quota sampling is a form of purposive sampling procedure.

Key concept 17.5
What is theoretical sampling?

According to Glaser and Strauss (1967: 45), theoretical sampling 'is the process of data collection for generating theory whereby the analyst jointly collects, codes, and analyzes his data and decides what data to collect next and where to find them, in order to develop his theory as it emerges. The process of data collection is *controlled* by the emerging theory, whether substantive or formal.' This definition conveys a crucial characteristic of theoretical sampling—namely, that it is an ongoing process rather than a distinct and single stage, as it is, for example, in probability sampling. Moreover, it is important to realize that it is not just people that are the 'objects' of sampling, as can be seen in a more recent definition: 'Data gathering driven by concepts derived from the evolving theory and based on the concept of "making comparisons", whose purpose is to go to places, people, or events that will maximize opportunities to discover variations among concepts and to densify categories in terms of their properties and dimensions' (Strauss and Corbin 1998: 201). For Charmaz (2000: 519), theoretical sampling is a 'defining property of grounded theory' and is concerned with the refinement of ideas, rather than boosting sample size.

qualitative research. Theoretical sampling is meant to be an alternative strategy. As they put it: 'Theoretical sampling is done in order to discover categories and their properties and to suggest the interrelationships into a theory. Statistical sampling is done to obtain accurate evidence on distributions of people among categories to be used in descriptions and verifications' (Glaser and Strauss 1967: 62).

Figure 17.3

The process of theoretical sampling

- General research question
- Sample theoretically
- Collect data
- Analyse data (concepts, categories)
- Theoretical saturation
- Generate hypotheses

Figure 17.3 outlines the main steps in theoretical sampling. The reference in Key concept 17.5 to 'places, people, or events' reminds us that, in ethnographic research, it is not just people who are being sampled but also events and contexts as well (see below).

In grounded theory, you carry on collecting data (observing, interviewing, collecting documents) until you have achieved *theoretical saturation* (see Key concept 17.6). This means that: successive interviews/observations have both formed the basis for the creation of a category and confirmed its importance; there is no need to continue with data collection in relation to that category or cluster of categories; instead, the researcher should move on and generate hypotheses out of the categories that are building up and then move on to collecting data in relation to these hypotheses. Proponents of grounded theory argue that there is a great deal of redundancy in statistical sampling. For example, committing yourself to interviewing x per cent of an organization's members may mean that you end up wasting time and resources because you could have confirmed the significance of a concept and/or its connections with other concepts by using a much smaller sample. Instead, grounded theory advocates that you sample in terms of what is relevant to and meaningful for your theory. The key is to ensure you sample so as to test your emerging theoretical ideas.

Key concept 17.6
What is theoretical saturation?

The key idea is that you carry on sampling theoretically until a category has been saturated with data. 'This means, until (a) no new or relevant data seem to be emerging regarding a category, (b) the category is well developed in terms of its properties and dimensions demonstrating variation, and (c) the relationships among categories are well established and validated' (Strauss and Corbin 1998: 212). In the language of grounded theory, a category operates at a somewhat higher level of abstraction than a concept in that it may group together several concepts that have common features denoted by the category. Theoretical sampling refers to the sampling, not just of people, but also of settings and events.

The ideas of theoretical sampling and theoretical saturation will be encountered again when grounded theory is examined in greater detail in the context of qualitative data analysis in Chapter 22.

Not just people

As was pointed out in the last section, in ethnographic research sampling is not just about people but also about other things. Hammersley and Atkinson (1995) mention time and context as units that need to be considered in the context of sampling. Attending to *time* means that the ethnographer must make sure that people or events are observed at different times of the day and different days of the week. To do otherwise risks drawing inferences about certain people's behaviour or about events that are valid only for mornings or for weekdays rather than weekends. It is impossible to be an ethnographer all the time for several reasons: need to take time out to write up notes; other commitments (work or domestic); and body imperatives (eating, sleeping, and so on). When the group in question operates a different cycle from the ethnographer's normal regime (such as night shifts in a hospital or going to nightclubs), the requirement to time sample may necessitate a considerable change of habit.

It can also be important to sample in terms of *context*. People's behaviour is influenced by contextual factors so that it is important to ensure that such behaviour is observed in a variety of locations. For example, one of the important features of research on football hooliganism is that, of course, those engaged in such activity are not full-time football hooligans. In order to understand the culture and world view of football hooligans, writers like Armstrong (1993) and Giulianotti (1995; Research in focus 17.2) had to ensure that they interacted with them not just around the time of football matches, but also in a variety of contexts (pubs, general socializing), which also meant at different times.

 # Field notes

Because of the frailties of human memory, ethnographers have to take notes based on their observations. These should be fairly detailed summaries of events and behaviour and the researcher's initial reflections on them. The notes need to specify key dimensions of whatever is observed or heard. There are some general principles.

- Write down notes, however brief, as quickly as possible after seeing or hearing something interesting.

- Write up full field notes at the very latest at the end of the day and include such details as location, who is involved, what prompted the exchange or whatever, date and time of the day, etc.

- Nowadays, people may prefer to use a digital recorder to record initial notes, but this may create a problem of needing to transcribe a lot of speech.

- Notes must be vivid and clear—you should not have to ask at a later date 'what did I mean by that?'

- You need to take copious notes, so, if in doubt, write it down. The notes may be of different types (see below).

Obviously, it can be very useful to take your notes down straight away—that is, as soon as something interesting happens. However, wandering around with a notebook and pencil in hand and scribbling notes down on a continuous basis runs the risk of making people self-conscious. It may be necessary, therefore, to develop strategies of taking small amounts of time out, though hopefully without generating the anxieties Ditton (1977) appears to have occasioned (see Research in focus 17.1).

To some extent, strategies for taking field notes will be affected by the degree to which the ethnographer enters the field with clearly delineated research questions. As noted in Chapter 16, most qualitative research adopts a general approach of beginning with general research questions (as specifically implied by Figure 16.1), but there is considerable variation in the degree to which this is the case. Obviously, when there is some specificity to a research question, ethnographers have to orient their observations to that research focus, but at the same time maintain a fairly open mind so that the element of flexibility that is such a strength of a qualitative research strategy is not eroded. Ditton (1977; Research in focus 17.1) provides an illustration of a very open-ended approach when he writes that his research 'was not set up to answer any empirical questions' (1977: 11). Similarly, in the context of her research on female drug users, Taylor (1993: 15) explains that in her early days in the field she tended to listen rather than talk because she 'did not know what questions [she] wanted to ask'. Armstrong (1993: 12) writes in connection with his research on football hooliganism that his research 'began without a focus' and that as a result 'he decided to record everything'. As a result, a typical Saturday 'would result in thirty sides of notes handwritten on A4 paper'. This period of open-endedness usually cannot last long, because there is the temptation to try to record the details of absolutely everything, which can be very trying. Usually the ethnographer will begin to narrow down the focus of his or her research and to match observations to the emerging research focus. This approach is implied by the sequence suggested by Figure 16.1, and can be seen in the account by Atkinson (1981; see Research in focus 17.5). For these reasons, ethnographers frequently try to narrow down their focus of interest and to devise specific research questions or relate their emerging findings to the social scientific literature (see Research in focus 17.6).

Thinking deeply 17.1
Research questions in ethnographic research

As I noted in Chapter 16, research questions in qualitative research, and in ethnographic research in particular, are usually open-ended, though the extent to which this is the case varies a great deal. Elijah Anderson (2006) has provided a fascinating account of the background to his participant observation research into the lives of black street corner men in Chicago in the 1970s (Anderson 1978). This study was undertaken by focusing on the lives and habits of clients of Jelly's—a drinking establishment that acted as both a bar and a store for the sale of alcoholic drinks. Anderson says that at the outset of his fieldwork, he 'had absolutely no idea where the research would lead' and had 'no explicit sociological problem or question' (2006: 40). Indeed, he writes that 'this open-ended approach was a conscious act', arguing that to go in with a pre-designed set of issues 'could preclude certain lines of enquiry that might prove valuable later' (2006: 40). Gradually, the research questions emerged: 'Why did men really come to and return to Jelly's corner? What did they seek to gain? What was the nature of the social order there? What was the basis for their social ranking?' (2006: 46).

Anderson's open-ended strategy can be interestingly contrasted with a study of taxi drivers in New York and Belfast whose data are described as 'of an ethnographic kind' (Gambetta and Hamill 2005: 18). The researchers were fundamentally interested in the sociological study of trust and sought to explore how taxi drivers establish whether prospective passengers that they might pick up are trustworthy. Taxi drivers are very vulnerable in many ways: the passenger may not pay or worse may rob the driver or even worse may rob and assault the driver. Therefore, they are forced to make more or less instant decisions about whether someone who hails them is trustworthy. Their **hypothesis** is worth quoting: *'drivers screen passengers looking for reliable signs of trust- or distrust-warranting properties*, in the sense that they look for signs that are too costly for a mimic to fake but affordable for the genuine article' (Gambetta and Hamill 2005: 11; emphasis in original).

To investigate this explicit research question, Gambetta and Hamill (2005: 18) conducted 'partially structured interviews and participant observation with drivers, dispatchers, and passengers'. Unlike Anderson's initially open-ended strategy, where research questions emerged in the course of the study, Gambetta and Hamill collected their data to examine the validity of their research question, which they also refer to as a hypothesis. Their findings are presented in order to shed light on this research question, and new research questions do not appear to have emerged in the course of the study.

On a personal note, I have an impression that an open-ended approach of the kind used by Anderson is less frequently seen than in the past. That is not to say that researchers veer towards the highly explicit formulation that we see in Gambetta and Hamill's study but that there is a greater tendency towards explicitness nowadays. I suspect that this is often to do with the expectations of research funding bodies when deciding whether to fund investigations and perhaps also to do with the expectations of journals. It may also be to do with the expectations of committees that review the ethical integrity of proposed projects, because securing ethical clearance forces the researcher to be clear about what he or she intends to do and why. However, this is an impression only—maybe it could be called a hypothesis!

For most ethnographers, the main equipment with which they will need to supply themselves in the course of observation will be a note pad and pen (see e.g. Armstrong 1993: 28, and Atkinson 1981; see Research in focus 17.5). A recording device like a digital voice recorder can be another useful addition to the participant observer's hardware, but, as suggested above, it is likely to increase radically the amount of transcription and is possibly more obtrusive than writing notes. Most ethnographers report that after a period of time they become less obtrusive to participants in social settings, who become familiar with their presence (e.g. Atkinson 1981: 128). Speaking into a recording device may rekindle an awareness of the ethnographer's presence. Also, in gatherings it may be difficult to use, because of the impact of extraneous noise. Photography can be an additional source of data and helps to stir the ethnographer's memory, but it is likely that some kinds of research (especially involving crime and deviance) will render the taking of photographs unworkable.

Research in focus 17.5
Taking field notes: encounters with doctors and patients in a medical school training programme

In the context of his research in a medical school, Atkinson (1981: 131–2) provides an account that strongly implies that ethnographers need to be flexible in their note-taking tactics:

> I found that my strategies for observation and recording changed naturally as the nature of the social scene changed. Whenever possible I attempted to make rough notes and jottings of some sort whilst I was in the field. Such notes were then amplified and added to later in the day when I returned to the office. The quantity and type of on the spot recording varied across recurrent types of situation. During 'tutorials', when one of the doctors taught the group in a more or less formal manner, or when there was some group discussion . . . then it seemed entirely natural and appropriate to sit among the students with my notebook on my knee and take notes almost continuously. At the other extreme, I clearly did not sit with my notebook and pen whilst I was engaged in casual conversations with students over a cup of coffee. Whereas taking notes is a normal thing to do, taking notes during a coffee break chat is not normal practice. . . . Less clear cut was my approach to the observation and recording of bedside teaching. On the whole I tried to position myself at the back of the student group and make occasional jottings: main items of information on the patients, key technical terms, and brief notes on the shape of the session (e.g. the sequence of topics covered, the students who were called on to perform and so on).

Research in focus 17.6
Narrowing the focus of an ethnography

Ruth Horowitz has written about the process of narrowing down the focus of her research on groups on the margins of society in Gerson and Horowitz (2002). As she puts it, she tends to be interested in such questions as:

> 'What is really going on' in such groups and communities? How do people make sense of their social worlds? How do they strike a balance between group membership and wider social participation? And finally, what limits and what helps create the social worlds of the people? (Gerson and Horowitz 2002: 202)

In her early research on young people in a very poor community in Chicago, she used these general research questions to guide her data collection but 'began to focus on specifying the sociological issues only after some time in the field' (Gerson and Horowitz 2002: 202). She found a great deal of variety in the ambitions, orientations, patterns of interaction, attitudes towards street life, and behaviour in different settings among the young people she observed. Horowitz began to ask questions about how well the world of these young people fitted with two prominent models used to explain the worlds of the poor. Her research questions about the degree of fit between these models and her data led her to conclude that the models 'failed to account for young people's creativity or for the struggles they mounted and the choices that they made in the face of great obstacles' (Gerson and Horowitz 2002: 202).

Types of field notes

Some writers have found it useful to classify the types of field notes that are generated in the process of conducting an ethnography. The following classification is based on the similar categories suggested by Lofland and Lofland (1995) and Sanjek (1990):

- *Mental notes*—particularly useful when it is inappropriate to be seen taking notes (for example, during the coffee breaks referred to by Atkinson in Research in focus 17.5).

- *Jotted notes* (also called *scratch notes*)—very brief notes written down on pieces of paper or in small notebooks to jog one's memory about events that should be written up later. Lofland and Lofland (1995: 90) refer to these as being made up of 'little phrases, quotes, key words, and the like'. They need to be jotted down inconspicuously, preferably out of sight, since detailed note taking in front of people may make them self-conscious. These are equivalent to the 'rough notes and jottings' that Atkinson refers to in Research in focus 17.5.

- *Full field notes*—as soon as possible make detailed notes, which will be your main data source. They should be written at the end of the day or sooner if possible. Write as promptly and as fully as possible. Write down information about events, people, conversations, etc. Write down initial ideas about interpretation. Record impressions and feelings. When

Atkinson (in Research in focus 17.5) refers to notes in which he 'amplified and added to' the jottings made during the day, he was producing full field notes. An example of a full field note is provided in Research in focus 17.7.

It is worth adding that field notes are often to do with the ethnographer as well as the social setting being observed. It is frequently in field notes that the ethnographer's presence is evident. We see this in the field note on page 413 from Punch's study of police work in which he confirms his (false) status as a plain clothes officer, and in the field note in Research in focus 17.7 when he lends support to letting the cyclist go. Precisely because they record the quotidian as observed and experienced by ethnographers, it is here that they come to the surface. In the finished work—the ethnography in the sense of a written account of a group and its culture—the ethnographer is frequently written out of the picture (Van Maanen 1988). A major difference here is that field notes, except for brief passages like those taken from Punch's work, are invariably for personal consumption (Coffey 1999), whereas the written ethnography is for public consumption and has to be presented as a definitive account of the social setting and culture in question. To keep on allowing the ethnographer to surface in the text risks conveying a sense of the account as an artifice rather than an authoritative chronicle. This issue will be addressed in further detail in Chapter 27.

Research in focus 17.7
A field note: police work in Amsterdam

Punch's (1979) ethnographic research on police work in Amsterdam was briefly mentioned above. One of the ideas he developed was the way in which police officers often cultivated distinctive styles of working. One of them, Anton, was inflexible and therefore disinclined to use his discretion (perhaps because he was new to the work), as the following passage from Punch's field notes suggests:

> Once Jan had been sitting inside for a couple of hours doing nothing and was desperate to get out. He was sent out in a car with a newcomer, Anton. The three of us stepped outside the station and immediately saw a young man cycling erratically the wrong way down the Warmoesstraat which is a one-way street. Anton stopped him, smelt his breath, and ordered him to leave the bike and walk home. The man refused and Anton threatened to take him inside and book him for being drunk on a bike [under an article normally applied to car-drivers and almost never used for cyclists]. Jan pleaded with Anton to let the man go so that we could get out on patrol. I also added support to Jan's plea. But Anton was adamant and took the youth inside where the brigadier talked the cyclist into seeing reason and proceeding by foot. (Punch 1979: 110–11)

The end

Knowing when to stop is not an easy or straightforward matter in ethnography. Because of its unstructured nature and the absence of specific hypotheses to be tested (other than those that might emerge during data collection and analysis), there is a tendency for ethnographic research to lack a sense of an obvious end point. But clearly ethnographic research does come to an end! It may be that there is an almost natural end to the research, such as in Waddington's study of a strike (see Research in focus 16.4), but this is a fairly rare occurrence. Sometimes, the rhythms of the ethnographer's occupational career or personal and family life will necessitate withdrawal from the field, or research funding commitments will bring fieldwork to a close. Such factors include: the end of a period of sabbatical leave; the need to write up and submit a doctoral thesis by a certain date; or funding for research drawing to a close. As regards family and personal commitments, for example, Taylor (1993) writes that one of the factors that was instrumental in her departure from the field was an illness of her youngest son that lasted many months.

Moreover, ethnographic research can be highly stressful for many reasons: the nature of the topic, which places the fieldworker in stressful situations (as in research on crime); the marginality of the researcher in the social setting and the need constantly to manage a front; and the prolonged absence from one's normal life that is often necessary. The ethnographer may feel that he or she has simply had enough. A further possibility that may start to bring about moves to bring fieldwork to a close is that the ethnographer may begin to feel that the research questions on which he or she has decided to concentrate are answered, so that there are no new data worth generating. The ethnographer may even feel a strong sense of déjà vu towards the end of data collection. Altheide (1980: 310) has written that his decision to leave the various news organizations in which he had conducted ethnographic research was often motivated by 'the recurrence of familiar situations and the feeling that little worthwhile was being revealed'. In the language of grounded theory, all the researcher's categories are thoroughly saturated, although Glaser and Strauss's approach would invite you to be certain that there are no new questions to be asked of the area you are investigating, or no new comparisons to be made.

The reasons for bringing ethnographic research to a close can involve a wide range of factors from the personal to matters of research design. Whatever the reason, disengagement has to be managed. For one thing, this means that promises must be kept, so that, if you promised a report to an organization as a condition of entry, that promise should not be forgotten. It also means that ethnographers must provide good explanations for their departure. Members of a social setting always know that the researcher is a temporary fixture, but over a long period of time, and especially if there was genuine participation in activities within that setting, people may forget that the ethnographer's presence is finite. The farewells have to be managed and in an orderly fashion. Also, the ethnographer's *ethical* commitments must not be forgotten, such as the need to ensure that persons and settings are anonymized—unless, of course, as sometimes happens, there has been an agreement that the nature of the social setting can be disclosed (as often occurs in the study of religious sects and cults).

Can there be a feminist ethnography?

This heading is in fact the title of a widely cited article by Stacey (1988). It is a rebuttal of the view that there is and/or can be a distinctively feminist ethnography that both draws on the distinctive strengths of ethnography and is informed by feminist tenets of the kind outlined at the end of Chapter 16. Reinharz (1992) sees feminist ethnography as significant in terms of feminism, because:

- it documents women's lives and activities, which were previously largely seen as marginal and subsidiary to men's;

- it understands women from their perspective, so that the tendency that 'trivializes females' activities and thoughts, or interprets them from the standpoint of men in the society or of the male researcher' (Reinharz 1992: 52), is militated against; and

- it understands women in context.

Similarly, Skeggs (2001: 430) has observed that ethnography, 'with its emphasis on experiences and the words, voice and lives of the participants', has been viewed by many feminist researchers as well suited to the goals of feminism. Reinharz's principles lay behind Mattley's (2006) choice of participant observation for collecting data on working for a sex fantasy phone line in order to explore the notion of emotional labour (see Research in focus 16.1 for a brief discussion of the emergence of this concept). She writes:

> I knew that as a feminist my goals were to understand the phone workers' experiences, to document their experiences using my own words and perspectives, and to understand how their emotional labor was a part of their work context. I also knew that

> understanding their experiences from their own point of view was important to challenge the dominant sociological view of sex workers as deviants, which has most often been written by male sociologists. (Mattley 2006: 143)

However, such commitments and practices go only part of the way. Of great significance to feminist researchers is the question of whether the research allows for a non-exploitative relationship between researcher and researched. One of the main elements of such a strategy is that the ethnographer does not treat the relationship as a one-way process of extracting information from others, but actually provides something in return.

Skeggs's (1994, 1997) account of her ethnographic research on young women, which was briefly mentioned in Chapter 16, represents an attempt to address this issue of a non-exploitative relationship when women conduct ethnographic research on other women (see Research in focus 17.8). Stacey (1988: 23), however, argues, on the basis of her fieldwork experience, that the various situations she encountered as a feminist ethnographer placed her 'in situations of inauthenticity, dissimilitude, and potential, perhaps inevitable betrayal, situations that I now believe are inherent in fieldwork method. For no matter how welcome, even enjoyable the fieldworker's presence may appear to "natives", fieldwork represents an intrusion and intervention into a system of relationships, a system of relationships that the researcher is far freer to leave'. Stacey also argues that, when the research is written up, it is the feminist ethnographer's interpretations and judgements that come through and that have authority. Skeggs responds to this general charge against feminist ethnography by acknowledging in the case of her own study that her academic career was undoubtedly enhanced by the research, but argues that Stacey's views construe women as victims. Instead, she argues:

> The young women were not prepared to be exploited; just as they were able to resist most things which did not promise economic or cultural reward, they were able to resist me. . . . They enjoyed the research.
> It provided resources for developing a sense of their self-worth. More importantly, the feminism of the research has provided a framework which they use to explain that their individual problems are part of a wider structure and not their personal fault.
> (Skeggs 1994: 88)

Similarly, Reinharz (1992: 74–5) argues that, although ethnographic fieldwork relationships may sometimes *seem* manipulative, a clear undercurrent of reciprocity often lies beneath them. The researcher, in other words, may offer help or advice to her research participants, or she may be exhibiting reciprocity by giving a public airing to normally marginalized voices (although the ethnographer is always the mouthpiece for such voices and may be imposing a particular 'spin' on them). Moreover, it seems extreme to abandon feminist ethnography on the grounds that the ethnographer cannot fulfil all possible obligations simultaneously. Indeed, this would be a recipe for the abandonment of all research, feminist or otherwise. What is also crucial is transparency —transparency in the feminist ethnographer's dealings with the women she studies and transparency in the account of the research process, both of which are a great strength in Skeggs's work. Nonetheless, it is clear that the question of whether there is or can be a feminist ethnography is a matter of ongoing debate.

Research in focus 17.8
A feminist ethnography

Skeggs (1997: 1) refers to 'the 83 White working-class women of this longitudinal ethnographic study, set in the North West of England' and writes that it was 'based on research conducted over a total period of 12 years including three years' full-time, in-the-field participant observation. It began when the women enrolled on a "caring" course at a local college and it follows their trajectories through the labour market, education and the family.'

The elements of a distinctively feminist ethnography can be seen in the following comments:

- 'This ethnography was politically motivated to provide space for the articulations and experiences of the marginalized' (Skeggs 1997: 23).

- The 'study was concerned to show how young women's experience of structure (their class and gender positioning) and institutions (education and the media) framed and informed their responses and how this process informed constructions of their own subjectivity' (Skeggs 1994: 74). This comment, like the previous one, reflects the commitment to documenting women's lives and allowing their experiences to come through, while also pointing to the significance of the understanding of women in context, to which Reinharz (1992) refers.

Skeggs also feels that the relationship with the women was not an exploitative one. For example, she writes that the research enabled the women's 'sense of self-worth' to be 'enhanced by being given the opportunity to be valued, knowledgeable and interesting' (Skeggs 1994: 81). She also claims she was able to 'provide a mouthpiece against injustices' and to listen 'to disclosures of violence, child abuse and sexual harassment' (Skeggs 1994: 81).

The rise of visual ethnography

One of the most striking developments in qualitative research in recent years has been the growth of interest in the use of visual materials. The use of such materials in social research is by no means new; for example, social anthropologists have made use of photographs of the tribes and villages in which they resided for many decades. In sociology, it was not uncommon to encounter articles that made use of photographs in the *American Journal of Sociology* at the end of the nineteenth and beginning of the twentieth centuries. However, from around the time of the First World War, their use fell away. One factor in this loss of interest in the use of photographs is likely to have been a feeling that their inclusion was inconsistent with the discipline's growing scientific pretensions. However, in recent years, there is a clear sense that the use of visual materials in social research has entered a new phase of interest that can be discerned in the number of books that appeared around the turn of the millennium on this area (Banks 2001; Pink 2001; Rose 2001).

Photographs did not disappear completely from the outputs of social scientists, of course. Particularly in book-length monographs, photographs could sometimes be found. For example, Blauner's (1964) well-known book on alienated work under different technological conditions contained several photographs that were used to illustrate each of the technologies. Of particular significance is that the photographs were accompanied by quite detailed captions that more or less informed readers of what they were seeing in the images. These photographs were essentially being presented as having uncontested meanings, which was very much in tune with the realist stance on visual images (see Thinking deeply 17.2 on the distinction between realist and reflexive approaches to visual materials and Thinking deeply 17.3 for more on issues relating to Blauner's use of photographs).

A distinction can be made between the use of visual materials that are *extant* and those that are produced more or less exclusively for the purposes of research. The former will be featured in Chapter 21 and take the form of such artefacts as people's collections of photographs and images in newspapers and magazines. In this chapter I will be emphasizing research-driven visual images and my main focus will be upon photographs. Visual images that are research driven may be taken either by the researcher or by the research participants themselves. In either case, the images may be used as a basis for what is often referred to as *photo-elicitation*, whereby the researcher uses the images as a springboard for discussion concerning the meaning and significance of the images (see Research in focus 17.9 for an example). Photo-elicitation is often employed in connection with extant images too, and this point will be addressed further in Chapter 21.

The distinction between extant and research-driven visual materials is not an entirely satisfactory one. For example, when researcher participants are asked to discuss items in their photograph collections, this is similar to asking participants to take photographs and then to discuss the images that are taken. However, in order to restrict the discussion of documents in Chapter 21 only to items that have *not* been produced for research purposes, the distinction is required.

It is also worth observing that, although the term 'visual ethnography' is becoming increasingly popular (e.g. Peñaloza 1999; Pink 2001), it is sometimes used in a way that does not imply the kind of sustained immersion in a social setting that has been taken in this chapter to be a feature of ethnography. Sometimes, the term is used to include interviews of the kind covered in Chapter 18 in which visual materials figure prominently. However, in order to avoid splitting visual resources and research methods across too many chapters, I have located the discussion of their use in qualitative research in this chapter.

In the discussion that follows, I will emphasize photographs, mainly because they are the visual medium that have received the greatest attention. There are a number of ways in which photographs have been employed by qualitative researchers.

- As an *aide-mémoire* in the course of fieldwork, in which context the images essentially become components of the ethnographer's field notes. This is how I have tended to use images in my own work (see Research in focus 17.9).

- As sources of data in their own right and not simply as adjuncts to the ethnographer's field notes (see Research in focus 17.11; see also Thinking deeply 17.3).

Research in focus 17.9
Researching Disneyization

In recent years, I have been intrigued by something that I call 'Disneyization', which refers to the process by which the principles associated with the Disney theme parks have permeated many aspects of modern society and economy. In my book on Disneyization (Bryman 2004a) I included several photographs that I felt illustrated the processes I was describing quite well. In addition to serving this role, the photographs were very helpful in acting as reminders of contexts that revealed the process of Disneyization for me. This was especially the case with an article I wrote on the Disneyization of McDonald's (Bryman 2003). At one point in this article I discussed the rather bizarre case of a themed McDonald's in Chicago that was themed on rock 'n' roll. I'd visited Chicago a year previously to give a paper at the American Sociological Association conference and took the opportunity to take some photographs of the restaurant. These images were very helpful in remembering the restaurant, although I did not use them for illustrative purposes in either the book or the article. Two of the images are presented here—Plate 17.1 shows the restaurant's exterior against the Chicago skyline and Plate 17.2 shows statues of three members of the Beatles, which were among many other artefacts that contributed to the musical theme.

Plate 17.1

Disneyization in pictures: a themed McDonald's

Plate 17.2

Disneyization in pictures: The Beatles in the themed McDonald's

- As prompts for discussion by research participants. Sometimes the photographs may be extant, and this kind of context will be examined in Chapter 21. In other contexts, the discussions may be based on photographs taken by the ethnographer or by research participants (see Research in focus 17.10) more or less exclusively for the purposes of the investigation. In the case of photographs that are taken by research participants and that form the basis for an interview or discussion, Pink (2004: 399) writes: 'By working with informants to produce images that are meaningful for them we can gain insights into their visual cultures and into what is important for them as individuals living in particular localities.'

Pink (2001) draws attention to two different ways in which visual images have been conceptualized in social research. She calls these the *realist* and *reflexive* approaches (see Thinking deeply 17.2). The latter approach to the visual is frequently collaborative, in the sense that research participants may be involved in decisions about what photographs should be taken and then how they should be interpreted. Further, there is a recognition of the fluidity of the meaning of images, implying that they can never be fixed and will always be viewed by different people in different ways. Thus, in Pink's research on Spanish bullfighters, the images she took of bullfights were interpreted by enthusiasts in terms of their performative qualities of the bullfighter. UK viewers of the images employed a different interpretive frame to do with animal rights and cruelty. Plate 17.3 presents an image, referred to as *The Bullfighter's Braid*, from Pink's research. It is taken of a female bullfighter and appealed to many connoisseurs of the sport, who read into it

Thinking deeply 17.2
Two stances on the role of visual images in ethnography

Pink (2001) draws an important distinction between two positions on visual materials. The traditional framework is a *realist* one (see Key concept 1.3 on **realism**) in which the photograph or video recording simply captures an event or setting that then becomes a 'fact' for the ethnographer to interpret along with his or her other data. The image and what it represents is essentially unproblematic and acts as a window on reality. This has been the dominant frame within which visual resources have been produced and analysed. Researchers who employ photographic images to illustrate their work or as adjuncts to their field notes typically operate within a realist frame of reference that treats the image as relatively unproblematic (see Research in focus 17.9 and Thinking deeply 17.3 for examples). In contrast, Pink draws attention to a position that she calls *reflexive*, which entails an awareness of and sensitivity to the ways in which the researcher as a person has an impact on what a photograph reveals. This sensitivity requires a grasp of the way that one's age, gender, background, and academic proclivities influence what is photographed, how it is composed, and the role that informants and others may have played in influencing the resulting image.

different artistic and other meanings and values. For Pink, it held additional significance in terms of her interests in gender and the broader discipline of social anthropology (see Pink 2001: 101 for more information about this photograph). Further examples of the use of visual resources in ethnographic contexts can be found in Thinking deeply 17.2 and Research in focus 17.10.

The various examples of the use of visual materials give a sense that they have great potential for ethnographers and qualitative researchers more generally. Their growing popularity should not entice readers into thinking that visual methods should necessarily be incorporated into their investigations: their use must be relevant to the research questions being asked. For her research on Niketown in Chicago, Peñaloza (1999; Research in focus 17.11) was interested in what she dubs 'spectacular consumption'—that is, turning what could otherwise be a mundane consumption event (purchasing sportswear) into a spectacle through the use of sporting images, sounds, and atmospheres. When she explored research questions to do with this topic (for example, the role of the environment in creating a sense of spectacular consumption), an approach that included photography was very appropriate, since spectacle is a visual phenomenon.

As sources of data, visual research methods require an ability on the part of the researcher to 'read' images in a manner that is sensitive to: the context in which they were generated; the potential for multiple meanings that

Plate 17.3

The Bullfighter's Braid

Copyright Sarah Pink. Reproduced with thanks.

Research in focus 17.10
Photographs in a study of the experience of homelessness

Radley *et al.* (2005) were interested in the ways in which homeless people visualize their lives. They were especially interested in how their lives are visualized in the context both of their hostels and on the streets of London. Following an initial interview, twelve homeless people were each given disposable cameras and asked to take photographs 'that represented their experience of being a homeless person. They were told that photographs could be of key times in their day, of typical activities and spaces, or of anything else that portrayed their situation' (Radley *et al.* 2005: 277). The films were developed shortly after the photographs were taken, and the participants were interviewed shortly after that. On each occasion, participants were asked about all the photographs and which ones best expressed their experience of being a homeless person. This approach to interviewing—namely, asking people to discuss photographs and their meaning and significance for them—is often referred to as the technique of *photo-elicitation*. Plates 17.4 and 17.5 provide examples of the kinds of photograph that were taken. The photograph in Plate 17.4 was taken by Rose (the names are pseudonyms) and shows the entrance to her day centre. For Rose, this photograph had significance because it is where she is welcomed and where she welcomes others and which provides her

Plate 17.4

Images of homelessness

Copyright Alan Radley, Darrin Hodgetts, and Andrea Cullen. Reproduced with thanks.

Plate 17.5

Images of homelessness

Copyright Alan Radley, Darrin Hodgetts, and Andrea Cullen. Reproduced with thanks.

with the opportunity to move between her two worlds—as someone who sleeps in the rough at night but who during the day is able to mix with others with more conventional lives in terms of having jobs and homes. The photograph in Plate 17.5 was taken by Mary, who, unlike Rose, did not sleep rough at night, as she made use of a hostel that was in fact close to Rose's day centre. For Mary, this photograph took on significance because it 'shows us a community of friends who share not only a place [referred to as The Wall situated on Vauxhall Bridge Road] but also an activity—drinking' (Radley *et al.* 2005: 283; note how the faces are blanked out to protect the individuals in the photographs). The photographs and the discussions of them by the participants provide insights into the experience of homelessness and how the homeless navigate an identity in a world in which homelessness is on the fringes of society.

may need to be worked through with research particip-ants; and, where the researcher is the source of the images, the significance of his or her own social position. In other words, the analyst of visual materials needs to be sceptical about the notion that a photograph provides an unproblematic depiction of reality. In addition, researchers will usually include non-visual research methods in their investigations (such as interviews). This leads to the question of the relative significance of words and images in the analysis of data and the presentation of findings. Since words are the traditional medium, it is easy to slip into seeing the visual as ancillary.

However, at the same time, Pink (2004) reminds us that visual research methods are never purely visual.

Research in focus 17.11
Visual ethnography? Just do it.

Peñaloza (1999) conducted what she calls a 'visual ethnographic' study of Niketown in Chicago. The Niketowns are huge stores that act as showcases for Nike's products and can be found in many large cities worldwide, including one in London on Oxford Street. She was interested in the store as a spectacle that has been designed specifically for the consumer and that is meant to create a sense of awe. Peñaloza (1999: 34) argues that an approach that included photography was well suited to her research, given her interest in the environment within which consumption occurred, 'particularly its architecture, furnishings, displays of artifacts, images, sounds and textures in relation to consumers' behaviors'. Her corpus of data included: 148 pages of field notes; 58 pages of entries in a **diary**; and 357 photographs. In addition, interviews were conducted with employees and consumers. Through her data, Peñaloza shows, for example, that the display of artefacts and images of revered athletes are deployed to transfer the sense of power and awe in which these individuals are held to Nike as a corporation.

Thinking deeply 17.3
Copyright and photographs

An interesting fairly early use of photographs can be found in Blauner's (1964) influential book on work in four different technological conditions. Blauner used photographs to illustrate each of the four technologies and the kinds of work with which each was associated. They are very memorable photographs, which were accompanied by a detailed description of the work beneath the image. I wanted to include a photograph very similar to the one in Plate 17.6 to demonstrate Blauner's use of photographs to illustrate assembly-line work in the automobile industry in the USA in the 1950s and early 1960s. Blauner's photograph had the title 'Subdivided jobs and restricted freedom' and was accompanied by a description of employees' work and the following comment: 'These men perform the identical tasks shown above all day long and may fasten from eight hundred to one thousand wheels in eight hours. The movement of the cars along the conveyor belt determines the pace of their work and kept them close to their stations, virtually "chained" to the assembly line' (Blauner 1964: 112). Thus, Blauner used the image to illustrate the work of assembly-line workers and was operating very much within a realist view of the role of the photograph. I write above that the Plate 17.6 is 'very similar', because it proved impossible to track the owner of the image. In Blauner's book the image he used is described as 'Courtesy of the Chrysler Corporation'. However, Chrysler's archivists could not find the photograph and therefore could not provide us with permission to use it. However, they were kind enough to allow me to use the image in Plate 17.6. This anecdote demonstrates some of the difficulties with the use of photographs in general and of older ones in particular.

Plate 17.6

The automobile assembly line

Copyright DaimlerChrysler Corporation. Used with permission.

There are two aspects to this point. First, as Pink points out, visual research methods are usually accompanied by other (often traditional) research methods like interviewing and observation. Second, the visual is almost always accompanied by the non-visual—words—that are the medium of expression for both the research participants and the researchers themselves.

Finally, visual research methods raise especially difficult issues of ethics, an area that is explored in Chapter 5. The Visual Sociology Group, a study group of the British Sociological Association (BSA), has provided a statement of ethical practice for researchers using visual research methods: http://www.visualsociology.org.uk/about/ethical_statement.php (accessed on 28 September 2007). This is a useful statement, which draws on the BSA's *Statement of Ethical Practice*, which was referred to

in Chapter 5. Here are some statements of ethical practice that are recommended:

> Researchers may want to discuss the status of the images with participants in order to clearly explain the dissemination strategy of the research project. In certain circumstances, the researcher(s) may want to create a written or verbal contract guaranteeing the participants ownership of the images produced. Under UK law copyright can be waived by participants and given to the researcher(s); however it is recommended that researchers read the current legislation or seek legal advice if taking this option (please note that the date of the creation of the image affects the legal status).

As far as possible participation in sociological research should be based on the freely given informed consent of those studied. This implies a responsibility on the sociologist to explain in appropriate detail, and in terms meaningful to participants, what the research is about, who is undertaking and financing it, why it is being undertaken, and how it is to be disseminated and used. Here again clarity about the status and ownership of visual data will benefit the participants and the reputation of the discipline.

As these points reveal, there is a special sensitivity to the use of visual materials, like photographs, in that the subjects who appear in them may have their images widely disseminated. It is important, therefore, to ensure that permission is gained from those whose images appear and that they are fully aware of the implications of that agreement. If you are considering using visual research methods, you should consult this statement of ethical practice.

Thinking deeply 17.4
When is a study ethnographic?

There is some debate about when it is and is not appropriate to refer to a qualitative investigation as an ethnography. In fact, one gets the impression that ethnography is almost a matter of degree. At one extreme, Nightingale (1989) has questioned whether it is appropriate to refer to supposedly ethnographic studies of media audiences as ethnographic. She argues that they are invariably ethnographic in name only in that there is little if any participant observation; instead, the researchers typically rely on semi-structured or **unstructured interviewing** or focus groups for their data. For writers like Emerson (1987) and Wolcott (1990*b*), a degree of immersion in the field is the touchstone of ethnography, with Emerson arguing that too often ethnographers do not spend enough time in the field. Indeed, my account of ethnography in Key concept 17.1 entails immersion in a social setting.

However, as I noted previously, ethnographers are rarely pure participant observers, in that they invariably conduct interviews or examine documents, thus raising the question of when it is appropriate to refer to a qualitative study as ethnographic. However, there may be circumstances when this requirement needs to be relaxed. A striking case in point is Gusterson's (1996: p. ix) 'ethnographic study of a nuclear weapons laboratory' in the USA. Because of the top-secret nature of work at this establishment and its sheer scale, participant observation in the conventional sense of prolonged immersion in the field was not possible. Gusterson (1996: 32) writes: 'I decided to mix formal interviews and the collection of documentary sources with a strategy of participant observation adapted to the demands and limitations of my own fieldwork situation. . . . I relied less on participant observation than most anthropologists in the field.' However, he did seek out as many employees as he could muster and he lived in the community in which the laboratory was located, participating in many of their core activities. Thus, while a study such as this may not exhibit the characteristics of a conventional ethnography of a workplace—because this option was not available to the researcher— Gusterson's determination to live among members of the community and to see the development of nuclear weapons through the eyes of those who worked there through interviews provides the investigation with many of the ingredients of an ethnography. What the study also suggests, along with the discussions of writers such as Emerson (1987) and Wolcott (1990*b*), is that whether a qualitative study is ethnographic is to a significant extent a matter of degree.

Key points

- Ethnography is a term that refers to both a method and the written product of research based on that method.
- The ethnographer is typically a participant observer who also uses non-observational methods and sources such as interviewing and documents.
- The ethnographer may adopt an overt or covert role, but the latter carries ethical difficulties.
- The method of access to a social setting will depend in part on whether it is a public or closed one.
- Key informants frequently play an important role for the ethnographer, but care is needed to ensure that their impact on the direction of research is not excessive.
- There are several different ways of classifying the kinds of role that the ethnographer may assume. These are not necessarily mutually exclusive.
- Sampling considerations differ from those addressed in the context of quantitative research, in that issues of representativeness are emphasized less.
- Field notes are important for prompting the ethnographer's memory.
- Feminist ethnography has become a popular approach to collecting data from a feminist standpoint, but there have been debates about whether there really can be a feminist ethnography.
- Visual materials such as photographs and video have attracted considerable interest among ethnographers in recent years, not just as adjuncts to data collection but as objects of interest in their own right.

Questions for review

- Is it possible to distinguish ethnography and participant observation?
- How does participant observation differ from structured observation?
- To what extent do participant observation and ethnography rely solely on observation?

Access

- 'Covert ethnography obviates the need to gain access to inaccessible settings and therefore has much to recommend it.' Discuss.
- Examine some articles in British sociology journals in which ethnography and participant observation figure strongly. Was the researcher in an overt or covert role? Was access needed to closed or open settings? How was access achieved?
- Is access to closed settings necessarily more difficult to achieve than to open settings?
- Does the problem of access finish once access to a chosen setting has been achieved?
- What might be the role of key informants in ethnographic research? Is there anything to be concerned about when using them?

Roles for ethnographers

- Compare Gold's and Gans's schemes for classifying participant observer roles.
- What is meant by going native?
- Should ethnographers be active or passive in the settings in which they conduct research?

Sampling

- What is snowball sampling?
- What is theoretical sampling?
- How crucial is the idea of theoretical saturation to theoretical sampling?

Field notes

- Why are field notes important for ethnographers?
- Why is it useful to distinguish between different types of field notes?

The end

- How do you decide when to complete the data collection phase in ethnographic research?

Can there be a feminist ethnography?

- What are the main ingredients of feminist ethnography?
- Assess Stacey's argument about whether feminist ethnography is possible in the light of Skeggs's research or any other ethnographic study that describes itself, or can be seen, as feminist.

The rise of visual ethnography

- What kinds of roles can visual materials play in ethnography?
- Do photographs provide unproblematic images of reality?

Online Resource Centre
http://www.oxfordtextbooks.co.uk/orc/brymansrm3e/

Visit the Online Resource Centre that accompanies this book to enrich your understanding of ethnography and participant observation. Consult web links, test yourself using multiple choice questions, and gain further guidance and inspiration from the Student Researcher's Toolkit.

Interviewing in qualitative research

Chapter outline

Chapter guide

This chapter is concerned with the interview in **qualitative research**. The term 'qualitative interview' is often used to capture the different types of interview that are used in qualitative research, and this is the term that I will use as a shorthand way of categorizing the different forms of qualitative research interview. Such interviews tend to be far less structured than the kind of interview associated with **survey research**, which was discussed in Chapter 8 in terms of **structured interviewing**. This chapter is concerned with individual interviews in qualitative research; the **focus group** method, which is a form of interview but with several people, is discussed in the next chapter. The two forms of qualitative interviewing discussed in this chapter are unstructured and **semi-structured interviewing**. The chapter explores:

- the differences between structured interviewing and qualitative interviewing;
- the main characteristics of and differences between unstructured and semi-structured interviewing; this entails a recognition that the two terms refer to extremes and that in practice a wide range of interviews with differing degrees of structure lie between the extremes;
- how to devise and use an **interview guide** for semi-structured interviewing;
- the different kinds of question that can be asked in an interview guide;
- the importance of recording and transcribing qualitative interviews;
- approaches to sampling in studies using qualitative interviews;
- the significance of qualitative interviewing in feminist research;
- the advantages and disadvantages of qualitative interviewing relative to **participant observation**.

Introduction

The interview is probably the most widely employed method in qualitative research. Of course, as we have seen in Chapter 17, **ethnography** usually involves a substantial amount of interviewing, and this factor undoubtedly contributes to the widespread use of the interview by qualitative researchers. However, it is the flexibility of the interview that makes it so attractive. Since ethnography entails an extended period of participant observation, which is very disruptive for researchers because of the sustained absence(s) required from work and/or family life, research based more or less exclusively on interviews is a highly attractive alternative for the collection of qualitative data. Interviewing, the **transcription** of interviews, and the analysis of **transcripts** are all very time-consuming, but they can be more readily accommodated into researchers' personal lives.

In Key concept 8.2, several different types of interview were briefly outlined. The bulk of the types outlined there—other than the structured interview and the standardized interview—are ones associated with qualitative research. *Focus groups* and *group interviewing* will be examined in the next chapter, and the remaining forms of interview associated with qualitative research will be explored at various points in this chapter. However, in spite of the apparent proliferation of terms describing types of interview in qualitative research, the two main types are the *unstructured interview* and the *semi-structured interview*. Researchers sometimes employ the term 'qualitative interview' to encapsulate these two types of interview. There is clearly the potential for considerable confusion here, but the types and definitions offered in Key concept 8.2 are meant to inject a degree of consistency of terminology.

Differences between the structured interview and the qualitative interview

Qualitative interviewing is usually very different from interviewing in quantitative research in a number of ways.

- The approach tends to be much less structured in qualitative research. In quantitative research, the approach is structured to maximize the reliability and validity of measurement of key concepts. It is also more structured because the researcher has a clearly specified set of research questions that are to be investigated. The structured interview is designed to answer these questions. Instead, in qualitative research, there is an emphasis on greater generality in the formulation of initial research ideas and on interviewees' own perspectives.

- In qualitative interviewing, there is much greater interest in the interviewee's point of view; in quantitative research, the interview reflects the researcher's concerns. This contrast is a direct outcome of the previous one.

- In qualitative interviewing, 'rambling' or going off at tangents is often encouraged—it gives insight into what the interviewee sees as relevant and important; in quantitative research, it is usually regarded as a nuisance and discouraged.

- In qualitative interviewing, interviewers can depart significantly from any schedule or guide that is being used. They can ask new questions that follow up interviewees' replies and can vary the order and even the wording of questions. In quantitative interviewing, none of these things should be done, because they will compromise the standardization of the interview process and hence the reliability and validity of measurement.

- As a result, qualitative interviewing tends to be flexible, responding to the direction in which interviewees take the interview and perhaps adjusting the emphases in the research as a result of significant issues that emerge in the course of interviews (see Research in focus 18.3 for an example). By contrast, quantitative interviews are typically inflexible, because of the need to standardize the way in which each interviewee is dealt with.

- In qualitative interviewing, the researcher wants rich, detailed answers; in structured interviewing, the interview is supposed to generate answers that can be coded and processed quickly.

- In qualitative interviewing, the interviewee may be interviewed on more than one and sometimes even several occasions (see Research in focus 18.1 for an example). In structured interviewing, unless the research is longitudinal in character, the person will be interviewed on one occasion only.

Research in focus 18.1
Unstructured interviewing

Malbon (1999: 33) describes his interviewing strategy for his research on 'clubbers' in the following way:

> Clubbers were usually interviewed twice, with the second interview happening after we had been clubbing together. Both interviews were very much 'conversational' in style and I avoided interview schedules, although all interviews were taped. The first interview was designed to achieve three main goals: to put the clubber at ease while also explaining fully and clearly in what ways I was hoping for help; to begin to sketch in details of the clubbers' clubbing preferences, motivations and histories; and to allow me an opportunity to decide how to approach the night(s) out that I would be spending with the clubber . . . The second interview provided a forum for what was invariably a more relaxed meeting than the first interview . . . The main content of the second interview consisted of comments, discussion, and questions about the club visits we had made together, and the nature of the night out as an experience. In the latter half of these second interviews, discussion occasionally diversified in scope to cover wider aspects of the clubbers' lives: their relationships to work or study, their relationships with friends and loved ones, their hopes and fears for the future and their impressions of a social life beyond and after clubbing.

Student experience
The advantages of semi-structured interviewing

The relatively unstructured nature of the semi-structured interview and its capacity to provide insights into how research participants view the world was important to Hannah Creane. Hannah was attracted to it because she was concerned not to 'pigeon-hole' people while she was researching childhood.

> The aim of my study was to explore the generational changes within childhood. I decided to interview nine people of several different generations about their childhood experiences, their opinions on the concept and construction of childhood, and their thoughts on childhood today. I chose to use semi-structured interviews because of the fact that they would allow me to gain the research I wanted without pigeon-holing the response of those I was interviewing.

To read more about Hannah's research experiences, go to the Online Resource Centre that accompanies this book at http://www.oxfordtextbooks.co.uk/orc/brymansrm3e/.

Asking questions in the qualitative interview

However, qualitative interviewing varies a great deal in the approach taken by the interviewer. The two major types were mentioned at the beginning of the chapter.

1. The almost totally *unstructured interview*. Here the researcher uses at most an *aide-mémoire* as a brief set of prompts to him- or herself to deal with a certain range of topics. There may be just a single question that the interviewer asks, and the interviewee is then allowed to respond freely, with the interviewer simply responding to points that seem worthy of being followed up. Unstructured interviewing tends to be very similar in character to a conversation (Burgess 1984). See Research in focus 18.1 for an illustration of an unstructured interview style.

2. A *semi-structured interview*. The researcher has a list of questions or fairly specific topics to be covered, often referred to as an *interview guide*, but the interviewee has a great deal of leeway in how to reply. Questions may not follow on exactly in the way outlined on the schedule. Questions that are not included in the guide may be asked as the interviewer picks up on things said by interviewees. But, by and large, all the questions will be asked and a similar wording will be used from interviewee to interviewee. Research in focus 18.2 and 18.3 provide examples of these features.

In both cases, the interview process is *flexible*. Also, the emphasis must be on how the interviewee frames and understands issues and events—that is, what the interviewee views as important in explaining and understanding events, patterns, and forms of behaviour. Thus, Leidner (1993: 238) describes the interviewing she carried out in a McDonald's restaurant as involving a degree of structure, but adds that the interviews also 'allowed room to pursue topics of particular interest to the workers'. Once again, we must remember that qualitative research is *not* quantitative research with the numbers missing. There is a growing tendency for semi-structured and unstructured interviewing to be referred to collectively as *in-depth interviews* or as *qualitative interviews*. The kinds of interviewing carried out in qualitative research are typical also of *life history* and *oral history* interviewing (see Key concept 18.1).

The two different types of interview in qualitative research are extremes, and there is quite a lot of variability between them (the example in Research in focus 18.2 seems somewhat more structured than that in Research in focus 18.3, for example, though both are illustrative of semi-structured interviewing), but most qualitative interviews are close to one type or the other. In neither case does the interviewer slavishly follow a schedule, as is

Research in focus 18.2
Semi-structured interviewing

Lupton (1996) was interested in investigating people's food preferences, and to this end her research entailed thirty-three semi-structured interviews conducted by four female interviewers (of whom she was one) living in Sydney in 1994. She writes:

> Interviewees were asked to talk about their favourite and most detested foods; whether they thought there was such a thing as 'masculine' or 'feminine' foods or dishes; which types of foods they considered 'healthy' or 'good for you' and which not; which types of foods they ate to lose weight and which they avoided for the same reason; memories they recalled about food and eating events from childhood and adulthood; whether they liked to try new foods; which foods they had tasted first as an adult; whether there had been any changes in the types of food they had eaten over their lifetime; whether they associated different types of food with particular times, places or people; whether they ever had any arguments about food with others; whether they themselves cooked and if they enjoyed it; whether they ate certain foods when in certain moods and whether they had any rituals around food. (Lupton 1996: 156, 158)

Research in focus 18.3
Flexibility in semi-structured interviewing

Like Lupton (Research in focus 18.2), Beardsworth and Keil (1992) were interested in food-related issues, and in particular in vegetarianism. They carried out seventy-three 'relatively unstructured interviews' in the East Midlands. They write that the interviews were

> guided by an inventory of issues which were to be covered in each session. As the interview programme progressed, interviewees themselves raised additional or complementary issues, and these form an integral part of the study's findings. In other words, the interview programme was not based upon a set of relatively rigid pre-determined questions and prompts. Rather, the open-ended, discursive nature of the interviews permitted an iterative process of refinement, whereby lines of thought identified by earlier interviewees could be taken up and presented to later interviewees. (Beardsworth and Keil 1992: 261–2)

done in quantitative research interviewing; but in semi-structured interviews the interviewer does follow a script to a certain extent. The choice of whether to veer towards one type rather than the other is likely to be affected by a variety of factors.

- Researchers who are concerned that the use of even the most rudimentary interview guide will not allow genuine access to the world views of members of a social setting or of people sharing common attributes are likely to favour an unstructured interview.

- If the researcher is beginning the investigation with a fairly clear focus, rather than a very general notion of wanting to do research on a topic, it is likely that the interviews will be semi-structured ones, so that the more specific issues can be addressed.

- If more than one person is to carry out the fieldwork, in order to ensure a modicum of comparability of interviewing style, it is likely that semi-structured interviewing will be preferred. See Research in focus 18.2 and 18.3 for examples.

- If you are doing multiple-case study research, you are likely to find that you will need some structure in order to ensure cross-case comparability. Certainly, all my qualitative research on different kinds of organization has entailed semi-structured interviewing, and it is not a coincidence that this is because most of it has been multiple-case study research (e.g. Bryman *et al.* 1994; see Research in focus 16.6; Bryman, Gillingwater, and McGuinness 1996).

Key concept 18.1
What are life history and oral history interviews?

Two special forms of the kind of interview associated with qualitative research are the *life history* and *oral history* interviews. The former is generally associated with the *life history method*, where it is often combined with various kinds of **personal documents** such as diaries, photographs, and letters. This method is often referred to alternatively as the *biographical method*. A **life history interview** invites the subject to look back in detail across his or her entire life course. It has been depicted as documenting 'the inner experience of individuals, how they interpret, understand, and define the world around them' (Faraday and Plummer 1979: 776). However, the life history method is very much associated with the life history interview, which is a kind of unstructured interview covering the totality of an individual's life. Thomas and Znaniecki, who are among the pioneers of the approach as a result of their early use of it in relation to Polish immigrants to the USA, regarded it as 'the *perfect* type of sociological material' (quoted in Plummer 1983: 64). Their use, in particular, of a solicited autobiography that was written for them by one Polish peasant is regarded as an exemplification of the method.

However, in spite of Thomas and Znaniecki's endorsement, while there was a trickle of studies using the approach over the years (a table in Plummer 1983 points to twenty-six life histories dating from Thomas and Znaniecki's research in the 1910s and the publication of Plummer's book), until the 1990s it was not a popular approach. It has tended to suffer because of an erroneous treatment of the life in question as a **sample** of one and hence of limited **generalizability**. However, it has certain clear strengths from the point of view of the qualitative researcher: its unambiguous emphasis on the point of view of the life in question and a clear commitment to the processual aspects of social life, showing how events unfold and interrelate in people's lives. The terms *life history* and *life story* are sometimes employed interchangeably, but Miller (2000: 19) suggests that the latter is an account someone gives about his or her life and that a life history dovetails a life story with other sources, such as diaries and letters (of the kind discussed in Chapter 21).

An example of the life history interview approach is provided by Lewis (1961: p. xxi) in the context of his research on the Sánchez family and their experiences of a Mexican slum:

> In the course of our interviews I asked hundreds of questions of [the five members of the Sánchez family] . . . While I used a directive approach to the interviews, I encouraged free association, and I was a good listener. I attempted to cover systematically a wide range of subjects: their earliest memories, their dreams, their hopes, fears, joys, and sufferings; their jobs; their relationship with friends, relatives, employers; their sex life; their concepts of justice, religion, and politics; their knowledge of geography and history; in short, their total world view of the world. Many of my questions stimulated them to express themselves on subjects which they might otherwise never have thought about.

Miller (2000) distinguishes between certain aspects of life history inteviews. One distinction has to do with age and life course effects. The former relates to the ageing process, in the sense of biological ageing and its effects and manifestations; life course effects are the patterned features associated with the stages of the life course. He also points to the need to distinguish cohort effects, which are the unique clusters of experiences associated with a specific generation.

An interesting use of the life history method is the research by Laub and Sampson (2004) in connection with the study referred to in Research in focus 2.13 (see also Research in focus 25.4). They approached their reconstruction of the lives of the 52 delinquents from the original study in two ways. First, they developed a form of life history calendar that provided their sample with a framework within which they could pinpoint major turning points in their lives, such as marriage, job change, and divorce. Second, they also conducted interviews that invited the 52 men to reflect on their life course. They write:

> Of particular interest were the questions regarding the participant's assessment of his own life, specifically whether he saw improvement or a worsening since childhood, adolescence, or young adulthood and the self-evaluation of turning points in one's own life course and the relationship to criminal activity and various life course transitions (e.g., marriage, divorce, military service, residential change, and the like). . . . By drawing on the men's own words, narratives helped us unpack mechanisms that connect salient life events across the life course, especially regarding personal choice and situational context. (Laub and Sampson 2004: 93, 94)

Through the collection of these data, the researchers were able to enhance their understanding of the significance of turning points in an individual's life that influence the likelihood of continued involvement in or desistance from crime.

Miller (2000) suggests there has been a resurgence of interest in recent years and Chamberlayne *et al.* (2000) argue that there has been a recent 'turn to biographical methods'. To a large extent, the revival of the approach derives from a growth of interest in the role and significance of agency in social life. The revival is largely associated with the growing use of life story interviews and especially those that are often referred to as *narrative interviews*. Moreover, the growing use of such interviews has come to be associated less and less with the study of a single life (or indeed just one or two lives) and increasingly with the study of several lives (see Research in focus 22.5).

Plummer (2001) draws a useful distinction between three types of life story:

1. *Naturalistic life stories*. These are life stories that occur whenever people reminisce or write autobiographies or diaries, or when job applicants write out letters of application and are interviewed.

2. *Researched life stories*. These are life stories that are solicited by researchers with a social scientific purpose in mind. Most research based on life history/story interviews, like that of Squire (2000), are of this kind.

3. *Reflexive and recursive life stories*. Such life stories recognize that the life story is always a construction in which the interviewer is implicated.

Atkinson (2004) observes that the length of the typical life story interview varies considerably but suggests that it usually comprises two or three sessions of between one hour and one-and-a-half hours each. He has provided a catalogue of questions that can be asked and divides these into groups. The following list of categories and sample questions are taken from Atkinson (1998: 43–53):

- *Birth and family of origin*. For example: 'How would you describe your parents?'
- *Cultural settings and traditions*. For example: 'Was your family different from others in the neighbourhood?'
- *Social factors*. For example: 'What were some of your struggles as a child?'
- *Education*. For example: 'What are your best memories of school?'
- *Love and work*. For example: 'How did you end up in the type of work you do or did?'
- *Historical events or periods*. For example: 'Do you remember what you were doing on any of the really important days in our history?'
- *Retirement*. For example: 'What is the worst part of being retired?'
- *Inner life and spiritual awareness*. For example: 'What are the stresses of being an adult?'
- *Major life themes*. For example: 'What are the crucial decisions in your life?'
- *Vision of the future*. For example: 'Is your life fulfilled yet?'
- *Closure questions*. For example: 'Do you feel that you have given a fair picture of yourself?'

An *oral history interview* is usually somewhat more specific in tone in that the subject is asked to reflect upon specific events or periods in the past. The emphasis is less upon the individual and his/her life than on the particular events in the past. It too is sometimes combined with other sources, such as documents. The chief problem with the oral history interview (which it shares with the life history interview) is the possibility of bias introduced by memory lapses and distortions (Grele 1998). On the other hand, oral history testimonies have allowed the voices to come through of groups that are typically marginalized in historical research (a point that also applies to life history interviews), either because of their lack of power or because they are typically regarded as unexceptional (Samuel 1976). Bloor (2002) has shown how oral history testimonies, collected in 1973 and 1974, of Welsh miners' experiences of pit life could be used to facilitate an understanding of how they sought collectively to make an impact on their health in the pits and to improve safety. Bloor draws lessons from these testimonies for social policies at the time he was writing.

Preparing an interview guide

The idea of an interview guide is much less specific than the notion of a structured interview schedule. In fact, the term can be employed to refer to the brief list of memory prompts of areas to be covered that is often employed in unstructured interviewing or to the somewhat more structured list of issues to be addressed or questions to be asked in semi-structured interviewing. What is crucial is that the questioning allows interviewers to glean the ways in which research participants view their social world and that there is flexibility in the conduct of the interviews. The latter is as much if not more to do with the conduct of the interview than with the nature of the interview guide as such.

In preparing for qualitative interviews, Lofland and Lofland (1995: 78) suggest asking yourself the question 'Just what about this thing is puzzling me?' This can be applied to each of the research questions you have generated or it may be a mechanism for generating some research questions. They suggest that your puzzlement can be stimulated by various activities: random thoughts in different contexts, which are then written down as quickly as possible; discussions with colleagues, friends, and relatives; and, of course, the existing literature on the topic. The formulation of the research question(s) should not be so specific that alternative avenues of enquiry that might arise during the collection of fieldwork data are closed off. Such premature closure of your research focus would be inconsistent with the process of qualitative research (Figure 16.1), with the emphasis on the world view of the people you will be interviewing, and with the approaches to qualitative data analysis like **grounded theory** that emphasize the importance of not starting out with too many preconceptions (see Chapter 22). Gradually, an order and structure will begin to emerge in your meanderings around your research question(s) and will form the basis for your interview guide.

You should also consider 'What do I need to know in order to answer each of the research questions I'm interested in?' This means trying to get an appreciation of what the interviewee sees as significant and important in relation to each of your topic areas. Thus, your questioning must cover the areas that you need but from the perspective of your interviewees. This means that, even though qualitative research is predominantly unstructured, it is rarely so unstructured that the researcher cannot at least specify a research focus.

Some basic elements in the preparation of your interview guide will be:

- create a certain amount of order on the topic areas, so that your questions about them flow reasonably well, but be prepared to alter the order of questions during the actual interview;

- formulate interview questions or topics in a way that will help you to answer your research questions (but try not to make them too specific);

- try to use a language that is comprehensible and relevant to the people you are interviewing;

- just as in interviewing in quantitative research, do not ask leading questions;

- remember to ensure that you ask or record 'facesheet' information of a general kind (name, age, gender, etc.) and a specific kind (position in company, number of years employed, number of years involved in a group, etc.), because such information is useful for contextualizing people's answers.

There are some practical details to attend to before the interview.

- Make sure you are familiar with the setting in which the interviewee works or lives or engages in the behaviour of interest to you. This will help you to understand what he or she is saying in the interviewee's own terms.

- Get hold of a good-quality recording machine and microphone. Qualitative researchers nearly always record and then transcribe their interviews. This procedure is important for the detailed analysis required in qualitative research and to ensure that the interviewees' answers are captured in their own terms. If you are taking notes, it is easy to lose the phrases and language used. Also, because the interviewer is supposed not to be following a strictly formulated schedule of questions of the kind used in structured interviewing, he or she will need to be responsive to the interviewee's answers so that it is possible to follow them

up. A good microphone is highly desirable, because many interviews are let down by poor recording.

- Make sure as far as possible that the interview takes place in a setting that is quiet (so there is no or little outside noise that might affect the quality of the recording) and private (so the interviewee does not have to worry about being overheard).

- Prepare yourself for the interview by cultivating as many of the criteria of a quality interviewer suggested by Kvale (1996) as possible (see Tips and skills 'Criteria of a successful interviewer').

- Interviewing is very demanding, and students who are new to the method sometimes understate the personal issues involved. It is worth conducting some pilot interviews, not just to test how well the interview flows but in order to gain some experience. As Tips and skills 'Interviewing for the first time' shows, it is better to be prepared for some of the unexpected contingencies that can arise in the course of an interview.

Student experience
On not leading interviewees

As noted in the list of bullet points concerning the preparation of an interview guide, it is important not to lead interviewees. Gareth Matthews describes how he was concerned not to lead the employers and managers in firms in the hospitality industry to focus on migrant workers. He wanted any discussion of migrant workers to come naturally from them. Here is how he went about it.

Also, I wanted to explore the nature of employers' recruitment decisions in terms of their perceptions of skill/attributes/attitudes that exist in the external labour market in both British workers and migrant workers, though without making it overly obvious that this was a primary line of enquiry. Therefore, while I did not want to mask the research aims from interviewees, I also did not want to alert them to focus on migrants, as I felt that this would prejudice their responses (I found that, in the first few interviews, employers were generally quite suspicious and, accordingly, quite defensive when speaking about these matters).

Therefore, I found it easier to focus on the notion of 'skill shortages' in the hospitality industry, by referring to the published information that points to a crisis in the sector with regards to finding workers with the appropriate attributes. This tended to [elicit] a detailed response on the nature of skills and the perceptions of British workers with regards to these skills. It was then easier to turn the discussion towards a focus on employers' recruitment of migrant workers and their perceptions of the attributes embodied in these workers vis-à-vis British workers. Also, this discussion made it possible to explore employers' perceptions of particular groups of migrant workers, and led to some very interesting (though worrying) findings with regards to employers' use of race and nationality as distinctive categories when making recruitment decisions.

To read more about Gareth's research experiences, go to the Online Resource Centre that accompanies this book at http://www.oxfordtextbooks.co.uk/orc/brymansrm3e/.

Tips and skills
Interviewing for the first time

The prospect of doing your first interview can be daunting. Also, it is easy to make some fundamental mistakes when you begin interviewing. An American study of postgraduates' experiences of a lengthy interview training course showed that novice interviewers were easily thrown out by a number of events or experiences in the course of the interview (Roulston *et al.* 2003). Their findings suggest five challenges that are worth bearing in mind when approaching your first interview(s).

1. *Unexpected interviewee behaviour or environmental problems.* These inexperienced interviewers were easily discomforted by responses or behaviour on the part of interviewees or by problems like noise in the vicinity of the interview. When you go into the interview, bear in mind that things may not go according to plan. Interviewees sometimes say things that are very surprising and some like to startle or even shock interviewers. Equally, there can be many distractions close to where the interview takes place. You clearly cannot plan for or have control over these things, but you can bear in mind that they might happen and try to limit their impact on you and on the course of the interview.

2. *Intrusion of own biases and expectations.* Roulston *et al.* report that some of the trainees were surprised when they read their transcripts how their own biases and expectations were evident in the ways they asked questions and followed up on replies.

3. *Maintaining focus in asking questions.* Students reported that they sometimes had difficulty probing answers, asking follow-up questions, and clarifying questions in a way that did not lose sight of the research topic and what the questions were getting at.

4. *Dealing with sensitive issues.* Some students asked questions that caused interviewees to become upset, and this response could have an adverse impact on the course of the interview. However, most students felt that they coped reasonably well with such emotionally charged situations.

5. *Transcription.* Many reported finding transcription difficult and time-consuming—more so than they had imagined.

There are, of course, many other possible issues that impinge on first-time interviewees. Many do not go away either, no matter how experienced you are. It is very difficult to know how to deal with some of these contingencies. However, it is worth bearing in mind that they arise and that their impact may be greatest when you begin interviewing.

After the interview, make notes about:

- how the interview went (was interviewee talkative, cooperative, nervous, well-dressed/scruffy, etc.?);

- where the interview took place;

- any other feelings about the interview (did it open up new avenues of interest?);

- the setting (busy/quiet, many/few other people in the vicinity, new/old buildings, use of computers).

These various guidelines suggest the series of steps in formulating questions for an interview guide in qualitative research presented in Figure 18.1.

Tips and skills
Criteria of a successful interviewer

Kvale (1996) has proposed a very useful list of ten criteria of a successful interviewer.

- *Knowledgeable*: is thoroughly familiar with the focus of the interview; pilot interviews of the kind used in survey interviewing can be useful here.
- *Structuring*: gives purpose for interview; rounds it off; asks whether interviewee has questions.
- *Clear*: asks simple, easy, short questions; no jargon.
- *Gentle*: lets people finish; gives them time to think; tolerates pauses.
- *Sensitive*: listens attentively to what is said and how it is said; is empathetic in dealing with the interviewee.
- *Open*: responds to what is important to interviewee and is flexible.
- *Steering*: knows what he or she wants to find out.
- *Critical*: is prepared to challenge what is said—for example, dealing with inconsistencies in interviewees' replies.
- *Remembering*: relates what is said to what has previously been said.
- *Interpreting*: clarifies and extends meanings of interviewees' statements, but without imposing meaning on them.

To Kvale's list I would add the following.

- *Balanced*: does not talk too much, which may make the interviewee passive, and does not talk too little, which may result in the interviewee feeling he or she is not talking along the right lines.
- *Ethically sensitive*: is sensitive to the ethical dimension of interviewing, ensuring the interviewee appreciates what the research is about, its purposes, and that his or her answers will be treated confidentially.

Tips and skills
Interviewees and distance

Sometimes you may need to contact interviewees who are a long way from you—perhaps even abroad. While interviewing in qualitative research is usually of the face-to-face kind, time and money restrictions may mean that you will need to interview such people in a less personal context. There are two possibilities. One is telephone interviewing. The cost of a telephone interview is much less than the cost involved in travelling long distances. Telephone interviewing in qualitative research is discussed in a separate section below. Another possibility is the online interview, in which the interview is conducted by email. This method is described in Chapter 26.

Kinds of questions

The kinds of questions asked in qualitative interviews are highly variable. Kvale (1996) has suggested nine different kinds of question. Most interviews will contain virtually all of them, although interviews that rely on lists of topics are likely to follow a somewhat looser format. Kvale's nine types of question are as follows.

1. *Introducing questions*: 'Please tell me about when your interest in *X* first began?'; 'Have you ever . . . ?'; 'Why did you go to . . . ?'.

Figure 18.1

Formulating questions for an interview guide

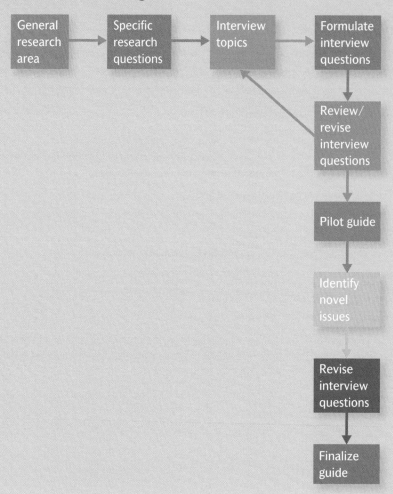

2. *Follow-up questions*: getting the interviewee to elaborate his or her answer, such as 'What do you mean by that?'; even 'Yeeees?' Kvale suggests that repeating significant words in an answer can stimulate further explanation. See Research in focus 18.4 for an example.

3. *Probing questions*: following up what has been said through direct questioning, such as 'Could you say some more about that?'; 'You said earlier that you prefer not to X. Could you say what kinds of things have put you off X?'; 'In what ways do you find X disturbing?'

4. *Specifying questions*: 'What did you do then?'; 'How did X react to what you said?'; 'What effect did X have on you?' See Research in focus 18.4 for an example.

5. *Direct questions*: 'Do you find it easy to keep smiling when serving customers?'; 'Are you happy with the way you and your husband decide how money should be spent?' Such questions are perhaps best left until towards the end of the interview, in order not to influence the direction of the interview too much.

6. *Indirect questions*: 'What do most people round here think of the ways that management treats its staff?', perhaps followed up by 'Is that the way you feel too?', in order to get at the individual's own view.

7. *Structuring questions*: 'I would now like to move on to a different topic.'

Research in focus 18.4
Using a semi-structured interview: research on female offenders

Davies (2000) has usefully described the course of her research on female offenders. Two factors seem to have been instrumental in her decision to employ semi-structured interviewing. First, she felt that her research questions—'exploring the types of crimes individuals engaged in and details of the ways in which they conducted them' (2000: 85)—were an important factor in her decision to use this method. A second factor was its consistency with the principles of feminist research, 'because such interviews seek not to be exploitative but to be appreciative of the position of women' (2000: 86). Davies interviewed female offenders, both in prison, which necessitated a lengthy series of negotiations about access, and in the community. The latter were selected through snowball sampling, whereby some willing interviewees put her in touch with others. Davies describes her interview strategy as follows: 'Most important is to listen, then prompt and encourage when appropriate without "leading", and to steer the discussion back on track if it appears to be heading down a less promising avenue' (2000: 91). At one point she employed as a follow-up question, repeating the interviewee's words, a tactic mentioned by Kvale (1996; see above), and then followed up the interviewee's reply with what Kvale calls a probing question:

PD   You mentioned security tags and foil?

F   It depended on the shops—some shops we would just . . . when we just started out we didn't know about the foil so we used ter take in a pair of wire clippers, take them off and dump them in the changing room but they made one hell of a crack—have you heard wire being cut? It made a hell of a bang so we just used ter take them off and shove them anywhere—yer know what I mean—somewhere they wouldn't be found like in a pocket of someone else's coat and . . . then we found out about the foil an we started doing that.

PD   How did you find out about that? (Davies 2000: 91)

Interviews were transcribed and written up within a day or two of taking place so that any particular nuances or impressions would not be forgotten.

8. *Silence*: allow pauses to signal that you want to give the interviewee the opportunity to reflect and amplify an answer.

9. *Interpreting questions*: 'Do you mean that your leadership role has had to change from one of encouraging others to a more directive one?'; 'Is it fair to say that what you are suggesting is that you don't mind being friendly towards customers most of the time, but when they are unpleasant or demanding you find it more difficult?'

As this list suggests, one of the main ingredients of the interview is listening—being very attentive to what the interviewee is saying or even not saying. It means that the interviewer is active without being too intrusive—a difficult balance. But it also means that, just because the interview is being recorded (the generally recommended practice whenever it is feasible), the interviewer cannot

take things easy. In fact, an interviewer must be very attuned and responsive to what the interviewee is saying and doing. This is also important because something like body language may indicate that the interviewee is becoming uneasy or anxious about a line of questioning. An ethically sensitive interviewer will not want to place undue pressure on the person he or she is talking to and will need to be prepared to cut short that line of questioning if it is clearly a source of concern.

It is also likely that the kinds of questions asked will vary in terms of the different stages of a qualitative interview. Charmaz (2002) distinguishes three types of questions in this connection. She was in fact writing in the context of interviewing for a project guided by grounded theory (see Chapter 22), but her suggestions have a more general applicability. She distinguishes:

- *Initial open-ended questions*: Examples are: 'What events led to . . . ?'; 'What was your life like prior to . . .?'; 'Is this organization typical of others you have worked in?'

- *Intermediate questions*: 'How did you feel about . . . when you first learned about it?'; 'What immediate impacts did . . . have on your life?'; 'What do you like most/least about working in this organization?'

- *Ending questions*: 'How have your views about . . . changed?; 'What advice would you give now to someone who finds that he or she must get experience . . . ?'; 'If you had your time again, would you choose to work for this organization?'

Most questions are likely to be of the intermediate kind in any interview guide, and in practice there is likely to be overlap between the three kinds. None the less, this is a useful distinction to bear in mind.

Remember as well that in interviews you are going to ask about different kinds of things, such as:

- values—of interviewee, of group, of organization;

- beliefs—of interviewee, of others, of group;

- behaviour—of interviewee, of others;

- formal and informal roles—of interviewee, of others;

- relationships—of interviewee, of others;

- places and locales;

- emotions—particularly of the interviewee, but also possibly of others;

- encounters;

- stories.

Try to vary the questioning in terms of types of question (as suggested by Kvale's nine types, which were outlined above) *and* the types of phenomena you ask about.

Vignette questions in qualitative interviews

It is also worth bearing in mind that, although there may be times when you want to ask fairly general questions, these are frequently best avoided. Mason (2002) counsels against the use of such questions, arguing that, when they are used, interviewees usually ask the interviewer to clarify what is meant by or to contextualize the question. Vignette questions may be used in qualitative interviewing as well as in structured interviewing (see Chapter 8) and represent one way of asking specific questions. In qualitative research, vignette questions can be employed to help to ground interviewees' views and accounts of behaviour in particular situations (Barter and Renold

1999). By presenting interviews with concrete and realistic scenarios, the researcher can elicit a sense of how certain contexts mould behaviour. Hughes (1998) employed the technique in a study of perceptions among drug injectors of HIV risk. This is a field of research in which context has been shown to be important, because injectors' willingness to engage in risky behaviour is influenced by situational factors. A scenario was produced that presented risk behaviour scenarios that two hypothetical drug injectors have to address. The vignette helped to reveal the kinds of behaviour interviewees felt that injectors *should* engage in (such as protected sex) and how they felt the hypothetical injectors *would* behave (such as unprotected sex in particular situations). Hughes argues that such an approach is particularly valuable with sensitive topics of this kind and for eliciting a range of responses to different contexts.

Photographs in qualitative interviews

A further way in which questioning in qualitative interviews may be grounded is through the use of photographs. The use of photographs in interviews was explored in the context of visual ethnography in Chapter 17 but is briefly covered here to present some further thoughts in the specific context of interviewing. The use of photographs in this way is often referred to as *photo elicitation*, which has been defined as 'the simple idea of inserting a photograph into a research interview' (Harper 2002: 13). Photographs that are part of the interviewee's collection or ones that he or she has taken for the purpose of the research may be used as a stimulus for questioning. Harper argues that using photographs (or indeed other visual media) in interviews may serve several useful roles:

- Images may help to ground the researcher's interview questions. The kinds of things in which social researchers are interested are often quite difficult for others to relate to. Using a photograph may help to provide both parties to the interview with a meaningful context for their discussion.

- Stimulating interviewees to engage visually with familiar settings and objects may help them to think about things that they take for granted in different ways.

- The use of photographs may stimulate the interviewee to remember people or events or situations that might otherwise have been forgotten.

However, Harper also reminds us that using photographs in qualitative interviews does not necessarily result in superior interviews. He cites the case of a study

Research in focus 18.5
A photo-elicitation study of inter-racial families

Twine (2006) discusses her use in several different countries of photo-elicitation interviews designed to explore racial consciousness in inter-racial families. In one study, she used family photographs to explore with 'white mothers of African-descent children' issues of cultural identity and the practices through which identity is generated, and how racial identities shift over time. The photographs were explored in terms of what was important about them to the interviewee. What the photographs in tandem with the interviews allowed her to reveal is that the images of apparent familial and racial harmony occluded an underlying opposition to the inter-racial partnership that was created. This opposition was found on both sides of the family. However, the use of both the photographs and the interview generated a balanced account in which the discord was tempered by considerable harmony. Referring to the particular photo-elicitation interview that is the focus of her article, Twine (2006: 507) writes: 'The photo-interview combined with my analysis of the photographs brought into sharp relief the emphasis that I had placed on conflicts, tensions and racial troubles while not considering the degree of social cohesion that existed.' Twine argues that the photographs provided an opportunity and pretext for the interviewees to reflect on the struggles of the past in relation to the present and to reframe their understanding of the significance of the photographs. What emerges is a balanced account of harmony and disharmony and of change in relationships in connection with the life course.

he conducted of farmers in the USA. The research sought to understand farmers' perspectives on a host of issues such as how they defined the land and the animals they nurtured and their views of such things as changes in farming technology. However, Harper writes that the photographs he took 'did not evoke deep reflections on the issues I was interested in' and 'did not *break the frame* of farmers' normal views' (Harper 2002: 20; emphasis in original). He suggests that the photographs may have been too familiar in appearance to farmers, in that they possibly resembled images that regularly appear in farming magazines. Harper found that, when he subsequently took aerial photographs and used historical ones, farmers were more reflective in their interviews. This experience from one of the leading exponents of the use of visual research methods reminds us that there is no way of guaranteeing interesting data in qualitative investigations and suggests that a preparedness to experiment when things do not go quite according to plan can pay dividends.

Using an interview guide: an example

Research in focus 18.6 is taken from an interview from a study of visitors to Disney theme parks (Bryman 1999). The study was briefly mentioned in Chapter 7 as an example of a snowball sampling procedure. The interviews were concerned to elicit visitors' interpretations of the

parks that had been visited. The interview is with a man who was in his sixties and his wife who was two years younger. They had visited Walt Disney World in Orlando, Florida, and were very enthusiastic about their visit.

The sequence begins with the interviewer asking what would be considered a 'direct question' in terms of the list of nine question types suggested by Kvale (1996) and outlined above. The replies are very bland and do little more than reflect the interviewees' positive feelings about their visit to Disney World. The wife acknowledges this when she says 'but I need to say more than that, don't I?' Interviewees frequently know that they are expected to be expansive in their answers. This sequence occurred around halfway through the interview, so the interviewees were primed by then into realizing that more details were expected. There is almost a tinge of embarrassment that the answer has been so brief and not very illuminating. The husband's answer is more expansive but not particularly enlightening.

There then follows the first of two important prompts by the interviewer. The husband's response is more interesting in that he now begins to answer in terms of the possibility that black people were under-represented in attractions like the American Adventure, which tells the story of America through tableaux and films via a debate between two audio-animatronic figures—Mark Twain and Benjamin Franklin. The second prompt yields further useful reflection, this time carrying the implication that Third World countries are under-represented in World Showcase in the Epcot Centre. The couple are clearly aware that it is the prompting that has made them provide these reflections when they say: 'Well thinking about it now, because I hadn't really given this any consideration before you started asking about it' and 'Well, like you, I hadn't thought of it like that before'. This is the whole point of prompting—to get the interviewee to think more about the topic and to provide the opportunity for a more detailed response. It is not a leading question, since the interviewees were not being asked 'Do you think that the Disney company fails to recognize the significance of black history (or ignores the Third World) in its presentation of different cultures?' There is no doubt that it is the prompts that elicit the more interesting replies, but that is precisely their role.

Research in focus 18.6
Part of the transcript of a semi-structured interview

Interviewer   OK. What were your views or feelings about the presentation of different cultures, as shown in, for example, Jungle Cruise or It's a Small World at the Magic Kingdom or in World Showcase at Epcot?

Wife   Well, I thought the different countries at Epcot were wonderful, but I need to say more than that, don't I?

Husband   They were very good and some were better than others, but that was down to the host countries themselves really, as I suppose each of the countries represented would have been responsible for their own part, so that's nothing to do with Disney, I wouldn't have thought. I mean some of the landmarks were hard to recognize for what they were supposed to be, but some were very well done. Britain was OK, but there was only a pub and a Welsh shop there really, whereas some of the other pavilions, as I think they were called, were good ambassadors for the countries they represented. China, for example, had an excellent 360 degree film showing parts of China and I found that very interesting.

Interviewer   Did you think there was anything lacking about the content?

Husband   Well I did notice that there weren't many black people at World Showcase, particularly the American Adventure. Now whether we were there on an unusual day in that respect I don't know, but we saw plenty of black Americans in the Magic Kingdom and other places, but very few if any in that World Showcase. And there was certainly little mention of black history in the American Adventure presentation, so maybe they felt alienated by that, I don't know, but they were noticeable by their absence.

Interviewer   So did you think there were any special emphases?

Husband   Well thinking about it now, because I hadn't really given this any consideration before you started asking about it, but thinking about it now, it was only really representative of the developed world, you know, Britain, America, Japan, world leaders many of them in technology, and there was nothing of the Third World there. Maybe that's their own fault, maybe they were asked to participate and didn't, but now that I think about it, that does come to me. What do you think, love?

Wife   Well, like you, I hadn't thought of it like that before, but I agree with you.

Recording and transcription

The point has already been made on several occasions that, in qualitative research, the interview is usually audio-recorded and transcribed whenever possible (see Tips and skills Why you should record and transcribe interviews). Qualitative researchers are frequently interested not just in *what* people say but also in the *way* that they say it. If this aspect is to be fully woven into an analysis, it is necessary for a complete account of the series of exchanges in an interview to be available. Also, because the interviewer is supposed to be highly alert to what is being said—following up interesting points made, prompting and probing where necessary, drawing attention to any inconsistencies in the interviewee's answers—it is best if he or she is not distracted by having to concentrate on getting down notes on what is said.

Tips and skills
Why you should record and transcribe interviews

With approaches that entail detailed attention to language, such as **conversation analysis** and **discourse analysis** (see Chapter 20), the recording of conversations and interviews is to all intents and purposes mandatory. However, researchers who use qualitative interviews and focus groups (see Chapter 19) also tend to record and then transcribe interviews. Heritage (1984: 238) suggests that the procedure of recording and transcribing interviews has the following advantages.

- It helps to correct the natural limitations of our memories and of the intuitive glosses that we might place on what people say in interviews.
- It allows more thorough examination of what people say.
- It permits repeated examinations of the interviewees' answers.
- It opens up the data to public scrutiny by other researchers, who can evaluate the analysis that is carried out by the original researchers of the data (that is, a **secondary analysis**).
- It therefore helps to counter accusations that an analysis might have been influenced by a researcher's values or biases.
- It allows the data to be reused in other ways from those intended by the original researcher—for example, in the light of new theoretical ideas or analytic strategies.

However, it has to be recognized that the procedure is very time-consuming. It also requires good equipment, usually in the form of a good-quality tape recorder and microphone but also, if possible, a transcription machine. Transcription also very quickly results in a daunting pile of paper. Also, recording equipment may be offputting for interviewees.

Tips and skills
Audio-recording interviews digitally

For years, the cassette tape recorder was the accepted medium for recording interviews and focus group sessions. In recent years, more and more researchers are using digital audio-recording devices, which can be played back on a computer with the appropriate software or on an MP3 player like an iPod. The chief advantage of a digital recording is that the recording is far superior, not least because the familiar 'hiss' that can usually be heard when playing back cassette tapes is eliminated. It is also possible to enhance the recordings so that background noise is filtered out. As a result of the superior sound quality, it is easier to transcribe interviews and also mistakes due to mishearing are less likely. Digital recordings can easily be backed up and can be played back again and again to listen to a portion that may be unclear without increasing any risk to the recording (doing this with tapes increases the chance of them snapping or of affecting the quality of the recording).

One further advantage, although one that may lie more in the future than in the present, is that it may be possible to use voice-recognition (voice-to-text) software to transcribe the interviews. This represents a massive saving on time. The problem is that, although such software is improving all the time, interviews are not an ideal medium for such software. This is because the software needs to be 'trained' to recognize a voice. However, an interview comprises as least two voices and a project will comprise several, and very often many, interviewees, which will make the process of 'training' very difficult. One solution is to back up the digital recording onto tape. This may seem a pointless thing to do, but it will result in a much crisper recording than if the interview had been recorded directly onto tape, and it is then possible to use a conventional transcribing machine. Transcribing machines replay a tape recording and have a pedal that transcribers can employ to start and stop recordings, so that they do not need to keep having to take their hands off the keyboard when transcribing. Also, if the person who is transcribing finds a certain word or portion of speech inaudible, they can use the digital recording to see if it has been picked up better on that recording. If a transcription machine is not going to be used, this issue does not arise, and the digital recorder represents the superior recording medium anyway. It should also be borne in mind that, regardless of the machine that is used, attending to such issues as using a high-quality microphone and seeking out a venue with as little extraneous noise as possible are still important to recording quality.

Some researchers have adapted to the use of speech-recognition software and the difficulty of getting interviewees voice-trained for the software by using their own voice to speak back all the recording into the microphone, so that their speech alone is processed by the software. They use a headset to listen to the recording and simultaneously speak what is said into the microphone, though it is necessary to keep on stopping and starting the recording that is being listened to.

Digital recordings are not without disadvantages. One is obviously the cost of the recording device. Second, digital audio files, like .wav ones, are huge, so that they require a lot of disk space for storage. Third, there are competing formats for both digital files and voice-to-text software, which can cause compatibility problems.

As with just about everything in conducting social research, there is a cost (other than the financial cost of recording equipment and tapes or disks), in that the use of a recorder may disconcert respondents, who become self-conscious or alarmed at the prospect of their words being preserved. Most people accede to the request for the interview to be recorded, though it is not uncommon for a small number to refuse (see Research in focus 18.7). When faced with refusal, you should still go ahead with the interview, as it is highly likely that useful information will still be forthcoming. This advice also applies to cases of a malfunction in recording equipment (again see Research in focus 18.7). Among those who do agree to be recorded, there will be some who will not get over their alarm at being confronted with a microphone. As a result, some interviews may not be as interesting as you might have hoped. In qualitative research, there is often quite a large amount of variation in the amount of time that interviews take. For example, in Chattoe and Gilbert's (1999) study of budgeting in what they call 'retired households', the twenty-six interviews they carried out lasted between thirty minutes and three hours; in the research in Research in focus 18.7, the twenty interviews varied between forty-five minutes and three hours. It should not be assumed that shorter interviews are necessarily inferior to longer ones, but very short ones that are a product of interviewee non-cooperation or anxiety about being recorded are likely to be less useful—though it is not being suggested that this applies to these researchers' shorter interviews. In the extreme, when an interview has produced very little of significance, it may not be worth the time and cost of transcription. Thankfully, such occasions are relatively unusual. If people do agree to be interviewed, they usually do so in a cooperative way and loosen up after initial anxiety about the microphone. As a result, even short interviews are often quite revealing.

Research in focus 18.7
Getting it taped and transcribed: an illustration of two problems

Rafaeli *et al.* (1997) conducted semi-structured interviews with twenty female administrators in a university business school in order to study the significance of dress at the workplace. They write:

> Everyone we contacted agreed to participate. Interviews took place in participants' offices or in a school lounge and lasted between 45 minutes and three hours. We recorded and transcribed all but two interviews: 1 participant refused to be taped, and the tape recorder malfunctioned during another interview. For interviews not taped, we recorded detailed notes. We assured all participants that their responses would remain confidential and anonymous and hired an outside contractor to transcribe the interviews. (Rafaeli *et al.* 1997: 14)

Even though, overall, this interview study was highly successful, generating eighteen interviews that were recorded and transcribed, it does show two kinds of problems qualitative interviewers can face—namely, hardware malfunctions and refusals to be recorded.

Tips and skills
Transcribing interviews

If you are doing research for a project or dissertation, you may not have the resources to pay for professional transcription, and, unless you are an accurate touch typist, it may take you a lot longer than the suggested five–six hours per hour of speech. If you have access to a transcription machine with a foot-operated stop–start mechanism, this will make the task of transcription somewhat easier. However, the important thing to bear in mind is that you must allow sufficient time for transcription and be realistic about how many interviews you are going to be able to transcribe in the time available.

The problem with transcribing interviews is that it is very time-consuming. It is best to allow around five–six hours for transcription for every hour of speech. Also, transcription yields vast amounts of paper, which you will need to wade through when analyzing the data. Beardsworth and Keil (1992: 262) report that their seventy-three interviews on vegetarianism (see Research in focus 18.3) generated 'several hundred thousand words of transcript material'. It is clear, therefore, that, while transcription has the advantage of keeping intact the interviewee's (and interviewer's) words, it does so by piling up the amount of text to be analysed. It is no wonder that writers like Lofland and Lofland (1995) advise that the analysis of qualitative data is not left until all the interviews have been completed and transcribed. To procrastinate may give the researcher the impression that he or she faces a monumental task. Also, there are good grounds for making analysis an ongoing activity, because it allows the researcher to be more aware of emerging themes that he or she may want to ask about in a more direct way in later interviews (see Research in focus 18.3 for an example). The preference for ongoing analysis is also very much recommended by proponents of approaches to qualitative data analysis like grounded theory (see Chapter 22).

Student experience
Handling large amounts of qualitative data

Rebecca Barnes found that she collected a large amount of data as a result of transcribing her recordings of semi-structured interviews but help was at hand! She writes:

> The sheer amount of data which I had collected (40 transcripts, averaging 30 pages each) was at first quite overwhelming, but using NVivo made it much more manageable.

*To read more about Rebecca's research experiences, go to the Online Resource Centre that accompanies this book at **http://www.oxfordtextbooks.co.uk/orc/brymansrm3e/**.*

Tips and skills
Conventions when using direct quotations from an interview

When transcribing an interview, it is important that the written text reproduces exactly what the interviewee said, word for word. For this reason, if there are parts of the interview that you can't hear properly on the tape recording, don't be tempted to guess or make them up, instead indicate in your transcript that there is a missing word or phrase—for example, by using the convention {???}. This helps to give the reader confidence in your data collection process. However, people rarely speak in fully formed sentences, they often repeat themselves and they may have verbal 'tics' in the form of a common word or phrase that is often repeated either through habit or just because they like it! So when it comes to writing up your research, when you will probably wish to quote directly from the interview transcripts, you may want to edit out some of these digressions for the sake of length and ease of understanding. However, you must make sure that you do not paraphrase the words of the speaker and then claim these as the actual words that were spoken, because this is misleading, and there is always the possibility that someone reading your work might suspect that people did not really speak in such a fluent way. The use of certain conventions when quoting from an interview transcript helps to overcome these problems.

- Use quotation marks to indicate that this is a direct quote or indicate this by consistently setting them out so they stand out from the main body text—for example, by indenting them or by using a different font, in a similar way to how you would quote at length from a book. This makes it immediately apparent to the reader that this is a direct quote and it enables you to differentiate between your presentation of the data and your analysis of it.

- If it is appropriate in relation to ethical considerations (see Chapter 5), indicate who is speaking in the quote, either introducing the speaker before the quote by saying something like 'As John put it', or 'Anne explained her reasons for this', or attribute the quote to the interviewee immediately afterwards—for example, by writing their pseudonym or [Interviewee 1] in square brackets.

- If you wish to quote the first sentence from a section of speech and then a sentence or two further on from the transcript, use the convention of three consecutive dots to indicate the break point.

- If an interviewee omits a word from a sentence that is a grammatical omission or if the interviewee refers to a subject in a way that does not make its meaning clear and you need to provide the readers with more contextual information so that they can understand the quote, use the convention of brackets or square brackets in which you insert the words you have added.

- Finally, one of the most difficult things about presenting interview data as part of your analysis is that it can take some effort and perseverance to create a smooth flow to the text because of the switches between your 'voice', as the researcher, and the 'voices' of the interviewees, which can make the text seem quite fragmented. For this reason it is important to introduce direct quotes before you present them and then take a sentence or two of your analysis to explain in your own words how you have interpreted them. In this way you construct a narrative that guides the reader through your data and shows why you have chosen the particular quotes you have as illustrative of particular themes or concepts.

It is easy to take the view that transcription is a relatively unproblematic translation of the spoken into the written word. However, given the reliance on transcripts in qualitative research based on interviews, the issue should not be taken lightly. Transcribers need to be trained in much the same way that interviewers do. Moreover, even among experienced transcribers, errors can creep in. Poland (1995) has provided some fascinating examples of mistakes in transcription that can be the result of many different factors (mishearing, fatigue, carelessness). For example, one transcript contained the following passage:

> I think unless we want to become like other countries, where people have, you know, democratic freedoms . . .

But the actual words on the audiotape were:

> I think unless we want to become like other countries, where people have no democratic freedoms . . .
> (Poland 1995: 294)

Steps clearly need to be taken to check on the quality of transcription.

It is also worth bearing in mind that it may not always be feasible to record interviews. Grazian (2003) conducted his ethnographic research into the manufacture of authentic blues music in Chicago blues clubs. He started out using a cassette recorder to record interviews with musicians and members of the audience but gave up. He writes that there were several reasons for giving up on the use of tape recorders, of which one was the following: 'I was observing settings where the combination of loud music and chattering customers made the level of background noise extremely high, and thus a recording device would have proved useless' (Grazian 2003: 246).

Tips and skills
Transcribing sections of an interview

Some interviews or at least large portions of them are sometimes not very useful, perhaps because interviewees are reticent or not as relevant to your research topic as you had hoped. There seems little point in transcribing material that you know is unlikely to be fruitful. This is a common experience among qualitative interviewers. Gerson and Horowitz (2002: 211) observe that some qualitative interviews are 'uninspiring and uninteresting', so if you do find some interviews or portions of them that are not terribly illuminating, you may not be alone in this respect. It may be that, for some of your interviews, it would be better to listen to them closely first, at least once or more usually twice and then transcribe only those portions that you think are useful or relevant. However, this may mean that you miss certain things or that you have to go back to the tapes at a later stage in your analysis to try and find something that emerges as significant only later on.

Student experience
The advantage of transcribing your own interviews

Rebecca Barnes chose to transcribe herself the recordings of her semi-structured interviews. She writes:

> I tape-recorded all interviews, and I then transcribed all the tapes myself. I chose to transcribe the interviews myself because, whilst it was an arduous and very time-consuming task, it offered great benefits in terms of bringing me closer to the data, and encouraging me to start to identify key themes, and to become aware of similarities and differences between different participants' accounts.

To read more about Rebecca's research experiences, go to the Online Resource Centre that accompanies this book at **http://www.oxfordtextbooks.co.uk/orc/brymansrm3e/**.

Flexibility in the interview

One further point to bear in mind is that you need to be generally flexible in your approach to interviewing in qualitative research. This advice is not just to do with needing to be responsive to what interviewees say to you and following up interesting points that they make. Such flexibility *is* important and is an important reminder that, with semi-structured interviewing, you should not turn the interview into a kind of structured interview but with **open questions**. Flexibility is important in such areas as varying the order of questions, following up leads, and clearing up inconsistencies in answers. Flexibility is important in other respects, such as coping with audio-recording equipment breakdown and refusals by interviewees to allow a recording to take place (see Research in focus 18.7). A further element is that interviewers often find that, as soon as they switch off their recording equipment, the interviewee continues to ruminate on the topic of interest and frequently will say more interesting things than in the interview. It is usually not feasible to switch the machine back on again, so try to take some notes either while the person is talking or as soon as possible after the interview. Such 'unsolicited accounts' can often be the source of revealing information or views (Hammersley and Atkinson 1995). This is certainly what Parker found in connection with his research on three British organizations—a National Health Service District Health Authority, a building society, and a manufacturing company—which was based primarily on semi-structured interviews: 'Indeed, some of the most valuable parts of the interview took place after the tape had been switched off, the closing intimacies of the conversation being prefixed with a silent or explicit "well, if you want to know what I really think . . .". Needless to say, a visit to the toilet to write up as much as I could remember followed almost immediately' (Parker 2000: 236).

Tips and skills
Keep the recorder going

Since interviewees sometimes 'open up' at the end of the interview, perhaps just when the recording device has been switched off, there are good grounds for suggesting that you should keep it switched on for as long as possible. So, when you are winding the interview down, don't switch off the tape recorder immediately.

Student experience
After the interview comments

Tips and skills 'Keep the recorder going' suggests that valuable material may be lost if you stop recording as soon as the formal interview is over. This has also been suggested by Warren *et al.* (2003) and was also mentioned by Hannah Creane.

> One of the main issues which arose for me was that often after I had completed my interview and stopped recording, other things were said that were relevant to the interview and were often very interesting, and so unfortunately not all these points were always in my findings.

Hannah mentioned this point when dealing with the issue of whether she had encountered any ethical difficulties in her research. This is interesting, because it raises the question of the ethical status of post-interview remarks. From the interviewee's point of view, they could be regarded as 'off the record'. One way of dealing with the ethics of post-interview remarks would be to ask the interviewee whether it is alright to use them for the research once proceedings have finally come to an end.

To read more about Hannah's research experiences, go to the Online Resource Centre that accompanies this book at ***http://www.oxfordtextbooks.co.uk/orc/brymansrm3e/***.

Telephone interviewing

Telephone interviewing is quite common in survey research, as was noted in Chapter 8. However, it has not been used a great deal in qualitative research. It is likely to have certain benefits when compared to face-to-face qualitative interviewing. One of these inevitably is cost, since it will be much cheaper to conduct qualitative interviews by telephone, just as it is with survey interviewing. It is likely to be especially useful for hard-to-reach groups and when interviewer safety is a consideration. Further, it may be that asking sensitive questions by telephone will be more effective, since interviewees may be less distressed about answering when the interviewer is not physically present.

There is some evidence that there are few differences in the kinds of response that one gets when asking questions by telephone rather than in person. Sturges and Hanrahan (2004) were conducting a study of visitors' and correctional officers' views concerning visiting jail inmates in California. Because of some difficulties associated with conducting the study, some respondents had to be interviewed by phone. This allowed a comparison of responses between the telephone and face-to-face interviews. Fifteen visitors were interviewed face-to-face and nineteen by telephone. Nine prison officers were interviewed—

six face-to-face and three by telephone. Sturges and Hanrahan concluded there were no noticeable differences between the responses given in that there were 'similarities in the quantity, nature and depth of responses' (Sturges and Hanrahan 2004: 113).

Certain issues about the use of telephone interviewing in qualitative research need to be borne in mind. Most obviously, it will not be appropriate to some groups of interviewees, such as those with no or limited access to telephones. Second, it is unlikely to work well with very long interviews. It is much easier for the interviewer to terminate a telephone interview than one conducted in person. This is especially significant for qualitative interviews, which often take a long time. Third, it is not possible to observe body language to see how interviewees respond in a physical sense to questions. Body language may be important because of the interviewer's ability to discern such things as discomfort, puzzlement, or confusion. It should also be borne in mind that there can be technical difficulties with recording interviews. Special equipment is needed and there is always the possibility that the line will be poor.

My colleagues and I used qualitative telephone interviews for a study of social policy researchers (Bryman *et al.* in press; Sempik *et al.* 2007). The interviews were designed to allow us to probe more deeply into researchers' views about research quality in the field of social policy following the use of an online **questionnaire**. The interviews were conducted by a researcher who had been appointed for this specific role. We found that interviewees were quite expansive in their replies and there were no significant recording problems. No comparison with in-person interviews of the kind conducted by Sturges and Hanrahan was carried out, but the detailed replies suggested that the method can generate detailed and considered replies of the kind typically sought by qualitative researchers. When the saving of time and travel costs is taken into account, given that the interviewees were widely dispersed in the UK, the method can certainly be regarded as highly efficient when viewed in relation to the large volume of data collected.

Sampling

Sampling issues in relation to qualitative research were introduced in Chapters 16 and 17. They are given a more specific treatment here because interviewing is probably the most widely used qualitative research method.

Very often, the lack of transparency that is sometimes a feature of qualitative research (referred to in Chapter 16) is particularly apparent in relation to sampling. It is sometimes more or less impossible to discern from researchers' accounts of their methods either *how* their interviewees were selected or *how many* there were of them. Often, qualitative researchers are clear that their samples are convenience or opportunistic ones, and, on other occasions, the reader suspects that this is the case. For the study referred to in Research in focus 18.2, Lupton (1996) used four interviewers, each of whom interviewed 'personal contacts'. The resort to convenience sampling is usually the product of such factors as the availability of certain individuals who are otherwise difficult to contact, such as homeless people (Wardhaugh 1996), or a belief that, because it aims to generate an in-depth analysis, issues of representativeness are less important in qualitative research than they are in quantitative research. Sometimes, convenience samples may be the result of restrictions placed on the researcher—for example, when members of an organization select interviewees rather than give the researcher a free rein to do so.

Sometimes, a probability sampling approach is employed. The research on organizational dress by Rafaeli *et al.* (1997; see Research in focus 18.7) employed such an approach. The authors write: 'First, we identified a stratified random sample of 20 people from the population of full-time, permanent administrative employees in the organization' (Rafaeli *et al.* 1997: 13–14). The stratifying criteria were administrative section and hierarchical level. A similar kind of sampling strategy occurs when a sample of interviewees is taken (sometimes randomly, sometimes by ensuring a 'spread' in terms of stratifying criteria) from a much larger sample generated for **social survey** purposes. This approach allows the researcher to sample purposively (if not randomly) and so ensures a wide range of characteristics of interviewees. King (1994) used this approach for a study of general practitioners who had taken part in a survey of GP referrals eighteen months earlier. Similarly, for their study of media representations of social science research, Fenton *et al.* (1998) carried out a **postal questionnaire** survey of social scientists who had received coverage of their research in the **content analysis** referred to in Research in focus 12.1. A total of 123 questionnaires were posted, and, of those returned, twenty social scientists were selected to be interviewed. The interviews were of a semi-structured kind.

Purposive sampling

Most writers on sampling in qualitative research based on interviews recommend that *purposive sampling* is conducted. Such sampling is essentially strategic and entails an attempt to establish a good correspondence between research questions and sampling. In other words, the researcher samples on the basis of wanting to interview people who are relevant to the research questions.

There are two general approaches to sampling. First, snowball sampling, which was discussed in Chapter 17, is sometimes used to contact groups of people for whom there is no **sampling frame**. This approach was employed in my study of visitors to Disney theme parks and by Beardsworth and Keil in their study of vegetarians (see Research in focus 18.8).

Research in focus 18.8
A snowball sample

For their study of vegetarians, Beardsworth and Keil (1992; see Research in focus 18.3) describe their sampling approach as follows:

> The drawing of a simple random sample in order to ensure statistical representativeness is clearly impossible in that it is not feasible to enumerate the total United Kingdom population of self-defined vegetarians. . . . For these reasons it was concluded that the only practicable mode of tracing suitable respondents would be through the use of 'snowball' sampling techniques. Quite clearly, such techniques cannot possibly claim to produce a statistically representative sample, since they rely upon the social contacts between individuals to trace additional respondents. (Beardsworth and Keil 1992: 261)

Through this sampling procedure, they were able to conduct seventy-three interviews.

Second, a theoretical sampling approach might be employed (see Key concept 17.5 and Figure 17.3). This approach entails sampling interviewees until your categories achieve theoretical saturation (see Key concept 17.6) and selecting further interviewees on the basis of your emerging theoretical focus. The approach is supposed to be an iterative one—that is, one in which there is a movement backwards and forwards between sampling and theoretical reflection, but it may be that the researcher feels that his or her categories achieve theoretical saturation at a relatively early stage. For example, for their research on organization dress, which was referred to in Research in focus 18.7, Rafaeli *et al.* (1997: 14) employed initially a stratified random sampling approach (see above), but then evaluated their data 'after completing interviews with the 20 individuals selected and concluded that, because we had reached theoretical saturation (Glaser and Strauss 1967), no additional interviews were necessary'. A sampling approach that is more in tune with Glaser and Strauss's (1967) idea of theoretical sampling is provided by Finch and Mason's (1990) account of their Family Obligations Project (see Research in focus 18.9).

Research in focus 18.9
Theoretical sampling in a study of family obligations

Finch and Mason's (1990: 26) Family Obligations Project was a study of 'patterns of support, aid and assistance . . . between adult kin' in Manchester. Initially, survey research, using a structured interview, was conducted and yielded nearly 1,000 completed interviews. A sample of these interviewees was then approached to be interviewed by semi-structured interview. The initial sample for this phase of the investigation was selected purposively—that is, with specific target subgroups in mind. These were divorced and/or remarried people and the youngest group at the time of the survey (18–24 years of age). Their rationale for this purposive selection is as follows: 'Since fieldwork was principally to be concerned with understanding the process of negotiation between relatives, we decided that it would be much more useful to focus upon individuals who might currently or recently have been involved in processes of negotiation and renegotiation of family relationships' (1990: 33).

Finch and Mason sampled five at a time from the total of each of these subgroups who were willing to be interviewed again (112 in the divorced/remarried subgroup and 117 young adults). Individuals were sampled using random numbers. In addition, the authors wanted to interview the kin groups of individuals from the initial social survey as providing examples of 'negotiations between relatives over issues concerning financial or material support' (1990: 38). They decided to conduct two further interviews with the focal person in a negotiation over family obligations and one interview with each of that person's relatives. However, the sampling strategy was based on the selection not of individuals as cases but of *situations*. In order to make the data comparable, they searched out individuals and their kin who had been identified in the survey— for example, as having moved back into their parents' home following a divorce. A further element in their sampling strategy was that the authors 'tried to keep an eye on the range of experiences that [they] were studying, and to identify any obvious gaps' (1990: 43). As a result of this ongoing 'stocktaking exercise', as they call it, they identified certain gaps in their data: men, because by and large they were the focus of interviews as part of kin networks rather than initial **key informants** in their own right; unemployed people, particularly because of high levels at the time of the research; ethnic minorities; social classes I, IV, and V; widows and widowers; and stepchildren and stepgrandparents. As Finch and Mason's experience shows, the process of theoretical sampling is not only one that gives priority to theoretical significance in sampling decisions, but is also one that forces researchers to sharpen their reflections on their findings during the fieldwork process.

The chief virtue of theoretical sampling is that the emphasis is upon using theoretical reflection on data as the guide to whether more data are needed. It therefore places a premium on theorizing rather than the statistical adequacy of a sample, which may be a limited guide to sample selection in many instances.

Student experience
Purposive sampling for a student project

Several of the students who completed questionnaires about their investigations used a form of purposive sampling when they were conducting qualitative research. Isabella Robbins provided a particularly detailed account of how she went about purposive sampling of mothers for her study of decision-making in relation to childhood vaccinations and the reasons for some of her choices.

Recruitment of participants was planned to take place in my own locality, for the pragmatic reason of fitting in the collection of fieldwork with my own complex obligations. I planned to recruit mothers with contrasting socio-economic profiles, the reason being, to help make key comparisons and test and develop theoretical propositions. My plan was to recruit twenty mothers from working-class and twenty mothers from middle-class profiles in order to yield approximately forty interviews. I acknowledge that assigning the profile of class is problematic, and even more so for women whose working status is interrupted by motherhood. Their socio-economic profiles were assigned based on the mothers' current or previous job using the National Statistics Socio-Economic Classification (NS-SEC) schema.

Vaccination rates are known to differ in terms of socio-demographic profiles. In line with this, I gained access to parent and toddler groups in identifiable working-class and middle-class areas of Nottingham . . . Mothers were recruited through Parent and Toddler groups in areas with socio-economic profiles. Names of the groups and their organizers were identified from a local council publication, supplemented by other publications offering information regarding services offered to parents and children in the locality.

One of the features that is striking about this account is that Isabella employed statistics about vaccination rates as a springboard for her choices of criteria of whom to interview.

*To read more about Isabella's research experiences, go to the Online Resource Centre that accompanies this book at **http://www.oxfordtextbooks.co.uk/orc/brymansrm3e/**.*

One of the problems that the qualitative researcher faces is that it is difficult to establish at the outset how many people will be interviewed if theoretical considerations guide selection. It is impossible to know, for example, how many people should be interviewed before theoretical saturation has been achieved. To a certain extent, this is not helped by the fact that the criteria for recognizing or establishing when or whether saturation has been achieved are rarely articulated in detail (Guest et al. 2006). Also, as an investigation proceeds, it may become apparent that groups will need to be interviewed who were not anticipated at the outset. Morse (2004a) gives the example of a study of sudden infant death syndrome, which was initially to focus on parents but which, as a result of interviews with them, had to be broadened to include professionals. This necessity arose because parents' accounts flagged the importance of there being uncertainty about which groups of professionals had primary responsibility in such circumstances. With probability sampling, such considerations can be specified taking into account the size of the population and time and cost constraints.

Student experience
The need for persistence

As noted in Chapter 17, getting access to organizations can be very difficult. This is likely to be the case for researchers wanting to conduct qualitative research based on interviews, as well as for participant observers. Gareth Matthews's account of trying to gain access to employers and managers of hospitality organizations suggests that this can be difficult and that it is necessary to allow a considerable amount of time.

I needed to gain access to employers and managers of 40 hospitality establishments while I was living in Brighton. Therefore, I wrote a letter to around 200 employers, which included a description of my research aims and a rough idea as to the content of the interview questions. The letter ended by saying something along the lines of 'I will telephone early next week to try to arrange an appropriate time for the interview'. The following Monday, I telephoned all these businesses, asking to speak to the manager or employer and, referring to the letter, I requested an interview.

This strategy was not really a success. First, as I did not know the names of the individual managers and employers, not many of the people I spoke to had opened or read the letter, as it was addressed to the 'manager'. Second, while some of those in small businesses had read the letter, and were relatively easy to get hold of on the phone, it was extremely difficult to speak to the managers of large hotels—partly because there are, of course, numerous 'managers' in these organizations.

In the end, it proved useful to draw up a spreadsheet with all the relevant data on each businesses—under 'name of business', 'address', 'telephone number', etc.—and to record the responses at particular times when I telephoned. This was a good way, first, to narrow down the list by deleting those who refused to be interviewed and, second, to keep track of when I had been told the manager/employer would be likely to be around to speak to.

I had some success with this approach, but I also found that it worked well simply to walk around Brighton asking managers and employers for interviews 'on the spot'. It seemed that, when not given the easy choice of arranging or postponing the interview (which they often subsequently forgot anyway), managers/employers were more likely to agree there and then, or to ask me to come back later on the same day.

It is also worth noting that both these strategies were far more successful in the winter than in the summer, which is unsurprising considering how busy hospitality businesses are during the holiday months.

Gareth's last point suggests that it is important to be sensitive to the nature of the organizations to which you are seeking to gain access.

To read more about Gareth's research experiences, go to the Online Resource Centre that accompanies this book at http://www.oxfordtextbooks.co.uk/orc/brymansrm3e/.

As a rule of thumb, however, the broader the scope of a qualitative study and the more comparisons between groups in the sample that are required, the more interviews will need to be carried out (Warren 2002; Morse 2004b). Taking the second of these two criteria, if several comparisons are likely to be wanted—between males and females, different age groups, different types of research participants in terms of locally relevant factors—a larger sample is likely to be necessary. Also, in a study of the experience of relationship breakdown, fewer respondents are likely to be necessary if the emphasis is on those who have been formally married as opposed to the more general category of being in a relationship. Nonetheless, Warren (2002: 99) makes the interesting remark that, for a qualitative interview study to be published, the minimum number of interviews required seems to be between twenty and thirty. This suggests that, although there is an emphasis on the importance of sampling purposively in qualitative research, minimum levels of acceptability operate, although there are almost certainly exceptions to Warren's rule (for example, very intensive interviews of the kind conducted in life story interviews, where there may be just one or two interviewees). Moreover, by no means all practitioners would agree with Warren's figure. Gerson and Horowitz (2002: 223) write that 'fewer than 60 interviews cannot support convincing conclusions and more than 150 produce too much material to analyse effectively and expeditiously'. In one sense, there is no necessary clash between Warren's twenty to thirty and Gerson and Horowitz's sixty: it may be that research does get published that 'cannot support convincing conclusions'! On the other hand, it does suggest how difficult it can be to try to specify minimum sample sizes. Instead, the size of sample that is able to support convincing conclusions is likely to vary somewhat from situation to situation in theoretical sampling terms. What is likely to be crucial is to justify rigorously any sample size. See Thinking deeply 18.1 for more on this issue.

Thinking deeply 18.1
Saturation and sample size

As noted in the text, it is very difficult to know in advance how many interviews you need to conduct if theoretical saturation (see Key concept 17.6) is employed as a principle for assessing the adequacy of a sample. Further, the criteria for deciding when theoretical saturation has been achieved are more or less absent. In response to these conundrums, Guest et al. (2006) conducted some experiments with data they had collected from in-depth interviews with women in two West African countries. They had conducted and transcribed sixty interviews. They analysed the process of what they call 'data saturation', which means the number of interviews 'needed to get a reliable sense of thematic exhaustion and variability within [their] data set' (Guest et al. 2006: 65). Interestingly, they found that, by and large, data saturation was achieved once around twelve transcripts had been thematically analysed. Taking the transcripts from just one of the two West African countries, by the time twelve interviews had been examined, 92 per cent of the codes used for this batch of transcripts had been generated. Also, the codes generally did not require significant revision after twelve interviews, implying that saturation of categories was arrived at quite quickly. However, as the authors note, their sample was relatively homogenous (women at high risk of contracting HIV), and the research was narrow in scope (how these women discuss sex). Consequently, it may be that saturation was achieved at an earlier point than with qualitative studies drawing on more heterogeneous samples and with broad research foci. The experiment is instructive in terms of implying that research based on qualitative interviews can be based on quite small samples, when theoretical saturation is used as a criterion for deciding on the adequacy of the sample. What is now needed are similar experiments with different samples and topics.

Feminist research and interviewing in qualitative research

Unstructured and semi-structured interviewing have become extremely prominent methods of data gathering within a feminist research framework. In part, this is a reflection of the preference for qualitative research among feminist researchers, but it also reflects a view that the kind of interview with which qualitative research is associated allows many of the goals of feminist research to be realized. Indeed, the view has been expressed that, 'whilst several brave women in the 1980s defended quantitative methods, it is nonetheless still the case that not just qualitative methods, but the in-depth face-to-face interview has become the paradigmatic "feminist method"' (Kelly *et al.* 1994: 34). This comment is enlightening because it implies that it is not simply that qualitative research is seen by many writers and researchers as more consistent with a feminist position than quantitative research, but that, specifically, qualitative interviewing is seen as especially appropriate. The point that is being made here is not necessarily that such interviewing is somehow more in tune with feminist values than, say, ethnography (especially since it is often an ingredient of ethnographic research). Instead, it could be that the intensive and time-consuming nature of ethnography means that, although it has great potential as an approach to feminist research (see Chapter 17), qualitative interviewing is often preferred because it is usually less invasive in these respects.

However, it is specifically interviewing of the kind conducted in qualitative research that is seen as having potential for a feminist approach, not the structured interview with which social survey research is associated. Why might one type of interview be consistent with a sensitivity to feminism and the other not? In a frequently cited article, Oakley outlines the following points about the standard survey interview.

- It is a one-way process—the interviewer extracts information or views from the interviewee.
- The interviewer offers nothing in return for the extraction of information. For example, interviewers using a structured interview do not offer information or their own views if asked. Indeed, they are typically advised not to do such things because of worries about contaminating their respondents' answers.

- The interviewer–interviewee relationship is a form of hierarchical or power relationship. Interviewers arrogate to themselves the right to ask questions, implicitly placing their interviewees in a position of subservience or inferiority.
- The element of power is also revealed by the fact that the structured interview seeks out information from the perspective of the researcher.
- Because of these points, the standard survey interview is inconsistent with feminism when women interview other women. This view arises because it is seen as indefensible for women to 'use' other women in these ways.

Instead of this framework for conducting interviews, feminist researchers advocate one that establishes:

- a high level of rapport between interviewer and interviewee;
- a high degree of reciprocity on the part of the interviewer;
- the perspective of the women being interviewed;
- a non-hierarchical relationship.

In connection with the reciprocity that she advocates, Oakley noted, for example, that, in her research on the transition to motherhood, she was frequently asked questions by her respondents. She argues that it was ethically indefensible for a feminist not to answer when faced with questions of a certain kind with which she was confronted (see page 212 for an illustration of this point). For Oakley, therefore, the qualitative interview was viewed as a means of resolving the dilemmas that she encountered as a feminist interviewing other women. However, as noted in previous chapters, while this broad adherence to a set of principles for interviewing in feminist research continues, it has been tempered by a greater recognition of the possible value of quantitative research.

An interesting dilemma that is perhaps not so easily resolved is the question of what feminist researchers should do when their own 'understandings and interpretations of women's accounts would either not be shared by some of them [i.e. the research participants], and/or

Student experience
Feminism and the choice of semi-structured interviews

The potential of the semi-structured interview for feminist researchers as a means of allowing women's voices to be heard and in their own words was important to Erin Sanders in the context of her research on sex workers in Thailand.

My feminist background influenced my decision to employ feminist research methods. I used in-depth, semi-structured interviews because I wanted the women I interviewed to be able to express their ideas and their thoughts in their own way—I wanted their voices and their stories to be heard, rather than my own words and ideas directing their thoughts.

To read more about Erin's research experiences, go to the Online Resource Centre that accompanies this book at http://www.oxfordtextbooks.co.uk/orc/brymansrm3e/.

represent a form of challenge or threat to their perceptions, choices and coping strategies' (Kelly *et al.* 1994: 37). It is the first type of situation that will be examined, at least in part, because, while it is of particular significance to feminist researchers, its implications are somewhat broader. It raises the tricky question of how far the commitment of seeing through the eyes of the people you study can and/or should be stretched. Two examples are relevant here. Reinharz (1992: 28–9) cites the case of an American study by Andersen (1981), who interviewed twenty 'corporate wives', who came across as happy with their lot and were supportive of feminism only in relation to employment discrimination. Andersen interpreted their responses to her questions as indicative of 'false consciousness'—in other words, she did not really believe her interviewees. When Andersen wrote an article on her findings, the women wrote a letter rejecting her account, affirming that women can be fulfilled as wives and mothers. A similar situation confronted Millen (1997: 4.6) when she interviewed thirty-two British female scientists using 'semi-structured, in-depth individual interviewing'. As she puts it:

> There was a tension between my interpretation of their reported experience as sex-based, and the meaning the participants themselves tended to attribute to their experience, since the majority of respondents did not analyse these experiences in terms of patriarchy or sex–gender systems, but

considered them to be individualised, or as 'just something that had to be coped with'. . . . From my external, academically privileged vantage point, it is clear that sexism pervades these professions, and that men are assumed from the start by other scientists to be competent scientists of status whilst women have to prove themselves, overcome the barrier of their difference before they are accepted. These women, on the other hand, did not generally view their interactions in terms of gendered social systems. There is therefore a tension between their characterisation of their experience and my interpretation of it . . . (Millen 1997: 5.6, 5.9)

Three interesting issues are thrown up by these two accounts. First, how can such a situation arise? This is an issue that pervades qualitative research that makes claims to reveal social reality as viewed by members of the setting in question. If researchers are genuinely seeing through others' eyes, the 'tension' to which Millen refers should not arise. However, it clearly can and does, and this strongly suggests that qualitative researchers are more affected by their own perspectives and research questions when collecting and analysing data than might be expected from textbook accounts of the research process. Second, there is the question of how to handle such a 'tension'—that is, how do you reconcile the two accounts? Andersen's (1981) solution to the tension she encountered was to reinterpret her findings in terms of the conditions that engender the contentment she un-covered. Third, given that feminist research is often concerned with wider political goals of emancipation, a tension between participants' world views and the researcher's position raises moral questions about the appropriateness of imposing an interpretation that is not shared by research participants themselves. Such an imposition could hardly be regarded as consistent with the principle of a non-hierarchical relationship in the interview situation.

Therefore, while qualitative interviewing has become a highly popular research method for feminist researchers because of its malleability into a form that can support the principles of feminism, interesting questions are raised in terms of the relationship between researchers' and participants' accounts. Such questions have a significance generally for the conduct of qualitative research.

Qualitative interviewing versus participant observation

The aim of this section is to compare the merits and limi-tations of interviewing in qualitative research with those of participant observation. These are probably the two most prominent methods of data collection in qualita-tive research, so there is some virtue in assessing their strengths, a debate that was first begun many years ago (Becker and Geer 1957; Trow 1957). In this section, interviewing is being compared to participant observa-tion rather than ethnography, because the latter invari-ably entails a significant amount of interviewing. So too does participant observation, but in this discussion I will be following the principle that I outlined in Key concept 17.1—namely, that the term will be employed to refer to the specifically observational activities in which the par-ticipant observer engages. As noted in Key concept 17.1, the term 'ethnography' is being reserved for the wide range of data collection activities in which ethnogra-phers engage—one of which is participant observation—along with the written account that is a product of those activities.

Advantages of participant observation in comparison to qualitative interviewing

The following is an examination of the ways in which par-ticipant observation exhibits advantages over qualitative interviewing.

Seeing through others' eyes

As noted in Chapters 1 and 16, seeing through others' eyes is one of the main tenets of qualitative research, but, on the face of it, the participant observer would seem to be better placed for gaining a foothold on social reality in this way. The researcher's prolonged immersion in a social setting would seem to make him or her better equipped to see as others see. The participant observer is in much closer contact with people for a longer period of time; also, he or she participates in many of the same kinds of activity as the members of the social setting being studied. Research that relies on interviewing alone is likely to entail much more fleeting contacts, though in qualitative research interviews can last many hours and re-interviewing is not unusual.

Learning the native language

Becker and Geer (1957) argued that the participant observer is in the same position as a social anthropologist visiting a distant land, in that in order to understand a cul-ture the language must be learned. However, it is not sim-ply the formal language that must be understood in the case of the kinds of social research in which a participant observer in a complex urban society engages. It is also very often the 'argot'—the special uses of words and slang that are important to penetrate that culture. Such an understanding is arrived at through the observation of language use.

The taken for granted

The interview relies primarily on verbal behaviour, and as such matters that interviewees take for granted are less likely to surface than in participant observation, where such implicit features in social life are more likely to be revealed as a result of the observer's continued presence and because of the ability to observe behaviour rather than just rely on what is said.

Deviant and hidden activities

Much of what we know about criminal and deviant sub-cultures has been gleaned from participant observation. These are areas that insiders are likely to be reluctant to talk about in an interview context alone. Understanding is again likely to come through prolonged interaction. Many of the examples in Chapter 17 entailed participant observation of criminal or deviant worlds, such as drug taking, violent gangs, pilferage, illegal commerce, and hooliganism. Ethnographers conducting participant observation are more likely to place themselves in situations in which their continued involvement allows them gradually to infiltrate such social worlds and to insinuate themselves into the lives of people who might be sensitive to outsiders. For similar reasons, participant observers have found that they are able to gain access to areas like patterns of resistance at work or to groups of people who support a deviant ideology, like the National Front.

Sensitivity to context

The participant observer's extensive contact with a social setting allows the context of people's behaviour to be mapped out fully. The participant observer interacts with people in a variety of different situations and possibly roles, so that the links between behaviour and context can be forged.

Encountering the unexpected and flexibility

It may be that, because of the unstructured nature of participant observation, it is more likely to uncover unexpected topics or issues. Except with the most unstructured forms of interview, the interview process is likely to entail some degree of closure as the interview guide is put together, which may blinker the researcher slightly. Also, participant observation may be more flexible because of the tendency for interviewers to instil an element of comparability (and hence a modicum of structure) in their questioning of different people. Ditton's (1977) decision at a very late stage in the data collection process to focus on pilferage in the bakery in which he was a participant observer is an example of this feature (Research in focus 17.1).

Naturalistic emphasis

Participant observation has the potential to come closer to a naturalistic emphasis, because the qualitative researcher confronts members of a social setting in their natural environments. Interviewing, because of its nature as a disruption of members' normal flow of events, even when it is at its most informal, is less amenable to this feature. It is unsurprising, therefore, that, when referring to naturalism as a tradition in qualitative research, Gubrium and Holstein (1997; see Key concept 16.1) largely refer to studies in which participant observation was a prominent component (e.g. Whyte 1955).

Advantages of qualitative interviewing in comparison to participant observation

The following is an examination of the ways in which qualitative interviewing exhibits advantages over participant observation.

Issues resistant to observation

It is likely that there is a wide range of issues that are simply not amenable to observation, so that asking people about them represents the only viable means of finding out about them within a qualitative research strategy. For example, consider Beardsworth and Keil's (1992) research on vegetarianism (see Research in focus 18.3 and 18.8). It is not really feasible for investigators to insinuate themselves into the lives of vegetarians in order to uncover issues like reasons for their conversion to this eating strategy. For most people, vegetarianism is a matter that surfaces only at certain points, such as meals and shopping. It is not really sensible or feasible to carry out participant observation in relation to something like this, which is clearly highly episodic.

Reconstruction of events

Qualitative research frequently entails the reconstruction of events by asking interviewees to think back over how a certain series of events unfolded in relation to a current situation. Beardsworth and Keil (1992; see Research in focus 18.3 and 18.8) employed the symbolic interactionist notion of *career* to gain an understanding of how people came to be vegetarians. Similarly, for their study of the impact of male unemployment McKee and Bell (1985; see Thinking deeply 2.4, and the reference to this work in Chapter 16) asked husbands and their wives to reconstruct events following unemployment. Yet another example is Pettigrew's (1985) research on Imperial Chemicals Industries (ICI), which entailed interviewing about contemporaneous events but also included 'retrospective interviewing', as Pettigrew (1985) calls it (see Research in focus 2.16). This reconstruction of events is something that cannot be accomplished through participant observation alone. See Research in focus 18.10 for a further example.

Research in focus 18.10
Information through interviews:
research on prostitution

McKeganey and Barnard (1996) have discussed their strategies for conducting research into prostitutes and their clients. Their research was based in a red light area in Glasgow. Their approach was largely that of observer-as-participant (see Figure 17.2), in that their research was based primarily on interviews with prostitutes and their clients, as well as some (frequently accidental) observation of interactions and overheard conversations. The interviews they conducted were especially important in gaining information in relation to such areas as: how the prostitutes had moved into this line of work; permitted and prohibited sex acts; links with drug use; experience of violence; and the management of identity. In the following passage, a prostitute reconstructs her movement into prostitution:

> I was 14 and I'd run away from home. I ended up down in London where I met a pimp. . . . He'd got me a place to stay, buying me things and everything and I ended up sleeping with him as well. . . . One night we got really drunk and stoned and he brought someone in. . . . [Then] after it happened I thought it was bad, I didn't like it but at least I was getting paid for it. I'd been abused by my granddad when I was 11 and it didn't seem a million miles from that anyway. (1996: 25)

One area of particular concern to McKeganey and Barnard was the spread of HIV/AIDS infection and its implications for prostitutes and their work. This area was specifically addressed in interviews. For example:

> I've got a couple of punters who'll say I'll give you so and so if you'll do it without [a condom]. But never, I always use a condom for anal sex, oral sex and even for hand jobs, there's no way I'll let them come anywhere near me. (1996: 66)

> You still get the bam-pots [idiots] asking for sex without. I had one the other night—I said, 'where have you been living—on a desert island?' (1996: 66)

Ethical considerations

There are certain areas that could be observed—albeit indirectly through hidden hardware like a microphone—but would raise ethical considerations. The research by McKeganey and Barnard (1996; see Research in focus 18.10) on prostitution furnishes an example of this. One of the areas they were especially interested in was negotiations between prostitutes and their clients over the use of condoms in the light of the spread of HIV/AIDS infection. It is not inconceivable that such transactions could have been observed with the aid of hidden hardware and it is possible that some prostitutes would have agreed to being wired up for this purpose. However, clients would not have been party to such agreements, so that ethical principles of informed consent and invasion of privacy would have been transgressed (see Key concept 5.1). As a result, the researchers relied on interview accounts of such negotiations or of prostitutes' stances on the matter

(see Research in focus 18.10), as well as the views of a small number of clients.

Reactive effects

The question of reactive effects is by no means a straightforward matter. As with structured observation (see Chapter 11), it might be anticipated that the presence of a participant observer would result in reactive effects (see Key concept 11.4). People's knowledge of the fact that they are being observed may make them behave less naturally. However, participant observers, like researchers using structured observation, typically find that people become accustomed to their presence and begin to behave more naturally the longer they are around. Indeed, members of social settings sometimes express surprise when participant observers announce their imminent departure when they are on the verge of disengagement. Interviewers clearly do not suffer from the same kind of problem, but it could be argued that the unnatural character of the interview encounter can also be regarded as a context within which reactive effects may emerge. Participant observation also suffers from the related problem of observers disturbing the very situation being studied, because conversations and interactions will occur in conjunction with the observer that otherwise would not happen. This is by no means an easy issue to resolve and it seems likely that both participant observation and qualitative interviewing set in motion reactive effects but of different kinds.

Less intrusive in people's lives

Participant observation can be very intrusive in people's lives in that the observer is likely to take up a lot more of their time than in an interview. Interviews in qualitative research can sometimes be very long and re-interviewing is not uncommon, but the impact on people's time will probably be less than having to take observers into account on a regular basis, though it is likely that this feature will vary from situation to situation. Participant observation is likely to be especially intrusive in terms of the amount of people's time taken up when it is in organizational settings. In work organizations, there is a risk that the rhythms of work lives will be disrupted.

Longitudinal research easier

One of the advantages of participant observation is that it is inherently longitudinal in character because the observer is present in a social setting for a period of time. As a result, change and connections between events can be observed. However, there are limits to the amount of time that participant observers can devote to being away from their normal routines. Consequently, participant observation does not usually extend much beyond two to three years in duration. When participant observation is being conducted into an area of research that is episodic rather than requiring continued observation, a longer time period may be feasible. Armstrong's (1993) research on football hooliganism, which was referred to several times in Chapters 16 and 17, entailed six years of participant observation, but, since football hooligans are not engaged full-time in this area of activity, the research did not require the researcher's continued absence from his work and other personal commitments. Interviewing can be carried out within a longitudinal research design somewhat more easily because repeat interviews may be easier to organize than repeat visits to participant observers' research settings, though the latter is not impossible (e.g. Burgess 1987, who revisited the compre-

hensive school in which he had conducted participant observation). Following up interviewees on several occasions is likely to be easier than returning to research sites on a regular basis.

Greater breadth of coverage

In participant observation, the researcher is invariably constrained in his or her interactions and observations to a fairly restricted range of people, incidents, and localities. Participant observation in a large organization, for example, is likely to mean that knowledge of that organization far beyond the confines of the department or section in which the observation is carried out is likely not to be very extensive. Interviewing can allow access to a wider variety of people and situations.

Specific focus

As noted in Chapter 16, qualitative research sometimes begins with a specific focus, and indeed Silverman (1993) has been critical of the notion that it should be regarded as an open-ended form of research. Qualitative interviewing would seem to be better suited to such a situation, since the interview can be directed at that focus and its associated research questions. Thus, the research by my colleagues and myself on the police had a very specific research focus in line with its Home Office funding—namely, conceptions of leadership among police officers (Bryman, Stephens, and A Campo 1996). The bulk of the data gathering was in two police forces and entailed the interviewing of police officers at all levels using a semi-structured interview guide. Because it had such a clear focus, it was more appropriate to conduct the research by interview rather than participant observation, since issues to do with leadership notions may not crop up on a regular basis, which would make observation a very extravagant method of data collection.

Overview

When Becker and Geer (1957: 28) proclaimed in the mid-twentieth century that the 'most complete form of the sociological datum . . . is the form in which the participant observer gathers it', Trow (1957: 33) reprimanded them for making such a universal claim and argued that 'the problem under investigation properly dictates the methods of investigation'. The latter view is very much the one taken in this book. Research methods are appropriate to researching some issues and areas but not others. The discussion of the merits and limitations of participant observation and qualitative interviews is meant simply to draw attention to some of the considerations that might be taken into account if there is a genuine opportunity to use one or the other in a study.

Equally, and to repeat an earlier point, the comparison is a somewhat artificial exercise, because participant observation is usually carried out as part of ethnographic research and as such it is usually accompanied by interviewing as well as other methods. In other words, participant observers frequently buttress their observations with methods of data collection that allow them access to important areas that are not amenable to observation. However, the aim of the comparison was to provide a kind of balance sheet in considering the strengths and limitations of a reliance on either participant observation or qualitative interview alone. Its aim is to draw attention to some of the factors that might be taken into account in deciding how to plan a study and even how to evaluate existing research.

Checklist

Issues to consider for your qualitative interview

○ Have you devised a clear and comprehensive/informative way of introducing the research to interviewees?

○ Does your interview guide clearly relate to your research questions?

○ Have you piloted the guide with some appropriate respondents?

○ Have you thought about what you will do if your interviewee does not turn up for the interview?

○ Does the guide contain a good mixture of different kinds of questions, such as probing, specifying, and direct questions?

○ Have you ensured that interviews will allow novel or unexpected themes and issues to arise?

○ Is your language in the questions clear, comprehensible, and free of unnecessary jargon?

○ Are your questions relevant to the people you are proposing to interview?

○ Does your interview guide include requests for information about the interviewee, such as his or her age, work experience, position in the firm?

○ Have your questions been designed to elicit reflective discussions so that interviewees are not tempted to answer in 'yes' or 'no' terms?

○ Do your questions offer a real prospect of seeing the world from your interviewees' point of view rather than imposing your own frame of reference on them?

○ Are you familiar with the setting(s) in which the interviews will take place?

○ Are you thoroughly familiar with and have you tested your recording equipment?

○ Have you thought about how you will present yourself in the interview, such as how you will be dressed?

○ Have you thought about how you will go about putting into operation the criteria of a good interviewer?

Key points

- Interviewing in qualitative research is typically of the unstructured or semi-structured kind.
- In qualitative research, interviewing may be the sole method in an investigation or may be used as part of an ethnographic study, or indeed in tandem with another qualitative method.
- Qualitative interviewing is meant to be flexible and to seek out the world views of research participants.
- If an interview guide is employed, it should not be too structured in its application and should allow some flexibility in the asking of questions.
- The qualitative interview should be recorded and then transcribed.
- As with ethnographic research, investigations using qualitative interviews tend not to employ random sampling to select participants.
- The qualitative interview has become an extremely popular method of data collection in feminist studies.
- Whether to use participant observation or qualitative interviews depends in large part on their relative suitability to the research questions being addressed. However, it must also be borne in mind that participant observers invariably conduct some interviews in the course of their investigations.

Questions for review

- Outline the main types of interview employed by qualitative researchers.

Differences between the structured interview and qualitative research interviews

- How does qualitative interviewing differ from structured interviewing?

Asking questions in the qualitative interview

- What are the differences between unstructured and semi-structured interviewing?
- Could semi-structured interviewing stand in the way of flexibility in qualitative research?
- What are the differences between life history and oral history interviews?
- What kinds of consideration need to be borne in mind when preparing an interview guide?
- What kinds of question might be asked in an interview guide?
- What kinds of skills does the interviewer need to develop in qualitative interviewing?
- Why is it important to record and transcribe qualitative interviews?
- What role might vignette questions play in qualitative interviewing?

Sampling

- Compare theoretical sampling and snowball sampling.

Feminist research and interviewing in qualitative research

- Why has the qualitative interview become such a prominent research method for feminist researchers?

- What dilemmas might be posed for feminist researchers using qualitative interviewing?

Qualitative interviewing versus participant observation

- Outline the relative advantages and disadvantages of qualitative interviewing and participant observation.

- Does one method seem more in tune with the preoccupations of qualitative researchers than the other?

 Online Resource Centre

http://www.oxfordtextbooks.co.uk/orc/brymansrm3e/

Visit the Online Resource Centre that accompanies this book to enrich your understanding of interviewing in qualitative research. Consult web links, test yourself using multiple choice questions, and gain further guidance and inspiration from the Student Researcher's Toolkit.

Focus groups

Chapter outline

Chapter guide

The **focus group** method is an interview with several people on a specific topic or issue. It has been used extensively in market research but has only relatively recently made inroads into social research. This chapter explores:

- the possible reasons for preferring focus group interviews to individual interviews of the kind discussed in the previous chapter;
- how focus groups should be conducted in terms of such features as the need for recording, the number and size of groups, how participants can be selected, and how direct the questioning should be;
- the significance of interaction between participants in focus group discussions;
- the suggestion that the focus group method fits particularly well with a feminist research approach;
- some practical difficulties with focus group sessions, such as the possible loss of control over proceedings and the potential for unwanted group effects.

Introduction

We are used to thinking of the interview as something that involves an interviewer and one interviewee. Most textbooks reinforce this perception by concentrating on individual interviews. The focus group technique is a method of interviewing that involves more than one, usually at least four, interviewees. Essentially it is a group interview. Some authors draw a distinction between the focus group and the group interview techniques. Three reasons are sometimes put forward to suggest a distinction.

- Focus groups typically emphasize a specific theme or topic that is explored in depth, whereas group interviews often span very widely.
- Sometimes group interviews are carried out so that the researcher is able to save time and money by carrying out interviews with a number of individuals simultaneously. However, focus groups are not carried out for this reason.
- The focus group practitioner is invariably interested in the ways in which individuals discuss a certain issue *as members of a group*, rather than simply as individuals. In other words, with a focus group the researcher will be interested in such things as how people respond to each other's views and build up a view out of the interaction that takes place within the group.

However, the distinction between the focus group method and the group interview is by no means clear-cut, and the two terms are frequently employed interchangeably. Nonetheless, the definition proposed in Key concept 19.1 provides a starting point.

Most focus group researchers undertake their work within the traditions of **qualitative research**. This means that they are explicitly concerned to reveal how the group participants view the issues with which they are confronted; therefore, the researcher will aim to provide a fairly unstructured setting for the extraction of their views and perspectives. The person who runs the focus groups session is usually called the *moderator* or *facilitator*, and he or she will be expected to guide each session but not to be too intrusive.

Another general point about the focus group method is that, while it is gaining in popularity at the moment, it is by no means a new technique. It has been used for many years in market research, where it is employed for such purposes as testing responses to new products and advertising initiatives (see Thinking deeply 19.1 for an example). In fact, there is a large literature within market research to do with the practices that are associated with focus group research and their implementation (e.g. Calder 1977).

Key concept 19.1
What is the focus group method?

The focus group method is a form of group interview in which: there are several participants (in addition to the moderator/facilitator); there is an emphasis in the questioning on a particular fairly tightly defined topic; and the accent is upon interaction within the group and the joint construction of meaning. As such, the focus group contains elements of two methods: the group interview, in which several people discuss a number of topics; and what has been called a focused interview, in which interviewees are selected because they 'are known to have been involved in a particular situation' (Merton *et al.* 1956: 3) and are asked about that involvement. The focused interview may be administered to individuals or to groups. Thus, the focus group method appends to the focused interview the element of interaction within groups as an area of interest and is more focused than the group interview.

Thinking deeply 19.1
The real and the unreal thing: focus groups in market research

On 23 April 1985 a product was launched that proved to be one of the greatest marketing blunders in business history. On that day, the Coca-Cola company not only launched what it called its New Coke, but it removed from sale the old one, on which the massive corporation had been built. New Coke was a flop and the public clamoured for the return of its predecessor, in spite of assurances from the company that people would get used to the new formula and get to like it better. Yet close attention to data drawn from focus group research that the company had commissioned in the lead-up to the launch of New Coke might have prevented the disaster from happening. In 1982 and 1983 focus group research was conducted across the USA. At one point in each session, local consumers were presented with a scenario in which they were told that a new formula for a certain product had been introduced and that the response to it was very favourable. The participants were then asked how *they* would feel when that product came to their town and replaced the traditional one. The response to the prospect of new, improved Budweiser beer and of Hershey chocolate bars being replaced was positive. However, when the replacement of Coke was being considered, the consumers became vehemently antagonistic to the idea. Taste tests had shown that consumers liked New Coke, but they had not been asked how they would feel if traditional Coke was taken off supermarket shelves. The focus groups made it clear how they would feel, but Coca-Cola's chief executive officer was determined to plough ahead, and his assistant, who liaised with the firm conducting the focus groups, chose to follow his boss's lead.

Sources: Pendergrast (1993) and Greising (1998).

One final general point to register is that there is growing interest in the use of online focus groups, which will be covered in the context of Internet-based research methods in Chapter 26. There is evidence that, although they tend to be shorter than comparable face-to-face focus groups, they can generate a considerable amount of relevant data for the researcher (Reid and Reid 2005). When this is viewed in relation to the saving in time travelling and cost for both researchers and participants, it is clear that this is a form of the method that is likely to be used more and more in the future.

Uses of focus groups

What are the uses of the focus group method? In many ways its uses are bound up with the uses of qualitative research in general, but, over and above these, the following points can be registered.

- The original idea for the focus group—the focused interview—was that people who were known to have had a certain experience could be interviewed in a relatively unstructured way about that experience. The bulk of the discussion by Merton *et al.* (1956) of the notion of the focused interview was in terms of individual interviews, but their book also considered the extension of the method into group interview contexts. Subsequently, the focus group has become a popular method for researchers examining the ways in which people in conjunction with one another construe the general topics in which the researcher is interested. One of the best-known studies using the method in the context of a social scientific topic is Morgan and Spanish's (1985) study of the ways in which people organize knowledge about health issues. Their special interest was the question of people's knowledge about who has heart attacks and why they have them. Thus, the emphasis was on how focus group participants make sense of the causation of heart attacks in terms of the knowledge they have picked up over the years. However, a major impetus for the growing use of focus groups in social research has been their intensive use in the field of media and cultural studies. The growing emphasis in these fields is on what is known as 'audience reception'— how audiences respond to television and radio programmes, films, newspaper articles, and so on (McGuigan 1992; Fenton *et al.* 1998: ch. 1). An influential study in this context was Morley's (1980) research on *Nationwide*, a British news programme shown in the early evening that was popular in the 1970s. Morley organized focus groups made up of specific categories of people (for example, managers, trade unionists, students) and showed them recordings of the programme. He found that the different groups arrived at somewhat divergent interpretations of the programmes they had watched, implying that meaning does not reside solely in the programmes but also in the ways in which they are watched and inter-

preted. This research and the increasing attention paid to audience reception set in motion a growth of interest in the use of the focus group method for the study of audience interpretations of cultural and media 'texts'.

- The technique allows the researcher to develop an understanding about *why* people feel the way they do. In a normal individual interview the interviewee is often asked about his or her reasons for holding a particular view, but the focus group approach offers the opportunity of allowing people to probe each other's reasons for holding a certain view. This can be more interesting than the sometimes predictable question-followed-by-answer approach of normal interviews. For one thing, an individual may answer in a certain way during a focus group, but, as he or she listens to others' answers, he or she may want to qualify or modify a view; or alternatively may want to voice agreement to something that he or she probably would not have thought of without the opportunity of hearing the views of others. These possibilities mean that focus groups may also be very helpful in the elicitation of a wide variety of different views in relation to a particular issue.

- In focus groups participants are able to bring to the fore issues in relation to a topic that they deem to be important and significant. This is clearly an aim of individual interviews too, but, because the moderator has to relinquish a certain amount of control to the participants, the issues that concern them can surface. This is clearly an important consideration in the context of qualitative research, since the viewpoints of the people being studied are an important point of departure.

- In conventional one-to-one interviewing, interviewees are rarely challenged; they might say things that are inconsistent with earlier replies or that patently could not be true, but we are often reluctant to point out such deficiencies. In the context of a focus group, individuals will often argue with each other and challenge each other's views. This process of arguing means that the researcher may stand a chance of ending up with more realistic accounts of what people think, because they are forced to think about and possibly revise their views.

- The focus group offers the researcher the opportunity to study the ways in which individuals collectively make sense of a phenomenon and construct meanings around it. It is a central tenet of theoretical positions like **symbolic interactionism** that the process of coming to terms with (that is, understanding) social phenomena is not undertaken by individuals in isolation from each other. Instead, it is something that occurs in interaction and discussion with others. In this sense, therefore, focus groups reflect the processes through which meaning is constructed in everyday life and to that extent can be regarded as more naturalistic (see Key concept 2.4 on the idea of **naturalism**) than individual interviews (Wilkinson 1998).

Conducting focus groups

There are a number of practical aspects of the conduct of focus group research that require some discussion.

Recording and transcription

As with interviewing for qualitative research, the focus group session will work best if it is recorded and subsequently transcribed. The following reasons are often used to explain this preference.

- One reason is the simple difficulty of writing down not only exactly what people say but also who says it. In an individual interview you might be able to ask the respondent to hold on while you write something down, but to do this in the context of an interview involving several people would be extremely disruptive.

- The researcher will be interested in who expresses views within the group, such as whether certain individuals seem to act as opinion leaders or dominate the discussion. This also means that there is an interest in ranges of opinions within groups; for example, in a session, does most of the range of opinion derive from just one or two people or from most of the people in the group?

- A major reason for conducting focus group research is the fact that it is possible to study the processes whereby meaning is collectively constructed within each session (see above). It would be very difficult to do this by taking notes, because of the need to keep track of *who* says what (see also previous point). If this element is lost, the dynamics of the focus group session would also be lost, and a major rationale for doing focus group interviews rather than individual ones would be undermined.

- Like all qualitative researchers, the focus group practitioner will be interested in not just what people say but *how* they say it, for example, the particular language that they employ. There is every chance that the nuances of language will be lost if the researcher has to rely exclusively on notes.

It should be borne in mind that transcribing focus group sessions is more complicated and hence more time-consuming than transcribing traditional interview recordings. This is because you need to take account of *who* is talking in the session, as well as what is said. This is sometimes difficult, since people's voices are not always easy to distinguish. Also, people sometimes talk over each other, which can make **transcription** even more difficult. In addition, it is extremely important to ensure that you equip yourself with a very high-quality microphone, which is capable of picking up voices, some of which may be quite faint, from many directions. Focus group **transcripts** always seem to have more missing bits because of lack of audibility than transcripts from conventional interviews.

Tips and skills
Transcription of a focus group interview

In Tips and skills 'Transcribing sections of an interview' (Chapter 18), I pointed out that it may not always be desirable or feasible to transcribe the whole of the interview. The same applies to focus group research, which is often more difficult and time-consuming to transcribe than personal interview recordings because of the number of speakers who are involved. The suggestions I made in Chapter 18 in relation to transcribing sections of an interview therefore apply equally well to focus group recordings.

How many groups?

How many groups do you need? Table 19.1 provides data on the number of groups and other aspects of the composition of focus groups in several studies based on this method and follows a similar table in Deacon, Pickering, Golding, and Murdock (1999) in taking the view that this is a helpful way of providing basic information on this issue. As Table 19.1 suggests, there is a good deal of variation in the numbers of groups used in the studies referred to, with a range from eight to fifty-two. However, there does seem to be a tendency for the range mainly to be from ten to fifteen.

Clearly, it is unlikely that just one group will suffice the needs of the researcher, since there is always the possibility that the responses are particular to that one group. Obviously, time and resources will be a factor, but there are strong arguments for saying that too many groups will be a waste of time. Calder (1977) proposes that, when the moderator reaches the point that he or she is able to anticipate fairly accurately what the next group is going to say, then there are probably enough groups already. This notion is very similar to the *theoretical saturation* criterion that was briefly introduced in Key concept 17.6. In other words, once your major analytic categories have been saturated, there seems little point in continuing, and so it would be appropriate to bring data collection to a halt. For their study of audience discussion programmes, Livingstone and Lunt (1994: 181; see Table 19.1) used this criterion: 'The number of focus groups was determined by continuing until comments and patterns began to repeat and little new material was generated.' When this point of theoretical saturation is reached, as an alternative to terminating data collection, there may be a case for moving on to an extension of the issues that have been raised in the focus group sessions that have been carried out.

One factor that may affect the number of groups is whether the researcher feels that the kinds and range of views are likely to be affected by socio-demographic factors such as age, gender, class, and so on. Many focus group researchers like to use stratifying criteria like these to ensure that groups with a wide range of features will be included. If so, a larger number of groups may be required to reflect the criteria. In connection with the research described in Research in focus 19.1, Kitzinger (1994) writes that a large number of groups was preferred, not because of concerns about the representativeness of the views gleaned during the sessions, but in order to capture as much diversity in perspectives as possible. However, it may be that high levels of diversity are not anticipated in connection with some topics, in which case a large number of groups could represent an unnecessary expense.

One further point to bear in mind when considering the number of groups is that more groups will increase the complexity of your analysis. For example, Schlesinger *et al.* (1992: 29; see Table 19.1) report that the fourteen tape-recorded sessions they organized produced over 1,400 pages of transcription. This pile of paper was accumulated from discussions in each group of an average of one hour for each of the four screenings of violence that session participants were shown. Although this means that the sessions were longer than is normally the case, it does demonstrate that the amount of data to analyse can be very large, even though a total of fourteen sessions may not sound a lot to someone unfamiliar with the workings of the method.

Table 19.1

Composition of groups in focus group research

Authors	Morgan and Spanish (1985)	Schlesinger et al. (1992)	Kitzinger (1993, 1994)	Livingstone and Lunt (1994)	Lupton (1997)	Macnaghten and Jacobs (1997)	Fenton et al. (1998)	Livingstone (2006); Livingstone and Bober (2003)	Warr (2005)
Area of research	Lay health beliefs concerning heart attacks	The responses of women to watching violence	Audience responses to media messages about AIDS	Audience responses to audience discussion programmes	Responses to controversies concerning diet and health	Public understanding of and identification with sustainable development	Audience responses to reporting of social science research	Children's use and experience of using the Internet	Expectations regarding intimate relationships in socio-economically disadvantaged contexts
Number of groups	9	14	52	12	12	8 (each group had 2 sessions)	14	14	8
Size range of groups	4–5	5–9	Not specified but appears to be 3–9 or 3–10	4–8	3–5	6–10	4–6	Not clear	4–9
Average (mean) size of groups	4.4	6.6	6.75	5.75	4.1	Approximately 8	5	4	Not clear
Stratifying criteria (if any)	None mentioned, but all participants needed to be aged 35–50 and those who had experienced a heart attack were excluded	Experience of violence, Scottish/English, ethnicity, class	No, but groups made up of specific groups (e.g. civil engineers, retirement club members, male prostitutes)	None mentioned	Gender	Age, ethnicity, gender, occupation/retired, rural/urban location	Gender, education, occupation (private/public sector)	Age, gender, and school	Gender
Natural groups?	No, but all participants were mature university students	Some	Yes	No	Yes	No	Some	Yes, but picked at random by teachers	Most

Research in focus 19.1
Focus group in action: AIDS in the Media Research Project

Focus group research on the representation of AIDS in the mass media was part of a larger project on this topic. The focus groups were concerned with the examination of the ways in which 'media messages are explored by audiences and how understandings of AIDS are constructed. We were interested not solely in what people thought but in *how* they thought and *why* they thought as they did' (Kitzinger 1994: 104).

Details of the groups are in Table 19.1. Since one goal of the research was to emphasize the role of interaction in the construction of meaning, it was important to provide a platform for enhancing this feature. Accordingly, 'instead of working with isolated individuals, or collections of individuals drawn together simply for the purposes of the research, we elected to work with pre-existing groups—people who already lived, worked or socialized together' (Kitzinger 1993: 272).

As a result, the groups were made up of such collections of people as a team of civil engineers working on the same site, six members of a retirement club, intravenous drug users, and so on. The sessions themselves are described as having been 'conducted in a relaxed fashion with minimal intervention from the facilitator—at least at first' (Kitzinger 1994: 106). Each session lasted approximately two hours and was tape-recorded.

Size of groups

How large should groups be? Morgan (1998a) suggests that the typical group size is six to ten members, although the numbers in Table 19.1, which admittedly is not randomly selected and is mainly British, imply that this calculation is slightly high in terms of both the range and the mean. One major problem faced by focus group practitioners is people who agree to participate but who do not turn up on the day. It is almost impossible to control for 'no-shows' other than consciously over-recruiting, a strategy that is sometimes recommended (e.g. Wilkinson 1999a: 188).

The question of 'no-shows' aside (which almost certainly accounts for the figures at the low end of the size ranges in Table 19.1), Morgan (1998a) recommends smaller groups when participants are likely to have a lot to say on the research topic. This is likely to occur when participants are very involved in or emotionally preoccupied with the topic. He also suggests smaller groups when topics are controversial or complex and when gleaning participants' personal accounts is a major goal. Morgan (1998a: 75) recommends larger groups when involvement with a topic is likely to be low or when the researcher wants 'to hear numerous brief suggestions'. However, I am not convinced that larger groups are

Tips and skills
Number of focus groups

Focus groups take a long time to arrange, and it takes a long time to transcribe the recordings that are made. It is likely that students will not be able to include as many focus group sessions for projects or dissertations as the studies cited in this chapter. You will, therefore, need to make do with a smaller number of groups in most instances. Make sure you are able to justify the number of groups you have chosen and why your data are still significant.

necessarily superior for topics in which participants have little involvement, since it may be more difficult to stimulate discussion in such a context. Larger groups may make it even more difficult if people are rather diffident about talking about a topic about which they know little or have little experience. A topic like media representations of social science research, which most people are unlikely to have much interest in or even to have thought about, could easily have resulted in a wall of silence in large groups (Fenton *et al.* 1998; see Table 19.1).

Level of moderator involvement

How involved should the moderator/facilitator be? In qualitative research, the aim is to get at the perspectives of those being studied. Consequently, the approach should not be intrusive and structured. Therefore, there is a tendency for researchers to use a fairly small number of very general questions to guide the focus group session. Moreover, there is a further tendency for moderators to allow quite a lot of latitude to participants, so that the discussion can range fairly widely. Obviously, if the discussion goes off at a total tangent it may be necessary to refocus the participants' attention, but even then it may be necessary to be careful, because what may appear to be digressions may in fact reveal something of interest to the group participants. The advantage of allowing a fairly free rein to the discussion is that the researcher stands a better chance of getting access to what individuals see as important or interesting. On the other hand, too much totally irrelevant discussion may prove too unproductive, especially in the commercial environment of market research. It is not surprising, therefore, that, as Wilkinson (1999*a*) observes, some writers on focus groups perceive the possibility that participants come to take over the running of a session from the moderator as a problem and offer advice on how to reassert control (e.g. Krueger 1988).

One way in which the moderator may need to be involved is in responding to specific points that are of potential interest to the research questions but that are not picked up by other participants. In the extract in Research in focus 19.2 from the study of the reception of media representations of social science research from Fenton *et al.* (1998), a group of men who have been in higher education and are in private-sector employment begin to talk about the differences between the natural and the social sciences.

Research in focus 19.2
Extract from a focus group showing no moderator involvement

In the following extract, three focus group participants engage in a discussion with no intervention or involvement on the part of the moderator. The participants are discussing how people view media reporting of social science research.

R1   Essentially with the pure sciences I get an end result. Whereas with the social sciences it's pretty vague because it's very, very subjective.

R2   I suppose for me the pure sciences seem to have more control of what they are looking at because they keep control of more. Because with social sciences there are many different aspects that could have an impact and you can't necessarily control them. So it seems more difficult to pin down and therefore to some extent controversial.

R3   Pure science is more credible because you've got control over test environments, you've got an ability to test and control factually the outcome and then establish relationships between different agents or whatever. I think in social science it's always subject to interpretation. . . . I think if you want to create an easy life and be unaccountable to anybody, to obtain funding and spend your time in a stress-free way then one of the best things to do is to work in funded research and one of the best areas to do it in is in social science. (Fenton *et al.* 1998: 127)

It is interesting to see the way in which a consensus about the social sciences is built up in this discussion with a particular emphasis on the lack of control in social research and on the supposed subjectivity of interpretation when compared to the 'pure' sciences. On other occasions, a little nudge from the moderator may be required when a particularly interesting point is not followed up by other participants. An example of this is provided in

Research in focus 19.3 'Extract from a focus group showing some moderator involvement' which is from the same research, but this time the focus group is made up of women in private-sector employment and whose education is up to GCSE level. They are talking about a news item reporting research on victims of crime but that includes a number of detailed case studies of individual experiences of being a victim.

Research in focus 19.3
Extract from a focus group showing some moderator involvement

In the following extract, three focus group participants engage in a discussion with only a little intervention or involvement on the part of the moderator. The participants are discussing how people view media reporting of social science research.

R1	That was easy and interesting.
[Moderator]	Why interesting? Why easy?
R2	Because it affects all of us.
R1	It was actually reading about what had happened to people. It wasn't all facts and figures. I know it was, but it has in the first sentence, where it says 'I turned the key and experienced a sinking feeling'. You can relate to that straight away. It's how you'd feel.
R3	She's in a flat and she hears noises—it's something that everyone does. Being on their own and they hear a noise. (Fenton *et al.* 1998: 129)

On this occasion, the moderator's intervention usefully allows the discussion to bring out the kinds of attributes that make for an easy and interesting media item on this topic. In particular, the participants feel that they can appreciate the media representation of social science research when it is something they can relate to and that an important way of doing this is the ability to use people's personal experiences as a lens through which the research can be viewed.

Clearly, the moderator has to straddle two positions: allowing the discussion to flow freely and intervening to bring out especially salient issues, particularly when group participants do not do so. This is not an easy conundrum to resolve, and each tactic—intervention and non-intervention—carries risks. The best advice is to err on the side of minimal intervention—other than to start the group on a fresh set of issues—but to intervene when the

group is struggling in its discussions or when it has not alighted on something that is said in the course of the session that appears significant for the research topic.

Selecting participants

Who can participate? Anyone for whom the topic is relevant can logically be an appropriate participant. Sometimes, certain topics do not require participants of a particular kind, so that there is little if any restriction on who might be appropriate. This is a fairly unusual situation and normally some restriction is required. For example, for their research on the organization of knowledge about heart attacks, Morgan and Spanish (1985: 257) recruited people in the 35–50 age range, since they 'would be likely to have more experience with informal discussions of our chosen topic', but they excluded anyone who had had a heart attack or who was uneasy about discussing the topic.

More often, as Table 19.1 suggests and as previously noted, a wide range of people is required, but they are organized into separate groups in terms of stratifying criteria, such as age, gender, education, occupation, and having or not having had a certain experience. Participants for each group can then be selected randomly or through some kind of snowball sampling method. The aim is to establish whether there is any systematic variation in the ways in which different groups discuss a matter. For example, in his research on the *Nationwide* news programme, Morley (1980) found that groups of managers interpreted the programmes they were shown in ways that were broadly consistent with the intentions of the programme producers, but that groups of trade unionists derived interpretations that were in opposition to those intentions. Such an inference can be derived only when focus group participation has been organized in terms of such stratifying criteria. Similarly, drawing on findings from their research into the responses of women to viewing violence, Schlesinger *et al.* (1992) derived a similar kind of conclusion. They showed their fourteen groups (see Table 19.1) four items: an episode of *Crimewatch UK* featuring some violence; an episode of *EastEnders* in which violence was incidental; a television drama, *Closing Ranks*, featuring marital violence; and the Hollywood movie *The Accused*, which contains an extremely vivid rape scene. Drawing on their findings concerning the groups' responses to these showings, the authors concluded:

> in general, the salience in any particular programme of ethnicity, class, or gender or a lived experience such as violence is greatest for those *most directly involved* and diminishes in importance with social distance. Having a particular experience or a particular background does significantly affect the interpretation of a given text. The four programmes screened are obviously open to various readings. However, on the evidence, *how* they are read is fundamentally affected by various socio-cultural factors and by lived experience. (Schlesinger *et al.* 1992: 168; emphases in original)

A slight variation on this approach can be seen in Kitzinger's (1994) study of reactions to media representations of AIDS (see Research in focus 19.1 and Table 19.1).

Her groups were made up of people in a variety of different situations. Some of these were what she calls 'general **population** groups' (for example, a team of civil engineers working on the same site), but others were made up of groups that might have a special interest in AIDS (for example, male prostitutes, intravenous drug users). However, the general point is that increasingly focus group practitioners try to discern patterns of variation by putting together groups with particular attributes or clusters of attributes.

A further issue in relation to the selection of group participants is whether to select people who are unknown to each other or to use natural groupings (for example, friends, co-workers, students on the same course). Some researchers prefer to exclude people who know each other on the grounds that pre-existing styles of interaction or status differences may contaminate the session. Not all writers accept this rule of thumb. Some prefer to select natural groups whenever possible. Kitzinger (1994; Research in focus 19.1 and Table 19.1) used groups made up of people who knew each other. The reason was that she wanted the discussions to be as natural as possible, and she felt that this quality would be enhanced through the use of members of what she calls 'pre-existing groups'. Holbrook and Jackson (1996; see Research in focus 19.4) report that, for their research on shopping centres, they initially tried to secure participants who did not know each other, but this strategy did not result in anybody coming forward. They then sought out participants from various clubs and social centres in the vicinity of the two North London shopping centres in which they were interested. They argue that, in view of their interest in research questions concerning shopping in relation to the construction of identity and how it relates to people's sense of place, recruiting people who knew each other was a highly appropriate strategy.

However, opting for a strategy of recruiting people entirely from natural groups is not always feasible, because of difficulties of securing participation. Fenton *et al.* (1998: 121), in the context of their research on the representation of social science research (Table 19.1), report that they preferred to recruit 'naturally occurring groups' but that 'this was not always achievable'. Morgan (1998a) suggests that one problem with using natural groups is that people who know each other well are likely to operate with taken-for-granted assumptions that they feel do not need to be brought to the fore. He suggests that, if it is important for the researcher to bring out such assumptions, groups of strangers are likely to work better.

Research in focus 19.4
Asking about shopping

For their research on the linkages between shopping, people's sense of place and locality, and the construction of identity (see Miller *et al.* 1998), Holbrook and Jackson (1996: 138) describe their questioning strategy as follows:

> We endeavoured to maintain spontaneity of discussion within the groups and only intervened when it was clear that the conversation was going off track, where there were unproductive silences or where there was continuous repetition of the same issue. Our interventions were mostly in the form of **open questions** on themes we had prepared beforehand, but we were careful that these questions should naturally fit with the general flow of conversation. The themes that we developed for our focus group discussion were as follows:

- Experiences of Wood Green Shopping City and Brent Cross Shopping Centre
- The differences between shopping on high streets and markets and going to a shopping centre
- Gender differences
- Shopping as pleasure, work or leisure
- Christmas shopping and shopping in sales.

Asking questions

An issue that is close to the question of the degree of involvement on the part of the moderator is the matter of how far there should be a set of questions that must be addressed. This issue is very similar to the considerations about how unstructured an interview should be in qualitative interviewing (see Chapter 18). Some researchers prefer to use just one or two very general questions to stimulate discussion, with the moderator intervening as necessary along the lines outlined above. For example, in their research on knowledge about heart attacks, Morgan and Spanish (1985) asked participants to discuss just two topics. One topic was 'who has heart attacks and why?'; here participants were encouraged to talk about people they knew who had had attacks. The second topic was 'what causes and what prevents heart attacks?'

However, other researchers prefer to inject somewhat more structure into the organization of the focus group sessions. An example of this is the research on the viewing of violence by women by Schlesinger *et al.* (1992; see Table 19.1). For example, in relation to the movie *The Accused*, the reactions of the audiences were gleaned through 'guiding questions' under five main headings, the first three of which had several more specific elements.

- Initially, the participants were given the opportunity to discuss the film in terms of such issues as: perceived purpose of the film; gratifications from the film; and realism and storyline.

- The questioning then moved on to reactions to the characters such as: Sarah Tobias (the woman who is raped); the three rapists; the female lawyer; and the male lawyers.

- Participants were then asked about their reactions to scenes, such as: the rape; the female lawyer's decision to change from not supporting Sarah Tobias's case to supporting it; and the winning of the case.

- Participants were asked about their reactions to the inclusion of the rape scene.

- Finally, they were asked about how they perceived the film's value, in particular whether the fact that it is American made a difference to their reactions.

While the research by Schlesinger *et al.* (1992) clearly contained quite a lot of specific questions to be addressed, the questions themselves were fairly general and were designed to ensure that there was some comparability between the focus group sessions in terms of gauging participants' reactions to each of the four programmes that were shown. Moreover, there was ample opportunity for moderators to react to points made in the course of the sessions. The authors write that 'due allowance was made for specific issues raised within a given group' (Schlesinger *et al.* 1992: 28). Moreover, the early questions were designed to generate initial reactions in a relatively open-ended way. Such a general approach to questioning, which is fairly common in focus group research, allows the researcher to navigate the channel between, on the one side, addressing the research questions and ensuring comparability between sessions, and, on the other side, allowing participants to raise issues they see as significant and in their own terms.

Clearly, there are different questioning strategies and approaches to moderating focus group sessions. Most seem to approximate to the one described in Research in focus 19.2, which lies in between the rather open-ended approach employed by Morgan and Spanish (1985) and the somewhat more structured one used by Schlesinger *et al.* (1992). Similarly, Macnaghten and Jacobs (1997) employed a 'topic guide' and grouped the topics to be covered into areas of discussion. Their middle-of-the-road approach in terms of the degree to which the questioning was structured can be seen in the following passage, in which a group of working women reveal a cynicism about governments and experts regarding the reality of environmental problems, a tendency that could also be seen in most of the other groups, which similarly preferred to rely on their own sensory experience (in this passage 'F' is 'female'):

F   They only tell us what they want us to know. And that's just the end of that, so we are left with a fog in your brain, so you just think—what have I to worry about? I don't know what they're on about.

Mod   So why do Government only tell us what they want us to hear?

F   To keep your confidence going. (All together)

Mod   So if someone provides an indicator which says the economy is improving you won't believe it?

F   They've been saying it for about 10 years, but where? I can't see anything!

F   Every time there's an election they say the economy is improving. (Macnaghten and Jacobs 1997: 18)

In this passage, we see an emphasis on the topic to be addressed but a capacity to pick up on what the group says. A rather structured approach to focus group questioning was used in a cross-national study of young Europeans' 'orientations to the present and future, with respect to their "careers" as partners, parents and workers' (Smithson and Brannen 2002: 14). The countries involved were Ireland, Norway, Portugal, Sweden, and the UK. Three hundred and twelve people participated in the research, but the number of groups and the number of participants in them varied considerably by country. The somewhat more structured approach to questioning can be seen in the fact that there were nineteen topic areas, each of which had several questions. For example, for the topic of 'jobs':

- What do you want from a job?
- What is important when you look for a job?
- Do you think it is important to support yourself?
- How do you expect to do that (job/state/spouse/other way)?
- Do you think it is different for women and men of your age?
- Do you expect to be in paid employment in five years' time/ten years' time? (Brannen *et al.* 2002: 190)

The more structured approach to questioning that seems to have occurred with these groups may have been the result of the demands of ensuring comparability between the sessions conducted in the different nations.

There is probably no one best way, and the style of questioning and moderating is likely to be affected by various factors, such as the nature of the research topic (for example, is it one that the researcher already knows a lot about, in which case a modicum of structure is feasible) and levels of interest and/or knowledge among participants in the research (for example, a low level of participant interest may require a somewhat more structured approach). Whichever strategy of questioning is employed, the focus group researcher should generally be prepared to allow at least some discussion that departs from the interview guide, since such debate may provide new and unexpected insights. A more structured approach to questioning might inhibit such spontaneity, but it is unlikely to remove it altogether.

Research in focus 19.5
Questioning in a focus group

Warr's (2005) study was concerned with notions of intimacy among predominantly socio-economically disadvantaged people in New Zealand. Most of her participants were aged between 18 and 29 years. Her questioning strategy was to begin with what she calls an 'icebreaker', which entailed asking participants about a popular movie that was on release at the time. Such an opening can be useful in stimulating initial thoughts on issues of intimacy, given the frequency with which relationships are emphasized in movies. This icebreaker was followed by the following questions:

'How do you know when you've in love?' 'How do you know when someone is in love with you?' 'In getting to know people, who makes the first move?' and How do you learn about sex and love?' To conclude, I would request participants to imagine the future in terms of whether they expected to settle down with someone, get married, or have children. The theme list posed very broad questions for discussion so there was plenty of scope for participants to pursue the topics in undirected ways and to introduce other issues as required. (Warr 2005: 156)

This approach clearly entailed using broad questions or topics as a means of stimulating discussion.

Beginning and finishing

It is recommended that focus group sessions begin with an introduction, whereby the moderators thank people for coming and introduce themselves, the goals of the research are briefly outlined, the reasons for recording the session are given, and the format of the focus group session is sketched out. It is also important to present some of the conventions of focus group participation, such as: only one person should speak at a time (perhaps explaining the problems that occur with recordings when people speak over each other); that all data will be treated confidentially and anonymized; the session is open and everyone's views are important; and the amount of time that will be taken up. During the introduction phase, focus group researchers also often ask participants to fill in forms providing basic socio-demographic information about themselves, such as age, gender, occupation, and where resident. Participants should then be encouraged to introduce themselves and to write out their first names on a card placed in front of them, so that everyone's name is known.

At the end, moderators should thank the group members for their participation and explain very briefly what will happen to the data they have supplied. If a further session is to be arranged, steps should be taken to co-ordinate this.

Group interaction in focus group sessions

Kitzinger (1994) has observed that reports of focus group research frequently do not take into account interaction within the group. This is surprising, because it is precisely the operation of social interaction and its forms and impact that would seem to distinguish the focus group session from the individual interview. Yet, as Kitzinger observes, very few publications based on focus group research cite or draw inferences from patterns of inter- action within the group. Wilkinson reviewed over 200 studies based on focus groups and published between 1946 and 1996. She concluded: 'Focus group data is most commonly presented as if it were one-to-one interview data, with interactions between group participants rarely reported, let alone analysed' (Wilkinson 1998: 112).

In the context of her research on AIDS in the mass media, Kitzinger (1994) drew attention to two types of interaction in focus groups: complementary and argumentative interactions. The former bring out the elements of the social world that provide participants' own frameworks of understanding. The discussion in Research in focus 19.2 brings out the agreement that emerges about the differences between the natural and the social sciences in people's minds. The discussion demonstrates broad agreement between the participants concerning such issues as the lack of control and the subjective nature of interpretation. Such a view is an emergent product of the interaction, with each participant building on the preceding remark. A similar sequence can be discerned in the following passage, which is taken from Morgan and Spanish's (1985: 414) research on heart attack victims:

No. 1   But I think maybe what we're saying here is that there's no one cause of heart attacks, there's no one type of person, there's probably umpteen different types of heart attacks and causes coming from maybe smoking, maybe obesity, maybe stress, maybe design fault, hereditary, overwork, change in life style. Any of these things in themselves could be . . .

No. 2   And when you start putting them in combination [unclear] be speeding up on yourself.

No. 3   Yeah, you may be really magnifying each one of these particular things.

No. 2   Yeah, and depending on how, and in each person that magnification is different. Some people can take a little stress without doing any damage, some people can take a little smoking, a little drinking, a little obesity, without doing any damage. But you take a little of each of these and put them together and you're starting to increase the chances of damage. And any one of these that takes a magnitude leap increases the chances.

This sequence from the transcript helpfully brings out the consensus that emerges around the question of who has heart attacks and why. No. 1 summarizes several factors that have been discussed; No. 2 then introduces the possible significance of some of these factors existing in combination; No. 3 agrees about the importance of combinations of factors; and No. 2 summarizes the position of the group on the salience of combinations of factors, raising at the same time the possibility that for each person there are unique combinations of factors that may be responsible for heart attacks.

However, as Kitzinger (1994) suggests, arguments in focus groups can be equally revealing. She suggests that moderators can play an important role in identifying differences of opinion and exploring with participants the factors that may lie behind them. Disagreement can provide participants with the opportunity to revise their opinions or to think more about the reasons why they hold the view that they do. By way of illustration, a passage from Schlesinger *et al.* (1992; see Table 19.1) is presented. The group is made up of English Afro-Caribbean women with no experience of violence. The debate is concerned with the rape scene in *The Accused* and reveals a misgiving that its inclusion may actually be exploiting sexual violence:

Speaker 1   I think . . . that they could've explained it. They could easily leave that rape scene.

Speaker 2   But it's like that other film we watched. You don't realise the full impact, like, the one we were watching, the first one [*Crimewatch*], until you've got the reconstruction.

Speaker 3   Yeah, but I think with that sort of film, it would cause more damage than it would good, I mean, if someone had been raped, would you like to have [to] sit through that again? (Schlesinger *et al.* 1992: 151–2)

The debate then continues to consider the significance of the scene for men:

Speaker 1   But you wouldn't miss anything, would you? What would you? All right, if you didn't watch that particular part, would you miss anything? You could still grasp it couldn't you?

Speaker 2   You could still grasp it but the enormous effect that it's had on us at the moment, it wouldn't be as drastic . . . without those.

Speaker 1   Yeah, but I'm thinking how would men see it? . . .

Speaker 3   That's what I'm saying, how would they view that scene?

Speaker 4   They couldn't believe it either, I mean, they didn't—they didn't think they were doing any wrong.

Speaker 1   Men would sit down and think, 'Well, she asked for it. She was enjoying it and look, the men around enjoyed it.' (Schlesinger *et al.* 1992: 152)

One factor, then, that seems to be behind the unease of some of the women about the inclusion of the vivid rape scene is that it may be enjoyed by men, rather than being found repulsive, and that they would identify with the onlookers in the film. This account has come about because of the discussion that is stimulated by disagreement within the group and allows a rounded account of women's reactions to the scene to be forged. As Kitzinger (1994) argues, drawing attention to patterns of interaction within focus groups allows the researcher to determine how group participants view the issues with which they are confronted in their own terms. The posing of questions by and agreement and disagreement among participants helps to bring out their own stances on these issues. The resolution of disagreements also helps to force participants to express the grounds on which they hold particular views.

As Warr's (2005) research on intimacy found, focus groups frequently reveal a mixture of agreement and disagreement among participants (see Table 19.1 and Research in focus 19.5 for more on this research). This feature allows the researcher to draw out the tensions associated with people's private beliefs in relation to wider public debates and expectations. This was of particular significance for Warr's interest in intimacy because of the difficulties involved in resolving disagreements about what is and is not appropriate in matters of love and sex. Warr argues that focusing on areas of agreement and disagreement in focus groups can be a useful starting point for the interpretation and analysis of the qualitative data that derive from them.

 # The focus group as a feminist method

The use of focus groups by feminist researchers has grown considerably in recent years, and Wilkinson (1998, 1999*b*) has argued that it has great potential in this regard. Three aspects of the method stand out in terms of their compatibility with the ethics and politics of feminism.

1. Focus group research is less artificial than many other methods, because, in emphasizing group interaction, which is a normal part of social life, it does not suffer from the problem of gleaning information in an unnatural situation. Moreover, the tendency of many focus group researchers to recruit participants from naturally occurring groups underpins the lower level of artificiality of the method, since people are able to discuss in situations that are quite normal for them. As a result, there is greater opportunity to derive understandings that chime with the 'lived experience' of women. However, not all writers accept the contention that focus groups are more naturalistic than individual interviews. Even when natural groups are used, gathering people to discuss a certain topic (such as a television programme) is not inherently naturalistic, because the social setting is to a significant extent contrived (Morrison 1998: 154–5). Indeed, completing questionnaires or being interviewed may appear more natural, because such instruments are fairly commonplace, whereas being asked to discuss in a group an issue not necessarily of one's choosing is less so.

2. Feminist researchers have expressed a preference for methods that avoid *decontextualization*—that is, that successfully study the individual within a social context. The tendency for most methods to treat the individual as a separate entity devoid of a social context is disliked by many feminist researchers who prefer to analyse 'the self as relational or as socially constructed' (Wilkinson 1999*b*: 229–30). Because the individual is very much part of a group in the focus group method, this tendency towards decontextualization is avoided.

3. As we have seen in previous chapters, feminist researchers are suspicious of research methods that are exploitative and create a power relationship between the female researcher and the female respondent. Wilkinson observes that the risk of this occurring is greatly reduced because focus group participants are able to take over much of the direction of the session from the moderator. Indeed, they may even subvert the goals of the session in ways that could be of considerable interest to the moderator. As a result, participants' points of view are much more likely to be revealed than in a traditional interview.

Wilkinson does not argue that focus groups or indeed any method can be described as inherently feminist. Instead, she argues that, because of these three features and when employed with a sensitivity towards feminist concerns, the focus group method has considerable potential as a tool of feminist research.

The kinds of argument put forward regarding the fit between the focus group method and feminist research have been extended to suggest they may have a further role in allowing the voices of highly marginalized groups of women to surface. Madriz (2000: 843) argues that, for a group like lower-socio-economic-class women of colour, focus groups constitute a relatively rare opportunity for them to 'empower themselves by making sense of their experience of vulnerability and subjugation'.

 # Limitations of focus groups

Focus groups clearly have considerable potential for research questions in which the processes through which meaning is jointly constructed is likely to be of particular interest. Indeed, it may be that, even when this is not a prominent emphasis, the use of the focus group method may be appropriate and even advantageous, since it allows participants' perspectives—an important feature of much qualitative research (see Chapter 16)—to be revealed in ways that are different from individual interviews (for example, through discussion, participants' questions, arguments, and so on). It also offers considerable potential for feminist researchers. What, then, might be its chief limitations?

- The researcher probably has less control over proceedings than with the individual interview. As we have seen, by no means all writers on focus groups perceive this as a disadvantage, and indeed feminist researchers often see it as an advantage. Kamberelis and Dimitriadis (2005) note that there is a tradition among some focus group researchers to value the method because it provides greater opportunity than most other methods for research participants to have some 'ownership' of the interview and the research process more generally. However, the question of control raises issues for researchers of how far they can allow a focus group to 'take over' the running of proceedings. There is clearly a delicate balance to be taken into account over how involved moderators should be and how far a set of prompts or questions should influence the conduct of a focus group, as some of the earlier discussions have suggested. What is not clear is the degree to which it is appropriate to surrender control of a focus group to its participants, especially when there is a reasonably explicit set of research questions to be answered, as is commonly the case, for example, in funded research.

- The data are difficult to analyse. A huge amount of data can be very quickly produced. Developing a strategy of analysis that incorporates both themes in what people say and patterns of interaction is not easy. Also, as previously pointed out, focus group recordings are particularly prone to inaudible elements, which affects transcription. However, studies like those of Kitzinger (1994) and Morgan and Spanish (1985) demonstrate that the examination of group interaction can be used to show how issues of thematic interest arise in the course of discussion.

- They are difficult to organize. Not only do you have to secure the agreement of people to participate in your study; you also need to persuade them to turn up at a particular time. Small payments, such as book or store tokens, are sometimes made to induce participation, but nonetheless it is common for people not to turn up. As a result, it is a common practice in focus group circles to over-recruit for each session on the grounds that at least one or two people will not turn up.

- The recordings are probably more time-consuming to transcribe than equivalent recordings of individual interviews, because of variations in voice pitch and the need to take account of who says what. For example, Bloor et al. (2001) suggest that a focus group session lasting one hour can take up to eight hours to transcribe, which is somewhat longer than would be likely in connection with an equivalent personal interview.

- There are problems with focus groups that are not encountered in individual interviews, most notably the tendency for two or more participants to speak at the same time. It is usually very difficult and often impossible to make sense of and therefore transcribe the portions of recordings where this has occurred.

Of course, moderators can ask participants not to speak at the same time, but in my experience it is difficult to prevent this from occurring in spite of constant warnings.

- There are possible problems of group effects. This includes the obvious problem of dealing with reticent speakers and with those who hog the stage! In this respect, they are a bit like tutorials. Krueger (1998: 59) suggests in relation to the problem of overly prominent participants that the moderator should make clear to the speaker and other group participants that other people's views are definitely required; for example, he suggests saying something like 'That's one point of view. Does anyone have another point of view?' As for those who do not speak very much, it is recommended that they are actively encouraged to say something. Also, as the well-known Asch experiments showed, an emerging group view may mean that a perfectly legitimate perspective held by just one individual may be suppressed (Asch 1951). There is also evidence that, as a group comes to share a certain point of view, group members come to think uncritically about it and to develop almost irrational attachments to it (Janis 1982). It is not known how far such group effects have an adverse impact on focus group findings, but it is clear that they cannot be entirely ignored. In this context, it would be interesting to know how far agreement among focus group participants is more frequently encountered than disagreement (I have a hunch that it is), since the effects to which both Asch and Janis referred would lead us to expect more agreement than disagreement in focus group discussions.

- Related to this last issue is the fact that, in group contexts, participants may be more prone to expressing culturally expected views than in individual interviews. Morgan (2002) cites the case of a study in which group interviews with boys discussing relationships with girls were compared with individual interviews with them on the same topic. In the latter they expressed a degree of sensitivity that was not present in the group context, where more macho views tended to be forthcoming. This suggests that, in the group interviews, the boys were seeking to impress others and were being influenced by the norms of their peer group. However, this does not render the group interview data questionable, because it may be precisely the gulf between privately and publicly held views that is of interest.

- Madriz (2000) proposes that there are circumstances when focus groups may not be appropriate, because of their potential for causing discomfort among participants. When such discomfort might arise, individual interviews are likely to be preferable. Situations in which unease might be occasioned are: when intimate details of private lives need to be revealed; when participants may not be comfortable in each other's presence (for example, bringing together people in a hierarchical relationship to each other); and when participants are likely to disagree profoundly with each other.

Checklist

Issues to consider for your focus group

○ Have you devised a clear and comprehensive way of introducing the research to participants?

○ Do the questions or topics you have devised allow you to answer all your research questions?

○ Have you piloted the guide with some appropriate respondents?

○ Have you devised a strategy for encouraging respondents to turn up for the focus group meeting?

○ Have you thought about what you will do if some participants do not turn up for the session?

○ Have you ensured that sessions will allow novel or unexpected themes and issues to arise?

○ Is your language in the questions clear and comprehensible?

○ Are your questions relevant to the people who are participating in the focus groups?

○ Have your questions been designed to elicit reflective discussions so that participants are not tempted to answer in 'yes' or 'no' terms?

○ Have your questions been designed to encourage group interaction and discussion?

○ Do your questions offer a real prospect of seeing the world from your interviewees' point of view rather than imposing your own frame of reference on them?

○ Are you familiar with the setting(s) in which the session will take place?

○ Are you thoroughly familiar with and have you tested your recording or audio-visual equipment?

○ Have you thought about how you will present yourself in the session, such as how you will be dressed?

○ Have you devised a strategy for dealing with silences?

○ Have you devised a strategy for dealing with participants who are reluctant to speak?

○ Have you devised a strategy for dealing with participants who speak too much and hog the discussion?

○ Do you have a strategy for how far you are going to intervene in the focus group discussion?

○ Do you have a strategy for dealing with the focus group if the discussion goes off in a tangent?

○ Have you tested out any aids that you are going to present to focus group participants (e.g. visual aids, segments of film, case studies)?

Key points

- The focus group is a group interview that is concerned with exploring a certain topic.
- The moderator generally tries to provide a relatively free rein to the discussion. However, there may be contexts in which it is necessary to ask fairly specific questions, especially when cross-group comparability is an issue.
- There is concern with the joint production of meaning.
- Focus group discussions need to be recorded and transcribed.
- There are several issues concerning the recruitment of focus group participants—in particular, whether to use natural groupings and whether to employ stratifying criteria.
- Group interaction is an important component of discussions.
- Some writers view focus groups as well suited to a feminist standpoint.

Questions for review

- Why might it be useful to distinguish between a focus group and a group interview?

Uses of focus groups

- What advantages might the focus group method offer in contrast to an individual qualitative interview?

Conducting focus groups

- How involved should the moderator be?
- Why is it necessary to record and transcribe focus group sessions?
- Are there any circumstances in which it might be a good idea to select participants who know each other?
- What might be the advantages and disadvantages of using an interview guide in focus group sessions?

Group interaction in focus group sessions

- Why might it be important to treat group interaction as an important issue when analysing focus group data?

The focus group as a feminist method

- Evaluate the argument that the focus group can be viewed as a feminist method.
- To what extent are focus groups a naturalistic approach to data collection?

Limitations of focus groups

- Does the potential for the loss of control over proceedings and for group effects damage the potential utility of the focus group as a method?
- How far do the greater problems of transcription and difficulty of analysis undermine the potential of focus groups?

Online Resource Centre

http://www.oxfordtextbooks.co.uk/orc/brymansrm3e/

Visit the Online Resource Centre that accompanies this book to enrich your understanding of focus groups. Consult web links, test yourself using multiple choice questions, and gain further guidance and inspiration from the Student Researcher's Toolkit.

Language in qualitative research

Chapter outline

Chapter guide

This chapter is concerned with two approaches to the examination of language: conversation analysis and discourse analysis. For the practitioners of both approaches, language is an object of interest in its own right and not simply a resource through which research participants communicate with researchers. The chapter explores:

- the roots of conversation analysis in ethnomethodology;
- some of its rules and principles;
- the assumptions of discourse analysis;
- some of its analytic strategies;
- points of difference between the two approaches.

Introduction

Language is bound to be of importance for social researchers. It is, after all, through language that we ask people questions in interviews and through which the questions are answered. Understanding language categories has been an important component of research involving participant observation, because knowing how words are used and the meanings of specific terms in the local vernacular (often called 'argot') is frequently viewed as crucial to an appreciation of how the social world being studied is viewed by its members.

In this chapter, however, two approaches will be examined that treat language as their central focal points. They are called conversation analysis (CA) and discourse analysis (DA). What is crucial about these approaches is that, unlike traditional views of the role of language in social research, they treat language as a topic rather than as a resource (admittedly a clichéd phrase). This means that language is treated as significantly more than a medium through which the business of social research is conducted (such as asking questions in interviews). It becomes a focus of attention in its own right. While CA and DA do not exhaust the range of possibilities for studying language as a topic, they do represent two of the most prominent approaches. Each has developed a technical vocabulary and set of techniques. This chapter will outline some of the basic elements of each of them and draw attention to some contrasting features.

Conversation analysis

The roots of CA lie in ethnomethodology, a sociological position developed in the USA under the general tutelage of Harold Garfinkel and Harvey Sacks, though it is the latter with whom CA is most associated. Ethnomethodology takes as its basic focus of attention 'practical, common-sense reasoning' in everyday life and as such is funda-

mentally concerned with the notion of social life as an accomplishment. Social order is seen not as a pre-existing force constraining individual action, but as something that is worked at and accomplished through interaction. Contrary to what its name implies, ethnomethodology is *not* a research methodology; it is the study of the methods employed in everyday life though which social order is accomplished. As Garfinkel (1967: p. vii) put it in his inimitable style:

in contrast to certain versions of Durkheim that teach that the objective reality of social facts is sociology's fundamental principle, the lesson is taken instead, and used as a study policy, that the objective reality of social facts *as* an ongoing accomplishment of the concerted activities of daily life, with the ordinary, artful ways of that accomplishment being by members known, used, and taken for granted, is, for members doing sociology, a fundamental phenomenon.

Two ideas are particularly central to ethnomethodology and find clear expression in CA: indexicality and reflexivity. The former means that the meaning of an act, which in CA essentially means spoken words or utterances including pauses and sounds, depends upon the context in which it is used. Reflexivity means that spoken words are constitutive of the social world in which they are located; in other words, the principle of reflexivity in ethnomethodology means that talk is not a 'mere' representation of the social world, so that it does much more than just stand for something else. In these ways, ethnomethodology fits fairly squarely with two aspects of

qualitative research—the predilection for a contextual understanding of action (see Chapter 16) and an ontological position associated with constructionism (see Chapter 1).

In the years following its initial introduction into sociology, ethnomethodological research split into two camps. One entailed drawing on traditional social research methods, albeit in perhaps a somewhat altered form, and on ethnography in particular (e.g. Cicourel 1968). The other, which is mainly associated with Sacks and his co-workers (e.g. Sacks *et al.* 1974), sought to conduct fine-grained analyses of talk in naturally occurring situations. Moreover, it is not just talk in itself that is the object of interest but talk as it occurs in and through social interaction. CA concerns itself with the organization of such talk in the context of interaction (see Key concept 20.1). In order to conduct such investigations, a premium was placed on the recording of naturally occurring conversations and their transcription for the purpose of intensive analysis of the sequences of interaction revealed in the subsequent transcripts. As such, CA is a multifaceted approach—part theory, part method of data acquisition, part method of analysis. The predilection for the analysis of talk gleaned from naturally occurring situations suggests that CA chimes with another preoccupation among qualitative researchers—namely, a commitment to naturalism (see Key concept 2.4).

Key concept 20.1
What is conversation analysis?

Conversation analysis (CA) is the fine-grained analysis of talk as it occurs in interaction in naturally occurring situations. The talk is recorded and transcribed so that the detailed analyses can be carried out. These analyses are concerned with uncovering the underlying structures of talk in interaction and as such with the achievement of order through interaction.

As the definition of CA in Key concept 20.1 and the preceding discussion suggest, CA takes from ethnomethodology a concern with the production of social order through and in the course of social interaction but takes conversation as the basic form through which that social order is achieved. The element of indexicality is

also evident, in that practitioners of CA argue that the meaning of words is contextually grounded, while the commitment to reflexivity is revealed in the view that talk is constitutive of the social context in which it occurs.

Conversation analysts have developed a variety of procedures for the study of talk in interaction. Psathas

(1995: 1) has described them as 'rigorous, systematic procedures' that can 'provide reproducible results'. Such a framework smacks of the commitment to the codification of procedures that generate valid, reliable, and replicable findings that are a feature of quantitative research. It is not surprising, therefore, that CA is sometimes described as having a positivist orientation. Thus, a cluster of features that are broadly in tune with qualitative research (contextual, naturalistic, studying the social world in its own terms and without prior theoretical commitments) are married to traits that are resonant of quantitative research. However, the emphasis on context in CA is somewhat at variance with the way in which contextual understanding is normally conceptualized in qualitative research. For CA practitioners, context refers to the specific here-and-now context of immediately preceding talk, whereas for most qualitative researchers it has a much wider set of resonances, which has to do with an appreciation of such things as the culture of the group within which action occurs. In other words, for most qualitative researchers action is to be understood in terms of the values, beliefs, and typical modes of behaviour of that group. This is precisely the kind of attribution from which CA practitioners are keen to refrain. It is no wonder, therefore, that writers like Gubrium and Holstein (1997) treat it as a separate tradition within qualitative research (see Key concept 16.1), while Silverman (1993) finds it difficult to fit CA into broad descriptions of the nature of qualitative research.

Assumptions of conversation analysis

An initial route into CA often begins with the analyst noticing something significant in or striking about the way that a speaker says something. This recognition then generates an emphasis on what that turn of phrase or whatever might be 'doing'—that is, what functions it serves. Clayman and Gill (2004) give the example, which was first noticed by Harvey Sacks, of the way in which children often begin a question by saying 'You know what, daddy [or whoever]?' when among adults. Their question invariably produces the reply 'What?' and thereby allows the child to find a slot in a sequence of conversation or to inaugurate such a sequence. The use of this strategy reflects children's desire to insinuate themselves in conversations as legitimate participants and indeed to be able to inaugurate sequences of the talk.

Once such a focus has been identified, conversation analysts typically follow certain basic assumptions. Heritage (1984, 1987) has proposed three such assumptions:

1. *Talk is structured*. Talk comprises invariant patterns—that is, it is structured. Participants are implicitly aware of the rules that underpin these patterns. As a result, conversation analysts eschew attempts to infer the motivations of speakers from what they say or to ascribe their talk to personal characteristics. Such information is unnecessary, since the conversation analyst is oriented to the underlying structures of action, as revealed in talk.

Research in focus 20.1
Conversation analysis in action showing a question and answer adjacency pair

Silverman (1994: 72) provides the following extract from a conversation between an HIV counsellor (*C*) at a clinic and a patient (*P*):

1. *C*: Can I just briefly ask why: you thought about having

2. an HIV test done:

3. *P*: .hh We:ll I mean it's something that you have these

4. I mean that you have to think about these da: ys, and

5. I just uh: m felt (0.8) <u>you</u>—you have had sex with

6. several people and you just don't want to go on (.)

7. not k<u>n</u>owing.

2. *Talk is forged contextually.* Action is revealed in talk and as such talk must be analysed in terms of its context. This means that we must seek to understand what someone says in terms of the talk that has preceded it and that therefore talk is viewed as exhibiting patterned sequences.

3. *Analysis is grounded in data.* Conversation analysts shun prior theoretical schemes and instead argue that characteristics of talk and of the constitutive nature of social order in each empirical instance must be induced out of data.

Heritage (1987: 258) has written: 'it is assumed that social actions work *in detail* and hence that the specific details of interaction cannot simply be ignored as insignificant without damaging the prospects for coherent and effective analyses.' This assumption represents a manifesto for the emphasis on fine-grained details (including length of pauses, prolongation of sounds, and so on) that is the hallmark of CA.

Transcription and attention to detail

As the third of the three assumptions associated with CA indicates, the approach requires the analyst to produce detailed transcripts of natural conversation. Consider the portion of transcript in Research in focus 20.1, which contains some of the basic notational symbols employed in CA.

.hh	h's preceded by a dot indicate an intake of breath. If no dot is present, it means breathing out.
We:ll	A colon indicates that the sound that occurs directly before the colon is prolonged. More than one colon means further prolongation (e.g. : : : :).
(0.8)	A figure in parentheses indicates the length of a period of silence, usually measured in tenths of one second. Thus, (0.8) signals eight-tenths of a second of silence.
<u>you</u> and k<u>n</u>owing	An underline indicates an emphasis in the speaker's talk.
(.)	Indicates a very slight pause.

The attention to detail in the sequence in Research in focus 20.1 is very striking and represents a clear difference from the way in which talk is normally treated by social researchers—for example, in their transcription conventions when analysing qualitative interviews. But what is significant in this sequence of talk?

Silverman (1994) draws two main inferences from the sequence in Research in focus 20.1. First, *P* initially tries to deflect any suggestion that there might be a special reason that she needs a test. As a result, the disclosure that she has been engaging in potentially risky behaviour is delayed. Second, *P*'s use of 'you' depersonalizes her behaviour. Silverman argues that sequences like these show how 'people receiving HIV counselling skilfully manage their talk about delicate topics' (1994: 75). The hesitations are designed by patients to establish that issues like these are not the subject of normal conversation; the rather general replies to questions are meant to indicate that the speaker is not the kind of person who will immediately launch into a discussion about difficult sexual matters with a stranger. Silverman suggests that the notion that the hesitancy and depersonalization on the part of *P* is to do with her embarrassment about talking about sex is 'severely limited' and that instead we find that 'the production and management of delicate topics is skilfully and co-operatively organized between professionals and clients' (1994: 76).

This analysis shows how attention to fine details is an essential ingredient of CA work. Pauses and emphases are not to be regarded as incidental or of little significance in terms of what the speaker is trying to achieve; instead, they are part of 'the specific details of interaction [that] cannot simply be ignored as insignificant', as Heritage put it in the quotation above.

Some basic tools of conversation analysis

The gradual accumulation of detailed analyses of talk in interaction has resulted in a recognition that there are recurring features of the ways in which that talk is organized. These features can be regarded as tools that can be applied to sequences of conversation. The following tools are presented merely to provide a flavour of the ways in which CA proceeds.

Turn-taking

One of the most basic ideas in CA is the notion that one of the ways in which order is achieved in everyday conversation is through turn-taking. This is a particularly important tool of conversation analysis, because it illustrates that talk depends on shared codes. If such codes did not exist, there would not be smooth transitions in conversation. In other words, there must be codes for indicating the ends of utterances.

Tips and skills
Don't collect too much data

If you are doing a project based on CA, do not be tempted to collect too much data. The real work of CA goes into the painstaking analysis that its underlying theoretical stance requires. It may be that just one or two portions of transcribed text will allow you to address your research questions using the technique.

Hutchby and Wooffitt (1998: 47) summarize this model as indicating that: '(1) turn-taking occurs; (2) one speaker tends to talk at a time; and (3) turns are taken with as little gap or overlap between them as possible'. This is not to say that turn-taking 'errors' do not occur. They manifestly do, as the discussion of *repair mechanisms* below suggests. One of the ways in which turn-taking is revealed is through the examination of *adjacency pairs*, which are the focus of the next subsection.

Adjacency pairs

The idea of the *adjacency pair* draws attention to the well-attested tendency for some kinds of activity as revealed in talk to involve two linked phases: a question followed by an answer, as in Research in focus 20.1; an invitation followed by a response (accept/decline); or a greeting followed by a returned greeting. The first phase invariably implies that the other part of the adjacency pair will be forthcoming—for example, that an invitation will be responded to. The second phase is of interest to the conversation analyst not just because it becomes a springboard for a response in its own right but because compliance with the putative normative structure of the pairing indicates an appreciation of how one is supposed to respond to the initial phase. In this way, 'intersubjective understandings' are continuously reinforced (Heritage 1987: 259–60). This is not to imply that the second phase will *always* follow the first; indeed, the response to a failure to comply with the expected response has itself been the focus of attention by conversation analysts.

Preference organization

While it is true to say that the second phase in an adjacency pair is always anticipated, some responses are clearly preferential to others. An example is that, when an invitation or a request is proffered, acceptance does not have to be justified, whereas a refusal does have to

be justified. A further example is that, when an attempt to be self-deprecating is provided, it will be met with disagreement rather than agreement. In each case, the former (acceptance, disagreement) is the *preferred response* and the latter (refusal, agreement) is the *dispreferred response*. Therefore, the preference structure is discovered by the conversation analyst through the response to an initial statement.

Speakers' awareness of the preference organization of such pairings has implications for the structure of a conversation. For example, Potter (1996: 59) contrasts a sequence in which an offer is met with a straightforward preferred response of acceptance—'thank you'—with the sequence in Research in focus 20.2, in which an invitation is declined (the dispreferred response).

Potter argues that this kind of response by *A* is fairly typical of acceptance rejections, which are, of course, dispreferred responses. Potter draws attention to several features that contrast strikingly with the unequivocal 'thank you' associated with the case of acceptance. For example, *A* delays the start of his or her response and fills it with 'hehh'. Also, the rejection is 'softened' by *A* saying that he or she doesn't 'think' he or she can make it and is accompanied by an explanation for failing to provide the preferred response. Moreover, Potter follows the admonition not to make inferences about speakers' motivations by observing that the notion of a preference structure is a feature of the talk not the motivations of the participants. After all, *A* may actually have preferred to accept the invitation but was prevented from doing so by a prior commitment. The key point is that the participants recognize the preference structure of this kind of adjacency pairing and this affects the form of their response (that is, hesitancy, acknowledgement of the invitation, and providing an explanation) in the case of declining the offer or an unelaborated (or barely elaborated) response in the case of acceptance.

Research in focus 20.2
Conversation analysis in action: a dispreferred response

1. *B*: Uh if you'd care to come over and visit a little while
2.   this morning I'll give you a cup of <u>co</u>ffee.
3. *A*: hehh
4.   Well
5.   that's awfully sweet of you,
6.   I don't think I can make it this morning. hh uhm
7.   I'm running an ad in the paper and—and uh I have to
8.   stay near the phone (Atkinson and Drew 1979: 58; quoted in Potter 1996: 59)

Accounts

A feature of the sequence in Research in focus 20.2 is that from line 7 onwards *A* formulates an account of why it is that the invitation cannot be accepted. As Potter observes, the account does two things: it establishes a reason for declining the invitation and depicts *A* as constrained by circumstances. The important feature to note in the treatment of accounts in CA is that they are analysed in context—that is, the form that they assume is handled as being occasioned by what precedes it (an invitation). Unlike the traditional view of accounts in sociology, a CA view of *A*'s account is to stress the importance of depicting it as allowing the invitation to be construed in a positive light even though it cannot be accepted, thereby allowing the relationship between the two parties not to be jeopardized. Moreover, in CA, accounts are not unusual phenomena to be deployed when things go wrong but are intrinsic to talk in a variety of situations. What is also striking about this sequence as an account is that it is in essence simply a description of a state of affairs (having an advertisement in the paper and as a result needing to stay close to the telephone in case there are calls). The factual nature of the account further allows the relationship between the two parties to be unharmed by *A*'s dispreferred response.

Repair mechanisms

Of course, things do go wrong in conversations, as occurs when turn-taking conventions are not followed so that there is overlapping of people talking. Silverman (1993: 132) notes several repair mechanisms, such as:

- when someone starts to speak before someone else has finished, the initial speaker stops talking before completing his or her turn;
- when a turn transfer does not occur at an appropriate point (for example, when someone does not respond to a question), the speaker may speak again, perhaps reinforcing the need for the other person to speak (for example, by reinforcing the question).

The crucial point to note about such repair mechanisms is that they allow the rules of turn-taking to be maintained in spite of the fact that they have been breached.

Overview

This review of CA can only scratch the surface of an approach that has developed a highly sophisticated way of studying talk in interaction. It has sometimes been suggested that it fails to capture body movements, but in recent times the use of video recordings has supplemented its tool kit of methods (e.g. Heath 1997). Also, there has been a growing use of CA in connection with the examination of talk in institutional settings such as organizations and mediation sessions.

The insistence of conversation analysts that it is important to locate understanding in terms of sequences of talk, and therefore to avoid making extraneous inferences about the meanings of that talk, marks CA as representing a somewhat different approach from much qualitative research. As we have seen in previous chapters, qualitative researchers often claim (perhaps erroneously from the perspective of CA) that they seek to achieve understanding from the perspective of those being studied. Conversation analysts claim to do this only in so far as that understanding can be revealed in the specific contexts of talk. To import elements that are not specifically grounded in the here and now of what has just been said during a conversation risks the implanting of understanding that is not grounded in participants' own terms (Schegloff 1997).

Two points seem relevant here. First, this is a somewhat limiting stance, in that it means that the attribution of motives and meanings as a result of an in-depth understanding of a culture is illegitimate. While an interpretative understanding of social action carries risks on misunderstanding, an approach that prohibits such speculation is potentially restrictive. Secondly, CA is contextual in that it locates understanding in the sequences of talk. However, for the participants of an exchange, much of their talk is informed by their mutual knowledge of contexts. The analyst is restricted from taking those additional components of the context into account if they are not specifically part of the organization of talk. Again, this admonition seems to restrict the analyst more than is desirable in many circumstances and to consign CA to a range of research questions that are amenable solely to the location of meaning in talk alone. On the other hand, CA reduces the risk about making unwarranted speculations about what is happening in social interaction and has contributed much to our understanding of the accomplishment of social order, which is one of the classic concerns of social theory.

 # Discourse analysis

Unlike CA, DA is an approach to language that can be applied to forms of communication other than talk. As such, it can be and has been applied to forms like texts, such as newspaper articles, and is in this respect more flexible than CA. Moreover, in DA there is much less of an emphasis on naturally occurring talk, so that talk in research interviews can be a legitimate target for analysis. However, DA should not be treated totally in opposition or contradistinction to CA, since it incorporates insights from it. In addition, DA incorporates insights from the work of continental philosophers like Michel Foucault (1926–84), for whom discourse was a term that denoted the way in which a particular set of linguistic categories relating to an object and the ways of depicting it frame the way we comprehend that object. The discourse forms a version of it. Moreover, the version of an object comes to *constitute* it. For example, a certain discourse concerning mental illness comes to make up our concepts of what mentally ill persons are like, the nature of their illness, how they should be treated, and who is legitimately entitled to treat them. The discourse then becomes a framework for the justification for the power of practitioners concerned with the mentally ill and for their treatment regimes. In this way, a discourse is much more than language as such: it is constitutive of the social world that is a focus of interest or concern. Foucault's approach was to take a broad-brush historical approach to the study of discourse. Discourse analysts, in integrating insights from CA, results in a much more fine-grained analysis of talk and texts than was a feature of Foucault's approach.

Unlike CA, which by and large reveals a uniformity based on an orthodoxy associated with certain classic statements concerning its core practices (e.g. Sacks *et al.* 1974), there are several different approaches that are labelled as DA (Potter 1997). The version to be discussed in this section is one that has been of special interest to social researchers and is associated with such writers as Potter (1997); Gilbert and Mulkay (1984); Potter and Wetherell (1987, 1994); and Billig (1992). This version of DA (see Key concept 20.2) has been described as exhibiting two distinctive features at the level of epistemology and ontology (Potter 1997).

Key concept 20.2
What is discourse analysis?

There is no one version of discourse analysis (DA). The version described in the main body of this section is one that has been of particular interest to social scientists and that can be applied to both naturally occurring and contrived forms of talk and to texts. According to Potter (1997: 146), DA 'emphasizes the way versions of the world, of society, events and inner psychological worlds are produced in discourse'. Language is depicted in discourse analysis as constituting or producing the social world; it is not simply a means of understanding that world, as it is in most quantitative and qualitative research methods.

In the next section, a variant of discourse analysis—*critical discourse analysis*—will be discussed. Critical discourse analysis, which is very influenced by the work of Michel Foucault, seeks to link language and its modes of use to the significance of power and social difference in society.

---

1. It is *anti-realist*; in other words, it denies that there is an external reality awaiting a definitive portrayal by the researcher and it therefore disavows the notion that any researcher can arrive at a privileged account of the aspect of the social world being investigated. Some discourse analysts, however, adopt a stance that is closer to a realist position, but most seem to be anti-realist in orientation.

2. It is *constructionist*; in other words, the emphasis is placed on the versions of reality propounded by members of the social setting being investigated and on the fashioning of that reality through their renditions of it (see Key concept 1.6). More specifically, the constructionist emphasis entails a recognition that discourse entails a selection from many viable renditions and that in the process a particular depiction of reality is built up.

Thus, discourse is not simply a neutral device for imparting meaning. People seek to accomplish things when they talk or when they write; DA is concerned with the strategies they employ in trying to create different kinds of effect. This version of DA is therefore action-oriented—that is, a way of getting things done. This is revealed in three basic discourse-analytic questions:

1. What is this discourse doing?

2. How is this discourse constructed to make this happen?

3. What resources are available to perform this activity? (Potter 2004: 609)

This action orientation is revealed in a study of the first few moments of telephone calls to a National Society for the Prevention of Cruelty to Children helpline. Through an analysis of these call openings, Potter and Hepburn (2004) show that these first few moments perform certain actions:

- They are the springboard for the caller specifying the details of his or her concerns.

- They seek to establish that the child protection officer who receives the call is someone who, as an expert, can verify the caller's concerns.

- The caller makes it clear that he or she is concerned but not so concerned or certain about the status of the situation as to contact the police.

- The child protection officer is able to treat the report as serious without having to presuppose the truth or seriousness of the report.

Thus, through an analysis of these brief moments of conversation, the flow of discourse achieves a number of objectives for both parties and is therefore action.

In addition, DA shares with CA a preference for locating contextual understanding in terms of the situational specifics of talk. As Potter (1997: 158) puts it, discourse analysts prefer to avoid making reference in their analyses to what he refers to as 'ethnographic particulars' and argues that instead they prefer 'to see things as things that are worked up, attended to and made relevant in interaction rather than being external determinants'. However, DA practitioners are less wedded to this principle than conversation analysts, in that the former sometimes show a greater preparedness to make reference to 'ethnographic particulars'.

Discourse analysts resist the idea of codifying their practices and indeed argue that such a codification is probably impossible. Instead, they prefer to see their style of research as an 'analytic mentality' and as such as 'a craft skill, more like bike riding or chicken sexing than following the recipe for a mild chicken rogan josh' (Potter 1997: 147–8). One useful point of departure for DA research that has been suggested by Gill (1996) following Widdicombe (1993) is to treat the way that something is said as being 'a solution to a problem' (Widdicombe 1993: 97; quoted in Gill 1996: 146). She also suggests adopting a posture of 'sceptical reading' (Gill 2000). This means searching for a purpose lurking behind the ways that something is said or presented. Gill has also proposed that DA can be usefully thought of as comprising four main themes, which are outlined in Thinking deeply 20.1.

Tips and skills
Using existing material

As some of the examples of DA show, you may well be able to employ the technique to illuminate issues of interest to you on materials that are in the public domain, such as speeches. In many cases, these will be available in electronic form. This means that you do not have to put a lot of effort into the collection of data, though it will still be necessary to seek out the materials. Instead, you can give greater emphasis to analysing the materials using the DA approach.

Thinking deeply 20.1
Four themes in discourse analysis

Gill (2000) has drawn attention to four prominent themes in DA.

1. *Discourse is a topic*. This means that discourse is a focus of enquiry itself and not just a means of gaining access to aspects of social reality that lie behind it. This view contrasts with a traditional research interview in which language is a way of revealing what interviewees think about a topic or their behaviour and the reasons for that behaviour.

2. *Language is constructive*. This means that discourse is a way of constituting a particular view of social reality. Moreover, in rendering that view, choices are made regarding the most appropriate way of presenting it and these will reflect the disposition of the person responsible for devising it.

3. *Discourse is a form of action*. As Gill (2000: 175) puts it, language is viewed 'as a practice in its own right'. Language is a way of accomplishing acts, such as attributing blame, presenting oneself in a particular way, or getting an argument across. Moreover, a person's discourse is affected by the context that he or she is confronting. Thus, your account of your reasons for wanting a job may vary according to whether you are addressing interviewees in a job interview, members of your family, or friends.

4. *Discourse is rhetorically organized*. This means that DA practitioners recognize that discourse is concerned with 'establishing one version of the world in the face of competing versions' (Gill 2000: 176). In other words, there is a recognition that we want to persuade others when we present a version of events or whatever.

The bulk of the exposition of DA that follows is based on two studies: research on scientists' discourse and the use of numbers in a television programme on cancer. In the case of the former, we will see that attention to scientists' discourse is a solution to problems of how to represent their practices in formal and informal settings; the study of the television programme demonstrates that the examination of discourse reveals how claims about facts can be boosted or undermined through the use of a language of quantification. A further element to be sensitive to is that, as Gill (1996), following Billig (1991), suggests, what is said is always a way of *not* saying something else. In other words, either total silence on a topic, or formulating an argument in a conversation or article in one way rather than in another way, is a crucial component of seeing discourse as a solution to a problem. As we will see, the silences about aspects of their procedures in the scientists' published papers are crucial to conveying a sense of the fixed, neutral nature of their findings; in the case of the television programme, conveying a quantitative argument in one way rather than in another way is crucial to undermining the credibility of claims about success in the treatment of cancer.

Potter and Wetherell (1994) suggest that there are two tendencies within the kind of DA work being discussed in this chapter, although they acknowledge that the distinction is somewhat artificial. One is the identification of 'the general resources that are used to construct discourse and enable the performance of particular actions' (1994: 48–9), which is concerned with identifying *interpretative repertoires*. The other is concerned to identify 'the detailed procedures through which versions are constructed and made to look factual' (1994: 49). We will now explore these two strands of DA.

Uncovering interpretative repertoires

In order to illustrate the idea of an *interpretative repertoire*, an influential study of scientists by Gilbert and Mulkay (1984) will be employed. This research is outlined in some detail in Research in focus 20.3. Gilbert and Mulkay noticed a distinct difference between the ways in which the scientists presented their work in formal contexts, most notably the scientific paper, and in informal contexts, such as in the interviews with the researchers. Such differences went far beyond rather predictable differences in tone of presentation, in that they also related to such areas as the depiction of the ways in which the findings emerged. For example, Gilbert and Mulkay noted an instance in which a scientific paper portrayed

Research in focus 20.3
Discourse analysis in action: the study of interpretative repertoires in scientists' discourse

Gilbert and Mulkay's (1984) research on scientists' discourse is concerned with the field of bioenergetics and in particular with the process whereby scientists working in this area come to understand a mechanism dubbed by them 'oxidative phosphorylation'. The main source of Gilbert and Mulkay's data derives from interviews with thirty-four researchers in this field. The interviews lasted between two-and-a-half and three hours on average. The authors describe the process of analysing the resulting data as follows:

> The interviews were tape-recorded and transcribed in full. We then read through the transcripts and copied those pages which included material relating to the topics which interested us. The passages from the interviews concerning each topic were placed together in 'topic files', so that we had convenient access to all the material on, for instance, consensus or diagrams and pictorial representations. We aimed to make each file as inclusive as possible so that no passage which could be read as dealing with a particular topic was omitted from its file. (Gilbert and Mulkay 1984: 19)

In addition, the authors drew on further sources, such as: privately circulated letters written by leading authorities in the field; the main articles in the field; and copies of the chief textbooks in the field.

a model as emerging out of the data, whereas in the research interview the rendition is one of reinterpreting the model, which in turn suggested seeing the existing data from a different perspective, which in turn suggested a new series of experiments. Similarly, Gilbert and Mulkay found that the sections of the scientific papers that described the experimental methodology portrayed the procedures in terms that suggested they were neutral operations that were largely independent of the scientist and could be replicated by anyone. In the research interviews, however, the scientists emphasized the operation of practical skills that are the product of experience and developing a 'feel' for experimental work. As one scientist put it:

> How could you write it up? It would be like trying to write a description of how to beat an egg. Or like trying to read a book on how to ski. You'd just get the wrong idea altogether. You've got to go and watch it, see it, do it. There's no substitute for it. These are *practical* skills. We all know that practical skills are not well taught by bits of paper. (Quoted in Gilbert and Mulkay 1984: 53)

Gilbert and Mulkay argue that in the formal context of the scientific paper an *empiricist repertoire* prevailed. This concept was derived from 'the observation that the texts of experimental papers display certain recurrent stylistic, grammatical and lexical features which appear to be coherently related' (1984: 55–6). The empiricist repertoire was revealed in such features as: an emphasis on procedural routines in the conduct of experiments, such that the findings appear as an inevitable, logical outcome; no mention of theoretical commitments on the part of authors; and an impersonal writing style with little or no mention of the authors' role in the production of the findings. By contrast, in the informal milieu of the research interview, a *contingent repertoire* was in operation. In this context, 'scientists presented their actions and beliefs as heavily dependent on speculative insights, prior intellectual commitments, personal characteristics, indescribable skills, social ties and group membership' (1984: 56). In other words, when describing their research within a contingent repertoire, scientists were much less likely to present their findings as the inevitable outcome of their experimental engagement with natural phenomena and were therefore far more likely to recog-

nize their own role in the production of scientific findings. Gilbert and Mulkay then go on to show that, when scientists disagree with the positions of other scientists, they describe their own work within an empiricist repertoire, in which their own findings take on the character of natural inevitability through the following of proper procedure, but of other scientists the work is described within a contingent repertoire, which shows up their competitors' errors as the product of prejudices, theoretical commitments, bias, and so on.

The notion of the interpretative repertoire is interesting because it brings out the idea that belief and action take place within templates that guide and influence the writer or speaker. The two repertoires discussed by Gilbert and Mulkay by no means exhaust the range of possibilities: Potter and Wetherell (1987), for example, suggest that a community repertoire was used in the context of a riot in Bristol in 1980 to cast light on events and beliefs. In the process, the police were cast in the role of *agents provocateurs* rather than as keepers of the peace. What is particularly striking about Gilbert and Mulkay's research, however, is that the two repertoires are employed by scientists but in different contexts (in formal or informal contexts, and whether describing their own or competitors' procedures). In a similar vein, Billig's (1992: 149) research on the ways in which people talk about the royal family suggested that, when referring to the role of newspapers in providing information about its members, two positions were frequently held and deployed on different occasions: 'the papers as the sources of lies and the papers as the source of knowledge'. Such a recognition of the almost simultaneous use of different repertoires brings to the fore the 'dilemmatic' nature of thinking in these and other environments (Billig *et al.* 1988).

Producing facts

As with the exposition of interpretative repertoires in DA, in this section a study will be employed as a lens through which to view the practice of discourse analytic research. On this occasion, the emphasis is upon the resources that are employed in conveying allegedly factual knowledge. The researchers were especially interested in the role of what they call *quantification rhetoric*, by which is meant the ways in which numerical and non-numerical statements are made to support or refute arguments. The interest in this issue lies in part in the importance of quantification in everyday life and in part in the tendency for many social scientists to make use of this strategy themselves (John 1992). The specific focus of the research was upon a study of a television programme shown on Channel 4 in April 1988 and entitled *Cancer: Your Money or Your Life* (Potter *et al.* 1991; Potter and Wetherell 1994). Among other things, the programme claimed to show that the huge amounts of money donated by the public to cancer charities are doing little to 'cure' the disease. The details of the materials used in the research and an outline of the process of analysis are provided in Research in focus 20.4. Research in focus 20.5 provides a key part of the transcript for the television programme itself.

In proceeding with an analysis of their data, such as the portions of transcript in Research in focus 20.5, Potter and Wetherell employed several devices.

Research in focus 20.4
Discourse analysis in action: producing facts through quantification rhetoric

The study of the representation of facts in the television programme *Cancer: Your Money or Your Life* (Potter *et al.* 1991; Potter and Wetherell 1994) used a variety of different sources:

- a video recording of the programme;
- the observations of one of the members of the team making the programme, who acted as a participant observer while it was being made;
- drafts of the script, shooting schedules, and recordings of editing sessions;
- the entire interviews with the various people interviewed for the programme (such as cancer research specialists and heads of charities);
- research interviews with some of the latter people;
- research interviews with some of the people involved in making the programme.

One of the phases of the analysis entailed the 'coding' of the various sources that had been collected. The authors tell us:

> We made a list of about a dozen keywords and phrases that related to the sequence—percentage, cure rates, death rates, 1 per cent, etc.—and then ran through each of the interview and interaction files, looking for them with a standard word-processor . . . Whenever we got a 'hit' we would read the surrounding text to see if it had relevance to our target sequence. When it did we would copy it across to an already opened coding file . . . noting the transcript page numbers at the same time. If we were not sure if the sequence was relevant we copied it anyway, for, unlike the sorts of coding that take place in traditional **content analysis**, the coding is not the analysis itself but a preliminary to make the task of analysis manageable. (Potter and Wetherell 1994: 52)

A prominent sequence used in the research is provided in Research in focus 20.5.

Research in focus 20.5
Sequence from the study of the television programme *Cancer: Your Money or Your Life is a TV programme*

The following sequence occurred roughly halfway through the programme, following interviews with cancer scientists who cast doubt on whether their research, much of it funded by charities, results in successful treatment:

> COMMENTARY: The message from these scientists is clear—exactly like the public—they hope their basic research will lead to cures in the future—although at the moment they can't say how this will happen. In the meantime, their aim is to increase scientific knowledge on a broad front and they're certainly achieving this. But do their results justify them getting so much of the money that has been given to help fight cancer? When faced with this challenge the first thing the charities point to are the small number of cancers which are now effectively curable.
>
> [on screen: DR NIGEL KEMP CANCER RESEARCH CAMPAIGN]
>
> KEMP: The outlook for individuals suffering from a number of types of cancer has been totally revolutionized. I mean for example—children suffering from acute leukaemia—in old days if they lived six months they were lucky—now more than half the children with leukaemia are cured. And the same applies to a number of other cancers—Hodgkin's Disease in young people, testicular tumours in young men, and we all know about Bob Champion's success [Champion was a prominent jockey who contracted testicular cancer, made a much-heralded recovery, won the Grand National, and even had a movie made about him]. (Potter and Wetherell 1994: 52–3)

At this point a table showing the annual incidence of thirty-four types of cancer begins to scroll on the screen. The total incidence is 243,000 and the individual incidences range from placenta (20) to lung (41,400). The three forms of cancer mentioned by Kemp and their levels of incidence are highlighted in yellow: childhood leukaemia (350), testis (1,000), and Hodgkin's Disease (1,400). The programme continues while the table is scrolling.

> COMMENTARY: But those three curable types are amongst the rarest cancers—they represent around 1 per cent of a quarter of a million cases of cancers diagnosed each year. Most deaths are caused by a small number of very common cancers.
>
> KEMP: We are well aware of the fact that erm once people develop lung cancer or stomach cancer or cancer of the bowel sometimes—the outlook is very bad and aaa obviously one is frustrated by the sss relatively slow rate of progress on the one hand but equally I think there are a lot of real opportunities and and positive signs that advances can be made—even in the more intractable cancers. (Potter and Wetherell 1994: 53)

Looking for rhetorical detail

Attention to rhetorical detail entails a sensitivity to the ways in which arguments are constructed. Thus, during the editing of the film, the programme makers' discourse suggested they were looking for ways to provide a convincing argument for their case that cancer remains largely intractable in spite of the money spent on it. The programme makers very consciously devised the strategy outlined in the discussion of 'using variation as a lever' of playing down the numerical significance of those cancers that are amenable to treatment. Moreover, Potter *et al.* (1991) point out that one element of their argumentative strategy is to employ a tactic they call a 'preformulation', whereby a possible counter-argument is discounted in the course of presenting an argument, as when the com-

mentary informs us: 'When faced with this challenge the first thing the charities point to are the small number of cancers which are now effectively curable.' Research in focus 20.6 examines a further rhetorical device that is employed in making a persuasive argument.

Research in focus 20.6
The extreme case formulation: the social construction of the asylum seeker

Discourse analysts have examined a variety of different rhetorical strategies through which arguments are formulated. One interesting form is known as the *extreme case formulation*. Potter (1996: 187) gives the example of someone who returns an item of clothing to a dry cleaner claiming it has been damaged by them might emphasize the significance of the claim by suggesting that the item is not simply new but 'brand new'. An interesting use of the concept can be found in connection with a study of letters to newspapers written by members of the general public in connection with 'asylum seekers', who were the focus of considerable controversy during the period the letters were written (March to September 2001). The researchers point to a 'striking predominance' of two rhetorical strategies in the discourse surrounding asylum seekers, of which the extreme case formulation was one (Lynn and Lea 2003: 446). Examples, with the extreme case formulation elements underlined, are:

> Perhaps if they learned to say no now and again instead of accepting <u>every freebie</u> that comes their way any resentment would melt away. (*Sun*)

> Asylum seekers who are genuine should have <u>no qualms</u> about being held in a reception centre. (*Daily Mail*)

> A solution to the problem of dispersing asylum-seekers is staring us in the face—namely, billet them free of charge on white liberals. That would have the advantage of both dispersing asylum-seekers widely and to areas with no social deprivation. White liberals will, of course be <u>only too happy to welcome them into their homes</u>. Indeed it is most odd that they have not been queuing up to offer their services. (*Independent*)

The extreme case formulation allows the writer to convey a position that is hostile to asylum seekers that simultaneously justifies that position. In essence, it acknowledges that a possibly extreme position is being presented that is unsympathetic to asylum seekers and that might even be viewed as racist, but uses the extreme case formulation in order to legitimize the position. It forms an important ingredient in the social construction of the asylum seeker as someone who is unfairly advantaged relative to UK citizens and who is a possible threat to the social order.

Rhetorical analysis is a mode of analysis that is often used in its own right. Researchers interested in rhetorical analysis emphasize the ways in which arguments are constructed either in speech or in written texts and the role that various linguistic devices (such as metaphor, ana-

logy, and irony) play in the formulation of arguments. Research in focus 20.7 provides an example of rhetorical analysis of textbooks in the field of marketing management to illustrate the approach.

Research in focus 20.7
The rhetoric of marketing management textbooks

An interesting application of rhetorical analysis is Hackley's (2003) rhetorical analysis of textbooks in the field of marketing management. This might not seem an obvious focus of interest for the social researcher but in fact these textbooks can be of considerable significance for researchers with an interest in consumption and consumerism, as marketing is very much to do with the strategies employed by companies to target consumers. Hackley notes that this field has spawned a huge number of books and that two publishers alone—Pearson Education and Macmillan—between them had over 200 titles in their UK catalogues in 2000. He explored the underlying rhetoric of a selection of these texts. Through his rhetorical exploration of these texts, Hackley uncovered several striking themes. He notes, for example, that 'theory' occupies a paradoxical position in these texts. It is both, as he puts it, 'aggrandized and despised' (Hackley 2003: 1332). It is aggrandized because the texts typically indicate that they will cover key theories but then theory is knocked down because it is seen to be impractical and not likely therefore to provide guides to action. They frequently use other terms such as 'tool', 'framework', and 'concept' rather than 'theory', because of its association with lofty ivory tower (and presumably irrelevant) reflection. Another rhetorical device noted is what Hackley calls 'bogus reflexivity', which occurs when the author of the marketing text notes limitations of typical work in the field but then proceeds to reaffirm the stance of much of that typical work. In other words, there is an acknowledgement of shortcomings, but those shortcomings are often held in abeyance so far as the writing of the text is concerned. For Hackley, the rhetorical examination of these texts provides an insight into managerialist ideology.

Using variation as a lever

The authors draw attention to the phrase '1 per cent of a quarter of a million' (see Research in focus 20.5), because it incorporates two quantitative expressions: a relative expression (a percentage) and an absolute frequency (quarter of a million). The change of the register of quantification is important, because it allows the programme makers to make their case about the low cure levels (just 1 per cent) compared with the large number of new cases of cancer. They could have pointed to the absolute number of people who are cured, but the impact would have been less. Also, the 1 per cent is not being contrasted with 243,000 but with quarter of a million. Not only does this citation allow the figure to grow by 7,000; a quarter of a million sounds larger.

Reading the detail

Discourse analysts incorporate the CA preference for attention to the details of discourse. For example, Potter and Wetherell suggest that the description of the three 'curable cancers' as 'amongst the rarest cancers' is deployed to imply that these are atypical cancers, so that it is unwise to generalize to all cancers from experiences with them.

Looking for accountability

Discourse analysts draw on CA practitioners' interest in and approach to accounts. The programme makers were concerned to be accountable for the position they took, and Potter and Wetherell's (1994: 61) transcript of an editing session suggests they were keen to ensure they could defend their inference about the 1 per cent. From the point of view of both CA and DA, the extracts presented in Research in focus 20.5 can and should be regarded as accounts. The editing session notes suggest that it is the credibility of the account that was of concern to the programme makers. For DA practitioners, the search for accountability entails attending to the details through which accounts are constructed.

Cross-referencing discourse studies

Potter and Wetherell suggest that reading other discourse studies is itself an important activity. First, it helps to sharpen the analytic mentality at the heart of DA. Second, other studies often provide insights that are suggestive for one's own data. They indicate that they were influenced by a study of market traders by Pinch and Clark (1986). This research showed that a kind of quantification rhetoric was often being used by the traders (though Pinch and Clark did not use this term) in order to convey a sense of value (such as selling a pen with a pencil). It appeared that something similar was occurring when the

table was being scrolled whereby the large number of cancers and the long list of types was being contrasted with the small number (three) of curable ones. Similarly, the 'extreme case formulation' in the context of asylum seekers discussed in Research in focus 20.6 could be compared to uses of this rhetorical device in other contexts and studies.

Critical discourse analysis

Critical discourse analysis (CDA) emphasizes the role of language as a power resource that is related to ideology and socio-cultural change. It draws in particular on the theories and approaches of Foucault (e.g. 1977), who sought to uncover the representational properties of discourse as a vehicle for the exercise of power through the construction of disciplinary practices, such as individual subjectivity and the operation of rules and procedures that enabled the construction of disciplinary practices that enable the construction of the self-disciplining subject. The notion of discourse is therefore defined more broadly than in fine-grained approaches, as this summary by Phillips and Hardy (2002: 3) illustrates:

> We define a discourse as an interrelated set of texts, and the practices of their production, dissemination, and reception, that brings an object into being . . . In other words, social reality is produced and made real

through discourses, and social interactions cannot be fully understood without reference to the discourses that give them meaning. As discourse analysts, then, our task is to explore the relationship between discourse and reality.

As the final part of this quotation indicates, CDA practitioners are more receptive than discourse analysts to the idea of a pre-existing material reality that constrains individual agency, and in particular to the epistemology of critical realism (see Key concept 1.3), arguing that discourses should be examined in relation to social structures, including the power relationships that are responsible for occasioning them (Reed 2000). Discourse is thus conceived as a 'generative mechanism' rather than as a self-referential sphere in which nothing of significance exists outside it, as Thinking deeply 20.2 explains.

Thinking deeply 20.2
Critical realism and the discourse of organization

Fairclough (2005) argues that a version of CDA based on critical realism (see Key concept 1.3) is of particular value to organization studies especially in relation to the study of organizational change. Fairclough (2005: 917) is sceptical of the anti-realist assumptions of some discourse analysts who reject objectivist conceptions of organization as social structure in favour of seeing it as 'an interactive accomplishment', according to a constructionist perspective (see Chapter 1). He quotes Mumby and Clair (1997: 181) as typical of the latter position when they say 'we suggest that organizations exist only in so far as their members create them through discourse'.

Instead, Fairclough recommends an approach that centres on the tension between organizational discourse and organizational structure. Therefore, a critical realist approach to discourse analysis involves not just analysing the discourse *per se* but also its relationship to non-discursive elements. This is particularly important in relation to the study of organizational change because, 'while change in discourse is a part of organizational change, and organizational change can often be understood partly in terms of the constructive effects of discourse on organizations, organizational change is not simply change in discourse' (Fairclough 2005: 931). Fairclough identifies four sets of organizational research issues that a critical realist approach to discourse analysis can address.

1. *Emergence*: founded on the notion that 'new' organizational discourses emerge 'through "reweaving" relations between existing discourses' (2005: 932).

2. *Hegemony*: focusing on how particular discourses become hegemonic in particular organizations and on 'how discourse figures within the strategies pursued by groups of social agents to change organizations in particular directions' (2005: 933).

3. *Recontextualization*: involving identification of the principles through which 'external' discourses are internalized within particular organizations.

4. *Operationalization*: focusing on how discourses are operationalized, transformed into new ways of acting and interacting, inculcated into new ways of being, or materialized, within organizations.

In an organizational context, one of the things that CDA practitioners seek to trace is how discourses are constructed and maintained in relation to certain phenomena, such as globalization (see Research in focus 20.8). Analysis seeks to reveal the meaning of a particular phenomenon by exploring how:

- the discourse came to have a particular meaning today when 40 or 50 years ago it may have had none or a quite different meaning;

- the discourse draws on and influences other discourses;

- the discourse is constructed through texts (such as academic articles or journalistic writing);

- the discourse gives meaning to social life and makes certain activities possible, desirable or inevitable;

- particular actors draw on the discourse to legitimate their positions and actions.

This list of analytic devices in CDA is based on Phillips and Hardy (2002: 8).

As the second point in the above list indicates, discourses are conceived of as drawing on and influencing other discourses; so, for example, the discourse of globalization might affect discourses on new technology, free trade and liberalism, or corporate social responsibility. However, this is not always a complementary process, as in some cases discourses compete with each other for dominance in what is termed *dialogical struggle* (Keenoy *et al.* 1997). An example of how the temporal evolution of

discourses can be traced analytically is provided in Research in focus 20.8 in relation to globalization. Critical discourse analysis thus involves exploring why some meanings become privileged or taken for granted and others become marginalized. In other words, discourse does not just provide an account of what goes on in organizations; it is also a process whereby meaning is created. This involves asking 'who uses language, how, why and when' (van Dijk 1997: 2).

Analysis of a particular *discursive event* is usually carried out according to a 'three-dimensional' framework, which proceeds as follows:

- examination of the actual content, structure, and meaning of the text under scrutiny (*the text dimension*);

- examination of the form of discursive interaction used to communicate meaning and beliefs (*the discursive practice dimension*);

- consideration of the social context in which the discursive event is taking place (*the social practice dimension*) (Grant *et al.* 2004: 11).

A further key concept within CDA is the notion of *intertextuality*. This draws attention to the notion of discourse as existing beyond the level of any particular discursive event on which analysis is focused. The notion of intertextuality thus enables a focus on the social and historical context in which discourse is embedded. Further examples of the use of CDA can be found in Research in focus 21.7 and 21.8.

Research in focus 20.8
A critical analysis of globalization discourses

Fairclough and Thomas (2004) examine the discourse of globalization in relation to the process of organizing. Outlining various debates between commentators on globalization, the authors argue that 'we should not be asking what globalization is, but why certain versions of it seem to dominate our thinking in relation to the issue of organization. At the same time we need to be sensitive to the changeability of discourse and to the diverse ways in which the discourse develops. In short, we should consider the potential diversity of the discourse, but also seek to explain why this potential is not necessarily realized' (2004: 380). Using key texts in the literature on globalization, the authors analyse the consultancy-led 'hyperglobalist' discourse, which positions globalization as a positive force that represents a valuable opportunity for managers of corporations. They also analyse prescriptive texts that tell managers how to handle the challenges of globalization in a variety of respects and contexts and review the tendency for the globalization to be constructed as a reified object rather than a process within the discourse. However, they also note that 'discourses that appear to be dominant and hegemonic may not be so' (2004: 394). Instead they inevitably contain weaknesses that can be exploited, giving rise to counter-discourses.

Overview

As the discussion of DA has emphasized on several occasions, DA draws on insights from CA. Particularly when analysing strings of talk, DA draws on conversation analytic insights into the ways in which interaction is realized in and through talk in interaction. The CA injunction to focus on the talk itself and the ways in which intersubjective meaning is accomplished in sequences of talk is also incorporated into DA. This is not easy to accomplish, and, when one reads articles based on DA, it sometimes seems as though the practitioners come perilously close to invoking speculations that do not seem to be directly discernible in the sequences being analysed—that is, speculations about 'ethnographic particulars' and hence about motives.

Sometimes, there is a more explicit recognition of the potential contribution of an appreciation of the ethnographic context. Edley and Wetherell (1997) report findings relating to a study conducted within a DA framework. The data were gathered from discussions held in three-person groups with 17–18-year-old boys in a UK school. The focus of the article was upon the construction of masculinity as it emerged in the course of the group discussions. However, one of the authors carried out observations within the school. This ethnographic research 'led

to the identification of divisions within friendship groups in the sixth form as a major participant concern connected with formulations of masculinity within the school' (Edley and Wetherell 1997: 207). One of the key components of the friendship structure was the division between rugby players and the rest. Edley and Wetherell show that an important component of the construction of masculinity during talk among the non-players is their antipathy towards the rugby players. In other words, they defined their masculinity in contradistinction to the concepts of masculinity associated with the rugby players. However, the key point is that it is clear that the periods of ethnographic observation at least in part informed the discourse analytic interpretation of the sequences of talk that had been recorded. Such research suggests that the proscription concerning the recourse to ethnographic particulars is honoured more by some discourse analysts than others. It is easy to see why: attention to ethnographic details may alert the analyst to nuances and understandings that are not directly entrenched in the flow of discourse.

DA is in certain respects a more flexible approach to language in social research than CA, because it is not solely concerned with the analysis of naturally occurring talk, since practitioners also use various kinds of documents and research interviews in their work. Also, it permits the intrusion of understandings of what is going on that are not specific to the immediacy of previous utterances. It is precisely this to which conversation analysts object, as when Schegloff (1997: 183) writes about DA: 'Discourse is too often made subservient to contexts not of its participants' making, but of its analysts' insistence.' For their part, discourse analysts object to the restriction that this injunction imposes, because it means that conversation analysts 'rarely raise their eyes from the next turn in the conversation, and, further, this is not an entire conversation or sizeable slice of social life but usually a tiny fragment' (Wetherell 1998: 402). Thus, for discourse analysts, phenomena like interpretative repertoires are very much part of the context within which talk occurs, whereas in CA they are inadmissible evidence. But it is here that we see the dilemma for the discourse analyst, for, in seeking to admit a broader sense of context (such as attention to interpretative repertoires in operation) while wanting to stick close to the conversation analysts' distaste for ethnographic particulars, they are faced with the uncertainty of just how far to go in allowing the inclusion of conversationally extraneous factors.

The anti-realist inclination of many DA practitioners has been a source of controversy, because the emphasis on representational practices through discourses sidelines any notion of a pre-existing material reality that can constrain individual agency. Reality becomes little more than that which is constituted in and through discourse. This lack of attention to a material reality that lies behind and underpins discourse has proved too abstracted for some social researchers and theorists. For example, writing from a critical realist position (see Key concept 1.3), Reed (2000) has argued that discourses should be examined in relation to social structures, such as power relationships, that are responsible for the occasioning of those discourses. Attention would additionally be focused on the ways in which discourses then work through existing structures. Discourse is thereby conceived as a 'generative mechanism' rather than as a self-referential sphere in which nothing of significance exists

outside it. Reed (2000: 529) provides an interesting example of such an alternative view:

> Discourses—such as the quantitatively based discourses of financial audit, quality control and risk management—are now seen as the generative mechanisms through which new regulatory regimes 'carried out' by rising expert groups—such as accountants, engineers and scientists—become established and legitimated in modern societies. What they represent is less important than what they do in facilitating a radical re-ordering of pre-existing institutional structures in favour of social groups who benefit from the upward mobility which such innovative regulatory regimes facilitate . . .
> (Reed 2000: 529)

As this passage suggests, while many DA practitioners are anti-realist, an alternative, realist position in relation to discourse is feasible. Such an alternative position is perhaps closer to the classic concerns of the social sciences than an anti-realist stance.

Many of these studies refer to their analysis of language using the term discourse. However, the extensive use of this term brings its own problems, because what different researchers understand the term discourse to mean varies considerably, and so does their approach to analysis. There is thus a danger, noted by Alvesson and Kärreman (2000), that the term 'discourse analysis' is too broad to be meaningful, authors treating the term as though it has a clear, broadly agreed-upon meaning that, just from reading this chapter, you will be able to see it does not. Hence 'discourse sometimes comes close to standing for everything, and thus nothing' (Alvesson and Kärreman 2000: 1128). However, the important thing to remember is that understanding how language is used is viewed by some researchers as crucial to understanding the social world, and the approaches examined in this chapter provide some tools through which language can be explored as a focus of attention in its own right.

Key points

- CA and DA approaches take the position that language is itself a focus of interest and not just a medium through which research participants communicate with researchers.
- CA is a systematic approach to conversation that locates action in talk.
- In CA, talk is deemed to be structured in the sense of following rules.
- Practitioners of CA seek to make inferences about talk that are not grounded in contextual details that are extraneous to talk.
- DA shares many features with CA but there are several different versions of it.
- DA can be applied to a wider variety of phenomena than CA, which is just concerned with naturally occurring talk.
- Discourse is conceived of as a means of conveying meaning.
- DA practitioners display a greater inclination to relate meaning in talk to contextual factors.

Questions for review

- In what ways does the role of language in conversation and discourse analysis differ from that which is typical in most other research methods?

Conversation analysis

- In what ways is CA fundamentally about the production of social order in interaction? Why are audio-recording and transcription crucial in CA?
- What is meant by each of the following: turn-taking; adjacency pair; preference organization; account; repair mechanism?
- How do the terms in the previous question relate to the production of social order?
- Evaluate Schegloff's argument that CA obviates the need to make potentially unwarranted assumptions about participants' motives.

Discourse analysis

- What is the significance of saying that DA is anti-realist and constructionist?
- What is an interpretative repertoire?
- What techniques are available to the discourse analyst when trying to understand the ways in which facts are presented through discourse?
- What is distinctive about critical DA?
- What are the chief points of difference between CA and DA?

Critical discourse analysis

- What key questions might a CDA practitioner ask in seeking to reveal the meaning of globalization discourses?
- Why is the notion of intertextuality important to CDA practitioners?

Online Resource Centre

http://www.oxfordtextbooks.co.uk/orc/brymansrm3e/

Visit the Online Resource Centre that accompanies this book to enrich your understanding of language in qualitative research. Consult web links, test yourself using multiple choice questions, and gain further guidance and inspiration from the Student Researcher's Toolkit.

Documents as sources of data

Chapter outline

Chapter guide

The term 'documents' covers a very wide range of different kinds of source. This chapter aims to reflect that variability by examining a wide range of different documentary sources that have been or can be used in qualitative research. In addition, the chapter touches on approaches to the analysis of such sources. The chapter explores:

- personal documents in both written form (such as diaries and letters) and visual form (such as photographs);
- official documents deriving from the state (such as public inquiries);
- official documents deriving from private sources (such as documents produced by organizations);
- mass-media outputs;
- virtual outputs, such as Internet resources;
- the criteria for evaluating each of the above sources;
- how far readers of documents are active or passive consumers of documents;
- three approaches to the analysis of documents: qualitative content analysis; semiotics; and hermeneutics.

Introduction

This chapter will be concerned with a fairly heterogeneous set of sources of data, such as letters, diaries, autobiographies, newspapers, magazines, and photographs. The emphasis is placed on documents that have not been produced at the request of a social researcher—instead, the objects that are the focus of this chapter are simply 'out there' waiting to be assembled and analysed. However, this is not to suggest that the fact that documents are available for the social researcher to work on renders them somehow less time-consuming or easier to deal with than primary data that need to be collected. On the contrary, the search for documents relevant to your research can often be a frustrating and highly protracted process. Moreover, once they are collected, considerable interpretative skill is required to ascertain the meaning of the materials that have been uncovered.

Documents of the kind referred to in this chapter are materials that:

- can be read (though the term 'read' has to be understood in a somewhat looser fashion than is normally the case when we come to visual materials, like photographs);

- have not been produced specifically for the purpose of social research;
- are preserved so that they become available for analysis; and
- are relevant to the concerns of the social researcher.

Documents have already been encountered in this book, albeit in a variety of contexts or guises. For example, the kinds of source upon which content analysis is often carried out are documents, such as newspaper articles. However, the emphasis in this chapter will be upon the use of documents in qualitative research. A further way in which documents have previously surfaced was in the brief discussion in Key concept 13.3, which noted that archive materials are one form of unobtrusive measure. Indeed, this points to an often-noted advantage of using documents of the kind discussed in this chapter—namely, they are non-reactive. This means that, because they have not been created specifically for the purposes of social research, the possibility of a reactive effect can be largely discounted as a limitation on the validity of data.

In discussing the different kinds of documents used in the social sciences, Scott (1990) has usefully distinguished between personal documents and official documents and has further classified the latter in terms of private as opposed to state documents. These distinctions will be employed in much of the discussion that follows. A further set of important distinctions made by Scott relate to the criteria for assessing the quality of documents. He suggests (Scott 1990: 6) four criteria.

1. *Authenticity*. Is the evidence genuine and of unquestionable origin?

2. *Credibility*. Is the evidence free from error and distortion?

3. *Representativeness*. Is the evidence typical of its kind, and, if not, is the extent of its untypicality known?

4. *Meaning*. Is the evidence clear and comprehensible?

This is an extremely rigorous set of criteria against which documents might be gauged, and frequent reference to them will be made in the following discussion.

Personal documents

This section discusses the nature of and issues involved in using a variety of kinds of personal documents that individuals produce and that are often used in social research.

Diaries, letters, and autobiographies

Diaries and letters have been used a great deal by historians but have not been given a great deal of attention by social researchers. The latter have tended to employ these as sources when they have been specifically elicited from their authors. The researcher-driven diary has been used as a method of data collection in both quantitative and qualitative research. A similar approach can be employed in relation to letters: for example, Ang (1985) placed an advertisement in a Dutch women's magazine asking readers to write to her about their reactions to and feelings about the American television series *Dallas*. She received forty-two letters in response to this advertisement. However, the kinds of diary and letter that are the focus of attention here are ones that have not been solicited by a researcher. Research in focus 21.1 and 21.2 provide examples of the use of personal documents in

Research in focus 21.1
Using historical personal documents: the case of Augustus Lamb

Dickinson (1993) provides an interesting account of the use of historical personal documents in the case of Augustus Lamb (1807–36), who was the only child of Lady Caroline Lamb and William Lamb, the second Viscount Melbourne. It is possible that Augustus suffered throughout his short life from epilepsy, though he seems to have suffered from other complaints as well. Dickinson was drawn to him because of her interest in nineteenth-century reactions to people with mental handicaps who were not institutionalized. In fact, Dickinson doubts whether the term 'mental handicap' is applicable to Augustus and suggests the somewhat milder description of having learning difficulties. The chief sources of data are 'letters from family and friends; letters to, about and (rarely) from Augustus' (Dickinson 1993: 122). These letters were found in collections at the Hertfordshire County Office, the British Museum, and Southampton University Library. Other sources used include: the record of the post-mortem examination of Augustus and extracts from the diary of Augustus' resident tutor and physician for the years 1817–21. Dickinson employs these materials to demonstrate the difficulty of arriving at a definitive portrayal of what Augustus was like. At the same time, she shows the difficulties that people around him experienced in coming to terms with his conditions, in large part because of the difficulty they experienced in finding a vocabulary that was consistent with his high social status.

social research in both historical and more contemporary contexts.

It is likely that the potential of letters in historical and social research is or will be fairly limited to a certain time period. As Scott (1990) observes, letter writing became a significant activity only after the introduction of an official postal service and in particular after the penny post in 1840. The emergence of the telephone as a prevalent form of communication may have limited the use of letter writing, and it is likely that the emergence of email communication, especially in so far as emails are not kept in electronic or printed form, is likely to mean that the role of letters has been declining for some time and may continue to do so. On the other hand, there is growing interest in emails in their own right among social researchers. For example, Sharf (1999) has reported how, while conducting research into rhetoric about breast cancer, she joined a listserv (a managed list of email addresses around a specific theme) on breast cancer and gradually realized that electronic communications had considerable potential for her research. Research involving the study of emails and other forms of Internet-based communication are examined further in Chapter 26.

Whereas letters are a form of communication with other people, diarists invariably write for themselves, but, when written for wider consumption, diaries are difficult to distinguish from another kind of personal document—the autobiography. Like letters and diaries, autobiographies can be written at the behest of the researcher, particularly in connection with life history stud-ies (see Key concept 18.1). When used in relation to the life history or biographical method, letters, diaries, and autobiographies (whether solicited or unsolicited) either can be the primary source of data or may be used as adjuncts to another source of data, such as life history or life story interviews. However, it is with extant (that is, unsolicited) documents that this chapter is primarily concerned.

The widespread distinction between biographies and autobiographies can sometimes break down. Walt Disney provides a case in point. As I have shown, Disney provided, in short articles he authored and in articles written by others, many snippets about his life (Bryman 1995). The first biography of Disney, written by his daughter, Diane Disney Miller (1956), would almost certainly have been fed information by its subject. Moreover, several writers have noted the 'sameness' about subsequent biographies. This feature can be attributed to the tight control by the Disney Archive, which is itself controlled by the Walt Disney Corporation. It is from the primary materials of this archive (letters, notes of meetings, and so on) that biographies would be fashioned. As a result, while Walt Disney never wrote an autobiography in the conventional meaning of the term, his hand and subsequently that of the company can be seen in the biographies that have been written.

When we evaluate personal documents, the *authenticity* criterion is clearly of considerable importance. Is the purported author of the letter or diary the real author? In the case of autobiographies, this has become a growing problem in recent years as a result of the increasing use of 'ghost' writers by the famous. But the same is potentially

Research in focus 21.2
Using contemporary personal documents

Jacobs (1967) analysed 112 suicide notes written by adults and adolescents in the Los Angeles area who had successfully committed suicide. The notes were acquired in the course of a study of attempts by adolescents to commit suicide. The author writes that he was impressed with the 'rational and coherent character' of the notes (1967: 62) and attempts what he describes as a 'phenomenological' analysis of them. This analysis entailed attending to 'the conscious deliberations that take place before the individual is able to consider and execute the act of suicide' (1967: 64). Jacobs found that the notes fell into six groups, such as notes referring to an illness, a category that in turn was of two types: those in which the writers begged forgiveness and those in which they did not.

true of other documents. For example, in the case of Augustus Lamb (Research in focus 21.1), Dickinson (1993: 126–7) notes that there are 'only three letters existing from Augustus himself (which we cannot be certain were written in Augustus's own hand, since the use of amanuenses was not uncommon)'. This remark raises the question of how far Augustus was in fact the author of the entirety of the letters, especially in the light of his apparent learning difficulties. Turning to the issue of *credibility*, Scott (1990) observes that there are at least two major concerns with respect to personal documents: the factual accuracy of reports and whether they do in fact report the true feelings of the writer. The case of Augustus Lamb, in which clear differences were found in views about him and his condition, suggests that the notion that there might be a definitive factually accurate account is at the very least problematic. Scott recommends a strategy of healthy scepticism regarding the sincerity with which the writer reports his or her true feelings. Famous people may be fully aware that their letters or diaries will be of considerable interest to others and may, therefore, have one eye firmly fixed on the degree to which they really reveal themselves in their writings, or alternatively ensure that they convey a 'front' that they want to project.

Letters have to be treated with similar caution, since they can frequently be exercises in reputation building. In the case of the suicide notes analysed by Jacobs (1967) (see Research in focus 21.2), although the notes themselves were found to be rational and coherent, it is possible that the individuals themselves were in a highly distressed state, so that it is not clear how far their true feelings were being revealed.

Representativeness is clearly a major concern for these materials. Since literacy was far lower in earlier times, letters, diaries, and autobiographies are likely to be the preserve of the literate and by and large the middle class. Moreover, since boys were often more likely to receive an education than girls, the voices of women tend to be under-represented in these documents. Women are also less likely to have had the self-confidence to write diaries and autobiographies. Therefore, such historical documents are likely to be biased in terms of authorship. A further problem is the selective survival of documents like letters. Why do any survive at all and what proportion are damaged, lost, or thrown away? We do not know, for example, how representative the 112 suicide notes analysed by Jacobs (1967; see Research in focus 21.2) are. Quite aside from the fact that only a relatively small percentage of suicide victims leave notes, it may be that notes are sometimes destroyed by family members. The ques-

tion of *meaning* is often rendered problematic by such things as damage to letters and diaries and the use by authors of abbreviations or codes that are difficult to decipher. Also, as Scott (1990) observes, letter-writers may leave much unsaid in their communications, because they share with their recipients common values and assumptions that are not revealed.

Visual objects

There is a growing interest in the visual in social research, a point that was highlighted in Chapter 17. The photograph is the most obvious manifestation of this trend, in that, rather than being thought of as incidental to the research process, photographs are becoming objects of interest in their own right (see Key concept 21.1). Once again, there is a distinction between photographs and other visual objects that are produced as part of fieldwork and that were discussed in Chapter 17 and those that are extant (which are the focus of attention here). One of the main ways in which photographs may be of interest to social research is in terms of what they reveal about families. As Scott (1990) observes, many family photographs are taken as a record of ceremonial occasions (weddings, christenings) and of recurring events such as Christmas, annual holidays, and wearing a new uniform at the start of the new school year. Scott refers to a distinction between three types of home photograph: *idealization*, which is a formal pose—for example, the wedding photograph or a photograph of the family in its finery; *natural portrayal*, which entails capturing actions as they happen, though there may be a contrived component to the photograph; and *demystification*, which entails capturing an image of the subject in an untypical (and often embarrassing) situation. Scott suggests that it is necessary to be aware of these different types in order not to be exclusively concerned with the superficial appearance of the images and so that we can probe beneath that surface. He writes:

> There is a great deal that photographs do not tell us about their world. Hirsch [1981: 42] argues, for example, that 'The prim poses and solemn faces which we associate with Victorian photography conceal the reality of child labour, women factory workers, whose long hours often brought about the neglect of their infants, nannies sedating their charges with rum, and mistresses diverting middle class fathers.' (Scott 1990: 195)

Key concept 21.1
What are the roles of photographs in social research?

Photographs may have a variety of roles in relation to social research. While Chapter 17 and the present chapter discuss them in relation to qualitative research, there is no reason why they cannot be employed in quantitative research, and some researchers have employed them in this connection. For example, photographs could be the focus of **content analysis** or might be employed as prompts in connection with **structured interviewing** or an **experiment**. However, the growing interest in photographs and visual materials more generally has tended to come from qualitative researchers. There is an important distinction between the use of *extant* photographs that have not been produced for the research and *research-generated* photographs that have been produced by the researcher or at the researcher's behest. Three prominent roles have been:

1. *Illustrative.* Photographs may have a role whereby they do little more than illustrate points and therefore enliven what might otherwise be a rather dry discussion of findings. In some classic reports of their findings by anthropologists, photographs seemed to have such a limited role. Gradually, some anthropologists began to experiment with forms of **ethnography** in which photographs had a more prominent position.

2. *As data.* Photographs may be viewed as data in their own right. When based on research-generated photographs, they become essentially part of the researcher's *field notes* (see Research in focus 17.11 for an example). When based on extant photographs, they become the main source of data about the field in which the researcher is interested. The examples in the text of this section by Sutton (1992; Research in focus 21.3) and Blaikie (2001) are examples of this kind of use.

3. *As prompts.* Photographs may be used as prompts to entice people to talk about what is represented in them. Both research-driven photographs (see Research in focus 17.10) and extant photographs may be used in this way. Sometimes, research participants may volunteer the use of their photographs for this kind of use. For example, Riches and Dawson (1998) found that, in interviews with bereaved parents, unsolicited photographs with their deceased children were often shown. These photographs were frequently shown by the parents to others, so that their use in interviews merged with their existing practices for handling their grief. In this case, the photographs were extant ones. Research in focus 17.10 provides an illustration of the use of photographs of the research-generated kind, in that they were taken at the instigation of the researchers who were interested in the experience of homelessness.

As Scott argues, this means not only that the photograph must not be taken at its face value when used as a research source; it is also necessary to have considerable additional knowledge of the social context to probe beneath the surface. In fact, one might wonder whether the photograph in such a situation can be of any use to a researcher at all. The researcher does not need the photograph to uncover the ills that formed the underbelly of Victorian society; its only purpose seems to be to suggest that there is a gap between the photographic image and the underlying reality. A similar kind of point is made by Sutton in Research in focus 21.3.

Scott sees the issue of *representativeness* as a particular problem for the analyst of photographs. As he suggests, the photographs that survive the passage of time—for example, in archives—are very unlikely to be representative. They are likely to have been subject to all sorts of hazards, such as damage and selective retention. The example provided in Research in focus 21.3 of photographs of visits to Disney theme parks suggests that the process of discarding photographs may be systematic. The other problem relates to the issue of what is *not* photographed, as suggested by the quotation by Hirsch, and Sutton's suggestion that unhappy events at Disney

Research in focus 21.3
Photographs of the Magic Kingdom

Sutton (1992) has noted a paradox about people's visits to Disney theme parks. On the one hand, the Magic Kingdom is supposed to be 'the happiest place on Earth', with employees ('cast members') being trained to enhance the experience. However, it is clear that some people do not enjoy themselves while visiting a park. The time spent in queues, in particular, was a gripe for Sutton, as it often is for other visitors ('guests') (Bryman 1995). Nonetheless, people expect their visit to be momentous and therefore take along their cameras (and increasingly camcorders, though Sutton does not make this point). Sutton argues that photographs distort people's memories of their visit. They take pictures that support their anticipation that the Disney theme parks are happy places, and, when they return home, they 'discard photographs that remind them of unpleasant experiences and keep photographs that remind them of pleasant experiences' (Sutton 1992: 283). In other words, positive feelings are a post-visit reconstruction that are substantially aided by one's photographs. As a result, Sutton argues, the photographs provide not accurate recollections of a visit but distorted ones.

theme parks may not be photographed at all. A sensitivity to what is not photographed can reveal the 'mentality' of the person(s) behind the camera. This is the point that Sutton is making: the absence of photographs depicting less happy experiences at the parks suggests something about how the prospect of a visit to a Disney theme park is viewed and therefore tells us something about the reach of an influential corporation in the culture industry. What is clear is that the question of representativeness is much more fundamental than the issue of what survives, because it points to the way in which the selective survival of photographs may be constitutive of a reality that family members (or others) seek to fashion. As in Sutton's example, that very manufactured reality may then become a focus of interest for the social researcher in its own right.

The real problem for the user of photographs is that of recognizing the different ways in which the image may be comprehended. Blaikie (2001) found some fascinating photographs in the local museums of the Northern Isles of Orkney and Shetland. These photographs derived from the work of local photographers and donated family albums. As Blaikie (2001: 347) observes, in the images themselves and the ways in which they are represented by the museums, the 'apparently raw "reality" of island culture has already been appropriated and ordered'. The problem for the researcher is then one of coming to terms with the image and what it can be taken to mean. As he notes, is the image of a crofter standing by his home suggestive of respectability or of poverty? Also, however the image is construed, should it be seen as having had the function for the photographer of providing a social commentary, or of depicting a disappearing way of life, or of merely providing an image with no obvious subtext? Any or a combination of these different narratives may be applicable, so does this mean that the photograph is a highly limited form of document for the social researcher? While acknowledging the diversity of interpretations that can be bestowed on the images he examined, Blaikie argues that, in his case, they provide a perspective on the emergence of modernity and the sense of loss of a past life, especially in terms of the ways in which they were organized by the museums. Coming to this kind of understanding requires a sensitivity to the contextual nature of images and the variety of interpretations that can be attributed to them.

Official documents deriving from the state

The state is the source of a great deal of information of potential significance for social researchers. It produces a great deal of statistical information, some of which was touched on in Chapter 13. In addition to such quantitative data, the state is the source of a great deal of textual material of potential interest, such as Acts of Parliament and official reports.

An interesting use of official documents is Turner's (1994) employment of the reports of public inquiries into three disasters, one of which—the fire at the Summerland Leisure Centre, Douglas, Isle of Man, in 1973—is a particular emphasis in his discussion. The report was published in 1974. Turner was primarily interested in the preconditions of the fire—the factors that were deemed by the inquiry to have led to the fire itself and to the way in which the handling of the incident produced such disastrous consequences (fifty deaths). In his initial analysis, which was based on a grounded theory approach, Turner aimed to produce a theoretical account of the fire's preconditions. Turner describes the process for this and the other two public inquiry reports he examined as one of slowly going through the details of the report. He describes the process as follows:

> I asked, for each paragraph, what names or 'labels for ideas' I needed in order to identify those elements, events or notions which were of interest to me in my broad and initially very unfocused concern to develop a theory of disaster preconditions. I then recorded each name or concept label on the top of a 5 inch by 8 inch card, together with a note of the source paragraph, and added further paragraph references to the card as I encountered additional instances of the concept identified. (Turner 1994: 198)

He ended up with 182 of these cards, which provided the raw materials for building his theoretical model. Similar sources were employed by Weick (1990) in his study of the Tenerife plane crash in 1977, in that he used an official report of the Spanish Ministry of Transport and Communication and a further report by the US-based Airline Pilots Association.

Similar kinds of materials but in a different context were employed by Abraham (1994) in connection with his research on the medical drug Opren. The research was concerned with the role of interests and values in scientists' evaluations of the safety of medicines. The author describes his sources as 'publicly available transcripts of the testimonies of scientists, including many employed in the manufacture of *Opren*, Parliamentary debates, questions and answers in *Hansard*, and leaflets, letters, consultation papers and other documentation disposed by the British regulatory authority in respect of its duties under the 1968 British Medicines Act' (Abraham 1994: 720). Abraham's research shows that there were inconsistencies in the scientists' testimonies, suggesting that interests play an important role in such situations. He also uses his findings to infer that the notion of a scientific ethos, which has been influential in the sociology of science, has limited applicability in areas of controversy in which interests come to the surface.

In terms of Scott's (1990) four criteria, such materials can certainly be seen as authentic and as having meaning (in the sense of being clear and comprehensible to the researcher), but the two other standards require somewhat greater consideration. The question of credibility raises the issue of whether the documentary source is biased. This is exactly the point of Abraham's (1994) research. In other words, such documents can be interesting precisely because of the biases they reveal. Equally, this point suggests that caution is necessary in attempting to treat them as depictions of reality. The issue of representativeness is complicated in that materials like these are in a sense unique, and it is precisely their official or quasi-official character that makes them interesting in their own right. There is also, of course, the question of whether the case itself is representative, but in the context of qualitative research this is not a meaningful question, because no case can be representative in a statistical sense. The issue is one of establishing a cogent theoretical account and possibly examining that account in other contexts. Turner (1994) in fact examined three disasters and noted many common factors that were associated with behaviour in crisis situations.

Official documents deriving from private sources

This is a very heterogeneous group of sources, but one type that has been used a great deal is company documents. Companies (and indeed organizations generally) produce many documents. Some of these are in the public domain, such as annual reports, mission statements, press releases, advertisements, and public relations material in printed form and on the World Wide Web. Other documents are not (or may not be) in the public domain, such as company newsletters, organizational charts, minutes of meetings, memos, internal and external correspondence, manuals for new recruits, and so on. Such materials are often used by organizational ethnographers as part of their investigations, but the difficulty of gaining access to some organizations means that many researchers have to rely on public-domain documents alone. Even if the researcher is an insider who has gained access to an organization, it may well be that certain documents that are not in the public domain will not be available to him or her. For his study of ICI, Pettigrew (1985; see Research in focus 2.16) was allowed access to company archives, so that, in addition to interviewing, he was allowed to examine 'materials on company strategy and personnel policy, documents relating to the birth and development of various company OD [organizational development] groups, files documenting the natural history of key organizational changes, and information on the recruitment and training of internal OD consultants, and the use made of external OD consultants' (Pettigrew 1985: 41).

Such information can be very important for researchers conducting case studies of organizations using such methods as participant observation or (as in Pettigrew's case) qualitative interviews. Other writers have relied more or less exclusively on documents. The study of the film director Alfred Hitchcock by Kapsis (1989) employed a combination of personal documents (notably correspondence) and official documents, such as production notes and publicity files (Research in focus 21.4).

Such documents need to be evaluated using Scott's four criteria. As with the materials considered in the previous section, documents deriving from private sources like companies are likely to be authentic and meaningful (in the sense of being clear and comprehensible to the researcher), though this is not to suggest that the analyst of documents should be complacent. Issues of credibility

and representativeness are likely to exercise the analyst of documents somewhat more.

People who write documents are likely to have a particular point of view that they want to get across. An interesting illustration of this simple observation is provided by a study of company documentation by Forster (1994). In the course of a study of career development issues in a major British retail company (referred to pseudonymously as TC), Forster carried out an extensive analysis of company documentation relating primarily to human resource management issues, as well as interviews and a questionnaire survey. Because he was able to interview many of the authors of the documents about what they had written, 'both the accuracy of the documents and their authorship could be validated by the individuals who had produced them' (Forster 1994: 155). In other words, the authenticity of the documents was confirmed, and it would seem that credibility was verified as well. However, Forster also tells us that the documents showed up divergent interpretations among different groupings of key events and processes:

> One of the clearest themes to emerge was the apparently incompatible interpretations of the same events and processes amongst the three sub-groups within the company—senior executives, HQ personnel staff and regional personnel managers. . . . These documents were not produced deliberately to distort or obscure events or processes being described, but their effect was to do precisely this. (Forster 1994: 160)

In other words, members of the different groupings expressed through the documents certain perspectives that reflected their positions in the organization. Consequently, although authors of the documents could confirm the content of those documents, the latter could not be regarded as 'free from error and distortion', as Scott (1990: 6) puts it. Therefore, documents cannot be regarded as providing objective accounts of a state of affairs. They have to be interrogated and examined in the context of other sources of data. As Forster's case suggests, the different stances that are taken up by the authors of documents can be used as a platform for

Research in focus 21.4
Constructing Alfred Hitchcock: personal and official documents

The focus of Kapsis's (1989) study of Alfred Hitchcock is the way in which a reputation is fashioned in popular culture. In particular, he emphasizes the way in which Hitchcock's reputation as a director changed in the 1960s and beyond from that of a popular entertainer to that of a celebrated maker of highly significant films. Kapsis's analysis emphasizes the importance of sponsors, such as the influential French director François Truffaut, in the process of re-evaluation of his work, as well as the part played by Hitchcock himself. The main source was the director's personal files, which had been lodged with the Academy of Motion Picture Arts and Sciences. This collection is made up of materials that could be described as both personal and official documents, as well as other sources:

- scripts, production notes, and publicity files;
- correspondence, especially between Hitchcock and Truffaut and with various arts organizations;
- fifty-two hours of taped interviews with Truffaut;
- speeches delivered between 1960 and 1975;
- newspaper and magazine clippings, especially reviews;
- interviews by Kapsis with various people associated with Hitchcock.

developing insights into the processes and factors that lie behind divergence. In this instance, the documents are interesting in bringing out the role and significance of subcultures within the organization.

Issues of representativeness are likely to loom large in most contexts of this kind. Did Forster have access to a totally comprehensive set of documents? It could be that some had been destroyed or that he was not allowed access to certain documents that were regarded as sensitive. The case of the documents relating to Alfred Hitchcock is particularly interesting in this regard (see Research in

focus 21.4). Hitchcock or possibly others may not have deposited documents that were less than favourable to his image. Since Kapsis's article is concerned with reputation building and particularly with the active part played by Hitchcock and others in the construction of his reputation as a significant film maker, the part played by documents that might have been less than supportive of this reputation would be of considerable importance. This is not to say that such documents necessarily exist but that doubts are bound to surface whenever there is uncertainty about the representativeness of sources.

Mass-media outputs

Newspapers, magazines, television programmes, films, and other mass media are potential sources for social scientific analysis. Of course, we have encountered these kinds of source before when exploring content analysis in Chapter 12. In addition to mass-media outputs being explored using a quantitative form of data analysis like

content analysis, such sources can also be examined so that their qualitative nature is preserved. Typically, such analysis entails searching for themes in the sources that are examined, but see the discussion on analysing documents below for a more detailed examination of this issue.

In Chapter 12, Beharrell's (1993) content analysis of AIDS/HIV in the British press was cited as an illustration of different aspects of content analysis on several occasions. However, in this particular publication, the content analysis served mainly as a backcloth to a detailed investigation of themes in media representations of the risk of heterosexual transmission of HIV. During the period of press coverage that Beharrell investigated, a key component of the British government's health education strategy concerning HIV transmission was to demonstrate the risks associated with heterosexual transmission and especially the heightened risks of unprotected sex. Beharrell shows through an examination of such sources as editorials and articles by specialist medical reporters that three newspapers—the *Sun*, *Daily Mail*, and *Daily Express*—were consistently opposed to the government's campaign. For example, the *Daily Mail*'s editorials criticized the strategy on the grounds that it did not target sufficiently the high-risk groups—homosexuals and intravenous drug users. By contrast, the *Daily Mirror* was broadly supportive of the campaign. For example, a feature article on the occasion of World AIDS Day in 1988 proclaimed: 'And what we must never forget is that there is still no cure or vaccine for AIDS. So the way to stop its spread is through information, education and changes in human behaviour. Only then will there be any hope of controlling this deadly scourge' (*Daily Mirror*, 1 Dec. 1988; quoted in Beharrell 1993: 226). The broadsheet newspapers, such as *The Times*, the *Independent*, and the *Guardian*, were, like the *Daily Mirror*, broadly supportive

of the government's strategy of a general educational programme. However, Beharrell also points to internal contradictions in newspapers' reporting, such as references to articles in tabloids like the *Sun* in the summer of 1991 warning of the risks of HIV infection among British tourists going abroad for sun, sea, and sex holidays. Research in focus 21.7 provides a further illustration of the qualitative interpretation of newspaper articles.

As Beharrell points out, his research shows that an examination of reporting like this brings out the difficulty of referring to the 'press' in an undifferentiated way, and even conventional distinctions between tabloids and broadsheets need to be treated with some caution following such evidence. It also points to some of the contradictions in reporting. A content analysis might have been able to bring out aspects of this set of findings, but the employment of a more fine-grained analysis allows a greater sensitivity to the nature and content of specific themes. Magazines provide similar potential, as the example in Research in focus 21.5 suggests.

Similar observations can frequently be made about films. Aitken (1998) has analysed five British documentary films made between 1929 and 1939. All the films are about or touch substantially upon work and organizations. As such, they could be regarded as telling us a great deal in a graphic way about these themes in the inter-war years. For example, one of the five films—*Night Mail* (1936)—provides an insight into the Royal Mail train delivery service and concentrates on the operation during one day and night. While a shift in emphasis was apparent

Research in focus 21.5
Aberdeen football fanzines

Giulianotti (1997) has written about the fanzines that emerged in connection with Aberdeen football club, which was one of the clubs that were the focus of his ethnographic research (see Research in focus 17.2). He shows how the fanzines, some of which were defunct by the time of his analysis, play a role in the creation of a sense of identity among supporters, especially during a period of footballing decline. He shows, for example, that 'the fanzines combine the more traditional sense of cultural differences from the rest of Scotland with the North-East's self-deprecating, often self-defeating humour' (Giulianotti 1997: 231). An illustration of this tendency is through the medium of the sheep. Rival fans insist that Aberdeen supporters have an interest in this creature that extends beyond its potential as a provider of food and wool. This is revealed in the repetitive chant of rival supporters: 'Sheepshagging bastards, You're only [etc.] . . .' (Giulianotti 1997: 220). This allegation of bestiality is turned by the supporters upon themselves in their fanzines, so that the sheep is frequently used in cartoons, and stories about sheep frequent their pages.

over the years the films were made, Aitken notes that they reveal a celebration of manual and craft skills but provide a less enthusiastic or at least ambivalent depiction of administrative routines and organizational structures. As such, the films cannot be regarded as providing a neutral record of work and organizations during this period. Instead, they probably tell us more about the ambivalence towards large corporations during their emergence over this period.

Authenticity issues are sometimes difficult to ascertain in the case of mass-media outputs. While the outputs can usually be deemed to be genuine, the authorship of articles is often unclear (for example, editorials, some magazine articles), so that it is difficult to know whether the account can be relied upon as being written by someone

in a position to provide an accurate version. Credibility is frequently an issue, but in fact, as the examples used in this section show, it is often the uncovering of error or distortion that is the objective of the analysis. Representativeness is rarely an issue for analyses of newspaper or magazine articles, since the corpus from which a sample has been drawn is usually ascertainable, especially when a wide range of newspapers is employed, as in Beharrel's (1993) investigation. However, it is difficult to know whether the films analysed by Aitken (1998) are typical. Finally, the evidence is usually clear and comprehensible but may require considerable awareness of contextual factors, such as the need for Giulianotti to be aware of the symbolic significance of sheep to Aberdeen football supporters (see Research in focus 21.5).

Virtual documents

There is one final type of document that ought to be mentioned—documents that appear on the Internet. The vastness of the Internet and its growing accessibility make it a likely source of documents for both quantitative and qualitative data analysis. Two kinds of virtual documents tend to be the focus of attention: websites and Internet postings to message boards or forums. As an example of the former, Aldridge (1998) examined both written consumer guides to personal finance published in the UK and several Internet websites. Through an analysis of such documents Aldridge extracts a number of themes that he sees as part of the 'promotional culture' in which we live. Examples of such themes are the necessity for members of the public to assume responsibility for their personal finances, particularly in the light of the reductions in welfare provision, and the notion of the professional–client relationship as an uncontentious one in which the client has the ability to ask informed questions. Research in focus 12.3 reports a study that examined cancer websites and postings using a combination of quantitative and qualitative styles of content analysis. Research in focus 26.1 provides an example of an analysis of websites advertising ecotourism.

There is clearly huge potential with the Internet as a source of documents, but Scott's criteria need to be kept in mind. First, authenticity: anyone could set up a website, so that such matters as financial advice may be given by someone who is not an authority, though Aldridge selected sites of relatively assured probity. Second, credibility: we need to be aware of possible distortions. For example, if we were studying advice about the purchase of shares, it is known that websites have been set up encouraging people to buy or sell particular stocks held by the website authors, so that the prices of stocks can be manipulated. Third, given the constant flux of the Internet, it is doubtful whether we could ever know how representative websites are on a certain topic. Finally, websites are notorious for a kind of Webspeak, so that it may be difficult to comprehend what is being said without considerable insider knowledge. The use of websites as a source of data for social researchers is given further attention in Chapter 26 in the section on 'The Internet as object of analysis'.

The world as text

There is one word that I have done my best to avoid using in the chapter so far—text. The word 'text' is frequently employed as a synonym for a term like 'written document'. We have clearly strayed from this association, in that photographs and films have been touched upon. But, in relatively recent times, the word 'text' has been applied to an increasingly wide range of phenomena, so that theme parks, landscapes, heritage attractions, technologies, and a wide range of other objects are treated as texts out of which a 'reading' can be fashioned (e.g. Grint and Woolgar 1997). Thus, in Barthes's (1972) influential collection of essays, objects as varied as wrestling matches, Citroën cars, and striptease acts are submitted to readings. In a sense, therefore, just about everything can be treated as a text and perhaps as a document.

Readers and audiences—active or passive?

In Chapter 19, mention was made of the interest in audience reception as a prominent area of enquiry in media and cultural studies. **Focus group** research has played an important role in providing access to the ways in which members of audiences read media and cultural texts, and some of the examples in Table 19.1 were concerned with this issue. The key point about such research is whether audiences/readers are active interpreters of what they see or hear. Do they passively derive the meanings that authors or designers infuse into their texts, or do they resist those meanings and arrive at resistant readings, or do they arrive at a middle point that incorporates both passive and active elements? Much research on this issue suggests, as with Morley's (1980) study, which was briefly referred to in Chapter 19, that audiences frequently come up with alternative readings to those that were intended by authors or designers (see Fenton *et al.* 1998 for a summary of some of this research). Although the idea of the 'active audience' has not gone unchallenged (e.g. McGuigan 1992), the stream of research has been very influential and has placed a question mark over the readings of texts by social scientists. This means that we have to be cautious in concluding that the interpretations offered by social scientists of texts, such as Giulianotti's (1997) study of fanzines or Aitken's (1998) examination of documentary films in the inter-war years, are going to be the same as those of another social scientist, or as those of the readers or audiences of these outputs. The social researcher is always providing his or her own 'spin' on the texts that are analysed. The same is true of all social science data: the conclusions you derive from your questionnaire or ethnographic data are always going to be a reflection of your own personal interpretation. However, the main point being made for the present is that caution is required when reading writers' renditions of texts of all kinds.

The reality of documents

An issue that has attracted attention only relatively recently and that has implications for the interpretation of documents (the focus of the next section) is that of the status of documents. It is clearly tempting to assume that documents reveal something about an underlying social reality, so that the documents that an organization generates (minutes of meetings, newsletters, mission statements, job definitions, etc.) are viewed as representations of the reality of that organization. In other words, we might take the view that such documents tell us something about what goes on in that organization and will help us to uncover such things as its culture or ethos. According to such a view, documents are windows onto social and organizational realities.

However, some writers have expressed scepticism about the extent to which documents can be viewed in these terms. Rather than view documents as ways of gaining access to an underlying reality, writers like Atkinson and Coffey (2004) argue that documents should be viewed as a distinct level of 'reality' in their own right.

Atkinson and Coffey argue that documents should be examined in terms of, on the one hand, the context in which they were produced and, on the other hand, their implied readership. When viewed in this way, documents are significant for what they were supposed to accomplish and who they are written for. They are written in order to convey an impression, one that will be favourable to the authors and those whom they represent. Moreover, any document should be viewed as linked to other documents, because invariably they refer to and/or are a response to other documents. Other documents form part of the context or background to the writing of a document. Atkinson and Coffey refer to the inter-connectedness of documents as *inter-textuality*.

The minutes of a meeting in an organization might be the kind of document that would interest a social scientist. On the face of it, they are a record of such things as: issues raised at the meeting; the discussion of those issues; views of the participants; and actions to be taken. As such, they might be deemed interesting for a social researcher for their ability to reveal such things as the culture of the organization or section responsible for the minutes, its preoccupations, and possible disputes among the meeting participants. However, precisely because the minutes are a document that are to be read not only by participants but also by others (members of other departments or of other organizations or in the case of a public-sector organization the minutes may be accessed by the public under the Freedom of Information Act), they are likely to be written with prospective scrutiny by others in mind. Disagreements may be suppressed and actions to be taken may reflect a desire to demonstrate that important issues are to be addressed rather than because of a genuine desire for acting on them. Also, the minutes are likely to be connected either explicitly or implicitly to other documents of that organization, such as previous minutes, mission statements, job definitions, organizational regulations, and various documents external to the organization (e.g. legislation). Further, following Atkinson and Coffey's suggestions, the minutes should be examined for the ways in which language is employed to convey the messages that are contained.

Atkinson and Coffey's central message is that documents have a distinctive **ontological** status, in that they form a separate reality, which they refer to as a 'documentary reality', and should not be taken to be 'transparent representations' of an underlying organizational or social reality. They go on to write: 'We cannot . . . learn through written records alone how an organization actually operates day by day. Equally, we cannot treat records—however "official"—as firm evidence of what they report' (Atkinson and Coffey 2004: 58).

Atkinson and Coffey's central point is that documents need to be recognized for what they are—namely, texts written with distinctive purposes in mind, and not as simply reflecting reality. This means that, if the researcher wishes to employ documents as a means of understanding aspects of an organization and its operations, it is likely that he or she will need to buttress an analysis of documents with other sources of data. In this context, it is interesting to reflect on Atkinson and Coffey's illustrative examination of a document—Cardiff University's submission to the Educational Panel for the 2001 Research Assessment Exercise (RAE). Currently, the research of UK universities is periodically assessed by panels organized around disciplines. It is a major feature of life in UK universities. Each unit of assessment (in this case Education) submits a document that records the activities of that unit and the publications of its members. The document and in particular the publications are then assessed by panels of peers. As Atkinson and Coffey (2004: 72) note: 'At one level, any reader of English could makes sense of them [the documents]. On the other hand, it takes somebody who knows about research in higher education, and academic life more generally, to grasp much more of the significance of the phrases that are contained in the documents . . .'. This is a significant observation: Atkinson and Coffey can make sense of these RAE documents in terms of what they tell as about academic life in UK universities and the role of external audits within them only because they are insiders to that process. They are like participant observers. As such, they are able to bolster their examination of the documents by drawing on their experiences of modern university life. In other words, they have additional data on which they can draw in helping them to understand what the documents reveal about UK universities and modern audit culture. Thus, if we want to treat documents as telling us something about an underlying reality, we are likely to need to employ other sources of data regarding that reality and the contexts within which the documents are produced (see Research in focus 21.6 for an example).

Research in focus 21.6
Documents and disaster

Diane Vaughan (1996) wrote an extremely highly regarded book on the *Challenger* accident. This disaster occurred in January 1986 when the Space Shuttle *Challenger* burst into flames just after its launch. Vaughan had been interested in what she calls the 'dark side' of organizations and wanted to use this dreadful incident as a **case study** for understanding the chain of individual and organization factors that preceded and led to the decision to launch the shuttle in spite of evidence of possible problems. A huge report was written by the Presidential Commission that was appointed to investigate the accident. This report might have been considered sufficient to provide insights into the issues in which she was interested, but Vaughan also examined various other sources: an archive of NASA documents; other investigations of the accident; US House of Representatives hearing transcripts; transcripts of 160 interviews with people involved with *Challenger* conducted by government investigators; risk assessment documents that were solicited by Vaughan under the US Freedom of Information Act; and numerous interviews conducted by Vaughan herself (Vaughan 2004).

However, as Vaughan (2006) points out, examining documents like Presidential Commission reports can be extremely illuminating about the kinds of issues that they emphasize and the kinds of ways in which the issues are framed. This is precisely the point Atkinson and Coffey (2004) make in connection with the notion that documents provide a distinctive take on reality in their own right. Vaughan (2006) examined three Commission Reports: the *Challenger* report; the *Columbia* Accident Investigation Board Report, which dealt with another space shuttle disaster that took place in February 2003; and the 9/11 Commission Report. She shows that each report was shaped by a dominant frame, which was respectively: an 'accident investigation frame'; a 'sociological frame'; and an 'historical/war frame' (2006: 304). Further, she notes that the 9/11 report located causation in what she calls 'regulatory failure' (2006: 300), which is to do with problems with the activities of the agencies charged with upholding national security. An effect of that attribution of causation is to absolve the President and to some extent US foreign policy of responsibility. This examination of documents in their own right implies that they can tell us about such things as how those responsible for reporting officially on major incidents construe the background and causal precedents of those incidents. As such, the reports are interesting as much for where responsibility is *not* perceived as lying. As Atkinson and Coffey remind us, what they cannot tell us is what actually led up to them.

Interpreting documents

Although it means straying into areas that are relevant to the next chapter, this section will briefly consider the question of how, if you are not using content analysis, you interpret documents. Three possible approaches are outlined: qualitative content analysis; semiotics; and hermeneutics. In addition to these, discourse analysis,

which was covered in Chapter 20, has been employed as an approach for analysing documents. Research in focus 21.7 provides an example of the use of critical discourse analysis in relation to the interpretation of one kind of document reviewed in this chapter—newspaper articles.

Research in focus 21.7
Using critical discourse analysis to interpret newspaper articles

Critical discourse analysis was introduced in Chapter 20 as an approach to the examination of language and its use that can be applied to a variety of different materials. Teo (2000) employed it in relation to news reporting in Australian newspapers. Teo's focus of interest was the ways in which racism surfaced or was neutralized in two of the main Sydney newspapers. He emphasized in particular nine articles to do with 5T, a young Vietnamese gang that is relatively openly involved in drug-dealing in a suburb of Sydney. Critical discourse analysis was a suitable approach to interpreting these documents because of its capacity to provide insights into the way in which language use produces and legitimates racism in the press. As Teo observes, the 'critical' element in critical discourse analysis invites attention to the ideological basis of a discourse that naturalizes and thereby renders acceptable stances like racism. He notes a variety of mechanisms that are employed to convey a particular position with regard to racism and the police service's war on drugs. For example, Teo refers to the linguistic device that he refers to as *generalization*, which occurs when a cluster of characteristics of an identified group of individuals is extended (i.e. generalized to) a wider set of individuals. For example, he finds:

> In the newspaper discourse under analysis, we observe a *generalization* of the crimes of the 5T . . . to a progressively wider group of people (Vietnamese, Southeast Asians and Asians). References to 'Vietnamese' and 'Asian' appears so consistently and frequently in relation to criminal activities of the 5T that it becomes almost an endemic part of the drug culture of Australia. (Teo 2000: 16)

Examples quoted include: 'three Vietnamese men gunned down', 'the tall youth of Asian appearance', and 'five other youths of Asian appearance' (Teo 2000: 17). Here, then, the use of a critical discourse analysis approach to these documents provides a means of gaining insight into the ideological foundations of racism.

Qualitative content analysis

This is probably the most prevalent approach to the qualitative analysis of documents. It comprises a searching-out of underlying themes in the materials being analysed and can be discerned in several of the studies referred to earlier, such as Beharrell (1993), Giulianotti (1997), and Aitken (1998). The processes through which the themes are extracted is often not specified in detail. The extracted themes are usually illustrated—for example, with brief quotations from a newspaper article or magazine. Seale (2002: 109) examined newspaper reports in which people with cancer are portrayed. One of the phases of his analysis entailed an 'NVivo coding exercise, in which sections of text concerning themes of interest were identified and retrieved'. He was especially interested in gender differences in how sufferers are represented and shows, for example, that stories

about men were much more likely to include certain themes, such as how a person's character is important in helping him deal with the disease. The procedures adopted by Turner (1994) in connection with his research on the Summerland disaster are an example of the search for themes in texts, although Turner provided greater detail about what he did than is often the case. Research in focus 21.8 provides an example of a thematic analysis that illustrates some of its ingredients.

Altheide (1996) has outlined an approach that he calls 'ethnographic content analysis' (which he contrasts with quantitative content analysis of the kind outlined in Chapter 12). Altheide's approach (which he refers to as ECA) represents a codification of certain procedures that might be viewed as typical of the kind of qualitative content analysis on which many of the studies referred to so far are based. He describes his approach as differing from traditional quantitative content analysis in that the

Research in focus 21.8
Discerning themes in cartoons

The study in this Research in focus feature relates to an unusual kind of document—cartoons. This is unusual because most documents on which social researchers carry out analyses are textual rather than visual. Nonetheless, the study provides an interesting illustration of the extraction of themes from documents.

As a component of their study of the Canadian refugee system, Phillips and Hardy (2002: 75–8; see also Hardy and Phillips 1999) analysed 127 cartoons that appeared in Canadian newspapers in the 1987–9 period. The cartoons were connected with the general issues of immigration and refugees. They describe this collection of cartoons as a data set that was waiting for a research question, implying that they had collected the cartoons without any guiding principles, other than that they should relate to immigration and refugees. On examining the cartoons, they began to appreciate that the cartoons represented broader societal constructions of the immigrant, and this realization informed their analyses of the documents into themes. Early on in their examination of the cartoons, they realized that most cartoons relate to one or more of the following four objects:

1. the refugee;
2. government;
3. immigration system; and
4. the public (this fourth category was not a common one).

Further analysis revealed that in relation to each of these objects distinctive themes could be discerned. Each of these themes reflects the different ways that each of the four objects were represented in the cartoons. For example, seven themes could be discerned in the ways in which the immigration system was represented in the cartoons:

1. as inconsistent (23);
2. as inadequate (17);
3. as too tough (12);
4. as too lenient (10);
5. as too slow (7);
6. as gullible (7);
7. as honourable (1).

Each theme was accompanied by a definition. For example, the immigration system as inconsistent was defined as: 'Certain groups, such as illegal immigrants, fraudulent refugees, or individuals with political connections, are treated preferentially' (Phillips and Hardy 2002: 77). Hardy and Phillips (1999) also provide data on the frequency with which each of these themes occurred. The figures in parentheses above represent the number of cartoons that depicted each of the themes relating to the immigration system.

Hardy and Phillips (1999) provide some illustrative cartoons. For example, the immigration system as too tough is illustrated by an apparent refugee family of a couple and young child arriving at a door with the sign 'Immigration Canada Refugee Assessment'. Instead of a welcome mat in front of the door is a mat inscribed 'GET LOST'.

This research was conducted within a discourse analysis orientation, which is revealed in the authors' interest in the way in which the category of refugee is constructed through discourse and images and how both governments and non-governmental organizations with an interest in immigrants and refugees drew upon these discursive resources. However, the main point is that thematic analysis is a common approach to analysing documents (and indeed interview transcripts) and that it can be applied in relation to different kinds of orientation to qualitative data.

researcher is constantly revising the themes or categories that are distilled from the examination of documents. As he puts it:

ECA follows a recursive and reflexive movement between concept development-sampling-data, collection-data, coding-data, and analysis-interpretation. The aim is to be systematic and analytic but not rigid. Categories and variables initially guide the study, but others are allowed and expected to emerge during the study, including an orientation to *constant discovery* and *constant comparison* of relevant situations, settings, styles, images, meanings, and nuances. (Altheide 1996: 16; emphases in original)

Thus, with ECA there is much more movement back and forth between conceptualization, data collection, analysis, and interpretation than is the case with the kind of content analysis described in Chapter 12. Quantitative content analysis typically entails applying predefined categories to the sources; ECA employs some initial cat-egorization, but there is greater potential for refinement of those categories and the generation of new ones. In addition, ECA emphasizes the context within which documents are generated, so that a study of newspaper reporting of violence requires an appreciation of new organizations and the work of journalists (Altheide, 2004).

Altheide (2004) describes the steps involved as requir-ing the researcher to:

- generate a research question;
- become familiar with the context within which the documents were/are generated;
- become familiar with a small number of documents (6–10);
- generate some categories that will guide the collection of data and draft a schedule for collecting the data in terms of the generated categories;
- test the schedule by using it for collecting data from a number of documents;
- revise the schedule and select further cases to sharpen it up.

Once this process has been gone through, the schedule can be employed for the collection of data from documents.

Qualitative content analysis as a strategy of searching for themes in one's data lies at the heart of the coding approaches that are often employed in the analysis of qualitative data and as such will be encountered again in the next chapter.

Semiotics

Semiotics is invariably referred to as the 'science of signs'. It is an approach to the analysis of symbols in everyday life and as such can be employed in relation not only to documentary sources but also to all kinds of other data because of its commitment to treating phenomena as texts. The main terms employed in semiotics are:

- the *sign*—that is, something that stands for something else;
- the sign is made up of: a *signifier* and the *signified*;
- the *signifier* is the thing that points to an underlying meaning (the term *sign vehicle* is sometimes used instead of *signifier*);
- the *signified* is the meaning to which the signifier points;
- a *denotative meaning* is the manifest or more obvious meaning of a signifier and as such indicates its function;
- a *sign-function* is an object that denotes a certain function;
- a *connotative meaning* is a meaning associated with a certain social context that is in addition to its denota-tive meaning;
- *polysemy* refers to a quality of signs—namely, that they are always capable of being interpreted in many ways;
- the *code* is the generalized meaning that interested parties may seek to instil in a sign; a code is sometimes also called a *sign system*.

Semiotics is concerned to uncover the hidden meanings that reside in texts as broadly defined. Consider, by way of illustration, the curriculum vitae (CV) in academic life. The typical CV that an academic will produce contains such features as: personal details; education; previous and current posts; administrative responsibilities and experience; teaching experience; research experience; research grants acquired; and publications. We can treat the CV as a system of interlocking signifiers that signify at the level of denotative meaning a summary of the individual's experience (its sign function) and at the connotative level an indication of an individual's value, particularly in connection with his or her prospective employability. Each CV is capable of being interpreted in different ways, as anyone who has ever sat in on a short-listing meeting for a lectureship can testify, and is therefore polysemic, but there is a code whereby certain attributes of CVs are seen as especially desirable and are therefore less contentious in terms of the attribution of meaning. Indeed, applicants for posts know this latter point and devise their CVs to amplify the desired qualities so that the CV becomes an autobiographical practice for the presentation of self, as Miller and Morgan (1993) have suggested.

Research in focus 21.9 provides an illustration of a study from a semiotic perspective of Disneyland as a text. The chief strength of semiotics lies in its invitation to the analyst to try to see beyond and beneath the apparent ordinariness of everyday life and its manifestations. The main difficulty one often feels with the fruits of a semiotic analysis is that, although we are invariably given a compelling exposition of a facet of the quotidian, it is difficult to escape a sense of the arbitrariness of the analysis provided. However, in all probability this sensation is unfair to the approach, because the results of a semiotic analysis are probably no more arbitrary than any interpretation of documentary materials or any other data, such as a thematic, qualitative content analysis of the kind described in the previous section. Indeed, it would be surprising if we were not struck by a sense of arbitrariness in interpretation, in view of the principle of polysemy that lies at the heart of semiotics.

Research in focus 21.9
A semiotic Disneyland

Gottdiener (1982; 1997: 108–15) has proposed that Disneyland in Los Angeles, California, can be fruitfully analysed through a semiotic analysis. In so doing, he was treating Disneyland as a text. One component of his analysis is that Disneyland's meaning 'is revealed by its oppositions with the quotidian—the alienated everyday life of residents of L.A.' (1982: 148). He identifies through this principle nine *sign systems* that entail a contrast between the park and its surrounding environment: transportation; food; clothing; shelter; entertainment; social control; economics; politics; and family. Thus, the first of these sign systems—transportation—reveals a contrast between the Disneyland visitor as pedestrian (walk in a group; efficient mass transportation, which is fun) and as passenger (car is necessary; poor mass transportation; danger on the congested freeways). A further component of his analysis entails an analysis of the **connotations** of the different 'lands' that make up the park. He suggests that each land is associated as a signifier with signifiers of capitalism, as follows:

- Frontierland—predatory capital
- Adventureland—colonialism/imperialism
- Tomorrowland—state capital
- New Orleans—venture capital
- Main Street—family capital. (Gottdiener 1982: 156)

Hermeneutics

Hermeneutics refers to an approach that was originally devised in relation to the understanding or interpretation of texts and of theological texts in particular. It has been influential in the general formulation of interpretivism as an epistemology (see Chapter 1, where the idea of hermeneutics was briefly encountered) and is more or less synonymous with Weber's notion of *Verstehen*. The central idea behind hermeneutics is that the analyst of a text must seek to bring out the meanings of a text from the perspective of its author. This will entail attention to the social and historical context within which the text was produced. An approach to the analysis of texts like qualitative content analysis can be hermeneutic when it is sensitive to the context within which texts were produced. Hermeneutics is seen by its modern advocates as a strategy that has potential in relation both to texts as documents and to social actions and other non-documentary phenomena.

Phillips and Brown (1993) and Forster (1994) separately identify an approach to the interpretation of company documents that they describe as a *critical hermeneutic* approach. A hermeneutic approach, because of its emphasis on the location of interpretation within a specific social and historical context, would seem to represent an invitation to ensure that the analyst of texts is fully conversant with that context. As such, the approach is likely to entail the collection and analysis of data that will allow an understanding in context to be forged. As noted previously, Forster's study of the company referred to as TC included interviews with senior managers and a questionnaire survey. For their study of the corporate image advertisements of a Canadian company that produces synthetic crude oil, Phillips and Brown also employed a large database of magazine and newspaper articles relating to the company, which supplied the authors with additional documentary materials. Forster's critical hermeneutic analysis entailed the interrogation of the documents and the extraction of themes from them by reference to his knowledge of the organizational context within which the documents and the people and events within them were located.

Phillips and Brown's somewhat more formal approach entailed the examination of the advertisements in terms of three 'moments'.

1. *The social–historical moment*, which involves 'an examination of the producer of the text, its intentional recipient, its referent in the world [i.e. what it refers to], and the context in which the text is produced, transmitted, and received' (1993: 1558).

2. *The formal moment*, which involves 'a formal analysis of the structural and conventional aspects of the text' (1993: 1563). This means that the texts must be examined in terms of the constituent parts of each text and the writing conventions employed. This phase can involve the use of any of several techniques, such as semiotics or discourse analysis (see Chapter 20). Phillips and Brown used the former of these.

3. *The interpretation–reinterpretation moment*, which 'involves the interpretation of the results of the first two moments' (1993: 1567); in other words, they are synthesized.

Through this strategy, Phillips and Brown show, for example, the ways in which the corporate image advertisements constitute an attempt to mobilize support for the company's activities from government (and from among the public who were unlikely to be familiar with the company) at a time of intense competition for funding, and to ward off environmental legislation. The approach has points of affinity with the idea of the active audience (see above), in that there is an emphasis on the reception of texts and as such the notion that there may be a plurality of interpretations of them.

The critical hermeneutic approach thus can draw on practices associated with qualitative content analysis and can fuse them with ways of formally approaching texts, such as semiotics. What is crucial is the linkage that is made between understanding the text from the point of view of the author and the social and historical context of its production. Indeed, in many respects, for a hermeneutic approach, the latter is a precondition of the former. Its appeal to qualitative researchers is that it is an approach to the analysis of documents (and indeed other data) that explicitly draws on two central tenets of the qualitative research strategy: an emphasis on the point of view of the author of the text and a sensitivity to context.

Checklist

Evaluating documents

Can you answer the following questions?

○ Who produced the document?

○ Why was the document produced?

○ Was the person or group that produced the document in a position to write authoritatively about the subject or issue?

○ Is the material genuine?

○ Did the person or group have an axe to grind and if so can you identify a particular slant?

○ Is the document typical of its kind and if not is it possible to establish how untypical it is and in what ways?

○ Is the meaning of the document clear?

○ Can you corroborate the events or accounts presented in the document?

○ Are there different interpretations of the document from the one you offer and if so what are they and why have you discounted them?

Key points

- Documents constitute a very heterogeneous set of sources of data, which include personal documents, official documents from both the state and private sources, and the mass media.

- Such materials can be the focus of both quantitative and qualitative enquiry, but the emphasis in this chapter has been upon the latter.

- Documents of the kinds considered may be in printed, visual, digital, or indeed any other retrievable format.

- For many writers, just about anything can be 'read' as a text.

- Criteria for evaluating the quality of documents are: authenticity; credibility; representativeness; and meaning. The relevance of these criteria varies somewhat according to the kind of document being assessed.

- There are several ways of analysing documents within qualitative research. In this chapter we have covered qualitative content analysis, semiotics, and hermeneutics.

Questions for review

- What is meant by a document?
- What are Scott's four criteria for assessing documents?

Personal documents

- Outline the different kinds of personal documents.
- How do they fare in terms of Scott's criteria?
- What might be the role of personal documents in relation to the life history or biographical method?
- What uses can family photographs have in social research?

Official documents deriving from the state

- What do the studies by Abraham and Turner suggest in terms of the potential for social researchers of official documents deriving from the state?
- How do such documents fare in terms of Scott's criteria?

Official documents deriving from private sources

- What kinds of documents might be considered official documents deriving from private sources?
- How do such documents fare in terms of Scott's criteria?

Mass-media outputs

- What kinds of documents are mass-media outputs?
- How do such documents fare in terms of Scott's criteria?

Virtual documents

- Do Internet documents and other virtual outputs raise special problems in terms of assessing them from the point of view of Scott's criteria?

The world as text

- Can anything be treated as a text?
- What is the significance of audiences in connection with textual readings by academics?

The reality of documents

- In what sense can documents provide evidence on which social researchers can draw as data?

Interpreting documents

- What is thematic analysis?
- How does qualitative content analysis differ from the kind of content analysis discussed in Chapter 12?
- What is a sign? How central is it to semiotics?

- What is the difference between denotative meaning and connotative meaning?
- What is a hermeneutic approach to documents?
- What lessons can be learned from the studies by Phillips and Brown and by Forster concerning the potential uses of a hermeneutic approach?

Online Resource Centre

http://www.oxfordtextbooks.co.uk/orc/brymansrm3e/

Visit the Online Resource Centre that accompanies this book to enrich your understanding of documents as sources of data. Consult web links, test yourself using multiple choice questions, and gain further guidance and inspiration from the Student Researcher's Toolkit.

Qualitative data analysis

Chapter outline

Chapter guide

Because qualitative data deriving from interviews or **participant observation** typically take the form of a large corpus of unstructured textual material, they are not straightforward to analyse. Moreover, unlike quantitative data analysis, clear-cut rules about how qualitative data analysis should be carried out have not been developed. In this chapter, some general approaches to qualitative data analysis will be examined, along with *coding*, which is the main feature of most of these approaches. The chapter explores:

- *analytic induction* as a general strategy of qualitative data analysis;
- *grounded theory* as a general strategy of qualitative data analysis; this is probably the most prominent of the general approaches to qualitative data analysis; the chapter examines its main features, processes, and outcomes, along with some of the criticisms that are sometimes levelled at the approach;
- *coding* as a key process in grounded theory and in approaches to qualitative data analysis more generally; it is the focus of an extended discussion in terms of what it entails and some of the limitations of a reliance on coding;
- the criticism that is sometimes made of coding in relation to qualitative data—namely, that it tends to fragment data; the idea of *narrative analysis* is introduced as an approach to data analysis that is gaining a growing following and that does not result in data fragmentation;
- the possibility of conducting a **secondary analysis** of other researchers' qualitative data is examined.

Introduction

One of the main difficulties with **qualitative research** is that it very rapidly generates a large, cumbersome database because of its reliance on prose in the form of such media as **field notes**, interview **transcripts**, or documents. Miles (1979) has described qualitative data as an 'attractive nuisance', because of the attractiveness of its richness but the difficulty of finding analytic paths through that richness. The researcher must guard against being captivated by the richness of the data collected, so that there is a failure to give the data wider significance for the social sciences. In other words, it is crucial to guard against failing to carry out a true analysis. This means that you must protect yourself against the condition Lofland (1971: 18) once called 'analytic interruptus'.

Yet, finding a path through the thicket of prose that makes up your data is not an easy matter and is baffling to many researchers confronting such data for the first time. 'What do I do with it now?' is a common refrain. In large

part, this is because, unlike the analysis of quantitative data, there are few well-established and widely accepted rules for the analysis of qualitative data. Although learning the techniques of quantitative data analysis may seem painful at the time, they do give you an unambiguous set of rules about how to handle your data. You still have to interpret your analyses, but at least there are relatively clear rules for getting to that point. Qualitative data analysis has not reached this degree of codification of analytic procedures, and many writers would argue that this is not necessarily desirable anyway (see Bryman and Burgess 1994*b* on this point). What *can* be provided are broad guidelines (see Okely 1994), and it is in the spirit of this suggestion that this chapter has been written.

This chapter has two main sections.

1. *General strategies of qualitative data analysis*. In this section, I consider two approaches to data analysis—analytic induction and grounded theory.

2. *Basic operations in qualitative data analysis*. This section entails a consideration in particular of *coding*.

In addition, I consider *narrative analysis*, which is an approach to qualitative data analysis, which is to a certain extent different in style from the emphasis on coding that can be seen in both grounded theory and the basic operations typically used by qualitative researchers, and the secondary analysis of qualitative data.

In the next chapter, the use of computers in qualitative data analysis will be outlined.

General strategies of qualitative data analysis

This section considers two strategies of analysis—analytic induction and grounded theory. They are probably the most frequently cited approaches, though others do exist (e.g. Williams 1976; Hycner 1985). By a general strategy of qualitative data analysis, I simply mean a framework that is meant to guide the analysis of data. As we will see, one of the ways in which qualitative and quantitative data analysis sometimes differ is that, with the latter, analysis invariably occurs after your data have been collected. However, as noted in Chapter 16, general approaches like grounded theory (and analytic induction) are often described as *iterative*—that is, there is a repetitive interplay between the collection and analysis of data. This means that analysis starts after some of the data have been collected, and the implications of that analysis then shape the next steps in the data collection process. Consequently, while grounded theory and analytic induction are described as strategies of analysis, they can also be viewed as strategies for the *collection* of data.

Analytic induction

The main steps in analytic induction are outlined in Figure 22.1. Analytic induction (see Key concept 22.1) begins with a rough definition of a research question, proceeds to a hypothetical explanation of that problem, and then continues on to the collection of data (examination of cases). If a case that is inconsistent with the hypothesis is encountered, the analyst *either* redefines the hypothesis so as to exclude the deviant or negative case *or* reformulates the hypothesis and proceeds with further data collection. If the latter path is chosen, if a further deviant case is found, the analyst must choose again between reformulation or redefinition.

Key concept 22.1
What is analytic induction?

Analytic induction is an approach to the analysis of data in which the researcher seeks universal explanations of phenomena by pursuing the collection of data until no cases that are inconsistent with a hypothetical explanation (deviant or negative cases) of a phenomenon are found.

As this brief outline suggests, analytic induction is an extremely rigorous method of analysis, because encountering a single case that is inconsistent with a hypothesis is sufficient to necessitate further data collection or a reformulation of the hypothesis. Nor should the alternative of reformulating the hypothetical explanation be regarded as a soft option, as is shown by Katz's (1982) study of poverty lawyers in Chicago. Katz was interested in finding some characteristics that distinguished those who stayed on for some time as lawyers to help the poor

Figure 22.1

The process of analytic induction

(in spite of the lower pay and status associated with such work) from those whose tenure was brief. He writes that 'the definition of the explanandum [the phenomenon to be explained] was changed from staying two years, to desiring to stay two years, to desiring to stay in a frustrating place, to involvement in a frustrating place, to involvement in an insignificant status . . .' (Katz 1982: 200). Each shift necessitated a reanalysis and reorganization of his data. The rigours of analytic induction have not endeared the approach to qualitative researchers, and most of the examples used in textbooks to illustrate analytic induction derive from the 1940s and early 1950s (Bryman and Burgess 1994a: 4). Katz's work is unusual in being a relatively recent example. Bloor (1978) used a version of analytic induction in a study of doctors' decisions about whether to recommend an adeno-tonscillectomy. His approach especially diverged from

the sequence described in Figure 22.1 in that a specific hypothesis was not formulated. An account using Bloor's approach can be found in Johnson (1998).

Two further problems with analytic induction are worth noting. First, the final explanations that analytic induction arrives at specify the conditions that are *sufficient* for the phenomenon occurring but rarely specify the *necessary* conditions. This means that analytic induction may find out why people of certain characteristics or in certain circumstances become drug addicts (the focus of one major analytic induction study by Lindesmith 1947), but it does not allow us to say why those particular people became addicts rather than others in the same situation with the same characteristics. Second, it does not provide useful guidelines (unlike grounded theory) as to how many cases need to be investigated before the absence of negative cases and the validity of the hypothetical explanation (whether reformulated or not) can be confirmed.

Grounded theory

Grounded theory (see Key concept 22.2) has become by far the most widely used framework for analysing qualitative data. The book that is the chief wellspring of the approach, *The Discovery of Grounded Theory: Strategies for Qualitative Research* by Barney G. Glaser and Anselm L. Strauss (published in 1967), must be one of the most widely cited books in the social sciences. However, providing a definitive account of the approach is by no means a straightforward matter for the following reasons.

- Glaser and Strauss developed grounded theory along different paths after the publication of the above book. Glaser felt that the approach to grounded theory that Strauss was promoting (most notably in Strauss 1987, and Strauss and Corbin 1990) was too prescriptive and emphasized too much the development of concepts rather than of theories (Glaser 1992). However, because of the greater prominence of Strauss's writ-

ings, his version is largely the one followed in the exposition below. There is, however, considerable controversy about what grounded theory is and entails (Charmaz 2000). It is not uncommon for users of grounded theory to indicate whether the version that they are following is the Glaserian or the Struassian approach.

- Straussian grounded theory has changed a great deal over the years. This is revealed in a constant addition to the tool chest of analytic devices that is revealed in his writings.

- Some writers have suggested that grounded theory is honoured more in the breach than in the observance, implying that claims are often made that grounded theory has been used but that evidence of this being the case is at best uncertain (Bryman 1988a: 85, 91; Locke 1996; Charmaz 2000). Sometimes the term is employed simply to imply that the analyst has grounded his or her theory in data, so that grounded theory is more or less synonymous with an inductive approach. Grounded theory is more than this and refers to a set of procedures that are described below. Referencing

Key concept 22.2
What is grounded theory?

In its most recent incarnation, grounded theory has been defined as 'theory that was derived from data, systematically gathered and analyzed through the research process. In this method, data collection, analysis, and eventual theory stand in close **relationship** to one another' (Strauss and Corbin 1998: 12). Thus, two central features of grounded theory are that it is concerned with the development of theory out of data and that the approach is iterative, or recursive, as it is sometimes called, meaning that data collection and analysis proceed in tandem, repeatedly referring back to each other.

As the discussion in this chapter shows, the two originators of the approach—Glaser and Strauss—eventually disagreed on the path that Strauss was taking grounded theory. A further complication is that there is a lack of agreement on what grounded theory is. To some writers it is a distinct method or approach to qualitative research in its own right; to others, it is an approach to the generation of theory. It is this second view of grounded theory that is taken in this chapter. Grounded theory is not a theory—it is an approach to the generation of theory out of data. Usually, 'data' is taken to refer to qualitative data, but grounded theory can be used in connection with different kinds of data. One final complication to be noted is that, although it has just been suggested that grounded theory is a strategy for generating theory out of data, in many cases, reports using a grounded theory approach generate **concepts** rather than theory as such.

academic publications is often part of a tactic of persuading readers of the legitimacy of one's work (Gilbert 1977), and this process can be discerned in the citation of grounded theory. Alternatively, researchers sometimes appear to have used just one or two features of grounded theory but refer to their having used the approach without qualification (Locke 1996). Against such a background, writing about the essential ingredients of grounded theory is not an easy matter.

It is not going to be possible to describe here grounded theory in all its facets; instead, its main features will be outlined. In order to organize the exposition, I find it helpful to distinguish between *tools* and *outcomes* in grounded theory.

Tools of grounded theory

Some of the tools of grounded theory have been referred to in previous chapters. Their location is indicated in the list that follows.

- *Theoretical sampling*—see Key concept 17.5.
- *Coding*—the key process in grounded theory, whereby data are broken down into component parts, which are given names. It begins soon after the collection of initial data. As Charmaz puts it: 'We grounded theorists code our emerging data as we collect it. . . . Unlike quantitative research that requires data to fit into *preconceived* standardized codes, the researcher's interpretations of data shape his or her emergent codes in grounded theory' (Charmaz 2000: 515; emphasis in original). In grounded theory, different types or levels of coding are recognized (see Key concept 22.3).

- *Theoretical saturation*—see Key concept 17.6. Theoretical saturation is a process that relates to two phases in grounded theory: the coding of data (implying that you reach a point where there is no further point in reviewing your data to see how well they fit with your concepts or categories) and the collection of data (implying that, once a concept or category has been developed, you may wish to continue collecting data to determine its nature and operation but then reach a point where new data are no longer illuminating the concept).

- *Constant comparison*—an aspect of grounded theory that was prominent in Glaser and Strauss (1967) and that is often referred to as a significant phase by practitioners, but that seems to be an implicit, rather than an explicit, element in more recent writings. It refers to a process of maintaining a close connection between data and conceptualization, so that the correspondence between concepts and categories with their indicators is not lost. More specifically, attention to the procedure of constant comparison enjoins the researcher constantly to compare phenomena being coded under a certain category so that a theoretical elaboration of that category can begin to emerge. Glaser and Strauss advised writing a *memo* (see below) on the category after a few phenomena had been coded. It also entails being sensitive to contrasts between the categories that are emerging.

Key concept 22.3
Coding in grounded theory

Coding is one of the most central processes in grounded theory. It entails reviewing transcripts and/or field notes and giving labels (names) to component parts that seem to be of potential theoretical significance and/or that appear to be particularly salient within the social worlds of those being studied. As Charmaz (1983: 186) puts it: 'Codes . . . serve as shorthand devices to *label, separate, compile,* and *organize* data' (emphases in original). Coding is a somewhat different process from coding in relation to quantitative data, such as survey data. With the latter, coding is more or less solely a way of managing data, whereas in grounded theory, and indeed in approaches to qualitative data analysis that do not subscribe to the approach, it is an important first step in the generation of theory. Coding in grounded theory is also somewhat more tentative than in relation to the generation of quantitative data, where there is a tendency to think in terms of data and codes as very fixed. Coding in qualitative data analysis tends to be in a constant state of potential revision and fluidity. The data are treated as potential **indicators** of concepts and the indicators are *constantly compared* (see under 'Tools of grounded theory') to see which concepts they best fit with. As Strauss (1987: 25) put it: 'Many indicators (behavioral actions/events) are examined comparatively by the analyst who then "codes" them, naming them as indicators of a class of events/behavioral actions.'

Strauss and Corbin (1990), drawing on their grounded theory approach, distinguish between three types of coding practice.

1. *Open coding*: 'the process of breaking down, examining, comparing, conceptualizing and categorizing data' (1990: 61); this process of coding yields concepts, which are later to be grouped and turned into categories.

2. *Axial coding*: 'a set of procedures whereby data are put back together in new ways after open coding, by making connections between categories' (1990: 96). This is done by linking codes to contexts, to consequences, to patterns of interaction, and to causes.

3. *Selective coding*: 'the procedure of selecting the core category, systematically relating it to other categories, validating those relationships, and filling in categories that need further refinement and development' (1990: 116). A *core category* is the central issue or focus around which all other categories are integrated. It is what Strauss and Corbin call the storyline that frames your account.

The three types of coding are really different levels of coding and each relates to a different point in the elaboration of categories in grounded theory. Not all grounded theory practitioners operate with this three-fold distinction, and indeed the notion of axial coding has been especially controversial because it is sometimes perceived as closing off too quickly in a project the open-endedness and exploratory character of coding in qualitative data analysis.

Charmaz (2006) prefers to distinguish between two main forms or phases of coding: *initial coding* and *selective* or *focused coding*. Initial coding tends to be very detailed and may even result in a code per line of text, whereby a code is assigned to every line of text to provide initial impressions of the data. It is crucial at this stage to be open-minded and to generate as many new ideas and hence codes as necessary to encapsulate the data. It is the qualitative researcher's first steps towards making sense of his or her data. Charmaz suggests that it is important in initial coding to recognize that, although codes will reflect the perspectives of research participants, when the qualitative researcher makes sense of the codes, he or she may end up viewing their social world somewhat differently from them. Focused coding entails emphasizing the most common codes and those that are seen as most revealing about the data. This means that some, if not many, initial codes will be dropped. As she puts it: 'Focused coding requires decisions about which initial codes make the most analytic sense to categorize your data incisively and completely' (Charmaz 2006: 57–8). New codes may be generated by combining initial codes. The data are then re-explored and re-evaluated in terms of these selected codes. In the same way as Strauss and Corbin (1990), Charmaz sees *axial coding* as a mechanism for bringing coherence to the coded data. As she observes, initial coding 'fractures data into separate pieces and distinct codes' (Charmaz 2006: 60). Axial coding entails reassembling the data by searching for connections between the categories that have emerged out of the coding.

Pidgeon and Henwood (2004) provide a useful example of the move from initial coding to a focused and then axial coding based on Henwood's study of adult mother–daughter relationships. Sixty interviews with mother–daughter dyads were conducted. They write:

> The initial coding led to the development of a long and varied, but highly unwieldy, list of instances under the label 'Relational Closeness'. The attributes that had been coded onto the card were initially glossed as attaching global value to the relationship. However, closer reading and comparison of the individual instances indicated a much more mixed view of the emotional intensity of the relationships, ranging from a welcome but painful sense of gratitude and debt to a stance of hypersensitivity and a desire to flee from a relationship which involved 'confinement' or 'smothering'. The inextricable link between the two concepts resulting from this subdivision was retained and coded through their respective labels 'Closeness' and 'Overcloseness'. This link then became a key stimulus and focus for conceptual development and reflection . . . (Pidgeon and Henwood 2004: 638)

Although there are slight differences in the way in which the phases of the coding process is supposed to occur in grounded theory according to its practitioners, there is a basic understanding of it as involving a movement from generating codes that stay close to the data to more selective and abstract ways of conceptualizing the phenomenon of interest.

Outcomes of grounded theory

The following are the products of different phases of grounded theory.

- *Concept(s)*—refers to labels given to discrete phenomena; concepts are referred to as the 'building blocks of theory' (Strauss and Corbin 1998: 101). Concepts are produced through *open coding* (see Key concept 22.3).

- *Category, categories*—a concept that has been elaborated so that it is regarded as representing real-world phenomena. As noted in Key concept 17.6, a category may subsume two or more concepts. As such, categories are at a higher level of abstraction than concepts. A category may become a *core category* around which the other categories pivot (see Key concept 22.3). Research in focus 22.1 provides a good example of the emergence of a core category.

- *Properties*—attributes or aspects of a category.

- *Hypotheses*—initial hunches about relationships between concepts.

- *Theory*—according to Strauss and Corbin (1998: 22): 'a set of well-developed categories . . . that are systematically related through statements of relationship to form a theoretical framework that explains some relevant social . . . or other phenomenon'. Since the inception of grounded theory, writings have pointed to two types or levels of theory: *substantive theory* and *formal theory*. The former relates to theory in a certain empirical instance or substantive area, such as occupational socialization. A formal theory is at a higher level of abstraction and has a wider range of applicability to several substantive areas, such as socialization in a number of spheres, suggesting that higher-level processes are at work. The generation of formal theory requires data collection in contrasting settings.

Research in focus 22.1
Categories in grounded theory

Orona's (1997) study of sufferers of Alzheimer's disease and in particular of their relatives exemplifies many features of grounded theory. Orona began her research with an interest in the decision-making process that led relatives to place sufferers in a home. She gradually realized from coding her interview transcripts that this was not a crucial feature for relatives, as she had anticipated, not least because many of them simply felt they had no choice. Instead, she was slowly taken by the significance for relatives of the 'identity loss' sufferers were deemed to experience. This gradually became her core category. She conducted further interviews in order to flesh this notion out and reread existing transcripts in the light of it. The link between indicators and category can be seen in relatives' references to the sufferer as 'gone', 'different', 'not the same person', and as a 'stranger'. Orona was able to unearth four major themes that emerged around the process of identity loss. The theme of 'temporality' was particularly significant in Orona's emerging theoretical reflections and was revealed in such comments in transcripts as:

> It was the *time of the year* when nobody goes in the yard anyway . . .
> At the *beginning* . . .
> It got much worse *later on*.
> *More and more*, he was leaning on me.
> *Before* she would never have been like that.
> She *used* to love coffee. (Orona 1997: 179–80)

In other words, such comments served as indicators that allowed the category 'temporality' to be built up. The issue of temporality was significant in Orona's emerging analysis, because it related to the core category of identity loss. Relatives sought to help sufferers maintain their identities. However, gradually, with the passage of time, crucial events meant that the relatives could no longer deny sufferers' identity loss.

The different elements can be portrayed in Figure 22.2. As with all diagrams, this is a representation, and it is particularly so in the case of grounded theory, because the existence of different versions of the approach does not readily permit a more definitive rendition. Also, it is difficult to get across diagrammatically the iterative nature of grounded theory—in particular its commitment to the idea that data collection and analysis occur in parallel. This is partly achieved in the diagram through the presence of arrows pointing in both directions in relation to certain steps. The figure implies the following.

- The researcher begins with a general research question (step 1).
- Relevant people and/or incidents are theoretically sampled (step 2).
- Relevant data are collected (step 3).
- Data are coded (step 4), which may at the level of open coding generate concepts (step 4a).
- There is a constant movement backwards and forwards between the first four steps, so that early coding suggests the need for new data, which results in the need to sample theoretically, and so on.
- Through a constant comparison of indicators and concepts (step 5) categories are generated (step 5a). The crucial issue is to ensure that there is a fit between indicators and concepts.
- Categories are saturated during the coding process (step 6).
- Relationships between categories are explored (step 7) in such a way that hypotheses about connections between categories emerge (step 7a).
- Further data are collected via theoretical sampling (steps 8 and 9).
- The collection of data is likely to be governed by the theoretical saturation principle (step 10) and by the testing of the emerging hypotheses (step 11), which leads to the specification of substantive theory (step 11a). See Research in focus 22.2 for an illustration.
- The substantive theory is explored using grounded theory processes in relation to different settings from that in which it was generated (step 12), so that formal theory may be generated (step 12a). A formal theory will relate to more abstract categories, which are not specifically concerned with the research area in question (e.g., chronically ill men, relatives of sufferers of Alzheimer's disease).

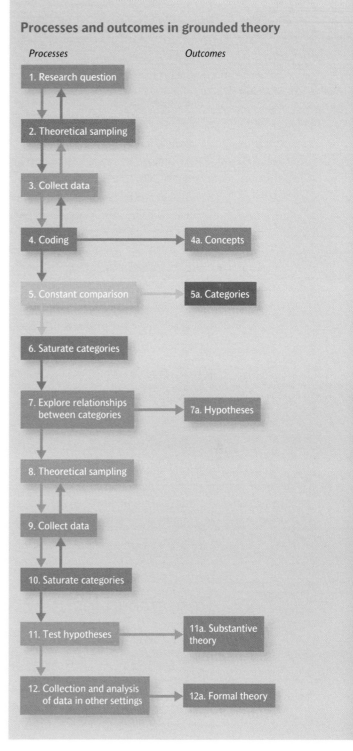

Figure 22.2

Processes and outcomes in grounded theory

Research in focus 22.2
Grounded theory in action

Charmaz's (1997) research is concerned with the identity dilemmas of men who have chronic (but not terminal) illnesses. She outlines very clearly the chief steps in her analysis.

- Interviews with men and a small number of women.
- Exploring the transcripts for gender differences.
- Searching for themes in the men's interviews and published personal accounts (e.g. autobiographies). An example is the notion of 'accommodation to uncertainty', as men find ways of dealing with the unpredictable paths of their illnesses.
- Building 'analytic categories from men's definitions of and taken-for-granted assumptions about their situations' (1997: 39). Of particular significance in her work is the idea of 'identity dilemmas'—that is, the ways in which men approach and possibly resolve the assault on their traditional self-images in terms of masculinity. She shows that men often used strategies to re-establish earlier selves, so that for many audiences their identity (at least in their own eyes) could be preserved.
- Further interviews designed to refine the categories.
- Rereading personal accounts of chronic illness with a particular focus on gender.
- Reading a new group of personal accounts.
- Making 'comparisons with women on selected key points' (1997: 39).

Charmaz provides a substantive theory that helps to explain the importance of notions of masculinity for the carving-out of an identity for chronically ill men.

Step 12 is relatively unusual in grounded theory, because researchers typically concentrate on a certain setting, although the investigation described in Research in focus 22.3 did examine other settings to explore the emerging concepts. A further way in which formal theory can be generated is through the use of existing theory and research in comparable settings.

Research in focus 22.3
Grounded theory in a study of consumer experiences of museums

Goulding (2008) has discussed the way in which she implemented grounded theory in the context of a study of how consumers experience museums, particularly so-called 'living' museums that seek to recreate the UK's industrial heritage. The approach she took was closer to Glaser's than to Strauss's version of grounded theory. Initially, she selected an open-air museum and interviewed the director and then conducted observations of parties of visitors, noting how they handled the attractions and exhibits. While these relatively unstructured observations were illuminating in terms of how visitors responded to the attractions, they did not generate insights into motivations, so Goulding conducted interviews with visitors to shed light on such things as their expectations and their perceptions of the exhibits. She conducted a line-by-line analysis of the interview transcripts, which generated a huge number of codes and words. She reduced this vast array of codes to themes that helped to understand her data, and this produced seven concepts, such as: the stimulation of nostalgia, the desire for education, and experience of alienation in the present. Each of these concepts had distinctive properties or dimensions. For example, the stimulation of nostalgia encapsulated in such things as a sense of retreat from the present and a 'rose-tinted' recollection of the past. However, Goulding felt that she had not saturated her concepts, so she collected new data in two new comparable but different sites. The same data collection approach was taken as with the original site but no new concepts were generated. However, the new data did allow her to reinforce her concepts and to produce a categorization of three types of visitor to such museums: existential, purist, and social. For example, existential visitors tended to exhibit high levels of the stimulation of nostalgia (one of the seven concepts derived from the data—see above) which was apparent from their position with regard to codes like 'selective recall', 'rose-tinted remembrance', a 'rejection of the present', and an 'ability to distort the past'.

Concepts and categories are perhaps the key elements in grounded theory. Indeed, it is sometimes suggested that, as a qualitative data analysis strategy, grounded theory works better for generating categories than theory. In part, this may be because studies purporting to use the approach often generate grounded *concepts* rather than grounded theory as such. Concepts and categories are nonetheless at the heart of the approach, and key processes such as coding, theoretical sampling, and theoretical saturation are designed to guide their generation.

Memos

One aid to the generation of concepts and categories is the *memo*. Memos in grounded theory are notes that researchers might write for themselves and for those with whom they work concerning such elements of grounded theory as coding or concepts. They serve as reminders about what is meant by the terms being used and provide the building blocks for a certain amount of reflection. Memos are potentially very helpful to researchers in helping them to crystallize ideas and not to lose track of their thinking on various topics. An illustration of a memo from research in which I was involved is provided in Research in focus 22.4.

Research in focus 22.4
A memo

In the course of research into the bus industry that I carried out with colleagues in the early 1990s (Bryman *et al.* 1996), we noticed that the managers we interviewed frequently referred to the notion that their companies had inherited features that derived from the running of those companies before deregulation. They often referred to the idea of inheriting characteristics that held them back in trying to meet the competitive environment they faced in the 1990s. As such, inheritance is what Strauss (1987) calls an 'in vivo code' (one that derives from the natural language of people in the social context being studied), rather than what he calls 'sociologically constructed codes', which are labels employing the analyst's own terminology. The following memo outlines the concept of inheritance, provides some illustrative quotations, and suggests some properties of the concept.

Memo for inheritance

Inheritance: many of our interviewees suggest that they have inherited certain company traits and traditions from the period prior to deregulation (i.e. pre-1985). It is a term that many of them themselves employed to denote company attributes that are not of their choosing but have survived from the pre-deregulation period. The key point about inheritance is that the inherited elements are seen by our interviewees as hindering their ability to respond to the changing environment of the post-deregulation era.

Inherited features include:

- expensive and often inappropriate fleets of vehicles and depots;
- the survival of attitudes and behaviour patterns, particularly among bus drivers, which are seen as inappropriate to the new environment (e.g. lack of concern for customer service) and which hinder service innovation;
- high wage rates associated with the pre-deregulation era; means that new competitors can enter the market while paying drivers lower wages.

Sample comments:

'We *inherited* a very high cost structure because of deregulation. 75% of our staff were paid in terms of conditions affected by [rates prior to deregulation]' (Commercial Director, Company B).

'I suppose another major weakness is that we are very tied by conditions and practices we've *inherited*' (Commercial Director, Company G).

'We have what we've *inherited* and we now have a massive surplus of double decks . . . We have to go on operating those' (Managing Director, Company B).

Managing Director of Company E said the company had inherited staff who were steeped in pre-deregulation attitudes, which meant that 'we don't have a staff where the message is "the customer is number one". We don't have a staff where that is emblazoned on the hearts and minds of everyone, far from it'.

Prepost-deregulation: interviewee makes a contrast between the periods before and after deregulation to show how they've changed. This shows in a sense the *absence* of inherited features and their possible impact; can refer to how the impact of possibly inherited features was negated or offset. For example, *X* referring to the recent end of the 3-week strike: 'there was no way we were going to give in to this sort of thing, this sort of blackmail. We just refused to move and the trade unions had never experienced that. It was all part of the change in culture following deregulation . . .'.

Inheriting constraints: such as staff on high wage rates and with inappropriate attitudes.

Inheriting surplus capacity: such as too many buses or wrong size.

Finding examples of grounded theory that reveal all its facets and stages is very difficult, and it is unsurprising that many expositions of grounded theory fall back on the original illustrations provided in Glaser and Strauss (1967). Many studies show some of its ingredients but not others. Research in focus 22.1 provides an illustration by one of Strauss's students that incorporates some key grounded theory features.

Criticisms of grounded theory

In spite of the frequency with which it is cited and the frequent lip-service paid to it, grounded theory is not without its limitations, of which the following can be briefly registered.

- Bulmer (1979) has questioned whether, as prescribed by the advocates of grounded theory, researchers can suspend their awareness of relevant theories or concepts until a quite late stage in the process of analysis. Social researchers are typically sensitive to the conceptual armoury of their disciplines, and it seems unlikely that this awareness can be put aside. Indeed, nowadays it is rarely accepted that theory-neutral observation is feasible. In other words, it is generally agreed that what we 'see' when we conduct research is conditioned by many factors, one of which is what we already know about the social world being studied (in terms both of social scientific conceptualizations and as members of society). Also, many writers might take the view that it is desirable that researchers are sensitive to existing conceptualizations, so that their investigations are focused and can build upon the work of others.

- Related to this first point is that, in many circumstances, researchers are required to spell out the possible implications of their planned investigation. For example, a lecturer making a bid for research funding or a student applying for funding for postgraduate research is usually required to demonstrate how his or her research will build upon what is already known or to demonstrate that he or she has a reasonably tightly defined research question, something that is also frequently disdained in grounded theory.

- There are practical difficulties with grounded theory. The time taken to transcribe recordings of interviews, for example, can make it difficult for researchers, especially when they have tight deadlines, to carry out a genuine grounded theory analysis with its constant interplay of data collection and conceptualization.

- It is somewhat doubtful whether grounded theory in many instances really results in *theory*. As previously suggested, it provides a rigorous approach to the generation of concepts, but it is often difficult to see what theory, in the sense of an explanation of something, is being put forward. Moreover, in spite of the frequent lip-service paid to the generation of formal theory, most grounded theories are substantive in character; in other words, they pertain to the specific social phenomenon being researched and not to a broader range of phenomena (though, of course, they *may* have such broader applicability).

- In spite of the large amount written on grounded theory, but perhaps because of the many subtle changes in its presentation, it is still vague on certain points, such as the difference between concepts and categories. For example, while Strauss and Corbin (1998: 73) refer to

theoretical sampling as 'sampling on the basis of emerging *concepts*' (emphasis added), Charmaz (2000: 519) writes that it is used to 'develop our emerging *categories*' (emphasis added). The term 'categories' is increasingly being employed rather than concepts, but such inconsistent use of key terms is not helpful to people trying to understand the overall process.

- Grounded theory is very much associated with an approach to data analysis that invites researchers to fragment their data by coding the data into discrete chunks. However, in the eyes of some writers, this kind of activity results in a loss of a sense of context and of narrative flow (Coffey and Atkinson 1996), a point to which I will return below.

- The presence of competing accounts of the ingredients of grounded theory does not make it easy to characterize it or to establish how to use it. This situation has been made even more problematic by Charmaz's (2000) suggestion that most grounded theory is objectivist and that an alternative, **constructionist** (she calls it *constructivist*) approach is preferable. She argues that the grounded theory associated with Glaser, Strauss, and Corbin is objectivist in that it aims to uncover a reality that is external to social actors. She offers an alternative, constructionist version that 'assumes that people create and maintain meaningful worlds through dialectical processes of conferring meaning on their realities and acting within them . . . Thus, social reality does not exist independent of human action' (Charmaz 2000: 521). Such a position stands in contrast to earlier grounded theory texts that 'imply that categories and concepts inhere within the data, awaiting the researcher's discovery. . . . Instead, a constructivist approach recognizes that the categories, concepts, and theoretical level of an analysis emerge from the researcher's interaction within the field and questions about the data' (Charmaz 2000: 522). One difficulty here is that the two meanings of constructionism referred to in Key concept 1.6 seem to be conflated. The first quotation refers to constructionism as an ontological position in relating to social objects and categories; the second is a reference to constructionism in relation to the nature of knowledge of the social world. It is certainly fair to suggest that Glaser, Strauss, and Corbin in their various writings neglect the role of the researcher in the generation of knowledge, but it is not clear that they are indifferent to the notion that social reality exists independently of social actors. Strauss was, after all, the lead of the study referred to on pages 19–20 concerning the hospital as a negotiated order, which was used as an illustration of constructionism (Strauss *et al.* 1973). Also, Orona's (1997) account of her grounded theory analysis of sufferers of Alzheimer's disease is described in a commentary on the research by Strauss and Corbin (1997*a*: 172) as a 'textbook exemplification' of the approach. Yet this study is concerned with the subjective experience of the disease (interpretivism) and with the *construction* of identity in everyday life. However, there is little doubt that there is considerable confusion currently about the nature of grounded theory.

Nonetheless, grounded theory probably represents the most influential general strategy for conducting qualitative data analysis, though how far the approach is followed varies from study to study. What can be said is that many of its core processes, such as coding, memos, and the very idea of allowing theoretical ideas to emerge out of one's data, have been hugely influential. Indeed, it is striking that one of the main developments in qualitative data analysis in recent years—computer-assisted qualitative data analysis—has implicitly promoted many of these processes, because the software programs have often been written with grounded theory in mind (Richards and Richards 1994; Lonkila 1995).

 # Basic operations in qualitative data analysis

Coding is the starting point for most forms of qualitative data analysis, although some writers prefer to call the process *indexing* rather than coding. The principles involved have been well developed by writers on grounded theory and others. Some of the considerations in developing codes, some of which are derived from Lofland and Lofland (1995), are as follows.

- Of what general category is this item of data an instance?
- What does this item of data represent?
- What is this item of data about?
- Of what topic is this item of data an instance?
- What question about a topic does this item of data suggest?
- What sort of answer to a question about a topic does this item of data imply?
- What is happening here?
- What are people doing?
- What do people say they are doing?
- What kind of event is going on?

Steps and considerations in coding

The following steps and considerations need to be borne in mind in preparation for and during coding.

- *Code as soon as possible*. It is well worth coding as you go along, as grounded theory suggests. This may sharpen your understanding of your data and help with theoretical sampling. Also, it may help to alleviate the feeling of being swamped by your data, which may happen if you defer analysis entirely until the end of the data collection period. At the very least, you should ensure that, if your data collection involves recording interviews, you begin transcription at a relatively early stage.

- *Read through your initial set of transcripts, field notes, documents, etc.*, without taking any notes or considering an interpretation; perhaps at the end jot down a few general notes about what struck you as especially interesting, important, or significant.

- *Do it again*. Read through your data again, but this time begin to make marginal notes about significant remarks or observations. Make as many as possible. Initially, they will be very basic—perhaps key words used by your respondents, names that you give to themes in the data. When you do this you are *coding*—generating an index of terms that will help you to interpret and theorize in relation to your data.

- *Review your codes*. Begin to review your codes, possibly in relation to your transcripts. Are you using two or more words or phrases to describe the same phenomenon? If so, remove one of them. Do some of your codes relate to concepts and categories in the existing literature? If so, might it be sensible to use these instead? Can you see any connections between the codes? Is there some evidence that respondents believe that one thing tends to be associated with or caused by something else? If so, how do you characterize and therefore code these connections?

- *Consider more general theoretical ideas in relation to codes and data*. At this point, you should be beginning to generate some general theoretical ideas about

Tips and skills
Coded text from the Disney project

Interviewer	OK. What were your views or feelings about the presentation of different cultures, as shown in, for example, Jungle Cruise or It's a Small World at the Magic Kingdom or in World Showcase at Epcot?	
Wife	Well, I thought the different countries at Epcot were wonderful, but I need to say more than that, don't I?	uncritical enthusiasm
Husband	They were very good and some were better than others, but that was down to the host countries themselves really, as I suppose each of the countries represented would have been responsible for their own part, so that's nothing to do with Disney, I wouldn't have thought.	not critical of Disney
	I mean some of the landmarks were hard to recognize for what they were supposed to be, but some were very well done. Britain was OK, but there was only a pub and a Welsh shop there really, whereas some of the other pavilions, as I think they were called, were good ambassadors for the countries they represented. China, for example, had an excellent 360 degree film showing parts of China and I found that very interesting.	content critique
Interviewer	Did you think there was anything lacking about the content?	
Husband	Well I did notice that there weren't many black people at World Showcase, particularly the American Adventure. Now whether we were there on an unusual day in that respect I don't know, but we saw plenty of black Americans in the Magic Kingdom and other places, but very few if any in that World Showcase.	visitors' ethnicity
	And there was certainly little mention of black history in the American Adventure presentation, so maybe they felt alienated by that, I don't know, but they were noticeable by their absence.	visitors' ethnicity
Interviewer	So did you think there were any special emphases?	
Husband	Well thinking about it now, because I hadn't really given this any consideration before you started asking about it, but thinking about it now, it was only really representative of the developed world, you know, Britain, America, Japan, world leaders many of them in technology, and there was nothing of the Third World there. Maybe that's their own fault, maybe they were asked to participate and didn't, but now that I think about it, that does come to me. What do you think, love?	nationality critique
Wife	Well, like you, I hadn't thought of it like that before, but I agree with you.	

Marginal codes (grouping right-hand column): "uncritical enthusiasm"; "not critical of Disney" and "content critique" grouped as **aesthetic critique**; "visitors' ethnicity" (×2) grouped as **ethnicity critique**; "nationality critique".

your data. Try to outline connections between concepts and categories you are developing. Consider in more detail how they relate to the existing literature. Develop hypotheses about the linkages you are making and go back to your data to see if they can be confirmed.

- Remember that *any one item or slice of data can and often should be coded in more than one way*.

- *Do not worry about generating what seem to be too many codes*—at least in the early stages of your analysis; some will be fruitful and others will not—the important thing is to be as inventive and imaginative as possible; you can worry about tidying things up later.

- *Keep coding in perspective*. Do not equate coding with analysis. It is part of your analysis, albeit an important one. It is a mechanism for thinking about the meaning of your data *and* for reducing the vast amount of data that you are facing (Huberman and Miles 1994). You must still interpret your findings, which means attending to issues like the significance of your coded material for the lives of the people you are studying, forging interconnections between codes, and reflecting on the overall importance of your findings for the research questions and the research literature that have driven your data collection.

Turning data into fragments

The coding of such materials as interview transcripts has typically entailed writing marginal notes on them and gradually refining those notes into codes. In this way, portions of transcripts become seen as belonging to certain names or labels. In the past, this process was accompanied by cutting and pasting in the literal sense of using scissors and paste. It entailed cutting up one's transcripts into files of chunks of data, with each file representing a code. The process of cutting and pasting is useful for data retrieval, though it is always important to make sure that you have ways of identifying the origins of the chunk of text (for example, name, position, date). Word-processing programs allow this to be done in a way that does not rely on your DIY skills so much (see Research in focus 20.4 for an account of this use of word-processing software). Nowadays CAQDAS software is increasingly being used to perform these tasks (see Chapter 23).

As Coffey and Atkinson (1996) observe, following Strauss and Corbin's account (1990) of grounded theory, codes should not be thought of purely as mechanisms for the fragmentation and retrieval of text. In other words, they can do more than simply manage the data you have gathered. For example, if we ask about the properties and interconnections between codes, we may begin to see that some of them may be dimensions of a broader phenomenon. For example, as shown in the next chapter (see especially Figure 23.1), 'ethnicity critique' came to be seen as a dimension of 'ideology critique', along with 'class critique' and 'gender critique'. In this way, we can begin to map the more general or formal properties of concepts that are being developed.

Tips and skills
Too many codes

The initial coding of a large corpus of data can generate an alarming number of codes. Charmaz (2004), for example, recommends as a first stage in coding for grounded theory 'line by line coding', whereby virtually every line in a transcript or other source of data will have a code attached to it. She argues that this process means that the qualitative researcher does not lose contact with his or her data and the perspectives and interpretations of those being studied. However, this process will almost certainly result in a proliferation of codes. This should not be alarming. What the analyst of qualitative data needs to do is ask questions about what these codes have in common so that they can be combined into higher-order and more abstract codes.

Problems with coding

One of the most commonly mentioned criticisms of the coding approach to qualitative data analysis is the possible problem of losing the context of what is said. By plucking chunks of text out of the context within which they appeared, such as a particular interview transcript, the social setting can be lost.

A second criticism of coding is that it results in a fragmentation of data, so that the narrative flow of what people say is lost (Coffey and Atkinson 1996). Sensitivity to this issue has been heightened by a growing interest in narrative analysis since the late 1980s (see Key concept 22.4). Riessman became concerned about the fragmentation of data that results from coding themes when she came to analyse data she had collected through structured interviews on divorce and gender. She writes:

Some [interviewees] developed long accounts of what had happened in their marriages to justify their divorces. I did not realize these were narratives until I struggled to code them. Applying traditional qualitative methods, I searched the texts for common thematic elements. But some individuals knotted together several themes into long accounts that had coherence and sequence, defying easy categorization. I found myself not wanting to fragment the long accounts into distinct thematic categories. There seemed to be a common structure beneath talk about a variety of topics. While I coded one interview, a respondent provided language for my trouble. As I have thought about it since, it was a 'click moment' in my biography as a narrative researcher . . . (Riessman 1993: p. vi)

Key concept 22.4
What is narrative analysis?

Narrative analysis is a term that covers quite a wide variety of approaches that are concerned with the search for and analysis of the stories that people employ to understand their lives and the world around them. It has become particularly prominent in connection with the life history or biographical approach (see Research in focus 22.5 for an example of this feature). However, as Research in focus 22.6 shows, narrative analysis is not exclusively concerned with the elucidation of life histories. As Roberts (2002) has observed, the term 'narrative analysis' is often employed to refer both to an approach—one that emphasizes the examination of the storied nature of human recounting of lives and events—and to the sources themselves—that is, the stories that people tell in recounting their lives. While there is little consensus on what narrative analysis entails, at the very least it entails a sensitivity to: the connections in people's accounts of past, present, and future events and states of affairs; people's sense of their place within those events and states of affairs; the stories they generate about them; and the significance of context for the unfolding of events and people's sense of their role within them. It is the ways that people organize and forge connections between events and the sense they make of those connections that provides the raw material of narrative analysis. Riessman (2004b) helpfully distinguishes four models of narrative analysis.

1. *Thematic analysis*: an emphasis on what is said rather than on how it is said.

2. *Structural analysis*: an emphasis on the way a story is related. Issues of content do not disappear but there is an emphasis on the use of narrative mechanisms for increasing the persuasiveness of a story.

3. *Interactional analysis*: an emphasis on the dialogue between the teller of a story and the listener. Especially prominent is the co-construction of meaning by the two parties, though content and form are by no means marginalized.

4. *Performative analysis*: an emphasis on narrative as a performance that explores the use of words and gestures to get across a story. This model of narrative analysis includes an examination of the response of an audience to the narrative.

Riessman's account is interesting because it suggests several possibilities: that the coding method of qualitative data analysis fragments data; that some forms of data may be unsuitable for the coding method; and that researchers can turn narrative analysis on themselves, since what she provides in this passage is precisely a narrative. Interest in narrative analysis certainly shows signs of growing and in large part this trend parallels the rebirth of interest in the life history approach (see Key concept 18.1). Nonetheless, the coding method is unlikely to become less prominent, because of several factors: its widespread acceptance in the research community; not all analysts are interested in research questions that lend themselves to the elicitation of narratives; the influence of grounded theory and its associated techniques; and the growing use and acceptance of computer software for qualitative data analysis, which frequently invites a coding approach.

Regardless of which analytical strategy you employ, what you must not do is simply say—'this is what my subjects said and did—isn't that incredibly interesting'. It may be reasonably interesting, but your work can acquire significance only when you theorize in relation to it. Many researchers are wary of this—they worry that, in the process of interpretation and theorizing, they may fail to do justice to what they have seen and heard; that they may contaminate their subjects' words and behaviour. This is a risk, but it has to be balanced against the fact that your findings acquire significance in our intellectual community only when you have reflected on, interpreted, and theorized your data. You are not there as a mere mouthpiece.

Thematic analysis

One of the most common approaches to qualitative data analysis entails what is often referred to as thematic analysis. However, unlike strategies like grounded theory or critical discourse analysis, this is not an approach to analysis that has an identifiable heritage or that has been outlined in terms of a distinctive cluster of techniques. Indeed, the search for themes is an activity that can be discerned in many if not most approaches to qualitative data analysis, such as grounded theory, critical discourse analysis, qualitative content analysis, and narrative analysis. Also, for some writers a theme is more or less the same as a code, whereas for others it transcends any one code and is built up out of groups of codes.

This does not appear to be a promising start, because, although qualitative researchers often claim to have employed thematic analysis, it is not an identifiable approach. Indeed, it did not appear as a separate section in either of the earlier editions of this book! Yet, as a simple exercise while writing this section, I did a search in the SSCI for 'thematic analysis' for the years 2000–7 inclusive and came up with 400 hits. The vast majority of these derived from references in abstracts to the article being based on 'thematic analysis'.

One general strategy for conducting a thematic analysis of qualitative data is provided by Framework, an approach that has been developed at the National Centre for Social Research in the UK. Framework is described as a 'matrix based method for ordering and synthesising data' (Ritchie *et al.* 2003: 219). The idea is to construct an index of central themes and subthemes, which are then represented in a matrix that closely resembles an SPSS spreadsheet with its display of cases and variables. The themes and subthemes are essentially recurring motifs in the text that are then applied to the data. The themes and subthemes are the product of a thorough reading and re-reading of the transcripts or field notes that make up the data. This framework is then applied to the data, which are organized initially into core themes, and the data are then displayed in terms of subthemes within the matrix and for each case. Taking the Disney project data described in Chapter 21, one of the main themes that was identified was 'Ideological critique'. This theme can be viewed as having a number of subthemes—class critique; ethnicity critique; gender critique; and nationality critique. Figure 22.3 is a matrix that draws on the coded text in Tips and skills 'Coded text from the Disney project' and that would be used for representing the data on the theme Ideological critique. The four subthemes are presented and the idea is to place brief snippets from the data into the appropriate cell. Thus, the passage in Tips and skills 'Coded text from the Disney project' provides the data for the insertion of some material into two of the cells for Interviewee 4. It also specifies the location within the transcript of the snippet(s) that are included in the cell. Ritchie *et al.* advise that, when inserting material into cells, the researcher should:

Figure 22.3

The Framework approach to thematic analysis

Theme: Ideological critique

	Class critique	**Ethnicity critique**	**Gender critique**	**Nationality critique**
Interviewee 1				
Interviewee 2				
Interviewee 3				
Interviewee 4		'saw plenty of black Americans' in MK 'but few if any in that World Showcase'. 'Little mention of black history' (Q14)		World Showcase 'only really representative of the developed world' (Q14)
Interviewee 5				

1. indicate where in the transcript the fragment comes from (I have used the question number);

2. keep the language of the research participant as far as possible;

3. try not to insert too much quoted material; and

4. use abbreviations in cells so that cells do not become too full.

As its name implies, this approach is meant to provide a framework for the thematic analysis of qualitative data and provides one way of thinking about how to manage themes and data. It does not necessarily tell the user how to identify themes, which, as the authors suggest, are likely to reflect the analyst's awareness of recurring ideas and topics in the data. When searching for themes, Ryan and Bernard (2003) recommend looking for:

- *repetitions*: topics that recur again and again;

- *indigenous typologies or categories*: local expressions that are either unfamiliar or are used in an unfamiliar way;

- *metaphors and analogies*: the ways in which participants represent their thoughts in terms of metaphors or analogies (they give the example of people describing their marriage as like 'the Rock of Gibraltar');

- *transitions*: the ways in which topics shift in transcripts and other materials;

- *similarities and differences*: exploring how interviewees might discuss a topic in different ways or differ from each other in certain ways or exploring whole texts like transcripts and asking how they differ;

- *linguistic connectors*: examining the use of words like 'because' or 'since', because such terms point to causal connections in the minds of participants;

- *missing data*: reflecting on what is *not* in the data by asking questions about what interviewees, for example, omit in their answers to questions;

- *theory-related material*: using social scientific concepts as a springboard for themes.

While thematic analysis lacks a clearly specified series of procedures, in spite of its prominence as a means of conducting qualitative data analysis, the Framework approach and Ryan and Bernard's suggestions provide some pointers about how to begin and to organize such an analysis.

Student experience
Thematic analysis of transcripts

Several of the students who had conducted qualitative research using interviews mentioned forms of analysis that were indicative of adopting a thematic approach. Rebecca Barnes writes that she sought to 'identify key themes', while Erin Sanders writes that she 'transcribed the interviews verbatim—and used NVivo to code the transcripts—looking for emerging and relevant themes'. Hannah Creane used a form of thematic analysis to understand her interviews on generational changes within childhood.

> Once the transcriptions were complete I then began to look at the responses for each individual question and then grouped together questions that looked at a similar element of childhood. I then used colour-coded spider diagrams and time lines with diagrammatic representation so that I could clearly see any emergent trends.

*To read more about Rebecca's, Erin's, and Hannah's research experiences, go to the Online Resource Centre that accompanies this book at **http://www.oxfordtextbooks.co.uk/orc/brymansrm3e/**.*

Student experience
Combining memos with thematic analysis

Isabella Robbins used memos as a means of elaborating her thematic analysis of her data. Her memos formed part of her discussions with her supervisor.

> I developed analytic memos, on each interview completed, throughout the data-collection period. These along with full verbatim transcripts and message board data were put into NVivo. I had ideas about the thematics before I used NVivo, so at the beginning a pen and paper were used in conjunction with NVivo. The themes that I was pulling from the data were consistent, and this felt reassuring. My supervisors were also involved with the analysis, in that I would report back with analytic memos and we discussed emerging themes, and I developed ideas and analysis from there.

*To read more about Isabella's research experiences, go to the Online Resource Centre that accompanies this book at **http://www.oxfordtextbooks.co.uk/orc/brymansrm3e/**.*

Narrative analysis

Narrative analysis, which was referred to in the previous section, is an approach to the elicitation and analysis of data that is sensitive to the sense of temporal sequence that people, as tellers of stories about their lives or events around them, detect in their lives and surrounding episodes and inject into their accounts. With narrative analysis, the focus of attention shifts from 'what actually happened?' to 'how do people make sense of what happened?'. Proponents of narrative analysis argue that most approaches to the collection and analysis of data neglect the fact that people perceive their lives in terms of continuity and process and that attempts to understand social life that are not attuned to this feature neglect the perspective of those being studied. Life history research (Key concept 18.1) is an obvious location for the application of a narrative analysis, but its use can be much broader than this. Mishler (1986: 77), for example, has argued for greater interest in 'elicited personal narratives'. In his view, and that of many others, the answers that people provide, in particular in qualitative interviews, can be viewed as stories that are potential fodder for a narrative analysis. In other words, narrative analysis relates not just to the life span but also to accounts relating to episodes and to the interconnections between them.

Some researchers apply narrative analysis to interview accounts. For example, in her account of her 'click moment' as a narrative researcher (see the long quotation in the previous section), Riessman describes how she applied narrative analysis to conventional interview transcript material and then began to uncover the stories her interviewees were telling her. In this case, Riessman was applying a narrative approach to materials that had been gathered in a conventional way for conventional purposes. Other researchers start out with the intention of conducting a narrative analysis and deliberately ask people to recount stories (e.g. Miller 2000). Thus, while stories can arise out of answers to questions that are not designed to elicit a narrative, certain kinds of question are especially likely to elicit them. Riessman (2004a) suggests that a question such as 'tell me what happened', followed up with 'and then what happened?', is much more likely to provide a narrative account than 'when did X happen?'. While some narrative researchers prefer simply to start people off by asking them to tell their story about an event, Riessman argues that it is usually necessary to keep asking follow-up questions to stimulate the flow of details and impressions. For example, in her study of divorce, she often asked 'Can you remember a time when . . . ?' and then followed it up with 'What happened that makes you remember that particular moment in your marriage?'. There are, then, two distinct ways of thinking about narrative analysis: for some researchers it is an approach to analysing different kinds of data; for others, it is this but, in addition, the researcher deliberately seeks to stimulate the telling of stories. The examples provided in Research in focus 22.5 and 22.6 are examples of the former.

Research in focus 22.5
HIV narratives

Squire (2000) conducted narrative interviews with 'thirty-four people infected or affected by HIV, who used HIV support groups for HIV positive people, and for workers, carers and volunteers in the HIV field'. Some were interviewed on more than one occasion. Interviewees were not directed to produce autobiographical narratives, but in the course of the interviews, many did so. For example, interviewees who were HIV-positive produced narratives of how the identities that were forged immediately after diagnosis were derived from a stigmatizing identity. However, with time, they forged identities based on acceptance and also a shift from not being involved with others towards communion with others who were similarly affected by the disease. Other narratives described by Squire include a *disengagement* narrative of seeking to get away from the illness and a *coming-out* narrative, which was one of finding ways of coming to terms with a gay sexual identity. With the latter, coming out about being HIV-positive inevitably meant for many gay men coming out about their sexuality to those who were not aware that they were gay. The dilemmas and concerns that this process occasioned, even though the concerns did not always have the negative impacts that were feared, was a key element in the coming-out narrative.

Research in focus 22.6
An example of organizational narratives in a hospital

Brown (1998) has examined the competing narratives involved in the aftermath of the introduction of a hospital information support system (HISS) at a British hospital trust referred to as 'The City'. The IT (information technology) implementation was largely seen as unsuccessful because of the absence of clear clinical benefits and cost over-runs. Drawing on his unstructured and **semi-structured interviews** with key actors regarding the IT implementation and its aftermath, Brown presents three contrasting narratives: the ward narrative; the laboratory narrative; and the implementation team's narrative, thereby presenting the perspectives of the main groups of participants in the implementation.

The three contrasting narratives provide a very clear sense of the organization as a political arena in which groups and individuals contest the legitimacy of others' interpretations of events. Thus, 'the representations of each group's narrative are described as vehicles for establishing its altruistic motives for embarking on the project, and for attributing responsibility for what had come to be defined as a failing project to others' (Brown 1998: 49).

Thus, while the three groups had similar motivations for participating in the initiative, largely in terms of the espousal of an ethic of patient care, they had rather different latent motivations and interpretations of what went wrong. In terms of the former, whereas the ward narrative implied a latent motivation to save doctors and nurses' time, the laboratory team emphasized the importance of retaining the existing IT systems, and the implementation team placed the accent on the possible advantages for their own careers, in large part by the increased level of dependence on their skills. In terms of the contrasting narratives of what went wrong, the ward narrative was to do with the failure of the implementation team to coordinate the initiative and meet deadlines, and the laboratory team emphasized the tendency for the implementation team not to listen or communicate. For their part, the implementation team's diagnosis was to do with the ward staff failing to communicate their needs, lack of cooperation from the laboratory staff, and poorly written software.

Research in focus 22.7
Narratives about the mantelpiece

Hurdley's (2006) interest in material culture led her to examine how people think about artefacts that are important to them. She interviewed 30 people and their families in Cardiff who had been identified in a **postal questionnaire** survey as likely to be appropriate research participants. Hurdley conducted her interviews in order to elicit narratives about the artefacts displayed on their mantelpieces. According to Hurdley (2006: 721): 'exploring the narratives about things emphasizes what mantelpiece displays (or other domestic display areas) are accomplishing in the home.'

Research participants were invited to tell stories about these items on display. These stories were usually contextualized by requesting interviewees to provide stories about their housing histories. Hurdley (2006: 721) writes:

Each object could . . . be made the subject of a narrative, as I asked individuals to tell me about the origins of the vase, or clock, or ornament. At other times, the information they had written in the questionnaires concerning childhood memories, or why they did not want a mantelpiece, suggested a narrative pathway. . . . Although the artefact on display remains materially the same, different stories, or different versions of the same story, can be related to it according to the specific identity its owner wishes to invoke in an interaction.

She goes on to show that the artefacts and the stories around them are not only a context within which identities can surface, but also identities that would not otherwise be obvious to the observer or possibly to the research participant.

Coffey and Atkinson (1996) argue that a narrative should be viewed in terms of the functions that the narrative serves for the teller. The aim of narrative interviews is to elicit interviewees' reconstructed accounts of connections between events and between events and contexts (see Research in focus 22.5 for an example). A narrative analysis will then entail a seeking-out of the forms and functions of narrative. Miller (2000) proposes that narrative interviews in life story or biographical research are far more concerned with eliciting the interviewee's perspective as revealed in the telling of the story of his or her life or family than with the facts of that life. There is a con-

cern with how that perspective changes in relation to different contexts. The interviewer is very much a part of the process in that he or she is fully implicated in the construction of the story for the interviewee. Research in focus 22.6 provides an example of the application of a narrative analysis approach to an environment that demonstrates its potential beyond the life story context (see also Thinking deeply 22.1). In this case, the author explores competing narratives in accounting for the failed implementation of an information technology system in a British hospital.

Thinking deeply 22.1
Narrative research in organizations

Rhodes and Brown (2005) conducted a review of the business and management literature on narrative analysis (one of which was the article in Research in focus 22.6). Their use of **narrative review** is consistent with the focus of their review, which was on a qualitative research method. They identify five principal research areas that narrative analysis has explored, assessing the theoretical value each has added.

1. *sensemaking*: focuses on the role of stories as a device through which people make sense of organizational events;

2. *communication*: explores how narratives are used to create and maintain organizational culture and power structure;

3. *learning/change*: analyses how stories help people to learn and subjectively make sense of change;

4. *politics and power*: considers the role of shared narratives in the control of organizational meaning;

5. *identity and identification*: focuses on the role of stories in creating and maintaining organizational identity.

They observe that this research has been beneficial to the field for several reasons. First, it has helped to focus attention on the temporal aspects of organizational life—how stories about organizational events express change and how the stories themselves change over time. Second, it stimulates reflection of the different and often divergent interpretations of organizational life. Third, it draws attention to the role and significance of language in constructing organizational realities.

Narrative analysis, then, is an approach to the analysis of qualitative data that emphasizes the stories that people employ to account for events. It can be applied to data that have been created through a variety of research methods (notably semi-structured and **unstructured interviewing** and participant observation), but it has also become a focus for an interviewing approach in its own right—that is, the narrative interview in which the researcher sets out to elicit stories. It is very much connected to a general increase in interest in narrative in social research. For example, as will be seen in connection with the writing of ethnographic research (see section on 'Writing ethnography' in Chapter 27), there has been a growing recognition of the nature of the ethnography (in the sense of the written product of a period of participant observation) as being a narrative that is designed to tell a story about a way of life.

As an approach to the analysis of qualitative data, narrative analysis has not gone uncriticized. Bury (2001), while noting the growing interest in *illness narratives* (stories that people tell about the causes of, in particular, chronic illnesses they and/or others experience and the impacts they have on their and others' lives), argues that there has been a tendency for narrative researchers to treat the stories they are told uncritically. For example, he suggests that the frequent recourse in illness narratives to coping with and normalizing chronic illness may in large part be to do with an attempt to convince the audience (for example, an interviewer or the reader of a book about someone's struggle with illness) of competence. It may therefore have more to do with signalling that one is not a failure in a society in which failure is frowned upon. Thus a narrative of coping with adversity in the form of a chronic illness may have more to do with wanting to be seen as a fully functioning member of society than a realistic account of coming-to-terms with a medical condition. However, as Bury recognizes, the social conditions that prompt such narratives and the form that the narratives take are themselves revealing. In drawing attention to the motives that may lie behind illness narratives, he is not seeking to undermine narrative analysis but to draw attention to the issue of what it is that narratives are supposed to be revealing to the researcher. A similar point could possibly be raised in connection with the studies of narrative in organizations referred to in Research in focus 22.6 and Thinking deeply 22.1. What is it that such studies reveal? Clearly, they draw attention to competing understandings of what goes on in organizations, but one might query how far the narratives reflect an underlying 'truth' about what happens or how far they reflect the divergent perspectives of different groups. In a sense, it does not matter: it is the perception that is typically important to people, but it may prove significant to the researcher in terms of how the stories should be interpreted.

Student experience
The use of narrative interviews

Isabella Robbins adopted a narrative interview approach for her study of parents' decision-making in connection with vaccination of their children. She did this by encouraging them to tell stories about the vaccinations.

In order to capture what I considered to be complex decision-making routes for some people contemplating childhood vaccination, I employed qualitative in-depth interviews as my main methodological route. In these interviews mothers were invited to explain how they came to their decisions regarding childhood vaccination. They were encouraged to tell the story of their child's/children's vaccination/s, and I took opportunities to follow up their talk. This narrative approach was supplemented towards the end of the interviews by inviting the mothers to respond to a series of informal vignettes, designed to elicit material relevant to foreshadowed and emerging themes.

To read more about Isabella's research experiences, go to the Online Resource Centre that accompanies this book at http://www.oxfordtextbooks.co.uk/orc/brymansrm3e/.

Secondary analysis of qualitative data

One final point to bear in mind is that this discussion of qualitative data analysis may have been presumed to be solely concerned with the analysis of data in which the analyst has played a part in collecting. However, in recent years, secondary analysis of qualitative data has become a growing focus of discussion and interest. While the secondary analysis of quantitative data has been on the research agenda for many years (see Chapter 13), similar use of qualitative data has only recently come to the fore. The general idea of secondary analysis was addressed in Key concept 13.1.

There is no obvious reason why qualitative data cannot be the focus of secondary analysis, though it is undoubtedly the case that such data do present certain problems that are not fully shared by quantitative data. The possible grounds for conducting a secondary analysis are more or less the same as those associated with quantitative data (see Chapter 13). In the context of qualitative data, it is possible that a secondary analysis will allow the researcher to mine data that were not examined by the primary investigators or that new interpretations may be possible (see Research in focus 22.8 for an example).

With such considerations in mind, Qualidata, an archival resource centre, was created in the UK in 1994. The centre is not a repository for qualitative data (unlike the Data Archive, which does house quantitative data); instead, it is concerned with 'locating, assessing and documenting qualitative data and arranging their deposit in suitable public archive repositories' (Corti *et al.* 1995). It has a very useful website: http://www.esds.ac.uk/qualidata/about/introduction.asp (accessed on 15 July 2007). Its

online catalogue—Qualicat—can be searched at the following address: http://www.qualidata.essex.ac.uk/search/qualicat.asp (accessed on 15 July 2007).

Qualidata acknowledges certain difficulties with the reuse of qualitative data, such as the difficulty of making settings and people anonymous and the ethical problems involved in such reuse associated with promises of confidentiality. Also, Hammersley (1997) has suggested that reuse of qualitative data may be hindered by the secondary analyst's lack of an insider's understanding of the social context within which the data were produced. This possible difficulty may hinder the interpretation of data but would seem to be more of a problem with ethnographic field notes than with interview transcripts. Such problems even seem to afflict researchers revisiting their own data many years after the original research had been carried out (Mauthner *et al.* 1998: 742). There are also distinctive ethical issues deriving from the fact that the original researcher(s) may not have obtained the consent of research participants for the analysis of data by others. This is a particular problem with qualitative data in view of the fact that it invariably contains detailed accounts of contexts and people that can make it difficult to conceal the identities of institutions and individuals in the presentation of raw data (as opposed to publications in which such concealment is usually feasible). Nonetheless, in spite of certain practical difficulties, secondary analysis offers rich opportunities, not least because the tendency for qualitative researchers to generate large and unwieldy sets of data means that much of the material remains under-explored.

Research in focus 22.8
A secondary analysis of qualitative data from the *Affluent Worker* study

Savage (2005) examined the field notes collected by researchers in the course of the *Affluent Worker* study in the 1960s (see e.g. Goldthorpe *et al.* 1968). This was an important project that explored questions concerning social class and work in Great Britain in this period. The findings in the monographs that emerged from the study emphasized the quantitative data collected from the **social survey**, and little use was made of the qualitative data that were collected in the course of the interviews. These qualitative data were deposited with Qualidata.

Savage re-examined some of the essentially qualitative field note data that were collected. Savage argues that, although a huge amount of qualitative data was generated through the *Affluent Worker* studies, very little of this part of the research made its way into publication. Instead the researchers focused on aspects of their data that could be quantified so that 'a huge amount of evocative material was "left on the cutting room floor"' (Savage 2005: 932). Savage uses the field notes, which contain many verbatim quotations from respondent interviews, to argue that rereading the field notes with a contemporary understanding of issues of money, power, and status indicates that the respondents had different understandings of class from Goldthorpe *et al.* that the researchers did not pick up on and this difference of understanding affected how the data were interpreted. Savage shows that many of the affluent workers struggled with the notion of 'class identity' and that the kinds of views that they held about class and related matters were not as different from other working-class groups as the authors' inferences about their survey data implied. His analysis also suggests greater continuity in individual identities between now and then than might have been expected. He shows how the interpretation of the data is affected by the researcher, in that the differences between his views of the data and those of the original researchers may in part be to do with different perspectives that are brought to bear on those data. This example of the secondary analysis of qualitative data indicates that new light can be shed on old data, but it also raises interesting methodological issues, in this case concerning how to disentangle inferences about change from the impact of looking at old data through new conceptual lenses.

Key points

- The collection of qualitative data frequently results in the accumulation of a large volume of information.

- Qualitative data analysis is not governed by codified rules in the same way as quantitative data analysis.

- There are different approaches to qualitative data analysis, of which grounded theory is probably the most prominent.

- Coding is a key process in most qualitative data analysis strategies, but it is sometimes accused of fragmenting and decontextualizing text.

- Narrative analysis is an approach that emphasises the stories that people tell in the course of interviews and other interactions with the qualitative researcher and that has become a distinctive strategy in its own right for the analysis of qualitative data.

- Secondary analysis of qualitative data is becoming a more prominent activity than in the past.

Questions for review

- What is meant by suggesting that qualitative data are an 'attractive nuisance'?

General strategies of qualitative data analysis

- What are the main ingredients of analytic induction?
- What makes it a rigorous method?

- What are the main ingredients of grounded theory?
- What is the role of coding in grounded theory and what are the different types of coding?
- What is the role of memos in grounded theory?
- Charmaz (2000: 519) has written that theoretical sampling 'represents a defining property of grounded theory'. Why do you think she feels this to be the case?
- What are some of the main criticisms of grounded theory?

Basic operations in qualitative data analysis

- Is coding associated solely with grounded theory?
- What are the main steps in coding?
- To what extent does coding result in excessive fragmentation of data?

Thematic analysis

- How far is there a codified scheme for conducting thematic analysis?
- How does the Framework approach help with a thematic analysis?
- What are the chief ways of identifying themes in qualitative data?

Narrative analysis

- To what extent does narrative analysis provide an alternative to data fragmentation?
- How does the emphasis on stories in narrative analysis provide a distinctive approach to the analysis of qualitative data?
- Can narrative analysis be applied to all kinds of qualitative interview?
- What is a narrative interview and how far does it differ from other kinds of qualitative interview?

Secondary analysis of qualitative data

- How feasible is it for researchers to analyse qualitative data collected by another researcher?

Online Resource Centre

http://www.oxfordtextbooks.co.uk/orc/brymansrm3e/

Visit the Online Resource Centre that accompanies this book to enrich your understanding of qualitative data analysis. Consult web links, test yourself using multiple choice questions, and gain further guidance and inspiration from the Student Researcher's Toolkit.

Computer-assisted qualitative data analysis: using NVivo

Chapter outline

Chapter guide

One of the most significant developments in qualitative research in the last twenty years is the emergence of computer software that can assist in the use of qualitative data analysis. This software is often referred to as computer-assisted (or computer-aided) qualitative data analysis software (CAQDAS). CAQDAS removes many if not most of the clerical tasks associated with the manual coding and retrieving of data. There is no industry leader among the different programs (in the sense that SPSS holds this position among quantitative data analysis software). This chapter introduces a relatively new entrant that is having a big impact—NVivo. It was developed out of an earlier program—NUD*IST—which is still available. This chapter explores:

- some of the debates about the desirability of CAQDAS;
- how to set up your research materials for analysis with NVivo;
- how to code using NVivo;
- how to retrieve coded text;
- how to create memos;
- basic computer operations in NVivo.

Introduction

One of the most notable developments in qualitative research in recent years has been the arrival of computer software that facilitates the analysis of qualitative data. Computer-assisted qualitative data analysis software, or CAQDAS as it is conventionally abbreviated, has been a growth area in terms of both the proliferation of programs that perform such analysis and the numbers of people using them. The term and its abbreviation were coined by Lee and Fielding (1991).

Most of the best-known programs are variations on the code-and-retrieve theme. This means that they allow the analyst to code text while working at the computer and to retrieve the coded text. Thus, if we code a large number of interviews, we can retrieve all those sequences of text to which a code (or combination of codes) was attached. This means that the computer takes over manual tasks associated with the coding process referred to in the previous chapter. Typically, the analyst would:

- go through a set of data marking sequences of text in terms of codes (coding); and
- for each code, collect together all sequences of text coded in a particular way (retrieving).

The computer takes over the physical task of writing marginal codes, making photocopies of transcripts or field notes, cutting out all chunks of text relating to a code, and pasting them together. CAQDAS does not automatically do these things: the analyst must still interpret his or her data, code, and then retrieve the data, but the computer takes over the manual labour involved (wielding scissors and pasting small pieces of paper together, for example).

Is CAQDAS like quantitative data analysis software?

One of the comments often made about CAQDAS is that it does not and cannot help with decisions about the coding of textual materials or about the interpretation of findings (Sprokkereef *et al.* 1995; Weitzman and Miles 1995). However, this situation is little different (if at all) from quantitative data analysis software. In quantitative research, the investigator sets out the crucial concepts and ideas in advance rather than generating them out of his or her data. Also, it would be wrong to represent the use of quantitative data analysis software like SPSS as purely mechanical: once the analyses have been performed, it is still necessary to interpret them. Indeed, the choice of variables to be analysed and the techniques of analysis to be employed are themselves areas in which a considerable amount of interpretative expertise is required. Creativity is required by both forms of software.

CAQDAS differs from the use of quantitative data analysis software largely in terms of the environment within which it operates.

No industry leader

With quantitative data analysis, SPSS is both widely known and used. It is not the only statistical software used by social researchers, but it is certainly dominant. It has competitors, such as Minitab, but SPSS is close to being the industry leader. No parallel situation exists with regard to CAQDAS. Up until the early 1990s, The Ethnograph was probably the best-known and most widely used CAQDAS. Lee and Fielding (1991: 11) report that, between March 1988 and January 1990, 1,600 copies of the software were sold. However, at that time more and more programs were coming onto the market: ten other programs were referred to in an appendix to the book in which Lee and Fielding's (1991) article appeared, and since then further programs have appeared. Seven years later, the situation had changed. The same authors observed that, in the UK, The Ethnograph 'seems . . . to have lost ground to both NUD*IST and Atlas/ti over the last few years. NUD*IST is now probably the package that most people at least know by name' (Fielding and Lee 1998: 15).

NUD*IST (Non-numerical Unstructured Data Indexing Searching and Theorizing) became very popular in the 1990s and has been built upon more recently with the emergence of QSR NUD*IST Vivo, known as NVivo. This software is the one featured in this chapter. It draws upon many features in NUD*IST, so that, if you have access to NUD*IST, most of what you read in this chapter will be applicable to you. If you are unsure about which software is likely to meet your needs, demonstration copies of many of the main packages (NVivo, ATLAS/ti and The Ethnograph) can be downloaded from these Internet sites:

www.qsrinternational.com

www.atlasti.com

www.qualisresearch.com

All three sites were accessed on 16 July 2007.

These demonstration copies are full working programs but you cannot save changes to the project work you carry out using them.

Lack of universal agreement about the utility of CAQDAS

Unlike quantitative data analysis, in which the use of computer software is both widely accepted and to all intents and purposes a necessity, among qualitative data analysts its use is by no means universally embraced. There are several concerns.

- Some writers are concerned that the ease with which coded text can be quantified, either within qualitative data analysis packages or by importing coded information into quantitative data analysis packages like SPSS, will mean that the temptation to quantify findings will prove irresistible to many researchers. As a result, there is a concern that qualitative research will then be colonized by the reliability and validity criteria of quantitative research (Hesse-Biber 1995).

- It has been suggested that CAQDAS reinforces and even exaggerates the tendency for the code-and-retrieve process that underpins most approaches to qualitative data analysis to result in a fragmentation of the textual materials on which researchers work (Weaver and Atkinson 1994). As a result, the narrative flow of interview transcripts and events recorded in field notes may be lost.

- It has also been suggested that the fragmentation process of coding text into chunks that are then retrieved and put together into groups of related fragments risks de-contextualizing data (Buston 1997; Fielding and Lee 1998: 74). Having an awareness of context is crucial to many qualitative researchers, and the prospect of this element being sidelined is not an attractive prospect.

- Catterall and Maclaran (1997) have argued on the basis of their experience that CAQDAS is not very suitable for focus group data because the code and retrieve function tends to result in a loss of the communication process that goes on when this method is used. Many writers view the interaction that occurs in focus groups as an important feature of the method (Kitzinger 1994).

- Stanley and Temple (1995) have suggested that most of the coding and retrieval features that someone is likely to need in the course of conducting qualitative data analysis are achievable through powerful word-processing software. They show how this can be accomplished using Word for Windows. The key point here is that the advantage of using such software is that it does not require a lengthy period of getting acquainted with the mechanics of its operations. Also, of course, if someone already has the necessary word-processing software, the possible cost of a CAQDAS program is rendered unnecessary.

- Researchers working in teams may experience difficulties in coordinating the coding of text when different people are involved in this activity (Sprokkereef *et al.* 1995).

- Coffey *et al.* (1994) have argued that the style of qualitative data analysis enshrined in most CAQDAS software (particularly the more prominent ones such as The Ethnograph, NUD*IST, and NVivo) is resulting in the emergence of a new orthodoxy. This arises because these programs presume and are predicated on a certain style of analysis—one based on coding and retrieving text—that owes a great deal to grounded theory. Coffey *et al.* argue that the emergence of a new orthodoxy is inconsistent with the growing flirtation with a variety of representational modes in qualitative research, partly as a result of the influence of postmodernism (see Chapter 27 for a discussion of these considerations).

On the other hand, several writers have sought to extol the virtues of such packages on a variety of grounds.

- Most obviously, CAQDAS can make the coding and retrieval process faster and more efficient.

- It has been suggested that new opportunities are offered. For example, Mangabeira (1995) has argued

on the basis of her experience with The Ethnograph that her ability to relate her coded text to what are often referred to as 'face-sheet variables' (socio-demographic and personal information, such as age, title of job, number of years in school education) offered new opportunities in the process of analysing her data. Thus, CAQDAS may be helpful in the development of explanations.

- It is sometimes suggested that CAQDAS enhances the transparency of the process of conducting qualitative data analysis. It is often noted that the ways in which qualitative data are analysed are unclear in reports of findings (Bryman and Burgess 1994b). CAQDAS may force researchers to be more explicit and reflective about the process of analysis.

- CAQDAS, like NVivo, invites the analyst to think about codes that are developed in terms of 'trees' of inter-related ideas. This can be a useful feature, in that it urges the analyst to consider possible connections between codes.

- Writers like Silverman (1985) have commented on the tendency towards anecdotalism in much qualitative research—that is, the tendency to use quotations from interview transcripts or field notes but with little sense of the prevalence of the phenomenon they are supposed to exemplify. CAQDAS invariably offers the opportunity to count such things as the frequency with which a form of behaviour occurred or a viewpoint was expressed in interviews. However, as previously noted, some qualitative researchers perceive risks in the opportunity offered for quantification of findings.

To use or not to use CAQDAS? If you have a very small data set, it is probably not worth the time and trouble navigating your way around new software. On the other hand, if you think you may use it on a future occasion, taking the time and trouble may be worth it. If you do not have easy access to CAQDAS, it is likely to be too expensive for your personal purchase, though the afore-mentioned Scolari Internet sites do outline student and educational discounts. It is also worth bearing in mind that learning new software does provide you with useful skills that may be transferable on a future occasion. By and large, I feel it is worthwhile, but you need to bear in mind some of the factors mentioned above in deciding whether to use it. The rest of this chapter provides an introduction to NVivo. It is based on my study of visitors to Disney theme parks, where I used NVivo as a tool to assist me in the process of qualitative data analysis.

Learning NVivo

This exposition of NVivo and its functions addresses just its most basic features. There may be features not covered here that you would find useful in your own work, so try to explore it. There is a very good help facility and tutorials have been included to assist learners. In the following account, as in Chapter 15, → signifies 'click once with the left-hand button of your mouse'—that is, select.

On opening NVivo, you will be presented with a welcome screen (Plate 23.1). This screen shows any existing NVivo projects and is the springboard for either opening one of the existing projects or starting a new one. If you are starting a new project, as in the example that follows, → **File** → **New Project**. The **New Project** dialog box appears and you are asked to provide a **Title** for your project. For this exercise, the title 'Disney Project1' was chosen. You are also asked to give a **Description** of the

project, though this is an optional feature. When you have done this, → **OK**.

You then need to import the documents you want to code. In this case, they will be interview transcripts from the project on visitors to Disney theme parks, referred to in Chapter 22. Other kinds of documents can be imported such as fieldwork notes. Earlier versions of NVivo could not import documents in Microsoft Word format (.doc), so that Word documents had to be converted into rich text format (.rtf) documents. This is not the case with NVivo 7, which is the release used for this chapter. NVivo 7 can accept documents in both rich text and Word formats. To import the documents, → **Documents** (below **Sources**) → **Project** → **Import Documents** . . . [opens the **Import Documents** dialog box] → **Browse** to locate the documents that are to be imported → select the documents to

Plate 23.1

The opening screen

Name	Filename	Modified
Disney Project	C:\Documents and Settings\Alan\My Docume	05/07/2006 12:14
Disney project 2	C:\Documents and Settings\Alan\My Docume	05/07/2006 12:16
Higher Education Leadership	C:\Documents and Settings\Alan\My Docume	26/06/2006 15:54
Volunteering	C:\Documents and Settings\All Users\Docum	10/03/2006 14:04

Plate 23.2

Stages in importing documents into NVivo

1. Select **Documents**

2. Select **Project** and then select **Import Documents . . .** This brings up the **Import Documents** dialog box

3. In the **Import Documents** dialog box, click on **Browse . . .** to locate the documents to be imported

4. Select the documents to be imported from the location identified in step 3

5. Click on **Open**. The selected documents will then be imported into NVivo

---

be imported → **Open** (see Plate 23.2 for the series of steps). The documents will then be visible in the Documents **List View**. Once the documents have been imported, they can be read and edited. All you need to do is to double-click on the yellow icon to the left of each interview in the **List View**.

Coding

Coding your data is obviously one of the key phases in the whole process of qualitative data analysis. For NVivo, coding is accomplished through nodes (see Key Concept 23.1).

Plate 23.3

The document viewer

To uncode at any point, highlight text to be uncoded and click here

Key concept 23.1
What is a node?

NVivo's help system in earlier releases defined coding as 'the process of marking passages of text in a project's documents with *nodes*' (emphasis added). Nodes are, therefore, the route by which coding is undertaken. In turn, a node is defined in the latest release as 'a collection of references about a specific theme, place, person or other area of interest'. When a document has been coded, the node will incorporate references to those portions of documents in which the code appears. Once established, nodes can be changed or deleted. Nodes can take different forms, but only two are covered in this chapter. First, there are *tree nodes*, whereby nodes are held in a treelike structure, implying connections between them. In this way, you can have groups (trees) of related nodes. The other type covered here is *free nodes*; these are independent of any tree.

There are several ways of going about the coding process in NVivo. The approach I took in relation to the coding of the Disney Project was to follow these steps.

- I read through the interviews both in printed form and in the Document viewer (Plate 23.3).

- I worked out some codes that seemed relevant to the documents.

- I went back into the documents and coded them using NVivo.

An alternative strategy is to code while browsing the documents.

Creating nodes

The nodes that I used that were relevant to the passage in Tips and skills Coded text from the Disney project in Chapter 22 are presented in Figure 23.1. Notice that there are two *free nodes* and three groups of *tree nodes*. The nodes and their associated numbers can be created in the following way.

Creating a free node

1. While in the **Navigation View** [this is the term used to describe the general screen shown in Plate 23.2] → **Nodes**

2. → **Free Nodes**

3. → **New** → **Free Node in This Folder** [opens the **New Free Node** dialog box—see Plate 23.4]

4. Enter the node **Name** [*not critical of Disney*] and a **Description** (the latter is optional)

5. → **OK**

Creating tree nodes

To create a tree node, the initial process is exactly the same as with a free node. In the following example, I will explain how to create the tree node *Class critique*, which is a branch of the tree node *Ideological critique*, which is itself a branch of the tree node *Critique* (see Figure 23.1). The following steps will generate this node.

Figure 23.1

Nodes used in the Disney project

Tree nodes

Critique
- Aesthetic critique
- Ideological critique
- Content critique
- Other critique

- Class critique
- Ethnicity critique
- Gender critique
- Nationality critique

Visitors
- Visitors' age
- Visitors' gender
- Visitors' class
- Visitors' ethnicity

Significance
- Educational significance
- Recreational significance
- Ideological significance
- Other significance

Free nodes

Uncritical enthusiasm   Not critical of Disney

Plate 23.4

Stages in creating a free node

2. Select Free Nodes

3. Select New and then Free Node in this Folder . . . which opens the **New Free Node** dialog box

1. Select Nodes

4. In the New Free Node dialog box enter the node **Name** and a **Description** (the latter is optional)

5. Click on OK

1. While in the **Navigation View** → **Nodes**

2. → **Tree Nodes**

3. → **New** → **Tree Node in This Folder . . .** [opens the **New Tree Node** dialog box—see Plate 23.5]

4. Enter the node **Name** [*Critique*] and a **Description** (the latter is optional). This node will form the initial root of the tree node.

5. → OK

6. → *Critique* in the Tree Node viewer

7. → **New** → **Tree Node in This Folder . . .** [opens the **New Tree Node** dialog box]

8. Enter the node **Name** [*Ideological critique*] and a **Description** (the latter is optional). This node will form a branch of the tree node. See Plate 23.5.

Plate 23.5

Stages in creating a tree node

2. Select **Tree Nodes**

3. Select **New** and then **Tree Node in this Folder . . .** which opens the **New Tree Node** dialog box

3a. If the tree node is a branch of an existing tree node, make sure the appropriate tree node has been selected

1. Select **Nodes**

4. In the **New Tree Node** dialog box enter the node **Name** and a **Description** (the latter is optional)

5. Click on **OK**

Plate 23.6

Using drag and drop to code

Highlight text to be coded and holding down the left-hand button of the mouse . . .

. . . drop it into the appropriate node, in this case *Uncritical enthusiasm*

9. → **OK**

10. → *Ideological critique* in the Tree Node viewer

11. → **New** → **Tree Node in This Folder . . .** [opens the **New Tree Node** dialog box]

12. Enter the node **Name** [*Class critique*] and a **Description** (the latter is optional). This node will form a branch of the tree node *Ideological critique*

13. → **OK**

Applying nodes in the coding process

Coding is carried out by applying nodes to segments of text. Once you have set up some nodes (and do remember

you can add and alter them at any time), assuming that you are looking at a document in the viewer, you can highlight the area of the document that you want to code and then right-click on the mouse while holding the cursor over the highlighted text. Then, → **Code** → **Code Selection at New Node**. This opens the **New Node** dialog box. The default is that it allows you to create a free node, but if you → **Select . . .** you have the opportunity to create a tree node and to locate it appropriately within a tree structure.

One of the easiest ways of coding in NVivo 7 is to drag and drop text into a node (see Plate 23.6). To do this, highlight the text to be coded and then, holding down the

Plate 23.7

Coding in NVivo

Select the appropriate node by clicking in the box by it

If you also want to code in terms of one or more tree nodes, click on this folder

left-hand button, drag the text over to the appropriate node.

An alternative is to highlight the text to be coded, right-click over the highlighted text, → **Code** → **Code Selection at Existing Nodes**, which opens the **Select Project Items** dialog box (see Plate 23.7). Tick the node(s) you want to use. If you do not see the node(s) you need, → the yellow folder that you need. To find a node within a tree, → the ⊞ sign next to a tree node. Thus, in the example in Plate 23.7, the tick by *Uncritical enthusiasm* will code the highlighted text at that node. If you also wanted to code it as a tree node, you would need to → yellow folder

at **Tree Nodes** and then find the appropriate root node or a branch of it by → the ⊞ sign. To *uncode* at any point, simply highlight the passage to be uncoded, and → the button with a red cross in it (see Plate 23.3). Alternatively, you can right-click on the highlighted text and select **Uncode**.

These instructions apply to the application of both free nodes and tree nodes.

Coding stripes

It is very helpful to be able to see the areas of text that have been coded and the nodes applied to them. NVivo

Plate 23.8

Coding stripes

has a very useful aid to this called *coding stripes*. Selecting this facility allows you to see multi-coloured stripes that represent portions of coded text and the nodes that have been used. Overlapping nodes do not represent a problem at all.

To activate this facility, → **View** and then → **Coding Stripes** → **Show Nodes Recently Coding Item**. Plate 23.8 shows these stripes. We can see that some segments have been coded at two or more nodes—such as *visitors ethnicity* and *ethnicity critique*. All the nodes that have been used are clearly displayed.

Searching text

Once you have coded your data, however preliminary that may be, you will want to conduct searches of your data at some point. A typical instance is that you are likely to want to retrieve all occurrences in your documents of a particular node. NVivo allows you very rapidly to trawl

through all your documents so that you will end up with all text that was coded at a particular node in all your documents. This is very easy to do in NVivo 7.

To search for occurrences of a single node

These steps describe how to conduct a search for sequences of text that have been coded in terms of the node *ethnicity critique*. The stages are outlined in Plate 23.9.

1. While in the **Navigation View** → **Nodes** [this opens the list of node folders in the top left-hand pane of Plate 23.9]

2. → 📁 at **Tree Nodes** [this generates a list of all tree nodes, as in Plate 23.9]

3. → on the ⊞ to the left of *Critique* [this brings up a list of all branches of the node *Critique*]

4. → on the ⊞ to the left of *Ideological critique* [this brings up a list of all branches of the node *Ideological critique*]

Plate 23.9

Stages in retrieving text from a tree node

2. Click on the **Tree Nodes** folder

1. Click on **Nodes**

3. Click on the + to bring up the branch(es) of the tree node you want to explore

---

5. → 🔎 to the left of *Nationality critique*

6. All instances of coded text at the node *Nationality critique* will appear at the bottom of the screen, as in Plate 23.10

To search for text coded in terms of a free node, the process is simpler in that you need to → the **Free Nodes** folder rather than the **Tree Nodes** folder and then → 🔎 to the left of the appropriate tree node.

To search for the intersection of two nodes

This section is concerned with searching for sequences of text that have been coded at two nodes: *aesthetic critique* and *not critical of Disney*. This type of search is known as a 'Boolean search'. It will locate text coded in terms of the two nodes together (that is, where they intersect), *not* text coded in terms of each of the two nodes. The following steps need to be followed:

Plate 23.10

Retrieving text from a tree node

Once you have brought up the appropriate node, in this case *nationality critique*, click here

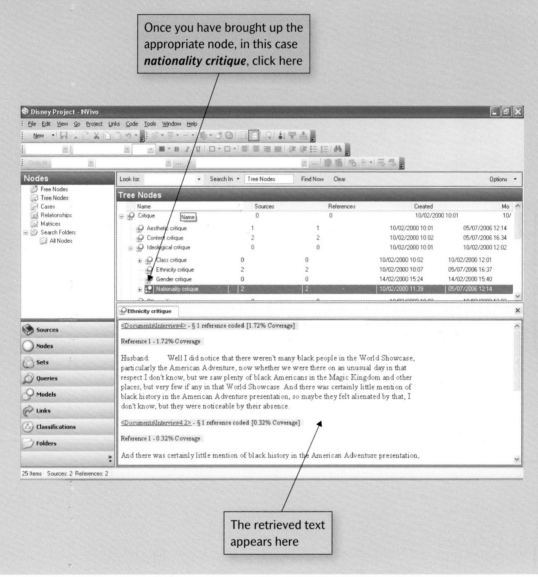

The retrieved text appears here

---

1. In the **Navigation View**, → **Queries** to the bottom left

2. → **New** on the toolbar in the top left

3. → **Coding Query in This Folder** [opens the **Coding Query** dialog box in Plate 23.11]

4. → **Coding Criteria** tab

5. → **Advanced** tab

6. In the **Define more criteria**: panel, → **Coded by** from drop-down menu

7. → **Select. . . .** You then need to choose the two nodes to be analysed

8. → Once the nodes have been selected, → **Add to List**

9. → **AND** from the drop-down menu

10. → **Run**

Plate 23.11

The Coding Query dialog box (searching for the intersection of two nodes)

1. Select **Coding Criteria** tab

2. Select **Advanced** tab

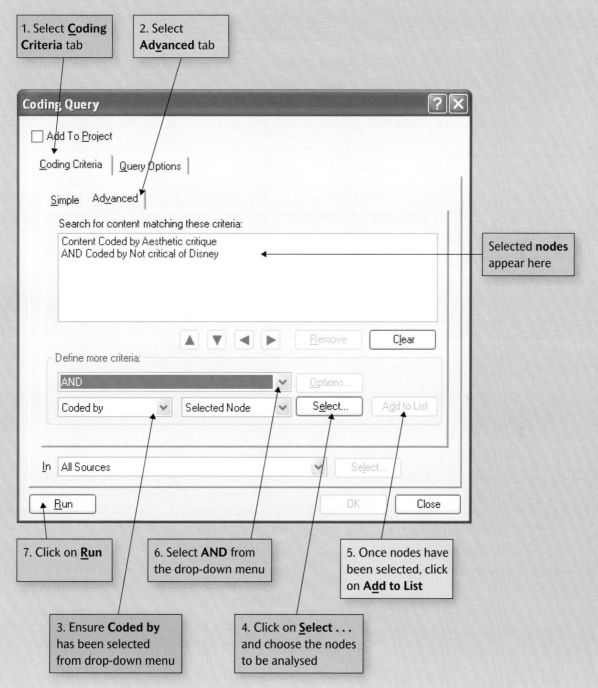

Selected **nodes** appear here

7. Click on **Run**

6. Select **AND** from the drop-down menu

5. Once nodes have been selected, click on **Add to List**

3. Ensure **Coded by** has been selected from drop-down menu

4. Click on **Select . . .** and choose the nodes to be analysed

Plate 23.12

The **Find Content** dialog box

To search for specific text

NVivo can also perform searches for specific words or phrases, often referred to as 'strings' in computer jargon. For example, to search for **Magic Kingdom**, the following steps would need to be taken:

1. On the menu bar at the top, → **Edit**

2. → **Find . . .** [opens the **Find Content** dialog box in Plate 23.12]

3. Insert **Magic Kingdom** to the right of **Text**

4. To the right of **Look in**, make sure **Text** has been selected

5. → **Find Next**

Text searching can be useful for the identification of possible in vivo codes. You would then need to go back to the documents to create nodes to allow you to code in terms of any in vivo codes.

Output

To find the results of coding at a particular node, → the **Nodes** button in the bottom left. This will bring up your node structure. Find the node that you are interested in and simply double-click on that node. This will bring up all text coded at that node along with information about which interview(s) the text comes from.

Memos

In Chapter 22 it was noted that one feature of the grounded theory approach to qualitative data analysis is the use of memos in which ideas and illustrations might be stored. Memos can be easily created in NVivo. The following steps, which are outlined in Plate 23.13, should be followed:

1. In the Navigation View, → **Sources**

2. Under **Sources** → **Memos**

Plate 23.13

Stages in creating a memo

2. Select **Memos**

3. Click on **New** and then **Memo in This Folder . . .** which opens the **New Memo** dialog box in Plate 23.14

1. Select **Sources**

3. → **New**

4. → **Memo in This Folder . . .** [opens the **New Memo** dialog box shown in Plate 23.14]

5. After Name, type in a name for the document (e.g.

gender critique memo). You can also provide a brief description of the document in the window to the right of Description, as in Plate 23.13

6. → **OK**

Plate 23.14

The New Memo dialog box

Saving an NVivo project

When you have finished working on your data, you will need to save it for future use. To do this, on the menu bar at the top, → **File** → **Save Project**. This will save all the work you have done. You will then be given the opportunity to exit NVivo or to create or open a project without worrying about losing all your hard work. You might also consider backing up the project. To do this, you will need to exit the project you are working on by → **File** → **Close Project**. This will take you to the Welcome screen. → **File** → **Copy** Project. The **Copy Project** dialog box will then be opened. This will allow you to specify the project you want to copy and where you want the backed up copy to be located—for example, on a flash memory drive.

Opening an existing NVivo project

To retrieve a project you have created, at the Welcome screen, → **File** → **Open Project**. This opens the **Open Project** dialog box. Search for and then select the project you want to work on. Then → **Open**.

You can also open a NUD*IST project, or one designed using an earlier release of NVivo, by selecting the appropriate project type from the drop-down menu to the right of **Files of type**.

Final thoughts

As with the chapter on SPSS (Chapter 15), a short chapter like this can provide help only with the most basic features of the software. In so doing, I hope that it will have given students who may be uncertain about whether CAQDAS is for them an impression of what the software is like. Doubtless, some readers will decide it is not for them and that the tried-and-tested scissors and paste will do the trick. On the other hand, the software warrants serious consideration because of its power and flexibility.

Student experience
The advantages of CAQDAS

Rebecca Barnes found NVivo extremely helpful in the context of analysing data from her semi-structured interviews concerning violence and abuse in same-sex partnerships. She began to use a thematic analysis of the transcripts to identify 'similarities and differences between different participants' accounts' and then decided to use NVivo. Although she found it time-consuming, it made many of the tasks associated with qualitative data analysis easier:

> I then used a computer software package for qualitative analysis called NVivo. This involved a process of indexing all the transcripts, in order to group together all the pieces of data that corresponded to a certain category or theme; for example, emotional abuse. Within the category of emotional abuse, there was then a more detailed breakdown of the types of emotional abuse, such as verbal abuse, or possessiveness. Like the transcribing, this was another time-consuming task, but, again, it offered huge rewards by increasing my familiarity with my data, and encouraging me to think analytically when naming and grouping codes. Although using NVivo required me to learn to use a new software package and to spend a substantial amount of time on the coding, it has saved me considerable time in the long term, as if I want to view all the data about a specific topic, such as verbal abuse, then rather than having to trawl back through forty transcripts, it only takes a few small mouse clicks! Once I had reached this stage, I started to make more concrete links between different themes, and I drew upon existing literature to examine the extent to which my findings supported or contradicted what is already known about both woman-to-woman partner abuse and heterosexual women's experiences of partner abuse.

To read more about Rebecca's research experiences, go to the Online Resource Centre that accompanies this book at http:www.oxfordtextbooks.co.uk/orc/brymansrm3e/.

Student experience
Reservations about CAQDAS

Gareth Matthews did not use CAQDAS because of problems of access to the software while in the field conducting his interviews. He describes his approach as follows:

> I started organizing my transcribed data into a spreadsheet, so as to feed my early results back into the interview schedule. As I continued to do this, I refined my 'codes' under different headings on the spreadsheet, and became very familiar with the content of the interviews. I think that, in reality, the process of conducting interviews, transcribing interviews, and then arranging the data under different headings results in the findings being lodged in the brain of the researcher.

However, he writes that he would advocate using a package because of the 'laboriousness' of the approach he took. He also feels that there are clear advantages to his approach because CAQDAS:

> carries the danger of the researcher becoming detached from the findings, and missing some of the less immediately obvious themes that come out of interviews (such as contradictions within the account of a respondent). By reading and rereading my interviews countless times, I was forced to become familiar with the technical content and more tacit meanings within the data set, and I feel that this helped me to find themes, as well as to refine my research instruments as I went along.

To read more about Gareth's research experiences, go to the Online Resource Centre that accompanies this book at http:www.oxfordtextbooks.co.uk/orc/brymansrm3e/.

Key points

- CAQDAS does not and cannot help with decisions about how to code qualitative data or how to interpret findings.
- CAQDAS can make many if not most of the clerical tasks associated with the manual coding and retrieving of data easier and faster.
- If you have a very small data set, it is probably not worth the time and trouble navigating your way around a new software program.
- If you have a larger data set, or are intending to use the software skills that you acquire on other research projects in the future, CAQDAS can be an invaluable tool.

Questions for review

Is CAQDAS like quantitative data analysis software?

- What are the main points of difference between CAQDAS and quantitative data analysis software like SPSS?
- Why is CAQDAS controversial?
- To what extent does CAQDAS help with qualitative data analysis?

Learning NVivo

- What is a node?
- What is the difference between a free node and a tree node?
- What is in vivo coding?
- Do nodes have to be set up in advance?
- In NVivo, what is the difference between a document and a memo?
- How do you go about searching for a single node and the intersection of two nodes?
- Why might it be useful to display coding stripes?
- How do you search for specific text?

Online Resource Centre

http://www.oxfordtextbooks.co.uk/orc/brymansrm3e/

Visit the Online Resource Centre that accompanies this book to enrich your understanding of computer-assisted qualitative data analysis. Consult web links, test yourself using multiple choice questions, and gain further guidance and inspiration from the Student Researcher's Toolkit.

Part Four

In Part Four we will explore areas that transcend the quantitative/ qualitative distinction. Chapter 24 invites readers to consider how useful the distinction is. This may seem a contrary thing to do, since the book has been organized around the quantitative/qualitative divide. However, the aim is to show that the distinction is not a hard-and-fast one. Chapter 25 considers the different ways in which quantitative and qualitative research can be combined. Such combinations are referred to as *mixed methods research*. Chapter 26 considers the growing possibilities for e-research and focuses on the use of the Internet both as a source of data and as a research method. Chapter 27 examines issues relating to the writing-up of social research and explores some features of good writing in both quantitative and qualitative research.

These chapters draw together certain issues from previous parts but also address others that have been raised already but this time are discussed in much greater depth.

Breaking down the quantitative/qualitative divide

Chapter outline

Chapter guide

This chapter is concerned with the degree to which the quantitative/qualitative divide should be regarded as a hard-and-fast one. It shows that, while there are many differences between the two research strategies, there are also many examples of research that transcend the distinction. One way in which this occurs is through research that combines quantitative and qualitative research, which is the focus of the next chapter. The present chapter is concerned with points of overlap between them. This chapter explores:

- aspects of qualitative research that can contain elements of the natural science model;
- aspects of quantitative research that can contain elements of interpretivism;
- the idea that research methods are more independent of epistemological and ontological assumptions than is sometimes supposed;
- ways in which aspects of the quantitative/qualitative contrast sometimes break down;
- studies in which quantitative and qualitative research are employed in relation to each other, so that qualitative research is used to analyse quantitative research and vice versa;
- the use of quantification in qualitative research.

Introduction

With this book structured so far around the distinction between quantitative and qualitative research, it might appear perverse to raise at this stage the prospect that the distinction might be overblown. The distinction has been employed so far for two main reasons.

1. There *are* differences between quantitative and qualitative research in terms of research strategy, and many researchers and writers on research methodology perceive this to be the case.

2. It is a useful means of organizing research methods and approaches to data analysis.

However, while epistemological and ontological commitments may be associated with certain research methods—such as the often-cited links between a natural science epistemology (in particular, positivism) and social survey research, or between an interpretivist epistemology (for example, phenomenology) and qualitative interviewing—the connections are not deterministic. In other words, while qualitative interviews may often reveal a predisposition towards or a reflection of an interpretivist and constructionist position, this is not always

the case, as an early example suggested (see the discussion of the study by Adler and Adler 1985 in Chapter 1). This means that the connections that were posited in Chapter 1 between epistemology and ontology, on the one hand, and research method, on the other, are best thought of as tendencies rather than as definitive connections. Such connections were implied by the suggestion that within each of the two research strategies—quantitative and qualitative—there is a distinctive mix of epistemology, ontology, and research methods (see Table 1.1). However, we cannot say that the use of a structured interview or self-completion questionnaire *necessarily* implies a commitment to a natural scientific model or that ethnographic research *must* mean an interpretivist epistemology. We should not be surprised at this: after all, quantitative research teaches us that it is rarely the case that we find perfect associations between variables. We should not be surprised, therefore, that the practice of social research similarly lacks absolute determinism.

Research methods are much more free-floating than is sometimes supposed. A method of data collection like participant observation can be employed in such a way that it is in tune with the tenets of constructionism, but equally it can be used in a manner that reveals an objectivist orientation. Also, it is easy to under-emphasize the significance of practical considerations in the way in which social research is conducted (though look again at Figure 1.3). Conducting a study of drug dealers by postal questionnaire may not be totally impossible, but it is unlikely to succeed in terms of yielding valid answers to questions.

In the rest of this chapter I will examine a variety of ways in which the contrast between quantitative and qualitative research should not be overdrawn.

 # The natural science model and qualitative research

One of the chief difficulties with the links that are frequently forged between issues of epistemology and matters of research method or technique is that they often entail a characterization of the natural sciences as necessarily or inherently positivist in orientation. There are three notable difficulties here.

1. There is no agreement on the epistemological basis of the natural sciences. As noted in Chapter 1, writers like Harré (1972) and Keat and Urry (1975) have argued that positivism is but one version of the nature of the natural sciences, *realism* being one alternative account (Bhaskar 1975).

2. If we assume that the practices of natural scientists are those that are revealed in their written accounts of what they do (and most of the discussions of the nature of the natural sciences do assume this), we run into a problem because studies by social researchers of scientists' practices suggest that there is often a disparity between their work behaviour and their writings. It is useful to recall in this connection the research by Gilbert and Mulkay (1984) cited in Chapter 20 (the section on 'Uncovering interpretative repertoires'), which suggested that the ways in which scientists talked about their work frequently revealed a different set of practices from those inscribed in their articles.

3. As Platt (1981) has argued, a term like 'positivist' has to be treated in a circumspect way, because, while it does refer to a distinctive characterization of scientific enquiry (see Key concept 1.2), it is also frequently employed in a polemical way. When employed in this manner, it is rarely helpful, because the term is usually a characterization (a negative one) of the work of others rather than of one's own work.

Quite aside from the difficulty of addressing the natural science model and positivism, there are problems with associating them solely with quantitative research.

Further, qualitative research frequently exhibits features that one would associate with a natural science model. This tendency is revealed in several ways:

- *Empiricist overtones*. Although empiricism (see Key concept 1.1) is typically associated with quantitative research, many writers on qualitative research display an equal emphasis on the importance of direct contact with social reality as the springboard for any investigation. Thus, writers on qualitative research frequently stress the importance of direct experience of social settings and fashioning an understanding of social worlds via that contact. The very idea that theory is to be grounded in data (see Chapter 22) seems to constitute a manifesto for empiricism, and it is unsurprising, therefore, that some writers claim to detect 'covert positivism' in qualitative research. Another way in which empiricist overtones are revealed is in the suggestion that social reality must be studied from the vantage point of research participants but that the only way to gain access to their interpretations is through extended contact with them, implying that meaning is accessible to the senses of researchers. The empiricism of qualitative research is perhaps most notable in conversation analysis, which was examined in Chapter 20. This is an approach that takes precise transcriptions of talk as its starting point and applies rules of analysis to such data. The analyst is actively discouraged from engaging in speculations about intention or context that might derive from an appreciation of the ethnographic particulars of the social setting.

- *A specific problem focus*. As noted in Chapter 16 in connection with the research by Hammersley *et al.* (1985), qualitative research can be employed to investigate quite specific, tightly defined research questions of the kind normally associated with a natural science model of the research process.

- *Hypothesis- and theory-testing*. Following on from the last point, qualitative researchers typically discuss hypothesis- and theory-testing in connection with hypotheses or theories generated in the course of conducting research, as in analytic induction or grounded theory. However, there is no obvious reason why this cannot occur in relation to previously specified hypotheses or theories. In fact, one of the best-known and most frequently cited articles on participant observation was written to show how to design a study using this method, 'which seeks to discover hypotheses as well as to test them' (Becker 1958: 652). The somewhat infamous research by Festinger *et al.* (1956) on a millenarian religious cult is a classic study that used participant observation, a technique associated with qualitative research, to test a theory. The theory had to do with the ways in which people respond when a belief that they zealously endorse is disconfirmed. The authors argued that it is possible to imagine a number of conditions that, if met, could result in the belief being held *more* fervently than previously after the belief had been shown to be flawed. When the authors learned of a local religious cult that believed that the end of the world was imminent, they felt that this group would provide an ideal opportunity for finding out how people respond to the falsification of a cherished belief. The researchers and some hired observers pretended to be converts and became members of the group. This membership afforded the opportunity for first-hand observation of levels of conviction and commitment among the cult's adherents and therefore for testing the theory. Clearly assuming that the prediction would not in fact come true, the researchers gathered data before the fateful day about members' levels of conviction and behaviour and then afterwards on their adaptation to the thwarted prophecy. It should be noted that this research violates certain ethical principles that were addressed in Chapter 5.

- *Realism*. Realism (Key concept 1.3) is one way in which the epistemological basis of the natural sciences has been construed. It has entered into the social sciences in a number of ways, but one of the most significant of these is Bhaskar's (1989) notion of *critical realism*. This approach accepts neither a constructionist nor an objectivist ontology and instead takes the view that the 'social world is reproduced and transformed in daily life' (Bhaskar 1989: 4). Social phenomena are produced by mechanisms that are real, but that are not directly accessible to observation and

are discernible only through their effects. For critical realism the task of social research is to construct hypotheses about such mechanisms and to seek out their effects. Fleetwood (2005) suggests that critical realism offers a more fruitful alternative to postmodernism (see Key concept 27.2), because it overcomes the ambiguity associated with postmodernism that stems from 'ontological exaggeration' of the role of language in determining reality. Critical realists occupy a middle position between positivism and postmodernism by claiming that an entity can exist independently of our knowledge of it, while also asserting that access to the social world is always mediated and thus subjective. Critical realists also believe in the notion of material entities that are said to be real if they have an effect on behaviour. In addition to the empirical domain of observable events, there is a real domain 'in which generative mechanisms capable of producing patterns of events reside' (Tsang and Kwan 1999: 762). Porter's (1993) critical realist ethnography is interesting in this connection (see Research in focus 24.1), because it demonstrates the use of ethnography in connection with an epistemological position that derives from the natural sciences. It also relates to the previous point in providing a further illustration of hypothesis-testing qualitative research.

In addition, writers on qualitative research sometimes distinguish stances on qualitative research that contain elements of both quantitative and qualitative research. Miller (2000), in connection with an examination of life history interviews (see Key concept 18.1), distinguishes three approaches to such research. One of these, which he calls 'neo-positivist', uses 'pre-existing networks of concepts . . . to make theoretically based predictions concerning people's experienced lives' (Miller 2000: 12). Therefore, one approach to the life history method, which is associated with qualitative rather than quantitative research, would seem to entail a theory-testing approach to the collection and analysis of qualitative data. A further illustration is Charmaz's (2000) suggestion that two approaches to grounded theory can be distinguished: objectivist and constructionist (she uses the term 'constuctivist'). She argues that, in spite of the differences that developed between Glaser (1992) and Strauss (e.g. Strauss and Corbin 1998), both held to the view of an objective, external reality. In other words, in the eyes of both the major writers on grounded theory, there is a social world beyond the researcher, whose job it is to reveal its nature and functioning.

Research in focus 24.1
Critical realist ethnography

A critical realist stance was employed by Porter (1993, 2002) in connection with an ethnographic study in a large Irish hospital in which the author was employed for three months as a staff nurse. Porter's interest was in the possible role of racism in this setting. He suggests that racism and professionalism were in operation such that the latter tempered the effects of the former in the context of interactions between doctors and nurses. Thus, racism and professionalism were conceptualized as generative structures—that is, mechanisms—that could be productive of certain kinds of effect. Two hypotheses were proposed: racism would play some part in the relationships between white staff and those from 'racialized minorities' and the 'occupational situation would affect the way in which racism was expressed' (Porter 1993: 599). Porter found that racism was not a significant factor in relationships between members of racialized minorities and the other staff. However, racism did manifest itself behind the backs of the racialized minorities in the form of racist remarks. Racism did not intrude into work relationships, because of the operation of the greater weight given to people's achievements and performance (such as qualifications and medical skills) rather than to their ascriptive qualities (that is, 'race') when judging members of professions. The emphasis on values associated with professionalism counteracted the potential role of those associated with racism. In part, this was due to the way in which Black or Asian doctors made a point of emphasizing their knowledge and qualifications during interaction so that their professional credentials were confirmed. Thus, 'racism can be seen as a tendency that is realised in certain circumstances, but exercised unrealised in others' (Porter 1993: 607). In terms of critical realism, one possible structural mechanism (racism) was countered by the operation of another structural mechanism (professional ideology). On certain occasions, the tension between these two mechanisms would surface—for example, when a Muslim doctor proceeded to conduct his religious observances on his knees in the middle of a hospital unit (Porter 2002).

Quantitative research and interpretivism

Qualitative research would seem to have a monopoly of the ability to study meaning. Its proponents essentially claim that it is only through qualitative research that the world can be studied through the eyes of the people who are studied. As Platt (1981: 87) observes, this contention seems rather at odds with the widespread study of attitudes in social surveys based on interviews and questionnaires. In fact, it would seem that quantitative researchers frequently address meanings. An example is the well-known concept of 'orientation to work' associated with the *Affluent Worker* research in the 1960s, which sought to uncover the nature and significance of the meanings that industrial workers bring with them to the workplace (Goldthorpe *et al*. 1968). Similarly, survey research by Stewart *et al*. (1980: 112) showed that clerks should not be treated as a unitary category and that 'the *meaning* of clerical work will not be the same for all engaged in it' (emphasis added).

The widespread inclusion of questions about attitudes in social surveys suggests that quantitative researchers are interested in matters of meaning. It might be objected that survey questions do not really tap issues of meaning because they are based on categories devised by the designers of the interview schedule or questionnaire.

Two points are relevant here. First, in the absence of **respondent validation** exercises, the notion that qualitative research is more adept at gaining access to the point of view of those being studied than quantitative research is invariably assumed rather than demonstrated. Qualitative researchers frequently claim to have tapped into participants' world views because of, for example, their extensive participation in the daily round of those they study, the length of time they spent in the setting being studied, or the lengthy and intensive interviews conducted. However, the explicit demonstration that interpretative understanding has been accomplished—for example, through respondent validation (see Key concept 16.3)—is rarely undertaken. Second, if the design of attitude questions is based on prior questioning that seeks to bring out the range of possible attitudinal positions on an issue, as in the research discussed in Research in focus 10.3, attitudinal questions may be better able to gain access to meaning.

Also, as Marsh (1982) has pointed out, the practice in much survey research of asking respondents the reasons for their actions implies that quantitative researchers are frequently concerned to uncover issues of meaning. For example, she cites Brown and Harris's (1978) research, which was based on a social survey, on the relationship between critical life events (such as loss of a job, death of husband) and depression. In this research, exploring the meaning of critical life events for respondents was a notable feature of the questioning. As Marsh (1982: 115) puts it, 'it is the *meaning* that these events have for the subjects that gives them their causal force in provoking an onset' (emphasis added). Examples such as these further point to the possibility that the gulf between quantitative and qualitative research is not as wide as is sometimes supposed.

Quantitative research and constructionism

It was noted in Chapter 1 that one keynote of constructionism is a concern with issues of representation, as these play an important role in the construction of the social world. Qualitative content analysis has played an important role in developing just such an understanding, just as discourse analysis has in relation to the social construction of events and meanings in newspaper reports and television programmes. However, it is easy to forget that conventional quantitative content analysis can also be useful in this way.

Lantz and Booth's (1998) research on the social construction of breast cancer (see Research in focus 1.7) provides an example of its use. As Research in focus 1.7 makes clear, much of their understanding of the representation of breast cancer derived from a qualitative content analysis of magazine articles, but they also employed a quantitative content analysis. For example, a content analysis of the photographs of women linked to each article revealed that 80 per cent are apparently of women

who are below the age of 50. Also, 85 per cent of the anecdotes and case stories related to women in this age group. This emphasis on younger women creates the impression that this is the age group that is at risk. This finding allowed Lantz and Booth to make an interesting connection between relative youth and lifestyles and behaviour that are conducive to breast cancer and that therefore is consistent with the 'blame the victim' theme that is conveyed (see Research in focus 1.7). In fact, fewer than 20 per cent of new cases of breast cancer are in women under 50, and the mean age at diagnosis is 65. Thus, the quantitative content analysis of the articles in terms of the ages of the women who are focused upon is inconsistent with the actual age of women when first diagnosed with the disease. In this way, content analysis played an important part in revealing the social construction of breast cancer.

More generally, this example shows how quantitative research can play a significant role in relation to a constructionist stance.

Research methods and epistemological and ontological considerations

If we review the argument so far, it is being suggested that:

- there are differences between quantitative and qualitative research in terms of their epistemological and ontological commitments, *but*

- the connection between research strategy, on the one hand, and epistemological and ontological commitments, on the other, is not deterministic. In other words, there is a *tendency* for quantitative and qualitative research to be associated with the epistemological and ontological positions outlined in Chapter 1 (for example, in Table 1.1), but the connections are not perfect.

However, some writers have suggested that research methods carry with them a cluster of epistemological and ontological commitments such that to elect to use a self-completion questionnaire is more or less simultaneously and inevitably to select a natural science model and an objectivist world view. Similarly, the use of participant observation is often taken to imply a commitment to interpretivism and constructionism. Such a view implies that research methods are imbued with specific clusters of epistemological and ontological commitments and can be seen in comments of the following kind: 'the choice and adequacy of a method embodies a variety of assumptions regarding the nature of knowledge and the methods through which that knowledge can be obtained, as well as a set of root assumptions about the nature of the phenomena to be investigated' (Morgan and Smircich 1980: 491). The difficulty with such a view is that, if we accept that there is no perfect correspondence between research strategy and matters of epistemology and ontology, the notion that a method is inherently or necessarily indicative of certain wider assumptions about knowledge and the nature of social reality begins to founder.

In fact, research methods are much more 'free-floating' in terms of epistemology and ontology than is often supposed. This can be particularly demonstrated by reference to historical and other studies of social research. For example, Snizek (1976) examined 1,434 articles published in sociology journals between 1950 and 1970. He based his analysis on Ritzer's (1975) suggestion that sociology is underpinned by three *paradigms*, a term that will be briefly explored again in Chapter 25 (see Key concept 25.1). Two of the paradigms—the 'social factist' and

the 'social definitionist' paradigms—correspond roughly to quantitative and qualitative research respectively. In his analysis, Snizek was unable to uncover an unambiguous pattern linking the grounding of an article in either of these two paradigms with the research methods used. Similarly, Platt's (1986) historical research on American sociology has suggested that the connection that is often forged between functionalism, which itself is often associated with positivism, and the social survey is greatly exaggerated. Her research suggested that 'the two originated independently, and that leading functionalists had no special propensity to use surveys and leading surveyors no special propensity for functionalism' (Platt 1986: 527). Moreover, Platt's general conclusion from her research on the use of research methods in American sociology between 1920 and 1960 is very revealing:

> research methods may on the level of theory, when theory is consciously involved at all, reflect intellectual *bricolage* or *post hoc* justifications rather than the consistent working through of carefully chosen fundamental assumptions. Frequently methodological choices are steered by quite other considerations, some of a highly practical nature, and there are independent methodological traditions with their own channels of transmission. . . . In many cases general theoretical/methodological stances are just stances: slogans, hopes, aspirations, not guidelines with clear implications that are followed in practice. (Platt 1996: 275)

Platt's conclusion again suggests that the notion that research methods reflect or reveal certain assumptions about knowledge and social reality has to be questioned. When the use of research methods in practice is examined, while tendencies may be discernible that link them to certain assumptions, the connections are not absolute.

A further aspect of the way in which research methods are much more autonomous than is sometimes supposed can be seen in the fact that the methods associated with both quantitative and qualitative research are often employed together within a single piece of research. This issue is the focus of Chapter 25.

Problems with the quantitative/ qualitative contrast

The contrasts between quantitative and qualitative research that were drawn in Chapter 16 suggest a somewhat hard-and-fast set of distinctions and differences (see in particular Table 16.1). However, there is a risk that this kind of representation tends to exaggerate the differences between them. A few of the distinctions will be examined to demonstrate this point.

Behaviour versus meaning

The distinction is sometimes drawn between a focus on behaviour and a focus on meanings. However, quantitative research frequently involves the study of meanings in the form of attitude scales (such as the Likert scaling technique) and other techniques. Qualitative researchers may feel that the tendency for attitude scales to be preformulated and imposed on research participants means that they do not really gain access to meanings. The key point being made here is that at the very least quantitative

researchers frequently *try* to address meanings. Also, somewhat ironically many of the techniques with which quantitative research is associated, most notably social survey research based on questionnaires and interviews, have been shown to relate poorly to people's actual behaviour (see, for example, Thinking deeply 11.2). Moreover, looking at the other side of the divide, qualitative research frequently, if not invariably, entails the examination of behaviour in context. Qualitative researchers often want to interpret people's behaviour in terms of the norms, values, and culture of the group or community in question. In other words, quantitative and qualitative researchers are typically interested in both what people do and what they think, but go about the investigation of these areas in different ways. Therefore, the degree to which the behaviour versus meaning contrast coincides with quantitative and qualitative research should not be overstated. See Thinking deeply 24.1 for further consideration of this point.

Thinking deeply 24.1
Quantitative and qualitative research and the study of class identities

One of the problems with the quantitative/qualitative contrast is that sometimes there is a tendency to polarize or exaggerate their respective capacities. The 'behaviour versus meaning' issue is an illustration of that tendency. Another interesting example can be discerned in relation to the use of surveys to investigate class identities. Savage *et al.* (2001) conducted in-depth interviews with residents in the Manchester area to explore the nature of class identities at the end of the twentieth century. The interviews show that there is an ambivalence about class identities: people's sense of class identity is weak but class is nonetheless relevant to them. The authors depict class as a resource that is drawn upon to forge identity. In the abstract to the article, the authors make an interesting remark: 'sociologists should not assume that there is any necessary significance in how respondents define their class identity in surveys' (Savage *et al.* 2001: 875). Payne and Grew (2005) queried the notion that a qualitative research approach to the study of class identities is necessarily superior to that deriving from surveys. They point out that such a view often arises because of the greater spontaneity and hence apparent naturalness of qualitative interviewing. Payne and Grew (2005: 907) suggest that these features are often exaggerated by sociologists, who also 'over-estimate the degree of rapport and shared meaning with their respondents'. Further, Sturridge (2007: 211) has argued that quantitative research in the form of the survey can have an important role in the study of class identities, namely 'to look at who expresses a sense of class identity and how this sense of class identity relates to other identities. This is the major strength which large-scale surveys have in the field, they are able to provide a social mapping of who expresses a sense of class belonging.' Sturridge conducted a secondary analysis of data from the 2003 British Social Attitudes Survey to explore class identities. In line with her comments about the opportunities that surveys afford, she found that a sense of working-class identity continues to be salient for some social groups and that men are much more likely to express this awareness. She also found that for some groups a sense of belonging to the working class is construed in terms of class opposition and that this reflects workplace orientations and experiences.

These reflections and findings suggest that there is a tendency to overstate the differences between quantitative and qualitative research in terms of certain inherent capacities and that this may result in a neglect of certain issues and research questions. In this instance, the view that survey research has little to offer the study of class identities could result in its potential to address important issues on this topic not being exploited.

Theory and concepts tested in research versus theory and concepts emergent from data

A further related point is that the suggestion that theory and concepts are developed prior to undertaking a study in quantitative research is something of a caricature that is true only up to a point. It reflects a tendency to characterize quantitative research as driven by a theory-testing approach. However, while experimental investigations probably fit this model well, survey-based studies are often more exploratory than this view implies. Although concepts have to be measured, the nature of their interconnections is frequently not specified in advance. Quantitative research is far less driven by a hypothesis-testing strategy than is frequently supposed. As a result, the analysis of quantitative data from social surveys is often more exploratory than is generally appreciated and consequently offers opportunities for the generation of theories and concepts. As one American survey researcher has commented in relation to a large-scale survey he conducted in the 1950s, but which has much relevance today: 'There are so many questions which might be asked, so many correlations which can be run, so many ways in which the findings can be organized, and so few rules or precedents for making these choices that a thousand different studies could come out of the same data' (Davis 1964: 232).

The common depiction of quantitative research as solely an exercise in testing preformulated ideas fails to appreciate the degree to which findings frequently suggest new departures and theoretical contributions. Reflecting on his career in social survey research, Glock provides the following example based on his research on the correlates of variation in church involvement in an American sample:

> It occurred to me and my collaborators that one or both of two things might be happening. The results might simply be a reflection of the fact that women, older persons, the familyless, and the less well-to-do have more time on their hands to become involved in the Church. Alternatively or in addition, it could be that these people become involved as a compensation for being deprived, relative to their counterparts, of access to the rewards of the larger society. The data, having suggested these explanations, did not afford a means to test them . . . Subsequently, I had the opportunity to test the theory with new data . . . (Glock 1988: 45–6)

Therefore, the suggestion that, unlike an interpretivist stance, quantitative research is solely concerned with the testing of ideas that have previously been formulated (such as hypotheses) fails to recognize the creative work that goes into the analysis of quantitative data and into the interpretation of findings. Equally, as noted above (see page 590), qualitative research can be used in relation to the testing of theories.

Numbers versus words

Even perhaps this most basic element in the distinction between quantitative and qualitative research is not without problems. Qualitative researchers sometimes undertake a limited amount of quantification of their data. Silverman (1984, 1985) has argued that some quantification of findings from qualitative research can often help to uncover the generality of the phenomena being described. While observing doctor–patient interactions in National Health Service and private oncology clinics, Silverman quantified some of his data in order to bring out the differences between the two types of clinic. Through this exercise he was able to show that patients in private clinics were able to have a greater influence over what went on in the consultations. However, Silverman warns that such quantification should reflect research participants' own ways of understanding their social world.

In any case, it has often been noted that qualitative researchers engage in 'quasi-quantification' through the use of terms such as 'many', 'often', and 'some' (see below). All that is happening in cases of the kind described by Silverman is that the researcher is injecting greater precision into such estimates of frequency.

Artificial versus natural

The artificial/natural contrast referred to in Table 16.1 can similarly be criticized. It is often assumed that, because much quantitative research employs research instruments that are applied to the people being studied (questionnaires, structured interview schedules, structured observation schedules, and so on), it provides an artificial account of how the social world operates. Qualitative research is often viewed as more naturalistic (see Key concept 2.4 on naturalism). Ethnographic research in particular would seem to exhibit this quality, because the participant observer studies people in their normal social worlds and contexts—in other words, as they go about normal activities. However, when qualitative research is based on interviews (such as semi- and unstructured interviewing and focus groups), the depiction 'natural' is possibly less applicable. Interviews still have to be arranged and interviewees have to be taken away from activities that they would otherwise be engaged in, even when the interviewing style is of the more conversational kind. We know very little about interviewees' reactions to and feelings about being interviewed. Phoenix (1994) reports on the responses of interviewees to in-depth interviews in connection with two studies—one concerned with mothers under the age of 20 and the other with the social identities of young people. While many of her interviewees apparently quite enjoyed being interviewed, it is equally clear that they were conscious of the fact that they had been engaged in interviews rather than conversations. This is revealed by the tendency in the replies quoted by Phoenix for some of the interviewees to disclose that they were aware that the experience was out of the ordinary. In the study of social identities, one black young woman is reported as saying that she liked the interview and added: 'I had the chance to explain how I feel about certain things and I don't really get the opportunity to do that much.' And another interviewee said it was a 'good interview' and added: 'I have never talked so much about myself for a long time, too busy talking about kids and their problems' (Phoenix 1994: 61). The interviews were clearly valuable in allowing to surface the perspectives of people whose voices are normally silent, but the point being made here is that the view that the methods associated with qualitative research are naturalistic is to exaggerate the contrast with the supposed artificiality of the research methods associated with quantitative research.

As noted in Chapter 19, focus group research is often described as more natural than qualitative interviewing because it emulates the way people discuss issues in real life. Natural groupings are often used to emphasize this element. However, whether this is how group participants view the nature of their participation is unclear. In particular, when it is borne in mind that people are sometimes strangers, have to travel to a site where the session takes place, are paid for their trouble, and frequently discuss topics they rarely if ever talk about, it is not hard to take the view that the naturalism of focus groups is assumed rather than demonstrated.

In participant observation, the researcher can be a source of interference that renders the research situation less natural than it might superficially appear to be. Whenever the ethnographer is in an overt role, a certain amount of reactivity is possible—even inevitable. It is difficult to estimate the degree to which the ethnographer represents an intrusive element that has an impact on what is found, but once again the naturalism of such research is often assumed rather than demonstrated, although it is admittedly likely that it will be less artificial than the methods associated with quantitative research. However, when the ethnographer also engages in interviewing (as opposed to casual conversations), the naturalistic quality is likely to be less pronounced.

These observations suggest that there are areas and examples of studies that lead us to question the degree to which the quantitative/qualitative contrast is a rigid one. Once again, this is not to suggest that the contrast is unhelpful, but that we should be wary of assuming that in writing and talking about quantitative and qualitative research we are referring to two absolutely divergent and inconsistent research strategies.

The mutual analysis of quantitative and qualitative research

One further way in which the barriers between quantitative and qualitative research might be undermined is by virtue of developments in which each is used as an approach to analyse the other.

A qualitative research approach to quantitative research

There has been a growing interest in the examination of the writings of quantitative researchers using some of the methods associated with qualitative research. In part, this trend can be seen as an extension of the growth of interest among qualitative researchers in the writing of ethnography, which can be seen in such work as Van Maanen (1988) and Atkinson (1990). The attention to quantitative research is very much part of this trend, because it reveals a concern in both cases with the notion that the written account of research not only constitutes the presentation of findings but is also an attempt to persuade the reader of the credibility of those findings. This is true of the natural sciences too; for example, in relation to the research by Gilbert and Mulkay (1984) discussed in Chapter 20, it was shown how the scientists employed an empiricist repertoire when writing up their findings. This writing strategy was used to show how proper procedures were followed in a systematic and linear way. However, Gilbert and Mulkay demonstrated that, when the scientists discussed in interviews how they did their research, it is clear that the process was suffused with the influence of factors to do with their personal biographies.

One way in which a qualitative research approach to quantitative research is manifested is through what Gephart (1988: 9) has called 'ethnostatistics', by which is meant 'the study of the construction, interpretation, and display of statistics in quantitative social research'. Gephart shows that there are a number of ways in which the idea of ethnostatistics can be realized, but it is with just one of these—approaching statistics as rhetoric—that I will be concerned here. Directing attention to the idea of statistics as rhetoric means becoming sensitive to the ways in which statistical arguments are deployed to bestow credibility on research for target audiences. More specifically, this means examining the language used in persuading audiences about the validity of research. Indeed, the very use of statistics itself can be regarded as a rhetorical device because the use of quantification means that social research can bestow upon itself the appearance of a natural science and thereby achieve greater legitimacy and credibility by virtue of that association (McCartney 1970; John 1992). Some of the rhetorical strategies identified by analysts are presented in Thinking deeply 27.2. However, the chief point being made here is that the nature of quantitative research can be illuminated by being approached from the vantage point of qualitative research.

A quantitative research approach to qualitative research

In Chapter 12, the research by Hodson (1996), which was based on the content analysis of workplace ethnographies, was given quite a lot of attention (see Research in focus 12.3). Essentially, Hodson's approach was to apply a quantitative research approach—in the form of content analysis—to qualitative research. This is a form of research that may have potential in other areas of social research in which ethnography has been a popular method, and as a result a good deal of ethnographic evidence has been built up. Hodson (1999) suggests that the study of social movements may be one such field; religious sects and cults may be yet another. Hodson's research is treated as a solution to the problem of making comparisons between ethnographic studies in a given area. One approach to synthesizing related qualitative studies is *meta-ethnography*, which is a qualitative research approach to such aggregation (Noblit and Hare 1988). However, whereas the practice of meta-ethnography is meant to be broadly in line with the goals of qualitative research, such as a commitment to interpretivism and a sensitivity to the social context, Hodson's approach is one that largely ignores contextual factors in order to explore relationships between variables that have been abstracted out of the ethnographies.

Certain key issues need to be resolved when conducting analyses of the kind carried out by Hodson. One relates to the issue of conducting an exhaustive literature search for suitable studies for possible inclusion. Hodson chose to analyse just books, rather than articles, because of the limited amount of information that can usually be included in the latter. Even then, criteria for the inclusion of a book needed to be stipulated. Hodson (1999: 22) employed three: 'The criteria for inclusion were (a) the book had to be based on ethnographic methods of observation over a period of at least 6 months, (b) the observations had to be in a single organization, and (c) the book had to focus on at least one clearly identified group of workers . . .'. The application of these criteria resulted in the exclusion of 279 out of 365 books uncovered. A second crucial area relates to the coding of the studies, which was briefly covered in Research in focus 12.3. Hodson stresses the importance of having considerable knowledge of the subject area, adopting clear coding rules, and pilot testing the coding schedule. In addition, he recommends checking the *reliability* of coding by having 10 per cent of the documents coded by two people. The process of coding was time-consuming, in that Hodson calculates that each book-length ethnography took forty or more hours to code.

This approach has many attractions, not the least of which is the impossibility of a quantitative researcher being able to conduct investigations in such a varied set of organizations. Also, it means that more data of much greater depth can be used than can typically be gathered by quantitative researchers. It also allows hypotheses deriving from established theories to be tested, such as the 'technological implications' approach, which sees technologies as having impacts on the experience of work (Hodson 1996). However, the loss of a sense of social context is likely to be unattractive to many qualitative researchers.

Of particular significance for this discussion is the remark that 'the fundamental contribution of the systematic analysis of documentary accounts is that it creates an analytic link between the in-depth accounts of professional observers and the statistical methods of quantitative researchers' (Hodson 1999: 68). In other words, the application of quantitative methods to qualitative research may provide a meeting ground for the two research strategies.

Quantification in qualitative research

As noted in Chapter 16, the numbers versus words contrast is perhaps the most basic in many people's minds when they think about the differences between quantitative and qualitative research. After all, it seems to relate in a most fundamental way to the very terms used to denote the two approaches, which seem to imply the presence and absence of numbers. However, it is simply not the case that there is a complete absence of quantification in qualitative research. As we will see in the next chapter, when qualitative researchers incorporate research methods associated with quantitative research into their investigations, a certain amount of quantification is injected into the research.

Quite aside from the issue of combining quantitative and qualitative research, three observations are worth making about quantification in the analysis and writing-up of qualitative data.

Thematic analysis

In Chapter 22 it was observed that one of the commonest approaches to qualitative data analysis is undertaking a search for themes in transcripts or field notes. However,

as Bryman and Burgess (1994b: 224) point out, the criteria employed in the identification of themes are often unclear. One possible factor that these authors suggest may be in operation is the frequency of the occurrence of certain incidents, words, phrases, and so on that denote a theme. In other words, a theme is more likely to be identified the more times the phenomenon it denotes occurs in the course of coding. This process may also account for the prominence given to some themes over others when writing up the fruits of qualitative data analysis. In other words, a kind of implicit quantification may be in operation that influences the identification of themes and the elevation of some themes over others. In fact, Ryan and Bernard (2003), as noted in Chapter 22, recommend the search for 'repetitions' as one of the ways in which themes may be identified.

Quasi-quantification in qualitative research

It has often been noted that qualitative researchers engage in 'quasi-quantification' through the use of terms such as 'many', 'frequently', 'rarely', 'often', and 'some'. In order to be able to make such allusions to quantity, the qualitative researcher should have some idea of the relative frequency of the phenomena being referred to. However, as expressions of quantities, they are imprecise, and it is often difficult to discern why they are being used at all. The alternative would seem to be to engage in a limited amount of quantification when it is appropriate, such as when an expression of quantity can bolster an argument. This point leads directly on to the next section.

Combating anecdotalism through limited quantification

One of the criticisms that is levelled against qualitative research is that the publications on which it is based are often anecdotal, giving the reader little guidance as to the prevalence of the issue to which the anecdote refers. The widespread use of brief sequences of conversation, snippets from interview transcripts, and accounts of encounters between people provides little sense of the prevalence of whatever such items of evidence are supposed to indicate. There is the related risk that a particularly striking statement by someone or an unexpected activity may have more significance attached to it than might be warranted in terms of its frequency.

Perhaps at least partly in response to these problems, qualitative researchers sometimes undertake a limited amount of quantification of their data. We can see this feature in Silverman's (1984, 1985) research on oncology clinics, which was referred to above. In their research on concepts of leadership employed by British police officers, Bryman, Stephens, and A Campo (1996) counted the frequency with which certain leadership styles were cited in interview transcripts. This exercise allowed them to demonstrate that the kind of leadership preferred by police officers was different from what was in vogue among theorists of leadership at the time. Gabriel (1998) describes how he studied organizational culture in a variety of organizations by collecting during interviews stories about the organizations in question. Computers and information technology were a particular focus of the stories elicited. Altogether 377 stories were collected in the course of 126 interviews in five organiza-

tions. Gabriel shows that the stories were of different types, such as: comic stories (which were usually a mechanism for disparagement of others); epic stories (survival against the odds); tragic stories (undeserved misfortune); gripes (personal injustices); and so on. He counted the number of each type: comic stories were the most numerous at 108; then epic stories (82); tragic stories (53); gripe stories (40); and so on. Themes in the stories were also counted, such as whether they involved a leader, a personal trauma, an accident, and so forth. In all these cases, the types of stories and the themes could have been treated in an anecdotal way, but the use of such simple counting conveys a clear sense of their relative prevalence.

Exercises like these can be used to counter the suggestion that is sometimes made that the approach to presenting qualitative data can be too anecdotal, so that readers are given too little sense of the *extent* to which certain beliefs are held or a certain form of behaviour occurs. All that is happening in such cases is that the researcher is injecting greater precision into estimates of frequency than can be derived from quasi-quantification terms. Moreover, it is not inconceivable that there might be greater use of limited amounts of quantification in qualitative research in the future as a result of the growing incursion of computers into qualitative data analysis (CAQDAS). Most of the major software programs include a facility that allows the analyst to produce simple counts of such things as the frequency with which a word or a coded theme occurs. In many cases, they can also produce simple cross-tabulations—for example, relating the occurrence of a coded theme to gender. Writing when CAQDAS was used far less than it is today, Ragin and Becker (1989: 54) concluded their review of the impact of microcomputers on sociologists' 'analytic habits' with the following remark: 'Thus, the microcomputer provides important technical means for new kinds of dialogues between ideas and evidence and, at the same time, provides a common technical ground for the meeting of qualitative and quantitative researchers.' The greater use of quantification by qualitative researchers may turn out to be one of the more significant areas for this 'meeting'.

Key points

- There are differences between quantitative and qualitative research but it is important not to exaggerate them.
- The connections between epistemology and ontology, on the one hand, and research methods, on the other, are not deterministic.
- Qualitative research sometimes exhibits features normally associated with a natural science model.
- Quantitative research aims on occasions to engage with an interpretivist stance.
- Research methods are more autonomous in relation to epistemological commitments than is often appreciated.
- The artificial/natural contrast that is often an element in drawing a distinction between quantitative and qualitative research is frequently exaggerated.
- A quantitative research approach can be employed for the analysis of qualitative studies and a qualitative research approach can be employed to examine the rhetoric of quantitative researchers.
- Some qualitative researchers employ quantification in their work.

Questions for review

- What is the nature of the link between research methods and epistemology?

The natural science model and qualitative research

- Are the natural sciences positivistic?
- To what extent can some qualitative research be deemed to exhibit the characteristics of a natural science model?

Quantitative research and interpretivism

- To what extent can some quantitative research be deemed to exhibit the characteristics of interpretivism?

Quantitative research and constructionism

- To what extent can some quantitative research be deemed to exhibit the characteristics of constructionism?

Research methods and epistemological and ontological considerations

- How far do research methods necessarily carry epistemological and ontological implications?

Problems with the quantitative/qualitative contrast

- Outline some of the ways in which the quantitative/qualitative contrast may not be as hard and fast as is often supposed.

The mutual analysis of quantitative and qualitative research

- What might some of the implications of Gilbert and Mulkay's concepts of interpretative repertoires be for the qualitative analysis of quantitative research?
- Assess the significance of ethnostatistics.
- Assess the significance of Hodson's research.

Quantification in qualitative research

- How far is quantification a feature of qualitative research?

Online Resource Centre

http://www.oxfordtextbooks.co.uk/orc/brymansrm3e/

Visit the Online Resource Centre that accompanies this book to enrich your understanding of breaking down the quantitative/qualitative divide. Consult web links, test yourself using multiple choice questions, and gain further guidance and inspiration from the Student Researcher's Toolkit.

Mixed methods research: combining quantitative and qualitative research

---

Chapter outline

Chapter guide

This chapter is concerned with **mixed methods research**—that is, research that combines **quantitative** and **qualitative research**. While this may seem a straightforward way of resolving and breaking down the divide between the two research strategies, it is not without controversy. Moreover, there may be practical difficulties associated with mixed methods research. This chapter explores:

- arguments against the combination of quantitative and qualitative research; two kinds of argument are distinguished and are referred to as the embedded methods and paradigm arguments;

- the suggestion that there are two versions of the debate about the possibility of combining quantitative and qualitative research: one that concentrates on methods of research and another that is concerned with **epistemological** issues;

- the different ways in which mixed methods research has been carried out;

- the need to recognize that mixed methods research is not inherently superior to research that employs a single **research strategy**.

Introduction

So far throughout the book an emphasis has been placed upon the strengths and weaknesses of the research methods associated with quantitative and qualitative research. One possible response to this kind of recognition is to propose combining them. After all, such a strategy would seem to allow the various strengths to be capitalized upon and the weaknesses offset somewhat. However, not all writers on research methods agree that such integration is either desirable or feasible. On the other hand, it is probably the case that the amount of combined research has been increasing since the early 1980s. Therefore, in discussing the combination of quantitative and qualitative research, this chapter will be concerned with three main issues:

1. an examination of the arguments against integrating quantitative and qualitative research;

2. the different ways in which quantitative and qualitative research have been combined;

3. an assessment of combined research, which asks whether it is necessarily superior to investigations relying on just one research strategy and whether there are any additional problems deriving from it.

The term 'mixed methods research' is used as a simple shorthand to stand for research that integrates quantitative and qualitative research within a single project. Of course, there is research that, for example, combines **structured interviewing** with **structured observation** or **ethnography** with **semi-structured interviewing**. However, these instances of the combination of research methods are associated with just one research strategy. By mixed methods research I am referring to research that combines research methods that cross the two research strategies. In the earlier editions of this book, I used the term 'mixed strategy research' to describe investigations combining quantitative and qualitative research. However, 'mixed methods research' has increasingly become the preferred term and in many ways better expresses the fact that in many cases, using both quantitative and qualitative research should involve a mixing of the research methods involved and not just using them in tandem. In other words, the quantitative and the qualitative data deriving from mixed methods research should be mutually illuminating. Indeed, mixed methods research has become something of a growth industry since the first edition of this book. Since *Social Research Methods* was first published, there have been numerous discussions of the approach, a handbook on it has been published (Tashakkori and Teddlie 2003) and a *Journal of Mixed Methods Research* has begun life. Just after I finished writing the second edition of this book, I conducted research specifically to do with the nature of mixed methods research (Bryman 2006a, 2006b). I have organized the section on 'Approaches to mixed methods research' below around some of my findings from that research project.

The argument against mixed methods research

The argument against mixed methods research tends to be based on either and sometimes both of two kinds of argument:

1. the idea that research methods carry epistemological commitments, and

2. the idea that quantitative and qualitative research are separate *paradigms*.

These two arguments will now be briefly reviewed.

The embedded methods argument

This first position, which was outlined in Chapter 24, implies that research methods are ineluctably rooted in epistemological and ontological commitments. Such a view of research methods can be discerned in statements like the following:

> every research tool or procedure is inextricably embedded in commitments to particular versions of the world and to knowing that world. To use a questionnaire, to use an attitude scale, to take the role of participant observer, to select a random sample, to measure rates of population growth, and so on, is to be involved in conceptions of the world which allow these instruments to be used for the purposes conceived. (Hughes 1990: 11)

According to such a position, the decision to employ, for example, participant observation is not simply about how to go about data collection but a commitment to an epistemological position that is inimical to positivism and that is consistent with interpretivism.

This kind of view of research methods has led some writers to argue that mixed methods research is not feasible or even desirable. An ethnographer may collect questionnaire data to gain information about a slice of social life that is not amenable to participant observation, but this does not represent an integration of quantitative and qualitative research, because the epistemological positions in which the two methods are grounded constitute irreconcilable views about how social reality should be studied. Smith (1983: 12, 13), for example, argues that each of the two research strategies 'sponsors different procedures and has different epistemological implications' and therefore counsels researchers not to 'accept the unfounded assumption that the methods are complementary'. Smith and Heshusius (1986: 8) criticize the integration of research strategies, because it ignores the assumptions underlying research methods and transforms 'qualitative inquiry into a procedural variation of quantitative inquiry'.

The chief difficulty with the argument that writers like Smith present is that, as was noted in Chapter 24, the idea that research methods carry with them fixed epistemological and ontological implications is very difficult to sustain. They are capable of being put to a wide variety of tasks.

The paradigm argument

The paradigm argument is closely related to the previous one. It conceives of quantitative and qualitative research as *paradigms* (see Key concept 25.1) in which epistemological assumptions, values, and methods are inextricably intertwined and are incompatible between paradigms (e.g. Guba 1985; Morgan 1998b). Therefore, when researchers combine participant observation with a questionnaire, they are not really combining quantitative and qualitative research, since paradigms are incommensurable—that is, they are incompatible: the integration is only at a superficial level and within a single paradigm.

The problem with the paradigm argument is that it rests, as with the embedded methods one, on contentions about the interconnectedness of method and epistemology in particular that cannot—in the case of social research—be demonstrated. Moreover, while Kuhn (1970) certainly argued that paradigms are incommensurable, it is by no means clear that quantitative and qualitative research are in fact paradigms. As suggested in Chapter 24, there are areas of overlap and commonality between them.

Key concept 25.1
What is a paradigm?

Kuhn's (1970) highly influential use of the term 'paradigm' derives from his analysis of revolutions in science. A paradigm is 'a cluster of beliefs and dictates which for scientists in a particular discipline influence what should be studied, how research should be done, [and] how results should be interpreted' (Bryman 1988a: 4). Kuhn depicted the natural sciences as going through periods of revolution, whereby normal science (science carried out in terms of the prevailing paradigm) is increasingly challenged by anomalies that are inconsistent with the assumptions and established findings in the discipline at that time. The growth in anomalies eventually gives way to a crisis in the discipline, which in turn occasions a revolution. The period of revolution is resolved when a new paradigm emerges as the ascendant one and a new period of normal science sets in. An important feature of paradigms is that they are *incommensurable*—that is, they are inconsistent with each other because of their divergent assumptions and methods. Disciplines in which no paradigm has emerged as pre-eminent, such as the social sciences, are deemed pre-paradigmatic, in that they feature competing paradigms. One of the problems with the term is that it is not very specific: Masterman (1970) was able to discern twenty-one different uses of it by Kuhn. Nonetheless, its use is widespread in the social sciences (e.g. Ritzer 1975; Guba 1985).

Thinking deeply 25.1
Stages in the development of mixed methods research

Creswell and Plano Clark (2007) have suggested that mixed methods research has proceeded through four stages.

1. A *formative period* during which various writers took tentative steps towards and lay the foundations for mixed methods approaches. This period corresponds roughly to a period spanning the 1950s through to the early 1980s.

2. A *paradigm debate period* during the 1970s and 1980s that responded to qualitative researchers' insistence that their style of investigation was based on different epistemological and ontological foundations from quantitative research. Because of this insistence, quantitative and qualitative research were viewed as not capable of integration. During this period, a number of writers challenged this view, arguing that mixed methods investigations were feasible and potentially could lead to superior findings. I am placed in this period, because in Bryman (1988a) I 'challenged the argument and began suggesting that a clear connection existed between the two traditions' (Creswell and Plano Clark 2007: 15).

3. A *procedural development period* beginning in the late 1980s and progressing into the twenty-first century that is concerned with how mixed methods studies could be designed. Morgan (1998*b*), whose work is referred to in Thinking deeply 25.3, belongs to this period.

4. An *advocacy* period that began in the present century and is concerned with the recognition of and development of mixed methods research as a distinctive approach, even as a movement. The arrival of a separate handbook for mixed methods researchers (Tashakkori and Teddlie 2003) and of the *Journal of Mixed Methods Research* are indicative of this development.

 # Two versions of the debate about quantitative and qualitative research

There would seem to be two different versions about the nature of quantitative and qualitative research, and these two different versions have implications in writers' minds about whether the two can be combined.

- An *epistemological version*, as in the embedded methods argument and the paradigm argument, sees quantitative and qualitative research as grounded in incompatible epistemological principles (and ontological ones too, but these tend not to be given as much attention). According to this version of their nature, mixed methods research is not possible.

- A *technical version*, which is the position taken by most researchers whose work is mentioned in the next section, gives greater prominence to the strengths of the data-collection and data-analysis techniques with which quantitative and qualitative research are each associated and sees these as capable of being fused. There is a recognition that quantitative and qualitative research are each connected with distinctive epistemological and ontological assumptions, but the connections are not viewed as fixed and ineluctable. Research methods are perceived, unlike in the epistemological version, as autonomous. A research method from one research strategy is viewed as capable of being pressed into the service of another. Indeed, in some instances, as will be seen in the next section, the notion that there is a 'leading' research strategy in a mixed methods investigation may not even apply in some cases.

The technical version about the nature of quantitative and qualitative research essentially views the two research strategies as compatible. As a result, mixed methods research becomes both feasible and desirable. It is in that spirit that we now turn to a discussion of the ways in which quantitative and qualitative research can be combined.

 # Approaches to mixed methods research

This section will be structured in terms of a classification I derived from conducting a **content analysis** of empirical articles in refereed journals in the social sciences (Bryman 2006*a*, 2006*b*). The classification has been changed slightly from the one presented in my earlier publications. Several other ways of classifying such investigations have been proposed by other authors, and two of these are presented in Thinking deeply 25.2 and 25.3.

Thinking deeply 25.2
Hammersley's classification of approaches to mixed methods research

Hammersley (1996) has proposed three approaches to mixed methods research.

1. *Triangulation*. This refers to the use of quantitative research to corroborate qualitative research findings or vice versa.

2. *Facilitation*. This approach arises when one research strategy is employed in order to aid research using the other research strategy.

3. *Complementarity*. This approach occurs when the two research strategies are employed in order that different aspects of an investigation can be dovetailed.

Thinking deeply 25.3
Morgan's classification of approaches to mixed methods research

Morgan (1998*b*) has proposed four approaches to mixed methods research. His classification is based on two criteria.

1. *The priority decision*. How far is a qualitative or a quantitative method the principal data-gathering tool?

2. *The sequence decision*. Which method precedes which? In other words, does the qualitative method precede the quantitative one or vice versa?

These criteria yield four possible types.

		Priority	
		Quantitative	*Qualitative*
Sequence	*Preliminary*	M1	M2
	Follow-up	M3	M4

This is an interesting approach to take, but the chief difficulty with this scheme is that it relies upon being able to identify both (*a*) that either quantitative or qualitative research had priority in research and (*b*) that one was preliminary to the other. This is not necessarily possible in all cases. Research in focus 25.2 provides an example of a research project that combined quantitative and qualitative research strategies through the use of several methods. However, no single method or research strategy was dominant.

Research in focus 25.1
Mixed methods research on mixed methods research

In 2003–4 I worked on a fellowship funded by the Economic and Social Research Council that focused on mixed methods research. There were two main components: a content analysis on articles reporting the findings of mixed methods research and interviews with mixed methods researchers. With the first component I was interested in the ways that quantitative and qualitative research are combined in published journal articles (Bryman 2006a). With the second component, I conducted semi-structured interviews with twenty mixed methods researchers because I was keen to glean an inside view of the research process. The findings from the two components of this project will be used for discussing mixed methods research in the rest of this chapter.

A content analysis of articles based on mixed methods research

One component of the research on mixed methods research described in Research in focus 25.1 was a content analysis of journal articles reporting the findings of mixed methods research. Journal articles do not encapsulate all possible contexts in which projects reporting mixed methods research might be found. Conference papers and books are other possible sites. However, journal articles are a major form of reporting findings and have the advantage that, in most cases, the peer review process provides a quality control mechanism. By contrast, conference papers and books are sometimes not peer reviewed. The approach to gleaning a **sample** was to search the Social Sciences Citation Index (SSCI) for articles in which relevant keywords or phrases such as 'quantitative' and 'qualitative', or 'multi(-)method', or 'mixed method', or 'triangulation' appeared in the title, keywords, or abstract. This means that the sample comprises articles that to some degree foreground the fact that the study is based on both quantitative and qualitative

research. During the search, the emphasis was on uncovering articles in five fields: sociology; social psychology; human, social and cultural geography; management and organizational behaviour; and media and cultural studies. The analysis was restricted to a ten-year period of 1994–2003. Judgements about whether articles fell within the purview of the investigation, in terms of whether they could be regarded as deriving from the five fields, were made on the basis of the journal title or information supplied in abstracts. In this way, a total of 232 articles was generated and content analysed.

A major focus of the content analysis was on the rationales proffered for combining quantitative and qualitative research. A coding scheme was developed for classifying the rationales given by authors of articles. This coding scheme was based on an extensive review of the kinds of reasons that are frequently given in both methodological writings and research articles for combining quantitative and qualitative research. The scheme provided for the rationales outlined in Thinking deeply 25.4. These can be thought of as ways of combining quantitative and qualitative research.

Thinking deeply 25.4
Ways of combining quantitative and qualitative research

1. *Triangulation* or greater **validity**—refers to the traditional view that quantitative and qualitative research might be combined to triangulate findings in order that they may be mutually corroborated. If the term was used as a synonym for integrating quantitative and qualitative research, it was not **coded** as triangulation.

2. *Offset*—refers to the suggestion that the research methods associated with both quantitative and qualitative research have their own strengths and weaknesses so that combining them allows the researcher to offset their weaknesses to draw on the strengths of both.

3. *Completeness*—refers to the notion that the researcher can bring together a more comprehensive account of the area of enquiry in which he or she is interested if both quantitative and qualitative research are employed.

4. *Process*—quantitative research provides an account of structures in social life but qualitative research provides sense of process.

5. **Different research questions**—this is the argument that quantitative and qualitative research can each answer different research questions, but this item was coded only if authors explicitly stated that they were doing this.

6. *Explanation*—one of the two research methods is used to help explain findings generated by the other.

7. *Unexpected results*—refers to the suggestion that quantitative and qualitative research can be fruitfully combined when one generates surprising results that can be understood by employing the other.

8. *Instrument development*—refers to contexts in which qualitative research is employed to develop questionnaire and scale items, for example, so that better wording or more comprehensive closed answers can be generated.

9. *Sampling*—refers to situations in which one approach is used to facilitate the sampling of respondents or cases.

10. *Credibility*—refers to suggestions that employing both approaches enhances the integrity of findings.

11. *Context*—refers to cases in which the combination is rationalized in terms of qualitative research providing contextual understanding coupled with either generalizable, externally valid findings or broad **relationships** among **variables** uncovered through a survey.

12. *Illustration*—refers to the use of qualitative data to illustrate quantitative findings, often referred to as putting 'meat on the bones' of 'dry' quantitative findings.

13. *Utility* or improving the usefulness of findings—refers to a suggestion, which is more likely to be prominent among articles with an applied focus, that combining the two approaches will be more useful to practitioners and others.

14. *Confirm and discover*—this entails using qualitative data to generate hypotheses and using quantitative research to test them within a single project.

15. *Diversity of views*—this includes two slightly different rationales—namely, combining researchers' and participants' perspectives through quantitative and qualitative research respectively and uncovering relationships between variables through quantitative research while also revealing meanings among research participants through qualitative research.

16. *Enhancement* or building upon quantitative/qualitative findings—this entails a reference to making more of or augmenting either quantitative or qualitative findings by gathering data using a qualitative or quantitative research approach.

17. *Other/unclear.*

18. *Not stated.*

Source: Bryman (2006*a*).

When coding each article, a distinction was made between *rationale* and *practice*. First, the rationale given by authors for combining the two approaches to data collection and/or analysis was coded. For this exercise, the reasons that had been given before the findings were presented were typically examined and coded. Then, the ways in which quantitative and qualitative research were actually combined were coded. In doing so, the coding reflected authors' reflections on what they felt had been gleaned from combining quantitative and qualitative

Table 25.1

Mixed methods research in practice		
Category	Rationale	Practice
	Number of articles (% of all 232 cases)	
Triangulation	29 (12.5)	80 (34.5)
Offset	7 (3)	4 (1.7)
Completeness	31 (13)	67 (28.9)
Process	5 (2.2)	6 (2.6)
Different research questions	13 (5.6)	10 (4.3)
Explanation	13 (5.6)	32 (13.8)
Unexpected results	0	2 (0.9)
Instrument development	18 (7.8)	21 (9.1)
Sampling	31 (13.4)	43 (18.5)
Credibility	2 (0.9)	5 (2.2)
Context	8 (3.4)	10 (4.3)
Illustration	4 (1.7)	53 (22.8)
Utility	2 (0.9)	2 (0.9)
Confirm and discover	9 (3.9)	15 (6.5)
Diversity of views	26 (11.2)	35 (15.1)
Enhancement	73 (31.5)	121 (52.2)
Other/unclear	8 (3.4)	14 (6.1)
Not stated	62 (26.7)	1 (0.4)

Source: Based on Bryman (2006*a*).

research and any ways in which the two were combined that were not reflected in authors' accounts. This is what is meant by *practice*. The purpose of discriminating between these two ways of thinking about the justification for mixed methods research was that authors' accounts of why they intended to combine quantitative and qualitative research might differ from how they actually combined them in practice.

Table 25.1 provides the number of articles classified in terms of each category of rationale and practice and their respective percentages of all 232 articles. The percentages add up to over 100% in the case of both rationale and practice because any article could be coded in terms of two or more categories. Interestingly, the number and percentage of articles within each category are usually higher for practice than for rationale. This occurs for two reasons. One is that the number of articles where the rationale is not stated falls from just over one-quarter to nearly zero. Second, researchers seem to find more uses for mixed methods research than they envisaged at the outset.

The bulk of the rest of this chapter will present some examples of each of these rationales for conducting mixed methods research. Some of the examples are ones that were in the sample on which the content analysis was based and some are not. In the latter category, I have included books, which were not included in the sample. One of the books I have included is a classic of British sociology. This is included in large part to register the point that, although mixed methods research has attracted a great deal of attention in recent years it is by no means new or novel. Each of the rationales may be thought of as an approach to conducting mixed methods research.

Approaches to combining quantitative and qualitative research in mixed methods research

This section of the chapter provides illustrations of each of the ways of combining quantitative and qualitative research in mixed methods research. Each of the rationales outlined in the previous section can be thought of as an approach to mixed methods research. This applies rather less obviously to two of the rationales—credibility and utility—but these have been included for the sake of completeness.

Triangulation

The idea of triangulation has been previously encountered in Key concept 16.4. When applied to the present context, it implies that the results of an investigation employing a method associated with one research strategy are cross-checked against the results of using a method associated with the other research strategy. It is an adaptation of the argument by writers like Webb *et al.* (1966) that confidence in the findings deriving from a study using a quantitative research strategy can be enhanced by using more than one way of measuring a concept.

An illustration of a study using a triangulation approach is an investigation by Hughes *et al.* (1997) of the consumption of 'designer drinks' by young people. The term 'designer drinks' is usually applied to a new range of fortified wines and strong white ciders that became popular in the UK in the 1990s. The authors used two main research methods:

1. *a qualitative research method*: eight focus groups with fifty-six children and young adults, with each discussion lasting around two hours;

2. *a quantitative research method*: a questionnaire administered in two parts to a multi-stage cluster sample of 824 12–17 year olds. The first part was conducted by interview and the second, which sought to elicit more sensitive information, was self-administered.

The overall tenor of the results of the combined use of the two research strategies was mutually reinforcing. The qualitative findings showed differences in attitudes towards designer drinks and other forms of alcoholic drink among young people of different ages: the youngest (12–13) tended to adopt a generally experimental approach; the 14- and 15-year-olds thought of drinking as a means of having fun and losing inhibitions and felt that designer drinks met their needs well; the oldest group (16- and 17-year-olds) were mainly concerned to appear mature and to establish relationships with the opposite sex, and tended to think of designer drinks as immature, as they were mainly seen by this age group as being targeted at younger drinkers. These connections with age were confirmed by the quantitative evidence, which also corroborated the suggestion from the qualitative evidence that the designer drinks were largely associated with a desire to get drunk.

In this research, two features are worth noting: the use of a triangulation strategy seems to have been planned by the researchers, and the two sets of results were broadly consistent. However, researchers may carry out mixed methods research for other purposes, but in the course of doing so discover that they have generated quantitative and qualitative findings on related issues, so that they can treat such overlapping findings as a triangulation exercise. Whether planned or unplanned, when a triangulation exercise is undertaken, the possibility of a failure to corroborate findings always exists. This raises the issue of what approach should be taken to inconsistent results. One approach is to treat one set of results as definitive, as Newby did in connection with his research on Suffolk farm workers. Newby (1977: 127) wrote that, when his survey and participant observation findings were inconsistent, he 'instinctively trusted the latter'. The greater richness and depth of participant observation findings, coupled with the ethnographer's greater proximity to the people studied, frequently inspire greater confidence in such data. However, simply and often arbitrarily favouring one set of findings over another is not an ideal approach to reconciling conflicting findings deriving from a triangulation exercise.

Deacon *et al.* (1998) provide an example of unplanned triangulation in that they gathered data through several quantitative and qualitative research methods (see Research in focus 25.2) but had not intended these to be deployed as part of a triangulation exercise. However, their analysis of their data revealed an inconsistency between some of the quantitative and qualitative data: the former (methods 2 and 3) suggested that journalists and social scientists enjoyed broadly consensual relationships with regard to the reporting of social science research in the media, but the qualitative findings (methods 4 and 5) suggested greater collision of approaches and values. Rather than opt for one set of findings as providing the more accurate view, the data were re-examined. For example, Deacon *et al.* show that a major component of the apparent discrepancy has to do with the tendency for social scientists who are answering survey questions about coverage of their own research (method 3) to reply in terms of a feeling of relief that it was not as bad as expected. However, in interviews (method 4), social scientists tend to make much more of what Deacon *et al.* call 'war stories'—that is, memorable and often highly wounding encounters with the media. Such encounters

Research in focus 25.2
Research methods used in a study of the reporting of social science research in the mass media

In their research on the reporting of social science research in the British mass media, Fenton *et al.* (1998; see also Deacon *et al.* 1998) employed several quantitative and qualitative methods:

1. content analysis of news and current affairs coverage (local and national newspapers, TV, and radio) (592 items); see Research in focus 12.1 for more on this aspect of the research;

2. **mail questionnaire** survey of social scientists' views about media coverage and their own practices (674 respondents);

3. mail questionnaire survey of social scientists who had received media coverage as identified in the content analysis (123 respondents);

4. semi-structured interviews with social scientists who had received coverage as identified in the content analysis (20 interviews);

5. semi-structured interviews with journalists identified in the content analysis (34 interviews);

6. semi-structured interviews with representatives of funding bodies and government (27 interviews);

7. tracking of journalists at conferences (3 conferences);

8. focus group analysis of audience reception of media items (13 focus groups); see Chapter 19 for more on this aspect of the research.

were not being depicted in the interviews as typical, but their general feelings about media coverage of social science research appeared to have been highly influenced by their bruising encounters. Thus, in general, the questionnaires revealed that social scientists were relatively pleased with the reporting of their research, but, when they were encouraged to reflect on specific problems in the past, the drift of their replies became more negative.

Offset

Offset was rarely encountered. It implies that the weaknesses of a quantitative or a qualitative method can be offset by including a qualitative or a quantitative method that has its own strengths. In the preamble to her account of mixed methods research on the benefits of adult learning, Hammond (2005: 240) has suggested that 'each approach has its own limitations or "imperfections", which can be compensated for by using an alternative method'. Similarly, the authors of the study referred to in Research in focus 25.6 write that the combination of methods helped 'to reduce the biases associated with each method and therefore improve our understanding of the cultural forces involved in child development' (Harkness *et al.*

2006: 78). One of the mixed methods research practitioners that I interviewed was explicit on this point:

> it seems to me that the only way you can begin to get close to the kind of methods that are reliable in natural scientific or engineering work is to use every tool you've got. You know, our tools are so inadequate and the material to which we're applying them is so slippery that you've got to use everything you have.

Completeness

Completeness indicates that a more complete answer to a research question or set of research questions can be achieved by including both quantitative and qualitative methods. It implies that the gaps left by one method (e.g. a quantitative one) can be filled by another (e.g. a qualitative one). One of its most common forms is when ethnographers employ structured interviewing or possibly a self-completion questionnaire, because not everything they need to know about is accessible through participant observation. This kind of need can arise for several reasons, such as the need for information that is not accessible to observation or to qualitative interviewing (for example, systematic information about social backgrounds of people in a particular setting), or the difficulty of gaining access to certain groups of people. For her research on the processes whereby people became Moonies (members of the Unification Church) in Britain, Barker (1984) relied mainly on participant observation and in-depth interviewing. However, she also conducted a number of questionnaire surveys of members. Sometimes, this was done to test hypotheses she had begun to formulate (see above on this use of mixed methods research), but often it was undertaken in order to acquire information on social class backgrounds and religious experiences prior to becoming a Moonie. Such information was not accessible through participant observation.

Lockyer (2006) employed a mixed methods approach for her study of humour. She was interested in the controversies that can arise in relation to humour. There were various components to her mixed methods examination of humour, including: a quantitative content analysis of readers' letters of complaint in *Private Eye* about offence caused to them concerning humour in the magazine; an examination of the discursive practices used in the magazine for managing complaints; a detailed linguistic analysis of some of the letters; libel cases brought against the magazine; and semi-structured interviews

with *Private Eye* journalists. Lockyer argues that the chief benefit of using a mixed methods approach is that an extremely comprehensive portrait of humour in this magazine (and the controversies surrounding that humour) is forthcoming. Thus, the content analysis provided a necessary overview of the issue, such as the topics that are particularly likely to produce complaints, while the examination of discursive strategies for managing complaints identified some of the rhetorical strategies used to do this (such as suggesting that the reader lacks a sense of humour). The intensive linguistic examination of some letters, which were selected from those that had been content analysed, showed the ways in which the criticism of humour is initiated. Lockyer shows, for example, that readers rarely baldly state that they have been caused offence and that they often provide a preamble to their letters that establishes that they greatly value *Private Eye* and thereby help to head off objections to their letters. Lockyer argues that humour is a complex social phenomenon, largely because of the ambiguities and controversies with which it is often, if not invariably, imbued. She suggests that complex objects of social scientific analysis like this require a variety of research tools to arrive at a comprehensive understanding.

A further example is provided by the investigation described in Research in focus 1.8 and 25.3.

Research in focus 25.3
Mixed methods research and foot and mouth disease

In Research in focus 1.8, a mixed methods study (Poortinga *et al.* 2004) that was carried out at the height of the Foot and Mouth Disease (FMD) outbreak in the UK was introduced as an example of a study that implies that quantitative and qualitative research can be combined. It was introduced at that point to illustrate the possibility of a mixed methods investigation.

The main rationale for the use of mixed methods research was in terms of completeness, in that the authors argue that a more comprehensive picture would be generated. In addition, the survey allowed focus group participants to be purposively sampled. In terms of rationale, therefore, following the categories outlined in Thinking deeply 25.4, completeness and sampling are the main uses of their mixed methods research. In terms of practice, six uses of mixed methods research could be discerned:

1. *Illustration.* The authors write that the focus group data were 'used to illustrate findings from the questionnaire' (Poortinga *et al.* 2004: 61).

2. *Completeness.* They write that the focus groups 'provided valuable additional information, especially on the reasons, rationalizations and arguments behind people's understanding of the FMD issue'.

3. *Triangulation.* Focus group findings 'reinforce' questionnaire findings (e.g. few worried about health impacts on people) and reveal concern about government policies in the handling of FMD rather than the disease itself. This implies that there was also an element of *enhancement*, as the qualitative findings augmented the quantitative ones by clarifying the nature of concern about the disease.

4. *Explanation.* The authors suggest that, in Bude, the high trust ratings of local sources of information and the low trust ratings of government 'may well be a judgement of where these sources are thought to stand in this debate. . . . the focus groups suggested that trust judgements might reflect the extent to which sources are believed to protect people and their interests' (Poortinga *et al.* 2004: 88).

5. *Sampling.* As previously noted, the survey allowed the focus group participants to be purposively sampled.

6. *Enhancement.* This occurs on several occasions in this article. See the section on 'Enhancement' below for more on this aspect.

Research in focus 25.4
Mixed methods research in the study of juvenile delinquency

An extremely unusual instance of mixed methods research is provided by the study referred to in Research in focus 2.13. Although the main data generated by Glueck and Glueck for this longitudinal study of juvenile delinquents in the USA were quantitative, a great deal of qualitative data were also collected (e.g. interviews with research participants and their families). For their **secondary analysis** of the quantitative data that Glueck and Glueck had compiled, Laub and Sampson (1998: 220) were concerned to uncover 'the main predictors of desistance from criminal careers over time'. They used the qualitative data to compile a life history analysis that, when merged with the quantitative findings, would 'provide a more complete portrait of criminal offending over the life course' (Laub and Sampson 1998: 221). With the life history analysis of the qualitative data, Laub and Sampson were concerned to explore changes over the life course and how environmental factors interacted with change over time for each person examined.

The results of the secondary quantitative analysis were used to identify suitable candidates for the in-depth analysis required by the life history study. For example, the quantitative data demonstrated that job stability predicted desistence from crime. Accordingly, they selected for the life history study: cases where there was a combination of high job stability and no arrest in adult life; cases where there was a combination of low job stability and arrest in adult life; and cases that were inconsistent with the pattern of job stability and desistence being related. The same was done for marital attachment, as the quantitative data showed that being married was associated with desistence. The authors write:

> our qualitative analysis was consistent with the hypothesis that the major turning points in the life courses of men who refrained from crime and deviance in adulthood were stable employment and good marriages. At the same time, we found that persistence in criminal behavior in adulthood often was the result of a developmental process of 'cumulative disadvantage' in which the negative influences of structural disadvantages (e.g., dropping out of school, having a criminal record or a dishonorable discharge from the military) persist throughout adult development. (Laub and Sampson 2004: 86)

In this way, the qualitative data were able to extend and amplify the quantitative findings. The cases that were inconsistent with the general pattern were also able to enhance the explanation: for example, the qualitative data suggested that alcohol abuse could offset the positive impact of marital attachment or job stability on desistence.

As noted in Research in focus 2.13, Laub and Sampson followed up fifty-two of the original participants at the age of 70. One reason was that they felt that Glueck and Glueck had emphasized 'behavioral continuity' and as a result, the qualitative data in particular were not suited to examining 'behavioral change in the lives of the participants' (Laub and Sampson 2004: 90). This is an interesting instance of the way in which the assumptions of researchers have an impact on the kinds of data that are collected. The researchers decided to conduct life history interviews with the fifty-two men for various reasons. Most notably, it would allow them to shed light on how involvement in and/or desistence from crime over time was related to their personal circumstances as well as to the wider social context. They elicited life history narratives for those who maintained an involvement in crime, those who desisted, and those who were in and out of criminal activity. The key contribution that these new qualitative data provided was the significance of turning points in their interviewees' lives:

> Changes in crime were associated in the narratives with a number of themes, including aging, employment, marriage, military service, excessive drinking, and personal choice. Of all the themes we have investigated, marriage turned up again and again in the narratives as a turning point. One former delinquent stated, 'If I hadn't met my wife at the time I did, I'd probably be dead.' (Laub and Sampson 2004: 95)

The significance of marriage as a turning point prompted the researchers to return to their quantitative data and to examine its importance. Their reanalysis of the data confirmed the importance of turning points and of marriage in particular.

Process

One of the contrasts suggested by Table 16.1 is that, whereas quantitative research tends to bring out a static picture of social life, qualitative research is more processual. The term 'static' can easily be viewed in a rather negative light. In fact, it is very valuable on many occasions to uncover regularities, and it is often the identification of such regularities that allows a processual analysis to proceed. A mixed methods research approach offers the prospect of being able to combine both elements. For example, both Lacey (1976) and Ball (1981) conducted ethnographic studies of schools, in which the chief purpose was to explore processes of selection and socialization. However, in addition both researchers employed sociometric questionnaires to examine pupils' friendship patterns. Such questionnaires ask respondents to indicate those people with whom they interact and the frequency of interaction. The use of these research instruments allowed the stability of pupils' friendship patterns to be explored. The study by Laub and Sampson in Research in focus 25.4 provides an illustration of the use of mixed methods research in terms of regularities and process.

A further illustration is provided by Miller's (1994) study of mass consumption in Trinidad. Miller's main method of data collection was through participant observation, but in addition he conducted questionnaire surveys of forty households in each of the four contrasting communities in which he conducted his ethnographic investigation. The surveys generated information on such issues as the stability of marriages in households, household composition, and the role of ethnicity in marriage. Such data allowed him to establish the structure of Trinidadian society. By contrast, the details of how, for example, mass consumption fits into the everyday life of Trinidadians and how they responded to consumer goods were gleaned from conversations, observations, and interviews with key informants.

A final illustration is a study by Holdsworth (2006) of university students' experiences of student life in terms of their residential status (whether living away from home or at home). For the quantitative data, undergraduates at four higher educational institutions around Greater Merseyside were contacted by email or by electronic bulletin board to complete a web-based questionnaire. Ten per cent of eligible students (3,282) completed the questionnaire. Qualitative interviews were then carried out with a sample of students who had signalled in their questionnaire responses that they were prepared to be interviewed. Interviewees were purposively sampled on the basis of answers they had given concerning such issues as gender, their residential status, and whether they were paying fees. In addition, six focus groups were conducted with prospective year 13 students at local schools and colleges. Holdsworth's theoretical framework for analysing her data was strongly influenced by the work of Bourdieu and in particular his concept of 'habitus'. The quantitative findings point strongly to clear differences in the student experience between those living at home and those living away. A thematic analysis of the interviews was designed 'to explore how students' habitus facilitates the process of fitting in and how the experience of leaving home is part of that process' (Holdsworth 2006: 505). Thus, while the quantitative data provide insight into broad differences between students, the qualitative data are used to explore the processes that lie behind the differences in experience revealed by the e-survey findings.

Different research questions

The research referred to in Research in focus 25.2 is an example of a research project in which quantitative and qualitative research were used in order to be able to answer different research questions.

- Questions about coverage, such as: how much coverage is there of social science research? What gets covered? Where? (method 1).

- Questions about the production of media items, such as: what kinds of attributes do journalists look for when thinking about whether to write an item on social science research? (methods 5 and 7).

- Questions about social scientists' attitudes to the media reporting of research in general (method 2) and to the reporting of their own research (methods 3 and 4). In addition, the research addressed social scientists' practices with regard to media coverage. Method 4 was designed to allow the findings deriving from method 3 to be elaborated and more fully understood.

- Questions about reception, such as: how do readers/viewers interpret media reporting of social science research? (method 8).

- Questions about the communication environment, such as: what are the policies of universities, government departments, and funding bodies concerning the media reporting of research? (method 6).

This form of mixed methods research entails making decisions about which kinds of research question are best answered using a quantitative research method and which by a qualitative research method and about how best to interweave the different elements, especially since, as suggested in the context of the discussion about triangulation, the outcomes of mixtures of methods are not always predictable.

Similarly, in my investigation of mixed methods research which is referred to in Research in focus 25.1, I had in mind different research questions for each of the two components of that investigation. With the content analysis, I wanted to know about the kinds of mixed methods research that is carried out in terms of issues such as: What kinds of research methods are employed in mixed methods research? Does the amount of mixed methods research vary by discipline? What are the reasons given for conducting mixed methods research? In the interviews, I was especially interested in questions such as: Do mixed methods researchers see the approach as generating distinctive problems that are separate from the quantitative and qualitative components? How did they feel about the state of mixed methods research? Did they experience problems of integrating the quantitative and the qualitative data?

Explanation

One of the problems that frequently confront quantitative researchers is how to explain relationships between variables. One strategy is to look for what is called an intervening variable, which is influenced by the independent variable but which in turn has an effect on the dependent variable. Thus, if we find a relationship between ethnicity and occupation, we might propose that education is one factor behind the relationship implying:

$$\text{ethnicity} \rightarrow \text{education} \rightarrow \text{occupation.}$$

This sequence implies that the variable ethnicity has an impact on people's education (for example, how much education people of different ethnic groups tend to undergo), which in turn has implications for the kinds of jobs that people of different ethnic groups attain. An alternative approach might be to seek to explore the relationship further by carrying out a qualitative study.

Rank (1989) used official statistics from one state in the USA to establish that women receiving the equivalent of social security benefits had low rates of fertility. Not only was the fertility rate lower than for the equivalent general population; the longer a woman received such benefits, the less likely she was to give birth. Why? Rank carried out fifty interviews with welfare recipients. The interviews dealt with such issues as 'family dynamics, employment, and the experience of getting on and off welfare' (Rank 1989: 298). Rank explains the relationship between the variables on the basis of these interviews, as follows: 'The economic, social, and psychological costs of becoming pregnant and having a child while on public assistance are perceived as clearly outweighing the benefits. It is argued that the economic and psychological stress that virtually all welfare recipients experience exerts a powerful effect on women's fertility behavior' (Rank 1989: 303). The inclusion of a qualitative research component thus allowed Rank to develop an explanation of his findings about rates of fertility among women receiving benefits.

A further illustration is provided by research on HIV-related risk behaviour among drug injectors by Barnard and Frischer (1995). Data from structured interviews with 503 injectors in Glasgow revealed that 'females report significantly higher levels of needle sharing, sexual activity and AIDS awareness than their male counterparts. Furthermore, women who are co-habiting with sexual partners who are themselves injectors are particularly likely to report high levels of risk behaviour and also AIDS awareness' (Barnard and Frischer 1995: 357). What are the factors that produced this pattern of relationships between gender, risk behaviour, and co-habitation? Semi-structured interviews with seventy-three injectors in Glasgow were also conducted. The authors suggest that the relationships between these variables 'can be explained by the tendency for women to be in sexual relationships with men who themselves inject and with whom they are unlikely to use condoms' (Barnard and Frischer 1995: 360). Once again, we see an instance of light being shed on relationships between variables derived from quantitative research by a related qualitative one.

Unexpected results

The outcomes of research are, as suggested by the last sentence, not always easy to anticipate. Although people sometimes cynically suggest that social scientists find what they want to find or that social scientists just convey the obvious, the capacity of the obvious to provide us with puzzling surprises should never be underestimated. When this occurs, employing a research method associated with the research strategy that was not used initially can be helpful. One context in which this might occur is when qualitative research is used as a salvage operation, when an anticipated set of results from a quantitative investigation fails to materialize (Weinholtz *et al.* 1995). Research in focus 25.5 provides an interesting illustration of this use of mixed methods research.

Research in focus 25.5
Using mixed methods research to solve a puzzle: the case of displayed emotions in convenience stores

An example of combining quantitative and qualitative research to solve a puzzle is Sutton and Rafaeli's (1988) study of the display of emotions in organizations. Following a traditional quantitative research strategy, based on their examination of studies like Hochschild (1983), Sutton and Rafaeli formulated a hypothesis suggesting a **positive relationship** between the display of positive emotions to retail shoppers (smiling, friendly greeting, eye contact) and the level of retail sales. In other words, we would expect that, when retail staff are friendly and give time to shoppers, sales will be better than when they fail to do so. Sutton and Rafaeli had access to data that allowed this hypothesis to be tested. The data derived from a study of 576 convenience stores in a national retail chain in the USA. Structured observation of retail workers provided the data on the display of positive emotions, and sales data provided information for the other variable. The hypothesis implied that there would be a positive relationship—that is, stores in which there was a more pronounced display of positive emotions would report superior sales. When the data were analysed, a relationship was confirmed, but it was found to be negative; that is, stores in which retail workers were *less* inclined to smile, be friendly, and so on tended to have better sales than those in which such emotions were in evidence. This was the reverse of what the authors had anticipated that they would uncover. Sutton and Rafaeli (1992: 124) considered restating their hypothesis to make it seem that they had found what they had expected, but fortunately resisted the temptation! Instead, they conducted a qualitative investigation of four case study stores to help understand what was happening.

This involved a number of methods: unstructured observation of interactions between staff and customers; semi-structured interviews with store managers; brief periods of participant observation; casual conversations with store managers, supervisors, executives, and others; and data gathered through posing as a customer in stores. The stores were chosen in terms of two criteria: high or low sales and whether staff typically displayed positive emotions. The qualitative investigation suggested that the relationship between the display of positive emotions and sales *was* negative, but that sales were likely to be a cause rather than a consequence of the display of emotions. This pattern occurred because, in stores with high levels of sales, staff were under greater pressure and encountered longer queues at checkouts. Staff therefore had less time and inclination for the pleasantries associated with the display of positive emotions. The quantitative data were then reanalysed with this alternative interpretation in mind and it was supported.

Thus, instead of the causal sequence being

Display of positive emotions → Retail sales

it was

Retail sales → Display of positive emotions

This exercise also highlights the main difficulty associated with inferring causal direction from a cross-sectional **research design**.

A somewhat different form of this category of mixed methods research occurs when researchers are interested in generating data that will allow them to address a specific research question or hypothesis but at the same time want to leave open the possibility of coming up with unanticipated findings. Usually, the quantitative research methods are deployed to address a specific hypothesis, while the usually more open-ended qualitative methods are designed to allow novel, unexpected findings to emerge. In the cross-cultural study described in Research in focus 25.6, the authors were concerned to address the hypothesis that 'parents structure and participate in activities with their children in ways that resonate with their cultural beliefs' (Harkness *et al.* 2006: 68). While both the quantitative and the qualitative research methods were seen as relevant to this hypothesis, the qualitative component threw up some unexpected findings. One of these was a cultural practice that had not been documented previously. The authors call this 'Swedish parent–child co-sleeping'. The researchers noted through interviews and informal home visits that, among Swedish families, children were spending a large amount of their night-times sleeping in their parents' bedrooms. This finding prompted the researchers to ask specific questions about this practice in later interviews, and questionnaires were devised to glean further details. The authors write: 'Close analysis of the Swedish co-sleeping findings, using both

qualitative and quantitative methods, provided a new way to access Swedish cultural models of the child and the family, particularly in relation to cultural ideas about gender and equality' (Harkness *et al.* 2006: 75). Also, the finding encouraged the researchers in the other countries to ask explicit questions about children and night-time behaviour.

Like unplanned triangulation, this category of mixed methods research is more or less impossible to plan for. It essentially provides the quantitative researcher with an alternative either to reconstruct a hypothesis or to file the results away (and probably never looking at them again) when findings are inconsistent with a hypothesis. It is probably not an option in all cases in which a hypothesis is not confirmed. There may also be instances in which a quantitative study could shed light on puzzling findings drawn from a qualitative investigation.

Instrument development

The in-depth knowledge of social contexts acquired through qualitative research can be used to inform the design of survey questions for structured interviewing and self-completion questionnaires. Pope and Mays (1995) point out that semi-structured interviewing took place before a British national survey on sexual attitudes and lifestyles (Wellings *et al.* 1994), so that the most appropriate sexual terms to be used in the survey questions

Research in focus 25.6
Mixed methods research in a cross-cultural investigation

Harkness *et al.* (2006) provide an interesting example of mixed methods research in relation to a seven-nation investigation of research into cultural context of children's development in home and school and transition from home to school. The seven nations were: Australia, Italy, the Netherlands, Poland, Spain, Sweden, and the USA.

Sixty families per nation were recruited, with the target children stratified in age groups up to age 8. Data were gleaned from parents through semi-structured interviews and week-long diaries dealing with their child's activities. These provided the qualitative component of the study. Parents also completed several questionnaires to do with areas such as: sources of advice and support; child's temperament; child's first contact with school; and child's qualities related to school success.

The combination of quantitative and qualitative research served several purposes for the researchers. The opportunity to use a triangulation approach, whereby they were able to test their central hypothesis that 'parents structure and participate in activities with their children that resonate with their cultural beliefs' through both quantitative and qualitative findings (Harkness *et al.* 2006: 68). Another key contribution of their mixed methods approach was that the qualitative findings informed the development of measures through the questionnaires, so that these 'would be reliable and valid for the various cultural sites' (Harkness *et al.* 2006: 69).

could be decided. The interviews revealed considerable misunderstanding about many terms. Similarly, Carlson *et al.* (1996) used ethnographic data that they had collected on needle sharing among drug injectors to inform the design of questions for a questionnaire survey of 276 users. Laurie and Sullivan (1991) report that, before the first wave of data collection for the British Household Panel Survey (see Research in focus 2.10), qualitative research was conducted through 'depth interviews' and 'group discussions'. One of the main purposes of this phase was 'to clarify terminologies and concepts about intra-household allocative processes in order to aid in the development of questions for the panel questionnaire' (Laurie and Sullivan 1991: 114). Walklate (2000) explains that, for her research on fear of crime and safety issues in two areas with high rates of crime, a survey using traditional questions about victimization was used. However, the questions were amended to reflect the local context following six months of gaining a detailed knowledge of the area through interviews, **ethnography**, and examination of local newspapers. Livingstone (2006) reports that the findings deriving from focus groups with children concerning their use of the Internet (see Table 19.1) were used to inform the content of questions concerning online privacy in a subsequent questionnaire survey. An example of the use of mixed methods research in the context of instrument development in a cross-cultural study can be found in Research in focus 25.6.

Sampling

One of the chief ways in which quantitative research can prepare the ground for qualitative research is through the selection of people to be interviewed. This can occur in several ways. In the case of the research on the reporting of social science research in the British mass media (see Research in focus 25.2), a content analysis of media content (method 1) was used as a source of data in its own right. However, it also served as a means of identifying journalists who had reported relevant research (method 5). In addition, replies to questions in the general survey of social scientists (method 2) were used to help identify two groups of social scientists—those with particularly high and those with low levels of media coverage of their research—who would then be interviewed with a semi-structured approach (method 4).

My colleagues and I used a similar approach in our study of social policy researchers' views about the quality of research in this field. We wrote:

> Telephone interviews were carried out with 28 interviewees who had indicated in the E-survey that they were willing to be interviewed. Ninety respondents had agreed to be interviewed and a purposive sampling method was used to select interviewees so that as many as possible of the different 'orientations' in attitudes to research and quality were represented in the sample. (Bryman *et al.* in press)

By 'orientations' was meant where the respondent stood on such issues as whether social policy research should be concerned with the advancement of knowledge or whether it should be concerned with the development of policy and practice. We wanted to ensure that, in our telephone interviews, we had a good representation of researchers in terms of their positions on this issue.

Jamieson (2000) reports that for a study of offending she administered a self-completion questionnaire to a sample of young men in which they reported criminal offences. On the basis of their replies, equal numbers of young men were interviewed using qualitative interviewing in each of three categories: those who did not offend; those who had offended but not recently; and persistent offenders. A similar use of mixed methods research can be seen in the example in Research in focus 25.3. Laub and Sampson (1998) in the study described in Research in focus 25.4 used quantitative data on criminal activity as a means of selecting people for further study.

Credibility

When credibility is the rationale for mixed methods research, the emphasis tends to be upon the symbolic virtues of the approach in terms of its capacity to bestow legitimacy on the research and its outputs. Milkman (1997: 192), for example, has suggested in the context of her research on a General Motors factory that the promise that she 'would produce "hard", quantitative data through survey research was what secured [her] access', even though she had no experience in this method. Milkman's predilection was towards a qualitative approach, relying mainly on semi-structured interviews with a variety of individuals and stakeholders in the factory, but she clearly felt including a quantitative component, in this case a survey, would secure the access she needed.

In this example, the researcher is using mixed methods research to gain credibility in the eyes of the organization in which she wanted to conduct her fieldwork. Sometimes mixed methods research is conducted because it is believed to have greater credibility among audiences.

These may be audiences of different kinds, such as: supervisors; dissertation examiners; research funding agencies; policy-makers; and potential readers. For example, Rocheleau (1995) included a questionnaire in conjunction with a qualitative study in the field of political ecology because she and her research team felt that the survey data would be more familiar and acceptable to policy-makers. She admits that the inclusion of the questionnaire in the research was 'cynical', as she puts it, because in fact she and her team felt that the qualitative data would be far more insightful. Similarly, when I conducted interviews with mixed methods researchers, some of my interviewees confessed that they sometimes used mixed methods research because they felt it would be more likely to get funded (Bryman 2007*b*). For example, one interviewee said:

> And also . . . and I don't know how true this is, but I think there's been a general perception . . . that the ESRC had . . . undergone quite a quantitative turn and that there was a great . . . there was a concern about the lack of quantitative research [a] concern about lack of quantitative skills and that they particularly kind of favoured projects that used mixed methods or had a strong quantitative component. And so, I tend to use them because strategically I think it's a good idea.

In other words, mixed methods research was more likely to be funded because it was perceived as having greater credibility among those responsible for funding social science research.

Context

The typical circumstance for this approach to mixing methods was for a qualitative study to provide the context for understanding broad-brush quantitative findings. An example is provided by research reported by Phillipson *et al.* (1999). The research was concerned with older people's experiences of community life in three English urban areas: Bethnal Green, Wolverhampton, and Woodford. Each of these areas had been the focus of earlier research on this general topic in the 1940s or 1950s. As such, this comparative case study research permitted a longitudinal element by allowing comparisons to be drawn with previous findings. A questionnaire survey of around 200 older people in each of these three locations was conducted and was designed to explore the extent of change since the earlier studies and such issues as experiences of assistance from neighbours. Qualitative interviews were conducted with 62 older people who had participated in the survey. In the qualitative interviews, questions were asked partly to allow contrasts with the earlier investigations but also in order to 'provide a context for the information about social networks gleaned from the survey' (Phillipson *et al.* 1999: 723). For example, at one point the authors present some statistical findings concerning whether people could find something they liked about their area. Most (79 per cent) could find something, but this varied quite a lot, with Woodford residents being more likely than Bethnal Green ones to be able to mention a feature they liked. However, the qualitative interviews provided insights into what it was about the areas that people liked. For example, having a community feeling was viewed positively, with one elderly woman in Woodford saying: 'More like a village. Everybody knows everyone else. It is very friendly' (Phillipson *et al.* 1999: 723). The authors note that Bethnal Green residents were especially likely to mention having roots in an area as being of particular significance, as when one woman said: 'It's my home, my roots are here now. It's what I'm used to . . . living here and working here for so many years' (Phillipson *et al.* 1999: 724). In this example, the qualitative findings allow the quantitative data to be contextualized. We understand the statistical data better because we have an appreciation of the nature of the areas in which the surveys were conducted and the motives and preferences of their members.

Illustration

In Research in focus 22.8, it was reported that in their classic study of affluent workers in Luton, Goldthorpe *et al.* (1968) collected a considerable amount of qualitative data in addition to the quantitative information that formed the main basis for their inferences about issues like the notion of an instrumental orientation to work. Savage (2005) reanalysed much of these qualitative data, but, as he notes, Goldthorpe and his colleagues did not totally ignore these data: they used the qualitative data to illustrate some of the themes arising from their quantitative findings. In the context of their discussion towards the end of their book on the industrial attitudes and behaviour of affluent workers, they wrote:

We present three 'case studies' which are taken from among those men in our sample who fell in the 'highly instrumental' category. These serve to show that the links which we have suggested between 'instrumentalism' and both geographical and social

mobility are not at any rate entirely fanciful but can rather be seen at work in the lives of particular individuals. In the first case the effects of geographical mobility appear to have been of greatest importance . . . (Goldthorpe *et al.* 1968: 168)

In the first of these case studies, we are told about 'Mr Doyle', who was from the Irish Republic: 'Through Irish friends he heard about the "big money" available in Luton and eventually he decided to move there and take a factory job.' He is quoted as saying that the tempo of the work is 'a bit of a strain' but that he has no intention of leaving his firm because 'the pay's very good here; there aren't many places where you could do better' (Goldthorpe *et al.* 1968: 169). Here we see, from one of the classics of British sociology, the use of qualitative research to illustrate (and perhaps in the process to illuminate) the quantitative survey findings.

Illustration was also a feature of the research reported in Research in focus 25.3, but, as noted elsewhere in this chapter, this illustration was often accompanied by enhancement, whereby the qualitative data qualified the questionnaire findings.

Utility

For some writers and researchers, mixed methods research is preferred because it is felt that it is more likely to generate findings that will have utility. This is more likely to be a concern among researchers in fields with a strong disposition towards findings being useful. For example, one of my interviewees said of mixed methods research: 'The main reason I use it and the main reason I will probably always put it on grant applications is because of the issues around needing to . . . generate data that's . . . suitable for policy-makers.' This interviewee went on to add: 'I think by doing both methods, it enables you . . . to speak to kind of policy audiences and to speak to academic audiences.' By way of further illustration of utility as a rationale for mixed methods research, Pernice (1996) conducted both quantitative and qualitative research on unemployed people in New Zealand. She found that the questionnaire date revealed that most members of the sample wanted a job. However, qualitative data gleaned from interviews revealed a more complex set of attitudes with regard to intentions towards employment. Many spoke about alternatives to paid employment that they were considering and also revealed in interviews a more nuanced set of attitudes towards employment than was being (or could be) revealed through the questionnaires. Pernice (1996: 348) argues that not only was her understanding of unemployment enhanced through mixed methods research, but also, 'if only quantitative approaches are taken, our understanding of unemployment will not be deep enough to formulate effective solutions'.

Confirm and discover

The most common form of this rationale for mixed methods research is that the inferences that are derived from a qualitative study are then subsequently tested with quantitative research. An example is a study by Tripp *et al.* (2002) of revenge in the workplace. Initially, 88 working MBA students in the USA were asked to give an account of two incidents in which the student or someone else had sought to gain revenge against another person. The revenge episodes were examined to establish the activities involved in taking revenge. The overriding finding was that symmetry between the initial episode and the revenge should be in line with each other. This symmetry has two elements: symmetry of consequences —the revenge should do the same amount of harm as the original wrongdoing; and symmetry of method—the way in which revenge is exacted should resemble that involved in the initial harm that was done. Drawing on this distinction, the researchers conducted a second study, using an experimental design, to test their prediction, which emerged out of the qualitative study, that 'the symmetry of consequences will influence individual judgments of revenge [and] symmetry of method should shape individual judgments about revenge' (Tripp *et al.* 2002: 972–3). In fact, the experiment did not entirely support these expectations. When revenge is symmetric in terms of consequences, the experiment showed that the vengeful act is viewed more positively. This was in line with the researchers' expectations. However, symmetry of method operated in a manner contrary to their expectations: vengeful acts were viewed *more* harshly when they were symmetric with the original harmful act.

Diversity of views

Sometimes, researchers want to gather two kinds of data: qualitative data that will allow them to gain access to the perspectives of the people they are studying; and quantitative data that will allow them to explore specific issues in which they are interested. When this occurs, they are seeking to explore an area in both ways, so that they can both adopt an unstructured approach to data collection in which participants' meanings are the focus of attention

and investigate a specific set of issues through the more structured approach of quantitative research. An example of this is Milkman's (1997) study of a General Motors car manufacturing plant in the USA.

She was interested in the nature of the labour process in the late twentieth century and whether new factory conditions were markedly different for car production workers from the negative portrayals of such work in the 1950s and early 1960s (e.g. Blauner 1964). As such, she was interested in the meaning of industrial work. She employed semi-structured interviews and focus groups with car production workers to elicit data relevant to this aspect of her work. However, in addition she had some specific interests in a 'buyout' plan that the company's management introduced in the mid-1980s after it had initiated a variety of changes to work practices. The plan gave workers the opportunity to give up their jobs for a substantial cash payment. In 1988 Milkman carried out a questionnaire survey of workers who had taken up the company's buyout offer. These workers were surveyed again the following year and in 1991. The reason for the surveys was that Milkman had some very specific interests in the buyout scheme, such as the reasons for workers taking the buyout, how they had fared since leaving General Motors, how they felt about their current employment, and differences between social groups (in particular, different ethnic groups) in current earnings relative to those at General Motors.

A further example is the research on school size differences that was referred to in Research in focus 11.1. One of the aims of this study was the exploration of the relationships between class size and various aspects of classrooms. As noted in Research in focus 11.1 and elsewhere in Chapter 11, Blatchford and his colleagues collected quantitative data, drawing on structured observation of classrooms and questionnaires. The data that were generated reflected the preoccupations of the research team. However, Blatchford (2005) reports that they also wanted to capture teachers' experiences and to that end conducted semi-structured interviews and conducted detailed case studies of particular classes. Further, the various qualitative findings relating to the differences between large and small classes influenced later questionnaires that were developed (a case of 'instrument development').

Enhancement

In the Poortinga *et al.* (2004) article on the Foot and Mouth Disease (FMD) crisis (see Research in focus 1.8

and 25.3), enhancement occurs on several occasions. For example, at one point the authors note that their focus group data regarding the perceived causes of the outbreak were more or less the same as the causes identified in their questionnaire survey. In this way, the quantitative and qualitative findings are being used for the purpose of *triangulation*. With both sets of data, three factors had been identified. However, they then qualify this finding by noting that, in the focus groups, 'the three factors were often used in combination. That is, the three factors were seen as being highly interconnected' (Poortinga *et al.* 2004: 87). Another example is when they note another correspondence between their quantitative and their qualitative data: 'The findings of the focus groups reinforce those of the questionnaire regarding general concern' (Poortinga *et al.* 2004: 78). However, they then go on to note that the picture from the focus groups is slightly more complex than if one relies on the survey data alone, and they quote a focus group participant to exemplify this point:

In terms of health impacts, people were worried that rotting carcasses of culled animals, which in some cases were not put onto a funeral pyre immediately, would spread various diseases, and also because of toxins being emitted from the fires. That is, people were more concerned about health risks arising from *government policy measures and handling of FMD* than about the *disease itself*.

I think a lot of people are genuinely concerned about the fires, the toxins coming out in the fires, that became quite an issue. And that is one of those things that we probably won't know if there is any kind of come back on it, we probably won't know for a few years and that is quite a concern. (Norwich, Male) (Poortinga *et al.* 2004: 78)

Research in focus 25.7 provides another example of enhancement.

Research in focus 25.7
Combining survey research and qualitative interviewing in a study of managers

Wajcman and Martin (2002) conducted survey research using a questionnaire on male and female managers (470 in total) in six Australian companies. The authors were interested in career orientations and attitudes. They also conducted semi-structured interviews with 136 managers in each company. The survey evidence showed that male and female managers were generally more similar than different in terms of most variables. Thus, contrary to what many people might have anticipated, women's career experiences and orientations were *not* distinctive. They then examined the qualitative interviews in terms of narratives of identity. Wajcman and Martin found that both male and female managers depicted their careers in 'market' terms (as needing to respond to the requirements of the managerial labour market to develop their skills, experience, and hence career). *But*, whereas, for men, narratives of career meshed seamlessly with narratives of domestic life, for women there was a disjuncture. Female managers found it much harder to reconcile managerial identities with domestic ones. They needed to opt for one. Thus, choices about career and family are still gendered. This research shows how a mixed methods research approach was able to reveal much more than could have been gleaned through one approach alone by collecting evidence on both career patterns and expectations and identities using research methods suited to each issue area.

Reflections on mixed methods research

There can be little doubt that mixed methods research is becoming far more common than when I first started writing about it (Bryman 1988*a*). Two particularly significant factors in prompting this development are:

1. a growing preparedness to think of research methods as techniques of data collection or analysis that are not as encumbered by epistemological and ontological baggage as is sometimes supposed, and

2. a softening in the attitude towards quantitative research among feminist researchers, who had previously been highly resistant to its use (see Chapter 16 for a discussion of this point).

Other factors are doubtlessly relevant, but these two developments do seem especially significant. An example of the operation of these factors can be found in an area of research that has been mentioned on several occasions in this book and that has predominantly been studied using qualitative research methods (in particular focus groups, see Chapter 19)—the study of audience reception of media and cultural texts. Some researchers in this area have called for a rethinking of the field's attitude to quantitative research. Some of the studies described in Table 19.1 are focus group studies of audience reception. This method, along with other qualitative methods (e.g. Ang 1985), has been the main data-collection approach employed in this field. Yet lingering unease among some practitioners of qualitative research in this area, particularly regarding issues to do with reliability and generalizability of findings, has led to some calls for a consideration of the possible use of quantitative research in tandem with qualitative methods (e.g. Schrøder 1999). However, it is important to realize that mixed methods research is not intrinsically superior to mono-method or mono-strategy research. It is tempting to think that mixed methods research is more or less inevitably superior to research that relies on a single method on the grounds that more and more varied findings are inevitably 'a good thing'. However, five points must be borne in mind.

1. Mixed methods research, like mono-method research, must be competently designed and conducted. Poorly conducted research will yield suspect findings no matter how many methods are employed.

2. Just like mono-method research, mixed methods research must be appropriate to the research questions or research area with which you are concerned. There is no point collecting more data simply on the basis that 'more is better'. Mixed methods research has to be dovetailed to research questions, just as all research methods must be. It is, after all, likely to consume considerably more time and financial resources than research relying on just one method.

3. Any research project has limited resources. Employing mixed methods research may dilute the research effort in any area, since resources would need to be spread.

4. By no means all researchers have the skills and training to carry out both quantitative and qualitative research, so that their 'trained incapacities' may act as a barrier to integration (Reiss 1968: 351). However, there is a growing recognition of the potential of mixed methods research, so that this point probably carries less weight than it did when Reiss was writing.

5. As far as possible, users of mixed methods research should explore what the combined set of findings indicate. Mixed methods researchers sometimes experience difficulties with the integration of the findings deriving from the quantitative and qualitative components of their research, and there are several reasons for this (Bryman 2007*c*; Bryman *et al.* 2007). Mixed methods research ideally should be more than the sum of its parts (O'Cathain *et al.* 2007).

In other words, mixed methods research should not be considered as an approach that is universally applicable or as a panacea. It *may* provide a better understanding of a phenomenon than if just one method had been used. It may also frequently enhance our confidence in our own or others' findings—for example, when a triangulation exercise has been conducted. It may even serve a tactical purpose of enhancing the credibility of an application for research funding or a publication, especially when it is borne in mind that some writers believe that mixed methods research has become methodologically fashionable (Sandelowski 2003). However, as I have tried to suggest with these final reflections, mixed methods research is subject to the same (or at least very similar) considerations and constraints as any research method or design.

Thinking deeply 25.5
Are the paradigm wars over?

The period during which many commentators viewed quantitative and qualitative research as based on incompatible assumptions is often referred to as the 'paradigm wars' (Hammersley 1992c; Oakley 1999) or the 'paradigm debate' (Creswell and Plano Clark 2007). The growing popularity of mixed methods research would seem to signal the end of the paradigm wars, as it is sometimes represented as having given way to pragmatism. Many of the contributors to Tashakkori and Teddlie's (2003) *Handbook* appear to be committed to a pragmatist position. However, there are signs that the paradigm wars have not entirely disappeared but have resurfaced in slightly different ways (Bryman 2007a). One of these is the growing predilection for **systematic reviews** of the literature, particularly in areas of the social sciences with a strong applied focus (see Key concept 4.1 and Research in focus 4.1 and the discussion in Chapter 4 of this approach to reviewing the literature). Several writers have noted that the proponents of systematic review advocate its use in terms of principles that are very much associated with quantitative research and its positivist foundations. They tend to attribute to it qualities such as reliability, **replicability**, transparency of procedures, and greater comprehensiveness, and suggest that it is more objective (Hammersley 2001; MacLure 2005). These attributes have strong affinities with quantitative research. In contrast, the critics of systematic review tend to emphasize what systematic review does *not* do and what traditional **narrative reviews** are capable of achieving. The critics of systematic review emphasize features of systematic review that are associated with qualitative research and its interpretivist foundations. They tend to emphasize the significance of interpretation in narrative literature reviews and the importance of understanding and locating findings within the entire study of which the findings are a part. They also suggest that systematic review neglects inter-textuality—the links between studies and their findings—whereas it is standard practice in a literature review to explore such links. The key point to register at this point is that this debate has several of the hallmarks of the paradigm arguments.

Key points

- While there has been a growth in the amount of mixed methods research, not all writers support its use.

- Objections to mixed methods research tend to be the result of a view that there are epistemological and ontological impediments to the combination of quantitative and qualitative research.

- There are several different ways of combining quantitative and qualitative research and of representing mixed methods research.

- The outcomes of combining quantitative and qualitative research can be planned or unplanned.

Questions for review

● What is mixed methods research?

The argument against mixed methods research

● What are the main elements of the embedded methods and paradigm arguments in terms of their implications for the possibility of mixed methods research?

Two versions of the debate about quantitative and qualitative research

● What are the main elements of the technical and epistemological versions of the debate about quantitative and qualitative research? What are the implications of these two versions of the debate for mixed methods research?

Approaches to mixed methods research

● What are the main differences between Hammersley's and Morgan's classifications of mixed methods research?

● What are the chief ways in which quantitative and qualitative research have been combined?

● Why might it be useful to distinguish between them?

● What is the logic of triangulation?

● Traditionally, qualitative research has been depicted as having a preparatory role in relation to quantitative research. To what extent do the different forms of mixed methods research reflect this view?

Reflections on mixed methods research

● Why has mixed methods research become more prominent?

● Is mixed methods research necessarily superior to single strategy research?

● To what extent does the rise of mixed methods research suggest that the paradigm wars are over?

Online Resource Centre

http://www.oxfordtextbooks.co.uk/orc/brymansrm3e/

Visit the Online Resource Centre that accompanies this book to enrich your understanding of mixed methods research. Consult web links, test yourself using multiple choice questions, and gain further guidance and inspiration from the Student Researcher's Toolkit.

E-research: using the Internet as object and method of data collection

Chapter guide

This chapter is concerned with the ways in which the Internet can be used in research. Most readers will be familiar with the Internet as a means of searching for material on topics for essays, for further reading, and for various other uses. It can be very valuable for such purposes, but this kind of activity is *not* the focus of this chapter. Instead, I will be concerned with the ways in which Internet websites can be used as objects of analysis in their own right and with the ways the Internet can be used as a means of collecting data, much like the post and the telephone. The main topics covered in this chapter are:

- World Wide Web sites or pages as objects of analysis;
- ethnographic study of the Internet;
- qualitative research using online focus groups;
- qualitative research using online personal interviews;
- online social surveys.

In the process of presenting these topics, I will draw comparisons with traditional methods wherever appropriate.

Introduction

There can be little doubting that the Internet and online communication have proliferated since the early 1990s and it would be surprising if this boom did not have implications for social research methods. Between January and April 2006, 13.9 million British households could access the Internet from home, representing 57 per cent of all households. This represented an increase of 2.9 million households since 2002 (a 26 per cent increase) and an increase of 0.6 million since the previous year (a 5 per cent increase) (http://www.statistics.gov.uk/pdfdir/inta0806.pdf (accessed on 12 June 2007)).

Use of the Internet is particularly high among university students, many of whom have been brought up with the technology and for whom it is a very natural medium. A survey of Internet use among American college students found particularly high rates of use in comparison with the population at large, with 86 per cent of students being regular users compared with 59 per cent of the population (Jones 2002). Nearly 80 per cent of university students felt that the Internet had had a positive impact on their college experience. The situation in the UK is

likely to be similar to that found in the USA. Given this background, it is plausible that many students will be drawn to the Internet as an environment within which to conduct social research.

The ongoing and burgeoning nature of the Internet and online communication makes it difficult to characterize this field and its impact on social research and its conduct in any straightforward and simple way. In this chapter, I will be concerned with the following areas of e-research:

- World Wide Web sites or pages as objects of analysis;
- using the World Wide Web or online communications as a means of collecting data from individuals and organizations.

In addition, I will address some of the broader implications and ramifications of the Internet for conducting social research.

While the choice of these two areas of online research and their classification is rather arbitrary and they tend to shade into each other somewhat, they provide the basis for a reasonably comprehensive overview in the face of a highly fluid field. This chapter does not consider the use of the Internet as an information resource or as a means of finding references. Some suggestions about the latter can be found in Chapter 4. The Internet is a vast information resource and has too many possible forms to be covered in a single chapter. Moreover, I advise caution about the use of such materials; while the Internet is a cornucopia of data and advice, it also contains a great deal of misleading and downright incorrect information. Healthy scepticism should guide your searches.

The Internet as object of analysis

Websites and webpages are potential sources of data in their own right and can be regarded as potential fodder for both quantitative and qualitative content analysis of the kind discussed in Chapters 12 and 21. Indeed, in the latter chapter, there is a section on 'virtual documents' that draws attention to websites as a form of document. Aldridge (1998), for example, examined both written consumer guides to personal finance published in the UK and several Internet websites. Through an analysis of such documents Aldridge extracted a number of themes that he saw as part of the 'promotional culture' in which we live. Examples of such themes are:

1. the necessity for members of the public to assume responsibility for their personal finances, particularly in the light of the reductions in welfare provision; and

2. the depiction of the professional–client relationship as unthreatening and relatedly as one in which the client may legitimately ask informed questions.

However, there are clearly difficulties with using websites as sources of data in this way. Four issues to consider when assessing the quality of documents were mentioned in Chapter 21. In addition to the issues raised there, the following additional observations are worth considering.

1. You will need to find the websites relating to your research questions. This is likely to mean trawling the web using a search engine such as Google. However, any search engine provides access to only a portion of the web. This is why Dorsey *et al.* (2004) used several search engines to find websites that promote ecologically sensitive tourism (see Research in focus 26.1), and even then there is evidence that the combined use of several search engines will allow access to only just under a half of the total population of websites (see Research in focus 26.2). While this means that the use of several search engines is highly desirable when seeking out appropriate websites, it has to be recognized not only that they will allow access to just a portion of the available websites but also that they may be a biased sample.

2. Related to this point, seeking out websites on a topic can only be as good as the keywords that are employed in the search process. The researcher has to be very patient to try as many relevant keywords as possible (and combinations of them—known as Boolean searches) and may be advised to ask other people (librarians, supervisors, etc.) to advise on whether the most appropriate ones are being used.

3. New websites are continually appearing and others disappearing. Researchers basing their investigations on websites need to recognize that their analyses may be based on websites that no longer exist and that new ones may have appeared since data collection was terminated.

4. Websites are also continually changing, so that an analysis may be based upon at least some websites that have been quite considerably updated.

5. The analysis of websites and webpages is a new field that is very much in flux. New approaches are being developed at a rapid rate. Some draw on ways of interpreting documents that were covered in Chapters 20 and 21, such as discourse analysis and qualitative content analysis. Others have been developed specificially in relation to the web, such as the examination of hyperlinks between websites and their significance (Schneider and Foot 2004).

Research in focus 26.1
Conducting an analysis of ecotourism websites

Dorsey *et al.* (2004) note that a growing interest in environmental issues in the West has been associated with a growth in 'ecotourism' and in cultural tourism. The former term denotes tourism to remote areas that is ecologically sensitive; cultural tourism reflects an interest in people and their cultures in relation to their ecosystems. They argue that the Internet has played a significant role in promoting these newer forms of tourism and were interested in the ways in which they are promoted on websites. Using several search engines, they searched for such websites. They emerged with seven websites that met their criteria for inclusion: well-established companies; a claim to offer 'sustainable' tours; culture emphasized for at least some of the tours; developing societies as the main destinations; plenty and a variety of information, including photographs; and a variety of destinations advertised.

Dorsey *et al.* submitted the websites to a detailed **narrative analysis** (see Key concept 22.4) guided by two research questions. First, do the companies advertising these tours on their websites do so in a manner consistent with the discourse of ecotourism and sustainable development? Second, does the online strategy of advertising these tours differ from traditional forms? Regarding the first research question, the researchers found that only two of the seven websites represented their tours in a manner consistent with the discourse of ecotourism and sustainable development. The others missed key elements of the discourse. Moreover, the authors found that most websites 'do not discuss the principles of sustainability and only rarely refer to the environmental dynamics of the communities and landscapes that are visited' (Dorsey *et al.* 2004: 774). As regards the second research question, the researchers found that there was little difference between online advertising of such tourism and what had been found by previous researchers who had examined the advertising of ecotourism in traditional media.

This is a study that has produced some interesting findings from an examination of websites. It provides useful findings for tourism researchers and for those with an interest in advertising and in the marketing of tourist destinations. It also provides an interesting use of previous findings, as reported in books and journals: the researchers did not conduct their own investigation of the advertising of ecotourism in traditional media in order to forge a comparison with their own findings regarding online advertising because they were able to employ previous findings generated by other researchers to do so.

Research in focus 26.2
Conducting an analysis of alternative websites

Ho *et al.* (2002) were interested in 'alternative websites' in Singapore against the backcloth of a country whose government has been concerned to facilitate the spread of online access as a means of building a knowledge-based economy capable of participating fully in a global economic order. The Singapore government is depicted as concerned to create a knowledge-based workforce with the skills and mindset capable of responding to and capitalizing upon the diffusion of new technologies. Alternative websites are in a sense a paradox because they have been facilitated by the spread of Internet access but at the same time challenge the status quo. Ho *et al.* chose to emphasize websites concerned with politics, religion, and alternative sexuality. The research was conducted over a four-month period and employed five search engines

(Yahoo, Alta Vista, Google, Infoseek, and Webcrawler) to trawl for suitable sites. The team of researchers used for each website a two-page report sheet to record information about:

(a) web-content in the form of 'alternative culture,' via recourse to complaints, criticisms, promotion of alternative values, practices and lifestyles; (b) the target audience: whether the site targets its own community or 'outsiders'; and (c) website characteristics which included guest book entries, links, sponsors, interactive functions, and evidence of Web-rings (clusters of inter-linked sites representing a general theme). (Ho *et al.* 2002: 135)

On the basis of their analyses, the authors proceeded to classify the different types of alternative website. For example, some were concerned with civil rights and used the Singapore constitution or general civil rights issues as the basis for advancing their position. Another type was made up of websites that sought to reduce or even purge censorship. Thus, while the Internet is often associated with technologies of surveillance and control, it also contains spaces in which surveillance and control can be resisted.

Most researchers who use documents as the basis for their work have to confront the issue that it is difficult to determine the universe or population from which they are sampling. Therefore, the problems identified here and in Chapter 21 are not entirely unique to websites. However, the rapid growth and speed of change in the web accentuate these kinds of problems for social researchers who are likely to feel that the experience is like trying to hit a target that not only continually moves but is in a constant state of metamorphosis. The crucial issue is to be sensitive to the limitations of the use of websites as material that can be content analysed, as well as to the opportunities they offer. Employing both printed and website materials, as Aldridge (1998) did, has the potential to bring out interesting contrasts in such sources and can also provide the basis for cross-validating sources.

It was noted in Chapters 17 and 21 that there has been a growing interest in visual materials. The use of images in websites is also potentially interesting. Crook and Light (2002) analysed the photographs in ten university prospectuses. The authors note that the images that accompany departmental entries often include photographs of students apparently studying but that they are rarely shown in the archetypal formal contexts of university learning, such as lectures or private study. Instead, they are usually shown in 'social' forms of learning where they are also active, engaged and frequently out of doors. The authors argue that these less typical learning contexts are chosen because of their capacity to connect with familiar routines for many applicants.

In addition, emails and other forms of Internet-based communications (such as listservs, discussion groups, and chat rooms) have been used as objects of analysis. For their study of online self-help and social support groups in the UK, Nettleton *et al.* (2002) examined online interactions in newsgroups, discussion lists, chat rooms, and so on. In a study of the use of email in two organizations, Brown and Lightfoot (2002) found that online communication was used in a manner that was strongly influenced by pre-existing, non-online forms of communication (such as memos) so that previous ways of working were not displaced. In addition, they note that email was often employed as a means of establishing who is responsible (and not responsible) for certain actions. As such, the internal politics of organizations in terms of establishing personal responsibility loomed large in the use of email.

In addition, it is important to bear in mind the four quality criteria recommended by Scott (1990) in connection with documents (see Chapter 21). Scott's suggestions invite us to consider quite why a website is constructed. Why is it there at all? Is it there for commercial reasons? Does it have an axe to grind? In other words, we should be no less sceptical about websites than about any other kind of document.

One final point to register is that, just like most documents, websites can be subjected to both qualitative and quantitative forms of analysis. The examples in Research in focus 26.1 and 26.2 involve a qualitative approach to the analysis, but it is worth looking back to Research in focus 12.3, which outlines a study that conducted a quantitative content analysis of postings to cancer support websites.

Tips and skills
Referring to websites

There is a growing practice in academic work that, when referring to websites, you should include the date you consulted them. This convention is very much associated with the fact that websites often disappear and frequently change, so that, if subsequent researchers wanted to follow up your findings, or even to check on them, they may find that they are no longer there or that they have changed. Citing the date you accessed or consulted the website may help to relieve any anxieties about someone not finding a website you have referred to or finding it has changed (e.g. **http://www.oxfordtextbooks.co.uk/orc/brymansrm3e/** (accessed on 3 July 2007)). This does mean, however, that you will have to keep a running record of the dates you consulted the websites to which you refer.

Using the Internet to collect data from individuals

In this section, I examine research methods that entail the use of either the web or online communications, such as email, as a platform for collecting data from individuals. At the time of writing, the bulk of the discussion concerned with this issue has emphasized four main areas:

1. an **ethnography** of the Internet;
2. qualitative research using online focus groups;
3. qualitative research using online personal interviews;
4. online social surveys.

These types of Internet-based research methods do not exhaust the full range of possibilities but they do represent recurring emphases in the emerging literature on this subject. All of them offer certain advantages over their traditional counterparts because:

- they are usually more economical in terms of time and money;
- they can reach large numbers of people very easily;
- distance is no problem, since the research participant only has to be accessible by computer—it does not matter whether he or she is in the same building or across the world;
- data can be collected and collated very quickly.

The chief general disadvantages tend to revolve around the following issues:

- access to the Internet is still nowhere near universal, so that certain people are likely to be inaccessible;
- invitations to take part in research may be viewed as just another nuisance email;
- loss of the personal touch—lack of rapport between interviewer and interviewee, inability to pick up visual or auditory cues;
- concerns among research participants about confidentiality of replies at a time of widespread anxiety about fraud and hackers.

More specific balance sheets of advantages and disadvantages relating to some of the individual e-research methods will be covered below.

There are two crucial distinctions that should be borne in mind when examining Internet-based research methods:

1. There is a distinction between *web-based* and *communication-based* methods. The former is a research method whereby data are collected through the Internet, for example, a **questionnaire** that forms a webpage and that the respondent then completes. A communication-based research method is one where email or a similar communication medium is the platform from which the data-collection instrument is launched.

2. There is a distinction between *synchronous* and *asynchronous* methods of data collection. The former occur in

real time. An example would be an interview in which an online interviewer asks a question and the respondent, who is also online, replies immediately, as in a chat room. An asynchronous method is not in real time so that there is no immediate response from the respondent, who is unlikely to be on online at the same time as the interviewer (or, if the respondent is on online, he or she is extremely unlikely to be in a position to reply immediately). An example would be an interview question posed by the interviewer in an email that is opened and answered by the respondent some time later, perhaps days or weeks later.

With these distinctions in mind I can now move on to examine the four main forms of online research methods previously identified.

An ethnography of the Internet?

Ethnography may not seem to be an obvious method for collecting data on Internet use. The image of the ethnographer is that of someone who visits places or locations such as communities and organizations. The Internet seems to go against the grain of ethnography, in that it seems a decidedly placeless space. In fact, as Hine (2000) has observed, conceiving of the Internet as a place—a cyberspace—has been one strategy for an ethnographic study of the Internet, and from this it is just a short journey to the examination of communities in the form of online communities or virtual communities. In this way, our concepts of place and space that are constitutive of the way in which we operate in the real world are grafted onto the Internet and its use. A further issue is that, as noted in Chapter 17, ethnography entails participant observation, but in cyberspace what is the ethnographer observing and in what is he or she participating?

Markham's (1998) approach to an ethnography of life on the Internet involved interviews. The interviews followed a period of 'lurking' (reading but not participating) in computer-mediated communication forums like chat rooms and MUDs (multi-user domains). The interviews allowed synchronous questioning and answering; in other words, the asking and answering of questions were in real time, rather than the kind of questioning and answering that might occur via email, where a question might be answered several hours or days later. She used an interview guide, and the interviews lasted between one hour and over four hours. Such interviews are a very real challenge for both interviewer and interviewee because neither party can pick up on visual cues (for example, puzzlement, anxiety) or auditory cues (sighs, groans).

One of Markham's interests lay in the reality or otherwise of online experiences. This can be seen in the following brief online interview sequence (Markham is Annette):

Annette: 'How real are your experiences in the Internet?'

Sherie: 'How real are experiences off the internet?' (Markham 1998: 115)

In fact, Markham notes how her notion of 'real' was different from that of her interviewees. For Markham 'real' or 'in real life' carried a connotation of genuineness or authenticity, but for her interviewees it was more to do with distinguishing experiences that occur offline. Indeed, Markham increasingly felt that her interviewees were questioning the validity of the dichotomous distinction between the real and the non-real, so far as online interaction was concerned. However, it is likely that these distinctions between life online and life offline will become less significant as younger people who are growing up with the Internet conduct large portions of their lives online. This development would have considerable implications for social researchers, since, for many research participants, the online world may become very naturalistic.

An interesting question about this research is—in what sense is it an ethnography? At one level, Markham was simply an interviewer who used a semi-structured interview guide to elicit information about the world view of her correspondents. At another level, she was indeed a participant in and observer of life online, although the life that she was participating in and observing was very much a product of her promptings, no matter how open the questions she asked and no matter how willing she was to allow her interviewees leeway in what they wanted to discuss. In much the same way that her interviewees were questioning the nature of reality, Markham's investigation invites us to question the nature of ethnography so far as research on the Internet is concerned.

Kendall (1999) was probably closer to the traditional concept of the ethnographer in that she describes her research as comprising three years of online participant observation in a MUD, as well as face-to-face interviews and attendance at face-to-face gatherings. Such research is probably closer to the conventional notion of ethnographic research in its use of several methods of data collection and a sense of participation in the lives of those being studied, as well as interviewing them. She was interested in issues to do with identity and the presentation of self online and interestingly found (among other things) that the participants 'privilege embodied experience over mediated experience' (Kendall 1999: 62).

A further example of the use of ethnography in relation to the study of online worlds can be found in Research in focus 26.3, which shows how the study of online discussion groups can be revealing about patterns of social relationships online.

Miller and Slater's (2000) ethnography of Internet use takes an approach that is rather more redolent of traditional ethnography than Markham's (see Research in focus 26.4). Its location in a particular place (Trinidad), its use of several methods of gathering data, and its commitment to observation (e.g. in cybercafés) are probably for many people closer to the traditional meanings of ethnography. As the authors put it: 'For us an ethnography does include participating, which may mean going on a chat line for the eight hours that informants will remain online, or participating in a room full of people playing networked Quake . . .' (Miller and Slater 2000: 22).

One of Miller and Slater's chief interests lay in the state of e-commerce in Trinidad. They found a situation in which there was considerable uncertainty at the time about how far to get into this business medium. There was recognition that the Internet should provide more than a means of advertising wares but little agreement beyond that. Thus, the clothing firms they studied recognized that the Internet could provide more than just a catalogue on a monitor screen, but the nature of any kind of alternative or additional interface represented an area of some uncertainty. Generally, however, consumers did little of their purchasing of goods on the Internet. Indeed, a Trinidadian cultural trait of seeking out things that are free would seem to militate against the use of the Internet for online purchasing.

A feature that is striking about all these studies from the point of view of anyone familiar with organizational behaviour research on technology is the way in which they treat the Internet as a technology as a 'given'. Recent thinking on technology and work has preferred to view technologies as texts that have 'interpretive flexibility' (Grint and Woolgar 1997). This notion means that the researcher needs to approach any technology through an examination of both the principles inscribed into it and how it is interpreted by users. Such a position is very much associated with the notion, previously encountered in Chapter 21, which suggests that the audiences of texts need to be the focus of attention as much as the texts themselves. Taking this position, Hine (2000: 9) locates the Internet 'as a product of culture: a technology that was produced by particular people with contextually situated goals and priorities. It is also a technology which is shaped by the ways in which it is marketed, taught and used'.

Research in focus 26.3
Participant observation in cyberspace

Kanayama (2003) describes her research on an online senior community in Japan as ethnographic and her own role as that of a 'participant observer'. She was interested in the nature of the virtual community that was formed out of an Internet group of senior citizens that had been founded in 1997. In the middle of 1999, there were 120 participants to the group, which is referred to as 'senior-ml'. Kanayama (2003: 274) describes her research approach as follows:

This study used participant observation to study all messages, which were posted on senior-ml from September 1999 to July 2000. I had participated in this group as a technical volunteer supporter for two years to help senior members use PCs and the internet, and subscribed to senior-ml, as did most technical volunteers of this group . . . I took a position as a non-active participant in the participant observation of this study. Many members, including representatives of the group, knew of the researcher's personal background. I also conducted in-depth interviews with six female and seven male members with their agreement by telephone . . .

Kanayama was interested in the experiences of the participants and particularly in patterns of interaction and the construction of online social relationships. She found that members of this virtual community were able to operate well with the medium and that they were able to construct real social relationships in cyberspace. As such they were able to provide a supportive environment for each other.

Research in focus 26.4
An ethnography of Internet use in Trinidad

Miller and Slater (2000) conducted ethnographic research on the use of the Internet in Trinidad. The first author had previously conducted research on the unfolding of modernity in Trinidad and drew on his prior research to help appreciate the context of the reception of the Internet in the country; Slater had previously conducted research on computer-mediated communication in the UK. This preamble is significant because it forms part of the authors' justification for describing their investigation as ethnographic. For Miller and Slater, an important component of ethnography is that it entails protracted involvement with the people one studies. In fact, the authors spent just five weeks in Trinidad for this study, so their prior experiences are invoked as a way of legitimizing the label 'ethnography'. Further, the authors consulted Internet websites on their return and interviewed Trinidadians in London and New York. They also maintained contact with informants after their return through email and 'chat'.

Overall, the following were the main methods:

1. Interviews 'largely devoted to the study of the political economy of the Internet, including businesses, the ISPs [Internet service providers] and government officers' (2000: 22).

2. Hanging around 'in cybercafés watching people go online and chatting with them. We also interviewed them more formally' (2000: 22).

3. Exploring with friends how the Internet had become intertwined with their lives.

4. A house-to-house survey in the same four areas in which Miller had previously conducted a similar investigation (see Chapter 25) to ascertain levels of Internet usage.

5. In-depth interviews with some of those contacted through the survey.

Like Markham, Miller and Slater found that the worlds of the Internet and of everyday life beyond the Internet are highly intertwined.

Hine describes her approach as one of 'virtual ethnography' (see Research in focus 26.5), which has a deliberate dual meaning: it is both an ethnography of being online—that is, of the virtual—and a virtual ethnography—that is, not quite an ethnography in any of the term's conventional settings. In particular, a virtual ethnography requires getting away from the idea that an ethnography is in or of a place in any traditional sense. It is also an ethnography of a domain that infiltrates other spaces and times of its participants, so that its boundedness is problematic to participants and analysts alike. As regards the issue of the interpretative flexibility of the Internet, Hine shows that there was some general agreement about its purposes as a technology. However, these purposes were not inscribed in the technology in the way that a technological determinist position might imply, but had arisen in the course of the use of the Internet. Moreover, Hine argues that the nature and capacities of the Internet have not become totally stabilized in the minds of participants and that gradual increments of change are likely in response to particular needs and purposes of participants.

Studies like these are clearly inviting us to consider the nature of the Internet as a domain for investigation, but they also invite us to consider the nature and the adapt-

ability of our research methods. In the examples discussed in this section, the question of what is and is not ethnography is given a layer of complexity that adds to the considerations about this issue that were referred to in Chapter 20. But these studies are also cases of using Internet-based research methods to investigate Internet use. Future online ethnographic investigations of issues unrelated to the Internet will give a clearer indication of the possibilities that the method offers.

Research in focus 26.5
Virtually an ethnography

Hine's (2000) research was concerned with the trial in 1997 in Boston of a British nanny (Louise Woodward) for the murder of the child in her charge, as well as the aftermath of the trial. Hine's data collection strategy included: searching out websites concerned with the case, which attracted a great deal of Internet interest; contacting web authors by email and asking a series of questions about their intentions, familiarity with the web, experiences, and so on; examining communication in newsgroups in which ten or more postings about the case had been made and posting a message in those groups; and contact with the official site that campaigned for Louise Woodward. In contacting web developers and newsgroup participants, Hine (2000: 78) writes:

> I introduced myself as a researcher in communications who was looking at the specific case of Louise Woodward on the Internet. I explained that I was concerned with how people got interested in the case, where they got their information from, and what they thought of the quality of information on newsgroups and web pages . . . I offered people a promise of confidentiality and the chance to check my own credentials through my website.

Hine did not receive a very good response to the newsgroup postings, which may reflect a tendency noticed by other researchers for newsgroup, MUD, listserv, and other participants to be sceptical about the use of their cyberdomains for research and suspicious about researchers who contact them. In her examination of newsgroup communication, Hine employed an approach that was heavily influenced by discourse analysis (see Chapter 20)—for example, by showing the discursive moves through which participants sought to construe the authenticity or factual nature of their information.

Research in focus 26.6
Researching cybercrime

Williams (2007) has conducted a great deal of research on cybercrime. His central research question is: 'what is the prevalence and nature of online deviant activity and how is it best regulated within online graphical communities? (Williams 2007: 457). He describes his research into Cyberworlds, an online social space that incorporates graphical representations and is an outgrowth of MUDs, which are text-based. Over a period of six months, Williams carried out more or less daily participant observation of this online community. He alerted community members through posted messages that he was a researcher studying them, an act that provoked a variety of responses. On the basis of their expressed concerns, Williams then decided in each case whether or not to continue his observations. As he notes, the ethical aspects of this process are not straight forward, as people are joining and leaving these online environments all the time. Once he had satisfied himself regarding the ethical issues, he joined Cyberworlds by becoming a citizen and using an online persona. He notes that one aspect of this virtual participant observation was easier than in conventional ethnography: he could take notes and use other data-collection devices without affecting the ongoing interaction in any way, since members were not able to see his offline actions.

One practical difficulty that was encountered related to the fact that Cyberworlds members are from a variety of countries, which, because of time differences, caused Williams problems relating to timing. In particular, the site is dominated by American members, who were coming online quite late in the day in terms of UK time. As a result, he says he was plagued with a nagging worry that he was missing something significant when he was not observing online. Eventually, he focused his observational activities on two 'worlds' that were well established. He describes his participant observation as entailing 'an overt but distanced approach . . . allowing for minimal interference and wide visual scope for observation' (Williams 2007: 463). His interests began to focus more and more on the language used (including the use of emoticons), such as turn-taking conventions. In addition, Williams carried out online focus groups with community members to gain an understanding of issues not amenable to observation. To recruit focus group participants, Williams sent out emails to over 1,000 individuals who were involved in relevant newsgroups. This procedure produced some concerned responses from newsgroup members who felt that their privacy had been violated. The focus groups were conducted asynchronously using a discussion list program. One interesting decision that Williams had to make was to choose what kind of virtual environment should be created as the 'venue' for the focus group (Stewart and Williams 2005).

Qualitative research using online focus groups

There is a crucial distinction between synchronous and asynchronous online focus groups. With the former, the focus group is in real time, so that contributions are made more or less immediately after previous contributions (whether from the moderator or other participants) among a group of participants all of whom are simultaneously online. Contributions can be responded to as soon as they are typed (and with some forms of software, the contributions can be seen as they are being typed). As Mann and Stewart (2000) observe, because several participants can type in a response to a contribution at the same time, the conventions of normal turn-taking in conversations are largely sidelined. If participants are in considerably different time zones, the organization of such groups can be slightly more difficult.

With asynchronous groups, focus group exchanges are not in real time. Email is one form of asynchronous communication that is sometimes used (see Research in focus 26.7 for an example). For example, the moderator might ask a question and then send the email containing it to focus group participants. The latter will be able to reply to the moderator and to other group members at some time in the future. Such groups get around the time zone problem and are probably easier than synchronous groups for participants who are not skilled at using the keyboard.

Conferencing software is used for synchronous groups and is often used for asynchronous groups as well. This may mean that focus group participants will require access to the software, which can be undesirable if the software needs to be loaded onto their computers. Participants may not feel confident about loading the software, and there may be compatibility problems with particular machines and operating systems.

Research in focus 26.7
An asynchronous focus group study

Adrianssens and Cadman (1999) report their experiences of conducting a market research exercise to explore the launch of an online share-trading platform in the UK. Participants were in two groups: one group of active shareholders (20 participants) and a second group of passive shareholders (10). They were identified through the MORI Financial Services database as 'upmarket shareholders who were also Internet users' (Adrianssens and Cadman 1999: 418–19). The participants who were identified were very geographically spread, so online focus groups were ideal. Questions were emailed to participants in five phases with a deadline for returning replies, which were then copied anonymously to the rest of the participants. The questions were sent in the body of the email, rather than as attachments, to solve problems of software incompatibility. After each phase, a summary document was produced and circulated to participants for comment, thus injecting a form of **respondent validation** into the project. The researchers found it difficult to ensure that participants kept to the deadlines, which in fact were rather tight, although it was felt that having a schedule of deadlines that was kept to as far as possible was helpful in preventing dropouts. The researchers felt that the group of active shareholders was too large to manage and suggest groups of no more than ten participants.

Selecting participants for online focus groups is potentially difficult, not least because they must normally have access to the necessary hardware and software. One possibility is to use questionnaires as a springboard for identifying possible participants. For their study of virtual communities concerned with consumption issues, Evans *et al.* (2001) used a combination of questionnaires (both paper and online) and focus groups made up of respondents to the questionnaires who had indicated a willingness to take further part in the research. The British focus groups were of the face-to-face kind, but, in addition, international respondents to the questionnaire who were prepared to be further involved in the research participated in an online focus group. Other sources of participants for online focus groups might involve postings on appropriate special interest websites or on such outlets as special interest bulletin boards or chat rooms.

The requisite number of participants is affected by the question of whether the online focus group is being conducted synchronously or asynchronously. Mann and Stewart (2000) advocate that, with the former type, the group should not be too large because it can make it difficult for some people to participate, possibly because of limited keyboard skills, and they recommend groups of between six and eight participants. Also, moderating the session can be more difficult with a large number. In asynchronous mode, such problems do not exist, and very

large groups can be accommodated—certainly much larger ones than could be envisaged in a face-to-face context, although Adrianssens and Cadman (1999) suggest that large groups can present research management problems.

Before starting the focus group, moderators are advised to send out a welcome message introducing the research and laying out some of the ground rules for the ongoing discussion. There is evidence that participants respond more positively if the researchers reveal something about themselves (Curasi 2001). This can be done in the opening message or by creating links to personal websites.

One problem with the asynchronous focus group is that moderators cannot be available online twenty-four hours a day, although it is not inconceivable that moderators could have a shift system to deal with this limitation. This lack of continuous availability means that emails or postings may be sent and responded to without any ability of the moderator to intervene or participate. This feature may not be a problem but could become so if offensive messages were being sent or if it meant that the discussion was going off at a complete tangent from which it would be difficult to redeem the situation. Further, because focus group sessions in asynchronous mode may go on for a long time, perhaps several days or even weeks, there is a greater likelihood of participants dropping out of the study.

Online focus groups are unlikely to replace their face-to-face counterparts. Instead, they are likely to be employed in connection with certain kinds of research topic and/or sample. As regards the latter, dispersed or inaccessible people are especially relevant to online focus group research. As Sweet (2001) points out, relevant topics are likely to be ones like those involving sensitive issues and ones concerned with Internet use; for example, Research in focus 26.7 and 26.8.

Research in focus 26.8
A synchronous focus group study

O'Connor and Madge (2001, 2003; see also Madge and O'Connor 2002) employed conferencing software in connection with a virtual focus group study of the use of online information for parents. The research was specifically concerned with one UK parenting website (**http://www.babyworld.co.uk** (accessed 1 October 2007)). Initially, the researchers set up a **web survey** (see later in the chapter for information about this technique) on the use of this website. When respondents sent in their questionnaire, they were thanked for their participation and asked to email the researchers if they were prepared to be interviewed in depth. Of the 155 respondents who returned questionnaires, 16 agreed to be interviewed. Interviewees were sent the software to install on their own machines. The researchers tried to ensure that each group was asked more or less the same questions, so the researchers worked in pairs whereby one cut and pasted questions into the discussion (or otherwise typed questions) and the other acted as a focus group moderator by thinking about the evolution of the discussion and about when and how to intervene. For each session, the researchers introduced themselves and asked participants to do likewise. In addition, they had placed descriptions and photographs of themselves on a website to which participants were directed. An important part of the process of building rapport was the fact that both of the researchers were mothers. One of the findings reported is that the greater anonymity afforded by the Internet gave participants greater confidence to ask embarrassing questions, a finding that has implications for online focus groups. This can be seen in the following extract:

Amy: I feel better askign BW [Babyworld] than my health visitor as they're not goign to see how bad I am at housekeeping!!!

Kerry: I feel the same. Like the HV [health visitor] is judging even though she says she isn't

Kerry: Although my HV has been a life line as I suffer from PND [post natal depression]

Amy: Also, there are some things that are so little that you don't want to feel like you're wasting anyone's time. Askign the HV or GP might get in the way of something mreo important, whereas sending an email, the person can answer it when convenient

Amy: My HV is very good, but her voice does sound patronising. I'msure she doesn't mean it, but it does get to me . . .

Kerry: Being anon means that you don't get embarassed asking about a little point or something personal (O'Connor and Madge 2001: 10.4)

It is striking that this brief extract reveals a good flow without intervention by the researchers. It contains several misspellings and mistakes (e.g. 'I'msure') but these are retained to preserve the reality of the interaction. The researchers did not have to transcribe the material because it was already in textual form. Also, the fact that participants appear to relish the anonymity of the Internet as a source of information has implications for online focus groups because it may be that participants find it easier to ask naive questions or to make potentially embarrassing comments than in face-to-face focus groups.

Tips and skills 'Advantages and disadvantages of online focus group and personal interviews compared to face-to-face interviews in qualitative research' summarizes the chief advantages and disadvantages of online relative to face-to-face focus groups. The discussion is combined with online personal interviews, which are the subject of the next section, since most of the elements in the balance sheet of advantages and disadvantages are the same.

Tips and skills
Advantages and disadvantages of online focus group and personal interviews compared to face-to-face interviews in qualitative research

This box summarizes the main advantages and disadvantages of online focus groups and personal interviews compared to their face-to-face counterparts. The two methods are combined because the tally of advantages and disadvantages applies more or less equally well to both of them.

Advantages

- Online interviews and focus groups are extremely cheap to conduct compared to comparable face-to-face equivalents. They are likely to take longer, however, especially when conducted asynchronously.

- Interviewees or focus group participants who would otherwise normally be inaccessible (e.g. because they are located in another country) or hard to involve in research (e.g. very senior executives, people with almost no time for participation) can more easily be involved.

- Interviewees and focus group participants are able to reread what they (and, in the case of focus groups, others) have previously written in their replies.

- People participating in the research may be better able to fit the interviews into their own time.

- People participating in the research do not have to make additional allowances for the time spent travelling to a focus group session.

- The interviews do not have to be audio-recorded, thus eliminating interviewee apprehension about speaking and being recorded.

- There is no need for **transcription**. This represents an enormous advantage because of time and cost involved in getting recorded interview sessions transcribed.

- Because of the previous point, the interview **transcripts** can be entered more or less immediately into a **CAQDAS** program of the kind introduced in Chapter 23.

- The transcripts of the interviews are more likely to be accurate because the problems that may arise from mishearing or not hearing at all what is said do not arise. This is a particular advantage with focus group discussions, because it can be difficult to establish who is speaking and impossible to distinguish what is said when participants speak at the same time.

- Focus group participants can employ pseudonyms so that their identity can be more easily concealed from others in the group. This can make it easier for participants to discuss potentially embarrassing issues or to divulge potentially unpopular views. It has also been suggested that electronic interviews may make the discussion of sensitive issues easier than in face-to-face interviews.

- In focus groups, shy or quiet participants may find it easier to come to the fore.

- Equally, in focus groups overbearing participants are less likely to predominate, but in synchronous groups variations in keyboard skills may militate slightly against equal participation.
- Participants are less likely to be influenced by characteristics such as the age, ethnicity, or appearance (and possibly even gender if pseudonyms are used) of other participants in a focus group.
- Similarly, interviewees and focus group participants are much less likely to be affected by characteristics of interviewers or moderators respectively, so that interviewer bias is less likely.
- When interviewees and participants are online at home, they are essentially being provided with an 'anonymous, safe and non-threatening environment' (O'Connor and Madge 2001: 11.2) that may be especially helpful to vulnerable groups.
- Similarly, researchers are not confronted with the potentially discomfiting experience of having to invade other people's homes or workplaces, which can themselves sometimes be unsafe environments.

Disadvantages

- Only people with access to online facilities and/or who find them relatively straightforward are likely to be in a position to participate.
- It can be more difficult for the interviewer to establish rapport and to engage with interviewees. However, when the topic is of interest to participants, this may not be a great problem.
- It can be difficult in asynchronous interviews to retain over a longer term any rapport that has been built up.
- Probing is more difficult though not impossible. Curasi (2001) reports some success in eliciting further information from respondents, but it is easier for interviewees to ignore or forget about the requests for further information or for expansion on answers given.
- Asynchronous interviews may take a very long time to complete depending on cooperativeness.
- With asynchronous interviews, there may be a greater tendency for interviewees to discontinue their participation than is likely to be the case with face-to-face interviews.
- There is less spontaneity of response, since interviewees can reflect on their answers to a much greater extent than is possible in a face-to-face situation. However, this can be construed as an advantage in some respects, since interviewees are likely to give more considered replies.
- There may be a tendency for **non-response** to be higher in online personal interviews.
- The researcher cannot be certain that the people who are interviewed are who they say they are (though this issue may apply on occasion to face-to-face interviews as well).
- In synchronous focus groups, variations in keyboard skills may make equal levels of participation difficult.
- Online interviews and focus groups from home require considerable commitment from interviewees and participants if they have to install software onto their computers and remain online for extended periods of time, thereby incurring expense (though it is possible to offer remuneration for such costs) and blocking their telephone lines.
- The interviewer/moderator may not be aware that the interviewee/participant is distracted by something and in such circumstances will continue to ask questions as if he or she had the person's full attention.
- Online connections may be lost, so research participants need to know what to do in the case of such an eventuality. Relatedly, longer-term breakdowns can undermine confidence and any momentum in interaction that has been built up.
- Interviewers cannot capitalize upon body language that might suggest puzzlement or in the case of focus groups a thwarted desire to contribute to the discussion.

Sources: Based on Clapper and Massey (1996); Adrianssens and Cadman (1999); Tse (1999); Mann and Stewart (2000); Curasi (2001); O'Connor and Madge (2001); Sweet (2001); Bampton and Cowton (2002); http://www.geog.le.ac.uk/orm/site/home.htm (accessed on 12 June 2007).

Qualitative research using online personal interviews

The issues involved in conducting online personal interviews for qualitative research are essentially the same as those to do with conducting online focus groups. In particular, the researcher must decide whether the interviews should take place in synchronous or asynchronous mode. The factors involved in deciding which to use are also largely the same, although issues to do with variable typing speed or computer-related knowledge among focus group participants will not apply.

Although online interviews run the risk relative to face-to-face interviews that the respondent is somewhat more likely to drop out of the exchange (especially in asynchronous mode, since the interviews can sometimes be very protracted), Mann and Stewart (2000: 138–9) suggest that in fact a relationship of mutual trust can be built up. This kind of relationship can make it easier for a longer-term commitment to the interview to be maintained, but also makes it easier for the researchers to go back to their interviewees for further information or reflections, something that is difficult to do with the face-to-face personal interview. The authors also suggest that it is important for interviewers to keep sending messages to respondents to reassure them that their written utterances are helpful and significant, especially since interviewing through the Internet is still an unfamiliar experience for most people.

A further issue for the online personal interviewer to consider is whether to send all the questions at once or to interview on the basis of a question followed by a reply. The problem with the former tactic is that respondents may read all the questions and reply only to those that they feel interested in or to which they feel they can make a genuine contribution, so that it is likely that asking one question at a time is likely to be more reliable. Bampton and Cowton (2002) report their experiences of conducting email interviews by sending questions in small batches. They argue that this approach took pressure off interviewees to reply quickly, gave them the opportunity to provide considered replies (although the authors recognize that there may be a loss of spontaneity), and gave the interviewers greater opportunity to respond to interviewees' answers.

There is evidence that prospective interviewees are more likely to agree to participate if their agreement is solicited prior to sending them questions and if the researcher uses some form of self-disclosure, such as directing the person being contacted to the researcher's website, which contains personal information, particularly information that might be relevant to the research issue (Curasi 2001; O'Connor and Madge 2001, 2003). The argument for obtaining prior agreement from interviewees before sending them questions to be asked is that unsolicited emails, often referred to as 'spamming', are regarded as a nuisance among online users and can result in an immediate refusal to take the message seriously.

Curasi (2001) conducted a comparison in which twenty-four online interviews carried out through email correspondence (and therefore asynchronous) were contrasted with twenty-four parallel face-to-face interviews. The interviews were concerned with shopping on the Internet. She found that:

- face-to-face interviewers were better able than online interviewers to maintain rapport with respondents;

- greater commitment and motivation are required for completing an online interview, but, because of this, replies were often more detailed and considered than with face-to-face interviews;

- online interviewers are less able to have an impact on whether the interview is successful or not because they are more remote;

- online interviewees' answers tend to be more considered and grammatically correct because they have more time to ponder their answers and because they can tidy them up before sending them. Whether this is a positive feature is debatable: there is the obvious advantage of a 'clean' transcript, but there may be some loss of spontaneity;

- follow-up probes could be carried out in online interviews, as well as in face-to-face ones.

On the other hand, Curasi also found that the worst interviews in terms of the amount of detail forthcoming were from online interviews. It may be that this and the other differences are to do with the fact that, whereas a qualitative face-to-face interview is *spoken*, the parallel online interview is *typed*. The full significance of this difference in the nature of the respondent's mode of answering has not been fully appreciated.

Some researchers have combined different types of interview in a single investigation. In addition to examining email and other forms of Internet-based communications for their study of online social support in the UK, Nettleton *et al.* (2002) interviewed fifty-one people involved in these communications. The interviewees were all approached by email after they had submitted relevant postings in the various lists that were being studied. In addition, some interviewees had responded to postings submitted by the research group. Some of these interviews were conducted face to face, some on the telephone, and still others online. One of the online interviews was with a woman in her 60s with ME. She brings across the importance of online social support for someone with this condition:

> The mailing list MECHAT . . . in particular has been a real lifeline. I check mail several times a day. I have been able to discuss things with people who understand . . . important as ME is an especially misunderstood illness . . . make new friends and share experiences and laughter . . . It is a real comfort if any trauma or upset occurs—death or illness of a loved one, relapse, relationship problems, or even just thoughtless remarks from folks who do not understand ME, which we would otherwise have to bear alone. (Nettleton *et al.* 2002: 183)

Thus far, most of the discussion of online personal interviewing assumes that the exchange is conducted entirely in a textual context (particularly by email). However, the webcam may offer further possibilities for synchronous online personal interviews should the technology become widespread. Such a development would make the online interview similar to a telephone interview, in that it is mediated by a technology, but also similar to an in-person interview, since those involved in the exchange would be able to see each other. However, one of the main advantages of the online interview would be lost, in that the respondent's answers would need to be transcribed, as in traditional qualitative interviewing.

At the time of writing, the possibilities associated with conducting online focus groups have probably attracted greater attention than online personal interviews, perhaps because the potential advantages are greater with the former. For example, with focus groups, a great deal of time and administration can be saved by online focus groups, whereas there is less comparable saving with online personal interviews unless a great deal of travel is involved.

Student experience
Using the Internet for supplementary data

Isabella Robbins wanted to interview mothers whose children had been vaccinated and those who had not been vaccinated. However, she found it difficult to find mothers in the latter group. This passage shows how she enlisted the Internet to help her to find supplementary data on mothers' decision-making in relation to the decision not to vaccinate their children, but it is also interesting and significant for her reliance on **theoretical saturation** (see Key concept 17.6).

> Recruitment of mothers was fairly straightforward in terms of the mothers who said they had vaccinated. However, recruiting mothers who had not vaccinated proved to be problematic. Essentially, because childhood vaccination is a moral issue, these mothers were careful about who they talked to about their resistance. They were a hard to get at community. With time running out I decided to use Internet message boards—from women/mothers forums—in order to supplement my data. This data helped to confirm that I had reached saturation. No new themes came out from it, but it provided some additional rich data.

To read more about Isabella's research experiences, go to the Online Resource Centre that accompanies this book at **http://www.oxfordtextbooks.co.uk/orc/brymansrm3e/**.

Online social surveys

There has been a considerable growth in the number of surveys being administered online. It is questionable whether the research instruments should be regarded as **structured interviews** (see Chapter 8) or as **self-completion questionnaires** (see Chapter 9)—in a sense they are both. So far as online social surveys are concerned there is a crucial distinction between surveys administered by email (email surveys) and surveys administered via the web (web surveys). In the case of the former, the questionnaire is sent via email to a respondent, whereas, with a web survey, the respondent is directed to a website in order to answer a questionnaire. Sheehan and Hoy (1999) suggest that there has been a tendency for email surveys to be employed in relation to 'smaller, more homogeneous on-line user groups', whereas web surveys have been used to study 'large groups of online users'.

Email surveys

With email surveys it is important to distinguish between **embedded and attached questionnaires sent by email**. In the case of the embedded questionnaire, the questions are to be found in the body of the email. There may be an introduction to the questionnaire followed by some marking that partitions the introduction from the questionnaire itself. Respondents have to indicate their replies using simple notations, such as an 'x', or they may be asked to delete alternatives that do not apply. If questions are open, they are asked to type in their answers. They then simply need to select the reply button to return their completed questionnaires to the researcher. With an attached questionnaire, the questionnaire arrives as an attachment to an email that introduces it. As with the embedded questionnaire, respondents must select and/or type their answers. To return the questionnaire, it must be attached to a reply email, although respondents may also be given the opportunity to fax or send the completed questionnaire by postal mail to the researcher (Sheehan and Hoy 1999).

The chief advantage of the embedded questionnaire is that it is easier for the respondent to return to the researcher and requires less computer expertise. Knowing how to read and then return an attachment requires a certain facility with handling online communication that is still not universally applicable. Also, the recipients' operating systems or software may present problems with reading attachments, while many respondents may refuse to open the attachment because of concerns about a virus. On the other hand, the limited formatting that is possible with most email software, such as using bold, variations in font size, indenting, and other features, makes the appearance of embedded questionnaires rather dull and featureless, although this limitation is rapidly changing. Furthermore, it is slightly easier for the respondent to type material into an attachment that uses well-known software like Microsoft Word, since, if the questionnaire is embedded in an email, the alignment of questions and answers may be lost.

Dommeyer and Moriarty (2000) compared the two forms of email survey in connection with an attitude study. The attached questionnaire was given a much wider range of embellishments in terms of appearance than was possible with the embedded one. Before conducting the survey, undergraduate students were asked about the relative appearance of the two formats. The attached questionnaire was deemed to be better looking, easier to complete, clearer in appearance, and better organized. The two formats were then administered to two random samples of students, all of whom were active email users. The researchers found a much higher response rate with the embedded than with the attached questionnaire (37 per cent versus 8 per cent), but there was little difference in terms of speed of response or whether questions were more likely to be omitted with one format rather than the other. Although Dommeyer and Moriarty (2000: 48) conclude that 'the attached e-mail survey presents too many obstacles to the potential respondent', it is important to appreciate that this study was conducted during what were still early days in the life of online surveys. It may be that, as prospective respondents become more adept at using online communication methods and as viruses become less of a threat (for example, as virus-checking software improves in terms of accessibility and cost), the concerns that led to the lower response rate for the attached questionnaire will be less pronounced. Also, the researchers do not appear to have established a prior contact with the students before sending out the questionnaires; it may be that the reaction to such an approach, which is frowned upon in the online community, may have been more negative in the case of the attached questionnaire format.

Web surveys

Web surveys operate by inviting prospective respondents to visit a website at which the questionnaire can be found and completed online. The web survey has an important advantage over the email survey in that it can use a much wider variety of embellishments in terms of appearance.

Plate 26.1 presents part of the questionnaire from the gym study from Chapter 14 in a web survey format and answered in the same way as in Tips and skills 'A completed and processed questionnaire'. Common features include 'radio buttons' (whereby the respondent makes a choice between closed question answers by clicking on a circle in which a dot appears—see question 1 in Plate 26.1) and pull-down menus of possible answers (see Plate 26.2). There are also greater possibilities in terms of the use of colour. With open questions, the respondent is invited to type directly into a boxed area (e.g. question 2 in Plate 26.1). It is worth noting at this juncture that there

Plate 26.1

Gym survey in web survey format

1. Are you male or female?

   ⦿ Male   ○ Female

2. How old are you?

   [21]

3. Which of the following best describes your main reason for going to the gym?
   Please select one only

   [Maintain or improve fitness ▾]   Other Answer: [_____]

4. When you go to the gym, how often to you use the cardiovascular equipment?

   ☑ Always   ☐ Usually   ☐ Rarely   ☐ Never

5. When you go to the gym, how often do you use the weights machines (including free weights)?

   ☑ Always   ☐ Usually   ☐ Rarely   ☐ Never

6. How frequently do you usually go to the gym?

   [2 or 3 days a week ▾]

Plate 26.2

A pull-down menu

3. Which of the following best describes your main reason for going to the gym?
Please select one only

| Maintain or improve fitness ▾ | Other Answer: [   ] |

— Select Answer —
Relaxation
Maintain or improve fitness
Lose weight
Meet others
Build strength

4. ...d to you use the cardiovascular equipment?

Rarely ☐ Never

is evidence that there is a problem with pull-down menus as a mechanism for presenting respondents with potential answers: when the list of possible answers is quite long, there is a tendency for respondents not to read the entire list and to choose one of the earlier answers (Couper *et al.* 2004). This implies that, for most instances, radio buttons will be preferable to pull-down menus when there are many possible answers. However, there is a trade-off here, in that pull-down menus have the advantage of taking up less room on the screen than radio buttons.

However, the advantages of the web survey are not just to do with appearance. The questionnaire can be designed so that when there is a filter question (e.g. 'if yes, go to question 12; if no, go to question 14'), it skips automatically to the next appropriate question. The questionnaire can also be programmed so that only one question ever appears on the screen or so that the respondent can scroll down and look at all questions in advance. Finally, respondents' answers can be automatically programmed to download into a database, thus eliminating the daunting coding of a large number of questionnaires. One of the chief problems with the web survey is that, in order to produce the attractive text and all the other features, the researcher will either have to be highly sophisticated in the use of HTML or will need to use one of a growing number of software packages that are designed to produce questionnaires with all the features that have been described.

Plates 26.1 and 26.2 were created using Survey Galaxy (http://www.surveygalaxy.com (accessed on 16 July 2007)), which my colleagues and I employed in a study of social policy researchers (Bryman *et al.* in press; Sempik *et al.* 2007). With commercial websites such as these, you can design your questionnaire online and then create a web address to which respondents can be directed in order to complete it. There is a fee for using this software. The fee will be affected by the number of respondents who complete the questionnaire and the length of time that the questionnaire is active. Each respondent's replies are logged and the entire data set can be retrieved once you decide the data-collection phase is complete. This means that there is no coding of replies and entering of data into your software. Not only does this save time; it also reduces the likelihood of errors in the processing of data.

Potential respondents need to be directed to the website containing the questionnaire. Research in focus 26.10 provides an example of the kind of approach that might be used. Where there are possible problems to do with restricting who may answer the questionnaire, it may be necessary to set up a password system to filter out people for whom the questionnaire is not appropriate.

Mixing modes of survey administration

The example in Research in focus 26.10 relates to a case in which a web survey is combined with a conventional self-administered questionnaire. When this occurs, there are two different modes of administration of the research instrument in operation. Mixed modes of administering a survey raise the question of whether the mode of administration matters; in other words, do you get different results when you administer a questionnaire online from when you administer it offline (for example, by handing a questionnaire or mailing it to respondents). Obviously, it would not be desirable to aggregate data from two different modes of administration if part of the variation in respondents' replies could be attributed to the way they received and completed the questionnaire. Equally, researchers using solely a web-based questionnaire need to know how far their findings are different from conventional modes of administration.

Experiments with different modes of administration are quite reassuring on this point. A study of self-reported illicit drug use among a large sample of US university students found that there were similar findings when the results from web- and paper-based questionnaire surveys were compared (McCabe 2004). The sample had been randomly assigned to either of the two modes of administration. Denscombe (2006) compared paper and web-based modes of administration of nearly identical questionnaires administered to young people at an East Midlands school. The questionnaire was concerned with perceptions of social issues. One batch of questions, which is explored in Denscombe's article, dealt with views about smoking. The findings confirmed McCabe's study in suggesting that there is little evidence that the mode of administration makes a significant difference to the findings. There was a lower incidence of self-reported smoking among those using the web-based questionnaire than those using the paper one. However, given the large number of items compared for a mode effect in Denscombe's study, it was likely that a small number would be found to exhibit a mode effect, so it would be unwise to read too much into this particular finding.

Given that the differences between modes of administration in surveys that combine a web-based mode with a conventional mode (such as a paper-based self-completion questionnaire) do not appear to be great, there is often a good case to be made for offering respondents an online option. A covering letter might draw prospective respondents' attention to a web-based option along with the necessary instructions for accessing it, so that those who prefer to work online are not put off responding to the questionnaire.

Sampling issues

Anyone who has read Chapter 7 must be wondering how the sampling principles described there might apply to online surveys. A major issue and limitation is that not everyone in any nation is online or has the technical abil-

ity to handle questionnaires online in either email or web formats. Certain other features of online communications make the issue more problematic, such as:

- many people have more than one email address;

- many people use more than one Internet service provider (ISP);

- a household may have one computer but several users;

- Internet users are a biased sample of the population in that they tend to be better educated, wealthier, younger, and not representative in ethnic terms (Couper 2000), although, as Internet access diffuses more and more, it is possible that some of these biases will become less prominent or even disappear;

- few sampling frames exist of the general online population and most of these are likely to be expensive to acquire since they are controlled by ISPs or may be confidential.

Such issues make the possibilities of conducting online surveys using probability sampling principles difficult to envisage. This is not to say that online surveys should not be considered. For example, in many organizations, most if not all non-manual workers are likely to be online and to be familiar with the details of using email and the Internet. Thus surveys of samples of online populations can be conducted using essentially the same probability sampling procedures. Similarly, surveys of members of commercially relevant online groups can be conducted using these principles. Smith (1997) conducted a survey of web presence providers (people or organizations that are involved in creating and maintaining web content). She acquired her sample from a directory of providers, which acted as her sampling frame. A further example of the use of a directory to generate a probability sample can be found in Research in focus 26.11. Research in focus 26.9 provides an interesting example of the use of a well-known website—*Friends Reunited*—as a means of finding people in the context of an unplanned longitudinal survey.

As Couper (2000: 485) notes of surveys of populations using probability sampling procedures: 'Intra-organizational surveys and those directed at users of the Internet were among the first to adopt this new survey technology. These restricted populations typically have no coverage problems or very high rates of coverage. Student surveys are a particular example of this approach that are growing in popularity.'

The chief problem with sampling strategies of the kind employed by Evans *et al.* (2001; see Research in focus

Research in focus 26.9
Using the web for an unplanned longitudinal survey: the case of *Friends Reunited*

One of the best-known websites in the UK in recent years has been *Friends Reunited* (**http://www.friendsreunited.co.uk** (accessed on 16 July 2007)). It is best known for its use as a platform for helping old school friends to meet each other once again. Power *et al.* (2005) report that in the mid-1990s they had received research funding to study the progress of young people who had been participants in an earlier study, when they were aged 12 or 13 years. In 2004 they received further funding to examine the same group when they would be in their early 30s. One of the main problems with following up research participants for a study such as this is finding them. *Friends Reunited* proved invaluable. Because *Friends Reunited* organizes its participants by school, it was relatively easy for the researchers to examine the *Friends Reunited* postings for each of the eighteen schools that had been involved in the project during the first wave of data collection. Also, because *Friends Reunited* organizes postings by the year the student left a school, the researchers could home in on the postings relating to particular years relevant to their sample. Further, because *Friends Reunited* participants tend to use their original names, tracking people who had changed their names (most obviously, because of marriage) made the process even easier. As a result, the researchers were able to find over 80 per cent of the original sample and over 90 per cent of those involved in the second wave of data collection.

The process of contacting people through *Friends Reunited* was not unproblematic, because the website does not allow direct communication with those who post messages. As the authors put it: 'This means that while you can send messages and inform people that they are part of a research cohort and you would like them to contact you, they then have to take the initiative and effort to locate you' (Power *et al.* 2005: 7). Further, as a result of the process of contacting participants through *Friends Reunited* and being contacted by them by email (once they had contacted the researchers), Power *et al.* point out that they became more reliant on the use of online questionnaires than they had originally anticipated.

26.10) is that we have no idea about the representativeness of those who answered the web survey questionnaire (though the same applies to the respondents to their paper-based questionnaire too). On the other hand, given that we have so little knowledge and understanding of online behaviour and attitudes relating to online issues, it could reasonably be argued that some information about these areas is a lot better than none at all, provided the limitations of the findings in terms of their **generalizability** is appreciated.

A further issue in relation to sampling and sampling-related error is the matter of *non-response* (see Key concept 7.1). There is growing evidence that online surveys typically generate lower response rates than **postal questionnaire** surveys (Tse 1998; Sheehan 2001). In the early years, response rates for email surveys were quite encouraging (Sheehan and Hoy 1999) but more recently they have been declining and are at lower levels than those

for most postal questionnaires (Sheehan 2001), though there are clear exceptions to this tendency (for example, see Research in focus 26.11). Two factors may account for this decline: the novelty of email surveys in the early years and a growing antipathy towards unsolicited emails among online communities. However, response rates can be boosted by following two simple strategies.

1. Contact prospective respondents before sending them a questionnaire. This is regarded as basic 'netiquette'.

2. As with postal questionnaire surveys, follow up non-respondents at least once.

The case for the first of these two strategies in boosting response rates is not entirely clear (Sheehan 2001) but seems to be generally advisable.

Crawford *et al.* (2001) report the results of a survey of students at the University of Michigan that experimented with a number of possible influences on the response rate.

Students in the sample were initially sent an email inviting them to visit the website, which allowed access, via a password, to the questionnaire. Some of those emailed were led to expect that the questionnaire would take 8–10 minutes to complete (in fact, it would take considerably longer); others were led to expect that it would take 20 minutes. As might be expected, those led to believe it would take longer were less likely to accept the invitation, resulting in a lower response rate for this group. However, Crawford *et al.* also found that those respondents who were led to believe that the questionnaire would take only 8–10 minutes were *more* likely to give up on the questionnaire part of the way through, resulting in unusable partially completed questionnaires in most cases. Interestingly, they also found that respondents were most likely to abandon their questionnaires part of the way through when in the middle of completing a series of open questions. The implications of this finding echo the advice in Chapter 9 that it is probably best to ask as few open questions in self-completion questionnaires as possible.

Further evidence regarding this survey suggests that having a progress indicator with a web survey can reduce the number of people who abandon the questionnaire part of the way through completion (Couper *et al.* 2001). A progress indicator is usually a diagrammatic representation of how far the respondent has progressed through the questionnaire at any particular point. Couper *et al.* also found that it took less time for respondents to complete related items (for example, a series of Likert items) when they appeared on a screen together than when they appeared singly. Respondents also seemed less inclined to omit related questions when they appeared together on a screen rather than singly.

However, it is important not be too sanguine about some of these findings. One difficulty with them is that the samples derive from populations whose members are not as different from one another as would almost certainly be found in samples deriving from general populations. Another is that it must not be forgotten that, as previously noted, access to the Internet is still not universal and there is evidence that those with web access differ from those without both in terms of personal characteristics and attitudinally. Fricker *et al.* (2005) compared the administration of a questionnaire by web survey and by telephone interview among a general US sample. They found that telephone interviewees were much more likely to complete the questionnaire (though it is possible if not probable that the same effect would have been noted if they had compared the web mode with a self-completion

mode). By contrast, telephone interviewees were more likely to omit questions by saying they had 'no opinion' than in the web administration, probably because respondents were prompted to answer if they failed to answer a question. One difficulty noted by Fricker *et al.* is that web respondents were more likely than telephone interviewees to give undifferentiated answers to series of questions like Likert items. In other words, they were more prone to response sets. Some of the questions were open questions inviting respondents to display their knowledge on certain issues. The researchers found that Web respondents took longer to answer the questions and were more likely to provide valid answers than the telephone interviewees.

These findings suggest that it is difficult and probably impossible, given their relative newness, to provide a definitive verdict on web surveys compared to traditional forms of survey administration. For one thing, it is difficult to separate out the particular formats that researchers use when experimenting with modes of administration from the modes themselves. It may be that if they had displayed web questions in a different manner, their findings would have been different—with obvious implications for how the web survey fares when compared with any of the traditional forms. Further, web surveys seem to work better than traditional survey forms in some respects better than others. On the day I was writing this (24 January 2007), I was sent my quotation of the day by http://www.quotationspage.com/qotd.html, which was written by the noted social theorist Thorstein Veblen. Apparently, he once wrote: 'The outcome of any serious research can only be to make two questions grow where only one grew before.' That is certainly true where developmental work on the web survey is concerned!

Tips and skills 'Advantages and disadvantages of online surveys compared to postal questionnaire surveys' summarizes the main factors to take into account when comparing online surveys with postal questionnaire surveys, and Table 26.1 compares the different methods of administering a survey.

Overview

Online surveys are clearly in their infancy but they have considerable potential. There is evidence that having a web survey or even an email option can boost response rates to postal questionnaires (Yun and Trumbo 2000). Several problems have been identified with web and email surveys but it is too early to dismiss them because methodologists are only beginning to get to grips with

Table 26.1

The strengths of email and web-based surveys in relation to other modes of survey administration

Issues to consider	Mode of survey administration				
	Email	Web	Face-to-face interview	Telephone interview	Postal questionnaire
Resource issues					
Is the cost of the mode of administration relatively low?	✓✓✓	✓ (unless access to low-cost software)	✓	✓✓	✓✓✓
Is the speed of the mode of administration relatively fast?	✓✓✓	✓✓✓	✓	✓✓✓	✓✓✓
Is the cost of handling a dispersed sample relatively low?	✓✓✓	✓✓✓	✓ (✓✓ if clustered)	✓✓✓	✓✓✓
Does the researcher require little technical expertise for devising a questionnaire?	✓✓	✓	✓✓✓	✓✓✓	✓✓✓
Sampling-related issues					
Does the mode of administration tend to produce a good response rate?	✓	✓	✓✓✓	✓✓	✓
Is the researcher able to control who responds (i.e. the person at whom it is targeted is the person who answers)?	✓✓	✓✓	✓✓✓	✓✓✓	✓✓
Is the mode of administration accessible to all sample members?	✓ (because of need for respondents to be accessible online)	✓ (because of need for respondents to be accessible online)	✓✓✓	✓✓	✓✓✓
Questionnaire issues					
Is the mode of administration suitable for long questionnaires?	✓✓	✓✓	✓✓✓	✓✓	✓✓
Is the mode of administration suitable for complex questions?	✓✓	✓✓	✓✓✓	✓	✓✓
Is the mode of administration suitable for open questions?	✓✓	✓✓	✓✓✓	✓✓	✓
Is the mode of administration suitable for filter questions?	✓	✓✓✓ (if allows jumping)	✓✓✓ (especially if CAPI used)	✓✓✓ (especially if CATI used)	✓
Does the mode of administration allow control over order questions are answered?	✓	✓	✓✓✓	✓✓✓	✓
Is the mode of administration suitable for sensitive questions?	✓✓✓	✓✓✓	✓	✓✓	✓✓✓
Is the mode of administration less likely to result in non-response to some questions?	✓✓	✓✓	✓✓✓	✓✓✓	✓✓
Does the mode of administration allow the use of visual aids?	✓✓	✓✓✓	✓✓✓	✓	✓✓✓
Answering context issues					
Does the mode of administration give respondents the opportunity to consult others for information?	✓✓✓	✓✓✓	✓✓	✓	✓✓✓

Table 26.1

Continued

Issues to consider	Mode of survey administration				
	Email	Web	Face-to-face interview	Telephone interview	Postal questionnaire
Does the mode of administration minimize the impact of interviewers' characteristics (gender, class, ethnicity)?	✓✓✓	✓✓✓	✓	✓✓	✓✓✓
Does the mode of administration minimize the impact of the social desirability effect?	✓✓✓	✓✓✓	✓	✓✓	✓✓✓
Does the mode of administration allow control over the intrusion of others in answering questions?	✓	✓	✓✓✓	✓✓	✓
Does the mode of administration minimize the need for respondents to have certain skills to answer questions?	✓ (because of need to have online skills)	✓ (because of need to have online skills)	✓✓✓	✓✓✓	✓✓
Does the mode of administration enable respondents to be probed?	✓✓	✓	✓✓✓	✓✓✓	✓

Notes: Number of ticks indicates the strength of the mode of administration of a questionnaire in relation to each issue. More ticks correspond to more advantages in relation to each issue. A single tick implies that the mode of administering a questionnaire does not fare well in terms of the issue in question. Three ticks imply that it does very well, but two ticks imply that it is acceptable. This table has been influenced by the author's own experiences and by Dillman (1978) and Czaja and Blair (1996).
CAPI is computer-assisted personal interviewing; CATI is computer-assisted telephone interviewing.

this approach to survey research and may gradually develop ways of overcoming the limitations that are being identified. Moreover, as I have pointed out, for certain kinds of populations and as more and more people and organizations go online, some of the sampling-related problems will diminish. As Yun and Trumbo (2000) observe: 'the electronic-only survey is advisable when resources are limited and the target population suits an electronic survey.'

It is also worth making the obvious point that, when conducting an online survey, you should bear in mind the principles about sampling, interview design, and question construction that were posed in Chapters 7 through 10 in particular. While online surveys are distinctive in certain ways, they require the same rigorous considerations that go into the design of conventional surveys that are conducted by postal questionnaire or by personal or telephone interview.

Research in focus 26.10
Combining a paper survey with a web survey

As part of their research into virtual communities concerned with consumption issues, Evans *et al.* (2001) carried out a survey using two methods of administration. First, they distributed a paper-based questionnaire at various locations at the University of Bristol and the University of West of England, Bristol, and at three cybercafés. Second, they used a web survey hosted by the Bristol Business School, which was linked via BBC Bristol Online and a cybercafé. The authors write: 'Invitations to respond to the on-line questionnaire were posted on several electronic lists within the two Bristol universities, and several international discussion lists' (Evans *et al.* 2001: 152). As a result of these two strategies, over 300 questionnaires were returned.

Tips and skills
Using Internet surveys to supplement traditional postal questionnaire surveys

There is a growing tendency for researchers who conduct postal questionnaire surveys to offer their respondents the opportunity to complete their questionnaires online (Couper 2000). This can be done by indicating in the covering letter that goes out with the postal questionnaire that they can have the questionnaire emailed to them or, if the questionnaire is accessible via the Internet, they can be directed to the web address. The advantage of doing this is that some of the samples of respondents may feel more comfortable completing the questionnaire online because of the long periods of time they spend online and it removes the need to return the questionnaire by post. There is the question of whether the mode of administration (postal as against online) influences the kinds of response received, but some research suggests that the impact of mode of administration is not great.

Research in focus 26.11
Sampling for an online survey

Cobanoglu *et al.* (2001) report the results of a study in which three different modes of survey administration were used: post, fax, and online. The questionnaires were administered to 300 hospitality professors in the USA who had been randomly sampled from the online directory of the Council on Hotel, Restaurant, and Institutional Education. The sampling was carried out only from those who had an email address. The 300 professors were randomly assigned to one of the three modes of survey administration. The authors write:

> For the web-based survey, an email message was sent to the professors along with a cover letter and the website address. The respondents were informed that they could request a paper copy of the survey should they have problems accessing the survey online. A unique website address was created for each respondent . . . (Cobanoglu *et al.* 2001: 447)

Compared with the postal administration of the questionnaire, the online administration achieved a higher response rate (26 per cent versus 44 per cent), a faster response speed, and was cheaper.

Tips and skills
Advantages and disadvantages of online surveys compared to postal questionnaire surveys

Here I summarize the main advantages and disadvantages of online surveys compared to postal questionnaire surveys. The tally of advantages and disadvantages in connection with online surveys relates to both email and web surveys. It should also be made clear that, by and large, online surveys and postal questionnaires suffer from one disadvantage relative to personal and telephone interviews—namely, that the researcher can never be certain that the person answering questions is who the researcher believes him or her to be.

Advantages

- *Low cost.* Even though postal questionnaire surveys are cheap to administer, there is evidence that email surveys in particular are cheaper. This is in part due to the cost of postage, paper, envelopes, and the time taken to stuff covering letters and questionnaires into envelopes with postal questionnaire surveys. However, with web surveys there may be start-up costs associated with the software needed to produce the questionnaire. But the low-cost advantage of Internet surveys increases as the sample size increases. When viewed in relation to the overall amount of time invested in conducting a survey, the cost advantage of an Internet survey over other modes of administration for small surveys is probably not as great as is often presumed.

- *Faster response.* Online surveys tend to be returned considerably more quickly than postal questionnaires.

- *Attractive formats.* With web surveys, there is the opportunity to use a wide variety of stylistic formats for presenting questionnaires and closed question answers. Also, automatic skipping when using filter questions and the possibility of immediate downloading of questionnaire replies into a database make this kind of survey quite attractive for researchers.

- *Mixed administration.* Online surveys can be combined with postal questionnaire surveys so that respondents have the option of replying by post or online. Moreover, the mode of administration does not seem to make a significant difference to the kinds of replies generated.

- *Unrestricted compass.* There are no constraints in terms of geographical coverage. The same might be said of postal questionnaire surveys, but the problems of sending respondents stamped-addressed envelopes that can be used in their own countries is overcome.

- *Fewer unanswered questions.* There is evidence that online questionnaires are completed with fewer unanswered questions than postal questionnaires, resulting in less **missing data**. However, there is also evidence of little difference between the two modes of administering surveys.

- *Better response to open questions.* To the extent that open questions are used, they tend to be more likely to be answered online and to result in more detailed replies.

Disadvantages

- *Low response rate.* Typically, response rates to online surveys are lower than those for comparable postal questionnaire surveys.

- *Restricted to online populations.* Only people who are available online can reasonably be expected to participate in an online survey. This restriction may gradually ease over time, but, since the online population differs in significant ways from the non-online population, it is likely to remain a difficulty. On the other hand, if online populations are the focus of interest, this disadvantage is unlikely to prove an obstacle.

- *Requires motivation.* Because online survey respondents must be online to answer the questionnaire, if they are having to pay for the connection and perhaps are tying up their telephone lines, they may need a higher level of motivation than postal questionnaire respondents. This suggests that the solicitation to participate must be especially persuasive.

- *Confidentiality and anonymity issues.* It is normal for survey researchers to indicate that respondents' replies will be confidential and that they will be anonymous. The same suggestions can and should be made with respect to online surveys. However, with email surveys, since the recipient must return the questionnaire either embedded within the message or as an attachment, respondents may find it difficult to believe that their replies really are confidential and will be treated anonymously. In this respect, web surveys may have an advantage over email surveys.

- *Multiple replies.* With web surveys, there is a risk that some people may mischievously complete the questionnaire more than once. There is much less risk of this with email surveys.

Sources: Based on Schaeffer and Dillman (1998); Tse (1998); Kent and Lee (1999); Sheehan and Hoy (1999); Cobanoglu *et al.* (2001); Fricker and Schonlau (2002); Denscombe (2006); **http://www.geog.le.ac.uk/orm/site/home.htm** (accessed on 3 July 2007).

Ethical considerations in Internet research

Conducting research by using the Internet as a method of data collection raises specific ethical issues which are only now starting to be widely discussed and debated. Some of these are related to the vast array of venues or environments in which these new forms of communication and possibilities for research occur, including weblogs, listservs or discussion groups, email, chat rooms, instant messaging, and newsgroups. The behaviour of Internet users is governed by 'netiquette', the conventions of politeness or definitions of acceptable behaviour that are recognized by online communities, as well as by service providers' acceptable use policies and by data protection legislation, and those contemplating using the Internet as a method of data collection should start by familiarizing themselves with these and by considering the general ethical principles discussed in Chapter 5. However, this section is concerned with the specific ethical issues raised by Internet research. One of the problems faced by social researchers wanting to use the Internet for data collection is that we are clearly in the middle of a huge growth in the amount of research being conducted in this way (Williams 2007). Not only is this trend creating the problem of over-researched populations who suffer from respondent fatigue; many of those involved in doing research with this new technology are not adhering to ethical principles. As a result, fatigue and suspicion are beginning to set in among prospective research participants, creating a less than ideal environment for future Internet researchers.

The Association of Internet Researchers recommends that researchers start by considering the ethical expectations established by the venue (http://www.aoir.org/reports/ethics.pdf (accessed on 12 June 2007)). For instance, is there a posted site polity that notifies users that the site is public and specifies the limits to privacy? Or are there mechanisms that users can employ to indicate that their exchanges are private? The more the venue is acknowledged to be public, the less obligation there is on the researcher to protect the confidentiality and anonymity of individuals using the venue, or to seek their informed consent. However, the distinction between public and private space on the Internet is blurred and contested. Hewson *et al.* (2003) suggest that data that have been deliberately and voluntarily made available in the public Internet domain, such as newsgroups, can be used by researchers without the need for informed

consent, provided anonymity of individuals is protected. In the course of her research on websites for female sex workers and their male clients, Sanders (2005) acted as a 'lurker', whereby she observed the activity on message boards without revealing her identity as a researcher, so that she was essentially a covert non-participant observer. She did not reveal her identity because she did not want to have an impact on participants' behaviour and did not want to trigger hostility that might adversely affect her research. Certainly, some researchers (e.g. Hudson and Bruckman 2004) have found that, although certain Internet venues might be considered by some to be public spaces, entering online environments and recording the conversation for research purposes can provoke hostile responses from users (Research in focus 26.12 and 26.13). In the case of the use of the *Friends Reunited* website (Research in focus 26.9), the researchers do not report irritation among respondents about being contacted through *Friends Reunited* because many remembered the previous contact with the researchers, though they do acknowledge that 'overuse of the website for research purposes might ultimately irritate members and lead to it being prohibited' (Power *et al.* 2005: 8).

Barnes (2004) identifies five types of Internet message, each presenting slightly different ethical concerns for anonymity, confidentiality, and informed consent.

1. *Messages exchanged in online public discussion lists.* A typical forum for these would be discussion groups, MUDs, or newsgroups. Although most group members see their messages as public, Barnes (2004) found that some consider them as private, despite having been sent statements upon joining the group indicating the public nature of the space. Barnes (2004) recommends as a general principle that the ideas of individuals who share their ideas on public lists should be attributed to their authors in the same way as you would attribute something they had written in a printed text under traditional copyright law. However, it is a good idea to check the welcoming messages of public discussion lists for guidance on how to cite email messages. Some discussion groups state that researchers must notify the group in advance of any research being undertaken. She advises that when researching any Internet group it is a good idea to contact members in advance and ask for permission to observe them.

2. *Messages exchanged in private discussions between individuals and on private lists.* Barnes (2004) suggests in this situation the names of the lists and participants should never be revealed. Further to protect individual identities, she recommends that messages are combined, all headers and signatures are removed, references to the exact type of forum being studied are not made, and behaviour is described in general terms in a composite personality type rather than by referring to specific messages that could be traced to particular individuals.

3. *Personal messages sent to the researcher.* In Barnes's (2004) research messages were sent on to her by a contact who had already deleted the names and email addresses of the original sender, but in any case she suggests that headers and signatures are removed to protect the authors' anonymity.

4. *Messages reposed and passed around the Internet.* Such messages include those that people forward on to other people and to discussion lists because they think they are interesting. They can contain the name of the original author or be distributed as anonymous email. If they are distributed anonymously, Barnes (2004) believes it is worth trying to find the original author so that they can be properly credited in a research publication. She advises emailing the author and asking for permission to use the message.

5. *Messages generated by computer programs.* This refers to messages generated by natural language computer programs that form the basis for interaction with people.

There may also be specific ethical considerations associated with certain types of research, such as virtual ethnography (see Research in focus 26.13).

Research in focus 26.12
Chat room users' responses to being studied

Hudson and Bruckman (2004) designed an experiment to understand how potential participants react to being invited to participate in an online study. This involved entering a number of online moderated chat rooms and informing the participants that they were recording them and then recording how they responded. They downloaded a list of available chat rooms on 'ICQ Chat' each evening at 9.50 p.m. Dividing the chat rooms by size from very small (2–4 participants) to large (30 or more participants), they then randomly selected sixteen chat rooms from each set, then subdivided these into groups of four. Each group of four chat rooms was sent a different message as follows:

- *No Message.* The researchers entered the chat room using the nickname 'Chat Study' and said nothing.
- *Recording Message.* The researchers entered the chatroom as 'Chat Study' and announced that they were recording the chat room for a study.
- *Opt Out Message.* The researchers entered the chat room in the same way as above but posted a message giving the participants the option not to be recorded.
- *Opt In Message.* The researchers entered the chat room in the same way as before but gave participants the option to volunteer to be recorded.

Using a sample of 525 chat rooms studied over a two-week period, Hudson and Bruckman found that posting a message about the study resulted in significant hostility, greatly increasing the likelihood of researchers being kicked out of the chat room by the moderator. Moreover, the likelihood of being kicked out of a chat room decreased as the number of participants in the chatroom increased. The reasons given for being kicked out included referring to the study as 'spamming' (unwanted electronic communication often involving some form of commercial advertising), objection to being studied, general requests to leave, and insults. When given a chance to opt in, only 4 of the 766 potential respondents actually did so. Hence, even when the option of fully informed consent was given, chat room participants still objected to being studied. The researchers conclude that 'these results suggest that obtaining consent for studying online chatrooms is impracticable' (Hudson and Bruckman 2004: 135). This example highlights the potential ethical difficulties in intruding on a pre-existing Internet communication venue for research purposes, even if it is considered to be a public space.

A further ethical issue relates to the principle of protecting research participants from harm (see Chapter 5) and the related issues of individual anonymity and confidentiality. Complete protection of anonymity is suggested by Stewart and Williams (2005) to be almost impossible in Internet research, since, in computer-mediated communication, information about the origin of a computer-generated message, revealed for instance in the header, is very difficult to remove. It is also more difficult to guarantee confidentiality, because the data are often accessible to other participants. In a similar vein, DeLorme *et al.* (2001) suggest that the Internet raises particular ethical concerns for qualitative researchers that arise from the difficulty of knowing who has access to information. For example, a message posted on an Internet discussion group can be accessed by any-

one who has a computer and an Internet connection. In addition, some Internet environments enable 'lurkers', people who listen to what is going on without making themselves identifiable. This makes it difficult for researchers to protect the confidentiality of data that they collect. A further concern arises from the potential for individuals to present a 'fake' identity during online interaction. If a research participant does this, it has implications for the validity of the data, but there is also potential for the researcher to deceive participants in the expectation that this will encourage them to respond more openly, for example, by pretending to be a man when conducting a focus group with all male participants. This is thus a form of covert research that, as discussed in Chapter 5, raises particular ethical issues because of the lack of informed consent.

Research in focus 26.13
Ethical issues in a virtual ethnography of change in the NHS

There have also been some attempts to highlight the ethical considerations associated with particular kinds of Internet research such as virtual ethnography. Smith (2004) was interested in organizational change and the role played by professionals in the NHS. While she was in the process of doing her research, she came across a listserv that was being used by British general practitioners (GPs) as a forum to discuss their feelings about the proposed reforms to the British health care system and their likely effects. She explains 'essentially, I had stumbled on a "setting" in which GPs were "talking" among themselves about the significance of the proposed health care reforms for them as individuals, for the wider profession and generally about the future of general practice in Britain' (2004: 225). The geographically dispersed nature of GPs' work meant that the list provided a unique opportunity for them to interact with each other. Smith argues that one of the advantages of such virtual methods is that it provides opportunity to conduct research with virtually no observer effects (see Research in focus 2.5). Therefore, her strategy was covert because, she explains, 'I anticipated difficulties in informing participants about my research without intruding in the ongoing interaction to an unacceptable extent' (2004: 232) and feared that this might also arouse hostility because of the way she observed that 'spam' messages were received unfavourably. For fifteen months she 'participated' in the list by receiving and reading messages daily without explicitly stating or explaining her presence to the majority of the listserv's members. A further difficulty in seeking informed consent arose from the nature of the list as an unmoderated forum; therefore there was no gatekeeper to whom she could address her request. Added to this, the membership of the list of around 500 members was in constant flux, so any single request for consent would have been impossible. Hence 'the only appropriate way to gain informed consent would be to repeatedly post requests to the entire list. Through my previous exposure to the list, however, I knew that such behavior was clearly out of line with accepted practice in this domain' (2004: 233).

However, as Smith explains: 'I am aware that in making the decision not to expound my presence on the list, I may face considerable ethical critique. My research appears analogous with the notion of "covert" research so demonized in the usual discussions of research ethics' (2004: 225). One of the ways in which she justifies this is through discussion of the features of her study that distinguish it from other studies of virtual interaction. She notes how her study examined interaction between participants who were not engaged in the kinds of 'fantasy interaction' associated with sexual or social virtual interaction. Therefore, Smith argues, her participants were not taking the opportunity to 'engage in behavior with which they would not be comfortable engaging as part of their "real" lives' (2004: 228). A further ethical justification of her research arises from the extent to which participants saw the list as a public rather than a private space. Hence, the warning posted to each member on subscription and at monthly intervals states 'MEMBERS ARE ADVISED TO CONSIDER COMMENTS POSTED TO LISTX TO BE IN THE PUBLIC DOMAIN' (2004: 229; capitalization in original). In addition, list members receive guidelines on the copyright implications of email messages, which state that comments posted to public lists are comparable to sending letters to a newspaper editor. Smith suggests that this provides justification for her 'electronic eavesdropping', since the ethical guidelines she was working to suggested that it was 'not necessary to explicitly seek permission for recording and analyzing publicly posted messages' because this is 'akin to conducting research in a marketplace, library or other public area, where observers are not necessarily expected to obtain informed consent from all present' (2004: 230).

A final ethical issue arising from the study concerns the principle of anonymity. Initially, Smith assumed she should protect the identity of participants when reporting her research findings, but through her involvement in the list she became aware that 'participants might wish to be "credited" for their postings' (2004: 234) because of the reaction when journalists used list messages without crediting the authors. However, despite this she felt that, because she had not sought informed consent from all list members, it would be wrong to do this.

These concerns have led some researchers to suggest that there is a need for an ethics code for Internet research. DeLorme *et al.* (2001) surveyed qualitative researchers to find out whether they felt there was a need for an ethics code for qualitative researchers using the Internet and, if so, what kinds of issues it should cover. A majority of respondents thought that there should be an ethics code for qualitative Internet research. When asked what their reasons were for believing this, researchers expressed a rationale based on principles, driven by a professional view of what constitutes good research, and a practical rationale, based on the belief that dishonest practices will discourage Internet users from taking part in future online studies and undermine the reputation of legitimate researchers who use the Internet. DeLorme *et al.* (2001) suggest that ethics codes designed by professional associations such as those discussed in Chapter 5 need to be revised to include an addendum that deals with these issues. However, the debates about the ethics of Internet research and the development of guidelines for researchers are ongoing, and, even though traditional ethical guidelines may need to be revised to reflect the ethical issues raised by Internet research, researchers should continue to be guided by the ethical principles discussed in Chapter 5.

Student experience
The ethics of Internet research

As noted in a Student experience feature earlier in this chapter, Isabella Robbins used Internet message boards to gain additional data on mothers whose children had not been vaccinated. She was concerned about the ethics of using these media, and this is how she dealt with the issues.

In terms of the ethics of using data from the Internet, I would argue that the Internet is in the realm of the public sphere. I decided that I did not want to contact the women on the message board, because I considered this forum did provide these women with a useful forum in which to debate difficult issues. I considered it unethical to break into that forum. I don't consider that what I was doing was covert. The message board had very visual reminders that the message board is a public space, warning women not to use names, addresses, and phone numbers (although some did). I did contact the press office of the message board, and they referred me to their terms and conditions of using the message board. This acknowledged that it is a public space, and that people using it take responsibility for that. They did not object to me using this data. I told them what I intended to do with it, and that the message board and data would be anonymysed.

 To read more about Isabella's research experiences, go to the Online Resource Centre that accompanies this book at http://www.oxfordtextbooks.co.uk/orc/brymansrm3e/.

Key points

- The growth in the use of the Internet offers significant opportunities for social researchers in allowing them access to a large and growing body of people.
- Many research methods covered elsewhere in this book can be adapted to online investigations.
- There is a distinction between research that uses websites as objects of analysis and research that uses the Internet to collect data from others.
- Online surveys may be of either of two major types: web surveys and email surveys.
- Most of the same considerations that go into designing research that is not online apply to e-research.
- Both quantitative and qualitative research can be adapted to e-research.
- There is growing concern about the ethical aspects of e-research.

Questions for review

The Internet as object of analysis

- In what ways might the analysis of websites pose particular difficulties that are less likely to be encountered in the analysis of non-electronic documents?

Using the Internet to collect data from individuals

- What are the chief ways of collecting data from individuals using the World Wide Web and online communications?
- What advantages do they have over traditional research methods for collecting such data?
- What disadvantages do they have in comparison with traditional research methods for collecting such data?
- What is the difference between web-based and communication-based research methods?

An ethnography of the Internet?

- How does ethnography need to be adapted in order to collect data on the use of the Internet?
- Does the study of the impact of the Internet necessarily mean that we end up as technological determinists?
- Are ethnographies of the Internet really ethnographic?

Qualitative research using online focus groups

- What is the significance of the distinction between synchronous and asynchronous focus groups?
- How different is the role of the moderator in online, as against face-to-face, focus groups?

Qualitative research using online personal interviews

- Can online personal interviews really be personal interviews? To what extent does the absence of direct contact mean that the online interview cannot be a true interview?

Online social surveys

- What is the significance of the distinction between email and web surveys?
- Are there any special circumstances in which embedded email questionnaires will be more likely to be effective than attached questionnaires?
- Do sampling problems render online social surveys too problematic to warrant serious consideration?
- Are response rates in online surveys worse or better than in traditional surveys?

Ethical considerations in Internet research

- What ethical issues are raised by using the Internet as a method of data collection?

Online Resource Centre

http://www.oxfordtextbooks.co.uk/orc/brymansrm3e/

Visit the Online Resource Centre that accompanies this book to enrich your understanding of e-research. Consult web links, test yourself using multiple choice questions, and gain further guidance and inspiration from the Student Researcher's Toolkit.

Writing up social research

Chapter outline

Chapter guide

It is easy to forget that one of the main stages in any research project, regardless of its size, is that it has to be written up. Not only is this how you will convey your findings, but being aware of the significance of writing is crucial, because your audience must be persuaded about the credibility and importance of your research. This chapter presents some of the characteristics of the writing-up of social research. The chapter explores:

- why writing, and especially good writing, is important to social research;
- using examples, how **quantitative** and **qualitative research** are composed;
- the influence and implications of **postmodernism** for writing;
- key issues raised by discussions about the writing of **ethnography**, an area in which discussions about writing have been especially prominent.

Introduction

The aim of this chapter is to examine some of the strategies that are employed in writing up social research. Initially, we will explore the question of whether quantitative and qualitative research reveal divergent approaches. As we will see, the similarities are frequently more striking and apparent than the differences. However, the main point of this chapter is to extract some principles of good practice that can be developed and incorporated into your own writing. This is an important issue, since many people find writing up research more difficult than carrying it out. On the other hand, many people treat the writing-up stage as relatively unproblematic. But no matter how well research is conducted, others (that is, your readers) have to be convinced about the credibility of the knowledge claims you are making. Good writing is therefore very much to do with developing your style so that it is *persuasive* and *convincing*. Flat, lifeless, uncertain writing does not have the power to persuade and convince. In exploring these issues, I will touch on rhetorical strategies in the writing of social research (see Thinking deeply 27.2). As Atkinson (1990: 2) has observed in relation to social research, 'the conventions of text and rhetoric are among the ways in which reality is *constructed*'. This chapter will review some of the ways in which social research is written up in a way that will provide some basic ideas about structuring your own written work if you have to produce something like a dissertation.

Key concept 27.1
What is rhetoric?

The study of rhetoric is fundamentally concerned with the ways in which attempts to convince or persuade an audience are formulated. We often encounter the term in a negative context, such as 'mere rhetoric' or the opposition of 'rhetoric and reality'. However, rhetoric is an essential ingredient of writing, because when we write our aim is to convince others about the credibility of our knowledge claims. To suggest that rhetoric should somehow be suppressed makes little sense, since it is in fact a basic feature of writing. The examination of rhetorical strategies in written texts based on social research is concerned with the identification of the techniques in those texts that are designed to convince and persuade.

Writing up your research

It is easy to neglect the writing stage of your work because of the difficulties that you often encounter in getting your research under way. But—obvious though this point is—your dissertation has to be written. Your findings must be conveyed to an audience, something that all of us who carry out research have to face. The first bit of advice is . . .

Start early

It is easy to take the view that the writing-up of your research findings is something that you can think about after you have collected and analysed your data. There is, of course, a grain of truth in this view, in that you could hardly write up your findings until you know what they are, which is something that you can know only once you have gathered and analysed your data. However, there are good reasons for beginning writing early on, since you might want to start thinking about such issues as how best to present and justify the research questions that are driving your research or how to structure the theoretical and research literature that will have been used to frame your research questions. Students often tend to underestimate the time that it will take to write up their research, so it is a good idea to allow plenty of time for this, especially if you are expecting your supervisor to read and comment on an early draft, since you will need to allow him or her a reasonable amount of time for this. A further reason why it is advisable to begin writing earlier rather than later is an entirely practical one: many people find it difficult to get started and employ (probably unwittingly) procrastination strategies to put off the inevitable. This tendency can result in the writing being left until the last minute and consequently rushed. Writing under this kind of pressure is not ideal. How you represent your findings and conclusions is a crucial stage in the research process. If you do not provide a convincing account of your research, you will not do justice to it.

Student experience
Writing up is difficult

Several of the students mentioned that they found writing up difficult. Gareth Matthews comments that he 'found this stage the most difficult'. Isabella Robbins admits that writing the chapters presenting her findings was 'the most difficult task of the Ph.D. process'. Having enough time for writing up is a common refrain in their questionnaires. Sarah Hanson's advice is:

> The only problem with a writing project of this size is time. As it is always against you, start early, and be organized, do one thing at a time. Work chronologically. Lecturers and markers like to see that you have gone on a journey of exploration into an interesting world and at the end have come out with something worthwhile that has changed your thinking and will hopefully challenge theirs.

*To read more about Gareth's, Isabella's, and Sarah's research experiences, go to the Online Resource Centre that accompanies this book at **http://www.oxfordtextbooks.co.uk/orc/brymansrm3e/**.*

Be persuasive

This point is crucial. Writing up your research is not simply a matter of reporting your findings and drawing some conclusions. Writing up your research will contain many other features, such as referring to the literature on which you drew, explaining how you did your research, and outlining how you conducted your analysis. But above all, you must be *persuasive*. This means that you must convince your readers of the credibility of your conclusions. Simply saying 'this is what I found; isn't it interesting' is not enough. You must persuade your readers that your findings and conclusion are significant and that they are plausible.

Get feedback

Try to get as much feedback on your writing as possible and respond positively to the points anyone makes about what they read. Your supervisor is likely to be the main source of feedback, but institutions vary in what supervisors are allowed to comment on. Provide your supervisor with drafts of your work to the fullest extent that regulations will allow. Give him or her plenty of time to provide feedback. There will be others like you who will want

your supervisor to comment on their work, and, if he or she feels rushed, the comments may be less helpful. Also, you could ask others on the same degree programme to read your drafts and comment on them. They may ask you to do the same. Their comments may be very useful, but, by and large, your supervisor's comments are the main ones you should seek out.

Avoid sexist, racist, and disablist language

Remember that your writing should be free of sexist, racist, and disablist language. The British Sociological Association provides very good general and specific advice about this issue, which can be found at http://www.britsoc.co.uk/equality/ (accessed on 16 July 2007).

Tips and skills
Non-sexist writing

One of the biggest problems (but by no means the only one) when trying to write in a non-sexist way is avoiding complex his/her formulations. The easiest way of dealing with this is to write in the plural in such circumstances. Consider, for example: 'I wanted to give each respondent the opportunity to complete the questionnaire in his or her own time and in a location that was convenient for him or her.' This is a rather tortuous sentence and, although grammatically correct, it could be phrased more helpfully as: 'I wanted to give respondents the opportunity to complete their questionnaires in their own time and in a location that was convenient for them.

Structure your writing

It may be that you have to write a dissertation of around 10,000–15,000 words for your degree. How might it be structured? The following is typical of the structure of a dissertation.

Title page

You should examine your institution's rules about what should be entered here.

Acknowledgements

You might want to acknowledge the help of various people, such as gatekeepers who gave you access to an

organization, people who have read your drafts and provided you with feedback, or your supervisor for his or her advice.

List of contents

Your institution may have recommendations or prescriptions about the form this should take.

An abstract

A brief summary of your dissertation. Not all institutions require this component, so check on whether it is required. Journal articles usually have abstracts, so you can draw on these for guidance on how to approach this task.

Introduction

The following are some points to consider when writing an introduction.

- You should explain what you are writing about and why it is important. Saying simply that it interests you because of a long-standing personal interest is not enough.

- You might indicate in general terms the theoretical approach or perspective you will be using and why.

- You should also at this point outline your research questions. In the case of dissertations based on qualitative research, it is likely that your research questions will be rather more open-ended than is the case with quantitative research. But do try to identify some research questions. A totally open-ended research focus is risky and can lead to the collection of too much data, and, when it comes to writing up, it can result in a lack of focus.

- The opening sentence or sentences are often the most difficult of all. Becker (1986) advises strongly against opening sentences that he describes as 'vacuous' and 'evasive'. He gives the example of 'This study deals with the problem of careers', and adds that this kind of sentence employs 'a typically evasive manœuvre, pointing to something without saying anything, or anything much, about it. *What* about careers?' (Becker 1986: 51). He suggests that such evasiveness often

occurs because of concerns about giving away the plot. In fact, he argues, it is much better to give readers a quick and clear indication of what is going to be meted out to them and where it is going.

Literature review

See Chapter 4 for more detailed advice on how to go about writing this chapter of your dissertation.

Research methods

The term 'research methods' is meant here as a kind of catch-all for several issues that need to be outlined: your research design; your sampling approach; how access was achieved if relevant; the procedures you used (such as, if you sent out a postal questionnaire, did you follow up non-respondents); the nature of your questionnaire, interview schedule, participant observation role, observation schedule, coding frame, or whatever (these will usually appear in an appendix, but you should comment on such things as your style of questioning or observation and why you asked the things you did); problems of non-response; note taking; issues of ongoing access and cooperation; coding matters; and how you proceeded with your analysis. When discussing each of these issues, you should describe and defend the choices that you made, such as why you used a postal questionnaire rather than a structured interview approach, or why you focused upon that particular population for sampling purposes.

Tips and skills
The importance of an argument

In my experience, one of the things that students find most difficult about writing up their research is the formulation of an argument. The writing-up of research should be organized around an argument that links all aspects of the research process from problem formulation, through literature review and the presentation of research methods, to the discussion and conclusion. Too often, students make a series of points without asking what the contribution of those points is to the overall argument that they are trying to present. Consider what your claim to knowledge is and try to organize your writing to support and enhance it. That will be your argument. Sometimes it is useful to think in terms of seeking to tell a story about your research and your findings. Try to avoid tangents and irrelevant material that may mean that your readers will lose the thread of your argument. If you are not able to supply a clear argument, you are very vulnerable to the 'so what?' question. Ask yourself: 'What is the key point or message that I want my readers to take away with them when they have finished reading my work?' If you cannot answer that simple question satisfactorily (and it may be worth trying it out on others), almost certainly you do not have an argument. The argument is a thread that runs through your dissertation (see Figure 27.1 for an illustration of this).

Figure 27.1

The role of an argument in a dissertation

Introduction	A
Literature review	R G
Research methods	U
Results	M E
Discussion	N
Conclusion	T

Results

In this chapter you present the bulk of your findings. If you intend to have a separate Discussion chapter, it is likely that the results will be presented with little commentary in terms of the literature or the implications of your findings. If there will be no Discussion chapter, you will need to provide some reflections on the significance of your findings for your research questions and for the literature. Bear these points in mind.

- Whichever approach you take, remember not to include *all* your results. You should present and discuss only those findings that relate to your research questions. This requirement may mean a rather painful process of leaving out many findings, but it is necessary, so that the thread of your argument is not lost (see Tips and skills 'The importance of an argument' for more on the significance of having a good argument).

- Your writing should point to particularly salient aspects of the tables, graphs, or other forms of analysis you present. Do not just summarize what a table shows; you should direct the reader to the component or components of it that are especially striking from the point of view of your research questions. Try to ask yourself what story you want the table to convey and try to relay that story to your readers.

- Another sin to be avoided is simply presenting a graph or table or a section of the transcript of a semi-structured interview or focus group session without

any comment whatsoever, because the reader is left wondering why you think the finding is important.

- When reporting quantitative findings, it is quite a good idea to vary wherever possible the method of presenting results—for example, provide a mixture of diagrams and tables. However, you must remember the lessons of Chapter 14 concerning the methods of analysis that are appropriate to different types of variable.

- A particular problem that can arise with qualitative research is that students find it difficult to leave out large parts of their data. As one experienced qualitative researcher has put it: 'The major problem we face in qualitative inquiry is not to get data, but to get rid of it!' (Wolcott 1990a: 18). He goes on to say that the 'critical task in qualitative research is not to accumulate all the data you can, but to "can" [i.e. get rid of] most of the data you accumulate' (Wolcott 1990a: 35). You simply have to recognize that much of the rich data you accumulate will have to be jettisoned. If you do not do this, any sense of an argument in your work is likely to be lost. There is also the risk that your account of your findings will appear too descriptive and lack an analytical edge. This is why it is important to use research questions as a focus and to orient the presentation of your findings to them. It is also important to keep in mind the theoretical ideas and the literature that have framed your work. The theory and literature that have influenced your thinking will also have shaped your research questions.

Student experience
Do not try to write up everything

You will not be able to write up everything that you have found. Sophie Mason recognized this. She writes:

> The great quantity of data meant that I had to use my own judgement as to what data was the most relevant to the aims of the research. I also had to be careful to use visual aids when using complicated statistics to emphasize the importance of the results.

Rebecca Barnes writes:

> Because so many important and interesting issues have emerged in the analysis of my data, I have had to be selective; I have chosen to do justice to a smaller number of themes, rather than resorting to superficial coverage of a larger number of themes.

*To read more about Sophie's and Rebecca's research experiences, go to the Online Resource Centre that accompanies this book at **http://www.oxfordtextbooks.co.uk/orc/brymansrm3e/**.*

Student experience
The importance of research questions, theory, and the literature in writing up findings

Several students mentioned how important it was for them to keep in mind their research questions and the theory and literature that were driving their research while writing up. For one thing, they help the student to decide which findings to include or to emphasize when writing up. Rebecca Barnes writes:

> I chose to have three chapters of my thesis that reported my findings, and I chose the themes that I would include in each of these chapters. These were not, however, set in stone, and have changed in a number of respects from when I first started to plan the writing-up. Each of these chapters addresses one of my main research questions or aims.

Erin Sanders writes: 'First I wrote down the main points and ideas I wanted to get across—and how my findings related to [my] research question.' Hannah Creane's writing-up of her findings was geared to her research questions.

> I grouped together questions and responses that concerned similar aspects within the childhood debate and formed three main chapters: What makes a child a child?; Childhood past times; and The child today. Within these chapters I interwove themes that emerged from the data and seemed to be present in most responses.

For Gareth Matthews the theoretical debates about the labour process were crucial: 'This has allowed me to frame my thesis theoretically, and to lay the foundations for a discussion of my empirical findings.'

*To read more about Rebecca's, Erin's, Hannah's, and Gareth's research experiences, go to the Online Resource Centre that accompanies this book at **http://www.oxfordtextbooks.co.uk/orc/brymansrm3e/**.*

- If you are writing a thesis—for example, for an M.Phil. or Ph.D. degree—it is likely that you will have more than one and possibly several chapters in which you present your results. Cryer (1996) recommends showing at the beginning of each chapter the particular issues that are being examined in the chapter. You should indicate which research question or questions are being addressed in the chapter and provide some signposts about what will be included in the chapter. In the conclusion of the chapter, you should make clear what your results have shown and draw out any links that might be made with the next results chapter.

Discussion

In the Discussion, you reflect on the implications of your findings for the research questions that have driven your research. In other words, how do your results illuminate your research questions? If you have specified hypotheses, the discussion will revolve around whether the hypotheses have been confirmed or not, and, if not, you might speculate about some possible reasons for and the implications of their refutation.

Conclusion

The main points here are as follows.

- A Conclusion is not the same as a summary. However, it is frequently useful to bring out in the opening paragraph of the Conclusion your argument thus far. This will mean relating your findings and your discussion of them to your research questions. Thus, your brief summary should be a means of hammering home to your readers the significance of what you have done.
- You should make clear the implications of your findings for your research questions.

- You might suggest some ways in which your findings have implications for theories relating to your area of interest.
- You might draw attention to any limitations of your research with the benefit of hindsight, but it is probably best not to overdo this element and provide examiners with too much ammunition that might be used against you!
- It is often valuable to propose areas of further research that are suggested by your findings.
- Two things to avoid are engaging in speculations that take you too far away from your data, or that cannot be substantiated by the data, and introducing issues or ideas that have not previously been brought up.

Appendices

In your appendices you might want to include such things as your questionnaire, coding frame, or observation schedule, letters sent to sample members, and letters sent to and received from gatekeepers where the cooperation of an organization was required.

References

Include here all references cited in the text. For the format of the References section you should follow whichever one is prescribed by your department. Nowadays, the format is usually a variation of the Harvard method, such as the one employed for this book.

Finally

Remember to fulfil any obligations you entered into, such as supplying a copy of your dissertation, if, for example, your access to an organization was predicated on providing one, and maintaining the confidentiality of information supplied and the anonymity of your informants and other research participants.

Student experience
Structure of the dissertation or thesis

Some of the students wrote up their work with a similar structure to the one that has been outlined in this section. Sophie Mason writes:

The research project was written in various stages and split into several different sections; these were as follows: Introduction and Aims, Literature Review, Research Design and Data Gathering, Data Analysis and Research Findings, Conclusions and Recommendations, Appendix and Bibliography.

Erin Sanders writes:

I wrote it in order, introduction, literature review, research design, findings, discussion, and conclusion. I took each section as if it were an essay in and of itself, and attempted to break it down into chunks so as not to get lost in a long document.

To read more about Sophie's and Erin's research experiences, go to the Online Resource Centre that accompanies this book at http://www.oxfordtextbooks.co.uk/orc/brymansrm3e/.

Tips and skills
Proof reading your dissertation

Before submitting your dissertation, make sure that it is spell-checked and check it for grammatical and punctuation errors. There are many useful guides and handbooks that can be used for this purpose. It may also be useful to ask someone else, such as a friend or family member, to proof read your work in case there are errors that you have missed. As well as being an important presentational issue, this will affect the ease with which your written work can be read and understood. It therefore has the potential to affect the quality of your dissertation significantly.

Writing up quantitative, qualitative, and mixed methods research

In the next three sections, research-based articles that have been published in journals are examined to detect some helpful features. One is based on quantitative research, one on qualitative research, and another on mixed methods research. The presentation of the quantitative and the qualitative research articles raises the question of whether practitioners of the two research strategies employ different writing approaches. It is sometimes suggested that they do, though, when I compared two articles based on research in the sociology of work, I found that the differences were less pronounced than I had anticipated on the basis of reading the literature on the topic (Bryman 1998). One difference that I have noticed is that, in journals, quantitative researchers often give more detailed accounts of their research design, research methods, and approaches to analysis than qualitative researchers. This is surprising, because, in books reporting their research, qualitative researchers provide detailed accounts of these areas. Indeed, the chapters in Part Three of this book rely heavily on these accounts. Wolcott (1990a: 27) has also noticed this

tendency: 'Our [qualitative researchers'] failure to render full and complete disclosure about our data-gathering procedures give our methodologically oriented colleagues fits. And rightly so, especially for those among them willing to accept our contributions if we would only provide more careful data about our data.' Being informed that a study was based on a year's participant observation or a number of semi-structured interviews is not enough to gain an acceptance of the claims to credibility that a writer might be wishing to convey.

However, this point aside, in the discussion that follows, although one article based on quantitative research and one based on qualitative research will be examined, we should not be too surprised if they turn out to be more similar than might have been expected. In other words, although we might have expected clear differences between the two in terms of their approaches to writing, the similarities are more noticeable than the differences.

In addition to looking at examples of writing in quantitative and qualitative research, I will examine the matter of how mixed methods research can be written up and explore some guidelines that are being proffered by practitioners. The approach to dealing with the mixed methods research article is slightly different from the other two in that I will begin with some general suggestions for writing up mixed methods research as this is an area that has not been given a great deal of attention.

Writing up quantitative research

To illustrate some of the characteristics of the way quantitative research is written up for academic journals, I will take the article by Kelley and De Graaf (1997) that was referred to on several occasions in Chapters 1, 2, 6, and 13 (see especially Research in focus 1.4 and 6.3). I am not suggesting that this article is somehow exemplary or representative, but rather that it exhibits some features that are often regarded as desirable qualities in terms of presentation and structure. The article is based on a secondary analysis of survey data on religion in fifteen nations and was accepted for publication in one of the most prestigious journals in sociology—the *American Sociological Review*, which is the official journal of the American Sociological Association. The vast majority of published articles in academic journals entail the blind refereeing of articles submitted. This means that an article will be read by two or three peers, who comment on the article and give the editors a judgement about its merits and hence whether it is worthy of publication. Most articles submitted are rejected. With highly prestigious journals, it is common for in excess of 90 per cent of articles to be rejected. It is unusual for an article to be accepted on its first submission. Usually, the referees will suggest areas that need revising and the author (or authors) is expected to respond to that feedback. Revised versions of articles are usually sent back to the referees for further comment, and this process may result in the author having to revise the draft yet again. It may even result in rejection. Therefore, an article like Kelley and De Graaf's is not just the culmination of a research process, but is also the outcome of a feedback process. The fact that it has been accepted for publication, when many others have been rejected, testifies to its merits as having met the standards of the journal. That is not to say it is perfect, but the refereeing process is an indication that it does possess certain crucial qualities.

Structure

The article has the following components, aside from the abstract:

1. introduction;
2. theory;
3. data;
4. measurement;
5. methods and models;
6. results;
7. conclusion.

Introduction

Right at the beginning of the introduction, the opening four sentences attempt to grab our attention, to give a clear indication of where the article's focus lies, and to provide an indication of the probable significance of the findings. This is what the authors write:

> Religion remains a central element of modern life, shaping people's world-views, moral standards, family lives, and in many nations, their politics. But in many Western nations, modernization and secularization may be eroding Christian beliefs, with profound consequences that have intrigued sociologists since Durkheim. Yet this much touted secularization may be overstated—certainly it varies widely among nations and is absent in the United States (Benson, Donahue, and Erickson 1989: 154–7; Felling, Peters, and Schreuder 1991; Firebaugh and Harley 1991; Stark and Iannaccone 1994). We explore the degree to which religious beliefs are passed on from generation to generation in different nations. (Kelley and De Graaf 1997: 639)

This is an impressive start, because, in just over 100 words, the authors set out what the article is about and its significance. Let us look at what each sentence achieves.

- The first sentence locates the article's research focus as addressing an important aspect of modern society that touches on many people's lives.

- The second sentence notes that there is variety among Western nations in the importance of religion and that the variations may have 'profound consequences'. But this sentence does more than the first sentence: it also suggests that this is an area that has been of interest to sociologists. To support this point, one of sociology's most venerated figures—Émile Durkheim— is mentioned.

- The third sentence suggests that there is a problem with the notion of secularization, which has been a research focus for many sociologists of religion. Several fairly recent articles are cited to support the authors' contention that there is a possibility that secularization is being exaggerated by some commentators. In this sentence, the authors are moving towards a rationale for their article that is more in terms of sociological concerns than pointing to social changes, which are the main concern of the two opening sentences.

- Then in the fourth sentence the authors set up their specific contribution to this area—the exploration of the passing-on of religious beliefs between generations.

So, by the end of four sentences, the contribution that the article is claiming to make to our understanding of religion in modern society has been outlined and situated within an established literature on the topic. This is quite a powerful start to the article, because the reader knows what the article is about and the particular case the authors are making for their contribution to the literature on the subject.

Theory

In this section, existing ideas and research on the topic of religious socialization are presented. The authors point to the impact of parents and other people on children's religious beliefs, but then assert that 'a person's religious environment is also shaped by factors other than their own and their parents' religious beliefs, and hence is a potential cause of those beliefs . . .' (Kelley and De Graaf 1997: 641). This suggestion is then justified, which prompts the authors to argue that 'prominent among these "unchosen" aspects of one's religious environment is birthplace' (1997: 641). Kelley and De Graaf's ruminations on this issue lead them to propose the first of three hypotheses, which is presented in Research in focus 1.4. This hypothesis stipulates that contextual factors have an impact on religious beliefs. This leads the authors to suggest in two related hypotheses that, in predominantly secular societies, family background will have a greater impact on a person's religious beliefs than in predominantly devout societies, because in the former parents and other family members are more likely to seek to isolate children from secular influences. However, in devout societies this insulation process is less necessary and the influence of national factors will be greater. Thus, we end up with very clear research questions, which have been arrived at by reflecting on existing ideas and research in this area.

Data

In this section, the authors outline the data they drew on for their research. This exposition entails a general outline of the data sets. The quotation on page 299 is taken from this commentary. The sampling procedures are outlined along with sample sizes and response rates.

Measurement

In this section, Kelley and De Graaf explain how the main concepts in their research were measured. The concepts were: *religious belief* (the questionnaire items used are in Research in focus 6.3); *parents' church attendance*; *secular and religious nations* (that is, the scoring procedure for indicating the degree to which a nation was religious or secular in orientation on a five-point scale); *other contextual characteristics of nations* (for example, whether a former Communist nation or not); and *individual characteristics* (for example, age and gender).

Methods and models

This is a very technical section, which outlines the different ways in which the relationships between the variables might be conceptualized and the implications of using different mutivariate analysis approaches for the ensuing findings.

Results

The authors provide a general description of their findings and then consider whether the hypotheses *are* supported. In fact, it turns out the hypotheses are supported. The significance of other contextual characteristics of nations and individual differences are separately explored.

Conclusion

In this final section, Kelley and De Graaf return to the issues that have been driving their investigation. These are the issues they had presented in the Introduction and Theory sections. They begin the section with a strong statement of their findings: 'The religious environment of a nation has a major impact on the beliefs of its citizens: People living in religious nations acquire, in proportion to the orthodoxy of their fellow citizens, more orthodox beliefs than those living in secular nations' (Kelley and De Graaf 1997: 654). They then reflect on the implications of the confirmation of their hypotheses for our understanding of the process of religious socialization and religious beliefs. They also address the implications of their findings for certain theories about religious beliefs in modern society, which were outlined in their Theory section:

> Our results also speak to the long-running debate about US exceptionalism (Warner 1993): They support the view that the United States is unusually religious. . . . Our results do not support Stark and Iannaccone's (1994) 'supply-side' analysis of differences between nations which argues that nations with religious monopolies have substantial unmet religious needs, while churches in religiously competitive nations like the United States do a better job of meeting diverse religious needs. (Kelley and De Graaf 1997: 655)

The final paragraph spells out some inferences about the ways in which social changes have an impact on levels of religious belief in a nation. The authors suggest that factors such as modernization and the growth of education depress levels of religious belief and that their impact tends to result in a precipitous rather than a gradual fall in levels of religiosity. In their final three sentences, they go on to write about societies undergoing such change:

> The offspring of devout families mostly remain devout, but the offspring of more secular families now strongly tend to be secular. A self-reinforcing spiral of secularization then sets in, shifting the nation's average religiosity ever further away from orthodoxy. So after generations of stability, religious belief declines abruptly in the course of a few generations to the modest levels seen in many Western nations. (Kelley and De Graaf 1997: 656)

It might be argued that these reflections are somewhat risky, because the data from which the authors derive their findings are cross-sectional in research design terms rather than longitudinal. They are clearly extrapolating from their scoring of the fifteen nations in terms of levels of modernization to the impact of social changes on national levels of religiosity. However, these final sentences make for a strong conclusion, which itself might form a springboard for further research.

Lessons

What lessons can be learned from Kelley and De Graaf's article? To some extent, these have been alluded to in the course of the above exposition, but they are worth spelling out.

- There is a clear attempt to grab the reader's attention with strong opening statements, which also act as signposts to what the article is about.
- The authors spell out clearly the rationale of their research. This entails pointing to the continued significance of religion in many societies and to the literature on religious beliefs and secularization.
- The research questions are spelled out in a very specific way. In fact, the authors present hypotheses that are a highly specific form of research question. As noted in Chapter 6, by no means all quantitative research is driven by hypotheses, even though outlines of the nature of quantitative research often imply that it is. Nonetheless, Kelley and De Graaf chose to frame their research questions in this form.
- The nature of the data, the measurement of concepts, the sampling, the research methods employed and the approaches to the analysis of the data are clearly and explicitly summarized in sections 3, 4, and 5.
- The presentation of the findings in section 6 is oriented very specifically to the research questions that drive the research.
- The conclusion returns to the research questions and spells out the implications of the findings for them and for the theories examined in section 2. This is an important element. It is easy to forget that you should think of the research process as closing a circle in which you must return unambiguously to your research questions. There is no point inserting extraneous findings if they do not illuminate your research questions. Digressions of this kind can be confusing to readers, who might be inclined to wonder about the significance of the extraneous findings.

We also see that there is a clear sequential process moving from the formulation of the research questions through the exposition of the nature of the data and the presentation of the findings to the conclusions. Each stage is linked to and follows on from its predecessor (but see Thinking deeply 27.1). The structure used by Kelley and De Graaf is based on a common one employed in the writing-up of quantitative research for academic journals in the social sciences. Sometimes there is a separate Discussion section that appears between the Results and the Conclusion. Another variation is that issues of measurement and analysis appear in the same section as the one dealing with research methods, but perhaps with distinct subheadings.

Thinking deeply 27.1
An empiricist repertoire?

At this point, it is worth recalling the discussion in Chapter 20 of Gilbert and Mulkay's (1984) research on scientists. The authors drew a distinction between an *empiricist repertoire* and a *contingent repertoire*. The former derived from 'the observation that the texts of experimental papers display certain recurrent stylistic, grammatical and lexical features which appear to be coherently related' (Gilbert and Mulkay 1984: 55–6). We should bear in mind that the same is true of papers written for social science journals. These too display certain features that suggest a certain inevitability to the outcome of the research. In other words, the reader is given a sense that, in following the rigorous procedures outlined in the article, the researchers logically arrived at their conclusions. The contingent repertoire, with its recognition of the role of the researcher in the production of findings, is far less apparent in scientists' published work. Thus, we have to recognize the possibility that the impression of a series of linked stages leading to an inescapable culmination is to a large extent a reconstruction of events designed to persuade referees (who, of course, use the same tactics themselves) of the credibility and importance of one's findings. This means that the conventions about writing up a quantitative research project, some of which are outlined in this chapter, are in many ways an invitation to reconstruct an investigation in a particular way. The whole issue of the ways in which the writing-up of research represents a means of persuading others of the credibility of one's knowledge claims has been a particular preoccupation among qualitative researchers (see below) and has been greatly influenced by the surge of interest in postmodernism. However, in Thinking deeply 27.2, some of the rhetorical strategies involved in writing up quantitative social research are outlined. Three points are worth making about these strategies in the present context. First, they are characteristic of the empiricist repertoire. Second, while the writing of qualitative research has been a particular focus in recent times (see below), some attention has also been paid to quantitative research. Third, when I compared the writing of quantitative and qualitative research articles, I found they were not as dissimilar in terms of rhetorical strategies as is sometimes proposed (Bryman 1998). However, I did find greater evidence of a management metaphor (see Thinking deeply 27.2), which is also evident in Kelley and De Graaf's article; for example, 'we excluded the deviant cases from our analysis' (1997: 646) and 'we divided the nations into five groups' (1997: 647).

Writing up qualitative research

Now we will look at an example of a journal article based on qualitative research. Again, I am not suggesting that the article is exemplary or representative, but that it exhibits some features that are often regarded as desirable qualities in terms of presentation and structure. The article is one that has been referred to in several previous chapters (especially Research in focus 2.10, 18.2, and 18.8): a study of vegetarianism by Beardsworth and Keil (1992). The study is based on semi-structured interviews and was published in the *Sociological Review*, a leading British journal.

Structure

The structure runs as follows:

1. introduction;
2. the analysis of the social dimensions of food and eating;
3. studies of vegetarianism;
4. the design of the study;
5. the findings of the study;
6. explaining contemporary vegetarianism;
7. conclusions.

What is immediately striking about the structure is that it is not dissimilar to Kelley and De Graaf's (1997). Nor should this be all that surprising. After all, a structure that runs

Introduction → Literature review → Research design/ methods → Results → Discussion → Conclusions is not obviously associated with one research strategy rather than the other. One difference from quantitative research articles is that the presentation of the results and the discussion of them are frequently rather more interwoven in qualitative research articles. We will see this in the case of Beardsworth and Keil's article. As with Kelley and De Graaf's article, we will examine the writing in terms of the article's structure.

Introduction

The first four sentences give us an immediate sense of what the article is about and where its focus lies:

> The purpose of this paper is to offer a contribution to the analysis of the cultural and sociological factors which influence patterns of food selection and food avoidance. The specific focus is contemporary vegetarianism, a complex of inter-related beliefs, attitudes and nutritional practices which has to date received comparatively little attention from social scientists. Vegetarians in western cultures, in most instances, are not life-long practitioners but converts. They are individuals who have subjected more traditional foodways to critical scrutiny, and subsequently made a deliberate decision to change their eating habits, sometimes in a radical fashion.
> (Beardsworth and Keil 1992: 253)

Like Kelley and De Graaf's, this is a strong introduction. We can look again at what each sentence achieves.

- The first sentence makes clear that the research is concerned with issues to do with the study of food.

- The second sentence provides us with the specific research focus—the study of vegetarianism—and makes a claim for our attention by suggesting that this is a topic that has been under-researched by sociologists. Interestingly, this is almost the opposite of the claim made by Kelley and De Graaf in their second sentence, in that they point to a line of sociological interest in religion going back to Durkheim. Each is a legitimate textual strategy for gaining the attention of readers.

- Our attention is jolted even more by an interesting assertion that begins to draw the reader into one of the article's primary themes—the idea of vegetarians as converts.

- The fourth sentence elaborates upon the idea of vegetarianism as being for most people an issue of choice rather than a tradition into which one is born.

Thus, after around 100 words, the reader has a clear idea of the focus of the research and has been led to anticipate that there is unlikely to be a great deal of pre-existing social research on this issue.

The analysis of the social dimensions of food and eating

This and the next section review existing theory and research in this area. In this section, the contributions of various social scientists to social aspects of food and eating are discussed. The literature reviewed acts as a backcloth to the issue of vegetarianism. Beardsworth and Keil (1992: 255) propose that their review of existing theory and research suggests that 'there exists a range of theoretical and empirical resources which can be brought to bear upon the issue of contemporary vegetarianism'. This point is important, as the authors note once again at the end of the section that vegetarianism has received little attention from social scientists.

Studies of vegetarianism

This section examines aspects of the literature on vegetarianism that has been carried out by social scientists or that has a social scientific angle. The review includes: opinion poll and survey data, which point to the likely percentage of vegetarians in the British population; debates about animal rights; sociological analysis of vegetarian ideas; and one study (Dwyer *et al.* 1974) of vegetarians in the USA carried out by a team of social scientists using survey research. In the final paragraph of this section, the authors indicate the contribution of some of the literature they have covered.

The design of the study

The first sentence of this section forges a useful link with the preceding one: 'The themes outlined above appear to warrant further investigation, preferably in a manner which allows for a much more richly detailed examination of motivations and experiences than is apparent in the study by Dwyer *et al.*' (Beardsworth and Keil 1992: 260). This opening gambit allows the authors to suggest that the literature in this area is scant and that there are many unanswered questions. Also, they distance themselves from the one sociological study of vegetarians, which in turn leads them to set up the grounds for preferring qualitative research. The authors then outline:

- who was to be studied and why;

- how respondents were recruited (see Research in focus 18.8) and the difficulties encountered;

- the semi-structured interviewing approach (see Research in focus 18.2) and the rationale for it;

- the number of people interviewed and the context in which the interviews took place;

- the approach to analysing the interview transcripts, which largely comprised the identification of themes.

The findings of the study

The chief findings are outlined under separate headings: respondents' characteristics; types of vegetarianism; the process of conversion; motivations; nutritional beliefs; social relations; and dilemmas. The presentation of the results is carried out so that there is some discussion of their meaning or significance in such a way as to lead onto the next section, which provides exclusively a discussion of them. For example, in the final sentence in the section reporting findings relating to nutritional beliefs, the authors write:

> Just as meat tended to imply strongly negative connotations for respondents, concepts like 'fruit' and 'vegetable' tended to elicit positive reactions, although less frequently and in a more muted form than might have been anticipated on the basis of the analysis of the ideological underpinnings of 'wholefoods' consumption put forward by Atkinson (1980, 1983), or on the basis of the analysis of vegetarian food symbolism advanced by Twigg (1983: 28). (Beardsworth and Keil 1992: 276)

In this way, the presentation of the results is pointing forward to some themes that are taken up in the following sections and demonstrates the significance of certain findings for some of the previously discussed literature.

Explaining contemporary vegetarianism

This section discusses the findings in the light of the study's research questions in connection with food selection and avoidance. The results are also related to many of the ideas encountered in the two sections dealing with the literature. The authors develop an idea emerging from their research, which they call 'food ambivalence'. This concept encapsulates for the authors the anxieties and paradoxes concerning food that can be discerned in the interview transcripts (for example, food can be construed both as necessary for strength and energy and simultaneously as a source of illness). Vegetarianism is in many respects a response to the dilemmas associated with food ambivalence.

Conclusions

In this section, the authors return to many of the ideas and themes that have driven their research. They spell out the significance of the idea of food ambivalence, which is probably the article's main contribution to research in this area. The final paragraph outlines the importance of food ambivalence for vegetarians, but the authors are careful not to imply that it is the sole reason for the adoption of vegetarianism. In the final sentence they write: 'However, for a significant segment of the population [vegetarianism] appears to represent a viable device for re-establishing some degree of peace of mind when contemplating some of the darker implications of the carefully arranged message on the dinner plate' (Beardsworth and Keil 1992: 290). This sentence neatly encapsulates one of the article's master themes—the idea of vegetarianism as a response to food ambivalence—and alludes through the reference to 'the carefully arranged message' to semiotic analyses of meat and food.

Lessons

As with Kelley and De Graaf's article, it is useful to review some of the lessons learned from this examination of Beardsworth and Keil's article.

- Just like the illustration of quantitative research writing, there are strong opening sentences, which attract our attention and give a clear indication of the nature and content of the article.

- The rationale of the research is clearly identified. To a large extent, this revolves around identifying the sociological study of food and eating as a growing area of research but noting the paucity of investigations of vegetarianism.

- Research questions are specified but they are somewhat more open-ended than in Kelley and De Graaf's article, which is in keeping with the general orientation of qualitative researchers. The research questions revolve around the issue of vegetarianism as a dietary choice and the motivations for that choice.

- The research design and methods are outlined and an indication is given of the approach to analysis. The section in which these issues are discussed demonstrates greater transparency than is sometimes the case with articles reporting qualitative research.

- The presentation and discussion of the findings in sections 5 and 6 are geared to the broad research questions that motivated the researchers' interest in vegetarianism. However, section 6 also represents the major opportunity for the idea of food ambivalence and its dimensions to be articulated. The inductive nature of qualitative research means that the concepts and theories that are generated from an investigation must be clearly identified and discussed, as in this case.

- The conclusion elucidates in a more specific way the significance of the results for the research questions. It also explores the implications of food ambivalence for vegetarians, so that one of the article's major theoretical contributions is clearly identified and emphasized.

Writing up mixed methods research

Partly because interest in and the practice of mixed methods research has gained momentum only in relatively recent times, it has few if any writing conventions. More particularly, it is difficult to say what an exemplary or model mixed methods research journal article might look like. To a certain extent, it is bound to borrow some of the conventions associated with writing up quantitative and qualitative research in terms of needing to start out with a research focus in the sense of a research problem and/or some research questions. Creswell and Tashakkori (2007: 108), the editors of the *Journal of Mixed Methods Research*, have suggested that 'good original/empirical mixed methods articles' should be:

- 'well-developed in both quantitative and qualitative components' (Creswell and Tashakkori 2007: 108); and

- 'more than reporting two distinct "strands" of quantitative and qualitative research; these studies must also integrate, link, or connect these "strands" in some way' (Creswell and Tashakkori 2007: 108).

They actually add a third feature of good mixed methods articles—namely, that they contribute to the literature on mixed methods research in some way. This seems a rather tall order for many writers and researchers, so that I would tend to emphasize the other two features.

The first implies that the quantitative and the qualitative components of a mixed methods article should be at the very least competently executed. This means that in terms of the fundamental criteria for conducting good quantitative and good qualitative research, mixed methods research should conform to both quantitative and qualitative research criteria. In terms of writing, it means that, for each of the components, it should be clear what the research questions were, how the sampling was done,

what the data collection technique(s) was or were, and how the data were analysed.

The second feature implies that a good mixed methods article will be more than the sum of its parts. This issue relates to a tendency that has been identified by some writers (e.g. Bryman 2007c; O'Cathain *et al.* 2007) for some mixed methods researchers not to make the best use of their quantitative and qualitative data, in that they often do not link the two sets of findings so that they extract the maximum yield from their study. As Creswell and Tashakkori (2007: 108) put it:

> The expectation is that, by the end of the manuscript, conclusions gleaned from the two strands are integrated to provide a fuller understanding of the phenomenon under study. Integration might be in the form of comparing, contrasting, building on, or embedding one type of conclusion with the other.

To some extent, when writing up the results from a mixed methods study, researchers might make it easier for themselves to get across the extra yield associated with their investigations if they make clear their rationales for including both quantitative and qualitative components in their overall research strategy. The issue of rationales for conducting mixed methods research is one that was addressed in Chapter 25.

Further advice on writing up mixed methods research can be found in suggestions in Creswell and Plano Clark's (2007: 161) delineation of a structure for a mixed methods journal article. They suggest that the structure should be along the following lines.

- *Introduction*. This would include such features as: a statement of the research problem or issue; an examination of the literature on the problem/issue; an examination of the problems with the prior literature, which might include indicating why a mixed methods approach would be beneficial perhaps because much of the previous research is based mainly on just quantitative or qualitative research; and the specific research questions.

- *Methods*. This would include such features as: indicating the rationale for the mixed methods approach; the type of mixed methods design (see e.g. Morgan's classification of approaches to mixed methods research in Thinking deeply 25.3); data collection and data analysis methods; and indications of how the quality of the data can be judged.

Tips and skills
Do not separate your quantitative from your qualitative findings

I have noticed that some students who conduct mixed methods investigations treat their quantitative and qualitative findings as separate domains, so that they present one set and then the other. In Ph.D. theses and Masters dissertations, this can take the form of separate chapters labelled something like 'survey findings' and 'qualitative interview findings'. This may not be a problem if the two (or more) sets of findings are then integrated in the Discussion sections or chapters. However, treating findings in this way does tend to encourage a view of the quantitative and the qualitative findings as separate spheres and may therefore militate against integration, which, as writers like Creswell and Tashakkori (2007) imply, is increasingly an expectation in mixed methods studies. Instead, try to think of the quantitative and the qualitative findings thematically across the two sets of results, so that the findings are presented in terms of substantive issues rather than in terms of different methods.

- *Results*. The quantitative and the qualitative findings might be presented either in tandem or sequentially, but, if the latter, they would need to be merged in the Discussion.

- *Discussion*. Summarize and explain results, emphasizing the significance of the mixed methods nature of the research and what is gained from the presence of both quantitative and qualitative findings; draw attention to any limitations of the investigation; and possibly suggest avenues for future research.

In terms of the overall structure, Creswell and Plano Clark's (2007) suggestions are more or less the same as for an article based on quantitative research or an article based on qualitative research (see above). It is in the need to outline the mixed methods nature of the research and to bring the two sets of findings together that the distinctiveness of a mixed methods journal article can be discerned.

An example of mixed methods writing

Many of these features can be seen in the study of the food-and-mouth crisis by Poortinga *et al.* (2004). This article has been previously encountered in Research in focus 1.8 and 25.3. It may be worth looking back at these two accounts as a reminder of the study. The following examination of the writing of this article is organized in terms of its structure.

Introduction

The article begins with a very strong and clear statement of the focus of the article and its methodological leanings:

Thirty years of empirical work on public perceptions have generated an impressive body of findings on attitudes to the consequences, benefits and institutional profiles of a range of important risk issues . . . However, much of the available research tends to have been conducted when the risk issues studied are not particularly salient in public debate. Although there is some evidence from opinion polling, risk perception studies are rarely conducted during a major risk crisis. The present study examines public attitudes to risk and its management during one such crisis: the 2001 Foot and Mouth Disease (FMD) epidemic in Britain. A mixed method study design was employed, specifically a quantitative survey conducted at the height of the epidemic followed up by qualitative focus groups comprising individuals who had participated in the survey. Recent studies have shown that combining different research methods can provide a more comprehensive view on risk issues than can any one methodology alone . . . (Poortinga *et al.* 2004: 73–4)

This opening passage accomplishes the following:

- It locates the study immediately in the literature on risk.

- It provides a justification for conducting the study at the time of the FMD crisis.

- It identifies itself as a mixed methods study *and* provides a rationale for a mixed methods approach.

The authors then go on to outline the structure of the article so that the reader has a route map for what is to come.

The British 2001 Foot and Mouth Crisis

The authors outline the origins of the crisis, its timing, its extent, and its effects. As a result, the reader is left with a clear understanding of the nature of the FMD crisis.

Government policy, trust, and public reactions to the FMD epidemic

This section provides a justification for the researchers' emphasis on the significance of trust in the government and its policies and draws attention to related literature on the topic. For example, the authors draw attention to a study of trust in relation to another food-related crisis in Britain, the BSE crisis:

> Losing trust, as occurred to the British government over the BSE (mad cow) crisis in the mid-1990s, may have far-reaching consequences (Slovic, 1993), as people become suspicious about new government policy interpreted in the light of earlier experiences, perhaps turning elsewhere for information and advice. So, it is vitally important to have some gauge of public response. Not only regarding perceptions of the FMD crisis as an event within society, but also as a test case of the impacts of government policy and industry responsiveness in the UK in the wake of the BSE crisis. (Poortinga *et al.* 2004: 75)

They then outline the nature of their study in broad-brush terms, pointing out that it comprised a survey and focus groups. The authors explain that they emphasized in their research four aspects of FMD and its management (see below) and that they were also keen to examine how perceptions of them differed between the two communities (see Research in focus 1.8).

Methodology

The discussion of the research design and research methods is divided into three sections.

1. *Study locations.* The two communities—Bude and Norwich—are examined, along with a justification for using these two communities, when they write that they wanted 'to find out more about differences in attitudes between communities that were differentially affected by the epidemic' (Poortinga *et al.* 2004: 75).

2. *The questionnaire survey.* The authors explain how and when the questionnaires were distributed in Bude and Norwich. They outline the kinds and formats of the questions that were asked. They provide the response rates for the two surveys and examine the comparability of the ensuing samples.

3. *Focus groups.* The authors explain that the focus group participants were selected from the questionnaire survey samples. They provide data on the numbers of participants and of focus groups, when they took place, and how long the sessions lasted. The topics for discussion are also summarized.

Results

The findings are organized into four numbered sections, each of which deals with one of the four aspects of FMD and its management that were indicated earlier in the article: public risk perceptions of FMD; blame; government handling of the FMD crisis; and trust in information about FMD. It is very striking that, when presenting data for each of the four aspects of FMD they explored, the authors present both the quantitative and the qualitative findings, examining how the two interrelate. For example, when discussing the first of the four aspects—public risk perceptions of FMD—they begin by presenting some questionnaire data about respondents' levels of concern about FMD. These questionnaire data derive from Likert items that asked about levels of agreement with statements like 'My main concerns about FMD are to do with the possible impacts on the health and welfare of animals'. A table is presented showing mean levels of agreement with this and five other items, with the data being presented for the whole sample, as well as for Bude and Norwich separately. They then present the focus group findings, noting that the 'findings of the focus groups reinforce those of the questionnaire regarding general concern' (Poortinga *et al.* 2004: 78). The focus groups found that participants were deeply concerned about the slaughter of animals and the rotting carcases, whereas the questionnaires did not pick up this point. The possible health effects of these rather than of the disease itself was a concern (the survey and the focus group results both suggest that there was a low level of concerns about the direct health effects of FMD).

Discussion

The Discussion section begins by outlining the rationale for the mixed methods study and what has been gleaned from it:

> The aim of this mixed methodology study was to investigate public reactions to the FMD epidemic, support for government policies to get FMD under control, and trust in information about FMD. More specifically, a quantitative survey and qualitative focus groups were conducted to examine how two separate communities that were affected to different degrees by the epidemic responded to the crisis. In this study, the focus groups were mainly used to illustrate the findings of the questionnaire. The focus groups provided valuable additional information, especially on the reasons, rationalizations and arguments behind people's understanding of the FMD issue. (Poortinga *et al.* 2004: 86)

Thus, the authors restate the mixed methods nature of the investigation and the rationale for the different components. They then proceed to provide a detailed summary of the main findings. This account of the key findings is set in the context of other crises, like the BSE crisis, and existing literature on crisis management. They reflect in some detail on the differences between Bude and Norwich. The final paragraph provides a very strong concluding statement:

> In conclusion, the combination of a questionnaire survey and a focus group study gave a comprehensive view on people's perceptions and responses to the 2001 FMD epidemic. The unique aspect of this study is that it has captured perceptions *during* the FMD crisis. Although it only gives a snapshot of public attitudes to risk and its management, it provided a vivid picture of people's perceptions and debates on FMD at the height of the epidemic. Further research may provide insight in the dynamics and the long-term effects of the disease. Some studies have shown that risk perception can be related to the amount of press coverage that is given to that particular risk (Renn *et al.* 1992). Additional studies

> may provide answers on how a range of different drivers, such as the media, policy measures, and local and individual events (see e.g. Pidgeon *et al.* 2003) take on various levels of importance for people's reaction to a crisis such as FMD. Taken as a whole, this study suggests that risk perceptions of a crisis are embedded in both local and national social contexts. (Poortinga *et al.* 2004: 89)

This final paragraph is significant and well crafted for several reasons:

- The first sentence restates the mixed methods nature of the study and that its primary rationale was to provide a 'comprehensive' overview of the topic.
- The major contribution of the research—that it was conducted in the course of the crisis—is suggested to the reader in the second sentence.
- The third sentence provides a brief indication of a limitation of the study ('only gives a snapshot') but then invites the reader not to dwell on this limitation by suggesting that the research 'provided a rich description'.
- The next three sentences suggest future potentially fruitful avenues for inquiry.
- The final sentence provides a final message for readers to take away with them, namely, that 'risk perceptions of a crisis are embedded in both local and national social contexts'.

This is a very strong final and concluding paragraph that leaves readers in no doubt about what the authors believe is the major contribution of their findings and which reminds them of the significance of the fact that it is a mixed methods study.

One feature of this article that is quite striking is that in terms of structure and overall approach it is quite similar to the quantitative and the qualitative research articles previously examined. Indeed, it was noted that the qualitative research article was not dissimilar to the quantitative one. In large part, these similarities can be attributed to the fact that there are general conventions about how findings should be written up for academic audiences, and these conventions act as a template for, and to some extent restrict, much academic writing. What *is* striking about the article by Poortinga *et al.* is their inclination to make as much of the mixed methods status and context of their research as possible, as recommended in the guidelines suggested by Creswell and Plano Clark (2007).

While attention to the writing-up of mixed methods research is an area that is in its infancy, the suggestions of writers mentioned above like Creswell and Tashakkori (2007) and Creswell and Plano Clark (2007) along with strong exemplars like the article by Poortinga *et al.* provide helpful pointers to the ways in which this task should be approached.

Student experience
Writer's block

Sometimes when writing we feel as though the words will not come out. Rebecca Barnes writes that, when this happened to her, it usually meant that she needed to return to her data to work out what exactly she was trying to say.

> There have been frustrating times when I have been unsure of what to write and have spent many hours staring at a largely blank computer screen. I have now realized that when I experience this, it is usually because I need to return to the data and spend more time planning what I want to say, how, and why it matters.

Isabella Robbins's response to similar problems was to try to write every day:

> Sometimes just getting words on the page is difficult. I have set myself the task of writing 1,000 words a day, no matter how incoherent they are. I can usually achieve this. I have tried to put the thesis into the realm of 'good enough' and 'the last part of my research training' rather than it being 'something exceptional'.

*To read more about Rebecca's and Isabella's research experiences, go to the Online Resource Centre that accompanies this book at **http://www.oxfordtextbooks.co.uk/orc/brymansrm3e/**.*

Postmodernism and its implications for writing

Postmodernism (see Key concept 27.2) is an extremely difficult idea to pin down. In one sense, it can be seen as a form of sensitivity—a way of seeing and understanding that results in a questioning of the taken-for-granted. It questions the very notion of the dispassionate social scientist seeking to uncover a pre-given external reality. Instead, postmodernists view the social scientist's account as only one among many ways of rendering social reality to audiences. The social world itself is viewed as a context out of which many accounts can be hewn. As a result, 'knowledge' of the social world is relative; any account is just one of many possible ways of rendering social reality. As Rosenau (1992: 8) puts it, postmodernists 'offer "readings" not "observations," "interpretations" not "findings" . . .'.

Key concept 27.2
What is postmodernism?

As noted in the main text, postmodernism is extremely difficult to pin down. Part of the problem is that, as an approach, postmodernism is at least two things. One is that it is an attempt to get to grips with the nature of modern society and culture. The other, which is the more relevant aspect for this book, is that it represents a way of thinking about and representing the nature of the social sciences and their claims to knowledge. In particular, it is a distinctive sensitivity regarding the representation of social scientific findings. Postmodernists tend to be deeply suspicious of notions that imply that it is possible to arrive at a definitive version of any reality. Reports of findings are viewed as versions of an external reality, so that the key issue becomes one of the plausibility of those versions rather than whether they are right or wrong in any absolute sense. Typically, writers of a postmodernist persuasion have less to say about data-collection issues than about the writing and representation of social science findings, though it is probably the case that they are more sympathetic to qualitative than quantitative research (Alvesson 2002). Indeed, postmodernists have probably been most influential in qualitative research when discussing the nature of ethnographic accounts and questioning the **ethnographer**'s implicit claim that he or she has provided a definitive account of a society. This thinking can be discerned in Van Maanen's (1988) implicit critique of 'realist tales' as he called them (Key concept 27.5).

For postmodernists, there can be no sense of an objective reality out there waiting to be revealed to and uncovered by social scientists. That reality is always going to be accessed through narratives in the form of research reports that provide representations. With this shift in orientation came an interest in the language employed in research reports, like written ethnographies, to reveal the devices researchers use to convey the definitiveness of their findings (Delamont and Atkinson 2004). Postmodernists tend to emphasize the notion of **reflexivity** (see Key concept 27.4), which posits the significance of the researcher for the research process and consequently the tentativeness of any findings presented in a research report (since the researcher is always implicated in his or her findings). As this account of postmodernism implies, postmodernists tend to be deeply suspicious of any view of research that implies that there are or can be accepted foundations to knowledge, as is suggested by positivists (see Key concept 1.2). Postmodernism is a deeply disruptive stance on social research, in that it problematizes and questions our capacity ever to know anything. Views vary on postmodernism's current appeal. Matthewman and Hoey (2006) depict its influence as having waned to a significant extent, while Bloland (2005) argues that it has had an impact on thinking in many fields in higher education and that this is especially noticeable among those who do not identify themselves as postmodernists.

One of the effects of the impact of postmodernism since the 1980s has been a growing interest in the writing of social science. For postmodernists, reporting findings in a journal article provides merely one version of the social reality that was investigated. Postmodernists mistrust the knowledge claims that are frequently boldly made when findings are reported and instead they adopt an attitude of investigating the bases and forms of those knowledge claims and the language that is used to represent them. This has led to what is described as a **linguistic turn** within the social sciences (Key concept 27.3). While the writing of all types of social science is potentially in the postmodernist's firing line, it has been the kinds of text produced by ethnographers that have been a particular focus of attention. This focus has led to a particular interest in the claims to ethnographic authority that are inscribed into ethnographic texts (Clifford 1983). The ethnographic text 'presumes a world out there (the real) that can be captured by a "knowing" author through the careful transcription and analysis of field materials (interviews, notes, etc.)' (Denzin 1994: 296). Postmodernism problematizes such accounts and their authority to represent a reality because there 'can never be a final, accurate representation of what was meant or said, only different textual representations of different experiences' (Denzin 1994: 296).

However, it would be wrong to depict the growing attention being focused on ethnographic writing as exclusively a product of postmodernism. Atkinson and Coffey (1995) have argued that there are other intellectual trends in the social sciences that have stimulated this interest. Writers in the area of theory and research known as the social studies of science have been concerned with the limitations of accepted distinctions between rhetoric and logic and between the observer and the observed (e.g. Gilbert and Mulkay 1984). The problematizing of these distinctions, along with doubts about the possibility of a neutral language through which the natural and social worlds can be revealed, opened the door for

an evaluation of scientific and social scientific writing. Some illustrations of these analyses can be discerned in Thinking deeply 27.1 and 27.2. Atkinson and Coffey also point to the antipathy within feminism towards the image of the neutral 'observer-author' who assumes a privileged stance in relation to members of the social setting being studied. This stance is regarded as revealing a position of domination of the observer-author over the observed that is inconsistent with the goals of feminism (see Chapter 16 for an elaboration of this general point). This concern has led to an interest in the ways in which privilege is conveyed in ethnographic texts and how voices, particularly of marginal groups, are suppressed.

Key concept 27.3
What is the linguistic turn?

Postmodernism can also be seen as the stimulus for the linguistic turn in the social sciences. The linguistic turn is based on the idea that language shapes our understanding of the world. Moreover, because knowledge is constructed through language, and language can never create an objective representation of external reality, meaning is uncontrollable and undiscoverable. This leads to a rejection of positivist scientists' claims to be able to produce reliable knowledge through a neutral process of exploration. Postmodernists argue that knowledge is never neutral and is constantly open to revision. They reject what they see as scientific 'grand' or 'meta' narratives that seek to explain the world from an objective viewpoint. Scientific investigation is thus suggested by postmodernists to be nothing more than a type of 'language game' (Rorty 1979) used by this particular community to produce localized understandings. Postmodernists have also suggested that certain methods can be more easily adapted to the linguistic turn, such as qualitative research and in particular ethnography, because it can be used to deconstruct claims to represent reality and can provide alternative versions of reality that attempt to blur the boundary between 'fact' and 'fiction' (Alvesson 2002). The impact of the linguistic turn can be seen in the growing use of various forms of **discourse analysis**, which was covered in Chapter 20. Discourse analysis has proved a particularly useful approach for unpacking the role of language in shaping particular versions of social reality.

Thinking deeply 27.2
Rhetorical strategies in writing up quantitative research

The rhetorical strategies used by quantitative researchers include the following.

- There is a tendency to remove the researcher from the text as an active ingredient of the research process in order to convey an impression of the objective nature of the findings—that is, as part of an external reality that is independent of the researcher (Gusfield 1976). Woolgar (1988) refers to this as an externalizing device.

- The researcher surfaces in the text only to demonstrate his or her ingenuity in overcoming obstacles (Bazerman 1987; Bryman 1998).

- Key figures in the field are routinely cited to bestow credibility on the research (McCloskey 1985).

- The research process is presented as a linear one to convey an air of inevitability about the findings arrived at (Gusfield 1976).

- Relatively strict rules are followed about what should be reported in published research and how it should be reported (Bazerman 1987).

- The use of a *management* metaphor is common in the presentation of findings in which the researcher is depicted as ingeniously '"designing" research, "controlling" variables, "managing" data, and "generating" tables' (Bryman 1998: 146). See Shapiro (1985–6) and Richardson (1990) on this point.

Note that the first two points are somewhat inconsistent. There is some evidence that disciplines within the social sciences differ in respect of their use of an impersonal style of writing. But it may well also be that it sometimes depends on what the writer is trying to do; for example, sometimes getting across a sense of one's cunning in overcoming practical difficulties can be just as useful as giving a sense of the external nature of the findings. Therefore, sometimes the style of presentation may vary somewhat.

Key concept 27.4
What is reflexivity?

Reflexivity has several meanings in the social sciences. The term is employed by ethnomethodologists to refer to the way in which speech and action are constitutive of the social world in which they are located; in other words, they do more than merely act as indicators of deeper phenomena (see Chapter 20). The other meaning of the term carries the connotation that social researchers should be reflective about the implications of their methods, values, biases, and decisions for the knowledge of the social world they generate. Relatedly, reflexivity entails a sensitivity to the researcher's cultural, political, and social context. As such, 'knowledge' from a reflexive position is always a reflection of a researcher's location in time and social space. This notion is especially explicit in Pink's (2001) formulation of a reflexive approach to the use of visual images (see Chapter 17) and in Plummer's (2001) delineation of a reflexive approach to life histories (see Key concept 18.1).

There has been evidence of a growing reflexivity in social research in the form of an industry of books that collect together inside stories of the research process that detail the nuts and bolts of research as distinct from the often sanitized portrayal in research articles. An early volume edited by Hammond (1964) paved the way for a large number of imitators (e.g. Bell and Newby 1977; Bell and Roberts 1984; Bryman 1988b), and the confessional tales referred to in Key concept 27.5 are invariably manifestations of this development. Therefore, the rise of reflexivity largely predates the growing awareness of postmodern thinking since the late 1980s. What distinguishes the reflexivity that has followed in the wake of postmodernism is a greater awareness and acknowledgement of the role of the researcher as part and parcel of the construction of knowledge. In other words, the reflexive attitude within postmodernism is highly critical of the notion that the researcher is someone who extracts knowledge from observations and conversations with others and then transmits knowledge to an audience. The researcher is viewed as implicated in the construction of knowledge through the stance that he or she assumes in relation to the observed and through the ways in which an account is transmitted in the form of a text. This understanding entails an acknowledgement of the implications and significance of the researcher's choices as both observer and writer.

However, reflexivity is a notoriously slippery concept. Lynch (2000) has complained that too often it is assumed that a reflexive position is somehow superior to an unreflexive one. The case for the superiority of reflexivity is rarely made. Moreover, he points out that the term has different meanings. One of these is methodological reflexivity, which comes closest to the kind of reflexivity that is being referred to in this chapter. However, this meaning has a number of sub-meanings, three of which are especially prominent in methodological writings.

1. *Philosophical self-reflection*: an introspection involving 'an inward-looking, sometimes confessional and self-critical examination of one's own beliefs and assumptions' (Lynch 2000: 29).

2. *Methodological self-consciousness*: taking account of one's relationships with those whom one studies.

3. *Methodological self-criticism*: the confessional style of ethnography (see Key concept 27.5), but Lynch notes that the injunction to be self-critical that is associated with such ethnographic writing is much more pervasive in academic disciplines.

The term 'reflexivity' has to be used with a degree of caution, as Lynch's discussion implies.

The concerns within these and other traditions (including postmodernism) have led to experiments in writing ethnography (Richardson 1994). An example is the use of a 'dialogic' form of writing that seeks to raise the profile of the multiplicity of voices that can be heard in the course of fieldwork. As Lincoln and Denzin (1994: 584) put it: 'Slowly it dawns on us that there may . . . be . . . not one "voice", but polyvocality; not one story, but many tales, dramas, pieces of fiction, fables, memories, histories, autobiographies, poems, and other texts to inform our sense of lifeways, to extend our understandings of the Other . . .'.

Manning (1995) cites, as an example of the postmodern preference for allowing a variety of voices to come through within an ethnographic text, the work of Stoller (1989), who conducted research in Africa. Manning (1995: 260) describes the text as 'periodically' dialogic in that it is 'shaped by interactions between informants or "the other" and the observer'. This postmodern preference for seeking out multiple voices and for turning the ethnographer into a 'bit player' reflects the mistrust among postmodernists of 'meta-narratives'—that is, positions or grand accounts that implicitly make claims about absolute truths and that therefore rule out the possibility of alternative versions of reality. On the other hand, 'mini-narratives, micro-narratives, local narratives are just stories that make no truth claims and are therefore more acceptable to postmodernists' (Rosenau 1992: p. xiii).

Postmodernism has also encouraged a growing reflexivity in considerations about the conduct of social research, and the growing interest in the writing of ethnography is very much a manifestation of this trend (see Key concept 27.4). This reflexivity can be discerned in the way in which many ethnographers have turned inwards to examine the truth claims inscribed in their own classic texts, which is the focus of the next section.

In the end, what postmodernism leaves us with is an acute sense of uncertainty. It raises the issue of how we can ever know or capture the social reality that belongs to others and in so doing it points to an unresolvable tension that will not go away and that is further revealed in the issues raised in the next section, because, to quote Lincoln and Denzin (1994: 582) again: 'On the one hand there is the concern for validity, or certainty in the text as a form of isomorphism and authenticity. On the other hand, there is the sure and certain knowledge that all texts are socially, historically, politically, and culturally located. We, like the texts we write, can never be transcendent.' At the same time, of course, such a view renders problematic the very idea of what social scientific knowledge is or comprises.

Writing ethnography

The term 'ethnography', as noted in Chapter 17, is interesting, because it refers both to a method of social research and to the finished product of ethnographic research. In other words, it is both something that is carried out in doing research and something that one reads. Thus, writing seems to be at the heart of the ethnographic enterprise. In recent years, the production of ethnographic texts has become a focus of interest in its own right. This means that there has been a growth of interest not just in how ethnography is carried out in the field but also in the rhetorical conventions employed in the production of ethnographic texts.

Ethnographic texts are designed to convince readers of the *reality* of the events and situations described, and the plausibility of the analyst's explanations. The ethnographic text must not simply present a set of findings: it must provide an 'authoritative' account of the group or culture in question. In other words, the ethnographer must convince us that he or she has arrived at an account of social reality that has strong claims to truth.

The ethnographic text is permeated by stylistic and rhetorical devices whereby the reader is persuaded to enter into a shared framework of facts and interpretations, observations and reflections. Just like the scientific paper and the kind of approach to writing found in reporting quantitative social research, the ethnographer typically works within a writing strategy that is imbued with *realism*. This simply means that the researcher presents an authoritative, dispassionate account that represents an external, objective reality. In this respect, there is very little difference between the writing styles of quantitative and qualitative researchers. Van Maanen (1988) calls ethnography texts that conform to these characteristics *realist tales*. These are the common type of ethnographic writing, though he distinguishes other types (see Key concept 27.5). However, the *form* that this realism takes differs. Van Maanen distinguishes four characteristics of realist tales: experiential authority; typical forms; the native's point of view; and interpretive omnipotence.

Key concept 27.5
Three forms of ethnographic writing

Van Maanen (1988) has distinguished three major types of ethnographic writing.

1. *Realist tales*—apparently definitive, confident, and dispassionate third-person accounts of a culture and of the behaviour of members of that culture. This is the most prevalent form of ethnographic writing.

2. *Confessional tales*—personalized accounts in which the ethnographer is fully implicated in the data-gathering and writing-up processes. These are warts-and-all accounts of the trials and tribulations of doing ethnography. They have become more prominent since the 1970s and reflect a growing emphasis on reflexivity in qualitative research in particular. Several of the sources referred to in Chapter 17 are confessional tales (e.g. Armstrong 1993; Hobbs 1993; Giulianotti 1995). However, confessional tales are more concerned with detailing how research was carried out than with presenting findings. Very often the confessional tale is told in one context (such as an invited chapter in a book of similar tales), but the main findings are written up in realist tale form.

3. *Impressionist tales*—accounts that place a heavy emphasis on 'words, metaphors, phrasings, and . . . the expansive recall of fieldwork experience' (Van Maanen 1988: 102). There is a heavy emphasis on stories of dramatic events that provide 'a representational means of cracking open the culture and the fieldworker's way of knowing it' (Van Maanen 1988: 102). However, as Van Maanen (1988: 106) notes, impressionist tales 'are typically enclosed within realist, or perhaps more frequently, confessional tales'.

Experiential authority

Just as in much quantitative research writing, the author disappears from view when writing ethnography. We are told what members of a group say and do, and they are the only people directly visible in the text. The author provides a narrative in which he or she is no longer to be seen. As a result, an impression is conveyed that the findings presented are what any reasonable, similarly placed researcher would have found. As readers, we have to accept that this is what the ethnographer saw and heard while working as a participant observer or whatever. The personal subjectivity of the author/ethnographer is essentially played down by this strategy. The possibility that the fieldworker may have his or her own biases or may have become too involved with the people being studied is suppressed. To this end, when writing up the results of their ethnographic work, authors play up their academic credentials and qualifications, their previous experience, and so on. All this enhances the degree to which the author's account can be relied upon. The author/ethnographer can then appear as a reliable witness.

A further element of experiential authority is that, when describing their methods, ethnographers invariably make a great deal of the intensiveness of the research that they carried out—they spent so many months in the field, had conversations and interviews with countless individuals, worked hard to establish rapport, and so on. These features are also added to by drawing the reader's attention to such hardships as the inconvenience of the fieldwork—the danger, the poor food, the disruptive effect on normal life, the feelings of isolation and loneliness, and so on. Also worth mentioning are the extensive quotations from conversations and interviews that invariably form part of the ethnographic report. These are also obviously important ingredients of the author's use of *evidence* to support points. However, they are a mechanism for establishing the credibility of the report in that they demonstrate the author's ability to encourage people to talk and so demonstrate that he or she achieved rapport with them. The copious descriptive details—of places, patterns of behaviour, contexts, and so on—can also be viewed as a means of piling on the sense of the author being an ideally placed witness for all the findings that have been uncovered.

Typical forms

The author often writes about typical forms of institutions or of patterns of behaviour. What is happening here is that the author is generalizing about a number of recurring features of the group in question to create a typical form that that feature takes. He or she may use examples based on particular incidents or people, but basically the emphasis is upon the general. For example, in Taylor's (1993) conclusion to her ethnographic research on female drug users, which was cited several times in Chapter 17, we encounter findings such as these: 'Yet the control exercised over women through the threat to remove their children highlights a major factor differentiating female and male drug users. Unlike male drug users, female drug users, like many other women, have two careers: one in the public sphere and one in the private, domestic sphere' (Taylor 1993: 154). This is meant to portray drug users in general, so that individuals are important only in so far as they represent such general tendencies.

The native's point of view

The point has been made several times that one of the distinguishing features of much qualitative research is the commitment to seeing through the eyes of the people being studied. This is an important feature for qualitative researchers because it is part of a strategy of getting at the meaning of social reality from the perspective of those being studied. However, it also represents an important element in creating a sense of authoritativeness on the part of the ethnographer. After all, claiming that he or she takes the native's point of view and sees through his or her eyes means that he or she is in an excellent position to speak authoritatively about the group in question. The very fact that the ethnographer has taken the native's point of view testifies to the fact that he or she is well placed to write definitively about the group in question. Realist tales frequently include numerous references to the steps taken by the ethnographer to get close to the people studied and his or her success in this regard. Thus, for her research on female drug users, Taylor (1993: 16) writes:

Events I witnessed or took part in ranged from the very routine (sitting around drinking coffee and eating junk food) to accompanying various women on visits to DSS [Department of Social Security] offices or to the HIV clinic; I accompanied them when they were in court, and even went flat-hunting with one woman. I went shopping with some, helping them choose clothes for their children and presents for their friends. I visited them in their homes, rehabilitation centres, and maternity wards, sat with them through withdrawals, watched them using drugs, and accompanied them when they went 'scoring' (buying drugs). (Taylor 1993: 16)

Similarly, referring to his study of a factory in a small Welsh community, Delbridge (1998: 19) writes:

I stood out like a sore thumb . . . My actual participation in the tasks which faced the workers helped to break down the barriers and several people approached me over the weeks and told me that when they actually saw me sitting there alongside them day after day they began to have some respect for what I was doing. It was important to be able to develop some shared ground.

He goes on to say:

the relationships developed over long hours working on the shop floor, chatting over lunch, moaning about the weather, and so on. In the close-knit village community, I soon got involved in long conversations about families, mine and theirs, which was a most unusual topic in the social world from which I had come. . . . the common ground we found in our family lives cemented relationships and founded them on something other than a student/subject basis. (Delbridge 1998: 20)

These passages are very effective in demonstrating how the ethnographer was able gradually to be transformed from an outsider to an insider with similar experiences and concerns. As such, his credibility as someone who can speak authoritatively about these workers and their lives is enhanced.

Interpretative omnipotence

When writing up an ethnography, the author rarely presents possible alternative interpretations of an event or pattern of behaviour. Instead, the phenomenon in question is presented as having a single meaning or significance, which the fieldworker alone has cracked. Indeed, the evidence provided is carefully marshalled to support the singular interpretation that is placed on the event or pattern of behaviour. We are presented with an inevitability. It seems obvious or inevitable that someone would draw the inferences that the author has drawn when faced with such clear-cut evidence.

These four characteristics of realist tales imply that what the researcher did as a researcher is only one part of creating a sense of having figured out the nature of a culture. It is also very much to do with how the researcher represents what he or she did through writing about ethnography. For the postmodernist position, any realist tale is merely one 'spin'—that is one version, that can be or has been formulated in relation to the culture in question.

Checklist

Issues to consider for writing up a piece of research

○ Have you clearly specified your research questions?

○ Have you clearly indicated how the literature you have read relates to your research questions?

○ Is your discussion of the literature critical and organized so that it is not just a summary of what you have read?

○ Have you clearly outlined your research design and your research methods, including:

    ○ why you chose a particular research design?

    ○ why you chose a particular research method?

    ○ how you selected your research participants?

- ○ whether there were any issues to do with cooperation (e.g. response rates)?
- ○ why you implemented your research in a particular way (e.g. how the interview questions relate to your research questions, why you observed participants in particular situations, why your focus group guide asked the questions in a particular way and order)?
- ○ if your research required access to an organization, how and on what basis was agreement for access forthcoming?
- ○ steps you took to ensure that your research was ethically responsible;
- ○ how you analysed your data?
- ○ any difficulties you encountered in the implementation of your research approach.

○ Have you presented your data in a manner that relates to your research questions?

○ Does your discussion of your findings show how they relate to your research questions?

○ Does your discussion of your findings show how they shed light on the literature that you presented?

○ Are the interpretations of the data that you offer fully supported with tables, figures, or segments from transcripts?

○ If you have presented tables and/or figures, are they properly labelled with a title and number?

○ If you have presented tables and/or figures, are they commented upon in your discussion?

○ Do your conclusions clearly allow the reader to establish what your research contributes to the literature?

○ Have you explained the limitations of your study?

○ Do your conclusions consist solely of a summary of your findings? If they do, rewrite them!

○ Do your conclusions make clear the answers to your research questions?

○ Does your presentation of the findings and the discussion allow a clear argument and narrative to be presented to the reader?

○ Have you broken up the text in each chapter with appropriate subheadings?

○ Does your writing avoid sexist, racist, and disablist language?

○ Have you included all appendices that you might need to provide (e.g. interview schedule, letters requesting access, communications with research participants)?

○ Have you checked that your list of references includes *all* the items referred to in your text?

○ Have you checked that your list of references follows precisely the style that your institution requires?

○ Have you followed your supervisor's suggestions when he or she has commented on your draft chapters?

○ Have you got people other than your supervisor to read your draft chapters for you?

○ Have you checked to ensure that there is not excessive use of jargon?

○ Do you provide clear signposts in the course of writing, so that readers are clear about what to expect next and why it is there?

○ Have you ensured that your institution's requirements for submitting projects are fully met in terms of such issues as word length (so that it is neither too long nor too short) and whether an abstract and table of contents are required?

○ Have you ensured that you do not quote excessively when presenting the literature?

○ Have you fully acknowledged the work of others so that you cannot be accused of plagiarism?

○ Is there a good correspondence between the title of your project and its contents?

○ Have you acknowledged the help of others where this is appropriate (e.g. your supervisor, people who may have helped with interviews, people who read your drafts)?

Key points

- Good writing is probably just as important as good research practice. Indeed, it is probably better thought of as a part of good research practice.

- Clear structure and statement of your research questions are important components of writing up research.

- Be sensitive to the ways in which writers seek to persuade us of their points of view.

- The study of rhetoric and writing strategies generally teaches us that the writings of scientists and social scientists do more than simply report findings. They are designed to convince and to persuade.

- The emphasis on rhetoric is not meant to imply that there is no external social reality; it merely suggests that our understanding of that reality is profoundly influenced by the ways it is represented by writers.

- While postmodernism has exerted a particular influence on this last point, writers working within other traditions have also contributed to it.

- The basic structure of and the writing strategies employed in most quantitative and qualitative research articles are broadly similar.

- We need to get away from the idea that rhetoric and the desire to persuade others of the validity of our work are somehow bad things. They are not. We all want to get our points across and to persuade our readers that we have got things right. The question is—do we do it well? Do we make the best possible case? We all have to persuade others that we have got the right angle on things; the trick is to do it well. So, when you write an essay or dissertation, do bear in mind the significance of your writing strategy.

Questions for review

- Why is it important to consider the ways in which social research is written up?

Writing up your research

- Why is it important to be clear about your main argument when writing up your findings?

Writing up quantitative research

- Read an article based on quantitative research in a British sociology journal. How far does it exhibit the same characteristics as Kelley and De Graaf's (1997) article?

- What is meant by rhetorical strategy? Why might rhetorical strategies be important in relation to the writing-up of social research?
- Do Kelley and De Graaf employ an empiricist repertoire?

Writing up qualitative research

- Read an article based on quantitative research in a British sociology journal. How far does it exhibit the same characteristics as Beardsworth and Keil's (1992) article?
- How far is the structure of Beardsworth and Keil's article different from Kelley and De Graaf's?

Writing up mixed methods research

- Read an article based on quantitative research in a British sociology journal. How far does it exhibit the same characteristics as the one by Poortinga *et al.*?

Postmodernism and its implications for writing

- Why has postmodernism produced a growth of interest in writing social research?
- What is reflexivity?

Writing ethnography

- How far is it true to say that ethnographic writing is typically imbued with realism?
- What forms of ethnographic writing other than realist tales can be found?
- What are the main characteristics of realist tales?

Online Resource Centre

http://www.oxfordtextbooks.co.uk/orc/brymansrm3e/

Visit the Online Resource Centre that accompanies this book to enrich your understanding of writing up social research. Consult web links, test yourself using multiple choice questions, and gain further guidance and inspiration from the Student Researcher's Toolkit.

Glossary

Terms appearing elsewhere in the Glossary are in **bold**.

Action research An approach in which the action researcher and a client collaborate in the diagnosis of a problem and in the development of a solution based on the diagnosis.

Ad libitum sampling A sampling approach in **structured observation** whereby whatever is happening at the moment that observation is due to occur is recorded.

Adjacency pair The tendency for certain kinds of activity in talk to be characterized by linked phases.

Analytic induction An approach to the analysis of qualitative data in which the researcher seeks universal explanations of phenomena by pursuing the collection of data until no cases that are inconsistent with a hypothetical explanation (deviant or negative cases) of a phenomenon are found.

Arithmetic mean Also known simply as the **mean**, this is the everyday average—namely, the total of a distribution of values divided by the number of values.

Asynchronous online interview or **focus group** Online interviews may be asynchronous or **synchronous**. In the case of the former, the transactions between participants are not in real time, so that there may be long spaces of time between interviewers' questions and participants' replies, and in the case of focus groups, between participants' contributions to the discussion.

Attached email survey A survey in which respondents are sent a questionnaire, which is received as an attachment by email. Compare with **embedded email survey**.

Behaviour sampling A sampling approach in **structured observation** whereby an entire group is watched and the observer records who was involved in a particular kind of behaviour.

Biographical method See **life history method**.

Bivariate analysis The examination of the relationship between two variables, as in **contingency tables** or **correlation**.

CAQDAS An abbreviation of Computer-Assisted (or -Aided) Qualitative Data Analysis Software.

Case study A **research design** that entails the detailed and intensive analysis of a single case. The term is sometimes extended to include the study of just two or three cases for comparative purposes.

Causality A concern with establishing causal connections between variables, rather than mere **relationships** between them.

Cell The point in a table, such as a **contingency table**, where the rows and columns intersect.

Census The enumeration of an entire **population**. Unlike a **sample**, which comprises a count of *some* units in a population, a census relates to *all* units in a population. Thus, if a **postal questionnaire** is mailed to every person in a town or to all members of a profession, the research should be characterized as a census.

Chi-square test Chi-square (χ^2) is a test of **statistical significance**, which is typically employed to establish how confident we can be that the findings displayed in a **contingency table** can be generalized from a **probability sample** to a **population**.

Closed question A question employed in an **interview schedule** or **self-completion questionnaire** that presents the respondent with a set of possible answers to choose from. Also called **fixed-choice question** and **pre-coded question**.

Cluster sample A sampling procedure in which at an initial stage the researcher samples areas (i.e. clusters) and then samples units from these clusters, usually using a **probability sampling** method.

Code, coding In **quantitative research**, codes act as tags that are placed on data about people or other units of analysis. The aim is to assign the data relating to each **variable** to groups, each of which is considered to be a category of the variable in question. Numbers are then assigned to each category to allow the information to be processed by the computer. In **qualitative research**, coding is the process whereby data are broken down into component parts, which are given names.

Coding frame A listing of the codes used in relation to the analysis of data. In relation to answers to a structured interview schedule or questionnaire, the coding frame will delineate the categories used in connection with each question. It is particularly crucial in relation to the coding of **open questions**. With **closed questions**, the coding frame is essentially incorporated into the pre-given answers, hence the frequent use of the term **pre-coded question** to describe such questions.

Coding manual In **content analysis**, this is the statement of instructions to coders that outlines all the possible categories for each dimension being coded.

Coding schedule In **content analysis**, this is the form onto which all the data relating to an item being coded will be entered.

Comparative design A **research design** that entails the comparison of two or more cases in order to illuminate existing theory or generate theoretical insights as a result of contrasting findings uncovered through the comparison.

Concept A name given to a category that organizes observations and ideas by virtue of their possessing common features.

Concurrent validity One of the main approaches to establishing **measurement validity**. It entails relating a measure to a criterion on which cases (e.g. people) are known to differ and that is relevant to the **concept** in question.

Connotation A term used in **semiotics** to refer to the principal and most manifest meaning of a **sign**. Compare with **denotation**.

Constant An attribute in terms of which cases do not differ. Compare with **variable**.

Constructionism, constructionist An **ontological** position (often also referred to as **constructivism**) that asserts that social phenomena and their meanings are continually being accomplished by social actors. It is antithetical to **objectivism** and **essentialism**.

Constructivism See **constructionism**.

Content analysis An approach to the analysis of documents and texts that seeks to quantify content in terms of predetermined categories and in a systematic and replicable manner. The term is sometimes used in connection with qualitative research as well—see **qualitative content analysis**.

Contingency table A table, comprising rows and columns, that shows the **relationship** between two **variables**. Usually, at least one of the variables is a **nominal variable**. Each cell in the table shows the frequency of occurrence of that intersection of categories of each of the two variables and usually a percentage.

Continuous recording A procedure in **structured observation** whereby observation occurs for extended periods so that the frequency and duration of certain types of behaviour can be carefully recorded.

Control group See **experiment**.

Convenience sample A sample that is selected because of its availability to the researcher. It is a form of **non-probability sample**.

Conversation analysis The fine-grained analysis of talk as it occurs in interaction in naturally occurring situations. The talk is recorded and **transcribed** so that the detailed analyses can be carried out. The analysis is concerned with uncovering the underlying structures of talk in interaction and as such with the achievement of order through interaction. Conversation analysis is grounded in **ethnomethodology**.

Correlation An approach to the analysis of relationships between **interval/ratio variables** and/or **ordinal variables** that seeks to assess the strength and direction of the relationship between the variables concerned. **Pearson's r** and **Spearman's rho** are both methods for assessing the level of correlation between variables.

Covert research A term frequently used in connection with **ethnographic** research in which the researcher does not reveal his or her true identity. Such research violates the ethical principle of **informed consent**.

Cramér's V A method for assessing the strength of the relationship between two variables, at least one of which must have more than two categories.

Critical discourse analysis A form of **discourse analysis** that emphasizes the role of language as a power resource that is related to ideology and socio-cultural change. It draws in particular on the theories and approaches of Foucault.

Critical realism A **realist** epistemology that asserts that the study of the social world should be concerned with the identification of the structures that generate that world.

Critical realism is critical because its practitioners aim to identify structures in order to change them, so that inequalities and injustices may be counteracted. Unlike a **positivist** epistemology, critical realism accepts that the structures that are identified may not be amenable to the senses. Thus, whereas **positivism** is **empiricist**, critical realism is not.

Cross-sectional design A **research design** that entails the collection of data on more than one case (usually quite a lot more than one) and at a single point in time in order to collect a body of quantitative or quantifiable data in connection with two or more variables (usually many more than two), which are then examined to detect patterns of association.

Deductive An approach to the relationship between theory and research in which the latter is conducted with reference to hypotheses and ideas inferred from the former. Compare with **inductive**.

Denotation A term used in **semiotics** to refer to the meanings of a **sign** associated with the social context within which it operates that are supplementary to and less immediately apparent than its **connotation**.

Dependent variable A **variable** that is causally influenced by another variable (i.e. an **independent variable**).

Diary A term that in the context of social research methods can mean different things. Three types of diary can be distinguished: diaries written or completed at the behest of a researcher; personal diaries that can be analysed as a **personal document**, but that were produced spontaneously; and diaries written by social researchers as a log of their activities and reflections.

Dichotomous variable A variable with just two categories.

Dimension Refers to an aspect of a **concept**.

Discourse analysis An approach to the analysis of talk and other forms of discourse that emphasizes the ways in which versions of reality are accomplished through language.

Distribution of values A term used to refer to the entire data relating to a **variable**. Thus, the ages of members of a **sample** represent the distribution of values for that variable for that sample.

Ecological fallacy The error of assuming that inferences about individuals can be made from findings relating to aggregate data.

Ecological validity A concern with the question of whether social scientific findings are applicable to people's everyday, natural social settings.

Embedded email survey A **social survey** in which respondents are sent an email that contains a **questionnaire**. Compare with **attached email survey**.

Empiricism An approach to the study of reality that suggests that only knowledge gained through experience and the senses is acceptable.

Epistemology, epistemological A theory of knowledge. It is particularly employed in this book to refer to a stance on what should pass as acceptable knowledge. See **positivism, realism**, and **interpretivism**.

Essentialism A position that has close affinities with naive **realism**. Essentialism suggests that objects have essences that denote their authentic nature. Compare with **constructionism**.

Eta A test of the strength of the **relationship** between two **variables**. The **independent variable** must be a **nominal variable** and the **dependent variable** must be an **interval variable** or **ratio variable**. The resulting level of correlation will always be positive.

Ethnographic content analysis See **qualitative content analysis**.

Ethnography, ethnographer Like **participant observation**, a research method in which the researcher immerses him- or herself in a social setting for an extended period of time, observing behaviour, listening to what is said in conversations both between others and with the fieldworker, and asking questions. However, the term has a more inclusive sense than participant observation, which seems to emphasize the observational component. Also, the term 'an ethnography' is frequently used to refer to the written output of ethnographic research.

Ethnomethodology A sociological perspective concerned with the way in which social order is accomplished through talk and interaction. It provides the intellectual foundations of **conversation analysis**.

Evaluation research Research that is concerned with the evaluation of real-life interventions in the social world.

Experiment A **research design** that rules out alternative explanations of findings deriving from it (i.e. possesses **internal validity**) by having at least (*a*) an experimental group, which is exposed to a treatment, and a control group, which is not, and (*b*) **random assignment** to the two groups.

Experimental group See **experiment**.

External validity A concern with the question of whether the results of a study can be generalized beyond the specific research context in which it was conducted.

Face validity A concern with whether an **indicator** appears to reflect the content of the **concept** in question.

Facilitator See **moderator**.

Factor analysis A statistical technique used for large numbers of **variables** to establish whether there is a tendency for groups of them to be inter-related. It is often used with **multiple-indicator measures** to see if the **indicators** tend to bunch to form one or more groups of indicators. These groups of indicators are called factors and must then be given a name.

Field notes A detailed chronicle by an **ethnographer** of events, conversations, and behaviour, and the researcher's initial reflections on them.

Field stimulation A study in which the researcher directly intervenes in and/or manipulates a natural setting in order to observe what happens as a consequence of that intervention.

Focal sampling A sampling approach in **structured observation** whereby a sampled individual is observed for a set period of time. The observer records all examples of whatever forms of behaviour are of interest.

Focus group A form of group interview in which: there are several participants (in addition to the **moderator/facilitator**); there is an emphasis in the questioning on a particular fairly tightly defined topic; and the emphasis is upon interaction within the group and the joint construction of meaning.

Frequency table A table that displays the number and/or percentage of units (e.g. people) in different categories of a variable.

Generalization, generalizability A concern with the **external validity** of research findings.

Grounded theory An approach to the analysis of qualitative data that aims to generate theory out of research data by achieving a close fit between the two.

Hermeneutics A term drawn from theology, which, when imported into the social sciences, is concerned with the theory and method of the interpretation of human action. It emphasizes the need to understand from the perspective of the social actor.

Hypothesis An informed speculation, which is set up to be tested, about the possible relationship between two or more variables.

Independent variable A **variable** that has a causal impact on another variable (i.e. a **dependent variable**).

Index See **scale**.

Indicator A measure that is employed to refer to a **concept** when no direct measure is available.

Inductive An approach to the relationship between theory and research in which the former is generated out of the latter. Compare with **deductive**.

Informed consent A key principle in social research ethics. It implies that prospective research participants should be given as much information as might be needed to make an informed decision about whether or not they wish to participate in a study.

Inter-coder reliability The degree to which two or more individuals agree about the **coding** of an item. Intercoder reliability is likely to be an issue in **content analysis, structured observation**, and when **coding** answers to **open questions** in research based on **questionnaires** or **structured interviews**.

Internal reliability The degree to which the indicators that make up a **scale** are consistent.

Internal validity A concern with the question of whether a finding that incorporates a causal relationship between two or more variables is sound.

Internet survey A very general term used to include any social survey conducted online. As such, it includes the **web survey** and the **attached email survey** and the **embedded email survey**.

Interpretative repertoire A collection of linguistic resources that are drawn upon in order to characterize and assess actions and events.

Interpretivism An **epistemological** position that requires the social scientist to grasp the subjective meaning of social action.

Interval variable A **variable** where the distances between the categories are identical across its range of categories.

Intervening variable A **variable** that is affected by another variable and that in turn has a causal impact on another variable. Taking an intervening variable into account often facilitates the understanding of the relationship between two variables.

Interview guide A rather vague term that is used to refer to the brief list of memory prompts of areas to be covered that is often employed in **unstructured interviewing** or to the somewhat more structured list of issues to be addressed or questions to be asked in **semi-structured interviewing**.

Interview schedule A collection of questions designed to be asked by an interviewer. An interview schedule is always used in a **structured interview**.

Intra-coder reliability The degree to which an individual differs over time in the **coding** of an item. Intra-coder reliability is likely to be an issue in **content analysis, structured observation**, and when **coding** answers to **open questions** in research based on **questionnaires** or **structured interviews**.

Key informant Someone who offers the researcher, usually in the context of conducting an **ethnography**, perceptive information about the social setting, important events, and individuals.

Life history interview Similar to the **oral history interview**, but the aim of this type of **unstructured interview** is to glean information on the entire biography of each respondent.

Life history method Also often referred to as the **biographical method**, this method emphasizes the inner experience of individuals and its connections with changing events and phases throughout the life course. The method usually entails **life history interviews** and the use of **personal documents** as data.

Likert scale A widely used format developed by Rensis Likert for asking attitude questions. Respondents are typically asked their degree of agreement with a series of statements that together form a **multiple-indicator** or **-item** measure. The scale is deemed then to measure the intensity with which respondents feel about an issue.

Linguistic turn A stance that is based on the notion that language shapes our understanding of the world, so that we cannot manufacture objective representations of an external reality.

Longitudinal research A **research design** in which data are collected on a **sample** (of people, documents, etc.) on at least two occasions.

Mail questionnaire Traditionally, this term has been synonymous with the **postal questionnaire** but with the arrival of email-based questionnaires (see **embedded email survey** and **attached email survey**), many writers prefer to refer to postal rather than mail questionnaires.

Mean See **arithmetic mean**.

Measure of central tendency A statistic, like the **arithmetic mean, median**, or **mode**, that summarizes a **distribution of values**.

Measure of dispersion A statistic, like the **range** or **standard deviation**, that summarizes the amount of variation in a **distribution of values**.

Measurement validity The degree to which a measure of a concept truly reflects that concept. See also **face validity** and **concurrent validity**.

Median The mid-point in a **distribution of values**.

Meta-analysis A form of **systematic review** that involves summarizing the results of a large number of quantitative studies and conducting various analytical tests to show whether or not a particular variable has an effect across the studies.

Meta-ethnography A form of **systematic review** that is used to achieve interpretative synthesis of **qualitative research** and other secondary sources thus providing a counterpart to **meta-analysis** in **quantitative research**. It can be used to synthesize and analyse information about a phenomenon that has been extensively studied.

Missing data Data relating to a case that are not available—for example, when a respondent in **social survey** research does not answer a question. These are referred to as 'missing values' in **SPSS**.

Mixed methods research A term that is increasingly employed to describe research that combines the use of both quantitative and qualitative research. The term can be employed to describe research that combines just quantitative research methods or that combines just qualitative research methods. However, in recent times, it has taken on this more specific meaning of combining quantitative and qualitative research methods.

Mode The value that occurs most frequently in a **distribution of values**.

Moderated relationship A **relationship** between two **variables** is said to be moderated when it holds for one category of a third variable but not for another category or other categories.

Moderator The person who guides the questioning of a **focus group**. Also called a **facilitator**.

Multiple-indicator measure A measure that employs more than one **indicator** to measure a **concept**.

Multivariate analysis The examination of relationships between three or more **variables**.

Narrative analysis An approach to the elicitation and analysis of data that is sensitive to the sense of temporal sequence that people, as tellers of stories about their lives or events around them, detect in their lives and surrounding episodes and inject into their accounts. However, the approach is not exclusive to a focus on life histories.

Narrative review An approach to reviewing the literature that is often contrasted nowadays with a **systematic review**. It tends to be less focused than a systematic review and seeks to arrive at a critical interpretation of the literature that it covers.

Naturalism A confusing term that has at least three distinct meanings: a commitment to adopting the principles of natural scientific method; being true to the nature of the phenomenon being investigated; and a style of research that seeks to minimize the intrusion of artificial methods of data collection.

Negative relationship A **relationship** between two **variables**, whereby as one increases the other decreases.

Nominal variable Also known as a **categorical variable**, this is a variable that comprises categories that cannot be rank ordered.

Non-manipulable variable A **variable** that cannot readily be manipulated either for practical or for ethical reasons and that therefore cannot be employed in an **experiment**.

Non-probability sample A sample that has not been selected using a random sampling method. Essentially, this implies that some units in the population are more likely to be selected than others.

Non-response A source of **non-sampling error** that occurs whenever some members of a sample refuse to cooperate, cannot be contacted, or for some reason cannot supply the required data.

Non-sampling error Differences between the **population** and the **sample** that arise either from deficiencies in the sampling approach, such as an inadequate **sampling frame** or **non-response**, or from problems such as poor question wording, poor interviewing, or flawed processing of data.

Null hypothesis A **hypothesis** of no relationship between two variables.

Objectivism An **ontological** position that asserts that social phenomena and their meanings have an existence that is independent of social actors. Compare with **constructionism**.

Observation schedule A device used in **structured observation** that specifies the categories of behaviour that are to be observed and how behaviour should be allocated to those categories.

Official statistics Statistics compiled by or on behalf of state agencies in the course of conducting their business.

Ontology, ontological A theory of the nature of social entities. See **objectivism** and **constructionism**.

Open question A question employed in an **interview schedule** or **self-completion questionnaire** that does not present the respondent with a set of possible answers to choose from. Compare with **closed question**.

Operational definition The definition of a **concept** in terms of the operations to be carried out when measuring it.

Operationism, operationalism A doctrine, mainly associated with a version of physics, that emphasizes the search for **operational definitions** of **concepts**.

Oral history interview A largely **unstructured interview** in which the respondent is asked to recall events from his or her past and to reflect on them.

Ordinal variable A variable whose categories can be rank ordered (as in the case of **interval** and **ratio variables**), but the distances between the categories are not equal across the range.

Outlier An extreme value in a distribution of values. If a **variable** has an extreme value—either very high or very low—the **arithmetic mean** or the **range** will be distorted by it.

Paradigm A term deriving from the history of science, where it was used to describe a cluster of beliefs and dictates that for scientists in a particular discipline influence what should be studied, how research should be done, and how results should be interpreted.

Participant observation Research in which the researcher immerses him- or herself in a social setting for an extended period of time, observing behaviour, listening to what is said in conversations both between others and with the fieldworker, and asking questions. Participant observation usually includes interviewing key informants and studying documents and as such is difficult to distinguish from **ethnography**. In this book, participant observation is employed to refer to the specifically observational aspect of ethnography.

Pearson's *r* A measure of the strength and direction of the **relationship** between two **interval/ratio variables**.

Personal documents Documents such as **diaries**, letters, and autobiographies that are not written for an official purpose. They provide first-person accounts of the writer's life and events within it.

Phenomenology A philosophy that is concerned with the question of how individuals make sense of the world around them and how in particular the philosopher should bracket out preconceptions concerning his or her grasp of that world.

Phi A method for assessing the strength of the **relationship** between two **dichotomous variables**.

Population The universe of units from which a **sample** is to be selected.

Positive relationship A **relationship** between two **variable**s, whereby as one increases the other increases as well.

Positivism An **epistemological** position that advocates the application of the methods of the natural sciences to the study of social reality and beyond.

Postal questionnaire A form of **self-completion questionnaire** that is sent to respondents and usually returned by them by mail.

Postmodernism A position that displays a distaste for master-narratives and for a **realist** orientation. In the context of research methodology, postmodernists display a preference for qualitative methods and a concern with the modes of representation of research findings.

Pre-coded question Another name for a **closed question**. The term is often preferred, because such a question removes the need for the application of a **coding frame** to the question after it has been answered. This is because the range of answers has been predetermined and a numerical **code** will have been pre-assigned to each possible answer. The term is particularly appropriate when the codes appear on the **questionnaire** or **interview schedule**.

Probability sample A sample that has been selected using **random sampling** and in which each unit in the population has a known probability of being selected.

Projective techniques A method involving the presentation of ambiguous stimuli to individuals, which are interpreted by the researcher to reveal the underlying characteristics of the individual.

QSR NVivo A **CAQDAS** package that derives from but goes beyond NUD*IST (Non-numerical Unstructured Data Indexing Searching and Theorizing).

Qualitative content analysis An approach to documents that emphasizes the role of the investigator in the construction of the meaning of and in texts. There is an emphasis on allowing categories to emerge out of data and on recognizing the significance for understanding the meaning of the context in which an item being analysed (and the categories derived from it) appeared.

Qualitative research Qualitative research usually emphasizes words rather than quantification in the collection and analysis of data. As a **research strategy** it is **inductivist**, **constructionist**, and **interpretivist**, but qualitative researchers do not always subscribe to all three of these features. Compare with **quantitative research**.

Quantitative research Quantitative research usually emphasizes quantification in the collection and analysis of data. As a **research strategy** it is **deductivist** and **objectivist** and incorporates a natural science model of the research process (in particular, one influenced by **positivism**), but quantitative researchers do not always subscribe to all three of these features. Compare with **qualitative research**.

Quasi-experiment A **research design** that is close to being an **experiment** but that does not meet the requirements fully and therefore does not exhibit complete **internal validity**.

Questionnaire A collection of questions administered to respondents. When used on its own, the term usually denotes a **self-completion questionnaire**.

Quota sample A **sample** that non-randomly samples a **population** in terms of the relative proportions of people in different categories. It is a type of **non-probability sample**.

Random assignment A term used in connection with **experiments** to refer to the random allocation of research participants to the experimental group and the control group.

Random sampling Sampling whereby the inclusion of a unit of a **population** occurs entirely by chance.

Range The difference between the maximum and the minimum value in a **distribution of values** associated with an **interval** or **ratio variable**.

Ratio variable An **interval variable** with a true zero point.

Reactivity, reactive effect A term used to describe the response of research participants to the fact that they know they are being studied. Reactivity is deemed to result in untypical behaviour.

Realism An epistemological position that acknowledges a reality independent of the senses that is accessible to the researcher's tools and theoretical speculations. It implies that the categories created by scientists refer to real objects in the natural or social worlds. See also **critical realism**.

Reflexivity A term used in research methodology to refer to a reflectiveness among social researchers about the implications for the knowledge of the social world they generate of their methods, values, biases, decisions, and mere presence in the very situations they investigate.

Relationship An association between two variables whereby the variation in one variable coincides with variation in another variable.

Reliability The degree to which a measure of a concept is stable.

Replication, replicability The degree to which the results of a study can be reproduced. See also **internal reliability**.

Representative sample A **sample** that reflects the population accurately, so that it is a microcosm of the **population**.

Research design This term is employed in this book to refer to a framework for the collection and analysis of data. A choice of research design reflects decisions about the priority being given to a range of dimensions of the research process (such as **causality** and **generalization**).

Research strategy A term used in this book to refer to a general orientation to the conduct of social research (see **quantitative research** and **qualitative research**).

Respondent validation Sometimes called *member validation*, this is a process whereby a researcher provides the people on whom he or she has conducted research with an account of his or her findings and requests feedback on that account.

Response set The tendency among some respondents to **multiple-indicator measures** to reply in the same way to each constituent item.

Rhetoric A concern with the ways in which appeals to convince or persuade are devised.

Sample The segment of the population that is selected for research. It is a subset of the **population**. The method of selection may be based on **probability sampling** or **non-probability sampling**.

Sampling error Differences between a **random sample** and the **population** from which it is selected.

Sampling frame The listing of all units in the **population** from which a **sample** is selected.

Scale A term that is usually used interchangeably with **index** to refer to a **multiple-indicator measure** in which the score a person gives for each component **indicator** is used to provide a composite score for that person.

Scan sampling A sampling approach in **structured observation** whereby an entire group of individuals is scanned at regular intervals and the behaviour of all of them is recorded at each occasion.

Secondary analysis The analysis of data by researchers who will probably not have been involved in the collection of those data for purposes that may not have been envisaged by those responsible for the data collection. Secondary analysis may entail the analysis of either quantitative data or qualitative data.

Self-administered questionnaire See **self-completion questionnaire**.

Self-completion questionnaire A **questionnaire** that the respondent answers without the aid of an interviewer. Sometimes called a **self-administered questionnaire**.

Semiotics The study/science of **signs**. An approach to the analysis of documents and other phenomena that emphasizes the importance of seeking out the deeper meaning of those phenomena. A semiotic approach is concerned to uncover the processes of meaning production and how signs are designed to have an effect upon actual and prospective consumers of those signs.

Semi-structured interview A term that covers a wide range of types. It typically refers to a context in which the interviewer has a series of questions that are in the general form of an **interview guide** but is able to vary the sequence of questions. The questions are frequently somewhat more general in their frame of reference from that typically found in a **structured interview** schedule. Also, the interviewer usually has some latitude to ask further questions in response to what are seen as significant replies.

Sensitizing concept A term devised by Blumer to refer to a preference for treating a **concept** as a guide in an investigation, so that it points in a general way to what is relevant or important. This position contrasts with the idea of an **operational definition**, in which the meaning of a concept is fixed in advance of carrying out an investigation.

Sign A term employed in **semiotics**. A sign is made up of a signifier (the manifestation of a sign) and the signified (that idea or deeper meaning to which the signifier refers).

Simple observation The passive and unobtrusive observation of behaviour.

Simple random sample A **sample** in which each unit has been selected entirely by chance. Each unit of the **population** has a known and equal probability of inclusion in the sample.

Snowball sample A **non-probability sample** in which the researcher makes initial contact with a small group of people who are relevant to the research topic and then uses these to establish contacts with others.

Social desirability bias A distortion of data that is caused by respondents' attempts to construct an account that conforms to a socially acceptable model of belief or behaviour.

Social survey See **survey research**.

Spearman's rho (ρ) A measure of the strength and direction of the **relationship** between two **ordinal variables**.

SPSS Originally, short for **S**tatistical **P**ackage for the **S**ocial **S**ciences, SPSS is a widely used computer program that allows quantitative data to be managed and analysed.

Spurious relationship A **relationship** between two **variables** is said to be spurious if it is being produced by the impact of a third variable on each of the two variables that form the spurious relationship. When the third variable is controlled, the relationship disappears.

Standard deviation A measure of dispersion around the **mean**.

Standard error of the mean An estimate of the amount that a sample mean is likely to differ from the population mean.

Statistical inference See **statistical significance (test of)**.

Statistical significance (test of) Allows the analyst to estimate how confident he or she can be that the results deriving from a study based on a randomly selected **sample** are generalizable to the **population** from which the sample was drawn. Such a test does not allow the researcher to infer that the findings are of substantive importance. The **chi-square test** is an example of this kind of test. The process of using a test of statistical significance to generalize from a sample to a population is known as **statistical inference**.

Stratified random sample A **sample** in which units are **randomly sampled** from a **population** that has been divided into categories (strata).

Structured interview A research interview in which all respondents are asked exactly the same questions in the same order with the aid of a formal **interview schedule**.

Structured observation Often also called **systematic observation**, structured observation is a technique in which the researcher employs explicitly formulated rules for the observation and recording of behaviour. The rules inform observers about what they should look for and how they should record behaviour.

Survey research A **cross-sectional design** in relation to which data are collected predominantly by **self-completion questionnaire** or by **structured interview** on more than one case (usually quite a lot more than one) and at *a single point in time* in order to collect a body of quantitative or quantifiable data in connection with two or more **variables** (usually many more than two), which are then examined to detect patterns of **relationship** between variables.

Symbolic interactionism A theoretical perspective in sociology and social psychology that views social interaction as taking place in terms of the meanings actors attach to action and things.

Synchronous online interview or **focus group** Online interviews may be **asynchronous** or synchronous. In the case of the latter, the transactions between participants are in real time, so that there there will be only brief time lapses between interviewers' questions and participants' replies, and in the case of focus groups, between participants' contributions to the discussion.

Systematic observation See **structured observation**.

Systematic review Systematic reviews are reviews of the literature that aim to provide an account of the literature in a domain that is comprehensive, capable of **replication**, and transparent in its approach. **Meta-analysis** and **meta-ethnography** are both forms of systematic review.

Systematic sample A **probability sampling** method in which units are selected from a **sampling frame** according to fixed intervals, such as every fifth unit.

Text A term that is used either in the conventional sense of a written work or in more recent years to refer to a wide range of phenomena. For example, in arriving at a **thick description**, Geertz refers to treating culture as a text.

Thematic analysis A term used in connection with the analysis of qualitative data to refer to the extraction of key themes in one's data. It is a rather diffuse approach with few generally agreed principles for defining core themes in data.

Theoretical sampling A term used mainly in relation to **grounded theory** to refer to sampling carried out so that emerging theoretical considerations guide the selection of cases and/or research participants. Theoretical sampling is supposed to continue until a point of **theoretical saturation** is reached.

Theoretical saturation In **grounded theory**, the point when emerging **concepts** have been fully explored and no new insights are being generated. See also **theoretical sampling**.

Thick description A term devised by Geertz to refer to detailed accounts of a social setting that can form the basis for the creation of general statements about a culture and its significance in people's social lives.

Time sampling A sampling method in **structured observation**, which entails using a criterion for deciding when observation will occur.

Transcription, transcript The written translation of a recorded **interview** or **focus group** session.

Triangulation The use of more than one method or source of data in the study of a social phenomenon so that findings may be cross-checked.

Trustworthiness A set of criteria advocated by some writers for assessing the quality of **qualitative research**.

Turn taking The notion from **conversation analysis** that order in everyday conversation is achieved through orderly taking of turns in conversations.

Univariate analysis The analysis of a single **variable** at a time.

Unobtrusive methods Methods that do not entail the awareness among research participants that they are being studied and that are therefore not subject to **reactivity**.

Unstructured interview An interview in which the interviewer typically has only a list of topics or issues, often called an **interview guide**, that are typically covered. The style of questioning is usually very informal. The phrasing and sequencing of questions will vary from interview to interview.

Validity A concern with the integrity of the conclusions that are generated from a piece of research. There are different aspects of validity. See, in particular, **measurement validity, internal validity, external validity**, and **ecological validity**. When used on its own, **validity** is usually taken to refer to **measurement validity**.

Variable An attribute in terms of which cases vary. See also **dependent variable** and **independent variable**. Compare with **constant**.

Web survey A **social survey** conducted so that respondents complete a **questionnaire** via a website.

References

Abraham, J. (1994), 'Bias in Science and Medical Knowledge: The Opren Controversy', *Sociology*, 28: 717–36.

Adler, P., and Adler, P. A. (1985), 'From Idealism to Pragmatic Detachment: The Academic Performance of College Athletes', *Sociology of Education*, 58: 241–50.

Adler, P. A. (1985), *Wheeling and Dealing: An Ethnography of an Upper-Level Drug Dealing and Smuggling Community* (New York: Columbia University Press).

Adriaenssens, C., and Cadman, L. (1999), 'An Adaptation of Moderated E-mail Focus Groups to Assess the Potential of a New Online (Internet) Financial Services Offer in the UK', *Journal of the Market Research Society*, 41: 417–24.

Aitken, I. (1998), 'The Documentary Film Movement: The Post Office Touches All Branches of Life', in J. Hassard and R. Holliday (eds.), *Organization-Representation: Work and Organization in Popular Culture* (London: Sage).

Alderson, P. (1998), 'Confidentiality and Consent in Qualitative Research', *Network: Newsletter of the British Sociological Association*, 69: 6–7.

Aldridge, A. (1998), 'Reproducing the Value of Professional Expertise in Post-Traditional Culture: Financial Advice and the Creation of the Client', *Cultural Values*, 2: 445–62.

Allison, G. T. (1971), *Essence of Decision: Explaining the Cuban Missile Crisis* (Boston: Little, Brown).

Altheide, D. L. (1980), 'Leaving the Newsroom', in W. Shaffir, R. A. Stebbins, and A. Turowetz (eds.), *Fieldwork Experience: Qualitative Approaches to Social Research* (New York: St Martin's Press).

—— (1996), *Qualitative Media Analysis* (Thousand Oaks, Calif.: Sage).

—— (2004), 'Ethnographic Content Analysis', in M. S. Lewis-Beck, A. Bryman, and T. F. Liao (eds.), *The Sage Encyclopedia of Social Science Research Methods* (3 vols.; Thousand Oaks, Calif.: Sage).

Altschuld, J. W., and Lower, M. A. (1984), 'Improving Mailed Questionnaires: Analysis of a 96 Percent Return Rate', in D. C. Lockhart (ed.), *Making Effective Use of Mailed Questionnaires* (San Francisco: Jossey-Bass).

Alvesson, M. (2002), *Postmodernism and Social Research* (Buckingham: Open University Press).

—— and Karreman, D. (2000) 'Varieties of Discourse: On the Study of Organization through Discourse Analysis', *Human Relations*, 53(9): 1125–49.

Anderson, E. (1978), *A Place on the Corner* (Chicago: University of Chicago Press).

—— (2006), 'Jelly's Place: An Ethnographic Memoir', in D. Hobbs and R. Wright (eds.), *The Sage Handbook of Fieldwork* (London: Sage).

Andersen, M. (1981), 'Corporate Wives: Longing for Liberation or Satisfied with the Status Quo?', *Urban Life*, 10: 311–27.

Ang, I. (1985), *Watching Dallas: Soap Opera and the Melodramatic Imagination* (London: Methuen).

Angell, E., Bryman, A., Ashcroft, R., and Dixon-Woods, M. (2008), 'Never Mind the Scientific Quality, Feel the Ethics?: An Analysis of Decision Letters by Research Ethics Committees and a Reflection', *Quality and Safety in Health Care*.

Arber, S., and Gilbert, G. N. (1989), 'Transitions in Caring: Gender, Life Course and the Care of the Elderly', in B. Bytheway, T. Keil, P. Allatt, and A. Bryman (eds.), *Becoming and Being Old: Sociological Approaches to Later Life* (London: Sage).

Armstrong, D., Gosling, A., Weinman, J., and Marteau, T. (1997), 'The Place of Inter-Rater Reliability in Qualitative Research: An Empirical Study', *Sociology*, 31: 597–606.

Armstrong, G. (1993), 'Like that Desmond Morris?', in D. Hobbs and T. May (eds.), *Interpreting the Field: Accounts of Ethnography* (Oxford: Clarendon Press).

—— (1998), *Football Hooligans: Knowing the Score* (Oxford: Berg).

Arnold, H. J., and Feldman, D. C. (1981), 'Social Desirability Response Bias in Self-Report Choice Situations', *Academy of Management Journal*, 24: 377–85.

Aronson, E., and Carlsmith, J. M. (1968), 'Experimentation in Social Psychology', in G. Lindzey and E. Aronson (eds.), *The Handbook of Social Psychology* (Reading, Mass.: Addison-Wesley).

Asch, S. E. (1951), 'Effect of Group Pressure upon the Modification and Distortion of Judgments', in H. Guetzkow (ed.), *Groups, Leadership and Men* (Pittsburgh: Carnegie Press).

Ashforth, B. E., Kreiner, G. E., Clark, M. A., and Fugate, M. (2007), 'Normalizing Dirty Work: Tactics for Countering Occupational Taint', *Academy of Management Journal*, 50: 149–74.

Atkinson, J. M., and Drew, P. (1979), *Order in Court: The Organization of Verbal Interaction in Judicial Settings* (London: Macmillan).

Atkinson, P. (1981), *The Clinical Experience* (Farnborough: Gower).

—— (1990), *The Ethnographic Imagination: Textual Constructions of Society* (London: Routledge).

—— and Coffey, A. (1995), 'Realism and its Discontents: On the Crisis of Cultural Representation in Ethnographic Texts', in B. Adam and S. Allan (eds.), *Theorizing Culture: An Interdisciplinary Critique after Postmodernism* (London: UCL Press).

—— —— (2004), 'Analysing Documentary Realities', in D. Silverman (ed.), *Qualitative Research: Theory, Method and Practice* (2nd edn.; London: Sage).

Atkinson, R. (2004), 'Life Story Interview', in M. S. Lewis-Beck, A. Bryman, and T. F. Liao (eds.), *The Sage Encyclopedia of Social Science Research Methods* (3 vols.; Thousand Oaks, Calif.: Sage).

—— (1998), *The Life Story Interview* (Beverly Hills, Calif.: Sage).

—— and Kintrea, K. (2001), 'Disentangling Area Effects: Evidence from Deprived and Non-Deprived Neighbourhoods', *Urban Studies* 38: 2277–98.

Baggini, J. (2007), *Welcome to Everytown* (London: Granta).

Bahr, H. M., Caplow, T., and Chadwick, B. A. (1983), 'Middletown III: Problems of Replication, Longitudinal Measurement, and Triangulation', *Annual Review of Sociology*, 9: 243–64.

Ball, S. J. (1981), *Beachside Comprehensive: A Case Study of Secondary Schooling* (Cambridge: Cambridge University Press).

—— (1984), 'Beachside Reconsidered: Reflections on a Methodological Apprenticeship', in R. G. Burgess (ed.), *The Research Process in Educational Settings: Ten Case Studies* (London: Falmer Press).

Bampton, R., and Cowton, C. J. (2002), 'The E-Interview', *Forum Qualitative Social Research*, 3(2), http://www.qualitative-research.net/fqs/.

Banks, M. (2001), *Visual Methods in Social Research* (London: Sage).

Barker, E. (1984), *The Making of a Moonie: Choice or Brainwashing?* (Oxford: Blackwell).

Barnard, M., and Frischer, M. (1995), 'Combining Quantitative and Qualitative Approaches: Researching HIV-Related Risk Behaviours among Drug Injectors', *Addiction Research*, 2: 351–62.

Barnes, S. (2004), 'Issues of Attribution and Identification in Online Social Research', in M. D. Johns, S.-L. S. Chen, and G. J. Hall (eds.), *Online Social Research* (New York: Peter Lang).

Barnett, R. (1994), 'Editorial', *Studies in Higher Education*, 19(2): 123–4.

Barter, C., and Renold, E. (1999), 'The Use of Vignettes in Qualitative Research', *Social Research Update*, 25.

Barthes, R. (1972), *Mythologies* (London: Jonathan Cape).

Bauman, Z. (1978), *Hermeneutics and Social Science: Approaches to Understanding* (London: Hutchison).

Baumgartner, R. M., and Heberlein, T. A. (1984), 'Applying Attitude Theories to the Return of Mailed Questionnaires', in D. C. Lockhart (ed.), *Making Effective Use of Mailed Questionnaires* (San Francisco: Jossey-Bass).

Bazerman, C. (1987), 'Codifying the Social Scientific Style: The APA *Publication Manual* as a Behaviorist Rhetoric', in J. S. Nelson, A. Megill, and D. N. McClosky (eds.), *The Rhetoric of the Human Sciences* (Madison: University of Wisconsin Press).

Beardsworth, A. (1980), 'Analysing Press Content: Some Technical and Methodological Issues', in H. Christian (ed.), *Sociology of Journalism and the Press* (Keele: Keele University Press).

—— and Bryman, A. (2004), 'Meat Consumption and Meat Avoidance among Young People: An 11-Year Longitudinal Study', *British Food Journal*, 106: 313–27.

—— and Keil, T. (1992), 'The Vegetarian Option: Varieties, Conversions, Motives and Careers', *Sociological Review*, 40: 253–93.

—— —— (1997), *Sociology on the Menu: An Invitation to the Study of Food and Society* (London: Routledge).

—— Bryman, A., Keil, T., Goode, J., Haslam, C., and Lancashire, E. (2002), 'Women, Men and Food: The Significance of Gender for Nutritional Attitudes and Choices', *British Food Journal*, 104: 470–91.

—— —— Ford, J., and Keil, T. (n.d.), ' "The Dark Figure" in Statistics of Unemployment and Vacancies: Some Sociological Implications', discussion paper, Department of Social Sciences, Loughborough University.

Bechhofer, F., Elliott, B., and McCrone, D. (1984), 'Safety in Numbers: On the Use of Multiple Interviewers', *Sociology*, 18: 97–100.

Becker, H. S. (1958), 'Problems of Inference and Proof in Participant Observation', *American Sociological Review*, 23: 652–60.

—— (1963), *Outsiders: Studies in the Sociology of Deviance* (New York: Free Press).

—— (1967), 'Whose Side are We On?', *Social Problems*, 14: 239–47.

—— (1970), 'Practitioners of Vice and Crime', in R. W. Habenstein (ed.), *Pathways to Data* (Chicago: Aldine).

—— (1982), 'Culture: A Sociological View', *Yale Review*, 71: 513–27.

—— (1986), *Writing for Social Scientists: How to Start and Finish Your Thesis, Book, or Article* (Chicago: University of Chicago Press).

—— and Geer, B. (1957), 'Participant Observation and Interviewing: A Comparison', *Human Organization*, 16: 28–32.

Beharrell, P. (1993), 'AIDS and the British Press', in J. Eldridge (ed.), *Getting the Message: News, Truth and Power* (London: Routledge).

Belk, R. W., Sherry, J. F., and Wallendorf, M. (1988), 'A Naturalistic Inquiry into Buyer and Seller Behavior at a Swap Meet', *Journal of Consumer Research*, 14: 449–70.

Bell, C. (1969), 'A Note on Participant Observation', *Sociology*, 3: 417–18.

—— and Newby, H. (1977), *Doing Sociological Research* (London: George Allen & Unwin).

—— and Roberts, H. (1984), *Social Researching: Politics, Problems, Practice* (London: Routledge & Kegan Paul).

Bell, E., and Bryman, A. (2007), 'The Ethics of Management Research: An Exploratory Content Analysis', *British Journal of Management* 18: 63–77.

Belson, W. A. (1981), *The Design and Understanding of Survey Questions* (Aldershot: Gower).

Berelson, B. (1952), *Content Analysis in Communication Research* (New York: Free Press).

Berthoud, R. (2000a), 'Introduction: the Dynamics of Social Change', in R. Berthoud and J. Gershuny (eds.), *Seven Years in the Lives of British Families: Evidence on the Dynamics of Social Change from the British Household Panel Survey* (Bristol: Policy Press).

—— (2000b), 'A Measure of Changing Health', in R. Berthoud and J. Gershuny (eds.), *Seven Years in the Lives of British Families: Evidence on the Dynamics of Social Change from the British Household Panel Survey* (Bristol: Policy Press).

Beynon, H. (1975), *Working for Ford* (Harmondsworth: Penguin).

Bhaskar, R. (1975), *A Realist Theory of Science* (Leeds: Leeds Books).

—— (1989), *Reclaiming Reality: A Critical Introduction to Contemporary Philosophy* (London: Verso).

Billig, M. (1991), *Ideology and Opinions: Studies in Rhetorical Psychology* (Cambridge: Cambridge University Press).

—— (1992), *Talking of the Royal Family* (London: Routledge).

—— Condor, S., Edwards, D., Gane, M., Middleton, D., and Radley, A. (1988), *Ideological Dilemmas: A Social Psychology of Everyday Thinking* (London: Sage).

Blaikie, A. (2001), 'Photographs in the Cultural Account: Contested Narratives and Collective Memory in the Scottish Islands', *Sociological Review*, 49: 345–67.

Blatchford, P. (2005), 'A Multi-Method Approach to the Study of School Size Differences', *International Journal of Social Research Methodology*, 8: 195–205.

—— Edmonds, S., and Martin, C. (2003), 'Class Size, Pupil Attentiveness and Peer Relations', *British Journal of Educational Psychology*, 73: 15–36.

Blauner, R. (1964), *Alienation and Freedom* (Chicago: University of Chicago Press).

Blaxter, M. (1990), *Health and Lifestyles* (London: Routledge).

Bloland, H. G. (2005), 'Whatever Happened to Postmodernism in Higher Education?', *Journal of Higher Education*, 76: 121–50.

Bloor, M. (1978), 'On the Analysis of Observational Data: A Discussion of the Worth and Uses of Inductive Techniques and Respondent Validation', *Sociology*, 12: 545–52.

—— (1997), 'Addressing Social Problems through Qualitative Research', in D. Silverman (ed.), *Qualitative Research: Theory, Method and Practice* (London: Sage).

—— (2002), 'No Longer Dying for a Living: Collective Responses to Injury Risks in South Wales Mining Communities, 1900–47', *Sociology*, 36: 89–105.

—— Frankland, S., Thomas, M., and Robson, K. (2001), *Focus Groups in Social Research* (London: Sage).

Blumer, H. (1954), 'What is Wrong with Social Theory?', *American Sociological Review*, 19: 3–10.

—— (1956), 'Sociological Analysis and the "Variable" ', *American Sociological Review*, 21: 683–90.

—— (1962), 'Society as Symbolic Interaction', in A. M. Rose (ed.), *Human Behavior and Social Processes* (London: Routledge & Kegan Paul).

Bogdan, R., and Taylor, S. J. (1975), *Introduction to Qualitative Research Methods: A Phenomenological Approach to the Social Sciences* (New York: Wiley).

Bond, S., and Sales, J. (2001), 'Household Work in the UK: An Analysis of the British Household Panel Survey 1994', *Work, Employment and Society*, 15: 233–50.

Bottomore, T. B., and Rubel, M. (1963), *Karl Marx: Selected Writings in Sociology and Social Philosophy* (Harmondsworth: Penguin).

Bourdieu, P. (1984), *Distinction: A Social Critique of the Judgement of Taste* (Cambridge, Mass. Harvard University Press).

Bradburn, N. A., and Sudman, S. (1979), *Improving Interview Method and Questionnaire Design* (San Francisco: Jossey-Bass).

Brannen, J., and Nilsen, A. (2006), 'From Fatherhood to Fathering: Tradition and Change Among British Fathers in Four-Generation Families', *Sociology*, 40: 335–52.

Brannen, J., Lewis, S., Nilsen, A., and Smithson, J. (2002), *Young Europeans, Work and Family: Futures in Transition* (London: Routledge).

Bridgman, P. W. (1927), *The Logic of Modern Physics* (New York: Macmillan).

Braverman, H. (1974), *Labor and Monopoly Capital: The Degradation of Work in the Twentieth Century* (London: Monthly Review Press).

Brayfield, A., and Rothe, H. (1951), 'An Index of Job Satisfaction', *Journal of Applied Psychology*, 35: 307–11.

Briggs, C. L. (1986), *Learning How to Ask: A Sociolinguistic Appraisal of the Role of the Interview in Social Science Research* (Cambridge: Cambridge University Press).

Britten, N. (2005), 'Welcome to Birmingham, the Rudest City in Britain', *Daily Telegraph*, 21 Oct., http://www.telegraph. co.uk/news/main.jhtml?xml=/news/2005/10/21/ nbrum21.xml&sSheet=/news/2005/10/21/ixhome.html.

Brown, A. D. (1998), 'Narrative, Politics and Legitimacy in an IT Implementation', *Journal of Management Studies*, 35: 35–58.

Brown, G. W., and Harris, T. W. (1978), *The Social Origins of Depression: A Study of Psychiatric Disorder in Women* (London: Tavistock).

Brown, S. D., and Lightfoot, G. (2002), 'Presence, Absence, and Accountability: E-mail and the Mediation of Organizational Memory', in S. Woolgar (ed.), *Virtual Society? Technology, Cyperbole, Reality* (Oxford: Oxford University Press).

Bruce, C. S. (1994), 'Research Students' Early Experiences of the Dissertation Literature Review', *Studies in Higher Education*, 19(2): 217–29.

Bryman, A. (1974), 'Sociology of Religion and Sociology of Elites', *Archives de sciences sociales des religions*, 38: 109–21.

—— (1988a), *Quantity and Quality in Social Research* (London: Routledge).

—— (1988b), *Doing Research in Organizations* (London: Routledge).

—— (1989a), *Research Methods and Organization Studies* (London: Routledge).

—— (1989b), 'The Value of Re-Studies in Sociology: The Case of Clergy and Ministers, 1971 to 1985', *Sociology*, 23: 31–54.

—— (1992), 'Quantitative and Qualitative Research: Further Reflections on their Integration', in J. Brannen (ed.), *Mixing Methods: Qualitative and Quantitative Research* (Aldershot: Avebury).

—— (1994), 'The Mead/Freeman Controversy: Some Implications for Qualitative Researchers', in R. G. Burgess (ed.), *Studies in Qualitative Methodology, Vol. 4* (Greenwich, Conn.: JAI Press).

—— (1995), *Disney and his Worlds* (London: Routledge).

—— (1998), 'Quantitative and Qualitative Research Strategies in Knowing the Social World', in T. May and M. Williams (eds.), *Knowing the Social World* (Buckingham: Open University Press).

—— (1999), 'Global Disney', in P. Taylor and D. Slater (eds.), *The American Century* (Oxford: Blackwell).

—— (2003), 'McDonald's as a Disneyized Institution: Global Implications', *American Behavioral Scientist*, 47: 154–67.

—— (2004a), *The Disneyization of Society* (London: Sage).

—— (2004b), 'Qualitative Research on Leadership: A Critical but Appreciative Review', *Leadership Quarterly*, 15: 729–69.

—— (2006a), 'Integrating Quantitative and Qualitative Research: How is it Done?', *Qualitative Research*, 6: 97–113.

—— (2006b), 'Paradigm Peace and the Implications for Quality', *International Journal of Social Research Methodology*, 9: 111–26.

—— (2007a), 'The End of the Paradigm Wars?', in P. Alasuutari, J. Brannen, and L. Bickman (eds.), *Handbook of Social Research* (London: Sage).

—— (2007b), 'The Research Question in Social Research: What is its Role?', *International Journal of Social Research Methodology*, 10: 5–20.

—— (2007c), 'Barriers to Integrating Quantitative and Qualitative Research', *Journal of Mixed Methods Research*, 1: 8–22.

—— (2008). *Social Research Methods* (3rd edn.; Oxford: Oxford University Press).

—— and Burgess, R. G. (1994a), 'Developments in Qualitative Data Analysis: An Introduction', in A. Bryman and R. G. Burgess (eds.), *Analyzing Qualitative Data* (London: Routledge).

—— —— (1994b), 'Reflections on Qualitative Data Analysis', in A. Bryman and R. G. Burgess (eds.), *Analyzing Qualitative Data* (London: Routledge).

—— —— (1999), 'Introduction: Qualitative Research Methodology—A Review', in A. Bryman and R. G. Burgess (eds.), *Qualitative Research* (London: Sage).

—— and Cramer, D. (2001), *Quantitative Data Analysis with SPSS Release 10 for Windows: A Guide for Social Scientists* (London: Routledge).

—— —— (2004), 'Constructing Variables', in M. Hardy and A. Bryman (eds.), *Handbook of Data Analysis* (London: Sage).

—— —— (2008), *Quantitative Data Analysis with SPSS 15: A Guide for Social Scientists* (London: Routledge).

—— Becker, S., and Sempik, J. (in press), 'Quality Criteria for Quantitative, Qualitative and Mixed Methods Research: The View from Social Policy', *International Journal of Social Research Methodology*.

—— Gillingwater, D., and McGuinness, I. (1996), 'Industry Culture and Strategic Response: The Case of the British Bus Industry', *Studies in Cultures, Organizations and Societies*, 2: 191–208.

—— Haslam, C., and Webb, A. (1994), 'Performance Appraisal in UK Universities: A Case of Procedural Compliance?', *Assessment and Evaluation in Higher Education*, 19: 175–88.

—— Stephens, M., and A Campo, C. (1996), 'The Importance of Context: Qualitative Research and the Study of Leadership', *Leadership Quarterly*, 7: 353–70.

Buckle, A., and Farrington, D. P. (1984), 'An Observational Study of Shoplifting', *British Journal of Criminology*, 24: 63–73.

—— —— (1994), 'Measuring Shoplifting by Systematic Observation', *Psychology, Crime and Law*, 1: 133–41.

Bulmer, M. (1979), 'Concepts in the Analysis of Qualitative Data', *Sociological Review*, 27: 651–77.

—— (1980), 'Why Don't Sociologists Make More Use of Official Statistics?', *Sociology*, 14: 505–23.

—— (1982), 'The Merits and Demerits of Covert Participant Observation', in M. Bulmer (ed.), *Social Research Ethics* (London: Macmillan).

—— (1984), 'Facts, Concepts, Theories and Problems', in M. Bulmer (ed.), *Social Research Methods* (London: Macmillan).

Burawoy, M. (1979), *Manufacturing Consent* (Chicago: University of Chicago Press).

—— (2003), 'Revisits: An Outline of a Theory of Reflexive Ethnography', *American Sociological Review*, 68: 645–79.

Burgess, R. G. (1983), *Inside Comprehensive Education: A Study of Bishop McGregor School* (London: Methuen).

—— (1984), *In the Field* (London: Allen & Unwin).

—— (1987), 'Studying and Restudying Bishop McGregor School', in G. Walford (ed.), *Doing Sociology of Education* (Lewes: Falmer).

Burman, M. J., Batchelor, S. A., and Brown, J. A. (2001), 'Researching Girls and Violence: Facing the Dilemmas of Fieldwork', *British Journal of Criminology*, 41: 443–59.

Burrell, I., and Leppard, D. (1994), 'Fall in Crime a Myth as Police Chiefs Massage the Figures', *Sunday Times*, 16 Oct.: 1, 5.

Bury, M. (2001), 'Illness Narratives: Fact or Fiction?', *Sociology of Health and Illness*, 23: 263–85.

Business Week (1973), 'The Public Clams up on Survey Takers', 15 Sept.: 216–20.

Buston, K. (1997), 'NUD*IST in Action: Its Use and its Usefulness in a Study of Chronic Illness in Young People', *Sociological Research Online*, 2, http://www.socresonline.org.uk/socresonline/2/3/6.html.

Butcher, B. (1994), 'Sampling Methods: An Overview and Review', *Survey Methods Centre Newsletter*, 15: 4–8.

Butler, T., and Robson, G. (2001), 'Social Capital, Gentrification and Neighbourhood Change in London: A Comparison of Three South London Neighbourhoods', *Urban Studies*, 38: 2145–62.

Calder, B. J. (1977), 'Focus Groups and the Nature of Qualitative Marketing Research', *Journal of Marketing Research*, 14: 353–64.

Camerer, C. F. (1997), 'Taxi Drivers and Beauty Contests', *Engineering and Science*, 60: 11–19.

Campbell, D. T. (1957), 'Factors Relevant to the Validity of Experiments in Social Settings', *Psychological Bulletin*, 54: 297–312.

Campbell, R., Pound, P., Pope, C., Britten, N., Pill, R., Morgan, M., and Donovan, J. (2003), 'Evaluating Meta-Ethnography: A Synthesis of Qualitative Research on Lay Experiences of Diabetes and Diabetes Care', *Social Science and Medicine*, 56: 671–84.

Carlson, R. G., Siegal, H. A., Wang, J., and Falck, R. A. (1996), 'Attitudes toward Needle "Sharing" among Injection Drug Users: Combining Qualitative and Quantitative Research Methods', *Human Organization*, 55: 361–9.

Catterall, M., and Maclaran, P. (1997), 'Focus Group Data and Qualitative Analysis Programs: Coding the Moving Picture as well as Snapshots', *Sociological Research Online*, 2, http://www.socresonline.org.uk/socresonline/2/1/6.html.

Cavendish, R. (1982), *Women on the Line* (London: Routledge & Kegan Paul).

Chamberlayne, P., Bornat, J., and Wengraf, T. (2000), 'Introduction: The Biographical Turn', in P. Chamberlayne, J. Bornat, and T. Wengraf (eds.), *The Turn to Biographical Methods in Social Science: Comparative Issues and Examples* (London: Routledge).

Charles, N., and Kerr, N. (1988), *Women, Food and Families* (Manchester: Manchester University Press).

Charlton, T., Gunter, B., and Coles, D. (1998), 'Broadcast Television as a Cause of Aggression?: Recent Findings from a Naturalistic Study', *Emotional and Behavioural Difficulties*, 3: 5–13.

—— Coles, D., Panting, C., and Hannan, A. (1999), 'Behaviour of Nursery Class Children before and after the Availability of Broadcast Television: A Naturalistic Study of Two Cohorts in a Remote Community', *Journal of Social Behavior and Personality*, 14: 315–24.

Charmaz, K. (1983), 'The Grounded Theory Method: An Explication and Interpretation', in R. M. Emerson (ed.), *Contemporary Field Research: A Collection of Readings* (Boston: Little, Brown).

—— (1991), *Good Days, Bad Days: The Self in Chronic Illness and Time* (New Brunswick, NJ: Rutgers University Press).

—— (1997), 'Identity Dilemmas of Chronically Ill Men', in A. Strauss and J. M. Corbin (eds.), *Grounded Theory in Practice* (Thousand Oaks, Calif.: Sage).

—— (2000), 'Grounded Theory: Objectivist and Constructivist Methods', in N. K. Denzin and Y. S. Lincoln (eds.), *Handbook of Qualitative Research* (2nd edn.; Thousand Oaks, Calif.: Sage).

Charmaz, K. (2002), 'Qualitative Interviewing and Grounded Theory Analysis', in J. F. Gubrium and J. A. Holstein (eds.), *Handbook of Interview Research: Context and Method* (Thousand Oaks, Calif.: Sage).

—— (2004), 'Grounded Theory', in M. S. Lewis-Beck, A. Bryman, and T. F. Liao (eds.), *The Sage Encyclopedia of Social Science Research Methods* (3 vols.; Thousand Oaks, Calif.: Sage).

—— (2006), *Constructing Grounded Theory: A Practical Guide through Qualitative Analysis* (London: Sage).

Chattoe, E., and Gilbert, N. (1999), 'Talking about Budgets: Time and Uncertainty in Household Decision Making', *Sociology*, 33: 85–103.

Chin, M. G., Fisak, B. Jr., and Sims, V. K. (2002), 'Development of the Attitudes toward Vegetarianism Scale', *Anthrozoös*, 15: 333–42.

Cicourel, A. V. (1964), *Method and Measurement in Sociology* (New York: Free Press).

—— (1968), *The Social Organization of Juvenile Justice* (New York: Wiley).

—— (1982), 'Interviews, Surveys, and the Problem of Ecological Validity', *American Sociologist*, 17: 11–20.

Clairborn, W. L. (1969), 'Expectancy Effects in the Classroom: A Failure to Replicate', *Journal of Educational Psychology*, 60: 377–83.

Clapper, D. L., and Massey, A. P. (1996), 'Electronic Focus Groups: A Framework for Exploration', *Information and Management*, 30: 43–50.

Clayman, S., and Gill, V. T. (2004), 'Conversation Analysis', in M. Hardy and A. Bryman (eds.), *Handbook of Data Analysis* (London: Sage).

Clifford, J. (1983), 'On Ethnographic Authority', *Representations*, 1: 118–46.

Cloward, R. A., and Ohlin, L. E. (1960), *Delinquency and Opportunity: A Theory of Delinquent Gangs* (New York: Free Press).

Cobanoglu, C., Ward, B., and Moreo, P. J. (2001), 'A Comparison of Mail, Fax and Web-Based Survey Methods', *International Journal of Market Research*, 43: 441–52.

Coffey, A. (1999), *The Ethnographic Self: Fieldwork and the Representation of Reality* (London: Sage).

—— and Atkinson, P. (1996), *Making Sense of Qualitative Data: Complementary Research Strategies* (Thousand Oaks, Calif.: Sage).

—— Holbrook, B., and Atkinson, P. (1994), 'Qualitative Data Analysis: Technologies and Representations', *Sociological Research Online*, 2, http://www.socresonline.org.uk/socresonline/1/1/4.html.

Cohen, S. (1973), *Folk Devils and Moral Panics: The Creation of the Mods and Rockers* (London: Paladin).

Coleman, C., and Moynihan, J. (1996), *Understanding Crime Data: Haunted by the Dark Figure* (Buckingham: Open University Press).

Coleman, J. S. (1958), 'Relational Analysis: The Study of Social Organization with Survey Methods', *Human Organization*, 16: 28–36.

Collins, M. (1997), 'Interviewer Variability: A Review of the Problem', *Journal of the Market Research Society*, 39: 67–84.

Collins, R. (1994), *Four Sociological Traditions* (rev. edn., New York: Oxford University Press).

Conger, J. A., and Kanungo, R. N. (1998), *Charismatic Leadership in Organizations* (Thousand Oaks, Calif.: Sage).

Converse, J. M., and Presser, S. (1986), *Survey Questions: Handcrafting the Standardized Questionnaire* (Beverly Hills, Calif.: Sage).

Cook, T. D., and Campbell, D. T. (1979), *Quasi-Experimentation: Design and Analysis for Field Settings* (Boston, Mass.: Houghton Mifflin).

Corti, L. (1993), 'Using Diaries in Social Research', *Social Research Update*, 2.

—— Foster, J., and Thompson, P. (1995), 'Archiving Qualitative Research Data', *Social Research Update*, 10.

Couper, M. P. (2000), 'Web Surveys: A Review of Issues and Approaches', *Public Opinion Quarterly*, 64: 464–94.

—— (2004), 'Internet Surveys', in M. S. Lewis-Beck, A. Bryman, and T. F. Liao (eds.), *The Sage Encyclopedia of Social Science Research Methods* (3 vols.; Thousand Oaks, Calif.: Sage).

—— and Hansen, S. E. (2002), 'Computer-Assisted Interviewing', in J. F. Gubrium and J. A. Holstein (eds.), *Handbook of Interview Research: Context and Method* (Thousand Oaks, Calif.: Sage).

—— Tourangeau, R., Conrad, F. G., and Crawford, S. D. (2004), 'What They See Is What We Get: Response Options for Web Surveys', *Social Science Computer Review*, 22: 111–27.

—— Traugott, M. W., and Lamias, M. J. (2001), 'Web Survey Design and Administration', *Public Opinion Quarterly*, 65: 230–53.

Coxon, A. P. M. (1994), 'Diaries and Sexual Behaviour: The Use of Sexual Diaries as Method and Substance in Researching Gay Men's Response to HIV/AIDS', in M. Boulton (ed.), *Challenge and Innovation: Methodological Advances in Social Research on HIV/AIDS* (London: Taylor & Francis).

Craig, G. (2004), 'Managing Safety in Policy Research', in S. Becker and A. Bryman (eds.), *Understanding Research for Social Policy and Practice: Themes, Methods, and Approaches* (Bristol: Policy Press).

—— Corden, A., and Thornton, P. (2000), 'Safety in Social Research', *Social Research Update*, issue 20, available at http://sru.soc.surrey.ac.uk/SRU29.html.

Cramer, D. (1998), *Fundamental Statistics for Social Research* (London: Routledge).

Crawford, S. D., Couper, M. P., and Lamias, M. J. (2001), 'Web Surveys: Perceptions of Burden', *Social Science Computer Review*, 19: 146–62.

Creswell, J., and Plano Clark, V. L. (2007), *Conducting and Designing Mixed Methods Research* (Thousand Oaks, Calif.: Sage).

—— and Tashakkori, A. (2007), 'Developing Publishable Mixed Methods Manuscripts', *Journal of Mixed Methods Research*, 1: 107–11.

Croll, P. (1986), *Systematic Classroom Observation* (London: Falmer Press).

—— and Moses, D. (1985), *One in Five: The Assessment and Incidence of Special Educational Needs* (London: Routledge & Kegan Paul).

Crompton, R., and Birkelund, G. (2000), 'Employment and Caring in British and Norwegian Banking', *Work Employment and Society*, 14: 331–52.

Crook, C., and Light, P. (2002), 'Virtual Society and the Cultural Practice of Study', in S. Woolgar (ed.), *Virtual Society? Technology, Cyperbole, Reality* (Oxford: Oxford University Press).

Cryer, P. (1996), *The Research Student's Guide to Success* (Buckingham: Open University Press).

Curasi, C. F. (2001), 'A Critical Exploration of Face-to-Face Interviewing vs. Computer-Mediated Interviewing', *International Journal of Market Research*, 43: 361–75.

Czaja, R., and Blair, J. (1996), *Designing Surveys: A Guide to Decisions and Procedures* (Thousand Oaks, Calif.: Sage).

Dale, A. (1987), 'The Effect of Life Cycle on Three Dimensions of Stratification', in A. Bryman, B. Bytheway, P. Allatt, and T. Keil (eds.), *Rethinking the Life Cycle* (London: Macmillan).

—— Arber, S., and Proctor, M. (1988), *Doing Secondary Analysis* (London: Unwin Hyman).

Daniel, W. W. (1968), *Racial Discrimination in Britain* (Harmondsworth: Penguin).

Davies, C. A. (1999), *Reflexive Ethnography: A Guide to Researching Selves and Others* (London: Routledge).

Davies, P. (2000), 'Doing Interviews with Female Offenders', in V. Jupp, P. Davies, and P. Francis (eds.), *Doing Criminological Research* (London: Sage).

Davies, R. B., Elias, P., and Penn, R. (1994), 'The Relationship between a Husband's Unemployment and his Wife's Participation in the Labour Force', in D. Gallie, C. Marsh, and C. Vogler (eds.), *Social Change and the Experience of Unemployment* (Oxford: Oxford University Press).

Davis, J. A. (1964), '*Great Books and Small Groups*: An Informal History of a National Survey', in P. Hammond (ed.), *Sociologists at Work* (New York: Basic Books).

Davis, S. N. (2003), 'Sex Stereotypes in Commercials Targeted toward Children: A Content Analysis', *Sociological Spectrum*, 23: 407–24.

Deacon, D., Bryman, A., and Fenton, N. (1998), 'Collision or Collusion? A Discussion of the Unplanned Triangulation of Quantitative and Qualitative Research Methods', *International Journal of Social Research Methodology*, 1: 47–63.

—— Fenton, N., and Bryman, A. (1999), 'From Inception to Reception: The Natural History of a News Item', *Media, Culture and Society*, 21: 5–31.

—— Pickering, M., Golding, P., and Murdock, G. (1999), *Researching Communications: A Practical Guide to Methods in Media and Cultural Analysis* (London: Arnold).

Delamont, S. (1976), 'Beyond Flanders' Fields: The Relationship of Subject-Matter and Individuality in Classroom Style', in M. Stubbs and S. Delamont (eds.), *Explorations in Classroom Observation* (Chichester: Wiley).

—— and Atkinson, P. (2004), 'Qualitative Research and the Postmodern Turn', in C. Hardy and A. Bryman (eds.), *Handbook of Data Analysis* (London: Sage).

—— and Hamilton, D. (1984), 'Revisiting Classroom Research: A Continuing Cautionary Tale', in S. Delamont (ed.), *Readings on Interaction in the Classroom* (London: Methuen).

Delbridge, R. (1998), *Life on the Line: The Workplace Experience of Lean Production and the 'Japanese' Model* (Oxford: Oxford University Press).

DeLorme, D. E., Zinkhan, G. M., and French, W. (2001), 'Ethics and the Internet: Issues Associated with Qualitative Research', *Journal of Business Ethics*, 33: 271–86.

Denscombe, M. (2006), 'Web-Based Questionnaires and the Mode Effect: An Evaluation Based on Completion Rates and Data Contents of Near-Identical Questionnaires Delivered in Different Modes', *Social Science Computer Review*, 24: 246–54.

Denzin, N. K. (1968), 'On the Ethics of Disguised Observation', *Social Problems*, 15: 502–4.

—— (1970), *The Research Act in Sociology* (Chicago: Aldine).

—— (1994), 'Evaluating Qualitative Research in the Poststructural Moment: The Lessons James Joyce Teaches us', *International Journal of Qualitative Studies in Education*, 7: 295–308.

—— and Lincoln, Y. S. (1994), 'Introduction: Entering the Field of Qualitative Research', in N. K. Denzin and Y. S. Lincoln (eds.), *Handbook of Qualitative Research* (Thousand Oaks, Calif.: Sage).

Denzin, N. K., and Lincoln, Y. S. (2000), *Handbook of Qualitative Research* (2nd edn.; Thousand Oaks, Calif.: Sage).

—— —— (2005a), *Handbook of Qualitative Research* (3rd edn.; Thousand Oaks, Calif.: Sage).

—— —— (2005b), 'Introduction: The Discipline and Practice of Qualitative Research', in N. K. Denzin and Y. S. Lincoln (eds.), *Handbook of Qualitative Research* (3rd edn.; Thousand Oaks, Calif.: Sage).

Department of Health (2005), *Research Governance Framework for Health and Social Care* (London: Department of Health).

Dickinson, H. (1993), 'Accounting for Augustus Lamb: Theoretical and Methodological Issues in Biography and Historical Sociology', *Sociology*, 27: 121–32.

Diener, E., and Crandall, R. (1978), *Ethics in Social and Behavioral Research* (Chicago: University of Chicago Press).

Dillman, D. A. (1978), *Mail and Telephone Surveys: The Total Design Method* (New York: Wiley).

—— (1983), 'Mail and Other Self-Administered Questionnaires', in P. H. Rossi, J. D. Wright, and A. B. Anderson (eds.), *Handbook of Survey Research* (Orlando, Fl.: Academic Press).

Dingwall, R. (1980), 'Ethics and Ethnography', *Sociological Review*, 28: 871–91.

Ditton, J. (1977), *Part-Time Crime: An Ethnography of Fiddling and Pilferage* (London: Macmillan).

Dixon-Woods, M., Angell, E., Ashcroft, R., and Bryman, A. (2007), 'Written Work: The Social Functions of Research Ethics Committee Letters', *Social Science and Medicine*, 65: 792–802.

Dohrenwend, B. P. (1966), 'Social Status and Psychiatric Disorder: An Issue of Substance and an Issue of Method', *American Sociological Review*, 31: 14–34.

Dommeyer, C. J., and Moriarty, E. (2000), 'Comparison of Two Forms of an E-Mail Survey: Embedded vs. Attached', *International Journal of Market Research*, 42: 39–50.

Dorsey, E. R., Steeves, H. L., and Porras, L. E. (2004), 'Advertising Ecotourism on the Internet: Commodifying Environment and Culture', *New Media and Society*, 6: 753–79.

Douglas, J. D. (1967), *The Social Meanings of Suicide* (Princeton: Princeton University Press).

—— (1976), *Investigative Social Research: Individual and Team Field Research* (Beverly Hills, Calif.: Sage).

Duncombe, J., and Marsden, D. (1993), 'Love and Intimacy: The Gender Division of Emotion and "Emotion Work"', *Sociology*, 27: 221–41.

Dunning, E., Murphy, P., and Williams, J. (1988), *The Roots of Football Hooliganism: An Historical and Sociological Study* (London: Routledge).

Durkheim, E. (1938), *The Rules of Sociological Method*, trans. S. A. Solovay and J. H. Mueller (New York: Free Press).

—— (1952), *Suicide. A Study In Sociology*, trans. J. A. Spaulding and G. Simpson (London: Routledge & Kegan Paul).

Dwyer, J. T., Mayer, L. D. V. H., Dowd, K., Kandel, R. F., and Mayer, J. (1974), 'The New Vegetarians: The Natural High?', *Journal of the American Dietetic Association*, 65: 529–36.

Dyer, W. G., and Wilkins, A. L. (1991), 'Better Stories, not Better Constructs, to Generate Better Theory: A Rejoinder to Eisenhardt', *Academy of Management Review*, 16: 613–19.

Edley, N., and Wetherell, M. (1997), 'Jockeying for Position: The Construction of Masculine Identities', *Discourse and Society*, 8: 203–17.

Edwards, R. (1979), *Contested Terrain* (New York: Basic Books).

Eisenhardt, K. M. (1989), 'Building Theories from Case Study Research', *Academy of Management Review*, 14: 532–50.

Elliott, C., and Ellingworth, D. (1997), 'Assessing the Representativeness of the 1992 British Crime Survey: The Impact of Sampling Error and Response Biases', *Sociological Research Online*, 2, http://www.socresonline.org.uk/socresonline/2/4/3.html.

Elliott, H. (1997), 'The Use of Diaries in Sociological Research on Health Experience', *Sociological Research Online*, 2, http://www.socresonline.org.uk/socresonline/2/2/7.html.

Emerson, R. M. (1987), 'Four Ways to Improve the Craft of Fieldwork', *Journal of Contemporary Ethnography*, 16: 69–89.

Erikson, K. T. (1967), 'A Comment on Disguised Observation in Sociology', *Social Problems*, 14: 366–73.

Evans, J., and Benefield, P. (2001), 'Systematic Reviews of Educational Research: Does the Medical Model Fit?', *British Educational Research Journal*, 27: 527–41.

Evans, M., Wedande, G., Ralston, L., and van 't Hul, S. (2001), 'Consumer Interaction in the Virtual Era: Some Qualitative Insights', *Qualitative Market Research*, 4: 150–9.

Fairclough, N. (2003), *Analysing Discourse: Textual Analysis for Social Research* (London: Routledge).

—— (2005), 'Peripheral Vision: Discourse Analysis in Organization Studies: The Case for Critical Realism', *Organization Studies*, 26: 915–39.

—— and Thomas, P. (2004), 'The Discourse of Globalization and the Globalization of Discourse', in D. Grant, C. Hardy, C. Oswick, and L. Putnam (eds.), *The Sage Handbook of Organizational Discourse* (London: Sage).

Faraday, A., and Plummer, K. (1979), 'Doing Life Histories', *Sociological Review*, 27: 773–98.

Fenton, N., Bryman, A., and Deacon, D. (1998), *Mediating Social Science* (London: Sage).

Ferrie, J., Shipley, M. J., Marmot, M. G., Stansfeld, S., and Smith, G. D. (1998), 'The Health Effects of Major

Organizational Change and Job Insecurity', *Social Science and Medicine*, 46: 343–54.

Festinger, L., Riecken, H. W., and Schachter, S. (1956), *When Prophecy Fails* (New York: Harper & Row).

Fielding, N. (1981), *The National Front* (London: Routledge & Kegan Paul).

—— (1982), 'Observational Research on the National Front', in M. Bulmer (ed.), *Social Research Ethics* (London: Macmillan).

—— and Lee, R. M. (1998), *Computer Analysis and Qualitative Research* (London: Sage).

Filmer, P., Phillipson, M., Silverman, D., and Walsh, D. (1972), *New Directions in Sociological Theory* (London: Collier-Macmillan).

Finch, J. (1984), ' "It's great to have someone to talk to": The Ethics and Politics of Interviewing Women', in C. Bell and H. Roberts (eds.), *Social Researching: Politics, Problems, Practice* (London: Routledge & Kegan Paul).

—— (1987), 'The Vignette Technique in Survey Research', *Sociology*, 21: 105–14.

—— and Hayes, L. (1994), 'Inheritance, Death and the Concept of the Home', *Sociology*, 28: 417–33.

—— and Mason, J. (1990), 'Decision Taking in the Field-Work Process: Theoretical Sampling and Collaborative Working', in R. G. Burgess (ed.), *Studies in Qualitative Methodology*, 2: 25–50.

Fine, G. A. (1996), 'Justifying Work: Occupational Rhetorics as Resources in Kitchen Restaurants', *Administrative Science Quarterly*, 41: 90–115.

Fisher, K., and Layte, R. (2004), 'Measuring Work–Life Balance using Time Diary Data', *Electronic International Journal of Time Use Research*, 1: 1–13, http://ffb.uni-lueneburg.de/eijtur/pdf/volumes/eIJTUR-1-1.pdf#pagemode=bookmark.

Flanders, N. (1970), *Analyzing Teacher Behavior* (Reading, Mass.: Addison-Wesley).

Fleetwood, S. (2005), 'Ontology in Organization and Management Studies: A Critical Realist Perspective', *Organization*, 12: 197–222.

Fletcher, J. (1966), *Situation Ethics* (London: SCM Press).

Flint, A., Clegg, S., and Macdonald, R. (2006), 'Exploring Staff Perceptions of Student Plagiarism', *Journal of Further and Higher Education*, 30: 145–56.

Flyvbjerg, B. (2003), 'Five Misunderstandings about Case Study Research', in C. Seale, G. Gobo, J. F. Gubrium, and D. Silverman (eds.), *Qualitative Research Practice* (London: Sage).

Foddy, W. (1993), *Constructing Questions for Interviews and Questionnaires: Theory and Practice in Social Research* (Cambridge: Cambridge University Press).

Forster, N. (1994), 'The Analysis of Company Documentation', in C. Cassell and G. Symon (eds.), *Qualitative Methods in Organizational Research* (London: Sage).

Foster, J. (1995), 'Informal Social Control and Community Crime Prevention', *British Journal of Criminology*, 35: 563–83.

Foucault, M. (1977), *Discipline and Punish* (Harmondsworth: Penguin).

Fowler, B., and Bielsa, E. (2007), 'The Lives We Choose to Remember: A Quantitative Analysis of Newspaper Obituaries', *Sociological Review*, 55: 203–26.

Fowler, F. J. (1993), *Survey Research Methods* (2nd edn.; Newbury Park, Calif.: Sage).

—— and Mangione, T. W. (1990), *Standardized Survey Interviewing: Minimizing Interviewer-Related Error* (Beverly Hills, Calif.: Sage).

Fox, J., and Fogelman, K. (1990), 'New Possibilities for Longitudinal Studies of Intergenerational Factors in Child Health and Development', in D. Magnusson and L. R. Bergman (eds.), *Data Quality in Longitudinal Research* (Cambridge: Cambridge University Press).

Frean, A. (1998), 'Children Read More after Arrival of TV', *The Times*, 29 Apr.: 7.

Frey, J. H. (2004), 'Telephone Surveys', in M. S. Lewis-Beck, A. Bryman, and T. F. Liao (eds.), *The Sage Encyclopedia of Social Science Research Methods* (3 vols.; Thousand Oaks, Calif.: Sage).

—— and Oishi, S. M. (1995), *How to Conduct Interviews by Telephone and in Person* (Thousand Oaks, Calif.: Sage).

Fricker, S., Galesic, M., Tourangeau, R., and Yan, T. (2005), 'An Experimental Comparison of Web and Telephone Surveys', *Public Opinion Quarterly*, 69: 370–92.

—— and Schonlau, M. (2002), 'Advantages and Disadvantages of Internet Research Surveys: Evidence from the Literature', *Field Methods*, 14: 347–67.

Gabriel, Y. (1998), 'The Use of Stories', in G. Symon and C. Cassell (eds.), *Qualitative Methods and Analysis in Organizational Research* (London: Sage).

Gallie, D. (1978), *In Search of the New Working Class: Automation and Social Integration within the Capitalist Enterprise* (Cambridge: Cambridge University Press).

Gallup, G. (1947), 'The Quintamensional Plan of Question Design', *Public Opinion Quarterly*, 11: 385–93.

Galton, M., Simon, B., and Croll, P. (1980), *Inside the Primary Classroom* (London: Routledge & Kegan Paul).

Gambetta, D., and Hamill, H. (2005), *Streetwise: How Taxi Drivers Establish their Customers' Trustworthiness* (New York: Russell Sage Foundation).

Gans, H. J. (1962), *The Urban Villagers* (New York: Free Press).

Gans, H. J. (1968), 'The Participant-Observer as Human Being: Observations on the Personal Aspects of Field Work', in H. S. Becker (ed.), *Institutions and the Person: Papers Presented to Everett C. Hughes* (Chicago: Aldine).

Garfinkel, H. (1967), *Studies in Ethnomethodology* (Englewood Cliffs, NJ: Prentice-Hall).

Geertz, C. (1973*a*), 'Thick Description: Toward an Interpretive Theory of Culture', in C. Geertz, *The Interpretation of Cultures* (New York: Basic Books).

—— (1973*b*), 'Deep Play: Notes on the Balinese Cockfight', in C. Geertz, *The Interpretation of Cultures* (New York: Basic Books).

Gephart, R. P. (1988), *Ethnostatistics: Qualitative Foundations for Quantitative Research* (Newbury Park, Calif.: Sage).

Gerson, K., and Horowitz, R. (2002), 'Observation and Interviewing: Options and Choices', in T. May (ed.), *Qualitative Research in Action* (London: Sage).

Gibson, N. (2004), 'Action Research', in M. S. Lewis-Beck, A. Bryman, and T. F. Liao (eds.), *The Sage Encyclopedia of Social Science Research Methods* (3 vols.; Thousand Oaks, Calif.: Sage).

Giddens, A. (1984), *The Constitution of Society* (Cambridge: Polity).

Gilbert, G. N. (1977), 'Referencing as Persuasion', *Social Studies of Science*, 7: 113–22.

—— and Mulkay, M. (1984), *Opening Pandora's Box: A Sociological Analysis of Scientists' Discourse* (Cambridge: Cambridge University Press).

Gill, R. (1996), 'Discourse Analysis: Practical Implementation', in J. T. E. Richardson (ed.), *Handbook of Qualitative Research Methods for Psychology and the Social Sciences* (Leicester: BPS Books).

—— (2000), 'Discourse Analysis', in M. W. Bauer and G. Gaskell (eds.), *Qualitative Researching with Text, Image and Sound* (London: Sage).

Giulianotti, R. (1995), 'Participant Observation and Research into Football Hooliganism: Reflections on the Problems of Entrée and Everyday Risks', *Sociology of Sport Journal*, 12: 1–20.

—— (1997), 'Enlightening the North: Aberdeen Fanzines and Local Football Identity', in G. Armstrong and R. Giulianotti (eds.), *Entering the Field: New Perspectives on World Football* (Oxford: Berg).

Gladney, A. P., Ayars, C., Taylor, W. C., Liehr, P., and Meininger, J. C. (2003), 'Consistency of Findings Produced by Two Multidisciplinary Tesearch Teams', *Sociology*, 37: 297–313.

Glasby, J., and Lester, H. (2005), 'On the Inside: A Narrative Review of Mental Health Inpatient Services', *British Journal of Social Work*, 35: 863–79.

Glaser, B. G. (1992), *Basics of Grounded Theory Analysis* (Mill Valley, Calif.: Sociology Press).

—— and Strauss, A. L. (1967), *The Discovery of Grounded Theory: Strategies for Qualitative Research* (Chicago: Aldine).

Glasgow University Media Group (1976), *Bad News* (London: Routledge & Kegan Paul).

Glock, C. Y. (1988), 'Reflections on Doing Survey Research', in H. J. O'Gorman (ed.), *Surveying Social Life* (Middletown, Conn.: Wesleyan University Press).

Glucksmann, M. (1994), 'The Work of Knowledge and the Knowledge of Women's Work', in M. Maynard and J. Purvis (eds.), *Researching Women's Lives from a Feminist Perspective* (London: Taylor & Francis).

Goffman, E. (1956), *The Presentation of Self in Everyday Life* (New York: Doubleday).

—— (1963), *Stigma: Notes on the Management of Spoiled Identity* (Harmondsworth: Penguin).

Gold, R. L. (1958), 'Roles in Sociological Fieldwork', *Social Forces*, 36: 217–23.

Golden-Biddle, K., and Locke, K. D. (1993), 'Appealing Work: An Investigation of How Ethnographic Texts Convince', *Organization Science*, 4: 595–616.

—— —— (1997), *Composing Qualitative Research* (Thousand Oaks, Calif.: Sage).

Goldthorpe, J. H., Lockwood, D., Bechhofer, F., and Platt, J. (1968), *The Affluent Worker: Industrial Attitudes and Behaviour* (Cambridge: Cambridge University Press).

Goode, E. (1996), 'The Ethics of Deception in Social Research: A Case Study', *Qualitative Sociology*, 19: 11–33.

Goode, W. J., and Hatt, P. K. (1952), *Methods of Social Research* (New York: McGraw Hill).

Gottdiener, M. (1982), 'Disneyland: A Utopian Urban Space', *Urban Life,* 11: 139–62.

—— (1997), *The Theming of America: Dreams, Visions and Commercial Spaces* (Boulder, Colo.: Westview Press).

Goulding, C. (2008), 'Grounded Theory Perspectives in Organizational Research', in D. Buchanan and A. Bryman (eds.), *Handbook of Organizational Research Methods* (London: Sage).

Gouldner, A. (1968), 'The Sociologist as Partisan', *American Sociologist*, 3: 103–16.

Grant, D., Hardy, C., Oswick, C., and Putnam, L. L. (2004), 'Introduction: Organizational Discourse: Exploring the Field', in D. Grant, C. Hardy, C. Oswick, and L. Putnam (eds.), *The Sage Handbook of Organizational Discourse* (London: Sage).

Grazian, D. (2003), *Blue Chicago: The Search for Authenticity in Urban Blues Clubs* (Chicago: University of Chicago Press).

Greene, J. C. (1994), 'Qualitative Program Evaluation: Practice and Promise', in N. K. Denzin and Y. S. Lincoln (eds.),

Handbook of Qualitative Research (Thousand Oaks, Calif.: Sage).

—— (2000), 'Understanding Social Programs through Evaluation', in N. K. Denzin and Y. S. Lincoln (eds.), *Handbook of Qualitative Research* (2nd edn.; Thousand Oaks, Calif.: Sage).

Greising, D. (1998), *I'd Like the World to Buy a Coke: The Life and Leadership of Robert Goizueta* (New York: Wiley).

Grele, R. J. (1998), 'Movement without Aim: Methodological and Theoretical Problems in Oral History', in R. Perks and A. Thomson (eds.), *The History Reader* (London: Routledge).

Griffin, J. H. (1961), *Black Like Me* (Boston: Houghton Mifflin).

Grint, K., and Woolgar, S. (1997), *The Machine at Work: Technology, Work and Organization* (Cambridge: Polity).

Groves, R. M., Fowler, F. J., Couper, M. P., Lepkowski, J. M., Singer, E., and Tourangeau, R. (2004), *Survey Methodology* (Hoboken, NJ: Wiley).

Guba, E. G. (1985), 'The Context of Emergent Paradigm Research', in Y. S. Lincoln (ed.), *Organization Theory and Inquiry: The Paradigm Revolution* (Beverly Hills, Calif.: Sage).

—— and Lincoln, Y. S. (1994), 'Competing Paradigms in Qualitative Research', in N. K. Denzin and Y. S. Lincoln (eds.), *Handbook of Qualitative Research* (Thousand Oaks, Calif.: Sage).

Gubrium, J. F., and Holstein, J. A. (1997), *The New Language of Qualitative Method* (New York: Oxford University Press).

Guest, G., Bunce, A., and Johnson, L. (2006), 'How Many Interviews are Enough? An Experiment with Data Saturation and Variability', *Field Methods*, 18: 59–82.

Guillemin, M., and Gillam, L. (2004), 'Ethics, Reflexivity, and "Ethically Important Moments" in Research', *Qualitative Inquiry*, 10: 261–80.

Gully, S., Incalcaterra, K., Joshi, A., and Beaubien, J. (2002), 'A Meta-Analysis of Team-Efficacy, Potency, and Performance: Interdependence and Level of Analysis as Moderators of Observed Relationships', *Journal of Applied Psychology*, 87(5): 819–32.

Gusfield, J. (1976), 'The Literary Rhetoric of Science: Comedy and Pathos in Drinking Driving Research', *American Sociological Review*, 41: 16–34.

Gusterson, H. (1996), *Nuclear Rites: A Weapons Laboratory at the End of the Cold War* (Berkely, Calif.: University of California Press).

Hackley, C. (2003), ' "We Are All Customers Now": Rhetorical Strategy and Ideological Control in Marketing Management Texts', *Journal of Management Studies*, 40: 1325–52.

Halford, S., Savage, M., and Witz, A. (1997), *Gender, Careers and Organisations: Current Developments in Banking, Nursing and Local Government* (London: Sage).

Halfpenny, P. (1979), 'The Analysis of Qualitative Data', *Sociological Review*, 27: 799–825.

Hall, W. S., and Guthrie, L. F. (1981), 'Cultural and Situational Variation in Language Function and Use-Methods and Procedures for Research', in J. L. Green and C. Wallatt (eds.), *Ethnography and Language in Educational Settings* (Norwood, NJ: Ablex).

Hamilton, A. (2006), 'London Fails Civility Test in Survey of World Cities', *The Times*, 20 June: 1.16.

Hammersley, M. (1989), *The Dilemma of Qualitative Method: Herbert Blumer and the Chicago Tradition* (London: Routledge).

—— (1992a), 'By what Criteria should Ethnographic Research be Judged?', in M. Hammersley, *What's Wrong with Ethnography* (London: Routledge).

—— (1992b), 'Deconstructing the Qualitative–Quantitative Divide', in M. Hammersley, *What's Wrong with Ethnography* (London: Routledge).

—— (1992c), 'The Paradigm Wars: Reports from the Front', *British Journal of Sociology of Education*, 13: 131–43.

—— (1996), 'The Relationship between Qualitative and Quantitative Research: Paradigm Loyalty versus Methodological Eclecticism', in J. T. E. Richardson (ed.), *Handbook of Research Methods for Psychology and the Social Sciences* (Leicester: BPS Books).

—— (1997), 'Qualitative Data Archiving: Some Reflections on its Prospects and Problems', *Sociology*, 31: 131–42.

—— (2001), 'On "Systematic" Reviews of Research Literatures: A "Narrative" Response to Evans and Benefield', *British Educational Research Journal*, 27: 543–54.

—— and Atkinson, P. (1995), *Ethnography: Principles in Practice* (2nd edn.; London: Routledge).

—— and Gomm, R. (2000), 'Bias in Social Research', in M. Hammersley (ed.), *Taking Sides in Social Research: Essays in Partisanship and Bias* (London: Routledge).

—— Scarth, J., and Webb, S. (1985), 'Developing and Testing Theory: The Case of Research on Pupil Learning', in R. G. Burgess (ed.), *Issues in Educational Research: Qualitative Methods* (London: Falmer).

Hammond, C. (2005), 'The Wider Benefits of Adult Learning: An Illustration of the Advantages of Multi-Method Research', *International Journal of Social Research Methodology*, 8: 239–55.

Hammond, P. (1964), *Sociologists at Work* (New York: Basic Books).

Hansen, A. (1995), 'Using Information Technology to Analyze Newspaper Content', in R. M. Lee (ed.), *Information Technology for the Social Scientist* (London: UCL Press).

Hantrais, L. (1996), 'Comparative Research Methods', *Social Research Update*, 13.

Hardy, C., and Phillips, N. (1999), 'No Joking Matter: Discursive Struggle in the Canadian Refugee System', *Organization Studies*, 20: 1–24.

Hardy, M., and Bryman, A. (2004), 'Introduction: Common Threads among Techniques of Data Analysis', in M. Hardy and A. Bryman (eds.), *Handbook of Data Analysis* (London: Sage).

Hargreaves, J., Lewis, I., and Speers, T. (n.d.), *Towards a Better Map: Science, the Public and the Media* (Swindon: ESRC).

Harkness, S., Moscardino, U., Bermúdez, M. R., Zylickz, P. O., Welles-Nyström, B., Blom, M., Parmar, P., Axia, G., Palacios, J., and Super, C. M. (2006), 'Mixed Methods in International Collaboration Research: The Experiences of the International Study of Parents, Children, and Schools', *Cross-Cultural Research*, 40: 65–82.

Harper, D. (2002), 'Talking about Pictures: A Case for Photo Elicitation', *Visual Studies*, 17: 13–26.

Harré, R. (1972), *The Philosophies of Science* (Oxford: Oxford University Press).

Haslam, C., and Bryman, A. (1994), 'The Research Dissemination Minefield', in C. Haslam and A. Bryman (eds.), *Social Scientists Meet the Media* (London: Routledge).

Hawkes, N. (2003), 'Close Shaves Beat Death by Whisker', *The Times*, 6 Feb.: 1.

—— (2006), 'Fat Children Dodge the Scales in Study of National Obesity', *The Times*, 21 Dec.: 24.

Hazelrigg, L. (2004), 'Inference', in M. Hardy and A. Bryman (eds.), *Handbook of Data Analysis* (London: Sage).

Heap, J. L., and Roth, P. A. (1973), 'On Phenomenological Sociology', *American Sociological Review*, 38: 354–67.

Heath, C. (1997), 'The Analysis of Activities in Face to Face Interaction Using Video', in D. Silverman (ed.), *Qualitative Research: Theory, Method and Practice* (London: Sage).

Heritage, J. (1984), *Garfinkel and Ethnomethodology* (Cambridge: Polity).

—— (1987), 'Ethnomethodology', in A. Giddens and J. H. Turner (eds.), *Social Theory Today* (Cambridge: Polity).

Hesse-Biber, S. (1995), 'Unleashing Frankenstein's Monster? The Use of Computers in Qualitative Research', *Studies in Qualitative Methodology*, 5: 25–41.

Hewson, C., Yule, P., Laurent, D., and Vogel, C. (2003), *Internet Research Methods: A Practical Guide for the Social and Behavioural Sciences* (London: Sage).

Hine, V. (2000), *Virtual Ethnography* (London: Sage).

Hirsch, J. (1981), *Family Photographs* (New York: Oxford University Press).

Ho, K. C., Baber, Z., and Khondker, H. (2002), 'Sites of Resistance: Alternative Websites and State–Society Relations', *British Journal of Sociology*, 53: 127–48.

Hobbs, D. (1988), *Doing the Business: Entrepreneurship, the Working Class and Detectives in the East End of London* (Oxford: Oxford University Press).

—— (1993), 'Peers, Careers, and Academic Fears: Writing as Field-Work', in D. Hobbs and T. May (eds.), *Interpreting the Field: Accounts of Ethnography* (Oxford: Clarendon Press).

—— Hadfield, P., Lister, S., and Winlow, S. (2003), *Bouncers: Violence and Governance in the Night-Time Economy* (Oxford: Oxford University Press).

Hochschild, A. R. (1983), *The Managed Heart* (Berkeley and Los Angeles: University of California Press).

Hodges, L. (1998), 'The Making of a National Portrait', *The Times Higher*, 20 Feb.: 22–3.

Hodson, R. (1996), 'Dignity in the Workplace under Participative Management', *American Sociological Review*, 61: 719–38.

—— (1999), *Analyzing Documentary Accounts* (Thousand Oaks, Calif.: Sage).

—— (2004), 'Work Life and Social Fulfillment: Does Social Affiliation at Work Reflect a Carrot or a Stick?', *Social Science Quarterly*, 85: 221–39.

Holbrook, A., Bourke, S., Fairburn, H., and Lovat, T. (2007), 'Examiner Comment on the Literature Review in Ph.D. Theses', *Studies in Higher Education*, 32: 337–56.

—— Green, M. C., and Krosnick, J. A. (2003), 'Telephone versus Face-to-Face Interviewing of National Probability Samples with Long Questionnaires: Comparisons of Respondent Satisficing and Social Desirability Response Bias', *Public Opinion Quarterly*, 67: 79–125.

Holbrook, B., and Jackson, B. (1996), 'Shopping Around: Focus Group Research in North London', *Area*, 28: 136–42.

Holdaway, S. (1982), ' "An Inside Job": A Case Study of Covert Research on the Police', in M. Bulmer (ed.), *Social Research Ethics* (London: Macmillan).

—— (1983), *Inside the British Police: A Force at Work* (Oxford: Blackwell).

Holdsworth, C. (2006), ' "Don't you think you're missing out, living at home?": Student Experiences and Residential Transitions', *Sociological Review*, 54: 495–519.

Holmes, L. (2004), 'Guidance for Ensuring Confidentiality and the Protection of Data', in S. Becker and A. Bryman (eds.), *Understanding Research for Social Policy and Practice: Themes, Methods, and Approaches* (Bristol: Policy Press).

Holsti, O. R. (1969), *Content Analysis for the Social Sciences and Humanities* (Reading, Mass.: Addison-Wesley).

Homan, R. (1991), *The Ethics of Social Research* (London: Longman).

—— and Bulmer, M. (1982), 'On the Merits of Covert Methods: A Dialogue', in M. Bulmer (ed.), *Social Research Ethics* (London: Macmillan).

Houghton, E. (1998), 'Sex is Good for You', *Guardian* (92 section), 20 Jan.: 14–15.

Howell, J. M., and Frost, P. J. (1989), 'A Laboratory Study of Charismatic Leadership', *Organizational Behavior and Human Decision Processes*, 43: 243–69.

Huberman, A. M., and Miles, M. B. (1994), 'Data Management and Analysis Methods', in N. K. Denzin and Y. S. Lincoln (eds.), *Handbook of Qualitative Research* (Thousand Oaks, Calif.: Sage).

Hudson, J. M., and Bruckman, A. S. (2004) '"Go Away": Participant Objections to Being Studied and the Ethics of Chatroom Research', *Information Society*, 20: 127–39.

Hughes, E. C. (1958), *Men and their Work* (Glencoe, Ill.: Free Press).

Hughes, G. (2000), 'Understanding the Politics of Criminological Research', in V. Jupp, P. Davies, and P. Francis (eds.), *Doing Criminological Research* (London: Sage).

Hughes, J. A. (1990), *The Philosophy of Social Research* (2nd edn.; Harlow: Longman).

Hughes, K., MacKintosh, A. M., Hastings, G., Wheeler, C., Watson, J., and Inglis, J. (1997), 'Young People, Alcohol, and Designer Drinks: A Quantitative and Qualitative Study', *British Medical Journal*, 314: 414–18.

Hughes, R. (1998), 'Considering the Vignette Technique and its Application to a Study of Drug Injecting and HIV Risk and Safer Behaviour', *Sociology of Health and Illness*, 20: 381–400.

Humphreys, L. (1970), *Tearoom Trade: Impersonal Sex in Public Places* (Chicago: Aldine).

Hurdley, R. (2006), 'Dismantling Mantelpieces: Narrative Identities and Materializing Culture in the Home', *Sociology*, 40: 681–98.

Hutchby, I., and Wooffitt, R. (1998), *Conversation Analysis* (Cambridge: Polity).

Hycner, R. H. (1985), 'Some Guidelines for the Phenomenological Analysis of Interview Data', *Human Studies*, 8: 279–303.

Israel, M., and Hay, I. (2004), *Research Ethics for Social Scientists* (London: Sage).

Jacobs, J. (1967), 'A Phenomenological Study of Suicide Notes', *Social Problems*, 15: 60–72.

Jagger, E. (1998), 'Marketing the Self, Buying an Other: Dating in a Post Modern, Consumer Society', *Sociology*, 32: 795–814.

—— (2005), 'Is Thirty the New Sixty? Dating, Age and Gender in a Postmodern, Consumer Society', *Sociology*, 39: 89–106.

Jamieson, J. (2000), 'Negotiating Danger in Fieldwork on Crime: A Researcher's Tale', in G. Lee-Treweek and S. Linkogle (eds.), *Danger in the Field: Risk and Ethics in Social Research* (London: Routledge).

Janis, I. L. (1982), *Groupthink: Psychological Studies of Policy Decisions and Fiascos* (2nd edn.; Boston: Houghton-Mifflin).

Jayaratne, T. E., and Stewart, A. J. (1991), 'Quantitative and Qualitative Methods in the Social Sciences: Current Feminist Issues and Practical Strategies', in M. M. Fonow and J. A. Cook (eds.), *Beyond Methodology: Feminist Scholarship as Lived Research* (Bloomington, Ind.: Indiana University Press).

Jenkins, G. D., Nader, D. A., Lawler, E. E., and Cammann, C. (1975), 'Standardized Observations: An Approach to Measuring the Nature of Jobs', *Journal of Applied Psychology*, 60: 171–81.

John, I. D. (1992), 'Statistics as Rhetoric in Psychology', *Australian Psychologist*, 27: 144–9.

Johnson, P. (1998), 'Analytic Induction', in G. Symon and C. Cassell (eds.), *Qualitative Methods and Analysis in Organizational Research* (London: Sage).

Jones, M. L. (2004), 'Application of Systematic Review Methods to Qualitative Research: Practical Issues', *Journal of Advanced Nursing*, 48: 271–8.

Jones, S. (2002), *The Internet Goes to College: How Students are Living in the Future with Today's Technology* (Washington: Pew Internet and American Life Project).

Jowell, R., Brook, L., Prior, G., and Taylor, B. (1992), *British Social Attitudes 1991 Survey* (London: Social and Community Planning Research).

Kamberelis, G., and Dimitriadis, G. (2005), 'Focus Groups: Strategic Articulations of Pedagogy, Politics, and Inquiry', in N. K. Denzin and Y. S. Lincoln (eds.), *Handbook of Qualitative Research* (3rd edn.; Thousand Oaks, Calif.: Sage).

Kamin, L. J. (1974), *The Science and Politics of IQ* (New York: Wiley).

Kanayama, T. (2003), 'Ethnographic Research on the Experience of Japanese Elderly People Online', *New Media and Society*, 5: 267–88.

Kapsis, R. E. (1989), 'Reputation Building and the Film Art World: The Case of Alfred Hitchcock', *Sociological Quarterly*, 30: 15–35.

Katz, J. (1982), *Poor People's Lawyers in Transition* (New Brunswick: Rutgers University Press).

Keat, R., and Urry, J. (1975), *Social Theory as Science* (London: Routledge & Kegan Paul).

Keenoy, T., Oswick, C., and Grant, D. (1997), 'Organizational Discourses: Text and Context', *Organization*, 2: 147–58.

Kelley, J., and De Graaf, N. D. (1997), 'National Context, Parental Socialization, and Religious Belief: Results from 15 Nations', *American Sociological Review*, 62: 639–59.

Kelly, L., Burton, S., and Regan, L. (1994), 'Researching Women's Lives or Studying Women's Oppression? Reflections on what Constitutes Feminist Research', in M. Maynard and J. Purvis (eds.), *Researching Women's Lives from a Feminist Perspective* (London: Taylor & Francis).

Kendall, L. (1999), 'Recontextualizing "Cyberspace": Methodological Considerations for On-line Research', in S. Jones (ed.), *Doing Internet Research: Critical Issues and Methods for Examining the Net* (Thousand Oaks, Calif.: Sage).

Kent, R., and Lee, M. (1999), 'Using the Internet for Market Research: A Study of Private Trading on the Internet', *Journal of the Market Research Society*, 41: 377–85.

Kimmel, A. J. (1988), *Ethics and Values in Applied Social Research* (Newbury Park, Calif.: Sage).

King, N. (1994), 'The Qualitative Research Interview', in C. Cassell and G. Symon (eds.), *Qualitative Methods in Organizational Research* (London: Sage).

Kirk, J., and Miller, M. L. (1986), *Reliability and Validity in Qualitative Research* (Newbury Park, Calif.: Sage).

Kitsuse, J. I., and Cicourel, A. V. (1963), 'A Note on the Use of Official Statistics', *Social Problems*, 11: 131–9.

Kitzinger, J. (1993), 'Understanding AIDS: Researching Audience Perceptions of Acquired Immune Deficiency Syndrome', in J. Eldridge (ed.), *Getting the Message: News, Truth and Power* (London: Routledge).

—— (1994), 'The Methodology of Focus Groups: The Importance of Interaction between Research Participants', *Sociology of Health and Illness*, 16: 103–21.

Knights, D., and Willmott, H. (1990), *Labour Process Theory* (London: Macmillan).

—— Willmott, H., and Collinson, D. (1985), *Job Redesign: Critical Perspectives on the Labour Process* (Aldershot: Gower).

Koeber, C. (2005), 'Introducing Multimedia Presentations and a Course Website to an Introductory Sociology Course: How Technology Affects Student Perceptions of Teaching Effectiveness', *Teaching Sociology*, 33: 285–300.

Krosnick, J. A., Holbrook, A. L., Berent, M. K., Carson, R. T., Hanemann, W. M., Kopp, R. J., Mitchell, R. C., Presser, S., Ruud, P. A., Smith, V. K., Moody, W. R., Green, M. C., and Conaway, M. (2002), 'The Impact of "No Opinion" Response Options on Data Quality: Non-Attitude Reduction or an Invitation to Satisfice?', *Public Opinion Quarterly*, 66: 371–403.

Krueger, R. A. (1988), *Focus Groups: A Practical Guide for Applied Research* (Newbury Park, Calif.: Sage).

—— (1998), *Moderating Focus Groups* (Thousand Oaks, Calif.: Sage).

Kuhn, T. S. (1970), *The Structure of Scientific Revolutions* (2nd edn.; Chicago: University of Chicago Press).

Kvale, S. (1996), *InterViews: An Introduction to Qualitative Research Interviewing* (Thousand Oaks, Calif.: Sage).

Lacey, C. (1976), 'Problems of Sociological Fieldwork: A Review of the Methodology of "Hightown Grammar" ', in M. Hammersley and P. Woods (eds.), *The Process of Schooling* (London: Routledge & Kegan Paul).

Lankshear, G. (2000), 'Bacteria and Babies: A Personal Reflection on Researcher's Risk in a Hospital', in G. Lee-Treweek and S. Linkogle (eds.), *Danger in the Field: Risk and Ethics in Social Research* (London: Routledge).

Lantz, P. M., and Booth, K. M. (1998), 'The Social Construction of the Breast Cancer Epidemic', *Social Science and Medicine*, 46: 907–18.

LaPiere, R. T. (1934), 'Attitudes vs. Actions', *Social Forces*, 13: 230–7.

Laub, J. H., and Sampson, R. J. (1998), 'Integrating Quantitative and Qualitative Data', in J. Z. Giele and G. H. Elder, Jr. (eds.), *Methods of Life Course Research* (Thousand Oaks, Calif.: Sage).

—— —— (2003), *Shared Beginnings, Divergent Lives: Delinquent Boys to Age 70* (Cambridge, Mass.: Harvard University Press).

—— —— (2004), 'Strategies for Bridging the Quantitative and Qualitative Divide: Studying Crime over the Life Course', *Research in Human Development*, 1: 81–99.

Laurie, H., and Gershuny, J. (2000), 'Couples, Work and Money', in R. Berthoud and J. Gershuny (eds.), *Seven Years in the Lives of British Families: Evidence on the Dynamics of Social Change from the British Household Panel Survey* (Bristol: Policy Press).

—— and Sullivan, O. (1991), 'Combining Quantitative and Qualitative Data in the Longitudinal Study of Household Allocations', *Sociological Review*, 39: 113–30.

Layder, D. (1993), *New Strategies in Social Research* (Cambridge: Polity).

Lazarsfeld, P. (1958), 'Evidence and Inference in Social Research', *Daedalus*, 87: 99–130.

Leake, J. (1998), 'Police Figures Hide Poor Clear-up Rate', *The Times*, 21 June: 1, 5.

LeCompte, M. D., and Goetz, J. P. (1982), 'Problems of Reliability and Validity in Ethnographic Research', *Review of Educational Research*, 52: 31–60.

Lee, R. M. (2000), *Unobtrusive Methods in Social Research* (Buckingham: Open University Press).

—— (2004), 'Danger in Research', in M. S. Lewis-Beck, A. Bryman, and T. F. Liao (eds.), *The Sage Encyclopedia of Social Science Research Methods* (3 vols.; Thousand Oaks, Calif.: Sage).

—— and Fielding, N. G. (1991), 'Computing for Qualitative Research: Options, Problems and Potential', in N. G. Fielding and R. M. Lee (eds.), *Using Computers in Qualitative Research* (London: Sage).

Lee-Treweek, G. (2000), 'The Insight of Emotional Danger: Research Experiences in a Home for the Elderly', in G. Lee-Treweek and S. Linkogle (eds.), *Danger in the Field: Risk and Ethics in Social Research* (London: Routledge).

Legge, K. (1995), *Human Resource Management: Rhetorics and Realities* (Basingstoke: Macmillan).

Leidner, R. (1993), *Fast Food, Fast Talk: Service Work and the Routinization of Everyday Life* (Berkeley and Los Angeles: University of California Press).

Leonard, M. (2004), 'Bonding and Bridging Social Capital: Reflections from Belfast', *Sociology*, 38: 927–44.

Letherby, G. (2003), *Feminist Research in Theory and Practice* (Buckingham: Open University Press).

Levitas, R., and Guy, W. (1996), 'Introduction', in R. Levitas and W. Guy (eds.), *Interpreting Official Statistics* (London: Routledge).

Lewis, O. (1961), *The Children of Sánchez* (New York: Vintage).

Liebling, A. (2001), 'Whose Side Are We On? Theory, Practice and Allegiances in Prisons Research', *British Journal of Criminology*, 41: 472–84.

Liebow, E. (1967), *Tally's Corner* (Boston, Mass.: Little, Brown).

Lincoln, Y. S., and Denzin, N. K. (1994), 'The Fifth Moment', in N. K. Denzin and Y. S. Lincoln (eds.), *Handbook of Qualitative Research* (Thousand Oaks, Calif.: Sage).

—— —— (2005), 'Epilogue: The Eighth and Ninth Moments—Qualitative Research in/and the Fractured Future', in N. K. Denzin and Y. S. Lincoln (eds.), *Handbook of Qualitative Research* (3rd edn.; Thousand Oaks, Calif.: Sage).

—— and Guba, E. (1985), *Naturalistic Inquiry* (Beverly Hills, Calif.: Sage).

—— and Tierney, W. G. (2004), 'Qualitative Research and Institutional Review Boards', *Qualitative Inquiry*, 10: 219–34.

Lindesmith, A. R. (1947), *Opiate Addiction* (Bloomington, Ind.: Principia Press).

Livingstone, S. (2006), 'Children's Privacy Online: Experimenting with Boundaries Within and Beyond the Family', in R. Kraut, M. Brynin and S. Kiesler (eds.), *Computers, Phones, and the Internet* (Oxford: Oxford University Press).

—— and Bober, M. (2003), *UK Children Go Online: Listening to Young People's Experiences*, London: LSE Report, http://personal.lse.ac.uk/bober/ UKChildrenGoOnlineReport1.pdf.

—— and Lunt, P. (1994), *Talk on Television: Audience Participation and Public Debate* (London: Routledge).

Locke, K. (1996), 'Rewriting *The Discovery of Grounded Theory* after 25 Years?', *Journal of Management Inquiry*, 5: 239–45.

Lockyer, S. (2006), 'Heard the One About . . . Applying Mixed Methods in Humour Research?', *International Journal of Social Research Methodology*, 9: 41–59.

Lofland, J. (1971), *Analyzing Social Settings: A Guide to Qualitative Observation and Analysis* (Belmont, Calif.: Wadsworth).

—— and Lofland, L. (1995), *Analyzing Social Settings: A Guide to Qualitative Observation and Analysis* (3rd edn.; Belmont, Calif.: Wadsworth).

Lonkila, M. (1995), 'Grounded Theory as an Emergent Paradigm for Computer-Assisted Qualitative Data Analysis', in U. Kelle (ed.), *Computer-Aided Qualitative Data Analysis* (London: Sage).

Lucas, R. (1997), 'Youth, Gender and Part-Time Work: Students in the Labour Process', *Work, Employment and Society*, 11: 595–614.

Lunt, P. K., and Livingstone, S. M. (1992), *Mass Consumption and Personal Identity* (Buckingham: Open University Press).

Lupton, D. (1996), *Food, the Body and the Self* (London: Sage).

Lynch, M. (2000), 'Against Reflexivity as an Academic Virtue and Source of Privileged Knowledge', *Theory, Culture and Society*, 17: 26–54.

Lynd, R. S., and Lynd, H. M. (1929), *Middletown: A Study in Contemporary American Culture* (New York: Harcourt, Brace).

—— —— (1937), *Middletown in Transition: A Study in Cultural Conflicts* (New York: Harcourt, Brace).

Lynn, N., and Lea, S. (2003), ' "A Phantom Menace and the New Apartheid": The Social Construction of Asylum Seekers in the United Kingdom', *Discourse and Society*, 14: 425–52.

McCabe, S. E. (2004), 'Comparison of Mail and Web Surveys in Collecting Illicit Drug Use Data: A Randomized Experiment', *Journal of Drug Education*, 34: 61–73.

McCall, M. J. (1984), 'Structured Field Observation', *Annual Review of Sociology*, 10: 263–82.

McCartney, J. L. (1970), 'On Being Scientific: Changing Styles of Presentation of Sociological Research', *American Sociologist*, 5: 30–5.

McClosky, D. N. (1985), *The Rhetoric of Economics* (Brighton: Wheatsheaf).

McGuigan, J. (1992), *Cultural Populism* (London: Routledge).

McKee, L., and Bell, C. (1985), 'Marital and Family Relations in Times of Male Unemployment', in B. Roberts, R. Finnegan, and D. Gallie (eds.), *New Approaches to Economic Life* (Manchester: Manchester University Press).

McKeever, L. (2006), 'Online Plagiarism Detection Services: Saviour or Scourge?', *Assessment of Evaluation in Higher Education*, 31: 155–65.

McKeganey, N., and Barnard, M. (1996), *Sex Work on the Streets* (Buckingham: Open University Press).

MacLure, M. (2005), ' "Clarity Bordering on Stupidity": Where's the Quality in Systematic Review?', *Journal of Education Policy*, 20: 393–416.

Macnaghten, P., and Jacobs, M. (1997), 'Public Identification with Sustainable Development: Investigating Cultural Barriers to Participation', *Global Environmental Change*, 7: 5–24.

McPhail, C., and Rexroat, C. (1979), 'Mead vs. Blumer: The Divergent Methodological Perspectives of Social Behaviorism and Symbolic Interactionism', *American Sociological Review*, 44: 449–67.

McVeigh, K. (2006), 'Damsels in Distress Given Cold Shoulder', *The Times*, 14 July: 15.

Madge, C., and O'Connor, H. (2002), 'On-Line with E-Mums: Exploring the Internet as a Medium of Research', *Area*, 34: 92–102.

Madriz, M. (2000), 'Focus Groups in Feminist Research', in N. K. Denzin and Y. S. Lincoln (eds.), *Handbook of Qualitative Research* (2nd edn.; Thousand Oaks, Calif.: Sage).

Maitlis, S., and Lawrence, T. B. (2007), 'Triggers and Enablers of Sensegiving in Organizations', *Academy of Management Journal*, 50: 57–84.

Malbon, B. (1999), *Clubbing: Dancing, Ecstasy and Vitality* (London: Routledge).

Malinowski, B. (1967), *A Diary in the Strict Sense of the Term* (London: Routledge & Kegan Paul).

Malkin, A. R., Wornian, K., and Chrisler, J. C. (1999), 'Women and Weight: Gendered Messages on Magazine Covers', *Sex Roles*, 40: 647–55.

Mangabeira, W. (1995), 'Qualitative Analysis and Microcomputer Software: Some Reflections on a New Trend in Sociological Research', *Studies in Qualitative Methodology*, 5: 43–61.

Mangione, T. W. (1995), *Mail Surveys: Improving the Quality* (Thousand Oaks, Calif.: Sage).

Mann, C., and Stewart, F. (2000), *Internet Communication and Qualitative Research: A Handbook for Researching Online* (London: Sage).

Manning, P. K. (1995), 'The Challenge of Postmodernism', in J. Van Maanen (ed.), *Representation in Ethnography* (Thousand Oaks, Calif.: Sage).

Maric, D. (2000), *Respect: Women and Popular Music* (New York: Taxere).

Markham, A. (1998), *Life Online: Researching the Real Experience in Virtual Space* (London and Walnut Creek, Calif.: AltaMira Press).

Marsh, C. (1982), *The Survey Method: The Contribution of Surveys to Sociological Explanation* (London: Allen & Unwin).

—— and Scarbrough, E. (1990), 'Testing Nine Hypotheses about Quota Sampling', *Journal of the Market Research Society*, 32: 485–506.

Marshall, G., and Rose, D. (1989), 'Reply to Saunders', *Network: Newsletter of the British Sociological Association*, 44: 4–5.

—— Newby, H., and Vogler, C. (1988), *Social Class in Modern Britain* (London: Unwin Hyman).

Martin, P., and Bateson, P. (1986), *Measuring Behaviour: An Introductory Guide* (Cambridge: Cambridge University Press).

Marx, G. T. (1997), 'Of Methods and Manners for Aspiring Sociologists: 37 Moral Imperatives', *American Sociologist*, 102–25.

Mason, J. (1994), 'Linking Qualitative and Quantitative Data Analysis', in A. Bryman and R. G. Burgess (eds.), *Analyzing Qualitative Data* (London: Routledge).

—— (1996), *Qualitative Researching* (London: Sage).

—— (2002), 'Qualitative Interviewing: Asking, Listening, Interpreting', in T. May (ed.), *Qualitative Research in Action* (London: Sage).

Masterman, M. (1970), 'The Nature of a Paradigm', in I. Lakatos and A. Musgrave (eds.), *Criticism and the Growth of Knowledge* (Cambridge: Cambridge University Press).

Matthewman, S., and Hoey, D. (2006), 'What Happened to Postmodernism?', *Sociology*, 40: 529–47.

Mattley, C. (2006), 'Aural Sex: The Politics and Moral Dilemmas of Studying the Social Construction of Fantasy', in D. Hobbs and R. Wright (eds.), *The Sage Handbook of Fieldwork* (London: Sage).

Matza, D. (1969), *Becoming Deviant* (Englewood Cliffs, NJ: Prentice-Hall).

Mauthner, N. S., Parry, O., and Backett-Milburn, K. (1998), 'The Data are Out There, or Are They? Implications for Archiving and Revisiting Qualitative Data', *Sociology*, 32: 733–45.

Mayhew, P. (2000), 'Researching the State of Crime: Local, National, and International Victim Surveys', in R. D. King and E. Wincup (eds.), *Doing Research on Crime and Justice* (Oxford: Oxford University Press).

Maynard, M. (1994), 'Methods, Practice and Epistemology: The Debate about Feminism and Research', in M. Maynard and J. Purvis (eds), *Researching Women's Lives from a Feminist Perspective* (London: Taylor & Francis).

—— (1998), 'Feminists' Knowledge and the Knowledge of Feminisms: Epistemology, Theory, Methodology and Method', in T. May and M. Williams (eds.), *Knowing the Social World* (Buckingham: Open University Press).

Mays, N., Pope, C., and Popay, J. (2005), 'Systematically Reviewing Qualitative and Quantitative Evidence to Inform Management and Policy-Making in the Health Field', *Journal of Health Services Research and Policy*, 10 (Supplement 1): S6–S20.

Mead, M. (1928), *Coming of Age in Samoa* (New York: Morrow).

Meltzer, B. N., Petras, J. W., and Reynolds, L. T. (1975), *Symbolic Interactionism: Genesis, Varieties and Criticism* (London: Routledge & Kegan Paul).

Menard, S. (1991), *Longitudinal Research* (Newbury Park, Calif.: Sage).

Merton, R. K. (1967), *On Theoretical Sociology* (New York: Free Press).

—— Fiske, M., and Kendall, P. L. (1956), *The Focused Interview: A Manual of Problems and Procedures* (New York: Free Press).

Midgley, C. (1998), 'TV Violence has Little Impact on Children, Study Finds', *The Times*, 12 Jan.: 5.

Mies, M. (1993), 'Towards a Methodology for Feminist Research', in M. Hammersley (ed.), *Social Research: Philosophy, Politics and Practice* (London: Sage).

Miles, M. B. (1979), 'Qualitative Data as an Attractive Nuisance', *Administrative Science Quarterly*, 24: 590–601.

Milgram, S. (1963), 'A Behavioral Study of Obedience', *Journal of Abnormal and Social Psychology*, 67: 371–8.

—— and Shotland, L. (1973), *Television and Antisocial Behavior: Field Experiments* (New York: Academic Press).

—— Mann, L., and Harter, S. (1965), 'The Lost Letter Technique: A Tool of Social Research', *Public Opinion Quarterly*, 29: 437–8.

Milkman, R. (1997), *Farewell to the Factory: Auto Workers in the Late Twentieth Century* (Berkeley and Los Angeles: University of California Press).

Millar, J. (2004), 'Systematic Reviews for Policy Analysis', in S. Becker and A. Bryman (eds.), *Understanding Research for Social Policy and Practice: Themes, Methods, and Approaches* (Bristol: Policy Press).

Millen, D. (1997), 'Some Methodological and Epistemological Issues Raised by Doing Feminist Research on Non-Feminist Women', *Sociological Research Online*, 2, http://www.socresonline.org.uk/socresonline/2/3/3.html.

Miller, D. (1994), *Modernity: An Ethnographic Approach: Dualism and Mass Consumption in Trinidad* (Oxford: Berg).

—— Jackson, P., Thrift, N., Holbrook, B., and Rowlands, M. (1998), *Shopping, Place and Identity* (London: Routledge).

—— and Slater, D. (2000), *The Internet: An Ethnographic Approach* (Oxford: Berg).

Miller, D., and Reilly, J. (1995), 'Making an Issue of Food Safety: The Media, Pressure Groups, and the Public Sphere', in D. Maurer and J. Sobal (eds.), *Food and Nutrition as Social Problems* (New York: Aldine de Gruyter).

Miller, D. Disney (1956), *The Story of Walt Disney* (New York: Dell).

Miller, N., and Morgan, D. (1993), 'Called to Account: The CV as an Autobiographical Practice', *Sociology*, 27: 133–43.

Miller, R. L. (2000), *Researching Life Stories and Family Histories* (London: Sage).

Miner-Rubino, K., Jayaratne, T. E., and Konik, J. (2007), 'Using Survey Research as a Quantitative Method for Feminist Social Change', in S. N. Hesse-Biber (ed.), *Handbook of Feminist Research: Theory and Praxis* (Thousand Oaks, Calif.: Sage).

Mintzberg, H. (1973), *The Nature of Managerial Work* (New York: Harper & Row).

Mishler, E. G. (1986), *Research Interviewing: Context and Narrative* (Cambridge, Mass.: Harvard University Press).

Mitchell, J. C. (1983), 'Case and Situation Analysis', *Sociological Review*, 31: 186–211.

Mitchell, T. (1985), 'An Evaluation of the Validity of Correlational Research Conducted in Organizations', *Academy of Management Review*, 10: 192–205.

Morgan, D. L. (1998*a*), *Planning Focus Groups* (Thousand Oaks, Calif.: Sage).

—— (1998*b*), 'Practical Strategies for Combining Qualitative and Quantitative Methods: Applications for Health Research', *Qualitative Health Research*, 8: 362–76.

—— (2002), 'Focus Group Interviewing', in J. F. Gubrium and J. A. Holstein (eds.), *Handbook of Interview Research: Context and Method* (Thousand Oaks, Calif.: Sage).

—— and Spanish, M. T. (1985), 'Social Interaction and the Cognitive Organization of Health-Relevant Behaviour', *Sociology of Health and Illness*, 7: 401–22.

Morgan, G., and Smircich, L. (1980), 'The Case for Qualitative Research', *Academy of Management Review*, 5: 491–500.

Morgan, R. (2000), 'The Politics of Criminological Research', in R. D. King and E. Wincup (eds.), *Doing Research on Crime and Justice* (Oxford: Oxford University Press).

Morley, D. (1980), *The 'Nationwide' Audience: Structure and Decoding* (London: British Film Institute).

Morrison, D. E. (1998), *The Search for a Method: Focus Groups and the Development of Mass Communication Research* (Luton: University of Luton Press).

Morse, J. M. (2004*a*), 'Purposive Sampling', in M. S. Lewis-Beck, A. Bryman, and T. F. Liao (eds.), *The Sage Encyclopedia of Social Science Research Methods* (3 vols.; Thousand Oaks, Calif.: Sage).

Morse, J. M. (2004*b*), 'Sampling in Qualitative Research', in M. S. Lewis-Beck, A. Bryman, and T. F. Liao (eds.), *The Sage Encyclopedia of Social Science Research Methods* (3 vols.; Thousand Oaks, Calif.: Sage).

Moser, C. A., and Kalton, G. (1971), *Survey Methods in Social Investigation* (London: Heinemann).

Mumby, D., and Clair, R. (1997), 'Organizational Discourse', in T. A. van Dijk (ed.) *Discourse as Social Interaction. Discourse Studies, Vol. 2: A Multidisciplinary Introduction* (Newbury Park, Calif.: Sage).

Nettleton, S., Pleace, N., Burrows, R., Muncer, S., and Loader, B. (2002), 'The Reality of Virtual Social Support', in S. Woolgar (ed.), *Virtual Society? Technology, Cyperbole, Reality* (Oxford: Oxford University Press).

Newby, H. (1977), 'In the Field: Reflections on the Study of Suffolk Farm Workers', in C. Bell and H. Newby (eds.), *Doing Sociological Research* (London: Allen & Unwin).

Nichols, T., and Beynon, H. (1977), *Living with Capitalism: Class Relations and the Modern Factory* (London: Routledge).

Nightingale, V. (1989), 'What's "Ethnographic" about Ethnographic Audience Research', *Australian Journal of Communication*, 16: 50–63.

Noblit, G. W., and Hare, R. D. (1988), *Meta-Ethnography: Synthesizing Qualitative Studies* (Newbury Park, Calif.: Sage).

Nordenmark, M., and Strandh, M. (1999), 'Towards a Sociological Understanding of Mental Well-Being among the Unemployed: The Role of Economic and Psychosocial Factors', *Sociology*, 33: 577–98.

Norris, C. (1993), 'Some Ethical Considerations on Fieldwork with the Police', in D. Hobbs and T. May (eds.), *Interpreting the Field: Accounts of Ethnography* (Oxford: Clarendon Press).

Oakley, A. (1981), 'Interviewing Women: A Contradiction in Terms', in H. Roberts (ed.), *Doing Feminist Research* (London: Routledge & Kegan Paul).

—— (1998), 'Gender, Methodology and People's Ways of Knowing: Some Problems with Feminism and the Paradigm Debate in Social Science', *Sociology*, 32: 707–31.

—— (1999), 'Paradigm Wars: Some Thoughts on a Personal and Public Trajectory'. *International Journal of Social Research Methodology*, 2: 247–54.

—— (2000), *Experiments in Knowing: Gender and Method in the Social Sciences* (Cambridge: Polity).

Oates, C. J., and McDonald, S. (2006), 'Recycling and the Domestic Division of Labour: Is Green Pink or Blue?', *Sociology*, 40: 417–33.

O'Cathain, A., Murphy, E., and Nicholl, J. (2007), 'Integration and Publication as Indicators of "Yield" from Mixed Methods Studies', *Journal of Mixed Methods Research*, 1: 147–63.

O'Connell Davidson, J. (1998), *Prostitution, Power and Freedom* (Cambridge: Polity).

—— and Layder, D. (1994), *Methods, Sex and Madness* (London: Routledge).

O'Connor, H., and Madge, C. (2001), 'Cyber-Mothers: Online Synchronous Interviewing using Conferencing Software', *Sociological Research Online*, 5, http://www.socresonline.org.uk/ 5/4/o'connor.html.

—— —— (2003), ' "Focus Groups in Cyberspace": Using the Internet for Qualitative Research', *Qualitative Market Research*, 6: 133–43.

Okely, J. (1994), 'Thinking through Fieldwork', in A. Bryman and R. G. Burgess (eds.), *Analyzing Qualitative Data* (London: Routledge).

Oppenheim, A. N. (1966), *Questionnaire Design and Attitude Measurement* (London: Heinemann).

—— (1992), *Questionnaire Design, Interviewing and Attitude Measurement* (London: Pinter).

O'Reilly, K. (2000), *The British on the Costa del Sol: Transnational Identities and Local Communities* (London: Routledge).

Orona, C. J. (1997), 'Temporality and Identity Loss due to Alzheimer's disease', in A. Strauss and J. M. Corbin (eds.), *Grounded Theory in Practice* (Thousand Oaks, Calif.: Sage).

Pace, L. A., and Livingston, M. M. (2005), 'Protecting Human Subjects in Internet Research', *International Journal of Business Ethics and Organization Studies*, 10: 35–41, http://ejbo.jyu.fi/pdf/ejbo_vol10_no1_pages_35-41.pdf.

Pahl, J. (1990), 'Household Spending, Personal Spending and the Control of Money in Marriage', *Sociology*, 24: 119–38.

Park, C. (2003), 'In Other (People's) Words: Plagiarism by University Students: Literature and Lessons', *Assessment and Evaluation in Higher Education*, 28: 471–88.

Parker, M. (2000), *Organizational Culture and Identity* (London: Sage).

Patrick, J. (1973), *A Glasgow Gang Observed* (London: Eyre-Methuen).

Patterson, M. G., West, M. A., Shackleton, V. J., Dawson, J. F., Lawthom, R., Maitlis, S., Robinson, D. L., and Wallace, A. M. (2005), 'Validating the Organizational Climate Measure: Links to Managerial Practices, Productivity and Innovation', *Journal of Organizational Behavior*, 26: 379–408.

Pawson, R., and Tilley, N. (1997), *Realistic Evaluation* (London: Sage).

Payne, G., and Grew, C. (2005), 'Unpacking "Class Ambivalence": Some Conceptual and Methodological Issues in Accessing Class Identities', *Sociology*, 39: 893–910.

Peel, E. (2004), 'Gaining Informed Consent', in S. Becker and A. Bryman (eds.), *Understanding Research for Social Policy and Practice: Themes, Methods, and Approaches* (Bristol: Policy Press).

Peñaloza, L. (1999), 'Just Doing It: A Visual Ethnographic Study of Spectacular Consumption Behavior at Nike Town', *Consumption, Market and Culture*, 2: 337–400.

Pendergrast, M. (1993), *For God, Country and Coca-Cola: The Unauthorized History of the World's Most Popular Soft Drink* (London: Weidenfeld & Nicolson).

Penn, R., Rose, M., and Rubery, J. (1994), *Skill and Occupational Change* (Oxford: Oxford University Press).

Peräkylä, A. (1997), 'Reliability and Validity in Research Based on Transcripts', in D. Silverman (ed.), *Qualitative Research: Theory, Method and Practice* (London: Sage).

Pernice, R. (1996), 'Methodological Issues in Unemployment Research: Quantitative and/or Qualitative Approaches?', *Journal of Occupational and Organizational Psychology*, 69: 339–49.

Pettigrew, A. (1985), *The Awakening Giant: Continuity and Change in Imperial Chemical Industries* (Oxford: Blackwell).

—— (1997), 'What is a Processual Analysis?', *Scandinavian Journal of Management*, 13: 337–48.

—— and Whipp, R. (1991), *Managing Change for Competitive Success* (Oxford: Blackwell).

Phelan, P. (1987), 'Comparability of Qualitative and Quantitative Methods: Studying Child Sexual Abuse in America', *Education and Urban Society*, 20: 35–41.

Phillips, D. L. (1973), *Abandoning Method* (San Francisco: Jossey-Bass).

Phillips, N., and Brown, J. L. (1993), 'Analyzing Communications in and around Organizations: A Critical Hermeneutic Approach', *Academy of Management Journal*, 36: 1547–76.

—— and Hardy, C. (2002), *Discourse Analysis: Investigating Processes of Social Construction* (London: Sage).

Phillipson, C., Bernard, M., Phillips, J., and Ogg, J. (1999), 'Older People's Experiences of Community Life: Patterns of Neighbouring in Three Urban Areas', *Sociological Review*, 47: 715–43.

Phoenix, A. (1994), 'Practising Feminist Research: The Intersection of Gender and "Race" in the Research Process', in M. Maynard and J. Purvis (eds.), *Researching Women's Lives from a Feminist Perspective* (London: Taylor & Francis).

Pidgeon, N., and Henwood, K. (2004), 'Grounded Theory', in M. Hardy and A. Bryman (eds.), *Handbook of Data Analysis* (London: Sage).

Pinch, T., and Clark, C. (1986), 'The Hard Sell: "Patter Merchanting" and the Strategic (Re)production and Local Management of Economic Reasoning in the Sales Routines of Market Pitchers', *Sociology*, 20: 169–91.

Pink, S. (2001), *Visual Ethnography* (London: Sage).

—— (2004), 'Visual Methods', in C. Seale, G. Gobo, J. F. Gubrium, and D. Silverman (eds.), *Qualitative Research Practice* (London: Sage).

Platt, J. (1981), 'The Social Construction of "Positivism" and its Significance in British Sociology, 1950–80', in P. Abrams, R. Deem, J. Finch, and P. Rock (eds.), *Practice and Progress: British Sociology 1950–1980* (London: George Allen & Unwin).

—— (1984), 'The *Affluent Worker* Revisited', in C. Bell and H. Roberts (eds.), *Social Researching: Politics, Problems, Practice* (London: Routledge & Kegan Paul).

—— (1986), 'Functionalism and the Survey: The Relation of Theory and Method', *Sociological Review*, 34: 501–36.

—— (1996), *A History of Sociological Research Methods in America 1920–1960* (Cambridge: Cambridge University Press).

Plummer, K. (1983), *Documents of Life: An Introduction to the Problems and Literature of a Humanistic Method* (London: Allen & Unwin).

—— (2001), 'The Call of Life Stories in Ethnographic Research', in P. Atkinson, A. Coffey, S. Delamont, J. Lofland, and L. Lofland (eds.), *Handbook of Ethnography* (London: Sage).

Podsakoff, P. M., and Dalton, D. R. (1987), 'Research Methodology in Organizational Studies', *Journal of Management*, 13: 419–44.

Poland, B. D. (1995), 'Transcription Quality as an Aspect of Rigor in Qualitative Research', *Qualitative Inquiry*, 1: 290–310.

Pollert, A. (1981), *Girls, Wives, Factory Lives* (London: Macmillan).

Polsky, N. (1967), *Hustlers, Beats and Others* (Chicago: Aldine).

Poortinga, W., Bickerstaff, K., Langford, I., Niewöhner, J., and Pidgeon, N. (2004), 'The British 2001 Foot and Mouth Crisis: A Comparative Study of Public Risk Perceptions, Trust and Beliefs about Government Policy in Two Communities', *Journal of Risk Research*, 7: 73–90.

Pope, C., and Mays, N. (1995), 'Reaching the Parts Other Methods Cannot Reach: An Introduction to Qualitative Methods in Health and Health Services Research', *British Medical Journal*, 311: 42–5.

Porter, S. (1993), 'Critical Realist Ethnography: The Case of Racism and Professionalism in a Medical Setting', *Sociology*, 27: 591–609.

—— (2002), 'Critical Realist Ethnography', in T. May (ed.), *Qualitative Research in Action* (London: Sage).

Potter, J. (1996), *Representing Reality: Discourse, Rhetoric and Social Construction* (London: Sage).

—— (1997), 'Discourse Analysis as a Way of Analysing Naturally Occurring Talk', in D. Silverman (ed.), *Qualitative Research: Theory, Method and Practice* (London: Sage).

—— (2004), 'Discourse Analysis', in M. Hardy and A. Bryman (eds.), *Handbook of Data Analysis* (London: Sage).

—— and Hepburn, A. (2004), 'The Analysis of NSPCC Call Openings', in S. Becker and A. Bryman (eds.), *Understanding*

Research for Social Policy and Practice: Themes, Methods, and Approaches (Bristol: Policy Press).

Potter, J., and Wetherell, M. (1987), *Discourse and Social Psychology: Beyond Attitudes and Behaviour* (London: Sage).

—— —— (1994), 'Analyzing Discourse', in A. Bryman and R. G. Burgess (eds.), *Analyzing Qualitative Data* (London: Routledge).

—— —— and Chitty, A. (1991), 'Quantification Rhetoric: Cancer on Television', *Discourse and Society*, 2: 333–65.

Powell, G. N., and Butterfield, D. A. (1997), 'Effect of Race on Promotions to Top Management in a Federal Department', *Academy of Management Journal*, 40: 112–28.

Power, S., Moss, G., Lewis, J., Whitty, G., and Edwards, T. (2005), 'Staying in Touch? The Potential of *Friends Reunited* as a Research Tool', *Research Intelligence*, 92: 6–8.

Psathas, G. (1995), *Conversation Analysis: The Study of Talk-in-Interaction* (Thousand Oaks, Calif.: Sage).

Punch, M. (1979), *Policing the Inner City: A Study of Amsterdam's Warmoesstraat* (London: Macmillan).

—— (1994), 'Politics and Ethics in Qualitative Research', in N. K. Denzin and Y. S. Lincoln (eds.), *Handbook of Qualitative Research* (Thousand Oaks, Calif.: Sage).

Radley, A., and Chamberlain, K. (2001), 'Health Psychology and the Study of the Case: From Method to Analytic Concern', *Social Science and Medicine*, 53: 321–32.

—— Hodgetts, D., and Cullen, A. (2005), 'Visualizing Homelessness: A Study in Photography and Estrangement', *Journal of Community and Applied Social Psychology*, 15: 273–95.

Rafaeli, A., Dutton, J., Harquail, C. V., and Mackie-Lewis, S. (1997), 'Navigating by Attire: The Use of Dress by Female Administrative Employees', *Academy of Management Journal*, 40: 9–45.

Ragin, C. C., and Becker, H. S. (1989), 'How the Microcomputer is Changing our Analytic Habits', in G. Blank *et al.* (eds.), *New Technology in Sociology: Practical Applications in Research and Work* (New Brunswick: Transaction Publishers).

Rank, M. R. (1989), 'Fertility among Women on Welfare: Incidence and Determinants', *American Sociological Review*, 54: 296–304.

Raz, A. E. (1999), *Riding the Black Ship: Japan and Tokyo Disneyland* (Cambridge, Mass.: Harvard University Press).

Reed, M. (2000), 'The Limits of Discourse Analysis in Organizational Analysis', *Organization*, 7: 524–30.

Reid, D. J., and Reid, F. J. M. (2005), 'Online Focus Groups: An In-depth Comparison of Computer-Mediated and Conventional Focus Group Discussions', *International Journal of Market Research*, 47: 131–62.

Reiner, R. (2000*a*), 'Crime and Control in Britain', *Sociology*, 34: 71–94.

—— (2000*b*), 'Police Research', in R. D. King and E. Wincup (eds.), *Doing Research on Crime and Justice* (Oxford: Oxford University Press).

Reinharz, S. (1992), *Feminist Methods in Social Research* (New York: Oxford University Press).

Reiss, A. J. (1968), 'Stuff and Nonsense about Social Surveys and Participant Observation', in H. S. Becker, B. Geer, D. Riesman, and R. S. Weiss (eds.), *Institutions and the Person: Papers in Memory of Everett C. Hughes* (Chicago: Aldine).

—— (1976), 'Systematic Observation of Natural Phenomena', in H. W. Sinaiko and L. A. Broedling (eds.), *Perspectives on Attitude Assessment: Surveys and their Alternatives* (Champaign, Ill.: Pendleton).

Rhodes, C., and Brown, A. D. (2005), 'Narrative, Organizations and Research', *International Journal of Management Research*, 7: 167–88.

Richards, L., and Richards, T. (1994), 'From Filing Cabinet to Computer', in A. Bryman and R. G. Burgess (eds.), *Analyzing Qualitative Data* (London: Routledge).

Richardson, L. (1990), 'Narrative and Sociology', *Journal of Contemporary Ethnography*, 19: 116–35.

—— (1994), 'Writing: A Method of Inquiry', in N. K. Denzin and Y. S. Lincoln (eds.), *Handbook of Qualitative Research* (Thousand Oaks, Calif.: Sage).

Riches, G., and Dawson, P. (1998), 'Lost Children, Living Memories: The Role of Photographs in Processes of Grief and Adjustment among Bereaved Parents', *Death Studies*, 22: 121–40.

Riessman, C. K. (1993), *Narrative Analysis* (Newbury Park, Calif.: Sage).

—— (2004*a*), 'Narrative Interviewing', in M. S. Lewis-Beck, A. Bryman, and T. F. Liao (eds.), *The Sage Encyclopedia of Social Science Research Methods* (3 vols.; Thousand Oaks, Calif.: Sage.)

—— (2004*b*), 'Narrative Analysis', in M. S. Lewis-Beck, A. Bryman, and T. F. Liao (eds.), *The Sage Encyclopedia of Social Science Research Methods* (3 vols.; Thousand Oaks, Calif.: Sage.)

Ritchie, J., Spencer, L., and O'Connor, W. (2003), 'Carrying out Qualitative Analysis', in J. Ritchie and J. Lewis (eds.), *Qualitative Research Practice: A Guide for Social Science Students and Researchers* (London: Sage).

Ritzer, G. (1975), 'Sociology: A Multiple Paradigm Science', *American Sociologist*, 10: 156–67.

Roberts, B. (2002), *Biographical Research* (Buckingham: Open University Press).

Rocheleau, D. (1995), 'Maps, Numbers, Text, and Context: Mixing Methods in Feminist Political Ecology', *Professional Geographer*, 47: 458–66.

Rojek, C. (1995), *Decentring Leisure: Rethinking Leisure Theory* (London: Sage).

Rorty, R. (1979), *Philosophy and the Mirror of Nature* (Princeton: Princeton University Press).

Rose, G. (2001), *Visual Methodologies* (London, Sage).

Rosenau, P. M. (1992), *Post-Modernism and the Social Sciences: Insights, Inroads, and Intrusions* (Princeton: Princeton University Press).

Rosenhan, D. L. (1973), 'On Being Sane in Insane Places', *Science*, 179: 350–8.

Rosenthal, R., and Jacobson, L. (1968), *Pygmalion in the Classroom: Teacher Expectation and Pupils' Intellectual Development* (New York: Holt, Rinehart & Winston).

Rosnow, R. L., and Rosenthal, R. (1997), *People Studying People: Artifacts and Ethics in Behaviorial Research* (New York: W. H. Freeman).

Roulston, K., deMarrais, K., and Lewis, J. (2003), 'Learning to Interview in the Social Sciences', *Qualitative Inquiry*, 9: 643–68.

Rubin, H. J., and Rubin, I. S. (1995), *Qualitative Interviewing: The Art of Hearing Data* (Thousand Oaks, Calif.: Sage).

Rubinstein, J. (1973), *City Police* (New York: Ballantine).

Russell, R., and Tyler, M. (2002), 'Thank Heaven for Little Girls: "Girl Heaven" and the Commercial Context of Feminine Childhood', *Sociology*, 36: 619–37.

Ryan, G. W., and Bernard, H. R. (2003), 'Techniques to Identify Themes', *Field Methods*, 15: 85–109.

Sacks, H., Schegloff, E. A., and Jefferson, G. (1974), 'A Simplest Systematics for the Organization of Turn-Taking in Conversation', *Language*, 50: 696–735.

Salancik, G. R. (1979), 'Field Stimulations for Organizational Behavior Research', *Administrative Science Quarterly*, 24: 638–49.

Sampson, H., and Thomas, M. (2003), 'Lone Researchers at Sea: Gender, Risk and Responsibility', *Qualitative Research*, 3: 165–89.

Samuel, R. (1976), 'Oral History and Local History', *History Workshop Journal*, 1: 191–208.

Sandelowski, M. (2003), 'Tables or Tableaux? The Challenges of Writing and Reading Mixed Methods Studies', in A. Tashakkori and C. Teddlie (eds.), *Handbook of Mixed Methods in Social and Behavioral Research* (Thousand Oaks, Calif.: Sage).

Sanders, T. (2005), 'Researching the Online Sex Work Community', in C. Hine (ed.), *Virtual Methods: Issues in Social Research on the Internet* (Oxford: Berg).

Sanjek, R. (1990), 'A Vocabulary for Fieldnotes', in R. Sanjek (ed.), *Fieldnotes: The Making of Anthropology* (Ithaca, NY: Cornell University Press).

Sarsby, J. (1984), 'The Fieldwork Experience', in R. F. Ellen (ed.), *Ethnographic Research: A Guide to General Conduct* (London: Academic Press).

Saunders, P. (1989), 'Left Write in Sociology', *Network: Newsletter of the British Sociological Association*, 44: 3–4.

Savage, M. (2005), 'Working-Class Identities in the 1960s: Revisiting the Affluent Worker Study', *Sociology*, 39: 929–46.

—— Bagnall, G., and Longhurst, B. (2001), 'Ordinary, Ambivalent and Defensive: Class Identities in the Northwest of England', *Sociology*, 35: 875–92.

Schaeffer, D. R., and Dillman, D. A. (1998), 'Development of a Standard E-Mail Methodology', *Public Opinion Quarterly*, 62: 378–97.

Schegloff, E. A. (1997), 'Whose Text? Whose Context?', *Discourse and Society*, 8: 165–87.

Schlesinger, P., Dobash, R. E., Dobash, R. P., and Weaver, C. K. (1992), *Women Viewing Violence* (London: British Film Institute).

Schneider, S. M., and Foot, K. A. (2004), 'The Web as an Object of Study', *New Media and Society*, 6: 114–22.

Schrøder, K. C. (1999), 'The Best of Both Worlds? Media Audience Research between Rival Paradigms', in P. Alasuutari (ed.), *Rethinking the Media Audience* (London: Sage).

Schuman, H., and Converse, J. (1971), 'The Effects of Black and White Interviewers on Black Responses in 1968', *Public Opinion Quarterly*, 35: 44–68.

—— and Presser, S. (1981), *Questions and Answers in Attitude Surveys: Experiments on Question Form, Wording, and Context* (San Diego, Calif.: Academic Press).

Schutz, A. (1962), *Collected Papers I: The Problem of Social Reality* (The Hague: Martinus Nijhof).

Scott, A. M. (1994), *Gender Segregation and Social Change: Men and Women in Changing Labour Markets* (Oxford: Oxford University Press).

Scott, J. (1990), *A Matter of Record* (Cambridge: Polity).

Seale, C. (1999), *The Quality of Qualitative Research* (London: Sage).

—— (2002) 'Cancer Heroics: A Study of News Reports with Particular Reference to Gender', *Sociology*, 36: 107–26.

—— Ziebland, S., and Charteris-Black, J. (2006), 'Gender, Cancer Experience and Internet Use: A Comparative Keyword Analysis of Interviews and Online Cancer Support Groups', *Social Science and Medicine*, 62: 2577–90.

Seeman, M. (1959), 'On the Meaning of Alienation', *American Sociological Review*, 24: 783–91.

Sempik, J., Becker, S., and Bryman, A. (2007), 'The Quality of Research Evidence in Social Policy: Consensus and Dissension among Researchers', *Evidence and Policy*, 3: 407–23.

Shapiro, M. (1985–6), 'Metaphor in the Philosophy of the Social Sciences', *Cultural Critique*, 2: 191–214.

Sharf, B. F. (1999), 'Beyond Nettiquette: The Ethics of Doing Naturalistic Discourse Research on the Internet', in S. Jones (ed.), *Doing Internet Research: Critical Issues and Methods for Examining the Net* (Thousand Oaks, Calif.: Sage).

Sharpe, K. (2000), 'Sad, Bad, and (Sometimes) Dangerous to Know: Street Corner Research with Prostitutes, Punters, and the Police', in R. D. King and E. Wincup (eds.), *Doing Research on Crime and Justice* (Oxford: Oxford University Press).

Shaw, C. R. (1930), *The Jack-Roller* (Chicago: University of Chicago Press).

Sheehan, K. (2001), 'E-Mail Survey Response Rates: A Review', *Journal of Computer-Mediated Communication*, 6, http://www.ascusc.org/jcmc/vol6/issue2/sheehan.html.

—— and Hoy, M. G. (1999), 'Using E-Mail to Survey Internet Users in the United States: Methodology and Assessment', *Journal of Computer-Mediated Communication*, 4, http://www.ascusc.org/jcmc/vol4/issue3/sheehan.html.

Shepherd, J., Harden, A., Rees, R., Brunton, G., Garcia, J., Oliver, S., and Oakley, A. (2006), 'Young People and Healthy Eating: A Systematic Review of Research on Barriers and Facilitators', *Health Education Review*, 21: 239–57.

Shuy, R. W. (2002), 'In-Person versus Telephone Interviewing', in J. F. Gubrium and J. A. Holstein (eds.), *Handbook of Interview Research: Context and Method* (Thousand Oaks, Calif.: Sage).

Silverman, D. (1984), 'Going Private: Ceremonial Forms in a Private Oncology Clinic', *Sociology*, 18: 191–204.

—— (1985), *Qualitative Methodology and Sociology: Describing the Social World* (Aldershot: Gower).

—— (1993), *Interpreting Qualitative Data: Methods for Analysing Qualitative Data* (London: Sage).

—— (1994), 'Analysing Naturally-Occurring Data on AIDS Counselling: Some Methodological and Practical Issues', in M. Boulton (ed.), *Challenge and Innovation: Methodological Advances in Social Research on HIV/AIDS* (London: Taylor & Francis).

—— (2000), *Doing Qualitative Research: A Practical Handbook* (London: Sage).

Singer, E. (2003), 'Exploring the Meaning of Consent: Participation in Research and Beliefs about Risks and Benefits', *Journal of Official Statistics*, 19: 273–85.

Skeggs, B. (1994), 'Situating the Production of Feminist Ethnography', in M. Maynard and J. Purvis (eds.), *Researching Women's Lives from a Feminist Perspective* (London: Taylor & Francis).

—— (1997), *Formations of Class and Gender* (London: Sage).

—— (2001), 'Feminist Ethnography', in P. Atkinson, A. Coffey, S. Delamont, J. Lofland, and L. Lofland (eds.), *Handbook of Ethnography* (London: Sage).

Smith, C. B. (1997), 'Casting the Net: Surveying an Internet Population', *Journal of Computer-Mediated Communication*, 3, http://www.ascusc.org/jcmc/vol3/issue1/yun.html.

Smith, D. J., and McVie, S. (2003), 'Theory and Method in the Edinburgh Study of Youth Transitions and Crime', *British Journal of Criminology*, 43: 169–95.

Smith, J. K. (1983), 'Quantitative versus Qualitative Research: An Attempt to Clarify the Issue', *Educational Researcher*, 12: 6–13.

—— and Heshusius, L. (1986), 'Closing down the Conversation: The End of the Quantitative-Qualitative Debate among Educational Enquirers', *Educational Researcher*, 15: 4–12.

Smith, K., and Joshi, H. (2002), 'The Millennium Cohort Study', *Population Trends*, 30–4.

Smith, K. M. Clegg (2004), ' "Electronic Eavesdropping": The Ethical Issues Involved in Conducting a Virtual Ethnography', in M. D. Johns, S. L. S. Chen, and G. J. Hall (eds.), *Online Social Research* (New York: Peter Lang), 223–37.

Smith, L. (1994), 'A Content Analysis of Gender Differences in Children's Advertising', *Journal of Broadcasting and Electronic Media*, 38: 323–37.

Smith, N., Lister, R., and Middleton, S. (2004), 'Longitudinal Qualitative Research', in S. Becker, and A. Bryman (eds.), *Understanding Research for Social Policy and Practice: Themes, Methods, and Approaches* (Bristol: Policy Press).

Smith, T. W. (1995), 'Trends in Non-Response Rates', *International Journal of Public Opinion Research*, 7: 157–71.

Smithson, J., and Brannen, J. (2002), 'Qualitative Methodology in Cross-National Research', in J. Brannen, S. Lewis, A. Nilsen, and J. Smithson (eds.), *Young Europeans, Work and Family: Futures in Transition* (London: Routledge).

Snizek, W. E. (1976), 'An Empirical Assessment of "Sociology: A Multiple Paradigm Science" [Ritzer, 1975]', *American Sociologist*, 11: 217–19.

Snyder, N., and Glueck, W. F. (1980), 'How Managers Plan: The Analysis of Managers' Activities', *Long Range Planning*, 13: 70–6.

Spencer, L., Ritchie, J., Lewis, J., and Dillon, L. (2003), *Quality in Qualitative Evaluation: A Framework for Assessing Research Evidence* (London: Government Chief Social Researcher's Office). Available at http://www.policyhub.gov.uk/docs/qqe_rep.pdf.

Spradley, J. P. (1979), *The Ethnographic Interview* (New York: Holt, Rinehart & Winston).

Sprokkereef, A., Larkin, E., Pole, C. J., and Burgess, R. G. (1995), 'The Data, the Team, and the Ethnograph', *Studies in Qualitative Methodology*, 5: 81–103.

Squire, C. (2000), 'Situated Selves, the Coming-out Genre and Equivalent Citizenship in Narratives of HIV', in P. Chamberlayne, J. Bornat, and T. Wengraf (eds.), *The Turn to Biographical Methods in Social Science: Comparative Issues and Examples* (London: Routledge).

Stacey, J. (1988), 'Can there be a Feminist Ethnography?', *Women's International Studies Forum*, 11: 21–7.

Stacey, M. (1960), *Tradition and Change: A Study of Banbury* (London: Oxford University Press).

Stake, R. E. (1995), *The Art of Case Study Research* (Thousand Oaks, Calif.: Sage).

Stanley, L., and Temple, B. (1995), 'Doing the Business? Evaluating Software Packages to Aid the Analysis of Qualitative Data Sets', *Studies in Qualitative Methodology*, 5: 169–97.

Stefani, L., and Carroll, J. (2001), 'A Briefing Note on Plagiarism', Assessment Series 10, http://www.sussex.ac.uk/tldu/documents/plag_ass0101.doc.

Stewart, K., and Williams, M. (2005), 'Researching Online Populations: The Use of Online Focus Groups for Social Research', *Qualitative Research*, 5: 395–416.

Stewart, S., Prandy, K., and Blackburn, R. M. (1980), *Social Stratification and Occupations* (London: Macmillan).

Stoller, P. (1989), *The Taste of Ethnographic Things* (Philadelphia: University of Pennsylvania Press).

Strauss, A. (1987), *Qualitative Analysis for Social Scientists* (New York: Cambridge University Press).

—— and Corbin, J. M. (1990), *Basics of Qualitative Research: Grounded Theory Procedures and Techniques* (Newbury Park, Calif.: Sage).

—— —— (1997*a*), 'Commentary [on Orona, 1997]', in A. Strauss and J. M. Corbin (eds.), *Grounded Theory in Practice* (Thousand Oaks, Calif.: Sage).

—— —— (1997*b*), *Grounded Theory in Practice* (Thousand Oaks, Calif.: Sage).

—— —— (1998), *Basics of Qualitative Research: Techniques and Procedures for Developing Grounded Theory* (Thousand Oaks, Calif.: Sage).

—— Schatzman, L., Ehrich, D., Bucher, R., and Sabshin, M. (1973), 'The Hospital and its Negotiated Order', in G. Salaman and K. Thompson (eds.), *People and Organizations* (London: Longman).

Sturges, J. E., and Hanrahan, K. J. (2004), 'Comparing Telephone and Face-to-Face Qualitative Interviewing: A Research Note', *Qualitative Research* 4: 107–18.

Sturridge, P. (2007), 'Class Belonging: A Quantitative Exploration of Identity and Consciousness', *British Journal of Sociology*, 58: 207–26.

Sudman, S., and Bradburn, N. M. (1982), *Asking Questions: A Practical Guide to Questionnaire Design* (San Francisco: Jossey-Bass).

Sullivan, O. (1996), 'Time Co-Ordination, the Domestic Division of Labour and Affective Relations: Time Use and the Enjoyment of Activities within Couples', *Sociology*, 30: 79–100.

—— (1997), 'Time Waits for no (Wo)man: An Investigation of the Gendered Experience of Domestic Time', *Sociology*, 31: 221–39.

Sutton, R. I. (1992), 'Feelings about a Disneyland Visit: Photography and the Reconstruction of Bygone Emotions', *Journal of Management Inquiry*, 1: 278–87.

—— and Rafaeli, A. (1988), 'Untangling the Relationship between Displayed Emotions and Organizational Sales: The Case of Convenience Stores', *Academy of Management Journal*, 31: 461–87.

—— —— (1992), 'How we Untangled the Relationship between Displayed Emotion and Organizational Sales: A Tale of Bickering and Optimism', in P. J. Frost and R. Stablein (eds.), *Doing Exemplary Research* (Newbury Park, Calif.: Sage).

Swain, J. (2004), 'The Resources and Strategies that 10–11-Year-Old Boys Use to Construct Masculinities in the School Setting', *British Educational Research Journal*, 30: 167–85.

Sweet, C. (2001), 'Designing and Conducting Virtual Focus Groups', *Qualitative Market Research*, 4: 130–5.

Tashakkori, A., and Teddlie, C. (2003), *Handbook of Mixed Methods in Social and Behavioral Research* (Thousand Oaks, Calif.: Sage).

Taylor, A. (1993), *Women Drug Users: An Ethnography of an Injecting Community* (Oxford: Clarendon Press).

Taylor, S. (1999), 'Covert Participant Observation: Unguarded Moments in Organizational Research', *Notework: The Newsletter of the Standing Conference on Organizational Symbolism*, May: 8–18.

Teitler, J. O., Reichman, N. E., and Sprachman, S. (2003), 'Costs and Benefits of Improving Response Rates for a Hard-to-Reach Population', *Public Opinion Quarterly*, 67: 126–38.

Teo, P. (2000), 'Racism in the News: A Critical Discourse Analysis of News Reporting in Two Australian Newspapers', *Discourse and Society*, 11: 7–49.

Thompson, P. (1989), *The Nature of Work* (2nd edn., London: Macmillan).

Tilley, N. (2000), 'Doing Realistic Evaluation of Criminal Justice', in V. Jupp, P. Davies, and P. Francis (eds.), *Doing Criminological Research* (London: Sage).

Tourangeau, R., and Smith, T. W. (1996), 'Asking Sensitive Questions: The Impact of Data Collection Mode, Question Format, and Question Context', *Public Opinion Quarterly*, 60: 275–304.

Tranfield, D., Denyer, D. and Smart, P. (2003) 'Towards a Methodology for Developing Evidence-Informed Management Knowledge by Means of Systematic Review', *British Journal of Management*, 14: 207–22.

Tripp, T. M., Bies, R. J., and Aquino, K. (2002), 'Poetic Justice or Petty Jealousy? The Aesthetics of Revenge', *Organizational Behavior and Human Decision Processes*, 89: 966–84.

Trow, M. (1957), 'Comment on "Participant Observation and Interviewing: A Comparison"', *Human Organization*, 16: 33–5.

Tsang and Kwan (1999), 'Replication and Theory Development in Organizational Science: A Critical Realist Perspective', *Academy of Management Review*, 24: 759–80.

Tse, A. C. B. (1998), 'Comparing the Response Rate, Response Speed and Response Quality of Two Methods of Sending Questionnaires: E-Mail vs. Mail', *Journal of the Market Research Society*, 40: 353–61.

—— (1999), 'Conducting Electronic Focus Group Discussions among Chinese Respondents', *Journal of the Market Research Society*, 41: 407–15.

Turnbull, C. (1973), *The Mountain People* (London: Cape).

Turner, B. A. (1994), 'Patterns of Crisis Behaviour: A Qualitative Inquiry', in A. Bryman and R. G. Burgess (eds.), *Analyzing Qualitative Data* (London: Routledge).

Twine, F. W. (2006), 'Visual Ethnography and Racial Theory: Family Photographs as Archives of Interracial Intimacies', *Ethnic and Racial Studies*, 29: 487–511.

Van den Hoonaard, W. (2001), 'Is Research Ethics Review a Moral Panic?', *Canadian Review of Sociology and Anthropology*, 38: 19–36.

van Dijk, T. A. (1997), 'Discourse as Interaction in Society', in T. A. Van Dijk (ed.), *Discourse as Social Interaction. Discourse Studies Vol. 2—A Multidisciplinary Introduction* (Newbury Park, Calif.: Sage).

Van Maanen, J. (1978), 'On Watching the Watchers', in P. Manning and J. Van Maanen (eds.), *Policing: The View from the Street* (Santa Monica, Calif.: Goodyear).

—— (1988), *Tales of the Field: On Writing Ethnography* (Chicago: University of Chicago Press).

—— (1991*a*), 'Playing Back the Tape: Early Days in the Field', in W. B. Shaffir and R. A. Stebbins (eds.), *Experiencing Fieldwork: An Inside View of Qualitative Research* (Newbury Park, Calif.: Sage).

—— (1991*b*), 'The Smile Factory: Work at Disneyland', in P. J. Frost, L. F. Moore, M. R. Louis, C. C. Lundberg, and J. Martin (eds.), *Reframing Organizational Culture* (Newbury Park, Calif.: Sage).

—— and Kolb, D. (1985), 'The Professional Apprentice: Observations on Fieldwork Roles in Two Organizational Settings', *Research in the Sociology of Organizations*, 4: 1–33.

Vaughan, D. (1996), *The Challenger Launch Decision: Risky Technology, Culture, and Deviance at NASA* (Chicago: University of Chicago Press).

—— (2004), 'Theorizing Disaster: Analogy, Historical Ethnography, and the *Challenger* Accident', *Ethnography*, 5: 315–47.

—— (2006), 'The Social Shaping of Commission Reports', *Sociological Forum*, 21: 291–306.

Vidich, A. R., and Bensman, J. (1968), *Small Town in Mass Society* (Princeton: Princeton University Press).

Vincent, N. (2006), *Self-Made Man: My Year Disguised as a Man* (London: Atlantic Books).

Voas, D., and Crockett, A. (2005), 'Religion in Britain: Neither Believing nor Belonging', *Sociology*, 39: 11–28.

Von Wright, G. H. (1971), *Explanation and Understanding* (London: Routledge).

Waddington, D. (1994), 'Participant Observation', in C. Cassell and G. Symon (eds.), *Qualitative Methods in Organizational Research* (London: Sage).

Wajcman, J., and Martin, B. (2002), 'Narratives of Identity in Modern Management: The Corrosion of Identity Difference?', *Sociology*, 36: 985–1002.

Walby, S., and Myhill, A. (2001), 'New Survey Methodologies in Researching Violence against Women', *British Journal of Criminology*, 41: 502–22.

Walklate, S. (2000), 'Researching Victims', in R. D. King and E. Wincup (eds.), *Doing Research on Crime and Justice* (Oxford: Oxford University Press).

Wall, R. (1989), 'The Living Arrangements of the Elderly in Europe in the 1980s', in B. Bytheway, T. Keil, P. Allatt, and A. Bryman (eds.), *Becoming and Being Old: Sociological Approaches to Later Life* (London: Sage).

Walsh, D. (1972), 'Sociology and the Social World', in P. Filmer, M. Phillipson, D. Silverman, and D. Walsh, *New Directions in Sociological Theory* (London: Collier-Macmillan).

Warde, A. (1997), *Consumption, Food and Taste* (London: Sage).

Wardhaugh, J. (1996), '"Homeless in Chinatown": Deviance and Social Control in Cardboard City', *Sociology*, 30: 701–16.

Warr, D. J. (2005), ' "It Was Fun . . . But We Don't Usually Talk about These Things": Analyzing Sociable Interaction in Focus Groups', *Qualitative Inquiry*, 11: 200–25.

Warren, C. A. B. (2002), 'Qualitative Interviewing', in J. F. Gubrium and J. A. Holstein (eds.), *Handbook of Interview Research: Context and Method* (Thousand Oaks, Calif.: Sage).

—— Barnes-Brus, T., Burgess, H., Wiebold-Lippisch, L., Hackney, J., Harkness, G., Kennedy, V., Dingwall, R., Rosenblatt, P. C., Ryen A., and Shuy, R. (2003), 'After the Interview', *Qualitative Sociology*, 26: 93–110.

Weaver, A., and Atkinson, P. (1995), *Microcomputing and Qualitative Data Analysis* (Aldershot: Avebury).

Webb, E. J., Campbell, D. T., Schwartz, R. D., and Sechrest, L. (1966), *Unobtrusive Measures: Nonreactive Measures in the Social Sciences* (Chicago: Rand McNally).

Weber, M. (1947), *The Theory of Social and Economic Organization*, trans. A. M. Henderson and T. Parsons (New York: Free Press).

Weick, K. E. (1990), 'The Vulnerable System: An Analysis of the Tenerife Air Disaster', *Journal of Management*, 16: 571–93.

Weinholtz, D., Kacer, B., and Rocklin, T. (1995), 'Salvaging Quantitative Research with Qualitative Data', *Qualitative Health Research*, 5: 388–97.

Weitzman, E. A., and Miles, M. B. (1995), *Computer Programs for Qualitative Data Analysis* (Thousand Oaks, Calif.: Sage).

Wellings, K., Field, J., Johnson, A., and Wadsworth, J. (1994), *Sexual Behaviour in Britain: The National Survey of Sexual Attitudes and Lifestyles* (Harmondsworth: Penguin).

Westergaard, J., Noble, I., and Walker, A. (1989), *After Redundancy: The Experience of Economic Insecurity* (Cambridge: Polity).

Westmarland, L. (2001), 'Blowing the Whistle on Police Violence: Ethics, Research and Ethnography', *British Journal of Criminology*, 41: 523–35.

Wetherell, M. (1998), 'Positioning and Interpretative Repertoires: Conversation Analysis and Post-Structuralism in Dialogue', *Discourse and Society*, 9: 387–412.

Whyte, W. F. (1955), *Street Corner Society* (2nd edn.; Chicago: University of Chicago Press).

Widdicombe, S. (1993), 'Autobiography and Change: Rhetoric and Authenticity of "Gothic" Style', in E. Burman and I. Parker (eds.), *Discourse Analytic Research: Readings and Repertoires of Text* (London: Routledge).

Wilkinson, S. (1998), 'Focus Groups in Feminist Research: Power, Interaction, and the Co-Production of Meaning', *Women's Studies International Forum*, 21: 111–25.

—— (1999a), 'Focus Group Methodology: A Review', *International Journal of Social Research Methodology*, 1: 181–203.

—— (1999b), 'Focus Groups: A Feminist Method', *Psychology of Women Quarterly*, 23: 221–44.

Williams, M. (2000), 'Interpretivism and Generalisation', *Sociology*, 34: 209–24.

Williams, M. (2007), 'Cybercrime and Online Methodologies', in R. King and E. Wincup (eds.), *Doing Research on Crime & Justice* (Oxford: Oxford University Press).

Williams, R. (1976), 'Symbolic Interactionism: Fusion of Theory and Research', in D. C. Thorns (ed.), *New Directions in Sociology* (London: David & Charles).

Willis, P. (1977), *Learning to Labour* (Farnborough: Saxon House).

Winch, P. (1958), *The Idea of a Social Science and its Relation to Philosophy* (London: Routledge & Kegan Paul).

Winkler, C. (1995), 'The Ethnography of the Ethnographer', in C. Nordstrom and A. C. G. M. Robben (eds.), *Fieldwork under Fire: Contemporary Studies of Violence and Survival* (Berkeley and Los Angeles: University of California Press).

Winlow, S., Hobbs, D., Lister, S., and Hadfield, P. (2001), 'Get Ready to Duck: Bouncers and the Realities of Ethnographic Research on Violent Groups', *British Journal of Criminology*, 41: 536–48.

Wolcott, H. F. (1990a), *Writing up Qualitative Research* (Newbury Park, Calif.: Sage).

—— (1990b), 'Making a Study "More Ethnographic"', *Journal of Contemporary Ethnography*, 19: 44–72.

Wolf, D. R. (1991), 'High Risk Methodology: Reflections on Leaving an Outlaw Society', in W. B. Shaffir and R. A. Stebbins (eds.), *Experiencing Fieldwork: An Inside View of Qualitative Research* (Newbury Park, Calif.: Sage).

Woolgar, S. (1988), *Science: The Very Idea* (Chichester: Ellis Horwood).

Wright, R., Brookman, F., and Bennett, T. (2006), 'The Foreground Dynamics of Street Robbery in Britain', *British Journal of Criminology*, 46: 1–15.

Yardley, L. (2000), 'Dilemmas in Qualitative Health Research', *Psychology and Health*, 15: 215–28.

Yin, R. K. (2003), *Case Study Research: Design and Methods* (3rd edn.; Thousand Oaks, Calif.: Sage).

Yun, G. W. and Trumbo, C. W. (2000), 'Comparative Response to a Survey Executed by Post, E-mail, and Web Form', *Journal of Computer-Mediated Communication*, 6, http://www.ascusc.org/jcmc/vol6/issue1/yun.html.

Zimmerman, D. H., and Wieder, D. L. (1977), 'The Diary: Diary-Interview Method', *Urban Life*, 5: 479–98.

Zukin, S. (1982), *Loft Living: Culture and Capital in Urban Change* (Baltimore, Md.: Johns Hopkins University Press).

Name index

Index

Please note that references to non-textual material such as figures or tables are in *italic* print